THE
ISTHMIAN FOOTBALL LEAGUE

THE
FIRST 100 YEARS

by

Nick Robinson

First published 2009

Published by:

The Isthmian Football League Limited
Triumph House,
Station Approach,
South Croydon CR2 0PL
United Kingdom

British Library Cataloguing in Publication Data.
A catalogue record for this book is available from the British Library.

ISBN 978 0 9562514 0 4

Typesetting and origination by:
Queensway Publishing Limited,
4 Centre Way, London N9 0AP

Printed and bound in the United Kingdom

THE FIRST 100 YEARS - CONTENTS

Acknowledgements

Introduction

Foreword by Alan Simpson, OBE

1 - A Concise History

2 - Founder Member Clubs - The Super Six

3 - Season by Season - Development of the League

4 - The Elite Eleven Clubs

5 - Off The Field

6 - The Dream Team

7 - Referees

8 - Representative Matches

9 - Sponsorship

10 - Success in FA Competitions

11 - League Cup Competitions

12 - The Complete Record

Statistics

Afterword by Jimmy Hill, MBE

Acknowledgements

I would like to record the great help I have received in compiling this book. Had I realised at the outset the amount of time I would commit to this task, I might have thought more before volunteering! The concept of the book was an easy one and the planning began well before the Centenary Season. However no-one connected with the book had any idea of the thousands of man hours which would be invested in researching and writing the copy and then laying out the book and inserting the images which also had to be sourced.

Inevitably when one compiles a list of thanks there is someone who slips through the net; so if you are reading this and feel that you have helped in the production of this book in some way, then my warmest thanks go to you and I apologise for not including you in this section. Mea culpa!

Mike Wilson has been an important cog in the machinery from the beginning. His experience in writing a number of books on non-league football and the statistical record of the League for many years was invaluable. He has contributed many programmes from his own collection, together with work as a writer; in editing and proof reading.

David Ballheimer joined the team as an experienced author and enthusiastic supporter of Hendon FC and has written significant parts of the book and added his own professional wisdom when we prepared the lay out.

Peter Butcher who, as a journalist, has reported upon more than 1,100 Isthmian League matches was our final proof reader and showed his expertise on the use of commas!

Lee Harding is Queensway Publishing and has assisted the League for many years with our printing requirements. His contribution to this book at the publishing stage cannot be underestimated. Indeed we would not have the professional publication which we now have without the many days spent in his company at his offices in North London where he showed us how to deal with widows and orphans and other matters of publishing nightmares! His dexterity with sizing our images, his skill in producing near perfect images from partially defective ones and his overall advice was much appreciated and I am sure that he will not have charged us the amount he should have done if we had paid at piece rate. Thank you Lee and may Braintree Town go on to greater heights under your guidance.

Alan Simpson was delighted to be asked to write the Foreword to this book and we are grateful to him; somehow the book would not have been the same without his contribution. Alan has been well known around "the Circuit" for decades. He is well known as patron of Hampton & Richmond Borough FC, so thank you Alan for your help and your friendship over the years and for the Foreword to this book.

Jimmy Hill was equally pleased to be asked to provide the Afterword and his connection with the League at the time of the commencement of sponsorship is not known by many people. His position as president of Corinthian-Casuals FC is not just in name but he is an enthusiastic supporter.

I could not have produced the Chapters on Sponsorship and Success in FA Competitions as easily without the help of Tony Williams. Tony is well known in non League circles having played in the League and having worked for Rothmans in the early days of Sponsorship. I have known Tony for over 30 years and was delighted when he agreed to help with this project.

Contributions were also received from Graeme Auger (Epping Town & Harlow Town); Robert Cavallini (Corinthian-Casuals); Nick Dugard (Wealdstone); Sadie Gordon (Woking); Simon Grigor (Harrow Borough); Ian Hollowell (Clapton); Neil Jensen (Hitchin Town); John Lawrence (Dulwich Hamlet); Len Llewellyn (Ilford); David McKnight (Wimbledon); Norman Moss and David Simpson (Walthamstow Avenue); Roger Reed (Enfield); John Shepperd (Oxford City); Kris Stewart (AFC Wimbledon); Dave Taverner and Peter Taylor (St. Albans City); Steve Tyler (Croydon); Robert Wooldridge and Ali Kazam (Kingstonian).

I have sourced many hundreds of images for this publication. Gavin Ellis of TGS Photo particularly assisted with images of players. Paul Claydon and the team at Groundtastic Magazine provided most of the pictures of grounds. Dave Twydell assisted with other images. The League Managers Association, City of London Metropolitan Archives and the Bucks Examiner were amongst many who gave permission to use images free of charge. I trust I have not breached the copyright of any image owner and if I have, please accept my apologies, and understand that this is a non-profit making venture.

The books *Non League* and *The FA Amateur Cup* by Bob Barton, and *The Complete Record of The FA Cup* by Mike Collett provided sources for research.

I had assistance from many individuals who contributed autobiographies but most important was the support of the Board of The Isthmian Football League Limited who have underwritten this venture. In particular I must mention Chairman Alan Turvey with whom I have worked for over twenty-five years. I am sure he would have liked this book to be produced sooner but he has always impressed on me the importance of quality. I hope that he, in particular, will be proud of this publication because he is "Mr Isthmian League".

There will undoubtedly be errors in a book of this size so, if you spot one, please let me know!

Nick Robinson

INTRODUCTION

Isthmian

An Isthmus is a narrow strip of land, bordered on two sides of water, and connects two larger land masses. The term Isthmus is pronounced Is-mus with the 'th' silent. The most famous isthmus is the land which connects the North and South American continents but we now think of the first isthmus as the Isthmus of Corinth, in Greece.

The Isthmian Games were organised in c581BC and were held at Corinth in the spring of every other year. They were part of the Olympiad in honour of Poseidon, the Greek god of the sea. The games included a variety of athletics, horse and chariot racing, and contests in music and poetry. The prize was a simple wreath of parsley, pine or ivy.

The "modern" Olympic Games began in 1896, the brainchild of Baron Pierre de Coubertin whose famous ideal was that it was not the winning that mattered but the taking part. This in turn led to the ideals of Greek amateur sportsmanship spreading to football. At the beginning of the twentieth century prominent administrators within the game set about creating a number of leagues to accommodate those who wanted to play the sport for the Corinthian ideal.

The new leagues introduced after that date maintained a link with Greek ideology by their names. We know of the Olympian, Hellenic (Greek for Greek!) Athenian, Spartan, Delphian, Corinthian, Parthenon, and Nemean Leagues. Most famously we have the **Isthmian Football League** which was formed on 8th March 1905. The motto of the League is *Honor Sufficit* (the honour is sufficient) and the League badge is a laurel wreath around a Greek "I". The laurel wreath was awarded to the victors of events in the ancient Olympic Games. The laurel wreath was registered by the League as a Trade Mark in 1996.

The Isthmian League has survived more than one hundred seasons. This book is a tribute to the League and all those who made it what it is today - the Clubs, the Players, and the League Officers, who, together with millions of spectators, created the first hundred years of history.

The information and statistics appear as they were at the end of the Centenary Season with updating, where appropriate.

Foreword

by Alan Simpson OBE: President, Hampton & Richmond Borough FC

It is a great honour to be asked to write the foreword to this celebration of one hundred years of the Isthmian League. My own lifelong love affair with football began a mere seventy years ago. Both sides of my family were connected with Stamford Bridge. My father and all my uncles were on the turnstiles, my grandfather was the chief programme seller, another of my uncles was on the ground staff and my mother and all my aunties worked on the Tote during greyhound meetings. The entire family were staunch Chelsea fans. Consequently there was no way I was going to support Chelsea.

But who? That was the question. All self-respecting six year olds had a team to support. One of my aforementioned uncles had given me a fantastic Christmas present. A set of photos of all the twenty two teams in the first division – in *colour*. Very rare in the thirties. My favourite colour was red so I put all the photos of the teams playing in red in a box, closed my eyes and picked one out. Brentford. Oh yes they were a first division side in those days.

And so I was a Brentford fan. I shudder when I think it could just have easily have been the hated Arsenal or Charlton Athletic, Sheffield United, Middlesbrough or even Sunderland. Not Manchester United or Liverpool. They were in the second division then.

So the die was cast and for the next thirty years my football habits were set in stone. Brentford whenever possible interspersed only by many visits to Fulham purely to watch the divine Johnny Haynes, for me the best footballer I ever saw.

But then in 1967 my whole life changed. One Saturday afternoon I was in my office working, too late to get to Brentford or Fulham. Needing my weekly injection of football I picked up the local paper. Football fixtures. Hampton v Crown and Manor. I didn't even know there was a club in Hampton. I drove up to the High Street two minutes away, and asked nine people, all locals, where the ground was. None of them knew. The tenth one did. "You're standing outside it mate. Just down that path." Down the winding path through a thick copse and there it was. Heaven. Like walking through the wardrobe and finding Narnia. I enjoyed the game and went into the rickety wooden clubhouse, had a drink and a sausage sizzling on the gas stove behind the bar, when I saw a blackboard on an easel. A football pitch divided into small squares. Five pounds a square for the Floodlight Fund.

I was so enchanted with the idea of this beautiful little ground floodlit that I found a committee member and donated a fiver. A week later I had a phone call from the Chairman asking if I would become President. Apparently it costs far more than a fiver to get a title these days. I gladly accepted thinking all I would have to do was turn out and give out the prizes at the annual dinner. How wrong can you be. I made the cardinal error of going to another match, then another one, then an away one. I was hooked. It has been Hampton home and away ever since. I haven't seen more than a dozen live professional games since then. Frankly if Hampton are playing Staines Town I wouldn't cross the road to watch Chelsea play Manchester United.

Hampton (and Richmond Borough as they are now) competed for many seasons in the Isthmian League and I have never enjoyed my football more. Until 1967 my experience of non-league was confined to occasional visits to my then local club Tooting and Mitcham at Sandy Lane where I came across a strange phenomenon. Every time a player hoofed a ball out of the ground the cry went up "Redhill!" Evidently a club famed for not messing about when defending. Thirty years later I was writing a film in Hollywood and went to the Los Angeles Coliseum to watch the Los Angeles Wolves play the San Francisco Bears in the North American Soccer League. Ten minutes in the San Francisco left back hoisted the ball into the stand whereupon a Mexican-American in front of me stood up and shouted "Redhill!" I always wondered if he knew why.

Another thing I shall never forget. I was there when the first ever Corinthian-Casual was sent off, this over seventy years after they were founded. It was against Hampton again at Sandy Lane. The then player manager Chris Kilby was sent off after fouling Hampton's Perry Tunesi, whereupon the Casuals had a quick committee meeting in the stand and the secretary went down to meet the culprit just as he reached the touchline ... and sacked him. In the boardroom afterwards the committee were beside themselves with shame. The magnificent Tiny, their Chairman, said he would have rather lost ten-nil than have such a calumny occur. Finally they apologised to the referee for his having to send one of their players off. Surely only in the Isthmian League.

I also love the other stories I have heard about the Casuals. This may be apocryphal – one of the Four Horsemen – but I was told that in the old days if they were awarded a penalty they were instructed to put it wide, and if in the unlikely event they conceded a penalty the goalkeeper was told to leave his goal and give an undefended kick. Sad to think that if they did that these days there would probably be a yellow card for dissent or for bringing the game into disrepute. I am afraid not all change is for the best.

And so a hundred years of Isthmian League football has come and gone. I have been privileged to watch a goodly part of it. I only wish I could watch the next hundred years. Obviously things will change, clubs will come and go, but I just hope that in the year 2105 when a defender boots a ball over the stand someone will stand up and shout "Redhill!"

CHAPTER ONE

A Concise History

It is not easy to summarise 100 years of any history into a few thousand words but over the next few pages we attempt to give an overview of what has happened to the League since the first meeting at Winchester House (pictured) in London up to the 100th season of the League.

Winchester House, Old Broad Street, where the League held its meetings from 1905 to 1965

In the late 19th century, the only competitive games for amateur clubs in the south of England came in the form of various cup competitions, with the majority of other fixtures being friendlies. At the suggestion of three stalwarts of the amateur game, Thomas Kirkup, Secretary of the London Football Association, George Clark, Honorary Treasurer of Ilford Football Club, and Frank Evans, Honorary Secretary of Clapton Football Club, a meeting was held at Winchester House, Old Broad Street, London, with representatives of the Casuals, Civil Service, Clapton, Ealing Association, Ilford, and London Caledonians to consider the formation of a strong amateur league. The representatives were all in favour and the Isthmian Football League was formed on 8 March 1905 and received official Football Association sanction on 31 March. The first letter from Mr Kirkup had been sent on 8 February, the first meeting held on 16 February and a second meeting held six days later to approve the proposal in principle. At a third meeting on 8 March Frank Evans of Clapton proposed, and Mr J M M Dallas of Civil Service seconded the formation of the League. A 51-day gestation period – almost certainly not achievable in the 21st century!

The League's motto then – as it remains today – was *honor sufficit* or "the honour suffices". In keeping with this ethos, it was agreed that no cup should be awarded to the champions, nor would there be any medals for players. Honour was the only reward. The League has always considered itself to be innovative and membership was by invitation only. It was a single division league and remained that way for almost seven decades. Continuity of membership was thus ensured.

STATEMENT OF ACCOUNTS, 1905-6.

RECEIPTS.	£	s.	d.	EXPENDITURE	£	s.	d.
Subscriptions— Six Clubs at £2 2s. od.	12	12	0	Hire of Room for Meetings .. .	1	0	0
				Printing and Stationery	5	0	1
				Postages and Petty Cash	1	2	3
				Balance—Cash in hands of Hon. Treas.	5	9	8
	£12	12	0		£12	12	0

HENRY J. HUBAND, *Hon. Treasurer.*

Examined with Vouchers and found correct—
O. O. HAYWARD (Clapton) } *Auditors.*
E. L. HOLLAND (Civil Service) }
16th May, 1906.

TABLE OF RESULTS, 1905-6.

	Played.	Won.	Drawn.	Lost.	Goals For.	Goals Agst.	Points.
London Caledonians	10	7	1	2	25	8	15
Clapton	10	6	1	3	11	13	13
Casuals	10	3	4	3	14	14	10
Civil Service	10	4	1	5	16	20	9
Ealing	10	3	2	5	15	19	8
Ilford	10	1	3	6	5	12	5

Financial and playing results for the inaugural season - not the most complex set of accounts and just £2.10 to play!

The first season went without undue problems, with London Caledonians becoming the inaugural champions. However, a major problem arose in the spring of 1907 when the Surrey County FA, Middlesex County FA and Football Association Council forced county associations to take over the government of professional clubs as well as amateur ones. This was met with stern resistance in the south of England and, in July 1907, the Amateur Football Association (later called Alliance) was formed to protect what the amateur clubs considered their rights. The AFA divorced itself from the other county associations and they decreed that their member clubs would not be allowed to play against professional clubs or even any amateur clubs still affiliated to the original FA. The upshot was that before the League's third season, three clubs, the Casuals, Civil Service and Ealing Association – who had all joined the AFA – resigned from the League. Their places were taken by Dulwich Hamlet, Oxford City and West Norwood *(below)*.

A season later, for 1908–09, the League decided to increase its membership to ten clubs and Bromley, Leytonstone, Nunhead and Shepherd's Bush accepted invitations to join. Bromley won the championship in their first two seasons, but resigned when asked to do so at the end of their third season. They had used a re-instated professional player which was not permitted at that time. Two clubs, Tunbridge Wells and Woking, accepted invitations to join the League for 1911–12, thereby increasing the membership to 11 clubs, a figure that remained constant until the outbreak of the First World War in 1914, although New Crusaders did replace Tunbridge Wells for the 1913–14 season. In the months before the First World War, the dispute between The FA and the AFA was resolved. On the pitch, London Caledonians completed a hat-trick of championships, a feat that would not be repeated until after the Second World War. The League was suspended on 4 September 1914 as a result of the outbreak of war.

GREENLEES CLAYMORE Rare Old Scotch WHISKY
Tired Natures Sweet Restorer.

ROBERT BALDWIN,
Stationer, Tobacconist & Newsagent

AGENT FOR—
John Bull Fountpens
" Telesco " Loose Leaf Books.
Hieratica Pads and Stationery.
etc., etc.

Always in Stock, a good selection of—
Letter Cases.
Note Cases.
Picture Post Cards.
Birthday Cards, etc., etc.

All Popular Brands of Cigarettes, Tobaccos & Cigars in Stock. A nice selection of Novels to choose from

669 HIGH ROAD, 669
Leytonstone, E. 11. (CLOSE TO GROUND).

M. SMITH,
Pork and Beef Butcher,
467, High Road,
LEYTONSTONE.

Best Quality Meat obtainable.
All Small Goods made on the Premises.

CLUB NOTES.

After an encouraging win over Luton Amateurs by 2-0, (A. Moule scoring the first goal of the season, and F. Spooner being responsible for the other point), we to-day turn our attention to the Isthmian League programme, and have Woking as visitors. There is sure to be a keen struggle for victory.

Unfortunately, the first match did not pass off without mishap, for G. Hardie was injured, and is unable to play to-day. We hope he will speedily recover.

Our Reserve Team made a good start last Saturday, and beat West Green by 1-0. To-day they are at Woking, and we wish them good luck. Their first home League game is, *v.* Oxford City Reserves, on September 20th.

Next Saturday we are at home to Civil Service in the League, and on Monday, Sept. 15th, at 5-30, we are at home to Ilford in the London Challenge Cup. Both these games should prove very attractive.

SATURDAY, SEPTEMBER 6th, 1919. Kick-off 3.30 p.m.

LEYTONSTONE v. WOKING
ISTHMIAN LEAGUE.

LEYTONSTONE.

RIGHT] GOAL. [LEFT
J. Munday
P. R. Ward S. F. Kennerley
F. H. Dunk J. E. Payne P. G. Burtenshaw
W. L. Kenhope A. S. Moule F. W. Spooner L. Coxhead J. C. Monaghan

O

E. Hodgeman H. Gowler G. Cochran G. Darcy G. H. Over
F. Cæsar H. J. Crane R. Rayer
F. E. Smith T. Bowey
H. J. Phillips
LEFT] GOAL. [RIGHT

WOKING.

Referee ... ... Mr. J. C. O'NEILL.

ISTHMIAN LEAGUE TABLES.

	Pld.	W.	D.	L.	Goals For	Goals Agt.	Pts.
Casuals	...	...	...	...	...	...	...
Civil Service ...	...	...	...	...	...	...	...
Clapton	...	...	...	...	...	...	...
Dulwich Hamlet	...	...	...	...	...	...	...
Ilford	...	...	...	...	...	...	...
Leytonstone ..	...	...	...	...	...	...	...
Lon. Caledonians	...	...	...	...	...	...	...
Nunhead ...	...	...	...	...	...	...	...
Oxford City ...	...	...	...	...	...	...	...
Tufnell Park ...	...	...	...	...	...	...	...
West Norwood ...	...	...	...	...	...	...	...
Woking	...	...	...	...	...	...	...

RESERVES SECTION.

	Pld.	W.	D.	L.	Goals For	Goals Agt.	Pts.
Civil Service	...	...	...	...	...	...	...
Clapton	...	...	...	...	...	...	...
Dulwich Hamlet	...	...	...	...	...	...	...
Ilford	...	...	...	...	...	...	...
Leytonstone ...	...	...	...	...	...	...	...
Lon. Caledonians	...	...	...	...	...	...	...
Nunhead ...	...	...	...	...	...	...	...
Oxford City ...	...	...	...	...	...	...	...
Tufnell Park ...	...	...	...	...	...	...	...
West Norwood ...	...	...	...	...	...	...	...
Woking	...	...	...	...	...	...	...

TOM SCOTT,
Hairdresser and Tobacconist,
448, HIGH ROAD,
LEYTONSTONE.
A few doors past the Fire Station.

"The BELL" INN,
HIGH ROAD, LEYTONSTONE.
(Adjoining the Fire Station).
Proprietor - - F. HILL.
HANDSOME CLUB AND CONCERT ROOM.
WINES AND SPIRITS OF THE BEST QUALITY.

GOSSLING & CO.,
Bespoke Tailors,
550, High Road,
LEYTONSTONE.
A. J. GOSSLING. G. H. KETTLE.
'Phone— Wanstead 381.

A programme from the start of the first season after the Great War - the game finished as a 2-2 draw

For the first full post-war season, 1919–20, the Isthmian League was much changed, with both New Crusaders and Shepherd's Bush deciding not to compete. Their places were taken by Casuals and Civil Service, who were both free to return to League competition after resolution of the AFA dispute, and Tufnell Park whose acceptance made the League a more manageable 12 clubs. Two more clubs arrived for the 1921–22 season, Wimbledon and Wycombe Wanderers, ensuring the League now had 14 members and a 26-match season. After St. Albans City had replaced West Norwood for 1923–24, the League enjoyed remarkable stability for 15 years. Kingstonian's arrival, following the departure of Civil Service for 1929–30, was the only change in membership until just before the Second World War.

In 1939, Casuals merged with Corinthians to form Corinthian-Casuals – the merged club continuing their membership of the League – and Romford as well as Walthamstow Avenue were elected to bring the membership to a total of 16 clubs. The 1939–40 season was brought to a premature halt after eight matches due to the declaration of war on 3 September 1939, almost exactly 25 years to the day that the League competition had been suspended in 1914.

The first post-Second World War season saw the League operating with the same number of Clubs as before the election of Romford and Walthamstow Avenue in 1939, namely 14. London Caledonians – six times champions – and Nunhead – twice winners – were not members. London Caledonians had actually resigned in July 1939 as a result of not being able to find a suitable ground on which to play. Sadly, Nunhead's Ivydale Road ground had been requisitioned for the War effort and their lease had expired during the hostilities. They were unable to find alternative accommodation.

The post-Second World War era was the heyday of amateur football and if the Northern League was where the cream of the northern clubs played, then the Isthmian League was the same in the south, although the Athenian League had a number of very strong clubs. However, after 1951–52, when Leytonstone completed a hat-trick of championships – and seven in nine playing seasons – Tufnell Park became the first Isthmian League club not to be re-elected after finishing at the foot of the table. They were replaced by Barking, while Bromley rejoined the League. This made for a rather unsatisfactory 15-strong set-up, a situation that was remedied by the 1956 arrival of Tooting & Mitcham United. At the end of the 1959–60 season, Romford elected to turn professional and their place in the League was taken by Maidstone United.

For the 1963–64 season, membership was increased to 20 with the addition of four of the strongest clubs from the Athenian League: Enfield, Hendon, Hitchin Town and Sutton United. After winning the championship that season, Wimbledon elected to turn professional and joined the Southern League and Wealdstone became the latest club from the Athenian League to transfer to the Isthmian. Membership then remained fairly static until 1971 when Maidstone United and Wealdstone turned professional, joining the Southern League, and were replaced by three more clubs from the Athenian League – Bishop's Stortford, Hayes and Walton & Hersham. In 1972 Leatherhead were admitted to increase membership to 22 clubs.

The Isthmian League remained innovative and at a Council Meeting held on 8 December 1972 a resolution was passed to introduce a second division with promotion and relegation for season 1973–74, the last season of the amateur/professional divide. At the same time, the League announced a sponsorship deal with tobacco company Rothmans and the League became known as the Rothmans Isthmian League. As a new idea to reward attacking football, Isthmian Clubs received a bonus – £40 – for any League victory by three goals or more. There was also prize money based on finishing positions in the table, but this came on the understanding that players did not misbehave. It seems incredible to those new to football, but in 1973–74, a Club that collected five cautions and a dismissal over the whole 42-game season would lose all prize money. Under Rothmans' patronage, the League was the first to adopt three points for a win and the first to use goal difference instead of goal average.

Rothmans' sponsorship ended after three seasons, and the League has been able to have a backer every season since. Michael Lawrie & Partners were the first to take on title sponsorship after Rothmans, followed by Berger Paints, Servowarm, Vauxhall, Diadora, ICIS and current sponsors Ryman. As part of their deal Vauxhall and the Isthmian League agreed to drop the Isthmian name from the League title. However, for ease of comprehension, generic names for the leagues (Southern, Northern Premier, Alliance/Conference, etc.) are used throughout this narrative.

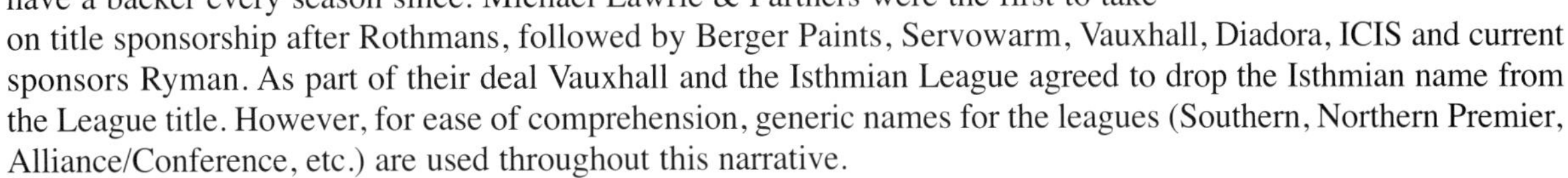

In 1974, the League created the Subsidiary Cup for the 16 Clubs in the new second division to give those Clubs additional matches. The following season the Cup was open to Clubs in Division One, on a voluntary basis (only ten clubs opted for the competition), but in its third season, and every season since, the League Cup Competition has been compulsory for all Clubs. For the 1977–78 season, this competition had its own sponsor, the electronics company Hitachi, and became known as The Hitachi Cup.

The League, whose second division had grown gradually to reach 22 clubs, expanded further in 1977–78, with a third division added. It was decided to rename the divisions Premier, One and Two, an innovation that was still 15 years away in the Football League.

Away from the Isthmian League, there was a ground-breaking change in non-league football. In 1979, the Northern Premier League and the Southern Football League provided the 20 Clubs which, under the leadership of Jim Thompson of Maidstone United, formed the Alliance Premier Football League, now known as the Football Conference. Initially, Isthmian Clubs did not join the new Competition but in 1981 Dagenham and Enfield joined to make their numbers up to 22. Subsequently the League became part of the pyramid of Non League Football with the proviso that promotion was not compulsory but would be available to any Club finishing in the top three places. No Club took promotion until 1985 when Wycombe Wanderers, finishing in third place behind Sutton United and Worthing, became the first Isthmian Club to join the Alliance.

Gradually the availability of promotion was restricted to only the Champion Club but in most years the League provided a club and received one back by relegation. As much as there was a wind of change in the organisation of football on a national scale, so there was inside the Isthmian League. From 1905 up to 1982 a Council of Clubs had existed, to which each member club contributed one delegate with one vote. The first change came about when the League expanded in 1977 to three divisions and the Clubs in the bottom division were only granted Associate Member status without full voting rights.

In 1981 the Council was disbanded in favour of a Management Committee comprising the Officers of the League and eight senior representatives of Full Member Clubs. This management structure remained in place until 1989 when the League incorporated as a Limited Company with the result that the Management Committee members became directors. The Isthmian League was the first league apart from the Football League to protect its Clubs by incorporation. The reasoning behind this was the increasingly litigious nature of society which could have resulted in the bankruptcy of the League or its Clubs.

At the same time the Isthmian League faced the simple reality that membership by invitation was no longer possible. Prior to this time, aspiring clubs had to make application for membership and some, like Farnborough Town FC, created memorable applications. There would be promotion and relegation to feeder leagues in the same way that there was between the divisions inside the League. At the end of the 1982–83 season, Harwich and Parkeston became the first Isthmian League club to be relegated. It went to the Athenian League. As there was a vacancy in the League only one club, St. Albans City, was relegated from Division One to Division Two. Newbury Town and Grays Athletic were promoted from the Athenian League to ensure 66 clubs competed in 1983–84. The arrangement with the Athenians did not last for long because during the following season they decided to go into "hibernation" and the Isthmian League expanded further in 1984–85 by regionalising its second division.

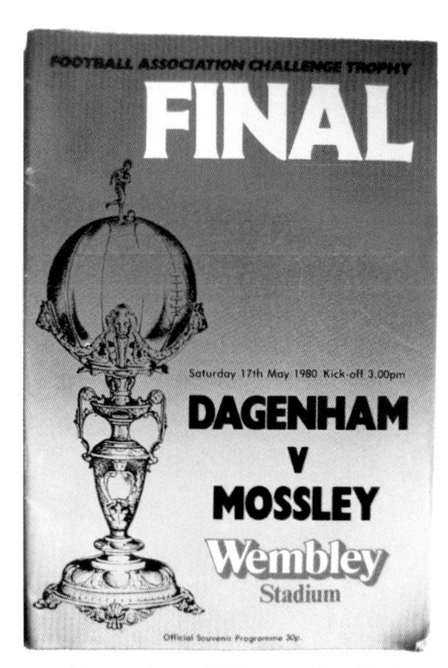

Dagenham FC were the first Isthmian winners of The FA Trophy.

Twenty clubs were added, 15 from the Athenian League, together with five clubs from various County Leagues. The League initiated a ground grading criterion to provide a standard which the new clubs applying for membership would need to meet. Subsequently all clubs in membership had to achieve the grading relative to their status and the grading was refined from time to time. This was expanded to encompass the whole of non-league football over the years and, today, no promotion is confirmed until the standards are met.

The first club to fall victim to these new standards was Staines Town. They finished 12th in the Premier Division but were demoted at the end of the 1983–84 season because they failed to carry out the requisite improvements. Tooting & Mitcham United were thereby saved from relegation. Corinthian–Casuals, as a merged club who had existed for 45 years without a ground of their own, were forced to resign from the League because they had transgressed the Rule which existed at that time not permitting ground sharing.

As part of the development of the pyramid, the Isthmians accepted feeder leagues. However, as the League had not committed to the pyramid at the outset, the feeder leagues available were the Combined Counties, Essex Senior, London Spartan and South Midlands Leagues. The other regional leagues had previously been accepted as feeders by the Southern Football League.

Changes took place at the bottom of the League in 1984–85 when Chertsey Town were relegated to the Combined Counties League despite the League not having a full complement of Clubs for the following season. A League Rule was hastily introduced to avoid this happening again. Epping Town did not complete their fixtures and became the first club to have their record expunged. Southwick and Vauxhall Motors were newcomers to the League for the 1985–86 season.

During the late eighties, the League introduced a paid administrator in the guise of Clive Moyse, having already appointed Chairman Alan Turvey as a full time Managing Director. In this way the League was able to meet the demands of 88 member clubs in running what they perceived was the best administered league in non-league football.

The regional divisions ended in 1991 when, at the Annual General Meeting that year, the Clubs decided that they would prefer to have four divisions in a straight line. This meant only three clubs would be relegated from Division One. The next few seasons saw remarkable stability with the promotion and relegation system working well at both ends apart from times when ground grading operated against clubs.

At the beginning of the new century attempts were made by the Conference to exclude the Isthmian League from the usual promotion so that they would only have a direct link with the Southern and Northern Premier Leagues. This led to a torrid few years and the most dramatic restructuring of football below the Football League since the abolition of the amateur player. The pyramid was restructured. In anticipation of this, and to ensure that the Isthmian Clubs were treated the same as their sister Clubs in the Southern League, the League voted to introduce regionalised divisions again, but this time at Division One level, with one major change: the Premier and both Division Ones would have 24 clubs – all of whom were Full Members – playing a 46-game campaign, while Division Two, who would be Associate Members with limited voting rights, had a membership of only 16 clubs.

Thus Divisions One and Two were reformed as North and South divisions. Division Two was now on an equal footing with the senior divisions of the three feeder leagues, the newly merged Spartan South Midlands, Essex Senior and Combined Counties Leagues. Promotion and relegation criteria were again amended, with the bottom four in the Premier Division going into one of the Division Ones, while the top two in both Division One North and South went up. The two lowest placed clubs in each of the regionalised divisions were replaced by the top two Clubs in Division Two and two Clubs from the remaining three feeder leagues. There was no relegation from Division Two.

In fact the regionalised Divisions One only lasted two seasons. In the background were attempts by the Football Conference to introduce a Second Division between their one Division of 22 clubs and the Premier Divisions of the Isthmian, Northern Premier and Southern Leagues. Many different proposals were put forward by various interested parties and The FA was called upon to make decisions.

The Isthmian League Board felt that the decisions being made were not in the best interests of the League, particularly doing away with the tripartite feeder structure involving the Isthmian League with their sister leagues, the Southern and Northern Premier Leagues. Initially the League was successful in persuading The FA not to change the structure but the Chairman of the relevant FA Committee, Alan Burbidge, was determined to

Ryman
football league
NEWS RELEASE

STATEMENT TO THE NON LEAGUE NEWSPAPER

The League has followed with interest the public debate which has ensued since the Football Conference's announcement on the 17th July 2000 concerning the restructuring of football.

The League are concerned and disappointed at some of the comments attributed to persons who are senior administrators in other leagues when interviewed on this matter.

To date the League has received no information from either the Football Conference, the Northern Premier League or the Southern Football League save for the nine line statement issued by the Conference. The Isthmian League understands no further information has been received by the Football Association.

On learning that a meeting of the three other leagues had been called for the 10th August the Chairman of the Isthmian League did telephone the Chairman of the Football Conference on the 1st August to ask for the opportunity to be in attendance. Subsequently he wrote on the 8th August after receiving no response. A letter was received on the 14th August, four days after the meeting, stating the other leagues did not deem it appropriate for the Isthmian League to be represented.

The League has long recognised the need for change, particularly with regard to league boundaries, and has been a prime mover in the debates on these matters. At meetings held during the 1999-2000 Season it was agreed by all parties that change was needed. After the Football Conference withdrew from the National Joint Liaison Committee the Isthmian, Northern Premier and Southern Leagues continued the discussions and agreed that this level of football would be best served by three leagues – based on the North, Midlands/South West and South East feeding into the Football Conference. It would now appear the other two leagues have changed their minds on this issue, but have given the Isthmian League no reasons why they have gone back on the original agreement. While the League is still prepared to meet with the other leagues to continue discussions it would appear the issue will be best dealt with by the Football Association – which is the ruling body of football in this country.

The actions proposed by the other leagues could have a devastating effect on football outside the Football League throughout the country. The need for a proper airing of all the issues is paramount as clubs and leagues plan for the future. Already the uncertainty of recent weeks is affecting clubs' chances of retaining existing sponsors and recruiting new ones.

The League firmly believes that any changes should be by evolution and not revolution. The support from other competitions – many outside the League's own feeder system – has been heartening. The Isthmian Management Committee fervently hopes full and frank discussions can see this matter resolved in the best interests of the game when the views of all involved have been made known. The League awaits further details of the proposals at the earliest opportunity, but cannot comment further on a plan on which it does not have the full facts.

ENDS 16th August 2000

Issued on behalf of the Isthmian League Management Committee
Any enquiries to Chairman and Managing Director Alan Turvey, telephone 01256 461789

www.isthmian.co.uk www.ryman.co.uk

push through a savage restructuring which would see more than 40 clubs forcibly moved from membership of the Isthmian League.

The Conference did not give up their fight and eventually a decision was taken to have a National Division of the Conference with two regionalised divisions underneath into which the three Premier Divisions of the three feeders would promote clubs.

A fourth step would exist with four divisions and beneath that there would be three further 'steps' as each level would now be known, to complete the structure of non league football. The Isthmian League was so incensed by what they saw as a plan to destroy the League that they took every step they could to oppose the plans and eventually went to an arbitration in the spring of 2004 but the Panel ruled against the League and so the new structure was put into place for season 2004–05, the 100th of the Isthmian Football League. Not an auspicious way in which to commemorate the Centenary of the League but perhaps a foundation for the next hundred years...

The original League Rules, from the first handbook, are now reproduced.

11

Rules.

1.—This Combination of Clubs shall be called the "ISTHMIAN FOOTBALL LEAGUE," and shall consist of not more than six (6) Amateur Clubs affiliated to an Association recognized by the Football Association.

2.—The Combination shall be governed by a Council consisting of a President, Chairman, Honorary Secretary, and Treasurer, and the Acting-Secretary of each Club. The President, Chairman, and Honorary Secretary and Treasurer need not be connected in any way with the Clubs constituting the Combination.

3.—The Annual General Meeting shall be held in April or May of each year, at which meeting the President, Chairman, Honorary Secretary and Treasurer, Appeals Committee, and Auditors shall be elected. Each Club shall be entitled to send two (2) representative members who shall have the power by a majority to exclude from the competition any Club whose conduct has in their opinion been objectionable. Special general meetings shall be convened at any time by order of the Council, or upon a requisition signed by the Secretaries of not less than three (3) Clubs forming the Combination.

4.—The annual subscription shall be Two Guineas (£2 2s.), payable immediately upon election. The Council may also call upon each Club to contribute equally such sum as may be necessary to meet any deficiency at the end

12

of the season. Any Club withdrawing from the Combination after accepting election at the annual meeting shall be held responsible for a share of any deficit for the season in question in the same proportion as those left in.

5.—No player shall be allowed to play for more than one competing Club in the Combination during any one season without the consent of the Council. Except during the months of September and October each player must have been a recognized playing member of the Club on behalf of which he proposes to compete for at least 28 days, or shall have previously played twice for his Club in the current season. A playing member is one who has been elected by his Club for at least twenty-eight days. The twenty-eight days' qualification is not necessary in the case of Clubs whose players consist solely of old boys of any public school. No reinstated professional shall be eligible to compete in the Combination save and except in cases where such player was a member of a competing Club previous to the 1st May, 1905. Any Club playing an ineligible man may have two (2) points deducted from its score, and shall also be liable to such fines as the Council may inflict.

6.—Where possible all dates for matches shall be arranged by mutual consent, including re-arranged dates from causes over which neither Club has control, failing which the Council shall decide. Priority of fixture shall be given to all Cup Competitions, and no Club shall be compelled to arrange for any match to

13

be played during the months of September or April, or upon any public holiday. Home and home matches shall be played, and each Club shall take its own gate receipts and pay its own expenses.

7.—All matches shall be played according to the laws of the game, and the Rules, Regulations and Bye-Laws of the Football Association. By arrangement between the Captains the duration of each match may be reduced to a period of not less than one hour, such arrangement to be notified to the Referee before the match.

8.—At the end of each season the Club scoring the highest number of points shall be declared the Champion Club. Should two (2) or more Clubs gain an equal number of points they shall, if practicable, meet on a neutral ground, to be selected by the Council for the purpose of deciding the Championship. The nett proceeds of such matches shall be divided in the following proportion, viz., two-thirds equally between the competing Clubs and one-third to the funds of the Combination. Should the above course be impracticable, the Championship shall be decided by goal average, the method of scoring in all matches shall be two (2) points for a win and one (1) for a draw. No cup, shield, medal or other trophy shall be provided or presented by the Combination.

9.—At the end of each season the two (2) Clubs which have scored the least number of points shall retire, but shall be eligible for re-election. Any club, other than the last two

14

(2), which shall be desirous of retiring from the Combination at the close of any season shall give written notice of such intention at least 28 days prior to the Annual General Meeting.

10.—Each Club must send the result of their matches to the Honorary Secretary, together with the names and initials of the players competing therein, within three (3) days of each match.

11.—Referees for all matches shall be appointed by the Council from an approved list to be kept by the Secretary. The Referee, in conjunction with the two Captains, shall have the power to decide as to the fit condition of the ground in all matches. In the event of the appointed Referee failing to appear the Captain may agree to a substitute on the field. The Referee's reasonable and actual out-of-pocket expenses, not exceeding seven shillings and sixpence (7/6), shall be defrayed by the home Club. No past or present member of any of the Clubs shall be eligible to officiate as Referee in any match.

12.—All protests, claims and complaints must be forwarded to the Honorary Secretary in duplicate, accompanied by a fee of ten shillings (10/-), within seven days of the match taking place, and shall be heard and determined by the Council.

13.—The Annual Balance Sheet of the Combination, duly audited, shall be presented at the Annual General Meeting, and a copy of such balance sheet shall be sent with the notice convening the meeting.

15

14.—The Secretary and Treasurer of each Club in the Combination shall sign the following agreement within one week of election :—

"We, the undersigned representatives of the .... Football Club do hereby agree on behalf of the said Club to become members of the 'ISTHMIAN FOOTBALL LEAGUE,' to conform to the Rules and Regulations of the Combination, and to abide by all decisions of the Council, subject to an appeal being made within five days to the Appeals Committee, such appeal to be accompanied by a deposit of £1 1s., which may be forfeited should the appeal be unsuccessful."

Signed,

.... *Treasurer.*

.... *Secretary.*

15.—No alteration shall be made to the Rules except at the Annual Meeting, or at a meeting specially convened for the purpose, and fourteen (14) days' notice must be given to the Honorary Secretary of any proposed alteration or addition, the same to be forwarded to each Club at least seven (7) days prior to the meeting.

16.—The Council shall have power to deal with any matters relating to the Combination as they think fit, and to provide for any contingency that may arise.

17.—All communications must be addressed to the Honorary Secretary and Treasurer, who shall conduct the correspondence of the Council.

The current League Rules are now in a form standardised with all other leagues outside the Football League and now fill more than 30 A5 pages!

CHAPTER TWO

Founder Member Clubs - The Super Six

The League was instituted on 8 March 1905 and officially sanctioned on 31 March 1905 with the first matches played on 9 September 1905. The Officers for 1905–06 were the President, Rt Hon Alfred Lyttleton, KC, MP; the Chairman, Percy A Timbs; the Hon Secretary and Treasurer, Henry J Huband; the Auditors, O O Hayward of Clapton and E L Holland of Civil Service. A Board of Appeal was established with three members of The Football Association: G S Sherrington, T H Kirkup and N Malcomson.

The three founders of the League were acknowledged to be Thomas Kirkup, Secretary of the London Football Association, George J Clarke of Ilford FC and Frank Evans of Clapton FC.

The six founder member Clubs which competed for the first Championship in 1905 were Casuals, Civil Service, Clapton, Ealing Association, Ilford and London Caledonians. Details of these Clubs are shown below and taken from the first handbook with a history of each Club.

THE CASUALS

Ground - Tufnell Park
Nearest Station - Junction Road (Midland R.)
Colours - Chocolate and Pink
Hon Secretary - S L King, The Elms, Rickmansworth

The Casuals FC can trace their existence back to 17 January 1878 when they encountered Upton Park in a friendly fixture, which they lost 2–0. Three further games can be traced in that initial season, followed by possibly eight the following season. The club appears to have been run on a very 'casual' basis at this point. A couple of games at the start of 1880–81 are all that can be traced until 1883 when the club was either reformed or established. An Old Etonian, F Bickley, and T W Blenkiron, a Cambridge Blue and Old Carthusian, are credited with being founder members and it is stated in an early report in the Charterhouse School magazine that it was a club for the old boys of Eton and Charterhouse. The famous chocolate and pink colours were adopted as they were Bickley's racing colours.

The Club, basing itself at Wandsworth Common, had its headquarters at the Surrey Hotel which still exists today, and looked strong from an organisational point of view. Casuals grew in strength over the following years and during 1886–87 the club first made an impact on the amateur football scene and reached the London Charity Cup final, losing 3–0 to the Swifts at The Oval. The same week, however, the club became joint holders of the London Senior Cup when, following a 1–1 draw against Old Westminsters, the replay was called off in farcical circumstances. Despite both teams being ready and willing to play, the game could not go ahead as someone had forgotten one vital ingredient ... the ball!! In 1887–88, Casuals again made both London FA finals losing what were both rematches from 1887. However, Casuals would win the London Charity Cup in 1891, 1894 and 1897.

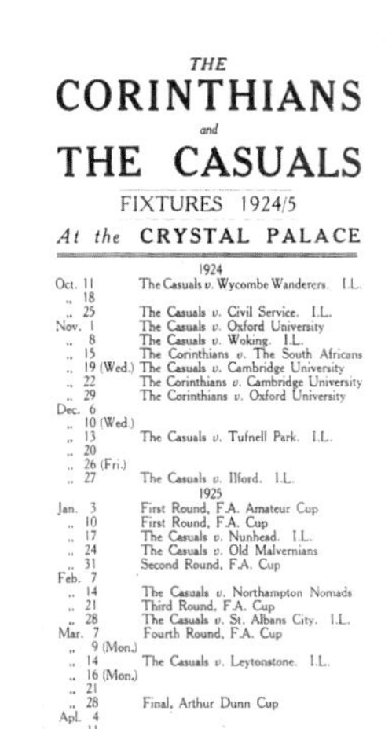
THE
CORINTHIANS
and
THE CASUALS
FIXTURES 1924/5
At the CRYSTAL PALACE

	1924
Oct. 11	The Casuals v. Wycombe Wanderers. I.L.
.. 18	
.. 25	The Casuals v. Civil Service. I.L.
Nov. 1	The Casuals v. Oxford University
.. 8	The Casuals v. Woking. I.L.
.. 15	The Corinthians v. The South Africans
.. 19 (Wed.)	The Casuals v. Cambridge University
.. 22	The Corinthians v. Cambridge University
.. 29	The Corinthians v. Oxford University
Dec. 6	
.. 10 (Wed.)	
.. 13	The Casuals v. Tufnell Park. I.L.
.. 20	
.. 26 (Fri.)	
.. 27	The Casuals v. Ilford. I.L.
	1925
Jan. 3	First Round, F.A. Amateur Cup
.. 10	First Round, F.A. Cup
.. 17	The Casuals v. Nunhead. I.L.
.. 24	The Casuals v. Old Malvernians
.. 31	Second Round, F.A. Cup
Feb. 7	
.. 14	The Casuals v. Northampton Nomads
.. 21	Third Round, F.A. Cup
.. 28	The Casuals v. St. Albans City. I.L.
Mar. 7	Fourth Round, F.A. Cup
.. 9 (Mon.)	
.. 14	The Casuals v. Leytonstone. I.L.
.. 16 (Mon.)	
.. 21	
.. 28	Final, Arthur Dunn Cup
Apl. 4	
.. 11	
.. 18	The Casuals v. Clapton. I.L.
.. 25	
May 2	The Casuals v. Oxford City. I.L.

(I.L. Denotes Isthmian League Match)

Ground Members Tickets admit to the Ground and Seats for all Corinthian and Casuals Matches (Cup Ties excepted). **PRICE, ONE GUINEA** (No Tax). All enquiries and applications for Tickets, which must be accompanied by a remittance, must be made to—
The Assistant Secretary, Corinthian F.C., Crystal Palace, S.E. 19

The Corinthian F.C. will take part in the F.A. Cup Competition and the Casuals F.C. in the F.A. Amateur Cup, Surrey Senior Cup, and the London Charity Cup Competitions.

Other Corinthian Matches with Prominent League Clubs will also be arranged

E. C. BAMBRIDGE, Hon. Sec., Corinthian F.C.
S. F. HEPBURN, Hon. Sec., The Casuals F.C.

In The FA Cup, the Club received a bye to the first round in 1890–91 – whereupon Aston Villa inflicted the club's record defeat, 13–1 – and 1891–92 losing to Stoke. In 1892–93, after battling through all the qualifying rounds, the club went out to Nottingham Forest 4–0. The most impressive achievement of this period was reaching the final of the inaugural FA Amateur Cup, losing by the odd goal in three to old adversaries Old Carthusians.

The new century started well for the Casuals as the club lifted the London Charity Cup in 1901, defeating Clapton in the final. Clapton got their revenge in the final of 1903, before Casuals defeated them in the finals of 1904 and 1905. In April 1905 the Casuals toured what would become Czechoslovakia and Hungary, defeating Slavia Prague and MTK of Budapest and winning all seven games played.

In 1905, Casuals embarked on an exciting new venture, league football, when they became founder members of the Isthmian League and at the same time relocated to a new ground at Junction Road, Tufnell Park. Casuals did not set the new League alight although during this time they were joint winners of the London Charity Cup in 1907 and runners up in 1906. Casuals did however, play a major part in the split of 1907 which saw a number of clubs leaving the jurisdiction of The FA after a dispute about professionalism and founding the Amateur Football Alliance and the Southern Amateur League. During their seven years in the top flight of the Southern Amateur League the Casuals' best placing was runners up in 1914, but they lifted the AFA Senior Cup twice in 1908 and 1913 and reached the final in 1909 and 1911.

Just prior to World War One, the split was resolved and Casuals rejoined the Isthmian League. On the resumption of organised football following the hostilities, M.M. Morgan-Owen called a meeting which led to the club restarting for the 1919–20 season, playing at the County Ground in Leyton. The club struggled, not helped by the constant relocation as they played at East Molesey Cricket Club in 1920–21 and St Joseph's Road, Guildford in 1921–22, before spending three years at the Crystal Palace *(pictured left is the team from the first game)* where possibly the first ground share took place as the Club shared with The Corinthians. The move to the old cup final ground, however, marked a resurgence in the club's fortunes under the guidance of secretary H.F. Dubuis and captain Miles Howell, both pictured in the team above. In 1923 the Casuals visited Spain and played two games against Atletico Bilbao, losing the first game 2–4 before sharing eight goals in the rematch.

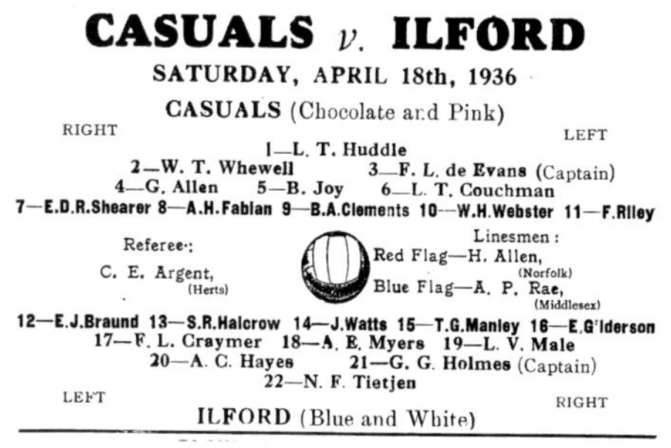

In 1925, mainly due to falling attendances at the Crystal Palace the club relocated to Richmond Road, the home of Kingstonian. This marked a run where the club was competitive for the last few years of the 1920s, before becoming a solid outfit for the majority of the 1930s. In 1926 the Casuals toured Portugal and held Benfica and Sporting Lisbon to draws. In 1930, Casuals won their first trophy for many years when Nunhead were defeated 2-0 in the Surrey Senior Cup Final. The crowning glory was the 1936 FA Amateur Cup win against Ilford *(teams right)*, with what has been argued to be the finest pre-war cup winning side. The club could call on many fine players during its history and included England internationals whose primary club was the Casuals in A G Topham and R Topham (v Wales 1894), R R Barker (v Wales 1895), F H Ewer (v France and Belgium 1924) and Bernard Joy, the last amateur to be capped by England in 1936.

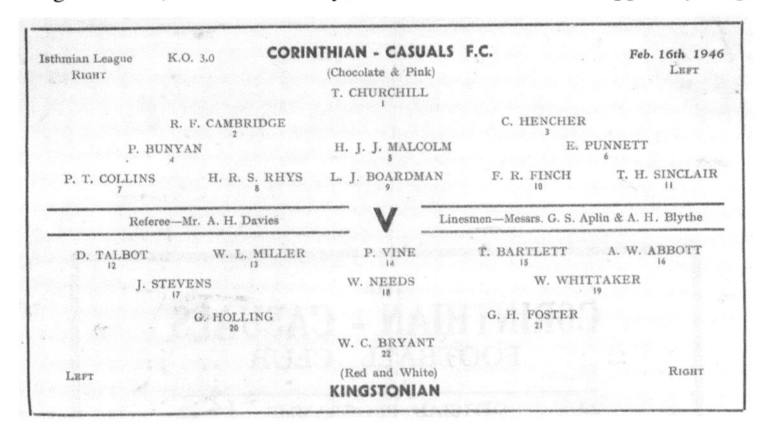

A merger with an even more famous amateur club, Corinthians, took place in 1939 but Corinthian–Casuals played only one game before the outbreak of the war. After the war, they maintained their Isthmian status until 1984 *(left, the team from the first season back)* although with League expansion they were relegated in both 1973 and 1978. In 1954 the club beat Epsom 2–0 to win the Surrey Senior Cup and in 1956 got to the Amateur Cup Final where they drew 1–1 with Bishop Auckland at Wembley. The Bishops won the replay 4–1. A year later another good run in the Amateur Cup saw the club reach the semi-final. After this high point the club slipped into a long decline, a rare moment of success seeing them reach The FA Cup 1st Round in 1965–66 but Watford won 5–1.

Some steady seasons were played out before new ground sharing rules created by the Isthmian League saw Casuals leave in 1983–84. Ironically the year this occurred was their best in quite a while; the club reached the first round proper of The FA Cup, holding Bristol City to a goalless draw at Dulwich Hamlet's ground before losing 4–0 in the replay. They also finished fifth in their division and reached the fifth round of The FA Vase. The club started to rebuild in the London Spartan League, winning the Senior Division in 1986 and being runners up in the Premier Division in 1993. A transfer to the Combined Counties League for 1996–97 saw a runners-up position achieved and with it promotion back to the Isthmian League. The first three seasons back in Isthmian Division Three saw the Club, now with its own ground at Tolworth, finish 10th, 11th and 10th again, winning a Best Disciplinary award in the Ryman League in 1999–2000. A dramatic improvement followed in 2000–01 when the Club missed promotion by three points in a rain affected season. In May 2001 the Casuals toured Brazil again and won the Sao Paulo Athletic Invitation Cup. Thanks to some astute thinking in 2001, the ground was improved to gain a Grade B award and due to circumstances elsewhere, this enabled Corinthian–Casuals to take their place in Isthmian League Division One, their highest standing since 1978.

CIVIL SERVICE

Ground - Kensal Rise
Nearest Station - Kensal Rise (N.L.R.)
Colours - White Shirts with Blue Knickers
Hon Secretary - J M M Dallas, Home Office, SW

The origins of the Civil Service FC are unclear although it appears the club were formed around 1863 with the original body splitting into two parts to become, respectively, the football club and the rugby club.

After a few further seasons the Club is found helping to make history by taking a leading part in the formation of the Football Association, and in 1871 competing in the first contest for The FA Cup with Barnes, Crystal Palace, Clapham Rovers, Donnington School, Hampstead Heathens, Harrow Chequers, Upton Park, The Wanderers, Hitchin Town, Maidenhead, Marlow, Queens Park (Glasgow), Reigate and Royal Engineers, although its name does not appear among the winners.

In 1892 the club was reorganised, a home ground secured at Norbury, and a series of home and away matches arranged with the best London and provincial clubs. After two seasons at Norbury, a ground subsequently held by Dulwich Hamlet was leased, followed after one season at Chiswick Park. In 1901 the Club moved to the White Hart Ground, Neasden. With the exception of The Corinthians it may be said that no club had done more towards the development of the game on the continent than Civil Service FC. From 1901, excluding the War period, the club regularly toured the continent up to 1925, when professional clubs began to take over the round. In recognition of this valuable pioneer work the club has been elected a life honorary member of both Slavia Prague and Real Madrid.

In 1902–03 the club was playing at Edmonton and succeeded in going right through the Amateur Cup up to the Southern semi-final, in which they were defeated by Oxford City in a replay. The Club also reached the divisional final of The FA Cup, losing to the professional club of Luton. In 1903–04 the club was playing at Wood Lane, Shepherd's Bush, and in The FA Cup met the professional club Fulham in the third round, holding them to a draw and only losing in the replay. In 1904–05, the club again reached the divisional final of The FA Cup, losing to Southall, then a professional club. In 1905–06, owing to Wood Lane being required for the Great Exhibition, the club migrated to the National Athletic ground, Kensal Rise.

CIVIL SERVICE
FOOTBALL CLUB.

AVENUE GROUND,
CRICKLEWOOD LANE.

Official Programme - ONE PENNY

The desirability of forming a good amateur league was being felt in London at this time, and the Civil Service FC took a leading part in forming the Isthmian League, the first of many successful amateur leagues in the South. In 1906–07, the Club again had a successful season, reaching the Southern Final of the Amateur Cup, losing to the eventual Cup winners, Clapton, by 1–0, and finishing fourth in the Isthmian League. In the season 1907–08, following the split of the amateur clubs from The FA, the Civil Service FC became members of the Amateur FA in the newly formed Southern Amateur League, which it took a big part in establishing.

From the point up to the time the split was healed in 1914, the club was playing at Stonebridge Park and on the ground of the South West Ham Cricket Club. During this period it had a very successful career, winning in 1909–10 both the AFA Senior and Junior Cups, the Middlesex Cup in 1907–08 and 1912–13, the Southern Amateur League championship in 1911–12 and 1913–14 and the AFA Junior Cup again in 1912–13.

In 1914, the Great War necessitated a complete cessation of the club's activities as practically all its players were members of the Civil Service Rifles and were mobilised at the outbreak of hostilities. After the Armistice, when the question of restarting the club arose, it was found that, owing to war casualties, very few of the old players were available and it is only right at this point to pay a sincere tribute to those of the club who gave to the country of their best in life and limb.

The ground question was acute. The club, however, was invited to rejoin the Isthmian League, the invitation was duly accepted and late in 1919 a fine playing pitch was obtained at the Hurlingham Polo ground. The club for the second time won the AFA Cup in 1919–20, beating Merton 4–2 in the final. For three years the club remained at Hurlingham ground until it moved to Hampstead Town FC on a sharing basis. This arrangement lasted until 1925, when the club became located at the new Civil Service Sports Ground at Chiswick.

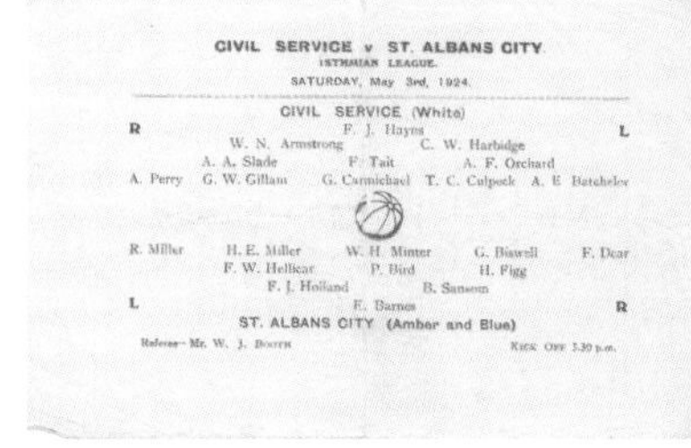

CIVIL SERVICE v ST. ALBANS CITY
ISTHMIAN LEAGUE.
SATURDAY, May 3rd, 1924.

CIVIL SERVICE (White)
R F. J. Hayns L
W. N. Armstrong C. W. Harbidge
A. A. Slade F. Tait A. F. Orchard
A. Perry G. W. Gillam G. Carmichael T. C. Culpeck A. E. Batchelor

R. Miller H. E. Miller W. H. Minter G. Biswell F. Dear
F. W. Hellicar P. Bird H. Figg
F. J. Holland B. Sanson
L F. Barnes R
ST. ALBANS CITY (Amber and Blue)

Kick Off 3.30 p.m.

Up to this point and for the first few seasons at Chiswick, the club had done well in the Isthmian League and had held its own but towards the end of the decade the absence of youth in the Service told its tale and in the season 1929–30 it was thought advisable to resign from the Isthmian League and seek readmission to the Southern Amateur League. Re-election was obtained, but the club was somewhat astonished at being required to compete in the third division. Nothing daunted, however, it set itself the task of getting to the first division in the minimum of two years and duly accomplished the feat together with that of winning a third AFA Cup. It remains in that league to this day.

CLAPTON
Ground - Spotted Dog, Upton
Nearest Station - Forest Gate (G.E.R.)
Colours - Red and White Stripes
Hon Secretary - H Edwards, 96 Lordship Road, Stoke Newington, N

In August 1877, a month after he had left school, Mr W R Davies invited a few young friends to his father's house at 11 Queensdown Road Clapton to discuss the question of forming a football club. The club they formed, the Downs Football Club, was soon renamed the Clapton Football Club. These enthusiasts attending the conference did not dream that they were laying down the foundation stone of an organisation that ten years later was destined to make history in the National Game and play such an inspiring part in the rapid association of Association Football in London and the South of England.

CLAPTON F.C. 1923-24
WINNERS OF F.A. AMATEUR CUP AND JOINT HOLDERS OF LONDON CHARITY CUP 1924

Back Row (L to R): B. Wilcox (Hon. Treas.), J.R. Cully (Vice-Pres.), F. Seymour (Committee), E.J. Caston (Vice-Pres.), W.C. Davis (Vice-Pres.), L.R. Sanderson (Committee), W. Edgley (Vice-Pres.), H. Cramp (Committee)
Middle Row (L to R): R.E. Solomon (Vice-Pres.), F.C.B. Lord (Vice-Pres.), E.F. Smith (Committee), C. Williams, E.A. Penstone, A. Moore, F.J.C. Blake, C.W. Cable, A. Andrews (Committee), A. Todd (Vice-Pres.)
Front Row (L to R): H. Martin (Trainer), A.N, Ryley, W.I. Bryant, S.C.J. Earle (Captain), F.K. Harvey (President), W.V.T. Gibbins, R.E. Potter, W. Barnard
Sitting: H.S. Groves (Hon. Secretary), H.B. Cordell (Hon. Secretary)

Ten years later, in 1888, the club migrated to its present headquarters, The Old Spotted Dog, and introduced a standard of play that created much public enthusiasm and led to many amateur organisations springing into existence in various parts of London. Later, when the friendly match became doomed, the Clapton officials took a leading part in the formation of the old Southern League of which Mr R H Clark, the then Clapton captain, was the first chairman.

It was the establishment of the Southern League, in which Clapton played such a prominent part, that paved the way for the rapid advancement of the game in the South. Apart from sharing in this progress at home, Clapton introduced the game of Association Football abroad by sending a team to Antwerp at Easter 1890 to meet a specially selected Belgium Eleven whom the Clapton players defeated by 7–0.

This was the first occasion on which an English club had visited the Continent and as Mr W A Clark, who was at the time Hon Treasurer, said: "We may take some credit for fostering the game, now so largely followed in most of the countries in Europe". The marked impression created by the skill of the Clapton players in the match against the Belgium Eleven caused a wave of enthusiasm for the game to spread all over the Continent and was followed by invitations from numerous continental clubs to English organisations to visit them at Easter.

The 1890 trip of Clapton to Belgium was the pioneer movement of amateur clubs' Easter tours abroad. While Clapton's endeavours in the cause of the advancement of Association Football, and subsequent achievements in Cup competitions, naturally delighted everyone associated with the club, what Claptonians past and present take the greatest pride in is that throughout the club's 120 plus years it has maintained a high reputation for sporting play.

Clapton FC were members of the Southern Football League from 1894 to 1896 and were then founder members of the Isthmian League in 1905.

They are the only club to remain in continuous membership of the League throughout its first 100 years and while their successes have been few and far between in recent years their enthusiasm and commitment has not shown any decrease.

Pictured right: Isthmian League action from Clapton's match with Romford in early 1950.

BROOKS AND JENNINGS (ROMFORD) FALL AGAINST CLAPTON

EALING ASSOCIATION
Ground - Gunnersbury Avenue, Ealing
Nearest Station - Mill Hill Park (D.R.)
Colours - Red and Green
Hon Secretary - M B Frere, 55 Grange Park, Ealing, W

Ealing Association was established in the autumn of 1891, with matches being played for their first two seasons on Ealing Common. Opponents included Barnet, Clapham Rovers, Vampires and several of the hospital sports clubs. For the 1894–95 season the club obtained a private ground at Gunnersbury Lane, Acton.

In 1895–96, Ealing Association progressed to the competition proper in both the London and Middlesex Cups and the latter trophy was won in 1896–97, when 3rd Grenadier Guards were defeated 2–1 in the final. The Acton ground was lost to building development and in 1898 the club moved to Gunnersbury Avenue, Ealing, with members' loans helping to provide first-class facilities including a pavilion and grandstand.

The Middlesex Charity Cup was inaugurated in 1901 and in both this competition and the Senior Cup Ealing lost 1–0 in the final, to Clapton Orient and Richmond Association respectively. The club had further success in reaching three finals of the Middlesex Charity Cup, losing 2–0 to West Hampstead in 1902–03, but defeating Shepherd's Bush 4-2 in 1903–04, before gaining revenge against West Hampstead 4–2 in 1904–05. In that same season, the Senior Cup was also won with London Caledonians beaten 2–1.

Ealing Association's most successful season, without a doubt, was 1903–04, when the club reached the Final of The FA Amateur Cup, recording victories against Southall, 4–0, Tunbridge Wells, 4–0 in a replay after a 3–3 draw, Norwich City 2–1 after a 0–0 draw and Cheshunt 2–0 in the semi-final at Slough. In the final, they travelled to Bradford to play Sheffield FC on Easter Monday and in front of 4,000 spectators were defeated 3–1, with Hebdon scoring the consolation goal for Ealing. The Ealing team on that great occasion was: Findlay, Blackburn, Fox, Wood, Mitchell, Pryce, Grice, Hebdon, Doll, Powell and Rogers.

EALING ASSOCIATION
(F.A., L.F.A. and M.C.F.A.)

Ground ... Gunnersbury Avenue, Ealing.
Nearest Station Mill Hill Park (D.R.)
Colours ... Red and Green.
Hon. Secretary M. B. Frere, 55, Grange Park, Ealing, W.

In 1905, the club were founder-members of the Isthmian League and in their first season finished fifth of six clubs with three wins, two draws, and five defeats, but this did include a double over eventual runners-up Clapton. In their second, and final, season the club again finished fifth, before resigning along with Casuals and Civil Service as a direct result of clubs leaving the Football Association after a dispute about professionalism. They assisted in the formation of the Amateur Football Alliance and the Southern Amateur League which was formed a few weeks later. The League was split into Divisions A and B, with Ealing Association grouped with Casuals, Civil Service, Croydon, Eastbourne, Ipswich Town, New Crusaders, Richmond Association and Townley Park.

Ealing Association remained in the Southern Amateur League until 1914, which is also the year they won the AFA Cup. They applied and were accepted by the Isthmian League for the 1914–15 season, however football was suspended between 1914–18 for the Great War. When football resumed, Ealing Association decided to rejoin the Southern Amateur League where they remained in that competition until 1971. During their time they won the Division One championship in 1927 and 1947, the AFA Cup 1921 and 1927.

In 1971 Ealing Association joined the Nemean Amateur League and were Division Two champions in 1974. The 1984–85 season proved to be the last season of the Nemean Amateur League and several of the clubs including Ealing Association joined the Southern Olympic League where success was limited. In 2002 the Southern Olympian League merged with the Old Boys League to form the Amateur Football Combination which is where this club is now playing in Division Four Western Section.

Above: the Ealing Association entry from the original Isthmian League handbook.

Right: their ground as it now is!

ILFORD

Ground - Newbury Park, Ilford
Nearest Station - Ilford (G.E.R.)
Colours - Blue and White Stripes
Hon Secretary - T H Randell, 101 St Mary's Road, Ilford, E

It is not surprising that the young men of Ilford in the 1880s should have decided that they would use their new found recreation time on a Saturday to play football. It was probably the "in thing" at the time. Less than 20 years old as an organised game and The FA Cup had been going for almost a decade, everywhere new teams were springing up. That was the setting for a group of young men to be playing a game of football on a field where now the Town Hall stands. The impromptu kick-about led to these men forming their own club. It was to be known as Ilford Alliance, there already being an "Ilford" in existence. The date was the 20 October 1881. There can be little doubt from Ilford Alliance's early records that the driving force behind the Club was the Porter family, who had considerable business interests in what was to become a rapidly growing town over the next half-century.

However they were not alone and the club was set up with the help of R Gilderson (whose son Eric played in the mighty teams of the late 1920s), W M Lusby, a well-known music-hall proprietor, who was the first President, and H Watts and C Stenning, later club secretary. Within a couple of years the original Ilford club had folded and, in the 1883–84 season, Ilford dropped the "Alliance" from their title. The first senior honour to come Ilford's way was the Essex Senior Cup in 1888.

Ilford FC - The FA Amateur Cup, London Senior Cup, Essex Senior Cup and the Ilford Hospital Shield winners in 1929

Ilford played a major part in the formation of three competitions as well as playing in the first ever FA Amateur Cup competition of 1893–94. Firstly for the 1894–95 season they became founder members of the Southern League, finishing fourth. In the next season, however, the competition took a determined step towards professionalism, which was not to the liking of the club. They finished bottom and immediately withdrew.

The Club was then invited to become inaugural members of the London League for 1896–97, where they played for two years until they switched to the South Essex League and then also played in the Metropolitan Amateur League. During these years the Club played at the Ilford Sports Ground, situated in Balfour Road, where many famous opponents visited Ilford – Millwall were once defeated in a London Senior Cup semi-final. During the period to 1901 the population of Ilford had risen to 42,000 and the village had given way to a booming town. Perhaps not surprising then that the Ilford Sports Ground fell into the hands of developers in what is now an area very close to the town centre, station and all other amenities. The demise of the Ilford Sports Ground led to Ilford's move to their home for three-quarters of a century: Lynn Road, Newbury Park. Old opponents Clapton were the first visitors, there was torrential rain, but Ilford won 2–1. Many famous clubs visited: Nottingham Forest, Northampton Town, Manchester City, Brentford and Aston Villa all came to Newbury Park.

It was the formation of the Isthmian League in 1905 that turned Ilford into one of the most respected amateur clubs in the country. The 1920s were arguably the best decade in the history of Ilford Football Club. They purchased Lynn Road *(pictured left)* and in successive seasons, 1921 and 1922, were League champions. In 1927–28 Ilford notched 134 goals in all competitions and a year later won The FA Amateur Cup at Highbury, beating Leyton, the holders, 3–1. They repeated their Amateur Cup win the following year, beating Bournemouth Gasworks Athletic 5–1 at West Ham United. In 1935–36 they again reached the Amateur Cup Final and in a thrilling match at Selhurst Park they drew 1–1 with fellow Isthmians Casuals. The replay at West Ham a fortnight later was lost 2–0.

After World War 2, in the 1950s, there were two major highlights. The first was a memorable win in the London Senior Cup Final against Hounslow Town on 8 May 1954 at Highbury; the second, four years later, resulted in Ilfordians swelling the Wembley crowd for the 1958 FA Amateur Cup Final against Woking to 70,000. Ilford, surprise finalists, started brightly but succumbed 3–0. In the 1960s there was little success for Ilford, and it wasn't until the last season of the Amateur Cup, in 1974, that the club tasted glory of any kind again. Ilford were again surprise finalists, but they lost 4–1 to Bishop's Stortford in the old competition that was to be replaced by The FA Vase and Trophy.

Two years later the Lynn Road ground was sold to Fairview Homes and the club sought a site in the north of the borough on the old Fairlop aerodrome. In the end there was not enough left of the original £325,000 sale money left to re-develop the site and members voted to merge with Leytonstone for the 1979–80 season.

In 1987 Ilford Football Club was reborn as an intermediate club by a group of dedicated former supporters. However, senior status and a place in the Essex Senior League was only achieved when Redbridge Council permitted the use of the Cricklefield Stadium for the 1996–97 season. Runners-up spot in the Essex Senior League in the 2003–04 season led to the club being offered a place in Ryman League Division Two for season 2004–05. With a sense of history and a desire to return to their spiritual home, the founders of the Isthmian League were absolutely delighted to be back in the competition as it celebrated its 100th season.

The 2004–05 season turned into a roller coaster ride in its second half with the Club finishing in the Champions spot after the last matches were played. Even after that day there was one more celebration as on May Day Monday 2005 the club lifted the Ryman League's Associate Members Trophy after a thrilling extra time win over Flackwell Heath. The Championship opened up the prospect of playing at step four of the national pyramid of football and with it a position in Division One East of the Southern League for season 2005–06. This move back to the first ever League that the club played in came to fruition on 13 August 2005.

LONDON CALEDONIANS

Ground - Tufnell Park
Nearest Station - Junction Road (Midland R.)
Colours - Black and White Stripes
Hon Secretary - T G Gibbons, 33 Rosemont Road, Richmond, SW

London Caledonians were formed in 1886 following a meeting at Anderton's Hotel in Fleet Street called together by H Scott MacPherson – a Scotsman – in 1886. Mr MacPherson and a few fellow countrymen conceived the idea of forming a football club which consisted of only Scottish players. They had a hard struggle in those early days as they failed to attract local support, although they did have some fine players and usually won their games with Old Westminster, Old Carthusians, Crusaders, Clapton, and Ilford on their first ground, Elm Farm, Walthamstow, and at the Essex County Ground, Leyton, where they subsequently moved. Their first cup success was in 1889–90 when they beat Crouch End in the final of the Middlesex Senior Cup. The ground at Leyton was where they achieved some of the club's notable cup successes as well as defeating a strong Blackburn Olympic team who a few seasons earlier had won The FA Cup.

In 1891 the club made a determined but not too successful effort to establish itself in South London when they secured the old "Greyhound" pitch at Dulwich Village. The bait of a £15 guarantee – considered most substantial in those days –even brought Aston Villa to Dulwich but alas, the gate was only £14 9s 6d.

On advice they migrated north – to Tufnell Park – where they shared the ground with the local club until it was claimed by their landlords in 1938. From the off it proved a successful move as there was a large Scottish community in the area and many of them started following the 'Caleys'.

Their best performance in the old days was a win in the London Charity Cup Final in 1896 over an Old Carthusian eleven that included the famous brothers PM and AM Walters at back, C Wreford-Brown at centre half, and O Smith in the forward line. During Easter 1898 the 'Caleys' sent a team to Paris to play a match against Le Club Francais. This was one of the first teams to visit the continent and on Easter Monday they defeated the local side before a large crowd. The Club subsequently visited Holland, Belgium and Denmark.

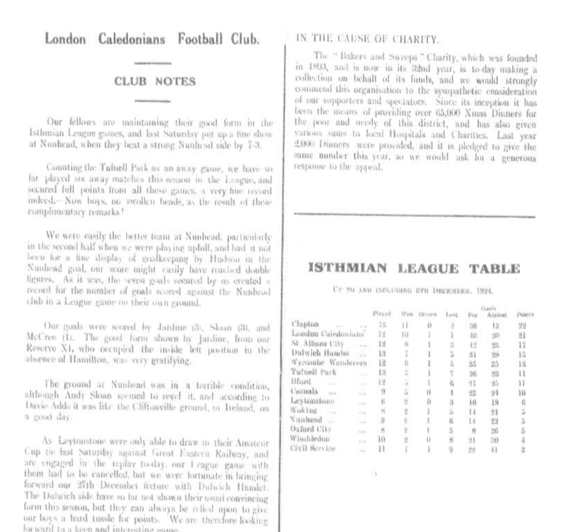
London Caledonians Football Club.

CLUB NOTES

Our fellows are maintaining their good form in the Isthmian League games, and last Saturday put up a fine show at Nunhead, when they beat a strong Nunhead side by 7-3.

Counting the Tufnell Park as an away game, we have so far played six away matches this season in the League, and secured full points from all these games, a very fine record indeed.—Now boys, no swollen heads, as the result of these complimentary remarks!

We were easily the better team at Nunhead, particularly in the second half when we were playing uphill, and had it not been for a fine display of goalkeeping by Hudson in the Nunhead goal, our score might easily have reached double figures. As it was, the seven goals secured by us created a record for the number of goals scored against the Nunhead club in a League game on their own ground.

Our goals were scored by Jardine (3), Sloan (3), and McCree (1). The good form shown by Jardine, from our Reserve XI, who occupied the inside left position in the absence of Hamilton, was very gratifying.

The ground at Nunhead was in a terrible condition, although Andy Sloan seemed to revel it, and according to Davie Adds it was like the Cliftonville ground, in Ireland, on a good day.

As Leytonstone were only able to draw in their Amateur Cup tie last Saturday against Great Eastern Railway, and are engaged in the replay to-day, our League game with them had to be cancelled, but we were fortunate in bringing forward our 27th December fixture with Dulwich Hamlet. The Dulwich side have so far not shown their usual convincing form this season, but they can always be relied upon to give our boys a hard tussle for points. We are therefore looking forward to a keen and interesting game.

IN THE CAUSE OF CHARITY.

The "Bakers and Sweeps" Charity, which was founded in 1893, and is now in its 32nd year, is to-day making a collection on behalf of its funds, and we would strongly commend this organisation to the sympathetic consideration of our supporters and spectators. Since its inception it has been the means of providing over 65,000 Xmas Dinners for the poor and needy of this district, and has also given various sums to local Hospitals and Charities. Last year 2,000 Dinners were provided, and it is pledged to give the same number this year, so we would ask for a generous response to the appeal.

ISTHMIAN LEAGUE TABLE

UP TO AND INCLUDING 6TH DECEMBER, 1924.

	Played	Won	Drawn	Lost	Goals For	Goals Against	Points
Clapton	13	11	0	2	36	13	22
London Caledonians	12	10	1	1	40	20	21
St. Albans City ...	12	8	1	3	42	23	17
Dulwich Hamlet ...	13	7	1	5	31	28	15
Wycombe Wanderers	12	6	1	5	35	25	13
Tufnell Park ...	13	5	1	7	26	23	11
Ilford	12	5	1	6	21	25	11
Casuals	9	5	0	4	23	24	10
Leytonstone ...	6	3	0	3	16	18	6
Woking	8	2	1	5	14	21	5
Nunhead	9	2	1	6	14	22	5
Oxford City ...	8	2	1	5	8	26	5
Wimbledon ...	10	2	0	8	21	30	4
Civil Service ...	11	1	1	9	22	41	3

Programme notes for Dulwich Hamlet's visit in 1924

London Caledonians were invited to join the newly-formed Isthmian League in 1905, and the Club were undoubtedly the most successful pre-war outfit, winning the inaugural League championship on four more occasions before the War, in 1906, 1908, 1912, 1913 and 1914 (Caleys were champions again in 1925), and runners-up in 1907 (with four further second-place finishes in 1921, 1926, 1928 and 1929) as well as numerous London and Middlesex cup competitions.

In 1907–08, besides winning the League championship, they secured the London Senior Amateur Cup for the second time, defeating Dulwich Hamlet in the final, with G A Sutherland scoring the winning goal. The following year the London Charity Cup was won for the third time. Among the players who assisted the club in their fruitful years were: R G Brebner, Tommy Burn, Johnnie Clunas, A Ewing, Charles Fairweather, T G Gibbons, A Grant, N Gray, G H How, Jimmy Hyslop, J A Laidlaw, J Laughland, J S McEachran, Bob McFarlane, J MacFarlane, Tommy Mason, W Melhuish, J M Mitchell, D Nisbet, W Porter, Andrew Ralston, J C Read, W J Reid, R D Robertson, T Robertson, CA Rutherford, F Sim, J Sim, Archie Strang, G A Sutherland, Charles Tennant, J Walton and J Dale Wilson. The first two of these named players represented England in numerous amateur internationals.

Most of the players joined up at the start of World War 1, many enlisting with the London Scottish regiment, so the Club closed down for the duration. They had to build a new team in 1919 as only four pre-war players, Ralston, Mitchell, Laughland, and Gaul, were available.

London Caledonians entertain Clapton during the 1930s

In 1923 came London Calendonians' greatest achievement when they lifted The FA Amateur Cup. Caleys beat Evesham United, 2–1 after extra time, in the Final at Crystal Palace before 14,132 spectators, with Jack McCubbin scoring the winning goal ten minutes into extra time. They had beaten Slough 10–2 in Round 1, then RAMC (Aldershot), Summerstown, and Ilford, before beating St. Albans City 2–0 at Kenilworth Road, Luton in the semi-final.

Andy Ralston, later Secretary of the Isthmian League, served the club for more than 25 years, and towards the close of his long playing career played in the early rounds of the Amateur Cup for the great London Caledonians side that won the trophy in 1923. That team included six amateur internationals: the famous brothers Basil and Eric Gates, Jimmy McCree and Ian Hamilton, all four of whom played for England; Andy Sloan, an Irish full international, and Bobby Noble of Scotland.

In The FA Cup, London Caledonians' best performance was when they reached the first round in 1912–13, defeating two professional teams – Chatham and Shrewsbury Town – before losing to Wolverhampton Wanderers 3–1, but Caleys were by no means outclassed. The following year London Caledonians were exempt to the first round and visited Huddersfield Town, where they were defeated 3–0.

The Club went into decline in the 1930s and, after losing their Tufnell Park ground in 1938, they shared Barking's Vicarage Field, as well as playing some matches at Park Royal Stadium during the 1938–39 season. London Caledonians resigned from the Isthmian League when they were unable to secure a new home although the club was still registering each year with the Football Association.

The Caleys' rule "All members of the club must be Scotsmen either by birth or parentage (father or mother)" accounts for the fact that so many of their players were eligible for English and Irish caps. The brothers Gates and Andy Sloan qualified for the Club through having Scottish mothers.

Basil and Eric Gates collected 15 England caps between them from 1920 to 1931, although they never played together in the same English side.

Andy Sloan possessed just that little extra amount of speed at critical moments that is needed to complete the make up of an ideal centre-forward.

His friends used to say that there was one corner of the net at Tufnell Park that was especially reserved for the opposing goalkeeper when Andy was on his mettle.

He led the Irish amateur attack against England for four successive seasons.

The London Caledonians championship-winning side of 1913

THE FIRST FIXTURES

The League commenced on 9 September 1905 with just two matches. Clapton entertained London Caledonians, winning by the only goal, whilst Civil Service travelled across London to play Ilford and won by the same score. We now reproduce the reports of the matches which appeared in the newspaper *The Sportsman*.

ISTHMIAN LEAGUE.

CLAPTON v. LONDON CALEDONIANS.

The above clubs played their first League match on Saturday at the Spotted Dog Grounds, Upton. The weather conditions were most unfavourable, rain falling incessantly, while the heavy going and greasy ball militated against good play. It was not surprising, therefore, that there was only a moderate attendance. The local supporters had the satisfaction of seeing Clapton win by a goal to love, which about indicated the difference in the respective merits of the teams on the day's play. The Scots were without McFarlane in goal, a trial being given to H. Allen, of the Regent-square Thistle, A. T. Ralston's old club. F. W. Sim was removed to the outside-right position, L. V. Simpson filling the vacancy at right half-back. Clapton played the same side, with one exception, that did so well against Townley Park, A. J. Seaton appearing at outside left in place of Rosei. Clapton kicked off against a strong wind, which blew straight down the ground, but the Scots were the first to press, Wilding having to save from Dale-Wilson. Porter shortly afterwards forced a corner, but nothing resulted, and then Seaton initiated a good run, Rance being too far behind to take his centre. After a spell of even play the Scots benefited by two free kicks. Porter, receiving from the first, made a splendid run, but was brought down near the corner flag and had to retire for ten minutes. The Scots, however, held their own, Ralston and Robertson being responsible for some good defensive work. The home forwards again attacked, and Allen had to concede a corner from a good shot by Eastwood. Following another corner to Clapton, which was sent behind, Ralston took a free kick for hands just outside the centre-line, and, kicking strongly, sent the ball behind a few yards from the goal posts. Just before the interval two corners fell to Clapton, but nothing resulted, and when the teams crossed over neither side had scored. Upon resuming, the Scots attacked strongly, Wilding having to negotiate shots from Gibbons and Dale-Wilson. A good round of passing by Eastwood, Russell, and Campbell transferred play to the other end, where Robertson had to concede a corner. The Scots' right, however, soon returned to the attack, three corners falling to them in as many minutes. Dale-Wilson was unfortunate in failing to find the net from the last, the ball just skimming the crossbar. Rance immediately after should have opened the scoring for Clapton, but Allen was hampered and the Scots were awarded a free kick just outside their goal. Eventually Rance scored after a good piece of passing by the home forwards. The Scots then made strenuous efforts to equalise, Wilding having to negotiate a difficult shot from Simpson. Each side pressed in turn, but in the last ten minutes Clapton assumed the upper hand and the visitors' defence was strongly tested. There was no further scoring, and a scrambling game resulted in a win for Clapton by one goal to love. The winners were stronger forward, Rance, Russell, Eastwood, and Seaton, considering the conditions, playing a good game throughout, whilst for the Scots Ralston and Robertson showed sound defence. Teams:

Clapton: J. Wilding (goal), A. K. Vickridge and R. Ewan (backs), H. Parkinson, L. Peel-Yates, and H. C. Hollis (half-backs), H. J. Eastwood, C. G. Russell, P. Campbell, C. S. Rance, and A. J. Seaton (forwards).

London Caledonians: H. Allen (goal), A. T. Ralston and R. D. Robertson (backs), L. V. Simpson, W. J. Reid, and A. F. Munro (half-backs), F. W. Sim, J. Dale-Wilson, T. G. Gibbons, J. C. Thomson, and W. Porter (forwards)

Referee: Mr G. Chambers.

ILFORD v. CIVIL SERVICE.

Played at Newbury Park, Ilford, on Saturday. Rain fell almost throughout the afternoon, but, considering the wretched conditions and the slippery nature of the ground, the game, which was witnessed by a moderate company, proved of a fairly interesting character. The Service won by a goal to love, and although the point was somewhat luckily obtained, the visitors, taking the play on the whole, were entitled to their victory. Ilford won the toss, and the Service right wing immediately became busy, a strong rush being well checked by Churchill. They came again, and A. Martin missed a good opportunity. Churchill was next prominent in pulling up Dwane and Warden in clever style, and then Daniels and Scott showed neat passing, but, after approaching the Ilford goal, they gave to the opposite wing, who sent the ball out. A capital run by Blake almost from end to end ended in Turner saving smartly by conceding a corner, which came to nothing. Robinson's goal was now in danger for some little time, but Andrews eventually cleared, although a shot by Marsh nearly found the net. The Service goal was again besieged, and play ruled exciting, Gaffney finally clearing. After a brief visit to the Ilford end, Barton ran clean up the centre, winding up by a hasty shot which went wide. Then Gaffney almost shot through his own goal through a mis-kick, and this escape was followed by the Civil Service left wing taking play to the other end in good style. Churchill mis-kicked in front of Miles, and Daniels promptly passed over to Dwane, who scored the only point of the match. Ilford had most of the game for a while after this, the reverse having stirred them up, and Turner twice saved in excellent style. Then Martin and Daniels caused Miles to toss out, and, following a spell of mid-field play, Blake shot finely, Andrews clearing in equally good fashion, and when Bryant seemed certain to score for the visitors a minute later, Martin dashed across and saved brilliantly. Immediately afterwards Dwane lost a good chance. Miles had to toss out a hot shot from Scott, and, following a free kick, Blake narrowly missed scoring for the home side, while Robinson showed himself a clever custodian by keeping out stinging shots from Barton and Marsh. At the interval the Service led by a goal to nil. Soon after crossing over Robinson had to fist out from Fairweather, who had gone centre forward. The home side generally brightened up and became very troublesome to the Service backs, while Marsh just failed to equalise. Blake struck the crossbar from a pass by Porter, and, the Service left changing ends, Copp shot into Miles's hands. Gaffney once pulled Marsh up finely, but Massey gave Robinson something to do. After this the Service had a lot the best of matters, Martin proving quite the hero of the Ilford team. But for his brilliant saves, the score must have been increased. Copp fed the visiting forwards nicely. A miss by Turner let in Bates, who gave to Marsh with practically an open goal, but in the excitement he sent wide, a rare opportunity to equalise being lost. Just before the close the Service goal was besieged. Shot after shot rained in, but somehow Robinson, Turner, Gaffney, and Andrews successfully dealt with them all, and the visitors won as stated above. Teams.

Ilford: D. Miles (goal), W. W. Martin and H. Churchill (backs), E. C. Porter, H. C. Massey, and C. Fairweather (half-backs), H. Marsh, J. T. Bates, Barton, W. A. White, and J. J. Blake (forwards).

Civil Service: G. W. Robinson (goal), T. E. F. Turner and J. J. Gaffney (backs), H. Bryant, C. H. Andrews, and H. Copp (half-backs), T. Dwane, C. C. Warden, A. Martin, W. P. Daniels, and J. J. Scott (forwards).

Referee: Mr H. Thompson.

FOOTBALL.

THE NEW AMATEUR LEAGUE.

Proceedings in the recently-formed Isthmian League, which is confined to the Casuals, Clapton Civil Service, Ilford, Ealing, and London Caledonians, were commenced on Saturday, when a couple of contests were decided. The most important was between Clapton and the Caledonians, and though the former had the choice of ground it was all they could do to win by a goal, which was scored late in the game, to nothing. The winners evidently miss the brothers Farnfield, as they were by no means well together, and both sides were heavily handicapped by the greasy turf. Robertson showed some very fine back play for the Scotsmen, and repeatedly neutralised the rushes of the home forwards. The defeat of Ilford, who last year were about the best of our regular club elevens, by Civil Service (1—0) caused some surprise. The winners, however, were somewhat lucky, and one must wait until they meet under more congenial surroundings before one can offer an opinion as to which is the better team. Ealing and the Casuals will meet next Saturday. By the way, Ealing who made a substantial profit on last year's working, are spending over £200 on improvements on their ground.

Left: the advent of the new League as reported in the press of the day.

Early team shots. Above: Civil Service FC. Below: The Casuals FC.

CHAPTER THREE

Season by Season - The Development of the League

The League has evolved from a six-Club configuration to one which has involved as many as 88 clubs. This chapter details how the League has developed from season to season; it concentrates on the League Championship itself rather than the Cup Competitions, which were not introduced until the 1970s.

PART ONE 1905–1939

1905–06 - The first ever games of the Isthmian League were played on 9 September 1905 with Civil Service beating Ilford 1–0 at Ilford whilst Clapton defeated London Caledonians at home by the same score. London Caledonians *(pictured left)* won the first championship by two points from Clapton, with Casuals and Civil Service finishing third and fourth, respectively. Ealing Association and Ilford, the two bottom clubs, retired from membership in accordance with League rules, but were both recommended for re-election at the Annual General Meeting. Cheshunt, Dulwich Hamlet, Luton Clarence New Crusaders, Shepherd's Bush and West Norwood all applied for membership but the League Council decided not to increase its numbers. Pictured right, the first League handbook.

		1	2	3	4	5	6
1	Casuals	*	2–0	1–1	1–3	3–1	1–1
2	Civil Service	2–3	*	1–2	1–0	2–2	5–3
3	Clapton	2–0	1–0	*	2–3	1–0	1–0
4	Ealing Association	2–2	2–4	4–0	*	1–1	0–4
5	Ilford	0–0	0–1	0–1	1–0	*	0–1
6	London Caledonians	2–1	5–0	4–0	3–0	2–0	*

		P	*W*	*D*	*L*	*F*	*A*	*Pts*
1	London Caledonians	10	7	1	2	25	8	15
2	Clapton	10	6	1	3	11	13	13
3	Casuals	10	3	4	3	14	14	10
4	Civil Service	10	4	1	5	16	20	9
5	Ealing Association	10	3	2	5	15	19	8
6	Ilford	10	1	3	6	5	12	5

1906–07 - Ilford, who had finished bottom in the inaugural season, were crowned champions in the second season, dropping only two points – drawing away to Clapton and Ealing Association. Inaugural champions London Caledonians finished runners-up. Clapton were third and Civil Service finished fourth. Ealing Association and Casuals occupied the bottom two positions and thus retired from membership, though both were re-elected for the 1907–08 season. Eastbourne and Croydon had also applied for membership, but their applications were rejected.

		1	2	3	4	5	6
1	Casuals	*	2–3	0–4	5–0	2–4	0–1
2	Civil Service	1–2	*	0–0	1–4	2–3	1–3
3	Clapton	1–1	4–0	*	3–1	1–1	1–2
4	Ealing Association	3–1	0–1	2–1	*	1–1	0–1
5	Ilford	4–1	1–0	2–0	5–0	*	3–2
6	London Caledonians	5–1	0–2	2–3	3–1	0–2	*

		P	*W*	*D*	*L*	*F*	*A*	*Pts*
1	Ilford	10	8	2	0	26	9	18
2	London Caledonians	10	6	0	4	19	14	12
3	Clapton	10	4	3	3	18	11	11
4	Civil Service	10	3	1	6	11	19	7
5	Ealing Association	10	3	1	6	12	22	7
6	Casuals	10	2	1	7	15	26	5

1907–08 - Before the 1907–08 season could start, problems within the Isthmian League regarding the status of amateur players and clubs came to a head and the infamous "split" took effect. Football in the South of England had been strictly amateur but, gradually, professional clubs were formed. The London County Football Association was reluctant to accept these professional clubs into their constitution, but eventually they did so. This led to several prominent amateur clubs resigning from the London FA and they subsequently formed the Amateur Football Association (later Alliance) but, on 31 March 1905, the AFA was declared illegal by The Football Association. At The FA's Annual General Meeting in 1907, a resolution was passed requiring all County FAs to accept professional clubs into membership. However, neither the Middlesex FA nor the Surrey FA were prepared to do this and they withdrew from their FA affiliation. This course of action led to the resignations of Casuals, Civil Service and Ealing Association, who opted to join the newly-formed Southern Amateur League. Percy Timbs tendered his resignation as Chairman of the Isthmian League, subsequently being elected as Treasurer of the Southern Amateur League, a position he would hold until 1948. The "split" would last for eight years.

A special meeting of the League was held on 31 July. Mr WA "Willie" Brown of London Caledonians succeeded Percy Timbs as Chairman, while Dulwich Hamlet, Oxford City and West Norwood were elected to the League to replace Casuals, Civil Service and Ealing Association. A late application from Leytonstone was rejected.

The Spartan Football League began competition in 1907–08. It had been formed by JR Schumacher, ably assisted by Thomas Kirkup, who had been involved in the formation of the Isthmian League two years earlier. Dulwich Hamlet were one of the Spartan League's founder members, but it was not unusual for a club to compete in more than one league. In February 1908 the Rt Hon. Alfred Lyttleton tendered his resignation as Isthmian League President. On 6 March 1908, at the invitation of JR Schumacher, the Spartan League's Hon Secretary, another special meeting was held, this one to consider amalgamating the Spartan and Isthmian Leagues for season 1908–09. After much discussion it was agreed that an amalgamation would be of benefit – providing it would not result in fixture congestion, bearing in mind the various cup competitions in which the clubs participated. This meeting was adjourned until 13 March, when there was further debate. The Spartan League were represented at this second meeting by J R Schumacher. The matter went to a vote and London Caledonians, Oxford City, Dulwich

Hamlet and West Norwood were all in favour of the scheme, but Clapton and Ilford were opposed to it. The Spartan League's membership was unanimous in support of the amalgamation, but the Isthmian League had made it clear they would not agree to the proposal unless all of their member clubs were in favour of it. Therefore, the amalgamation proposal was rejected. On the field, in a very close season, London Caledonians emerged victorious, winning their second championship. They finished one point ahead of Clapton, Ilford and Oxford City who all had eleven points. Dulwich Hamlet and West Norwood – fifth and sixth, respectively – were re-elected to the League. At the Annual General Meeting, a proposal was made to increase the Isthmian League's membership to ten clubs for season 1908–09. It was adopted, and Bromley, Leytonstone, Shepherd's Bush *(programme below)* and Nunhead all joined from the Spartan League.

	1	2	3	4	5	6
1 Clapton	*	1–0	2–2	2–1	5–0	8–1
2 Dulwich Hamlet	1–1	*	2–5	3–0	4–0	4–1
3 Ilford	5–3	3–0	*	3–4	3–0	4–0
4 London Caledonians	2–1	0–0	4–3	*	1–1	5–0
5 Oxford City	2–1	3–0	5–0	2–1	*	5–2
6 West Norwood	0–0	4–1	2–0	0–2	3–2	*

	P	*W*	*D*	*L*	*F*	*A*	*Pts*
1 London Caledonians	10	5	2	3	20	15	12
2 Clapton	10	4	3	3	24	14	11
3 Ilford	10	5	1	4	28	22	11
4 Oxford City	10	5	1	4	20	20	11
5 Dulwich Hamlet	10	3	2	5	15	18	8
6 West Norwood	10	3	1	6	13	31	7

1908–09 - Defending champions London Caledonians found it tough in the new ten-team Isthmian League, and had to apply for re-election along with basement club West Norwood. Bromley won the championship in their first year by one point from fellow newcomers Leytonstone, whilst Ilford were third for a second consecutive season and Dulwich *(pictured right)* fourth. London Caledonians and West Norwood were both re-elected for 1909–10 season, although Wimbledon, Tufnell Park, Woking, Woolwich Polytechnic and Upton Park made unsuccessful applications for membership.

	1	2	3	4	5	6	7	8	9	10
1 Bromley	*	3–1	1–0	4–3	3–2	4–0	4–3	1–4	0–0	7–1
2 Clapton	1–0	*	2–3	1–1	1–2	3–2	2–4	2–2	3–1	3–1
3 Dulwich Hamlet	2–3	2–4	*	5–3	0–1	3–0	3–1	3–4	3–1	4–1
4 Ilford	2–0	2–0	1–0	*	1–1	3–1	2–1	1–1	7–4	2–0
5 Leytonstone	3–2	2–2	3–0	1–1	*	5–3	0–1	5–1	1–3	4–1
6 London Caledonians	1–0	2–2	1–1	4–0	3–6	*	0–1	1–0	1–2	1–1
7 Nunhead	2–4	1–2	2–2	2–4	3–1	1–1	*	0–1	3–1	0–4
8 Oxford City	1–3	0–2	0–2	3–1	0–1	2–2	1–2	*	5–2	1–2
9 Shepherd's Bush	1–0	3–0	0–3	1–2	3–2	0–0	2–1	1–1	*	1–9
10 West Norwood	2–3	1–3	2–3	7–1	3–3	0–2	1–3	1–2	3–0	*

	P	*W*	*D*	*L*	*F*	*A*	*Pts*
1 Bromley	18	11	1	6	42	20	23
2 Leytonstone	18	9	4	5	43	31	22
3 Ilford	18	9	4	5	37	36	22
4 Dulwich Hamlet	18	9	2	7	39	30	20
5 Clapton	18	8	4	6	32	32	20
6 Oxford City	18	6	4	8	29	32	16
7 Nunhead	18	7	2	9	31	35	16
8 Shepherd's Bush	18	6	3	9	26	44	15
9 London Caledonians	18	4	6	8	25	34	14
10 West Norwood	18	5	2	11	40	43	12

LEYTONSTONE FOOTBALL CLUB.
SEASON. 1909-10.
WINNERS OF LONDON CHARITY CUP AND WEST HAM CHARITY CUP
FINALISTS ESSEX SENIOR CUP SEMI-FINALISTS LONDON SENIOR CUP

1909–10 - This season was another close affair with only three points separating the top four clubs. Bromley won a second consecutive championship, by two points from Clapton and Nunhead. Ilford finished fourth, three points clear of Dulwich Hamlet. The bottom two clubs – West Norwood and Shepherd's Bush – had to retire from membership, but both were re-elected at the Annual General Meeting. Woking also applied to join, but the League decided not to increase its membership. JR Schumacher approached the League Council with the possibility of forming a second division – including automatic promotion and relegation – for the 1910–11 season, but eight of the ten member Clubs rejected the proposal, fearing that the level of football would suffer.

	1	2	3	4	5	6	7	8	9	10
1 Bromley	*	2–0	1–0	1–0	1–0	3–0	1–1	8–0	1–0	2–0
2 Clapton	0–0	*	6–0	0–1	3–3	6–0	5–2	2–2	11–0	8–1
3 Dulwich Hamlet	2–1	0–2	*	1–0	2–1	3–2	1–0	2–2	3–0	3–1
4 Ilford	1–0	0–2	0–0	*	4–2	1–0	0–0	2–0	3–0	6–1
5 Leytonstone	2–1	4–3	3–2	4–2	*	1–2	2–7	5–0	4–2	2–2
6 London Caledonians	2–2	1–3	2–2	0–2	2–0	*	0–8	2–0	1–1	1–0
7 Nunhead	1–1	0–0	2–1	2–1	4–2	2–1	*	6–1	4–0	5–1
8 Oxford City	0–2	2–1	2–1	1–1	5–3	1–2	2–0	*	2–3	5–0
9 Shepherd's Bush	0–2	0–1	0–0	2–5	2–4	3–1	3–4	2–2	*	3–4
10 West Norwood	1–3	1–3	1–3	1–2	2–2	2–0	4–1	3–1	3–2	*

	P	*W*	*D*	*L*	*F*	*A*	*Pts*
1 Bromley	18	11	4	3	32	10	26
2 Clapton	18	10	4	4	56	19	24
3 Nunhead	18	10	4	4	49	26	24
4 Ilford	18	10	3	5	31	17	23
5 Dulwich Hamlet	18	8	4	6	26	26	20
6 Leytonstone	18	7	3	8	44	46	17
7 Oxford City	18	5	4	9	28	45	14
8 London Caledonians	18	5	3	10	19	40	13
9 West Norwood	18	5	2	11	28	52	12
10 Shepherd's Bush	18	2	3	13	23	55	7

1910–11 - In another close race for the League championship, Clapton came out on top, pipping Leytonstone by one point for their first Isthmian title. Dulwich Hamlet finished third. West Norwood – for the third successive season – had to apply for re-election along with London Caledonians. However, late in the season, a protest was lodged by Ilford regarding the eligibility of N A Wood of Bromley, a former professional footballer whose amateur status had been reinstated. A similar objection by Clapton followed although no formal protest was made. The League's Rules at this time excluded reinstated amateurs so Ilford's protest was upheld and the League Council deducted four points from Bromley's total. They also requested that the club resign from membership at the end of the season. At the Annual General Meeting, the bottom two, West Norwood and London Caledonians, were both re-elected to membership. The League Council agreed to increase League membership to 11 clubs and Woking gained election by 13 votes to 3 with Barking, Barnet Alston, Catford Southend, Chelmsford, Chesham Town, Enfield, Northern Nomads, Old Kingstonians, Romford United, Summerstown, Tunbridge Wells and Woolwich Polytechnic also applying. However, Tunbridge Wells were later elected to replace Bromley who had been forced to resign.

		1	2	3	4	5	6	7	8	9	10
1	Bromley	*	2–0	0–2	3–0	1–2	4–0	2–2	2–2	2–1	2–0
2	Clapton	5–1	*	2–0	3–1	1–1	0–2	3–0	5–1	2–0	3–0
3	Dulwich Hamlet	0–0	1–1	*	0–1	4–1	6–1	3–2	1–1	2–0	3–3
4	Ilford	1–1	1–2	4–1	*	1–2	4–2	0–1	6–2	0–2	6–0
5	Leytonstone	3–0	1–2	4–0	3–4	*	5–1	1–0	5–2	2–1	3–0
6	London Caledonians	2–1	0–0	0–2	1–1	1–3	*	0–2	2–3	0–1	1–3
7	Nunhead	0–0	2–4	0–1	2–3	0–4	6–1	*	8–4	5–4	1–1
8	Oxford City	1–2	3–4	1–0	4–3	2–1	2–1	1–0	*	1–1	1–1
9	Shepherd's Bush	3–1	0–0	1–2	2–1	7–1	2–2	3–0	0–1	*	2–1
10	West Norwood	3–7	3–2	0–0	0–4	3–5	0–1	1–1	1–0	4–1	*

		P	*W*	*D*	*L*	*F*	*A*	*Pts*
1	Clapton	18	11	4	3	39	19	26
2	Leytonstone	18	12	1	5	47	30	25
3	Dulwich Hamlet	18	8	5	5	28	22	21
4	Oxford City	18	7	4	7	32	43	18
5	Ilford	18	8	1	9	41	32	17
6	Shepherd's Bush	18	7	3	8	31	27	17
7	Bromley*	18	8	4	6	32	27	16
8	Nunhead	18	5	4	9	32	36	14
9	West Norwood	18	4	5	9	24	43	13
10	London Caledonians	18	3	3	12	18	45	9

**Bromley four points deducted*

1911–12 - London Caledonians won their third championship, gaining 29 points from the new 20-match League programme. Caleys finished four points clear of Ilford and Nunhead, with Dulwich Hamlet fourth on 21 points and West Norwood – outside the bottom two for the first time in their five seasons in the League – fifth on goal average. At the bottom end of the table, which was also decided by the final matches of the season, Shepherd's Bush and Leytonstone escaped re-election with Oxford City and debutants Tunbridge Wells occupying those places.

On 1 May 1912, League Champions elect London Caledonians met the Rest of the League – which consisted of Amateur Internationals – in aid of the Titanic Fund, at Tufnell Park. Three days later, the Isthmian League met the Spartan League, at Aylesbury United FC, for the same cause, which raised a total of £26.00 for the fund. The Titanic had sunk in the Atlantic Ocean, during its maiden voyage, on 15 April with the loss of more than 1,500 lives.

Woking FC, pictured during 1912.

At the Annual General meeting Oxford City and Tunbridge Wells were both re-elected, although there were unsuccessful applications from Barking, Barnet Alston, Kingston-upon-Thames and Luton Clarence.

		1	2	3	4	5	6	7	8	9	10	11
1	Clapton	*	1–5	2–2	1–1	1–0	1–2	2–0	5–1	2–1	1–0	3–3
2	Dulwich Hamlet	3–1	*	0–3	1–0	1–2	2–2	0–0	4–2	2–0	0–2	4–0
3	Ilford	1–4	1–0	*	3–1	1–1	2–1	2–0	3–0	1–0	2–2	4–0
4	Leytonstone	1–3	2–0	2–0	*	3–3	0–1	3–1	0–0	3–0	4–1	3–3
5	London Caledonians	3–1	0–0	3–2	4–0	*	2–0	3–1	4–3	1–1	1–0	1–1
6	Nunhead	4–4	1–2	2–0	2–2	5–1	*	1–1	1–0	2–0	1–0	3–1
7	Oxford City	2–0	3–1	1–3	6–1	1–1	0–0	*	2–4	6–2	5–1	0–1
8	Shepherd's Bush	1–1	1–1	1–3	4–1	2–2	3–1	3–3	*	9–0	0–0	2–1
9	Tunbridge Wells	2–1	1–0	1–0	0–0	0–1	0–1	2–0	6–2	*	3–3	1–1
10	West Norwood	3–2	0–6	1–2	3–0	0–2	4–1	4–1	3–1	4–3	*	4–2
11	Woking	2–1	1–1	2–1	2–1	2–4	4–5	2–0	8–0	1–0	1–3	*

		P	*W*	*D*	*L*	*F*	*A*	*Pts*
1	London Caledonians	20	11	7	2	39	25	29
2	Ilford	20	11	3	6	37	24	25
3	Nunhead	20	10	5	5	36	30	25
4	Dulwich Hamlet	20	8	5	7	33	23	21
5	West Norwood	20	9	3	8	38	38	21
6	Clapton	20	7	5	8	37	37	19
7	Woking	20	7	5	8	38	41	19
8	Shepherd's Bush	20	5	6	9	39	49	16
9	Leytonstone	20	5	6	9	28	38	16
10	Oxford City	20	5	5	10	33	36	14
11	Tunbridge Wells	20	5	4	11	23	40	14

1912–13 - For the second successive season London Caledonians won the championship, this time losing only one match. Leytonstone, who just missed re-election the previous season, were runners-up, ahead of Nunhead on goal average.

The bottom two clubs were Tunbridge Wells and West Norwood – both were forced to apply for re-election. However, due to West Norwood's poor performances – their fifth bottom-two finish in the six seasons since securing election in 1907 – and the state of Tunbridge Wells' ground, the League Council decided to conduct the re-election proceedings by ballot. Barking, Enfield, Guildford, Hampstead Town, Kingston-upon-Thames, Metrogas, New Crusaders, Old Kingstonians, St. Leonard's Amateurs, South Western Railway and Summerstown all applied for membership. The ballot result was: *West Norwood 17 votes, New Crusaders 16 votes, Tunbridge Wells 1 vote.*

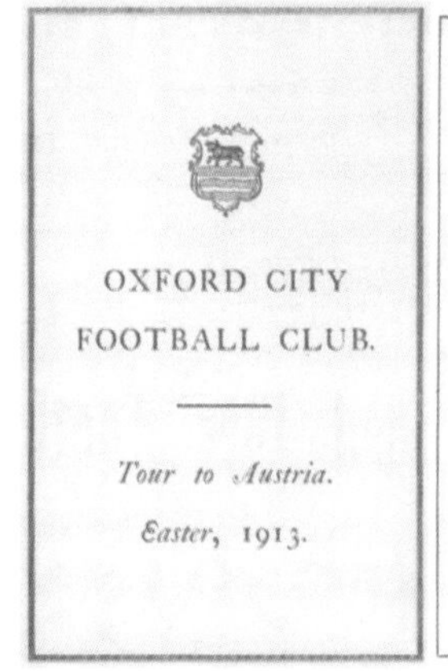

OXFORD CITY

FOOTBALL CLUB.

Tour to Austria.

Easter, 1913.

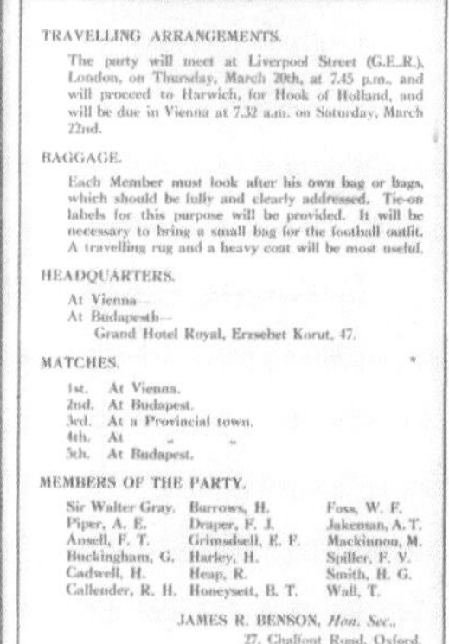

TRAVELLING ARRANGEMENTS.

The party will meet at Liverpool Street (G.E.R.), London, on Thursday, March 20th, at 7.45 p.m., and will proceed to Harwich, for Hook of Holland, and will be due in Vienna at 7.32 a.m. on Saturday, March 22nd.

BAGGAGE.

Each Member must look after his own bag or bags, which should be fully and clearly addressed. Tie-on labels for this purpose will be provided. It will be necessary to bring a small bag for the football outfit. A travelling rug and a heavy coat will be most useful.

HEADQUARTERS.

At Vienna—

At Budapesth—

Grand Hotel Royal, Erzsebet Korut, 47.

MATCHES.

1st. At Vienna.

2nd. At Budapest.

3rd. At a Provincial town.

4th. At " "

5th. At Budapest.

MEMBERS OF THE PARTY.

Sir Walter Gray.	Burrows, H.	Foss, W. F.
Piper, A. E.	Draper, F. J.	Jakeman, A. T.
Ansell, F. T.	Grimsdsell, E. F.	Mackinnon, M.
Buckingham, G.	Harley, H.	Spiller, F. V.
Cadwell, H.	Heap, R.	Smith, H. G.
Callender, R. H.	Honeysett, B. T.	Wall, T.

JAMES R. BENSON, *Hon. Sec.*,
27, Chalfont Road, Oxford.

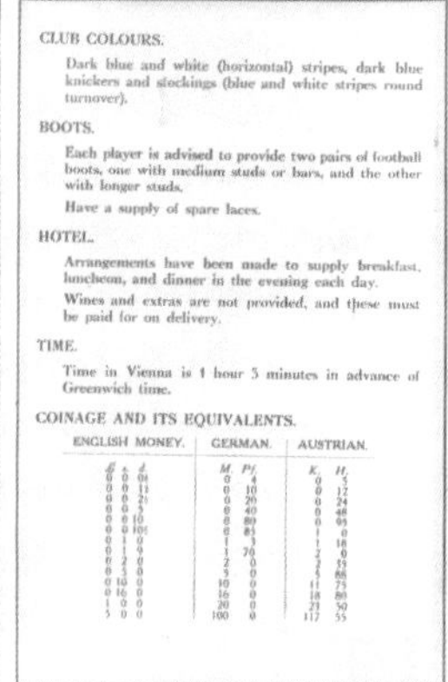

CLUB COLOURS.

Dark blue and white (horizontal) stripes, dark blue knickers and stockings (blue and white stripes round turnover).

BOOTS.

Each player is advised to provide two pairs of football boots, one with medium studs or bars, and the other with longer studs.

Have a supply of spare laces.

HOTEL.

Arrangements have been made to supply breakfast, luncheon, and dinner in the evening each day.

Wines and extras are not provided, and these must be paid for on delivery.

TIME.

Time in Vienna is 1 hour 5 minutes in advance of Greenwich time.

COINAGE AND ITS EQUIVALENTS.

ENGLISH MONEY.	GERMAN.	AUSTRIAN.
[illegible]	[illegible]	[illegible]

None of the other applicants received a single vote, so New Crusaders replaced Tunbridge Wells for the 1913–14 season.

		1	2	3	4	5	6	7	8	9	10	11
1	Clapton	*	2–0	2–2	0–0	0–2	0–2	0–1	1–1	2–0	2–2	2–1
2	Dulwich Hamlet	0–0	*	1–2	1–4	0–1	2–1	4–0	2–3	2–1	3–0	2–2
3	Ilford	4–2	1–6	*	1–3	1–2	1–1	3–0	2–3	1–1	1–0	3–1
4	Leytonstone	1–0	1–2	3–2	*	0–0	7–1	6–1	1–0	5–0	3–1	1–3
5	London Caledonians	2–0	3–1	2–0	2–0	*	1–1	2–2	2–1	1–1	3–1	5–0
6	Nunhead	0–0	2–0	1–2	2–0	1–0	*	1–0	2–3	2–0	2–0	5–3
7	Oxford City	0–1	1–1	0–0	2–1	2–2	2–5	*	1–1	2–0	2–1	3–3
8	Shepherd's Bush	1–3	1–4	1–1	0–0	1–3	0–3	0–1	*	5–0	2–1	1–5
9	Tunbridge Wells	0–2	2–0	4–0	1–3	0–1	1–0	4–1	3–1	*	2–2	0–1
10	West Norwood	1–1	1–3	2–0	1–2	0–1	1–2	1–2	2–0	3–0-	*	1–2
11	Woking	0–3	0–0	2–0	0–4	0–3	0–2	3–0	1–1	2–2	4–2	*

		P	*W*	*D*	*L*	*F*	*A*	*Pts*
1	London Caledonians	20	14	5	1	38	12	33
2	Leytonstone	20	12	3	5	45	20	27
3	Nunhead	20	12	3	5	36	23	27
4	Clapton	20	7	7	6	23	20	21
5	Dulwich Hamlet	20	8	4	8	34	28	20
6	Woking	20	7	5	8	33	40	19
7	Oxford City	20	6	6	8	23	39	18
8	Ilford	20	6	5	9	27	37	17
9	Shepherd's Bush	20	5	5	10	26	38	15
10	Tunbridge Wells	20	5	4	11	22	36	14
11	West Norwood	20	3	3	14	23	37	9

1913–14 - For the third year running London Caledonians won the League championship, this time by two points from Nunhead, with Ilford finishing third. Woking finished bottom with West Norwood, again, in the other re-election position. West Norwood and Woking were unanimously elected at the Annual General Meeting, along with Ealing Association, who returned after a seven-year absence due to the "split", making a 12-team League. Merton, Old Kingstonians, Redhill, St. Albans City and Tooting Town had also applied for membership, but they were rejected. At the AGM, it was agreed to form a Reserve Section for member Clubs, but membership would not be compulsory.

	1	2	3	4	5	6	7	8	9	10	11
1 Clapton	*	1–3	0–0	4–1	0–1	1–1	2–1	3–0	0–1	3–2	1–1
2 Dulwich Hamlet	3–1	*	0–1	1–0	4–2	1–2	0–0	3–1	4–2	1–0	3–0
3 Ilford	2–1	3–1	*	4–1	3–3	5–2	2–2	3–1	7–1	4–1	4–0
4 Leytonstone	1–0	0–0	2–6	*	2–6	0–0	2–0	3–2	4–0	3–1	1–0
5 London Caledonians	3–0	3–1	3–2	2–2	*	1–1	1–1	4–0	5–1	10–1	5–0
6 New Crusaders	0–3	1–0	8–0	1–0	0–2	*	2–4	4–0	0–0	4–1	3–1
7 Nunhead	2–0	2–2	3–1	2–0	2–2	5–2	*	6–1	6–1	1–1	3–2
8 Oxford City	4–2	2–1	2–1	0–1	3–0	3–1	5–2	*	4–1	3–2	7–1
9 Shepherd's Bush	0–2	0–0	2–1	0–0	0–1	2–1	1–3	3–2	*	2–0	4–1
10 West Norwood	1–3	0–2	1–1	3–2	0–0	0–4	0–2	1–0	4–0	*	7–0
11 Woking	0–2	1–4	1–2	0–4	0–1	1–2	0–2	0–2	0–3	2–1	*

	P	*W*	*D*	*L*	*F*	*A*	*Pts*
1 London Caledonians	20	12	6	2	55	23	30
2 Nunhead	20	11	6	3	49	27	28
3 Ilford	20	11	4	5	52	35	26
4 Dulwich Hamlet	20	10	4	6	34	22	24
5 New Crusaders	20	10	3	7	40	30	23
6 Oxford City	20	10	0	10	42	42	20
7 Leytonstone	20	8	4	8	29	32	20
8 Clapton	20	8	3	9	29	27	19
9 Shepherd's Bush	20	7	2	11	24	46	16
10 West Norwood	20	4	3	13	27	47	11
11 Woking	20	1	1	18	11	61	3

1914–15 to 1918 - The Isthmian League, as with most other leagues, suspended their competition in early September, the League shutting down on 4 September. The London League and the South Essex League did operate, but only for the 1914–15 season. Most Clubs had a large number of members available to play and several competed in cup matches and unofficial leagues. Both London Caledonians and Dulwich Hamlet had a large number of players in the forces, but other clubs including Leytonstone, Ilford, Nunhead and Ealing Association did not appear to be as severely affected.

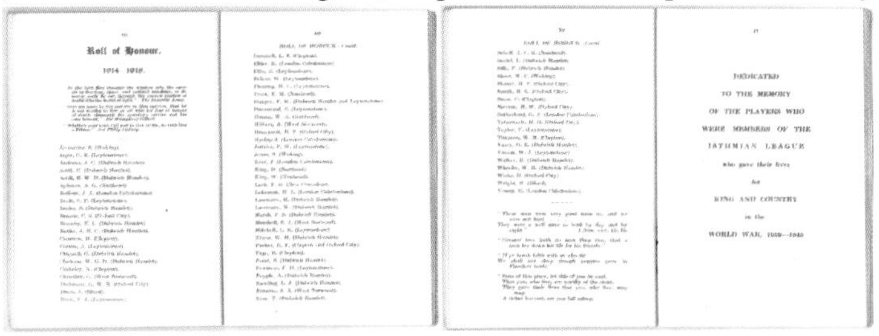

1919 UNOFFICIAL COMPETITION - The Isthmian League Council called a meeting on 18 December 1918 to arrange a competition to complete the 1918–19 season, although it would remain unofficial for the benefit of records. Of the 12 clubs in membership in 1914–15, Clapton, Dulwich Hamlet, Ilford, Leytonstone, and Nunhead indicated they would compete; Oxford City and Woking – who cited the difficulty in travelling to matches due to inadequate railway facilities – West Norwood and London Caledonians all declined to participate, while New Crusaders had disbanded, and no information was forthcoming from either Ealing Association or Shepherd's Bush. Clapton played their home matches at Ilford and Leytonstone as theirs was used by a company - Silley Weir's. Leytonstone went on to win the competition by one point from runners-up Ilford, followed by Dulwich Hamlet, Nunhead and Clapton.

	1	2	3	4	5
1 Clapton	*	3–3	0–7	0–4	2–2
2 Dulwich Hamlet	6–4	*	1–1	1–4	3–0
3 Ilford	2–2	2–4	*	1–0	3–0
4 Leytonstone	5–1	1–0	2–3	*	5–1
5 Nunhead	6–2	2–1	7–3	0–0	*

	P	*W*	*D*	*L*	*F*	*A*	*Pts*
1 Leytonstone	8	5	1	2	21	7	11
2 Ilford	8	4	2	2	22	16	10
3 Dulwich Hamlet	8	3	2	3	19	17	8
4 Nunhead	8	3	2	3	18	19	8
5 Clapton	8	0	3	5	14	35	3

At the Annual General Meeting, Casuals, Civil Service and Tufnell Park were invited to join the League to fill the vacancies created by the disbanded New Crusaders and Shepherd's Bush – although the former did play one last match in 1922 – and Ealing Association who opted to re-join the Southern Amateur League. Aquarius, Bromley, Catford Southend, Charlton Athletic, Chiswick Town, Civil Service, Custom House, Enfield, Guildford, Hampstead Town, Metrogas and St. Albans City had all shown interest in joining the Isthmian League for the first post-war season, but their applications were rejected.

1919–20 - The first official post-war season turned out to be the closest fought championship to date, with eventual champions Dulwich Hamlet winning their first title on goal average from Nunhead. Tufnell Park finished a creditable third, five points behind the champions, in their first season. Ilford took fourth place on goal average, ahead of Oxford City. West Norwood and Casuals were the bottom two and had to seek re-election. Although both clubs were re-elected, Casuals – who had arrived late for several matches and not always with a full complement of players – were only re-elected on the basis that an improvement must be made. Barking Town, Slough, Sutton United and Wycombe Wanderers had also applied but it was decided to keep League membership at 12 Clubs.

	1	2	3	4	5	6	7	8	9	10	11	12
1 Casuals	*	3–2	1–2	0–3	0–6	0–9	0–0	2–4	1–5	0–1	2–0	0–2
2 Civil Service	1–2	*	3–0	1–2	2–4	6–2	0–4	1–1	3–3	2–2	3–0	2–0
3 Clapton	8–2	3–1	*	0–4	0–2	5–3	1–1	2–4	2–4	0–0	1–1	3–2
4 Dulwich Hamlet	8–1	2–1	2–1	*	3–0	1–1	6–0	3–0	5–1	0–1	2–1	2–1
5 Ilford	12–1	2–3	0–2	1–5	*	4–2	2–1	2–3	3–1	3–6	2–2	4–1
6 Leytonstone	5–1	3–0	2–0	1–1	1–2	*	0–2	3–1	5–0	5–1	4–0	2–2
7 London Caledonians	5–1	0–1	1–0	1–0	1–3	1–0	*	0–2	3–3	0–1	3–1	1–3
8 Nunhead	1–1	1–0	3–2	0–0	3–0	3–0	0–2	*	4–2	3–0	4–0	3–0
9 Oxford City	4–0	4–0	2–1	3–2	1–2	5–0	3–2	3–3	*	3–2	4–1	5–3
10 Tufnell Park	2–0	2–1	5–0	+-+	1–4	4–0	1–2	2–2	2–4	*	0–0	2–1
11 West Norwood	3–2	0–2	0–3	0–5	0–4	1–0	1–0	1–2	3–1	1–7	*	2–2
12 Woking	5–0	0–0	1–2	1–2	3–1	3–2	1–2	0–1	4–2	1–3	0–1	*

	P	*W*	*D*	*L*	*F*	*A*	*Pts*
1 Dulwich Hamlet	22	15	3	4	58	16	33
2 Nunhead	22	14	5	3	48	26	33
3 Tufnell Park	22	12	4	6	45	32	28
4 Ilford	22	13	1	8	63	42	27
5 Oxford City	22	12	3	7	63	51	27
6 London Caledonians	22	10	3	9	32	30	23
7 Leytonstone	22	8	3	11	50	43	19
8 Clapton	22	8	3	11	38	44	19
9 Civil Service	22	7	4	11	35	40	18
10 Woking	22	6	3	13	36	42	15
11 West Norwood	22	5	4	13	19	53	14
12 Casuals	22	3	2	17	20	88	8

NOTE: Dulwich Hamlet v. Tufnell Park was played for four points.

1920–21 - Ilford won the League Championship for the second time by a five-point margin from London Caledonians and Tufnell Park, with Nunhead fourth. Casuals and West Norwood again occupied the bottom two positions and had to retire from membership, but both were duly re-elected at the Annual General Meeting. It was decided to increase the League membership to 14 clubs for the 1921–22 season, and 11 clubs applied for the two places. Wimbledon and Wycombe Wanderers were elected unanimously, while Barking Town, Chesham United, Grays Athletic, Great Eastern Railway, Guildford, Hampstead Town, Slough, Southend Corinthians and Sutton United were the unsuccessful applicants.

Kingstonians v. West Norwood F.C.
SURREY CHARITY SHIELD.
TEAMS.
KINGSTONIANS. Red and White Hoops, Blue Knickers.
RIGHT. LEFT.
1. R. CARROLL.
2. B. J. ROLLO 3. R. LEE
4. A. J. YATES 5. A. E. PALMER 6. W. J. KNIGHT
Kick-off, 2.30 p.m.
S. A. DAVENPORT 20. A. W. SMITH 21. A. E. HOLT 22.
T. P. DAVIS 23. E. SCHMID 24.
LEFT O. C. McGILL 25. RIGHT
WEST NORWOOD. Black and White Hoops.

Right: The teams for West Norwood's County Cup match at Kingstonian.

	1	2	3	4	5	6	7	8	9	10	11	12
1 Casuals	*	2–1	3–3	2–6	3–9	3–2	2–3	1–4	0–4	0–3	4–1	1–1
2 Civil Service	4–1	*	3–3	0–3	1–3	1–1	0–0	2–4	0–2	1–3	0–0	1–2
3 Clapton	2–2	0–0	*	1–0	1–3	2–1	1–0	2–7	2–2	1–1	7–1	1–0
4 Dulwich Hamlet	8–1	5–1	6–1	*	5–3	0–0	0–0	2–1	1–1	3–1	1–0	2–0
5 Ilford	2–1	3–1	8–0	2–1	*	2–1	1–1	4–0	3–0	4–1	5–0	7–0
6 Leytonstone	3–1	2–2	4–0	5–1	1–1	*	1–3	3–3	3–0	2–0	1–0	2–0
7 London Caledonians	6–0	2–2	5–1	0–0	2–0	2–0	*	6–1	4–1	0–1	1–0	2–0
8 Nunhead	5–1	4–0	0–0	2–1	2–2	3–1	1–0	*	4–2	0–1	4–2	2–0
9 Oxford City	9–1	2–1	3–1	4–1	1–1	3–1	1–3	2–1	*	4–1	4–1	3–0
10 Tufnell Park	5–0	2–1	2–0	2–2	0–1	1–0	3–1	1–1	3–2	*	4–1	3–0
11 West Norwood	4–1	0–3	0–2	1–10	1–2	0–1	0–2	0–4	2–6	0–4	*	1–1
12 Woking	2–1	1–3	1–2	2–2	1–4	1–1	0–2	0–0	4–0	0–1	0–2	*

	P	W	D	L	F	A	Pts
1 Ilford	22	16	4	2	70	24	36
2 London Caledonians	22	13	5	4	45	17	31
3 Tufnell Park	22	14	3	5	43	24	31
4 Nunhead	22	12	5	5	53	33	29
5 Dulwich Hamlet	22	11	6	5	60	30	28
6 Oxford City	22	12	3	7	56	38	27
7 Leytonstone	22	8	6	8	36	29	22
8 Clapton	22	7	7	8	33	52	21
9 Civil Service	22	3	7	12	28	45	13
10 Woking	22	3	5	14	16	43	11
11 Casuals	22	3	3	16	31	87	9
12 West Norwood	22	2	2	18	18	67	6

1921–22 - The season no doubt belonged to Ilford, who retained the League Championship, two points ahead of runners-up Dulwich Hamlet. London Caledonians finished a creditable third, seven points clear of fourth–placed Nunhead. Wimbledon, in their first season, and Casuals, who failed to win a match, had to retire from membership and subsequently applied for re-election. At the Annual General Meeting, both Wimbledon and Casuals were re-elected, while unsuccessful applications had been received from East Ham United, Farnham Breweries, Grays Athletic, Leyton, Millwall United, Slough and Windsor & Eton. The annual accounts showed a healthy balance of £148.

	1	2	3	4	5	6	7	8	9	10	11	12	13	14
1 Casuals	*	2–2	2–4	2–9	2–8	1–2	2–2	0–5	0 4	0 2	2 3	0 8	1 2	2 6
2 Civil Service	3–0	*	1–0	0–4	1–1	0–2	1–2	2–2	0–0	+-+	4–1	5–3	1–1	2–1
3 Clapton	4–2	1–1	*	1–3	1–2	1–0	0–1	3–3	5–1	5–1	3–1	1–2	2–0	3–2
4 Dulwich Hamlet	5–0	7–0	+-+	*	1–1	1–0	0–0	6–2	5–0	1–1	1–1	2–0	2–0	7–0
5 Ilford	3–2	4–1	0–2	1–1	*	3–1	1–0	2–0	4–2	2–0	5–2	1–0	4–2	9–1
6 Leytonstone	2–0	3–3	1–2	1–1	2–0	*	2–1	1–3	1–4	4–4	2–1	3–2	0-1	4–3
7 London Caledonians	3–1	1–0	1–0	2–1	4–1	1–0	*	2–0	0–1	2–1	0–0	3–2	4–2	3–0
8 Nunhead	8–0	1–2	2–2	0–2	1–2	4–2	1–0	*	6–0	5–0	4–1	1–1	2–1	2–3
9 Oxford City	4–0	1–2	1–3	5–0	0–2	5–1	1–0	3–1	*	0–2	3–0	4–2	5–2	2–1
10 Tufnell Park	3–0	4–1	4–1	1–1	3–1	1–1	0–0	2–2	4–0	*	4–0	3–2	1–2	0–1
11 West Norwood	2–1	3–1	5–0	2–0	0–1	2–2	1–5	0–1	1–0	5–2	*	2–2	4–4	2–1
12 Wimbledon	4–0	1–2	6–0	1–0	1–6	1–2	1–2	1–2	2–1	0–0	4–2	*	1–2	3–4
13 Woking	2–1	1–3	2–4	1–1	1–1	2–1	0–1	1–6	0–0	2–1	1–0	1–1	*	3–1
14 Wycombe Wndrs.	7–2	2–2	2–3	2–4	3–1	1–1	2–1	2–1	3–1	1–0	4–2	7–1	1–3	*

NOTE: Clapton v Dulwich Hamlet and Tufnell Park v Civil Service were each played for four points.

Above: a member of the Oxford City team that drew with Norwich City in The FA Cup during season 1921-22.

	P	W	D	L	F	A	Pts
1 Ilford	26	17	4	5	66	34	38
2 Dulwich Hamlet	26	14	8	4	65	24	36
3 London Caledonians	26	16	4	6	41	21	36
4 Nunhead	26	12	5	9	65	41	29
5 Clapton	26	13	3	10	51	46	29
6 Tufnell Park	26	10	7	9	44	39	27
7 Oxford City	26	12	2	12	48	47	26
8 Wycombe Wndrs.	26	12	2	12	61	64	26
9 Civil Service	26	9	8	9	40	48	26
10 Woking	26	10	6	10	39	49	26
11 Leytonstone	26	9	6	11	41	48	24
12 West Norwood	26	8	5	13	43	57	21
13 Wimbledon	26	7	4	15	52	56	18
14 Casuals	26	0	2	24	25	107	2

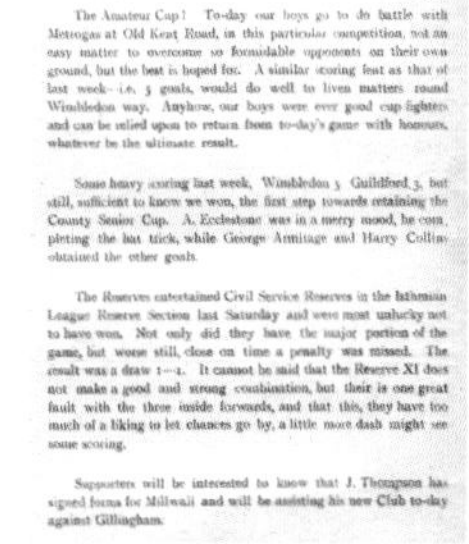

CLUB NOTES.

First Team Fixtures. Reserve Team Fixtures.

Isthmian League Table. Isthmian League Table.

Left: extracts from a Wimbledon programme during the season.

1922–23 - Clapton secured their first championship since 1911 when they won the title by two points from Nunhead. London Caledonians finished third for the second season running, while previous champions Ilford were fourth. Oxford City and West Norwood retired from membership. West Norwood were applying for re-election for the ninth time in their 11 seasons as members of the Isthmian League – and in 1922 they had avoided re-election by a solitary place. This application proved to be unlucky for the Bantams as St. Albans City were invited to take their place. They had also suffered problems with their ground and had played their home matches on opponents' grounds, something which did not meet with League Council approval. The voting at the Annual General Meeting was as follows: *Oxford City 24, St. Albans City 19, West Norwood 4*. Interest to join was also shown by Bromley and Kingstonian but their applications were not considered by the League Council.

	1	2	3	4	5	6	7	8	9	10	11	12	13	14
1 Casuals	*	0–2	3–4	4–4	3–2	2–2	3–0	1–0	2–0	7–1	8–0	1–2	0–0	2–2
2 Civil Service	2–7	*	3–1	2–6	1–1	4–4	0–0	2–0	1–1	2–0	3–2	2–1	1–2	4–1
3 Clapton	4–1	1–0	*	1–1	1–1	0–0	2–1	1–4	6–0	1–1	2–2	1–0	1–0	3–1
4 Dulwich Hamlet	2–2	0–0	0–1	*	5–1	1–1	0–3	2–3	2–2	2–1	8–1	4–3	6–1	3–0
5 Ilford	4–1	0–0	0–0	0–1	*	4–0	0–1	2–2	4–2	2–1	4–1	4–2	7–1	5–1
6 Leytonstone	2–1	1–1	1–1	4–1	2–1	*	0–4	1–2	3–1	3–4	2–1	1–0	5–3	1–0
7 London Caledonians	5–1	1–1	1–3	1–0	1–0	1–1	*	1–1	4–2	2–1	3–0	0–0	2–1	0–2
8 Nunhead	2–4	1–1	1–0	1–1	0–1	3–1	2–1	*	5–1	2–1	1–2	1–0	2–2	1–5
9 Oxford City	1–2	1–0	2–3	4–2	0–2	5–1	2–2	1–3	*	1–0	3–2	5–2	3–3	4–5
10 Tufnell Park	3–3	3–1	1–4	2–1	4–0	2–0	0–3	0–1	3–0	*	5–0	3–2	2–2	0–1
11 West Norwood	0–3	0–4	0–2	0–6	1–1	3–2	1–1	0–4	0–0	1–1	*	0–1	4–0	1–0
12 Wimbledon	0–3	1–0	3–5	2–0	3–2	7–2	0–2	0–1	4–0	1–1	4–1	*	0–3	4–2
13 Woking	4–1	0–1	1–2	2–1	2–7	0–3	2–1	0–2	4–2	1–1	2–0	1–3	*	1–1
14 Wycombe Wndrs.	3–4	1–1	5–1	2–1	2–2	4–2	1–2	1–7	3–2	3–0	1–2	5–4	9–4	*

Above: action from Nunhead's 2-1 victory over Tufnell Park in 1923.

Season 1922-23	P	W	D	L	F	A	PTS
1 Clapton	26	15	7	4	51	33	37
2 Nunhead	26	15	5	6	52	32	35
3 London Caledonians	26	13	7	6	43	26	33
4 Ilford	26	11	7	8	57	38	29
5 Casuals	26	12	5	9	68	51	29
6 Civil Service	26	9	10	7	39	36	28
7 Wycombe Wndrs.	26	11	4	11	61	61	26
8 Dulwich Hamlet	26	9	7	10	60	44	25
9 Leytonstone	26	9	7	10	45	56	25
10 Tufnell Park	26	9	5	12	41	45	23
11 Wimbledon	26	10	2	14	49	50	22
12 Woking	26	7	6	13	42	67	20
13 Oxford City	26	6	5	15	45	68	17
14 West Norwood	26	5	5	16	25	71	15

Above: Tufnell Park FC early in their Isthmian career.

Above: St. Albans City – Isthmian League Champions 1923-24 Back row; Bert Sansom, Ted Barnes, Fred Holland. Middle row; Edward Keightley, Percy Bird, Harold Figg, Fred Hellicar, WJ Green (hon.sec), Sid Duller. Front row; Fred Dear, George Biswell, Wilfred Minter, Ted Miller, Redvers Miller. Photograph taken 24 April 1924, St. Albans City 4-1 London Caledonians.

1923–24 - St. Albans City won the League championship in their first season, three points clear of Dulwich Hamlet with Clapton and Wycombe Wanderers third and fourth, respectively. Oxford City – for the second year running – and Leytonstone had to retire from membership, although both clubs were re-elected at the Annual General Meeting. Applications to join the League for 1924–25 were received from Grays Athletic, Great Eastern Railway (Romford), Leyton, London Welsh and Walthamstow Avenue but although the applications were considered none were recommended for membership. It was decided by the League Council to provide a suitable flag, bearing League colours, to be presented to the League champions at the end of each season. This custom only ceased at the end of the hundredth season by which time very few clubs had flagpoles and the art of flying a flag was an outdated one.

Right: the Ilford programme from 1924-25 season.

	1	2	3	4	5	6	7	8	9	10	11	12	13	14
1 Casuals	*	5–2	1–3	0–4	6–2	1–2	3–2	3–0	4–1	0–4	4–1	8–3	5–1	6–2
2 Civil Service	2–1	*	2–1	2–0	2–1	1–0	2–2	4–1	3–0	0–3	2–5	3–2	6–3	6–0
3 Clapton	2–3	1–1	*	0–1	4–2	5–2	3–1	3–2	5–1	4–4	2–0	4–1	6–2	2–3
4 Dulwich Hamlet	1–0	0–0	2–2	*	3–2	6–1	2–1	4–0	4–0	0–4	1–0	1–0	0–0	4–2
5 Ilford	1–3	3–1	1–1	2–2	*	4–3	1–1	1–2	6–0	1–0	2–2	6–0	3–0	1–8
6 Leytonstone	0–1	2–1	2–3	0–2	2–2	*	3–4	2–2	3–2	0–0	2–1	2–1	1–0	2–3
7 London Caledonians	2–1	4–1	3–1	1–1	3–2	4–3	*	2–1	3–0	2–1	0–2	3–1	4–2	4–0
8 Nunhead	4–0	2–2	2–4	0–0	1–1	4–1	1–0	*	3–3	0–0	6–1	0–2	2–1	2–2
9 Oxford City	3–1	2–4	0–1	1–3	5–0	4–1	0–1	0–2	*	3–6	3–1	3–1	11–2	6–1
10 St. Albans City	3–1	2–1	2–2	2–3	3–2	5–2	4–1	3–0	5–1	*	5–1	3–2	1–0	5–0
11 Tufnell Park	0–1	1–2	3–5	1–0	0–2	4–0	0–3	0–2	7–1	1–3	*	1–0	3–1	0–1
12 Wimbledon	3–2	1–0	3–5	2–3	3–2	3–1	3–0	2–0	1–1	2–3	4–0	*	1–1	1–1
13 Woking	1–1	1–1	2–1	1–0	2–3	2–1	4–1	0–0	1–0	0–0	0–2	1–1	*	1–6
14 Wycombe Wndrs.	5–4	4–1	4–3	4–2	2–3	3–3	7–1	5–2	5–2	9–1	1–1	8–0	2–2	*

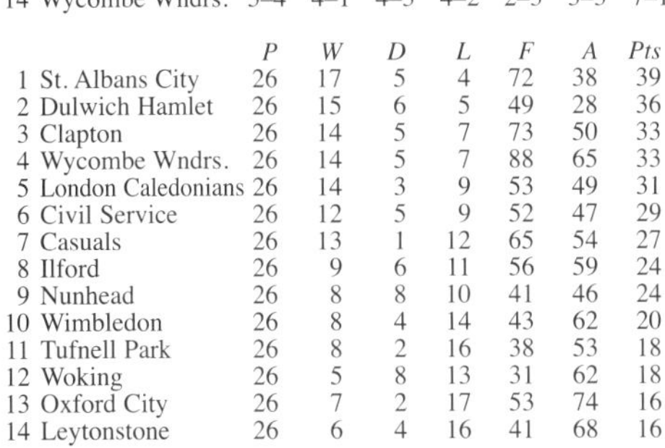

	P	W	D	L	F	A	Pts
1 St. Albans City	26	17	5	4	72	38	39
2 Dulwich Hamlet	26	15	6	5	49	28	36
3 Clapton	26	14	5	7	73	50	33
4 Wycombe Wndrs.	26	14	5	7	88	65	33
5 London Caledonians	26	14	3	9	53	49	31
6 Civil Service	26	12	5	9	52	47	29
7 Casuals	26	13	1	12	65	54	27
8 Ilford	26	9	6	11	56	59	24
9 Nunhead	26	8	8	10	41	46	24
10 Wimbledon	26	8	4	14	43	62	20
11 Tufnell Park	26	8	2	16	38	53	18
12 Woking	26	5	8	13	31	62	18
13 Oxford City	26	7	2	17	53	74	16
14 Leytonstone	26	6	4	16	41	68	16

Below: St. Albans City pictured prior to a fixture away to Tufnell Park on 15 September 1923 when a Wilfred Minter hat-trick secured the Saints' first League victory.

1924–25 - London Caledonians secured their sixth Isthmian League championship, finishing two points in front of Clapton who in turn had a five-point advantage of third-placed St. Albans City. Tufnell Park – the best of three teams on 26 points – finished fourth, but they were only six points ahead of Oxford City, who had to apply for re-election for a third consecutive season, and eight behind St. Albans. Woking, who last applied for re-election in 1914, finished bottom of the table with just 13 points. Aldershot Traction Company, Erith & Belvedere, Leyton and Northampton Nomads all made applications to join the League and Bromley and Kingstonian both indicated they would accept an invitation. The League Council, however, re-elected Oxford and Woking for the following season.

	1	2	3	4	5	6	7	8	9	10	11	12	13	14
1 Casuals	*	4–3	2–3	2–1	0–0	2–1	4–5	0–7	3–4	3–0	0–2	3–1	6–1	5–3
2 Civil Service	3–2	*	2–3	1–2	0–3	2–2	2–5	1–1	3–1	2–1	1–1	2–6	3–1	0–3
3 Clapton	3–0	3–4	*	2–4	1–0	3–2	1–3	1–0	4–1	4–2	2–2	3–0	8–1	2–1
4 Dulwich Hamlet	0–2	3–2	0–2	*	0–1	5–1	2–2	0–2	0–0	0–2	3–0	4–2	2–2	0–4
5 Ilford	2–0	0–2	0–1	2–1	*	4–2	1–4	2–2	2–0	0–0	3–0	3–1	6–0	5–1
6 Leytonstone	2–1	5–2	1–2	6–2	2–0	*	2–2	2–4	2–1	1–0	0–2	4–3	5–3	2–1
7 London Caledonians	0–1	6–3	0–2	1–1	5–1	4–0	*	4–0	1–1	2–1	2–2	2–0	1–0	3–0
8 Nunhead	1–4	0–1	1–2	3–3	1–4	3–1	3–7	*	2–0	0–0	4–0	1–1	3–1	3–0
9 Oxford City	1–3	1–5	0–3	4–2	4–2	2–4	1–5	2–0	*	0–5	3–1	2–0	5–0	3–2
10 St. Albans City	5–3	6–3	3–2	6–1	6–2	2–1	1–3	2–1	5–0	*	3–2	0–1	5–2	4–0
11 Tufnell Park	3–1	2–1	0–3	2–0	3–0	4–0	2–4	1–0	6–0	0–1	*	5–1	3–1	1–2
12 Wimbledon	2–0	2–3	1–3	1–3	1–1	4–0	1–3	0–2	4–0	3–2	3–1	*	1–0	4–5
13 Woking	6–1	0–1	2–0	0–3	1–0	4–5	0–1	2–0	0–1	0–1	0–0	1–3	*	4–2
14 Wycombe Wndrs.	0–3	1–1	2–1	5–0	4–2	1–2	4–1	2–1	7–1	3–6	3–2	1–4	1–1	*

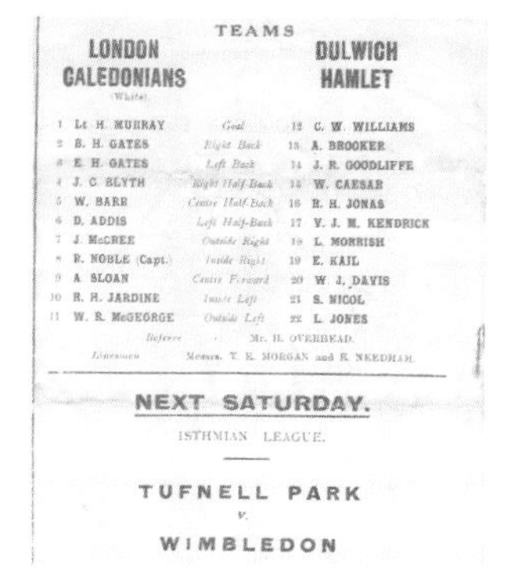

Above: the teams for the 1-1 draw between London Caledonians and Dulwich Hamlet.

Left: Nunhead FC between the two wars.

Season 1924-25	P	W	D	L	F	A	PTS
1 London Caledonians	26	18	5	3	76	36	41
2 Clapton	26	19	1	6	64	34	39
3 St. Albans City	26	16	2	8	69	39	34
4 Tufnell Park	26	11	4	11	47	41	26
5 Ilford	26	11	4	11	46	42	26
6 Leytonstone	26	12	2	12	55	63	26
7 Casuals	26	12	1	13	55	58	25
8 Wycombe Wndrs.	26	11	2	13	58	61	24
9 Civil Service	26	10	4	12	52	64	24
10 Nunhead	26	9	5	12	45	43	23
11 Wimbledon	26	10	2	14	50	54	22
12 Dulwich Hamlet	26	8	5	13	42	57	21
13 Oxford City	26	9	2	15	38	71	20
14 Woking	26	5	3	18	33	67	13

1925–26 - The championship went to Dulwich Hamlet, who clinched their second title, four points clear of London Caledonians, the defending champions. Clapton were third, with Wycombe Wanderers fourth. At the other end of the table, Oxford City – again – had to retire from membership, this time along with Civil Service.

Despite applications from Great Eastern Railway (Romford), Grays Athletic and Leyton, the two resigning clubs were re-elected. Bromley and Kingstonian were again interested had an invitation to join the League been forthcoming. Although they only finished in fourth position, Wycombe Wanderers scored 97 goals, the highest number scored in one season so far.

The League Council also suffered a double blow in its ranks. Chairman WA Brown resigned his position in February owing to ill-health and Sir Arthur Holmes was elected to succeed him. Then Referees Secretary JR Schumacher resigned, also due to ill-health; he was replaced by an active referee, Stanley Rous, at the Annual General Meeting.

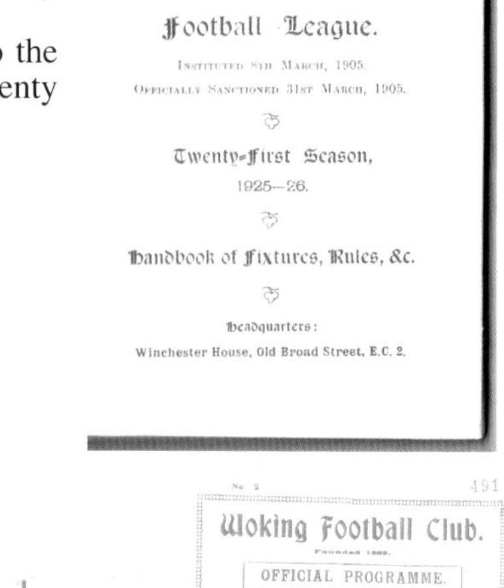

Messrs Brown and Schumacher were honoured for their contribution to the Isthmian League by being made the first Life Members. Only a further twenty men were accorded this honour in the first hundred years.

	1	2	3	4	5	6	7	8	9	10	11	12	13	14
1 Casuals	*	6–0	0–1	2–3	3–2	1–2	2–5	2–1	4–2	2–5	0–0	3–5	1–1	1–1
2 Civil Service	3–5	*	2–5	3–11	3–1	3–1	2–4	0–1	0–1	3–5	4–1	0–5	1–1	6–5
3 Clapton	8–1	5–0	*	3–0	3–3	4–1	0–0	3–2	3–1	5–1	2–2	2–3	3–4	2–1
4 Dulwich Hamlet	4–1	4–1	0–4	*	2–4	2–1	2–1	2–0	2–0	3–1	5–0	6–3	7–5	3–1
5 Ilford	1–0	5–3	6–0	0–1	*	6–1	7–1	0–2	5–3	4–3	2–0	5–1	3–1	4–6
6 Leytonstone	2–1	9–1	3–0	2–3	5–3	*	5–3	7–1	1–2	1–3	2–4	6–0	8–1	4–1
7 London Caledonians	4–1	2–0	3–1	5–2	6–0	2–1	*	2–3	7–1	5–2	1–0	4–2	1–0	9–1
8 Nunhead	3–0	3–0	4–1	1–5	4–2	1–2	3–5	*	2–1	1–1	2–1	1–0	3–0	0–1
9 Oxford City	2–1	2–1	1–0	0–2	2–4	3–2	3–1	1–2	*	3–6	2–3	2–4	3–4	7–2
10 St. Albans City	1–4	1–2	1–1	2–3	5–1	7–2	1–0	3–3	6–0	*	1–1	3–0	4–0	4–1
11 Tufnell Park	0–2	1–0	1–3	3–3	1–3	0–2	0–4	0–0	3–0	0–2	*	2–1	3–2	2–4
12 Wimbledon	3–2	6–1	0–2	1–2	4–1	6–2	0–1	1–4	2–2	2–1	1–3	*	4–5	2–4
13 Woking	1–1	4–0	1–2	1–2	3–3	2–0	1–0	1–1	3–2	3–3	1–4	4–3	*	3–5
14 Wycombe Wndrs.	1–2	5–4	9–1	4–1	7–6	3–3	4–5	2–1	6–2	4–4	4–1	9–2	6–4	*

	P	*W*	*D*	*L*	*F*	*A*	*Pts*
1 Dulwich Hamlet	26	20	1	5	80	49	41
2 London Caledonians	26	18	1	7	81	44	37
3 Clapton	26	14	4	8	64	50	32
4 Wycombe Wndrs.	26	14	3	9	97	83	31
5 St. Albans City	26	12	6	8	76	54	30
6 Nunhead	26	13	4	9	49	43	30
7 Ilford	26	13	2	11	81	70	28
8 Leytonstone	26	12	1	13	75	63	25
9 Woking	26	8	6	12	56	73	22
10 Tufnell Park	26	8	5	13	36	53	21
11 Casuals	26	8	4	14	48	61	20
12 Wimbledon	26	9	1	16	61	77	19
13 Oxford City	26	8	1	17	48	76	17
14 Civil Service	26	5	1	20	43	99	11

Right: the Woking programme for their game with champions Dulwich Hamlet, which the visitors won 2-1.

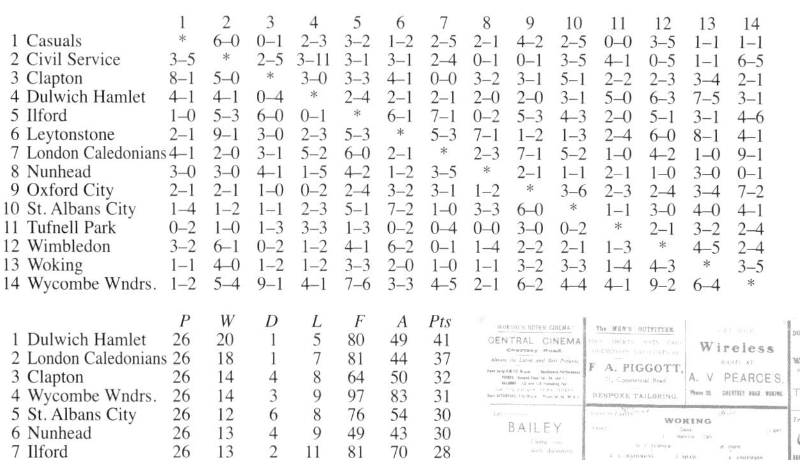

1926–27 - St. Albans City raced to the championship, matching Dulwich Hamlet's year-old record of 20 wins, and finishing seven points clear of runner-up Ilford, scoring 96 goals in the process.

Wimbledon finished third, their highest League position, and Nunhead were fourth. Casuals and Civil Service, who retired from membership as the bottom clubs in the League, were both unanimously re-elected at the Annual General Meeting, despite applications from Bromley and Grays Athletic.

Above: Harold Figg – St. Albans City 1919-20 to 1932-33 (370 app, 56 goals).

	1	2	3	4	5	6	7	8	9	10	11	12	13	14
1 Casuals	*	1–0	2–1	1–0	1–7	3–3	3–2	1–2	1–0	1–3	2–0	2–1	1–1	1–3
2 Civil Service	1–2	*	2–3	2–3	1–4	1–2	3–2	0–0	4–0	0–5	1–4	0–3	2–4	6–0
3 Clapton	4–3	2–2	*	0–1	6–3	3–1	4–3	1–2	1–1	2–1	1–2	2–6	3–3	4–3
4 Dulwich Hamlet	3–3	4–2	3–0	*	3–4	3–2	1–3	2–2	6–0	0–1	2–1	2–2	1–3	8–1
5 Ilford	3–1	6–2	1–0	3–1	*	10–0	0–2	1–0	3–1	1–0	3–2	2–10	5–3	5–1
6 Leytonstone	3–1	1–4	5–1	3–2	0–2	*	2–8	3–2	3–1	0–4	3–2	1–0	6–3	4–1
7 London Caledonians	2–1	2–2	0–0	2–1	1–0	6–1	*	0–0	2–2	2–0	2–2	1–4	2–2	3–0
8 Nunhead	6–0	1–1	0–3	2–2	4–2	4–0	3–1	*	2–1	1–2	1–0	2–2	8–0	3–2
9 Oxford City	7–1	1–5	1–6	5–3	1–2	3–1	2–3	2–1	*	1–1	2–2	1–0	2–2	2–1
10 St. Albans City	13–1	3–0	6–4	3–0	5–2	4–1	2–1	4–2	6–1	*	3–0	3–1	5–2	9–0
11 Tufnell Park	4–1	1–2	4–0	3–1	0–4	1–4	3–1	0–0	2–3	2–1	*	4–1	0–4	2–2
12 Wimbledon	4–1	2–1	4–0	0–6	3–2	2–1	4–1	2–2	5–2	5–2	3–1	*	2–3	3–0
13 Woking	2–1	5–1	0–3	5–1	5–0	4–2	2–2	0–1	3–2	2–4	2–0	0–2	*	5–1
14 Wycombe Wndrs.	3–1	4–3	1–4	5–1	4–1	3–2	3–4	1–0	6–2	2–6	6–3	3–1	3–3	*

	P	*W*	*D*	*L*	*F*	*A*	*Pts*
1 St. Albans City	26	20	1	5	96	34	41
2 Ilford	26	17	0	9	76	57	34
3 Wimbledon	26	15	3	8	72	45	33
4 Nunhead	26	11	8	7	51	33	30
5 Woking	26	12	6	8	68	60	30
6 London Caledonians	26	11	7	8	58	47	29
7 Clapton	26	11	4	11	58	60	26
8 Leytonstone	26	11	1	14	54	78	23
9 Dulwich Hamlet	26	9	4	13	60	58	22
10 Wycombe Wndrs.	26	10	2	14	59	86	22
11 Tufnell Park	26	8	4	14	45	55	20
12 Oxford City	26	7	5	14	46	72	19
13 Casuals	26	8	3	13	37	78	19
14 Civil Service	26	6	4	16	48	65	16

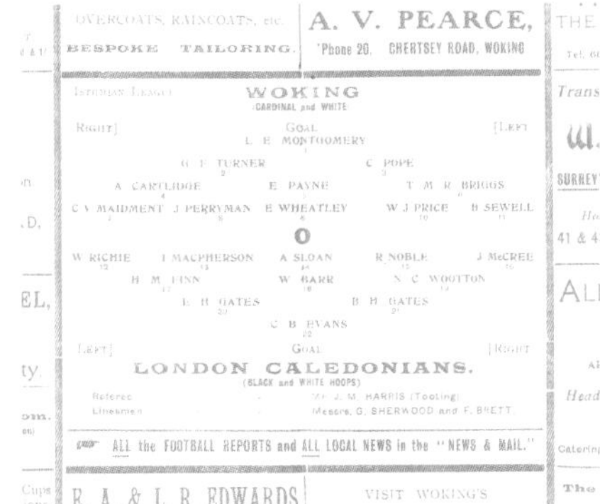

Left: the teams from Woking's 2-2 draw with London Caledonians.

1927–28 - The 1927–28 championship was a much closer affair, with St. Albans City retaining their title by two points from London Caledonians, who finished one point ahead of Ilford with Woking, in turn, a further point adrift in fourth.

Civil Service had to retire from membership for the third successive season along with Tufnell Park. Grays Athletic made an application to join the League, but at the Annual General Meeting the League Council recommended that Civil Service and Tufnell Park should be re-elected.

It was also agreed that, as from 1928–29, the League should not be a closed corporation. Effectively, it meant that it would be the Clubs who voted on applications to join the League – rather than taking recommendations from the League Council – and if Clubs believed the applicants would be of benefit to the League, then they should be elected.

	1	2	3	4	5	6	7	8	9	10	11	12	13	14
1 Casuals	*	8–0	1–1	2–2	2–5	2–1	0–0	6–1	1–1	2–5	3–0	4–3	2–2	1–3
2 Civil Service	4–2	*	2–2	1–1	3–3	1–3	2–2	2–0	1–0	2–1	2–1	0–2	2–8	3–1
3 Clapton	4–4	3–1	*	0–2	3–3	7–1	1–2	0–2	2–1	4–1	2–2	1–2	1–1	2–0
4 Dulwich Hamlet	4–0	10–2	1–1	*	1–4	1–1	2–2	5–2	1–2	2–3	3–2	4–0	2–0	2–1
5 Ilford	2–0	1–3	5–1	3–2	*	3–0	0–5	4–1	2–0	5–3	2–2	3–2	2–3	5–0
6 Leytonstone	5–0	0–1	4–3	4–0	0–4	*	1–2	1–4	3–1	0–2	7–2	1–0	4–1	2–1
7 London Caledonians	0–1	3–1	2–0	1–1	2–1	4–1	*	4–1	2–2	6–4	4–0	1–4	1–2	2–2
8 Nunhead	2–3	5–0	0–0	4–2	1–4	5–2	2–0	*	0–1	2–3	6–1	2–0	3–1	3–1
9 Oxford City	2–2	2–0	1–0	1–1	4–2	3–0	0–4	0–0	*	1–4	2–3	2–1	4–5	1–1
10 St. Albans City	2–2	4–1	1–2	1–1	1–1	5–2	2–1	5–0	8–0	*	7–1	2–2	4–2	6–1
11 Tufnell Park	0–1	1–0	2–3	1–1	2–3	0–2	2–2	1–5	5–0	1–4	*	1–4	2–0	1–2
12 Wimbledon	3–2	4–1	1–4	2–0	3–0	0–2	2–2	1–2	2–1	3–3	4–2	*	5–1	6–1
13 Woking	2–1	6–1	1–1	5–3	7–4	3–4	2–2	4–0	4–1	3–0	5–2	2–1	*	1–1
14 Wycombe Wndrs.	4–2	3–2	4–4	4–2	3–1	1–2	2–7	3–4	3–3	3–5	8–1	4–0	3–1	*

Above: Nunhead's programme for their game against Ilford which they lost 4-1.

	P	*W*	*D*	*L*	*F*	*A*	*Pts*
1 St. Albans City	26	15	5	6	86	50	35
2 London Caledonians	26	12	9	5	63	38	33
3 Ilford	26	14	4	8	72	54	32
4 Woking	26	13	5	8	72	56	31
5 Nunhead	26	13	2	11	57	54	28
6 Wimbledon	26	12	3	11	57	48	27
7 Leytonstone	26	13	1	12	53	56	27
8 Clapton	26	8	10	8	52	47	26
9 Dulwich Hamlet	26	8	9	9	56	49	25
10 Casuals	26	8	8	10	54	58	24
11 Wycombe Wndrs.	26	9	5	12	60	69	23
12 Oxford City	26	7	7	12	36	57	21
13 Civil Service	26	8	4	14	37	78	20
14 Tufnell Park	26	4	4	18	38	82	12

Left: Leytonstone's edition for their game against Woking which also finished 4-1, to the Stones.

1928–29 - In a close-fought championship, Nunhead came out on top. They won their first title, by two points from London Caledonians and near neighbours Dulwich Hamlet, with Wimbledon fourth. Woking finished 13th and Civil Service bottom, six points adrift. Both clubs had to resign in accordance with League rules, but while the Cardinals applied for re-election at the Annual General meeting, Civil Service opted not to, confirming their resignation from League membership. They returned to the Southern Amateur League. A number of applications were received to replace Civil Service and in an election involving Bromley, Hampstead Town and Kingstonian it was the Ks who secured the majority of the vote. Great Eastern Railway (Romford), Grays Athletic, Maidenhead United, Redhill and Romford had also shown keen interest but these clubs were not considered suitable for membership.

The League President, the Rt. Hon. Earl of Rosebery – Archibald Primrose, British Prime Minister 1894–95 – passed away on 21 May 1929. It was agreed to recommend to the Annual General Meeting that his eldest son – the 6th Earl of Rosebery – should be elected to succeed to his father as League President.

	1	2	3	4	5	6	7	8	9	10	11	12	13	14
1 Casuals	*	0–0	4–2	1–3	3–1	2–4	0–1	1–2	4–0	4–0	1–3	0–3	0–2	1–1
2 Civil Service	3–6	*	1–2	1–5	1–2	4–1	1–0	2–4	2–2	2–4	1–2	2–2	2–4	2–4
3 Clapton	5–1	3–1	*	2–3	2–2	2–2	1–1	0–0	4–4	0–4	5–0	0–1	2–1	3–5
4 Dulwich Hamlet	1–0	1–1	3–1	*	0–2	3–1	4–1	2–2	7–1	4–0	1–1	0–0	4–0	6–0
5 Ilford	6–7	1–2	2–3	2–0	*	5–1	2–0	1–2	3–4	5–0	3–2	2–2	4–0	6–2
6 Leytonstone	4–2	6–2	1–5	2–1	0–5	*	2–1	2–3	4–0	2–2	4–1	2–2	3–2	3–1
7 London Caledonians	4–1	2–0	1–4	2–1	2–0	12–0	*	2–2	5–1	6–0	1–2	4–2	2–0	1–1
8 Nunhead	0–2	2–0	1–2	1–0	0–0	3–2	1–1	*	0–2	2–1	3–3	3–2	1–2	3–2
9 Oxford City	7–1	5–2	5–3	1–0	4–3	6–2	1–4	0–1	*	5–1	2–3	2–3	1–1	4–1
10 St. Albans City	3–2	6–0	4–1	4–6	3–0	4–2	0–2	2–3	4–0	*	2–2	4–3	3–2	2–0
11 Tufnell Park	2–3	3–2	3–1	1–2	1–3	2–3	0–2	0–3	2–0	8–2	*	1–1	3–1	3–2
12 Wimbledon	1–1	1–1	1–4	1–1	5–1	6–0	5–4	2–4	5–1	3–3	3–3	*	4–2	2–0
13 Woking	2–2	1–0	1–3	3–3	2–4	1–0	1–2	0–1	2–1	2–5	0–5	5–3	*	1–0
14 Wycombe Wndrs.	0–0	2–4	3–0	3–4	4–2	2–3	1–2	2–0	4–2	3–0	4–2	4–3	7–1	*

	P	*W*	*D*	*L*	*F*	*A*	*Pts*
1 Nunhead	26	15	6	5	47	35	36
2 London Caledonians	26	15	4	7	65	33	34
3 Dulwich Hamlet	26	14	6	6	65	34	34
4 Wimbledon	26	9	10	7	66	54	28
5 Ilford	26	12	3	11	67	52	27
6 Clapton	26	11	5	10	60	55	27
7 Tufnell Park	26	11	5	10	58	55	27
8 St. Albans City	26	12	3	11	63	69	27
9 Leytonstone	26	11	3	12	56	79	25
10 Wycombe Wndrs.	26	10	3	13	58	60	23
11 Oxford City	26	10	3	13	61	71	23
12 Casuals	26	8	5	13	49	60	21
13 Woking	26	8	3	15	39	65	19
14 Civil Service	26	4	5	17	39	71	13

OFFICIAL PROGRAMME. 1d.
Leytonstone Football Club.
Members of F.A., L.F.A., E.C.F.A., and ISTHMIAN LEAGUE.
CLUB NOTES.
WILLIAMSONS, LTD.
High-Class Catering and Confectionery.
LUNCHEON & DINING ROOMS. TEAS & LIGHT REFRESHMENTS.
The best cup of tea 2d. freshly made for each customer.
664 & 666, HIGH ROAD, LEYTONSTONE.

Right: Leytonstone's programme for their 2-2 draw with St. Albans City.

1929–30 - Nunhead secured back-to-back championships, winning the title by five points from Dulwich Hamlet, with debutants Kingstonian finishing a creditable third, one point ahead of Ilford. At the other end of the table London Caledonians, Leytonstone and Tufnell Park all finished level on points with Caleys escaping re-election by virtue of a better goal average (it was 0.0015 of a goal better than Leytonstone and 0.022 better than Tufnell Park). At the Annual General meeting, an application from Hampstead Town proved unsuccessful as Leytonstone and Tufnell Park were both re-elected.

	1	2	3	4	5	6	7	8	9	10	11	12	13	14
1 Casuals	*	5–0	2–3	5–3	1–1	5–3	5–0	1–1	2–1	1–0	1–1	2–3	2–2	2–2
2 Clapton	2–1	*	3–3	1–5	1–2	1–4	2–3	0–1	5–1	2–2	2–1	1–3	3–1	7–1
3 Dulwich Hamlet	2–2	3–0	*	3–2	1–0	3–1	5–3	1–2	3–0	5–0	6–0	2–0	0–0	7–0
4 Ilford	7–0	1–1	1–2	*	1–3	3–2	5–2	2–1	7–1	3–0	1–0	5–3	5–1	2–1
5 Kingstonian	2–1	2–2	3–2	3–4	*	5–2	5–0	3–1	1–2	1–1	3–0	1–3	2–0	2–0
6 Leytonstone	2–5	2–0	1–3	1–4	3–2	*	2–6	1–2	1–1	3–1	0–0	1–3	6–1	2–0
7 London Caledonians	1–0	1–3	2–5	2–5	1–3	0–1	*	2–4	1–0	0–3	1–1	6–2	3–0	2–1
8 Nunhead	1–0	3–1	2–2	4–3	2–0	2–0	3–2	*	2–0	7–1	4–0	3–1	3–0	3–1
9 Oxford City	3–1	1–2	2–0	6–3	1–1	2–3	2–1	2–5	*	2–1	6–4	2–1	4–1	1–0
10 St. Albans City	2–2	4–2	1–6	1–5	2–4	4–2	2–3	2–2	5–2	*	5–1	4–3	5–3	3–2
11 Tufnell Park	0–1	3–1	1–1	0–3	0–3	4–0	1–1	1–2	2–1	2–3	*	2–2	1–1	2–0
12 Wimbledon	3–0	1–4	5–2	7–1	1–2	2–2	3–2	1–4	0–1	6–2	4–2	*	2–4	3–1
13 Woking	3–1	1–0	4–4	9–3	5–1	5–1	4–2	5–4	4–1	4–0	0–3	6–1	*	2–2
14 Wycombe Wndrs.	3–2	2–1	2–0	1–0	0–2	4–2	2–2	4–1	4–1	4–0	2–3	4–1	6–0	*.

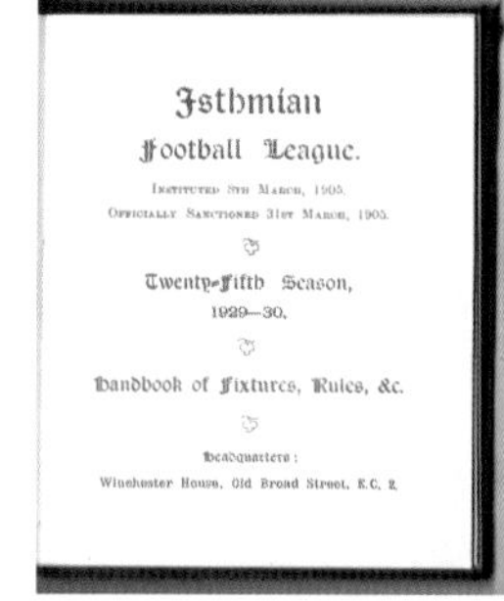
Isthmian
Football League.
Instituted [illegible] March, 1905.
Officially Sanctioned 31st March, 1905.
Twenty-Fifth Season,
1929—30.
Handbook of Fixtures, Rules, &c.
Headquarters:
Winchester House, Old Broad Street, E.C. 2.

	P	*W*	*D*	*L*	*F*	*A*	*Pts*
1 Nunhead	26	19	3	4	69	36	41
2 Dulwich Hamlet	26	15	6	5	74	39	36
3 Kingstonian	26	15	4	7	57	37	34
4 Ilford	26	16	1	9	84	60	33
5 Woking	26	11	5	10	66	65	27
6 Wimbledon	26	11	2	13	64	66	24
7 Wycombe Wndrs.	26	10	4	12	49	52	24
8 Casuals	26	8	7	11	50	51	23
9 Oxford City	26	10	3	13	45	60	23
10 St. Albans City	26	9	4	13	54	77	22
11 Clapton	26	8	4	14	47	57	20
12 London Caledonians	26	8	3	15	49	69	19
13 Leytonstone	26	8	3	15	48	68	19
14 Tufnell Park	26	6	7	13	35	54	19

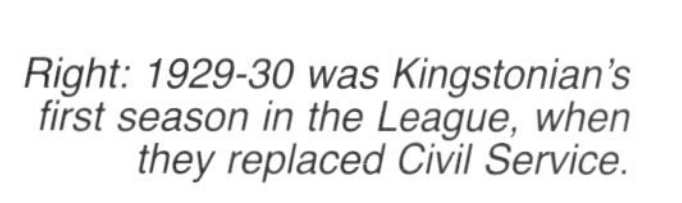
Right: 1929-30 was Kingstonian's first season in the League, when they replaced Civil Service.

1930–31 - Wimbledon won their first Isthmian League Championship by nine points, and with a new record of 42 points out of a maximum of 52, from Dulwich Hamlet, who were again runners-up, with Wycombe Wanderers in third. Wycombe's total of 30 points was actually only eight more than Woking, who were in 12th spot. Leytonstone and Clapton were both rather detached at the bottom of the table – six and four points respectively behind the Cardinals – but they were re-elected. Cambridge Town, Hampstead Town, Maidenhead United, Bromley and Walthamstow Avenue all made unsuccessful applications.

	1	2	3	4	5	6	7	8	9	10	11	12	13	14
1 Casuals	*	6–2	1–1	3–2	6–1	5–1	0–0	2–1	4–2	2–2	5–3	2–3	1–2	3–0
2 Clapton	3–5	*	1–5	1–2	2–3	2–2	1–1	4–0	0–1	3–6	3–2	1–3	8–4	5–1
3 Dulwich Hamlet	3–3	3–2	*	3–3	2–2	2–1	3–1	2–2	2–4	1–0	3–1	0–1	1–4	2–2
4 Ilford	5–3	2–2	1–3	*	0–3	4–3	7–2	8–2	4–0	3–3	5–1	2–2	4–5	0–2
5 Kingstonian	3–1	1–6	2–2	1–5	*	5–2	4–0	1–0	2–4	4–0	1–3	1–2	6–2	2–0
6 Leytonstone	1–3	4–2	0–2	2–4	6–0	*	0–2	2–5	2–0	5–2	1–2	0–0	2–2	1–3
7 London Caledonians	3–1	2–1	2–2	4–1	2–2	1–3	*	0–2	1–2	1–1	1–1	3–1	0–1	1–0
8 Nunhead	2–2	4–0	0–1	4–1	5–0	2–2	3–2	*	0–0	3–4	4–0	1–3	2–1	2–1
9 Oxford City	2–0	3–3	0–1	3–0	4–1	2–1	0–1	2–0	*	1–2	1–2	2–2	1–1	0–5
10 St. Albans City	4–5	4–2	1–4	0–0	3–1	3–1	5–3	3–0	2–4	*	2–2	3–7	2–4	4–2
11 Tufnell Park	2–0	0–2	2–2	4–1	2–0	3–1	2–2	2–1	3–1	1–2	*	1–2	1–3	3–3
12 Wimbledon	5–4	3–2	0–0	3–2	1–1	4–0	7–2	2–0	4–1	2–2	2–0	*	4–3	3–1
13 Woking	0–1	2–3	0–1	2–2	0–2	1–2	0–3	4–2	3–1	4–4	5–2	2–3	*	0–1
14 Wycombe Wndrs.	3–3	6–1	3–1	2–2	4–0	4–1	3–3	5–2	2–2	1–3	8–0	1–0	4–1	*

	P	*W*	*D*	*L*	*F*	*A*	*Pts*
1 Wimbledon	26	18	6	2	69	37	42
2 Dulwich Hamlet	26	12	9	5	51	39	33
3 Wycombe Wndrs.	26	12	6	8	67	45	30
4 Casuals	26	12	6	8	71	56	30
5 St. Albans City	26	11	7	8	67	66	29
6 Ilford	26	10	6	10	70	62	26
7 Oxford City	26	10	5	11	43	48	25
8 London Caledonians	26	8	8	10	43	53	24
9 Kingstonian	26	10	4	12	49	64	24
10 Tufnell Park	26	9	5	12	45	61	23
11 Nunhead	26	9	4	13	49	54	22
12 Woking	26	9	4	13	56	63	22
13 Clapton	26	7	4	15	62	75	18
14 Leytonstone	26	6	4	16	46	65	16

Oxford City v London Caledonians, note the players are numbered from 1 to 22.

1931–32 - Wimbledon's second consecutive Isthmian League championship was a very close-run thing. They finished a point ahead of nearest challengers Ilford, with Dulwich Hamlet two points adrift in third, but ahead only on goal average from Wycombe Wanderers. Woking and London Caledonians, the retiring clubs, were both re-elected despite strong applications from Maidenhead United, Barnet and Hampstead Town. The Caleys went through a miserable season, collecting only two wins and 11 points.

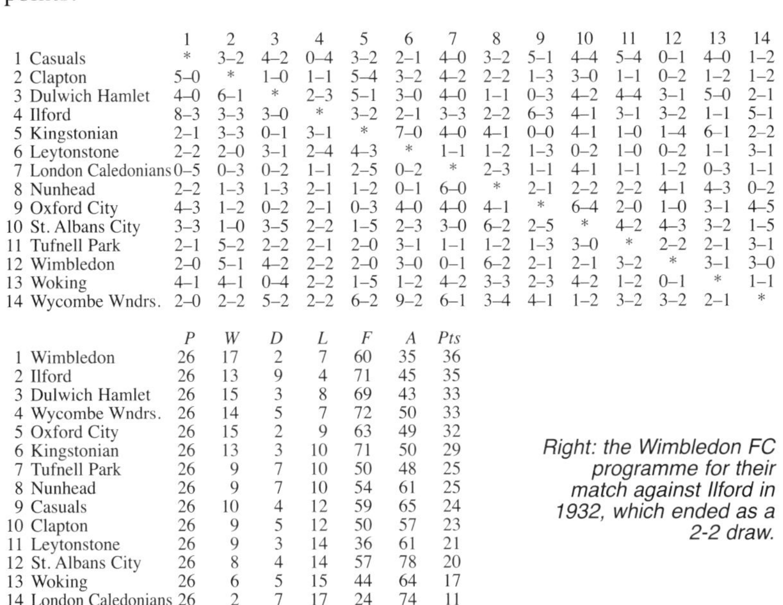

	1	2	3	4	5	6	7	8	9	10	11	12	13	14
1 Casuals	*	3–2	4–2	0–4	3–2	2–1	4–0	3–2	5–1	4–4	5–4	0–1	4–0	1–2
2 Clapton	5–0	*	1–0	1–1	5–4	3–2	4–2	2–2	1–3	3–0	1–1	0–2	1–2	1–2
3 Dulwich Hamlet	4–0	6–1	*	2–3	5–1	3–0	4–0	1–1	0–3	4–2	4–4	3–1	5–0	2–1
4 Ilford	8–3	3–3	3–0	*	3–2	2–1	3–3	2–2	6–3	4–1	3–1	3–2	1–1	5–1
5 Kingstonian	2–1	3–3	0–1	3–1	*	7–0	4–0	4–1	0–0	4–1	1–0	1–4	6–1	2–2
6 Leytonstone	2–2	2–0	3–1	2–4	4–3	*	1–1	1–2	1–3	0–2	1–0	0–2	1–1	3–1
7 London Caledonians	0–5	0–3	0–2	1–1	2–5	0–2	*	2–3	1–1	4–1	1–1	1–2	0–3	1–1
8 Nunhead	2–2	1–3	1–3	2–1	1–2	0–1	6–0	*	2–1	2–2	2–2	4–1	4–3	0–2
9 Oxford City	4–3	1–2	0–2	2–1	0–3	4–0	4–0	4–1	*	6–4	2–0	1–0	3–1	4–5
10 St. Albans City	3–3	1–0	3–5	2–2	1–5	2–3	3–0	6–2	2–5	*	4–2	4–3	3–2	1–5
11 Tufnell Park	2–1	5–2	2–2	2–1	2–0	3–1	1–1	1–2	1–3	3–0	*	2–2	2–1	3–1
12 Wimbledon	2–0	5–1	4–2	2–2	2–0	3–0	0–1	6–2	2–1	2–1	3–2	*	3–1	3–0
13 Woking	4–1	4–1	0–4	2–2	1–5	1–2	4–2	3–3	2–3	4–2	1–2	0–1	*	1–1
14 Wycombe Wndrs.	2–0	2–2	5–2	2–2	6–2	9–2	6–1	3–4	4–1	1–2	3–2	3–2	2–1	*

	P	*W*	*D*	*L*	*F*	*A*	*Pts*
1 Wimbledon	26	17	2	7	60	35	36
2 Ilford	26	13	9	4	71	45	35
3 Dulwich Hamlet	26	15	3	8	69	43	33
4 Wycombe Wndrs.	26	14	5	7	72	50	33
5 Oxford City	26	15	2	9	63	49	32
6 Kingstonian	26	13	3	10	71	50	29
7 Tufnell Park	26	9	7	10	50	48	25
8 Nunhead	26	9	7	10	54	61	25
9 Casuals	26	10	4	12	59	65	24
10 Clapton	26	9	5	12	50	57	23
11 Leytonstone	26	9	3	14	36	61	21
12 St. Albans City	26	8	4	14	57	78	20
13 Woking	26	6	5	15	44	64	17
14 London Caledonians	26	2	7	17	24	74	11

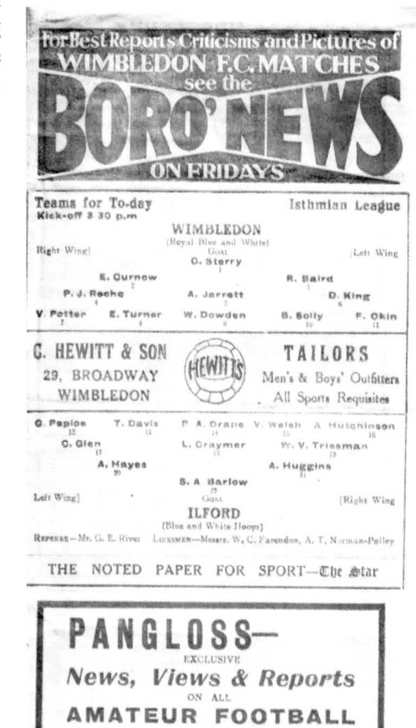

For Best Reports Criticisms and Pictures of
WIMBLEDON F.C. MATCHES
see the
BORO' NEWS
ON FRIDAYS

Teams for To-day — Isthmian League
Kick-off 3 30 p.m

WIMBLEDON
(Royal Blue and White)
Right Wing] — Goal — [Left Wing
C. Sterry 1
E. Curnow 2 — R. Baird 3
P. J. Roche 4 — A. Jarrett 5 — D. King 6
V. Potter 7 — E. Turner 8 — W. Dowden 9 — B. Solly 10 — F. Okin 11

G. HEWITT & SON
29, BROADWAY
WIMBLEDON
HEWITT'S
TAILORS
Men's & Boys' Outfitters
All Sports Requisites

G. Peploe 12 — T. Davis 13 — P. A. Drane 14 — V. Welsh 15 — A. Hutchinson 16
C. Glen 17 — L. Craymer 18 — W. V. Triesman 19
A. Hayes 20 — A. Huggins 21
S. A. Barlow 22
Left Wing] — Goal — [Right Wing
ILFORD
(Blue and White Hoops)
Referee—Mr. G. E. River — Linesmen—Messrs. W. C. Farendon, A. T. Norman-Polley

THE NOTED PAPER FOR SPORT—The Star

PANGLOSS—
EXCLUSIVE
News, Views & Reports
ON ALL
AMATEUR FOOTBALL
ONLY IN THE
News Chronicle

Newsome & Co., Printers, 17, Victoria Crescent, Broadway, Wimbledon.

Right: the Wimbledon FC programme for their match against Ilford in 1932, which ended as a 2-2 draw.

1932–33 - Dulwich Hamlet, who had finished either second or third in four consective seasons, finally secured the League championship, albeit on goal average from Leytonstone, four points ahead of third-placed Kingstonian, with Ilford a similar distance behind in fourth position. Defending Champions Wimbledon slipped to 13th position and had to retire from membership, along with London Caledonians who more than doubled their win total from 1931–32, but still finished bottom by five points. Both the Dons and Caleys were re-elected without difficulty at the Annual General Meeting because there had been no applications for new members.

The League suffered a blow when the former Referees & Fixture Secretary and life member Dick Schumacher died on 6 June.

		1	2	3	4	5	6	7	8	9	10	11	12	13	14
1	Casuals	*	5–0	2–3	2–3	0–3	1–2	1–0	0–0	4–0	4–1	0–1	4–2	5–3	2–1
2	Clapton	2–1	*	0–5	3–5	4–3	1–1	4–2	4–0	1–1	1–3	3–1	3–2	5–1	3–0
3	Dulwich Hamlet	3–1	0–0	*	2–1	5–2	2–3	1–1	4–1	4–2	2–1	4–2	6–2	2–2	3–2
4	Ilford	2–1	0–1	3–0	*	1–0	6–3	2–1	5–1	3–2	3–2	0–4	1–4	1–0	5–3
5	Kingstonian	0–1	5–1	1–0	6–3	*	6–3	8–3	7–1	0–4	7–3	3–2	6–1	1–3	3–1
6	Leytonstone	0–1	3–2	2–2	1–0	2–0	*	8–1	2–2	4–1	4–3	1–1	2–0	3–1	2–1
7	London Caledonians	0–1	3–3	3–2	2–1	0–1	0–1	*	1–4	0–0	0–1	2–1	1–3	3–0	2–0
8	Nunhead	1–0	5–0	2–3	2–4	1–1	1–4	7–0	*	0–0	1–0	3–0	1–1	2–1	0–0
9	Oxford City	0–3	4–2	2–2	2–1	1–1	4–2	2–2	1–0	*	4–2	2–1	2–5	5–1	0–3
10	St. Albans City	3–2	3–2	0–4	2–1	2–4	0–2	7–4	4–2	3–1	*	2–1	4–1	1–6	4–0
11	Tufnell Park	0–4	3–4	2–2	3–1	3–0	1–6	2–1	0–1	4–1	2–1	*	2–1	4–0	2–2
12	Wimbledon	3–1	2–1	5–0	1–4	1–3	1–3	1–1	2–0	2–6	2–2	2–6	*	5–1	2–3
13	Woking	1–0	1–1	3–4	5–3	2–1	3–1	1–1	4–3	2–1	3–0	2–3	2–2	*	5–1
14	Wycombe Wndrs.	2–2	6–0	0–6	5–1	1–5	2–1	2–1	2–1	2–1	0–3	3–0	2–2	3–0	*

		P	*W*	*D*	*L*	*F*	*A*	*Pts*
1	Dulwich Hamlet	26	15	6	5	71	45	36
2	Leytonstone	26	16	4	6	66	43	36
3	Kingstonian	26	15	2	9	77	49	32
4	Ilford	26	14	0	12	60	58	28
5	Casuals	26	12	2	12	48	36	26
6	Tufnell Park	26	11	3	12	51	51	25
7	St. Albans City	26	12	1	13	57	63	25
8	Clapton	26	10	5	11	51	65	25
9	Oxford City	26	9	6	11	49	54	24
10	Woking	26	10	4	12	53	61	24
11	Wycombe Wndrs.	26	10	4	12	47	56	24
12	Nunhead	26	8	6	12	42	50	22
13	Wimbledon	26	8	5	13	55	67	21
14	London Caledonians	26	5	6	15	35	64	16

Above: the Dulwich Hamlet programme for their match with Tufnell Park in 1932 - unusually for the Champion Hill club on blue paper!

Left: the Kingstonian side which finished third at the end of 1932-33.

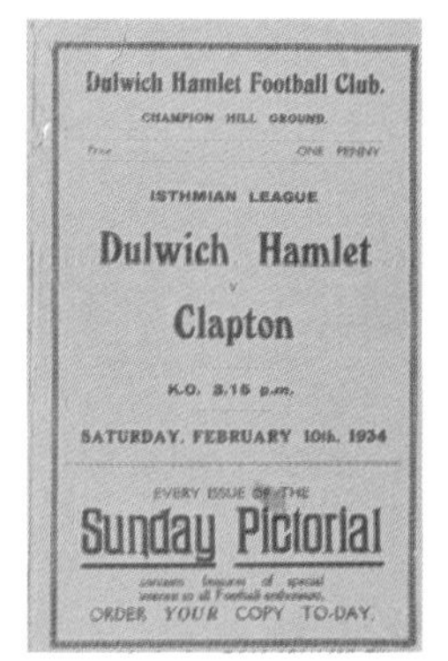

1933–34 - Kingstonian won their first League championship by two points from nearest challengers and 1933 champions Dulwich Hamlet. Wimbledon, who as defending champions had been forced to apply for re-election the previous year, yo-yoed back to third, ahead of Tufnell Park on goal average. The bottom two, Woking and Clapton, were both re-elected although applications were received from Epsom Town, Golders Green (previously Hampstead Town), Hitchin Town, Leyton, Maidenhead United, Metropolitan Police and Walthamstow Avenue.

Three Isthmian officials were appointed to high offices away from the League: Secretary Henry Huband was elected Treasurer of The Football Association in 1934 and, away from football, was appointed by the Lord Chancellor as a Justice of the Peace in the County of London; Stanley Rous was compelled to resign his position as Referees & Fixture Secretary of the League because of his appointment as Secretary of The FA, but he was subsequently elected as a life member of the Isthmian League; and League Vice-Chairman Andrew Ralston was also elected to The FA Council.

Above left: Dulwich Hamlet's programme for their game with Clapton, which the Essex side won 2-1.

		1	2	3	4	5	6	7	8	9	10	11	12	13	14
1	Casuals	*	6–1	1–3	3–1	2–2	3–1	1–2	1–0	4–3	2–0	3–0	3–3	2–0	2–0
2	Clapton	2–1	*	2–0	1–2	2–2	0–3	1–1	1–1	0–0	1–2	4–1	1–3	4–0	1–1
3	Dulwich Hamlet	2–0	1–2	*	2–3	5–1	4–1	2–1	1–1	2–0	6–1	2–2	3–1	6–1	2–0
4	Ilford	1–2	3–2	2–1	*	3–1	1–1	6–2	3–2	3–1	3–1	1–3	2–1	4–1	2–1
5	Kingstonian	0–0	2–2	2–2	3–1	*	5–2	6–1	4–2	3–2	7–1	3–1	2–3	3–0	7–2
6	Leytonstone	1–0	5–2	2–1	8–0	1–4	*	2–1	3–0	1–0	5–1	3–3	0–2	3–2	2–2
7	London Caledonians	0–0	1–0	2–6	1–0	1–1	0–1	*	0–0	2–2	2–2	0–0	0–0	4–0	2–0
8	Nunhead	0–1	3–2	0–2	2–1	1–4	3–1	2–0	*	2–0	8–0	1–2	1–1	3–0	5–0
9	Oxford City	2–2	4–2	1–3	2–3	0–2	6–0	4–0	4–2	*	0–0	1–4	0–5	4–1	2–1
10	St. Albans City	0–4	4–1	5–0	2–4	2–0	0–3	2–0	2–2	2–1	*	0–1	3–3	4–2	4–2
11	Tufnell Park	2–0	2–0	1–1	3–3	1–5	4–2	0–3	4–1	3–1	7–1	*	4–3	1–0	3–0
12	Wimbledon	1–2	7–0	2–2	3–1	2–2	2–0	6–0	0–1	2–1	1–0	0–1	*	4–4	4–1
13	Woking	2–1	5–1	1–4	1–4	1–5	0–3	6–1	2–4	2–3	5–4	4–2	0–2	*	3–1
14	Wycombe Wndrs.	3–1	2–0	1–5	6–3	2–4	2–1	1–2	5–1	6–1	5–1	8–0	1–2	4–0	*

		P	*W*	*D*	*L*	*F*	*A*	*Pts*
1	Kingstonian	26	15	7	4	80	42	37
2	Dulwich Hamlet	26	15	5	6	68	36	35
3	Wimbledon	26	13	7	6	63	35	33
4	Tufnell Park	26	14	5	7	55	50	33
5	Ilford	26	15	2	9	60	56	32
6	Casuals	26	13	5	8	47	32	31
7	Leytonstone	26	13	3	10	55	48	29
8	Nunhead	26	10	5	11	48	44	25
9	London Caledonians	26	7	8	11	29	51	22
10	Wycombe Wndrs.	26	9	2	15	57	60	20
11	St. Albans City	26	8	4	14	44	75	20
12	Oxford City	26	7	4	15	45	57	18
13	Clapton	26	5	6	15	35	62	16
14	Woking	26	6	1	19	43	81	13

Above: Tufnell Park's programme for their match against Leytonstone.

Below: the League Handbook for the 1934-35 season.

1934–35 - League Secretary Henry Huband announced that he would stand down at the end of the season due to his commitments with The Football Association. Sidney Donaldson succeeded Stanley Rous as Referees & Fixture Secretary.

On the pitch, Wimbledon won the League championship, three points clear of Oxford City, with Leytonstone third on goal average. Goal average also separated fourth and fifth, Dulwich Hamlet and Tufnell Park. At the bottom, Wycombe Wanderers and Casuals, who retired from membership, were both re-elected; no applications for membership were received. Also at the Annual General Meeting, the recently retired League Secretary Huband was elected as the fourth life member of the League.

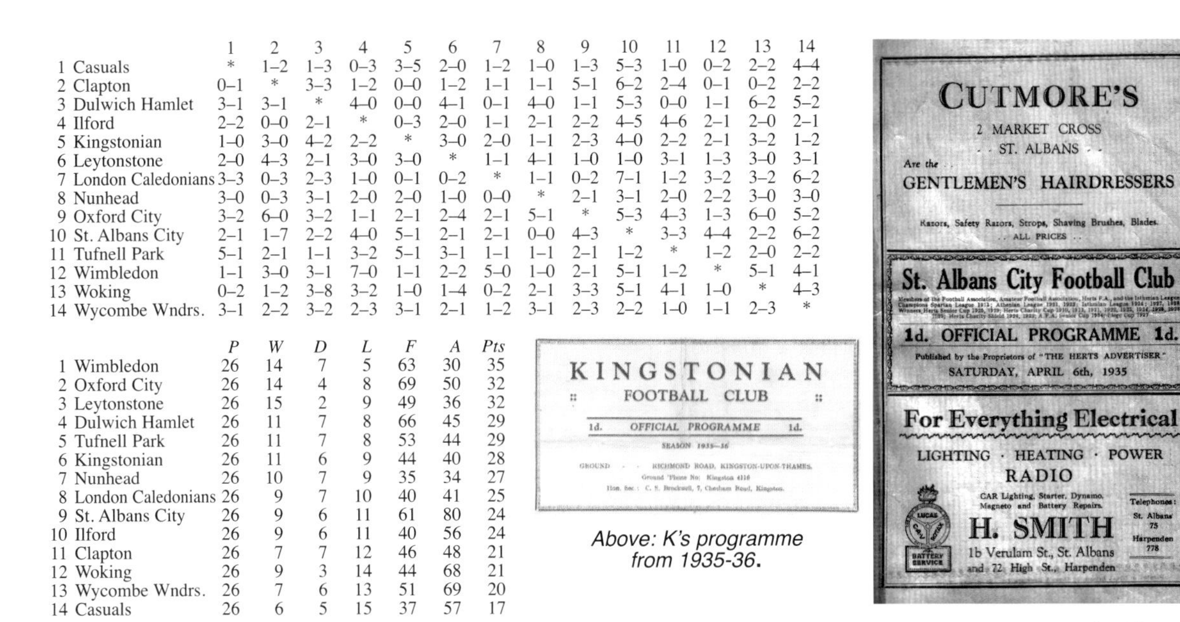

	1	2	3	4	5	6	7	8	9	10	11	12	13	14
1 Casuals	*	1–2	1–3	0–3	3–5	2–0	1–2	1–0	1–3	5–3	1–0	0–2	2–2	4–4
2 Clapton	0–1	*	3–3	1–2	0–0	1–2	1–1	1–1	5–1	6–2	2–4	0–1	0–2	2–2
3 Dulwich Hamlet	3–1	3–1	*	4–0	0–0	4–1	0–1	4–0	1–1	5–3	0–0	1–1	6–2	5–2
4 Ilford	2–2	0–0	2–1	*	0–3	2–0	1–1	2–1	2–2	4–5	4–6	2–1	2–0	2–1
5 Kingstonian	1–0	3–0	4–2	2–2	*	3–0	2–0	1–1	2–3	4–0	2–2	2–1	3–2	1–2
6 Leytonstone	2–0	4–3	2–1	3–0	3–0	*	1–1	4–1	1–0	1–0	3–1	1–3	3–0	3–1
7 London Caledonians	3–3	0–3	2–3	1–0	0–1	0–2	*	1–1	0–2	7–1	1–2	3–2	3–2	6–2
8 Nunhead	3–0	0–3	3–1	2–0	2–0	1–0	0–0	*	2–1	3–1	2–0	2–2	3–0	3–0
9 Oxford City	3–2	6–0	3–2	1–1	2–1	2–4	2–1	5–1	*	5–3	4–3	1–3	6–0	5–2
10 St. Albans City	2–1	1–7	2–2	4–0	5–1	2–1	2–1	0–0	4–3	*	3–3	4–4	2–2	6–2
11 Tufnell Park	5–1	2–1	1–1	3–2	5–1	3–1	1–1	1–1	2–1	1–2	*	1–2	2–0	2–2
12 Wimbledon	1–1	3–0	3–1	7–0	1–1	2–2	5–0	1–0	2–1	5–1	1–2	*	5–1	4–1
13 Woking	0–2	1–2	3–8	3–2	1–0	1–4	0–2	2–1	3–3	5–1	4–1	1–0	*	4–3
14 Wycombe Wndrs.	3–1	2–2	3–2	2–3	3–1	2–1	1–2	3–1	2–3	2–2	1–0	1–1	2–3	*

	P	*W*	*D*	*L*	*F*	*A*	*Pts*
1 Wimbledon	26	14	7	5	63	30	35
2 Oxford City	26	14	4	8	69	50	32
3 Leytonstone	26	15	2	9	49	36	32
4 Dulwich Hamlet	26	11	7	8	66	45	29
5 Tufnell Park	26	11	7	8	53	44	29
6 Kingstonian	26	11	6	9	44	40	28
7 Nunhead	26	10	7	9	35	34	27
8 London Caledonians	26	9	7	10	40	41	25
9 St. Albans City	26	9	6	11	61	80	24
10 Ilford	26	9	6	11	40	56	24
11 Clapton	26	7	7	12	46	48	21
12 Woking	26	9	3	14	44	68	21
13 Wycombe Wndrs.	26	7	6	13	51	69	20
14 Casuals	26	6	5	15	37	57	17

Above: K's programme from 1935-36.

Above: St. Albans City programme cover v Leytonstone. 6 April 1935.

1935–36 - Vice-Chairman Andrew Ralston was elected to succeed Henry Huband as League Secretary with Sid Meadows assuming the role of Vice-Chairman. Wimbledon retained the championship, finishing seven points clear of Casuals, whose second-place was their best-ever position – just a season after finishing bottom. Ilford were in third place, four points behind Casuals, with Dulwich Hamlet a point further back in fourth. Kingstonian ended up bottom of the table just behind Leytonstone, whose drop from third place in 1935 was almost as precipitous as Casuals' rise. The retiring clubs were both re-elected as, yet again, no other clubs applied for membership.

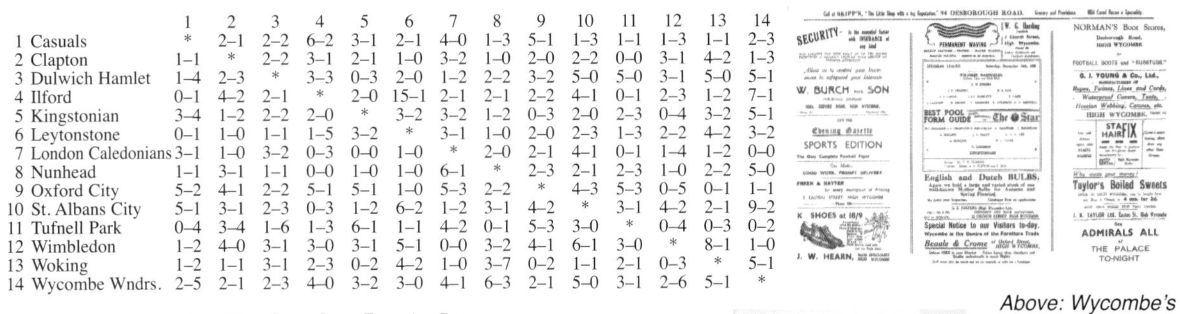

	1	2	3	4	5	6	7	8	9	10	11	12	13	14
1 Casuals	*	2–1	2–2	6–2	3–1	2–1	4–0	1–3	5–1	1–3	1–1	1–3	1–1	2–3
2 Clapton	1–1	*	2–2	3–1	2–1	1–0	3–2	1–0	2–0	2–2	0–0	3–1	4–2	1–3
3 Dulwich Hamlet	1–4	2–3	*	3–3	0–3	2–0	1–2	2–2	3–2	5–0	5–0	3–1	5–0	5–1
4 Ilford	0–1	4–2	2–1	*	2–0	15–1	2–1	2–1	2–2	4–1	0–1	2–3	1–2	7–1
5 Kingstonian	3–4	1–2	2–2	2–0	*	3–2	3–2	1–2	0–3	2–0	2–3	0–4	3–2	5–1
6 Leytonstone	0–1	1–0	1–1	1–5	3–2	*	3–1	1–0	2–0	2–3	1–3	2–2	4–2	3–2
7 London Caledonians	3–1	1–0	3–2	0–3	0–0	1–0	*	2–0	2–1	4–1	0–1	1–4	1–2	0–0
8 Nunhead	1–1	3–1	1–1	0–0	1–0	1–0	6–1	*	2–3	2–1	2–3	1–0	2–2	5–0
9 Oxford City	5–2	4–1	2–2	5–1	5–1	1–0	5–3	2–2	*	4–3	5–3	0–5	0–1	1–1
10 St. Albans City	5–1	3–1	2–3	0–3	1–2	6–2	1–2	3–1	4–2	*	3–1	4–2	2–1	9–2
11 Tufnell Park	0–4	3–4	1–6	1–3	6–1	1–1	4–2	0–1	5–3	3–0	*	0–4	0–3	0–2
12 Wimbledon	1–2	4–0	3–1	3–0	3–1	5–1	0–0	3–2	4–1	6–1	3–0	*	8–1	1–0
13 Woking	1–2	1–1	3–1	2–3	0–2	4–2	1–0	3–7	0–2	1–1	2–1	0–3	*	5–1
14 Wycombe Wndrs.	2–5	2–1	2–3	4–0	3–2	3–0	4–1	6–3	2–1	5–0	3–1	2–6	5–1	*

Above: Wycombe's programme for their home game with Kingstonian, which Wanderers won 3-2.

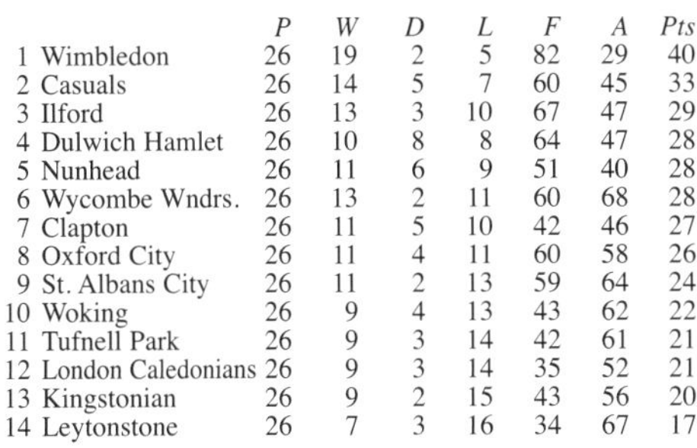

	P	*W*	*D*	*L*	*F*	*A*	*Pts*
1 Wimbledon	26	19	2	5	82	29	40
2 Casuals	26	14	5	7	60	45	33
3 Ilford	26	13	3	10	67	47	29
4 Dulwich Hamlet	26	10	8	8	64	47	28
5 Nunhead	26	11	6	9	51	40	28
6 Wycombe Wndrs.	26	13	2	11	60	68	28
7 Clapton	26	11	5	10	42	46	27
8 Oxford City	26	11	4	11	60	58	26
9 St. Albans City	26	11	2	13	59	64	24
10 Woking	26	9	4	13	43	62	22
11 Tufnell Park	26	9	3	14	42	61	21
12 London Caledonians	26	9	3	14	35	52	21
13 Kingstonian	26	9	2	15	43	56	20
14 Leytonstone	26	7	3	16	34	67	17

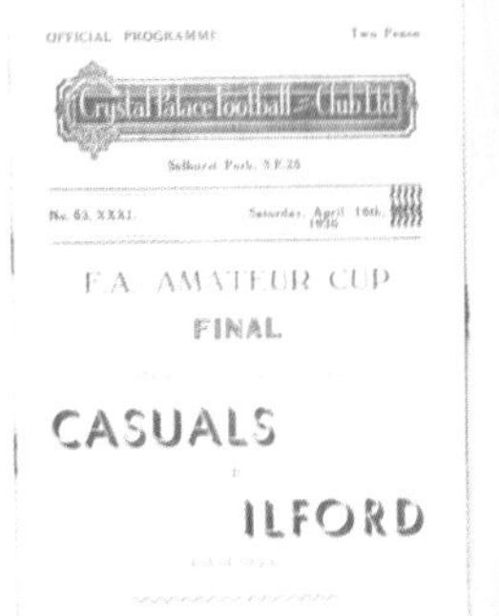

Left: the 1936 FA Amateur Cup Final and replay programmes for the ties involving The Casuals and Ilford, which The Casuals won.

1936–37 - In January 1937 Finchley Football Club proposed an amalgamation of the Isthmian, Athenian, Spartan and London Leagues into a Greater London Amateur League. Although some clubs in the Isthmian League were in favour of a form of amalgamation, none favoured the scheme as submitted. After much discussion it was decided that the League Council was unable to support the proposal. Another special meeting was held at which the League stated that no transfers of players between member Clubs would be granted after 31 December of each year.

The unpredictable nature of the League season was proved yet again as the bottom two in 1936, Leytonstone and Kingstonian, finished in the top three. The Ks took the League title by two points from Nunhead, with Leytonstone a point behind and Ilford in fourth. With no applications received for membership, the bottom two clubs, Tufnell Park and London Caledonians, both retired and were re-elected.

Right: a cartoon from the Amateur Cup Final programme in 1936.

	1	2	3	4	5	6	7	8	9	10	11	12	13	14
1 Casuals	*	4–3	0–4	1–4	4–1	1–5	2–1	1–1	2–2	4–0	2–0	2–3	3–3	4–0
2 Clapton	2–1	*	0–2	0–0	1–3	1–1	3–1	3–1	4–3	2–1	2–2	2–1	1–1	0–0
3 Dulwich Hamlet	1–2	2–0	*	2–2	1–2	3–0	3–0	2–1	2–2	8–0	2–1	1–1	4–2	1–5
4 Ilford	0–2	4–3	4–6	*	11–0	1–4	6–0	4–0	10–0	5–0	4–0	0–0	2–0	6–0
5 Kingstonian	2–0	7–0	1–0	3–2	*	5–1	2–0	1–1	4–2	2–1	5–1	6–1	3–0	2–2
6 Leytonstone	6–0	2–0	2–2	2–1	5–0	*	6–0	2–0	5–1	2–0	1–1	4–0	6–0	5–2
7 London Caledonians	1–3	1–2	3–1	1–3	0–0	1–2	*	0–7	3–3	2–1	2–1	1–2	0–2	2–0
8 Nunhead	4–0	2–0	1–1	0–2	6–2	2–0	7–0	*	5–2	1–0	6–1	3–2	5–1	5–3
9 Oxford City	3–2	2–1	1–5	2–2	1–3	8–2	1–0	0–4	*	3–2	4–8	3–3	4–3	2–1
10 St. Albans City	2–0	3–2	6–4	3–1	1–2	4–4	1–4	3–1	2–3	*	0–0	2–0	2–4	4–1
11 Tufnell Park	1–2	2–3	4–4	4–3	0–5	2–3	1–1	0–3	3–1	2–2	*	1–3	5–2	2–2
12 Wimbledon	3–0	3–2	0–2	2–2	0–1	0–1	1–0	1–5	6–3	2–2	5–0	*	7–3	2–2
13 Woking	4–3	1–3	2–1	2–4	0–1	5–0	1–1	1–4	2–0	2–1	4–0	3–3	*	3–2
14 Wycombe Wndrs.	2–1	1–2	6–0	2–3	2–0	2–0	5–1	0–2	5–0	1–1	3–1	2–1	4–2	*

	P	*W*	*D*	*L*	*F*	*A*	*Pts*
1 Kingstonian	26	18	3	5	63	43	39
2 Nunhead	26	17	3	6	77	32	37
3 Leytonstone	26	16	4	6	71	42	36
4 Ilford	26	14	5	7	86	39	33
5 Dulwich Hamlet	26	12	6	8	64	48	30
6 Wycombe Wndrs.	26	10	5	11	55	52	25
7 Wimbledon	26	9	7	10	52	53	25
8 Clapton	26	10	5	11	42	51	25
9 Casuals	26	10	3	13	46	58	23
10 Woking	26	9	4	13	53	69	22
11 Oxford City	26	8	5	13	56	89	21
12 St. Albans City	26	7	5	14	44	62	19
13 Tufnell Park	26	4	7	15	43	74	15
14 London Caledonians	26	5	4	17	26	66	14

Right: Clapton's programme against Ilford during 1936-37 - a goal-less draw.

Left: Oxford City's programme for their game with St. Albans City.

1937–38 - Leytonstone won the League championship by three points from Ilford with Tufnell Park five points further back in third and Nunhead in fourth position. St. Albans City and Woking occupied the bottom two positions but as there were no applications for membership the two retiring clubs were both re-elected.

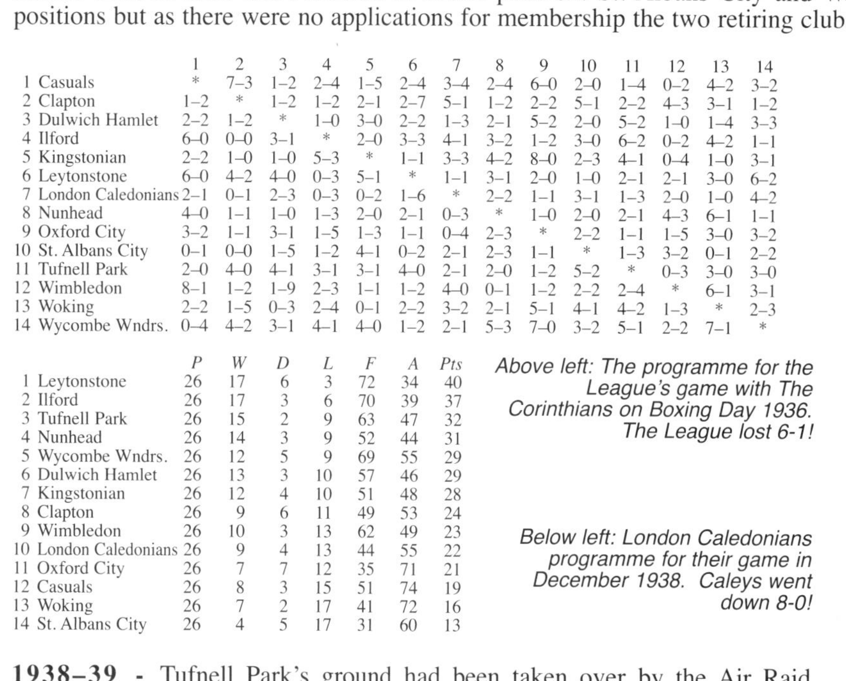

	1	2	3	4	5	6	7	8	9	10	11	12	13	14
1 Casuals	*	7–3	1–2	2–4	1–5	2–4	3–4	2–4	6–0	2–0	1–4	0–2	4–2	3–2
2 Clapton	1–2	*	1–2	1–2	2–1	2–7	5–1	1–2	2–2	5–1	2–2	4–3	3–1	1–2
3 Dulwich Hamlet	2–2	1–2	*	1–0	3–0	2–2	1–3	2–1	5–2	2–0	5–2	1–0	1–4	3–3
4 Ilford	6–0	0–0	3–1	*	2–0	3–3	4–1	3–2	1–2	3–0	6–2	0–2	4–2	1–1
5 Kingstonian	2–2	1–0	1–0	5–3	*	1–1	3–3	4–2	8–0	2–3	4–1	0–4	1–0	3–1
6 Leytonstone	6–0	4–2	4–0	0–3	5–1	*	1–1	3–1	2–0	1–0	2–1	2–1	3–0	6–2
7 London Caledonians	2–1	0–1	2–3	0–3	0–2	1–6	*	2–2	1–1	3–1	1–3	2–0	1–0	4–2
8 Nunhead	4–0	1–1	1–0	1–3	2–0	2–1	0–3	*	1–0	2–0	2–1	4–3	6–1	1–1
9 Oxford City	3–2	1–1	3–1	1–5	1–3	1–1	0–4	2–3	*	2–2	1–1	1–5	3–0	3–2
10 St. Albans City	0–1	0–0	1–5	1–2	4–1	0–2	2–1	2–3	1–1	*	1–3	3–2	0–1	2–2
11 Tufnell Park	2–0	4–0	4–1	3–1	3–1	4–0	2–1	2–0	1–2	5–2	*	0–3	3–0	3–0
12 Wimbledon	8–1	1–2	1–9	2–3	1–1	1–2	4–0	0–1	1–2	2–2	2–4	*	6–1	3–1
13 Woking	2–2	1–5	0–3	2–4	0–1	2–2	3–2	2–1	5–1	4–1	4–2	1–3	*	2–3
14 Wycombe Wndrs.	0–4	4–2	3–1	4–1	4–0	1–2	2–1	5–3	7–0	3–2	5–1	2–2	7–1	*

	P	*W*	*D*	*L*	*F*	*A*	*Pts*
1 Leytonstone	26	17	6	3	72	34	40
2 Ilford	26	17	3	6	70	39	37
3 Tufnell Park	26	15	2	9	63	47	32
4 Nunhead	26	14	3	9	52	44	31
5 Wycombe Wndrs.	26	12	5	9	69	55	29
6 Dulwich Hamlet	26	13	3	10	57	46	29
7 Kingstonian	26	12	4	10	51	48	28
8 Clapton	26	9	6	11	49	53	24
9 Wimbledon	26	10	3	13	62	49	23
10 London Caledonians	26	9	4	13	44	55	22
11 Oxford City	26	7	7	12	35	71	21
12 Casuals	26	8	3	15	51	74	19
13 Woking	26	7	2	17	41	72	16
14 St. Albans City	26	4	5	17	31	60	13

Above left: The programme for the League's game with The Corinthians on Boxing Day 1936. The League lost 6-1!

Below left: London Caledonians programme for their game in December 1938. Caleys went down 8-0!

1938–39 - Tufnell Park's ground had been taken over by the Air Raid Precautions authorities and, as trenches had been dug on the pitch, the Club was unable to use its ground. As a result, it was agreed that Tufnell Park's home matches would be played on their opponents' grounds.

For the second time in three seasons, a proposal to the AILS board meeting to amalgamate the four (Athenian, Isthmian, London and Spartan) leagues was again put forward. Put to a vote amongst their member clubs, the Isthmian voted 11–3 against. Nunhead, whilst against amalgamation, was in favour of the formation of a second division with promotion and relegation. This was put forward to the Isthmian League Annual General Meeting but, after much discussion before a vote, it was decided that the proposal would be dropped.

Leytonstone regained the championship, with Ilford again second, although this time by just two points. Kingstonian finished third and Dulwich Hamlet fourth, three and five points, respectively, behind Leytonstone. Three teams were adrift at the foot of the table, but Oxford City avoided a bottom-two finish on goal difference ahead of Tufnell Park, who with London Caledonians were re-elected at the Annual General Meeting. In May 1939 Casuals Football Club announced that they were to merge with the Corinthian Football Club to form a new club, Corinthian-Casuals.

At the AGM, however, it was agreed to increase League membership from 14 to 16 Clubs for the 1939–40 season, including Corinthian-Casuals. Although applications were received from Chesham United, Hersham, Metropolitan Police, Epsom and Hastings & St. Leonards, it was decided to strengthen the League by inviting Romford and Walthamstow Avenue from the Athenian League. This was agreed by the League Council.

	1	2	3	4	5	6	7	8	9	10	11	12	13	14
1 Casuals	*	2–3	1–1	0–2	1–2	1–4	4–0	2–3	4–1	2–1	3–1	4–3	0–3	4–2
2 Clapton	3–4	*	5–1	1–3	5–1	2–3	3–0	1–1	5–2	2–1	5–1	5–6	3–1	3–0
3 Dulwich Hamlet	5–1	2–1	*	3–1	0–0	2–1	3–0	3–1	5–0	3–1	4–0	2–0	4–1	4–1
4 Ilford	1–1	7–3	3–1	*	2–2	0–3	2–0	2–0	6–2	3–0	1–0	1–1	5–2	0–0
5 Kingstonian	3–2	2–1	2–1	4–1	*	3–0	8–1	1–2	3–1	4–0	3–0	0–0	4–0	2–0
6 Leytonstone	2–0	2–1	1–2	1–2	3–1	*	3–1	3–1	3–1	5–0	6–1	4–0	4–1	3–3
7 London Caledonians	1–1	3–4	0–0	0–8	2–3	0–2	*	0–6	3–2	2–2	2–3	1–0	2–0	2–2
8 Nunhead	1–1	2–2	3–2	2–1	3–0	1–2	2–1	*	0–0	2–1	2–2	2–5	2–0	3–4
9 Oxford City	0–2	3–6	2–2	1–5	3–5	2–3	5–1	2–1	*	3–4	1–3	3–8	2–1	2–2
10 St. Albans City	2–3	3–0	1–1	0–2	3–0	2–2	4–0	1–1	1–1	*	1–2	3–0	3–1	1–0
11 Tufnell Park	1–4	2–4	1–4	0–6	1–3	0–0	1–0	2–7	1–3	1–4	*	0–6	2–2	2–4
12 Wimbledon	3–4	5–0	3–2	0–1	1–3	4–4	6–1	2–1	3–1	4–3	7–2	*	5–1	9–3
13 Woking	1–1	2–1	2–1	1–2	1–3	0–2	2–1	3–1	2–1	1–0	1–0	1–4	*	5–1
14 Wycombe Wndrs.	2–2	2–0	0–2	4–1	5–0	1–2	5–2	1–4	5–0	5–2	4–4	4–3	2–0	*

	P	*W*	*D*	*L*	*F*	*A*	*Pts*
1 Leytonstone	26	18	4	4	68	32	40
2 Ilford	26	17	4	5	68	32	38
3 Kingstonian	26	17	3	6	62	39	37
4 Dulwich Hamlet	26	15	5	6	60	32	35
5 Wimbledon	26	14	3	9	88	56	31
6 Nunhead	26	11	6	9	54	44	28
7 Casuals	26	11	6	9	54	51	28
8 Clapton	26	12	2	12	69	61	26
9 Wycombe Wndrs.	26	10	6	10	62	62	26
10 St. Albans City	26	8	5	13	44	50	21
11 Woking	26	9	2	15	35	56	20
12 Oxford City	26	4	4	18	44	84	12
13 Tufnell Park	26	4	4	18	33	87	12
14 London Caledonians	26	3	4	19	26	81	10

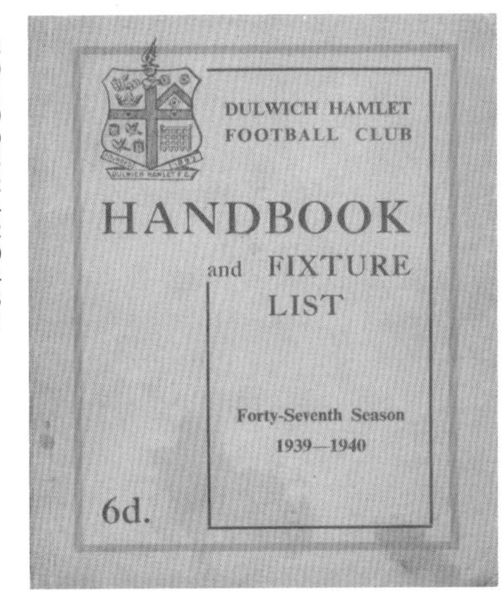

Right: The Dulwich Hamlet handbook for the ill-fated 1939-40 campaign.

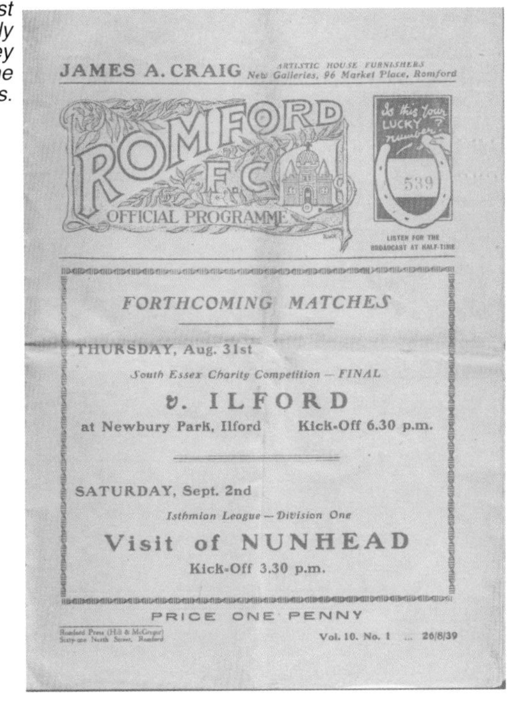

Below right: Romford's programme against Ilford on 26 August 1939, the only League match they played prior to the outbreak of hostilities.

1939–40 - Much happened between the Annual General Meeting and the season kicking off. First, London Caledonians sent a letter to the League for their July Council meeting, notifying them that, as they had failed to secure a ground for the forthcoming season, they would be resigning and probably disbanding too. The League Council expressed their regret at the Club's plight and it was agreed to have 15 clubs for the forthcoming season. Tufnell Park – who had also lost the use of their ground – announced that they had been offered the use of the Golders Green FC ground, an offer they had accepted. The very real threat of war was hanging over the country as the season commenced and the following matches were played:

26th August 1939: *Corinthian–Casuals 1, Oxford C 0;*
Leytonstone 4, Clapton 2;
Nunhead 0, Tufnell Park 1; Romford 2, Ilford 0;
Walthamstow Avenue 2, Dulwich Hamlet 2;
Wimbledon 2, Kingstonian 3;
Wycombe Wanderers 4, Woking 0.

2nd September 1939: *Dulwich Hamlet 2, Leytonstone 3.*

On 3 September Britain declared war on Germany and following this the League suspended operations, almost 25 years to the day after the onset of the Great War had caused a similar suspension.

DEDICATED TO THE MEMORY OF THE PLAYERS WHO WERE MEMBERS OF THE ISTHMIAN FOOTBALL LEAGUE
who gave their lives for
KING AND COUNTRY
in
WORLD WARS
1914-18 1939-45

PART TWO 1945 – 1973

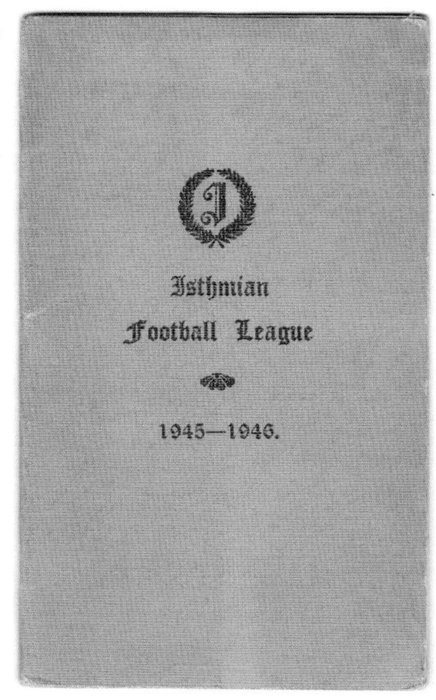

1945–46 - The ceasefire in Europe came into effect in the spring of 1945, so clubs had to act quickly in preparation for the 1945–46 season. Nunhead, who did not have a home ground, had no option but to withdraw from the coming season. Late applications were received from Walton-on-Thames, Epsom Town and Hastings & St. Leonards, but these were unanimously turned down and it was agreed to operate the League with 14 clubs. The first post-war season began in August and ended with Walthamstow Avenue – who had been elected in 1939, but played just one fixture before the League was suspended – securing the championship and setting a new League record by scoring 100 goals. They finished two points clear of Oxford City, who equalled their best-ever finish in the Isthmian League. Romford – elected with Walthamstow – finished third, three points clear of Dulwich Hamlet.

The bottom two clubs, St. Albans City and Kingstonian were both re-elected at the Annual General Meeting. Off the field, League Chairman Sir Arthur W. Holmes tendered his resignation on 5 January 1946, and Henry Huband was proposed and seconded to act as Chairman for the remainder of the season. Former Chairman WA Brown passed away in February 1940. Nunhead tendered their resignation from the League at a Council Meeting on 5 April. Applications to replace Nunhead were received from Epsom Town, Grays Athletic, Post Office Engineers and Metropolitan Police, but the League Council decided that the League should remain with 14 clubs. A proposal to increase membership from 14 to 16 clubs was defeated. Also at the AGM, Mr Huband was elected as Chairman of the League on a more permanent basis.

	1	2	3	4	5	6	7	8	9	10	11	12	13	14
1 Clapton	*	1–3	1–5	0–3	6–0	2–4	2–7	1–2	3–0	1–0	2–1	3–0	3–0	6–0
2 Corinthian-Casuals	2–2	*	2–4	0–3	3–0	1–4	1–4	3–5	2–0	4–2	0–5	4–3	2–2	1–4
3 Dulwich Hamlet	4–2	4–3	*	0–2	3–2	1–0	3–3	0–2	4–0	3–0	1–6	4–0	2–0	3–1
4 Ilford	2–1	3–2	3–2	*	1–4	5–3	1–4	1–1	4–1	1–6	2–5	3–2	4–3	2–5
5 Kingstonian	1–3	2–3	2–2	3–1	*	1–2	5–3	3–6	0–3	0–2	0–5	5–1	0–2	3–7
6 Leytonstone	3–2	0–4	3–2	2–3	3–2	*	0–4	5–0	4–2	2–2	0–5	3–1	2–2	10–5
7 Oxford City	2–0	2–2	4–1	5–1	7–2	2–3	*	6–0	4–0	4–3	2–0	5–1	2–2	3–1
8 Romford	1–0	8–3	1–2	6–1	1–1	5–2	2–2	*	3–2	8–0	3–2	6–1	5–2	3–3
9 St. Albans City	3–2	4–4	3–1	3–3	3–3	2–0	0–3	3–1	*	4–3	0–4	4–4	1–1	3–5
10 Tufnell Park	2–2	4–1	4–2	4–0	1–4	7–3	0–2	5–2	9–2	*	1–3	1–0	2–2	3–0
11 Walthamstow Ave.	3–1	7–2	9–0	1–5	6–0	5–2	4–1	6–2	8–0	1–0	*	3–2	1–0	3–0
12 Wimbledon	3–3	4–2	4–1	2–1	2–1	6–0	3–3	1–0	2–2	1–1	0–2	*	1–5	4–3
13 Woking	2–1	1–3	0–3	2–1	7–0	3–0	1–1	2–4	4–1	1–3	2–1	3–3	*	5–4
14 Wycombe Wndrs.	9–1	5–1	2–6	4–0	3–3	1–1	2–6	2–6	4–2	2–6	3–4	4–1	1–2	*

	P	*W*	*D*	*L*	*F*	*A*	*Pts*
1 Walthamstow Ave.	26	21	0	5	100	31	42
2 Oxford City	26	17	6	3	91	40	40
3 Romford	26	15	3	8	83	59	33
4 Dulwich Hamlet	26	14	2	10	63	59	30
5 Tufnell Park	26	12	4	10	70	55	28
6 Woking	26	10	7	9	56	51	27
7 Ilford	26	12	2	12	56	71	26
8 Leytonstone	26	11	3	12	61	75	25
9 Wycombe Wndrs.	26	9	3	14	80	88	21
10 Wimbledon	26	7	6	13	52	72	20
11 Corinthian-Casuals	26	8	4	14	58	83	20
12 Clapton	26	8	3	15	51	62	19
13 St. Albans City	26	6	6	14	48	85	18
14 Kingstonian	26	6	3	17	48	86	15

Right: the Walthamstow Avenue programme for their first post-war match, they beat St. Albans 8-0! Below: the first season for the newly merged Corinthian-Casuals.

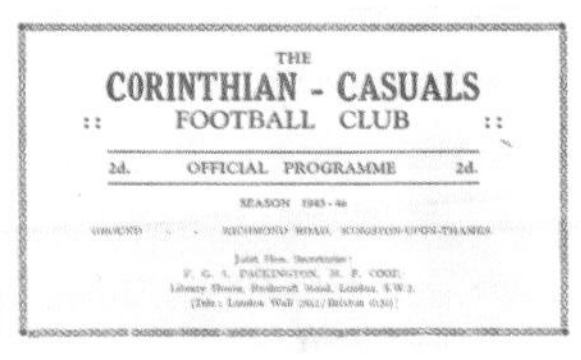

1946–47 - Leytonstone, champions in 1938 and 1939, won the second post-war championship by three points from Dulwich Hamlet. Romford finished third for the second consecutive season, ahead of previous champions Walthamstow Avenue. St. Albans City – for the second season running – had to apply for re-election, along with Corinthian-Casuals. Both Clubs were re-elected. Applications for the 1947–48 season were received from Harwich & Parkeston and Metropolitan Police, but it was agreed to have the same constitution.

	1	2	3	4	5	6	7	8	9	10	11	12	13	14
1 Clapton	*	1–1	1–1	2–2	0–1	1–3	0–3	1–4	2–1	1–1	0–4	2–0	1–1	8–2
2 Corinthian-Cas	2–2	*	0–2	1–2	0–1	0–5	1–6	3–5	3–1	2–3	2–4	0–1	0–2	3–2
3 Dulwich Hamlet	1–0	7–0	*	5–1	1–3	5–2	3–2	7–2	4–1	2–1	2–1	5–2	5–0	1–1
4 Ilford	2–1	3–3	0–6	*	5–2	2–4	3–3	2–2	7–2	2–3	3–5	6–0	3–2	7–2
5 Kingstonian	3–0	6–2	3–5	4–1	*	1–1	2–1	2–4	2–1	1–2	2–3	4–2	0–0	2–1
6 Leytonstone	4–2	10–1	7–1	2–0	3–1	*	4–1	2–0	3–1	3–3	0–3	5–1	8–1	4–0
7 Oxford City	1–1	3–0	3–1	5–4	1–2	2–1	*	3–5	2–4	6–1	2–1	2–2	6–1	2–1
8 Romford	1–2	3–0	2–1	7–3	3–3	0–4	4–3	*	4–2	5–1	0–0	6–0	5–1	2–2
9 St. Albans City	3–2	1–5	3–1	2–2	6–0	1–7	2–2	2–2	*	2–0	2–1	0–11	3–0	2–4
10 Tufnell Park	4–5	2–1	2–4	1–0	3–0	0–2	3–3	1–4	3–0	*	0–5	2–2	2–2	4–3
11 Walthamstow Ave.	6–3	1–2	2–4	3–0	4–0	1–2	0–0	3–3	4–1	5–0	*	2–1	2–1	2–2
12 Wimbledon	7–1	3–1	1–2	7–2	6–4	1–4	1–4	0–0	2–2	2–1	2–1	*	3–0	2–2
13 Woking	0–0	3–2	1–1	2–2	1–1	2–1	1–3	1–0	4–0	2–1	1–0	2–6	*	1–2
14 Wycombe Wndrs.	1–2	1–1	5–1	2–2	1–2	5–1	3–1	3–3	2–2	5–1	2–1	4–3	5–2	*

Below: Ilford's programme for the match against St. Albans City in November 1946, which the Essex club won 7-2.

	P	W	D	L	F	A	Pts
1 Leytonstone	26	19	2	5	92	36	40
2 Dulwich Hamlet	26	17	3	6	78	46	37
3 Romford	26	13	8	5	76	52	34
4 Walthamstow Ave.	26	13	4	9	64	37	30
5 Oxford City	26	12	6	8	70	51	30
6 Kingstonian	26	12	4	10	52	57	28
7 Wycombe Wndrs.	26	9	8	9	63	62	26
8 Wimbledon	26	10	5	11	68	64	25
9 Ilford	26	7	7	12	66	78	21
10 Tufnell Park	26	8	5	13	45	69	21
11 Woking	26	7	7	12	34	62	21
12 Clapton	26	6	8	12	41	59	20
13 St. Albans City	26	7	5	14	47	79	19
14 Corinthian-Casuals	26	4	4	18	36	80	12

Right: the club notes from Oxford City's programme for the 3-2 victory over St. Albans City on April 3rd 1948.

OFFICIAL PROGRAMME Price 2d

Oxford City Football Club

SEASON 1947-1948

Founded 1882

Winners of Amateur Cup 1906
Finalists " 1903
Finalists " 1913

Members of the Football Association
Oxfordshire F.A.
Isthmian League
Amateur F.A.

Old White House, Abingdon Road, Oxford. Tel. 18891.

President: Alderman J. R. BENSON, M.A.

Hon. Sec.: Mr. A. E. EDENS
55 BLACKFRIARS ROAD, OXFORD
Telephone 77606

Hon. Treasurer: Mr. R. F. HILL
7 Salisbury Crescent, Oxford

Assistant Secretary: Mr. G. F. WYATT
374 Marston Road, Oxford

Committee: Coun. E. A. Smewin, W. Jakeman, A. Haynes, J. Guilfoyle, H. W. Jones, G. Arlett, N. Crowder, E. Holton.

For to-day's game with St. Albans City we make several changes from the side which played on Easter Monday. Butler, former Abingdon Town player, replaces Ron Buckingham at outside-right, and Bill Barrett makes his first appearance in the First XI at centre-forward. Keith Savins is resting the injury he sustained on Monday and Peter Stone takes over the left-back position. The Hertfordshire Club have not had a particularly successful season, but can be relied upon to produce fast constructive football, and we anticipate seeing a good game this afternoon following the goalless draw at St. Albans on Good Friday.

Of the Senior Cup Final little need be said except that once again the absence of a first time shot in the forward line proved very expensive. Collectively everybody on our side may be said to have acquitted themselves well, with special mention to Ernie Ryman as being the best man on either side, and Aubrey Oakey, who relieved dangerous situations on a number of occasions, in spite of being severely shaken up early in the game and again in the second half. Headington were best served by Tony Harper, always dangerous at centre-forward, Jack Ramsden who played a captain's game at left-back, and Gerry Woodward in goal, though Gerry can count himself fortunate that the crossbar intervened on four occasions when he was well beaten. We hope that we may have the opportunity of a further meeting in the Hospital Cup.

Last Saturday's Reserve game with Woking was productive of two very welcome points, but was somewhat marred by an injury to Bill Breakspear, who was taken to the Radcliffe Infirmary for treatment of a damaged shoulder ligament. Charlie Carr, last minute selection at inside left, took over the jersey and kept a clean sheet, though his unorthodox style was something to marvel at. Without a game to-day, the Reserves visit Woking in the return game next Thursday evening.

1947–48 - Leytonstone retained their championship in a close finish, with only three points separating the top four clubs. Runners-up were Kingstonian, with Walthamstow Avenue and Dulwich Hamlet third and fourth, respectively. Clapton had to apply for re-election for the first time since 1934 and Corinthian-Casuals, who finished bottom in successive seasons, were both duly re-elected. Cambridge Town, Harwich & Parkeston and Metropolitan Police had applied to join the League for 1948–49 but it was again decided to keep membership at 14 clubs.

L W S Guy resigned as Hon Assistant Referees and Fixture Secretary because he had moved to Norfolk. He was succeeded by Donald McKenzie.

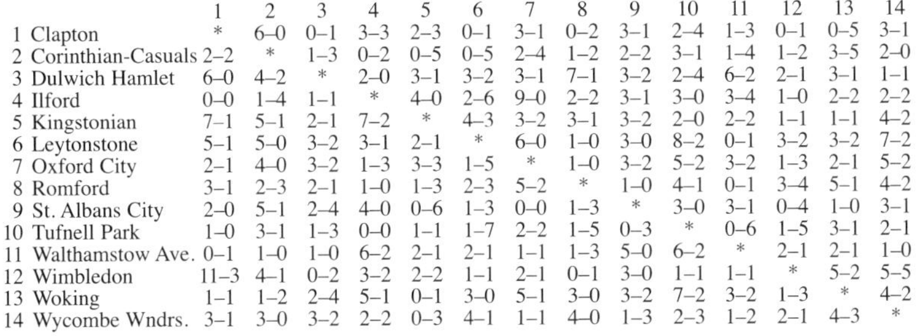

	1	2	3	4	5	6	7	8	9	10	11	12	13	14
1 Clapton	*	6–0	0–1	3–3	2–3	0–1	3–1	0–2	3–1	2–4	1–3	0–1	0–5	3–1
2 Corinthian-Casuals	2–2	*	1–3	0–2	0–5	0–5	2–4	1–2	2–2	3–1	1–4	1–2	3–5	2–0
3 Dulwich Hamlet	6–0	4–2	*	2–0	3–1	3–2	3–1	7–1	3–2	2–4	6–2	2–1	3–1	1–1
4 Ilford	0–0	1–4	1–1	*	4–0	2–6	9–0	2–2	3–1	3–0	3–4	1–0	2–2	2–2
5 Kingstonian	7–1	5–1	2–1	7–2	*	4–3	3–2	3–1	3–2	2–0	2–2	1–1	1–1	4–2
6 Leytonstone	5–1	5–0	3–2	3–1	2–1	*	6–0	1–0	3–0	8–2	0–1	3–2	3–2	7–2
7 Oxford City	2–1	4–0	3–2	1–3	3–3	1–5	*	1–0	3–2	5–2	3–2	1–3	2–1	5–2
8 Romford	3–1	2–3	2–1	1–0	1–3	2–3	5–2	*	1–0	4–1	0–1	3–4	5–1	4–2
9 St. Albans City	2–0	5–1	2–4	4–0	0–6	1–3	0–0	1–3	*	3–0	3–1	0–4	1–0	3–1
10 Tufnell Park	1–0	3–1	1–3	0–0	1–1	1–7	2–2	1–5	0–3	*	0–6	1–5	3–1	2–1
11 Walthamstow Ave.	0–1	1–0	1–0	6–2	2–1	2–1	1–1	1–3	5–0	6–2	*	2–1	2–1	1–0
12 Wimbledon	11–3	4–1	0–2	3–2	2–2	1–1	2–1	0–1	3–0	1–1	1–1	*	5–2	5–5
13 Woking	1–1	1–2	2–4	5–1	0–1	3–0	5–1	3–0	3–2	7–2	3–2	1–3	*	4–2
14 Wycombe Wndrs.	3–1	3–0	3–2	2–2	0–3	4–1	1–1	4–0	1–3	2–3	1–2	2–1	4–3	*

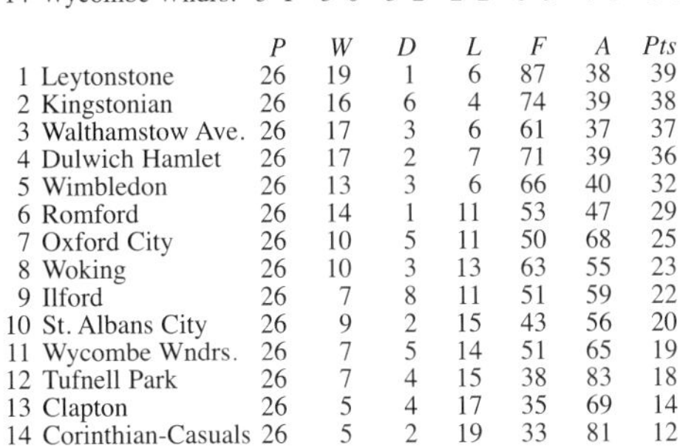

	P	W	D	L	F	A	Pts
1 Leytonstone	26	19	1	6	87	38	39
2 Kingstonian	26	16	6	4	74	39	38
3 Walthamstow Ave.	26	17	3	6	61	37	37
4 Dulwich Hamlet	26	17	2	7	71	39	36
5 Wimbledon	26	13	3	6	66	40	32
6 Romford	26	14	1	11	53	47	29
7 Oxford City	26	10	5	11	50	68	25
8 Woking	26	10	3	13	63	55	23
9 Ilford	26	7	8	11	51	59	22
10 St. Albans City	26	9	2	15	43	56	20
11 Wycombe Wndrs.	26	7	5	14	51	65	19
12 Tufnell Park	26	7	4	15	38	83	18
13 Clapton	26	5	4	17	35	69	14
14 Corinthian-Casuals	26	5	2	19	33	81	12

Left: Walthamstow Avenue's programme for their game against Corinthian Casuals, which they won 1-0.

Right: the Dulwich Hamlet programme for their match with Ilford, which the South London club won 2-0.

1948–49 - Goal average decided the 1948–49 League championship, with Dulwich Hamlet pipping Walthamstow Avenue to secure their first title for 16 years. Wimbledon were two points behind in third place, with Ilford fourth. St. Albans City had two points deducted for fielding ineligible players – J Chappell and H Rawlings, neither of whom were qualified to play in the League. Clapton again had to apply for re-election along with Tufnell Park, who only won one game, but both were re-elected at the Annual General Meeting.

Earlier in the season, Maidstone United had applied to join the Isthmian League. However, after much discussion at the Council Meeting held on 22 April, it was decided to recommend to the AGM to keep 14 clubs in the constitution. It was announced at the AGM that League Secretary & Treasurer Andrew Ralston would be resigning. Hon. Referees & Fixture Secretary Sidney Donaldson was elected to succeed Ralston as Secretary & Treasurer, with Donald McKenzie assuming the role of Hon. Referees & Fixture Secretary.

	1	2	3	4	5	6	7	8	9	10	11	12	13	14
1 Clapton	*	2–5	2–2	0–0	1–2	2–0	0–0	1–3	0–2	2–1	0–1	0–2	3–5	3–2
2 Corinthian-Casuals	0–3	*	1–1	1–2	2–4	2–1	2–4	0–4	4–1	4–0	0–4	3–4	4–2	1–2
3 Dulwich Hamlet	2–0	1–1	*	5–3	1–0	6–1	1–0	1–2	3–2	3–0	1–3	4–0	0–1	7–0
4 Ilford	7–0	0–1	3–1	*	2–2	1–2	2–1	3–1	6–1	3–1	2–3	3–1	1–0	2–1
5 Kingstonian	4–0	0–2	1–4	1–4	*	2–2	1–0	1–2	4–1	1–0	2–2	1–1	2–1	2–1
6 Leytonstone	2–2	6–0	1–2	1–0	3–2	*	3–1	2–0	1–1	2–2	3–1	1–1	3–0	0–1
7 Oxford City	2–1	6–1	1–0	0–3	2–1	3–1	*	4–1	3–3	3–1	2–0	1–1	3–2	2–1
8 Romford	3–1	0–1	1–1	1–1	2–3	2–3	2–0	*	2–1	3–3	1–2	0–1	4–6	4–1
9 St. Albans City	4–2	0–4	1–1	1–0	2–1	0–2	1–2	4–0	*	4–1	3–3	1–1	1–4	2–3
10 Tufnell Park	2–0	0–1	0–1	0–1	1–3	2–2	0–6	2–3	2–2	*	0–3	0–2	2–3	2–2
11 Walthamstow Ave.	1–3	3–0	2–2	4–1	3–1	0–2	1–1	2–3	5–1	2–1	*	3–2	5–1	3–1
12 Wimbledon	5–2	4–2	1–2	1–2	2–0	3–2	4–1	6–0	1–0	4–1	3–1	*	2–1	9–1
13 Woking	3–1	3–4	1–4	2–1	4–2	2–3	0–0	3–1	1–0	6–3	2–5	4–2	*	4–2
14 Wycombe Wndrs.	1–1	2–1	3–4	4–3	2–0	3–0	1–0	1–2	4–1	4–1	0–3	5–1	1–3	*

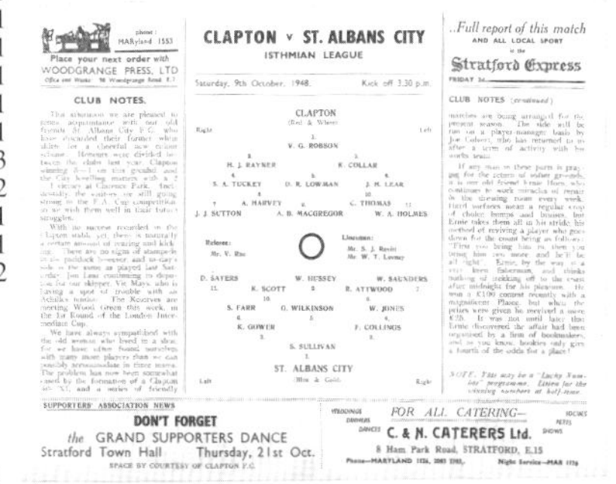

Right: the Club Notes and line-ups from Clapton's 0-2 defeat by St. Albans City.

	P	W	D	L	F	A	Pts
1 Dulwich Hamlet	26	15	6	5	60	31	36
2 Walthamstow Ave.	26	16	4	6	65	38	36
3 Wimbledon	26	15	4	7	64	41	34
4 Ilford	26	14	3	9	56	36	31
5 Oxford City	26	13	5	8	48	34	31
6 Leytonstone	26	12	6	8	49	41	30
7 Woking	26	14	1	11	64	59	29
8 Romford	26	11	3	12	47	54	25
9 Kingstonian	26	10	4	12	43	47	24
10 Corinthian-Casuals	26	11	2	13	47	59	24
11 Wycombe Wndrs.	26	11	2	13	49	61	24
12 St. Albans City*	26	6	6	14	40	60	18
13 Clapton	26	5	5	16	32	61	15
14 Tufnell Park	26	1	5	20	28	70	7

**St. Albans C 2 points deducted.*

Right: the programme from champions Leytonstone v Oxford City in December 1949, which the home side won 5-2 - note the interesting kick-off time!

1949–50 - Leytonstone won their third title in four seasons when they took the championship by one point from nearest challengers Wimbledon, with Kingstonian and Walthamstow Avenue third and fourth respectively. Corinthian-Casuals had to apply for re-election for the third time in four seasons, along with Tufnell Park, who had applied the previous year. Both clubs were successful in their re-election. However, Tufnell Park, who had lost the use of their ground, amalgamated with Edmonton Borough, who were members of the London League. The new Tufnell Park Edmonton Club was accepted into the Isthmian League. It was announced at the Council Meeting on 24 February that life member and past Chairman & Treasurer Andrew Ralston had passed away. At the Annual General Meeting, it was again decided to keep a 14-club constitution, although an A Section (for third teams) was formed for the benefit of clubs with a surplus of players. The founder clubs of the A section were: Clapton, Corinthian-Casuals, Ilford, Leytonstone, Tufnell Park Edmonton, Walthamstow Avenue, Wimbledon, Woking and Wycombe Wanderers.

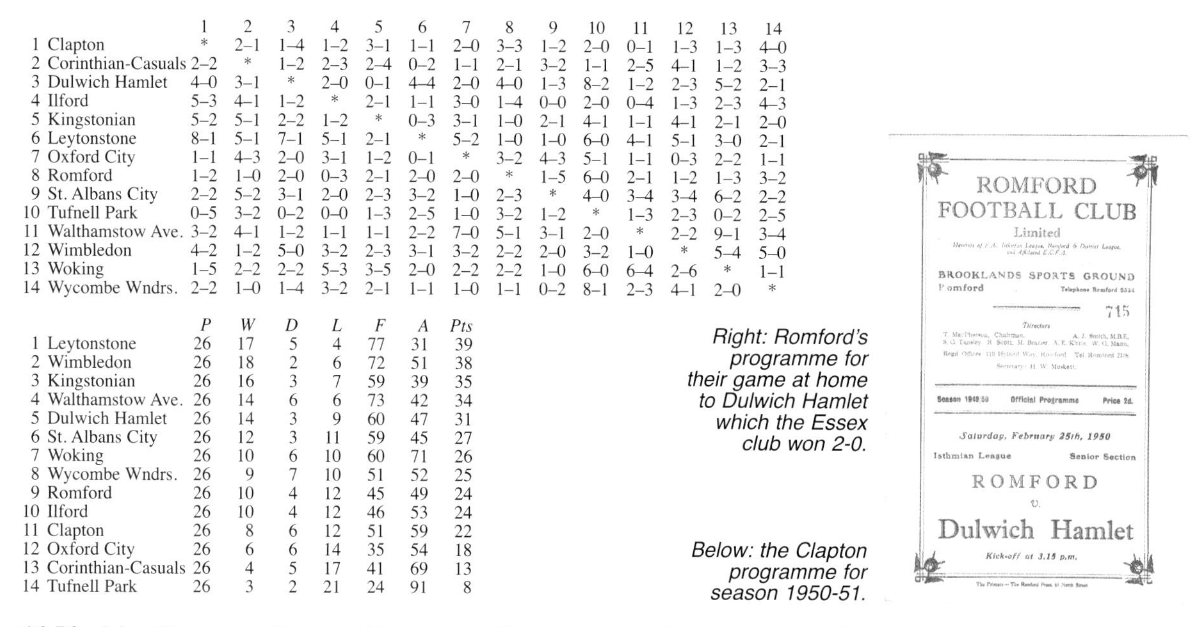

	1	2	3	4	5	6	7	8	9	10	11	12	13	14
1 Clapton	*	2–1	1–4	1–2	3–1	1–1	2–0	3–3	1–2	2–0	0–1	1–3	1–3	4–0
2 Corinthian-Casuals	2–2	*	1–2	2–3	2–4	0–2	1–1	2–1	3–2	1–1	2–5	4–1	1–2	3–3
3 Dulwich Hamlet	4–0	3–1	*	2–0	0–1	4–4	2–0	4–0	1–3	8–2	1–2	2–3	5–2	2–1
4 Ilford	5–3	4–1	1–2	*	2–1	1–1	3–0	1–4	0–0	2–0	0–4	1–3	2–3	4–3
5 Kingstonian	5–2	5–1	2–2	1–2	*	0–3	3–1	1–0	2–1	4–1	1–1	4–1	2–1	2–0
6 Leytonstone	8–1	5–1	7–1	5–1	2–1	*	5–2	1–0	1–0	6–0	4–1	5–1	3–0	2–1
7 Oxford City	1–1	4–3	2–0	3–1	1–2	0–1	*	3–2	4–3	5–1	1–1	0–3	2–2	1–1
8 Romford	1–2	1–0	2–0	0–3	2–1	2–0	2–0	*	1–5	6–0	2–1	1–2	1–3	3–2
9 St. Albans City	2–2	5–2	3–1	2–0	2–3	3–2	1–0	2–3	*	4–0	3–4	3–4	6–2	2–2
10 Tufnell Park	0–5	3–2	0–2	0–0	1–3	2–5	1–0	3–2	1–2	*	1–3	2–3	0–2	2–5
11 Walthamstow Ave.	3–2	4–1	1–2	1–1	1–1	2–2	7–0	5–1	3–1	2–0	*	2–2	9–1	3–4
12 Wimbledon	4–2	1–2	5–0	3–2	2–3	3–1	3–2	2–2	2–0	3–2	1–0	*	5–4	5–0
13 Woking	1–5	2–2	2–2	5–3	3–5	2–0	2–2	2–2	1–0	6–0	6–4	2–6	*	1–1
14 Wycombe Wndrs.	2–2	1–0	1–4	3–2	2–1	1–1	1–0	1–1	0–2	8–1	2–3	4–1	2–0	*

	P	W	D	L	F	A	Pts
1 Leytonstone	26	17	5	4	77	31	39
2 Wimbledon	26	18	2	6	72	51	38
3 Kingstonian	26	16	3	7	59	39	35
4 Walthamstow Ave.	26	14	6	6	73	42	34
5 Dulwich Hamlet	26	14	3	9	60	47	31
6 St. Albans City	26	12	3	11	59	45	27
7 Woking	26	10	6	10	60	71	26
8 Wycombe Wndrs.	26	9	7	10	51	52	25
9 Romford	26	10	4	12	45	49	24
10 Ilford	26	10	4	12	46	53	24
11 Clapton	26	8	6	12	51	59	22
12 Oxford City	26	6	6	14	35	54	18
13 Corinthian-Casuals	26	4	5	17	41	69	13
14 Tufnell Park	26	3	2	21	24	91	8

Right: Romford's programme for their game at home to Dulwich Hamlet which the Essex club won 2-0.

Below: the Clapton programme for season 1950-51.

1950–51 - The season began with some sombre news when it was announced that George Clarke, a co-founder and life member of the Isthmian League, had passed away on 28 August 1950. Leytonstone retained their League championship – matching London Caledonians' record of six titles – in stunning style. They set a new points record for a 26-game season with 43 and they finished nine points clear of East London rivals Walthamstow Avenue. Romford finished third one point behind the Avenue and Wimbledon fourth. Clapton had to apply for re-election for the third time in four seasons along with the amalgamated Tufnell Park Edmonton club, who also had been forced to re-apply as Tufnell Park after each of the previous two seasons. Clapton were re-elected without objection but Tufnell Park Edmonton – due to their recent poor record – were only re-elected by ballot with the result being seven votes to five in favour of re-election.

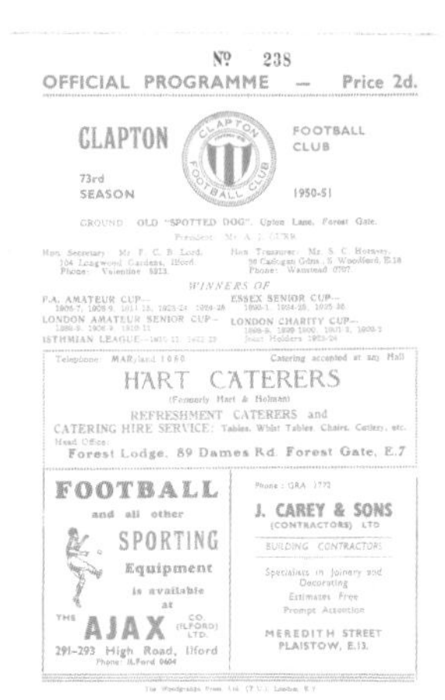

	1	2	3	4	5	6	7	8	9	10	11	12	13	14
1 Clapton	*	2–0	1–3	0–0	5–1	1–1	0–0	2–1	0–2	0–1	0–2	1–5	1–4	2–1
2 Corinthian-Casuals	5–0	*	2–5	2–3	2–1	0–2	1–4	7–1	1–0	3–1	6–3	0–2	1–2	4–0
3 Dulwich Hamlet	3–1	5–1	*	3–2	3–1	0–4	2–1	2–3	2–0	0–1	2–0	3–1	3–0	6–3
4 Ilford	2–0	1–2	1–0	*	2–0	1–2	2–1	2–2	1–1	0–1	2–3	2–1	4–1	2–0
5 Kingstonian	1–2	0–7	3–1	4–0	*	1–2	2–0	1–3	0–1	6–0	2–0	1–1	3–2	1–2
6 Leytonstone	5–4	3–0	3–0	4–0	6–0	*	4–2	1–2	3–0	3–1	1–3	3–1	3–2	3–0
7 Oxford City	3–3	3–4	3–0	2–4	2–2	1–7	*	2–4	2–1	3–0	3–2	1–3	3–2	2–2
8 Romford	1–0	0–3	1–3	1–2	5–2	1–1	3–0	*	3–1	2–0	1–4	3–0	2–2	7–3
9 St. Albans City	2–0	2–3	1–1	3–0	1–2	0–2	2–1	2–0	*	3–2	2–1	1–0	1–1	0–2
10 Tufnell Park Edm	1–2	1–2	0–2	2–3	1–2	0–3	4–3	1–2	0–1	*	0–3	2–2	1–6	0–1
11 Walthamstow Ave.	1–0	5–1	1–1	1–1	1–1	1–1	2–0	2–1	2–0	4–2	*	5–1	4–2	3–1
12 Wimbledon	0–0	3–2	2–1	6–1	3–2	3–0	5–0	2–3	3–0	4–1	4–1	*	2–2	4–1
13 Woking	2–0	2–1	4–1	1–5	2–2	2–3	3–2	2–4	2–2	8–1	2–1	3–0	*	2–2
14 Wycombe Wndrs.	3–2	9–2	3–2	2–1	0–5	0–2	1–3	0–2	2–3	5–0	0–2	0–0	3–4	*

	P	W	D	L	F	A	Pts
1 Leytonstone	26	20	3	3	72	26	43
2 Walthamstow Ave.	26	15	4	7	57	37	34
3 Romford	26	15	3	8	58	47	33
4 Wimbledon	26	13	5	8	58	39	31
5 Dulwich Hamlet	26	14	2	10	54	43	30
6 Woking	26	11	6	9	65	55	28
7 Ilford	26	12	4	10	44	45	28
8 Corinthian-Casuals	26	13	0	13	62	60	26
9 St. Albans City	26	11	4	11	32	36	26
10 Kingstonian	26	9	4	13	46	54	22
11 Wycombe Wndrs.	26	8	3	15	46	64	19
12 Oxford City	26	7	4	15	47	65	18
13 Clapton	26	6	5	15	29	50	17
14 Tufnell Park Edm	26	4	1	21	24	73	9

Tufnell Park FC amalgamated with Edmonton Borough FC (London League) to form Tufnell Park Edmonton.

Left: Romford's programme for their Essex Senior Cup tie against Walthamstow Avenue. Right: the programme from Kingstonian v Tufnell Park Edmonton in the visitors' last season in the League.

1951–52 - Leytonstone were again victorious, securing a record seventh League championship and third in a row, albeit only on goal average from Wimbledon, with Walthamstow Avenue two points behind in third and Romford a creditable fourth. Oxford City had to apply for re-election for the first time since 1926 and were comfortably re-elected. Sadly, Tufnell Park Edmonton, who again finished bottom, tendered their resignation from the League. The League Council agreed to increase membership to 15 clubs and Bromley – who last played in 1911, when they were forced to resign – were invited to fill Tufnell Park Edmonton's position. Barking and Walton & Hersham were both proposed and seconded to fill the remaining vacancy and, after much discussion, a vote was taken. It was very close, but Barking won the ballot by eight votes to seven. There were other unsuccessful applicants: Aylesbury United, Erith & Belvedere, Eton Manor, Slough Town and Woodford Town. Cyril Evans, the Hon. Secretary of Tufnell Park Edmonton, who had served on the League Council for 21 years, was made a life member in recognition of his service to the League. It was also noted that S J Meadows (life member), C Wreford Brown, and T Kirkup (founder) had all passed away during the season.

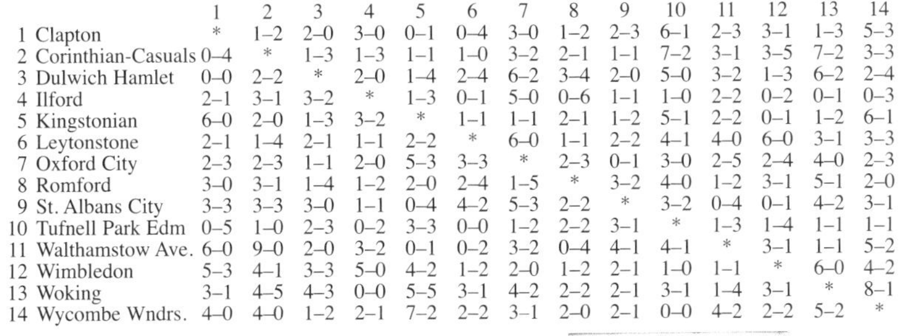

	1	2	3	4	5	6	7	8	9	10	11	12	13	14
1 Clapton	*	1–2	2–0	3–0	0–1	0–4	3–0	1–2	2–3	6–1	2–3	3–1	1–3	5–3
2 Corinthian-Casuals	0–4	*	1–3	1–3	1–1	1–0	3–2	2–1	1–1	7–2	3–1	3–5	7–2	3–3
3 Dulwich Hamlet	0–0	2–2	*	2–0	1–4	2–4	6–2	3–4	2–0	5–0	3–2	1–3	6–2	2–4
4 Ilford	2–1	3–1	3–2	*	1–3	0–1	5–0	0–6	1–1	1–0	2–2	0–2	0–1	0–3
5 Kingstonian	6–0	2–0	1–3	3–2	*	1–1	1–1	2–1	1–2	5–1	2–2	0–1	1–2	6–1
6 Leytonstone	2–1	1–4	2–1	1–1	2–2	*	6–0	1–1	2–2	4–1	4–0	6–0	3–1	3–3
7 Oxford City	2–3	2–3	1–1	2–0	5–3	3–3	*	2–3	0–1	3–0	2–5	2–4	4–0	2–3
8 Romford	3–0	3–1	1–4	1–2	2–0	2–4	1–5	*	3–2	4–0	1–2	3–1	5–1	2–0
9 St. Albans City	3–3	3–3	3–0	1–1	0–4	4–2	5–3	2–2	*	3–2	0–4	0–1	4–2	3–1
10 Tufnell Park Edm	0–5	1–0	2–3	0–2	3–3	0–0	1–2	2–2	3–1	*	1–3	1–4	1–1	1–1
11 Walthamstow Ave.	6–0	9–0	2–0	3–2	0–1	0–2	3–2	0–4	4–1	4–1	*	3–1	1–1	5–2
12 Wimbledon	5–3	4–1	3–3	5–0	4–2	1–2	2–0	1–2	2–1	1–0	1–1	*	6–0	4–2
13 Woking	3–1	4–5	4–3	0–0	5–5	3–1	4–2	2–2	2–1	3–1	1–4	3–1	*	8–1
14 Wycombe Wndrs.	4–0	4–0	1–2	2–1	7–2	2–2	3–1	2–0	2–1	0–0	4–2	2–2	5–2	*

Below: the programme from the match between Woking and Dulwich Hamlet on 15 March 1952, which Woking won by the odd goal in seven.

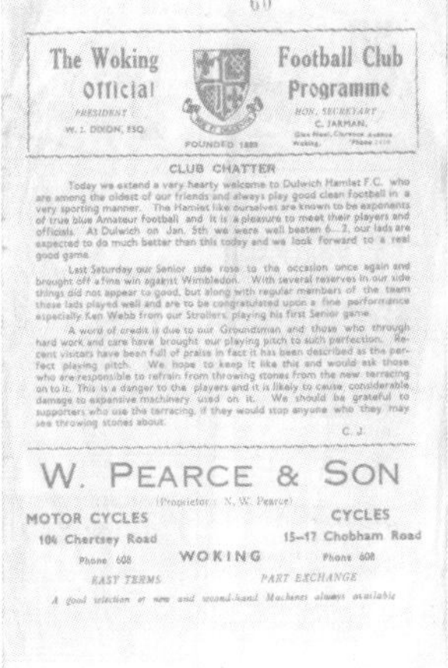

	P	W	D	L	F	A	Pts
1 Leytonstone	26	13	9	4	63	36	35
2 Wimbledon	26	16	3	7	65	44	35
3 Walthamstow Ave.	26	15	4	7	71	43	34
4 Romford	26	14	4	8	61	42	32
5 Kingstonian	26	11	7	8	62	48	29
6 Wycombe Wndrs.	26	12	5	9	64	59	29
7 Woking	26	11	5	10	60	71	27
8 Dulwich Hamlet	26	11	4	11	60	53	26
9 Corinthian-Casuals	26	11	4	11	55	66	26
10 St. Albans City	26	9	7	10	48	53	24
11 Ilford	26	8	5	13	32	47	21
12 Clapton	26	9	2	15	50	59	20
13 Oxford City	26	6	3	17	50	72	15
14 Tufnell Park Edm	26	2	6	18	25	73	10

Left: Barking's programme for their game with Leytonstone which finished as a 2-2 draw.

1952–53 - Henry Huband, who had served the Isthmian League since its inception in 1905 as Secretary, Chairman and President passed away. Vice-Chairman George Drane succeeded him as Chairman, at least for the remainder of the season. The championship went to another East London side, as Walthamstow Avenue broke Leytonstone's dominance by clinching the title, six points clear of Bromley, who were in turn four ahead of Leytonstone in third, with Wimbledon a further point adrift. Oxford City and Clapton, who occupied the two re-election places, were both duly elected at the Annual General Meeting. However, earlier in the season, Eastbourne United applied in the hope that a vacancy might occur. The League Council agreed to keep the constitution to 15 clubs. Also at the AGM, Max Woosnam was elected President of the League, while Sidney Donaldson succeeded the late Mr Huband as Chairman. Donald McKenzie was elected Hon Secretary & Treasurer and A W Peacock replaced him as Hon Referees & Fixture Secretary.

	1	2	3	4	5	6	7	8	9	10	11	12	13	14	15
1 Barking	*	1–0	2–2	2–2	5–1	2–3	0–3	2–2	2–0	0–2	2–0	1–1	1–1	0–2	3–0
2 Bromley	1–0	*	2–2	2–0	3–2	3–3	1–0	5–0	2–0	1–3	5–1	6–0	5–1	6–0	3–1
3 Clapton	0–2	2–6	*	3–3	2–4	0–4	0–1	0–5	3–0	1–3	1–2	0–4	1–0	0–0	1–3
4 Corinthian-Casuals	3–3	1–2	1–0	*	1–5	0–4	1–1	1–1	2–0	0–1	0–1	0–0	2–0	5–2	4–0
5 Dulwich Hamlet	2–0	2–1	1–0	4–1	*	1–5	5–2	2–2	8–1	2–1	0–1	0–2	2–0	4–3	3–1
6 Ilford	3–1	1–4	2–0	2–2	1–2	*	2–1	0–1	1–2	1–2	1–1	0–1	2–3	6–3	4–0
7 Kingstonian	2–0	2–1	3–1	4–3	3–0	5–1	*	5–3	3–3	2–2	1–2	1–1	2–1	1–0	1–2
8 Leytonstone	1–2	3–0	4–1	1–2	2–0	2–1	3–1	*	5–0	4–0	4–0	4–4	1–0	0–0	0–1
9 Oxford City	2–0	1–0	6–2	0–2	2–4	2–5	1–3	2–3	*	2–2	3–2	0–1	1–4	2–3	0–3
10 Romford	2–5	1–1	1–1	2–2	0–3	3–1	4–4	4–2	2–0	*	1–1	1–0	1–4	7–2	8–0
11 St. Albans City	3–3	0–3	2–1	1–1	2–2	3–2	2–1	0–3	4–3	4–2	*	1–2	1–3	2–1	1–3
12 Walthamstow Ave.	1–0	3–0	2–0	4–2	3–0	3–2	2–0	1–0	4–1	1–1	3–0	*	3–2	1–0	4–0
13 Wimbledon	8–0	1–1	2–1	3–0	1–0	2–2	5–1	0–0	7–0	3–1	1–2	0–2	*	5–3	6–1
14 Woking	4–2	3–4	3–1	4–1	2–1	4–0	1–1	1–3	4–3	2–3	3–3	3–0	0–4	*	2–3
15 Wycombe Wndrs.	0–1	1–3	3–1	4–3	5–2	4–0	3–5	3–1	6–0	3–2	2–1	0–0	1–1	1–2	*

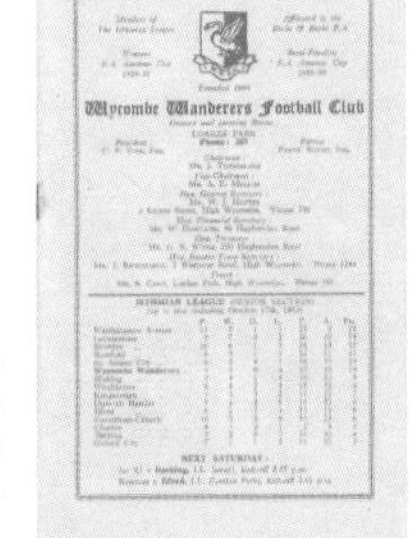

Right: the Wycombe Wanderers programme from 1953.

	P	*W*	*D*	*L*	*F*	*A*	*Pts*
1 Walthamstow Ave.	28	19	6	3	53	25	44
2 Bromley	28	17	4	7	71	35	38
3 Leytonstone	28	14	6	8	60	38	34
4 Wimbledon	28	14	5	9	68	37	33
5 Kingstonian	28	13	6	9	62	50	32
6 Dulwich Hamlet	28	15	2	11	62	52	32
7 Romford	28	12	8	8	62	52	32
8 Wycombe Wndrs.	28	14	2	12	54	62	30
9 St. Albans City	28	11	6	11	43	57	28
10 Barking	28	9	7	12	42	51	25
11 Ilford	28	10	4	14	59	57	24
12 Woking	28	10	4	14	57	72	24
13 Corinthian-Casuals	28	7	9	12	45	56	23
14 Oxford City	28	5	2	21	37	87	12
15 Clapton	28	2	5	21	27	71	9

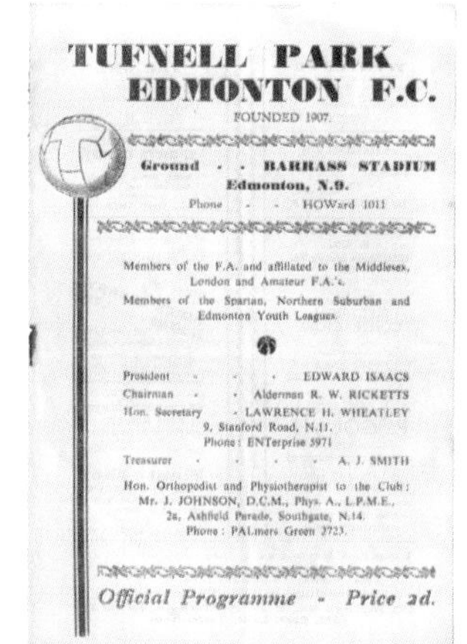

Right: the programme from Corinthian-Casuals' London Senior Cup tie at Tufnell Park Edmonton after the North London side had left the League.

1953–54 - Bromley earned one more point in this season than they had in 1952–53, but it was good enough for a six-point winning margin over defending champions Walthamstow Avenue. Wycombe Wanderers had an inferior goal average to the Avenue and thus were third, while Ilford ended up a respectable fourth, just a point behind the other two. At the other end of the table, Oxford City applied for re-election for the third time in succession along with Wimbledon who had by far their worst post-war season, although both clubs were re-elected at the Annual General Meeting.

	1	2	3	4	5	6	7	8	9	10	11	12	13	14	15
1 Barking	*	1–4	2–3	3–2	5–4	0–3	2–2	1–5	6–1	2–1	3–2	0–3	4–1	3–0	2–1
2 Bromley	8–0	*	3–1	3–0	2–3	2–1	5–2	3–2	4–0	7–1	4–2	0–2	2–1	2–0	2–1
3 Clapton	1–0	2–0	*	1–0	2–1	0–2	4–1	2–3	1–1	2–1	3–3	2–1	1–0	2–2	2–0
4 Corinthian-Casuals	3–2	5–2	6–0	*	0–0	1–2	1–1	2–1	1–1	2–0	2–2	1–3	2–2	5–1	2–3
5 Dulwich Hamlet	2–2	0–0	2–1	1–3	*	2–2	2–2	1–3	3–1	2–0	2–2	3–1	5–0	1–3	2–1
6 Ilford	0–1	1–2	3–1	2–2	5–3	*	2–1	0–5	0–0	2–1	3–0	2–1	3–2	1–4	2–2
7 Kingstonian	5–4	1–3	3–0	5–0	1–2	4–2	*	1–2	3–1	1–5	1–2	2–1	2–2	0–1	4–2
8 Leytonstone	1–2	4–0	2–2	0–1	1–2	1–1	7–3	*	1–1	0–1	3–1	3–1	0–0	4–2	2–1
9 Oxford City	6–3	3–4	4–1	1–6	3–4	2–4	3–3	2–3	*	1–3	0–1	0–1	2–1	3–2	0–4
10 Romford	2–4	2–3	3–1	2–1	1–0	2–2	8–3	4–3	2–2	*	1–3	0–2	3–2	7–0	1–1
11 St. Albans City	4–1	3–2	3–1	1–2	4–1	1–1	1–1	5–1	2–1	3–1	*	2–2	1–3	1–2	1–0
12 Walthamstow Ave.	8–0	2–1	2–2	0–0	2–1	3–1	1–1	1–0	8–1	2–2	4–1	*	4–0	0–0	0–1
13 Wimbledon	2–1	2–2	4–0	1–5	2–4	0–0	3–1	1–1	5–3	1–1	3–1	0–0	*	0–3	0–1
14 Woking	6–4	2–2	4–3	1–3	1–0	0–0	0–2	3–0	4–3	1–0	4–1	3–0	2–3	*	0–3
15 Wycombe Wndrs.	4–1	1–4	0–1	3–1	7–2	1–1	5–3	4–0	4–3	1–2	3–1	1–0	5–2	5–3	*

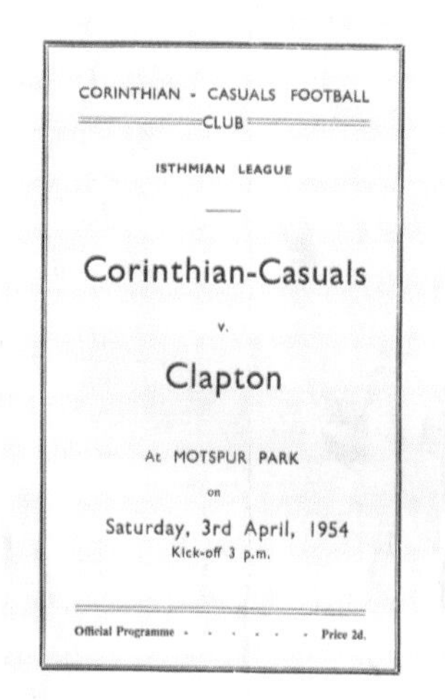

	P	*W*	*D*	*L*	*F*	*A*	*Pts*
1 Bromley	28	18	3	7	76	45	39
2 Walthamstow Ave.	28	13	7	8	55	30	33
3 Wycombe Wndrs.	28	15	3	10	65	44	33
4 Ilford	28	11	10	7	48	44	32
5 Corinthian-Casuals	28	12	7	9	59	44	31
6 Woking	28	13	4	11	54	58	30
7 Leytonstone	28	12	5	11	58	48	29
8 St. Albans City	28	11	6	11	54	55	28
9 Dulwich Hamlet	28	11	6	11	55	57	28
10 Romford	28	11	5	12	57	54	27
11 Clapton	28	11	5	12	42	56	27
12 Barking	28	11	2	15	59	84	24
13 Kingstonian	28	8	7	13	59	71	23
14 Wimbledon	28	7	8	13	43	59	22
15 Oxford City	28	4	6	18	49	84	14

Right above: the programme from Corinthian-Casuals' match with Clapton at Motspur Park in April 1954.

Right: The programme for the Clapton match against Walthamstow Avenue in April 1955.

Right below: the teams as they were printed in the programme. The Avenue won the match by the only goal.

1954–55 - The Isthmian League's Golden Jubilee championship went to Walthamstow Avenue, who took the title by four points from St. Albans City, with Bromley in third place and Wycombe Wanderers fourth. Dulwich Hamlet had a disastrous campaign, having to apply for re-election – for the first time since their inaugural season of 1907–08 – along with Romford, making their first application. Both clubs were re-elected.

A Fiftieth Anniversary Dinner was held at the Café Royal on 1 March 1955, attended by 420 guests. At the Annual General meeting, apart from the re-election of Romford and Dulwich Hamlet, the main item of business was agreeing to keep the League's constitution at 15 clubs for the 1955–56 season.

	1	2	3	4	5	6	7	8	9	10	11	12	13	14	15
1 Barking	*	1–3	1–3	3–2	3–4	1–0	1–2	0–2	4–0	0–0	3–1	1–2	4–2	5–1	2–0
2 Bromley	1–3	*	5–0	1–0	1–0	3–3	2–0	7–1	5–2	3–0	0–1	4–3	4–0	5–0	0–2
3 Clapton	0–1	1–2	*	3–2	1–1	0–2	1–2	0–1	4–0	1–4	1–0	0–1	2–0	5–2	1–1
4 Corinthian-Casuals	4–1	2–4	4–1	*	3–1	1–4	3–2	0–2	8–1	1–0	1–3	0–6	1–2	7–4	1–3
5 Dulwich Hamlet	2–4	1–2	1–2	1–3	*	2–2	2–0	2–0	1–3	4–1	1–1	1–2	0–2	2–1	5–3
6 Ilford	1–2	0–1	2–2	7–2	3–1	*	3–1	2–1	2–2	3–0	6–1	4–2	2–3	3–2	0–2
7 Kingstonian	2–0	2–1	1–4	0–0	2–2	0–0	*	4–0	3–1	1–1	0–2	1–4	5–4	4–2	1–1
8 Leytonstone	1–3	0–4	2–2	2–0	1–4	0–3	3–0	*	2–0	2–0	1–2	1–2	3–1	2–4	2–1
9 Oxford City	2–1	2–1	0–3	2–0	2–1	3–0	3–4	1–0	*	5–2	1–2	3–8	3–0	3–3	1–0
10 Romford	0–2	1–0	3–1	1–1	1–1	0–3	2–2	1–1	0–0	*	1–2	2–3	1–1	6–9	7–3
11 St. Albans City	3–1	2–2	1–0	3–0	3–1	4–2	3–0	1–1	5–2	4–2	*	1–2	0–3	5–1	3–2
12 Walthamstow Ave.	7–1	3–1	1–0	2–1	4–3	4–3	2–2	0–1	4–0	7–1	1–0	*	0–1	3–0	4–2
13 Wimbledon	3–1	0–1	4–2	1–2	3–1	1–2	1–2	3–1	5–0	1–1	1–3	2–3	*	1–3	1–3
14 Woking	1–4	4–1	4–0	0–0	3–2	3–1	6–2	3–1	2–1	4–4	1–4	1–0	9–1	*	2–4
15 Wycombe Wndrs.	1–2	0–2	2–1	5–1	4–1	2–1	3–2	1–1	4–0	8–1	4–1	1–0	3–0	3–0	*

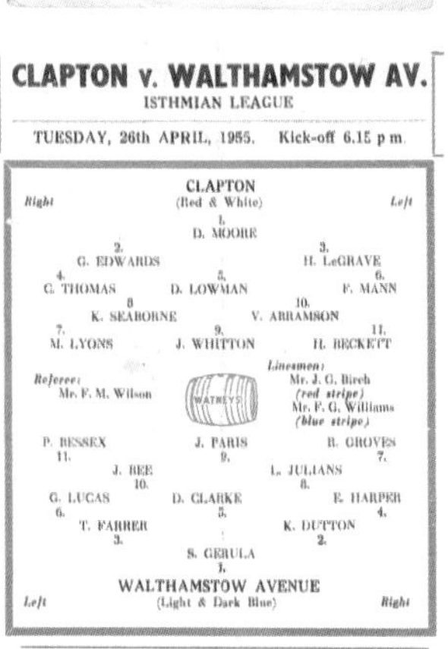

	P	W	D	L	F	A	Pts
1 Walthamstow Ave.	28	21	1	6	80	38	43
2 St. Albans City	28	18	3	7	61	41	39
3 Bromley	28	18	2	8	66	34	38
4 Wycombe Wndrs.	28	16	3	9	68	43	35
5 Ilford	28	13	5	10	64	46	31
6 Barking	28	15	1	12	55	51	31
7 Woking	28	12	3	13	75	79	27
8 Kingstonian	28	10	7	11	47	57	27
9 Leytonstone	28	10	4	14	35	51	24
10 Oxford City	28	10	3	15	43	74	23
11 Clapton	28	9	4	15	41	50	22
12 Wimbledon	28	10	2	16	48	62	22
13 Corinthian-Casuals	28	9	3	16	50	65	21
14 Dulwich Hamlet	28	7	5	16	48	60	19
15 Romford	28	4	10	14	43	73	18

Right: the St. Albans City side which finished as runners-up in 1954-55.

1955–56 - Wycombe Wanderers won their first Isthmian championship since joining the League in 1921. They did so in style, finishing twelve points ahead of Bromley, Leytonstone, Woking and Barking, who finished second to fifth, respectively, on goal average. Romford had to apply for re-election again, behind Dulwich Hamlet on goal average too, but they were only seven points behind runners-up Bromley in an incredibly congested table. St. Albans City were the only club who finished adrift of the main pack and the Saints propped up the table 10 points behind Romford. Both clubs were re-elected, and Tooting & Mitcham United were granted membership as the League Council agreed to expand the Isthmian League's constitution to 16 clubs.

	1	2	3	4	5	6	7	8	9	10	11	12	13	14	15
1 Barking	*	2–1	1–1	0–0	0–2	2–2	1–0	0–2	0–3	0–0	3–1	1–0	0–0	1–0	3–4
2 Bromley	2–2	*	3–0	0–1	3–2	1–1	3–3	2–1	3–1	7–0	1–0	2–1	5–3	1–2	2–3
3 Clapton	2–1	1–3	*	1–1	2–2	0–1	4–1	0–0	5–1	1–3	3–2	0–0	3–0	1–2	0–2
4 Corinthian-Casuals	7–2	1–2	2–2	*	3–1	6–2	0–3	2–3	1–0	0–2	1–1	0–0	3–1	4–5	0–0
5 Dulwich Hamlet	0–3	1–4	4–3	1–4	*	3–1	6–6	0–2	1–2	1–2	3–1	1–2	2–0	3–4	2–4
6 Ilford	0–1	1–1	0–3	3–1	2–2	*	1–3	4–2	1–1	2–2	2–0	2–1	2–2	3–1	0–3
7 Kingstonian	1–2	5–1	3–2	4–3	1–3	0–1	*	2–0	5–2	4–3	4–2	2–1	4–2	4–2	2–2
8 Leytonstone	2–2	1–0	4–0	2–1	2–2	2–2	3–3	*	2–2	1–1	2–0	1–3	4–0	4–0	2–1
9 Oxford City	3–0	0–0	1–1	1–1	1–3	1–0	4–0	3–2	*	1–3	4–4	2–1	3–2	3–3	1–3
10 Romford	1–2	0–0	0–1	1–3	1–2	1–5	2–1	2–1	0–2	*	2–2	4–0	5–4	1–3	1–3
11 St. Albans City	2–1	0–0	0–0	1–6	3–3	1–2	1–1	1–2	2–1	1–1	*	1–3	3–4	1–2	1–1
12 Walthamstow Ave.	2–4	5–2	5–1	4–1	2–2	1–2	5–1	4–1	4–1	0–2	2–0	*	1–3	2–1	2–4
13 Wimbledon	2–4	1–2	0–3	4–2	5–1	4–2	1–0	0–1	3–1	1–0	2–0	2–1	*	2–1	1–0
14 Woking	1–3	2–1	3–5	4–1	1–2	2–0	2–2	2–0	2–3	1–0	4–3	2–6	5–1	*	2–2
15 Wycombe Wndrs.	4–0	3–2	3–0	6–1	3–0	5–0	5–2	5–1	3–0	6–2	2–2	0–3	4–1	1–3	*

	P	W	D	L	F	A	Pts
1 Wycombe Wndrs.	28	19	5	4	82	36	43
2 Bromley	28	12	7	9	54	43	31
3 Leytonstone	28	12	7	9	50	44	31
4 Woking	28	14	3	11	62	60	31
5 Barking	28	12	7	9	41	45	31
6 Kingstonian	28	12	6	10	67	64	30
7 Walthamstow Ave.	28	13	3	12	61	45	29
8 Ilford	28	10	8	10	44	52	28
9 Oxford City	28	10	7	11	48	55	27
10 Clapton	28	9	8	11	45	48	26
11 Wimbledon	28	12	2	14	51	62	26
12 Corinthian-Casuals	28	9	7	12	56	56	25
13 Dulwich Hamlet	28	9	6	13	55	67	24
14 Romford	28	9	6	13	42	55	24
15 St. Albans City	28	2	10	16	36	62	14

Right above: the programme from Corinthian-Casuals' FA Amateur Cup Final with Bishop Auckland.

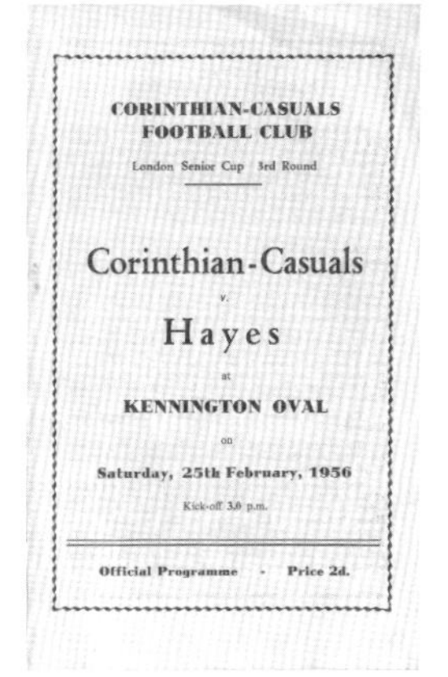

Right: the programme from Corinthian-Casuals' match with Hayes at the Kennington Oval in February 1956.

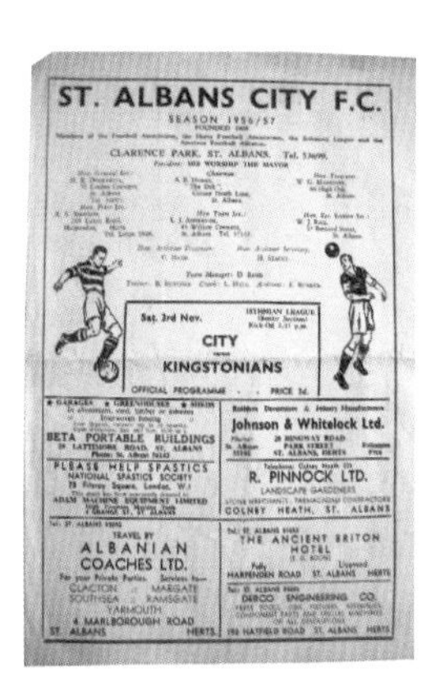

Right below: St. Albans City's programme for their game with Kingstonian in November 1956 which finished 1-1.

1956–57 - Life member Cyril Evans – formerly secretary of Tufnell Park and Tufnell Park Edmonton and a League Council member for more than two decades starting in the inter-war years – passed away early in the season. Wycombe Wanderers retained their title in a much more closely fought championship. They finished one point clear of Woking who enjoyed their most successful season since entering the Isthmian League in 1911. Bromley, runners-up in 1956, slipped one place to third, four points behind the Cardinals, but two clear of Oxford City who achieved their best League position since 1946. Corinthian-Casuals finished bottom and had to apply for re-election, along with Barking, whose 15th-place finish was their worst since joining the League in 1952. Both clubs were subsequently re-elected at the Annual General Meeting.

	1	2	3	4	5	6	7	8	9	10	11	12	13	14	15	16
1 Barking	*	5–2	2–1	2–0	1–0	3–3	2–3	1–1	0–1	1–2	3–5	2–2	3–1	1–1	2–5	2–2
2 Bromley	4–1	*	3–1	3–2	3–2	5–1	3–0	1–4	9–3	2–1	1–2	0–3	2–3	2–0	4–2	6–2
3 Clapton	2–1	2–2	*	1–1	3–2	1–4	2–3	0–3	2–3	7–1	1–0	1–2	1–1	0–1	2–1	1–1
4 Corinthian-Casuals	3–1	4–0	2–2	*	1–3	0–1	1–2	1–1	3–1	3–4	1–3	1–3	3–2	2–4	3–2	1–3
5 Dulwich Hamlet	2–1	2–1	4–2	2–1	*	3–1	4–1	3–0	1–2	5–1	6–1	1–1	1–1	4–1	3–6	1–3
6 Ilford	4–1	2–2	1–1	5–0	3–2	*	3–3	4–0	2–0	1–0	3–0	1–1	0–0	2–1	1–5	1–4
7 Kingstonian	4–3	2–2	6–3	7–1	0–1	3–3	*	2–2	4–1	5–2	4–1	0–0	4–1	2–2	2–3	0–6
8 Leytonstone	4–1	1–4	0–0	0–2	3–2	1–2	8–2	*	2–0	1–2	1–0	0–2	2–3	2–1	0–1	1–0
9 Oxford City	1–2	2–2	2–0	4–1	1–0	5–1	4–2	0–0	*	10–1	4–2	5–2	1–0	3–2	3–1	0–0
10 Romford	0–1	2–3	0–0	4–0	3–1	2–4	2–2	3–1	1–5	*	3–4	1–0	0–2	1–0	1–7	1–2
11 St. Albans City	2–1	5–3	1–1	1–2	4–2	7–1	1–1	4–2	3–1	2–3	*	1–3	1–2	5–0	1–0	1–2
12 Tooting & M Utd	1–1	1–4	1–2	3–2	1–1	0–0	5–1	1–2	3–0	3–1	1–1	*	2–2	3–3	0–1	1–1
13 Walthamstow Ave.	4–0	0–1	0–1	1–1	5–1	3–2	1–1	1–1	2–1	1–1	2–3	1–0	*	1–2	3–1	2–3
14 Wimbledon	2–1	1–1	1–2	4–2	0–5	2–0	2–4	3–2	3–0	1–3	3–0	2–4	1–2	*	3–2	1–4
15 Woking	4–1	3–1	7–1	6–0	1–0	6–0	4–1	2–4	5–0	3–3	7–1	5–0	2–0	6–0	*	3–2
16 Wycombe Wndrs.	6–2	1–2	3–5	3–2	2–1	4–3	4–1	2–1	1–2	4–4	7–0	5–4	4–1	0–0	5–3	*

	P	W	D	L	F	A	Pts
1 Wycombe Wndrs.	30	18	6	6	86	53	42
2 Woking	30	20	1	9	104	47	41
3 Bromley	30	16	5	9	78	60	37
4 Oxford City	30	16	3	11	65	57	35
5 Ilford	30	12	8	10	59	65	32
6 Tooting & M Utd	30	10	11	9	53	48	31
7 Kingstonian	30	11	9	10	72	77	31
8 Walthamstow Ave.	30	11	8	11	48	46	30
9 Dulwich Hamlet	30	13	3	14	65	54	29
10 St. Albans City	30	13	3	14	62	71	29
11 Leytonstone	30	11	6	13	50	50	28
12 Clapton	30	9	9	12	48	59	27
13 Wimbledon	30	10	5	15	47	66	25
14 Romford	30	10	5	15	53	81	25
15 Barking	30	7	6	17	48	72	20
16 Corinthian-Casuals	30	7	4	19	46	78	18

Left: the Tooting & Mitcham programme for their match with Ilford in their championship-winning season.

Right: the programme from Wimbledon's 'house-warming party' to welcome Tooting & Mitcham United to the League in April 1956.

1957–58 - In just their second season as members of the Isthmian League, Tooting & Mitcham United brought the title to South London, four points clear of runners-up Wycombe Wanderers. Walthamstow Avenue were third, a further three points adrift, but they had four in hand on Bromley, who had yet to finish lower than fourth in the League. At the other end of the table, Ilford had to apply for re-election for the first time since the League's inaugural season, along with Romford whose re-election application was their second in three seasons. Both clubs were re-elected at the Annual General Meeting. In January, Ilford FC proposed a change in the League's structure, with a more competitive approach, including promotion and relegation. The proposal suggested an amalgamation with another league – such as the Athenian League – to create a second division. The proposal was not seconded, so it could not be brought forward for discussion at the Annual General Meeting. However, it did lead a discussion on suggestions submitted by clubs after the May Council Meeting.

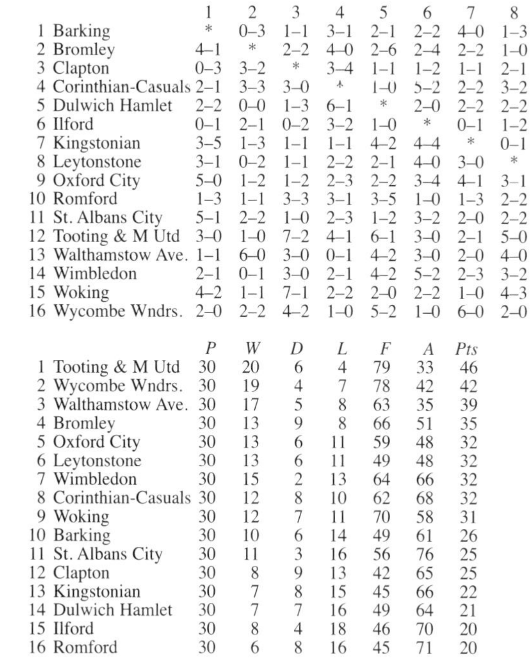

	1	2	3	4	5	6	7	8	9	10	11	12	13	14	15	16
1 Barking	*	0–3	1–1	3–1	2–1	2–2	4–0	1–3	2–2	2–2	3–1	1–3	1–0	5–1	0–2	0–2
2 Bromley	4–1	*	2–2	4–0	2–6	2–4	2–2	1–0	4–2	5–1	4–1	0–1	3–3	1–2	6–1	3–2
3 Clapton	0–3	3–2	*	3–4	1–1	1–2	1–1	2–1	1–1	2–1	1–1	1–0	1–3	0–2	2–1	3–4
4 Corinthian-Casuals	2–1	3–3	3–0	*	1–0	5–2	2–2	3–2	3–1	2–5	1–4	2–2	2–0	2–2	4–2	4–4
5 Dulwich Hamlet	2–2	0–0	1–3	6–1	*	2–0	2–2	2–2	0–3	2–2	1–2	0–1	0–2	0–3	2–0	2–1
6 Ilford	0–1	2–1	0–2	3–2	1–0	*	0–1	1–2	2–3	2–1	5–2	1–3	0–1	4–4	0–3	1–3
7 Kingstonian	3–5	1–3	1–1	1–1	4–2	4–4	*	0–1	2–3	1–0	1–2	1–3	0–0	2–3	3–2	5–2
8 Leytonstone	3–1	0–2	1–1	2–2	2–1	4–0	3–0	*	2–0	2–0	3–1	1–1	0–3	1–0	3–1	1–0
9 Oxford City	5–0	1–2	1–2	2–3	2–2	3–4	4–1	3–1	*	4–1	4–1	2–2	1–2	0–1	1–0	1–1
10 Romford	1–3	1–1	3–3	3–1	3–5	1–0	1–3	2–2	1–2	*	3–1	0–0	1–2	3–1	3–3	0–2
11 St. Albans City	5–1	2–2	1–0	2–3	1–2	3–2	2–0	2–2	0–2	2–0	*	4–0	3–1	3–4	6–3	1–4
12 Tooting & M Utd	3–0	1–0	7–2	4–1	6–1	3–0	2–1	5–0	3–0	5–1	5–0	*	4–3	4–1	3–1	1–1
13 Walthamstow Ave.	1–1	6–0	3–0	0–1	4–2	3–0	2–0	4–0	0–2	1–1	4–0	2–1	*	5–1	2–1	1–0
14 Wimbledon	2–1	0–1	3–0	2–1	4–2	5–2	2–3	3–2	0–1	5–1	2–1	3–4	3–2	*	2–5	1–2
15 Woking	4–2	1–1	7–1	2–2	2–0	2–2	1–0	4–3	1–1	1–3	6–1	1–1	2–2	5–1	*	2–1
16 Wycombe Wndrs.	2–0	2–2	4–2	1–0	5–2	1–0	6–0	2–0	4–2	6–0	7–1	2–1	4–1	3–1	0–4	*

	P	W	D	L	F	A	Pts
1 Tooting & M Utd	30	20	6	4	79	33	46
2 Wycombe Wndrs.	30	19	4	7	78	42	42
3 Walthamstow Ave.	30	17	5	8	63	35	39
4 Bromley	30	13	9	8	66	51	35
5 Oxford City	30	13	6	11	59	48	32
6 Leytonstone	30	13	6	11	49	48	32
7 Wimbledon	30	15	2	13	64	66	32
8 Corinthian-Casuals	30	12	8	10	62	68	32
9 Woking	30	12	7	11	70	58	31
10 Barking	30	10	6	14	49	61	26
11 St. Albans City	30	11	3	16	56	76	25
12 Clapton	30	8	9	13	42	65	25
13 Kingstonian	30	7	8	15	45	66	22
14 Dulwich Hamlet	30	7	7	16	49	64	21
15 Ilford	30	8	4	18	46	70	20
16 Romford	30	6	8	16	45	71	20

Right: the programme from Romford's game against Kingstonian in January 1958, which they lost 3-1.

Below: the Woking programme from 1958.

Below: the programme from St. Albans City's match with Ilford in February 1959, which Ilford won 1-0.

1958–59 - Wimbledon secured the title, six points clear of Dulwich Hamlet, with Wycombe Wanderers a point behind in third place and Oxford City four, two points behind the Chairboys. Corinthian-Casuals finished bottom for the second time in three seasons, but they were re-elected at the Annual General Meeting. However, Romford, who finished next to bottom, had already resigned from membership because the Club had decided to turn professional and join the Southern League. A proposal by Corinthian-Casuals, seconded by Woking, not to fill the vacancy created by Romford was rejected. Instead an invitation was made to Maidstone United, which was accepted by the Kent club. Three other Kent clubs, Chatham Town, Whitstable and Faversham Town, had made earlier applications to join the League – Chatham and Whitstable had decided to revert to amateur football – but these were rejected by the League Council. Bromley and Walthamstow Avenue were invited to join the Eastern Counties League but both declined to do so.

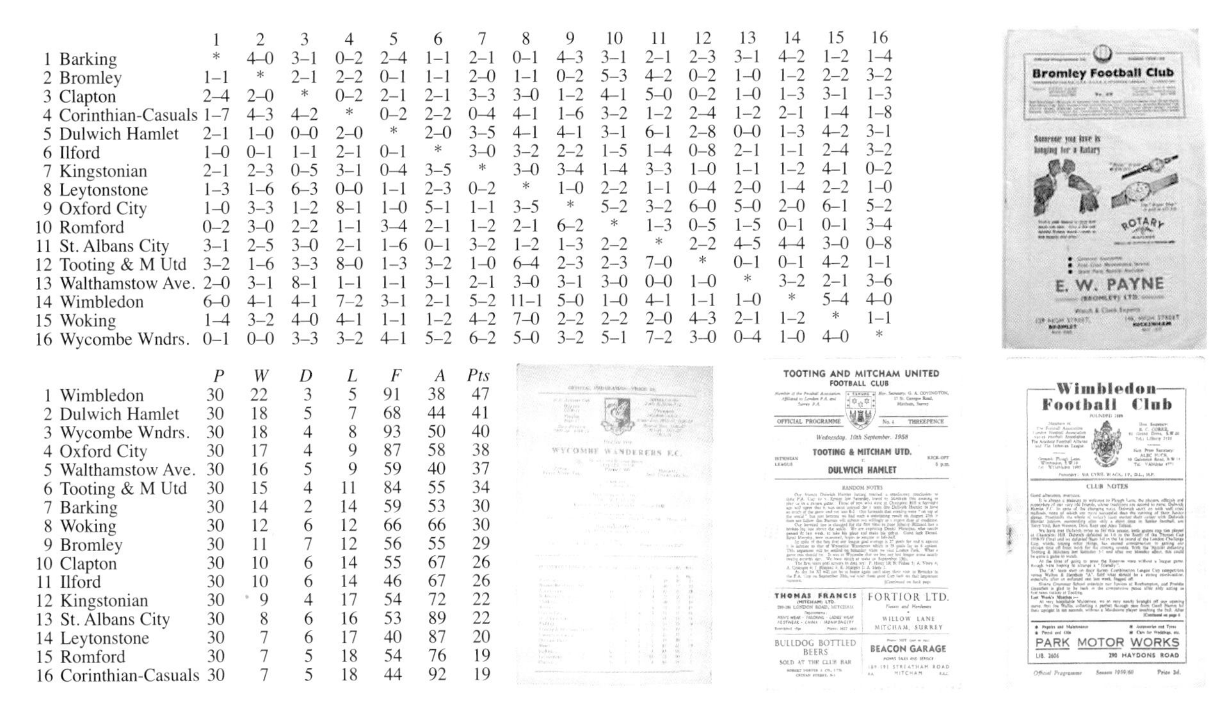

	1	2	3	4	5	6	7	8	9	10	11	12	13	14	15	16
1 Barking	*	4–0	3–1	0–2	2–4	1–1	2–1	0–1	4–3	3–1	2–1	2–3	3–1	4–2	1–2	1–4
2 Bromley	1–1	*	2–1	2–2	0–1	1–1	2–0	1–1	0–2	5–3	4–2	0–2	1–0	1–2	2–2	3–2
3 Clapton	2–4	2–0	*	0–2	2–1	2–1	3–3	3–0	1–2	4–1	5–0	0–2	1–0	1–3	3–1	1–3
4 Corinthian-Casuals	1–7	4–3	4–2	*	0–2	2–2	0–4	4–1	1–6	3–2	1–2	2–4	1–2	2–1	1–4	1–8
5 Dulwich Hamlet	2–1	1–0	0–0	2–0	*	2–0	3–5	4–1	4–1	3–1	6–1	2–8	0–0	1–3	4–2	3–1
6 Ilford	1–0	0–1	1–1	2–1	0–1	*	3–0	3–2	2–2	1–5	1–4	0–8	2–1	1–1	2–4	3–2
7 Kingstonian	2–1	2–3	0–5	3–1	0–4	3–5	*	3–0	3–4	1–4	3–3	1–0	1–1	1–2	4–1	0–2
8 Leytonstone	1–3	1–6	6–3	0–0	1–1	2–3	0–2	*	1–0	2–2	1–1	0–4	2–0	1–4	2–2	1–0
9 Oxford City	1–0	3–3	1–2	8–1	1–0	5–1	1–1	3–5	*	5–2	3–2	6–0	5–0	2–0	6–1	5–2
10 Romford	0–2	3–0	2–2	1–1	3–4	2–1	1–2	2–1	6–2	*	1–3	0–5	1–5	0–1	0–1	3–4
11 St. Albans City	3–1	2–5	3–0	2–1	1–6	0–1	3–2	1–2	1–3	2–2	*	2–2	4–5	4–4	3–0	0–8
12 Tooting & M Utd	3–2	1–6	3–3	8–0	1–3	3–2	1–0	6–4	2–3	2–3	7–0	*	0–1	0–1	4–2	1–1
13 Walthamstow Ave.	2–0	3–1	8–1	1–1	1–1	3–1	2–1	3–0	3–1	3–0	0–0	1–0	*	3–2	2–1	3–6
14 Wimbledon	6–0	4–1	4–1	7–2	3–1	2–1	5–2	11–1	5–0	1–0	4–1	1–1	1–0	*	5–4	4–0
15 Woking	1–4	3–2	4–0	4–1	1–1	1–2	4–2	7–0	2–2	2–2	2–0	4–3	2–1	1–2	*	1–1
16 Wycombe Wndrs.	0–1	0–0	3–3	3–2	4–1	5–2	6–2	5–0	3–2	5–1	7–2	3–0	0–4	1–0	4–0	*

	P	*W*	*D*	*L*	*F*	*A*	*Pts*
1 Wimbledon	30	22	3	5	91	38	47
2 Dulwich Hamlet	30	18	5	7	68	44	41
3 Wycombe Wndrs.	30	18	4	8	93	50	40
4 Oxford City	30	17	4	9	87	58	38
5 Walthamstow Ave.	30	16	5	9	59	40	37
6 Tooting & M Utd	30	15	4	11	84	55	34
7 Barking	30	14	2	14	59	53	30
8 Woking	30	12	6	12	66	66	30
9 Bromley	30	11	7	12	56	55	29
10 Clapton	30	10	6	14	55	67	26
11 Ilford	30	10	6	14	46	67	26
12 Kingstonian	30	9	4	17	54	72	22
13 St. Albans City	30	8	6	16	53	89	22
14 Leytonstone	30	7	6	17	40	87	20
15 Romford	30	7	5	18	54	76	19
16 Corinthian-Casuals	30	7	5	18	44	92	19

1959–60 - The League championship remained in South London, but this time it was Tooting & Mitcham United who secured the title, repelling a strong challenge from Wycombe Wanderers. In the end, the teams were separated by a single point, with Wimbledon taking third place ahead of Kingstonian on goal average, two points behind. Two of the League's founder members, Ilford and Clapton, occupied the bottom two spots and thus had to apply for re-election. Both clubs were re-elected at the Annual General Meeting.

	1	2	3	4	5	6	7	8	9	10	11	12	13	14	15	16
1 Barking	*	2–1	2–1	1–4	0–5	1–3	0–0	1–0	2–1	1–1	0–0	4–0	1–0	0–4	0–1	2–1
2 Bromley	5–0	*	8–2	3–1	2–2	3–0	3–1	1–0	0–2	3–3	5–4	1–2	1–1	4–0	1–2	2–4
3 Clapton	2–0	0–1	*	0–1	2–3	1–1	1–2	0–2	6–2	1–5	2–1	1–1	2–2	2–4	0–4	1–8
4 Corinthian-Casuals	3–1	0–7	2–1	*	1–5	7–2	0–6	2–0	6–2	5–1	4–2	3–2	1–1	1–2	1–0	4–0
5 Dulwich Hamlet	4–1	3–4	6–0	3–2	*	7–1	0–2	1–1	3–1	1–1	2–1	3–1	0–1	0–0	2–0	1–2
6 Ilford	1–0	1–1	1–0	0–4	1–3	*	1–2	1–1	1–2	2–2	1–2	2–2	2–0	2–6	5–1	0–2
7 Kingstonian	4–0	2–2	2–0	1–2	1–0	6–1	*	5–1	1–1	2–0	1–2	4–2	5–2	1–0	5–3	0–3
8 Leytonstone	1–0	1–3	4–0	1–4	0–2	2–0	7–3	*	3–1	1–2	1–1	1–1	1–3	1–0	1–3	0–0
9 Maidstone United	2–2	1–0	4–1	1–2	6–4	4–1	3–5	1–3	*	2–0	1–2	3–0	0–0	0–1	5–2	2–3
10 Oxford City	6–3	1–2	5–0	1–2	4–0	4–3	3–2	1–0	1–1	*	1–1	2–2	1–0	1–1	2–2	3–1
11 St. Albans City	3–1	0–2	3–2	1–0	3–0	6–0	3–0	4–0	1–3	2–1	*	2–5	3–3	0–3	2–2	2–1
12 Tooting & M Utd	6–1	3–3	5–1	5–2	1–1	1–0	3–2	0–0	3–0	3–1	5–0	*	2–2	4–1	4–1	5–1
13 Walthamstow Ave.	3–0	4–0	1–0	4–1	1–1	1–1	2–3	1–1	1–1	3–2	3–1	0–1	*	1–0	2–0	4–0
14 Wimbledon	2–0	2–1	6–0	5–1	2–0	3–0	2–1	2–4	1–0	7–0	2–2	0–1	3–0	*	2–4	2–1
15 Woking	5–0	0–5	1–1	0–2	1–3	2–0	6–1	2–4	3–0	1–1	3–0	0–3	1–1	0–2	*	3–5
16 Wycombe Wndrs.	6–4	2–0	5–2	3–1	4–0	10–0	2–0	1–1	2–1	3–1	5–0	1–2	3–1	4–1	1–1	*

Right: the Official Handbook from Ilford Football Club for the 1959-60 campaign.

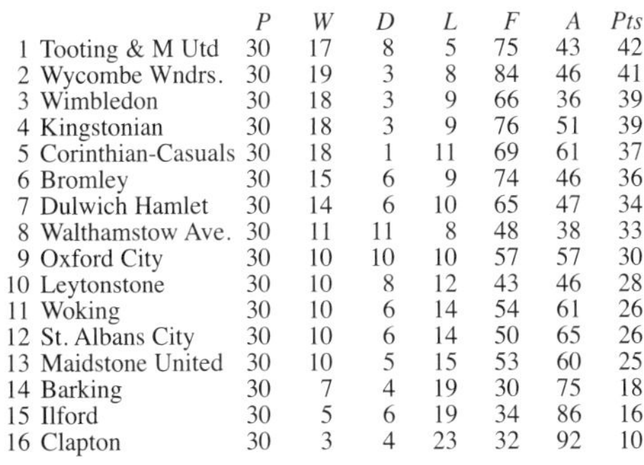

	P	*W*	*D*	*L*	*F*	*A*	*Pts*
1 Tooting & M Utd	30	17	8	5	75	43	42
2 Wycombe Wndrs.	30	19	3	8	84	46	41
3 Wimbledon	30	18	3	9	66	36	39
4 Kingstonian	30	18	3	9	76	51	39
5 Corinthian-Casuals	30	18	1	11	69	61	37
6 Bromley	30	15	6	9	74	46	36
7 Dulwich Hamlet	30	14	6	10	65	47	34
8 Walthamstow Ave.	30	11	11	8	48	38	33
9 Oxford City	30	10	10	10	57	57	30
10 Leytonstone	30	10	8	12	43	46	28
11 Woking	30	10	6	14	54	61	26
12 St. Albans City	30	10	6	14	50	65	26
13 Maidstone United	30	10	5	15	53	60	25
14 Barking	30	7	4	19	30	75	18
15 Ilford	30	5	6	19	34	86	16
16 Clapton	30	3	4	23	32	92	10

Below: Wimbledon's Plough Lane ground during the 1960-61 campaign.

1960–61 - Bromley held off a stern challenge from Walthamstow Avenue before taking the League championship for the fourth time by a solitary point, with Wimbledon three points behind in third, but they were, in turn four ahead of South London rivals Dulwich Hamlet. Clapton collected the "wooden spoon" for the second consecutive season, and they were joined in applying for re-election by Barking, who swapped places with Ilford from the previous season. Both clubs were successful in their applications at the Annual General Meeting.

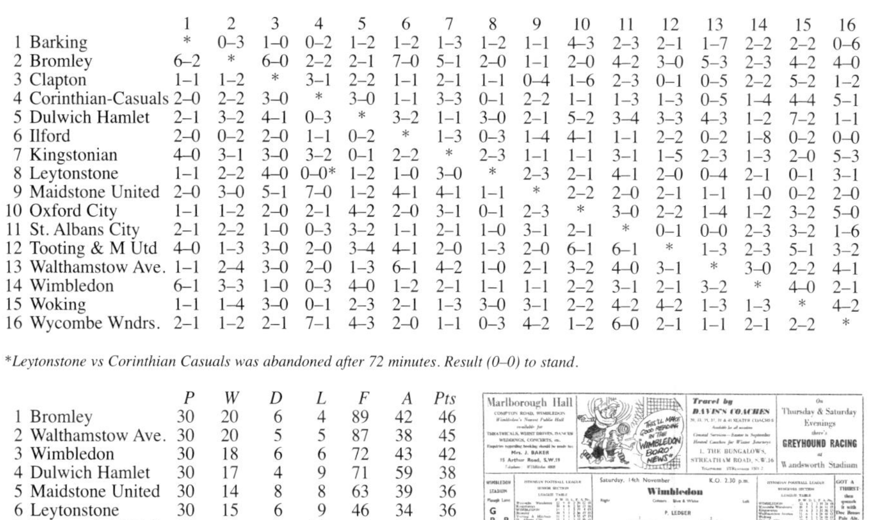

	1	2	3	4	5	6	7	8	9	10	11	12	13	14	15	16
1 Barking	*	0–3	1–0	0–2	1–2	1–2	1–3	1–2	1–1	4–3	2–3	2–1	1–7	2–2	2–2	0–6
2 Bromley	6–2	*	6–0	2–2	2–1	7–0	5–1	2–0	1–1	2–0	4–2	3–0	5–3	2–3	4–2	4–0
3 Clapton	1–1	1–2	*	3–1	2–2	1–1	2–1	1–1	0–4	1–6	2–3	0–1	0–5	2–2	5–2	1–2
4 Corinthian-Casuals	2–0	2–2	3–0	*	3–0	1–1	3–3	0–1	2–2	1–1	1–3	1–3	0–5	1–4	4–4	5–1
5 Dulwich Hamlet	2–1	3–2	4–1	0–3	*	3–2	1–1	3–0	2–1	5–2	3–4	3–3	4–3	1–2	7–2	1–1
6 Ilford	2–0	0–2	2–0	1–1	0–2	*	1–3	0–3	1–4	4–1	1–1	2–2	0–2	1–8	0–2	0–0
7 Kingstonian	4–0	3–1	3–0	3–2	0–1	2–2	*	2–3	1–1	1–1	3–1	1–5	2–3	1–3	2–0	5–3
8 Leytonstone	1–1	2–2	4–0	0–0*	1–2	1–0	3–0	*	2–3	2–1	4–1	2–0	0–4	2–1	0–1	3–1
9 Maidstone United	2–0	3–0	5–1	7–0	1–2	4–1	4–1	1–1	*	2–2	2–0	2–1	1–1	1–0	0–2	2–0
10 Oxford City	1–1	1–2	2–0	2–1	4–2	2–0	3–1	0–1	2–3	*	3–0	2–2	1–4	1–2	3–2	5–0
11 St. Albans City	2–1	2–2	1–0	0–3	3–2	1–1	2–1	1–0	3–1	2–1	*	0–1	0–0	2–3	3–2	1–6
12 Tooting & M Utd	4–0	1–3	3–0	2–0	3–4	4–1	2–0	1–3	2–0	6–1	6–1	*	1–3	2–3	5–1	3–2
13 Walthamstow Ave.	1–1	2–4	3–0	2–0	1–3	6–1	4–2	1–0	2–1	3–2	4–0	3–1	*	3–0	2–2	4–1
14 Wimbledon	6–1	3–3	1–0	0–3	4–0	1–2	2–1	1–1	1–1	2–2	3–1	2–1	3–2	*	4–0	2–1
15 Woking	1–1	1–4	3–0	0–1	2–3	2–1	1–3	3–0	3–1	2–2	4–2	4–2	1–3	1–3	*	4–2
16 Wycombe Wndrs.	2–1	1–2	2–1	7–1	4–3	2–0	1–1	0–3	4–2	1–2	6–0	2–1	1–1	2–1	2–2	*

**Leytonstone vs Corinthian Casuals was abandoned after 72 minutes. Result (0–0) to stand.*

	P	W	D	L	F	A	Pts
1 Bromley	30	20	6	4	89	42	46
2 Walthamstow Ave.	30	20	5	5	87	38	45
3 Wimbledon	30	18	6	6	72	43	42
4 Dulwich Hamlet	30	17	4	9	71	59	38
5 Maidstone United	30	14	8	8	63	39	36
6 Leytonstone	30	15	6	9	46	34	36
7 Tooting & M Utd	30	14	3	13	69	51	31
8 Wycombe Wndrs.	30	12	5	13	63	61	29
9 St. Albans City	30	12	4	14	45	72	28
10 Oxford City	30	10	7	13	59	59	27
11 Corinthian-Casuals	30	9	9	12	49	59	27
12 Kingstonian	30	10	6	14	55	61	26
13 Woking	30	10	6	14	58	71	26
14 Ilford	30	5	8	17	30	69	18
15 Barking	30	3	8	19	30	76	14
16 Clapton	30	3	5	22	25	77	11

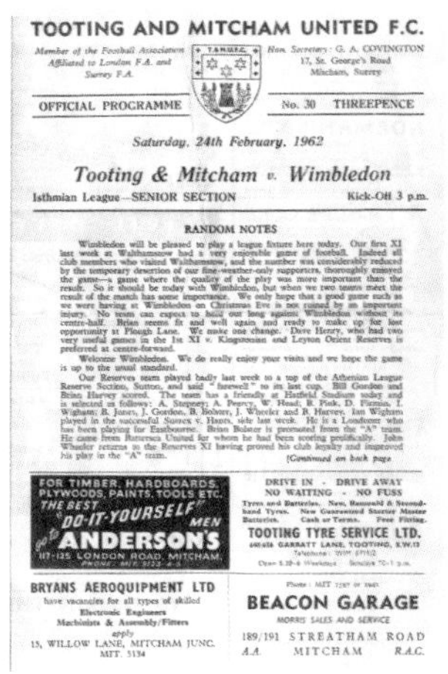

Above: programme from Tooting & Mitcham United's home match with Wimbledon in February 1962, which the visitors won by three goals to one.

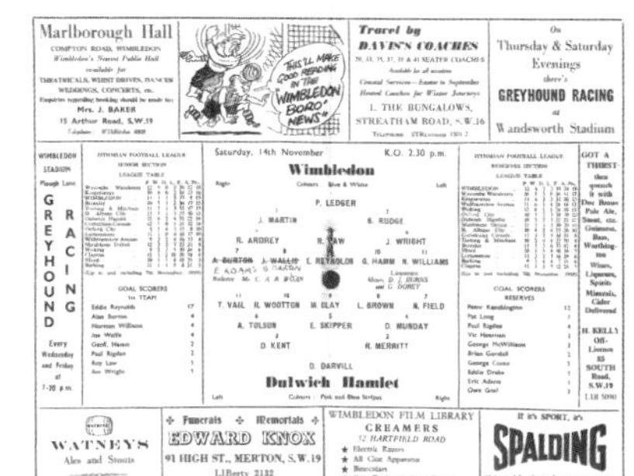

Left: The teams for Wimbledon's 2-0 victory over Dulwich Hamlet. Nice to see Woking stalwart Phil Ledger in goal!

1961–62 - Wimbledon won their sixth Isthmian League championship, finishing three points clear of runners-up Leytonstone, who enjoyed their best finish for nine seasons. Walthamstow Avenue were third, five points behind the "Stones", while Kingstonian were a point further behind in fourth place. Clapton avoided a third consecutive bottom-place finish, but again had to apply for re-election, along with Maidstone United, whose application was a first. Both clubs retained their membership at the Annual General Meeting. Applications to join the League were received from Maidenhead United and Dagenham, but these were rejected by the League Council.

	1	2	3	4	5	6	7	8	9	10	11	12	13	14	15	16
1 Barking	*	3–3	2–0	2–3	3–2	0–3	2–1	1–4	1–1	1–0	2–1	1–3	0–2	1–3	1–1	2–2
2 Bromley	0–1	*	4–1	2–1	0–2	3–3	2–3	4–2	3–0	3–2	0–4	1–0	1–4	2–1	2–2	2–3
3 Clapton	2–3	2–3	*	2–2	2–2	2–4	2–1	2–2	2–4	0–1	1–1	2–1	1–0	1–1	1–1	3–2
4 Corinthian-Casuals	1–0	2–1	2–1	*	1–2	2–0	0–6	1–3	3–0	1–1	2–2	1–3	0–3	1–0	2–2	4–2
5 Dulwich Hamlet	2–3	5–2	4–3	1–1	*	0–2	2–3	1–3	2–0	1–1	5–0	2–3	0–2	1–2	3–1	2–3
6 Ilford	2–2	1–3	1–2	0–0	1–3	*	3–2	1–4	0–1	4–0	3–1	3–2	1–3	0–2	1–1	2–5
7 Kingstonian	3–2	2–0	2–1	3–1	0–2	2–2	*	1–5	6–0	4–0	2–4	5–3	1–0	1–2	1–2	1–1
8 Leytonstone	1–1	3–1	2–1	1–1	6–1	1–0	2–1	*	1–0	3–3	2–1	2–3	0–0	1–0	2–0	3–1
9 Maidstone United	2–0	3–1	1–3	3–1	2–2	2–2	1–3	1–2	*	0–1	3–2	1–1	1–4	0–1	2–3	1–2
10 Oxford City	4–0	5–1	2–0	3–1	1–2	3–3	2–3	4–0	1–1	*	5–0	2–0	1–1	0–6	4–1	3–2
11 St. Albans City	0–0	3–0	3–2	3–0	4–2	4–1	1–2	2–1	2–2	2–2	*	1–3	2–1	3–1	0–2	0–0
12 Tooting & M Utd	8–1	1–1	1–1	3–1	5–0	2–1	0–0	1–1	2–0	1–1	1–1	*	4–2	1–3	5–1	2–2
13 Walthamstow Ave.	2–0	2–1	5–0	0–2	2–1	1–0	0–0	1–1	1–0	3–0	4–4	1–1	*	0–0	1–1	3–1
14 Wimbledon	4–0	3–0	5–1	0–2	3–0	2–2	3–1	7–0	1–1	1–1	0–0	5–1	3–2	*	5–1	2–0
15 Woking	3–3	1–2	2–1	2–3	1–3	2–2	2–2	1–3	5–1	0–2	4–3	3–0	2–1	0–1	*	3–0
16 Wycombe Wndrs.	1–2	3–1	3–3	0–2	6–0	2–2	1–3	2–0	1–0	4–1	2–1	1–1	2–0	0–1	3–1	*

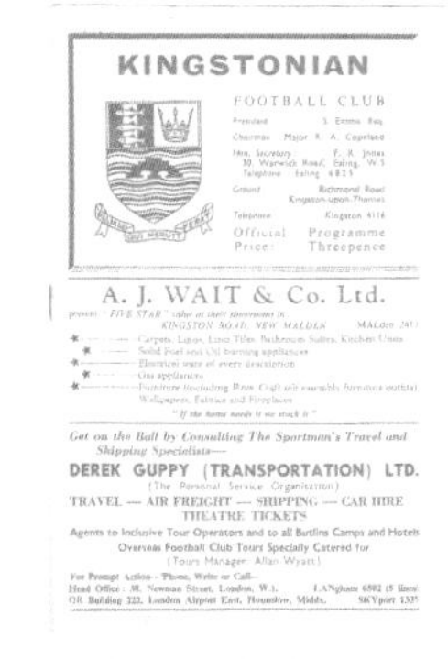

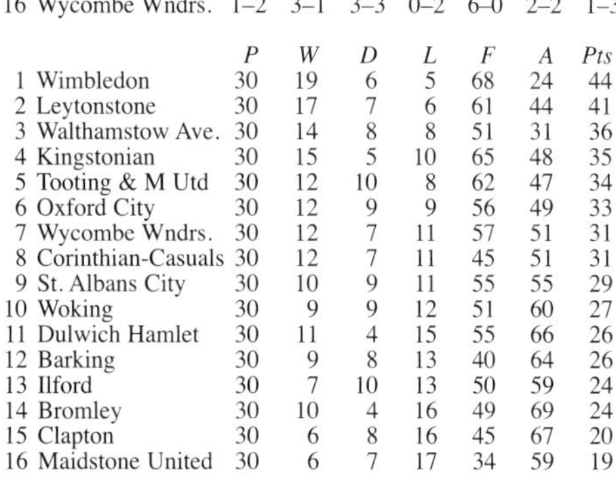

	P	W	D	L	F	A	Pts
1 Wimbledon	30	19	6	5	68	24	44
2 Leytonstone	30	17	7	6	61	44	41
3 Walthamstow Ave.	30	14	8	8	51	31	36
4 Kingstonian	30	15	5	10	65	48	35
5 Tooting & M Utd	30	12	10	8	62	47	34
6 Oxford City	30	12	9	9	56	49	33
7 Wycombe Wndrs.	30	12	7	11	57	51	31
8 Corinthian-Casuals	30	12	7	11	45	51	31
9 St. Albans City	30	10	9	11	55	55	29
10 Woking	30	9	9	12	51	60	27
11 Dulwich Hamlet	30	11	4	15	55	66	26
12 Barking	30	9	8	13	40	64	26
13 Ilford	30	7	10	13	50	59	24
14 Bromley	30	10	4	16	49	69	24
15 Clapton	30	6	8	16	45	67	20
16 Maidstone United	30	6	7	17	34	59	19

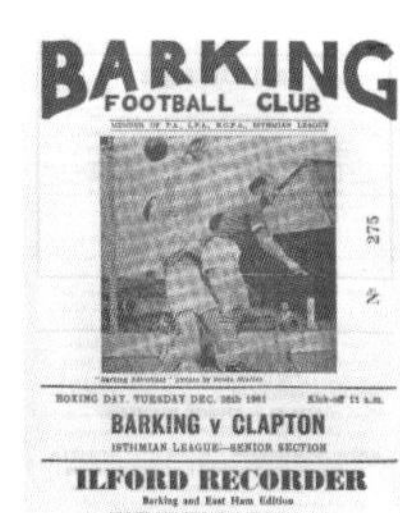

Right above: the programme from Kingstonian v Walthamstow Avenue.

Right: Ilford's programme from season 1961-62.

Left: the programme for Barking's 2-0 Boxing Day victory over Clapton.

1962–63 - Wimbledon achieved back-to-back championships – and, with Leytonstone and London Caledonians, a joint-record seven titles – when they finished two points clear of nearest challengers Kingstonian, with Tooting & Mitcham United a further two points behind in third place and Ilford another point adrift in fourth. This was Ilford's best finish in almost a decade. Dulwich Hamlet and Corinthian-Casuals slipped into the bottom two and had to apply for re-election; both were duly re-elected.

A proposal from both Bromley and Tooting & Mitcham United – recommending the Isthmian League increased its membership from 16 to 20 clubs – was passed by 12 votes to four. Woking, however, proposed an amendment to expand the League to only 18 clubs, but this was defeated by a similar 12–4 margin.

Seven clubs – Barnet, Enfield, Finchley, Hendon (formerly Hampstead Town and Golders Green), Hitchin Town, Sutton United and Wealdstone – were invited to apply to join the League, with the final four gaining inclusion following a ballot of the member clubs at a League Council Meeting prior to the Annual General Meeting.

Ballot Result	*1st ballot*	*2nd ballot*	*3rd ballot*	*4th ballot*
Barnet	8	9	10	12
Enfield	17	-	-	-
Finchley	8	7	8	-
Hendon	10	10	10	14
Hitchin Town	10	9	12	14
Sutton United	17	-	-	-
Wealdstone	10	5	-	-

The four successful Clubs – Enfield, Hendon, Hitchin Town and Sutton United – thus were invited to join the League. They accepted their invitations and were duly elected at the AGM. At the same time, citing the increase in membership, the Isthmian League decided to abolish the positions of Vice-Chairman, Hon Referees & Fixture Secretary and Assistant Referees & Fixture Secretary. The new positions were Hon Fixture Secretary, Hon Referees Secretary and Hon Assistant Referees Secretary, and Messrs AW Peacock, FM Wilson and MI Whittingham, respectively, were elected at the AGM.

Above: Sutton United's programme from their first Isthmian season.

	1	2	3	4	5	6	7	8	9	10	11	12	13	14	15	16
1 Barking	*	2–2	2–1	2–1	3–1	0–1	1–1	1–1	0–2	2–0	3–1	0–1	0–0	2–2	0–2	1–1
2 Bromley	0–0	*	2–0	2–1	2–2	2–3	1–3	2–2	1–3	2–0	4–1	2–1	4–1	1–2	3–2	4–4
3 Clapton	0–3	0–0	*	3–1	2–0	3–1	1–4	2–0	1–2	1–5	0–1	1–1	1–2	0–3	4–2	0–3
4 Corinthian-Casuals	2–2	1–4	2–0	*	1–2	0–1	2–2	3–2	0–1	3–3	2–3	0–0	1–2	0–2	2–1	1–3
5 Dulwich Hamlet	0–3	1–3	0–1	0–1	*	2–1	2–2	0–1	0–3	2–3	2–6	1–3	1–1	0–4	1–1	4–3
6 Ilford	3–1	3–0	2–1	2–0	4–1	*	2–1	4–1	1–1	6–1	1–0	0–2	3–1	4–0	3–4	7–1
7 Kingstonian	3–2	5–0	0–0	3–0	5–1	5–1	*	5–0	2–1	3–1	1–1	3–0	1–1	1–3	6–1	4–3
8 Leytonstone	3–1	4–1	2–0	2–1	2–0	2–0	1–2	*	2–0	3–2	2–1	1–1	1–1	1–1	4–2	1–2
9 Maidstone United	4–1	1–1	3–0	5–1	2–0	6–3	1–1	1–1	*	1–1	2–1	0–1	0–1	1–1	0–1	6–1
10 Oxford City	0–1	3–2	7–0	1–0	2–3	2–5	1–1	3–1	3–0	*	3–2	2–2	1–2	1–1	3–3	1–1
11 St. Albans City	1–1	1–2	1–1	3–0	2–1	2–2	1–2	3–2	0–1	5–2	*	1–2	4–1	2–2	5–0	3–0
12 Tooting & M Utd	5–0	2–2	3–0	2–0	3–0	2–1	4–2	2–4	7–3	1–0	3–0	*	1–3	2–2	4–0	2–1
13 Walthamstow Ave.	3–2	1–4	3–1	6–0	2–1	2–3	0–1	1–1	5–0	5–2	2–1	2–2	*	0–1	1–0	1–1
14 Wimbledon	3–1	0–0	9–1	5–1	2–0	1–2	4–1	4–1	3–3	5–1	4–1	3–2	4–0	*	4–0	5–1
15 Woking	5–1	0–2	2–4	3–0	2–1	0–1	0–5	2–0	1–1	1–1	0–1	2–2	0–1	0–2	*	3–2
16 Wycombe Wndrs.	1–1	2–2	5–1	4–1	1–1	0–0	1–4	2–0	4–2	0–0	1–0	1–2	2–0	3–2	2–2	*

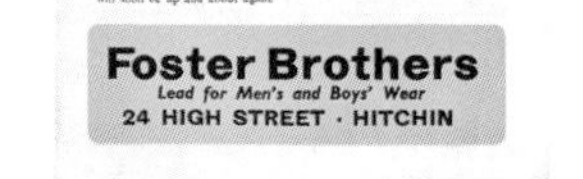

Right: a programme from Hitchin Town's first Isthmian campaign.

	P	*W*	*D*	*L*	*F*	*A*	*Pts*
1 Wimbledon	30	19	8	3	84	33	46
2 Kingstonian	30	18	8	4	79	37	44
3 Tooting & M Utd	30	17	8	5	65	37	42
4 Ilford	30	19	3	8	70	44	41
5 Walthamstow Ave.	30	14	7	9	51	44	35
6 Maidstone United	30	13	8	9	56	45	34
7 Bromley	30	12	10	8	57	51	34
8 Leytonstone	30	12	7	11	48	50	31
9 Wycombe Wndrs.	30	10	10	10	56	61	30
10 St. Albans City	30	11	5	14	54	49	27
11 Barking	30	8	10	12	39	50	26
12 Oxford City	30	8	9	13	55	64	25
13 Woking	30	8	6	16	42	66	22
14 Clapton	30	7	4	19	30	71	18
15 Dulwich Hamlet	30	4	5	21	30	71	13
16 Corinthian-Casuals	30	4	4	22	28	71	12

Below: Enfield's first Isthmian League programme.

Below: Hendon's first Isthmian League programme.

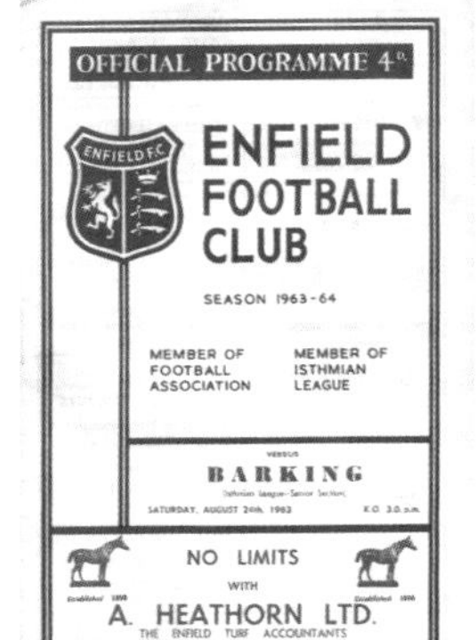

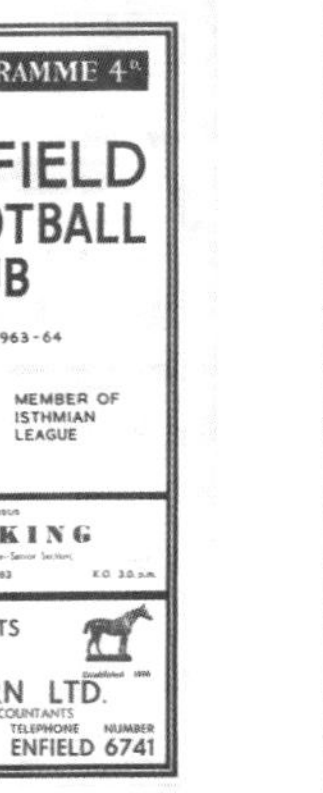

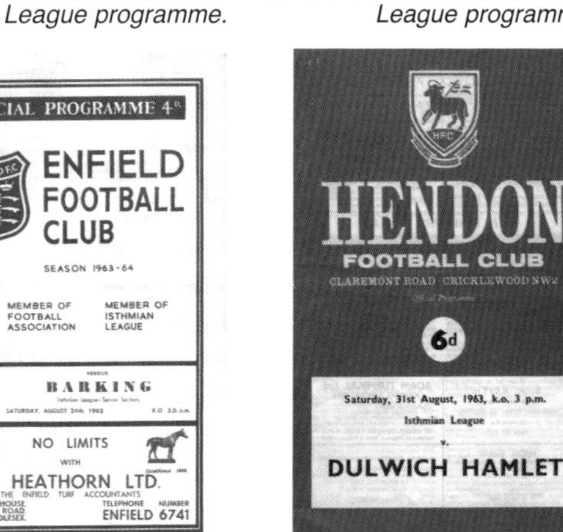

1963–64

Before the new season started, it was announced that The A.S.C.L.I.D. (Athenian, Spartan, Corinthian, London, Isthmian & Delphian) Advisory Board would be disbanded because it could no longer serve any useful function.

In what proved to be their final season as members, Wimbledon completed a hat-trick of League championships, and passed Leytonstone's record of seven League titles. Hendon, in their debut season, did not disappoint their supporters by finishing as runners-up, six points behind Wimbledon. They did have the consolation of a League record by scoring 124 goals. Kingstonian finished third, two points behind Hendon but a point ahead of another debutant, Sutton United. Dulwich Hamlet and Clapton, who occupied the two bottom places, were both re-elected at the Annual General Meeting. Clapton also set an unwanted record by conceding 120 goals in the season.

In the light of their hat-trick of championships, Wimbledon decided to turn professional and join the Southern League. There were applications received from Barnet, Croydon Amateurs, Erith & Belvedere, Finchley, Hertford Town and Wealdstone. Barnet, Finchley and Wealdstone – the three unsuccessful clubs in the ballot for membership for the 1963–64 season – were proposed and seconded for the vacancy, which would be decided in the usual way, by ballot. Wealdstone came top of the ballot and they were recommended for election at the Annual General Meeting. The result of the ballot was:

Wealdstone - 11 Barnet - 6 Finchley - 6

At the AGM, Donald McKenzie was elected Chairman, succeeding Sidney Donaldson, with J McCulloch assuming the role of Referees Secretary, from FM Wilson. SW Donaldson and AW Peacock, in recognition of their services to the Isthmian League since 1934 and 1951, respectively, were elected life members.

		1	2	3	4	5	6	7	8	9	10	11	12	13	14	15	16	17	18	19	20
1	Barking	*	1–0	1–2	1–0	1–1	1–2	1–1	2–1	0–4	2–1	1–1	2–2	2–2	4–1	1–0	2–0	0–0	0–4	0–0	2–3
2	Bromley	1–0	*	5–0	3–1	1–1	2–3	0–2	1–2	2–2	1–2	5–1	3–0	2–2	3–3	2–4	2–2	0–1	1–2	4–1	3–1
3	Clapton	3–4	0–0	*	0–4	1–2	0–0	1–2	1–1	1–2	0–3	0–4	0–5	3–1	1–5	2–2	1–3	0–3	1–1	1–4	2–6
4	Corinthian-Casuals	3–2	2–0	3–0	*	3–2	2–2	1–0	1–2	1–3	2–4	1–2	1–2	2–2	1–2	0–2	4–2	1–2	0–2	2–2	3–1
5	Dulwich Hamlet	3–0	2–3	3–0	1–3	*	2–2	1–9	2–1	0–1	1–2	2–3	3–2	2–5	0–2	0–1	0–4	2–2	0–3	0–0	3–3
6	Enfield	3–2	3–3	5–0	4–0	4–1	*	1–0	4–2	3–3	0–1	2–2	0–1	4–1	5–0	5–1	3–0	1–0	2–2	5–1	2–2
7	Hendon	3–1	5–0	4–0	7–0	10–1	1–3	*	8–2	2–0	0–1	5–1	1–3	2–2	0–0	5–0	0–2	6–3	3–0	5–1	2–1
8	Hitchin Town	1–0	3–2	5–3	3–1	2–1	0–3	0–5	*	7–2	2–0	0–1	2–0	1–0	2–3	0–3	2–2	0–2	2–3	3–3	4–1
9	Ilford	1–0	5–1	6–0	3–0	2–3	3–4	1–7	3–3	*	1–3	1–1	4–0	1–0	1–2	3–1	4–1	3–2	1–1	1–0	4–1
10	Kingstonian	5–2	0–2	3–2	6–1	5–1	5–3	0–4	6–2	7–1	*	3–2	4–2	1–0	2–3	3–3	3–2	4–2	2–4	7–0	4–2
11	Leytonstone	2–4	0–1	3–0	5–0	0–0	2–1	1–4	3–0	2–1	0–0	*	2–0	0–4	1–2	3–0	2–2	4–2	1–1	5–2	2–4
12	Maidstone United	0–0	3–1	2–1	4–0	4–0	0–3	0–2	4–3	2–0	0–3	0–0	*	1–6	3–2	3–2	0–1	1–0	1–1	3–2	3–2
13	Oxford City	3–1	3–0	5–0	2–2	0–0	3–0	3–0	4–0	2–2	4–0	3–0	4–2	*	2–0	2–0	4–1	5–2	3–2	2–2	0–3
14	St. Albans City	2–3	2–2	3–1	2–0	1–1	1–1	0–4	4–1	1–0	2–2	3–1	2–2	1–2	*	1–1	0–0	1–1	1–2	0–0	4–1
15	Sutton United	2–1	1–4	6–1	3–1	3–3	4–3	1–2	4–2	5–0	1–1	2–0	4–2	6–1	5–0	*	2–1	3–1	3–2	5–1	2–1
16	Tooting & M Utd	2–0	5–1	2–0	6–1	3–1	1–1	1–1	6–1	5–0	3–2	3–2	1–1	1–0	3–0	2–0	*	3–1	3–4	3–0	0–0
17	Walthamstow Ave.	3–0	4–1	3–1	1–3	1–1	1–4	2–1	7–0	1–1	1–2	3–2	3–2	3–0	2–1	2–3	0–1	*	0–2	5–1	0–0
18	Wimbledon	2–0	2–1	3–1	1–0	6–1	3–0	2–1	4–2	6–2	1–0	3–0	3–2	3–1	0–0	0–5	1–0	2–1	*	3–0	1–0
19	Woking	3–0	1–0	2–0	2–1	0–0	0–4	1–6	1–2	0–0	2–0	4–0	2–2	1–3	0–4	0–4	2–0	3–1	1–5	*	2–0
20	Wycombe Wndrs.	2–2	3–1	4–1	4–1	4–0	3–1	0–4	0–1	2–3	1–3	2–5	1–1	2–4	3–1	3–5	3–1	1–2	2–0	2–1	*

		P	*W*	*D*	*L*	*F*	*A*	*Pts*
1	Wimbledon	38	27	6	5	87	44	60
2	Hendon	38	25	4	9	124	38	54
3	Kingstonian	38	24	4	10	100	62	52
4	Sutton United	38	23	5	10	99	64	51
5	Enfield	38	20	10	8	96	56	50
6	Oxford City	38	20	8	10	90	55	48
7	Tooting & M Utd	38	19	8	11	78	51	46
8	St. Albans City	38	14	12	12	62	63	40
9	Ilford	38	16	8	14	75	79	40
10	Maidstone United	38	15	8	15	65	71	38
11	Walthamstow Ave.	38	15	6	17	70	66	36
12	Leytonstone	38	14	8	16	66	71	36
13	Wycombe Wndrs.	38	13	6	19	74	80	32
14	Hitchin Town	38	14	4	20	67	100	32
15	Bromley	38	11	8	19	64	75	30
16	Barking	38	10	9	19	46	69	29
17	Woking	38	10	9	19	48	88	29
18	Corinthian-Casuals	38	10	4	24	52	92	24
19	Dulwich Hamlet	38	6	12	20	47	97	24
20	Clapton	38	2	5	31	31	120	9

Right: Wycombe Wanderers programme for their 2-2 draw at home to Barking.

Below left: A Barking programme against Enfield from 1964. The Southbury Road club won 3-0.

Below right: A Corinthian-Casuals programme against Walthamstow Avenue from 1964. The East London club won 1-0.

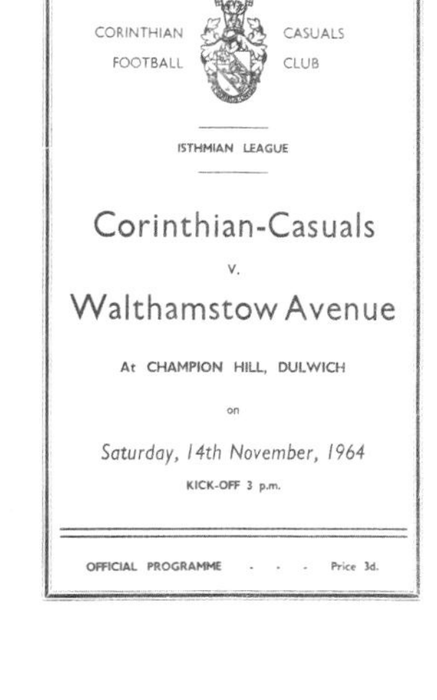

1964–65 - For the first and only time in Isthmian League history, the championship was decided under League Rule 8, as a result of which Enfield and Hendon had to meet in a play-off to decide the championship. The two Middlesex rivals had finished on 63 points, Enfield winning 29 of 38 matches, while Hendon lost just three times in the whole campaign; Hendon scored 25 more goals than the "E's", but conceded 14 more than Enfield's 35. The title decider, played at Dulwich Hamlet's Champion Hill ground, went Hendon's way, 4–1. the previous season's runners-up thus going one better. The four goals in the playoff raised Hendon's goal total for the season to a new record of 127. Kingstonian finished seven points adrift in third while Leytonstone were fourth, a further three points behind. Clapton, for the fifth time in six seasons, applied for re-election along with Woking, whose previous application had come in 1938. Both were duly re-elected. Isthmian League President Max Woosnam notified the League Council that due to ill-heath, he would neither be able to attend further meetings nor any matches and announced he would not stand for re-election as President for the following season. Sidney Donaldson was nominated and elected as Mr Woosnam's successor.

		1	2	3	4	5	6	7	8	9	10	11	12	13	14	15	16	17	18	19	20
1	Barking	*	1–1	1–0	1–2	0–2	0–3	1–2	5–2	2–1	1–2	2–4	1–1	2–3	0–1	2–2	5–0	1–1	1–3	5–1	2–2
2	Bromley	4–1	*	1–1	0–0	4–1	1–5	0–3	2–0	2–0	4–1	2–1	5–0	1–1	1–1	2–1	1–1	3–1	2–2	6–3	0–2
3	Clapton	4–3	1–4	*	1–4	1–4	1–3	2–3	2–3	1–2	2–3	1–4	0–0	1–2	2–1	0–1	0–1	0–3	0–2	2–0	0–3
4	Corinthian-Casuals	1–2	2–1	1–2	*	2–0	1–7	1–3	1–0	1–2	0–4	2–0	2–1	0–1	1–4	3–2	2–0	0–1	5–5	2–2	2–2
5	Dulwich Hamlet	2–1	1–2	2–4	0–1	*	0–1	0–3	0–0	0–0	1–4	1–4	1–0	2–2	1–3	1–2	1–0	5–1	1–2	3–0	0–1
6	Enfield	1–1	3–1	3–0	2–1	6–0	*	2–2	2–0	2–1	0–2	3–0	4–0	2–1	1–0	2–0	6–1	3–1	3–1	5–0	4–0
7	Hendon	5–2	4–0	3–1	6–0	2–0	0–0	*	2–0	3–1	2–2	1–1	5–0	7–1	3–0	5–1	4–2	4–3	2–1	7–4	9–2
8	Hitchin Town	0–2	2–2	3–0	4–4	3–2	0–3	0–1	*	4–0	1–0	2–2	1–1	2–3	1–1	2–2	1–0	2–1	4–0	5–0	3–1
9	Ilford	6–2	1–1	1–1	2–1	1–0	3–1	0–0	0–0	*	1–2	0–2	1–2	0–2	0–2	2–7	2–2	0–1	2–2	2–0	1–0
10	Kingstonian	2–0	2–2	5–0	1–1	3–2	1–2	2–1	4–0	2–1	*	3–2	6–1	1–1	3–1	2–2	2–3	0–1	2–1	6–0	3–1
11	Leytonstone	3–1	7–1	3–0	4–1	3–2	4–2	6–3	3–2	7–0	3–0	*	5–0	2–0	3–3	2–0	4–4	2–1	3–1	4–2	8–1
12	Maidstone United	0–0	1–1	1–5	0–1	1–2	3–2	1–3	0–2	7–0	1–2	2–4	*	1–3	4–1	0–2	2–1	3–1	2–2	2–1	2–1
13	Oxford City	0–2	5–0	3–0	2–1	5–2	1–2	1–1	3–4	5–2	0–2	3–1	5–2	*	0–1	4–0	2–1	1–0	1–1	1–1	4–0
14	St. Albans City	4–0	3–1	3–0	1–1	1–1	0–1	2–2	1–1	2–0	0–1	2–2	1–0	3–1	*	0–0	0–1	1–0	3–0	6–0	2–1
15	Sutton United	4–0	5–0	2–1	3–1	2–0	1–1	1–2	1–4	4–2	0–0	2–1	3–2	0–0	1–2	*	2–2	5–2	3–1	4–1	2–1
16	Tooting & M.Utd	1–2	4–2	3–0	1–1	4–2	0–2	1–2	4–2	5–0	2–0	2–1	4–3	0–4	2–1	1–1	*	5–0	1–3	4–0	1–1
17	Walthamstow Ave.	2–2	3–5	3–1	1–2	4–1	0–5	0–3	2–1	3–1	1–1	4–3	4–3	1–0	3–2	3–1	0–1	*	2–1	3–3	2–1
18	Wealdstone	4–0	7–2	4–0	4–2	3–1	3–3	3–6	2–1	5–3	2–5	3–1	1–0	0–1	3–0	1–1	2–1	5–0	*	6–0	4–2
19	Woking	1–3	0–3	1–3	3–2	1–1	0–1	2–3	3–0	4–0	1–3	1–3	1–0	1–3	0–1	1–3	1–0	2–1	2–1	*	1–3
20	Wycombe Wndrs.	3–1	3–1	2–3	3–1	2–0	2–3	3–2	6–0	2–2	1–1	2–3	2–0	2–1	1–3	1–1	1–6	3–3	0–3	6–1	*

	P	W	D	L	F	A	Pts
1 Hendon*	38	28	7	3	123	49	63
2 Enfield	38	29	5	4	98	35	63
3 Kingstonian	38	24	8	6	86	44	56
4 Leytonstone	38	24	5	9	115	62	53
5 Oxford City	38	20	7	11	76	51	47
6 St. Albans City	38	18	9	11	63	43	45
7 Sutton United	38	17	11	10	74	57	45
8 Wealdstone	38	19	6	13	93	68	44
9 Bromley	38	14	11	13	71	80	39
10 Tooting & M Utd	38	15	7	16	71	66	37
11 Hitchin Town	38	13	9	16	61	66	35
12 Walthamstow Ave.	38	15	5	18	63	82	35
13 Wycombe Wndrs.	38	13	7	18	70	85	33
14 Corinthian-Casuals	38	13	7	18	56	77	33
15 Barking	38	10	8	20	58	80	28
16 Ilford	38	8	8	22	43	89	24
17 Maidstone United	38	8	6	24	49	86	22
18 Dulwich Hamlet	38	8	5	25	45	79	21
19 Clapton	38	8	3	27	43	91	19
20 Woking	38	7	4	27	45	113	18

** Championship determined by Play-Off (Rule 8 applied).*

Left: the Play-Off programme which determined the 1964-65 champions. The game, played at Champion Hill, Dulwich, saw Hendon prevail over Middlesex neighbours Enfield by four goals to one.

Below: the League handbook for the 1965-66 season.

1965–66 - Leytonstone equalled Wimbledon's record of eight League championships when they secured the title, two points clear of defending title-holders Hendon, with Enfield third, three points behind, but ahead of Wycombe Wanderers only on goal average. Clapton and Dulwich Hamlet, who had occupied two of the bottom three positions for four consecutive seasons, had to apply for re-election at the Annual General Meeting, and both were successful.

Max Woosnam, whose ill health had forced his resignation as Isthmian League President after 11 years in 1965, passed away. Hornchurch & Upminster applied to join the League should a vacancy occur, but it was decided that the League's constitution would remain at 20 clubs. Also at the AGM, it was agreed that it would no longer be necessary for the bottom two clubs in the Isthmian League to have to apply for re-election. It is interesting to note that in the Isthmian League's 50 completed official seasons of play, only two clubs – Tunbridge Wells and West Norwood – were ever balloted out of the League (although a few did not apply for re-election before a ballot was needed).

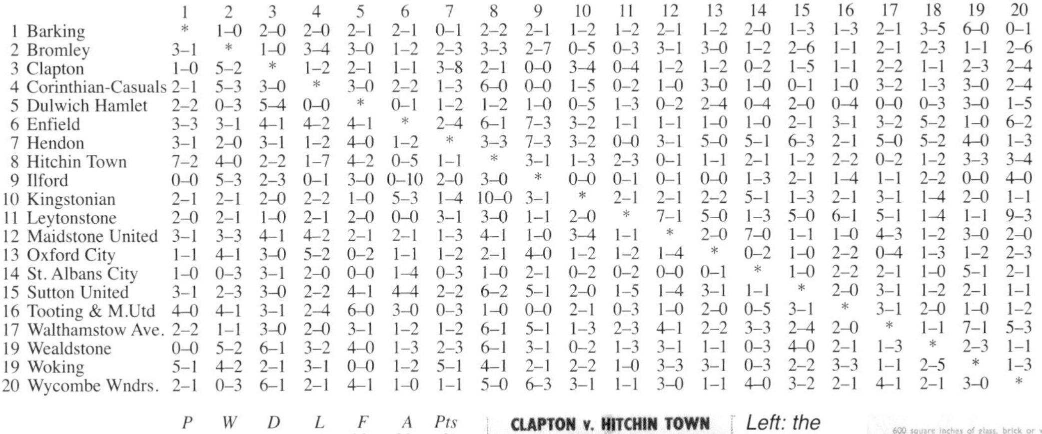

	1	2	3	4	5	6	7	8	9	10	11	12	13	14	15	16	17	18	19	20
1 Barking	*	1–0	2–0	2–0	2–1	2–1	0–1	2–2	2–1	1–2	1–2	2–1	1–2	2–0	1–3	1–3	2–1	3–5	6–0	0–1
2 Bromley	3–1	*	1–0	3–4	3–0	1–2	2–3	3–3	2–7	0–5	0–3	3–1	3–0	1–2	2–6	1–1	2–1	2–3	1–1	2–6
3 Clapton	1–0	5–2	*	1–2	2–1	1–1	3–8	2–1	0–0	3–4	0–4	1–2	1–2	0–2	1–5	1–1	2–2	1–1	2–3	2–4
4 Corinthian-Casuals	2–1	5–3	3–0	*	3–0	2–2	1–3	6–0	0–0	1–5	0–2	1–0	3–0	1–0	0–1	1–0	3–2	1–3	3–0	2–4
5 Dulwich Hamlet	2–2	0–3	5–4	0–0	*	0–1	1–2	1–2	1–0	0–5	1–3	0–2	2–4	0–4	2–0	0–4	0–0	0–3	3–0	1–5
6 Enfield	3–3	3–1	4–1	4–2	4–1	*	2–4	6–1	7–3	3–2	1–1	1–1	1–0	1–0	2–1	3–1	3–2	5–2	1–0	6–2
7 Hendon	3–1	2–0	3–1	1–2	4–0	1–2	*	3–3	7–3	3–2	0–0	3–1	5–0	5–1	6–3	2–1	5–0	5–2	4–0	1–3
8 Hitchin Town	7–2	4–0	2–2	1–7	4–2	0–5	1–1	*	3–1	1–3	2–3	0–1	1–1	2–1	1–2	2–2	0–2	1–2	3–3	3–4
9 Ilford	0–0	5–3	2–3	0–1	3–0	0–10	2–0	3–0	*	0–0	0–1	0–1	0–0	1–3	2–1	1–4	1–1	2–2	0–0	4–0
10 Kingstonian	2–1	2–1	2–0	2–2	1–0	5–3	1–4	10–0	3–1	*	2–1	2–1	2–2	5–1	1–3	2–1	3–1	1–4	2–0	1–1
11 Leytonstone	2–0	2–1	1–0	2–1	2–0	0–0	3–1	3–0	1–1	2–0	*	7–1	5–0	1–3	5–0	6–1	5–1	1–4	1–1	9–3
12 Maidstone United	3–1	3–3	4–1	4–2	2–1	2–1	1–3	4–1	1–0	3–4	1–1	*	2–0	7–0	1–1	1–0	4–3	1–2	3–0	2–0
13 Oxford City	1–1	4–1	3–0	5–2	0–2	1–1	1–2	2–1	4–0	1–2	1–2	1–4	*	0–2	1–0	2–2	0–4	1–3	1–2	2–3
14 St. Albans City	1–0	0–3	3–1	2–0	0–0	1–4	0–3	1–0	2–1	0–2	0–2	0–0	0–1	*	1–0	2–2	2–1	1–0	5–1	2–1
15 Sutton United	3–1	2–3	3–0	2–2	4–1	4–4	2–2	6–2	5–1	2–0	1–5	1–4	3–1	1–1	*	2–0	3–1	1–2	2–1	1–1
16 Tooting & M.Utd	4–0	4–1	3–1	2–4	6–0	3–0	0–3	1–0	0–0	2–1	0–3	1–0	2–0	0–5	3–1	*	3–1	2–0	1–0	1–2
17 Walthamstow Ave.	2–2	1–1	3–0	2–0	3–1	1–2	1–2	6–1	5–1	1–3	2–3	4–1	2–2	3–3	2–4	2–0	*	1–1	7–1	5–3
19 Wealdstone	0–0	5–2	6–1	3–2	4–0	1–3	2–3	6–1	3–1	0–2	1–3	3–1	1–1	0–3	4–0	2–1	1–3	*	2–3	1–1
19 Woking	5–1	4–2	2–1	3–1	0–0	1–2	5–1	4–1	2–1	2–2	1–0	3–3	3–1	0–3	2–2	3–3	1–1	2–5	*	1–3
20 Wycombe Wndrs.	2–1	0–3	6–1	2–1	4–1	1–0	1–1	5–0	6–3	3–1	1–1	3–0	1–1	4–0	3–2	2–1	4–1	2–1	3–0	*

	P	W	D	L	F	A	Pts
1 Leytonstone	38	27	7	4	98	33	61
2 Hendon	38	27	5	6	111	55	59
3 Enfield	38	24	8	6	104	54	56
4 Wycombe Wndrs.	38	25	6	7	100	65	56
5 Kingstonian	38	24	5	9	94	55	53
6 Wealdstone	38	20	6	12	90	64	46
7 Maidstone United	38	19	6	13	74	61	44
8 St. Albans City	38	19	5	14	57	56	43
9 Sutton United	38	17	7	14	83	72	41
10 Tooting & M Utd	38	16	7	15	65	58	39
11 Corinthian-Casuals	38	17	5	16	74	67	39
12 Woking	38	12	10	16	60	83	34
13 Walthamstow Ave.	38	12	9	17	81	75	33
14 Oxford City	38	10	9	19	49	72	29
15 Barking	38	10	7	21	51	72	27
16 Bromley	38	10	5	23	69	101	25
17 Ilford	38	7	10	21	50	84	24
18 Hitchin Town	38	6	8	24	57	118	20
19 Clapton	38	5	6	27	46	103	16
20 Dulwich Hamlet	38	5	5	28	30	95	15

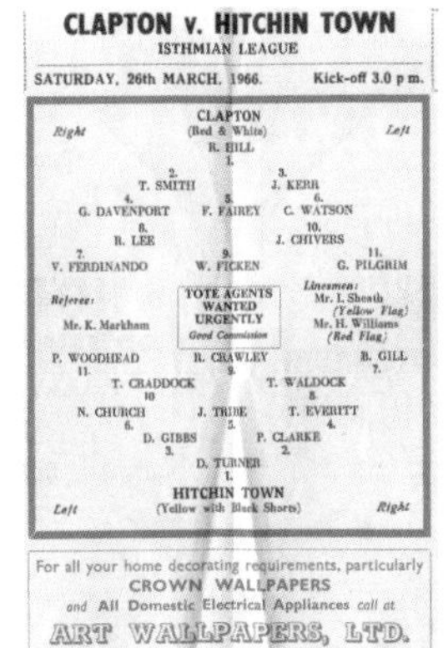

Left: the teams from Clapton's match with Hitchin Town.

Right: The programme from Woking's programme v Sutton United in October 1965 which ended as a 2-2 draw.

1966–67 - Sutton United secured their first Isthmian League championship, ending three points clear of runners-up Walthamstow Avenue, with a further two points each separating Wycombe Wanderers in third and Enfield in fourth. Dulwich Hamlet, with only three wins, finished bottom twelve points adrift from Hitchin Town. Clapton – who enjoyed their best finish since 1958–59 – had floodlighting installed at their Spotted Dog Ground. This meant that all 20 member Clubs were equipped with floodlights.

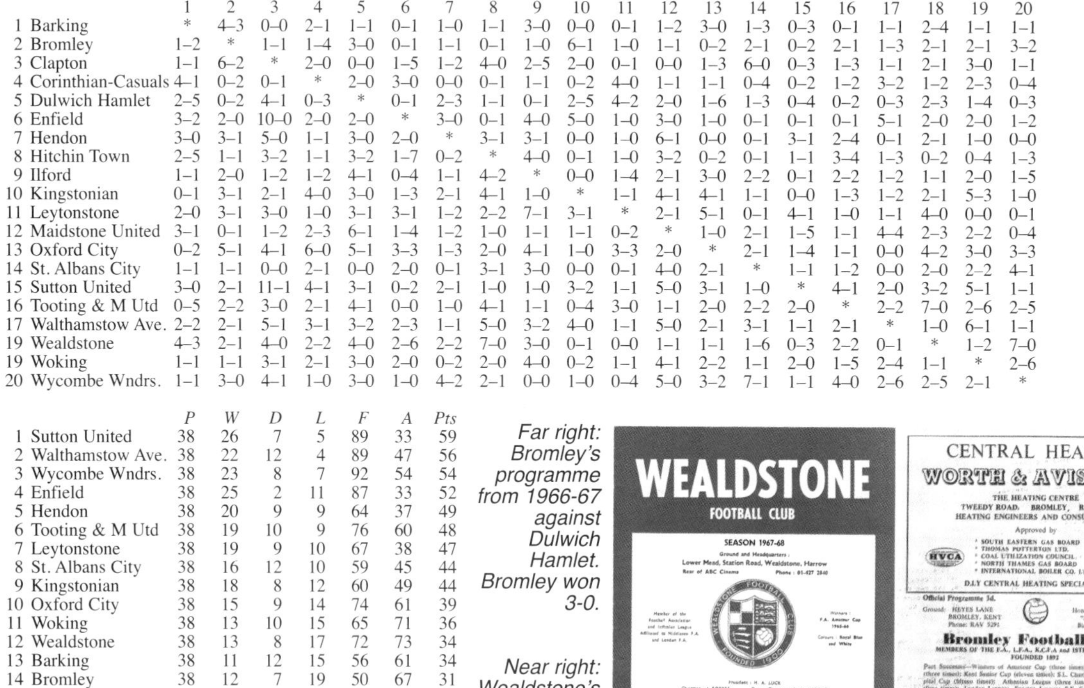

	1	2	3	4	5	6	7	8	9	10	11	12	13	14	15	16	17	18	19	20
1 Barking	*	4–3	0–0	2–1	1–1	0–1	1–0	1–1	3–0	0–0	0–1	1–2	3–0	1–3	0–3	0–1	1–1	2–4	1–1	1–1
2 Bromley	1–2	*	1–1	1–4	3–0	0–1	1–1	0–1	1–0	6–1	1–0	1–1	0–2	2–1	0–2	2–1	1–3	2–1	2–1	3–2
3 Clapton	1–1	6–2	*	2–0	0–0	1–5	1–2	4–0	2–5	2–0	0–1	0–0	1–3	6–0	0–3	1–3	1–1	2–1	3–0	1–1
4 Corinthian-Casuals	4–1	0–2	0–1	*	2–0	3–0	0–0	0–1	1–1	0–2	4–0	1–1	1–1	0–4	0–2	1–2	3–2	1–2	2–3	0–4
5 Dulwich Hamlet	2–5	0–2	4–1	0–3	*	0–1	2–3	1–1	0–1	2–5	4–2	2–0	1–6	1–3	0–4	0–2	0–3	2–3	1–4	0–3
6 Enfield	3–2	2–0	10–0	2–0	2–0	*	3–0	0–1	4–0	5–0	1–0	3–0	1–0	0–1	0–1	0–1	5–1	2–0	2–0	1–2
7 Hendon	3–0	3–1	5–0	1–1	3–0	2–0	*	3–1	3–1	0–0	1–0	6–1	0–0	0–1	3–1	2–4	0–1	2–1	1–0	0–0
8 Hitchin Town	2–5	1–1	3–2	1–1	3–2	1–7	0–2	*	4–0	0–1	1–0	3–2	0–2	0–1	1–1	3–4	1–3	0–2	0–4	1–3
9 Ilford	1–1	2–0	1–2	1–2	4–1	0–4	1–1	4–2	*	0–0	1–4	2–1	3–0	2–2	0–1	2–2	1–2	1–1	2–0	1–5
10 Kingstonian	0–1	3–1	2–1	4–0	3–0	1–3	2–1	4–1	1–0	*	1–1	4–1	4–1	1–1	0–0	1–3	1–2	2–1	5–3	1–0
11 Leytonstone	2–0	3–1	3–0	1–0	3–1	3–1	1–2	2–2	7–1	3–1	*	2–1	5–1	0–1	4–1	1–0	1–1	4–0	0–0	0–1
12 Maidstone United	3–1	0–1	1–2	2–3	6–1	1–4	1–2	1–0	1–1	1–1	0–2	*	1–0	2–1	1–5	1–1	4–4	2–3	2–2	0–4
13 Oxford City	0–2	5–1	4–1	6–0	5–1	3–3	1–3	2–0	4–1	1–0	3–3	2–0	*	2–1	1–4	1–1	0–0	4–2	3–0	3–3
14 St. Albans City	1–1	1–1	0–0	2–1	0–0	2–0	0–1	3–1	3–0	0–0	0–1	4–0	2–1	*	1–1	1–2	0–0	2–0	2–2	4–1
15 Sutton United	3–0	2–1	11–1	4–1	3–1	0–2	2–1	1–0	1–0	3–2	1–1	5–0	3–1	1–0	*	4–1	2–0	3–2	5–1	1–1
16 Tooting & M Utd	0–5	2–2	3–0	2–1	4–1	0–0	1–0	4–1	1–1	0–4	3–0	1–1	2–0	2–2	2–0	*	2–2	7–0	2–6	2–5
17 Walthamstow Ave.	2–2	2–1	5–1	3–1	3–2	2–3	1–1	5–0	3–2	4–0	1–1	5–0	2–1	3–1	1–1	2–1	*	1–0	6–1	1–1
19 Wealdstone	4–3	2–1	4–0	2–2	4–0	2–6	2–2	7–0	3–0	0–1	0–0	1–1	1–1	1–6	0–3	2–2	0–1	*	1–2	7–0
19 Woking	1–1	1–1	3–1	2–1	3–0	2–0	0–2	2–0	4–0	0–2	1–1	4–1	2–2	1–1	2–0	1–5	2–4	1–1	*	2–6
20 Wycombe Wndrs.	1–1	3–0	4–1	1–0	3–0	1–0	4–2	2–1	0–0	1–0	0–4	5–0	3–2	7–1	1–1	4–0	2–6	2–5	2–1	*

	P	*W*	*D*	*L*	*F*	*A*	*Pts*
1 Sutton United	38	26	7	5	89	33	59
2 Walthamstow Ave.	38	22	12	4	89	47	56
3 Wycombe Wndrs.	38	23	8	7	92	54	54
4 Enfield	38	25	2	11	87	33	52
5 Hendon	38	20	9	9	64	37	49
6 Tooting & M Utd	38	19	10	9	76	60	48
7 Leytonstone	38	19	9	10	67	38	47
8 St. Albans City	38	16	12	10	59	45	44
9 Kingstonian	38	18	8	12	60	49	44
10 Oxford City	38	15	9	14	74	61	39
11 Woking	38	13	10	15	65	71	36
12 Wealdstone	38	13	8	17	72	73	34
13 Barking	38	11	12	15	56	61	34
14 Bromley	38	12	7	19	50	67	31
15 Clapton	38	10	8	20	49	92	28
16 Ilford	38	8	10	20	43	77	26
17 Corinthian-Casuals	38	9	7	22	45	68	25
18 Maidstone United	38	6	10	22	43	90	22
19 Hitchin Town	38	8	6	24	39	89	22
20 Dulwich Hamlet	38	3	4	31	33	107	10

Far right: Bromley's programme from 1966-67 against Dulwich Hamlet. Bromley won 3-0.

Near right: Wealdstone's edition for their 3-0 victory over Corinthian-Casuals.

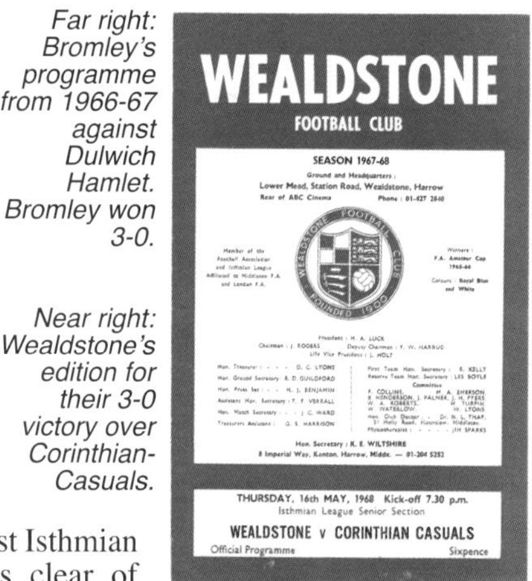

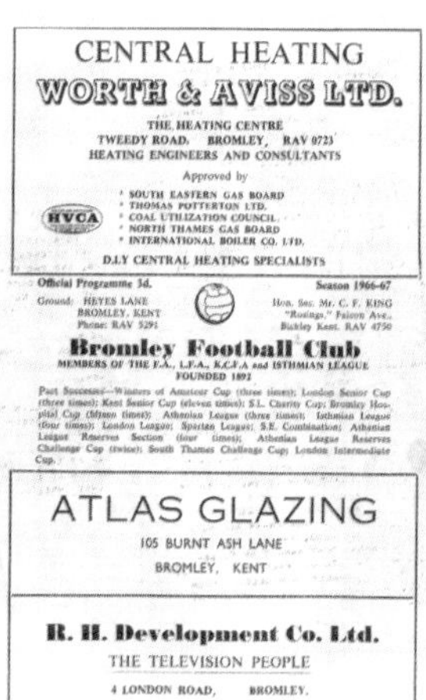

1967–68 - Enfield comfortably won their first Isthmian League championship, finishing nine points clear of runners-up Sutton United. The 'E's' lost only four League matches out of 38. Hendon, three points behind Sutton, claimed third spot ahead of Leytonstone, thanks to a superior goal average. At the other end of the table, Maidstone United conceded a new League record of 131 goals, managed to gain only ten points, and finished 11 behind Ilford. A proposal from Bromley to create a knock-out floodlit competition open exclusively to member clubs did not receive support from the League Council.

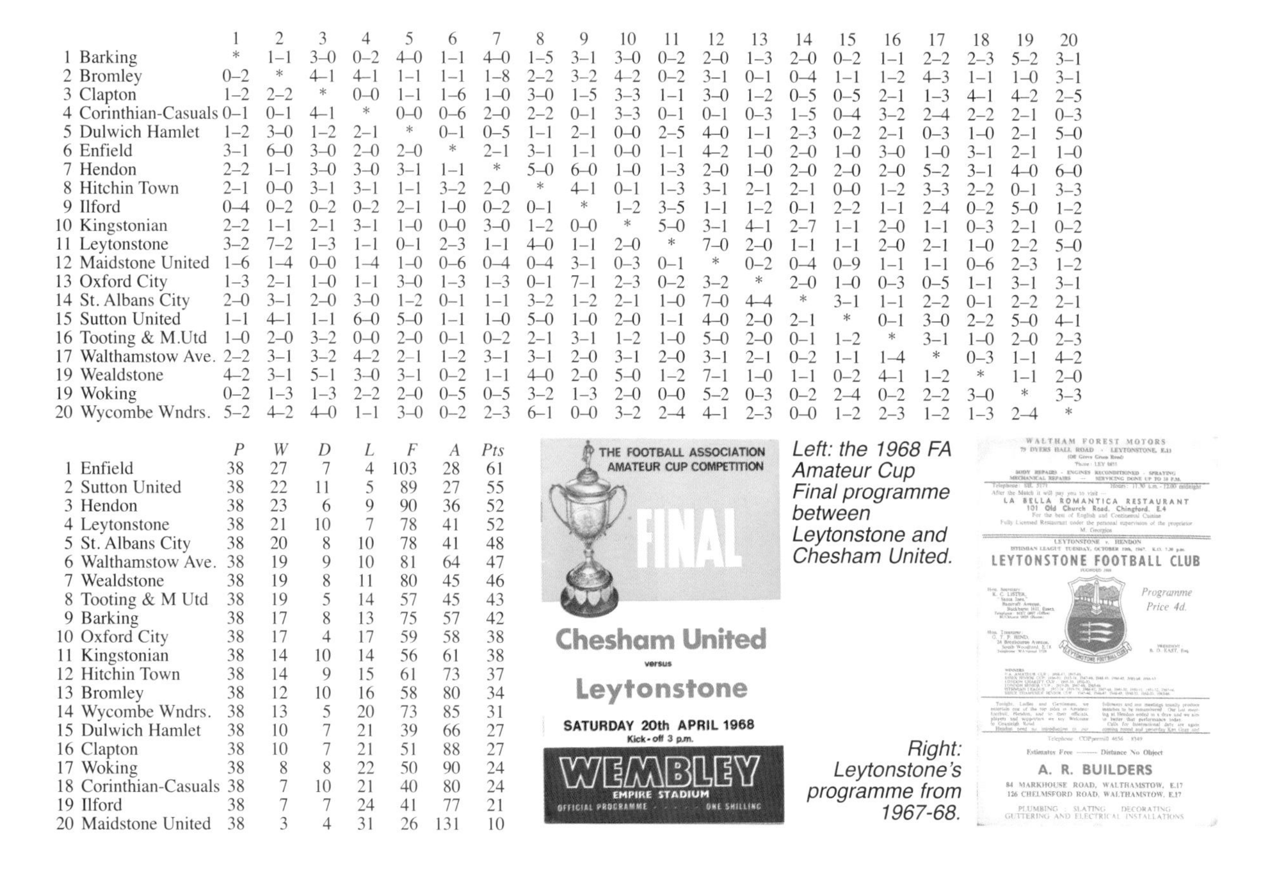

	1	2	3	4	5	6	7	8	9	10	11	12	13	14	15	16	17	18	19	20
1 Barking	*	1–1	3–0	0–2	4–0	1–1	4–0	1–5	3–1	3–0	0–2	2–0	1–3	2–0	0–2	1–1	2–2	2–3	5–2	3–1
2 Bromley	0–2	*	4–1	4–1	1–1	1–1	1–8	2–2	3–2	4–2	0–2	3–1	0–1	0–4	1–1	1–2	4–3	1–1	1–0	3–1
3 Clapton	1–2	2–2	*	0–0	1–1	1–6	1–0	3–0	1–5	3–3	1–1	3–0	1–2	0–5	0–5	2–1	1–3	4–1	4–2	2–5
4 Corinthian-Casuals	0–1	0–1	4–1	*	0–0	0–6	2–0	2–2	0–1	3–3	0–1	0–1	0–3	1–5	0–4	3–2	2–4	2–2	2–1	0–3
5 Dulwich Hamlet	1–2	3–0	1–2	2–1	*	0–1	0–5	1–1	2–1	0–0	2–5	4–0	1–1	2–3	0–2	2–1	0–3	1–0	2–1	5–0
6 Enfield	3–1	6–0	3–0	2–0	2–0	*	2–1	3–1	1–1	0–0	1–1	4–2	1–0	2–0	1–0	3–0	1–0	3–1	2–1	1–0
7 Hendon	2–2	1–1	3–0	3–0	3–1	1–1	*	5–0	6–0	1–0	1–3	2–0	1–0	2–0	2–0	2–0	5–2	3–1	4–0	6–0
8 Hitchin Town	2–1	0–0	3–1	3–1	1–1	3–2	2–0	*	4–1	0–1	1–3	3–1	2–1	2–1	0–0	1–2	3–3	2–2	0–1	3–3
9 Ilford	0–4	0–2	0–2	0–2	2–1	1–0	0–2	0–1	*	1–2	3–5	1–1	1–2	0–1	2–2	1–1	2–4	0–2	5–0	1–2
10 Kingstonian	2–2	1–1	2–1	3–1	1–0	0–0	3–0	1–2	0–0	*	5–0	3–1	4–1	2–7	1–1	2–0	1–1	0–3	2–1	0–2
11 Leytonstone	3–2	7–2	1–3	1–1	0–1	2–3	1–1	4–0	1–1	2–0	*	7–0	2–0	1–1	1–1	2–0	2–1	1–0	2–2	5–0
12 Maidstone United	1–6	1–4	0–0	1–4	1–0	0–6	0–4	0–4	3–1	0–3	0–1	*	0–2	0–4	0–9	1–1	1–1	0–6	2–3	1–2
13 Oxford City	1–3	2–1	1–0	1–1	3–0	1–3	1–3	0–1	7–1	2–3	0–2	3–2	*	2–0	1–0	0–3	0–5	1–1	3–1	3–1
14 St. Albans City	2–0	3–1	2–0	3–0	1–2	0–1	1–1	3–2	1–2	2–1	1–0	7–0	4–4	*	3–1	1–1	2–2	0–1	2–2	2–1
15 Sutton United	1–1	4–1	1–1	6–0	5–0	1–1	1–0	5–0	1–0	2–0	1–1	4–0	2–0	2–1	*	0–1	3–0	2–2	5–0	4–1
16 Tooting & M.Utd	1–0	2–0	3–2	0–0	2–0	0–1	0–2	2–1	3–1	1–2	1–0	5–0	2–0	0–1	1–2	*	3–1	1–0	2–0	2–3
17 Walthamstow Ave.	2–2	3–1	3–2	4–2	2–1	1–2	3–1	3–1	2–0	3–1	2–0	3–1	2–1	0–2	1–1	1–4	*	0–3	1–1	4–2
19 Wealdstone	4–2	3–1	5–1	3–0	3–1	0–2	1–1	4–0	2–0	5–0	1–2	7–1	1–0	1–1	0–2	4–1	1–2	*	1–1	2–0
19 Woking	0–2	1–3	1–3	2–2	2–0	0–5	0–5	3–2	1–3	2–0	0–0	5–2	0–3	0–2	2–4	0–2	2–2	3–0	*	3–3
20 Wycombe Wndrs.	5–2	4–2	4–0	1–1	3–0	0–2	2–3	6–1	0–0	3–2	2–4	4–1	2–3	0–0	1–2	2–3	1–2	1–3	2–4	*

	P	*W*	*D*	*L*	*F*	*A*	*Pts*
1 Enfield	38	27	7	4	103	28	61
2 Sutton United	38	22	11	5	89	27	55
3 Hendon	38	23	6	9	90	36	52
4 Leytonstone	38	21	10	7	78	41	52
5 St. Albans City	38	20	8	10	78	41	48
6 Walthamstow Ave.	38	19	9	10	81	64	47
7 Wealdstone	38	19	8	11	80	45	46
8 Tooting & M Utd	38	19	5	14	57	45	43
9 Barking	38	17	8	13	75	57	42
10 Oxford City	38	17	4	17	59	58	38
11 Kingstonian	38	14	10	14	56	61	38
12 Hitchin Town	38	14	9	15	61	73	37
13 Bromley	38	12	10	16	58	80	34
14 Wycombe Wndrs.	38	13	5	20	73	85	31
15 Dulwich Hamlet	38	10	7	21	39	66	27
16 Clapton	38	10	7	21	51	88	27
17 Woking	38	8	8	22	50	90	24
18 Corinthian-Casuals	38	7	10	21	40	80	24
19 Ilford	38	7	7	24	41	77	21
20 Maidstone United	38	3	4	31	26	131	10

Left: the 1968 FA Amateur Cup Final programme between Leytonstone and Chesham United.

Right: Leytonstone's programme from 1967-68.

1968–69 - There was sad news early in the season. On 15 October 1968, League President and past player, referee, Chairman, Secretary & Treasurer Sidney Donaldson passed away suddenly.

The championship stayed at Southbury Road as Enfield, who scored 103 goals and amassed 61 points, retained their title. This time it was a bit closer as only five points separated them from runners-up Hitchin Town, who enjoyed their best of their six seasons as League members. The previous season's runners-up, Sutton United, ended up three points behind Hitchin in third, while Wycombe Wanderers were fourth, one behind the Surrey club. Ilford, for the second season on the trot, finished second-bottom, with only 20 points, but this was 12 better than Corinthian-Casuals mustered in their 38-match campaign.

A proposal by St. Albans City to increase membership from 20 to 32 clubs, formed of two 16-club divisions, was rejected by the League Council. The vote was 13–7 against the proposal. A second proposal, by Wycombe Wanderers, that the League be increased from 20 to 22 clubs was also rejected.

	1	2	3	4	5	6	7	8	9	10	11	12	13	14	15	16	17	18	19	20
1 Barking	*	3–0	2–0	7–0	1–1	3–7	1–2	3–1	3–0	0–1	0–1	2–0	2–1	1–1	2–1	2–1	4–1	0–2	6–0	0–0
2 Bromley	3–2	*	1–0	2–2	1–1	1–4	2–4	0–0	5–1	2–4	0–1	5–1	1–1	0–3	0–1	4–2	1–3	0–4	0–4	0–1
3 Clapton	0–0	4–1	*	3–1	6–0	0–6	3–2	1–3	3–1	2–0	1–3	1–5	0–2	1–3	1–3	2–4	2–0	1–3	1–1	0–0
4 Corinthian-Casuals	0–1	0–5	0–2	*	3–1	0–3	1–4	1–2	1–1	0–3	0–5	1–3	2–4	0–1	0–4	4–5	2–2	0–5	2–1	0–2
5 Dulwich Hamlet	2–0	2–2	1–1	2–1	*	0–8	1–2	0–3	2–4	0–3	2–1	0–2	0–0	1–4	0–2	1–1	1–1	2–1	1–0	0–2
6 Enfield	3–1	0–0	1–0	4–0	3–0	*	0–0	1–1	0–0	1–1	1–0	6–0	3–0	2–1	1–0	1–0	4–1	4–0	4–1	4–2
7 Hendon	2–2	4–0	5–0	3–0	2–1	2–2	*	0–1	1–2	1–0	3–2	2–1	4–2	2–1	2–1	2–1	1–2	2–2	3–0	1–2
8 Hitchin Town	2–2	2–0	4–2	6–0	1–0	3–2	2–0	*	4–3	3–2	4–0	1–1	1–1	1–1	3–1	0–2	2–1	0–0	2–0	3–2
9 Ilford	0–1	1–1	0–5	2–0	2–0	0–2	0–1	0–1	*	0–0	1–1	0–2	0–2	1–2	0–4	1–4	2–1	1–1	0–2	1–2
10 Kingstonian	0–3	2–4	4–1	3–0	0–0	0–0	3–0	0–2	3–1	*	0–4	4–2	2–3	1–1	1–4	2–1	3–1	0–0	2–0	3–0
11 Leytonstone	4–2	7–0	0–0	4–0	0–3	0–1	0–1	2–0	3–2	2–1	*	2–0	5–4	1–2	1–3	0–2	6–0	1–3	3–0	1–2
12 Maidstone United	0–2	1–2	1–1	0–0	4–2	1–5	1–2	0–2	1–1	3–1	0–0	*	1–3	2–2	1–2	3–1	1–3	0–2	1–0	3–1
13 Oxford City	1–4	4–1	3–2	3–0	3–1	3–1	0–1	0–1	3–0	2–2	4–1	6–0	*	3–1	0–5	3–2	2–0	2–2	3–0	2–2
14 St. Albans City	0–3	3–1	5–0	2–0	5–0	1–4	3–2	7–0	4–1	2–1	2–0	3–0	2–2	*	2–2	0–1	1–1	1–1	2–2	2–0
15 Sutton United	4–0	2–1	1–0	2–0	1–1	2–0	0–0	0–0	6–1	4–1	3–0	3–0	4–0	1–1	*	0–0	7–1	0–2	2–3	0–1
16 Tooting & M.Utd	0–1	2–1	1–1	5–0	2–1	2–3	2–0	0–2	2–0	1–4	2–2	2–1	2–0	2–2	0–0	*	3–2	4–1	4–3	2–2
17 Walthamstow Ave.	0–1	4–2	4–0	2–0	1–0	0–3	2–1	1–1	0–0	0–1	1–4	1–1	0–0	0–0	0–4	2–1	*	1–2	0–0	3–4
19 Wealdstone	0–0	6–1	4–3	4–1	1–0	1–3	1–2	1–1	1–0	3–2	1–2	1–1	4–1	3–2	2–2	1–1	0–4	*	2–1	2–0
19 Woking	1–2	5–2	0–2	4–1	2–1	0–6	1–3	1–2	2–3	2–1	0–1	1–0	2–3	0–0	1–1	1–1	0–0	2–3	*	2–3
20 Wycombe Wndrs.	4–0	4–0	1–0	8–0	1–0	1–0	2–0	3–0	1–0	1–1	2–1	2–3	3–0	1–0	0–1	0–0	4–1	0–1	4–0	*

	P	*W*	*D*	*L*	*F*	*A*	*Pts*
1 Enfield	38	27	7	4	103	28	61
2 Hitchin Town	38	23	10	5	67	41	56
3 Sutton United	38	22	9	7	83	29	53
4 Wycombe Wndrs.	38	23	6	9	70	37	52
5 Wealdstone	38	20	11	7	73	48	51
6 Hendon	38	22	5	11	69	47	49
7 St. Albans City	38	17	13	8	75	44	47
8 Barking	38	20	7	11	69	46	47
9 Oxford City	38	18	8	12	76	64	44
10 Tooting & M Utd	38	16	10	12	68	55	42
11 Leytonstone	38	18	4	16	71	53	40
12 Kingstonian	38	15	8	15	62	56	38
13 Walthamstow Ave.	38	10	10	18	47	71	30
14 Maidstone United	38	10	8	20	47	75	28
15 Clapton	38	10	7	21	52	76	27
16 Woking	38	8	7	23	45	77	23
17 Bromley	38	8	7	23	52	95	23
18 Dulwich Hamlet	38	6	9	23	31	77	21
19 Ilford	38	6	8	24	33	77	20
20 Corinthian-Casuals	38	2	4	32	23	120	8

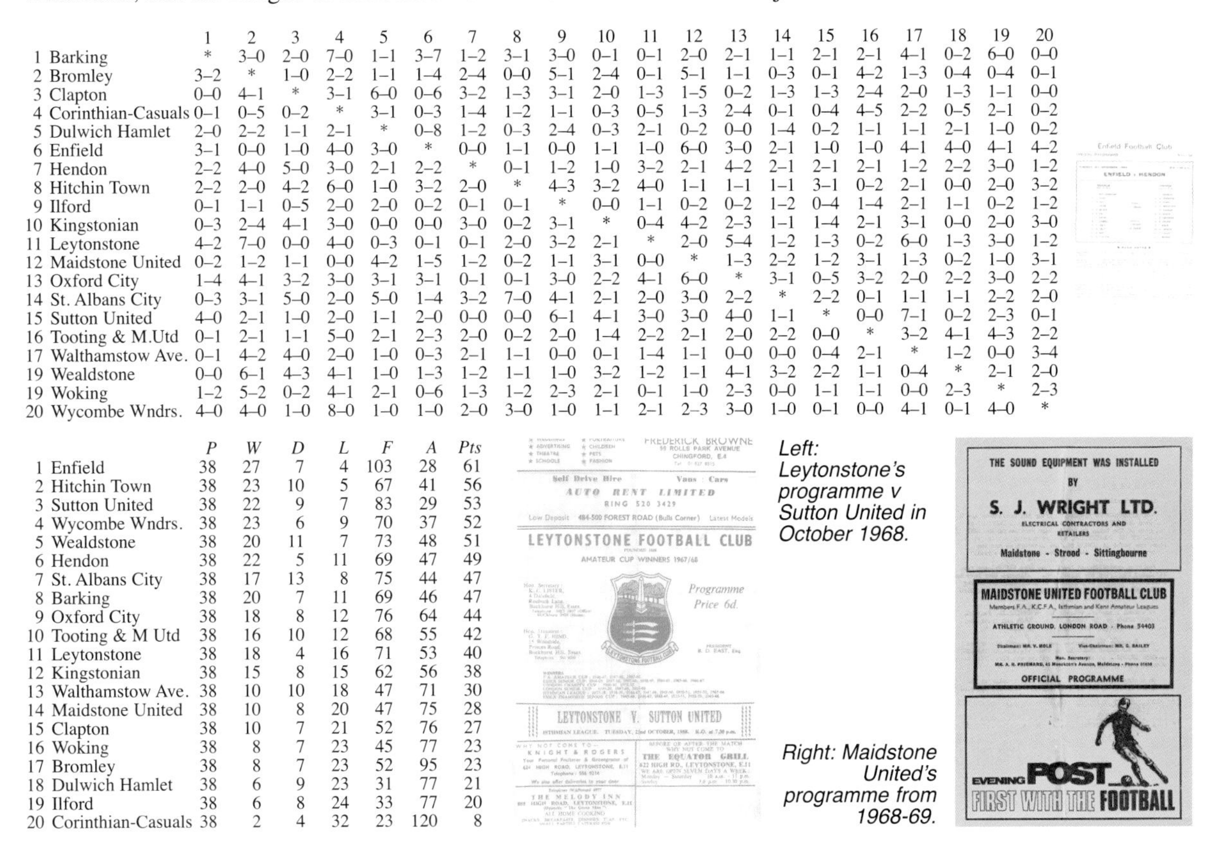

Left: Leytonstone's programme v Sutton United in October 1968.

Right: Maidstone United's programme from 1968-69.

1969–70 - Enfield became the fourth club to win the League championship in three successive seasons, emulating London Caledonians in 1912–14, Leytonstone 1950–52 and Wimbledon 1962–64. This was their closest title yet, with only one point separating them from runners-up Wycombe Wanderers. Sutton United finished third for the second season running, four behind Wycombe, but they had six in hand on the team in fourth spot, Barking – which was their best position since they had joined the League in 1952. Bromley finished bottom of the table, conceding 111 goals, with Corinthian-Casuals, the previous season's wooden spoonists, just above them.

At a Special General Meeting, called on 9 January 1970, it was agreed that one substitute could be used, whether replacing an injured player or for tactical reasons. This updated the law originally introduced into football from the 1967–68 season; it had stated previously that a substitute could only replace an injured player, but the amendment moved the Isthmian League into line with most of football.

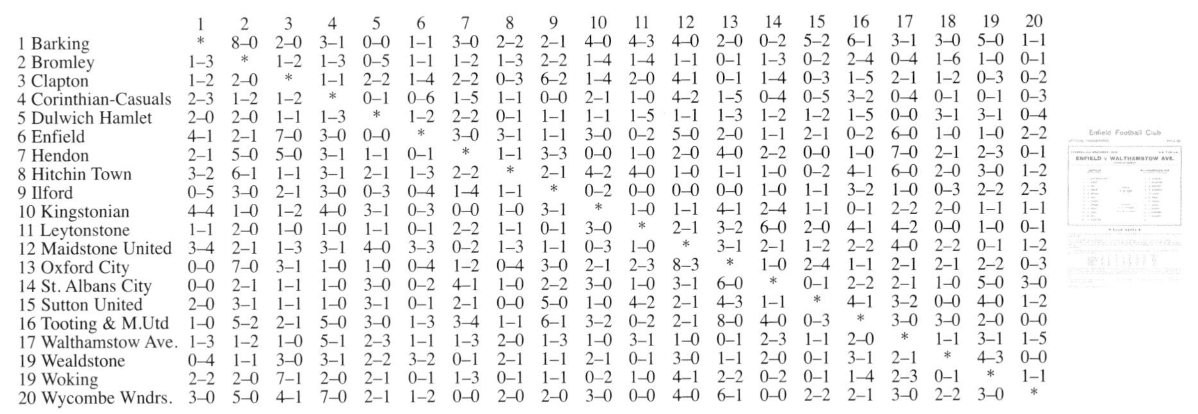

	1	2	3	4	5	6	7	8	9	10	11	12	13	14	15	16	17	18	19	20
1 Barking	*	8–0	2–0	3–1	0–0	1–1	3–0	2–2	2–1	4–0	4–3	4–0	2–0	0–2	5–2	6–1	3–1	3–0	5–0	1–1
2 Bromley	1–3	*	1–2	1–3	0–5	1–1	1–2	1–3	2–2	1–4	1–4	1–1	0–1	1–3	0–2	2–4	0–4	1–6	1–0	0–1
3 Clapton	1–2	2–0	*	1–1	2–2	1–4	2–2	0–3	6–2	1–4	2–0	4–1	0–1	1–4	0–3	1–5	2–1	1–2	0–3	0–2
4 Corinthian-Casuals	2–3	1–2	1–2	*	0–1	0–6	1–5	1–1	0–0	2–1	1–0	4–2	1–5	0–4	0–5	3–2	0–4	0–1	0–1	0–3
5 Dulwich Hamlet	2–0	2–0	1–1	1–3	*	1–2	2–2	0–1	1–1	1–1	1–5	1–1	1–3	1–2	1–2	1–5	0–0	3–1	3–1	0–4
6 Enfield	4–1	2–1	7–0	3–0	0–0	*	3–0	3–1	1–1	3–0	0–2	5–0	2–0	1–1	2–1	0–2	6–0	1–0	1–0	2–2
7 Hendon	2–1	5–0	5–0	3–1	1–1	0–1	*	1–1	3–3	0–0	1–0	2–0	4–0	2–2	0–0	1–0	7–0	2–1	2–3	0–1
8 Hitchin Town	3–2	6–1	1–1	3–1	2–1	1–3	2–2	*	2–1	4–2	4–0	1–0	1–1	1–0	0–2	4–1	6–0	2–0	3–0	1–2
9 Ilford	0–5	3–0	2–1	3–0	0–3	0–4	1–4	1–1	*	0–2	0–0	0–0	0–0	1–0	1–1	3–2	1–0	0–3	2–2	2–3
10 Kingstonian	4–4	1–0	1–2	4–0	3–1	0–3	0–0	1–0	3–1	*	1–0	1–1	4–1	2–4	1–1	0–1	2–2	2–0	1–1	1–1
11 Leytonstone	1–1	2–0	1–0	1–0	1–1	0–1	2–2	1–1	0–1	3–0	*	2–1	3–2	6–0	2–0	4–1	4–2	0–0	1–0	0–1
12 Maidstone United	3–4	2–1	1–3	3–1	4–0	3–3	0–2	1–3	1–1	0–3	1–0	*	3–1	2–1	1–2	2–2	4–0	2–2	0–1	1–2
13 Oxford City	0–0	7–0	3–1	1–0	1–0	0–4	1–2	0–4	3–0	2–1	2–3	8–3	*	1–0	2–4	1–1	2–1	2–1	2–2	0–3
14 St. Albans City	0–0	2–1	1–1	1–0	3–0	0–2	4–1	1–0	2–2	3–0	1–0	3–1	6–0	*	0–1	2–2	2–1	1–0	5–0	3–0
15 Sutton United	2–0	3–1	1–1	1–0	3–1	0–1	2–1	0–0	5–0	1–0	4–2	2–1	4–3	1–1	*	4–1	3–2	0–0	4–0	1–2
16 Tooting & M.Utd	1–0	5–2	2–1	5–0	3–0	1–3	3–4	1–1	6–1	3–2	0–2	2–1	8–0	4–0	0–3	*	3–0	3–0	2–0	0–0
17 Walthamstow Ave.	1–3	1–2	1–0	5–1	2–3	1–1	1–3	2–0	1–3	1–0	3–1	1–0	0–1	2–3	1–1	2–0	*	1–1	3–1	1–5
19 Wealdstone	0–4	1–1	3–0	3–1	2–2	3–2	0–1	2–1	1–1	2–1	0–1	3–0	1–1	2–0	0–1	3–1	2–1	*	4–3	0–0
19 Woking	2–2	2–0	7–1	2–0	2–1	0–1	1–3	0–1	1–1	0–2	1–0	4–1	2–2	0–2	0–1	1–4	2–3	0–1	*	1–1
20 Wycombe Wndrs.	3–0	5–0	4–1	7–0	2–1	1–2	0–0	2–0	2–0	3–0	0–0	4–0	6–1	0–0	2–2	2–1	3–0	2–2	3–0	*

Above: Enfield programmes.

	P	W	D	L	F	A	Pts
1 Enfield	38	27	8	3	91	26	62
2 Wycombe Wndrs.	38	25	11	2	85	24	61
3 Sutton United	38	24	9	5	75	35	57
4 Barking	38	21	9	8	93	47	51
5 Hendon	38	19	12	7	77	44	50
6 St. Albans City	38	21	8	9	69	40	50
7 Hitchin Town	38	19	10	9	71	40	48
8 Tooting & M Utd	38	19	5	14	88	62	43
9 Leytonstone	38	17	7	14	57	41	41
10 Wealdstone	38	15	10	13	53	48	40
11 Oxford City	38	15	7	16	61	78	37
12 Kingstonian	38	13	9	16	55	57	35
13 Ilford	38	8	15	15	42	73	31
14 Dulwich Hamlet	38	8	12	18	46	66	28
15 Woking	38	10	7	21	46	69	27
16 Walthamstow Ave.	38	11	5	22	52	81	27
17 Clapton	38	9	7	22	45	87	25
18 Maidstone United	38	7	8	23	48	84	22
19 Corinthian-Casuals	38	6	3	29	30	99	15
20 Bromley	38	3	4	31	28	111	10

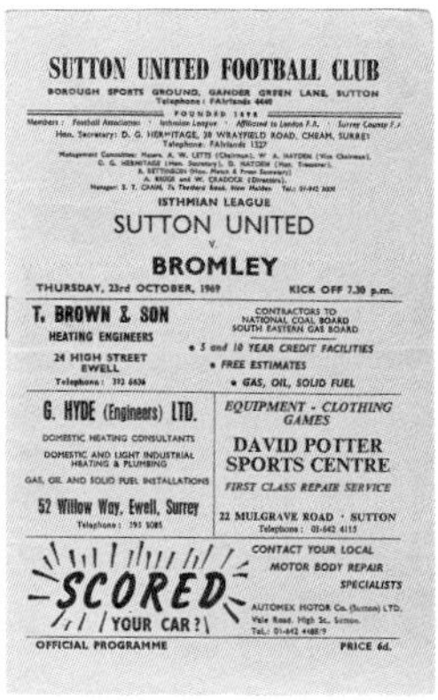

Right: Dulwich Hamlet's programme from 1969-70.

Left: The Sutton United programme from the same season.

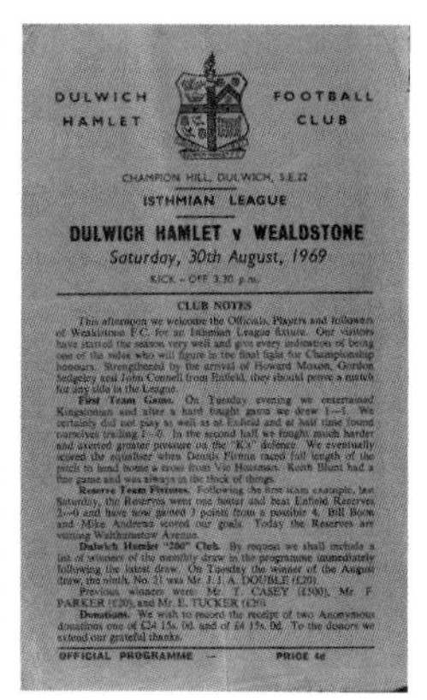

Below: Wealdstone's programme for the visit of Wycombe Wanderers, which The Stones lost 6-1.

1970–71 - Another close championship race was decided in Wycombe Wanderers' favour. They eventually overcame Sutton United by one point to secure their first title since 1957. St. Albans City were five points further back in third place, but one clear of defending champions Enfield, who finished fourth. Clapton and Corinthian–Casuals finished in the bottom two positions.

As exciting as the League season had been, there was plenty of other business carried out at administrator level.

Firstly, during the season, the Secretary of the Southern Football League gave notice, in accordance with Football Association regulations, of his intention to approach 13 Isthmian League clubs with a view of inviting them to join the Southern League for the 1971–72 season. Although the majority of clubs were not interested in the idea of leaving the Isthmian League, Maidstone United and Wealdstone announced that they were both to turn professional and join the Southern League.

This created two vacancies in the Isthmian League and there were a number of applications to fill them. The applications came from: Alton Town, Aveley, Bishop's Stortford, Dagenham, Harwich & Parkeston, Hayes, Hornchurch, Leatherhead, Leighton Town, Southall, Tilbury and Walton & Hersham. Some clubs later withdrew their applications, while others did not meet the satisfactory ground criteria for membership. The League Council decided that the three remaining applicants would be decided in two ballots. The voting in the two ballots was as follows: *Bishop's Stortford 17, Walton & Hersham 17, Hayes 16.*

The League Council, therefore, recommended Bishop's Stortford and Walton & Hersham to the Annual General Meeting to replace Maidstone United and Wealdstone. However, at the AGM, it was agreed to allow a maximum membership of 22 clubs, so Hayes were also elected to increase membership to 21 clubs.

Secondly, the first meeting of a sub-committee set up to deal with the future of amateur football in general, and the Isthmian League, in particular, was held on 18 December 1970. It created an agenda for items to be discussed at future meetings and these included the possible formation of a second division of the Isthmian League, increasing the League from twenty to 22 clubs, the re-introduction of the re-election process for the two bottom clubs and the introduction of a cup competition exclusively for member clubs.

FM Wilson, who served as a League officer since 1960, first as Hon Assistant Referees & Fixture Secretary, then Hon Referees Secretary and also Hon Secretary & Treasurer, was elected a life member of the League in recognition of his services.

	1	2	3	4	5	6	7	8	9	10	11	12	13	14	15	16	17	18	19	20
1 Barking	*	7–0	2–1	4–0	5–1	1–2	0–3	1–2	0–4	2–2	3–1	5–3	4–2	0–2	1–2	4–0	1–2	2–0	4–1	2–3
2 Bromley	0–4	*	3–0	1–1	4–1	1–1	1–4	0–0	1–3	2–1	3–1	2–0	0–4	1–0	1–3	3–0	1–1	1–0	0–1	0–4
3 Clapton	0–4	3–5	*	2–3	1–1	2–5	0–6	1–2	0–1	0–4	1–5	1–1	0–3	0–3	1–4	2–1	1–1	3–0	2–4	0–1
4 Corinthian-Casuals	2–3	0–1	1–2	*	0–0	0–4	0–8	3–3	1–1	1–2	1–3	1–2	0–6	0–2	0–4	1–5	0–1	1–4	1–5	0–4
5 Dulwich Hamlet	0–2	2–0	1–0	0–1	*	0–3	0–4	1–0	4–2	1–0	0–1	3–2	0–2	0–0	1–2	1–1	0–0	0–1	1–2	1–1
6 Enfield	1–0	2–0	0–0	3–1	1–0	*	2–0	1–0	0–1	2–0	2–1	1–0	1–0	1–2	0–2	1–0	4–2	4–0	3–0	1–1
7 Hendon	0–0	3–0	4–0	1–0	2–0	0–0	*	6–1	3–2	2–0	3–2	5–0	1–2	3–1	1–1	1–2	1–2	1–1	2–3	1–3
8 Hitchin Town	3–2	1–0	3–0	0–0	1–1	1–1	1–4	*	1–2	4–1	1–2	2–1	1–2	0–2	1–2	1–1	0–3	0–1	2–0	1–2
9 Ilford	1–3	1–0	3–0	3–1	3–1	1–5	1–1	3–1	*	0–0	3–2	1–1	4–1	0–0	0–2	1–0	1–2	2–1	3–0	0–2
10 Kingstonian	2–2	1–0	3–0	4–0	5–2	0–5	1–0	3–3	2–3	*	1–1	5–0	1–2	0–2	1–4	0–4	1–1	1–2	2–3	2–1
11 Leytonstone	2–1	6–0	1–1	3–0	4–0	0–0	1–1	2–1	2–1	2–1	*	4–1	0–0	0–0	1–3	1–2	2–2	2–2	3–0	2–2
12 Maidstone United	0–3	3–0	1–1	2–2	2–2	2–6	1–2	0–1	1–4	1–2	1–2	*	0–1	1–1	0–1	2–4	1–2	1–0	0–1	1–4
13 Oxford City	3–1	0–0	5–1	2–0	0–1	0–2	0–0	0–1	3–3	2–2	1–2	1–2	*	0–0	0–1	3–2	3–4	2–1	1–1	1–1
14 St. Albans City	3–0	4–1	7–1	0–0	6–0	2–0	0–0	4–0	2–2	3–0	2–1	4–2	1–1	*	4–2	3–1	4–2	5–0	0–1	2–0
15 Sutton United	4–2	2–1	1–0	3–0	3–2	1–0	2–0	1–1	0–2	5–0	3–1	1–2	2–0	0–2	*	2–0	2–1	2–1	2–1	0–1
16 Tooting & M Utd	0–1	1–1	1–2	2–1	0–0	1–2	1–1	0–2	1–5	1–0	1–2	0–2	1–0	0–7	1–1	*	2–1	2–0	1–0	0–0
17 Walthamstow Ave.	4–6	2–0	0–1	5–0	0–0	0–1	2–2	1–1	1–3	1–2	2–0	0–1	2–0	1–1	0–2	4–0	*	4–1	1–1	1–1
18 Wealdstone	1–3	4–0	2–2	0–0	2–1	1–0	1–1	1–2	2–0	1–1	0–1	3–2	0–0	0–3	0–2	2–2	3–2	*	3–0	1–6
19 Woking	2–2	4–0	4–0	5–0	2–1	0–0	1–3	1–0	3–1	2–0	1–1	1–0	2–0	2–1	1–2	1–1	0–1	1–2	*	0–2
20 Wycombe Wndrs.	1–2	2–0	5–1	3–0	1–0	1–0	2–1	4–1	1–3	4–0	3–1	5–0	3–0	3–2	4–0	5–2	3–2	2–1	2–0	*

	P	W	D	L	F	A	Pts
1 Wycombe Wndrs.	38	28	6	4	93	32	62
2 Sutton United	38	29	3	6	76	35	61
3 St. Albans City	38	23	10	5	87	26	56
4 Enfield	38	24	7	7	67	24	55
5 Ilford	38	21	7	10	74	51	49
6 Hendon	38	18	11	9	81	37	47
7 Barking	38	20	4	14	89	59	44
8 Leytonstone	38	17	10	11	68	50	44
9 Woking	38	18	6	14	57	50	44
10 Walthamstow Ave.	38	14	11	13	63	52	39
11 Oxford City	38	13	10	15	51	48	36
12 Hitchin Town	38	12	9	17	46	60	33
13 Wealdstone	38	12	8	18	45	64	32
14 Tooting & M Utd	38	11	9	18	44	66	31
15 Kingstoniian	38	11	8	19	53	71	30
16 Bromley	38	10	6	22	34	77	26
17 Dulwich Hamlet	38	7	10	21	30	66	24
18 Maidstone United	38	7	6	25	42	84	20
19 Clapton	38	5	7	26	33	101	17
20 Corinthian-Casuals	38	2	8	28	23	103	12

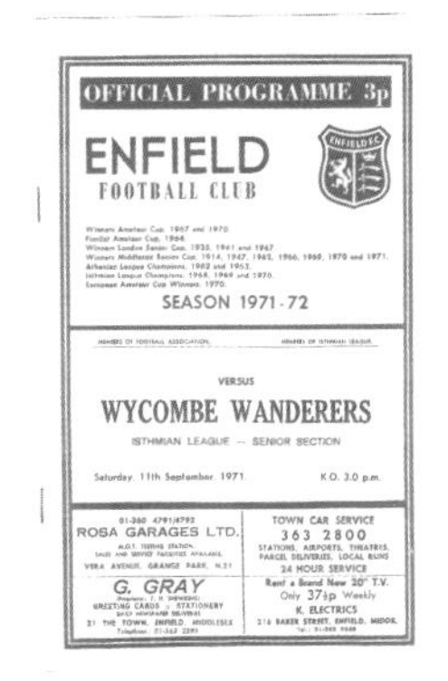

Left: Enfield's programme for their match with Wycombe Wanderers, which The E's lost 4-0.

Below: Wycombe's game with The Rest in 1972.

Below: Clapton's programme from 1971-72 against Hendon, days after their FA Amateur Cup Final victory.

1971–72 - Wycombe Wanderers retained their championships, this time by five points from Enfield, with Walton & Hersham – in their first season – edging out Hendon for third place on goal average, both clubs four points behind the E's. Dulwich Hamlet and Corinthian-Casuals occupied the bottom two positions.

At the Annual General Meeting Leatherhead were elected as members, which gave the Isthmian League their full complement of 22 clubs. Also at the AGM, Donald McKenzie, who had retired as Chairman, was elected a life member of the League in recognition of his long and outstanding service. Barry East, previously the Vice-Chairman, succeeded Mr McKenzie as Chairman, with Frank Wilson taking over the role of Vice-Chairman.

	1	2	3	4	5	6	7	8	9	10	11	12	13	14	15	16	17	18	19	20	21
1 Barking	*	1–2	2–2	2–0	2–1	2–1	2–0	0–2	0–1	4–2	1–2	2–1	3–1	1–5	1–0	2–1	5–0	2–0	1–0	0–2	2–1
2 Bishop's Stortford	0–0	*	4–0	3–1	2–0	2–0	1–2	1–2	2–0	3–1	2–2	1–0	1–3	2–1	2–0	3–1	2–1	0–1	1–0	1–0	0–1
3 Bromley	1–1	1–3	*	6–1	2–0	2–0	0–4	2–0	2–2	1–1	3–1	0–1	1–1	2–2	2–1	1–2	5–1	3–1	0–0	2–1	1–2
4 Clapton	2–1	1–2	3–0	*	2–0	2–2	0–2	3–0	0–4	2–4	2–2	1–0	2–2	0–3	0–2	0–1	4–2	1–2	2–3	1–3	0–7
5 Corinthian-Casuals	0–1	3–2	0–3	0–0	*	0–2	0–3	0–1	0–4	2–4	3–3	1–1	2–1	0–0	0–1	0–4	0–1	1–3	0–3	1–1	0–4
6 Dulwich Hamlet	1–2	0–1	0–1	2–2	2–1	*	2–5	1–1	0–3	0–0	1–2	2–2	2–0	2–4	2–1	1–1	2–2	1–1	0–1	0–2	0–4
7 Enfield	3–0	1–1	3–1	7–0	6–0	4–1	*	3–3	1–1	2–1	4–0	6–1	2–1	1–0	1–0	0–3	4–3	0–0	0–3	1–0	0–4
8 Hayes	4–1	0–1	1–2	4–0	1–0	2–2	0–1	*	2–1	0–0	0–2	1–1	2–2	2–2	3–0	2–2	3–1	2–4	1–1	2–1	0–0
9 Hendon	3–0	0–0	1–1	6–0	8–0	6–1	1–0	1–0	*	2–0	3–3	1–0	4–1	0–0	0–2	3–2	3–0	4–1	1–1	2–0	0–1
10 Hitchin Town	4–2	2–1	5–4	5–1	4–1	0–0	1–1	1–0	1–1	*	1–2	0–0	3–1	0–4	3–1	0–3	5–0	2–1	1–1	2–2	0–3
11 Ilford	3–0	1–0	1–0	3–1	4–1	2–1	2–0	1–1	1–2	1–0	*	2–1	1–2	0–2	0–1	0–1	1–1	0–1	1–0	1–1	1–3
12 Kingstonian	0–2	1–2	2–2	6–0	1–0	2–1	1–2	0–1	0–1	1–2	3–3	*	1–1	1–1	1–1	4–2	2–0	2–0	1–4	1–1	0–1
13 Leytonstone	2–2	0–1	2–3	1–3	9–0	2–1	0–2	1–0	0–1	0–1	0–3	0–3	*	2–1	0–3	1–2	3–0	1–1	1–0	1–0	0–0
14 Oxford City	1–3	0–1	3–3	1–1	0–1	2–1	3–3	1–0	4–0	1–3	0–2	2–0	1–2	*	1–4	1–2	4–0	0–0	0–4	1–2	1–4
15 St. Albans City	1–2	1–4	2–0	2–1	3–1	3–0	2–2	2–0	3–4	2–0	4–2	4–0	3–1	8–0	*	2–1	2–0	2–2	0–1	2–1	1–0
16 Sutton United	4–2	2–1	3–1	2–0	3–0	0–0	0–0	2–0	1–1	4–0	0–0	3–0	3–1	4–0	1–1	*	5–1	3–1	0–3	1–1	1–2
17 Tooting & M Utd	0–5	1–1	1–2	2–2	3–1	0–0	0–1	1–1	0–1	3–4	2–1	2–2	0–0	1–3	0–2	1–1	*	3–1	1–3	2–0	0–4
18 Walthamstow Ave.	2–5	0–1	1–4	10–2	4–1	3–1	1–5	1–3	3–1	1–3	0–4	0–2	0–1	0–1	0–1	1–1	3–0	*	0–1	5–3	1–1
19 Walton & Hersham	3–0	2–0	2–0	2–1	4–0	3–0	1–3	3–1	0–1	2–0	1–1	1–1	3–0	2–2	3–0	2–1	3–0	0–1	*	0–0	2–0
20 Woking	1–0	3–1	0–1	4–1	3–0	2–0	1–4	0–1	1–1	2–2	1–1	1–3	4–0	4–1	1–3	1–4	1–2	1–1	0–1	*	0–4
21 Wycombe Wndrs.	2–1	1–3	3–0	8–0	5–0	6–0	0–1	0–1	1–0	4–0	2–0	2–0	3–1	6–2	4–1	3–0	1–0	2–0	2–0	1–0	*

	P	W	D	L	F	A	Pts
1 Wycombe Wndrs.	40	31	3	6	102	20	65
2 Enfield	40	26	8	6	90	41	60
3 Walton & Hersham	40	24	8	8	69	25	56
4 Hendon	40	23	10	7	79	35	56
5 Bishop's Stortford	40	24	5	11	61	37	53
6 Sutton United	40	21	10	9	77	43	52
7 St. Albans City	40	23	4	13	74	47	50
8 Ilford	40	17	11	12	62	52	45
9 Barking	40	20	4	16	65	61	44
10 Hitchin Town	40	17	10	13	68	66	44
11 Bromley	40	16	10	14	67	64	42
12 Hayes	40	14	12	14	50	48	40
13 Oxford City	40	13	9	18	67	74	35
14 Woking	40	11	10	19	52	58	32
15 Kingstonian	40	10	12	18	49	59	32
16 Walthamstow Ave.	40	12	8	20	58	71	32
17 Leytonstone	40	11	8	21	48	68	30
18 Tooting & M Utd	40	6	9	25	38	93	21
19 Clapton	40	7	7	26	45	118	21
20 Dulwich Hamlet	40	4	12	24	35	81	20
21 Corinthian-Casuals	40	3	4	33	21	116	10

Left: Woking's programme for the 1971-72 campaign.

Below: Wycombe Wanderers were 1970-71 and 1971-72 champions.

(Back) Wharton, Goldsworthy, Delaney (Capt.), Faulkner, Maskell, Maclean, Holt, Williams
(Middle) B.R.Lee (Man.),Nobbs,Rundle,Fuschillo, Searle, Gale, Bremer, Powell, Pritchard, Blunt, T.Thomas,J.Reardon(Asst.Man.)
(Front) Hutchinson, Anthony, Crump (Sec.), Seymour (President), Adams (Patron), Smethurst (Chairman),
R.N. Lee (Treasurer), Horseman, Baker (Front sitting) Sheppard (Attendant)

1972–73 - Hendon won their first championship since 1965 when they took the title by a record margin of 13 points – losing only two games in the process – from nearest challengers Walton & Hersham, who themselves had done well in their first two seasons. Leatherhead completed their debut season five points behind Walton in third place, but ahead of Wycombe Wanderers on goal average. At the bottom were Clapton and Corinthian–Casuals, with the latter occupying a bottom-two place for a fifth consecutive season. On 12 May 1973, League champions Hendon beat their Northern League counterparts Blyth Spartans 2–0 *(see programme right)* in front of 2,285 spectators at Claremont Road. League Chairman Barry East donated trophies, as well as £1,000 for the game; £550 would go to the winners with £300 to the losers with balance of £150 divided between the two leagues.

The biggest change in the constitution of the Isthmian League, arguably since its formation, came into being during this season. At the League Council meeting, held on 8 December 1972, it was agreed to form a second division of 16 clubs from the commencement of the 1973–74 season. In addition, there would be promotion and relegation of two clubs up and down at the conclusion of season that followed. For the 1973–74 season, the existing 22 Clubs in membership would form Division One and Division Two would consist of the following 16 clubs, subject to their acceptance and election at the Annual General Meeting:

Aveley, Carshalton Athletic, Chesham United, Dagenham, Finchley, Hampton, Harlow Town, Harwich & Parkeston, Hertford Town, Horsham, Maidenhead United, Slough Town, Southall, Staines Town, Tilbury and Wokingham Town

Ten other clubs made applications, namely: Cheshunt, Erith & Belvedere, Grays Athletic, Hornchurch, Hounslow, Leyton, Marlow, Redhill, Wembley and Witney Town. Their applications for membership were unsuccessful.

At the AGM, the 16 new clubs were elected to the new Division Two. It was obvious, with the expansion of the League, there would be significantly more work for the League's officers and it was therefore proposed that A W Peacock would act as Hon Treasurer and former League referee Eddie Bray as Hon Assistant Referees Secretary. K Sharp succeeded W Varrell as Registration Secretary. Mr Varrell had resigned because he had numerous other commitments.

League Chairman Barry East and the secretary of Bromley FC, Charlie King, had kindly agreed to donate jointly the championship flag. It was also agreed to award a Division One Champions' trophy, to be held by the champion club for one season. There would also be a Division One Champions' trophy – which was kindly donated by Andrew Letts of Sutton United – and 15 medals would be struck for the players.

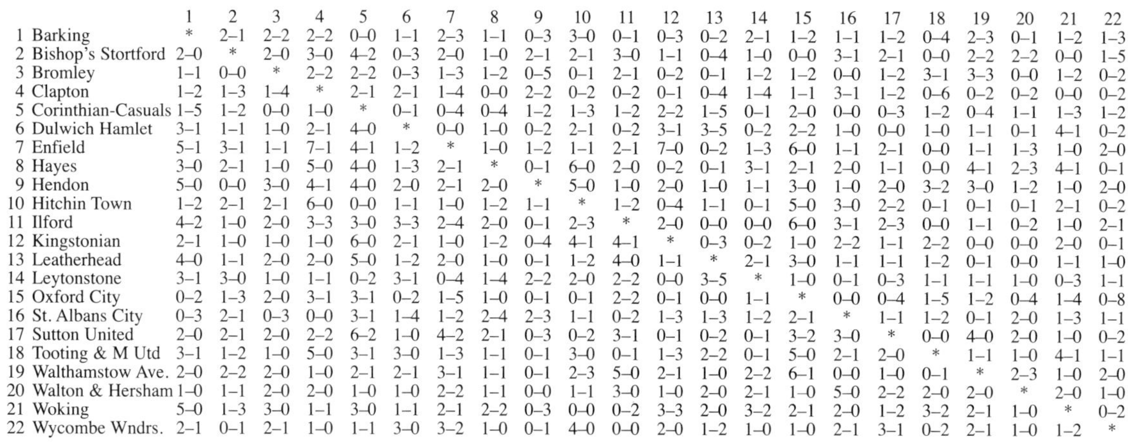

	1	2	3	4	5	6	7	8	9	10	11	12	13	14	15	16	17	18	19	20	21	22
1 Barking	*	2–1	2–2	2–2	0–0	1–1	2–3	1–1	0–3	3–0	0–1	0–3	0–2	2–1	1–2	1–1	1–2	0–4	2–3	0–1	1–2	1–3
2 Bishop's Stortford	2–0	*	2–0	3–0	4–2	0–3	2–0	1–0	2–1	2–1	3–0	1–1	0–4	1–0	0–0	3–1	2–1	0–0	2–2	2–2	0–0	1–5
3 Bromley	1–1	0–0	*	2–2	2–2	0–3	1–3	1–2	0–5	0–1	2–1	0–2	0–1	1–2	1–2	0–0	1–2	3–1	3–3	0–0	1–2	0–2
4 Clapton	1–2	1–3	1–4	*	2–1	2–1	1–4	0–0	2–2	0–2	0–2	0–1	0–4	1–4	1–1	3–1	1–2	0–6	0–2	0–2	0–0	0–2
5 Corinthian-Casuals	1–5	1–2	0–0	1–0	*	0–1	0–4	0–4	1–2	1–3	1–2	2–2	1–5	0–1	2–0	0–0	0–3	1–2	0–4	1–1	1–3	1–2
6 Dulwich Hamlet	3–1	1–1	1–0	2–1	4–0	*	0–0	1–0	0–2	2–1	0–2	3–1	3–5	0–2	2–2	1–0	0–0	1–0	1–1	0–1	4–1	0–2
7 Enfield	5–1	3–1	1–1	7–1	4–1	1–2	*	1–0	1–2	1–1	2–1	7–0	0–2	1–3	6–0	1–1	2–1	0–0	1–1	1–3	1–0	2–0
8 Hayes	3–0	2–1	1–0	5–0	4–0	1–3	2–1	*	0–1	6–0	2–0	0–2	0–1	3–1	2–1	2–0	1–1	0–0	4–1	2–3	4–1	0–1
9 Hendon	5–0	0–0	3–0	4–1	4–0	2–0	2–1	2–0	*	5–0	1–0	2–0	1–0	1–1	3–0	1–0	2–0	3–2	3–0	1–2	1–0	2–0
10 Hitchin Town	1–2	2–1	2–1	6–0	0–0	1–1	1–0	1–2	1–1	*	1–2	0–4	1–1	0–1	5–0	3–0	2–2	0–1	0–1	0–1	2–1	0–2
11 Ilford	4–2	1–0	2–0	3–3	3–0	3–3	2–4	2–0	0–1	2–3	*	2–0	0–0	0–0	6–0	3–1	2–3	0–0	1–1	0–2	1–0	2–1
12 Kingstonian	2–1	1–0	1–0	1–0	6–0	2–1	1–0	1–2	0–4	4–1	4–1	*	0–3	0–2	1–0	2–2	1–1	2–2	0–0	0–0	2–0	0–1
13 Leatherhead	4–0	1–1	2–0	2–0	5–0	1–2	2–0	1–0	0–1	1–2	4–0	1–1	*	2–1	3–0	1–1	1–1	1–2	0–1	0–0	1–1	1–0
14 Leytonstone	3–1	3–0	1–0	1–1	0–2	3–1	0–4	1–4	2–2	2–0	2–2	0–0	3–5	*	1–0	0–1	0–3	1–1	1–1	1–0	0–3	1–1
15 Oxford City	0–2	1–3	2–0	3–1	3–1	0–2	1–5	1–0	0–1	0–1	2–2	0–1	0–0	1–1	*	0–0	0–4	1–5	1–2	0–4	1–4	0–8
16 St. Albans City	0–3	2–1	0–3	0–0	3–1	1–4	1–2	2–4	2–3	1–1	0–2	1–3	1–3	1–2	2–1	*	1–1	1–2	0–1	2–0	1–3	1–1
17 Sutton United	2–0	2–1	2–0	2–2	6–2	1–0	4–2	2–1	0–3	0–2	3–1	0–1	0–2	0–1	3–2	3–0	*	0–0	4–0	2–0	1–0	0–2
18 Tooting & M Utd	3–1	1–2	1–0	5–0	3–1	3–0	1–3	1–1	0–1	3–0	0–1	1–3	2–2	0–1	5–0	2–1	2–0	*	1–1	1–0	4–1	1–1
19 Walthamstow Ave.	2–0	2–2	2–0	1–0	2–1	2–1	3–1	1–1	0–1	2–3	5–0	2–1	1–0	2–2	6–1	0–0	1–0	0–1	*	2–3	1–0	2–0
20 Walton & Hersham	1–0	1–1	2–0	2–0	1–0	1–0	2–2	1–1	0–0	1–1	3–0	1–0	2–0	2–1	1–0	5–0	2–2	2–0	2–0	*	2–0	1–0
21 Woking	5–0	1–3	3–0	1–1	3–0	1–1	2–1	2–2	0–3	0–0	0–2	3–3	2–0	3–2	2–1	2–0	1–2	3–2	2–1	1–0	*	0–2
22 Wycombe Wndrs.	2–1	0–1	2–1	1–0	1–1	3–0	3–2	1–0	0–1	4–0	0–0	2–0	1–2	1–0	1–0	2–1	3–1	0–2	2–1	1–0	1–2	*

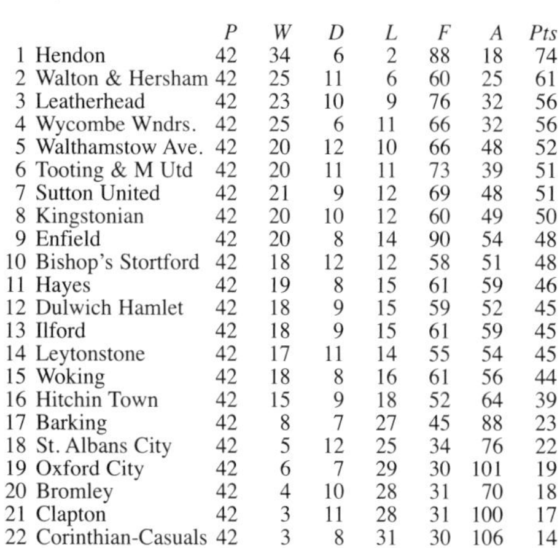

	P	*W*	*D*	*L*	*F*	*A*	*Pts*
1 Hendon	42	34	6	2	88	18	74
2 Walton & Hersham	42	25	11	6	60	25	61
3 Leatherhead	42	23	10	9	76	32	56
4 Wycombe Wndrs.	42	25	6	11	66	32	56
5 Walthamstow Ave.	42	20	12	10	66	48	52
6 Tooting & M Utd	42	20	11	11	73	39	51
7 Sutton United	42	21	9	12	69	48	51
8 Kingstonian	42	20	10	12	60	49	50
9 Enfield	42	20	8	14	90	54	48
10 Bishop's Stortford	42	18	12	12	58	51	48
11 Hayes	42	19	8	15	61	59	46
12 Dulwich Hamlet	42	18	9	15	59	52	45
13 Ilford	42	18	9	15	61	59	45
14 Leytonstone	42	17	11	14	55	54	45
15 Woking	42	18	8	16	61	56	44
16 Hitchin Town	42	15	9	18	52	64	39
17 Barking	42	8	7	27	45	88	23
18 St. Albans City	42	5	12	25	34	76	22
19 Oxford City	42	6	7	29	30	101	19
20 Bromley	42	4	10	28	31	70	18
21 Clapton	42	3	11	28	31	100	17
22 Corinthian-Casuals	42	3	8	31	30	106	14

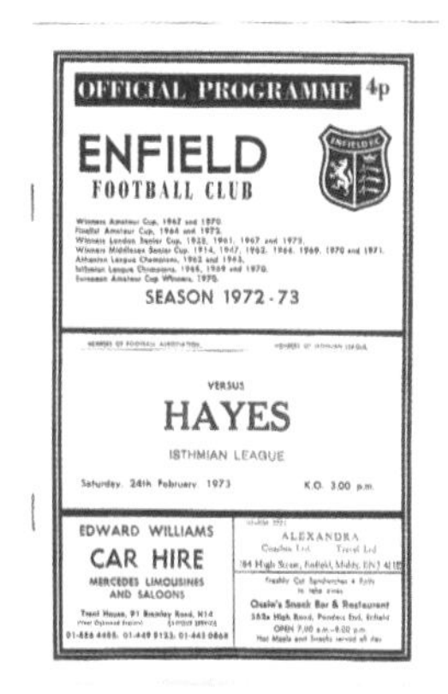

Left: Enfield's programme for their match with Hayes, which The E's won 1-0.
Below: the teams from Dulwich Hamlet's 3-1 win over Kingstonian, with Brian Robinson, subsequent League Treasurer, as referee.

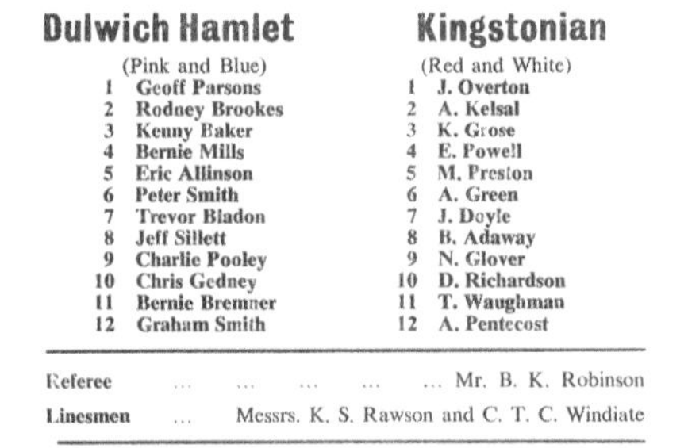

Dulwich Hamlet	Kingstonian
(Pink and Blue)	(Red and White)
1 Geoff Parsons	1 J. Overton
2 Rodney Brookes	2 A. Kelsal
3 Kenny Baker	3 K. Grose
4 Bernie Mills	4 E. Powell
5 Eric Allinson	5 M. Preston
6 Peter Smith	6 A. Green
7 Trevor Bladon	7 J. Doyle
8 Jeff Sillett	8 B. Adaway
9 Charlie Pooley	9 N. Glover
10 Chris Gedney	10 D. Richardson
11 Bernie Bremner	11 T. Waughman
12 Graham Smith	12 A. Pentecost

Referee ... ... Mr. B. K. Robinson
Linesmen ... Messrs. K. S. Rawson and C. T. C. Windiate

Below: programmes from 1972-73 - Leatherhead's first season.

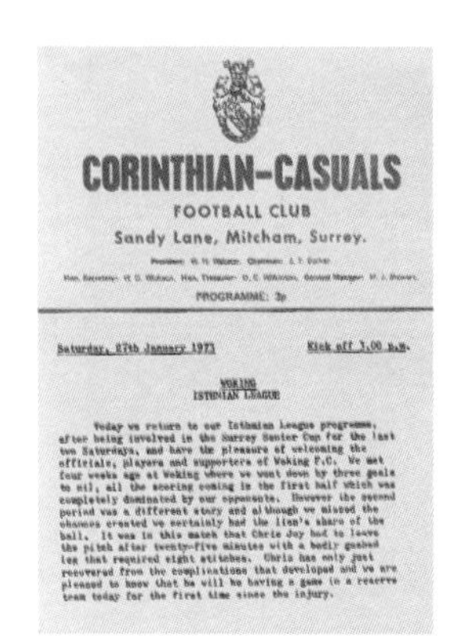

PART THREE: 1973 – 2005

1973–74 - This season was to be the last as an amateur football league as The Football Association abolished amateurism and professionals and amateurs alike were deemed as simply "players". This meant the end of The FA Amateur Cup competition and in the final Final, two members of the League - Bishop's Stortford and Ilford - contested the tie: a fitting end to a magnificent competition.

The first season of the Isthmian League sponsored by Rothmans also saw a change in the points system with three points awarded for a win instead of the two points which had existed since the formation of the League; clubs still earned one point for a draw.

Early in the season, The FA drew up proposals for the regionalisation of football below the Football League. The proposal was to merge the Southern and Northern Premier Leagues into a national division with three regionalised divisions, Northern, Midland and Southern, which it was hoped would result in promotion and relegation and would in the future involve the Rothmans Isthmian League and other leagues feeding into the regionalised divisions. The Isthmian League responded that under no circumstances would they be interested in participating in the scheme. The plan died completely when the Southern and Northern Premier Leagues decided not to merge.

BISHOP'S STORTFORD 1973-74

Left to Right: Back Row: Ted Hardy (manager), Tony Bass, Paul Scott, John Still, Alan Cherry, Terry Moore, Martin Smith, Paul Webb, Ron Duke (coach), David Jones (trainer). Front Row: Roy Mitchell, Dennis Murphy, John Payne, John Dear, Dave Lawrence (captain), Peter Leakey, Ray Coombes, Tony Gibson.

The Bishop's Stortford team that reached the last FA Amateur Cup Final in April 1974.

In a closely fought championship between the top three clubs, Wycombe Wanderers secured the championship two points ahead of runners-up Hendon with Bishop's Stortford third, a point behind the 'Greens'. Fourth placed Dulwich Hamlet were a further ten points adrift. The first clubs to suffer relegation to Division Two were St. Albans City and Corinthian-Casuals, with the latter finishing bottom the previous three years. In Division Two Dagenham were inaugural champions and were promoted with runners-up Slough Town to Division One. Southall and Wokingham Town who occupied the re-election positions were both re-elected at the Annual General Meeting. It was agreed to increase Division Two to eighteen clubs and Boreham Wood were invited to fill one of the vacancies with the remaining vacancy to be decided by ballot. Cheshunt, Croydon (who dropped their "Amateurs" second name in 1973), Edmonton & Haringey, Erith & Belvedere, Grays Athletic, Harrow Borough, Hoddesdon Town, Hornchurch, Hounslow, Leyton, Marlow, Redhill, Ware and Wembley all applied, and it was Croydon who secured election to the League.

Division I	1	2	3	4	5	6	7	8	9	10	11	12	13	14	15	16	17	18	19	20	21	22
1 Barking	*	0–1	1–0	4–0	2–2	3–1	3–1	1–1	1–1	1–1	2–0	1–2	2–1	0–1	2–2	2–2	1–1	1–0	1–1	6–1	2–0	0–0
2 Bishop's Stortford	4–0	*	3–0	4–0	6–0	1–1	1–1	0–0	0–3	3–0	5–0	3–1	2–1	1–2	3–1	1–0	1–1	3–0	5–1	2–0	2–1	2–0
3 Bromley	0–3	0–1	*	5–0	4–1	0–2	0–2	1–1	0–2	0–2	3–1	1–1	0–6	1–1	5–0	1–1	0–5	1–0	0–3	2–3	0–4	0–2
4 Clapton	0–1	1–7	1–1	*	0–3	0–5	4–1	0–5	0–7	2–3	1–0	1–3	2–4	0–3	1–2	2–1	0–2	0–4	2–0	1–4	1–4	2–3
5 Corinthian-Casuals	0–1	0–2	1–4	1–2	*	0–2	1–2	0–3	0–2	1–2	0–3	1–2	1–3	1–3	1–3	1–2	2–2	1–2	0–2	0–1	0–3	0–4
6 Dulwich Hamlet	2–1	0–1	5–1	3–0	1–2	*	2–2	1–1	2–1	0–0	2–2	1–2	2–1	2–1	0–0	3–0	0–1	2–0	3–0	4–2	2–0	1–1
7 Enfield	3–0	0–3	1–0	3–0	3–1	2–1	*	0–3	0–1	4–0	1–0	1–1	4–2	2–1	0–0	0–1	0–1	1–1	1–3	0–1	2–2	0–0
8 Hayes	3–0	0–1	3–1	7–0	1–0	1–3	2–1	*	0–0	1–1	0–1	1–0	2–0	0–0	3–0	3–0	2–2	1–0	3–1	1–2	0–0	0–3
9 Hendon	0–0	1–0	2–0	3–0	3–0	1–1	3–1	2–0	*	2–1	1–0	0–0	1–0	2–0	1–1	3–0	1–0	2–0	1–1	0–0	2–0	2–1
10 Hitchin Town	2–4	0–3	2–1	4–0	5–1	0–3	4–0	2–2	1–2	*	1–3	0–2	0–4	2–0	2–0	4–1	1–1	4–3	1–1	2–2	0–2	2–1
11 Ilford	1–0	1–1	0–0	2–0	6–0	0–1	2–0	2–1	0–2	2–2	*	2–0	2–4	1–1	1–0	2–0	1–1	2–1	0–0	0–3	3–0	1–3
12 Kingstonian	2–1	0–0	0–0	2–3	4–0	1–2	1–1	2–3	0–0	4–2	2–3	*	1–1	2–0	1–1	1–0	1–1	0–1	1–1	1–0	0–1	0–0
13 Leatherhead	5–1	3–0	1–2	0–3	2–1	1–0	2–1	1–2	0–1	2–0	1–0	0–0	*	2–0	0–0	3–0	5–0	2–1	0–3	3–0	3–1	1–1
14 Leytonstone	2–1	0–1	2–0	6–0	3–1	2–2	3–2	2–0	2–1	1–0	0–2	1–1	1–0	*	2–0	1–0	5–1	3–1	0–0	1–0	4–1	1–2
15 Oxford City	1–0	1–0	0–0	1–1	1–0	2–0	2–1	1–1	0–1	0–4	2–0	2–1	1–1	1–1	*	2–0	1–0	1–0	0–0	3–3	2–2	1–0
16 St. Albans City	0–0	0–0	3–0	2–4	1–0	0–2	1–1	1–2	1–1	2–4	0–2	1–4	1–3	0–3	2–2	*	0–1	3–4	1–2	2–3	0–3	0–3
17 Sutton United	3–2	1–1	1–0	1–1	1–1	1–2	0–2	1–1	0–0	2–2	0–2	1–0	0–1	3–0	1–3	3–0	*	2–2	3–1	0–2	2–0	0–2
18 Tooting & M Utd	3–2	0–1	1–1	5–0	2–1	0–1	1–0	1–1	2–2	4–0	1–5	1–0	1–4	1–1	0–0	2–0	1–1	*	3–0	1–2	1–0	0–3
19 Walthamstow Ave.	0–1	0–1	2–1	2–0	1–3	1–1	0–0	1–0	1–2	1–1	0–2	1–1	2–4	0–2	2–1	2–1	1–2	4–1	*	2–2	1–2	0–4
20 Walton & Hersham	1–1	1–1	2–0	4–1	1–1	0–1	1–0	4–1	1–0	1–2	0–0	4–0	0–0	0–0	2–1	3–0	2–1	0–2	0–0	*	2–1	4–1
21 Woking	2–0	2–1	2–1	2–0	3–1	2–1	1–1	0–0	1–1	2–1	0–2	1–0	0–4	3–2	1–3	2–0	2–1	2–1	2–1	3–2	*	1–0
22 Wycombe Wndrs.	5–2	2–0	7–0	4–0	7–0	1–1	2–1	4–3	2–0	2–1	2–1	1–0	2–0	3–0	1–0	7–0	0–0	2–2	3–1	2–2	3–2	*

Division I	*P*	*W*	*D*	*L*	*F*	*A*	*Pts*
1 Wycombe Wand	42	27	9	6	96	34	90
2 Hendon	42	25	13	4	63	20	88
3 Bishop's Stortford	42	26	9	7	78	26	87
4 Dulwich Hamlet	42	22	11	9	71	38	77
5 Leatherhead	42	23	6	13	81	44	75
6 Walton & Hersham	42	20	12	10	68	50	72
7 Woking	42	22	6	14	63	55	72
8 Leytonstone	42	20	9	13	63	44	69
9 Ilford	42	20	8	14	60	44	68
10 Hayes	42	17	14	11	65	43	65
11 Oxford City	42	15	16	11	45	47	61
12 Sutton United	42	13	16	13	51	52	55
13 Hitchin Town	42	15	10	17	68	73	55
14 Barking	42	14	12	16	57	58	54
15 Kingstonian	42	12	15	15	47	46	51
16 Tooting & M Utd	42	14	9	19	57	62	51
17 Enfield	42	13	11	18	50	57	50
18 Walthamstow Ave.	42	11	13	18	46	62	46
19 Bromley	42	7	9	26	37	81	30
20 Clapton	42	8	3	31	36	128	27
21 St. Albans City	42	4	7	31	30	92	19
22 Corinthian-Casuals	42	3	4	35	31	107	13

ILFORD F.C. 1973-74

Left to Right: Back Row: Tony Turley, Tony King, Denis Bowhill, Paul James, Peter Drabwell, John Butterfield, Peter Anderson. Front Row: Ray Carvill, Dave Gulver, Micky Bennett, Paddy Betson (Captain), Roger Day, Jeff Bookman and Andy McDermid.

The Ilford team that reached the last FA Amateur Cup Final.

Division II	1	2	3	4	5	6	7	8	9	10	11	12	13	14	15	16
1 Aveley	*	1–2	1–1	1–2	4–0	5–1	3–1	2–1	3–0	0–3	3–0	0–0	4–1	5–0	1–0	1–0
2 Carshalton Athletic	1–0	*	3–6	1–1	0–1	5–0	4–5	0–4	1–0	1–1	2–0	1–1	2–2	0–0	1–4	0–0
3 Chesham United	0–1	3–0	*	1–3	3–2	0–0	0–4	3–2	2–1	1–0	1–2	1–2	3–0	2–1	2–0	4–0
4 Dagenham	1–2	4–0	4–0	*	4–1	4–0	2–1	3–1	2–0	3–0	1–1	2–1	2–0	2–0	1–1	4–1
5 Finchley	0–1	0–2	0–2	1–2	*	1–1	1–0	0–3	0–2	0–1	2–3	1–0	1–0	1–1	1–3	5–1
6 Hampton	0–0	3–0	1–3	0–3	1–1	*	2–0	2–2	1–1	3–4	1–0	0–1	1–1	2–3	2–1	1–1
7 Harlow Town	2–4	2–1	1–2	2–3	1–1	1–1	*	1–1	1–3	1–1	0–0	1–1	1–0	0–2	0–1	3–2
8 Harwich & Parkst.	2–1	3–0	1–1	0–0	2–0	1–0	1–1	*	1–3	1–1	1–1	0–1	1–1	2–2	1–3	3–1
9 Hertford Town	2–0	1–0	3–2	2–1	1–1	2–0	0–1	2–0	*	3–1	0–1	2–1	1–0	1–0	3–2	5–1
10 Horsham	1–1	3–1	3–5	0–2	1–1	4–0	1–1	1–0	1–1	*	0–1	1–0	6–0	1–0	3–4	4–0
11 Maidenhead Utd	1–1	2–0	1–1	2–1	5–0	3–3	1–0	1–0	1–1	2–0	*	0–1	3–0	1–1	0–1	2–2
12 Slough Town	2–1	2–0	3–3	2–3	2–1	1–0	1–0	4–0	2–0	1–0	3–0	*	4–0	1–1	3–1	1–0
13 Southall	0–1	0–0	1–4	1–0	2–2	0–5	0–0	0–2	1–3	0–1	1–1	0–0	*	2–0	2–0	2–2
14 Staines Town	1–0	1–1	1–0	1–2	2–1	1–0	2–1	1–2	0–2	1–1	3–0	0–2	1–0	*	1–3	5–2
15 Tilbury	3–1	1–4	0–0	0–2	0–2	0–1	5–0	2–3	1–0	0–0	0–0	2–0	1–0	3–1	*	0–0
16 Wokingham Town	0–2	0–1	2–5	0–4	2–1	2–1	2–1	3–5	1–1	1–3	1–1	2–3	0–0	1–1	1–5	*

Division II	P	W	D	L	F	A	Pts
1 Dagenham	30	22	4	4	68	23	70
2 Slough Town	30	18	6	6	46	23	60
3 Hertford Town	30	17	5	8	46	29	56
4 Chesham United	30	16	6	8	61	43	54
5 Aveley	30	16	5	9	50	28	53
6 Tilbury	30	14	5	11	47	36	47
7 Maidenhead Utd	30	12	11	7	36	30	47
8 Horsham	30	12	9	9	47	35	45
9 Harwich & Parkst.	30	11	9	10	46	41	42
10 Staines Town	30	10	8	12	34	41	38
11 Carshalton Athletic	30	8	8	14	34	51	32
12 Hampton	30	6	10	14	33	51	28
13 Harlow Town	30	6	9	15	33	48	27
14 Finchley	30	6	7	17	29	52	25
15 Southall	30	3	10	17	17	52	19
16 Wokingham Town	30	3	8	19	30	74	17

Above right: Hayes programme for their game with Woking in April 1973, which finished goalless.

Right: The Ilford programme from their game with Dulwich Hamlet, which the visitors won 1-0.

Right: programme for the Surrey Senior Cup Final at Walton & Hersham in May 1975.

1974–75 - Wycombe Wanderers secured back-to-back championship successes by virtue of superior goal average from Enfield in the tightest championship since 1965, with newly-promoted Dagenham third, six points behind. Tooting & Mitcham United finished in fourth, five points behind the Daggers. Walton & Hersham and Bromley both suffered relegation. In Division Two Staines Town were crowned champions whilst Southall, who the previous season had to apply for re-election, were promoted as runners-up. The bottom two in Division One, Aveley and Corinthian-Casuals, were not required to apply for re-election as the League had decided to increase its membership to 22 clubs.

The following 19 clubs applied for membership of the Isthmian League for the 1975–76 season: Addlestone & Weybridge, Cheshunt, Edmonton & Haringey, Egham Town, Erith & Belvedere, Eton Manor, Grays Athletic, Harrow Borough, Hoddesdon Town, Hornchurch, Letchworth Town, Lewes, Leyton, Marlow, Molesey, Rainham Town, Redhill, Ware and Wembley. A ballot was conducted which resulted as follows:

Wembley - 47, Ware - 40, Harrow Borough - 39, Hornchurch - 18, Letchworth Town - 12, Lewes - 11, Erith & Belvedere - 7, Cheshunt - 4, Marlow - 4, Leyton - 3, Egham - 2, Grays Athletic - 2, Edmonton & Haringey - 1, Hoddesdon Town - 1, Molesey - 1

Addlestone, Rainham Town and Redhill did not secure any votes while Eton Manor's application was not considered as they did not have a ground of their own. Wembley, Ware and Harrow Borough were recommended for election. However, it was decided to hold a second ballot for the fourth place. The four clubs receiving the next most votes were in the race and it finished as follows:

Hornchurch - 17, Letchworth Town - 11, Erith & Belvedere - 10, Lewes - 10

The League Council decided on a third vote, this time on a show of hands, to decide between Letchworth Town and Hornchurch. The result of this vote was Hornchurch 25, Letchworth Town 14.

Division I	1	2	3	4	5	6	7	8	9	10	11	12	13	14	15	16	17	18	19	20	21	22
1 Barking	*	2–2	2–0	0–1	1–2	0–5	1–2	3–6	1–3	2–1	0–2	4–1	2–1	1–1	0–2	1–0	2–4	0–1	5–0	3–1	2–1	1–1
2 Bishop's Stortford	2–1	*	3–0	2–1	0–2	0–2	3–1	2–2	2–1	0–1	2–3	3–1	0–1	2–0	1–3	2–1	3–0	1–5	0–2	1–0	2–2	1–1
3 Bromley	0–3	1–3	*	1–1	1–2	0–4	0–1	1–2	0–2	3–1	0–5	3–2	1–1	2–0	0–3	1–5	1–2	0–1	1–3	1–0	0–0	0–7
4 Clapton	2–2	1–0	1–2	*	1–3	3–2	0–3	2–1	1–0	3–2	0–2	2–1	0–8	3–0	1–2	0–5	1–0	1–3	2–1	5–0	1–0	1–2
5 Dagenham	3–2	4–0	4–1	2–0	*	4–1	0–2	2–1	4–1	7–0	1–1	1–0	1–1	3–2	3–0	1–2	3–0	1–1	2–0	8–1	2–1	1–0
6 Dulwich Hamlet	2–0	3–0	3–1	2–0	2–2	*	0–1	1–1	3–1	2–1	0–0	4–0	2–1	2–0	3–1	0–4	3–2	0–1	3–1	2–0	1–1	0–0
7 Enfield	3–0	1–0	2–0	3–0	4–1	1–1	*	1–0	5–0	2–1	1–0	4–0	0–1	2–1	3–1	0–0	0–0	4–1	1–1	5–0	1–0	2–2
8 Hayes	0–0	1–0	1–0	1–1	2–2	2–2	0–2	*	2–1	1–2	0–4	0–1	2–1	2–2	0–1	0–2	2–0	1–3	1–1	2–2	2–0	1–2
9 Hendon	2–2	1–0	1–0	1–1	1–2	0–1	0–1	1–1	*	1–0	2–2	1–2	2–2	1–0	2–1	3–2	3–1	2–4	2–1	4–2	4–1	1–2
10 Hitchin Town	3–1	2–4	2–1	3–1	1–0	2–2	2–2	2–1	1–1	*	1–0	3–1	1–1	1–0	1–1	2–1	1–2	3–3	1–0	3–4	3–1	0–1
11 Ilford	4–0	1–1	6–1	4–1	0–1	1–0	3–4	1–1	5–4	1–1	*	4–2	3–1	2–0	1–0	1–2	2–0	4–1	3–1	3–0	6–2	0–2
12 Kingstonian	1–0	2–4	0–1	5–0	3–1	0–1	0–1	2–1	1–2	1–1	1–3	*	0–2	0–2	0–2	1–1	2–1	1–1	0–1	2–0	1–3	3–2
13 Leatherhead	5–1	2–0	3–0	3–0	1–2	3–1	1–0	1–0	1–1	3–1	2–1	2–2	*	2–0	2–1	4–0	2–3	1–1	2–1	3–0	3–2	2–1
14 Leytonstone	0–3	0–1	5–0	2–1	1–0	0–3	0–2	1–0	3–0	4–1	2–2	0–1	2–0	*	2–2	1–0	2–4	1–2	1–1	2–0	1–0	0–2
15 Oxford City	3–3	1–0	4–0	2–1	1–0	0–1	1–1	1–1	1–0	1–1	2–2	2–0	1–4	0–1	*	1–0	0–4	2–1	2–0	6–0	1–3	0–1
16 Slough Town	1–2	1–3	3–0	2–0	2–3	0–1	0–1	2–3	1–2	6–1	2–1	3–2	2–1	2–0	2–1	*	3–0	1–1	1–0	2–3	0–1	1–1
17 Sutton United	1–1	0–1	2–0	4–1	1–3	2–0	1–2	0–1	4–1	0–1	3–0	3–2	1–0	1–0	3–3	1–0	*	1–1	1–1	2–1	2–0	2–2
18 Tooting & M Utd	4–0	2–1	2–0	9–0	3–2	0–3	0–2	2–1	2–0	2–0	0–1	2–0	0–0	2–1	2–1	2–1	2–1	*	1–4	2–1	2–0	1–1
19 Walthamstow Ave.	1–0	4–1	6–0	4–2	1–2	0–3	0–4	4–2	2–0	1–1	1–3	0–2	1–2	0–0	2–4	0–0	2–1	0–1	*	3–0	3–0	0–2
20 Walton & Hersham	0–2	1–3	1–0	2–0	0–5	1–1	2–0	5–1	2–1	1–0	1–6	0–1	0–5	2–1	0–0	0–2	1–5	0–3	2–2	*	1–4	0–4
21 Woking	2–0	1–1	4–1	3–2	0–3	0–2	2–1	1–1	0–3	1–2	2–2	0–1	1–1	3–1	2–1	3–3	2–1	1–2	0–0	2–0	*	0–4
22 Wycombe Wndrs.	5–1	3–0	8–0	2–1	1–0	1–1	0–0	2–2	5–0	2–0	3–3	2–0	1–0	5–1	2–1	1–0	3–2	2–1	1–0	1–0	3–0	*

Division I	P	W	D	L	F	A	Pts
1 Wycombe Wand	42	28	11	3	93	30	95
2 Enfield	42	29	8	5	78	26	95
3 Dagenham	42	28	5	9	95	44	89
4 Tooting & M Utd	42	25	9	8	78	46	84
5 Dulwich Hamlet	42	24	10	8	75	38	82
6 Leatherhead	42	23	10	9	83	42	79
7 Ilford	42	23	10	9	98	51	79
8 Oxford City	42	17	9	16	63	56	60
9 Slough Town	42	17	6	19	68	52	57
10 Sutton United	42	17	6	19	68	63	57
11 Bishop's Stortford	42	17	6	19	56	64	57
12 Hitchin Town	42	15	10	17	57	71	55
13 Hendon	42	15	7	20	59	74	52
14 Walthamstow Ave.	42	13	9	20	56	62	48
15 Woking	42	12	10	20	53	73	46
16 Hayes	42	10	14	18	52	66	44
17 Barking	42	12	8	22	57	81	44
18 Leytonstone	42	12	7	23	42	61	43
19 Kingstonian	42	13	4	25	48	73	43
20 Clapton	42	12	4	26	46	96	40
21 Walton & Hersham	42	9	4	29	37	108	31
22 Bromley	42	6	3	33	25	110	21

Below: The Enfield FC handbook for 1974/75.

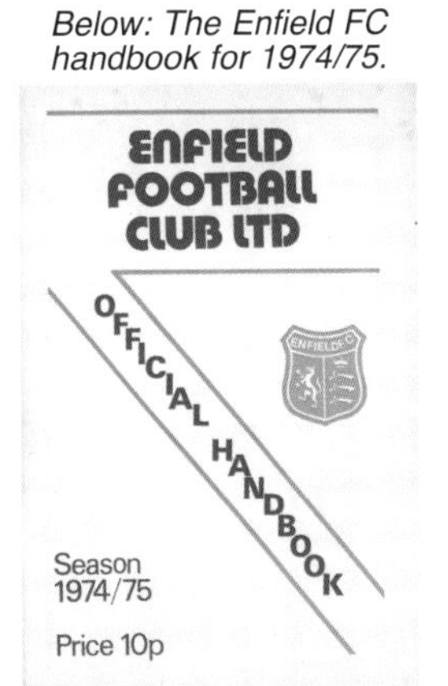

Below: Slough Town's programme from 1974-75.

Division II	1	2	3	4	5	6	7	8	9	10	11	12	13	14	15	16	17	18
1 Aveley	*	2–1	0–2	3–1	0–5	0–0	2–0	1–0	2–0	0–1	1–1	2–2	2–1	2–2	2–3	2–1	1–2	0–3
2 Boreham Wood	1–1	*	4–1	1–1	1–0	1–1	0–1	0–0	1–1	1–2	2–1	1–1	1–2	2–1	2–0	0–1	1–2	3–2
3 Carshalton Athletic	3–2	2–2	*	2–1	1–1	0–0	2–2	1–1	0–1	1–0	1–0	3–1	0–4	0–0	1–2	0–6	1–2	2–0
4 Chesham United	5–0	1–1	1–2	*	4–3	0–1	2–0	1–0	4–0	4–1	1–2	4–3	1–0	2–0	1–0	1–0	4–0	1–1
5 Corinthian-Casuals	1–0	1–2	1–0	0–1	*	2–2	2–2	0–3	1–2	2–0	1–1	0–4	1–0	1–1	2–3	0–2	0–5	1–0
6 Croydon	3–1	0–0	0–2	2–3	2–2	*	2–1	1–1	4–1	1–0	1–3	5–1	1–2	1–3	0–1	2–1	0–3	1–1
7 Finchley	1–0	2–2	2–2	4–2	2–3	2–2	*	2–1	1–0	1–2	1–1	2–1	1–2	0–1	3–1	0–1	1–2	1–1
8 Hampton	3–1	2–1	3–1	1–0	2–2	1–2	0–1	*	3–2	3–0	3–0	0–1	3–0	1–1	0–1	0–0	1–1	2–1
9 Harlow Town	3–3	1–1	3–0	4–2	1–0	0–2	5–0	2–1	*	3–0	2–1	2–0	1–3	3–1	3–5	2–0	2–1	2–0
10 Harwich & Parkst.	3–1	3–1	3–1	1–1	4–0	1–3	3–1	1–0	5–0	*	0–2	2–0	1–1	0–0	2–0	1–4	3–1	3–1
11 Hertford Town	2–0	1–0	0–2	1–1	1–3	3–1	1–1	2–1	0–3	1–2	*	3–1	2–1	1–2	0–2	0–5	1–2	1–2
12 Horsham	5–0	2–0	3–1	0–2	1–0	4–2	2–0	2–0	0–0	1–0	2–1	*	1–1	1–1	2–3	0–2	5–3	3–1
13 Maidenhead Utd	2–0	2–2	2–1	0–3	1–0	2–3	0–1	1–4	1–0	1–1	2–0	1–3	*	0–1	2–0	2–0	1–1	0–0
14 St. Albans City	2–0	3–3	1–1	1–0	0–0	1–0	1–0	4–1	0–0	2–0	3–0	1–2	0–1	*	1–0	2–1	2–1	0–1
15 Southall	0–1	2–1	3–1	1–2	0–0	3–1	2–0	0–1	1–0	4–1	1–0	3–2	3–0	2–2	*	2–0	1–0	2–0
16 Staines Town	3–0	6–1	1–0	1–0	2–0	2–2	2–0	4–1	2–0	0–1	2–0	1–0	1–0	6–0	2–1	*	2–1	2–0
17 Tilbury	1–1	0–0	3–0	2–1	4–0	4–0	3–0	2–0	2–0	1–2	0–1	2–1	0–0	4–1	4–1	2–0	*	3–1
18 Wokingham Town	0–1	0–1	2–1	1–0	5–0	3–0	0–0	3–1	0–2	1–3	0–0	0–2	1–0	0–1	0–2	0–2	1–0	*

Division II	P	W	D	L	F	A	Pts
1 Staines Town	34	23	2	9	65	23	71
2 Southall	34	20	3	11	55	41	63
3 Tilbury*	34	19	5	10	64	36	60
4 Harwich & Parkst.	34	18	4	12	52	44	58
5 Chesham United	34	17	6	11	59	39	57
6 St. Albans City	34	15	11	8	42	37	56
7 Harlow Town	34	16	6	12	53	47	54
8 Horsham	34	16	5	13	59	49	53
9 Maidenhead Utd	34	17	7	14	38	40	46
10 Hampton	34	12	7	15	44	42	43
11 Croydon	34	11	10	13	48	55	43
12 Hertford Town	34	10	7	17	35	52	37
13 Boreham Wood	34	7	15	12	41	49	36
14 Wokingham Town	34	10	6	18	32	43	36
15 Finchley	34	9	9	16	36	53	36
16 Carshalton Athletic	34	9	9	16	38	58	36
17 Aveley	34	9	7	18	34	63	34
18 Corinthian-Casuals	34	8	9	17	35	59	33

** Tilbury had 2 points deducted.*

Above right: Boreham Wood's programme for the 1974-75 season.

Left: the Bromley programme from the same season.

Right: Dagenham's programme from that season.

1975–76 - Enfield, narrow runners-up the previous season, clinched the title by five points from defending champions Wycombe Wanderers. Dagenham were again third, only a point behind the Chairboys, while Ilford enjoyed an excellent season, finishing five points adrift of Dagenham in fourth. At the other end of the table Oxford City and Clapton were relegated – with the latter only winning three matches all season.

In Division Two Tilbury amassed 102 points to win the title, four points clear of runners-up Croydon, who went through the whole League season undefeated, but they did draw 14 of their matches. This was only the second time in the entire 100 years when a club did not lose a League match - the first occasion was 1906-07 when Ilford only played ten matches. This emphasises the achievement of Croydon and the fact that they were only runners-up must have been a source of frustration.

Action from Enfield's 1-0 victory over Hendon at Southbury Road.

Hertford Town and Corinthian-Casuals, the bottom two clubs, both successfully applied for re-election at the Annual General Meeting, although Corinthian-Casuals – who had finished bottom of their division for six straight seasons – were warned that if they finished in a re-election position in 1976–77 they would probably not get re-elected. There were 13 applicants to join the League, including Egham Town, Erith & Belvedere, Hounslow, Molesey and Rainham Town, but a proposal to further expand League membership was rejected.

1975-76 Division I	1	2	3	4	5	6	7	8	9	10	11	12	13	14	15	16	17	18	19	20	21	22
1 Barking	*	3–1	3–0	1–2	2–1	1–1	3–0	1–2	1–0	1–1	1–0	1–2	0–1	2–1	1–0	2–1	2–1	2–3	1–1	2–1	1–0	1–2
2 Bishop's Stortford	0–0	*	4–0	2–0	1–3	2–3	0–0	1–3	1–2	0–0	0–0	3–2	2–0	2–0	1–0	1–1	1–0	5–2	0–2	1–0	2–2	2–2
3 Clapton	4–3	0–1	*	0–3	0–2	0–3	0–1	0–1	0–2	1–2	1–3	0–7	1–1	1–0	0–1	1–2	0–1	1–4	0–1	0–3	1–5	0–0
4 Dagenham	3–4	2–1	5–0	*	1–0	1–0	4–2	3–2	1–0	0–1	1–1	2–2	1–1	3–0	3–0	4–0	3–0	3–2	2–1	1–4	2–2	1–0
5 Dulwich Hamlet	3–2	1–0	2–0	2–1	*	2–3	1–1	0–2	0–2	3–0	3–1	4–0	2–0	1–0	2–0	0–1	2–1	1–1	0–1	0–0	1–0	0–1
6 Enfield	5–1	2–0	8–0	1–2	4–1	*	2–1	1–0	1–1	1–0	0–1	1–2	2–0	1–0	2–2	3–1	3–0	0–0	3–2	4–0	1–0	0–0
7 Hayes	5–1	2–0	1–0	0–2	1–0	2–4	*	1–1	1–1	0–0	2–2	2–2	1–1	1–1	1–1	2–2	0–0	0–0	1–0	0–0	1–2	0–1
8 Hendon	2–0	1–0	2–2	1–0	0–0	1–2	0–1	*	2–1	2–0	0–1	1–0	1–0	5–0	2–0	4–2	1–1	1–2	3–0	1–1	0–0	2–0
9 Hitchin Town	1–1	0–1	5–1	1–5	1–4	0–3	0–0	0–0	*	1–4	1–3	1–0	1–0	2–2	2–1	1–2	0–2	1–1	1–1	3–0	2–1	2–0
10 Ilford	2–1	1–0	3–0	2–2	2–1	2–2	2–1	4–0	0–0	*	1–0	1–0	0–1	2–0	2–0	1–0	2–0	3–1	1–1	2–0	2–1	1–3
11 Kingstonian	3–2	2–2	3–1	1–7	0–5	0–3	1–4	0–0	1–2	1–3	*	3–3	2–1	3–0	2–1	2–1	2–1	0–4	1–3	1–2	3–1	0–1
12 Leatherhead	2–1	1–1	2–0	3–1	2–2	1–0	0–0	0–1	2–0	3–1	3–3	*	2–0	1–0	0–0	2–1	2–0	2–2	3–1	0–2	0–1	1–0
13 Leytonstone	0–0	0–2	3–1	1–1	1–3	0–1	2–0	3–1	2–0	1–2	2–2	3–0	*	0–2	0–2	0–0	3–0	0–5	0–5	1–2	0–1	1–2
14 Oxford City	3–1	0–1	0–2	0–1	2–1	0–2	1–1	0–2	3–1	0–2	0–2	0–2	0–3	*	2–0	0–0	1–0	1–0	0–2	2–3	1–2	4–1
15 Slough Town	2–1	1–0	5–0	3–1	1–0	0–2	1–1	0–2	1–1	1–1	4–1	2–0	2–0	2–1	*	2–0	0–0	0–0	1–1	1–1	4–1	4–3
16 Southall & E Boro	3–0	2–3	5–0	1–2	0–1	0–0	0–1	2–2	2–1	3–1	4–1	1–2	0–1	1–2	1–4	*	0–1	1–2	2–1	1–1	5–1	1–1
17 Staines Town	2–1	1–0	1–0	0–3	2–1	0–0	0–0	1–1	0–0	1–0	3–0	5–0	3–1	4–1	1–1	0–2	*	1–0	3–0	3–0	1–0	0–1
18 Sutton United	3–2	2–2	1–0	0–3	2–5	2–2	3–2	1–3	0–2	0–1	1–0	3–0	3–0	0–1	3–2	7–1	0–2	*	0–3	3–1	1–1	3–1
19 Tooting & M Utd	0–1	1–1	4–1	3–1	2–1	5–0	3–1	2–2	4–1	1–1	2–0	0–3	2–2	1–1	1–0	3–0	1–1	2–2	*	2–1	2–0	0–1
20 Walthamstow Ave.	2–0	1–3	2–0	2–3	0–3	2–4	2–1	1–0	0–1	2–1	1–0	0–2	1–1	0–0	2–2	2–1	0–1	0–0	1–0	*	1–1	2–5
21 Woking	0–3	1–0	2–0	2–1	0–2	1–2	0–1	3–1	2–1	2–0	6–1	2–2	1–1	4–0	0–3	3–3	0–1	0–1	2–4	3–1	*	1–2
22 Wycombe Wndrs.	4–0	1–1	5–0	6–2	0–1	2–1	2–1	4–2	1–0	1–1	4–0	1–0	4–3	0–0	0–1	1–0	2–1	2–1	3–2	0–0	1–1	*

Division I	P	W	D	L	F	A	Pts
1 Enfield	42	26	9	7	83	38	87
2 Wycombe Wand	42	24	10	8	71	41	82
3 Dagenham	42	25	6	11	89	55	81
4 Ilford	42	22	10	10	58	39	76
5 Dulwich Hamlet	42	22	5	15	67	41	71
6 Hendon	42	20	11	11	60	41	71
7 Tooting & M Utd	42	19	11	12	73	49	68
8 Leatherhead	42	19	10	13	63	53	67
9 Staines Town	42	19	9	14	46	37	66
10 Slough Town	42	17	12	13	58	45	63
11 Sutton United	42	17	11	14	71	60	62
12 Bishop's Stortford	42	15	12	15	51	47	57
13 Walthamstow Ave.	42	14	11	17	47	60	53
14 Woking	42	14	9	19	58	62	51
15 Barking	42	15	6	21	57	70	51
16 Hitchin Town	42	13	11	18	45	57	50
17 Hayes	42	10	19	13	44	48	49
18 Kingstonian	42	13	8	21	53	87	47
19 Southall & E Boro	42	11	9	22	56	69	42
20 Leytonstone	42	10	10	22	41	63	40
21 Oxford City	42	9	8	25	29	65	35
22 Clapton	42	3	3	36	19	112	12

Southall & Ealing Borough previously Southall.

Below left: Harrow Borough's programme for their first season.

Below right: The 1975-76 season saw Oxford City introduce a continental style newspaper as their matchday programme.

JARRETT & CORDERY

L. MARTELL LTD.

HARROW BOROUGH FOOTBALL CLUB

Debenhams of Harrow Ltd

01-427 4300

ONLY 5 MINUTES FROM HARROW-ON-THE-HILL STATION

OXFORD CITY news

H & L TEXTILES

Makers of fine curtains.

WELCOME! to Oxford City Football Club

by JOHN SHEPPERD

Editor, Oxford City News

JOHN WOODLEY, A MAN OF MANY TALENTS

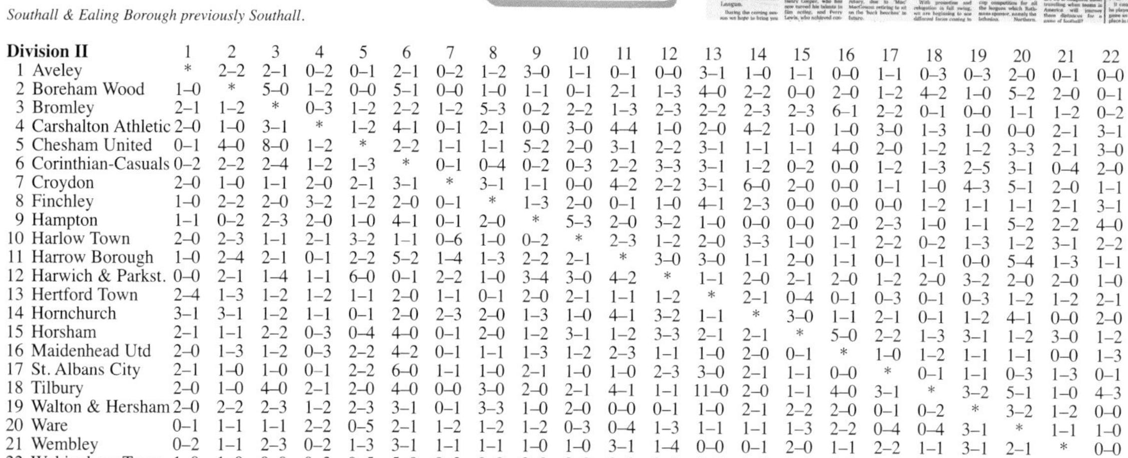

Division II	1	2	3	4	5	6	7	8	9	10	11	12	13	14	15	16	17	18	19	20	21	22
1 Aveley	*	2–2	2–1	0–2	0–1	2–1	0–2	1–2	3–0	1–1	0–1	0–0	3–1	1–0	1–1	0–0	1–1	0–3	0–3	2–0	0–1	0–0
2 Boreham Wood	1–0	*	5–0	1–2	0–0	5–1	0–0	1–0	1–1	0–1	2–1	1–3	4–0	2–2	0–0	2–0	1–2	4–2	1–0	5–2	2–0	0–1
3 Bromley	2–1	1–2	*	0–3	1–2	2–2	1–2	5–3	0–2	2–2	1–3	2–3	2–2	2–3	2–3	6–1	2–2	0–1	0–0	1–1	1–2	0–2
4 Carshalton Athletic	2–0	1–0	3–1	*	1–2	4–1	0–1	2–1	0–0	3–0	4–4	1–0	2–0	4–2	1–0	1–0	3–0	1–3	1–0	0–0	2–1	3–1
5 Chesham United	0–1	4–0	8–0	1–2	*	2–2	1–1	1–1	5–2	2–0	3–1	2–2	3–1	1–1	1–1	4–0	2–0	1–2	1–2	3–3	2–1	3–0
6 Corinthian-Casuals	0–2	2–2	2–4	1–2	1–3	*	0–1	0–4	0–2	0–3	2–2	3–3	3–1	1–2	0–2	0–0	1–2	1–3	2–5	3–1	0–4	2–0
7 Croydon	2–0	1–0	1–1	2–0	2–1	3–1	*	3–1	1–1	0–0	4–2	2–2	3–1	6–0	2–0	0–0	1–1	1–0	4–3	5–1	2–0	1–1
8 Finchley	1–0	2–2	2–0	3–2	1–2	2–0	0–1	*	1–3	2–0	0–1	1–0	4–1	2–3	0–0	0–0	0–0	1–2	1–1	1–1	2–1	3–1
9 Hampton	1–1	0–2	2–3	2–0	1–0	4–1	0–1	2–0	*	5–3	2–0	3–2	1–0	0–0	0–0	2–0	2–3	1–0	1–1	5–2	2–2	4–0
10 Harlow Town	2–0	2–3	1–1	2–1	3–2	1–1	0–6	1–0	0–2	*	2–3	1–2	2–0	3–3	1–0	1–1	2–2	0–2	1–3	1–2	3–1	2–2
11 Harrow Borough	1–0	2–4	2–1	0–1	2–2	5–2	1–4	1–3	2–2	2–1	*	3–0	3–0	1–1	2–0	1–1	0–1	1–1	0–0	5–4	1–3	1–1
12 Harwich & Parkst.	0–0	2–1	1–4	1–1	6–0	0–1	2–2	1–0	3–4	3–0	4–2	*	1–1	2–0	2–1	2–0	1–2	2–0	3–2	2–0	2–0	1–0
13 Hertford Town	2–4	1–3	1–2	1–2	1–1	2–0	1–1	0–1	2–0	2–1	1–1	1–2	*	2–1	0–4	0–1	0–3	0–1	0–3	1–2	1–2	2–1
14 Hornchurch	3–1	3–1	1–2	1–1	0–1	2–0	2–3	2–0	1–3	1–0	4–1	3–2	1–1	*	3–0	1–1	2–1	0–1	1–2	4–1	0–0	2–0
15 Horsham	2–1	1–1	2–2	0–3	0–4	4–0	0–1	2–0	1–2	3–1	1–2	3–3	2–1	2–1	*	5–0	2–2	1–3	3–1	1–2	3–0	1–2
16 Maidenhead Utd	2–0	1–3	1–2	0–3	2–2	4–2	0–1	1–1	1–3	1–2	2–3	1–1	1–0	2–0	0–1	*	1–0	1–2	1–1	1–1	0–0	1–3
17 St. Albans City	2–1	1–0	1–0	0–1	2–2	6–0	1–1	1–0	2–1	1–0	1–0	2–3	3–0	2–1	1–1	0–0	*	0–1	1–1	0–3	1–3	0–1
18 Tilbury	2–0	1–0	4–0	2–1	2–0	4–0	0–0	3–0	2–0	2–1	4–1	1–1	11–0	2–0	1–1	4–0	3–1	*	3–2	5–1	1–0	4–3
19 Walton & Hersham	2–0	2–2	2–3	1–2	2–3	3–1	0–1	3–3	1–0	2–0	0–0	0–1	1–0	2–1	2–2	2–0	0–1	0–2	*	3–2	1–2	0–0
20 Ware	0–1	1–1	1–1	2–2	0–5	2–1	1–2	1–2	1–2	0–3	0–4	1–3	1–1	1–1	1–3	2–2	0–4	0–4	3–1	*	1–1	1–0
21 Wembley	0–2	1–1	2–3	0–2	1–3	3–1	1–1	1–1	1–0	1–0	3–1	1–4	0–0	0–1	2–0	1–1	2–2	1–1	3–1	2–1	*	0–0
22 Wokingham Town	1–0	1–0	0–0	0–3	0–5	5–0	0–3	0–0	3–2	3–0	2–2	3–0	0–0	1–1	1–1	0–0	2–1	2–2	0–0	1–0	1–1	*

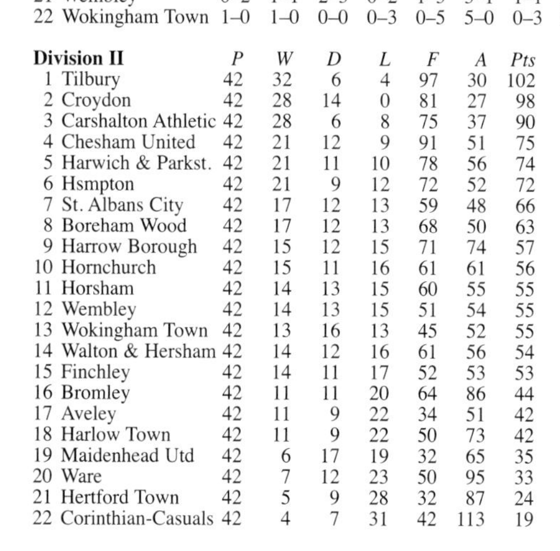

Division II	P	W	D	L	F	A	Pts
1 Tilbury	42	32	6	4	97	30	102
2 Croydon	42	28	14	0	81	27	98
3 Carshalton Athletic	42	28	6	8	75	37	90
4 Chesham United	42	21	12	9	91	51	75
5 Harwich & Parkst.	42	21	11	10	78	56	74
6 Hsmpton	42	21	9	12	72	52	72
7 St. Albans City	42	17	12	13	59	48	66
8 Boreham Wood	42	17	12	13	68	50	63
9 Harrow Borough	42	15	12	15	71	74	57
10 Hornchurch	42	15	11	16	61	61	56
11 Horsham	42	14	13	15	60	55	55
12 Wembley	42	14	13	15	51	54	55
13 Wokingham Town	42	13	16	13	45	52	55
14 Walton & Hersham	42	14	12	16	61	56	54
15 Finchley	42	14	11	17	52	53	53
16 Bromley	42	11	11	20	64	86	44
17 Aveley	42	11	9	22	34	51	42
18 Harlow Town	42	11	9	22	50	73	42
19 Maidenhead Utd	42	6	17	19	32	65	35
20 Ware	42	7	12	23	50	95	33
21 Hertford Town	42	5	9	28	32	87	24
22 Corinthian-Casuals	42	4	7	31	42	113	19

Although pipped for the 1975-76 championship, the Croydon team became the first team in seventy years to remain unbeaten throughout a campaign and suffered just one caution in 42 matches!

1976–77 - Early in the season Rothmans Ltd made a decision to withdraw their sponsorship of the Isthmian League at the end of 1976–77 for economic reasons.

A sub-committee on the future of the Rothmans Isthmian League, at their meeting in November, agreed to recommend to the League Council that a third division be formed. After a long discussion the League Council voted and agreed, 43–1, to form a third division for 1977–78 consisting of not more than 18 clubs.

A total of 38 clubs applied to join the new division and, after ground inspections, the following clubs were recommended for election at the Annual General Meeting: Camberley Town, Cheshunt, Eastbourne United, Egham Town, Epping Town, Epsom & Ewell, Farnborough Town, Feltham, Hemel Hempstead, Letchworth Garden City, Lewes, Metropolitan Police, Milton Keynes City, Molesey, Rainham Town, Tring Town, Willesden and Worthing. Milton Keynes City later withdrew their application and although several more clubs were interested in joining the League, the League Council decided to operate with only 17 clubs. It was decided that from 1977–78, the divisions would be named Premier Division, Division One and Division Two.

On the field, the top three in the Division One championship race were the same for the third consecutive season, with the 1975–76 finishing order being repeated. Enfield thus retained their title – their fifth championship – from runners-up Wycombe Wanderers, a point behind, with Dagenham in third, four points adrift. Hendon finished in fourth, while Tilbury – in their first year in the top division – finished a creditable fifth. At the bottom, Dulwich Hamlet and Ilford suffered relegation to Division Two, being replaced by Division Two champions Boreham Wood, who obtained 103 points, and runners-up Carshalton Athletic. With a new third division being introduced, the bottom two clubs, Finchley and Ware, were both re-elected at the Annual General Meeting.

Division I	1	2	3	4	5	6	7	8	9	10	11	12	13	14	15	16	17	18	19	20	21	22
1 Barking	*	5–2	0–1	0–1	1–1	0–1	1–2	1–1	0–1	1–0	1–0	3–1	1–0	3–0	3–0	2–2	2–1	2–2	2–3	2–1	1–2	0–2
2 Bishop's Stortford	2–2	*	2–2	0–0	1–2	2–0	2–1	1–0	2–3	0–1	0–1	2–3	0–2	1–2	1–1	1–1	2–0	2–2	5–0	1–2	1–2	1–1
3 Croydon	2–1	4–1	*	1–0	2–1	0–0	4–0	0–0	1–3	1–0	1–2	0–2	0–0	0–0	1–1	1–0	1–2	0–0	2–2	2–1	0–2	1–0
4 Dagenham	4–2	6–0	5–0	*	3–1	3–2	3–2	1–1	4–0	1–1	5–1	1–0	0–1	1–0	2–1	2–2	2–0	0–1	5–1	0–1	0–0	2–1
5 Dulwich Hamlet	0–2	5–1	3–1	0–1	*	2–3	1–2	0–3	4–2	2–0	1–1	1–3	1–3	0–1	0–1	1–2	2–2	1–1	2–4	1–1	2–1	0–1
6 Enfield	1–0	1–0	2–0	1–1	2–0	*	2–1	1–1	2–0	1–1	4–1	2–0	1–1	1–1	4–0	2–1	1–0	1–2	3–1	1–0	1–0	0–2
7 Hayes	2–4	0–1	1–0	1–1	1–1	0–3	*	2–2	3–0	1–0	0–0	1–0	2–0	3–2	3–1	0–2	1–2	3–1	0–0	0–3	1–1	0–1
8 Hendon	0–3	1–2	1–0	2–1	0–1	3–1	2–1	*	0–3	0–0	1–0	2–1	0–1	2–1	0–3	2–0	3–0	4–1	0–0	3–1	1–1	3–0
9 Hitchin Town	1–0	1–0	1–2	3–0	3–2	0–1	1–0	0–0	*	5–2	4–2	1–1	2–1	0–3	2–2	0–2	2–1	0–3	3–2	1–1	2–0	1–2
10 Ilford	2–2	0–0	3–0	1–2	0–2	0–2	2–1	0–3	1–3	*	1–0	0–2	1–2	0–1	1–2	1–4	1–0	0–1	0–4	3–2	1–0	1–1
11 Kingstonian	1–2	2–0	1–0	1–3	0–1	1–1	3–3	2–0	3–0	1–1	*	0–1	2–0	0–1	3–0	2–1	0–1	0–0	2–0	0–1	1–0	1–3
12 Leatherhead	1–1	2–0	1–0	0–0	1–2	1–1	4–3	3–1	3–0	4–0	0–1	*	1–2	3–0	3–2	0–2	3–1	1–2	1–1	2–0	0–1	0–0
13 Leytonstone	2–0	1–2	1–3	2–1	4–0	1–1	1–1	0–1	2–1	5–0	3–2	2–1	*	0–0	1–2	3–2	3–1	1–2	1–1	1–4	1–0	1–3
14 Slough Town	3–0	2–1	1–1	1–1	2–0	1–3	0–0	0–2	0–1	2–1	3–0	2–1	2–1	*	3–2	0–1	2–1	0–1	1–1	0–0	4–2	3–2
15 Southall & E Boro	2–2	3–4	2–1	1–0	2–1	0–2	3–0	1–2	1–0	0–1	2–1	1–4	3–1	2–0	*	1–1	2–0	0–0	0–0	3–0	0–1	1–2
16 Staines Town	1–1	2–0	1–0	0–3	1–0	1–1	1–2	3–1	1–5	0–1	3–0	1–0	0–0	1–1	1–1	*	0–1	2–2	1–0	1–1	1–0	1–1
17 Sutton United	1–0	1–1	0–0	3–3	0–2	1–2	2–0	2–0	1–0	0–1	2–2	1–2	1–1	1–0	1–0	0–1	*	0–2	0–0	2–1	1–2	1–0
18 Tilbury	0–1	1–1	0–0	0–2	1–0	2–0	3–1	2–2	2–2	3–1	1–3	1–0	3–3	1–4	4–0	2–0	2–0	*	0–1	0–2	2–0	0–2
19 Tooting & M Utd	7–3	1–2	3–2	3–1	3–2	1–2	4–1	2–1	5–0	5–2	4–2	2–1	4–0	3–0	3–0	1–2	2–4	3–1	*	2–4	1–1	2–3
20 Walthamstow Ave.	0–3	2–0	2–0	0–2	1–1	0–1	3–0	3–5	3–1	3–0	1–0	1–3	1–1	0–2	2–1	2–0	1–0	2–0	1–1	*	1–2	3–2
21 Woking	2–3	1–2	0–1	0–5	0–2	2–2	2–2	2–4	1–1	0–0	2–0	2–0	3–3	1–0	1–2	1–1	0–2	2–2	5–0	1–3	*	0–3
22 Wycombe Wndrs.	3–0	2–2	3–0	1–2	3–1	0–0	0–1	1–0	0–1	4–0	2–0	1–1	1–0	1–0	2–0	3–2	3–0	0–0	4–2	4–0	1–0	*

Division I	*P*	*W*	*D*	*L*	*F*	*A*	*Pts*
1 Enfield	42	24	12	6	63	34	84
2 Wycombe Wand	42	25	8	9	71	34	83
3 Dagenham	42	23	10	9	80	39	79
4 Hendon	42	19	10	13	60	48	67
5 Tilbury	42	18	13	11	57	49	67
6 Tooting & M Utd	42	18	10	14	85	72	64
7 Walthamstow Ave.	42	19	7	16	61	55	64
8 Slough Town	42	18	9	15	51	46	63
9 Hitchin Town	42	19	6	17	60	66	63
10 Leatherhead	42	18	7	17	61	47	61
11 Staines Town	42	16	13	13	52	48	61
12 Leytonstone	42	16	11	15	59	57	59
13 Barking	42	16	9	17	63	61	57
14 Southall & E Boro	42	15	8	19	52	64	53
15 Croydon	42	13	10	19	38	52	49
16 Sutton United	42	14	7	21	40	55	49
17 Kingstonian	42	13	7	22	45	60	46
18 Hayes	42	12	10	20	49	69	46
19 Woking	42	11	12	19	47	61	45
20 Bishop's Stortford	42	11	11	20	51	71	44
21 Dulwich Hamlet	42	11	8	23	52	68	41
22 Ilford	42	10	8	24	32	73	38

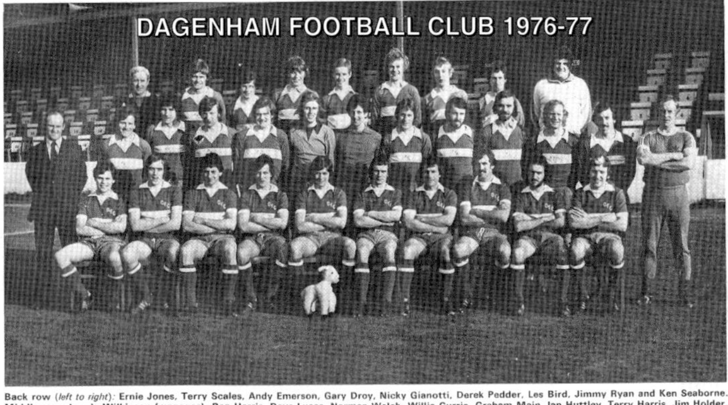

Back row (*left to right*): Ernie Jones, Terry Scales, Andy Emerson, Gary Droy, Nicky Gianotti, Derek Pedder, Les Bird, Jimmy Ryan and Ken Seaborne.
Middle row: Laurie Wilkinson (manager), Reg Harris, Dave Lucas, Norman Welch, Willie Currie, Graham Main, Ian Huttley, Terry Harris, Jim Holder, Joe Dunwell, Frank Saul, Ken Gray and Brian Kelly.
Front row: John Roche, Paul Currie, Peter Wellman, Paul Madden, Denis Moore (captain), John Borland, Jim Lye, Nevil Fox, Lewis Brook and Mal Harkin.

Division II	1	2	3	4	5	6	7	8	9	10	11	12	13	14	15	16	17	18	19	20	21	22
1 Aveley	*	0–1	1–0	0–0	2–0	1–0	2–1	0–1	0–1	2–1	0–2	2–3	1–1	1–0	0–0	2–0	2–3	0–1	1–0	1–1	0–2	1–0
2 Boreham Wood	1–0	*	2–0	0–0	3–2	3–1	3–0	1–0	2–1	1–0	1–0	4–1	6–1	3–0	5–1	2–0	1–0	2–1	1–0	3–1	2–1	0–1
3 Bromley	2–3	1–3	*	0–1	2–0	5–0	1–1	3–0	1–1	5–1	1–1	1–3	1–0	3–1	1–1	4–0	2–1	2–2	4–1	4–1	0–0	0–0
4 Carshalton Athletic	3–0	1–0	3–1	*	4–0	6–1	6–0	3–1	1–1	2–0	1–0	0–0	2–0	2–2	1–1	3–1	0–3	5–2	4–2	2–0	2–1	2–0
5 Chesham United	4–5	1–1	1–2	1–1	*	1–0	1–0	4–0	0–4	1–0	2–0	2–3	2–2	1–1	1–0	3–0	2–0	1–0	0–1	2–2	0–2	1–1
6 Clapton	2–1	0–2	0–2	2–2	2–2	*	1–3	0–0	0–4	3–1	0–2	1–2	1–0	2–2	4–1	1–3	1–1	1–3	2–0	2–5	1–2	0–2
7 Corinthian-Casuals	4–2	0–2	1–1	2–2	1–2	4–0	*	3–0	1–0	1–2	1–4	4–0	0–2	3–2	1–3	1–0	1–2	0–3	0–1	4–1	1–2	2–6
8 Finchley	1–1	1–3	1–2	0–1	1–1	1–1	2–0	*	0–0	1–1	2–2	2–3	0–3	1–2	2–3	1–1	3–2	1–0	3–3	1–1	1–0	1–1
9 Hampton	3–0	2–2	0–1	0–2	0–0	1–0	2–0	4–1	*	2–1	1–0	1–3	3–0	2–1	3–1	3–2	2–0	0–0	1–1	4–3	0–2	1–1
10 Harlow Town	1–1	1–2	2–0	0–1	1–2	1–1	0–3	2–1	1–2	*	0–0	1–1	1–0	2–1	0–3	1–0	0–4	0–1	1–3	1–0	0–1	1–1
11 Harrow Borough	2–1	1–0	0–3	1–1	3–2	1–0	3–0	5–1	1–0	2–3	*	3–1	4–1	2–1	3–0	1–1	3–0	0–0	1–2	5–0	2–1	1–1
12 Harwich & Parkst.	2–2	0–2	2–3	1–1	2–2	3–0	7–2	3–0	1–2	5–1	0–5	*	7–1	3–0	4–0	4–0	3–1	3–1	0–1	4–0	2–2	3–0
13 Hertford Town	3–2	1–1	0–2	1–2	0–3	2–0	1–1	3–1	0–1	0–2	0–2	1–1	*	0–1	4–1	1–1	1–0	0–3	2–0	1–1	2–3	1–1
14 Hornchurch	2–0	1–2	1–0	2–0	0–1	3–3	1–0	1–1	1–0	2–1	2–3	0–1	4–1	*	0–1	6–0	1–2	2–1	3–0	0–1	0–2	2–0
15 Horsham	2–1	1–0	2–2	0–2	7–3	2–1	0–1	3–1	2–1	1–2	1–1	1–0	2–0	1–2	*	4–1	3–0	1–0	2–0	3–0	3–1	2–0
16 Maidenhead Utd	3–0	0–2	1–2	0–1	1–2	1–1	0–1	3–1	3–1	1–1	2–1	1–2	1–1	0–1	1–3	*	0–1	0–1	2–2	3–0	1–0	0–2
17 Oxford City	0–1	1–0	1–1	2–0	1–4	4–1	2–1	3–0	2–1	9–0	2–3	3–1	2–0	3–3	2–0	1–1	*	1–1	0–1	3–1	3–2	2–1
18 St. Albans City	1–3	0–3	1–3	0–5	5–1	2–1	0–1	3–0	3–2	2–2	1–1	4–1	1–0	0–2	0–1	1–0	1–1	*	2–0	4–0	1–1	1–1
19 Walton & Hersham	2–2	1–2	1–0	1–1	1–0	1–2	0–0	2–0	2–1	4–0	1–1	0–1	3–1	1–0	2–0	3–0	3–0	1–2	*	4–1	3–4	0–5
20 Ware	2–4	1–3	0–1	1–0	0–1	0–1	1–1	0–0	1–2	1–2	0–3	2–4	0–5	0–1	0–2	3–0	1–3	2–2	2–2	*	1–2	5–2
21 Wembley	2–0	0–1	4–2	3–2	2–3	3–2	2–1	3–1	0–1	2–1	5–2	2–2	4–2	2–4	3–1	2–0	1–1	1–1	2–1	4–1	*	2–2
22 Wokingham Town	2–1	1–2	1–0	0–2	3–1	2–1	3–0	2–0	2–1	2–0	1–1	0–1	6–0	1–1	0–1	0–1	1–1	1–1	0–0	2–0	2–1	*

1976-77 Division II	P	W	D	L	F	A	Pts
1 Boreham Wood	42	33	4	5	80	26	103
2 Carshalton Athletic	42	25	12	5	80	33	87
3 Harwich & Parkst.	42	23	8	11	93	61	77
4 Wembley	42	23	8	11	82	58	77
5 Harrow Borough	42	21	12	9	78	44	75
6 Horsham	42	23	5	14	67	56	74
7 Bromley	42	20	10	12	71	46	70
8 Oxford City	42	20	8	14	73	55	68
9 Hampton	42	20	8	14	62	45	68
10 Wokingham Town	42	16	14	12	60	44	62
11 Hornchurch	42	18	7	17	62	53	61
12 Chesham United	42	17	10	15	63	66	61
13 St. Albans City	42	16	12	14	59	53	60
14 Walton & Hersham	42	17	9	16	57	56	60
15 Aveley	42	14	8	20	49	62	50
16 Corinthian-Casuals	42	13	6	23	52	75	45
17 Harlow Town	42	11	8	23	39	77	41
18 Hertford Town	42	9	9	24	45	80	36
19 Maidenhead Utd	42	8	8	26	36	73	32
20 Clapton	42	7	9	28	43	87	30
21 Finchley	42	5	13	24	36	82	28
22 Ware	42	5	8	29	43	98	23

LEATHERHEAD F.C.

1977-78

Back Row *(left to right)* Dave Wall (coach), John Deary (physiotherapist), John Bailey, Colin Brooks, John Swannell, Dave Reid, Paul Whittaker, John Baker, Billy Salkeld, John Cooper, Billy Miller (manager).
Front Row *(left to right)* John Doyle, Micky Cook, Chris Kelly, Dennis Malley (captain), Ray Eaton, Barrie Davies, Kevin Mansell.

1977–78 - Enfield made a tremendous start to the season and never looked back, completing a hat-trick of championships, accumulating 110 points with just two defeats in the campaign, the first in which the top flight was called the *Premier* Division. Enfield had beaten Hendon's fine record of thirty-four wins and six draws five years previously. The nearest challengers to the E's this time were Dagenham, who enjoyed their best season to date in finishing runners-up, albeit 31 points adrift of the Southbury Road club. Wycombe Wanderers, the previous two seasons' runners-up, finished third, four points behind the Daggers, but one ahead of Tooting & Mitcham United. Southall & Ealing Borough, after just two seasons in the top division, were relegated, along with Bishop's Stortford. In Division One Dulwich Hamlet – relegated in 1977 – made an immediate return to the top flight, claiming the championship by ten points from runners-up Oxford City, with Bromley missing promotion by one point in third place. Hornchurch and Corinthian–Casuals, with the latter only managing three wins from their 42-match programme, were the first clubs to suffer relegation to the newly formed Division Two. Epsom & Ewell won the inaugural Division Two championship, five points clear of Metropolitan Police who were also promoted to Division One. The bottom two clubs, Epping Town and Willesden, successfully applied for re-election at the Annual General Meeting, and they were joined by new members Hungerford Town, as Division Two expanded to 18 clubs.

Premier Division	1	2	3	4	5	6	7	8	9	10	11	12	13	14	15	16	17	18	19	20	21	22
1 Barking	*	5–1	2–0	0–2	2–3	1–2	1–2	0–1	3–0	1–2	1–3	4–1	2–0	3–1	4–0	4–0	2–4	2–2	2–0	2–1	1–3	2–3
2 Bishop's Stortford	0–1	*	1–2	2–3	1–3	2–4	1–4	1–1	0–3	1–4	3–0	0–0	1–0	1–0	2–1	1–0	1–2	1–3	0–1	1–1	1–3	0–1
3 Boreham Wood	2–2	1–1	*	1–2	1–0	2–4	0–1	3–2	1–0	2–0	2–2	0–0	3–1	1–2	0–0	1–0	1–4	2–0	0–3	0–1	0–1	0–5
4 Carshalton Athletic	2–1	6–1	3–1	*	4–0	1–2	1–2	1–0	1–2	1–0	2–2	2–1	2–2	0–1	1–2	3–2	3–1	0–0	1–1	1–2	1–2	1–1
5 Croydon	3–0	0–0	1–2	1–2	*	0–0	0–1	2–0	3–0	3–1	0–0	1–2	1–1	2–0	2–2	4–1	3–2	0–1	0–1	1–2	3–6	1–2
6 Dagenham	3–3	3–1	1–0	2–0	3–1	*	2–3	1–0	0–1	3–1	5–1	3–1	3–1	2–0	0–0	2–0	1–0	0–2	4–1	2–0	2–1	1–2
7 Enfield	3–1	3–1	2–0	2–1	2–2	3–0	*	3–1	2–0	2–0	3–0	2–0	3–0	2–0	1–0	2–1	4–0	3–0	3–1	1–0	3–2	3–0
8 Hayes	0–2	0–0	3–2	0–0	0–1	2–1	0–2	*	1–1	1–0	2–0	2–0	2–1	2–1	3–1	1–1	0–0	3–2	2–2	2–1	0–3	1–0
9 Hendon	2–3	2–0	1–0	5–0	0–1	3–1	0–4	2–1	*	0–2	0–1	1–1	4–0	0–1	1–1	1–1	2–1	3–0	0–2	1–1	1–1	1–2
10 Hitchin Town	3–0	1–0	3–0	0–0	0–1	2–2	3–2	3–0	2–3	*	1–0	2–0	1–0	2–1	0–1	2–1	0–0	3–2	1–3	4–1	1–1	1–3
11 Kingstonian	0–1	2–0	2–2	1–2	1–3	1–2	1–1	0–0	1–0	0–1	*	2–3	2–2	1–1	3–0	1–2	2–3	0–2	0–1	1–2	3–1	1–1
12 Leatherhead	1–1	1–0	1–0	3–0	2–3	3–0	1–2	1–0	4–1	1–1	3–1	*	4–1	1–1	5–1	2–0	2–2	2–1	0–1	0–0	4–1	1–0
13 Leytonstone	1–1	4–2	1–2	1–0	1–3	3–3	1–1	1–2	0–3	0–4	1–1	0–0	*	2–3	0–0	2–1	2–0	1–2	2–2	1–1	1–1	2–0
14 Slough Town	1–0	3–2	3–4	4–1	1–3	1–2	1–3	2–1	1–0	1–4	2–1	3–1	1–1	*	0–0	1–2	1–1	2–2	1–3	1–0	0–1	0–3
15 Southall & E Boro	0–5	0–1	1–1	2–2	3–1	0–0	0–0	0–1	1–1	2–3	1–3	0–0	3–1	0–3	*	1–2	2–1	1–2	2–3	2–3	2–2	0–3
16 Staines Town	2–3	0–0	1–2	0–0	1–1	2–2	0–1	0–0	1–0	2–2	0–0	1–0	1–2	1–0	2–1	*	1–1	3–0	1–0	1–1	1–0	1–3
17 Sutton United	2–2	1–2	0–0	1–0	1–2	1–0	1–6	4–1	4–2	3–0	1–1	3–0	1–0	1–1	3–2	2–2	*	2–1	0–1	2–1	1–0	1–0
18 Tilbury	2–2	5–1	1–2	0–0	0–0	1–4	2–2	1–1	0–2	3–3	1–1	2–0	1–2	4–0	1–3	3–1	1–4	*	1–1	1–1	0–1	2–3
19 Tooting & M Utd	2–1	1–0	0–1	3–4	0–1	1–0	0–3	3–2	2–0	2–2	1–0	1–2	0–0	1–1	2–0	2–2	2–1	2–0	*	2–3	2–0	1–2
20 Walthamstow Ave.	1–2	1–1	4–2	4–1	2–0	0–1	2–1	2–2	1–5	3–2	3–0	1–4	3–2	4–1	2–2	0–1	1–1	2–1	1–3	*	3–3	1–0
21 Woking	4–1	4–1	0–2	1–1	0–0	4–5	0–2	2–1	1–2	0–1	0–1	0–3	0–0	3–1	1–1	2–4	1–2	2–0	3–2	0–1	*	1–1
22 Wycombe Wndrs.	1–0	3–0	3–0	3–2	1–1	3–0	0–1	0–2	2–1	1–1	3–0	1–1	1–0	1–3	3–2	4–0	1–1	0–2	0–2	0–0	0–0	*

Premier Division	P	W	D	L	F	A	Pts
1 Enfield	42	35	5	2	96	27	110
2 Dagenham	42	24	7	11	78	55	79
3 Wycombe Wand	42	22	9	11	66	41	75
4 Tooting & M Utd	42	22	8	12	64	49	74
5 Hitchin Town	42	20	9	13	69	53	69
6 Sutton United	42	18	12	12	66	57	66
7 Leatherhead	42	18	11	13	62	48	65
8 Croydon	42	18	10	14	61	52	64
9 Walthamstow Ave.	42	17	12	13	64	61	63
10 Barking	42	17	7	18	76	66	58
11 Carshalton Athletic	42	15	11	16	60	62	56
12 Hayes	42	15	11	16	46	53	56
13 Hendon	42	16	7	19	57	55	55
14 Woking	42	14	11	17	62	62	53
15 Boreham Wood	42	15	8	19	48	65	53
16 Slough Town	42	14	8	20	52	69	50
17 Staines Town	42	12	13	17	46	60	49
18 Tilbury	42	11	12	19	57	68	45
19 Kingstonian	42	8	13	21	43	65	37
20 Leytonstone	42	7	15	20	44	71	36
21 Southall & E Boro	42	6	15	21	43	74	33
22 Bishop's Stortford	42	7	8	27	36	83	29

Above: Hornchurch's programme from 1977-78.

Right: The E's programme from their record breaking 1977-78 season when their 35 wins and 5 draws accumulated 110 points, a record yet to be bettered.

Division I	1	2	3	4	5	6	7	8	9	10	11	12	13	14	15	16	17	18	19	20	21	22
1 Aveley	*	1–1	0–2	0–0	2–0	0–2	0–2	1–0	1–1	0–3	3–2	2–3	1–0	2–1	1–1	1–2	0–2	1–0	1–3	2–0	2–3	3–2
2 Bromley	3–0	*	2–0	5–0	2–1	0–1	1–1	0–0	2–0	3–1	0–0	4–1	2–1	0–0	0–4	1–1	4–1	2–1	1–1	4–1	1–3	1–0
3 Chesham United	2–4	3–1	*	0–0	2–1	2–0	2–2	2–2	0–0	1–1	1–5	0–0	1–0	3–1	2–1	0–0	3–3	0–1	4–0	5–1	1–2	2–2
4 Clapton	1–2	2–4	1–2	*	0–0	0–3	3–0	3–1	1–4	1–3	1–2	1–2	2–2	1–0	0–1	0–3	1–1	1–2	0–1	2–3	2–0	3–1
5 Corinthian-Casuals	2–2	1–3	0–0	0–2	*	2–1	2–3	0–2	0–1	1–2	0–2	2–2	1–0	0–0	1–2	1–2	1–1	2–3	1–2	1–1	4–2	0–1
6 Dulwich Hamlet	4–0	0–0	4–0	3–0	5–0	*	3–0	2–0	2–0	1–0	4–1	1–0	5–0	0–2	0–0	0–0	2–1	2–1	3–3	4–0	2–1	2–1
7 Finchley	1–0	0–1	0–3	0–3	2–0	0–4	*	1–0	2–1	3–0	2–2	2–0	1–1	1–2	1–1	1–1	0–5	1–1	0–2	0–0	0–2	0–0
8 Hampton	2–1	1–2	2–2	2–1	1–1	0–2	1–0	*	3–1	1–1	0–0	1–1	2–0	2–1	1–2	0–2	2–1	1–1	1–2	2–1	0–1	0–2
9 Harlow Town	4–0	1–1	1–0	1–2	2–0	1–4	1–0	1–2	*	1–0	2–1	3–3	4–0	3–1	2–0	1–0	1–2	4–1	0–1	5–0	3–0	3–1
10 Harrow Borough	2–0	1–1	3–0	3–0	2–2	0–0	0–1	2–4	2–1	*	3–2	1–0	3–0	1–1	0–2	1–0	0–5	1–3	0–1	0–1	1–1	0–2
11 Harwich & Parkst.	2–1	2–4	4–2	3–0	4–2	2–2	2–2	4–3	1–0	1–1	*	1–1	1–1	1–3	1–1	1–2	2–1	1–1	1–5	2–2	1–2	2–0
12 Hertford Town	1–0	0–2	3–3	3–0	3–0	1–1	0–1	2–2	1–1	2–1	3–1	*	4–0	2–0	0–1	0–1	2–0	1–0	0–0	2–2	1–0	1–1
13 Hornchurch	1–2	0–2	4–5	1–2	2–1	0–4	1–1	2–2	1–1	0–0	6–1	2–1	*	4–1	1–2	0–0	0–2	1–3	1–1	3–1	3–2	0–2
14 Horsham	0–2	0–3	1–2	1–0	2–0	1–2	1–0	0–2	2–0	0–4	1–1	0–2	1–0	*	2–2	0–1	0–1	0–0	2–1	0–0	2–0	2–3
15 Ilford	1–3	1–1	3–1	3–1	3–1	1–1	1–0	1–0	1–1	2–1	1–1	1–0	1–1	1–1	*	2–2	2–1	2–1	0–2	3–2	0–3	0–0
16 Maidenhead Utd	2–3	0–1	2–0	1–1	3–3	0–3	2–2	1–1	1–2	3–4	2–1	1–0	1–0	3–0	0–1	*	0–1	2–1	1–1	2–1	4–0	2–2
17 Oxford City	2–0	3–1	3–1	2–1	3–1	1–0	3–2	1–0	5–1	1–2	1–0	1–2	2–0	0–2	3–0	3–1	*	0–1	1–1	5–0	6–1	3–2
18 St. Albans City	3–1	1–1	3–2	1–0	4–0	1–1	2–2	1–0	4–0	2–3	2–0	1–1	3–0	2–1	5–0	6–0	1–2	*	2–1	4–0	2–0	2–2
19 Walton & Hersham	3–1	2–1	1–0	4–1	3–2	1–2	0–1	0–1	0–0	0–2	2–1	1–1	5–1	1–0	2–3	4–1	2–0	1–2	*	1–1	3–0	1–0
20 Ware	1–1	1–1	3–2	2–4	4–2	0–3	4–2	2–0	0–3	3–3	3–4	4–2	2–3	2–2	1–2	1–2	1–2	2–2	0–0	*	1–2	4–2
21 Wembley	1–0	1–2	1–4	4–1	3–0	0–5	6–1	1–1	1–0	0–1	4–1	2–3	0–4	1–2	0–1	1–1	0–3	0–3	0–3	4–3	*	1–2
22 Wokingham Town	6–0	2–3	2–2	2–1	2–1	2–1	4–0	1–1	0–1	1–0	2–1	2–0	3–0	1–0	0–0	2–0	1–1	4–3	1–1	0–0	2–0	*

Division I	P	W	D	L	F	A	Pts
1 Dulwich Hamlet	42	28	9	5	91	25	93
2 Oxford City	42	26	5	11	85	44	83
3 Bromley	42	23	13	6	74	41	82
4 Walton & Hersham	42	22	11	9	69	41	77
5 Ilford	42	21	14	7	57	47	77
6 St. Albans City	42	22	10	10	83	46	76
7 Wokingham Town	42	19	12	11	68	48	69
8 Harlow Town	42	19	8	15	63	49	65
9 Harrow Borough	42	17	10	15	59	54	61
10 Maidenhead Utd	42	16	13	13	55	54	61
11 Hertford Town	42	15	14	13	57	51	59
12 Chesham United	42	14	13	15	69	70	55
13 Hampton	42	13	13	16	49	53	52
14 Harwich & Parkst.	42	12	13	17	68	79	49
15 Wembley	42	15	3	24	56	82	48
16 Horsham	42	12	10	20	41	57	46
17 Finchley	42	11	13	18	41	68	46
18 Aveley	42	13	7	22	47	75	46
19 Ware	42	8	13	21	61	95	37
20 Clapton	42	10	6	26	46	78	36
21 Hornchurch	42	8	10	24	47	81	34
22 Corinthian-Casuals	42	3	10	29	40	88	19

Right: The cover of the 1977-78 Wokingham Town matchday programme.

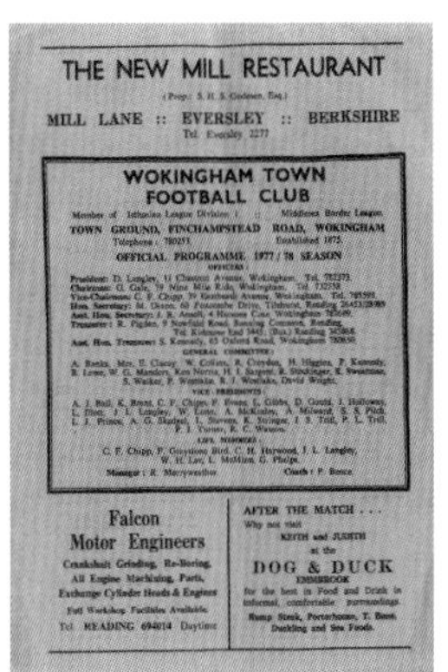

Left: The Clapton matchday programme in their centenary season. Clapton lost to eventual champions Dulwich Hamlet by three goals to nil.

Division II	1	2	3	4	5	6	7	8	9	10	11	12	13	14	15	16	17
1 Camberley Town	*	0–0	2–1	3–3	0–1	0–1	0–1	2–2	1–0	3–1	0–3	2–3	0–0	1–1	1–5	5–1	1–3
2 Cheshunt	0–2	*	0–2	0–0	1–2	2–1	1–4	1–1	4–0	3–2	1–3	1–2	2–1	3–2	2–2	1–4	0–1
3 Eastbourne United	1–1	2–2	*	0–1	1–2	1–4	1–4	2–1	0–0	1–1	2–3	1–1	1–2	1–0	0–0	2–3	0–1
4 Egham Town	3–0	2–1	2–2	*	5–3	1–3	0–1	1–0	0–0	1–2	4–1	0–1	3–0	3–0	2–3	0–1	0–0
5 Epping Town	0–0	3–2	0–2	2–2	*	0–2	1–2	0–1	0–2	0–4	3–3	0–3	0–2	1–2	1–1	1–0	2–1
6 Epsom & Ewell	1–1	4–0	5–1	1–0	4–1	*	0–3	2–0	0–0	2–2	2–0	1–0	4–2	0–1	0–3	4–2	1–0
7 Farnborough Town	5–0	0–3	1–0	2–3	2–3	2–0	*	8–2	4–2	2–2	0–2	1–2	0–1	1–0	2–2	5–1	2–1
8 Feltham	0–0	1–0	1–2	0–0	3–2	1–2	0–0	*	2–0	1–4	1–2	0–2	1–1	1–2	0–1	2–0	0–1
9 Hemel Hempstead	1–0	2–0	0–1	2–3	4–2	1–3	0–2	1–2	*	2–3	1–1	0–3	0–0	4–0	0–0	3–1	0–2
10 Letchworth G City	3–2	3–1	1–2	5–0	2–1	2–3	4–2	1–1	6–4	*	3–2	1–2	2–1	0–0	0–3	2–2	4–1
11 Lewes	1–2	3–3	2–2	0–1	2–1	0–1	2–5	3–1	2–1	1–1	*	2–0	1–2	2–0	1–0	2–0	1–1
12 Metropolitan Police	1–0	1–2	0–1	0–1	3–1	1–1	2–0	0–1	3–0	1–1	2–0	*	2–1	2–2	3–2	3–3	2–1
13 Molesey	0–0	4–0	1–0	0–0	0–0	3–2	2–1	3–1	1–0	1–0	1–1	2–1	*	1–1	0–1	1–0	4–0
14 Rainham Town	2–1	0–1	3–1	0–3	2–1	0–3	1–2	1–1	2–1	0–0	3–2	0–2	0–3	*	2–0	3–1	3–1
15 Tring Town	1–1	3–0	2–3	0–0	2–1	2–2	0–1	1–0	1–1	2–2	4–1	2–3	1–2	2–0	*	8–1	2–0
16 Willesden	1–0	0–4	3–4	0–6	3–1	1–3	1–2	3–1	0–0	0–2	1–2	0–2	0–5	1–4	0–6	*	1–2
17 Worthing	3–1	3–2	1–0	1–2	1–1	1–3	1–1	1–1	1–1	1–1	2–1	0–0	2–0	4–5	0 0	2–3	*

ISTHMIAN LEAGUE

DIVISION ONE

Harwich and Parkeston Football Club

FOUNDED 1877

Official Programme
Price 5p

Above: Harwich & Parkeston's matchday programme

Division II	P	W	D	L	F	A	Pts
1 Epsom & Ewell	32	21	5	6	65	34	68
2 Metropolitan Police	32	19	6	7	53	30	63
3 Farnborough Town	32	19	4	9	68	40	61
4 Molesey	32	17	8	7	47	27	59
5 Egham Town	32	15	9	8	52	34	54
6 Tring Town	32	14	11	7	62	32	53
7 Letchworth G City	32	14	11	7	67	48	53
8 Lewes	32	13	7	12	52	51	46
9 Rainham Town	32	13	6	13	42	50	45
10 Worthing	32	11	9	12	40	45	42
11 Eastbourne United	32	10	8	14	40	50	38
12 Cheshunt	32	9	6	17	43	60	33
13 Feltham	32	7	9	16	30	49	30
14 Camberley Town	32	6	11	15	32	49	29
15 Hemel Hempstead	32	6	9	17	33	50	27
16 Epping Town	32	7	6	19	37	64	27
17 Willesden	32	7	3	22	38	88	24

Left: Hugh Burbidge in action for Epping Town against Molesey in 1978, Epping lost 2-0.

1978–79 - This season saw the formation of the Alliance Premier Football League, a national semi-professional league comprising 20 clubs – 13 from the Southern League Premier Division and seven from the Northern Premier League.

Berger Paints Ltd had agreed to sponsor the Isthmian League and Isthmian League Youth Cup for two years, with an option for a third. In other sponsorship news, Dylon International Ltd agreed to sponsor, initially for three years, the Isthmian League Charity Shield – an annual match between the Premier Division champions and League Cup winners. However, as Enfield had been successful in both competitions in 1977–78, the inaugural Shield was contested by Enfield and Premier Division runners-up Dagenham. Enfield prevailed 2–1.

Barking won their first Isthmian League championship by 12 points from local rivals Dagenham with Enfield in third and newly-promoted Dulwich Hamlet fourth, four and six points, respectively, behind the Daggers.

Leytonstone and Kingstonian occupied the bottom two places and were relegated to Division One, from where champions Harlow Town and runners-up Harrow Borough gained promotion. St. Albans City and Southall & Ealing Borough both suffered a second relegation – with the latter suffering this fate in consecutive seasons. In Division Two Farnborough Town, who were only formed in 1967, continued their progress with the championship, while near neighbours Camberley Town were runners-up and gained the other promotion place. Willesden again had to apply for re-election, as did Corinthian-Casuals, and both were re-elected at the Annual General Meeting.

The League again expanded its membership – this time by one club – for 1979–80. Several clubs made applications and three were nominated for a card vote, The result of this ballot was as follows:

Barton Rovers 22, Billericay Town 11, Dorking Town 10

The League Council, therefore, invited Barton Rovers to join the League. However, at the Annual General Meeting it was announced that Ilford FC and Leytonstone FC had agreed to merge and would be known as Ilford & Leytonstone FC – they would compete in Division One. As a result of this merger, St. Albans City were spared relegation to Division Two. In addition to Barton Rovers' election as proposed by the League Council, proposers and seconders were found to allow Billericay Town and Dorking to be invited to join the League, increasing the membership of Division Two to 20 clubs.

Eddie Bray resigned his positions as both Hon Secretary and Hon Referees Secretary. Alan Turvey succeeded him as Hon Secretary and John Williams assumed the role of Hon Referees Secretary.

Premier Division	1	2	3	4	5	6	7	8	9	10	11	12	13	14	15	16	17	18	19	20	21	22
1 Barking	*	3–1	2–0	1–0	2–3	1–1	2–3	5–3	1–0	5–2	1–0	2–0	1–0	3–1	4–1	1–1	2–1	2–2	4–2	1–2	1–0	2–2
2 Boreham Wood	1–2	*	1–1	0–2	0–1	0–2	0–2	1–0	3–1	2–0	2–1	2–3	1–3	2–4	1–0	1–1	0–1	5–0	1–1	3–1	2–4	1–1
3 Carshalton Athletic	1–1	2–2	*	1–0	0–3	1–1	0–3	0–5	1–0	0–0	1–1	1–1	5–1	3–0	1–1	2–2	3–2	2–0	0–0	1–0	0–4	2–3
4 Croydon	0–4	1–2	0–0	*	3–2	2–3	1–1	1–0	1–3	1–1	1–0	2–1	2–1	3–1	4–2	2–1	4–0	4–1	1–1	2–0	1–3	3–0
5 Dagenham	0–3	0–0	4–3	3–0	*	0–2	2–6	4–1	1–1	3–1	3–2	2–1	0–1	5–0	2–1	3–1	0–2	2–0	1–0	5–4	5–3	1–0
6 Dulwich Hamlet	0–0	9–2	1–1	1–0	0–1	*	0–2	2–1	2–1	2–2	4–0	0–0	1–0	5–2	2–0	2–1	2–0	1–1	1–2	1–0	4–1	3–1
7 Enfield	1–1	0–0	2–0	2–1	2–0	2–0	*	1–1	1–2	4–0	4–1	2–0	2–0	1–1	0–1	3–0	1–0	2–1	0–2	4–4	1–1	1–4
8 Hayes	2–2	2–1	1–1	0–2	1–3	0–0	1–1	*	1–0	1–1	2–0	1–0	2–2	3–1	1–1	0–0	1–1	1–3	2–5	1–1	1–1	0–1
9 Hendon	0–1	1–1	2–1	5–2	3–0	0–1	1–1	2–0	*	3–2	2–2	1–1	3–0	0–0	3–2	1–1	1–0	1–1	3–2	1–1	1–2	1–0
10 Hitchin Town	6–2	1–1	0–1	0–0	1–3	1–1	2–1	5–1	0–1	*	1–1	1–0	5–1	2–2	1–2	1–1	0–2	4–1	0–1	2–0	1–0	2–1
11 Kingstonian	1–1	1–2	2–2	1–3	1–1	0–0	0–1	0–1	1–1	1–1	*	1–1	0–1	2–0	0–1	0–1	1–1	1–2	1–0	2–4	1–3	0–2
12 Leatherhead	2–0	0–1	1–2	0–2	1–1	1–2	0–1	1–1	0–0	3–1	4–1	*	2–0	3–0	1–1	3–0	5–2	3–0	3–0	1–0	2–0	1–2
13 Leytonstone	1–3	1–2	3–0	0–1	0–3	0–1	0–3	1–2	0–1	2–3	1–1	1–0	*	1–3	0–3	2–1	0–4	2–2	0–0	1–0	2–2	1–2
14 Oxford City	1–2	0–1	3–0	0–3	2–3	3–2	0–1	1–0	1–0	1–3	2–1	3–2	0–0	*	1–1	3–2	2–2	0–2	4–3	1–0	0–2	0–3
15 Slough Town	2–4	2–0	2–0	0–0	2–0	3–2	2–1	0–0	2–1	4–1	3–1	1–2	2–1	1–0	*	1–1	1–0	0–0	5–0	3–2	1–2	0–0
16 Staines Town	0–2	4–0	1–1	0–2	0–2	1–1	1–0	0–0	0–0	4–1	3–3	0–1	0–1	2–0	1–2	*	0–2	1–2	1–1	1–1	1–3	2–1
17 Sutton United	1–2	2–2	2–0	3–0	0–2	0–3	1–1	2–0	2–0	1–0	4–0	1–2	1–0	0–0	2–2	5–1	*	1–0	0–1	0–1	3–0	1–1
18 Tilbury	2–3	2–1	4–3	3–3	2–2	2–0	0–2	0–1	1–1	3–2	0–0	1–2	4–2	3–2	0–1	1–0	4–0	*	1–2	2–5	2–1	0–1
19 Tooting & M Utd	0–2	2–0	1–1	0–0	3–1	1–1	1–2	0–0	1–3	3–0	1–1	3–0	2–1	0–3	1–1	0–0	1–0	2–2	*	1–0	0–1	2–0
20 Walthamstow Ave.	1–4	1–2	4–1	1–0	4–1	1–2	2–1	1–1	1–2	0–1	0–1	1–3	1–0	2–1	1–0	4–1	1–5	4–1	0–1	*	0–6	2–0
21 Woking	2–3	1–0	3–2	3–1	3–4	1–1	1–0	1–1	2–2	3–1	2–0	0–0	2–2	4–1	0–0	2–0	3–3	2–2	2–2	1–1	*	1–1
22 Wycombe Wndrs.	1–4	1–0	0–2	0–0	1–1	1–0	0–0	3–2	5–0	2–0	2–1	2–0	2–0	2–0	0–1	1–1	1–2	2–0	3–1	1–2	3–1	*

Premier Division	*P*	*W*	*D*	*L*	*F*	*A*	*Pts*
1 Barking	42	28	9	5	92	50	93
2 Dagenham	42	25	6	11	83	63	81
3 Enfield	42	22	11	9	69	37	77
4 Dulwich Hamlet	42	21	13	8	69	39	76
5 Slough Town	42	20	12	10	61	44	72
6 Wycombe Wand	42	20	9	13	59	44	69
7 Woking	42	18	14	10	79	59	68
8 Croydon	42	19	9	14	61	51	66
9 Hendon	42	16	14	12	55	48	62
10 Leatherhead	42	17	9	16	57	45	60
11 Sutton United	42	17	9	16	62	51	60
12 Tooting & M Utd	42	15	14	13	52	52	59
13 Walthamstow Ave.	42	15	6	21	61	69	51
14 Tilbury	42	13	11	18	60	76	50
15 Boreham Wood	42	13	10	19	50	67	49
16 Hitchin Town	42	12	11	19	59	71	47
17 Carshalton Athletic	42	10	16	16	49	69	46
18 Hayes	42	9	18	15	45	58	45
19 Oxford City	42	12	7	23	50	80	43
20 Staines Town	42	6	16	20	40	64	34
21 Leytonstone	42	8	7	27	36	75	31
22 Kingstonian	42	3	15	24	35	72	24

Left: the Carshalton Athletic matchday programme from 1978-79 season.

Right: the Willesden edition from the same season.

Division I	1	2	3	4	5	6	7	8	9	10	11	12	13	14	15	16	17	18	19	20	21	22
1 Aveley	*	1–1	2–1	3–2	4–1	0–1	1–0	0–2	3–0	1–3	2–1	0–2	1–2	3–0	2–0	1–5	2–0	2–1	2–0	3–2	1–2	2–1
2 Bishop's Stortford	1–0	*	1–1	2–1	3–0	2–1	2–3	0–2	2–0	1–0	2–1	1–1	5–1	3–0	2–0	3–1	3–1	5–1	0–2	1–0	2–0	3–2
3 Bromley	1–1	2–1	*	4–0	4–3	3–0	1–1	4–2	0–0	0–0	1–4	1–1	1–2	1–2	1–2	3–1	5–1	1–1	4–0	3–0	4–0	0–1
4 Chesham United	0–1	1–2	1–1	*	3–0	2–0	1–0	2–1	1–3	0–0	0–2	0–2	0–2	1–2	0–0	0–1	2–0	1–1	0–2	0–0	2–2	3–1
5 Clapton	3–1	0–1	1–4	3–1	*	1–3	3–1	1–2	2–4	3–1	2–3	1–4	0–3	2–1	2–5	1–1	1–1	1–0	3–2	1–1	2–3	1–2
6 Epsom & Ewell	3–0	0–2	0–4	3–0	1–1	*	4–0	1–1	1–2	4–1	1–1	3–1	1–2	3–1	1–0	3–1	4–0	4–0	2–0	4–1	0–0	1–0
7 Finchley	2–2	0–0	0–0	2–1	3–5	3–2	*	1–1	1–2	1–4	1–1	1–2	1–3	1–0	1–4	1–1	3–2	1–1	0–1	0–0	0–1	0–2
8 Hampton	1–2	0–0	1–2	1–1	1–0	4–0	2–2	*	0–1	1–3	4–0	1–3	0–2	3–0	0–1	2–1	2–1	1–0	3–0	2–2	0–0	0–1
9 Harlow Town	3–1	4–1	2–0	2–1	0–0	0–0	2–1	0–0	*	4–0	2–2	2–1	2–0	5–1	3–0	0–0	8–0	3–0	3–0	3–1	3–1	0–3
10 Harrow Borough	4–2	1–1	2–1	1–1	3–0	3–1	3–1	2–1	1–2	*	4–3	1–1	3–1	2–2	2–1	0–2	1–2	2–1	2–0	2–0	0–2	3–0
11 Harwich & Parkst.	3–0	2–1	4–1	1–2	0–1	5–1	4–0	2–1	0–1	0–1	*	0–1	1–0	1–1	2–3	4–1	6–1	3–0	4–0	3–2	1–0	1–2
12 Hertford Town	1–0	2–0	1–1	0–2	1–2	1–0	3–0	2–1	1–2	0–4	3–1	*	1–1	2–0	1–3	0–0	2–0	2–0	4–0	0–0	1–2	2–1
13 Horsham	2–1	2–1	2–1	2–0	2–2	1–0	2–1	2–0	0–2	1–1	1–2	1–1	*	2–0	0–1	1–0	0–0	1–2	3–3	3–1	1–0	2–0
14 Ilford	1–1	1–0	0–2	1–2	1–6	2–1	0–1	2–4	2–3	3–4	1–3	2–0	2–1	*	0–5	0–2	5–1	2–1	1–1	1–2	1–0	0–3
15 Maidenhead Utd	0–1	1–1	1–4	2–0	3–1	1–0	1–1	1–2	1–4	1–1	3–1	1–2	3–2	1–0	*	1–0	3–2	1–0	1–1	3–0	2–1	3–1
16 Metropolitan Police	2–0	2–3	0–1	2–2	1–1	1–3	0–0	2–3	1–2	0–1	2–0	1–1	1–0	1–2	1–2	*	3–0	1–2	0–0	2–1	1–1	6–0
17 Southall & E Boro	3–1	1–1	0–2	3–1	0–3	3–2	1–2	0–1	0–6	2–3	0–4	1–1	1–2	1–2	1–2	1–5	*	5–2	1–2	1–6	0–2	2–3
18 St. Albans City	2–2	0–3	1–3	3–1	1–2	2–2	5–4	1–3	1–1	0–3	1–5	1–2	1–2	1–0	1–3	1–1	5–0	*	0–1	0–1	0–1	3–2
19 Walton & Hersham	4–1	0–3	1–1	2–3	0–2	2–4	2–0	1–1	0–2	1–3	1–2	1–1	1–3	0–1	0–1	2–2	1–0	5–0	*	2–0	0–3	1–1
20 Ware	2–1	1–1	2–1	1–3	0–1	1–1	0–0	0–1	0–2	0–4	2–1	1–0	1–2	1–1	0–1	0–0	1–0	4–0	3–2	*	4–3	2–3
21 Wembley	0–1	1–1	1–1	2–1	0–0	2–1	1–1	0–0	0–2	0–3	4–4	0–1	1–0	3–1	2–2	5–1	1–1	1–0	0–1	6–0	*	1–1
22 Wokingham Town	2–2	0–0	4–0	3–1	5–2	0–2	1–1	1–1	2–1	1–3	0–2	1–4	1–1	0–3	3–2	1–2	3–1	2–0	1–2	1–0	2–2	*

Division I	P	W	D	L	F	A	Pts
1 Harlow Town	42	31	7	4	93	32	100
2 Harrow Borough	42	26	8	8	85	49	86
3 Maidenhead Utd	42	25	6	11	72	50	81
4 Bishop's Stortford	42	22	11	9	68	40	77
5 Horsham	42	23	7	12	63	47	76
6 Hertford Town	42	21	11	10	62	41	74
7 Harwich & Parkst.	42	22	5	15	90	57	71
8 Bromley	42	18	12	12	76	50	66
9 Hampton	42	17	11	14	59	47	62
10 Epsom & Ewell	42	18	7	17	69	57	61
11 Wembley	42	15	14	13	57	50	59
12 Aveley	42	17	6	19	57	67	57
13 Wokingham Town*	42	17	8	17	64	68	56
14 Clapton	42	15	8	19	67	80	53
15 Metropolitan Police	42	12	13	17	58	55	49
16 Walton & Hersham	42	12	9	21	47	71	45
17 Ilford	42	13	5	24	48	80	44
18 Ware	42	11	10	21	46	69	43
19 Chesham United	42	11	9	22	46	66	42
20 Finchley	42	7	15	20	43	74	36
21 St. Albans City	42	7	7	28	43	90	28
22 Southall & E Boro	42	5	5	32	41	114	20

** Wokingham Town had three points deducted.*

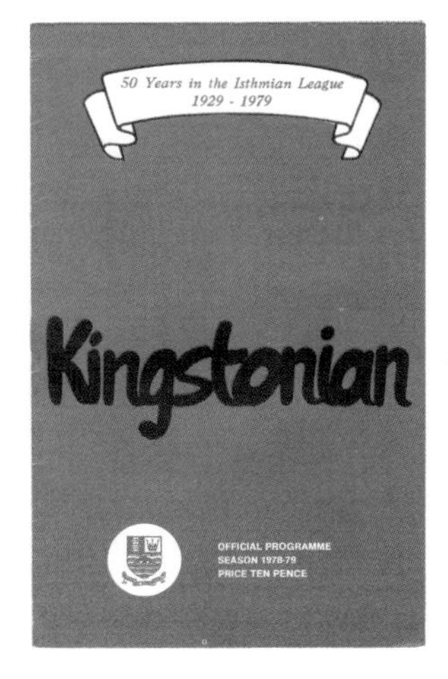

Left: the Kingstonian programme celebrating their half centenary of membership in 1979.

Right: the Chesham United programme for 1979-80.

Division II	1	2	3	4	5	6	7	8	9	10	11	12	13	14	15	16	17	18
1 Camberley Town	*	2–0	3–0	4–0	2–0	2–2	1–0	1–0	0–0	4–0	2–1	0–0	1–2	2–2	1–0	2–0	7–0	2–0
2 Cheshunt	2–0	*	2–0	1–0	2–2	1–0	0–2	0–1	0–1	1–1	1–1	2–0	4–2	2–3	1–0	2–2	1–0	0–1
3 Corinthian-Casuals	1–5	1–1	*	1–0	0–0	1–1	2–0	0–3	0–3	1–3	1–3	0–3	2–4	0–1	0–3	0–0	2–1	1–1
4 Eastbourne United	2–3	3–1	4–1	*	0–0	1–0	1–0	0–0	1–0	0–1	3–0	3–0	1–3	0–1	1–0	3–0	2–3	2–1
5 Egham Town	1–1	1–3	4–0	6–0	*	0–1	1–2	0–1	3–2	2–1	2–2	1–3	1–3	2–1	0–0	0–1	1–1	2–3
6 Epping Town	1–2	1–0	3–1	1–2	0–0	*	1–2	2–0	2–0	2–0	4–0	2–4	2–0	2–2	2–2	4–3	2–0	3–0
7 Farnborough Town	3–4	4–1	2–1	2–0	3–2	3–1	*	1–1	2–1	3–2	4–1	3–0	1–0	2–1	4–0	2–1	4–3	6–1
8 Feltham	2–1	4–5	0–2	3–1	0–1	2–0	1–3	*	2–2	1–1	1–2	1–1	1–3	1–0	1–2	2–0	2–0	1–0
9 Hemel Hempstead	0–2	2–2	3–2	0–1	2–1	2–0	1–2	0–1	*	3–1	3–3	2–1	1–0	2–2	1–0	1–2	0–0	2–0
10 Hornchurch	2–1	1–1	2–1	3–1	1–0	2–1	0–3	0–2	0–1	*	1–0	1–1	2–3	1–1	0–3	2–1	1–1	2–3
11 Hungerford Town	0–1	2–1	2–1	1–1	2–2	1–2	0–3	1–3	1–3	3–1	*	3–1	4–0	0–2	1–4	3–0	5–3	1–0
12 Letchworth G City	2–1	2–1	3–0	1–3	4–1	2–2	1–1	2–1	0–0	2–2	1–0	*	3–1	3–4	1–1	2–0	4–0	2–1
13 Lewes	1–2	4–1	0–0	2–1	1–1	2–0	2–5	3–2	2–2	3–1	3–1	1–2	*	2–2	3–2	2–0	4–2	1–0
14 Molesey	1–1	2–1	1–0	2–0	4–1	1–2	0–0	1–1	1–0	3–2	0–0	1–0	1–1	*	3–2	2–0	2–1	1–0
15 Rainham Town	1–1	1–0	1–0	0–0	3–3	3–0	2–0	0–3	0–0	1–1	2–1	0–0	0–3	1–1	*	2–1	0–5	3–1
16 Tring Town	2–3	1–0	0–0	1–3	2–1	0–1	0–1	0–1	1–1	3–0	2–3	3–2	1–1	1–3	0–1	*	1–2	2–2
17 Willesden	2–5	0–1	1–0	1–4	2–5	2–2	1–2	1–1	2–4	2–1	0–0	2–2	1–3	0–2	0–2	0–0	*	0–4
18 Worthing	2–2	2–2	2–1	2–3	1–1	1–0	0–2	0–1	0–0	4–0	0–0	3–1	0–1	0–1	2–0	2–2	1–2	*

Below: the Bishop's Stortford edition for 1979-80.

Division II	P	W	D	L	F	A	Pts
1 Farnborough Town	34	26	3	5	77	34	81
2 Camberley Town	34	21	8	5	71	32	71
3 Molesey	34	19	11	4	55	33	68
4 Lewes	34	19	6	9	66	50	63
5 Feltham	34	16	7	11	47	36	55
6 Letchworth G City	34	14	10	10	56	48	52
7 Eastbourne United	34	16	4	14	47	45	52
8 Hemel Hempstead	34	13	11	10	46	37	50
9 Epping Town	34	14	7	13	49	44	49
10 Rainham Town	34	13	10	11	42	41	49
11 Cheshunt	34	11	8	15	43	49	41
12 Hungerford Town	34	11	8	15	48	58	41
13 Worthing	34	9	8	17	40	50	35
14 Hornchurch	34	9	8	17	39	62	35
15 Egham Town	34	7	12	15	48	54	33
16 Tring Town	34	6	8	20	33	56	26
17 Willesden	34	6	8	20	41	77	26
18 Corinthian-Casuals	34	4	7	23	23	65	19

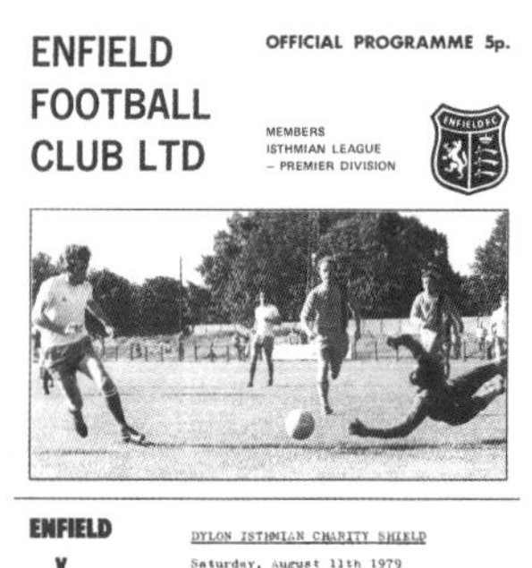

Left: the Enfield programme against Barking for the Dylon Charity Shield, the Mayesbrook Park club won 1-0.

Below: the Hungerford Town programme for their FA Vase Semi Final First Leg against Guisborough Town.

1979–80 - Before the season started, Ilford & Leytonstone FC decided that they would be known as Leytonstone Ilford FC. Furthermore, The Football Association instructed Dorking Town to compete in the Kingsmead Athenian League and not in Isthmian League Division Two.

The Premier Division championship was won by Enfield – their eighth title – by three points from Walthamstow Avenue. Dulwich Hamlet improved one position on their previous season's fourth place, two points behind the Avenue. They had six points in hand of Sutton United in fourth place. Oxford City were relegated back to Division One after just two seasons in the top flight. They were joined by basement-dwellers Tilbury, who also had two points deducted. In Division One, Leytonstone Ilford enjoyed their first year as a merged club, winning the championship by 17 points from Bromley, who took the second promotion place by two points from Maidenhead United and Bishop's Stortford. Horsham, who only gained 22 points and conceded 113 goals, were relegated to Division Two along with Harwich & Parkeston who also had a point deducted from their total. It should be said that neither penalty affected Tilbury or Harwich's final position. In Division Two, Billericay Town enjoyed a fantastic first season in the League, romping away with the championship also by 17 points and scoring 100 goals in their 36-match programme. Runners-up Lewes secured the second promotion place, eight points clear of Hungerford Town. The bottom two clubs, Hemel Hempstead and Corinthian-Casuals, were both re-elected at the Annual General Meeting. Dorking Town were elected to the League to increase Division Two's membership to 20 clubs. Basildon United, Chalfont St. Peter, Edgware, Leyton-Wingate and Redhill also applied to join the League, but they were unsuccessful, the League voting not to expand beyond 64 clubs.

Isthmian League President, Donald MacKenzie, passed away during the season and, at the Annual General Meeting, Chairman Barry East was invited to succeed him.

1979-80

Premier Division	1	2	3	4	5	6	7	8	9	10	11	12	13	14	15	16	17	18	19	20	21	22
1 Barking	*	0–1	3–0	3–1	1–1	1–1	1–1	0–0	2–3	5–1	1–2	5–0	1–1	3–1	3–1	2–1	2–1	2–0	5–2	0–0	4–3	2–1
2 Boreham Wood	0–4	*	0–2	0–3	1–1	0–1	1–1	2–0	1–4	2–2	1–1	1–1	3–2	2–0	3–2	3–0	0–2	2–0	0–1	1–5	2–3	0–0
3 Carshalton Athletic	3–0	3–1	*	2–0	1–4	0–1	0–2	3–2	1–3	1–2	2–1	0–3	1–4	2–1	1–1	2–1	1–2	1–3	1–2	0–2	2–1	0–1
4 Croydon	0–0	0–1	0–1	*	1–2	1–2	0–3	1–2	1–1	1–1	4–0	1–0	0–2	1–2	2–0	3–0	0–0	1–4	0–1	1–1	6–3	0–1
5 Dagenham	1–1	1–1	2–1	1–0	*	1–1	0–2	5–3	3–1	3–2	3–1	3–3	4–2	2–0	0–2	4–1	1–0	3–1	3–0	1–3	2–2	1–1
6 Dulwich Hamlet	4–0	2–1	1–0	2–0	2–1	*	3–2	1–2	1–1	3–0	1–1	4–1	1–0	1–1	1–1	0–0	0–0	5–0	2–2	2–1	1–0	2–1
7 Enfield	2–0	1–0	3–1	1–1	3–2	1–1	*	1–1	2–0	2–0	2–2	3–0	2–0	3–0	5–0	2–0	2–0	3–0	0–1	3–3	0–1	2–0
8 Harlow Town	4–2	3–1	1–1	2–1	0–2	3–3	1–1	*	2–0	0–3	2–2	2–2	1–0	1–1	2–1	0–2	1–1	0–1	3–5	0–1	1–1	2–1
9 Harrow Borough	3–1	2–1	1–1	1–1	2–2	1–0	0–2	1–0	*	1–0	0–0	0–0	0–0	2–0	1–1	3–0	1–1	1–0	2–0	1–2	2–2	1–2
10 Hayes	0–2	0–0	0–2	1–4	2–2	0–1	0–2	0–0	2–2	*	2–1	0–2	0–0	0–4	0–1	0–1	2–2	2–0	2–0	1–3	0–3	1–0
11 Hendon	1–1	2–2	3–1	0–1	1–0	0–3	0–1	0–1	3–2	1–0	*	1–1	2–1	4–0	0–1	3–1	1–1	2–1	1–2	1–2	3–0	2–2
12 Hitchin Town	0–1	3–1	0–0	3–2	4–3	1–1	3–1	1–0	0–1	1–0	1–0	*	3–0	1–1	1–1	1–2	3–3	2–2	2–1	0–2	3–1	2–3
13 Leatherhead	2–0	0–1	1–2	0–0	1–2	0–0	1–2	0–1	1–4	2–1	1–1	4–1	*	2–0	3–0	2–1	1–3	0–0	3–0	1–1	0–1	2–2
14 Oxford City	1–4	2–1	2–2	2–1	1–1	1–2	1–2	2–1	3–5	2–3	0–1	1–1	0–2	*	0–0	2–0	0–2	3–1	2–1	2–1	0–3	0–5
15 Slough Town	2–1	2–1	2–1	2–1	0–1	1–1	0–2	1–3	2–2	2–1	2–1	10–0	2–2	1–1	*	1–0	0–3	1–3	1–2	0–1	2–2	2–1
16 Staines Town	0–3	0–2	2–1	1–0	0–1	2–3	1–0	0–1	0–3	2–3	2–0	1–0	4–1	1–2	2–0	*	1–1	3–2	1–1	1–0	1–1	4–1
17 Sutton United	2–1	5–2	1–1	1–0	2–0	0–1	2–0	2–1	1–1	0–2	2–0	0–0	2–1	3–0	3–1	1–0	*	3–0	4–1	0–1	0–3	1–1
18 Tilbury	1–0	0–1	3–1	0–4	2–6	1–1	0–0	1–0	0–2	1–4	2–2	1–2	1–1	2–2	1–3	2–2	0–4	*	0–3	1–1	0–0	0–2
19 Tooting & M Utd	1–0	1–1	0–2	2–3	3–2	0–2	0–2	1–0	1–1	0–2	1–0	0–0	2–1	5–1	5–2	1–0	2–1	3–0	*	2–0	3–0	1–2
20 Walthamstow Ave.	1–3	4–1	4–0	2–2	1–5	3–0	3–0	2–2	2–1	2–2	0–1	4–2	2–3	2–1	3–0	3–1	2–0	7–0	4–0	*	2–4	2–1
21 Woking	0–0	2–3	7–0	1–1	0–0	1–1	2–1	3–1	2–1	2–1	3–1	1–1	3–0	5–1	4–0	2–3	1–3	3–2	1–3	0–1	*	0–0
22 Wycombe Wndrs.	1–2	1–2	4–1	5–1	0–0	2–1	0–4	2–3	5–0	3–1	1–1	1–0	3–1	5–3	1–0	4–0	2–2	2–2	0–0	1–1	1–1	*

Premier Division	*P*	*W*	*D*	*L*	*F*	*A*	*Pts*
1 Enfield	42	25	9	8	74	32	84
2 Walthamstow Ave.	42	24	9	9	87	48	81
3 Dulwich Hamlet	42	21	16	5	66	37	79
4 Sutton United	42	20	13	9	67	40	73
5 Dagenham	42	20	13	9	82	56	73
6 Tooting & M Utd	42	21	6	15	62	59	69
7 Barking	42	19	10	13	72	51	67
8 Harrow Borough	42	17	15	10	64	51	66
9 Woking	42	17	13	12	78	59	64
10 Wycombe Wand	42	17	13	12	72	53	64
11 Harlow Town	42	14	12	16	55	61	54
12 Hitchin Town	42	13	15	14	55	69	54
13 Hendon	42	12	13	17	50	57	49
14 Slough Town	42	13	10	19	54	71	49
15 Boreham Wood	42	13	10	19	50	69	49
16 Staines Town	42	14	6	22	46	67	48
17 Hayes	42	12	9	21	48	68	45
18 Leatherhead	42	11	11	20	51	60	44
19 Carshalton Athletic	42	12	7	23	48	78	43
20 Croydon	42	10	10	22	51	59	40
21 Oxford City	42	10	9	23	49	87	39
22 Tilbury*	42	7	11	24	41	90	30

**Tilbury had two points deducted.*

DULWICH HAMLET FOOTBALL CLUB
1979 - 80 Season
Back Row (L to R) Stuart Scott (Coach), Mark Denton, Paul Edwards, Kimm Connett, Steve Bowtell, Tony Davies, Rod Brookes, Danny Godwin, Tony White, Jeff Brittain (Physio)
Front Row—seated (L to R) Martin Lewis, Steve Rogers, Ossie Bayram, Alan Smith (Manager), Tony James, Kevin Wallis, George Borg

Division I	1	2	3	4	5	6	7	8	9	10	11	12	13	14	15	16	17	18	19	20	21	22
1 Aveley	*	4–0	1–5	0–1	1–1	2–1	2–0	2–2	1–4	3–0	0–0	0–0	4–0	1–0	0–2	0–1	0–0	1–0	1–1	1–2	0–2	0–2
2 Bishop's Stortford	3–0	*	4–3	1–0	0–0	6–0	2–2	0–3	2–1	3–1	2–0	4–2	5–0	0–2	2–1	2–2	4–0	1–1	2–0	2–1	2–1	2–2
3 Bromley	2–0	0–0	*	2–2	3–0	4–0	5–1	2–1	2–0	3–0	2–2	2–0	6–1	1–1	0–2	1–3	2–0	2–1	2–1	4–1	2–2	6–1
4 Camberley Town	0–0	1–0	1–1	*	0–1	0–0	2–0	0–1	1–0	1–3	1–0	2–1	2–1	0–1	0–1	1–3	0–1	3–0	3–0	0–1	0–2	0–2
5 Chesham United	1–1	1–4	2–1	1–1	*	2–1	3–2	2–2	0–1	2–2	6–0	2–2	4–1	1–1	0–2	3–1	2–1	0–1	1–1	2–2	3–0	1–0
6 Clapton	1–0	1–4	1–0	1–2	1–2	*	0–2	2–1	2–2	3–0	4–0	2–0	4–0	0–1	1–3	0–3	0–4	1–4	0–6	3–2	4–0	1–0
7 Epsom & Ewell	3–2	0–1	0–0	1–1	2–5	3–0	*	0–1	2–0	4–1	0–2	5–3	2–0	1–4	0–1	0–0	4–0	2–0	1–3	2–1	2–0	0–2
8 Farnborough Town	4–1	2–1	2–1	1–1	0–1	0–1	1–1	*	2–3	4–1	4–2	3–1	3–0	3–5	1–2	1–4	2–2	2–3	0–2	2–3	3–0	2–1
9 Finchley	1–0	3–0	0–1	0–1	1–1	1–0	0–0	1–2	*	1–0	1–1	0–2	2–0	1–2	1–5	2–1	2–2	1–0	1–2	2–1	0–2	2–1
10 Hampton	0–1	1–2	2–4	1–2	2–2	3–2	0–1	0–1	2–1	*	2–1	2–1	2–3	1–2	0–2	2–2	1–0	3–1	0–0	0–0	3–2	0–1
11 Harwich & Parkst.	2–5	0–2	3–0	1–3	2–3	2–1	0–2	2–0	3–0	1–0	*	1–2	4–2	1–3	1–1	1–2	2–3	2–4	1–3	2–2	1–1	3–0
12 Hertford Town	1–1	1–1	2–2	1–1	2–3	2–0	1–3	2–0	3–1	3–0	1–3	*	4–1	1–0	5–2	2–4	0–2	3–3	2–3	0–0	1–1	3–2
13 Horsham	0–1	1–1	0–4	1–1	0–2	0–2	1–4	0–4	1–1	1–3	2–0	0–5	*	0–1	1–4	0–7	0–1	0–4	0–3	0–1	1–0	2–1
14 Kingstonian	3–0	2–1	0–4	0–3	2–0	2–1	1–0	2–0	1–0	0–0	5–0	0–3	1–3	*	0–0	4–1	1–1	1–0	2–4	1–0	1–0	0–0
15 Leytonstone Ilford	0–1	2–0	2–2	2–0	1–0	5–2	3–2	2–1	3–2	3–1	1–0	3–1	3–0	2–1	*	3–0	2–0	2–1	3–0	2–0	1–0	1–1
16 Maidenhead Utd	1–1	2–1	1–4	1–0	2–1	2–0	2–1	0–1	0–0	0–4	3–0	4–0	6–1	0–1	1–0	*	4–0	1–1	3–0	3–0	0–0	1–0
17 Metropolitan Police	1–1	2–3	1–3	1–0	1–0	0–1	0–2	0–3	3–0	2–3	0–2	3–2	3–0	1–0	2–1	2–3	*	1–1	1–4	1–0	1–2	0–3
18 St. Albans City	3–0	0–1	1–1	0–2	2–3	1–0	4–0	2–2	2–0	2–3	2–1	2–0	4–1	2–2	0–0	1–1	2–2	*	1–0	3–0	0–0	1–1
19 Walton & Hersham	1–1	2–0	0–1	2–1	2–0	2–2	0–1	0–1	1–3	4–2	0–1	0–1	0–0	1–1	1–2	1–3	1–1	0–0	*	3–1	1–1	0–0
20 Ware	2–1	0–1	1–0	0–0	2–2	0–1	2–4	0–1	1–1	1–1	4–0	2–2	2–1	2–1	2–3	2–0	1–0	0–1	1–1	*	1–4	0–0
21 Wembley	1–3	0–1	1–2	0–3	0–1	3–1	0–0	1–0	3–1	1–3	3–0	1–0	2–1	3–1	1–2	1–0	2–0	0–2	0–4	0–0	*	1–0
22 Wokingham Town	1–1	0–1	0–1	2–0	3–1	1–0	1–0	1–1	0–0	1–2	2–1	3–3	0–2	1–0	1–1	1–3	1–0	1–2	2–1	3–1	0–2	*

Division I	*P*	*W*	*D*	*L*	*F*	*A*	*Pts*
1 Leytonstone Ilford	42	31	6	5	83	35	99
2 Bromley	42	24	10	8	93	44	82
3 Maidenhead Utd	42	24	8	10	81	46	80
4 Bishop's Stortford	42	24	8	10	74	47	80
5 Kingstonian	42	22	8	12	59	44	74
6 Chesham United	42	18	13	11	68	56	67
7 St. Albans City	42	17	13	12	65	47	64
8 Farnborough Town	42	19	7	16	70	57	64
9 Epsom & Ewell	42	18	7	17	62	57	61
10 Camberley Town	42	16	10	16	43	38	58
11 Walton & Hersham	42	15	12	15	61	50	57
12 Wembley	42	16	8	18	46	52	56
13 Wokingham Town	42	14	11	17	45	49	53
14 Hertford Town	42	13	11	18	71	74	50
15 Aveley	42	12	13	17	45	55	49
16 Hampton	42	14	7	21	57	74	49
17 Finchley	42	13	9	20	44	59	48
18 Metropolitan Police	42	13	8	21	46	67	47
19 Ware	42	11	12	19	45	61	45
20 Clapton	42	14	3	25	48	77	45
21 Harwich & Parkst.*	42	11	6	25	51	84	38
22 Horsham	42	6	4	32	29	113	22

** Harwich & Parkeston had one point deducted.*
Ilford FC and Leytonstone FC amalgamated to form Leytonstone & Ilford FC

CLAPTON F.C. 1979-80

Back Row: W. Tingle *(Chairman)*, L.Piatkowski, A. Shirley, J. Gormley, C. Flynn, A. Atkinson, J. Holt, M. McShea.
Front Row: T. Flynn, S. Faldo, M. Cleaver, L. Ashworth, D. Gill, T. Davis.

Clapton during season 1979/80.

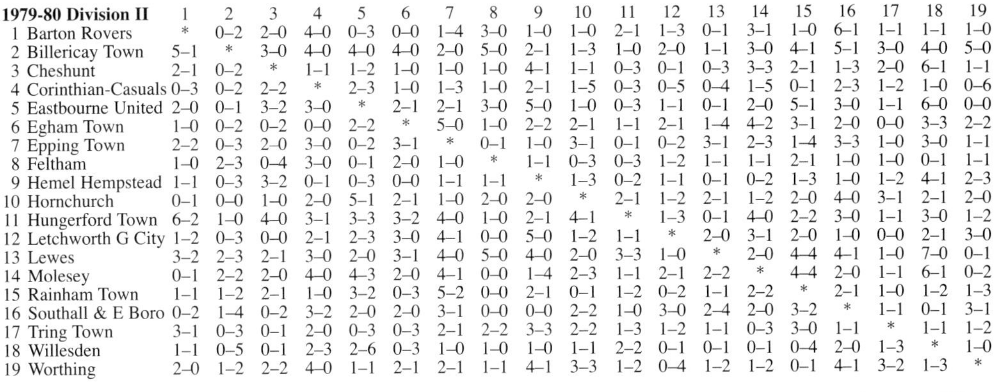

1979-80 Division II	1	2	3	4	5	6	7	8	9	10	11	12	13	14	15	16	17	18	19
1 Barton Rovers	*	0–2	2–0	4–0	0–3	0–0	1–4	3–0	1–0	1–0	2–1	1–3	0–1	3–1	1–0	6–1	1–1	1–1	1–0
2 Billericay Town	5–1	*	3–0	4–0	4–0	4–0	2–0	5–0	2–1	1–3	1–0	2–0	1–1	3–0	4–1	5–1	3–0	4–0	5–0
3 Cheshunt	2–1	0–2	*	1–1	1–2	1–0	1–0	1–0	4–1	1–1	0–3	0–1	0–3	3–3	2–1	1–3	2–0	6–1	1–1
4 Corinthian-Casuals	0–3	0–2	2–2	*	2–3	1–0	1–3	1–0	2–1	1–5	0–3	0–5	0–4	1–5	0–1	2–3	1–2	1–0	0–6
5 Eastbourne United	2–0	0–1	3–2	3–0	*	2–1	2–1	3–0	5–0	1–0	0–3	1–1	0–1	2–0	5–1	3–0	1–1	6–0	0–0
6 Egham Town	1–0	0–2	0–2	0–0	2–2	*	5–0	1–0	2–2	2–1	1–1	2–1	1–4	4–2	3–1	2–0	0–0	3–3	2–2
7 Epping Town	2–2	0–3	2–0	3–0	0–2	3–1	*	0–1	1–0	3–1	0–1	0–2	3–1	2–3	1–4	3–3	1–0	3–0	1–1
8 Feltham	1–0	2–3	0–4	3–0	0–1	2–0	1–0	*	1–1	0–3	0–3	1–2	1–1	1–1	2–1	1–0	1–0	0–1	1–1
9 Hemel Hempstead	1–1	0–3	3–2	0–1	0–3	0–0	1–1	1–1	*	1–3	0–2	1–1	0–1	0–2	1–3	1–0	1–2	4–1	2–3
10 Hornchurch	0–1	0–0	1–0	2–0	5–1	2–1	1–0	2–0	2–0	*	2–1	1–2	2–1	1–2	2–0	4–0	3–1	2–1	2–0
11 Hungerford Town	6–2	1–0	4–0	3–1	3–3	3–2	4–0	1–0	2–1	4–1	*	1–3	0–1	4–0	2–2	3–0	1–1	3–0	1–2
12 Letchworth G City	1–2	0–3	0–0	2–1	2–3	3–0	4–1	0–0	5–0	1–2	1–1	*	2–0	3–1	2–0	1–0	0–0	2–1	3–0
13 Lewes	3–2	2–3	2–1	3–0	2–0	3–1	4–0	5–0	4–0	2–0	3–3	1–0	*	2–0	4–4	4–1	1–0	7–0	0–1
14 Molesey	0–1	2–2	2–0	4–0	4–3	2–0	4–1	0–0	1–4	2–3	1–1	2–1	2–2	*	4–4	2–0	1–1	6–1	0–2
15 Rainham Town	1–1	1–2	2–1	1–0	3–2	0–3	5–2	0–0	2–1	0–1	1–2	0–2	1–1	2–2	*	2–1	1–0	1–2	1–3
16 Southall & E Boro	0–2	1–4	0–2	3–2	2–0	2–0	3–1	0–0	0–0	2–2	1–0	3–0	2–4	2–0	3–2	*	1–1	0–1	3–1
17 Tring Town	3–1	0–3	0–1	2–0	0–3	0–3	2–1	2–2	3–3	2–2	1–3	1–2	1–1	0–3	3–0	1–1	*	1–1	1–2
18 Willesden	1–1	0–5	0–1	2–3	2–6	0–3	1–0	1–0	1–0	1–1	2–2	0–1	0–1	0–1	0–4	2–0	1–3	*	1–0
19 Worthing	2–0	1–2	2–2	4–0	1–1	2–1	2–1	1–1	4–1	3–3	1–2	0–4	1–2	1–2	0–1	4–1	3–2	1–3	*

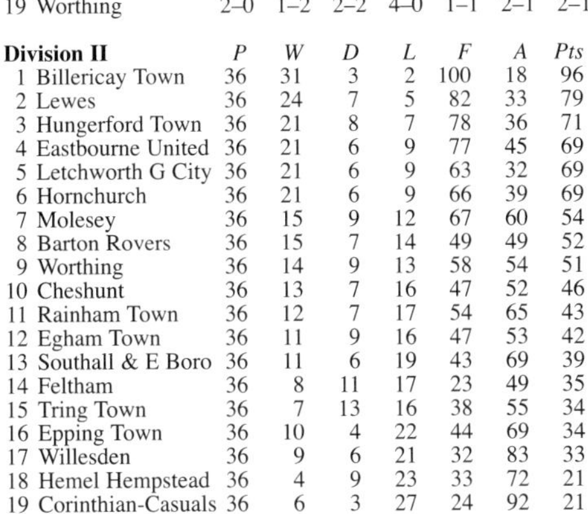

Division II	*P*	*W*	*D*	*L*	*F*	*A*	*Pts*
1 Billericay Town	36	31	3	2	100	18	96
2 Lewes	36	24	7	5	82	33	79
3 Hungerford Town	36	21	8	7	78	36	71
4 Eastbourne United	36	21	6	9	77	45	69
5 Letchworth G City	36	21	6	9	63	32	69
6 Hornchurch	36	21	6	9	66	39	69
7 Molesey	36	15	9	12	67	60	54
8 Barton Rovers	36	15	7	14	49	49	52
9 Worthing	36	14	9	13	58	54	51
10 Cheshunt	36	13	7	16	47	52	46
11 Rainham Town	36	12	7	17	54	65	43
12 Egham Town	36	11	9	16	47	53	42
13 Southall & E Boro	36	11	6	19	43	69	39
14 Feltham	36	8	11	17	23	49	35
15 Tring Town	36	7	13	16	38	55	34
16 Epping Town	36	10	4	22	44	69	34
17 Willesden	36	9	6	21	32	83	33
18 Hemel Hempstead	36	4	9	23	33	72	21
19 Corinthian-Casuals	36	6	3	27	24	92	21

Right: the Harrow Borough matchday programme from 1979-80.

Left: the Farnborough View from the same campaign.

Below: the Dagenham programme from 1980-81.

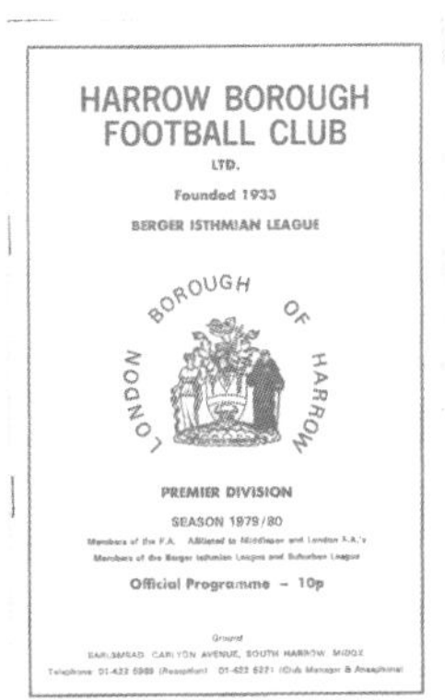

1980–81 - The Premier Division championship was decided on the final day of the season when Slough Town won their first Isthmian League title by two points from Enfield, with Wycombe Wanderers and newly-promoted Leytonstone & Ilford third and fourth, respectively. The most spectacular recovery of the season was Hendon who were bottom of the League in February and continued to move up the table to eventually finish in sixth. With Enfield and Dagenham leaving the Isthmian to join the Alliance Premier League, the bottom two teams, Boreham Wood and Woking, escaped relegation. In Division One it was a two-horse race for most of the season with Billericay Town continuing their success and securing the championship by three points from Bishop's Stortford, with Epsom & Ewell a respectable third. At the foot of the table Camberley Town and Finchley were both relegated to Division Two. In Division Two Feltham were crowned champions by just one point from Hornchurch, with Hungerford Town, who recovered from a poor start to the season, in third. At the Annual General Meeting it was confirmed that Enfield and Dagenham would be joining the Alliance Premier League and that Willesden had also resigned. An application had been received from Bognor Regis Town to join the League from the Southern League and it was proposed, seconded and voted by 51 votes for to 15 against that they would be elected to Division One. There were four vacancies in Division Two and five clubs including the two forced to apply for re-election – Molesey and Corinthian–Casuals – were subsequently proposed and seconded

The voting was by ballot, with Newbury Town the unlucky club. The results were as follows: *Windsor & Eton 64, Molesey 63, Basildon United 58, Corinthian–Casuals 56, Newbury Town 4.*

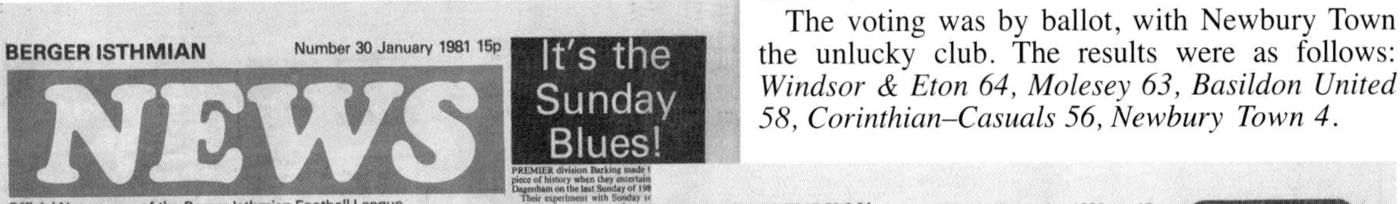

BERGER ISTHMIAN Number 30 January 1981 15p

NEWS

Official Newspaper of the Berger Isthmian Football League

It's the Sunday Blues!

Gigi Peronace

ISTHMIAN AND SOUTHERN TO FORM 'SUPER' LEAGUE

AN exciting set of proposals have been drawn up which could lead to the cream of the Isthmian and Southern Leagues forming a new "super" league the season after next.

BERGER ISTHMIAN No. 29 December 1980 15p

NEWS

Official Newspaper of the Berger Isthmian Football League

ISTHMIAN FURY OVER ALLIANCE APPROACH

Inside your News

A MAN WITH MAGIC HANDS — Page 3

ENFIELD TAKE FIVES TITLE — Page 4

F.A. CUP FIRST ROUND SPECIAL — Page 5

SPOTLIGHT ON CHESHUNT — Pages 6 & 7

Pictured above and to the right, copies of the popular and innovative Isthmian News, which was circulated monthly to each member club during the Berger sponsorship.

1980-81

Premier Division	1	2	3	4	5	6	7	8	9	10	11	12	13	14	15	16	17	18	19	20	21	22
1 Barking	*	3–2	2–2	0–0	0–0	1–3	2–3	4–2	0–2	1–1	1–0	1–3	2–3	2–1	5–4	1–1	0–2	3–3	0–1	0–3	1–3	2–0
2 Boreham Wood	2–2	*	0–1	0–0	0–3	1–0	2–1	0–2	1–1	0–1	1–0	1–3	0–3	2–1	3–3	1–0	2–2	1–1	0–0	1–1	2–1	0–4
3 Bromley	4–0	1–1	*	4–3	3–1	1–0	1–3	0–2	1–1	3–1	2–0	2–2	2–0	3–1	1–2	1–1	2–0	1–4	2–1	1–1	5–0	3–2
4 Carshalton Athletic	1–2	1–0	3–1	*	1–0	2–4	0–3	0–2	3–1	1–3	3–0	2–1	2–1	5–4	3–4	0–3	1–0	1–1	1–4	3–3	2–1	1–1
5 Croydon	3–0	1–1	0–0	2–1	*	1–1	1–1	1–2	2–1	1–0	0–1	3–0	1–1	1–1	1–3	1–1	1–1	3–1	1–2	6–3	2–1	2–3
6 Dagenham	1–4	3–0	2–0	2–1	2–1	*	2–2	1–0	1–1	3–3	0–0	1–0	2–0	1–2	1–3	0–2	2–2	1–4	5–1	1–0	4–0	5–0
7 Dulwich Hamlet	2–0	3–2	2–2	1–0	1–1	3–3	*	1–2	3–0	0–1	0–1	2–3	2–0	0–0	2–2	0–1	2–2	1–3	1–0	1–2	3–2	2–2
8 Enfield	2–1	4–0	1–0	1–2	1–0	1–1	2–0	*	6–1	3–1	0–1	0–3	2–5	4–0	0–0	0–0	1–1	1–1	3–3	2–1	3–1	2–0
9 Harlow Town	0–0	1–1	0–1	2–3	2–1	0–2	1–3	2–2	*	1–0	1–2	1–1	3–1	2–2	0–0	1–1	0–0	1–1	0–2	0–2	3–1	1–3
10 Harrow Borough	2–1	2–1	2–0	1–1	0–0	3–3	4–1	1–0	4–1	*	2–2	1–1	0–4	0–1	1–2	2–0	1–0	1–2	2–0	1–0	0–0	1–1
11 Hayes	1–2	0–3	3–0	3–1	2–1	1–0	2–0	1–1	2–1	0–1	*	3–1	0–0	1–2	1–1	0–0	0–1	1–1	2–4	0–1	1–0	2–1
12 Hendon	1–3	1–3	2–0	1–1	1–0	4–1	1–2	0–3	1–1	1–0	0–1	*	3–0	0–0	3–2	1–1	4–2	4–1	2–0	0–2	0–2	0–1
13 Hitchin Town	2–2	4–1	5–1	3–0	1–2	2–6	2–0	2–2	0–1	2–0	0–1	2–3	*	1–1	0–2	1–0	3–4	1–2	1–2	1–0	3–1	0–0
14 Leatherhead	1–1	1–2	3–0	2–0	0–0	1–2	0–0	0–3	0–2	0–0	0–3	1–1	1–0	*	1–0	0–2	1–0	0–1	0–1	1–0	0–0	1–1
15 Leytonstone Ilford	1–1	1–1	2–1	3–0	0–1	4–3	3–2	1–0	2–4	2–2	1–1	2–0	1–1	5–1	*	3–3	1–1	1–3	1–0	0–1	1–3	0–1
16 Slough Town	1–0	1–0	2–1	6–0	4–0	3–3	5–1	0–0	2–2	1–0	3–0	1–2	0–0	1–0	2–1	*	3–1	3–2	2–1	3–0	1–1	2–1
17 Staines Town	0–1	3–2	1–3	4–1	1–1	0–1	2–0	1–3	1–3	0–6	4–0	2–3	1–1	0–1	0–2	0–2	*	3–0	1–0	4–0	1–0	2–1
18 Sutton United	3–1	2–2	3–4	2–1	2–1	1–0	1–5	2–3	4–4	4–1	4–0	2–2	6–2	0–0	1–0	1–2	1–3	*	0–0	2–0	3–1	2–0
19 Tooting & M Utd	1–2	3–1	1–1	1–2	0–0	1–0	1–0	1–2	1–2	2–1	0–1	4–1	1–1	0–1	1–4	2–1	1–2	1–1	*	1–0	2–0	1–2
20 Walthamstow Ave.	2–3	2–1	3–2	2–2	2–3	3–1	1–1	1–8	2–1	2–0	2–4	0–4	0–4	2–1	0–2	0–2	3–2	0–2	1–1	*	0–1	2–2
21 Woking	1–1	1–2	1–0	1–2	1–1	3–1	1–1	1–2	0–1	1–2	1–0	0–0	0–1	1–2	1–4	2–0	0–3	2–1	2–0	1–0	*	0–4
22 Wycombe Wndrs.	2–0	1–0	5–0	2–0	2–0	4–4	4–1	1–1	1–0	3–2	3–1	1–2	2–0	0–0	0–2	1–4	1–0	3–1	1–0	5–0	4–0	*

Premier Division	*P*	*W*	*D*	*L*	*F*	*A*	*Pts*
1 Slough Town	42	23	13	6	73	34	82
2 Enfield	42	23	11	8	81	43	80
3 Wycombe Wand	42	22	9	11	76	49	75
4 Leytonstone Ilford	42	19	12	11	78	57	69
5 Sutton United	42	19	12	11	82	65	69
6 Hendon	42	18	10	14	66	58	64
7 Dagenham	42	17	11	14	79	66	62
8 Hayes	42	18	8	16	45	50	62
9 Harrow Borough	42	16	11	15	57	52	59
10 Bromley	42	16	9	17	63	69	57
11 Staines Town	42	15	9	18	60	61	54
12 Tooting & M Utd	42	15	8	19	49	53	53
13 Hitchin Town	42	14	10	18	64	62	52
14 Croydon	42	12	15	15	51	51	51
15 Dulwich Hamlet	42	13	12	17	62	67	51
16 Leatherhead	42	12	14	16	36	50	50
17 Carshalton Athletic	42	14	8	20	57	82	50
18 Barking*	42	13	12	17	58	72	49
19 Harlow Town	42	11	15	16	53	66	48
20 Walthamstow Ave.	42	13	7	22	50	81	46
21 Boreham Wood	42	10	13	19	46	69	43
22 Woking+	42	11	7	24	40	69	37

** Barking had two points deducted.*
+ Woking had three points deducted.

HARLOW
TOWN FOOTBALL CLUB LTD
BERGER ISTHMIAN LEAGUE · PREMIER DIV.
Official Match Day Magazine 1980-81

Left: Harlow Town's matchday programme from 1980-81.
Below: Wycombe Wanderers edition for the same season.

Wycombe Wanderers
Football Club
DULWICH HAMLET
Saturday 14th November 1981
Loakes Park
High Wycombe
3 p.m.
OFFICIAL PROGRAMME

Division I	1	2	3	4	5	6	7	8	9	10	11	12	13	14	15	16	17	18	19	20	21	22
1 Aveley	*	1–3	0–2	1–2	2–0	0–0	2–3	0–2	1–3	0–1	5–0	2–0	1–2	3–1	4–1	1–0	0–0	3–0	0–0	3–1	2–0	0–2
2 Billericay Town	1–0	*	0–1	2–0	0–1	2–1	2–2	1–0	1–0	4–2	3–0	2–1	3–1	2–1	1–3	0–1	1–0	1–1	3–2	2–0	2–1	2–1
3 Bishop's Stortford	3–0	0–1	*	1–0	0–0	5–2	0–0	1–0	6–0	1–0	1–1	1–0	3–0	3–0	3–1	2–1	3–6	2–0	3–1	3–0	1–0	0–0
4 Camberley Town	0–3	1–2	2–1	*	1–0	2–2	0–2	2–2	1–0	1–3	0–1	1–2	1–2	0–3	0–1	2–1	3–1	0–1	1–2	3–1	0–1	1–1
5 Chesham United	3–0	1–0	0–1	4–2	*	6–3	0–1	1–3	3–4	1–2	2–1	0–1	6–4	2–0	3–0	0–0	1–2	2–0	0–2	0–0	2–1	0–0
6 Clapton	2–2	0–3	0–4	3–1	0–1	*	3–1	0–0	1–0	1–2	1–1	2–1	3–2	2–1	1–4	0–1	3–1	1–1	3–1	2–2	2–1	3–2
7 Epsom & Ewell	3–1	2–2	1–1	5–1	0–2	4–0	*	2–0	1–1	1–1	2–1	2–2	2–0	1–0	3–2	2–0	0–0	5–0	2–0	0–1	1–1	1–1
8 Farnborough Town	3–2	1–1	0–1	3–1	1–1	3–0	1–0	*	2–1	0–0	5–1	0–0	3–2	3–0	1–0	2–2	3–1	5–1	0–1	2–2	1–0	2–0
9 Finchley	1–0	1–3	0–2	0–1	2–1	4–1	0–2	0–3	*	0–2	2–2	1–1	0–0	0–2	1–3	1–3	1–1	1–3	0–0	0–2	0–1	1–1
10 Hampton	2–1	1–3	0–1	2–2	2–1	2–0	1–1	0–2	0–0	*	1–1	1–2	1–1	1–2	1–1	2–0	0–1	0–1	0–0	1–0	0–1	2–1
11 Hertford Town	0–0	0–1	2–1	3–0	3–4	1–1	1–4	1–3	1–0	0–0	*	1–1	4–1	1–5	0–0	2–1	1–0	1–0	0–0	1–0	0–1	0–0
12 Kingstonian	0–0	1–0	0–3	1–0	4–2	4–1	1–2	2–3	3–1	4–1	2–0	*	4–0	2–1	1–0	2–3	0–2	4–0	1–1	0–0	1–3	1–0
13 Lewes	5–3	1–0	0–3	5–3	0–1	3–2	1–5	0–2	1–1	1–0	2–3	6–0	*	1–1	2–1	1–0	5–2	3–1	2–0	4–0	0–1	3–3
14 Maidenhead Utd	2–0	1–1	1–0	1–1	1–4	0–1	2–5	1–2	1–2	2–0	1–0	0–1	1–2	*	1–1	0–2	2–0	2–2	2–1	2–1	2–1	3–0
15 Metropolitan Police	1–0	0–2	0–5	3–2	3–3	3–0	0–2	2–3	1–0	0–2	1–0	2–4	0–0	1–1	*	2–0	3–0	4–2	2–0	3–0	0–0	0–1
16 Oxford City	1–1	0–1	1–1	3–0	0–2	5–0	0–1	1–1	5–0	1–1	1–3	1–2	3–0	3–3	2–0	*	2–0	3–2	1–1	4–0	3–2	5–1
17 St. Albans City	2–1	1–2	2–1	5–1	6–2	1–0	2–1	3–2	5–2	2–1	3–2	1–0	3–2	3–1	2–3	1–1	*	3–0	3–1	3–3	3–0	3–1
18 Tilbury	1–4	0–1	2–3	1–1	3–2	2–0	0–2	1–4	1–1	3–2	0–1	0–1	2–0	0–2	0–4	0–3	0–4	*	2–0	2–2	1–2	2–1
19 Walton & Hersham	0–0	1–2	1–2	2–0	0–0	1–0	1–0	1–0	3–3	2–2	4–0	0–1	2–4	3–1	0–1	0–3	2–1	4–3	*	1–0	0–0	1–1
20 Ware	0–1	0–1	1–3	5–0	2–0	0–4	1–2	0–0	3–1	2–2	2–1	1–1	2–3	1–2	2–0	2–3	1–3	0–0	1–1	*	3–2	2–2
21 Wembley	1–3	2–3	0–3	5–1	3–0	2–1	1–1	1–1	2–0	3–2	2–3	1–1	0–0	0–1	1–3	2–0	0–1	0–1	1–1	0–3	*	1–4
22 Wokingham Town	1–1	0–0	2–3	1–1	4–0	4–1	0–3	2–1	1–0	2–0	2–1	4–3	7–0	3–2	2–1	2–1	3–2	0–0	2–2	1–1	4–0	*

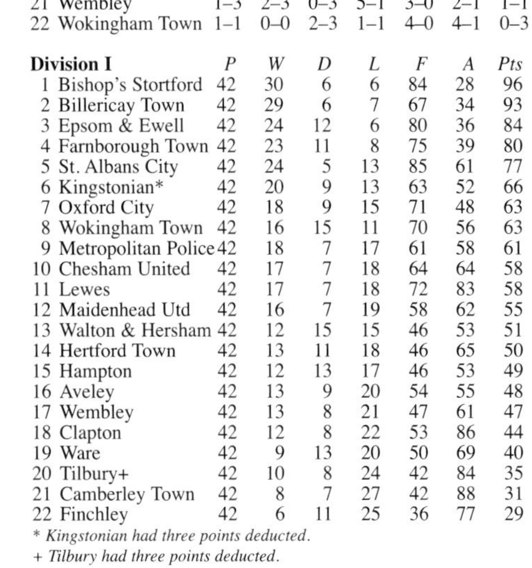

Division I	*P*	*W*	*D*	*L*	*F*	*A*	*Pts*
1 Bishop's Stortford	42	30	6	6	84	28	96
2 Billericay Town	42	29	6	7	67	34	93
3 Epsom & Ewell	42	24	12	6	80	36	84
4 Farnborough Town	42	23	11	8	75	39	80
5 St. Albans City	42	24	5	13	85	61	77
6 Kingstonian*	42	20	9	13	63	52	66
7 Oxford City	42	18	9	15	71	48	63
8 Wokingham Town	42	16	15	11	70	56	63
9 Metropolitan Police	42	18	7	17	61	58	61
10 Chesham United	42	17	7	18	64	64	58
11 Lewes	42	17	7	18	72	83	58
12 Maidenhead Utd	42	16	7	19	58	62	55
13 Walton & Hersham	42	12	15	15	46	53	51
14 Hertford Town	42	13	11	18	46	65	50
15 Hampton	42	12	13	17	46	53	49
16 Aveley	42	13	9	20	54	55	48
17 Wembley	42	13	8	21	47	61	47
18 Clapton	42	12	8	22	53	86	44
19 Ware	42	9	13	20	50	69	40
20 Tilbury+	42	10	8	24	42	84	35
21 Camberley Town	42	8	7	27	42	88	31
22 Finchley	42	6	11	25	36	77	29

** Kingstonian had three points deducted.*
+ Tilbury had three points deducted.

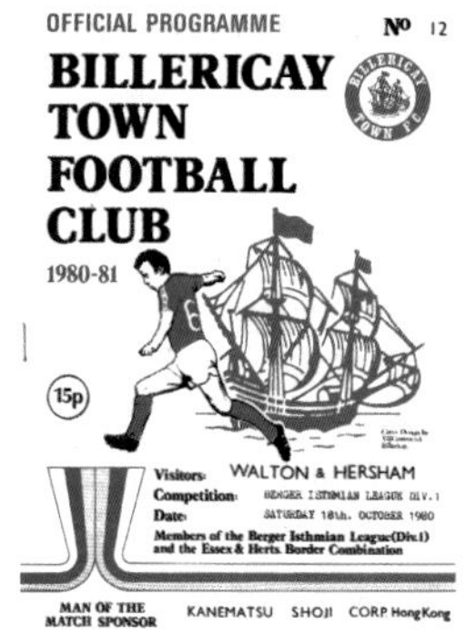

Left: the Billericay Town programme for 1980-81.

Right: the programme for the Five-a-Side Championship played at Wembley Arena for the Prince Philip Cup, a competition organised by the then Chairman and President Mr Barry East.

1980-81 Division II	1	2	3	4	5	6	7	8	9	10	11	12	13	14	15	16	17	18	19	20
1 Barton Rovers	*	0–1	1–1	0–0	5–0	2–0	0–0	0–2	2–1	3–0	1–0	1–0	0–0	3–3	2–0	0–0	3–2	3–0	1–2	0–0
2 Cheshunt	0–1	*	2–0	1–1	1–1	5–0	2–1	1–1	0–0	3–0	1–1	1–0	0–3	0–0	5–1	1–0	1–2	2–1	0–1	2–4
3 Corinthian-Casuals	0–4	0–1	*	0–2	2–1	2–3	0–2	1–4	1–7	0–2	0–3	0–2	0–4	0–3	1–1	0–2	1–1	0–2	2–2	1–4
4 Dorking Town	2–1	1–1	5–0	*	3–2	2–2	1–0	1–3	1–2	1–0	0–3	0–1	2–1	1–2	1–1	1–1	1–1	0–1	0–0	2–2
5 Eastbourne United	0–0	1–3	3–0	2–1	*	1–1	3–2	1–2	2–1	4–2	2–2	2–1	1–4	0–1	5–2	1–2	0–3	1–1	1–3	0–1
6 Egham Town	1–0	0–3	0–0	3–1	2–0	*	1–0	1–3	2–2	2–1	1–3	2–4	3–1	2–0	3–0	0–1	1–3	0–1	0–5	2–2
7 Epping Town	0–3	1–2	4–0	2–1	0–0	2–0	*	0–1	2–0	0–0	0–2	1–0	1–2	0–3	1–0	1–1	0–1	2–1	2–3	1–1
8 Feltham	1–0	1–0	1–1	1–0	2–2	0–0	4–0	*	5–0	2–1	1–2	2–0	0–0	1–1	1–1	2–0	4–1	4–0	1–0	0–0
9 Harwich & Parkst.	0–4	2–2	2–1	0–0	1–4	0–0	0–1	0–2	*	1–1	1–2	2–0	1–1	1–3	0–0	1–1	3–2	3–2	8–1	3–0
10 Hemel Hempstead	1–6	3–1	2–0	0–2	0–3	2–2	4–2	3–1	3–1	*	0–2	2–1	0–1	1–0	2–0	2–1	0–1	1–2	1–0	2–2
11 Hornchurch	1–0	1–4	7–0	1–0	3–3	2–0	0–1	2–0	1–0	2–2	*	4–0	0–0	2–1	4–0	2–1	1–0	1–3	3–1	0–3
12 Horsham	0–0	1–2	2–0	1–2	7–2	2–0	2–0	0–1	2–0	1–0	1–2	*	1-	0–3	3–0	1–0	0–0	1–0	1–3	1–0
13 Hungerford Town	2–2	0–0	6–0	4–1	4–1	3–0	2–0	1–1	1–0	2–0	0–0	2–0	*	5–0	5–2	2–1	3–0	4–1	3–0	1–1
14 Letchworth G City	0–1	0–0	3–1	0–1	2–2	2–4	0–2	0–1	2–3	2–0	1–0	1–0	2–1	*	3–1	1–0	1–1	2–0	2–0	0–2
15 Molesey	0–1	0–3	2–0	2–3	0–2	1–2	1–0	0–1	1–0	0–3	1–2	1–1	0–1	0–1	*	2–2	3–4	0–3	2–2	1–2
16 Rainham Town	0–0	1–2	0–0	0–0	1–2	0–0	3–2	0–1	2–3	0–0	3–2	3–1	3–1	2–1	1–0	*	1–1	1–1	2–1	1–3
17 Southall	1–3	0–1	1–0	0–2	3–2	2–1	0–0	2–2	0–3	0–1	0–2	1–2	1–1	1–0	3–3	2–2	*	0–0	2–0	1–0
18 Tring Town	1–4	0–1	1–0	1–3	2–1	0–2	1–1	1–3	2–2	0–5	0–2	2–1	3–2	1–2	0–2	0–5	3–1	*	1–1	1–2
19 Willesden	1–3	1–0	2–2	2–1	1–1	0–1	1–2	1–2	1–1	0–0	2–3	1–2	0–6	0–1	10–0	2–0	1–3	4–0	*	1–3
20 Worthing	2–1	2–2	1–0	1–1	4–0	4–1	4–1	6–1	1–2	3–0	1–4	2–4	1–3	0–0	0–0	3–0	0–1	2–1	5–1	*

Division II	*P*	*W*	*D*	*L*	*F*	*A*	*Pts*
1 Feltham	38	24	10	4	65	30	82
2 Hornchurch	38	25	6	7	74	35	81
3 Hungerford Town	38	23	10	5	84	29	79
4 Barton Rovers	38	19	11	8	61	25	68
5 Worthing	38	19	11	8	74	43	68
6 Cheshunt	38	19	11	8	57	33	68
7 Letchworth G City	38	18	7	13	49	40	61
8 Southall	38	14	11	13	48	52	53
9 Dorking Town	38	13	12	13	47	45	51
10 Horsham	38	16	3	19	47	47	51
11 Hemel Hempstead	38	14	7	17	47	54	49
12 Egham Town	38	13	9	16	45	62	48
13 Harwich & Parkst.	38	12	11	15	57	58	47
14 Rainham Town	38	11	13	14	44	45	46
15 Epping Town	38	12	7	19	37	50	43
16 Eastbourne United	38	11	10	17	59	75	43
17 Willesden	38	11	8	19	57	68	41
18 Tring Town	38	11	6	21	40	71	39
19 Molesey	38	4	9	25	31	83	21
20 Corinthian-Casuals	38	1	8	29	17	95	11

Southall were previously Southall & Ealing Borough.

Below left: the Boreham Wood matchday programme from 1981-82.

Below right: the Billericay Town Club Handbook for the same season.

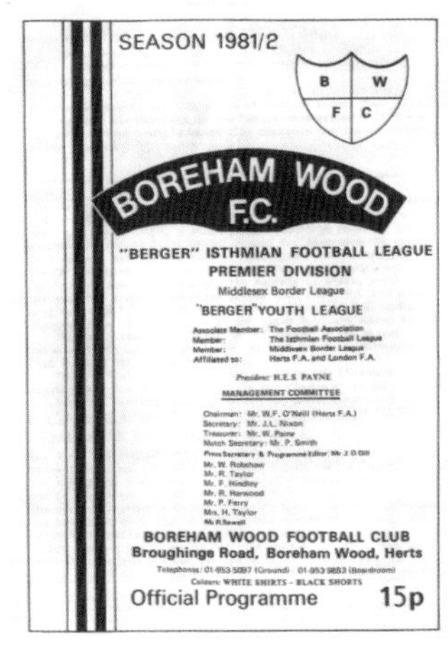

1981–82 - Berger Paints Ltd announced that it would not renew its sponsorship after the 1981–82 season. Also from 1981–82, the Isthmian League champions could move up to the Alliance Premier League. Leytonstone & Ilford emerged as champions, however they opted to remain with the Isthmian League. Sutton United finished runners-up, with Wycombe Wanderers third and Staines Town fourth. The top three clubs all lost 11 games, but Leytonstone & Ilford won 26 and drew five to finish eight points clear of Sutton. At the other end of the table Harlow Town were relegated to Division One, along with Boreham Wood. In Division One, Wokingham Town won the championship by 13 points from League newcomers Bognor Regis Town who also gained promotion from the 21-club Division, by two points from Oxford City. Clapton and Ware were both relegated to Division Two. The Division Two title went to Worthing, who were 11 points clear of Cheshunt, who were also promoted to Division One. This was also the first season when the bottom club would be relegated to the Athenian League after an agreement of promotion and relegation between the leagues. Camberley Town went down to the Athenian League, swapping places with Leyton-Wingate, the Athenian League champions. However, Uxbridge, who finished third in the Athenian League, were also accepted into the League's constitution for the 1982–83 season.

League Chairman Barry East stood down as Chairman at the end of the season, but continued as President. League Secretary Alan Turvey succeeded Barry East as Chairman whilst Nick Robinson was appointed League Secretary.

Premier Division	1	2	3	4	5	6	7	8	9	10	11	12	13	14	15	16	17	18	19	20	21	22
1 Barking	*	0–0	2–1	1–0	2–3	0–0	2–3	3–1	1–2	3–0	0–3	5–0	1–2	3–1	0–1	0–0	2–1	1–1	1–2	1–1	0–2	1–1
2 Billericay Town	0–1	*	1–1	0–6	1–1	1–1	1–3	0–0	2–0	3–1	1–0	1–2	3–1	0–0	2–1	0–1	0–0	0–1	0–0	1–1	2–2	2–0
3 Bishop's Stortford	3–1	1–2	*	1–0	4–2	1–4	1–1	0–1	1–0	2–1	1–2	1–0	0–1	3–4	1–2	1–2	2–0	0–4	2–0	2–1	1–1	2–0
4 Boreham Wood	3–0	0–0	2–1	*	6–0	0–1	1–2	1–2	1–3	0–3	1–1	1–1	2–2	0–2	2–0	1–1	1–1	0–2	0–1	2–2	1–0	0–1
5 Bromley	1–2	2–1	0–1	1–1	*	4–0	1–2	1–3	2–1	0–0	1–5	1–2	4–2	2–0	2–1	4–0	0–1	1–2	1–0	1–3	2–3	1–2
6 Carshalton Athletic	2–2	1–0	2–0	2–3	1–3	*	2–1	4–2	2–1	1–3	2–2	1–0	2–2	2–2	1–3	1–2	0–1	3–0	0–2	0–5	1–0	0–3
7 Croydon	1–2	0–3	0–2	0–0	3–2	6–0	*	2–1	1–0	0–0	1–0	1–2	3–0	0–1	2–3	1–1	0–2	2–1	0–0	0–0	0–0	0–1
8 Dulwich Hamlet	0–1	5–0	2–1	1–1	2–1	3–0	1–3	*	2–4	0–0	3–2	1–1	1–1	0–2	0–4	2–4	0–2	0–0	0–2	1–1	1–0	2–0
9 Harlow Town	1–1	3–1	2–2	1–0	1–1	1–2	1–4	2–1	*	1–4	1–0	1–2	4–1	1–1	1–1	1–1	0–0	1–2	0–0	3–3	3–1	1–1
10 Harrow Borough	1–1	2–1	1–2	1–1	5–1	3–0	1–0	6–1	5–1	*	3–3	0–0	1–1	0–0	1–2	2–2	3–2	1–0	3–2	2–0	2–1	2–3
11 Hayes	1–1	1–1	5–0	1–3	2–1	0–1	1–0	0–0	0–1	1–4	*	0–2	1–0	0–0	4–1	2–1	0–0	1–1	0–1	3–0	2–2	2–0
12 Hendon	0–2	0–0	5–0	3–3	2–2	3–1	2–3	0–1	2–1	2–0	2–1	*	1–1	0–2	1–4	0–0	1–2	1–1	0–0	1–1	3–1	1–1
13 Hitchin Town	1–0	1–1	0–2	2–0	0–0	3–4	1–4	1–0	1–1	2–1	0–2	3–1	*	2–1	1–3	0–4	3–0	2–4	0–1	1–5	2–2	4–2
14 Leatherhead	1–2	1–1	1–2	1–0	1–2	3–0	0–0	1–1	5–2	2–1	1–0	2–1	2–1	*	2–1	0–0	3–0	1–1	2–2	2–3	3–0	1–2
15 Leytonstone Ilford	3–1	1–0	2–1	5–0	3–0	2–1	4–1	3–1	4–2	1–3	4–0	5–2	3–0	1–1	*	2–1	1–1	1–2	2–1	3–0	2–1	2–2
16 Slough Town	0–0	0–1	4–0	3–2	1–3	3–2	0–0	0–1	2–0	1–1	4–1	0–2	0–3	1–0	1–0	*	1–0	2–0	5–2	4–1	0–0	3–3
17 Staines Town	3–1	1–1	1–0	1–0	3–1	3–1	3–2	0–1	2–1	1–1	2–3	2–4	2–1	3–0	1–0	2–4	*	1–1	2–1	2–1	3–1	0–1
18 Sutton United	1–1	2–0	4–1	2–0	2–1	4–4	3–1	0–3	2–0	0–2	0–1	5–1	0–0	2–0	1–3	2–1	1–0	*	2–1	5–2	3–0	2–1
19 Tooting & M Utd	2–4	3–1	1–0	1–0	5–0	1–1	3–1	0–0	2–0	2–2	1–2	1–0	3–1	2–0	2–2	3–0	0–3	1–0	*	1–0	1–2	0–3
20 Walthamstow Ave.	2–0	1–4	3–2	3–1	2–0	1–4	3–0	1–0	3–0	3–1	2–0	1–0	2–3	5–2	2–0	4–1	0–1	3–1	2–0	*	5–1	3–1
21 Woking	0–0	0–2	0–0	1–1	1–7	4–1	2–4	1–0	2–0	5–2	0–3	1–2	2–2	2–0	2–4	1–1	0–2	4–2	2–4	3–0	*	2–1
22 Wycombe Wndrs.	0–0	2–0	2–1	1–0	0–0	3–0	3–1	3–0	2–0	1–2	2–0	3–1	2–1	1–3	2–1	3–2	1–1	0–3	1–1	2–0	0–0	*

1981-82

Premier Division	P	W	D	L	F	A	Pts
1 Leytonstone Ilford	42	26	5	11	91	52	83
2 Sutton United	42	22	9	11	72	49	75
3 Wycombe Wand	42	21	10	11	63	48	73
4 Staines Town	42	21	9	12	58	45	72
5 Walthamstow Ave.	42	21	7	14	81	62	70
6 Harrow Borough	42	18	13	11	77	55	67
7 Tooting & M Utd	42	19	10	13	58	47	67
8 Slough Town	42	17	13	12	64	54	64
9 Leatherhead	42	16	12	14	57	52	60
10 Hayes	42	16	10	16	58	52	58
11 Croydon	42	16	9	17	59	57	57
12 Barking	42	14	14	14	53	51	56
13 Hendon	42	13	13	16	56	65	52
14 Dulwich Hamlet	42	14	10	18	47	59	52
15 Bishop's Stortford	42	15	5	22	50	70	50
16 Carshalton Athletic	42	14	8	20	58	86	50
17 Billericay Town	42	11	16	15	41	50	49
18 Hitchin Town	42	12	11	19	56	77	47
19 Bromley	42	13	7	22	63	79	46
20 Woking	42	11	13	18	57	75	46
21 Harlow Town	42	10	11	21	50	73	41
22 Boreham Wood	42	8	13	21	47	58	37

Left: the Carshalton Athletic matchday programme from season 1981-82. The Robins defeated the Hamlet by four goals to two.

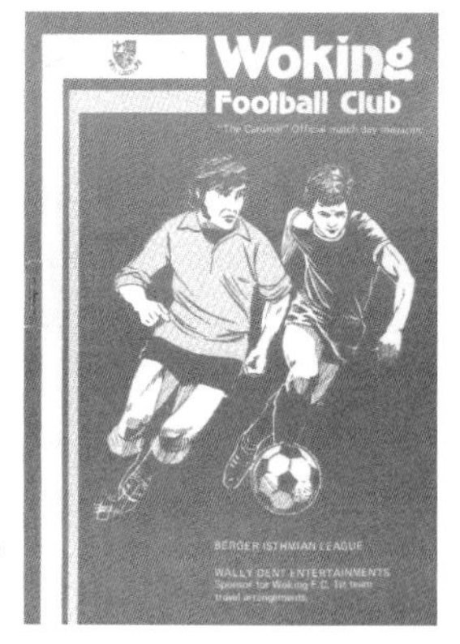

Right: the Woking programme from the same season.

Division I	1	2	3	4	5	6	7	8	9	10	11	12	13	14	15	16	17	18	19	20	21
1 Aveley	*	2–0	2–1	2–2	1–0	3–0	1–2	2–1	1–0	2–0	0–0	1–4	2–1	0–0	0–2	0–3	1–0	2–2	2–1	0–0	1–2
2 Bognor Regis Tn	3–0	*	1–1	2–1	1–0	0–0	3–0	3–0	1–1	0–0	3–0	3–0	0–2	1–0	3–3	1–2	1–1	1–2	2–1	1–0	2–0
3 Chesham United	3–2	0–2	*	1–0	0–1	2–1	1–3	1–0	1–2	0–0	0–1	1–2	1–1	0–0	0–3	2–1	1–1	3–0	1–0	0–2	0–5
4 Clapton	0–1	0–1	2–2	*	2–1	2–0	1–0	2–0	1–2	1–1	2–2	0–1	1–0	1–2	1–3	0–3	1–2	0–0	4–2	2–4	1–3
5 Epsom & Ewell	1–0	1–1	3–1	1–0	*	1–2	1–0	0–2	2–1	0–2	1–2	0–1	1–1	0–1	1–0	1–2	1–0	1–1	5–0	0–0	1–3
6 Farnborough Town	0–2	0–2	4–2	4–3	3–5	*	3–1	0–0	2–0	6–0	1–3	1–1	3–0	3–0	1–2	1–1	2–2	5–0	4–1	3–0	1–2
7 Feltham	5–0	1–0	3–0	1–0	2–1	1–1	*	2–0	1–3	0–2	2–1	2–3	0–2	1–1	0–2	4–0	1–1	2–1	1–1	3–2	1–2
8 Hampton	2–1	2–0	2–1	1–0	0–0	0–1	4–3	*	1–2	2–0	4–3	1–1	4–0	0–2	2–2	4–1	0–0	1–0	2–2	1–3	0–2
9 Hertford Town	2–3	1–2	3–1	4–2	1–1	2–2	1–2	1–0	*	1–1	1–1	1–0	2–1	1–0	1–3	3–1	5–1	1–1	3–0	1–3	0–1
10 Hornchurch	1–1	1–2	0–0	3–1	1–1	2–3	1–1	1–0	0–0	*	0–2	1–2	2–1	1–1	3–1	1–0	1–1	3–2	2–1	2–0	1–2
11 Kingstonian	1–0	1–4	2–1	4–1	3–2	1–0	1–1	0–1	1–2	3–1	*	5–2	2–0	0–1	0–2	2–1	2–2	2–0	3–0	0–0	1–0
12 Lewes	2–0	4–1	4–5	1–0	1–2	3–4	1–4	2–1	1–1	4–1	3–1	*	2–1	1–1	2–1	0–2	2–0	1–1	4–2	1–3	1–3
13 Maidenhead Utd	2–2	0–2	1–1	3–0	1–4	2–2	2–3	3–0	0–4	1–1	1–0	3–4	*	2–2	2–1	2–0	2–1	2–1	3–2	1–1	0–2
14 Metropolitan Police	2–0	1–2	2–0	1–0	2–1	4–1	1–1	2–2	4–3	0–0	1–0	4–2	4–1	*	2–0	3–0	2–1	3–1	7–1	5–3	0–3
15 Oxford City	2–1	1–1	6–0	5–1	1–1	1–0	1–2	3–1	2–0	1–2	3–2	0–0	1–1	3–1	*	2–2	2–2	3–2	4–0	2–2	0–3
16 St. Albans City	1–1	1–2	0–2	1–1	1–2	3–1	1–2	1–2	2–0	1–0	0–0	1–1	5–0	2–2	0–0	*	1–2	1–2	1–0	2–2	3–2
17 Tilbury	1–3	0–4	3–1	3–4	1–4	2–0	0–0	1–1	0–0	1–1	3–2	2–1	2–1	4–2	1–5	1–2	*	0–1	0–2	0–1	2–2
18 Walton & Hersham	1–1	0–0	1–1	4–0	0–2	0–0	0–3	0–0	2–1	1–2	1–0	2–1	1–0	1–2	2–3	0–4	3–2	*	0–2	1–4	0–4
19 Ware	3–1	0–2	0–3	2–1	1–3	0–5	0–1	0–3	0–2	0–1	1–0	0–5	1–2	1–2	0–3	0–1	0–1	1–6	*	1–3	0–1
20 Wembley	2–2	3–3	2–0	1–1	1–0	0–0	1–2	0–3	2–2	0–0	5–1	1–2	1–1	4–5	1–1	3–1	1–1	1–0	6–0	*	1–2
21 Wokingham Town	3–0	1–2	3–0	1–2	1–0	1–1	2–1	4–2	4–1	4–0	3–2	3–0	2–0	0–0	1–2	1–0	1–1	0–0	5–0	2–0	*

Division I	P	W	D	L	F	A	Pts
1 Wokingham Town	40	29	5	6	86	30	92
2 Bognor Regis Tn	40	23	10	7	65	34	79
3 Metropolitan Police	40	22	11	7	75	48	77
4 Oxford City	40	21	11	8	82	47	74
5 Feltham	40	20	8	12	65	49	68
6 Lewes	40	19	7	14	73	66	64
7 Hertford Town	40	16	10	14	62	54	58
8 Wembley	40	14	15	11	69	55	57
9 Farnborough Town	40	15	11	14	71	57	56
10 Epsom & Ewell	40	16	8	16	53	44	56
11 Kingstonian	40	16	7	17	57	56	55
12 Hampton	40	15	9	16	52	52	54
13 Hornchurch	40	13	15	12	42	50	54
14 Aveley	40	14	10	16	46	58	54
15 St. Albans City	40	14	9	17	55	55	51
16 Maidenhead Utd	40	11	10	19	49	70	43
17 Tilbury	40	9	15	16	49	66	42
18 Walton & Hersham	40	10	11	19	43	65	41
19 Chesham United	40	9	9	22	41	71	36
20 Clapton	40	9	7	24	44	75	34
21 Ware	40	5	2	33	29	105	17

Above: Kingstonian were still using their former Richmond Road ground in 1982.

Division II	1	2	3	4	5	6	7	8	9	10	11	12	13	14	15	16	17	18	19	20	21
1 Barton Rovers	*	1–0	2–1	1–3	3–0	2–1	2–0	0–1	2–0	2–2	0–1	1–1	1–0	1–0	3–1	3–0	5–1	3–0	2–1	0–1	1–1
2 Basildon United	0–2	*	6–0	0–0	0–2	1–0	3–0	7–1	4–2	3–0	2–2	0–1	3–1	1–0	0–1	2–3	2–2	4–2	2–0	2–3	0–1
3 Camberley Town	0–7	0–9	*	1–2	0–3	0–3	0–4	0–2	0–1	2–0	1–1	0–3	1–5	0–3	2–4	0–2	0–2	1–0	0–1	0–3	0–6
4 Cheshunt	3–1	4–0	6–0	*	1–1	1–1	2–0	2–0	2–0	1–0	3–4	0–1	4–0	3–2	2–0	6–2	1–1	2–0	1–1	3–0	0–2
5 Corinthian-Casuals	0–0	2–1	2–0	4–0	*	3–1	1–2	1–0	2–1	3–1	0–1	1–0	2–1	4–2	2–1	4–3	2–4	4–1	1–1	2–2	2–0
6 Dorking Town	1–0	0–1	4–0	0–3	3–0	*	1–1	1–0	4–2	1–1	1–0	1–1	1–1	1–1	3–1	0–0	2–1	1–1	2–0	1–3	0–0
7 Eastbourne United	0–2	0–0	3–0	0–2	1–3	2–2	*	1–1	1–1	2–3	1–1	0–0	2–1	1–7	1–3	4–2	1–1	0–3	1–3	1–1	1–2
8 Egham Town	2–2	1–1	10–1	0–2	1–3	1–1	0–2	*	1–1	0–1	5–1	3–0	0–0	2–3	0–0	3–1	2–1	0–2	2–3	0–2	0–3
9 Epping Town	0–4	0–1	2–0	0–0	2–2	2–2	1–0	1–0	*	1–2	1–1	4–2	2–0	1–2	1–1	3–1	1–0	1–1	3–1	0–2	0–1
10 Finchley	2–1	1–0	2–1	2–3	1–1	0–2	0–2	3–2	2–0	*	0–1	1–1	1–1	1–1	2–1	1–1	3–2	1–2	4–3	2–1	1–2
11 Harwich & Parkst.	2–0	2–0	5–1	0–0	1–1	4–1	3–3	2–1	2–0	3–2	*	1–0	1–0	2–0	1–3	0–2	2–3	1–0	1–1	1–2	0–1
12 Hemel Hempstead	1–1	1–0	7–1	1–3	1–0	1–1	5–0	1–1	0–1	2–0	2–0	*	2–1	0–1	2–3	1–3	2–1	0–0	1–2	3–0	1–1
13 Horsham	1–3	0–1	2–0	0–3	1–1	1–0	2–2	1–4	0–0	2–1	1–1	1–3	*	3–1	0–4	1–0	2–3	2–0	2–0	0–2	0–5
14 Hungerford Town	2–0	1–0	6–1	2–0	0–0	4–2	3–3	3–0	3–2	2–2	2–2	2–0	6–0	*	1–1	3–0	2–2	1–1	4–1	4–0	1–1
15 Letchworth G City	0–2	3–1	3–1	1–0	0–2	1–1	3–1	0–1	0–0	3–3	1–1	1–3	6–1	0–1	*	2–4	6–0	2–2	1–1	4–1	0–1
16 Molesey	1–1	5–2	2–0	0–2	3–0	0–2	1–2	1–3	4–2	2–1	3–5	1–2	1–2	1–3	1–2	*	2–0	0–0	0–1	1–1	1–2
17 Rainham Town	0–2	1–2	1–3	2–3	2–2	1–1	2–1	2–2	1–2	2–1	0–5	2–1	1–1	0–5	0–1	1–2	*	3–1	0–0	0–3	2–1
18 Southall	0–0	0–1	2–0	1–0	1–1	0–0	0–4	2–1	1–2	1–0	0–1	1–0	4–1	1–0	0–0	0–0	0–1	*	1–1	2–0	1–0
19 Tring Town	0–1	2–1	3–3	0–3	3–0	1–2	3–0	0–2	3–3	1–3	0–2	2–2	1–1	0–3	2–2	1–1	1–5	1–0	*	2–2	1–4
20 Windsor & Eton	2–0	1–0	4–0	0–2	3–2	1–1	1–0	1–0	2–1	3–4	3–0	4–0	0–1	1–2	4–1	1–2	3–1	1–1	3–1	*	1–0
21 Worthing	0–1	3–1	7–0	2–1	1–1	1–0	2–1	6–1	5–1	4–0	0–0	3–0	6–2	1–0	1–0	4–2	5–0	1–1	7–0	2–1	*

1981-82 Division II	P	W	D	L	F	A	Pts
1 Worthing	40	29	6	5	95	25	93
2 Cheshunt	40	25	7	8	79	33	82
3 Hungerford Town*	40	22	10	8	89	42	74
4 Barton Rovers	40	22	8	10	65	32	74
5 Windsor & Eton	40	22	6	12	69	49	72
6 Corinthian-Casuals	40	19	12	9	67	50	69
7 Harwich & Parkst.	40	19	12	9	64	47	69
8 Letchworth G City	40	15	11	14	67	55	56
9 Dorking Town	40	13	17	10	52	44	56
10 Hemel Hempstead	40	15	9	16	54	49	54
11 Basildon United	40	16	5	19	64	51	53
12 Finchley	40	14	9	17	57	68	51
13 Southall	40	12	14	14	36	42	50
14 Epping Town	40	12	11	17	48	62	47
15 Molesey	40	13	7	20	61	73	46
16 Egham Town	40	11	9	20	56	64	42
17 Rainham Town	40	11	9	20	53	83	42
18 Tring Town	40	9	13	18	49	78	40
19 Eastbourne United	40	9	12	19	51	73	39
20 Horsham	40	10	9	21	42	79	39
21 Camberley Town	40	3	2	35	21	140	11

** Hungerford Town had two points deducted.*

Below right: the programme insert for the new League sponsorship in 1982. For every Servowarm central heating system installed as a direct result of this leaflet, £50 was paid to the named club.

Below: the Ware programme for 1982-83.

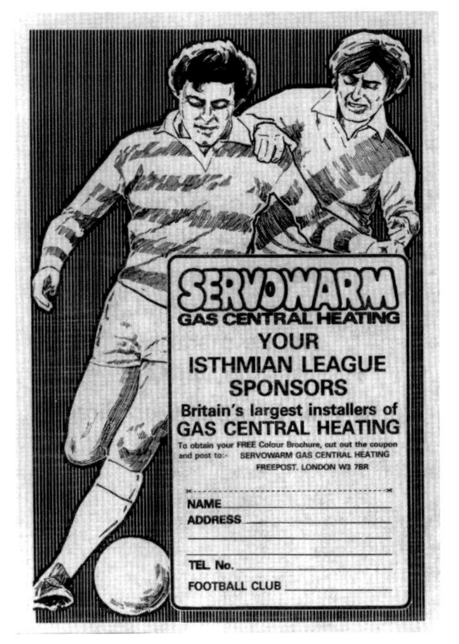

1982–83 - At the start of the season, the League did not have a major sponsor, however a major sponsorship deal was reached with Servowarm Gas Central Heating which was announced in October for a package worth over £32,000 for this season with an option for a further two years.Wycombe Wanderers won the League Championship for the seventh time when they secured their first title since 1975 from the previous year's champions Leytonstone & Ilford by four points with Harrow Borough third just ahead of Hayes. Woking and Leatherhead, with the latter conceding 121 goals, struggled to find any form all season and were both relegated to Division One. In Division One Worthing won their second successive championship and gained promotion to the Premier Division with Harlow Town just pipping Farnborough Town for the other promotion spot. With just twenty-one clubs in Division One bottom club St. Albans City were the only club relegated to Division Two. In Division Two founder-members of the League Clapton, who in recent years had struggled to find league form, had something to cheer when they won the Division Two championship and subsequent promotion to Division One. Division One runners-up Windsor & Eton were also promoted whilst at the other end of the table Harwich & Parkeston were relegated to the Athenian League by having an inferior goal difference to Horsham. Athenian League champions and runners-up Newbury Town and Grays Athletic respectively were promoted to Division Two to give 22 clubs in each division for the first time.

Premier Division	1	2	3	4	5	6	7	8	9	10	11	12	13	14	15	16	17	18	19	20	21	22
1 Barking	*	1–0	2–2	0–0	0–4	2–2	2–0	0–1	1–2	1–0	0–0	0–2	4–0	0–3	1–1	1–1	2–1	1–2	3–0	3–0	1–0	3–2
2 Billericay Town	2–0	*	1–0	1–0	0–2	1–1	1–0	1–0	1–2	1–0	5–0	3–1	0–0	0–1	0–0	3–0	0–2	2–1	1–1	2–2	1–1	1–2
3 Bishop's Stortford	5–0	1–2	*	2–3	0–1	1–2	0–2	1–0	3–2	2–4	2–3	2–1	4–2	0–4	0–0	0–0	2–2	3–1	0–0	2–0	3–1	3–1
4 Bognor Regis Tn	2–0	4–0	0–0	*	0–0	3–2	1–6	1–0	3–1	1–1	2–0	0–3	1–0	2–1	2–0	2–3	2–1	2–0	2–0	0–0	1–1	0–4
5 Bromley	0–0	1–1	0–1	2–1	*	4–1	2–1	1–2	0–0	2–4	0–0	0–0	2–0	1–1	0–0	2–1	2–3	0–2	2–2	2–0	0–0	0–3
6 Carshalton Athletic	4–1	2–1	5–2	0–1	0–1	*	5–1	1–1	1–1	0–2	1–0	2–2	2–2	3–1	2–2	1–2	1–5	1–0	1–1	3–0	0–1	0–1
7 Croydon	2–1	0–2	2–1	2–2	2–0	0–1	*	1–4	0–1	0–0	2–1	1–1	3–1	1–0	1–1	2–3	0–0	1–0	1–2	4–1	3–0	2–0
8 Dulwich Hamlet	2–0	3–3	2–2	2–1	3–2	0–1	1–1	*	3–1	0–0	1–5	2–1	1–0	2–1	1–0	2–1	1–3	2–1	2–0	1–1	1–2	2–1
9 Harrow Borough	0–0	4–0	4–0	2–1	3–3	2–0	4–3	4–2	*	2–1	3–1	5–1	3–0	1–2	1–0	2–1	5–3	2–2	3–1	2–0	1–0	4–2
10 Hayes	1–2	1–0	1–1	1–0	0–0	2–0	2–1	1–2	1–0	*	2–0	1–2	3–1	2–2	2–1	2–1	4–3	1–0	2–0	3–1	1–0	4–1
11 Hendon	2–1	1–0	1–2	1–0	0–1	2–4	2–4	0–0	3–1	2–1	*	0–1	4–0	0–0	3–0	6–2	0–2	0–0	4–1	2–0	2–0	3–4
12 Hitchin Town	1–1	0–3	0–2	2–0	0–2	1–0	1–1	3–1	1–1	0–2	1–6	*	2–2	0–2	1–3	2–1	1–4	1–1	2–0	1–2	1–2	0–3
13 Leatherhead	0–1	1–2	1–2	0–2	1–5	1–0	2–5	2–3	1–5	1–1	1–2	1–4	*	1–5	0–1	1–0	1–4	0–8	0–2	2–1	2–1	0–3
14 Leytonstone Ilford	0–0	2–2	1–0	1–0	4–2	2–0	3–2	2–0	3–2	0–0	1–0	4–1	2–0	*	2–1	2–1	0–2	0–1	2–0	2–0	2–0	2–3
15 Slough Town	1–1	2–1	2–0	2–0	1–2	4–0	0–0	0–0	4–2	0–1	6–0	1–1	5–1	1–0	*	1–1	6–0	5–0	7–2	3–0	0–1	2–3
16 Staines Town	2–2	4–1	1–0	0–2	1–0	1–3	1–1	1–1	2–2	2–1	2–4	3–1	2–2	1–1	0–2	*	4–5	1–1	0–1	5–1	1–0	1–1
17 Sutton United	1–1	1–1	1–0	1–1	3–0	1–0	3–4	2–2	2–3	2–0	4–2	4–2	11–1	2–3	0–2	4–0	*	3–1	1–1	1–2	2–4	1–2
18 Tooting & M Utd	3–1	2–1	2–5	1–2	2–1	2–0	0–2	1–1	0–4	4–2	0–0	3–2	2–1	1–3	2–1	5–0	2–2	*	2–0	2–1	1–1	1–0
19 Walthamstow Ave.	1–2	1–2	0–1	4–1	2–1	1–1	2–1	1–1	2–0	2–2	0–1	1–0	3–2	0–1	0–1	3–1	2–3	2–2	*	5–2	0–1	1–1
20 Woking	0–1	0–2	0–0	0–2	2–1	0–1	1–2	0–2	0–2	1–2	1–4	1–2	2–1	1–1	1–1	2–3	0–1	1–2	0–1	*	1–0	0–2
21 Wokingham Town	1–2	0–2	0–1	0–3	2–0	1–4	1–0	0–0	2–1	0–1	2–1	2–0	3–0	2–2	0–2	0–2	2–0	1–2	0–0	0–2	*	1–1
22 Wycombe Wndrs.	2–2	4–1	1–3	1–0	1–0	1–0	2–1	2–2	2–1	0–1	1–0	2–0	5–0	1–0	1–1	4–3	2–0	3–0	2–0	1–0	1–1	*

Premier Division	P	W	D	L	F	A	Pts
1 Wycombe Wand	42	26	7	9	79	47	85
2 Leytonstone Ilford	42	24	9	9	71	39	81
3 Harrow Borough	42	24	7	11	91	58	79
4 Hayes	42	23	9	10	63	41	78
5 Sutton United	42	20	8	14	96	71	68
6 Dulwich Hamlet	42	18	14	10	59	52	68
7 Slough Town	42	18	13	11	73	36	67
8 Bognor Regis Tn	42	19	8	15	53	48	65
9 Tooting & M Utd	42	18	9	15	65	62	63
10 Billericay Town	42	17	10	15	54	51	61
11 Croydon	42	17	9	16	68	58	60
12 Hendon	42	18	6	18	68	61	60
13 Bishop's Stortford	42	17	9	16	61	58	60
14 Barking	42	14	14	14	47	55	56
15 Bromley	42	14	12	16	51	50	54
16 Carshalton Athletic	42	15	9	18	58	60	54
17 Wokingham Town	42	13	9	20	37	51	48
18 Walthamstow Ave.	42	12	11	19	48	64	47
19 Staines Town	42	12	11	19	62	79	47
20 Hitchin Town	42	11	9	22	49	77	42
21 Woking	42	6	6	30	30	79	24
22 Leatherhead	42	4	5	33	35	121	17

Bishop's Stortford travelled to First Division Middlesbrough in the Third Round of The FA Cup and drew 2-2.

1982-83 Division I	1	2	3	4	5	6	7	8	9	10	11	12	13	14	15	16	17	18	19	20	21
1 Aveley	*	0-0	2-0	0-0	1-0	4-4	4-1	1-2	0-1	5-1	1-2	3-2	1-1	2-0	0-0	2-0	1-0	2-1	3-2	0-1	1-0
2 Boreham Wood	2-0	*	0-1	3-0	0-0	4-0	3-1	3-0	0-3	2-1	4-0	2-4	1-0	1-1	1-0	3-4	5-0	2-1	2-0	1-0	1-2
3 Chesham United	4-2	2-1	*	2-2	1-3	0-0	0-1	2-1	4-2	1-2	1-0	1-0	1-3	0-1	2-0	0-0	0-3	2-1	0-0	0-3	0-2
4 Cheshunt	2-0	1-2	3-0	*	2-0	0-2	0-1	2-0	2-2	1-1	1-0	1-2	3-0	0-0	1-0	0-1	1-3	1-0	0-0	0-2	1-2
5 Epsom & Ewell	1-0	1-2	3-2	0-0	*	2-3	0-0	1-2	1-2	0-0	1-1	2-1	2-0	1-1	1-1	0-0	5-0	2-2	2-3	0-0	4-2
6 Farnborough Town	3-1	1-0	3-1	2-0	2-0	*	0-0	3-4	1-1	2-2	2-0	4-0	3-1	1-0	5-0	1-1	2-0	2-0	0-0	1-0	1-2
7 Feltham	2-0	1-2	0-3	2-2	1-1	0-0	*	0-2	2-3	0-1	1-1	1-3	4-0	2-0	2-1	2-1	1-0	2-3	4-1	0-1	0-0
8 Hampton	4-0	1-1	2-0	3-3	2-0	1-1	1-1	*	0-1	2-2	1-1	1-3	1-0	8-2	2-4	0-1	4-4	0-1	2-1	2-0	0-0
9 Harlow Town	3-1	2-2	0-1	3-2	2-0	2-0	2-1	2-2	*	2-2	3-1	0-0	3-0	6-1	2-3	1-1	2-0	1-0	1-4	4-2	2-2
10 Hertford Town	2-1	1-0	0-0	3-2	3-1	3-2	1-0	4-1	3-2	*	2-0	0-0	3-2	2-2	1-0	1-3	4-2	1-1	1-0	1-0	0-0
11 Hornchurch	2-3	2-1	1-4	1-0	0-3	2-1	0-0	1-0	1-2	1-2	*	0-2	2-1	4-1	1-1	0-2	1-0	2-1	2-4	2-2	0-1
12 Kingstonian	2-0	1-0	3-0	0-0	1-0	1-1	1-2	2-3	2-1	4-0	1-1	*	1-1	2-2	0-2	0-3	2-3	1-1	0-1	0-2	3-2
13 Lewes	1-1	2-0	1-0	1-0	2-1	1-3	2-2	0-0	1-4	1-3	0-3	1-0	*	0-1	2-3	1-1	1-1	0-2	2-1	3-2	2-3
14 Maidenhead Utd	1-0	1-2	5-1	1-2	3-0	0-2	0-4	2-1	2-4	2-5	2-4	2-1	1-1	*	0-2	3-4	2-2	0-1	3-2	2-2	2-1
15 Metropolitan Police	5-1	0-1	4-1	2-1	1-2	2-2	3-1	2-0	4-3	4-3	1-1	1-1	2-1	6-1	*	1-2	7-2	1-0	3-2	3-3	1-1
16 Oxford City	3-0	1-1	4-2	3-0	0-0	0-0	1-1	2-1	2-2	2-5	7-0	2-2	0-1	3-2	2-1	*	2-0	2-0	0-2	4-3	2-4
17 St. Albans City	2-1	4-1	1-3	0-0	1-0	0-3	3-0	1-2	1-1	3-1	3-1	2-2	2-3	1-1	0-1	1-1	*	0-1	0-2	0-1	3-3
18 Tilbury	1-2	2-1	1-1	0-0	0-0	1-0	0-0	0-1	1-4	2-0	4-0	2-0	2-3	2-1	1-1	0-0	0-1	*	1-2	2-2	0-2
19 Walton & Hersham	2-2	0-1	1-0	1-2	0-3	2-3	4-0	2-3	1-1	4-1	2-1	1-1	1-2	0-3	2-1	4-1	3-0	2-1	*	3-2	1-0
20 Wembley	2-3	0-2	4-0	3-3	1-1	1-1	2-1	2-0	0-2	2-2	3-2	0-1	3-2	2-2	2-1	1-2	2-0	1-2	3-2	*	0-1
21 Worthing	0-1	1-2	5-0	1-0	4-0	0-2	2-1	2-0	2-0	2-0	3-1	2-1	4-1	3-1	1-2	1-0	6-3	2-0	2-0	3-0	*

Division I	P	W	D	L	F	A	Pts
1 Worthing	40	25	6	9	76	39	81
2 Harlow Town	40	21	11	8	84	55	74
3 Farnborough Town	40	20	13	7	69	39	73
4 Hertford Town	40	20	11	9	70	61	71
5 Oxford City	40	19	13	8	70	49	70
6 Boreham Wood	40	21	6	13	62	42	69
7 Metropolitan Police	40	19	9	12	77	57	66
8 Walton & Hersham	40	17	6	17	65	59	57
9 Hampton	40	15	10	15	62	60	55
10 Wembley	40	14	10	16	62	61	52
11 Aveley	40	15	7	18	52	62	52
12 Kingstonian	40	13	12	15	53	53	51
13 Tilbury	40	12	10	18	41	47	46
14 Feltham	40	11	12	17	45	54	45
15 Chesham United	40	13	6	21	43	70	45
16 Epsom & Ewell	40	10	14	16	44	49	44
17 Lewes	40	12	8	20	47	71	44
18 Cheshunt	40	10	13	17	41	49	43
19 Hornchurch	40	11	8	21	45	74	41
20 Maidenhead Utd	40	10	10	20	57	87	40
21 St. Albans City	40	10	9	21	52	79	37

Left: the Bishop's Stortford matchday programme from season 1982-83.

Right: Basildon United's programme from the same season.

Division II	1	2	3	4	5	6	7	8	9	10	11	12	13	14	15	16	17	18	19	20	21	22
1 Barton Rovers	*	1-1	3-1	5-3	7-1	4-1	0-2	4-0	0-1	5-1	2-1	1-0	1-1	2-0	0-1	2-1	2-1	3-2	0-2	0-2	4-1	1-3
2 Basildon United	1-2	*	0-0	0-0	2-1	2-1	2-2	2-0	5-1	3-0	5-1	1-0	1-1	1-1	0-1	1-3	7-0	4-0	3-0	3-1	5-0	1-1
3 Clapton	2-0	3-2	*	2-0	4-0	3-1	5-1	4-2	5-0	7-1	1-0	5-0	3-0	1-1	0-2	0-3	2-1	3-1	5-3	1-0	2-0	3-1
4 Corinthian-Casuals	1-1	1-2	4-0	*	2-0	5-0	3-0	3-0	4-3	5-1	1-2	6-0	0-1	3-0	1-2	3-1	1-0	5-2	2-2	1-2	4-1	0-1
5 Dorking Town	1-3	3-4	2-1	0-2	*	2-0	0-0	4-0	2-0	3-1	0-0	2-3	0-4	0-4	0-0	2-1	3-1	2-1	2-1	1-3	2-1	3-4
6 Eastbourne United	0-0	0-1	1-2	0-2	0-0	*	1-3	0-0	0-1	4-2	2-1	2-0	1-4	2-0	0-1	0-5	6-3	1-3	4-2	0-4	2-0	1-2
7 Egham Town	1-2	3-2	1-1	2-3	2-1	3-2	*	5-1	3-0	0-0	0-0	1-1	1-0	1-3	2-7	3-1	6-0	5-1	2-1	3-2	2-1	0-2
8 Epping Town	1-3	1-4	1-5	0-3	0-1	2-2	0-2	*	2-2	2-1	0-0	2-0	0-3	1-1	0-3	0-0	1-2	2-0	0-3	1-2	1-0	0-2
9 Finchley	1-3	0-3	1-1	0-0	1-1	0-2	0-1	0-2	*	2-2	1-1	1-3	3-2	0-1	0-7	1-1	1-1	0-0	1-2	0-2	1-0	0-2
10 Harwich & Parkst.	0-3	1-4	0-3	0-3	2-2	2-3	1-4	4-0	4-0	*	1-2	2-1	0-6	0-0	1-6	0-3	0-2	3-4	0-3	2-4	1-1	0-4
11 Hemel Hempstead	1-2	1-1	1-2	0-2	0-1	2-0	3-3	0-1	1-0	8-1	*	1-1	2-1	2-2	1-1	2-1	1-3	1-0	1-1	1-1	2-0	1-0
12 Horsham	0-1	0-2	0-1	0-5	1-3	2-1	0-1	1-0	2-2	0-2	2-0	*	1-3	1-2	0-4	0-5	2-2	1-4	1-3	0-2	0-0	0-5
13 Hungerford Town	0-3	0-0	2-1	2-0	3-1	4-0	4-0	1-0	4-0	4-1	2-1	3-1	*	0-0	1-3	2-2	2-0	3-0	1-1	1-0	5-0	1-1
14 Letchworth G City	0-1	3-3	2-4	4-1	1-1	2-1	5-2	2-0	1-0	3-1	1-2	0-0	0-3	*	2-1	2-0	4-1	6-2	1-0	0-0	3-2	1-2
15 Leyton-Wingate	2-2	0-1	1-3	2-0	4-0	6-1	4-2	0-0	5-0	1-1	5-0	10-2	1-2	0-2	*	4-3	2-0	1-1	1-1	2-2	4-0	2-1
16 Molesey	0-3	0-0	0-1	0-1	0-3	1-2	0-2	3-1	5-0	2-2	2-1	4-1	0-0	1-1	2-1	*	3-1	2-1	0-3	1-1	4-1	4-1
17 Rainham Town	1-0	1-3	0-1	1-3	0-3	3-3	1-0	3-1	3-1	4-0	2-1	2-2	2-1	0-1	0-5	2-1	*	1-2	1-3	0-3	1-2	0-2
18 Southall	4-7	2-2	4-0	2-1	2-2	7-0	2-0	2-0	2-1	4-0	3-0	5-1	1-0	4-2	1-0	1-1	2-6	*	1-1	0-3	2-1	1-3
19 Tring Town	1-2	4-5	3-2	2-0	1-0	3-3	1-1	3-2	4-0	3-0	2-2	4-0	2-1	1-1	1-3	0-3	6-0	3-1	*	2-0	2-1	0-1
20 Uxbridge	1-1	1-0	1-3	2-2	5-0	7-2	2-1	0-0	0-0	4-0	2-2	2-0	1-1	3-1	2-1	0-1	0-1	1-0	1-1	*	4-1	1-1
21 Ware	2-0	1-1	0-2	0-6	1-1	3-2	2-3	3-2	1-1	0-1	0-3	1-0	1-0	0-0	0-5	0-2	2-3	1-3	0-3	3-4	*	0-1
22 Windsor & Eton	2-0	0-2	0-1	3-3	3-0	5-0	0-1	6-0	2-1	8-0	1-1	3-2	3-3	3-2	3-0	4-1	3-1	1-1	4-2	1-2	3-0	*

Division II	P	W	D	L	F	A	Pts
1 Clapton	42	30	4	8	96	46	94
2 Windsor & Eton	42	27	7	8	98	43	88
3 Barton Rovers	42	26	6	10	86	48	84
4 Leyton-Wingate	42	25	8	9	111	41	83
5 Basildon United	42	23	13	6	92	42	82
6 Uxbridge	42	22	12	8	80	42	78
7 Hungerford Town	42	22	10	10	82	39	76
8 Corinthian-Casuals	42	23	6	13	95	48	75
9 Egham Town	42	21	8	13	77	67	71
10 Tring Town	42	20	10	12	86	59	70
11 Letchworth G City*	42	18	13	11	68	53	66
12 Southall	42	18	7	17	81	80	61
13 Molesey	42	17	9	16	73	56	60
14 Dorking Town	42	15	9	18	56	75	54
15 Hemel Hempstead	42	12	14	16	53	59	50
16 Rainham Town	42	14	4	24	57	94	46
17 Eastbourne United	42	10	6	26	54	104	36
18 Epping Town	42	6	8	28	29	89	26
19 Ware	42	6	6	30	34	97	24
20 Finchley	42	4	12	26	28	92	24
21 Horsham	42	5	7	30	32	106	22
22 Harwich & Parkst.	42	5	7	30	42	130	22

** Letchworth Garden City had 1 point deducted.*

EPPING TOWN
FOOTBALL CLUB
(Founded 1888)
SEASON 1982-3
OFFICIAL PROGRAMME

Left: Epping Town's programme for season 1982-83.

Right: the Barton Rovers matchday programme from season 1982-83.

1983–84 - In the Premier Division Harrow Borough had an excellent season by winning their first League championship from nearest challengers Worthing who despite winning their opening seven matches could not sustain their challenge for a third successive championship and had to settle for second place. Slough Town had an improved season, finishing third, closely followed by Sutton United, Hayes and Hitchin Town.

At the foot of the table Bromley were relegated to Division One whilst Staines Town were also relegated due to not meeting the strict ground grading criteria, thus reprieving Tooting & Mitcham United.

In Division One a close fought championship resulted in Windsor & Eton gaining the champions trophy whilst Epsom & Ewell were runners-up closely followed by Wembley, Maidenhead United and Boreham Wood. Feltham who finished nineteen points adrift at the bottom was relegated to Division Two with Cheshunt.

In Division Two Basildon United who led the division for the best part of the season won the championship by just a point from runners-up St. Albans City who gained immediate promotion following their relegation the previous season. The bottom four clubs, Horsham, Ware, Eastbourne United and Finchley were only separated by one point, however the League was to expand by adding another division to its ranks the following season.

A total of 25 clubs applied for membership of which 19 were accepted into the competition, namely Banstead Athletic, Berkhamsted Town, Bracknell Town, Camberley Town, Chalfont St. Peter, Chertsey Town, Flackwell Heath, Harefield United, Haringey Borough, Heybridge Swifts, Kingsbury Town, Marlow, Petersfield United, Royston Town, Ruislip Manor, Saffron Walden Town, Stevenage Borough, Whyteleafe and Wolverton Town with the majority from the Athenian League which turned out to be that competition's last playing season.

The six clubs not accepted, following second ground inspections, were Burnham, Edgware Town, Fleet Town, Hoddesdon Town, Redhill and Thatcham Town. It was agreed that Division Two would be split geographically into Division Two North of 21 clubs and Division Two South of 20 clubs.

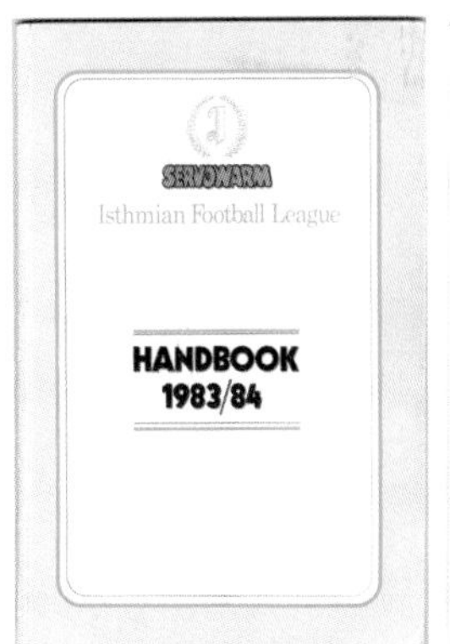

Above: Feltham's programme for 1983-84, the League's handbook for the season and Wembley's issue for that campaign.

Premier Division	1	2	3	4	5	6	7	8	9	10	11	12	13	14	15	16	17	18	19	20	21	22
1 Barking	*	2–0	1–1	0–1	3–0	2–4	0–2	2–3	1–0	3–2	0–1	1–3	0–2	1–2	1–0	0–0	1–1	1–1	3–1	2–1	2–0	0–0
2 Billericay Town	1–0	*	3–2	3–0	1–1	1–1	1–0	2–3	1–1	4–1	1–2	0–1	0–0	3–2	0–3	2–4	1–0	3–0	2–1	0–2	2–2	1–2
3 Bishop's Stortford	2–2	1–3	*	1–2	2–1	2–1	2–1	1–0	4–2	1–2	0–3	1–2	2–1	0–0	2–1	2–0	2–0	1–0	1–1	0–3	3–4	2–0
4 Bognor Regis Tn	1–2	3–0	0–2	*	1–0	2–0	1–0	3–1	2–0	1–1	1–1	1–1	3–2	1–1	2–2	1–1	2–1	1–2	1–0	1–4	2–3	1–2
5 Bromley	1–2	0–2	1–1	1–1	*	0–0	0–1	1–0	3–3	0–1	0–0	1–0	0–0	0–1	3–3	1–0	0–3	0–2	1–3	1–0	0–5	0–2
6 Carshalton Athletic	1–2	0–1	0–2	3–2	3–2	*	0–0	1–1	3–2	1–1	0–3	0–1	1–0	1–2	1–2	4–0	0–0	1–2	1–3	1–2	3–4	3–2
7 Croydon	3–2	3–3	0–1	3–0	2–0	3–2	*	2–0	1–2	0–3	2–2	3–1	1–2	0–1	2–2	1–1	0–3	2–1	4–0	2–2	2–4	0–1
8 Dulwich Hamlet	4–3	1–1	2–0	0–0	1–2	2–2	2–0	*	2–0	0–1	1–0	1–2	1–2	2–0	4–6	0–2	2–0	0–3	5–2	1–1	1–1	1–1
9 Harlow Town	0–0	3–0	1–2	4–2	2–1	2–1	2–0	0–1	*	0–0	2–3	0–1	1–1	1–2	3–2	2–1	0–0	2–2	0–1	3–2	3–2	3–5
10 Harrow Borough	2–2	3–1	1–1	2–2	2–0	1–2	1–0	3–3	5–1	*	2–0	1–0	2–1	1–0	1–0	2–1	0–0	3–2	2–0	2–2	2–1	1–1
11 Hayes	3–4	4–0	2–2	1–0	0–0	1–0	1–1	0–0	0–1	1–2	*	1–0	2–0	2–3	2–1	2–2	0–1	2–0	2–0	2–1	1–1	2–0
12 Hendon	2–2	0–0	0–0	5–2	8–1	0–1	0–0	3–0	2–2	3–3	1–1	*	1–2	4–0	0–1	3–0	1–3	1–0	1–2	0–2	3–0	2–1
13 Hitchin Town	2–1	1–0	2–2	1–1	2–1	3–2	1–1	0–0	0–2	1–3	1–1	1–0	*	1–0	1–1	2–1	2–2	3–1	1–0	4–3	2–1	0–0
14 Leytonstone-Ilford	2–2	3–5	2–0	2–4	3–0	1–4	1–2	0–2	1–1	0–2	1–2	2–0	1–1	*	0–2	0–2	1–2	0–0	5–1	1–0	2–2	1–2
15 Slough Town	1–1	2–0	1–1	3–2	0–0	2–1	5–1	2–4	2–2	0–2	1–0	3–1	5–1	2–1	*	1–2	1–0	1–0	2–0	0–1	2–4	3–0
16 Staines Town	1–1	0–1	2–1	3–2	0–3	3–0	4–1	4–5	3–4	0–1	2–1	0–0	2–1	0–2	2–3	*	1–1	3–1	2–1	0–4	2–4	1–1
17 Sutton United	2–1	3–0	3–2	1–1	3–0	2–0	0–1	1–2	3–1	0–1	1–2	5–1	3–3	1–1	2–0	1–2	*	4–1	3–4	2–0	2–1	2–1
18 Tooting & M Utd	1–1	3–0	0–0	0–0	0–5	4–5	0–2	1–1	0–1	2–1	1–0	0–2	3–3	4–0	3–0	1–1	1–2	*	1–2	1–2	0–2	0–0
19 Walthamstow Ave.	0–2	0–1	1–0	5–2	1–1	1–1	1–0	1–2	2–1	2–2	2–1	2–2	2–2	2–1	0–2	1–2	0–0	0–0	*	2–2	4–0	0–2
20 Wokingham Town	3–2	5–1	3–1	2–3	5–1	2–2	0–2	3–0	1–1	1–2	2–1	3–0	2–0	0–2	0–0	3–2	1–1	2–3	0–0	*	4–1	2–2
21 Worthing	4–0	4–2	1–1	1–2	2–0	2–2	1–1	2–0	4–1	2–2	0–0	1–2	2–1	3–2	2–1	5–2	2–1	1–1	3–2	2–0	*	2–2
22 Wycombe Wndrs.	3–2	4–0	2–2	2–2	1–0	2–0	2–0	3–0	1–2	0–1	1–1	1–2	0–2	2–2	1–2	0–2	2–2	2–2	1–0	1–0	5–1	*

Premier Division	*P*	*W*	*D*	*L*	*F*	*A*	*Pts*
1 Harrow Borough	42	25	13	4	73	42	88
2 Worthing	42	20	11	11	89	72	71
3 Slough Town	42	20	9	13	73	56	69
4 Sutton United	42	18	12	12	67	45	66
5 Hayes	42	17	13	12	56	41	64
6 Hitchin Town	42	16	15	11	58	57	63
7 Wycombe Wand	42	16	14	12	63	52	62
8 Wokingham Town*	42	18	10	14	78	55	61
9 Hendon	42	17	10	15	62	51	61
10 Dulwich Hamlet	42	16	11	15	61	64	59
11 Bishop's Stortford	42	15	13	14	56	57	58
12 Harlow Town	42	15	11	16	64	70	56
13 Bognor Regis Tn	42	14	13	15	62	69	55
14 Staines Town	42	15	9	18	63	72	54
15 Billericay Town	42	15	8	19	53	73	53
16 Barking	42	13	13	16	60	64	52
17 Croydon	42	14	10	18	52	58	52
18 Walthamstow Ave.	42	13	10	19	53	67	49
19 Leytonstone Ilford	42	13	9	20	54	67	48
20 Carshalton Athletic	42	11	10	21	59	72	43
21 Tooting & M Utd	42	10	13	19	50	63	43
22 Bromley	42	7	11	24	33	72	32

** Wokingham Town had three points deducted.*

Above: Harrow Borough's championship winning squad from1983-84.

1983-84 Division I	1	2	3	4	5	6	7	8	9	10	11	12	13	14	15	16	17	18	19	20	21	22
1 Aveley	*	0–2	3–1	4–0	1–2	2–1	3–1	1–0	2–0	2–2	1–0	2–1	0–0	0–0	2–0	1–1	3–0	1–1	1–4	1–2	0–2	2–5
2 Boreham Wood	1–0	*	0–1	0–0	2–0	3–1	2–1	5–0	4–2	2–0	5–2	3–0	0–4	1–2	4–0	0–0	0–1	2–0	1–1	1–0	4–0	5–0
3 Chesham United	2–0	2–2	*	4–0	4–1	2–4	1–1	3–0	2–1	2–2	3–0	0–1	3–1	0–2	3–0	2–0	3–0	1–1	1–0	1–1	3–1	1–2
4 Cheshunt	3–0	3–2	1–3	*	1–1	0–2	2–0	3–0	1–1	2–3	1–1	0–0	0–3	1–0	1–0	4–0	1–1	2–0	1–0	0–1	1–3	5–0
5 Clapton	0–3	2–3	2–0	1–3	*	0–0	0–1	4–1	0–0	1–2	1–0	1–1	2–1	1–0	1–3	0–2	1–0	4–1	3–1	0–0	0–4	3–1
6 Epsom & Ewell	3–2	2–1	3–1	3–1	2–1	*	2–2	1–2	0–0	2–0	2–1	3–2	2–0	1–1	2–1	0–3	3–2	1–1	2–0	2–1	4–0	2–1
7 Farnborough Town	2–1	1–1	1–2	1–0	0–1	1–2	*	6–0	3–0	5–1	5–1	2–2	1–8	3–2	3–2	4–0	1–1	2–0	3–2	0–2	1–3	4–0
8 Feltham	0–0	3–1	1–2	1–0	1–1	0–5	0–2	*	0–5	1–2	1–2	0–0	1–0	3–3	1–0	1–5	0–5	1–2	2–0	0–1	0–5	2–0
9 Hampton	0–0	0–2	0–1	3–0	4–1	0–0	0–0	3–0	*	4–0	4–1	0–1	2–3	1–1	1–1	4–2	3–0	1–1	3–0	1–5	1–1	2–1
10 Hertford Town	1–0	3–1	1–0	0–0	3–0	0–3	2–1	4–0	0–2	*	3–0	1–3	2–2	1–2	0–1	1–2	2–1	0–0	1–1	1–1	0–1	0–7
11 Hornchurch	1–3	1–0	1–1	2–0	2–1	0–0	1–1	2–1	0–1	0–1	*	1–1	0–0	1–3	1–0	3–2	1–3	1–2	4–0	0–0	1–0	1–3
12 Kingstonian	3–2	1–2	2–2	2–1	2–2	1–0	1–4	2–1	0–0	0–2	0–1	*	2–4	1–1	0–2	0–5	2–0	0–1	1–3	0–4	1–2	1–2
13 Leatherhead	0–0	2–1	3–1	0–0	1–1	2–1	0–2	6–0	1–2	0–2	2–3	0–1	*	2–2	2–2	0–1	1–7	6–2	6–0	0–2	1–0	1–1
14 Lewes	0–1	1–0	3–1	0–1	1–4	2–3	2–2	1–0	2–4	1–1	1–0	3–2	1–0	*	1–2	2–1	1–0	0–0	1–1	1–4	0–7	3–1
15 Maidenhead Utd	2–0	3–0	3–1	4–1	2–1	2–0	0–1	4–1	1–2	5–1	3–0	0–2	1–0	0–0	*	3–1	1–0	4–1	1–0	3–0	1–1	3–3
16 Metropolitan Police	2–1	0–1	1–0	4–1	1–1	3–0	1–2	3–2	4–0	5–3	2–1	0–2	0–1	3–0	0–0	*	1–2	5–2	0–5	1–1	4–1	2–1
17 Oxford City	0–0	1–1	0–0	2–0	1–1	1–1	3–3	3–1	3–0	0–1	0–1	3–1	0–1	3–0	0–1	1–4	*	4–0	2–1	0–1	1–2	3–1
18 Tilbury	0–1	1–0	1–0	3–1	2–1	0–1	1–1	2–0	1–3	0–0	4–2	2–1	2–1	2–0	0–1	2–0	6–1	*	3–1	0–5	3–2	0–0
19 Walton & Hersham	0–0	4–3	4–1	2–1	1–1	3–2	3–0	3–1	0–3	3–2	0–0	2–0	0–0	2–1	1–3	1–7	0–0	2–0	*	0–1	2–0	0–3
20 Wembley	4–0	2–3	0–1	1–0	3–0	1–1	2–2	2–0	1–1	5–2	1–2	0–1	1–0	0–0	0–0	1–0	1–2	0–0	3–1	*	1–0	2–0
21 Windsor & Eton	3–0	0–0	2–0	4–1	4–0	4–2	1–0	4–1	3–0	2–1	1–1	3–1	4–0	3–2	1–1	2–0	3–0	5–3	0–0	2–1	*	2–0
22 Woking	1–3	0–3	5–2	2–1	2–1	1–2	2–2	3–1	0–1	3–2	0–0	0–2	1–2	1–0	2–1	5–1	1–0	0–1	2–2	2–1	1–1	*

Division I	P	W	D	L	F	A	Pts
1 Windsor & Eton	42	26	7	9	89	44	85
2 Epsom & Ewell	42	23	9	10	73	51	78
3 Wembley	42	21	11	10	65	32	74
4 Maidenhead Utd	42	22	8	12	67	42	74
5 Boreham Wood	42	22	7	13	74	43	73
6 Farnborough Town	42	18	12	12	78	60	66
7 Hampton	42	18	12	12	65	49	66
8 Metropolitan Police	42	20	5	17	79	64	65
9 Chesham United	42	18	8	16	64	57	62
10 Tilbury	42	17	10	15	54	64	61
11 Leatherhead	42	15	10	17	67	56	55
12 Aveley	42	15	10	17	49	53	55
13 Woking	42	16	7	19	66	73	55
14 Hertford Town	42	15	9	18	56	73	54
15 Oxford City	42	14	9	19	57	56	51
16 Lewes	42	13	12	17	49	65	51
17 Walton & Hersham	42	13	10	19	52	70	49
18 Hornchurch	42	13	10	19	43	63	49
19 Kingstonian	42	13	9	20	47	67	48
20 Clapton	42	12	11	19	49	67	47
21 Cheshunt	42	12	8	22	45	64	44
22 Feltham	42	7	4	31	31	106	25

Left: Rainham Town's programme for season 1983-84.

Right: the Dorking matchday programme from the same campaign.

Division II	1	2	3	4	5	6	7	8	9	10	11	12	13	14	15	16	17	18	19	20	21	22
1 Barton Rovers	*	2–4	0–0	3–1	4–2	0–1	1–1	1–0	2–3	2–1	2–1	1–0	0–1	0–0	1–1	1–0	2–0	2–6	2–3	1–1	0–2	2–2
2 Basildon United	3–1	*	4–0	2–0	2–0	5–0	0–1	3–0	1–0	1–0	2–0	3–2	1–0	2–0	0–0	0–2	2–0	1–0	1–1	1–3	1–0	4–0
3 Corinthian-Casuals	3–0	0–0	*	2–1	2–0	1–1	1–2	2–0	0–4	0–0	4–0	0–2	2–0	1–2	1–2	3–1	3–1	2–2	2–0	1–0	1–0	4–0
4 Dorking	1–0	0–2	2–2	*	1–0	2–1	1–2	2–0	1–1	2–4	5–0	1–0	0–1	0–2	4–0	2–1	1–2	1–0	2–3	1–0	3–3	2–0
5 Eastbourne United	0–2	1–2	0–1	0–5	*	1–1	0–1	3–2	0–1	1–2	2–1	0–1	2–1	0–4	2–3	0–1	3–2	1–3	2–1	0–1	0–0	5–0
6 Egham Town	1–2	0–0	1–1	1–1	2–0	*	1–1	2–1	1–3	3–4	3–0	0–1	2–3	2–1	3–1	3–1	2–1	1–2	0–0	2–2	2–0	2–0
7 Epping Town	1–0	0–4	1–1	1–2	2–1	1–2	*	1–0	3–3	2–2	3–3	1–1	2–2	2–1	1–0	2–3	10–0	0–1	0–2	1–2	0–1	3–0
8 Finchley	0–3	0–3	0–2	0–2	2–1	0–2	0–0	*	1–0	0–2	0–1	0–2	0–0	1–4	2–2	2–2	2–0	1–1	0–1	0–2	1–0	2–2
9 Grays Athletic	5–1	0–1	3–1	0–2	2–1	2–1	1–1	4–1	*	3–2	1–0	2–2	1–3	2–7	3–3	3–2	0–0	0–1	1–2	0–1	0–1	3–0
10 Hemel Hempstead	0–3	0–2	2–3	2–0	0–1	1–1	2–2	3–1	0–1	*	0–0	4–5	0–1	3–0	1–0	1–2	3–1	1–2	0–2	2–3	2–2	1–2
11 Horsham	1–2	1–7	3–4	1–4	1–1	1–2	0–1	1–2	2–5	0–4	*	0–3	0–2	1–2	0–1	2–1	2–0	0–1	2–0	0–5	0–2	1–0
12 Hungerford Town	1–0	1–2	1–1	2–1	5–0	0–1	1–2	1–1	2–1	4–1	4–1	*	9–0	1–2	2–2	3–1	9–1	1–1	0–1	1–1	2–2	5–2
13 Letchworth G City	2–0	0–5	0–3	1–2	5–1	1–1	1–2	1–0	1–0	0–0	3–0	0–2	*	0–1	1–1	1–0	0–1	0–3	5–4	0–1	1–1	5–2
14 Leyton-Wingate	4–0	1–1	0–1	4–0	4–0	2–0	2–1	3–0	1–1	4–1	2–0	1–2	3–0	*	3–1	3–1	6–1	1–2	3–2	1–0	3–1	4–1
15 Molesey	1–1	0–0	1–4	1–2	4–1	1–0	0–0	1–1	2–2	2–1	3–6	1–5	2–0	1–2	*	2–1	3–2	1–2	0–2	2–1	0–1	1–3
16 Newbury Town	1–0	1–3	0–2	0–2	1–0	0–0	2–1	1–1	3–1	2–1	4–2	0–3	1–1	1–5	2–2	*	5–1	2–3	4–2	1–2	1–2	3–1
17 Rainham Town	0–2	0–3	2–5	1–4	3–2	0–1	2–2	3–2	0–1	1–1	2–0	1–1	1–0	0–4	1–3	1–3	*	0–4	0–2	1–4	0–1	1–1
18 St. Albans City	1–1	3–2	2–2	2–0	6–1	2–2	2–1	2–0	3–4	4–1	5–0	2–2	3–2	2–0	1–1	4–1	1–0	*	3–0	3–0	2–2	5–1
19 Southall	2–1	2–3	3–1	4–0	6–0	3–3	0–0	2–1	0–1	1–1	2–4	3–0	3–1	3–0	0–2	5–1	2–1	1–2	*	3–3	1–1	3–1
20 Tring Town	5–4	0–0	1–2	1–2	2–0	1–1	1–1	3–1	0–2	2–0	5–0	1–1	3–0	1–1	3–0	5–1	7–1	4–1	3–1	*	1–1	2–1
21 Uxbridge	2–0	5–1	0–0	1–0	2–1	0–0	0–1	5–0	0–0	1–2	1–0	1–1	1–0	2–3	0–0	1–0	4–0	2–3	0–0	1–1	*	5–2
22 Ware	0–2	0–4	3–4	1–1	7–0	0–4	1–1	2–0	1–2	0–5	2–2	1–3	0–2	0–1	0–5	3–0	1–3	1–2	3–1	1–5	0–4	*

Division II	P	W	D	L	F	A	Pts
1 Basildon United	42	30	7	5	88	27	97
2 St. Albans City	42	29	9	5	100	46	96
3 Leyton-Wingate	42	29	4	9	97	41	91
4 Tring Town	42	23	8	11	89	44	80
5 Corinthian-Casuals	42	23	11	8	75	47	80
6 Hungerford Town	42	21	12	9	94	47	75
7 Uxbridge	42	18	15	9	61	36	69
8 Grays Athletic	42	20	9	13	72	57	69
9 Dorking	42	21	5	16	66	54	68
10 Southall*	42	20	8	14	79	60	65
11 Egham Town	42	16	15	11	59	49	63
12 Epping Town	42	15	16	11	61	50	61
13 Molesey	42	13	14	15	59	68	53
14 Barton Rovers	42	15	8	19	54	64	53
15 Letchworth G City	42	15	7	20	48	66	52
16 Newbury Town	42	14	5	23	60	82	47
17 Hemel Hempstead	42	12	9	21	63	69	45
18 Rainham Town	42	7	5	30	38	114	26
19 Finchley	42	5	9	28	28	78	24
20 Eastbourne United	42	7	3	32	36	98	24
21 Ware	42	6	6	30	48	114	24
22 Horsham+	42	7	4	31	40	104	23

Left: the Eastbourne United matchday programme from season 1983-84.

Right: the cover of the Southall programme from the same season.

** Southall had two points deducted.*
+ Horsham had three points deducted.
Dorking previously Dorking Town.

1984–85 - During the close season Corinthian-Casuals were forced to resign from the League as they did not have a suitable home ground which met the ground grading criteria set by the League. As a result, Division Two would operate with nineteen clubs.

Sutton United captured the Premier Division championship for the first time since 1967 when they beat Windsor & Eton at Gander Green Lane on the last Saturday in April in one of the worst seasons for matches postponed or abandoned due to severe weather conditions. Worthing for the second successive season were runners-up, four points behind the champions with Wycombe Wanderers third and Wokingham Town who were fourth, their best position since gaining promotion

Left: the Stevenage Borough matchday programme from season 1984-85.

Below: the Croydon programme for their game with Hayes which the visitors won 1-0.

At the foot of the table Harlow Town who only won five matches were relegated to Division One and were joined by Leytonstone & Ilford. Farnborough Town secured the Division One championship and were promoted to the Premier Division along with Kingstonian who joined them at the expense of Leatherhead who had points deducted for a registration irregularity.

The bottom four clubs were relegated to the regionalised Second Divisions, namely Woking, Metropolitan Police, Clapton and Hertford Town. In Division Two North Leyton-Wingate won the championship with Finchley, despite having one point deducted, finishing runners-up and also being promoted. Epping Town had their playing record expunged from the League table and were not re-elected at the Annual General Meeting. This was due to a suspension by the Essex County Football Association, a poor administrative record during the latter part of the season and the failure to fulfil two fixtures. Although they were subsequently played, their final fixture against Heybridge Swifts was not.

In Division Two South the championship was smoother with Grays Athletic taking the title five points clear of runners-up Uxbridge, who also gained promotion and Molesey, third. At the bottom Chertsey Town were relegated to the Combined Counties League after just one season with just two wins from their 36 match programme.

At the Annual General Meeting, Yeovil Town, relegated from the Gola League, replaced Wycombe Wanderers who, despite finishing third in the Premier Division, became the first Isthmian club to rise to the Gola League, whilst Southwick and Vauxhall Motors were elected to fill vacancies to give 20 clubs in Divisions Two North and South.

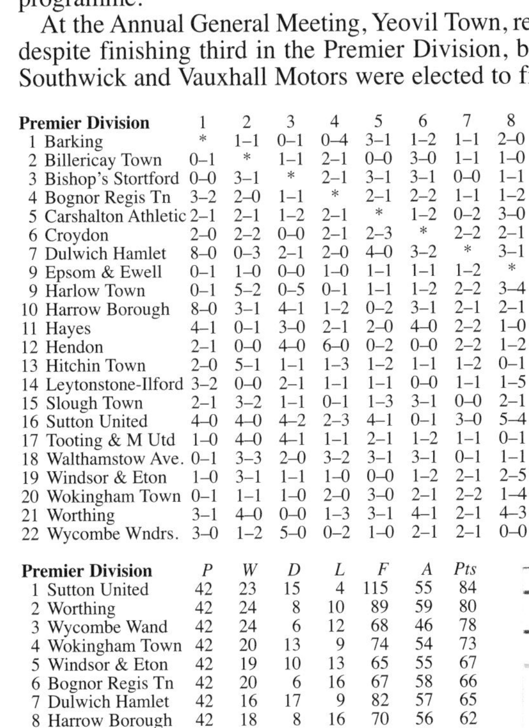

Premier Division	1	2	3	4	5	6	7	8	9	10	11	12	13	14	15	16	17	18	19	20	21	22
1 Barking	*	1–1	0–1	0–4	3–1	1–2	1–1	2–0	1–1	2–0	3–0	2–0	2–1	1–3	2–2	2–2	0–1	1–0	1–0	2–2	1–3	1–2
2 Billericay Town	0–1	*	1–1	2–1	0–0	3–0	1–1	1–0	3–1	2–5	3–1	1–1	1–4	2–0	4–1	4–4	1–1	0–3	0–0	2–1	0–0	0–1
3 Bishop's Stortford	0–0	3–1	*	2–1	3–1	3–1	0–0	1–1	0–2	0–1	1–0	1–4	2–2	2–1	3–1	0–3	0–2	2–3	1–2	2–1	3–2	0–1
4 Bognor Regis Tn	3–2	2–0	1–1	*	2–1	2–2	1–1	1–2	1–1	0–2	2–0	2–1	6–2	3–1	3–2	1–2	3–0	0–2	1–0	1–0	1–2	3–2
5 Carshalton Athletic	2–1	2–1	1–2	2–1	*	1–2	0–2	3–0	2–0	1–1	2–1	1–3	0–1	1–2	4–3	2–2	2–0	1–2	2–1	1–2	0–1	3–3
6 Croydon	2–0	2–2	0–0	2–1	2–3	*	2–2	2–1	0–0	4–1	0–1	3–0	0–1	5–1	2–1	1–1	1–2	2–1	5–1	0–2	2–2	1–1
7 Dulwich Hamlet	8–0	0–3	2–1	2–0	4–0	3–2	*	3–1	5–1	0–0	5–3	2–2	1–1	2–3	4–1	1–1	6–1	0–0	2–1	2–3	4–3	0–2
9 Epsom & Ewell	0–1	1–0	0–0	1–0	1–1	1–1	1–2	*	2–2	2–0	1–3	1–1	3–0	0–0	2–2	1–2	1–1	2–2	4–4	1–1	2–1	1–2
9 Harlow Town	0–1	5–2	0–5	0–1	1–1	1–2	2–2	3–4	*	1–4	1–2	0–0	0–1	0–2	3–1	1–1	1–1	3–2	0–4	2–2	0–2	0–1
10 Harrow Borough	8–0	3–1	4–1	1–2	0–2	3–1	2–1	2–1	3–0	*	0–3	1–1	1–2	0–1	3–1	2–2	4–1	1–0	1–1	3–0	1–0	2–3
11 Hayes	4–1	0–1	3–0	2–1	2–0	4–0	2–2	1–0	0–3	2–0	*	3–1	3–4	0–0	2–1	2–4	3–2	2–0	1–2	0–2	0–1	1–0
12 Hendon	2–1	0–0	4–0	6–0	0–2	0–0	2–2	1–2	2–2	2–1	0–0	*	2–2	0–0	1–2	2–2	1–1	2–2	0–0	1–2	2–3	0–2
13 Hitchin Town	2–0	5–1	1–1	1–3	1–2	1–1	1–2	0–1	1–1	1–1	2–2	1–1	*	2–1	1–1	0–2	1–1	1–1	2–0	1–1	1–2	1–4
14 Leytonstone-Ilford	3–2	0–0	2–1	1–1	1–1	0–0	1–1	1–5	2–1	0–0	0–1	0–1	1–0	*	0–2	0–3	3–2	0–2	0–1	0–5	1–3	2–0
15 Slough Town	2–1	3–2	1–1	0–1	1–3	3–1	0–0	2–1	3–1	3–1	0–0	0–0	3–0	1–1	*	3–1	3–1	4–1	0–3	2–4	0–2	2–2
16 Sutton United	4–0	4–0	4–2	2–3	4–1	0–1	3–0	5–4	7–1	0–0	3–1	7–3	4–1	4–0	1–1	*	1–1	6–0	2–0	2–2	2–2	1–0
17 Tooting & M Utd	1–0	4–0	4–1	1–1	2–1	1–2	1–1	0–1	2–1	1–0	1–0	2–2	3–1	7–2	1–4	1–3	*	1–1	1–2	1–0	1–4	1–2
18 Walthamstow Ave.	0–1	3–3	2–0	3–2	3–1	3–1	0–1	1–1	5–0	2–3	1–1	1–5	1–0	2–0	1–1	1–5	2–1	*	1–1	2–3	3–0	0–2
19 Windsor & Eton	1–0	3–1	1–1	1–0	0–0	1–2	2–1	2–5	4–1	2–3	1–1	2–1	3–3	1–0	1–1	0–3	0–2	2–1	*	5–1	2–1	1–0
20 Wokingham Town	0–1	1–1	1–0	2–0	3–0	2–1	2–2	1–4	3–1	3–1	1–0	4–0	1–1	2–1	3–2	2–2	1–1	1–1	0–1	*	3–2	2–0
21 Worthing	3–1	4–0	0–0	1–3	3–1	4–1	2–1	4–3	3–0	2–1	3–3	4–2	2–1	4–0	3–2	2–2	1–2	1–2	3–2	1–1	*	2–1
22 Wycombe Wndrs.	3–0	1–2	5–0	0–2	1–0	2–1	2–1	0–0	5–1	2–0	1–0	1–3	2–0	1–0	3–1	3–2	2–3	1–0	0–4	1–1	1–1	*

Premier Division	*P*	*W*	*D*	*L*	*F*	*A*	*Pts*
1 Sutton United	42	23	15	4	115	55	84
2 Worthing	42	24	8	10	89	59	80
3 Wycombe Wand	42	24	6	12	68	46	78
4 Wokingham Town	42	20	13	9	74	54	73
5 Windsor & Eton	42	19	10	13	65	55	67
6 Bognor Regis Tn	42	20	6	16	67	58	66
7 Dulwich Hamlet	42	16	17	9	82	57	65
8 Harrow Borough	42	18	8	16	70	56	62
9 Hayes	42	17	8	17	60	56	59
10 Tooting & M Utd	42	16	11	15	64	66	59
11 Walthamstow Ave.	42	15	11	16	64	65	56
12 Croydon*	42	15	12	15	62	63	54
13 Epsom & Ewell	42	13	14	15	65	62	53
14 Slough Town	42	13	12	17	69	74	51
15 Carshalton Athletic	42	14	8	20	55	68	50
16 Bishop's Stortford	42	12	12	18	48	67	48
17 Hendon	42	9	19	14	62	65	46
18 Billericay Town+	42	11	14	17	53	74	46
19 Barking	42	13	7	22	43	75	46
20 Hitchin Town	42	10	15	17	55	70	45
21 Leytonstone-Ilford	42	11	10	21	37	72	43
22 Harlow Town	42	5	12	25	45	95	27

** Croydon had three points deducted.*
+ Billericay Town had one point deducted.

Left: the Hendon matchday programme from season 1984-85.

Right: the Royston Town edition from the same season.

1984-85 Division I	1	2	3	4	5	6	7	8	9	10	11	12	13	14	15	16	17	18	19	20	21	22
1 Aveley	*	1–1	1–3	2–1	0–4	4–2	0–3	2–1	2–1	0–3	1–1	0–3	4–2	3–1	1–0	2–2	1–1	2–0	4–4	0–1	1–1	0–1
2 Basildon United	1–0	*	1–2	1–0	1–5	0–0	1–0	2–0	0–0	3–1	0–2	3–2	3–1	1–0	3–1	1–1	2–0	1–0	1–2	1–0	0–1	2–3
3 Boreham Wood	6–3	2–5	*	1–1	1–2	2–1	1–2	1–1	1–3	3–1	0–3	1–1	0–3	2–3	1–3	0–1	1–3	2–1	1–4	2–1	0–1	4–1
4 Bromley	1–0	3–0	4–1	*	1–0	2–0	1–2	2–1	2–1	2–1	0–1	0–3	6–3	0–1	1–2	0–4	1–1	3–1	6–2	0–1	1–0	3–1
5 Chesham United	4–1	3–2	2–1	2–0	*	2–0	0–3	1–2	1–1	2–0	1–0	1–2	1–0	2–0	5–1	3–1	0–2	2–0	1–1	1–3	1–1	4–0
6 Clapton	4–3	2–0	0–5	2–0	2–1	*	0–1	2–2	1–1	2–3	1–3	1–7	1–2	2–2	1–7	0–3	3–3	1–1	1–9	1–1	0–2	3–2
7 Farnborough Town	1–0	2–1	5–3	2–2	1–3	2–0	*	5–0	10–1	1–1	0–1	2–3	3–0	3–1	4–0	2–2	3–2	1–0	0–3	6–2	1–0	3–0
8 Hampton	0–1	3–2	4–2	5–1	2–2	5–1	0–2	*	3–0	3–2	0–0	1–4	1–1	0–0	2–1	3–1	1–1	0–2	4–1	2–4	5–0	1–2
9 Hertford Town	2–8	2–2	1–2	1–1	0–0	3–3	0–3	2–0	*	0–0	0–1	2–3	1–4	1–2	1–1	1–0	0–3	4–1	0–1	0–1	0–0	2–1
10 Hornchurch	0–1	1–0	4–1	0–0	0–4	2–1	2–5	2–1	2–0	*	1–2	0–4	0–1	2–0	3–0	1–4	3–2	2–0	3–3	1–0	1–2	0–2
11 Kingstonian	3–1	2–1	2–0	2–2	1–2	2–1	2–2	0–2	5–0	3–0	*	1–1	1–0	0–2	2–2	1–0	2–0	0–1	2–0	2–2	0–3	3–2
12 Leatherhead	7–0	1–3	3–4	3–3	1–0	3–1	1–1	1–3	3–0	4–1	2–0	*	1–1	5–0	2–2	3–1	2–1	3–0	2–5	1–2	1–0	5–1
13 Lewes	0–1	2–0	1–1	1–3	2–2	10–0	1–1	0–3	4–1	5–0	0–3	4–2	*	2–1	2–2	2–0	0–3	0–2	1–2	2–0	1–1	0–1
14 Maidenhead Utd	4–2	3–1	3–3	1–3	3–2	1–1	1–3	4–0	3–1	1–3	0–1	1–1	1–3	*	2–1	4–1	1–0	1–1	5–3	0–0	1–2	0–1
15 Metropolitan Police	4–3	3–2	0–4	1–2	2–1	3–3	1–1	1–4	2–1	3–4	2–2	1–4	2–2	0–3	*	2–2	0–3	2–1	2–2	0–2	2–0	1–1
16 Oxford City	0–1	1–1	3–2	0–1	2–3	5–0	0–4	0–0	4–1	1–0	0–1	1–1	6–0	1–1	1–0	*	3–1	2–0	1–1	1–2	1–0	2–0
17 St. Albans City	1–2	1–2	0–1	5–3	1–1	3–1	2–0	2–1	1–0	1–1	2–1	5–2	3–1	1–0	2–1	3–2	*	1–1	2–2	1–1	1–2	3–3
18 Staines Town	2–1	1–0	1–2	1–1	0–0	9–2	0–2	1–1	1–0	1–1	1–1	1–3	2–2	2–0	6–3	1–0	3–1	*	1–1	3–1	2–1	4–1
19 Tilbury	1–0	2–2	0–1	2–1	3–2	1–1	4–0	0–0	2–0	2–0	0–0	3–3	1–2	2–1	2–1	0–0	1–3	1–2	*	4–1	0–2	5–2
20 Walton & Hersham	1–2	0–0	0–0	2–1	0–1	3–0	0–7	0–3	5–1	1–0	2–4	3–2	4–0	0–1	0–1	1–1	2–4	0–2	4–2	*	1–4	0–0
21 Wembley	0–0	2–0	0–0	1–1	1–0	3–2	1–1	2–3	4–0	0–1	2–1	1–1	3–0	2–4	1–1	2–0	2–1	1–0	0–1	4–0	*	2–3
22 Woking	0–1	3–2	4–2	3–5	1–4	1–0	2–1	2–2	4–1	3–2	0–3	0–3	0–2	0–2	3–1	1–1	1–3	0–0	3–1	1–6	0–2	*

Division I	*P*	*W*	*D*	*L*	*F*	*A*	*Pts*
1 Farnborough Town	42	26	8	8	101	45	86
2 Kingstonian	42	23	10	9	67	39	79
3 Leatherhead*	42	23	10	9	109	61	76
4 Chesham United	42	22	8	12	78	46	74
5 Wembley	42	20	10	12	59	40	70
6 St. Albans City	42	19	10	13	79	60	67
7 Tilbury	42	18	13	11	86	68	67
8 Bromley	42	18	9	15	71	64	63
9 Hampton	42	17	11	14	75	62	62
10 Staines Town	42	16	11	15	59	53	59
11 Maidenhead Utd	42	17	8	17	65	64	59
12 Walton & Hershm+	42	16	8	18	60	69	55
13 Aveley	42	16	7	19	62	78	55
14 Oxford City	42	14	12	16	62	53	54
15 Lewes	42	15	9	18	70	72	54
16 Basildon United	42	15	8	19	55	61	53
17 Boreham Wood	42	15	7	20	72	83	52
18 Hornchurch	42	15	6	21	55	74	51
19 Woking	42	15	6	21	60	91	51
20 Metropolitan Police	42	10	12	20	65	92	42
21 Clapton	42	5	11	26	50	124	26
22 Hertford Town	42	5	10	27	36	97	25

** Leatherhead had three points deducted.*
+ Walton & Hersham had one point deducted.

Left: the Staines Town matchday programme from season 1984-85.

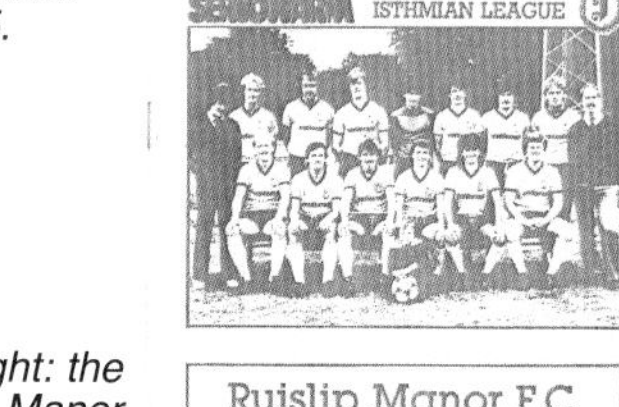

Right: the Ruislip Manor edition from the same season.

Division II North	1	2	3	4	5	6	7	8	9	10	11	12	13	14	15	16	17	18	19	20	21
1 Barton Rovers	*	2–2	2–3	3–0	6–0	1–2	0–1	1–5	2–1	3–1	0–2	1–0	3–1	0–1	1–1	1–1	1–1	1–2	0–1	3–1	1–1
2 Berkhamsted Town	1–0	*	2–2	0–0	3–3	0–1	1–0	3–0	2–0	0–2	2–1	1–0	0–0	3–3	0–1	2–1	0–0	1–2	1–1	4–0	2–0
3 Chalfont St Peter	2–0	2–2	*	1–1	2–0	0–2	1–2	1–1	6–0	1–0	2–0	4–0	7–1	0–2	5–1	0–1	1–1	0–2	1–1	4–1	1–0
4 Cheshunt	1–1	1–2	1–0	*	2–0	0–2	1–1	1–0	1–4	1–0	0–1	3–1	1–3	3–2	1–3	3–0	0–2	1–3	1–0	1–2	4–0
5 Epping Town	0–1	1–2	2–1	1–1	*	1–0	1–1	0–5	2–1	2–0	1–1	1–1	0–0	0–7	0–2	0–3	1–2	3–0	0–2	0–1	1–2
6 Finchley	2–0	0–1	1–1	1–0	1–0	*	0–1	3–1	1–1	0–2	2–0	2–0	2–0	0–0	2–1	1–0	1–0	3–1	2–0	1–4	0–0
7 Flackwell Heath	0–2	4–0	2–1	2–0	0–1	0–2	*	3–2	2–2	2–0	0–1	1–0	1–1	0–1	1–3	1–1	2–2	3–1	0–0	3–1	3–0
8 Harefield United	2–1	1–2	1–1	1–3	1–3	2–2	1–1	*	0–1	1–2	0–0	2–0	1–3	2–7	3–2	0–1	1–0	2–0	1–4	3–4	1–2
9 Haringey Borough	1–0	1–1	0–3	2–7	1–4	0–6	0–0	1–0	*	1–2	1–5	0–0	2–2	1–3	2–2	2–1	0–2	0–1	1–1	1–3	1–2
10 Hemel Hempstead	0–2	1–1	1–4	2–2	0–1	1–3	0–0	3–3	1–1	*	0–1	3–3	0–2	1–4	1–2	5–0	1–0	2–3	2–0	4–1	1–1
11 Heybridge Swifts	6–0	1–0	2–0	2–0	x-x	0–1	1–1	4–1	2–0	1–0	*	1–1	0–1	3–3	2–2	6–0	1–1	3–1	3–2	5–0	2–1
12 Kingsbury Town	1–0	1–1	1–3	1–2	1–0	3–3	1–2	2–0	0–0	1–2	1–2	*	2–4	2–0	4–2	1–2	0–1	0–2	2–2	5–2	1–2
13 Letchworth G City	1–1	1–0	1–2	3–5	1–1	1–1	2–1	5–1	3–1	0–4	1–0	2–0	*	0–1	5–2	2–3	1–3	1–0	0–4	3–2	4–1
14 Leyton-Wingate	3–2	5–1	1–1	3–1	0–1	1–0	2–1	6–2	2–2	6–2	0–1	0–4	2–1	*	3–1	1–1	2–2	3–0	3–4	4–1	4–1
15 Marlow	1–0	1–3	0–1	0–2	1–1	1–3	0–2	2–1	3–2	4–0	2–2	2–3	3–3	2–3	*	4–2	0–3	0–5	2–0	3–2	1–3
16 Royston Town	1–0	1–0	2–2	3–2	0–0	0–3	0–2	1–1	1–1	1–0	1–1	3–1	2–3	1–3	3–2	*	1–4	1–1	2–5	2–0	2–1
17 Saffron Walden Tn	7–0	3–0	2–0	1–0	2–0	4–2	2–1	3–0	3–0	1–0	0–1	2–0	1–0	1–3	2–3	2–3	*	3–0	3–1	1–0	5–1
18 Stevenage Borough	2–1	2–1	1–0	2–0	2–4	0–3	3–2	2–2	4–0	2–1	3–1	5–2	2–0	0–4	1–1	9–0	2–2	*	1–1	2–0	4–0
19 Tring Town	1–1	1–1	2–0	2–1	1–0	0–0	3–2	4–1	2–1	5–0	1–3	6–0	5–1	0–0	2–0	1–1	2–1	1–2	*	2–0	2–1
20 Ware	2–3	0–6	0–6	0–1	0–3	3–4	0–2	0–0	1–4	1–0	1–1	0–6	3–1	1–5	0–2	2–0	0–0	1–4	0–3	*	1–1
21 Wolverton Town	1–0	0–1	1–3	1–0	2–3	1–2	2–2	0–5	2–0	0–2	1–3	2–3	0–3	2–2	3–2	2–1	0–2	2–2	0–4	0–0	*

Division II North	*P*	*W*	*D*	*L*	*F*	*A*	*Pts*
1 Leyton-Wingate	38	24	9	5	98	50	81
2 Finchley*	38	24	8	6	66	31	79
3 Heybridge Swifts	38	22	9	7	71	33	75
4 Stevenage Borough	38	23	6	9	79	49	75
5 Saffron Walden Tn	38	22	8	8	73	31	74
6 Tring Town	38	19	11	8	76	41	68
7 Chalfont St. Peter	38	17	10	11	72	41	61
8 Flackwell Heath	38	16	11	11	54	40	59
9 Berkhamsted Town	38	15	12	11	50	42	57
10 Letchworth G City	38	17	6	15	66	69	57
11 Royston Town	38	13	9	16	47	77	48
12 Cheshunt	38	14	5	19	52	57	47
13 Marlow	38	13	6	19	64	81	45
14 Hemel Hempstead	38	11	7	20	49	64	40
15 Barton Rovers	38	9	8	21	40	62	35
16 Wolverton Town	38	9	8	21	38	77	35
17 Kingsbury Town	38	9	7	22	53	72	34
18 Harefield United	38	7	9	22	51	81	30
19 Haringey Borough	38	6	12	20	38	79	30
20 Ware	38	7	5	26	40	100	26

** Finchley had one point deducted.*
The record of Epping Town was expunged.

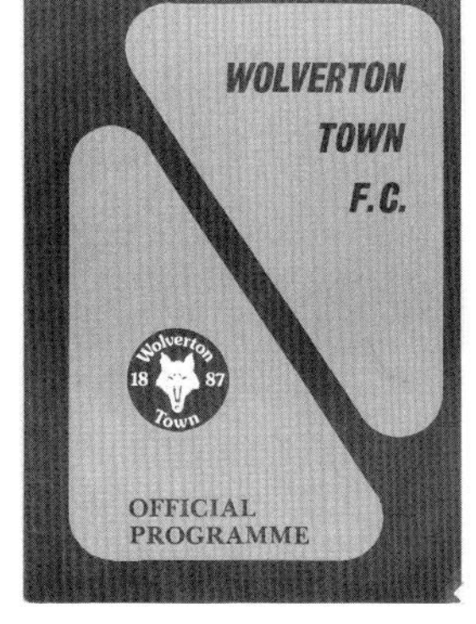

Left: the Wolverton Town edition from the same season.

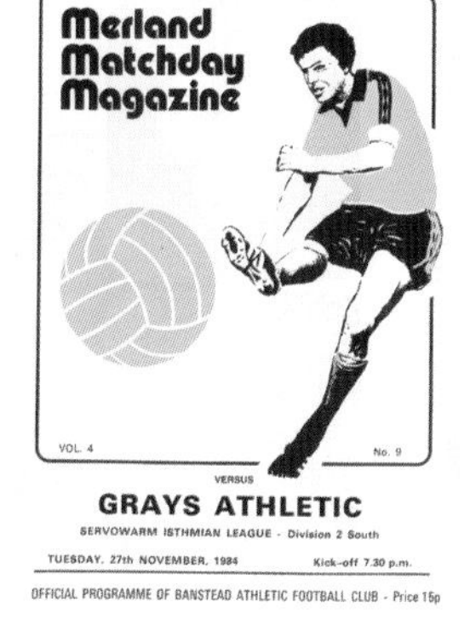

Right: the Banstead Athletic matchday programme from season 1984-85.

1984-85

Division II South	1	2	3	4	5	6	7	8	9	10	11	12	13	14	15	16	17	18	19
1 Banstead Athletic	*	1–1	0–1	6–1	3–3	2–2	0–0	3–2	0–0	1–0	0–2	4–3	3–0	3–2	1–2	3–6	2–4	2–3	2–1
2 Bracknell Town	4–1	*	0–1	3–1	4–4	1–1	0–1	2–1	0–3	3–1	4–1	1–1	0–1	2–1	2–3	0–0	0–1	0–4	3–0
3 Camberley Town	2–3	0–2	*	0–0	0–1	1–1	0–0	1–1	2–4	0–0	1–1	3–3	6–1	1–0	1–1	2–1	0–2	0–0	0–6
4 Chertsey Town	0–3	0–3	0–2	*	1–2	0–5	1–2	2–2	0–4	0–3	1–6	0–3	2–4	3–2	0–3	1–0	0–1	0–0	1–6
5 Dorking	0–2	1–1	1–0	2–0	*	1–1	2–1	4–0	0–2	0–2	0–2	2–2	4–1	1–0	1–1	0–0	1–0	0–0	0–0
6 Eastbourne United	2–3	1–4	4–3	6–0	0–1	*	2–3	1–1	1–6	2–1	1–3	0–2	4–0	4–0	4–1	2–2	0–1	1–2	4–2
7 Egham Town	1–1	2–1	2–0	2–1	3–1	5–1	*	1–2	1–0	0–2	4–0	2–3	2–0	0–1	1–2	1–1	2–1	0–1	0–0
8 Feltham	0–4	1–4	2–1	3–1	1–0	3–0	3–2	*	0–0	0–1	1–4	0–3	1–1	2–0	2–1	2–2	1–2	0–0	1–1
9 Grays Athletic	3–0	2–1	3–1	5–0	4–1	1–3	4–0	1–1	*	0–0	2–2	4–2	3–0	3–0	2–1	1–1	5–0	0–0	1–1
10 Horsham	4–2	2–1	3–2	2–1	2–2	0–0	0–2	2–0	1–1	*	0–1	1–3	0–1	1–2	1–1	1–2	4–0	0–2	0–0
11 Hungerford Town	3–1	2–0	2–5	5–3	2–0	2–1	2–1	3–3	0–1	3–0	*	1–1	1–2	1–1	4–1	2–1	4–1	4–2	1–1
12 Molesey	0–1	1–0	2–0	1–0	1–0	4–0	1–1	2–0	1–2	2–0	1–0	*	0–3	2–1	3–0	3–0	1–4	0–3	3–1
13 Newbury Town	0–1	0–1	0–1	3–0	1–2	1–1	1–2	1–1	0–2	0–2	1–1	0–3	*	1–1	0–0	2–3	2–1	0–2	0–3
14 Petersfield United	4–2	0–0	3–0	2–0	4–2	2–8	2–1	0–3	1–2	0–3	2–1	0–2	2–3	*	2–2	0–1	2–1	0–7	1–4
15 Rainham Town	5–1	1–3	2–2	6–0	2–2	3–0	1–2	0–0	1–4	2–2	0–2	2–1	2–2	2–1	*	0–1	6–1	0–5	1–2
16 Ruislip Manor	1–1	1–2	0–1	4–0	2–1	1–0	2–2	1–2	0–4	1–1	1–0	3–1	3–1	1–1	1–0	*	1–2	2–0	0–1
17 Southall	0–0	2–0	1–2	3–2	2–2	1–1	1–0	4–1	1–4	2–1	4–2	0–1	2–1	3–0	1–2	3–0	*	0–2	1–0
18 Uxbridge	4–1	5–0	2–2	11–0	2–0	3–1	0–2	1–1	0–1	0–0	1–1	2–0	2–0	4–0	2–0	4–1	3–0	*	1–0
19 Whyteleafe	4–0	0–1	0–0	3–1	1–1	6–1	2–3	2–0	2–0	0–1	0–0	1–0	5–1	4–1	2–1	2–1	2–1	1–1	*

Above: the Harefield United programme for 1984-85.

Division II South	*P*	*W*	*D*	*L*	*F*	*A*	*Pts*
1 Grays Athletic	36	24	9	3	84	25	81
2 Uxbridge	36	22	10	4	81	20	76
3 Molesey	36	20	5	11	62	42	65
4 Hungerford Town	36	18	9	9	71	49	63
5 Whyteleafe	36	17	10	9	66	34	61
6 Egham Town	36	17	7	12	54	42	58
7 Southall	36	18	3	15	54	57	57
8 Bracknell Town	36	15	7	14	54	48	52
9 Banstead Athletic	36	14	8	14	63	70	50
10 Horsham	36	13	10	13	44	39	49
11 Ruislip Manor	36	13	10	13	58	61	44
12 Dorking	36	12	11	13	45	50	47
13 Rainham Town	36	12	8	16	58	61	44
14 Feltham	36	10	13	13	44	58	43
15 Camberley Town	36	10	12	14	44	54	42
16 Eastbourne United	36	10	9	17	66	72	39
17 Petersfield United	36	9	5	22	41	80	32
18 Newbury Town+	36	8	7	21	35	69	16
19 Chertsey Town*	36	2	3	31	23	118	6

+ Newbury Town had 15 points deducted.
** Chertsey Town had three points deducted.*

Below: St. Albans City – Isthmian League Division One champions 1985-86: Back row; Steve Perrin, Iain Dowie, Terry Benning, Mark Pearson, Bob Dowie, Neil Jeffrey, Alan Paradise, John Mitchell (manager). Front row; Nigel Wilson, Steve Oliver, John Watt, Mick O'Shea, Gary Keen, Martin Gurney.

1985–86 - In an exciting finish to the season Sutton United retained the Premier Division championship by four points despite losing to nearest challengers Yeovil Town 2–0 at the end of April in front of over 5,000 spectators. Sutton United decided to join the GM Vauxhall Conference – formerly the Gola League – replacing Wycombe Wanderers who were relegated after a single season. Farnborough Town finished third, fourteen points behind the 'Glovers', whilst Croydon enjoyed their highest League position, finishing in fourth place. At the other end of the table a close finish saw Carshalton Athletic escape the drop by one point which resulted in Billericay Town and Epsom & Ewell being relegated to Division One. The Division One championship was decided on the final day of the season. St. Albans City won 7–1 at Lewes to secure the championship on goal-difference from Bromley, with Wembley two points behind in third.

At the foot of the table the four relegated clubs, Hornchurch, Chesham United, Harlow Town and Aveley would all go to Division Two North by switching Chalfont St. Peter and Harefield United to Division Two South. In Division Two North it was a two-horse race with Stevenage Borough pipping Kingsbury Town for the championship, whilst newcomers Southwick secured the Division Two South title by two points from runners-up Bracknell Town.

At the Annual General Meeting elected clubs were Chertsey Town, who returned to Division Two South after one season, with Collier Row and Wivenhoe Town joining Division Two North which gave 22 clubs in Division Two North and 21 clubs in Division South - a total League membership of 87 clubs. With just one vacancy remaining which it was hoped would be filled for the start of the 1986–87 season then promotion and relegation with the feeder leagues could be more than just a possibility.

Premier Division	1	2	3	4	5	6	7	8	9	10	11	12	13	14	15	16	17	18	19	20	21	22
1 Barking	*	0–0	2–2	0–2	3–0	1–2	1–1	2–1	2–3	2–0	1–0	2–0	1–1	1–2	4–3	0–2	1–2	1–0	2–2	1–2	3–0	0–0
2 Billericay Town	2–1	*	0–0	3–3	3–3	1–1	2–1	0–0	1–2	1–1	1–2	1–4	1–0	1–3	2–3	1–2	3–4	0–2	3–1	3–1	2–3	0–2
3 Bishop's Stortford	2–1	0–0	*	4–0	2–1	2–1	0–1	2–1	0–1	1–0	0–2	3–2	2–0	2–0	0–3	0–6	2–1	2–0	2–5	3–2	0–1	0–1
4 Bognor Regis Tn	0–1	1–0	1–1	*	6–0	0–2	3–1	1–1	0–1	4–1	3–0	1–1	0–2	3–3	3–0	2–0	2–1	3–2	0–1	2–1	0–3	3–1
5 Carshalton Athletic	3–1	1–2	1–2	1–2	*	0–2	2–0	2–1	1–0	0–1	2–0	1–1	2–3	0–0	1–1	1–4	1–2	1–1	2–1	1–0	3–1	1–1
6 Croydon	0–1	2–1	2–0	2–0	2–1	*	1–1	3–1	3–2	1–3	1–0	1–1	2–0	4–1	1–0	1–0	0–4	2–3	5–2	2–0	3–4	4–1
7 Dulwich Hamlet	1–1	1–3	2–5	3–1	2–1	1–1	*	5–3	2–1	1–4	1–0	0–0	1–0	2–3	0–1	1–2	2–2	1–1	1–2	1–0	2–2	1–1
8 Epsom & Ewell	3–0	0–2	0–2	1–0	2–2	1–2	0–3	*	0–1	1–3	1–0	5–3	3–3	3–2	2–1	2–2	1–2	1–2	2–3	2–4	3–3	2–2
9 Farnborough Town	0–0	4–0	1–0	2–1	4–2	0–2	6–1	2–3	*	6–0	1–1	5–0	6–0	0–0	2–1	3–2	2–3	3–2	2–1	0–1	3–2	1–2
10 Harrow Borough	0–0	1–1	3–1	3–2	3–2	2–1	3–0	3–0	1–3	*	1–0	3–2	2–0	1–3	4–2	0–3	1–1	2–2	4–1	1–1	3–2	3–2
11 Hayes	1–1	2–2	0–0	1–2	1–1	0–0	0–2	0–0	2–0	2–1	*	1–1	1–1	4–1	0–1	1–1	2–1	2–1	0–0	3–1	0–3	0–1
12 Hendon	2–1	4–2	1–1	1–0	2–3	0–2	1–3	3–0	1–5	1–3	0–0	*	2–3	1–1	1–1	1–2	1–1	1–2	2–0	1–2	2–2	1–2
13 Hitchin Town	0–0	2–2	1–1	2–1	1–1	1–1	1–2	2–1	1–1	3–2	2–2	2–2	*	0–0	0–1	2–1	0–0	2–0	1–2	0–2	4–1	1–3
14 Kingstonian	2–0	2–2	1–1	2–1	1–0	0–2	1–2	2–2	2–2	1–0	0–0	3–0	2–0	*	1–1	2–4	2–1	2–1	2–3	2–2	1–1	0–1
15 Slough Town	2–0	4–3	1–0	1–0	2–1	0–0	1–2	4–4	2–3	0–0	0–2	1–4	1–2	3–2	*	0–1	4–1	1–0	3–1	1–1	3–1	2–3
16 Sutton United	1–1	3–2	4–1	6–0	2–2	3–2	6–1	3–1	1–1	2–0	3–1	3–0	4–1	2–0	4–1	*	0–0	3–3	5–0	5–0	0–0	3–1
17 Tooting & M Utd	3–1	3–2	1–2	1–0	2–2	0–4	3–4	2–2	2–2	1–4	2–0	0–1	1–0	1–1	2–3	1–5	*	2–2	1–3	3–2	4–2	0–2
18 Walthamstow Ave.	3–2	2–0	1–3	5–2	2–2	1–0	7–2	2–2	0–5	3–2	0–0	0–2	3–3	0–1	1–2	0–1	0–0	*	4–1	0–0	4–2	2–2
19 Windsor & Eton	1–0	2–3	0–0	3–2	3–3	2–0	1–0	2–1	1–2	0–3	0–0	4–0	1–4	1–0	0–0	0–3	2–1	1–0	*	0–3	1–0	2–2
20 Wokingham Town	1–1	2–0	2–2	1–2	2–0	2–3	1–2	3–1	2–1	1–2	0–2	3–3	3–0	0–0	4–0	1–3	3–1	2–2	2–0	*	3–3	2–1
21 Worthing	0–1	2–1	6–2	2–2	3–1	2–0	2–3	2–3	1–1	4–0	0–0	0–2	2–1	0–1	2–1	0–2	0–2	2–2	3–1	1–2	*	2–5
22 Yeovil Town	3–1	1–0	2–0	3–2	5–1	5–0	3–1	3–0	1–0	2–2	2–1	2–1	3–1	1–2	3–4	2–0	3–0	2–1	2–1	3–0	5–0	*

1985-86

Premier Division	*P*	*W*	*D*	*L*	*F*	*A*	*Pts*
1 Sutton United	42	29	8	5	109	39	95
2 Yeovil Town	42	28	7	7	92	48	91
3 Farnborough Town	42	23	8	11	90	50	77
4 Croydon	42	23	7	12	70	50	76
5 Harrow Borough	42	21	8	13	76	66	71
6 Slough Town	42	18	8	16	66	68	62
7 Bishop's Stortford	42	17	10	15	55	61	61
8 Kingstonian	42	15	15	12	57	56	60
9 Dulwich Hamlet	42	17	9	16	64	79	60
10 Wokingham Town	42	16	10	16	67	64	58
11 Windsor & Eton	42	17	7	18	58	75	58
12 Tooting & M Utd	42	14	11	17	65	76	53
13 Walthamstow Ave.	42	12	14	16	69	70	50
14 Worthing	42	13	10	19	72	82	49
15 Bognor Regis Tn*	42	15	6	21	63	70	48
16 Hayes	42	10	17	15	36	42	47
17 Hitchin Town	42	11	14	17	53	69	47
18 Barking	42	11	13	18	45	55	46
19 Hendon	42	10	13	19	59	77	43
20 Carshalton Athletic	42	9	13	20	56	79	40
21 Billericay Town	42	9	12	21	59	78	39
22 Epsom & Ewell	42	8	12	22	63	90	36

** Bognor Regis Town had three points deducted.*

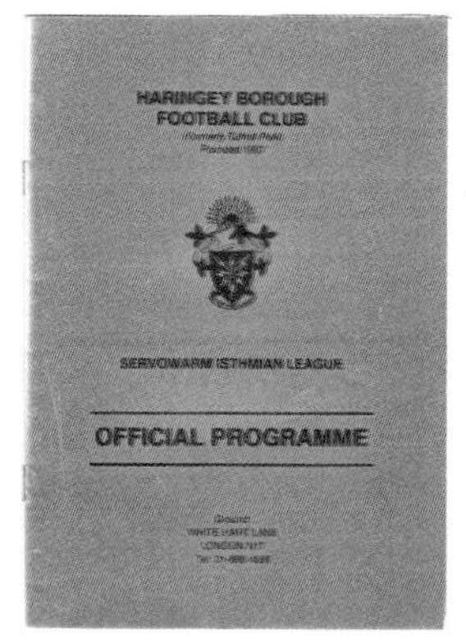

Left: the Haringey Borough matchday programme from season 1985-86.

Right: the Epsom & Ewell programme from the same campaign.

Division I	1	2	3	4	5	6	7	8	9	10	11	12	13	14	15	16	17	18	19	20	21	22
1 Aveley	*	2–0	0–3	0–3	1–2	2–2	1–3	1–1	0–2	1–2	0–1	1–4	3–4	2–3	2–1	1–3	2–3	3–3	0–3	0–1	2–1	0–2
2 Basildon United	3–4	*	3–1	1–2	4–0	1–1	1–2	1–2	2–1	1–1	1–0	1–2	0–1	0–2	3–1	2–2	3–1	1–0	1–1	1–3	0–3	1–1
3 Boreham Wood	1–1	2–0	*	0–0	2–0	0–0	1–1	2–0	2–2	2–1	2–1	0–2	2–1	1–1	2–1	2–3	1–1	3–5	0–0	3–1	1–1	1–4
4 Bromley	5–1	1–1	1–1	*	1–0	0–1	0–0	1–0	2–1	1–0	4–2	1–1	2–1	3–0	2–0	1–2	1–0	2–0	1–0	1–0	1–0	1–0
5 Chesham United	1–4	2–3	2–1	2–4	*	1–0	1–4	1–1	0–1	0–2	1–0	2–1	0–3	4–1	2–2	0–4	1–4	0–1	3–0	3–1	0–2	2–2
6 Finchley	3–1	2–2	1–1	3–2	4–1	*	5–2	1–2	2–0	1–1	4–1	2–2	0–3	2–0	0–1	1–1	0–2	1–2	3–0	1–1	2–0	1–1
7 Grays Athletic	4–3	0–2	1–1	1–4	2–0	2–2	*	2–3	0–1	3–0	3–0	0–1	1–3	2–3	2–1	3–0	3–3	2–3	2–3	1–2	1–1	1–0
8 Hampton	2–0	2–1	3–2	2–1	1–1	2–0	2–2	*	2–3	2–0	1–2	2–0	3–1	1–1	1–0	0–1	3–3	0–2	4–2	0–1	2–0	1–1
9 Harlow Town	2–3	4–1	1–1	0–1	2–3	0–0	1–1	1–2	*	1–1	1–1	2–2	2–5	1–3	4–3	2–3	2–2	0–0	1–2	1–1	2–2	0–2
10 Hornchurch	0–0	3–1	2–2	1–3	1–2	4–2	1–4	1–1	1–1	*	0–1	4–1	0–0	1–0	0–1	0–2	1–1	1–0	2–0	1–2	3–0	0–1
11 Leatherhead	2–0	1–3	0–1	3–2	1–1	4–2	5–1	0–1	1–1	2–0	*	6–1	1–2	1–1	0–3	1–0	1–2	4–0	0–1	1–0	4–1	0–2
12 Lewes	2–0	3–1	0–1	0–2	2–3	1–1	1–5	0–3	2–0	0–0	1–0	*	3–1	2–1	2–1	3–2	1–7	1–0	0–4	2–0	4–1	1–3
13 Leyton-Wingate	2–1	3–0	3–3	3–2	2–0	0–0	1–0	2–1	3–0	2–1	2–2	2–0	*	1–2	1–1	0–2	0–3	2–0	3–2	2–4	1–1	1–4
14 Leytonstone-Ilford	0–2	1–1	1–1	3–0	3–1	1–1	1–1	1–1	1–3	1–1	4–1	0–3	1–5	*	2–1	1–1	0–2	0–3	4–0	1–1	2–2	2–1
15 Maidenhead Utd	2–2	4–0	1–2	0–2	3–1	3–0	3–0	0–1	1–1	1–2	3–4	2–0	0–3	2–2	*	2–3	1–2	3–3	2–1	1–0	2–1	0–2
16 Oxford City	3–1	1–2	1–0	2–2	1–2	1–1	1–1	0–1	2–1	2–0	2–1	0–0	1–1	4–0	2–0	*	3–1	4–2	5–3	2–1	3–0	0–2
17 St. Albans City	3–2	3–1	1–3	2–1	2–1	2–0	2–0	2–2	3–2	4–2	6–2	3–3	1–1	4–1	3–1	0–3	*	1–1	3–0	2–1	1–1	0–1
18 Staines Town	5–2	2–1	0–4	2–2	1–1	1–2	2–1	0–2	2–0	2–0	2–0	2–1	1–1	2–1	1–2	3–0	4–0	*	3–2	0–3	3–2	1–1
19 Tilbury	2–4	0–0	2–1	1–1	4–0	2–2	1–2	0–1	1–2	1–0	2–2	3–2	0–2	2–2	3–2	0–0	0–0	4–1	*	2–1	5–1	0–0
20 Uxbridge	4–1	3–0	2–3	1–0	3–1	1–4	1–1	1–0	2–1	5–1	1–1	1–0	3–1	0–2	1–0	4–0	1–3	1–1	1–0	*	1–2	0–0
21 Walton & Hersham	3–2	2–0	1–0	2–0	3–1	4–1	5–1	4–2	1–0	2–1	3–2	1–3	1–0	0–0	1–1	2–2	2–4	4–2	1–1	2–3	*	1–2
22 Wembley	2–1	0–1	2–0	1–2	3–2	1–0	3–1	0–0	1–0	0–1	0–0	3–1	2–2	0–1	1–2	1–1	2–0	1–0	1–0	0–0	3–1	*

Division I	*P*	*W*	*D*	*L*	*F*	*A*	*Pts*
1 St. Albans City	42	23	11	8	92	61	80
2 Bromley	42	24	8	10	68	41	80
3 Wembley	42	22	12	8	59	30	78
4 Oxford City	42	22	11	9	75	51	77
5 Hampton	42	21	11	10	63	45	74
6 Leyton-Wingate	42	21	10	11	77	56	73
7 Uxbridge	42	20	8	14	64	49	68
8 Staines Town	42	18	10	14	69	66	64
9 Boreham Wood	42	15	16	11	62	54	61
10 Walton & Hersham	42	16	10	16	68	71	58
11 Lewes	42	16	8	18	61	75	56
12 Leytonstone-Ilford	42	13	15	14	57	67	54
13 Finchley	42	12	17	13	61	59	53
14 Grays Athletic	42	13	11	18	69	75	50
15 Leatherhead	42	14	8	20	62	68	50
16 Tilbury	42	13	11	18	60	66	50
17 Maidenhead Utd	42	13	7	22	61	67	46
18 Basildon United	42	12	9	21	52	72	45
19 Hornchurch	42	11	11	20	44	59	44
20 Chesham United	42	12	6	24	51	87	42
21 Harlow Town	42	8	14	20	53	70	38
22 Aveley	42	8	6	28	59	98	30

Left: Windsor & Eton's FA Cup First Round tie at home to Torquay United in November 1985.

Right: the programme from Southall's FA Vase Quarter-Final tie at home to Stevenage Borough.

Division II North	1	2	3	4	5	6	7	8	9	10	11	12	13	14	15	16	17	18	19	20
1 Barton Rovers	*	0–1	0–3	3–2	1–1	1–1	2–1	1–2	1–2	3–1	1–2	2–1	0–1	1–3	5–1	0–2	2–1	3–0	0–2	0–3
2 Berkhamsted Town	0–0	*	0–1	1–1	1–0	1–1	2–0	2–1	2–2	2–0	0–1	0–1	2–3	1–2	3–4	1–0	2–0	3–1	0–5	0–0
3 Chalfont St Peter	1–1	3–3	*	0–1	1–2	1–2	1–1	2–1	5–2	0–0	1–4	2–1	2–0	2–2	1–3	0–2	0–1	1–1	2–0	0–0
4 Cheshunt	1–2	1–0	0–0	*	1–1	1–2	0–1	2–0	1–1	0–1	1–2	4–0	6–1	3–1	3–0	0–3	1–0	2–1	1–0	2–1
5 Clapton	3–2	3–0	2–5	0–6	*	4–2	1–1	0–0	0–3	2–5	0–3	0–2	2–0	0–2	1–2	0–3	3–2	0–3	4–1	1–0
6 Harefield United	1–1	1–2	0–3	0–1	6–1	*	0–2	1–1	1–3	3–3	0–3	3–3	3–6	1–1	1–1	0–0	0–1	2–1	4–1	2–2
7 Haringey Borough	1–2	2–1	0–1	3–0	1–1	0–3	*	1–2	2–0	2–1	1–4	1–0	0–1	0–1	1–1	0–1	2–1	2–2	1–0	1–1
8 Hemel Hempstead	2–2	0–1	1–1	2–2	4–2	2–1	2–0	*	3–2	0–1	0–4	1–2	2–1	1–1	1–2	1–2	1–1	1–3	4–3	1–0
9 Hertford Town	2–1	4–0	0–1	1–1	0–4	2–0	1–2	2–1	*	0–0	0–4	1–0	7–1	3–0	3–0	2–1	3–4	2–1	0–0	1–0
10 Heybridge Swifts	2–1	0–1	3–0	0–1	3–0	4–2	2–1	2–1	1–3	*	4–2	0–0	1–2	2–1	0–0	1–2	2–0	2–1	3–0	1–1
11 Kingsbury Town	0–1	3–2	1–1	3–2	3–1	1–1	1–0	1–1	1–0	2–2	*	1–0	3–0	2–1	1–1	1–1	2–0	2–3	2–0	4–0
12 Letchworth G City	0–2	3–1	3–0	2–1	2–2	1–0	0–2	3–1	0–0	0–1	0–0	*	3–5	0–0	2–2	1–0	1–2	3–2	0–4	0–1
13 Rainham Town	3–2	0–3	1–3	0–0	3–1	1–2	0–4	4–1	3–2	3–1	0–5	0–4	*	1–1	0–0	1–3	2–1	1–0	0–3	1–1
14 Royston Town	1–2	4–2	2–2	0–1	2–0	3–1	3–2	0–0	0–2	2–4	2–4	2–1	2–1	*	1–1	0–1	3–3	0–0	1–1	2–1
15 Saffron Walden Tn	2–1	2–1	1–2	1–1	2–0	5–1	1–2	2–4	4–2	2–3	2–3	0–3	3–1	0–4	*	0–1	1–1	1–1	2–1	2–2
16 Stevenage Borough	4–1	1–2	3–0	1–2	5–4	3–0	4–1	2–0	1–0	3–1	2–1	1–0	6–1	3–3	2–0	*	0–0	3–0	0–0	1–0
17 Tring Town	1–1	0–0	3–1	1–1	2–0	3–0	3–1	2–0	0–1	1–1	2–2	2–1	5–0	2–2	1–3	0–0	*	0–1	3–1	4–1
18 Vauxhall Motors	2–0	1–0	0–1	3–3	3–0	1–3	1–4	6–1	1–1	1–3	1–0	5–1	4–1	1–2	0–3	0–2	2–2	*	4–4	0–2
19 Ware	2–1	0–0	1–0	1–2	5–5	2–2	3–2	1–2	2–0	0–1	0–3	1–1	3–2	3–1	2–1	0–1	1–1	1–1	*	0–2
20 Wolverton Town	2–1	1–2	2–3	1–2	5–0	0–3	1–1	1–2	1–0	1–3	1–3	0–1	0–3	2–1	3–3	0–3	1–2	0–0	2–2	*

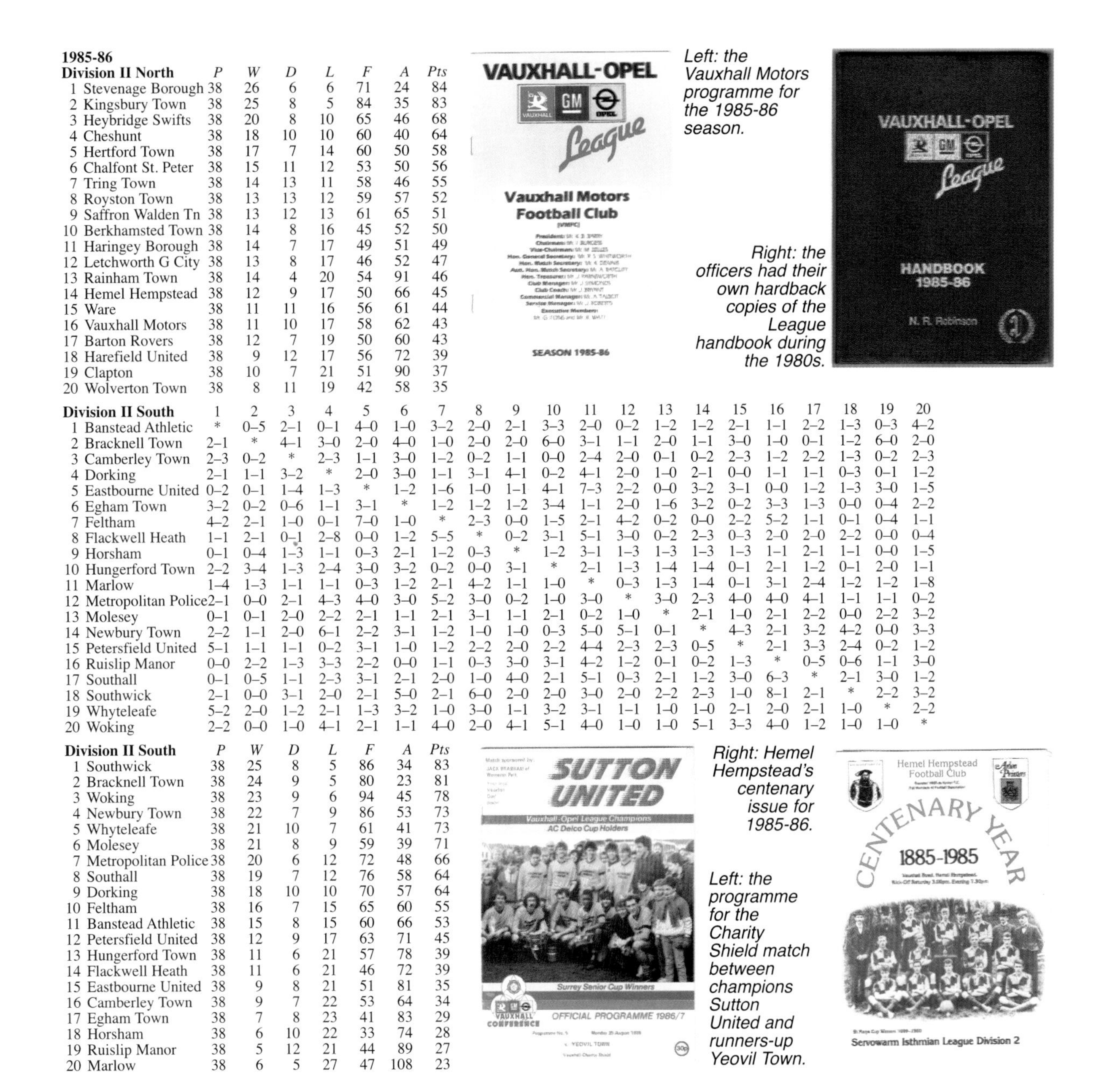

1985-86

Division II North	P	W	D	L	F	A	Pts
1 Stevenage Borough	38	26	6	6	71	24	84
2 Kingsbury Town	38	25	8	5	84	35	83
3 Heybridge Swifts	38	20	8	10	65	46	68
4 Cheshunt	38	18	10	10	60	40	64
5 Hertford Town	38	17	7	14	60	50	58
6 Chalfont St. Peter	38	15	11	12	53	50	56
7 Tring Town	38	14	13	11	58	46	55
8 Royston Town	38	13	13	12	59	57	52
9 Saffron Walden Tn	38	13	12	13	61	65	51
10 Berkhamsted Town	38	14	8	16	45	52	50
11 Haringey Borough	38	14	7	17	49	51	49
12 Letchworth G City	38	13	8	17	46	52	47
13 Rainham Town	38	14	4	20	54	91	46
14 Hemel Hempstead	38	12	9	17	50	66	45
15 Ware	38	11	11	16	56	61	44
16 Vauxhall Motors	38	11	10	17	58	62	43
17 Barton Rovers	38	12	7	19	50	60	43
18 Harefield United	38	9	12	17	56	72	39
19 Clapton	38	10	7	21	51	90	37
20 Wolverton Town	38	8	11	19	42	58	35

Left: the Vauxhall Motors programme for the 1985-86 season.

Right: the officers had their own hardback copies of the League handbook during the 1980s.

Division II South	1	2	3	4	5	6	7	8	9	10	11	12	13	14	15	16	17	18	19	20
1 Banstead Athletic	*	0–5	2–1	0–1	4–0	1–0	3–2	2–0	2–1	3–3	2–0	0–2	1–2	1–2	2–1	1–1	2–2	1–3	0–3	4–2
2 Bracknell Town	2–1	*	4–1	3–0	2–0	4–0	1–0	2–0	2–0	6–0	3–1	1–1	2–0	1–1	3–0	1–0	0–1	1–2	6–0	2–0
3 Camberley Town	2–3	0–2	*	2–3	1–1	3–0	1–2	0–2	1–1	0–0	2–4	2–0	0–1	0–2	2–3	1–2	2–2	1–3	0–2	2–3
4 Dorking	2–1	1–1	3–2	*	2–0	3–0	1–1	3–1	4–1	0–2	4–1	2–0	1–0	2–1	0–0	1–1	1–1	0–3	0–1	1–2
5 Eastbourne United	0–2	0–1	1–4	1–3	*	1–2	1–6	1–0	1–1	4–1	7–3	2–2	0–0	3–2	3–1	0–0	1–2	1–3	3–0	1–5
6 Egham Town	3–2	0–2	0–6	1–1	3–1	*	1–2	1–2	1–2	3–4	1–1	2–0	1–6	3–2	0–2	3–3	1–3	0–0	0–4	2–2
7 Feltham	4–2	2–1	1–0	0–1	7–0	1–0	*	2–3	0–0	1–5	2–1	4–2	0–2	0–0	2–2	5–2	1–1	0–1	0–4	1–1
8 Flackwell Heath	1–1	2–1	0–1	2–8	0–0	1–2	5–5	*	0–2	3–1	5–1	3–0	0–2	2–3	0–3	2–0	2–0	2–2	0–0	0–4
9 Horsham	0–1	0–4	1–3	1–1	0–3	2–1	1–2	0–3	*	1–2	3–1	1–3	1–3	1–3	1–3	1–1	2–1	1–1	0–0	1–5
10 Hungerford Town	2–2	3–4	1–3	2–4	3–0	3–2	0–2	0–0	3–1	*	2–1	1–3	1–4	1–4	0–1	2–1	1–2	0–1	2–0	1–1
11 Marlow	1–4	1–3	1–1	1–1	0–3	1–2	2–1	4–2	1–1	1–0	*	0–3	1–3	1–4	0–1	3–1	2–4	1–2	1–2	1–8
12 Metropolitan Police	2–1	0–0	2–1	4–3	4–0	3–0	5–2	3–0	0–2	1–0	3–0	*	3–0	2–3	4–0	4–0	4–1	1–1	1–1	0–2
13 Molesey	0–1	0–1	2–0	2–2	2–1	1–1	2–1	3–1	1–1	2–1	0–2	1–0	*	2–1	1–0	2–1	2–2	0–0	2–2	3–2
14 Newbury Town	2–2	1–1	2–0	6–1	2–2	3–1	1–2	1–0	1–0	0–3	5–0	5–1	0–1	*	4–3	2–1	3–2	4–2	0–0	3–3
15 Petersfield United	5–1	1–1	1–1	0–2	3–1	1–0	1–2	2–2	2–0	2–2	4–4	2–3	2–3	0–5	*	2–1	3–3	2–4	0–2	1–2
16 Ruislip Manor	0–0	2–2	1–3	3–3	2–2	0–0	1–1	0–3	3–0	3–1	4–2	1–2	0–1	0–2	1–3	*	0–5	0–6	1–1	3–0
17 Southall	0–1	0–5	1–1	2–3	3–1	2–1	2–0	1–0	4–0	2–1	5–1	0–3	2–1	1–2	3–0	6–3	*	2–1	3–0	1–2
18 Southwick	2–1	0–0	3–1	2–0	2–1	5–0	2–1	6–0	2–0	2–0	3–0	2–0	2–2	2–3	1–0	8–1	2–1	*	2–2	3–2
19 Whyteleafe	5–2	2–0	1–2	2–1	1–3	3–2	1–0	3–0	1–1	3–2	3–1	1–1	1–0	1–0	2–1	2–0	2–1	1–0	*	2–2
20 Woking	2–2	0–0	1–0	4–1	2–1	1–1	4–0	2–0	4–1	5–1	4–0	1–0	1–0	5–1	3–3	4–0	1–2	1–0	1–0	*

Division II South	P	W	D	L	F	A	Pts
1 Southwick	38	25	8	5	86	34	83
2 Bracknell Town	38	24	9	5	80	23	81
3 Woking	38	23	9	6	94	45	78
4 Newbury Town	38	22	7	9	86	53	73
5 Whyteleafe	38	21	10	7	61	41	73
6 Molesey	38	21	8	9	59	39	71
7 Metropolitan Police	38	20	6	12	72	48	66
8 Southall	38	19	7	12	76	58	64
9 Dorking	38	18	10	10	70	57	64
10 Feltham	38	16	7	15	65	60	55
11 Banstead Athletic	38	15	8	15	60	66	53
12 Petersfield United	38	12	9	17	63	71	45
13 Hungerford Town	38	11	6	21	57	78	39
14 Flackwell Heath	38	11	6	21	46	72	39
15 Eastbourne United	38	9	8	21	51	81	35
16 Camberley Town	38	9	7	22	53	64	34
17 Egham Town	38	7	8	23	41	83	29
18 Horsham	38	6	10	22	33	74	28
19 Ruislip Manor	38	5	12	21	44	89	27
20 Marlow	38	6	5	27	47	108	23

Right: Hemel Hempstead's centenary issue for 1985-86.

Left: the programme for the Charity Shield match between champions Sutton United and runners-up Yeovil Town.

1986–87 - After one season back in the League following relegation from the GM Vauxhall Conference, Wycombe Wanderers returned as champions – though with no team dropping down, they were replaced by Basingstoke Town, who transferred from the Southern League. The Chairboys were the first club for ten years to gain 100 points and scored 103 goals. For the second consecutive season Yeovil Town had to settle for runners-up, finishing two points behind, while Slough Town and Hendon, who were both well behind the top two, finished third and fourth respectively. Walthamstow Avenue were relegated for the first time since joining the League, along with Worthing. After a two-year absence, Leytonstone & Ilford returned to the Premier Division as Division One champions, by thirteen points from near neighbours Leyton-Wingate, who were promoted as runners-up. The two clubs promoted from Division Two South the previous year, Southwick and Bracknell Town, finished third and fourth. At the foot of the table, on the final day of the season, Tilbury and Epsom & Ewell joined already relegated Maidenhead United and Finchley in occupying the bottom four spots. In Division Two the North Division was won by Chesham United, with Wolverton Town promoted as runners-up; Woking, meanwhile, clinched the South title from Marlow on goal difference. Finchley and Tilbury went into Division Two North, along with newly-elected Witham Town – from the Essex Senior League – to replace basement-dwellers Cheshunt, who had resigned from the League. In Division Two South relegated Epsom & Ewell and Maidenhead United were joined by Yeading from the London-Spartan League thus bringing a full complement of 88 clubs in membership.

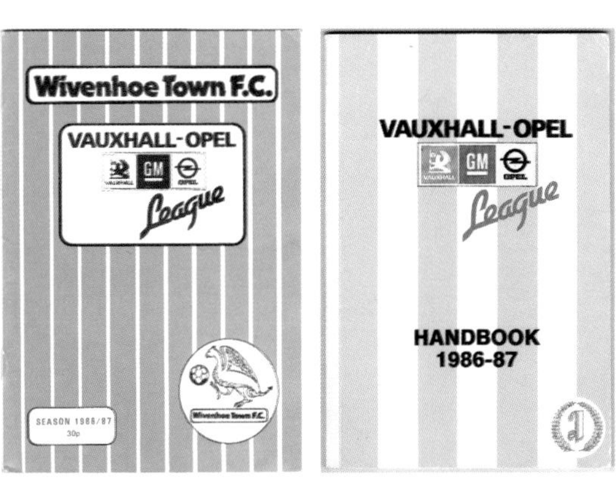

Above: Wivenhoe Town's programme for 1986-87 and the League's handbook for the same campaign.

1986-87

Premier Division	1	2	3	4	5	6	7	8	9	10	11	12	13	14	15	16	17	18	19	20	21	22
1 Barking	*	4–0	1–1	3–0	1–1	1–1	1–0	5–1	2–0	2–1	2–2	2–1	0–0	0–2	4–4	0–0	6–0	0–0	2–0	8–2	3–4	1–1
2 Bishop's Stortford	3–2	*	1–1	2–2	2–2	3–1	1–0	2–2	0–0	0–0	2–2	0–4	0–0	2–0	2–1	4–1	6–0	1–1	4–1	2–0	1–4	1–0
3 Bognor Regis Tn	0–2	2–0	*	3–2	3–0	0–0	3–2	3–0	1–3	2–0	1–2	1–1	2–3	2–0	0–0	2–1	8–1	3–2	1–3	1–1	1–2	1–0
4 Bromley	2–4	3–1	1–2	*	3–1	2–0	2–1	3–2	0–1	2–2	1–0	1–0	2–1	2–2	0–0	1–0	1–1	1–1	1–1	4–3	0–4	0–2
5 Carshalton Athletic	2–1	0–0	4–3	1–1	*	2–2	2–1	3–1	1–1	1–2	0–1	0–2	1–3	1–3	0–1	1–0	2–1	3–1	1–0	4–1	0–2	2–3
6 Croydon	4–1	1–0	2–1	3–0	1–0	*	1–2	0–3	1–1	1–0	2–4	1–0	1–0	4–0	1–1	0–2	2–0	0–1	0–0	2–1	1–0	0–1
7 Dulwich Hamlet	2–0	2–4	6–6	2–0	0–1	2–0	*	2–2	1–0	0–1	1–4	3–1	0–1	3–1	0–3	0–2	5–2	1–1	2–3	1–3	1–4	0–1
8 Farnborough Town	0–3	4–2	2–4	6–3	1–0	1–1	1–1	*	3–2	3–1	0–3	2–1	2–2	1–0	0–1	2–2	2–0	3–3	2–0	3–2	0–0	1–2
9 Harrow Borough	4–2	2–1	0–1	0–3	3–2	1–2	1–1	5–0	*	1–2	3–0	2–0	0–0	1–3	4–0	2–2	5–0	2–1	2–0	4–0	2–1	1–1
10 Hayes	3–0	0–0	2–3	3–2	1–1	1–1	2–1	2–2	1–1	*	0–3	1–0	2–1	0–5	1–4	3–1	1–0	2–1	2–3	1–1	0–2	1–3
11 Hendon	0–1	1–2	2–4	3–0	1–0	3–1	0–1	1–2	0–3	2–0	*	2–1	2–0	2–1	0–4	0–0	3–2	0–0	0–0	2–2	2–3	1–1
12 Hitchin Town	2–2	2–0	4–2	1–2	4–1	1–0	0–0	3–1	1–2	3–1	1–4	*	0–5	1–1	0–2	3–1	6–1	0–5	1–3	4–0	1–2	0–2
13 Kingstonian	0–3	3–3	1–2	2–4	0–1	4–2	0–0	0–0	1–2	2–0	0–1	1–1	*	5–3	2–1	1–0	3–0	3–1	1–0	1–1	0–1	0–1
14 St. Albans City	0–2	1–2	2–0	3–3	2–2	0–0	2–2	0–1	2–1	2–2	1–3	2–3	1–0	*	0–2	2–1	2–1	4–0	3–1	2–1	1–4	0–0
15 Slough Town	1–1	1–0	1–1	1–3	3–2	0–1	2–1	3–1	3–0	0–1	2–1	3–0	2–0	3–0	*	1–0	1–0	3–1	5–2	2–3	0–3	0–1
16 Tooting & M Utd	1–1	0–1	3–3	0–1	0–0	0–1	3–1	1–2	0–1	3–0	1–3	1–0	1–0	1–0	0–1	*	3–0	3–0	1–4	1–0	0–0	0–1
17 Walthamstow Ave.	1–1	1–1	1–4	1–3	1–4	2–2	3–3	3–0	0–1	3–0	0–1	1–2	0–2	0–4	0–2	0–1	*	0–2	0–2	0–2	1–2	0–4
18 Windsor & Eton	2–0	0–0	1–0	0–0	3–2	2–1	1–1	0–0	0–0	0–0	0–1	2–0	0–1	3–0	3–1	0–0	1–1	*	1–0	1–0	1–5	1–0
19 Wokingham Town	3–1	2–0	0–1	1–0	1–0	0–2	0–2	1–0	0–1	0–0	1–2	2–0	1–3	0–1	1–3	3–1	2–3	1–1	*	1–2	0–1	1–1
20 Worthing	0–0	2–6	0–5	1–1	3–4	2–3	2–5	0–3	2–1	2–2	0–2	2–0	1–4	4–2	1–1	1–3	2–3	2–1	2–3	*	0–3	2–2
21 Wycombe Wndrs.	2–1	0–0	2–1	3–0	4–0	3–1	4–1	1–2	0–0	2–1	5–0	1–0	3–2	3–0	1–1	4–0	7–1	4–1	2–0	4–2	*	0–1
22 Yeovil Town	3–0	2–0	0–0	4–1	1–0	0–1	0–2	1–2	3–2	2–0	2–1	2–1	2–0	1–1	2–0	4–0	2–1	3–1	3–0	5–0	2–1	*

Premier Division	*P*	*W*	*D*	*L*	*F*	*A*	*Pts*
1 Wycombe Wand	42	32	5	5	103	32	101
2 Yeovil Town	42	28	8	6	71	27	92
3 Slough Town	42	23	8	11	70	44	77
4 Hendon	42	22	7	13	67	53	73
5 Bognor Regis Tn	42	20	10	12	85	61	70
6 Harrow Borough	42	20	10	12	68	44	70
7 Croydon	42	18	10	14	51	48	64
8 Barking	42	16	14	12	76	56	62
9 Farnborough Town	42	17	11	14	66	72	62
10 Bishop's Stortford	42	15	15	12	62	57	60
11 Bromley	42	16	11	15	63	72	59
12 Kingstonian	42	16	9	17	58	50	57
13 Windsor & Eton	42	13	15	14	47	52	54
14 St. Albans City	42	14	9	19	61	70	51
15 Carshalton Athletic	42	13	9	20	55	68	48
16 Wokingham Town	42	14	6	22	47	61	48
17 Hayes	42	12	12	18	45	68	48
18 Dulwich Hamlet	42	12	10	20	62	71	46
19 Tooting & M Utd	42	12	9	21	41	53	45
20 Hitchin Town	42	13	5	24	56	69	44
21 Worthing	42	8	9	25	58	107	33
22 Walthamstow Ave.	42	4	6	32	36	113	18

Right: Yeovil Town's matchday programme from their second season when they again finished as runners-up. Yeovil lost the match 0-2.

Left: the Wycombe Wanderers edition from the same season.

Division I	1	2	3	4	5	6	7	8	9	10	11	12	13	14	15	16	17	18	19	20	21	22
1 Basildon United	*	2–1	2–1	2–0	0–3	4–2	2–2	3–1	0–0	1–0	0–3	1–2	1–1	1–1	3–1	0–3	1–1	2–2	1–0	1–0	1–1	3–4
2 Billericay Town	1–0	*	0–2	0–0	3–1	2–2	2–4	0–2	3–2	1–1	2–0	0–4	0–0	0–1	2–2	1–2	0–0	3–2	5–0	0–2	2–0	0–0
3 Boreham Wood	1–2	1–1	*	2–0	1–0	0–2	0–0	1–0	6–2	1–0	2–1	1–0	0–1	1–0	0–1	0–2	4–0	5–1	4–2	2–1	1–1	1–1
4 Bracknell Town	1–1	1–0	6–0	*	2–1	3–0	5–1	1–3	2–2	1–0	2–1	1–3	3–2	5–0	0–0	3–0	2–0	3–1	1–0	3–3	0–1	4–1
5 Epsom & Ewell	0–1	2–0	2–0	0–3	*	1–1	2–0	1–0	1–3	0–1	1–1	0–2	1–2	1–0	0–1	2–0	2–2	2–2	3–2	0–2	2–1	1–1
6 Finchley	1–1	0–3	3–1	2–4	1–2	*	2–2	1–0	1–4	0–0	0–2	0–1	0–4	0–2	0–0	2–3	0–2	1–4	1–2	2–4	3–0	1–1
7 Grays Athletic	2–1	1–1	0–4	1–2	4–2	2–1	*	1–1	4–0	7–1	3–2	2–0	2–1	4–1	3–2	1–1	1–1	1–1	2–0	5–2	1–0	2–0
8 Hampton	3–0	1–0	0–2	1–0	1–0	3–1	1–2	*	3–1	1–3	1–2	1–3	1–2	4–2	2–1	1–2	0–1	1–1	0–0	1–2	2–1	0–0
9 Kingsbury Town	1–2	1–5	0–0	0–5	6–0	3–1	3–1	3–2	*	1–1	1–0	0–0	1–2	2–0	1–0	0–2	2–1	2–1	2–1	0–4	1–1	0–2
10 Leatherhead	1–0	2–1	3–0	2–1	2–0	2–1	1–1	1–2	0–2	*	3–1	0–7	1–0	2–1	2–0	1–1	0–1	1–1	3–1	0–1	0–0	0–1
11 Lewes	0–3	0–0	3–1	1–4	2–0	7–1	3–1	2–1	1–0	1–1	*	0–1	1–4	2–0	4–2	2–1	0–0	2–1	1–1	0–1	0–2	2–0
12 Leytonstone-Ilford	3–1	1–0	1–2	2–1	2–0	2–1	1–0	2–1	2–0	0–0	3–2	*	0–0	5–1	2–0	2–1	2–0	1–0	3–0	3–4	4–0	0–1
13 Leyton-Wingate	2–0	0–0	2–0	1–1	4–0	0–0	3–2	2–1	2–1	2–0	3–2	0–1	*	2–0	2–1	0–0	2–2	0–0	2–0	3–0	4–0	2–2
14 Maidenhead Utd	3–4	0–1	1–2	0–0	1–0	0–1	1–0	1–2	0–2	1–2	1–0	0–1	1–3	*	1–1	5–1	3–1	0–1	3–0	0–1	0–1	3–0
15 Oxford City	2–1	1–3	1–0	3–2	1–2	7–1	2–1	5–0	1–3	2–3	6–1	1–1	1–3	1–2	*	1–3	1–1	0–2	0–0	3–3	4–3	0–2
16 Southwick	2–1	3–2	3–1	4–6	2–2	3–0	1–2	0–4	3–1	1–0	3–0	2–2	0–1	4–4	2–0	*	1–0	4–5	1–0	3–2	5–3	0–2
17 Staines Town	1–0	0–1	0–0	0–1	0–3	1–1	2–0	0–1	0–3	1–1	1–0	0–1	1–0	3–1	5–3	0–2	*	1–0	1–1	1–0	2–0	0–2
18 Stevenage Borough	1–4	4–2	0–1	1–3	1–0	0–2	2–2	0–3	1–4	2–0	2–0	0–1	0–0	4–0	2–2	4–1	3–3	*	1–2	1–0	1–2	0–1
19 Tilbury	0–1	2–5	2–1	1–4	1–0	4–3	2–0	1–2	3–3	0–0	3–0	0–2	1–2	5–0	0–3	1–1	0–1	1–0	*	1–2	2–1	2–1
20 Uxbridge	2–1	1–3	0–3	3–3	2–2	1–1	0–2	3–1	0–1	1–0	1–1	1–3	0–0	2–0	3–1	0–2	1–1	2–1	0–2	*	2–1	1–0
21 Walton & Hersham	3–3	0–0	1–4	1–2	4–0	1–1	2–3	0–1	2–3	1–3	1–0	3–2	2–1	0–3	0–0	2–3	2–0	2–2	1–0	0–0	*	3–2
22 Wembley	1–0	2–1	4–0	1–1	3–2	2–0	3–1	1–1	1–2	0–1	1–2	1–0	1–1	4–0	1–0	0–2	3–2	0–3	3–0	1–0	4–3	*

Division I	*P*	*W*	*D*	*L*	*F*	*A*	*Pts*
1 Leytonstone-Ilford	42	30	5	7	78	29	95
2 Leyton-Wingate	42	23	13	6	68	31	82
3 Bracknell Town	42	24	9	9	92	48	81
4 Southwick	42	23	7	12	80	66	76
5 Wembley	42	21	9	12	61	47	72
6 Grays Athletic	42	19	10	13	76	64	67
7 Kingsbury Town	42	20	7	15	69	67	67
8 Boreham Wood	42	20	6	16	59	52	66
9 Uxbridge	42	18	9	15	60	59	63
10 Leatherhead	42	17	11	14	45	48	62
11 Hampton	42	18	5	19	57	55	59
12 Basildon United	42	16	10	16	58	60	58
13 Billericay Town	42	14	12	16	57	52	54
14 Staines Town	42	13	13	16	40	51	52
15 Lewes	42	15	6	21	55	65	51
16 Stevenage Borough	42	12	11	19	61	67	47
17 Oxford City	42	11	10	21	64	72	43
18 Walton & Hersham	42	11	10	21	53	74	43
19 Tilbury	42	12	7	23	46	70	43
20 Epsom & Ewell	42	12	7	23	44	68	43
21 Maidenhead Utd	42	11	4	27	44	76	37
22 Finchley	42	6	11	25	44	90	29

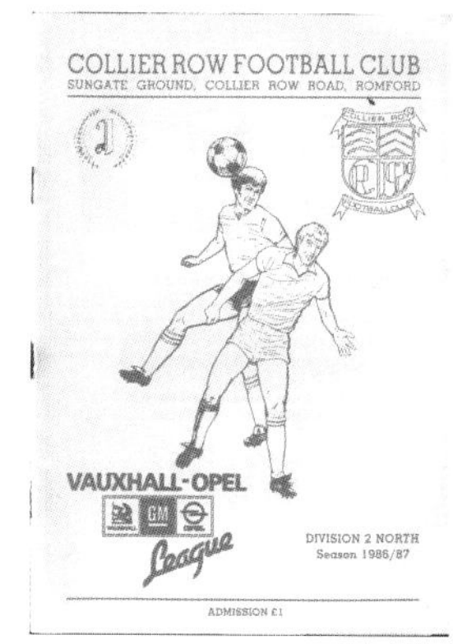

Left: Collier Row's matchday programme from their first home match as League members against Aveley, which they drew 1-1.

Right: the Leyton-Wingate programme from 1986-87.

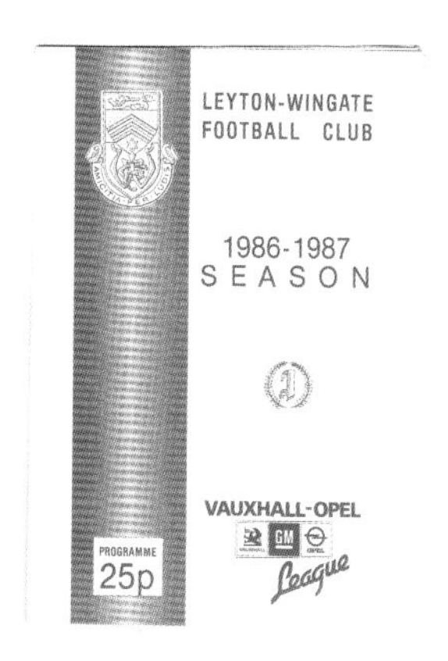

1986-87

Division II North	1	2	3	4	5	6	7	8	9	10	11	12	13	14	15	16	17	18	19	20	21	22
1 Aveley	*	0–1	0–0	0–1	3–1	2–0	3–1	1–4	1–0	3–1	0–1	1–0	2–0	5–0	3–1	2–0	1–1	2–1	3–1	1–0	3–0	2–1
2 Barton Rovers	3–3	*	2–1	1–2	1–0	1–0	3–1	1–1	2–0	2–0	1–2	3–0	3–2	0–1	2–0	2–0	2–0	1–0	0–2	0–0	2–0	1–2
3 Berkhamsted Town	1–1	2–1	*	1–3	1–1	1–1	0–0	0–2	4–2	4–1	0–0	3–2	3–2	0–0	2–0	1–1	2–4	1–1	1–1	3–3	4–0	4–0
4 Chesham United	1–1	2–1	3–0	*	3–0	3–0	2–1	1–0	3–1	3–1	2–2	2–2	0–1	1–0	1–0	4–2	2–1	1–2	2–1	2–1	3–0	0–2
5 Cheshunt	0–4	1–2	1–4	2–2	*	1–2	0–2	1–5	1–0	1–1	1–3	0–3	0–0	2–3	1–3	4–2	1–2	0–2	2–1	1–0	2–5	0–2
6 Clapton	1–1	0–0	3–0	3–1	1–1	*	1–0	1–5	1–1	0–1	1–0	1–2	3–3	1–2	2–2	7–0	0–0	0–2	2–0	0–4	1–1	3–0
7 Collier Row	1–1	4–0	1–0	0–1	4–3	6–2	*	0–0	1–0	2–0	1–3	1–0	0–3	5–3	2–0	2–1	3–1	1–5	1–2	1–3	1–0	0–0
8 Haringey Borough	1–1	1–1	2–1	2–3	5–1	3–0	4–0	*	1–0	1–1	1–0	0–2	2–1	1–2	4–0	5–0	1–0	0–1	0–1	1–1	1–1	2–2
9 Harlow Town	3–1	0–0	1–0	1–1	2–0	1–0	1–3	2–5	*	0–2	1–0	0–2	1–1	3–0	2–1	0–0	2–3	2–1	2–1	1–3	2–0	0–1
10 Hemel Hempstead	1–2	1–0	2–2	0–3	5–1	0–2	1–2	0–0	2–3	*	0–0	1–2	1–1	1–5	4–1	2–1	0–3	2–1	0–3	0–1	2–0	2–2
11 Hertford Town	4–0	1–1	4–3	2–1	3–0	1–0	1–3	3–4	0–0	0–1	*	2–0	1–1	3–4	0–1	0–0	0–0	2–1	1–4	0–1	0–1	0–0
12 Heybridge Swifts	3–5	1–0	1–1	3–1	2–1	2–0	0–0	2–3	0–0	2–1	1–1	*	2–1	3–0	3–2	4–0	3–0	1–3	2–2	2–2	2–1	2–1
13 Hornchurch	1–1	0–1	2–2	1–2	2–1	3–1	2–1	0–4	2–2	1–1	2–2	4–1	*	2–1	2–0	2–0	0–0	0–2	1–0	2–0	2–2	0–0
14 Letchworth G City	3–0	2–2	4–1	1–1	5–2	1–0	3–1	1–2	2–0	1–1	2–2	1–4	0–1	*	1–1	2–2	1–1	1–0	3–0	1–1	3–0	0–3
15 Rainham Town	0–0	1–3	2–0	1–0	5–1	3–0	2–1	3–2	2–2	2–0	2–3	1–1	1–1	0–2	*	4–1	2–3	0–4	0–4	0–1	0–1	0–0
16 Royston Town	1–1	0–1	1–1	0–2	1–3	2–1	1–6	0–3	2–2	4–4	0–1	1–7	2–2	1–6	2–2	*	1–6	1–4	0–1	2–0	1–1	0–3
17 Saffron Walden Tn	1–2	1–0	0–0	2–4	3–0	0–1	4–1	1–1	0–0	2–1	1–1	1–1	2–0	0–3	1–1	4–0	*	0–2	1–1	2–1	0–2	0–0
18 Tring Town	2–2	1–1	2–1	0–1	3–0	2–2	2–0	0–2	3–1	6–0	3–0	0–5	1–2	3–1	1–3	0–1	3–1	*	0–2	0–2	2–1	0–0
19 Vauxhall Motors	2–0	1–0	3–4	2–4	3–1	0–0	4–0	1–2	0–2	1–1	1–0	1–1	4–3	2–2	1–1	0–1	1–1	1–1	*	3–0	0–3	0–1
20 Ware	1–0	1–1	0–1	1–2	4–2	1–0	0–4	1–1	1–0	2–0	1–2	3–4	2–1	1–0	0–1	1–0	4–0	1–1	2–1	*	0–1	0–2
21 Wivenhoe Town	3–3	2–0	1–2	5–2	1–1	3–1	0–2	1–1	1–2	3–1	2–1	3–1	3–3	1–2	1–1	1–1	1–2	2–0	4–2	2–0	*	1–2
22 Wolverton Town	2–1	0–0	3–0	1–3	9–1	1–0	3–1	1–1	1–0	2–2	4–0	0–0	3–0	2–2	5–1	5–1	2–1	2–1	2–0	2–0	0–0	*

Division II North	*P*	*W*	*D*	*L*	*F*	*A*	*Pts*
1 Chesham United	42	28	6	8	81	48	90
2 Wolverton Town	42	23	14	5	74	32	83
3 Haringey Borough	42	22	13	7	86	40	79
4 Heybridge Swifts	42	21	11	10	81	54	74
5 Aveley	42	19	13	10	68	50	70
6 Letchworth G City	42	19	11	12	77	62	68
7 Barton Rovers	42	18	11	13	49	39	65
8 Tring Town	42	19	7	16	69	49	64
9 Collier Row	42	19	5	18	67	65	62
10 Ware	42	17	8	17	51	50	59
11 Saffron Walden Tn	42	14	14	14	56	54	56
12 Wivenhoe Town	42	15	11	16	61	61	56
13 Vauxhall Motors	42	15	10	17	61	57	55
14 Hornchurch	42	13	16	13	60	60	55
15 Hertford Town	42	14	13	15	52	53	55
16 Berkhamsted Town	42	12	16	14	62	64	52
17 Harlow Town	42	13	11	18	45	55	50
18 Rainham Town	42	12	11	19	53	70	47
19 Clapton	42	10	11	21	45	63	41
20 Hemel Hempstead	42	9	12	21	48	77	39
21 Royston Town	42	4	12	26	37	109	24
22 Cheshunt	42	5	6	31	43	114	21

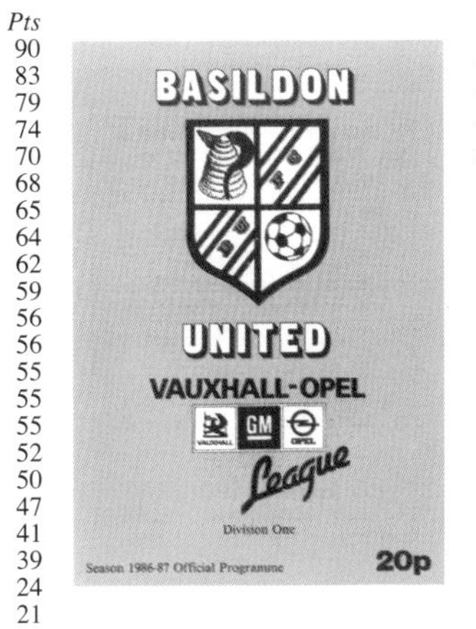

Left: the Basildon United matchday programme from season 1986-87.

Right: The Metropolitan Police programme for their game at home to Eastbourne United which they lost 4-1.

Division II South	1	2	3	4	5	6	7	8	9	10	11	12	13	14	15	16	17	18	19	20	21
1 Banstead Athletic	*	1–4	2–3	2–1	2–2	2–2	0–2	0–1	0–0	1–1	3–0	1–1	2–3	0–2	2–1	2–0	1–1	1–1	3–0	1–1	0–2
2 Camberley Town	0–1	*	1–3	0–2	1–2	1–3	0–1	1–0	1–0	0–0	4–2	2–2	2–1	1–2	0–2	2–9	5–0	1–2	2–0	2–1	0–1
3 Chalfont St Peter	1–1	4–0	*	2–2	2–1	3–4	3–3	2–2	2–0	4–2	2–1	1–0	0–1	0–2	2–0	1–1	1–2	1–3	1–0	2–1	1–3
4 Chertsey Town	3–1	3–1	0–0	*	1–1	2–5	3–1	0–1	1–0	0–0	1–2	2–2	3–1	0–0	4–0	0–2	1–0	1–1	0–0	3–1	3–2
5 Dorking	2–1	4–1	0–3	1–1	*	3–2	5–1	1–0	1–0	0–0	2–1	3–0	1–1	1–1	3–0	2–0	5–0	4–1	3–0	9–0	2–0
6 Eastbourne United	3–2	1–2	1–0	1–3	1–2	*	0–2	1–3	6–0	0–0	3–1	0–0	0–2	1–3	1–0	1–1	3–2	3–3	3–0	2–0	0–0
7 Egham Town	2–1	2–1	1–4	1–2	0–1	0–3	*	0–3	2–1	2–1	2–0	1–0	1–0	2–2	0–0	2–1	2–1	1–3	3–4	0–1	0–5
8 Feltham	6–1	3–1	2–0	3–0	0–1	3–1	1–0	*	2–0	3–1	3–0	3–1	0–2	1–2	8–0	8–3	1–0	3–0	2–0	0–0	0–3
9 Flackwell Heath	1–1	4–2	0–0	1–3	1–1	2–1	1–2	1–2	*	1–0	2–1	2–0	0–4	0–2	0–3	0–0	1–0	1–3	3–0	1–1	1–2
10 Harefield United	1–0	5–3	0–0	2–0	0–2	1–1	3–3	1–0	2–1	*	0–0	1–1	3–3	1–0	5–0	1–0	1–2	1–1	1–0	1–1	0–3
11 Horsham	1–1	4–3	2–0	0–0	1–0	2–1	2–0	0–1	1–1	3–0	*	0–1	0–1	2–2	1–0	4–0	1–0	1–2	5–2	0–0	0–5
12 Hungerford Town	2–0	2–1	0–1	2–0	1–1	2–2	2–0	0–1	1–1	0–1	0–2	*	1–0	3–0	2–4	1–1	2–2	2–2	5–0	1–0	1–1
13 Marlow	1–0	2–1	2–1	0–1	0–1	3–1	4–1	1–0	4–0	1–0	2–1	0–1	*	2–0	3–0	1–1	0–2	3–2	2–0	5–2	5–3
14 Metropolitan Police	2–1	1–2	1–1	3–0	1–3	1–4	2–0	1–1	2–1	2–5	3–1	2–2	1–3	*	1–1	3–3	2–0	1–1	1–1	1–0	0–3
15 Molesey	0–0	0–2	1–2	0–3	0–0	2–2	1–1	3–2	1–1	2–3	3–1	1–3	0–3	0–6	*	2–2	2–2	0–6	0–3	2–2	1–3
16 Newbury Town	1–1	1–3	3–0	1–2	2–1	1–1	1–3	2–1	3–3	1–0	1–1	0–2	0–2	2–2	1–2	*	1–2	1–1	0–3	0–2	1–3
17 Petersfield United	2–2	1–4	4–0	1–3	0–1	0–1	3–0	0–3	0–1	1–6	2–7	4–2	0–2	4–2	0–0	2–2	*	2–1	0–0	1–2	0–5
18 Ruislip Manor	3–2	5–2	0–1	1–0	0–0	2–0	5–0	1–0	4–0	0–0	2–0	2–0	3–4	0–0	2–0	7–1	4–0	*	2–1	4–0	0–3
19 Southall	0–2	0–0	2–1	1–2	1–1	0–7	1–1	0–3	0–1	1–2	0–1	0–2	0–2	1–4	1–2	1–0	3–1	1–2	*	1–2	0–2
20 Whyteleafe	2–0	4–2	3–4	0–0	0–2	1–0	2–0	3–1	0–0	1–0	2–2	1–1	0–0	2–7	1–1	3–1	1–1	1–3	6–0	*	1–1
21 Woking	0–0	8–1	1–1	1–0	3–3	2–0	4–0	0–2	2–0	3–1	5–1	2–4	1–2	5–0	5–0	5–0	3–0	4–0	5–0	1–1	*

Division II South	*P*	*W*	*D*	*L*	*F*	*A*	*Pts*
1 Woking	40	27	7	6	110	32	88
2 Marlow	40	28	4	8	78	36	88
3 Dorking	40	24	12	4	78	30	84
4 Feltham	40	25	3	12	79	34	78
5 Ruislip Manor	40	22	10	8	85	47	76
6 Chertsey Town	40	18	11	11	56	44	65
7 Metropolitan Police	40	16	13	11	70	61	61
8 Chalfont St. Peter	40	17	10	13	60	55	61
9 Hungerford Town	40	14	14	12	55	48	56
10 Harefield United	40	14	14	12	53	47	56
11 Eastbourne United	40	15	10	15	72	59	55
12 Whyteleafe	40	12	15	13	52	63	51
13 Horsham	40	14	8	18	54	61	50
14 Egham Town	40	14	6	20	45	77	48
15 Camberley Town	40	13	3	24	62	89	42
16 Flackwell Heath	40	9	11	20	34	63	38
17 Banstead Athletic	40	7	15	18	44	61	36
18 Petersfield United	40	9	8	23	45	84	34
19 Molesey	40	7	12	21	37	89	33
20 Newbury Town	40	6	14	20	51	83	32
21 Southall	40	6	6	28	28	85	24

Left: the Aveley programme for season 1986-87.

Right: the Chalfont St. Peter programme from the same season.

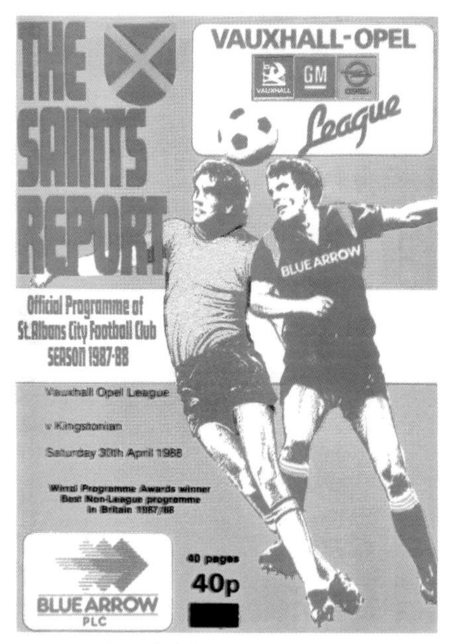

1987–88 - It was third time lucky for Yeovil Town as they secured the League championship after finishing runners-up the previous two years and return to the GM Vauxhall Conference. Yeovil won the title by a fifteen point margin from runners-up Bromley closely followed by Slough Town, Leytonstone & Ilford, Wokingham Town and Hayes. At the foot of the table Basingstoke Town in their first season were relegated to Division One along with Hitchin Town. In Division One it was virtually a two-horse race between Marlow and Grays Athletic who both gained record points with the Bucks club clinching the title on the final day of the season. Relegated to Division One were Wolverton Town, who only obtained twelve points from their forty-two match programme, Stevenage Borough, Billericay Town and Bracknell Town with the latter having narrowly missed promotion the previous season. In Division Two North the top three clubs were from Essex with Wivenhoe Town, in only their second season in the League, crowned champions whilst Collier Row, also in their second season, were runners-up and Tilbury were third. Division Two went to the final Saturday of the season, Chalfont St. Peter pipping Metropolitan Police and Dorking to the title with the former gaining promotion by virtue of a better goal difference. The basement clubs of the regionalised Division Twos played a relegation play-off with Hertford Town successful over the two-legged match with Petersfield United. However due to insufficient clubs being eligible for promotion, Petersfield United were reprieved. At the Annual General Meeting Dagenham were elected to replace champions Yeovil Town. In Division One Walthamstow Avenue resigned and would eventually be part of the Leytonstone & Ilford set-up and as a result Bracknell Town would not be relegated to Division Two South. In Division Two North Purfleet were elected from the Essex Senior League; however Edgware Town's application was rejected.

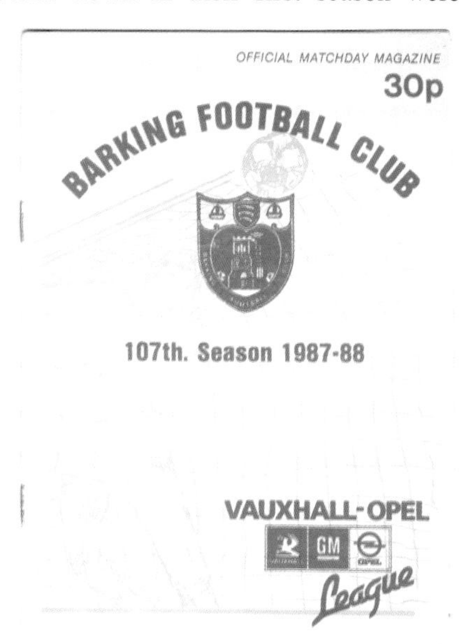

Premier Division	1	2	3	4	5	6	7	8	9	10	11	12	13	14	15	16	17	18	19	20	21	22
1 Barking	*	1–1	1–1	0–1	0–1	0–1	0–0	2–1	5–0	0–1	1–2	3–0	3–1	1–3	0–1	2–1	1–0	1–0	2–2	1–0	2–2	1–2
2 Basingstoke Town	0–0	*	3–1	1–1	2–1	1–2	1–1	1–1	2–2	1–3	1–3	2–0	1–1	2–1	0–2	1–1	1–1	0–3	1–1	2–2	0–2	1–0
3 Bishop's Stortford	1–0	2–0	*	3–0	5–3	1–0	2–1	0–1	1–5	2–1	0–3	1–0	0–0	5–1	0–2	1–2	2–3	1–1	0–1	2–1	2–0	1–2
4 Bognor Regis Tn	1–3	0–1	1–0	*	0–3	0–3	1–2	3–0	0–2	1–1	0–2	1–0	4–2	1–0	1–1	2–1	1–0	0–2	2–0	0–1	1–1	2–1
5 Bromley	5–1	1–0	2–3	3–0	*	2–0	2–0	0–0	4–2	1–0	1–1	1–0	3–2	2–0	1–2	2–2	1–2	2–1	2–0	2–1	3–0	2–1
6 Carshalton Athletic	2–0	4–2	1–0	3–0	0–1	*	0–1	2–2	0–0	2–0	0–1	1–1	5–0	1–1	1–1	2–3	1–1	1–1	1–0	2–3	0–0	0–0
7 Croydon	1–1	2–1	1–0	0–1	0–1	1–0	*	2–2	3–0	1–2	2–2	1–3	0–0	0–1	0–1	1–0	1–0	0–1	1–2	0–0	1–1	1–2
8 Dulwich Hamlet	0–1	4–0	2–2	0–3	3–1	0–1	0–1	*	1–4	1–2	0–1	1–2	5–0	0–0	2–1	1–3	1–0	1–0	3–3	1–1	1–2	1–1
9 Farnborough Town	4–1	1–1	3–1	2–0	1–0	1–1	1–1	1–1	*	2–1	0–1	2–3	2–0	1–0	4–0	0–0	1–0	4–1	2–2	0–0	1–2	0–1
10 Harrow Borough	1–0	2–2	1–1	1–1	1–0	0–1	2–1	2–1	1–1	*	2–3	2–2	1–0	0–1	1–2	0–1	3–1	1–3	4–0	1–1	1–0	1–0
11 Hayes	2–3	3–1	2–0	0–1	2–0	0–2	1–1	0–2	1–2	1–0	*	3–2	1–0	3–1	4–0	2–1	1–1	3–1	0–0	1–1	2–1	0–0
12 Hendon	1–0	2–0	2–2	1–1	0–3	2–2	3–0	0–2	5–2	5–1	1–0	*	3–2	2–0	0–1	5–1	1–1	1–4	1–0	1–1	1–1	0–0
13 Hitchin Town	0–0	3–0	1–3	1–0	0–0	2–0	2–1	1–0	4–1	2–2	0–5	4–1	*	1–1	1–2	3–1	0–3	1–6	0–1	0–1	2–3	0–4
14 Kingstonian	1–1	0–0	2–1	4–2	0–1	0–2	0–0	2–2	1–1	2–2	2–0	1–1	2–0	*	0–0	3–1	2–1	1–0	3–0	0–1	2–5	2–3
15 Leytonstone-Ilford	1–1	2–2	2–0	1–1	0–0	3–0	3–1	4–0	2–0	2–2	2–0	1–3	0–1	0–1	*	1–2	1–0	3–0	1–2	3–1	1–2	1–0
16 Leyton-Wingate	1–1	4–0	2–3	3–1	0–3	0–1	2–4	0–1	1–2	1–1	0–0	0–2	2–0	0–1	0–1	*	2–1	1–1	3–1	3–0	3–2	2–1
17 St. Albans City	5–2	2–1	2–2	1–0	0–5	3–1	3–0	4–1	3–2	0–1	2–1	2–1	2–1	1–3	3–4	3–2	*	1–3	2–4	2–1	1–2	1–2
18 Slough Town	2–0	1–1	0–0	0–1	1–0	0–1	1–0	2–0	3–1	3–1	1–1	0–0	1–0	3–1	3–2	1–1	3–0	*	4–1	1–0	3–1	2–2
19 Tooting & M Utd	5–2	0–0	0–1	2–2	2–2	0–0	2–2	1–0	3–0	0–2	5–3	2–0	4–3	0–0	0–0	0–2	1–0	2–0	*	0–0	0–1	1–2
20 Windsor & Eton	1–0	4–0	1–1	2–2	1–1	1–1	1–1	2–0	1–2	5–2	4–1	1–1	2–1	2–0	1–1	2–1	3–0	1–0	2–2	*	2–0	3–1
21 Wokingham Town	2–0	2–0	1–0	2–1	1–0	2–0	1–2	2–1	0–1	2–0	2–0	2–3	2–3	2–1	0–0	3–2	3–2	0–3	1–2	1–1	*	3–0
22 Yeovil Town	0–0	2–0	1–1	1–0	3–0	4–1	3–1	4–0	2–0	2–0	2–0	3–0	1–1	2–0	2–1	2–0	0–0	2–1	2–3	2–0	1–0	*

Premier Division	*P*	*W*	*D*	*L*	*F*	*A*	*Pts*
1 Yeovil Town	42	24	9	9	66	34	81
2 Bromley	42	23	7	12	68	40	76
3 Slough Town	42	21	9	12	67	41	72
4 Leytonstone-Ilford	42	20	11	11	59	43	71
5 Wokingham Town	42	21	7	14	62	52	70
6 Hayes	42	20	9	13	62	48	69
7 Windsor & Eton	42	16	17	9	59	43	65
8 Farnborough Town	42	17	11	14	63	60	62
9 Carshalton Athletic	42	16	13	13	49	41	61
10 Hendon	42	16	12	14	62	58	60
11 Tooting & M Utd	42	15	14	13	57	59	59
12 Harrow Borough	42	15	11	16	53	58	56
13 Bishop's Stortford	42	15	10	17	55	58	55
14 Kingstonian	42	14	12	16	47	53	54
15 St. Albans City	42	15	6	21	60	69	51
16 Bognor Regis Tn	42	14	9	19	41	57	51
17 Leyton-Wingate	42	14	8	20	58	64	50
18 Croydon	42	11	13	18	40	52	46
19 Barking	42	11	12	19	44	57	45
20 Dulwich Hamlet	42	10	11	21	46	64	41
21 Hitchin Town	42	10	8	24	46	79	38
22 Basingstoke Town	42	6	17	19	37	71	35

Left: the Yeading matchday programme from season 1987-88.

Right: the programme for the Charity Shield match between League champions Wycombe and League Cup Winners Bognor.

1987-88 Division I	1	2	3	4	5	6	7	8	9	10	11	12	13	14	15	16	17	18	19	20	21	22
1 Basildon United	*	2–1	1–2	2–1	3–1	1–3	1–0	0–0	1–1	1–2	1–1	4–0	1–1	0–4	0–1	4–0	3–2	3–0	1–0	0–3	4–0	0–4
2 Billericay Town	1–3	*	0–5	2–2	3–2	2–1	0–0	2–2	1–3	2–1	0–2	2–4	1–1	0–0	1–1	2–2	3–0	1–0	1–4	2–1	5–0	3–2
3 Boreham Wood	0–0	3–0	*	0–1	3–2	0–2	3–0	1–1	2–0	3–2	1–2	2–0	0–1	0–1	0–1	1–0	3–1	1–0	0–0	2–5	2–0	4–3
4 Bracknell Town	3–1	1–1	1–7	*	0–1	1–2	2–4	0–1	0–2	0–5	1–2	1–1	2–1	0–3	0–1	2–1	2–2	1–2	2–5	3–2	2–0	3–1
5 Chesham United	2–0	6–1	1–2	1–1	*	0–1	2–4	3–3	1–2	0–3	2–2	1–1	2–0	0–4	1–3	1–2	0–0	1–1	1–2	1–1	5–0	1–3
6 Grays Athletic	1–0	3–1	4–2	2–0	3–1	*	1–0	4–0	1–0	3–1	3–1	2–1	1–1	1–1	4–0	1–1	1–0	3–1	0–0	0–1	3–0	1–0
7 Hampton	0–2	0–1	1–1	3–1	0–5	0–1	*	2–2	2–2	1–3	0–1	2–4	3–1	1–0	5–1	0–0	2–0	2–1	0–1	0–2	3–1	4–1
8 Kingsbury Town	1–2	2–0	2–2	2–2	4–0	0–1	2–1	*	1–1	0–3	1–4	0–2	3–4	2–1	1–1	1–1	1–1	0–0	2–0	2–4	3–1	1–2
9 Leatherhead	1–3	1–1	1–1	4–2	1–2	1–3	0–1	1–1	*	4–0	0–1	2–1	1–0	1–1	2–0	3–1	1–0	1–3	0–0	0–0	4–1	2–1
10 Lewes	1–1	6–1	0–1	3–3	2–2	1–1	1–1	3–3	0–4	*	2–2	1–3	2–0	0–1	3–0	1–2	2–3	1–1	1–2	1–3	3–0	2–2
11 Marlow	3–1	2–2	2–0	1–0	5–1	1–2	0–3	3–1	4–1	5–2	*	2–1	1–2	3–2	0–1	2–0	4–3	4–2	1–0	3–0	4–0	2–1
12 Oxford City	3–1	1–2	3–1	3–0	0–0	1–1	4–1	2–2	2–0	3–6	0–3	*	2–3	6–3	2–2	2–2	0–4	0–0	1–1	2–4	4–1	5–1
13 Southwick	2–2	2–1	0–1	2–0	1–3	0–1	2–1	1–3	3–1	1–1	3–4	1–0	*	0–0	2–1	1–2	0–0	2–2	4–0	1–1	3–0	1–1
14 Staincs Town	3–1	3–1	0–0	1–0	2–3	0–1	0–1	2–2	3–1	5–4	1–3	6–0	2–1	*	1–0	0–1	1–1	1–0	4–2	3–3	4–0	1–0
15 Stevenage Borough	0–2	2–3	0–0	0–1	2–1	0–2	0–1	1–2	1–1	1–1	0–2	0–0	0–7	3–1	*	0–1	1–2	1–1	0–2	0–2	3–0	2–0
16 Uxbridge	1–1	1–0	0–1	1–1	0–2	1–1	0–0	2–0	1–1	0–0	0–1	0–0	3–1	1–1	1–2	*	0–0	1–0	0–0	0–1	6–0	0–2
17 Walthamstow Ave.	3–3	3–1	2–0	3–1	1–2	0–1	1–3	2–0	0–4	2–4	0–5	2–1	1–1	0–0	2–0	0–1	*	2–0	1–2	0–3	1–1	0–0
18 Walton & Hersham	2–1	3–1	1–2	1–1	4–0	0–0	1–1	1–1	1–0	2–1	3–3	2–2	1–1	0–0	1–0	2–0	1–0	*	0–0	2–0	4–0	2–2
19 Wembley	0–1	1–1	0–1	1–3	2–1	3–3	0–0	2–1	3–2	1–1	0–4	2–0	1–0	2–0	1–0	1–1	0–1	1–2	*	4–0	3–0	1–2
20 Woking	3–1	3–1	2–0	1–2	2–0	1–1	2–3	2–3	1–0	4–3	1–2	3–0	4–0	0–2	1–1	4–3	4–2	2–0	3–0	*	6–0	1–1
21 Wolverton Town	0–3	4–3	0–3	0–1	2–7	0–1	1–1	0–2	0–4	0–2	0–2	0–2	2–0	1–2	1–3	2–0	1–2	0–2	0–3	1–3	*	1–4
22 Worthing	1–3	3–1	2–2	2–4	1–1	0–3	0–2	2–1	2–3	3–2	0–1	4–1	5–1	2–1	3–0	2–1	0–3	0–1	0–1	0–2	2–2	*

Division I	*P*	*W*	*D*	*L*	*F*	*A*	*Pts*
1 Marlow	42	32	5	5	100	44	101
2 Grays Athletic	42	30	10	2	74	25	100
3 Woking	42	25	7	10	91	52	82
4 Boreham Wood	42	21	9	12	65	45	72
5 Staines Town	42	19	11	12	71	48	68
6 Wembley	42	18	11	13	54	46	65
7 Basildon United	42	18	9	15	65	58	63
8 Walton & Hersham	42	15	16	11	53	44	61
9 Hampton	42	17	10	15	59-	54	61
10 Leatherhead	42	16	11	15	64	53	59
11 Southwick	42	13	12	17	59	63	51
12 Oxford City	42	13	12	17	70	77	51
13 Worthing	42	14	8	20	67	73	50
14 Kingsbury Town	42	11	17	14	62	69	50
15 Walthamstow Ave.	42	13	11	18	53	63	50
16 Lewes	42	12	13	17	83	77	49
17 Uxbridge	42	11	16	15	41	47	49
18 Chesham United	42	12	10	20	69	77	46
19 Bracknell Town	42	12	9	21	54	80	45
20 Billericay Town	42	11	11	20	58	88	44
21 Stevenage Borough	42	11	9	22	36	64	42
22 Wolverton Town	42	3	3	36	23	124	12

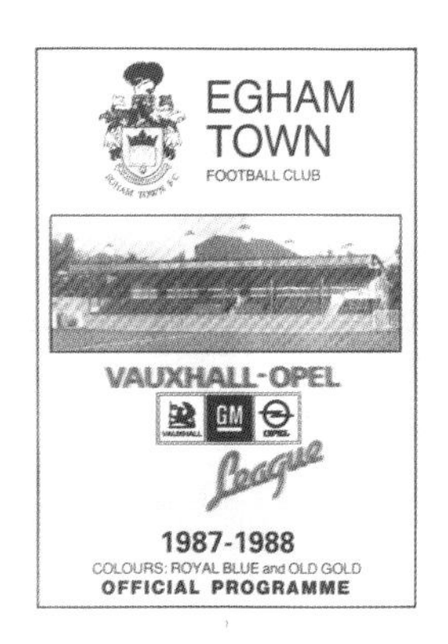

Left: the Egham Town matchday programme from season 1987-88.

Right: the programme for Yeovil's FA Cup First Round tie at Worcester City in November 1987.

Division II North	1	2	3	4	5	6	7	8	9	10	11	12	13	14	15	16	17	18	19	20	21	22
1 Aveley	*	3–0	2–3	0–1	7–1	2–1	0–1	1–1	1–1	2–1	0–1	0–2	0–2	2–1	2–0	0–1	1–1	1–1	1–1	2–3	0–4	0–1
2 Barton Rovers	2–0	*	0–1	2–0	0–0	3–0	1–0	0–0	3–1	0–3	2–0	3–3	0–2	1–2	1–0	1–0	0–0	2–3	1–3	2–0	3–2	1–4
3 Berkhamsted Town	4–0	1–1	*	1–1	1–1	2–3	1–5	2–2	3–0	4–0	3–2	1–0	1–0	1–1	2–0	3–0	3–0	2–0	2–1	1–2	1–1	1–1
4 Clapton	3–3	1–0	2–0	*	1–0	0–1	3–0	0–3	5–0	1–5	1–0	2–0	2–1	1–0	1–2	1–0	0–0	1–0	3–3	1–3	2–2	3–2
5 Collier Row	3–0	4–0	3–0	1–1	*	4–3	5–1	1–5	5–1	2–0	2–0	2–2	3–0	2–1	3–0	3–0	1–0	3–1	2–2	1–1	1–0	1–1
6 Finchley	4–0	2–0	1–2	4–1	0–0	*	2–2	1–1	0–1	2–0	1–1	2–0	1–0	3–2	0–1	6–0	1–1	4–0	0–1	2–1	0–0	3–0
7 Haringey Borough	0–0	3–1	1–2	3–0	0–3	0–2	*	2–0	2–2	0–3	1–0	1–1	2–0	1–2	2–1	0–1	0–2	0–4	1–1	2–2	0–1	0–3
8 Harlow Town	1–0	3–0	0–0	3–1	0–0	1–1	3–3	*	0–1	3–1	2–1	0–1	4–2	0–1	1–1	4–1	0–1	5–0	1–1	1–1	0–0	1–0
9 Hemel Hempstead	2–3	0–2	1–0	0–0	0–0	0–0	0–4	1–1	*	3–2	2–2	1–0	0–0	3–0	0–3	2–0	1–0	0–4	1–2	2–3	0–0	0–2
10 Hertford Town	1–1	2–2	0–0	1–2	0–1	0–6	2–0	0–2	0–3	*	1–3	3–4	0–1	0–0	3–1	1–0	0–3	2–3	0–1	1–2	1–5	0–5
11 Heybridge Swifts	2–1	1–1	2–0	1–1	1–0	2–1	3–2	1–1	2–0	1–0	*	3–1	1–1	1–1	2–0	2–0	2–2	3–1	0–0	2–1	0–1	0–1
12 Hornchurch	2–2	1–0	3–2	1–1	0–0	0–2	4–0	2–2	0–0	3–2	3–2	*	1–1	1–1	1–0	3–2	2–2	3–1	2–2	1–1	0–2	2–2
13 Letchworth G City	2–1	0–1	2–1	2–0	1–2	4–2	2–1	1–0	2–0	3–2	1–1	1–2	*	1–0	4–1	2–0	2–1	1–3	0–2	3–2	3–1	1–4
14 Rainham Town	3–2	1–2	1–2	1–1	3–0	3–3	1–2	0–1	2–0	6–0	0–2	3–1	3–1	*	2–1	2–2	2–2	0–1	1–1	2–2	3–3	0–3
15 Royston Town	0–1	2–0	2–2	1–1	0–4	1–1	5–4	0–4	1–2	1–0	2–1	5–2	1–1	2–1	*	0–0	1–0	1–0	0–1	1–2	2–2	2–3
16 Saffron Walden Tn	0–0	0–0	2–1	1–0	3–0	1–0	2–0	0–2	3–1	2–1	0–0	0–1	1–0	1–3	0–1	*	2–1	2–1	1–1	2–2	1–4	1–2
17 Tilbury	0–0	2–2	3–0	1–1	0–2	3–2	2–1	1–0	4–1	3–2	4–0	1–0	3–0	2–2	3–2	5–0	*	1–1	1–0	1–0	0–1	2–2
18 Tring Town	2–0	1–0	3–6	2–2	1–0	1–0	2–1	1–4	1–2	3–1	0–1	3–0	3–1	3–4	3–0	3–0	0–0	*	0–0	2–2	1–2	1–3
19 Vauuxhall Motors	1–0	1–1	1–1	3–0	0–2	6–0	1–1	1–0	2–2	1–2	0–2	1–0	3–1	2–1	0–1	0–2	0–1	1–3	*	1–1	2–1	1–1
20 Ware	0–0	2–0	1–1	1–1	1–2	1–0	3–5	1–0	0–0	1–0	2–2	2–0	1–3	1–0	1–0	2–0	1–1	4–0	1–3	*	0–6	3–2
21 Witham Town	1–1	3–1	0–4	1–1	1–1	2–0	1–0	0–2	2–1	1–2	2–2	3–0	3–1	4–0	1–1	4–0	0–1	0–5	0–1	2–2	*	0–1
22 Wivenhoe Town	4–0	3–1	2–3	7–0	0–0	4–0	4–0	3–3	5–0	5–0	5–1	1–1	4–3	2–1	6–3	2–0	2–0	2–1	1–1	0–1	0–0	*

Division II North	*P*	*W*	*D*	*L*	*F*	*A*	*Pts*
1 Wivenhoe Town	42	26	10	6	105	42	88
2 Collier Row	42	22	13	7	71	39	79
3 Tilbury	42	18	15	9	61	40	69
4 Berkhamsted Town	42	19	12	11	71	53	69
5 Harlow Town	42	17	16	9	67	36	67
6 Ware	42	17	15	10	63	58	66
7 Witham Town	42	17	14	11	69	47	65
8 Vauxhall Motors	42	16	17	9	56	42	65
9 Heybridge Swifts	42	17	13	12	56	50	64
10 Tring Town	42	18	6	18	69	67	60
11 Letchworth G City	42	18	5	19	59	64	59
12 Finchley	42	16	10	16	67	54	58
13 Clapton	42	14	15	13	50	62	57
14 Hornchurch	42	13	15	14	56	65	54
15 Barton Rovers	42	13	10	19	43	60	49
16 Rainham Town	42	12	12	18	63	66	48
17 Royston Town	42	13	8	21	49	70	47
18 Saffron Walden Tn	42	13	7	22	34	67	46
19 Hemel Hempstead	42	11	12	19	38	71	45
20 Haringey Borough	42	11	8	23	54	78	41
21 Aveley	42	8	13	21	42	65	37
22 Hertford Town	42	8	4	30	45	92	28

Left: the programme from Wokingham Town's FA Trophy Semi-Final Second Leg against Telford United in April 1988.

Right: the particularly attractive Vauxhall Motors edition for the 1987-88 season.

1987-88

Division II South	1	2	3	4	5	6	7	8	9	10	11	12	13	14	15	16	17	18	19	20	21	22
1 Banstead Athletic	*	4–1	0–1	0–3	1–2	0–5	2–0	1–2	1–2	4–0	0–2	2–4	0–3	0–2	0–1	0–2	1–1	2–2	2–2	1–0	0–0	2–1
2 Camberley Town	1–0	*	1–0	1–5	1–4	0–0	0–2	1–3	0–0	4–2	2–4	0–1	0–0	0–1	0–0	2–0	2–3	3–2	0–1	1–3	2–3	0–5
3 Chalfont St Peter	4–1	4–1	*	1–1	1–1	1–0	1–0	0–2	3–1	3–1	2–1	4–1	0–1	1–0	1–1	2–1	4–2	4–0	1–2	3–0	1–1	0–1
4 Chertsey Town	2–0	3–0	1–2	*	2–2	4–1	0–2	1–2	1–0	2–0	2–1	3–0	3–0	0–1	0–0	0–2	0–0	2–1	0–1	1–0	2–2	4–3
5 Dorking	4–0	4–1	0–2	0–1	*	4–2	0–0	3–2	0–3	6–0	2–1	2–0	3–1	2–1	1–1	0–0	3–0	3–1	4–0	2–0	1–0	3–1
6 Eastbourne United	0–0	3–0	0–2	2–1	2–2	*	0–0	0–2	2–2	1–1	0–1	1–0	2–2	1–3	0–1	2–0	4–1	2–2	1–0	1–0	1–2	2–3
7 Egham Town	2–0	1–4	1–1	1–0	0–1	2–3	*	2–1	0–2	1–0	0–0	1–1	0–1	1–1	1–3	0–0	6–0	1–0	1–1	0–1	0–3	1–2
8 Epsom & Ewell	1–0	3–1	1–4	0–1	1–1	0–1	3–0	*	0–0	5–1	2–2	3–1	1–0	2–0	4–3	2–0	4–0	5–1	1–6	1–0	2–2	0–0
9 Feltham	2–1	1–1	2–3	0–2	0–0	2–2	0–1	0–0	*	2–0	6–2	2–2	4–0	2–1	1–1	3–0	3–0	2–1	1–0	4–0	2–2	4–3
10 Flackwell Heath	3–0	2–2	1–5	2–3	1–3	2–4	0–1	1–2	0–3	*	0–1	1–0	1–1	0–2	1–1	3–1	1–1	1–0	1–1	1–4	3–3	2–0
11 Harefield United	2–0	3–4	1–0	0–2	1–1	2–3	1–3	1–2	1–0	2–1	*	0–2	0–3	1–1	0–1	0–0	5–0	3–1	0–1	2–0	0–3	2–0
12 Horsham	0–3	4–0	0–1	0–1	0–6	1–4	3–1	1–1	0–1	1–2	1–2	*	1–3	1–1	0–1	2–0	0–2	2–1	1–0	1–1	0–3	0–1
13 Hungerford Town	2–1	4–1	3–4	4–0	2–3	0–2	2–2	2–1	1–3	1–0	0–1	3–1	*	3–3	0–1	1–4	2–1	2–0	2–0	1–1	3–0	0–0
14 Maidenhead Utd	3–1	3–1	3–0	2–3	0–3	0–1	2–2	3–1	1–0	2–2	2–0	2–2	0–1	*	1–2	1–1	0–0	3–0	3–0	1–2	1–0	1–2
15 Metropolitan Police	5–0	2–2	1–1	2–0	0–0	2–2	2–0	1–1	1–1	4–0	2–0	0–0	2–1	2–2	*	2–0	0–0	6–1	4–0	3–1	2–1	1–1
16 Molesey	1–0	2–3	1–1	0–0	0–0	2–3	1–0	0–0	1–4	2–1	2–1	2–3	0–1	0–3	0–1	*	2–2	0–0	1–3	2–1	1–0	0–2
17 Newbury Town	1–1	3–0	0–6	0–1	1–2	1–0	2–1	0–0	1–1	3–1	1–2	0–1	0–1	2–2	2–4	2–3	*	1–1	0–2	1–1	2–1	0–5
18 Petersfield United	1–1	1–0	0–4	0–2	1–0	1–2	1–2	2–3	0–2	3–1	1–3	2–3	2–4	3–4	0–6	2–4	1–1	*	1–2	2–1	0–6	2–1
19 Ruislip Manor	5–1	2–4	0–1	3–0	2–3	2–3	2–1	1–1	4–0	3–1	0–1	0–0	1–3	5–1	1–4	3–1	1–0	1–2	*	4–1	0–3	2–0
20 Southall	1–0	0–0	0–0	3–1	3–2	2–1	0–0	0–2	0–2	1–0	4–3	0–1	0–2	1–2	0–3	4–2	0–2	3–0	0–6	*	1–1	2–1
21 Whyteleafe	2–0	3–1	0–2	4–1	1–2	3–1	2–2	2–1	2–1	4–1	2–2	2–2	3–0	2–3	4–0	1–1	3–1	1–0	0–1	4–3	*	1–5
22 Yeading	3–1	3–3	0–0	2–2	2–1	1–0	6–3	3–1	0–3	4–0	1–2	1–1	2–0	1–1	1–1	2–0	3–0	3–3	2–3	5–0	1–2	*

Division II South	*P*	*W*	*D*	*L*	*F*	*A*	*Pts*
1 Chalfont St. Peter	42	26	9	7	81	35	87
2 Metropolitan Police	42	23	17	2	80	32	86
3 Dorking	42	25	11	6	86	39	86
4 Feltham	42	21	12	9	74	41	75
5 Epsom & Ewell	42	21	11	10	71	49	74
6 Chertsey Town	42	22	7	13	63	47	73
7 Whyteleafe	42	20	11	11	84	55	71
8 Hungerford Town	42	21	7	14	66	54	70
9 Ruislip Manor	42	21	5	16	74	57	68
10 Yeading	42	19	10	13	83	56	67
11 Maidenhead Utd	42	18	12	12	69	54	66
12 Eastbourne United	42	18	10	14	67	57	64
13 Harefield United	42	18	6	18	59	60	60
14 Egham Town	42	12	12	18	45	55	48
15 Horsham	42	12	10	20	45	66	46
16 Southall	42	13	7	22	45	72	46
17 Molesey	42	11	11	20	42	63	44
18 Newbury Town	42	8	13	21	40	81	37
19 Camberley Town	42	9	9	24	51	94	36
20 Flackwell Heath	42	6	8	28	42	96	26
21 Banstead Athletic	42	6	7	29	34	81	25
22 Petersfield United	42	6	7	29	45	102	25

RELEGATION PLAY-OFF

1st leg: Petersfield United 0, Hertford Town 2; 2nd leg: Hertford Town 1, Petersfield United 1. Hertford Town won 3–1 on aggregate.

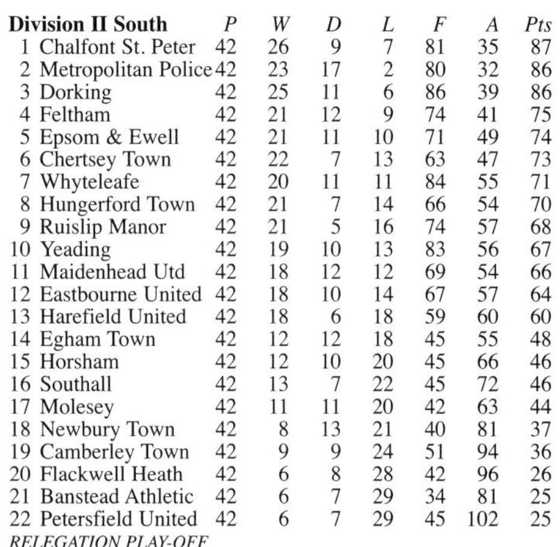

Left: the 1988 League Dinner brochure.

Below: Leytonstone-Ilford celebrated their championship by beating nearest challengers Farnborough Town by five goals to three at Green Pond Road to secure the title by eight points.

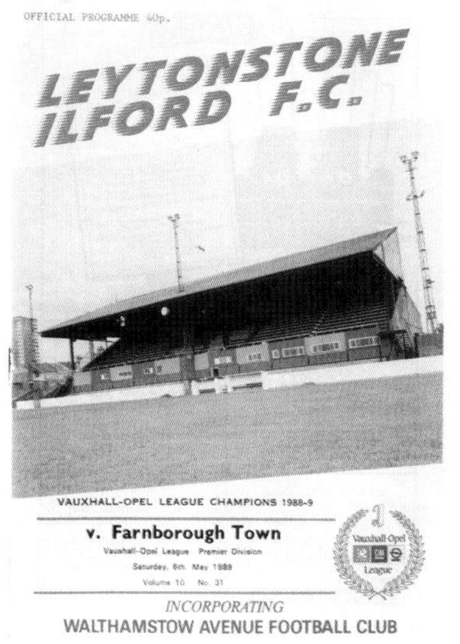

1988–89 - Prior to the commencement of the season Oxford City, who had ongoing problems with the lease of their White House ground, were suspended for the playing season and the position would be reviewed at the end of the season; as a result Division One would operate with 21 clubs.

Leytonstone-Ilford secured the League championship by eight points from nearest challengers Farnborough Town. The club, however, could not take their place in the GM Vauxhall Conference due to ground grading and their place went to the Hampshire club. Slough Town finished third for the second successive year. At the foot of the table South London's Tooting & Mitcham United and Croydon were both relegated to Division One. In Division One it was a three-horse race between Staines Town, Basingstoke Town and Woking and the title was decided on the last day of the season when Staines Town were champions four points clear of runners-up Basingstoke Town who themselves were two points ahead of Woking. With only 21 clubs in Division One, only three were relegated to the Division Twos, Collier Row, Bracknell Town and Basildon United. In Division Two North Harlow Town emerged as champions with newcomers Purfleet – only formed in 1985 – runners-up. In Division Two South Dorking were champions and were joined in promotion to Division One by runners-up Whyteleafe.

During the season an Extraordinary General Meeting was convened concerning the operation of Haringey Borough, who had been transferred from Division Two North to Division Two South. The club were expelled from membership and the League operated with 86 clubs.

A Special General Meeting was arranged in June 1989 to discuss the affairs of Wolverton Town (MK). For playing ineligible players in several of their matches, the League docked the club nine points. A vote was then taken by ballot to consider their continued membership of the League. The result was 48 votes in favour of expulsion and 5 against.

At an extraordinary meeting on 13 June 1989 it was unanimously agreed that the League be incorporated as a company limited by guarantee. At the Annual General Meeting, Aylesbury United – relegated from the GM Vauxhall Conference – replaced Farnborough Town. It was announced that League champions Leytonstone-Ilford FC had incorporated Walthamstow Avenue FC and the new club name would be Redbridge Forest, with their home matches played at Dagenham FC. Oxford City, who had requested a suspension at the start of the season, resigned from the League as they were without a home ground.

Abingdon Town, from the London-Spartan League, and Malden Vale, from the Combined Counties League, were elected to fill the vacancies and were placed in Division Two South. Newport County, who had been placed in liquidation, were elected into the League, subject to the consent of the liquidator. However, the club could not take their place and League membership for 1989–90 would be 87 clubs.

1988-89

Premier Division	1	2	3	4	5	6	7	8	9	10	11	12	13	14	15	16	17	18	19	20	21	22
1 Barking	*	4–0	0–0	2–2	0–1	1–1	0–1	0–0	2–2	1–0	3–1	2–2	0–1	0–0	0–1	1–0	0–0	1–0	1–0	2–1	2–3	1–0
2 Bishop's Stortford	0–1	*	1–3	2–1	0–1	3–0	3–3	1–0	0–1	1–0	2–0	3–2	3–2	0–1	1–0	1–2	1–1	1–1	4–0	2–1	4–1	1–2
3 Bognor Regis Tn	1–0	0–4	*	0–3	1–1	1–0	0–1	2–2	3–2	0–1	1–1	2–1	2–0	0–1	0–0	2–0	1–2	1–0	1–0	2–1	0–0	1–0
4 Bromley	1–2	2–0	1–2	*	1–1	3–2	3–3	1–2	4–0	0–0	1–1	1–1	0–1	1–1	0–2	1–1	6–0	0–1	0–1	3–1	1–1	2–1
5 Carshalton Athletic	0–1	1–2	2–1	1–1	*	1–0	3–1	2–0	1–2	0–1	0–0	1–0	1–0	0–0	0–0	1–0	3–0	5–1	0–0	2–1	1–1	1–0
6 Croydon	1–2	0–3	0–1	0–3	1–1	*	1–1	1–0	0–1	0–1	0–0	0–2	1–1	0–2	0–3	0–0	1–0	0–2	0–2	0–3	0–3	2–0
7 Dagenham	1–2	0–2	0–0	0–4	2–1	5–2	*	1–2	1–2	2–3	2–1	0–0	1–2	3–2	1–4	1–1	0–2	1–1	0–1	0–0	0–1	3–0
8 Dulwich Hamlet	1–1	1–3	2–2	1–1	1–2	2–1	2–1	*	2–4	1–2	2–2	0–0	4–2	0–1	0–2	3–0	1–2	1–0	1–0	1–1	1–1	5–1
9 Farnborough Town	1–0	2–2	3–0	1–0	4–4	5–1	4–1	3–1	*	3–0	2–0	4–1	0–2	0–3	0–2	3–0	4–1	2–1	2–6	1–0	1–0	3–4
10 Grays Athletic	2–2	4–3	5–0	2–2	0–2	1–0	2–0	1–2	1–2	*	5–0	1–2	0–0	2–2	2–2	3–2	4–2	1–0	2–1	2–1	0–0	2–1
11 Harrow Borough	2–3	1–2	4–0	2–0	0–4	0–3	3–3	2–1	1–1	1–0	*	1–2	1–2	0–3	1–1	1–2	3–2	0–2	1–2	2–1	3–0	1–2
12 Hayes	3–1	1–1	2–0	2–1	2–0	1–1	0–3	1–0	1–1	3–1	2–4	*	4–2	0–1	1–0	3–1	0–2	2–0	0–1	2–0	2–2	2–2
13 Hendon	2–2	1–0	1–1	1–1	2–4	2–1	2–2	1–1	0–1	1–1	0–0	1–1	*	0–0	2–2	1–1	4–1	2–1	1–1	1–0	1–1	0–3
14 Kingstonian	2–0	3–2	1–0	1–0	1–0	3–2	1–1	1–1	1–2	0–0	1–2	0–3	7–0	*	4–1	0–1	2–0	3–0	0–1	0–2	1–0	1–2
15 Leytonstone-Ilford	2–0	3–2	3–0	4–0	3–1	4–1	2–1	1–0	5–3	1–1	3–1	2–1	1–4	2–0	*	1–1	1–1	1–0	1–0	3–2	0–0	2–2
16 Leyton-Wingate	3–2	1–0	0–2	0–0	1–1	2–0	1–0	1–1	2–2	2–2	3–3	0–2	9–1	1–1	0–2	*	4–0	1–0	1–1	0–0	0–4	0–1
17 Marlow	0–0	1–2	0–1	0–1	2–2	3–0	0–2	1–7	3–3	0–2	1–1	0–0	1–1	2–2	1–4	3–1	*	1–2	0–2	3–0	2–3	2–2
18 St. Albans City	1–0	2–2	1–1	1–1	1–1	5–1	0–0	1–4	2–0	0–1	3–2	1–3	0–1	0–0	0–0	2–4	4–0	*	1–4	4–0	1–0	1–2
19 Slough Town	1–0	0–2	3–0	4–1	1–1	4–0	0–2	3–2	0–3	2–0	1–1	2–0	4–0	2–0	2–0	1–3	2–0	4–3	*	4–1	0–1	3–0
20 Tooting & M Utd	1–1	3–2	0–2	0–3	0–3	2–1	2–1	1–0	1–3	1–1	1–1	0–3	1–2	2–0	0–1	0–2	3–2	2–1	2–3	*	2–0	1–3
21 Windsor & Eton	2–3	1–2	0–1	0–3	0–1	1–1	0–1	1–0	0–0	2–2	3–1	1–1	2–0	2–0	0–3	2–0	1–3	3–2	3–2	5–0	*	1–1
22 Wokingham Town	2–3	2–0	0–0	0–1	1–1	1–1	6–1	2–0	2–2	0–1	3–1	1–0	1–1	0–1	0–1	1–1	0–1	0–2	1–1	7–0	1–0	*

Premier Division	*P*	*W*	*D*	*L*	*F*	*A*	*Pts*
1 Leytonstone-Ilford	42	26	11	5	76	36	89
2 Farnborough Town	42	24	9	9	85	61	81
3 Slough Town	42	24	6	12	72	42	78
4 Carshalton Athletic	42	19	15	8	59	36	72
5 Grays Athletic	42	19	13	10	62	47	70
6 Kingstonian	42	19	11	12	54	37	68
7 Bishop's Stortford	42	20	6	16	70	56	66
8 Hayes	42	18	12	12	61	47	66
9 Bognor Regis Tn	42	17	11	14	38	49	62
10 Barking	42	16	13	13	49	45	61
11 Wokingham Town	42	15	11	16	60	54	56
12 Hendon	42	13	17	12	51	68	56
13 Windsor & Eton	42	14	13	15	52	50	55
14 Bromley	42	13	15	14	61	48	54
15 Leyton-Wingate	42	13	15	14	55	56	54
16 Dulwich Hamlet	42	12	12	18	58	57	48
17 St. Albans City	42	12	9	21	51	59	45
18 Dagenham	42	11	12	19	53	68	45
19 Harrow Borough	42	9	13	20	53	75	40
20 Marlow	42	9	11	22	48	83	38
21 Tooting & M Utd	42	10	6	26	41	81	36
22 Croydon	42	4	9	29	27	81	21

THE TEAMS

LEYTONSTONE ILFORD
(Red & Blue Striped Shirts)
(Royal Blue Shorts)
(Light Blue Socks)

1. Dave MALLETT
2. Warren BARTON
3. Paul WATTS
4. Alan CAMPBELL
5. Mark DENTON
6. Joe SIMMONDS
7. Martin COATES
8. Lawrence HOLMES
9. Terry SULLIVAN
10. Frank COLES
11. Micky DINGWALL
12. Lincoln MANDERSON
13. Dave BENSTED

BARKING
(White Shirts)
(White Shorts)
(White Socks)

1. Lee HARMSWORTH
2. Billy GOLDSTONE
3. Adrian LEMOINE
4. Steve MOSELY
5. Steve HATTER
6. Perry CONEY
7. Micky ENGWELL
8. Mark KANE
9. John CAMPBELL
10. Andy WALLACE
11. David COLLYMORE
12. Neil SATCHELL
14. Mark WOODS

Referee: Mr. Graham Poll (Hitchin)
Linesmen: Mr. A. Porter (Red & Yellow Flag)
Mr. P. McPherson (Yellow Flag)

MATCH BALL SPONSOR:

Today's Match Ball has been sponsored by Club Trustee Mr. GEORGE WARD. Our thanks to George for his kind donation. We hope to see him here this afternoon so that we may personally thank him for this donation.

COMING FIXTURES

Vauxhall-Opel League Premier Division
v. CROYDON
Friday 24th. March 1989 (Good Friday) K.O. 3.00pm.

Left: the two team line-ups from the Leytonstone-Ilford v. Barking match including a young Warren Barton and refereed by an equally young Graham Poll!

The home side won 2-0 on their way to the League Championship.

Division I	1	2	3	4	5	6	7	8	9	10	11	12	13	14	15	16	17	18	19	20	21
1 Basildon United	*	0–2	0–1	2–3	1–2	2–2	1–0	1–2	1–1	0–3	0–1	2–3	1–1	0–0	0–2	1–0	1–3	1–2	1–2	1–2	2–3
2 Basingstoke Town	3–0	*	2–0	3–1	2–0	7–0	1–0	4–1	1–1	4–0	2–1	1–2	3–0	2–1	2–2	2–1	0–1	3–0	3–2	1–1	1–1
3 Boreham Wood	2–0	2–2	*	5–0	3–1	2–1	5–0	1–1	1–2	1–1	1–1	1–3	1–2	3–3	0–2	2–0	2–0	0–4	0–1	2–3	2–1
4 Bracknell Town	1–1	0–2	0–3	*	3–0	1–0	1–2	3–1	0–1	2–0	0–1	0–2	2–3	1–3	0–1	2–3	1–2	0–1	1–0	0–0	5–1
5 Chalfont St. Peter	2–0	1–4	3–2	4–0	*	2–1	2–2	0–3	0–2	1–4	1–3	4–0	1–1	0–0	0–3	2–4	0–1	3–1	2–2	1–3	4–1
6 Chesham United	2–0	3–4	0–1	4–1	4–4	*	2–0	3–0	0–1	0–0	1–0	2–1	1–4	5–2	0–2	0–0	0–0	0–1	0–1	0–5	1–1
7 Collier Row	1–0	0–3	2–2	1–0	0–1	1–3	*	2–2	0–3	1–1	1–1	1–3	3–0	3–0	1–1	1–2	0–2	2–3	0–3	0–2	3–1
8 Hampton	0–0	0–0	0–0	0–0	3–2	1–0	2–1	*	0–3	1–2	1–4	0–0	1–0	3–4	0–2	0–1	1–3	1–0	1–3	0–2	1–1
9 Hitchin Town	0–3	2–0	2–0	1–1	5–1	2–0	6–1	2–1	*	1–0	3–0	1–0	1–1	2–2	2–1	1–0	2–1	0–1	0–3	1–1	1–0
10 Kingsbury Town	6–1	0–2	0–2	2–1	2–2	5–1	1–2	2–1	3–1	*	3–0	0–1	1–0	2–0	2–1	2–1	1–2	1–1	1–0	0–1	3–1
11 Leatherhead	1–2	2–4	3–1	3–0	3–0	6–4	0–2	1–1	1–0	1–2	*	2–2	1–1	1–1	0–1	1–2	0–0	1–0	4–0	0–1	4–5
12 Lewes	2–1	0–3	2–2	3–1	3–2	2–2	6–0	3–1	1–0	1–4	3–0	*	2–0	1–0	0–1	2–1	2–1	4–1	0–1	0–2	3–0
13 Metropolitan Police	3–0	0–3	0–1	2–1	1–2	1–0	1–0	3–2	0–0	0–2	2–0	3–3	*	2–2	1–5	5–3	1–3	2–1	1–2	1–2	2–2
14 Southwick	5–0	0–3	0–1	1–0	1–0	0–4	1–1	1–0	1–4	2–1	0–1	0–0	4–0	*	0–1	0–2	2–2	1–2	0–0	0–2	1–1
15 Staines Town	4–1	1–1	2–1	3–0	5–0	1–1	5–0	1–1	1–0	0–0	2–0	3–0	3–0	1–1	*	1–2	2–0	2–0	2–1	1–0	5–3
16 Uxbridge	0–0	0–0	3–0	1–1	0–1	3–1	3–1	1–1	2–2	2–1	0–0	2–1	1–0	2–3	1–2	*	1–3	2–0	1–3	0–4	2–1
17 Walton & Hersham	2–0	2–1	0–0	1–0	3–1	0–1	3–0	1–1	0–2	0–0	3–0	0–1	3–1	2–0	2–2	1–0	*	5–0	0–2	1–3	1–2
18 Wembley	0–2	1–0	0–2	3–1	0–0	1–1	2–1	0–0	0–0	2–1	3–2	0–2	1–3	1–1	0–2	2–3	1–0	*	1–0	0–5	4–3
19 Wivenhoe Town	5–1	4–2	1–0	2–2	2–0	2–0	3–0	2–0	2–1	0–3	0–1	3–3	2–1	1–1	2–1	2–4	0–1	0–2	*	0–3	1–0
20 Woking	1–0	3–0	4–1	1–2	2–2	0–2	3–1	2–1	1–1	1–0	2–1	2–2	1–1	1–0	1–1	1–2	0–1	0–1	0–0	*	3–1
21 Worthing	2–3	0–2	0–1	1–0	2–2	0–2	1–0	1–1	0–0	0–3	1–4	4–3	1–2	0–0	2–1	1–2	2–0	1–2	0–2	1–1	*

Division I	*P*	*W*	*D*	*L*	*F*	*A*	*Pts*
1 Staines Town	40	26	9	5	79	29	87
2 Basingstoke Town	40	25	8	7	85	36	83
3 Woking	40	24	10	6	72	30	82
4 Hitchin Town	40	21	11	8	60	32	74
5 Wivenhoe Town	40	22	6	12	62	44	72
6 Lewes	40	21	8	11	72	54	71
7 Walton & Hersham	40	21	7	12	56	36	70
8 Kingsbury Town	40	20	7	13	65	41	67
9 Uxbridge	40	19	7	14	60	54	64
10 Wembley	40	18	6	16	45	58	60
11 Boreham Wood	40	16	9	15	57	52	57
12 Leatherhead	40	14	8	18	56	58	50
13 Metropolitan Police	40	13	9	18	52	68	48
14 Chesham United	40	12	9	19	54	67	45
15 Southwick	40	9	15	16	44	58	42
16 Chalfont St. Peter	40	11	9	20	56	82	42
17 Hampton	40	7	14	19	37	62	35
18 Worthing*	40	8	10	22	49	80	32
19 Collier Row	40	8	7	25	37	82	31
20 Bracknell Town	40	8	6	26	38	70	30
21 Basildon United	40	6	7	27	34	77	25

** Worthing had two points deducted.*

HUNGERFORD TOWN FOOTBALL CLUB

THE BVROVGH OF HVNGERFORD

VAUXHALL-OPEL League

Left: the Hungerford Town programme from season 1988-89.

Boro View

SPONSORED BY: WINDOWARM QUALITY GLAZED PRODUCTS

Leytonstone/Ilford
Vauxhall-Opel League
Premier Division
Monday, 27th March (3.00pm)

Official Programme
1988-89
50 Pence

Club Sponsors

Right: the Farnborough Town programme from the same season.

1988-89

Division II North	1	2	3	4	5	6	7	8	9	10	11	12	13	14	15	16	17	18	19	20	21	22
1 Aveley	*	2–1	3–0	0–3	3–1	0–1	2–1	2–0	2–2	1–1	1–1	0–1	2–1	3–2	1–2	0–0	1–0	1–0	1–2	1–1	1–0	1–1
2 Barton Rovers	3–1	*	3–0	0–1	2–2	1–1	2–0	2–1	0–1	2–0	1–1	2–2	1–1	2–1	1–0	1–1	1–0	4–1	0–0	2–0	2–1	2–1
3 Berkhamsted Town	1–1	2–1	*	0–1	3–3	1–1	2–3	2–1	1–3	0–2	2–2	4–0	2–0	3–1	0–2	2–0	1–1	3–3	2–1	1–3	2–0	2–4
4 Billericay Town	2–0	1–2	6–1	*	1–1	2–1	3–1	1–1	3–2	2–0	1–0	1–2	2–4	3–1	0–3	3–0	0–0	1–2	2–1	1–2	1–1	3–1
5 Clapton	0–1	0–2	0–1	1–1	*	2–2	1–0	1–0	1–3	3–1	2–0	3–0	4–3	2–1	1–1	1–1	2–1	2–1	2–0	1–0	3–1	3–2
6 Harlow Town	3–0	4–1	1–4	1–0	3–0	*	3–0	1–2	1–1	3–0	2–2	1–4	0–0	2–1	2–0	3–1	3–2	0–2	3–0	1–1	1–0	1–0
7 Hemel Hempstead	2–0	1–0	1–2	1–2	1–4	1–4	*	0–0	2–0	2–1	0–0	1–1	2–1	0–1	1–1	2–2	4–1	2–1	3–1	2–1	2–0	1–0
8 Hertford Town	0–2	3–0	1–1	1–1	2–1	0–0	2–0	*	3–1	2–2	0–0	3–0	1–1	2–0	1–0	1–1	3–0	2–0	4–2	1–3	0–3	2–1
9 Heybridge Swifts	2–0	1–0	1–0	2–0	1–0	1–3	2–0	2–0	*	2–1	3–0	0–1	1–0	1–0	1–1	1–2	5–0	1–1	2–0	6–0	2–1	2–0
10 Hornchurch	1–1	2–0	0–0	3–3	1–2	1–3	0–3	2–0	2–2	*	5–0	0–1	0–1	1–1	2–2	1–1	2–2	0–1	1–1	3–2	0–3	1–1
11 Letchworth G City	0–1	1–1	0–1	1–3	2–6	1–4	1–1	2–2	0–0	1–1	*	0–2	0–1	0–1	1–1	1–1	0–3	2–2	0–3	1–2	2–4	0–3
12 Purfleet	2–0	0–0	1–1	6–1	2–1	2–0	1–2	2–1	3–2	0–0	1–1	*	0–2	2–0	1–1	2–2	3–0	0–0	1–0	3–0	0–1	2–1
13 Rainham Town	2–3	2–2	3–1	0–0	1–0	1–1	0–1	0–4	0–0	2–4	0–3	1–1	*	2–3	1–1	1–3	1–1	0–1	1–1	1–0	0–0	3–1
14 Royston Town	0–1	1–3	0–3	2–1	0–1	0–3	1–1	1–0	2–2	2–1	0–0	2–0	2–1	*	1–4	0–4	1–0	0–1	2–1	0–2	2–5	4–0
15 Saffron Walden Tn	1–1	3–1	2–1	0–2	1–1	1–5	3–3	2–2	0–2	1–3	1–1	2–3	2–2	3–3	*	0–0	0–1	2–1	1–2	1–3	2–4	2–3
16 Stevenage Borough	3–0	3–0	5–1	0–1	2–1	2–3	2–0	3–5	3–0	1–3	2–1	2–3	3–2	2–2	2–0	*	1–1	4–4	3–0	2–1	3–1	3–1
17 Tilbury	2–3	1–3	0–1	1–0	0–0	0–5	1–0	3–2	2–0	1–2	1–0	0–0	1–1	0–0	1–1	2–3	*	1–2	0–1	2–0	2–1	5–0
18 Tring Town	0–0	2–1	0–0	0–1	1–1	0–2	2–1	0–1	2–0	1–0	3–0	3–1	2–0	3–1	4–0	1–1	1–0	*	3–2	2–2	1–0	2–0
19 Vauxhall Motors	2–1	0–0	3–1	3–1	2–1	0–1	2–3	0–0	0–0	1–1	0–1	0–1	1–0	2–1	1–0	1–2	0–3	4–0	*	3–2	3–1	4–1
20 Ware	1–3	2–1	3–0	2–2	3–0	0–1	1–1	1–0	1–0	0–3	2–3	0–0	2–2	0–1	2–1	0–4	4–3	0–4	2–0	*	4–1	3–0
21 Witham Town	4–3	1–2	2–1	1–1	2–2	0–1	2–1	2–2	4–2	1–2	1–2	1–2	2–1	2–0	4–1	2–0	2–6	0–1	2–2	1–1	*	3–0
22 Wolverton T (MK)	0–4	2–3	2–1	1–1	1–2	1–2	2–2	1–4	1–2	3–3	0–0	0–1	1–3	3–2	0–2	0–4	0–2	1–4	1–1	0–1	1–2	*

Division II North	*P*	*W*	*D*	*L*	*F*	*A*	*Pts*
1 Harlow Town	42	27	9	6	83	38	90
2 Purfleet	42	22	12	8	60	42	78
3 Tring Town	42	22	10	10	65	44	76
4 Stevenage Borough	42	20	13	9	84	55	73
5 Heybridge Swifts	42	21	9	12	64	43	72
6 Billericay Town	42	19	11	12	65	52	68
7 Clapton	42	18	11	13	65	56	65
8 Barton Rovers	42	18	11	13	58	50	65
9 Aveley	42	18	10	14	54	52	64
10 Hertford Town*	42	16	13	13	62	49	59
11 Ware	42	17	8	17	60	65	59
12 Hemel Hempstead	42	16	10	16	55	58	58
13 Witham Town	42	16	7	19	69	67	55
14 Vauxhall Motors	42	15	9	18	53	57	54
15 Berkhamsted Town	42	14	10	18	57	70	52
16 Hornchurch	42	11	16	15	59	61	49
17 Tilbury	42	13	10	19	53	60	49
18 Royston Town	42	12	7	23	46	72	43
19 Rainham Town	42	9	15	18	49	62	42
20 Saffron Walden Tn	42	8	16	18	54	72	40
21 Letchworth G City	42	4	18	20	34	71	30
22 Wolverton T (MK)+	42	5	7	30	42	95	13

** Hertford Town had two points deducted.*
+ Wolverton Town (MK) had nine points deducted.
Wolverton Town (Milton Keynes) previously Wolverton Town.

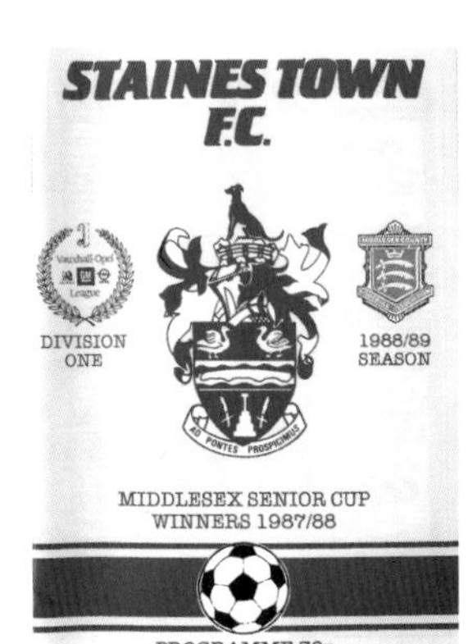

Left: the Staines Town matchday programme from season 1988-89.

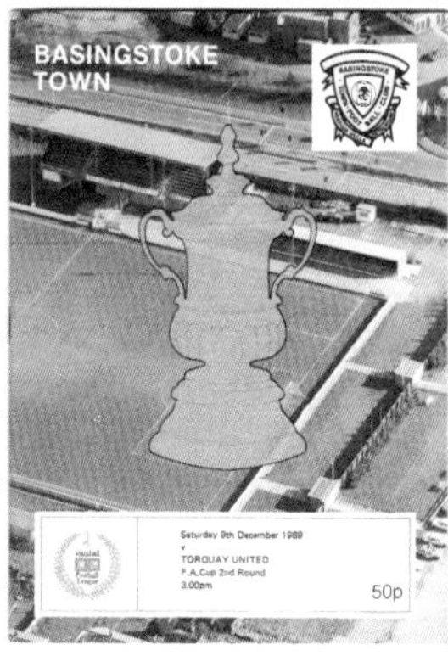

Right: the Basingstoke programme for their FA Cup tie against Torquay United in December 1989. The Camrose club lost by the odd goal in five.

Division II South	1	2	3	4	5	6	7	8	9	10	11	12	13	14	15	16	17	18	19	20	21
1 Banstead Athletic	*	2–2	2–3	0–2	0–4	4–0	1–2	3–1	1–2	2–0	3–4	0–2	0–0	0–2	0–0	1–0	3–0	2–0	0–0	2–4	0–0
2 Camberley Town	0–3	*	0–4	2–3	1–3	2–1	2–0	2–1	2–0	0–0	0–2	1–2	2–2	2–2	1–2	3–2	2–0	0–1	0–5	0–3	3–1
3 Chertsey Town	2–0	0–3	*	1–2	1–1	2–0	1–0	1–2	2–2	0–2	2–2	1–1	1–0	4–4	0–0	4–0	2–0	1–0	1–1	1–6	0–2
4 Dorking	8–1	5–0	4–2	*	1–1	4–2	3–0	0–2	3–1	1–2	0–1	3–1	1–1	5–1	2–2	5–2	5–1	2–1	5–0	2–0	3–0
5 Eastbourne United	0–2	2–0	2–0	2–4	*	1–3	5–3	3–1	0–1	1–1	0–1	2–1	2–2	5–2	4–0	1–1	3–1	0–2	7–0	0–1	1–2
6 Egham Town	1–0	1–2	1–2	1–4	5–1	*	1–2	0–0	0–3	1–0	3–0	1–1	3–2	0–0	1–1	3–0	3–2	1–0	2–3	1–3	3–0
7 Epsom & Ewell	3–0	3–0	2–1	0–1	0–1	2–1	*	4–0	1–4	0–0	1–0	3–0	1–3	1–1	2–3	1–0	3–3	0–1	0–2	1–1	2–0
8 Feltham	3–0	3–1	3–0	1–3	2–2	0–1	1–1	*	2–4	5–0	0–0	3–0	4–0	2–3	0–0	1–3	2–1	1–3	2–1	0–0	3–1
9 Finchley	2–0	1–0	1–1	0–3	3–0	0–3	3–2	0–1	*	2–1	4–3	4–1	1–1	3–0	0–0	3–1	1–1	2–1	3–1	2–1	2–1
10 Flackwell Heath	1–1	0–1	2–3	0–2	4–1	0–1	3–1	0–1	0–0	*	1–0	1–1	1–1	0–3	1–1	0–3	5–0	1–2	3–0	2–2	1–0
11 Harefield United	1–2	2–4	2–0	2–3	4–0	3–0	1–2	1–1	1–0	2–0	*	0–0	0–2	2–0	0–0	2–0	2–1	0–3	1–3	0–1	2–0
12 Horsham	0–2	1–1	0–0	1–2	0–4	2–2	1–3	0–2	2–1	2–2	1–2	*	1–1	1–2	0–2	3–0	2–2	0–2	1–1	0–2	3–1
13 Hungerford Town	2–0	0–0	4–1	0–1	1–0	2–2	1–1	4–2	2–1	2–3	3–1	1–2	*	1–0	3–1	1–0	2–1	1–1	3–1	0–1	0–2
14 Maidenhead Utd	1–2	0–1	0–0	1–4	0–0	3–0	0–1	1–1	0–3	3–2	0–0	2–0	0–2	*	0–0	1–1	2–1	1–0	0–2	3–2	1–1
15 Molesey	1–0	2–1	0–1	2–1	1–0	3–0	3–1	3–1	2–0	1–1	3–2	0–1	4–0	2–1	*	3–0	2–0	0–0	2–0	1–2	2–1
16 Newbury Town	2–2	2–0	1–1	0–4	3–3	1–0	0–1	0–3	0–0	1–0	0–1	4–0	0–0	2–0	3–0	*	3–1	1–2	1–4	2–2	1–2
17 Petersfield United	2–1	0–3	0–0	0–1	3–2	1–0	0–1	0–1	0–1	0–4	1–1	1–1	0–1	0–0	2–3	1–4	*	1–2	2–0	2–4	2–4
18 Ruislip Manor	2–2	2–0	2–2	0–1	0–1	1–3	1–1	3–0	2–2	1–3	0–2	0–0	0–1	2–1	3–3	0–1	6–1	*	4–0	0–0	2–0
19 Southall	0–2	0–2	0–4	0–3	1–1	1–1	2–0	1–0	0–0	0–2	0–2	2–0	0–3	3–1	1–1	2–1	0–2	0–1	*	2–2	1–1
20 Whyteleafe	3–2	5–2	2–1	1–1	3–1	0–1	1–1	3–0	3–2	0–2	1–2	4–0	0–0	2–1	2–1	2–1	4–0	2–1	6–0	*	2–0
21 Yeading	2–2	3–2	2–2	0–2	0–1	0–1	3–2	0–0	0–6	1–0	0–2	1–1	3–0	1–1	4–1	2–0	1–0	3–2	1–1	1–3	*

Division II South	*P*	*W*	*D*	*L*	*F*	*A*	*Pts*
1 Dorking	40	32	4	4	109	35	100
2 Whyteleafe	40	25	9	6	86	41	84
3 Finchley	40	21	9	10	70	45	72
4 Molesey	40	19	13	8	58	42	70
5 Harefield United	40	19	7	14	56	45	64
6 Hungerford Town	40	17	13	10	55	45	64
7 Ruislip Manor	40	16	9	15	56	43	57
8 Feltham	40	16	9	15	58	53	57
9 Epsom & Ewell	40	16	8	16	55	55	56
10 Egham Town	40	16	7	17	54	58	55
11 Eastbourne United	40	15	9	16	68	61	54
12 Chertsey Town	40	13	14	13	55	58	53
13 Flackwell Heath	40	13	11	16	51	49	50
14 Camberley Town	40	15	5	20	51	70	50
15 Yeading*	40	13	9	18	47	63	46
16 Banstead Athletic	40	12	8	20	50	65	44
17 Maidenhead Utd	40	10	13	17	44	61	43
18 Southall	40	11	10	19	41	73	43
19 Newbury Town	40	11	8	21	47	65	41
20 Horsham	40	7	14	19	36	68	35
21 Petersfield United	40	5	7	28	36	87	22

** Yeading had two points deducted.*

Left: the Wolverton matchday programme from season 1988-89.

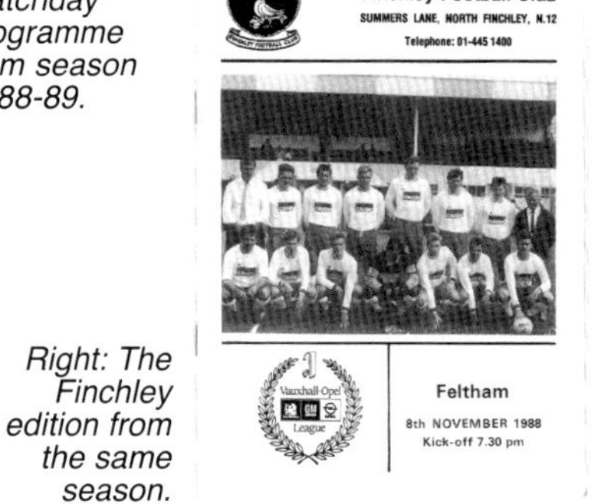

Right: The Finchley edition from the same season.

1989–90 - Slough Town were League champions in their centenary season, securing the championship in their last game at Bromley with a late winning goal and promotion to the GM Vauxhall Conference. Wokingham Town enjoyed their best position in the League as runners-up followed by Aylesbury United in their first season, Kingstonian and Grays Athletic. At the other end Bromley and Dulwich Hamlet both suffered relegation to Division One with the former going down on goal-difference from Barking. In Division One Wivenhoe Town, who gained one hundred points, clinched the title with Woking, who just missed out on promotion the previous year, two points behind as runners-up. In Division Two North the promoted clubs were champions Heybridge Swifts and runners-up Aveley while Yeading, champions, and runners-up Molesey provided the promoted clubs replacing the four relegated clubs from Division One, namely Hampton, Leatherhead, Purfleet and Kingsbury Town. Basement clubs in Division Two North and South, Letchworth Garden City and Horsham, met at the end of the season in a two leg relegation play-off with Horsham winning on aggregate and retaining their League place, whilst Letchworth Garden City were relegated to the South Midlands League. At the Annual General Meeting Enfield, relegated from the GM Vauxhall Conference, were elected to replace champions Slough Town. Cove from the Combined Counties League and Edgware Town from the London-Spartan League were elected to fill the vacancy in Division Two and the place vacated by relegated Letchworth Garden City, thus bringing League membership to 88 clubs. The top clubs in the previous season's Premier Division were invited to take part in the Premier Inter League Challenge Cup, sponsored by Clubcall.

Premier Division	1	2	3	4	5	6	7	8	9	10	11	12	13	14	15	16	17	18	19	20	21	22
1 Aylesbury United	*	3–0	1–0	2–1	5–0	1–2	4–1	4–0	3–1	0–0	3–0	4–0	4–0	1–1	1–1	1–1	3–1	0–1	3–1	3–0	3–1	1–3
2 Barking	0–0	*	1–1	1–2	2–2	1–0	2–1	0–4	0–3	1–2	1–1	2–1	0–0	1–1	0–3	4–1	1–3	2–0	1–1	3–3	1–1	2–3
3 Basingstoke Town	0–0	2–1	*	0–0	2–1	2–0	2–0	3–1	7–0	1–1	1–0	3–1	3–2	1–2	1–1	3–0	4–0	3–1	1–3	3–1	0–0	1–2
4 Bishop's Stortford	0–3	0–4	1–0	*	0–1	2–0	3–1	1–0	1–2	0–2	1–1	3–5	5–0	0–1	2–1	2–1	3–4	3–2	0–1	1–0	0–2	1–2
5 Bognor Regis Tn	0–2	3–2	1–1	2–3	*	2–2	2–0	1–1	2–1	0–0	0–0	1–1	0–3	0–0	0–1	0–2	1–6	3–1	1–3	1–3	0–4	0–2
6 Bromley	0–4	0–2	0–1	2–2	0–0	*	1–0	2–5	2–0	0–1	1–1	2–0	1–4	1–1	0–2	1–1	1–1	1–1	0–1	3–0	1–1	1–5
7 Carshalton Athletic	1–0	4–2	2–2	1–2	3–1	1–0	*	2–0	0–1	1–2	3–3	3–0	3–1	2–0	2–0	0–1	5–1	1–2	4–4	3–1	1–1	0–2
8 Dagenham	1–0	1–1	3–2	1–0	0–1	1–0	0–2	*	1–1	0–0	3–0	2–1	1–1	2–0	1–0	6–1	2–2	1–3	0–3	1–1	0–0	2–2
9 Dulwich Hamlet	0–2	1–1	0–1	0–3	1–1	0–0	0–1	0–0	*	2–2	0–2	0–4	3–6	0–4	1–3	0–1	0–3	2–1	2–3	1–3	0–0	0–2
10 Grays Athletic	2–1	2–1	2–3	1–1	2–0	3–0	0–1	0–0	2–1	*	4–0	2–1	3–0	3–1	1–0	2–0	1–1	0–1	1–1	4–3	3–0	0–2
11 Harrow Borough	1–5	3–1	3–1	2–3	1–0	2–1	0–1	1–2	4–1	4–2	*	2–0	0–2	1–3	0–2	1–1	0–0	3–2	1–5	3–2	1–3	1–4
12 Hayes	1–1	6–1	1–0	0–0	2–0	4–1	0–1	0–0	2–1	2–2	1–1	*	3–1	0–1	1–3	4–1	0–2	2–0	1–1	0–1	3–1	2–3
13 Hendon	1–1	1–0	2–1	0–1	0–1	0–2	3–1	2–1	1–0	3–0	0–1	0–2	*	3–0	0–1	0–0	2–2	1–0	1–1	1–4	2–2	0–0
14 Kingstonian	1–1	3–2	5–0	6–0	3–3	4–2	3–2	4–3	1–0	4–2	2–1	1–0	3–0	*	2–3	4–2	3–1	4–2	1–2	3–0	2–0	4–2
15 Leyton-Wingate	1–3	2–1	4–1	0–3	1–1	3–1	1–0	0–1	1–0	1–1	1–0	2–2	2–3	1–0	*	0–0	2–1	0–1	1–2	2–4	1–3	2–1
16 Marlow	0–3	4–1	3–1	1–3	2–0	0–0	3–0	0–0	2–1	0–1	3–1	2–2	1–2	1–1	0–1	*	0–2	1–1	0–0	1–3	1–0	0–0
17 Redbridge Forest	1–2	3–1	4–0	3–1	0–2	0–1	3–1	1–1	2–1	2–1	3–1	1–2	1–1	1–2	0–1	2–1	*	1–1	2–0	1–1	1–1	1–1
18 St. Albans City	0–1	3–1	1–1	2–1	0–0	2–0	1–2	0–1	1–1	1–2	2–1	3–0	2–1	0–0	2–0	1–1	1–0	*	0–3	0–2	2–4	1–2
19 Slough Town	1–2	4–2	2–1	1–1	0–0	1–0	3–2	0–1	2–0	2–0	4–0	1–0	3–1	2–1	3–2	3–0	5–0	3–3	*	1–0	1–1	2–0
20 Staines Town	0–3	4–1	0–2	0–2	1–2	2–0	2–3	0–2	1–0	0–0	3–1	2–2	0–2	0–4	1–0	1–0	0–1	1–1	0–4	*	0–1	0–1
21 Windsor & Eton	2–1	1–1	0–2	0–2	2–1	4–0	0–0	1–2	1–2	0–0	1–1	0–1	3–0	1–1	0–0	0–2	4–1	1–0	0–1	0–3	*	3–0
22 Wokingham Town	1–1	2–1	2–1	1–0	2–0	1–0	0–1	0–0	1–1	2–0	1–1	1–1	1–1	2–0	1–0	1–0	1–0	2–0	1–1	2–0	3–1	*

Premier Division	*P*	*W*	*D*	*L*	*F*	*A*	*Pts*
1 Slough Town	42	27	11	4	85	38	92
2 Wokingham Town	42	26	11	5	67	34	89
3 Aylesbury United	42	25	9	8	86	30	84
4 Kingstonian	42	24	9	9	87	51	81
5 Grays Athletic	42	19	13	10	59	44	70
6 Dagenham	42	17	15	10	54	43	66
7 Leyton-Wingate	42	20	6	16	54	48	66
8 Basingstoke Town	42	18	9	15	65	55	63
9 Bishop's Stortford	42	19	6	17	60	59	63
10 Carshalton Ath.*	42	19	5	18	63	59	59
11 Redbridge Forest	42	16	11	15	65	62	59
12 Hendon	42	15	10	17	54	63	55
13 Windsor & Eton	42	13	15	14	51	47	54
14 Hayes	42	14	11	17	61	59	53
15 St. Albans City	42	13	10	19	49	59	49
16 Staines Town	42	14	6	22	53	69	48
17 Marlow	42	11	13	18	42	59	46
18 Harrow Borough	42	11	10	21	51	79	43
19 Bognor Regis Tn	42	9	14	19	37	67	41
20 Barking	42	7	11	24	53	86	32
21 Bromley	42	7	11	24	32	69	32
22 Dulwich Hamlet	42	6	8	28	32	80	26

**Carshalton Athletic had three points deducted.*
Leytonstone-Ilford amalgamated with Walthamstow Ave to form Redbridge Forest.

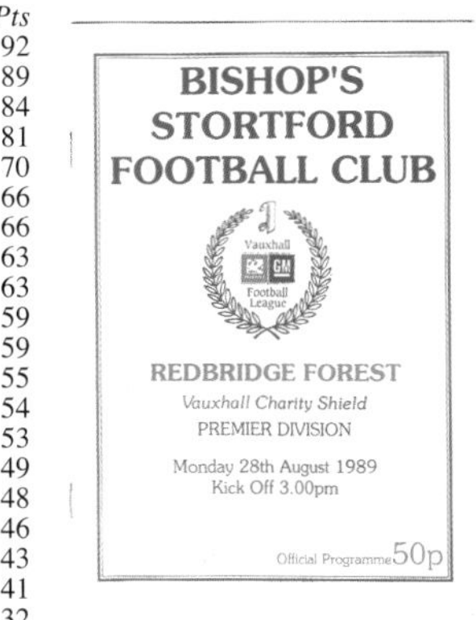

Left: the programme for the 1989 Charity Shield between League Champions Leytonstone-Ilford, who became Redbridge Forest, and League Cup winners Bishop's Stortford.

Right: the Wokingham Town matchday programme from season 1989-90.

1989-90 Division I	1	2	3	4	5	6	7	8	9	10	11	12	13	14	15	16	17	18	19	20	21	22
1 Boreham Wood	*	2–1	2–0	2–1	0–2	1–1	1–3	0–1	3–2	3–0	1–5	1–1	1–1	0–0	0–0	1–0	3–1	3–2	2–2	1–1	0–4	2–1
2 Chalfont St. Peter	1–0	*	0–0	1–1	0–2	3–1	4–1	0–5	3–1	2–2	2–1	1–0	3–0	0–0	1–0	2–2	0–2	0–4	1–2	2–1	1–1	0–2
3 Chesham United	2–2	2–1	*	1–1	0–1	0–1	1–0	1–1	2–2	1–0	4–1	2–1	2–0	2–0	0–0	1–5	0–1	1–0	0–1	0–1	2–4	2–1
4 Croydon	0–0	2–1	2–0	*	0–1	1–1	0–1	1–1	3–0	3–3	0–3	1–1	3–1	0–0	1–0	1–2	1–1	0–2	0–0	0–1	0–2	0–0
5 Dorking	2–0	2–3	2–1	2–0	*	3–0	1–1	0–0	2–1	1–1	2–2	0–1	5–1	0–0	3–0	2–1	1–1	1–2	3–2	1–2	0–0	1–1
6 Hampton	0–1	2–0	1–2	1–0	1–0	*	0–2	0–1	1–0	0–0	0–1	1–2	1–1	1–2	4–2	1–1	0–0	0–1	2–2	0–3	0–1	0–1
7 Harlow Town	1–1	1–2	5–1	0–0	0–0	1–1	*	0–1	4–0	0–2	3–1	2–2	0–1	0–3	0–1	3–1	3–2	3–2	2–2	1–2	2–2	4–1
8 Hitchin Town	2–2	2–0	1–0	2–1	3–1	2–1	1–1	*	1–1	2–0	1–0	2–0	0–1	0–0	3–0	3–0	1–0	2–1	0–1	1–3	1–3	2–1
9 Kingsbury Town	0–1	0–0	0–0	4–1	1–4	4–1	0–3	1–1	*	2–0	0–1	2–2	1–0	2–3	0–1	2–2	0–3	2–2	3–1	0–1	1–3	2–1
10 Leatherhead	2–3	1–0	0–1	0–1	0–2	0–0	1–2	0–3	2–0	*	1–1	1–0	2–1	1–4	2–3	0–2	1–1	1–2	1–2	0–1	0–2	1–3
11 Lewes	2–1	0–1	0–1	1–3	2–2	0–0	0–2	1–2	3–3	0–0	*	0–1	2–2	0–0	3–1	3–1	2–4	3–1	4–1	0–0	0–3	0–1
12 Metropolitan Police	3–1	1–1	1–5	2–1	2–1	0–1	0–1	1–1	1–0	1–1	3–0	*	1–0	0–4	1–2	4–2	0–4	2–0	0–0	1–3	3–3	2–1
13 Purfleet	1–2	2–2	0–0	3–0	0–4	1–0	2–3	1–1	0–5	2–0	1–3	1–2	*	2–3	0–0	0–1	1–2	2–1	0–1	1–2	0–1	0–0
14 Southwick	1–0	0–2	1–1	3–1	2–0	3–1	0–0	0–0	6–0	3–0	1–0	2–0	2–1	*	1–0	0–0	3–2	1–0	4–0	1–1	1–1	1–1
15 Tooting & M Utd	0–1	0–0	2–0	0–0	2–1	0–0	0–1	0–4	1–1	0–0	3–1	1–1	4–0	5–1	*	0–3	2–1	2–1	0–0	2–1	2–2	2–1
16 Uxbridge	2–2	0–0	1–2	1–2	0–3	0–0	2–2	0–2	1–0	3–0	0–3	2–0	3–1	0–4	0–0	*	0–1	2–6	0–1	0–3	2–3	1–1
17 Walton & Hersham	1–4	1–1	0–0	1–5	2–1	0–0	1–0	2–1	1–0	4–2	0–0	2–1	3–0	1–2	4–0	2–1	*	4–1	1–1	1–3	1–1	3–0
18 Wembley	1–2	1–1	1–1	1–1	1–3	3–1	0–0	0–0	1–2	3–1	0–1	0–1	3–0	2–3	2–2	2–1	1–0	*	0–0	1–5	0–3	1–2
19 Whyteleafe	3–2	2–3	2–2	1–1	1–1	0–1	5–2	1–1	3–0	2–3	2–2	1–3	1–2	1–1	1–0	0–2	0–3	1–1	*	0–4	0–0	1–2
20 Wivenhoe Town	3–2	3–1	3–1	3–2	1–1	2–1	0–0	1–0	3–0	4–0	2–1	2–2	2–0	1–1	0–1	5–2	4–1	4–1	4–1	*	1–2	3–1
21 Woking	1–2	4–1	1–0	5–0	3–0	2–0	4–0	3–0	3–0	6–0	6–0	1–0	4–0	1–0	2–0	6–1	3–1	2–1	0–1	1–2	*	2–1
22 Worthing	2–2	3–2	0–2	2–2	0–2	2–0	2–0	0–2	3–0	1–2	3–2	2–4	2–0	0–1	3–1	1–2	0–2	2–2	2–1	1–3	2–1	*

Division I	P	W	D	L	F	A	Pts
1 Wivenhoe Town	42	31	7	4	94	36	100
2 Woking	42	30	8	4	102	29	98
3 Southwick	42	23	15	4	68	30	84
4 Hitchin Town	42	22	13	7	60	30	79
5 Walton & Hersham	42	20	10	12	68	50	70
6 Dorking	42	19	12	11	66	41	69
7 Boreham Wood	42	17	13	12	60	59	64
8 Harlow Town	42	16	13	13	60	53	61
9 Metropolitan Police	42	16	11	15	54	59	59
10 Chesham United	42	15	12	15	46	49	57
11 Chalfont St. Peter	42	14	13	15	50	59	55
12 Tooting & M Utd	42	14	13	15	42	51	55
13 Worthing	42	15	8	19	56	63	53
14 Whyteleafe	42	11	16	15	50	65	49
15 Lewes	42	12	11	19	55	65	47
16 Wembley	42	11	10	21	57	68	43
17 Croydon	42	9	16	17	43	57	43
18 Uxbridge	42	11	10	21	52	75	43
19 Hampton	42	8	13	21	28	51	37
20 Leatherhead	42	7	10	25	34	77	31
21 Purfleet	42	7	8	27	33	78	29
22 Kingsbury Town*	42	8	10	24	45	78	25

** Kingsbury Town had nine points deducted.*

Left: the Chesham United matchday programme from season 1989-90.

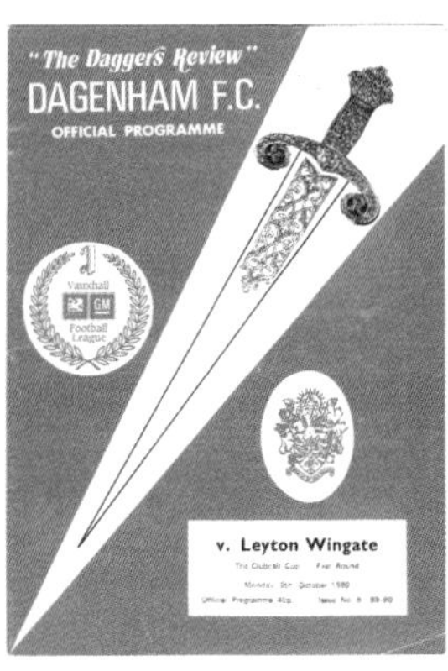

Right: the programme from the ClubCall Cup First Round tie between Dagenham and Leyton-Wingate.

Division II North	1	2	3	4	5	6	7	8	9	10	11	12	13	14	15	16	17	18	19	20	21	22
1 Aveley	*	3–0	0–1	3–1	0–0	0–0	0–0	1–1	1–1	1–1	1–0	0–0	3–0	3–1	3–0	2–2	1–1	3–2	4–1	0–0	0–0	1–0
2 Barton Rovers	3–1	*	0–0	1–3	0–0	1–0	1–2	1–0	1–0	1–2	0–1	3–0	3–1	3–1	2–0	0–0	0–2	1–0	2–2	1–0	2–0	1–0
3 Basildon United	1–2	0–1	*	2–3	1–0	0–0	1–1	3–3	4–0	0–1	1–1	0–0	0–0	2–2	0–1	1–1	1–1	2–1	1–0	1–1	0–2	1–1
4 Berkhamsted Town	2–1	2–2	0–2	*	1–4	0–2	0–1	1–1	2–2	2–2	0–3	0–3	2–0	2–1	0–2	3–0	2–2	0–1	2–0	0–3	2–2	2–2
5 Billericay Town	0–3	4–2	1–1	2–0	*	0–4	2–1	0–0	1–1	4–0	0–1	0–2	1–2	5–0	1–1	2–1	0–0	0–2	0–1	1–2	5–0	0–3
6 Clapton	1–2	0–2	0–0	1–1	2–2	*	0–2	2–1	1–1	3–2	0–2	1–2	3–1	1–2	4–1	1–1	2–0	3–0	0–1	3–0	2–0	3–0
7 Collier Row	0–3	1–3	0–2	1–3	2–1	0–0	*	1–1	2–1	1–1	0–1	0–0	2–0	0–3	1–4	0–3	0–0	1–3	2–1	1–1	1–0	5–1
8 Finchley	0–1	0–3	0–2	2–1	1–1	2–3	0–3	*	1–0	0–3	2–3	1–2	4–0	1–0	5–1	1–1	0–4	2–1	0–3	1–1	2–3	1–0
9 Hemel Hempstead	1–1	1–0	3–1	2–1	1–0	4–0	1–1	4–1	*	1–4	1–4	3–1	1–1	0–1	2–2	0–0	0–4	3–1	1–1	1–1	0–3	1–1
10 Hertford Town	1–1	1–0	0–0	6–0	4–0	4–2	0–3	1–1	3–2	*	3–1	2–0	3–1	5–1	1–2	5–2	2–3	2–2	4–1	4–3	1–0	2–0
11 Heybridge Swifts	1–1	2–1	1–0	0–0	5–0	0–0	0–2	5–0	4–0	0–0	*	0–1	0–0	1–0	0–1	6–0	1–0	6–1	4–1	5–1	0–2	3–1
12 Hornchurch	0–0	2–4	1–1	0–0	1–1	1–0	1–0	4–2	1–1	0–2	1–4	*	1–1	4–3	3–4	1–2	0–2	2–3	0–2	1–2	1–4	2–1
13 Letchworth G City	0–3	2–3	0–1	2–2	0–1	0–0	0–0	3–0	0–1	0–4	0–2	0–3	*	1–1	0–3	0–0	0–0	1–2	1–3	0–1	2–1	1–0
14 Rainham Town	0–0	2–1	1–2	1–1	1–2	1–1	3–0	0–2	2–4	1–1	2–2	1–0	0–2	*	0–2	2–3	1–1	0–1	2–1	0–3	1–2	1–0
15 Royston Town	0–1	0–4	1–1	2–0	1–3	1–2	2–1	2–3	3–3	1–2	1–2	2–2	1–3	2–2	*	1–2	0–0	0–0	2–1	2–2	2–4	2–2
16 Saffron Walden Tn	1–4	2–0	2–2	2–0	2–0	2–2	0–2	1–0	2–0	3–2	2–0	3–1	3–2	2–0	1–2	*	1–2	1–2	1–3	1–1	0–5	2–1
17 Stevenage Borough	0–3	2–0	3–3	0–0	1–0	5–0	0–1	2–0	2–1	2–1	2–2	1–0	0–0	1–1	4–0	4–1	*	1–1	1–1	3–1	4–1	0–0
18 Tilbury	0–2	1–2	4–1	0–1	5–2	0–0	0–0	2–1	3–3	1–3	1–1	2–0	1–0	3–1	3–0	3–3	0–1	*	3–1	0–1	5–0	1–0
19 Tring Town	0–4	0–1	2–3	0–0	0–1	0–0	0–0	2–3	2–2	1–2	0–1	1–1	5–0	3–0	0–5	2–1	1–3	0–2	*	1–3	1–2	1–1
20 Vauxhall Motors	0–2	3–1	1–2	4–1	2–0	0–0	0–1	3–1	1–2	3–3	0–1	0–2	1–1	2–1	1–2	2–1	1–3	0–1	3–0	*	0–2	0–0
21 Ware	1–2	1–1	1–1	0–0	0–1	0–0	1–0	1–1	2–3	1–1	0–2	1–1	3–1	1–3	0–1	2–1	0–3	1–2	0–1	0–0	*	2–2
22 Witham Town	0–1	1–2	1–2	1–1	1–1	2–1	1–1	0–2	3–0	0–1	0–1	4–1	0–1	2–2	1–1	4–1	1–0	2–2	2–1	1–1	1–2	*

Division II North	P	W	D	L	F	A	Pts
1 Heybridge Swifts	42	26	9	7	79	29	87
2 Aveley	42	23	16	3	68	24	85
3 Hertford Town	42	24	11	7	92	51	83
4 Stevenage Borough	42	21	16	5	70	31	79
5 Barton Rovers	42	22	6	14	60	45	72
6 Tilbury	42	20	9	13	68	54	69
7 Basildon United	42	13	20	9	50	44	59
8 Collier Row	42	15	13	14	43	45	58
9 Royston Town	42	15	11	16	60	73	56
10 Saffron Walden Tn	42	15	11	16	60	73	56
11 Vauxhall Motors	42	14	13	15	55	54	55
12 Clapton*	42	13	16	13	50	46	54
13 Ware	42	14	11	17	53	59	53
14 Hemel Hempstead	42	12	15	15	58	70	51
15 Billericay Town	42	13	11	18	49	58	50
16 Hornchurch	42	12	12	18	49	64	48
17 Berkhamsted Town	42	9	16	17	44	68	43
18 Finchley	42	11	10	21	50	75	43
19 Tring Town	42	10	9	23	48	70	39
20 Witham Town	42	8	14	20	44	56	38
21 Rainham Town	42	9	11	22	48	75	38
22 Letchworth G City	42	7	12	23	30	68	33

** Clapton had one point deducted.*

Left: the Southwick edition from the same season.

Right: the Bracknell Town matchday programme from season 1989-90.

1989-90

Division II South	1	2	3	4	5	6	7	8	9	10	11	12	13	14	15	16	17	18	19	20	21
1 Abingdon Town	*	5–3	2–0	1–0	1–0	4–0	2–1	2–1	4–2	3–2	2–0	1–1	2–2	1–0	1–0	0–0	2–0	7–0	1–1	0–1	2–3
2 Banstead Athletic	0–1	*	1–1	7–1	0–2	0–0	1–0	0–1	4–1	2–2	1–0	1–0	1–0	3–0	0–1	0–2	1–3	0–1	1–2	0–0	0–1
3 Bracknell Town	0–3	1–1	*	2–3	0–2	1–2	0–2	0–3	3–1	7–0	1–0	1–0	0–1	2–3	3–1	0–2	0–2	1–1	0–0	0–2	2–3
4 Camberley Town	2–1	1–0	0–0	*	1–0	1–1	1–2	0–0	4–0	3–2	0–1	1–3	4–1	0–3	0–1	0–7	2–0	3–3	1–2	2–0	0–2
5 Chertsey Town	1–2	3–1	0–0	0–0	*	1–2	2–0	1–1	4–1	1–3	1–3	1–1	2–2	2–6	2–0	2–1	1–0	2–0	0–1	1–2	2–3
6 Eastbourne United	0–0	1–2	1–2	2–0	1–2	*	1–1	1–0	0–1	2–0	1–3	2–1	2–1	1–1	2–2	3–5	0–1	3–1	0–4	2–0	1–1
7 Egham Town	0–1	0–0	4–0	1–1	3–2	3–2	*	1–1	1–0	0–2	0–1	3–0	0–0	0–1	4–1	0–1	1–0	2–2	1–1	2–2	0–1
8 Epsom & Ewell	3–0	1–1	2–3	1–0	1–2	3–1	0–0	*	0–2	2–2	0–2	4–1	1–0	0–2	0–1	0–0	0–1	2–1	0–5	0–2	1–2
9 Feltham	1–3	2–1	1–0	2–2	1–1	2–1	1–1	0–3	*	3–4	0–1	3–1	2–0	0–1	1–0	1–4	0–3	1–3	3–2	0–1	2–1
10 Flackwell Heath	2–1	1–1	3–1	1–0	4–2	1–1	1–1	1–1	0–2	*	2–0	3–0	1–1	3–0	3–1	1–1	0–2	4–0	1–0	3–5	0–2
11 Harefield United	1–1	0–1	1–1	2–0	0–3	3–0	0–1	2–3	1–1	3–3	*	1–0	0–1	0–1	0–1	3–2	0–0	3–2	0–0	0–1	3–2
12 Horsham	0–2	0–1	0–0	0–2	0–1	1–4	0–1	0–3	3–0	0–0	0–4	*	2–2	1–3	2–4	1–2	0–1	1–2	2–3	0–2	0–1
13 Hungerford Town	1–0	3–2	0–3	3–3	3–2	1–1	0–0	3–1	2–0	3–2	0–0	2–1	*	1–3	1–1	2–1	1–1	4–0	1–1	2–1	0–1
14 Maidenhead Utd	0–0	1–2	0–0	1–0	1–1	1–0	0–0	1–0	5–2	4–3	0–0	1–1	2–0	*	2–3	1–1	0–0	5–2	0–0	1–0	2–1
15 Malden Vale	0–0	0–2	2–0	1–3	1–0	0–3	1–0	0–5	2–0	1–2	1–1	0–1	1–1	0–6	*	0–2	2–0	3–0	0–2	0–1	0–5
16 Molesey	2–0	1–0	0–1	2–0	3–0	1–1	2–0	3–1	4–1	2–2	1–0	2–1	1–1	0–0	3–0	*	1–1	2–1	3–1	0–0	1–0
17 Newbury Town	1–2	1–0	1–0	1–0	3–1	5–1	1–1	3–0	3–2	1–0	1–0	0–1	2–4	2–1	1–1	2–1	*	2–0	0–2	1–1	1–2
18 Petersfield United	1–1	1–3	2–4	2–0	2–2	2–1	0–1	3–2	2–2	3–0	3–2	2–1	0–0	0–4	2–2	0–3	1–2	*	0–2	0–2	1–3
19 Ruislip Manor	4–1	2–0	2–0	2–2	1–1	2–0	1–0	0–0	3–1	1–0	2–1	1–1	0–1	1–1	2–0	2–2	2–0	0–1	*	1–0	2–3
20 Southall	0–1	1–2	2–0	4–1	1–0	2–0	1–0	4–0	2–2	1–3	3–0	2–0	2–1	1–0	0–1	0–3	0–1	4–0	2–0	*	1–2
21 Yeading	3–1	3–0	1–0	2–0	2–0	3–0	4–1	1–2	0–0	1–2	3–2	1–1	2–2	5–2	4–0	1–2	2–0	7–1	1–0	1–0	*

Division II South	*P*	*W*	*D*	*L*	*F*	*A*	*Pts*
1 Yeading	40	29	4	7	86	37	91
2 Molesey	40	24	11	5	76	30	83
3 Abingdon Town	40	22	9	9	64	39	75
4 Ruislip Manor	40	20	12	8	60	32	72
5 Maidenhead Utd	40	20	12	8	66	39	72
6 Southall	40	22	5	13	56	33	71
7 Newbury Town	40	21	7	12	50	36	70
8 Flackwell Heath	40	16	11	13	69	65	59
9 Hungerford Town	40	14	16	10	54	51	58
10 Egham Town	40	12	14	14	39	38	50
11 Banstead Athletic	40	14	8	18	46	47	50
12 Harefield United	40	13	9	18	44	46	48
13 Chertsey Town	40	13	9	18	53	58	48
14 Epsom & Ewell	40	13	9	18	49	54	48
15 Malden Vale	40	13	7	20	36	67	46
16 Eastbourne United	40	11	10	19	47	65	43
17 Camberley Town	40	11	9	20	44	66	42
18 Feltham	40	11	7	22	47	80	40
19 Bracknell Town	40	10	9	21	40	57	39
20 Petersfield United	40	10	8	22	48	93	38
21 Horsham	40	4	8	28	29	70	20

Left: the Flackwell Heath matchday programme from season 1989-90.

Right: the programme for Basingstoke Town's ClubCall Cup tie against Staines Town.

RELEGATION PLAY-OFF
FIRST LEG: Letchworth Garden City 1, Horsham 2;
SECOND LEG: Horsham 1, Letchworth Garden City 0. Horsham won 3–1 on aggregate.
Letchworth Garden City were relegated to the South Midlands League.

Left: the Malden Vale programme from season 1989-90.

Right: the programme for Letchworth Garden City's play-off match with Horsham.

1990–91 - Redbridge Forest, having been turned down by the Vauxhall Conference as Leytonstone-Ilford in 1989, were this time successful having settled in at Dagenham FC where there were major improvements to bring their ground up to standard. Redbridge Forest, managed by John Still, secured the championship by four points from Enfield who were managed by Peter Taylor. Aylesbury United finished third for the second year running while Woking enjoyed their first season in the top division by finishing in fourth place. Wivenhoe Town also had an enjoyable first season in the Premier Division while two other Essex clubs, Barking and Leyton-Wingate, were relegated. In Division One Chesham United were promoted to the Premier Division for the first time in their history while runners-up Bromley gained an immediate return following relegation the previous year. Relegated to Division Two were Metropolitan Police and Sussex clubs Southwick, Lewes and Worthing with the latter conceding a record 157 goals. In the regionalised Division Twos Stevenage Borough romped away with the championship by scoring 122 goals and gaining 107 points as well as having a 100% home record which was a first in the League's history for a forty-two match programme. Joining Stevenage Borough in Division One were Vauxhall Motors who were runners-up while a much closer league in the South division saw Abingdon Town clinch the championship five points clear of runners-up Maidenhead United. Egham Town finished third. At the bottom end of the Division Two tables Tring Town in Division Two North and Camberley Town in Division Two South both only won one League game all season. It was announced that Vauxhall Motors would be ending their sponsorship of the League at the conclusion of the season. The company had sponsored the League for six years.

At the Annual General Meeting Sutton United, relegated from the Vauxhall Conference, replaced champions Redbridge Forest. A reorganisation in Division Two was agreed when the top clubs of Division Two North and South would form Division Two while the remainder would play in Division Three with three clubs being promoted and relegated throughout the divisions. Basildon United had resigned due to the extra travelling involved while Finchley merged with Wingate and subsequently resigned, opting to join the South Midlands League where Wingate had been members. Thame United from the South Midlands League were elected to Division Three leaving that division with 21 clubs. Division Two South club Feltham had merged with Hounslow Town and would be known as Feltham & Hounslow Borough.

1990-91

Premier Division	1	2	3	4	5	6	7	8	9	10	11	12	13	14	15	16	17	18	19	20	21	22
1 Aylesbury United	*	2–1	3–0	1–0	4–1	3–2	2–1	1–0	1–0	6–1	4–0	2–0	3–0	3–0	2–0	3–1	3–0	2–2	1–2	1–2	2–3	3–1
2 Barking	3–2	*	4–2	0–5	0–2	0–2	0–2	1–1	0–1	0–2	2–1	1–1	0–2	0–0	0–8	0–1	3–3	1–1	1–1	1–4	0–1	0–0
3 Basingstoke Town	1–1	3–2	*	3–2	2–5	0–4	4–0	0–4	2–1	1–1	2–4	2–4	2–0	0–1	0–2	1–2	0–4	1–0	1–1	0–1	0–6	2–2
4 Bishop's Stortford	0–2	3–2	1–1	*	0–2	3–2	1–0	0–0	1–1	2–0	4–2	0–0	1–1	3–1	1–4	1–2	0–1	3–0	1–3	1–2	2–0	1–0
5 Bognor Regis Tn	1–1	0–1	3–1	1–0	*	1–1	2–0	1–2	0–3	1–1	0–1	1–1	1–3	0–0	1–2	2–4	1–2	1–1	1–1	0–2	0–2	1–0
6 Carshalton Athletic	3–5	4–0	2–4	3–1	4–0	*	0–3	0–2	3–1	2–2	2–0	1–0	3–2	2–2	0–0	1–1	0–4	2–0	1–0	2–1	2–2	1–2
7 Dagenham	3–2	0–0	5–2	0–0	0–2	1–3	*	1–3	2–2	1–3	4–0	3–2	2–2	1–0	1–2	1–1	2–2	4–0	2–2	2–2	0–1	1–1
8 Enfield	1–1	2–2	2–0	0–0	4–0	2–0	1–1	*	3–0	6–1	3–1	4–0	3–0	3–1	3–0	0–3	1–1	0–0	1–0	2–0	2–0	2–1
9 Grays Athletic	4–1	5–1	5–3	1–2	2–0	1–0	3–2	0–2	*	0–2	1–0	2–0	2–1	1–1	3–1	0–2	3–0	1–3	1–0	2–2	1–1	0–1
10 Harrow Borough	2–2	3–4	0–1	2–1	1–3	1–3	4–1	2–4	1–3	*	1–2	1–3	0–2	2–1	2–0	2–3	1–1	2–1	3–3	1–3	0–1	3–3
11 Hayes	2–2	2–1	2–3	2–0	0–0	1–1	1–0	0–3	0–2	2–0	*	3–1	0–0	3–0	0–0	2–0	1–2	2–0	3–0	0–1	4–1	4–1
12 Hendon	1–1	0–1	1–2	1–1	0–3	0–2	1–2	1–1	0–1	1–1	1–0	*	3–1	3–3	0–2	2–0	2–2	0–1	0–0	2–3	3–1	1–0
13 Kingstonian	0–0	5–1	5–2	2–2	4–1	3–1	2–0	4–1	5–1	2–0	0–1	2–1	*	3–1	1–1	2–2	5–2	2–0	1–1	3–1	4–2	1–1
14 Leyton-Wingate	0–4	2–0	1–2	0–3	3–1	1–3	1–4	1–4	1–2	1–0	1–2	0–2	2–2	*	0–2	1–2	3–0	1–2	2–0	1–2	0–4	1–4
15 Marlow	3–3	3–1	2–0	3–1	5–0	5–1	3–0	1–1	1–0	3–1	0–2	1–3	1–1	1–0	*	1–2	0–0	2–1	0–0	1–1	1–1	0–1
16 Redbridge Forest	0–4	2–1	2–0	1–0	1–0	2–1	1–0	2–1	1–1	1–0	1–0	2–0	2–0	7–4	5–1	*	2–1	2–0	3–0	2–0	0–1	2–4
17 St. Albans City	1–2	1–2	1–1	2–3	1–1	2–1	2–4	0–1	0–3	1–0	1–2	3–0	3–4	2–1	0–4	1–2	*	2–2	0–1	1–0	1–2	2–2
18 Staines Town	0–1	1–2	2–1	0–0	1–2	0–4	5–1	1–1	1–3	2–0	2–3	1–2	0–3	2–1	2–2	2–1	3–3	*	1–0	1–2	0–7	1–1
19 Windsor & Eton	1–2	2–1	1–0	1–0	2–0	3–2	1–2	0–3	1–0	0–5	1–4	0–1	1–3	6–2	1–0	1–2	2–0	2–1	*	3–2	2–1	0–2
20 Wivenhoe Town	1–1	2–1	3–3	0–4	1–2	1–3	1–1	0–1	3–1	2–3	3–0	1–3	6–1	1–1	1–1	0–1	1–1	3–0	2–2	*	4–4	2–1
21 Woking	3–1	0–0	0–2	0–0	3–0	2–4	1–0	2–1	1–1	4–0	4–0	2–0	0–0	3–0	4–1	0–0	2–0	5–1	0–0	1–0	*	4–0
22 Wokingham Town	0–0	1–0	3–0	0–0	3–0	3–2	0–2	0–2	1–1	1–0	2–1	2–1	0–2	0–1	2–2	1–1	1–4	1–1	5–0	4–0	0–2	*

Premier Division	*P*	*W*	*D*	*L*	*F*	*A*	*Pts*
1 Redbridge Forest	42	29	6	7	74	43	93
2 Enfield	42	26	11	5	83	30	89
3 Aylesbury United	42	24	11	7	90	47	83
4 Woking	42	24	10	8	84	39	82
5 Kingstonian	42	21	12	9	86	57	75
6 Grays Athletic	42	20	8	14	66	53	68
7 Marlow	42	18	13	11	72	49	67
8 Hayes	42	20	5	17	60	57	65
9 Carshalton Athletic	42	19	7	16	80	67	64
10 Wivenhoe Town	42	16	11	15	69	66	59
11 Wokingham Town	42	15	13	14	58	54	58
12 Windsor & Eton	42	15	10	17	48	63	55
13 Bishop's Stortford	42	14	12	16	54	49	54
14 Dagenham	42	13	11	18	62	68	50
15 Hendon	42	12	10	20	48	62	46
16 St. Albans City	42	11	12	19	60	74	45
17 Bognor Regis Tn	42	12	8	22	44	71	44
18 Basingstoke Town	42	12	7	23	57	95	43
19 Staines Town*	42	10	10	22	46	79	39
20 Harrow Borough	42	10	8	24	57	84	38
21 Barking	42	8	10	24	41	85	34
22 Leyton-Wingate	42	7	7	28	44	91	28

** Staines Town had one point deducted.*

Left: Dagenham take on the team with which they were soon to merge. The game finished all square at 1-1.

Right: the programme for Redbridge Forest's match with Aylesbury United, which the visitors won 4-0.

Division I	1	2	3	4	5	6	7	8	9	10	11	12	13	14	15	16	17	18	19	20	21	22
1 Aveley	*	0–0	1–1	4–1	1–1	1–2	4–1	2–2	2–2	2–1	1–1	1–2	2–1	0–1	2–0	0–1	3–0	2–0	1–1	1–2	5–1	1–0
2 Boreham Wood	0–2	*	1–2	1–0	2–3	0–1	1–2	2–2	0–0	3–1	1–2	3–1	3–0	3–2	0–0	1–0	4–1	2–1	0–2	0–2	3–2	2–1
3 Bromley	2–3	3–0	*	1–1	2–0	3–0	0–3	0–0	3–2	0–0	3–1	5–1	2–0	1–0	1–1	1–1	2–1	1–0	3–0	1–1	3–0	1–0
4 Chalfont St. Peter	1–0	3–1	0–0	*	1–0	2–1	4–2	1–0	2–1	1–1	0–3	3–0	2–0	0–1	1–0	1–1	0–2	0–1	2–1	0–1	3–1	1–4
5 Chesham United	3–1	2–1	0–1	3–2	*	4–0	2–0	2–0	2–1	5–1	0–0	5–2	1–3	0–2	8–1	0–0	0–1	2–1	1–1	7–2	8–0	2–2
6 Croydon	0–5	1–2	0–0	2–1	0–4	*	2–0	1–3	2–4	1–0	1–1	1–0	0–5	0–3	1–0	0–4	0–2	1–3	2–1	3–0	2–1	1–3
7 Dorking	0–3	1–0	0–0	5–0	0–3	0–0	*	2–4	1–0	4–0	5–2	3–0	4–2	4–3	2–1	2–4	0–1	2–2	0–2	0–1	4–0	3–2
8 Dulwich Hamlet	1–1	1–0	0–1	1–0	1–3	1–2	4–1	*	1–3	1–2	0–2	0–0	2–1	0–0	4–0	0–1	3–0	0–2	3–3	0–2	9–0	0–0
9 Harlow Town	4–1	2–0	3–0	0–1	0–3	0–2	0–3	1–1	*	1–1	1–3	3–2	2–0	4–1	1–0	1–1	1–1	3–1	0–4	4–3	6–2	0–1
10 Heybridge Swifts	0–2	0–0	0–2	2–1	0–2	2–2	1–2	0–1	0–4	*	1–4	5–0	1–1	1–2	0–0	3–0	1–2	1–0	0–1	2–0	0–0	2–1
11 Hitchin Town	2–0	1–2	0–0	2–0	1–1	6–3	1–4	2–3	1–0	3–1	*	2–0	2–1	2–0	6–1	0–2	4–0	0–1	2–1	2–0	9–1	0–1
12 Lewes	1–2	0–0	3–4	1–2	1–4	1–2	3–2	5–2	2–2	0–2	1–1	*	1–3	2–1	0–0	1–2	0–1	2–3	0–1	1–0	4–1	1–5
13 Metropolitan Police	0–4	0–1	3–1	1–2	0–3	5–1	2–3	1–3	0–2	0–2	0–2	0–1	*	1–1	4–0	1–3	1–2	1–1	2–3	0–2	2–0	4–1
14 Molesey	0–1	3–1	1–2	2–0	1–3	1–0	3–0	0–1	4–2	1–0	0–0	2–0	1–0	*	4–1	1–0	1–0	0–3	1–1	2–0	3–0	1–1
15 Southwick	0–2	2–0	1–0	2–1	1–0	2–0	3–5	1–1	1–2	0–2	3–0	0–0	2–2	2–4	*	1–3	1–0	0–2	5–2	0–1	8–3	2–0
16 Tooting & M Utd	0–0	1–0	2–2	2–5	1–1	1–2	1–1	2–1	0–0	2–0	2–1	1–1	2–1	1–3	5–1	*	5–0	4–4	1–1	0–1	5–1	0–2
17 Uxbridge	0–3	0–1	1–1	0–2	0–3	3–0	1–4	0–1	1–0	3–3	1–0	1–2	1–1	1–2	0–1	1–3	*	1–0	1–2	0–1	4–1	0–1
18 Walton & Hersham	3–1	2–1	1–1	2–0	0–0	4–0	2–1	2–2	3–1	0–2	4–0	3–1	3–0	3–1	2–1	1–3	0–2	*	3–3	0–2	4–0	1–1
19 Wembley	1–2	0–1	0–1	2–3	3–4	3–0	0–0	3–1	1–3	0–0	0–2	0–1	2–1	2–1	0–1	3–0	1–1	1–2	*	2–2	4–0	1–1
20 Whyteleafe	2–1	1–1	1–3	2–4	0–2	3–0	1–0	1–2	3–1	0–1	1–1	1–0	2–1	2–1	1–1	0–2	2–1	1–0	1–1	*	10–0	1–3
21 Worthing	0–4	1–1	2–0	2–2	0–4	0–4	1–2	0–5	0–3	1–3	0–0	1–3	2–3	0–4	0–1	0–2	0–6	0–3	3–2	0–2	*	0–3
22 Yeading	2–1	2–1	1–2	5–0	0–1	1–1	1–0	2–0	4–3	4–1	3–4	2–2	1–1	1–0	3–1	2–0	0–1	1–0	1–0	2–1	4–1	*

Division I	*P*	*W*	*D*	*L*	*F*	*A*	*Pts*
1 Chesham United	42	27	8	7	102	37	89
2 Bromley	42	22	14	6	62	37	80
3 Yeading	42	23	8	11	75	45	77
4 Aveley	42	21	9	12	76	43	72
5 Hitchin Town	42	21	9	12	78	50	72
6 Tooting & M Utd	42	20	12	10	71	48	72
7 Walton & Hersham	42	21	8	13	73	48	71
8 Molesey	42	22	5	15	65	46	71
9 Whyteleafe	42	21	6	15	62	53	69
10 Dorking	42	20	5	17	78	67	65
11 Chalfont St. Peter	42	19	5	18	56	63	62
12 Dulwich Hamlet	42	16	11	15	67	54	59
13 Harlow Town	42	17	8	17	73	64	59
14 Boreham Wood	42	15	8	19	46	53	53
15 Wembley	42	13	12	17	62	59	51
16 Uxbridge	42	15	5	22	45	61	50
17 Croydon	42	15	5	22	44	85	50
18 Heybridge Swifts	42	13	10	19	46	59	49
19 Southwick	42	13	8	21	49	75	47
20 Lewes	42	10	8	24	49	82	38
21 Metropolitan Police	42	9	6	27	55	76	33
22 Worthing	42	2	4	36	28	157	10

Left: Division One champions Chesham United's programme for the 1990-91 season.

Right: the programme for Aylesbury United's FA Cup First Round tie against Walsall.

1990-91

Division II North	1	2	3	4	5	6	7	8	9	10	11	12	13	14	15	16	17	18	19	20	21	22
1 Barton Rovers	*	5–0	1–2	0–1	2–0	0–0	3–1	5–1	2–1	0–0	0–1	3–0	1–1	2–1	1–1	2–1	0–2	2–2	0–0	0–1	2–0	2–1
2 Basildon United	1–0	*	0–4	0–0	3–2	0–0	1–3	3–2	1–1	1–1	2–0	3–4	2–2	2–0	1–5	0–1	2–2	2–3	3–2	2–2	0–4	0–1
3 Berkhamsted Town	2–0	1–1	*	1–0	1–1	2–1	1–2	2–1	2–1	0–1	0–0	1–0	2–2	1–0	1–1	7–1	0–0	1–0	1–0	1–1	1–1	1–1
4 Billericay Town	2–0	1–0	3–0	*	1–1	0–1	3–1	0–1	2–2	4–2	4–0	3–1	1–3	1–1	1–2	4–2	0–1	1–2	5–0	3–2	1–0	2–1
5 Clapton	0–1	1–4	4–2	0–1	*	1–1	2–3	4–2	1–4	2–3	1–2	1–2	0–0	1–1	3–2	2–2	0–5	5–2	1–0	0–0	1–2	3–3
6 Collier Row	1–3	3–1	4–1	1–1	3–0	*	1–0	1–0	3–1	1–1	1–1	1–2	0–2	1–4	1–1	1–3	0–3	3–0	3–3	1–4	1–3	2–0
7 Edgware Town	3–1	4–0	0–2	1–1	3–0	6–1	*	6–3	2–3	0–3	2–0	2–0	1–2	0–1	1–1	3–0	1–4	5–3	5–0	3–0	1–0	0–1
8 Finchley	1–3	0–4	1–3	0–2	4–1	0–2	0–1	*	0–3	4–3	0–4	2–5	1–2	1–2	1–5	1–3	0–6	1–4	1–1	3–3	2–4	2–3
9 Hemel Hempstead	0–0	3–1	1–1	1–0	1–1	1–1	2–1	4–0	*	0–3	1–0	1–0	2–2	0–1	1–4	1–1	2–1	1–3	0–0	1–1	2–2	0–0
10 Hertford Town	2–4	5–2	1–0	0–1	3–1	0–2	0–0	2–1	0–1	*	3–2	0–1	1–3	2–1	0–1	2–2	0–0	0–2	3–2	1–3	2–1	4–4
11 Hornchurch	3–1	0–0	1–3	0–1	2–2	0–4	3–3	2–2	1–2	2–3	*	4–2	1–3	0–2	2–1	1–1	1–3	1–0	2–1	1–4	2–5	4–1
12 Kingsbury Town	1–1	3–2	1–0	0–3	0–2	0–1	1–0	1–3	3–1	2–4	3–1	*	3–2	1–0	1–1	3–1	2–2	5–2	1–1	0–2	0–1	2–1
13 Purfleet	2–2	0–2	1–2	1–1	2–1	3–1	3–0	1–0	1–3	4–0	1–1	3–1	*	1–0	2–2	0–0	1–3	0–2	2–2	0–3	3–3	1–0
14 Rainham Town	2–0	0–1	0–1	5–4	1–0	2–1	0–1	0–0	2–1	2–0	4–2	1–2	1–1	*	1–0	1–0	0–1	2–1	2–1	1–2	2–2	1–1
15 Royston Town	1–2	3–3	2–2	1–2	3–0	2–2	1–1	2–2	0–3	2–1	4–2	1–1	1–2	3–2	*	2–2	2–3	3–1	5–0	2–1	2–0	0–1
16 Saffron Walden Tn	4–4	3–2	5–1	2–0	0–3	4–4	4–1	1–0	1–1	3–3	1–0	4–4	2–1	0–3	1–1	*	1–0	0–2	3–1	3–1	2–3	1–1
17 Stevenage Borough	3–0	3–1	4–0	2–0	7–1	2–1	3–2	7–0	6–0	1–0	7–0	2–1	3–0	3–2	2–1	3–1	*	4–0	5–1	4–0	2–0	2–0
18 Tilbury	6–0	6–1	2–1	0–1	0–1	1–2	1–1	2–2	1–3	1–1	1–2	2–3	2–1	1–0	2–2	0–2	2–3	*	1–0	1–1	3–4	0–1
19 Tring Town	1–3	0–3	2–4	0–5	1–2	0–2	1–1	0–1	0–3	1–2	1–1	2–2	0–3	0–2	1–3	0–1	0–3	1–3	*	0–2	1–0	1–3
20 Vauxhall Motors	4–1	5–2	2–1	1–3	6–1	2–0	1–0	1–2	2–1	2–1	2–1	0–0	1–1	2–0	1–0	2–0	2–2	4–1	3–1	*	2–2	1–2
21 Ware	0–2	3–1	0–1	1–1	6–0	2–0	3–0	2–0	2–1	2–2	2–0	2–0	2–1	0–2	3–1	2–3	2–0	2–1	1–0	0–1	*	1–1
22 Witham Town	2–0	2–1	1–0	1–0	2–1	1–3	5–2	2–2	1–1	2–4	3–0	3–0	1–2	2–2	2–1	4–0	0–3	4–1	3–1	1–2	1–3	*

Division II North	*P*	*W*	*D*	*L*	*F*	*A*	*Pts*
1 Stevenage Borough	42	34	5	3	122	29	107
2 Vauxhall Motors	42	24	10	8	82	50	82
3 Billericay Town	42	22	8	12	70	41	74
4 Ware	42	22	8	12	78	51	74
5 Berkhamsted Town	42	19	11	12	60	51	68
6 Witham Town	42	19	10	13	70	59	67
7 Purfleet	42	17	14	11	68	57	65
8 Rainham Town	42	19	7	16	57	46	64
9 Hemel Hempstead	42	16	14	12	62	56	62
10 Barton Rovers	42	17	10	15	61	58	61
11 Saffron Walden Tn	42	16	13	13	72	77	61
12 Collier Row	42	16	11	15	63	63	59
13 Kingsbury Town	42	17	8	17	64	72	59
14 Edgware Town	42	17	7	18	73	65	58
15 Hertford Town	42	16	10	16	69	70	58
16 Royston Town	42	14	15	13	78	62	57
17 Tilbury	42	14	6	22	70	79	48
18 Basildon United	42	11	10	21	61	90	43
19 Hornchurch	42	10	9	23	53	87	39
20 Clapton*	42	9	10	23	54	93	34
21 Finchley+	42	6	7	29	50	112	24
22 Tring Town	42	1	9	32	30	99	12

Left: the programme for Wokingham Town's FA Cup tie at Wycombe in October 1990.

Right: the programme for the Kingstonian FA Trophy tie at home to Barrow in March 1990.

** Clapton had three points deducted. + Finchley had one point deducted.*
NB Clubs finishing between 3rd and 11th formed Division Two whilst the remainder formed Division Three, apart from Basildon U and Finchley who resigned.

Division II South	1	2	3	4	5	6	7	8	9	10	11	12	13	14	15	16	17	18	19	20	21	22
1 Abingdon Town	*	2–0	0–1	11–0	1–0	4–0	3–0	2–1	4–0	4–0	2–1	2–0	3–0	3–0	6–1	1–1	0–1	0–0	2–1	2–0	0–1	1–2
2 Banstead Athletic	3–3	*	5–1	3–0	2–0	3–1	0–0	1–5	0–2	2–1	0–0	1–1	1–2	0–3	2–5	2–0	0–0	2–1	0–2	4–1	0–4	0–0
3 Bracknell Town	1–2	0–2	*	3–0	0–3	2–2	1–0	0–2	1–5	0–0	3–1	0–1	2–2	4–0	1–1	1–2	0–3	0–1	1–3	3–1	3–6	0–1
4 Camberley Town	0–4	0–1	4–5	*	0–8	2–1	0–3	1–3	1–1	0–1	1–2	0–5	1–4	2–2	0–5	0–7	1–4	1–4	0–6	0–3	2–3	1–3
5 Chertsey Town	0–1	2–2	2–4	1–1	*	5–2	1–1	0–4	2–0	3–1	1–1	1–0	2–2	0–1	2–2	4–3	4–3	1–2	1–3	2–1	0–1	2–0
6 Cove	1–2	1–3	4–1	3–0	1–3	*	1–0	0–4	0–1	1–0	3–5	1–3	4–1	0–2	2–3	0–5	1–1	0–2	1–2	4–0	1–1	0–2
7 Eastbourne United	1–1	1–1	4–3	3–1	1–7	3–2	*	0–4	2–0	3–1	4–2	0–2	0–4	2–0	2–2	2–1	2–4	0–1	1–2	3–1	1–2	1–3
8 Egham Town	1–1	1–3	0–1	8–1	1–0	4–0	2–2	*	3–0	1–0	3–2	1–2	1–0	2–0	2–1	2–0	0–2	2–0	1–1	7–0	1–0	1–1
9 Epsom & Ewell	0–1	3–2	1–2	0–0	1–0	2–2	4–0	1–3	*	1–1	1–0	3–2	2–0	1–3	2–2	2–0	1–2	1–2	0–1	3–0	1–0	0–0
10 Feltham	2–3	0–0	4–0	2–1	1–4	0–2	3–1	3–4	0–4	*	3–2	1–0	0–2	1–1	1–1	2–1	3–4	0–1	1–2	2–0	1–1	2–0
11 Flackwell Heath	1–3	2–0	1–1	1–0	2–2	0–2	5–1	1–4	0–0	1–2	*	0–0	2–3	1–1	2–2	2–2	0–1	0–3	2–1	2–0	1–5	0–0
12 Hampton	1–4	1–1	2–2	0–0	3–1	0–1	11–1	1–1	0–0	2–1	1–1	*	0–1	0–2	1–1	0–2	1–1	1–0	0–0	5–0	0–2	2–1
13 Harefield United	2–2	2–0	7–1	2–0	2–2	2–2	3–1	4–2	0–0	2–1	4–1	0–3	*	3–0	2–1	2–1	0–3	2–1	2–1	3–2	1–0	2–2
14 Horsham	0–3	0–0	3–2	5–0	0–1	5–0	5–0	2–3	3–0	3–0	0–1	1–1	0–2	*	1–2	2–1	0–1	1–4	1–0	1–2	2–2	1–1
15 Hungerford Town	1–2	1–2	3–2	4–1	1–1	6–1	3–0	2–2	1–1	4–2	4–1	2–1	1–2	5–2	*	1–0	1–1	1–3	1–3	1–3	2–0	0–3
16 Leatherhead	1–2	2–2	4–0	5–1	5–0	1–1	2–0	1–2	1–1	4–0	0–1	0–0	1–2	2–0	3–2	*	1–1	1–1	1–0	5–1	2–3	1–4
17 Maidenhead Utd	1–3	2–0	2–1	2–0	1–0	5–1	2–0	2–1	4–0	3–0	5–0	1–2	2–2	2–0	3–1	1–2	*	3–0	0–0	3–0	2–0	1–0
18 Malden Vale	1–0	2–2	2–1	2–0	3–1	5–0	3–1	0–3	2–0	3–0	1–0	2–1	1–1	2–0	2–3	3–3	0–2	*	1–2	2–0	1–0	2–3
19 Newbury Town	0–0	1–2	1–2	5–1	2–3	2–0	2–2	2–0	0–2	1–1	0–4	0–0	2–1	3–0	0–0	2–0	3–2	2–0	*	3–1	1–3	4–3
20 Petersfield United	0–3	1–3	2–2	3–1	4–2	0–1	5–3	1–4	0–1	0–0	0–4	0–4	1–1	1–3	0–3	0–2	0–2	1–2	0–1	*	0–6	0–4
21 Ruislip Manor	0–2	4–0	3–1	3–0	4–1	1–1	2–0	2–3	2–0	7–1	3–0	2–0	3–2	3–2	0–0	0–1	2–0	2–3	1–2	7–0	*	2–1
22 Southall	1–0	2–1	5–1	2–2	2–1	1–0	7–1	3–1	1–1	1–0	6–1	2–2	1–0	4–0	2–1	2–5	0–0	0–1	1–2	5–0	2–0	*

Division II South	*P*	*W*	*D*	*L*	*F*	*A*	*Pts*
1 Abingdon Town	42	29	7	6	95	28	94
2 Maidenhead Utd	42	28	8	6	85	33	92
3 Egham Town	42	27	6	9	100	46	87
4 Malden Vale	42	26	5	11	72	44	83
5 Ruislip Manor	42	25	5	12	93	44	80
6 Southall	42	23	10	9	84	43	79
7 Harefield United	42	23	10	9	81	56	79
8 Newbury Town	42	23	8	11	71	45	77
9 Hungerford Town	42	16	13	13	84	69	61
10 Leatherhead	42	17	9	16	82	55	60
11 Banstead Athletic	42	15	13	14	58	62	58
12 Hampton	42	14	15	13	62	43	57
13 Epsom & Ewell	42	15	12	15	49	50	57
14 Chertsey Town	42	15	9	18	76	72	54
15 Horsham	42	14	7	21	58	67	49
16 Flackwell Heath	42	11	11	20	56	78	44
17 Bracknell Town	42	11	7	24	60	97	40
18 Feltham	42	10	8	24	45	80	38
19 Cove	42	10	7	25	51	94	37
20 Eastbourne United	42	10	7	25	53	109	37
21 Petersfield United	42	6	3	33	35	119	21
22 Camberley Town	42	1	6	35	27	143	9

Left: the programme for Champions Abingdon Town's key Division 2 South match against Runners-up Maidenhead Utd, which the visitors won 1-0.

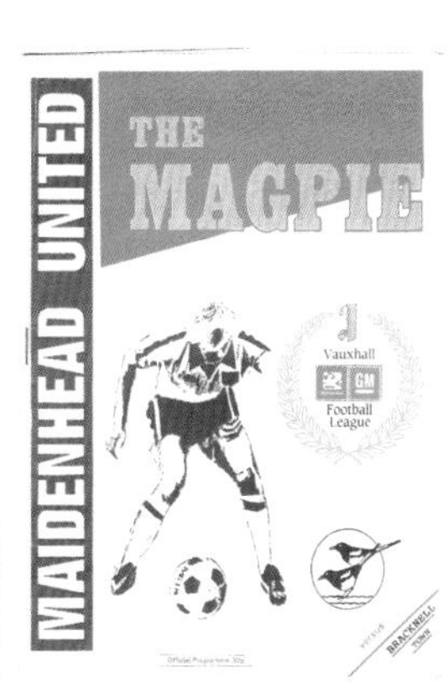

Right: Maidenhead United's programme from 1990.

NB Clubs finishing between 3rd and 11th formed Division Two whilst the remainder and newly elected Thame U formed Division Three.

1991–92 - It was announced that Diadora UK would be the new sponsors of the League.

During the close season Vauxhall Motors were excluded from membership of the League as they had an artificial pitch laid at their ground and as this was not acceptable by the League the club could not continue its membership, therefore Division One would operate with 21 clubs.

After their successful season the previous year Woking went one better and under the guidance of Manager Geoff Chapple secured the Premier Division championship by 18 points and subsequent promotion to the GM Vauxhall Conference. For the second successive year Enfield were runners-up, nine points ahead of Sutton United and Chesham United (in their first season in the top division) who finished third and fourth respectively. Only one Club, Bishop's Stortford, was relegated to Division One as the GM Vauxhall Conference did not relegate a club to the League and Dagenham had decided to merge with Redbridge Forest and play in the GM Vauxhall Conference. In Division One Stevenage Borough secured successive championships whilst runners-up Yeading and Dulwich Hamlet, who just pipped Boreham Wood, were promoted to the Premier Division. Heybridge Swifts, Whyteleafe and Aveley were given a reprieve as there was no relegation to Division Two. Returning to Division One after a gap of two years, Purfleet won the Division Two championship nine points clear of runners-up Lewes with Billericay Town claiming the other promotion place.

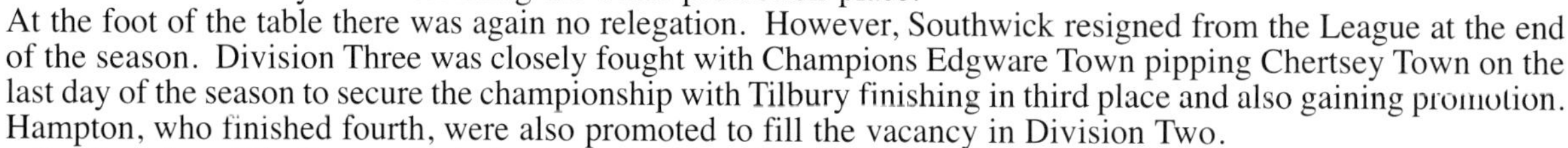
At the foot of the table there was again no relegation. However, Southwick resigned from the League at the end of the season. Division Three was closely fought with Champions Edgware Town pipping Chertsey Town on the last day of the season to secure the championship with Tilbury finishing in third place and also gaining promotion. Hampton, who finished fourth, were also promoted to fill the vacancy in Division Two.

Southwick and Eastbourne United, who had both resigned from the League, were given permission to return to the Sussex County League.

At the Annual General Meeting East Thurrock United (Essex Senior League), Northwood (London-Spartan League) and Leighton Town (South Midlands League) as well as Aldershot Town, who were formed a few months earlier by supporters of the former Football League club Aldershot FC, were accepted. The application of Farnham Town (Combined Counties League) was accepted providing their ground work was completed by 31 December. They would ground share with Aldershot Town in the interim. An application received from Romford was rejected.

Premier Division	1	2	3	4	5	6	7	8	9	10	11	12	13	14	15	16	17	18	19	20	21	22
1 Aylesbury United	*	2–1	0–0	1–1	1–2	0–0	1–2	1–1	1–1	3–1	7–1	0–0	4–1	0–1	1–0	2–0	0–1	4–4	4–0	1–1	0–4	4–0
2 Basingstoke Town	0–0	*	1–1	1–1	1–1	1–2	2–2	2–2	1–2	1–2	0–1	4–2	0–1	1–0	2–0	1–1	2–0	0–2	0–2	5–1	0–3	3–3
3 Bishop's Stortford	1–0	0–1	*	1–2	2–3	1–0	0–0	0–4	0–1	3–0	2–0	1–1	3–2	1–3	0–2	1–1	1–2	0–2	1–1	1–2	1–2	1–5
4 Bognor Regis Tn	2–2	1–2	1–1	*	0–0	1–0	0–6	1–0	0–1	2–2	2–2	3–4	1–4	2–2	0–1	2–4	2–2	0–0	0–1	3–0	1–1	1–3
5 Bromley	0–0	2–0	1–0	1–4	*	3–1	0–1	0–0	0–1	2–3	0–2	0–0	1–1	0–2	0–0	2–0	1–1	2–2	0–1	2–1	0–2	0–0
6 Carshalton Athletic	1–0	2–1	2–2	4–0	5–1	*	3–0	0–3	1–1	2–1	1–0	3–1	5–4	4–4	2–1	1–2	1–3	2–1	0–0	0–2	0–2	3–2
7 Chesham United	0–2	2–1	2–1	1–3	1–0	4–0	*	0–1	0–2	2–2	1–0	2–2	0–0	3–2	3–0	3–1	4–0	1–0	0–0	2–1	0–0	4–0
8 Dagenham	2–4	2–2	3–0	4–1	1–1	1–1	3–0	*	2–1	2–0	5–2	3–3	0–1	1–2	4–1	0–0	1–0	0–0	2–2	2–2	0–0	0–1
9 Enfield	2–2	0–2	1–0	3–1	0–1	2–1	3–2	3–5	*	2–2	3–0	2–0	1–0	4–0	0–2	3–1	0–0	3–1	0–0	1–0	1–0	0–2
10 Grays Athletic	3–3	1–0	3–1	1–2	5–1	2–1	1–3	2–1	0–4	*	0–0	0–0	0–0	1–2	1–2	2–0	1–1	0–2	0–0	4–1	0–2	1–1
11 Harrow Borough	0–4	5–1	3–2	4–1	2–1	1–2	1–1	2–2	1–2	0–2	*	2–4	1–1	1–1	2–1	2–2	6–1	1–1	3–1	1–0	1–3	1–2
12 Hayes	0–0	0–1	1–0	4–1	1–3	2–2	0–0	4–0	2–0	4–0	1–1	*	3–0	0–0	1–3	0–1	0–1	0–2	0–2	0–2	2–2	0–3
13 Hendon	1–2	0–2	0–1	3–1	4–1	1–1	2–3	0–1	1–0	1–2	2–2	1–0	*	4–1	1–2	0–1	5–0	0–6	1–1	2–0	0–5	2–1
14 Kingstonian	0–1	0–1	2–3	3–1	0–2	1–2	3–1	2–2	3–0	4–1	3–1	2–1	5–0	*	4–1	3–5	0–2	0–0	2–0	3–0	1–2	1–2
15 Marlow	0–0	2–4	1–0	2–1	0–4	4–1	3–0	2–0	0–1	1–0	1–0	1–1	4–0	2–1	*	0–0	4–0	1–0	1–1	1–2	0–3	1–1
16 St. Albans City	3–3	1–1	3–2	2–3	4–2	2–0	1–2	1–2	1–2	1–2	6–0	0–0	1–1	2–2	2–0	*	1–2	1–2	1–2	1–2	1–1	0–3
17 Staines Town	0–0	4–1	2–2	0–1	0–1	1–2	1–5	2–2	0–1	0–1	0–0	0–0	1–3	1–2	1–0	1–2	*	1–3	0–3	3–0	0–2	1–3
18 Sutton United	1–2	1–2	2–2	5–0	1–1	2–0	1–1	5–3	0–1	5–0	1–1	3–2	4–2	2–2	3–2	2–3	1–2	*	4–1	4–2	2–0	5–0
19 Windsor & Eton	2–3	1–3	2–2	1–0	2–1	1–2	1–2	0–1	2–3	1–2	4–0	1–2	1–4	3–0	0–0	2–3	3–1	2–2	*	4–1	0–3	1–0
20 Wivenhoe Town	0–3	4–1	1–0	4–0	3–2	2–4	1–0	4–0	1–1	1–1	1–4	2–0	2–1	2–0	1–3	1–2	3–0	0–1	0–3	*	1–7	2–0
21 Woking	2–1	5–0	3–0	3–1	1–2	3–0	2–1	3–1	5–0	1–0	2–0	4–1	1–1	3–1	0–1	4–1	2–2	1–0	2–0	2–0	*	0–1
22 Wokingham Town	4–0	1–1	0–0	3–1	1–4	0–0	1–0	1–1	2–0	3–1	1–1	5–2	2–1	0–1	2–3	4–1	1–3	3–3	0–1	6–0	0–3	*

Premier Division	*P*	*W*	*D*	*L*	*F*	*A*	*Pts*
1 Woking	42	30	7	5	96	25	97
2 Enfield	42	24	7	11	59	45	79
3 Sutton United	42	19	13	10	88	51	70
4 Chesham United	42	20	10	12	67	48	70
5 Wokingham Town	42	19	10	13	73	58	67
6 Marlow	42	20	7	15	56	50	67
7 Aylesbury United	42	16	17	9	69	46	65
8 Carshalton Athletic	42	18	8	16	64	67	62
9 Dagenham	42	15	16	11	70	59	61
10 Kingstonian	42	17	8	17	71	65	59
11 Windsor & Eton	42	15	11	16	56	56	56
12 Bromley	42	14	12	16	51	57	54
13 St. Albans City	42	14	11	17	66	70	53
14 Basingstoke Town	42	14	11	17	56	65	53
15 Grays Athletic	42	14	11	17	53	68	53
16 Wivenhoe Town	42	16	4	22	56	81	52
17 Hendon	42	13	9	20	59	73	48
18 Harrow Borough	42	11	13	18	58	78	46
19 Hayes	42	10	14	18	52	63	44
20 Staines Town	42	11	10	21	43	73	43
21 Bognor Regis Tn	42	9	11	22	51	89	38
22 Bishop's Stortford	42	7	12	23	41	68	33

Left: the programme for Bognor Regis Town's 1-0 victory over Dagenham in March 1992.

Right: the Petersfield United programme for their fixture at home to Eastbourne United.

1991-92 Division I	1	2	3	4	5	6	7	8	9	10	11	12	13	14	15	16	17	18	19	20	21
1 Abingdon Town	*	3–0	2–2	1–2	1–0	1–0	2–0	2–1	2–1	7–1	2–2	0–0	1–2	3–2	4–0	1–1	1–2	1–0	1–0	0–3	1–3
2 Aveley	0–1	*	2–1	1–2	2–0	0–4	2–0	2–5	0–4	0–0	1–0	1–5	1–0	1–1	0–4	0–2	0–4	1–0	0–2	0–1	0–2
3 Barking	1–0	5–1	*	2–0	1–0	3–3	2–1	2–0	0–1	1–0	0–2	2–2	2–0	1–1	1–3	0–3	0–1	0–1	1–1	2–1	1–1
4 Boreham Wood	2–0	4–0	1–1	*	4–2	3–0	3–3	1–1	0–1	0–0	3–0	3–1	1–0	2–1	0–3	4–0	3–0	2–3	1–2	2–2	0–1
5 Chalfont St. Peter	1–3	1–2	1–2	1–1	*	1–1	3–2	1–2	2–0	4–1	1–1	1–2	0–1	2–0	0–0	2–0	2–1	1–1	1–2	2–1	2–4
6 Croydon	0–0	1–0	1–3	0–1	4–3	*	3–2	0–4	0–0	1–0	2–0	2–0	1–0	0–1	0–1	1–1	1–2	0–3	0–1	2–3	0–3
7 Dorking	3–0	3–1	2–2	0–1	2–3	1–0	*	3–1	0–3	1–2	4–0	3–3	0–2	0–2	3–1	1–3	0–3	3–0	2–1	0–2	1–1
8 Dulwich Hamlet	1–1	2–0	3–0	1–0	2–3	6–1	3–4	*	1–0	3–0	3–1	1–0	2–1	0–1	0–1	1–1	2–1	2–2	1–0	1–1	0–0
9 Harlow Town	1–3	2–3	0–2	0–1	1–3	2–1	0–2	2–0	*	0–1	2–1	2–1	2–2	0–1	0–2	2–2	1–5	2–3	2–5	1–1	1–3
10 Heybridge Swifts	0–1	2–1	1–1	2–3	2–4	2–0	1–3	0–2	1–1	*	0–0	1–3	0–3	0–2	0–3	2–3	2–0	0–0	1–3	3–1	0–2
11 Hitchin Town	1–1	5–2	1–0	2–1	1–3	1–1	1–2	0–1	1–0	1–0	*	3–1	2–0	1–1	1–1	0–1	2–0	0–0	4–0	2–0	1–0
12 Leyton-Wingate	1–0	4–2	0–3	0–3	0–2	1–0	1–2	1–1	0–0	2–0	1–3	*	1–2	0–0	2–2	2–1	4–0	1–3	2–1	3–0	1–0
13 Maidenhead Utd	1–2	3–2	4–0	0–2	3–1	0–1	1–3	0–1	3–3	1–1	1–3	3–2	*	1–2	0–3	0–3	2–1	1–2	0–0	1–2	0–2
14 Molesey	0–2	2–1	4–0	0–1	2–1	2–4	0–3	0–4	1–1	3–1	2–4	0–0	1–3	*	1–1	2–1	4–1	0–3	1–2	2–1	2–4
15 Stevenage Borough	4–1	5–0	2–0	2–0	5–1	4–2	2–1	1–1	7–1	3–1	2–0	4–1	2–0	3–2	*	2–0	2–0	3–2	2–0	4–0	2–2
16 Tooting & M Utd	2–1	3–0	1–1	0–1	1–3	3–2	2–2	2–2	2–3	2–0	0–0	1–0	2–1	0–0	3–1	*	2–0	0–0	0–1	3–1	0–1
17 Uxbridge	1–2	1–0	0–0	2–3	2–0	1–0	1–1	1–2	1–3	1–1	1–1	0–2	2–2	2–3	1–3	1–1	*	2–1	0–0	2–0	0–3
18 Walton & Hersham	1–1	4–2	3–2	2–1	1–2	2–0	2–2	0–1	2–2	0–0	2–1	1–1	2–2	0–1	2–3	1–1	4–0	*	0–1	4–1	2–2
19 Wembley	2–1	3–1	2–1	1–0	2–2	1–0	2–0	3–2	1–0	0–1	3–2	2–1	1–2	0–2	0–1	1–3	0–1	3–0	*	1–1	0–0
20 Whyteleafe	1–3	1–1	1–3	2–2	2–0	2–3	0–1	1–4	1–3	1–3	0–2	1–1	0–2	1–1	0–1	1–0	1–1	0–3	1–3	*	1–1
21 Yeading	2–1	3–0	1–0	0–1	5–0	4–2	3–2	0–1	3–0	4–0	0–2	0–0	2–2	6–2	4–0	1–1	1–2	2–0	2–1	5–2	*

Division I	*P*	*W*	*D*	*L*	*F*	*A*	*Pts*
1 Stevenage Borough	40	30	6	4	95	37	96
2 Yeading	40	24	10	6	83	34	82
3 Dulwich Hamlet	40	22	9	9	71	40	75
4 Boreham Wood	40	22	7	11	65	40	73
5 Wembley	40	21	6	13	54	43	69
6 Abingdon Town	40	19	8	13	60	47	65
7 Tooting & M Utd	40	16	13	11	57	45	61
8 Hitchin Town	40	17	10	13	55	45	61
9 Walton & Hersham	40	15	13	12	62	50	58
10 Molesey	40	16	9	15	55	61	57
11 Dorking	40	16	7	17	68	65	55
12 Barking	40	14	11	15	51	54	53
13 Chalfont St. Peter	40	15	6	19	62	70	51
14 Leyton-Wingate	40	13	11	16	53	56	50
15 Uxbridge	40	13	8	19	47	62	47
16 Maidenhead Utd	40	13	7	20	52	61	46
17 Harlow Town	40	11	9	20	50	70	42
18 Croydon	40	11	6	23	44	68	39
19 Heybridge Swifts	40	8	9	23	33	71	33
20 Whyteleafe	40	7	10	23	42	78	31
21 Aveley	40	8	3	29	33	95	27

Left: the programme for Croydon's home match against Stevenage Borough.

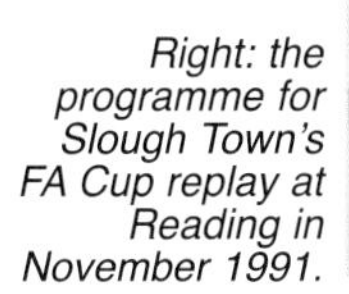

Right: the programme for Slough Town's FA Cup replay at Reading in November 1991.

Division II	1	2	3	4	5	6	7	8	9	10	11	12	13	14	15	16	17	18	19	20	21	22
1 Banstead Athletic	*	1–1	2–2	1–0	0–0	2–1	1–1	0–1	2–1	2–3	3–1	0–1	7–1	3–3	0–0	3–4	1–2	4–1	2–0	1–1	0–1	0–2
2 Barton Rovers	0–2	*	2–1	0–0	0–1	2–0	0–3	2–1	0–3	0–1	2–1	2–1	1–1	1–2	1–1	1–1	2–3	5–1	3–0	3–0	1–1	3–0
3 Berkhamsted Town	3–1	4–1	*	2–3	1–2	1–3	1–2	2–3	1–0	0–0	0–3	3–0	1–0	1–1	0–1	2–5	1–4	2–0	5–1	4–0	2–0	3–0
4 Billericay Town	2–0	4–0	2–0	*	2–2	1–1	0–0	4–1	0–3	1–1	3–0	3–2	7–0	0–2	1–1	4–3	2–1	1–0	4–0	1–0	4–1	3–1
5 Egham Town	3–1	2–1	1–1	1–4	*	1–1	3–1	1–3	0–1	3–1	2–1	4–2	1–1	3–4	1–1	3–2	1–1	5–0	5–4	1–1	5–1	1–3
6 Harefield United	1–2	0–2	1–1	0–3	0–3	*	4–0	0–1	2–3	2–1	0–0	2–1	2–0	2–4	2–3	0–0	0–1	1–1	5–2	1–2	1–0	0–1
7 Hemel Hempstead	4–1	0–1	1–0	0–1	1–2	2–0	*	1–3	2–1	1–1	3–1	1–1	6–1	1–1	1–0	2–0	0–1	4–0	0–2	6–3	0–1	2–2
8 Hungerford Town	0–0	1–1	2–1	2–0	1–3	2–1	2–2	*	0–0	0–0	2–0	1–0	1–1	1–2	2–0	2–1	1–1	1–2	2–1	0–2	0–1	4–1
9 Leatherhead	0–1	1–0	0–2	1–0	0–3	1–0	4–0	1–0	*	1–1	1–0	0–1	4–0	3–1	1–0	0–3	0–0	4–0	2–1	1–2	2–0	3–0
10 Lewes	2–2	1–0	3–2	2–1	0–0	1–0	2–0	2–1	0–1	*	1–1	2–2	5–0	1–3	0–0	0–2	4–0	3–0	0–0	2–1	1–0	9–1
11 Malden Vale	1–0	1–2	1–0	3–0	4–1	4–0	2–0	2–0	1–2	2–3	*	1–1	3–0	0–2	1–1	1–1	4–1	1–1	2–0	3–1	1–2	2–1
12 Metropolitan Police	3–2	0–0	3–0	1–2	3–3	4–1	1–0	3–2	2–1	0–3	2–2	*	0–0	1–2	2–0	1–0	2–2	6–1	4–1	3–0	5–1	1–0
13 Newbury Town	1–3	3–5	1–1	1–1	2–1	0–1	1–2	0–2	2–2	0–3	0–4	0–1	*	0–6	1–3	1–2	1–7	1–0	0–3	1–3	2–4	1–2
14 Purfleet	2–0	5–0	3–1	0–1	4–3	2–2	1–1	1–2	1–1	2–3	1–0	1–3	4–1	*	2–1	2–0	1–2	2–0	4–0	1–1	1–1	2–1
15 Rainham Town	2–1	2–1	0–0	0–1	0–1	5–1	0–1	0–1	2–1	1–1	1–1	1–1	3–0	1–2	*	2–3	3–2	3–0	0–1	2–1	1–2	3–2
16 Ruislip Manor	1–0	1–3	0–1	0–1	2–0	1–0	2–2	3–0	3–0	0–1	2–1	3–1	3–0	1–4	1–1	*	1–1	3–0	1–0	4–1	2–0	2–1
17 Saffron Walden Tn	1–1	1–2	2–0	1–0	1–1	1–0	0–1	4–0	2–4	2–4	4–2	3–2	1–2	1–2	2–2	3–3	*	2–2	5–0	0–4	3–3	3–1
18 Southall	1–2	2–1	1–1	0–1	1–2	1–3	0–3	2–4	0–4	0–1	0–0	0–4	4–0	0–4	0–0	1–0	2–3	*	7–1	1–0	2–3	2–0
19 Southwick	1–6	0–3	0–1	0–2	2–5	2–1	1–3	1–0	0–6	0–2	0–3	1–2	1–2	1–2	0–2	0–4	0–2	0–2	*	1–0	0–2	0–4
20 Ware	1–3	4–1	1–1	1–1	1–0	0–2	1–0	2–0	3–1	0–0	1–1	2–0	3–0	1–4	0–2	2–2	1–2	0–0	9–1	*	1–2	0–1
21 Witham Town	1–2	2–4	0–0	4–0	1–0	1–3	0–2	2–0	1–1	0–1	1–1	2–3	0–0	2–0	4–2	1–1	1–6	4–0	0–0	2–0	*	1–1
22 Worthing	1–4	5–1	1–1	5–4	1–1	1–0	1–1	5–1	1–2	2–2	0–0	3–0	4–1	0–4	2–0	2–1	3–2	4–1	1–0	0–1	0–0	*

Division II	*P*	*W*	*D*	*L*	*F*	*A*	*Pts*
1 Purfleet	42	27	8	7	97	48	89
2 Lewes	42	23	14	5	74	36	83
3 Billericay Town	42	24	8	10	75	44	80
4 Leatherhead	42	23	6	13	68	40	75
5 Ruislip Manor	42	20	9	13	74	51	69
6 Egham Town	42	19	12	11	81	62	69
7 Metropolitan Police	42	20	9	13	76	58	69
8 Saffron Walden Tn	42	19	11	12	86	67	68
9 Hemel Hempstead	42	18	10	14	63	50	64
10 Hungerford Town	42	18	7	17	53	58	61
11 Barton Rovers	42	17	8	17	61	64	59
12 Worthing	42	17	8	17	67	72	59
13 Witham Town	42	16	11	15	56	61	59
14 Banstead Athletic	42	16	10	16	69	58	58
15 Malden Vale	42	15	12	15	63	48	57
16 Rainham Town	42	14	13	15	53	48	55
17 Ware	42	14	9	19	58	62	51
18 Berkhamsted Town	42	13	11	18	56	57	50
19 Harefield United	42	11	7	24	47	66	40
20 Southall	42	8	7	27	39	93	31
21 Southwick	42	6	2	34	29	115	20
22 Newbury Town	42	4	8	30	30	117	20

Left: the programme for Chesham United's Loctite Cup tie against Woking.

Right: the 1991-92 programme for Edgware Town.

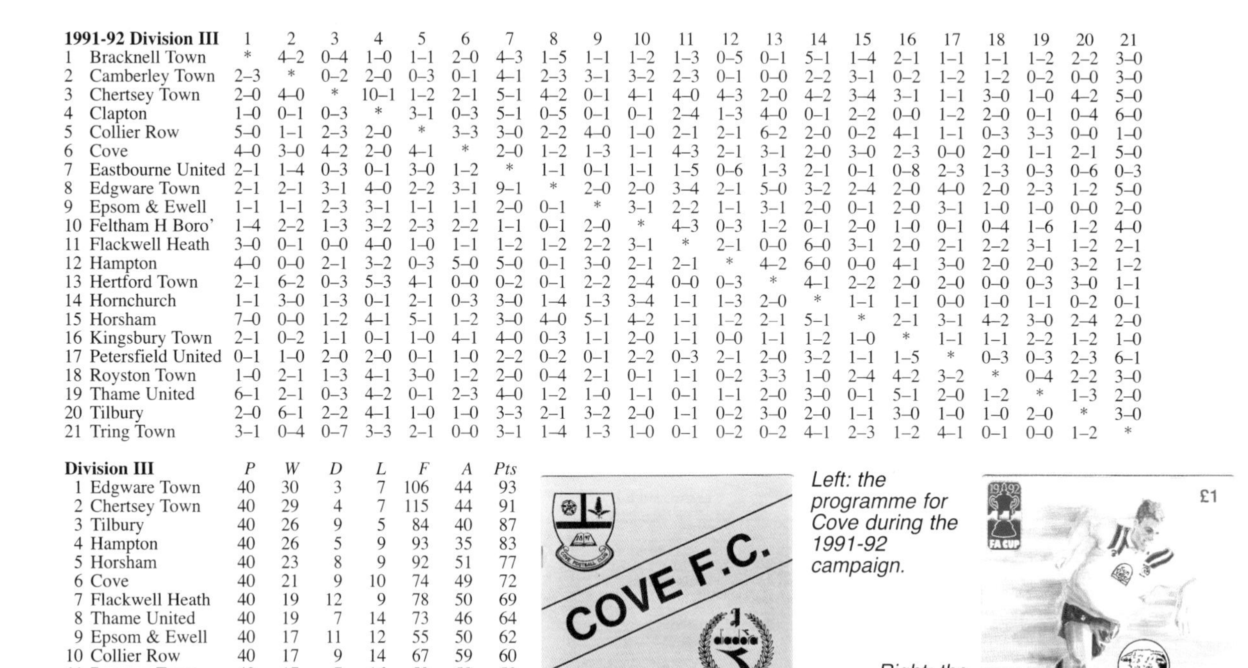

1991-92 Division III	1	2	3	4	5	6	7	8	9	10	11	12	13	14	15	16	17	18	19	20	21
1 Bracknell Town	*	4–2	0–4	1–0	1–1	2–0	4–3	1–5	1–1	1–2	1–3	0–5	0–1	5–1	1–4	2–1	1–1	1–1	1–2	2–2	3–0
2 Camberley Town	2–3	*	0–2	2–0	0–3	0–1	4–1	2–3	3–1	3–2	2–3	0–1	0–0	2–2	3–1	0–2	1–2	1–2	0–2	0–0	3–0
3 Chertsey Town	2–0	4–0	*	10–1	1–2	2–1	5–1	4–2	0–1	4–1	4–0	4–3	2–0	4–2	3–4	3–1	1–1	3–0	1–0	4–2	5–0
4 Clapton	1–0	0–1	0–3	*	3–1	0–3	5–1	0–5	0–1	0–1	2–4	1–3	4–0	0–1	2–2	0–0	1–2	2–0	0–1	0–4	6–0
5 Collier Row	5–0	1–1	2–3	2–0	*	3–3	3–0	2–2	4–0	1–0	2–1	2–1	6–2	2–0	0–2	4–1	1–1	0–3	3–3	0–0	1–0
6 Cove	4–0	3–0	4–2	2–0	4–1	*	2–0	1–2	1–3	1–1	4–3	2–1	3–1	2–0	3–0	2–3	0–0	2–0	1–1	2–1	5–0
7 Eastbourne United	2–1	1–4	0–3	0–1	3–0	1–2	*	1–1	0–1	1–1	1–5	0–6	1–3	2–1	0–1	0–8	2–3	1–3	0–3	0–6	0–3
8 Edgware Town	2–1	2–1	3–1	4–0	2–2	3–1	9–1	*	2–0	2–0	3–4	2–1	5–0	3–2	2–4	2–0	4–0	2–0	2–3	1–2	5–0
9 Epsom & Ewell	1–1	1–1	2–3	3–1	1–1	1–1	2–0	0–1	*	3–1	2–2	1–1	3–1	2–0	0–1	2–0	3–1	1–0	1–0	0–0	2–0
10 Feltham H Boro'	1–4	2–2	1–3	3–2	2–3	2–2	1–1	0–1	2–0	*	4–3	0–3	1–2	0–1	2–0	1–0	0–1	0–4	1–6	1–2	4–0
11 Flackwell Heath	3–0	0–1	0–0	4–0	1–0	1–1	1–2	1–2	2–2	3–1	*	2–1	0–0	6–0	3–1	2–0	2–1	2–2	3–1	1–2	2–1
12 Hampton	4–0	0–0	2–1	3–2	0–3	5–0	5–0	0–1	3–0	2–1	2–1	*	4–2	6–0	0–0	4–1	3–0	2–0	2–0	3–2	1–2
13 Hertford Town	2–1	6–2	0–3	5–3	4–1	0–0	0–2	0–1	2–2	2–4	0–0	0–3	*	4–1	2–2	2–0	2–0	0–0	0–3	3–0	1–1
14 Hornchurch	1–1	3–0	1–3	0–1	2–1	0–3	3–0	1–4	1–3	3–4	1–1	1–3	2–0	*	1–1	1–1	0–0	1–0	1–1	0–2	0–1
15 Horsham	7–0	0–0	1–2	4–1	5–1	1–2	3–0	4–0	5–1	4–2	1–1	1–2	2–1	5–1	*	2–1	3–1	4–2	3–0	2–4	2–0
16 Kingsbury Town	2–1	0–2	1–1	0–1	1–0	4–1	4–0	0–3	1–1	2–0	1–1	0–0	1–1	1–2	1–0	*	1–1	1–1	2–2	1–2	1–0
17 Petersfield United	0–1	1–0	2–0	2–0	0–1	1–0	2–2	0–2	0–1	2–2	0–3	2–1	2–0	3–2	1–1	1–5	*	0–3	0–3	2–3	6–1
18 Royston Town	1–0	2–1	1–3	4–1	3–0	1–2	2–0	0–4	2–1	0–1	1–1	0–2	3–3	1–0	2–4	4–2	3–2	*	0–4	2–2	3–0
19 Thame United	6–1	2–1	0–3	4–2	0–1	2–3	4–0	1–2	1–0	1–1	0–1	1–1	2–0	3–0	0–1	5–1	2–0	1–2	*	1–3	2–0
20 Tilbury	2–0	6–1	2–2	4–1	1–0	1–0	3–3	2–1	3–2	2–0	1–1	0–2	3–0	2–0	1–1	3–0	1–0	1–0	2–0	*	3–0
21 Tring Town	3–1	0–4	0–7	3–3	2–1	0–0	3–1	1–4	1–3	1–0	0–1	0–2	0–2	4–1	2–3	1–2	4–1	0–1	0–0	1–2	*

Division III	P	W	D	L	F	A	Pts
1 Edgware Town	40	30	3	7	106	44	93
2 Chertsey Town	40	29	4	7	115	44	91
3 Tilbury	40	26	9	5	84	40	87
4 Hampton	40	26	5	9	93	35	83
5 Horsham	40	23	8	9	92	51	77
6 Cove	40	21	9	10	74	49	72
7 Flackwell Heath	40	19	12	9	78	50	69
8 Thame United	40	19	7	14	73	46	64
9 Epsom & Ewell	40	17	11	12	55	50	62
10 Collier Row	40	17	9	14	67	59	60
11 Royston Town	40	17	7	16	59	58	58
12 Kingsbury Town	40	12	10	18	54	61	46
13 Hertford Town	40	12	10	18	55	73	46
14 Petersfield United	40	12	9	19	45	67	45
15 Camberley Town	40	11	8	21	52	69	41
16 Feltham & H Boro	40	11	2	22	53	78	40
17 Bracknell Town	40	10	7	23	48	90	37
18 Hornchurch	40	8	7	25	40	87	31
19 Tring Town	40	9	4	27	35	94	31
20 Clapton	40	9	3	28	47	93	30
21 Eastbourne United	40	5	5	30	34	121	20

Left: the programme for Cove during the 1991-92 campaign.

Right: the programme for Woking's FA Cup Third Round replay at Hereford United, which Woking lost 2-1 after extra time.

Feltham FC and Hounslow FC (Southern League) amalgamated to form Feltham & Hounslow Borough FC

1992–93 - At the start of the season Harlow Town could not fulfil their fixtures and therefore did not take their place in Division One. The club were subsequently suspended for the season and the position would be reviewed at the end of the season. Farnham Town, elected to Division Three at the Annual General Meeting, did not take their place which resulted in Divisions One and Three having twenty-one and twenty clubs respectively.

The Premier Division championship was virtually a two-horse race between Chesham United and St. Albans City who both scored over one hundred goals with the former enjoying a twenty-three match undefeated run to clinch the title on the final day of the season. Both Chesham United and St. Albans City, for different reasons, did not seek promotion to the GM Vauxhall Conference. Staines Town, Windsor & Eton and Bognor Regis Town were relegated; Staines and Bognor had been reprieved the previous year.

In Division One, although the promoted clubs, Hitchin Town, Molesey and Dorking, were known for some time, the championship was not decided until the final day of the season with Hitchin Town ahead of Molesey who enjoyed their most successful season in their history. As Division One was one club short only two clubs were relegated to Division Two: Lewes and Aveley. In Division Two Worthing, relegated in 1991, returned to Division One as champions, being joined by Ruislip Manor and Berkhamsted Town who just beat local rivals Hemel Hempstead for the third promotion spot. Harefield United and Southall, who shared Harefield's ground, were relegated to Division Three.

St. Albans City – Isthmian League Premier Division runners-up 1992-93. Back row; Steve Ketteridge, Martin Gurney, Gary Westwood, Shaun Brett, Martin Duffield, Steve Clark, Roy of the Rovers (sponsor), Allan Cockram, Kevin Mudd, Paul Price, Peter Hayward (physio), John Mitchell (manager). Front row; John Colfer, Dean Williams, Jimmy King, Bradley Anderson, Roy Edwards, Peter Risley, Steve Scott.

Aldershot Town, in their first season, won the Division Three championship with two weeks of the season remaining and were only defeated twice during their thirty-eight match programme. Joining Aldershot Town in Division Two were runners-up Thame United, in only their second season in membership, and Collier Row, who beat off the challenge of Leighton Town and Cove for the final promotion place. At the foot of the table Feltham & Hounslow Borough occupied bottom place eleven points adrift of Petersfield United who resigned from the League at the end of the season.

At the Annual General Meeting Harlow Town's suspension was lifted and the club re-admitted to the League, albeit in Division Three. Cheshunt (London Spartan League) and Oxford City (South Midlands League) – the latter after a five-year absence – were elected into membership; an application from Peppard was rejected.

1992-93

Premier Division	1	2	3	4	5	6	7	8	9	10	11	12	13	14	15	16	17	18	19	20	21	22
1 Aylesbury United	*	1–1	2–0	6–1	3–2	1–4	0–2	1–1	1–2	0–1	1–1	1–1	2–0	0–3	3–2	5–3	1–2	0–4	3–0	1–2	1–0	1–1
2 Basingstoke Town	1–2	*	0–0	1–1	0–1	0–0	2–1	4–0	4–0	0–0	1–0	1–1	0–0	2–1	1–2	1–1	0–0	1–1	3–0	1–1	5–0	0–6
3 Bognor Regis Tn	4–5	1–3	*	3–2	0–6	0–4	2–2	0–6	4–1	1–2	1–2	0–2	3–4	1–5	2–6	0–0	1–1	1–1	0–1	2–0	2–2	1–4
4 Bromley	1–2	1–0	3–0	*	0–4	2–2	2–2	0–5	2–3	1–3	1–1	1–0	0–2	0–1	1–3	4–1	1–2	1–1	1–2	3–0	0–2	1–0
5 Carshalton Athletic	1–0	0–0	2–0	0–2	*	1–1	2–2	1–2	2–1	1–1	1–1	3–1	3–0	3–2	3–5	2–1	3–1	2–1	1–3	3–1	1–1	1–1
6 Chesham United	2–1	2–1	6–1	0–0	5–1	*	4–0	0–1	3–2	2–2	1–0	4–0	2–1	4–3	2–2	1–0	7–1	7–0	1–0	2–1	3–1	3–0
7 Dulwich Hamlet	0–1	0–0	2–2	1–1	1–7	1–4	*	1–2	2–0	1–2	1–2	2–1	2–1	1–1	0–5	2–0	0–2	0–2	0–0	5–0	2–1	0–1
8 Enfield	3–1	4–1	6–2	2–0	2–1	0–1	1–2	*	2–1	0–1	2–3	0–2	2–2	1–4	0–2	4–1	1–0	1–0	6–0	4–0	3–0	4–1
9 Grays Athletic	2–1	3–2	2–1	4–1	2–2	2–0	0–0	3–2	*	2–1	1–0	0–0	1–1	1–2	3–0	1–1	2–1	1–3	0–0	2–1	2–0	3–0
10 Harrow Borough	2–3	0–0	2–0	0–2	2–4	0–3	1–1	1–0	0–0	*	2–2	1–1	2–0	2–5	3–6	2–2	3–1	4–3	0–0	0–0	4–1	3–0
11 Hayes	4–0	1–3	2–0	3–3	0–4	1–3	0–0	0–1	1–1	2–2	*	1–1	2–3	2–1	0–0	4–0	0–1	2–2	7–1	2–1	4–2	0–0
12 Hendon	1–1	0–0	1–0	1–1	1–2	2–1	2–1	0–0	0–1	1–2	2–0	*	1–0	0–0	2–2	1–1	1–2	1–1	2–0	1–1	1–1	3–3
13 Kingstonian	7–1	1–1	0–0	2–2	0–2	0–1	2–2	2–3	1–0	2–1	1–1	2–4	*	2–0	1–3	3–1	0–2	0–1	3–0	0–1	3–1	2–0
14 Marlow	3–4	0–0	1–2	2–2	0–5	1–4	0–1	1–1	1–1	1–2	1–2	3–0	1–1	*	1–1	5–2	2–3	1–1	0–2	5–1	3–2	1–2
15 St. Albans City	1–0	4–1	2–1	4–0	3–2	1–1	3–1	0–0	2–1	1–2	1–0	2–1	2–0	5–1	*	2–2	2–1	2–2	2–1	3–0	7–2	1–1
16 Staines Town	1–4	0–1	3–0	2–3	0–3	0–2	1–1	2–2	6–0	1–0	0–1	3–3	1–0	1–4	2–1	*	2–2	1–1	3–0	1–2	0–1	2–0
17 Stevenage Borough	1–3	0–2	4–1	0–1	3–2	1–0	2–4	0–3	6–1	0–0	1–2	4–1	2–0	2–0	1–2	1–2	*	1–0	0–1	1–0	1–1	2–0
18 Sutton United	4–0	1–0	0–0	3–1	3–1	0–1	2–0	3–2	1–1	2–1	1–2	0–2	1–1	2–1	3–1	2–4	1–1	*	5–2	3–0	2–0	2–2
19 Windsor & Eton	2–3	1–0	2–2	0–1	1–4	2–5	2–2	1–3	3–3	0–1	2–3	1–2	1–0	1–2	0–3	3–1	2–4	0–3	*	1–1	1–2	0–2
20 Wivenhoe Town	2–1	3–2	4–1	1–0	0–4	0–4	0–1	0–4	0–2	3–0	3–1	2–0	2–3	2–1	0–2	1–1	0–0	1–3	2–0	*	1–0	1–3
21 Wokingham Town	0–2	3–1	1–3	1–1	2–2	0–0	3–1	0–3	2–0	1–1	5–0	2–2	0–4	2–2	1–3	2–2	3–0	3–3	3–1	2–0	*	2–2
22 Yeading	2–1	1–2	2–1	0–0	1–1	1–2	0–2	3–5	2–3	4–0	1–2	1–3	1–2	0–0	1–2	0–1	2–2	4–0	1–0	0–0	2–4	*

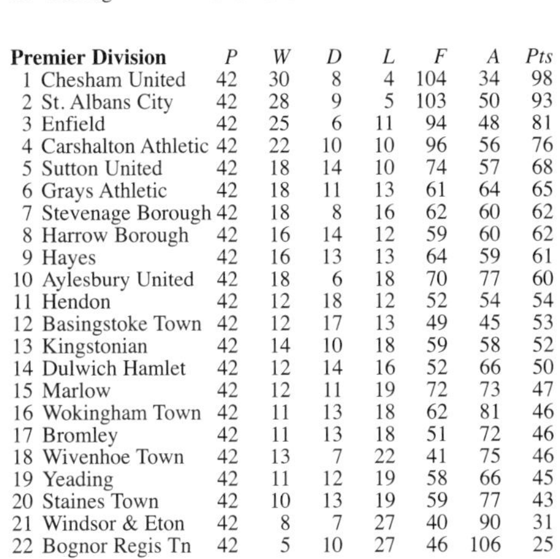

Premier Division	*P*	*W*	*D*	*L*	*F*	*A*	*Pts*
1 Chesham United	42	30	8	4	104	34	98
2 St. Albans City	42	28	9	5	103	50	93
3 Enfield	42	25	6	11	94	48	81
4 Carshalton Athletic	42	22	10	10	96	56	76
5 Sutton United	42	18	14	10	74	57	68
6 Grays Athletic	42	18	11	13	61	64	65
7 Stevenage Borough	42	18	8	16	62	60	62
8 Harrow Borough	42	16	14	12	59	60	62
9 Hayes	42	16	13	13	64	59	61
10 Aylesbury United	42	18	6	18	70	77	60
11 Hendon	42	12	18	12	52	54	54
12 Basingstoke Town	42	12	17	13	49	45	53
13 Kingstonian	42	14	10	18	59	58	52
14 Dulwich Hamlet	42	12	14	16	52	66	50
15 Marlow	42	12	11	19	72	73	47
16 Wokingham Town	42	11	13	18	62	81	46
17 Bromley	42	11	13	18	51	72	46
18 Wivenhoe Town	42	13	7	22	41	75	46
19 Yeading	42	11	12	19	58	66	45
20 Staines Town	42	10	13	19	59	77	43
21 Windsor & Eton	42	8	7	27	40	90	31
22 Bognor Regis Tn	42	5	10	27	46	106	25

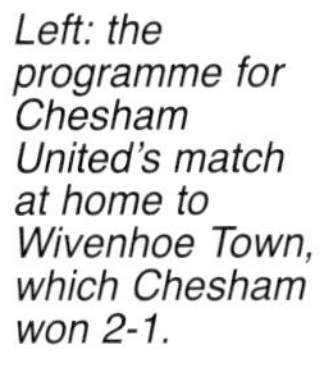

Left: the programme for Chesham United's match at home to Wivenhoe Town, which Chesham won 2-1.

Right: the 1992-93 programme for Hertford Town.

Division I	1	2	3	4	5	6	7	8	9	10	11	12	13	14	15	16	17	18	19	20	21
1 Abingdon Town	*	4–1	1–2	4–1	1–1	2–1	5–1	1–1	1–1	2–5	0–1	4–0	2–2	0–0	0–2	3–3	1–1	0–1	2–1	2–0	4–2
2 Aveley	1–5	*	2–2	0–2	1–0	0–2	2–1	1–3	1–3	2–2	1–1	4–0	1–3	3–3	2–3	0–2	2–2	0–0	1–4	0–1	2–1
3 Barking	1–0	2–1	*	1–1	1–2	1–0	2–1	1–2	0–2	1–2	0–0	1–2	3–1	1–0	0–5	0–2	0–1	1–1	1–1	1–1	0–1
4 Billericay Town	0–1	2–0	3–2	*	4–0	2–2	4–0	3–2	1–3	2–1	0–2	1–1	1–3	3–0	2–2	2–0	3–0	2–1	4–2	1–1	3–1
5 Bishop's Stortford	0–1	3–0	5–1	4–1	*	1–0	1–1	2–0	1–2	2–1	0–1	6–0	3–3	0–0	1–2	1–0	2–1	4–1	2–0	0–1	3–2
6 Boreham Wood	2–1	3–0	5–1	2–1	0–1	*	2–2	0–1	0–0	1–1	0–1	2–0	1–1	2–2	0–0	0–0	0–4	0–1	0–2	0–2	1–1
7 Chalfont St. Peter	2–2	2–2	3–0	2–0	2–2	1–1	*	1–1	2–2	0–1	0–1	4–1	1–1	1–1	1–1	2–2	2–1	0–1	0–2	2–1	1–1
8 Croydon	0–0	1–2	1–0	0–4	3–2	4–3	2–4	*	1–1	5–0	0–3	2–2	2–2	3–3	0–3	0–5	2–1	1–1	1–2	1–0	4–2
9 Dorking	0–1	4–2	7–0	2–1	1–0	0–2	4–1	2–1	*	2–1	1–0	5–0	2–1	1–0	1–2	0–1	3–1	1–0	4–0	1–3	2–3
10 Heybridge Swifts	1–2	1–2	2–1	1–2	0–1	1–1	0–2	3–0	0–2	*	0–7	1–2	2–3	0–1	2–1	0–1	1–2	1–0	3–3	1–0	2–1
11 Hitchin Town	1–1	3–0	3–2	2–1	2–3	1–0	6–0	2–0	1–2	1–0	*	1–0	2–0	1–1	2–0	3–1	2–1	2–1	1–2	0–0	3–0
12 Lewes	0–3	0–1	1–2	2–0	2–1	0–0	1–1	3–0	1–1	1–3	0–2	*	1–0	0–0	3–5	0–1	0–2	2–0	2–2	0–3	0–2
13 Leyton	0–0	1–2	2–1	0–1	2–2	0–1	1–0	2–1	0–2	0–0	2–0	0–0	*	1–1	2–4	4–1	2–0	4–4	1–1	0–3	5–0
14 Maidenhead Utd	0–0	1–0	3–4	3–1	0–2	1–1	2–2	1–0	0–1	0–0	2–3	4–0	1–0	*	0–0	2–2	1–1	1–0	3–1	0–0	3–0
15 Molesey	2–1	1–2	2–0	4–1	0–0	1–2	4–0	4–2	1–1	3–1	0–0	0–1	2–0	2–0	*	2–1	2–2	4–0	2–0	1–1	5–1
16 Purfleet	0–1	2–1	2–0	2–2	2–0	1–0	0–0	3–1	2–2	3–0	1–2	3–1	3–0	2–0	3–2	*	1–1	3–3	0–0	2–1	1–1
17 Tooting & M Utd	5–0	1–0	6–1	2–0	0–1	0–0	1–0	6–0	1–0	1–1	2–0	6–1	1–1	3–0	1–1	0–4	*	3–2	2–1	1–1	2–6
18 Uxbridge	0–1	4–1	2–0	3–2	1–1	1–4	3–2	3–2	1–2	2–1	1–2	1–1	1–1	1–1	1–1	1–1	0–2	*	0–0	2–3	2–0
19 Walton & Hersham	2–2	6–0	1–2	0–2	0–0	3–0	1–1	0–1	3–0	2–2	2–1	1–2	4–1	2–1	0–2	1–3	0–0	1–0	*	1–0	3–2
20 Wembley	3–2	3–1	1–1	3–0	1–1	0–1	2–0	1–0	1–1	0–2	1–1	1–1	0–2	1–2	0–1	2–1	1–0	0–0	1–1	*	0–0
21 Whyteleafe	0–2	3–1	2–2	0–1	1–2	1–2	3–0	3–3	2–2	1–1	1–0	4–0	4–2	5–1	1–2	1–0	1–1	1–3	2–0	0–0	*

Division I	*P*	*W*	*D*	*L*	*F*	*A*	*Pts*
1 Hitchin Town	40	25	7	8	67	29	82
2 Molesey	40	23	11	6	81	38	80
3 Dorking	40	23	9	8	73	40	78
4 Purfleet	40	19	12	9	67	42	69
5 Bishop's Stortford	40	19	10	11	63	42	67
6 Abingdon Town	40	17	13	10	65	47	64
7 Tooting & M Utd	40	17	12	11	68	46	63
8 Billericay Town	40	18	6	16	67	61	60
9 Wembley	40	14	15	11	44	34	57
10 Walton & Hersham	40	14	12	14	58	54	54
11 Boreham Wood	40	12	14	14	44	43	50
12 Maidenhead Utd	40	10	18	12	45	50	48
13 Leyton	40	11	14	15	56	61	47
14 Whyteleafe	40	12	10	16	63	71	46
15 Uxbridge	40	11	13	16	50	59	46
16 Heybridge Swifts	40	11	9	20	47	65	42
17 Croydon	40	11	9	20	54	82	42
18 Chalfont St. Peter	40	7	17	16	48	70	38
19 Barking	40	10	8	22	42	80	38
20 Lewes	40	9	10	21	34	80	37
21 Aveley	40	9	7	24	45	87	34

Leyton previously Leyton-Wingate.

Left: the programme for Leyton's match at home to Lewes, which finished goal-less.

Right: the programme for Hayes' FA Cup tie at Brighton & Hove Albion which the Church Road club lost 2-0.

1992-93 Division II	1	2	3	4	5	6	7	8	9	10	11	12	13	14	15	16	17	18	19	20	21	22
1 Banstead Athletic	*	2–2	0–1	0–1	1–2	1–2	1–1	5–2	1–1	8–0	4–2	2–0	1–0	0–1	4–1	1–2	1–0	1–0	4–1	2–2	0–0	0–3
2 Barton Rovers	1–0	*	1–1	2–2	3–0	0–0	1–0	0–0	0–3	3–0	0–0	0–3	0–1	0–1	1–1	2–1	2–2	1–1	0–2	3–2	1–1	0–2
3 Berkhamsted Town	1–1	2–0	*	4–0	3–3	1–2	6–1	1–0	1–3	2–2	2–1	1–0	1–2	2–1	2–1	1–0	3–1	6–3	3–0	2–0	0–3	1–2
4 Chertsey Town	1–2	0–1	5–1	*	5–1	0–3	2–1	3–0	1–0	7–2	2–1	1–3	1–3	1–1	2–4	2–1	2–3	5–0	6–1	2–3	1–1	1–2
5 Edgware Town	1–1	2–1	0–3	4–0	*	1–0	4–1	6–1	2–2	4–1	1–1	1–1	3–1	1–2	2–2	0–1	1–2	4–4	2–3	5–2	4–1	1–2
6 Egham Town	0–2	0–0	1–1	1–2	2–5	*	1–2	1–3	6–4	1–1	3–2	0–2	2–0	1–1	2–0	1–3	2–0	3–2	2–1	1–3	3–3	2–5
7 Hampton	0–0	2–0	0–2	1–3	3–3	2–3	*	2–2	1–0	1–0	3–2	0–1	1–3	0–0	2–0	1–1	1–0	0–2	7–0	3–1	3–0	3–0
8 Harefield United	3–2	0–2	0–0	0–2	1–2	1–0	0–1	*	1–1	0–1	0–1	0–3	0–2	2–2	2–0	0–1	0–1	0–0	3–0	1–4	1–2	0–4
9 Hemel Hempstead	1–1	3–0	0–1	2–1	2–0	2–0	1–0	1–0	*	3–0	1–1	2–1	1–0	3–2	4–2	1–4	3–0	4–3	2–1	1–0	0–0	0–0
10 Hungerford Town	0–5	2–0	0–1	1–0	1–1	0–2	0–3	1–3	1–6	*	2–1	0–0	1–0	1–0	1–4	0–0	0–1	1–0	1–4	2–1	1–3	1–1
11 Leatherhead	0–0	3–1	5–0	0–1	5–3	4–0	3–3	2–0	1–1	3–0	*	2–2	1–1	1–2	0–1	0–2	1–2	3–0	3–0	0–2	2–1	0–2
12 Malden Vale	3–0	2–2	3–4	0–0	2–1	1–0	1–1	0–1	3–2	5–1	1–2	*	3–1	1–2	1–2	1–2	2–0	2–3	3–1	4–3	3–0	2–1
13 Metropolitan Police	4–1	4–2	3–0	0–1	0–2	5–0	4–0	2–1	3–1	4–1	1–1	3–1	*	4–1	4–0	1–1	1–3	3–2	5–1	5–1	0–1	0–1
14 Newbury Town	1–1	2–2	0–2	2–2	1–0	0–0	3–1	0–1	2–2	0–0	2–2	2–1	3–0	*	3–2	0–0	1–1	1–0	0–1	1–1	0–0	3–1
15 Rainham Town	2–0	3–0	2–4	2–2	0–2	1–3	1–2	3–0	2–3	3–0	0–1	0–0	2–4	1–2	*	0–2	0–4	2–2	1–3	0–4	1–1	1–1
16 Ruislip Manor	1–1	4–0	4–0	1–0	3–1	0–0	1–1	2–1	1–0	1–0	5–0	2–0	0–0	1–1	2–1	*	3–2	4–0	8–0	0–3	2–2	3–2
17 Saffron Walden Tn	0–2	2–0	2–1	2–2	2–0	2–0	1–0	1–0	1–1	1–2	1–2	2–2	1–0	2–3	0–0	1–1	*	3–0	0–1	4–0	3–0	3–2
18 Southall	0–3	0–3	0–2	0–5	1–0	0–2	0–1	3–0	0–7	1–1	0–2	0–3	3–6	3–0	0–4	1–2	1–1	*	1–0	2–4	2–1	1–2
19 Tilbury	3–2	2–1	0–3	1–3	0–4	1–1	1–1	0–3	4–4	3–4	3–2	3–3	0–1	4–2	2–1	1–2	2–2	0–0	*	1–0	2–2	1–3
20 Ware	2–1	2–0	0–2	0–3	4–1	2–3	2–2	2–2	2–3	2–3	1–1	0–3	1–1	1–1	1–1	1–1	1–1	2–1	2–0	*	1–1	3–4
21 Witham Town	2–2	2–2	1–1	1–3	1–2	1–4	0–1	0–2	0–0	2–0	2–1	2–3	2–0	1–0	0–0	1–3	0–2	7–0	1–1	1–0	*	1–5
22 Worthing	2–1	4–0	2–2	2–1	2–2	4–0	3–0	6–0	2–3	3–1	3–1	2–3	2–2	1–1	5–2	2–0	3–1	5–1	3–0	1–0	3–2	*

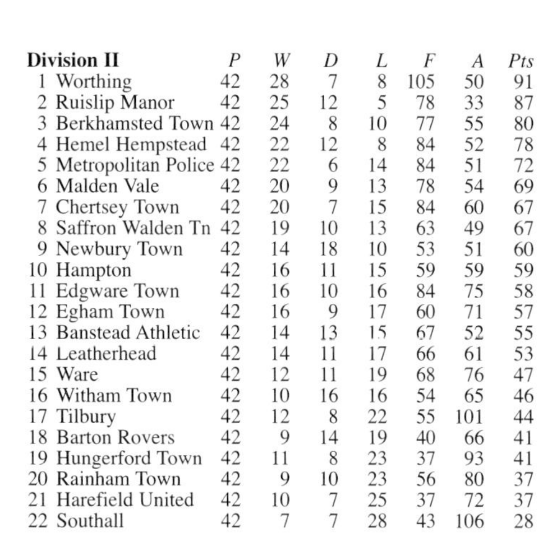

Division II	*P*	*W*	*D*	*L*	*F*	*A*	*Pts*
1 Worthing	42	28	7	8	105	50	91
2 Ruislip Manor	42	25	12	5	78	33	87
3 Berkhamsted Town	42	24	8	10	77	55	80
4 Hemel Hempstead	42	22	12	8	84	52	78
5 Metropolitan Police	42	22	6	14	84	51	72
6 Malden Vale	42	20	9	13	78	54	69
7 Chertsey Town	42	20	7	15	84	60	67
8 Saffron Walden Tn	42	19	10	13	63	49	67
9 Newbury Town	42	14	18	10	53	51	60
10 Hampton	42	16	11	15	59	59	59
11 Edgware Town	42	16	10	16	84	75	58
12 Egham Town	42	16	9	17	60	71	57
13 Banstead Athletic	42	14	13	15	67	52	55
14 Leatherhead	42	14	11	17	66	61	53
15 Ware	42	12	11	19	68	76	47
16 Witham Town	42	10	16	16	54	65	46
17 Tilbury	42	12	8	22	55	101	44
18 Barton Rovers	42	9	14	19	40	66	41
19 Hungerford Town	42	11	8	23	37	93	41
20 Rainham Town	42	9	10	23	56	80	37
21 Harefield United	42	10	7	25	37	72	37
22 Southall	42	7	7	28	43	106	28

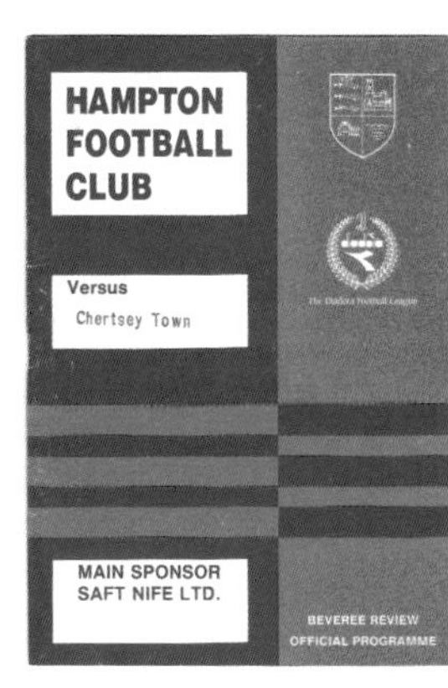

Left: the programme for Hampton's match at home to Chertsey Town, which they lost 3-1.

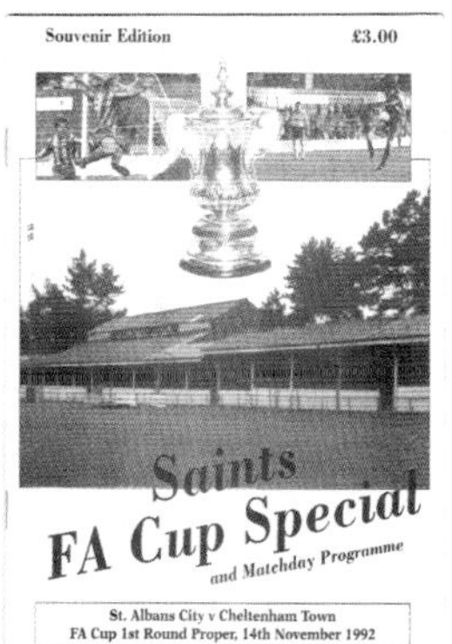

Right: the programme for St. Albans City's FA Cup tie at home to Cheltenham Town.

Division III	1	2	3	4	5	6	7	8	9	10	11	12	13	14	15	16	17	18	19	20
1 Aldershot Town	*	2–2	6–1	4–2	1–1	1–1	1–0	1–1	2–0	3–1	0–0	5–2	3–2	4–0	2–1	4–0	3–0	1–0	2–1	4–0
2 Bracknell Town	3–3	*	3–3	1–3	1–1	0–1	2–3	2–0	2–1	0–4	5–2	0–0	1–1	0–2	0–4	0–0	0–0	0–1	2–4	2–2
3 Camberley Town	1–3	0–0	*	1–0	0–1	1–2	0–3	0–1	2–1	0–2	0–2	1–2	2–2	0–1	0–3	1–4	1–1	1–1	0–2	0–4
4 Clapton	2–1	1–2	1–4	*	0–3	2–1	1–2	1–3	1–2	0–6	2–3	2–1	1–3	1–1	1–2	0–1	4–0	3–4	5–1	1–0
5 Collier Row	1–2	5–1	1–0	0–0	*	1–1	3–1	5–1	2–0	3–1	0–0	0–0	1–0	2–2	2–4	5–0	3–0	0–1	0–0	0–0
6 Cove	1–3	3–2	2–0	1–0	3–1	*	3–1	4–3	6–0	1–0	3–1	1–5	3–0	2–1	0–1	0–0	1–1	3–0	2–3	3–0
7 East Thurrock Utd	0–1	2–2	4–2	2–0	0–2	1–1	*	3–0	4–2	1–4	3–0	1–3	3–2	2–2	2–3	4–1	1–1	2–1	1–4	3–1
8 Epsom & Ewell	1–2	0–2	0–3	1–1	1–0	2–2	1–1	*	1–1	1–1	2–3	2–2	3–0	5–3	1–4	2–5	2–4	1–1	0–1	0–1
9 Feltham & H Boro'	1–3	3–5	1–3	4–1	0–4	0–1	0–1	1–3	*	1–4	2–3	2–2	0–5	1–5	2–7	3–5	3–2	3–2	0–5	3–1
10 Flackwell Heath	3–6	0–4	4–0	4–2	3–4	0–3	3–1	0–0	4–1	*	3–3	1–2	2–1	1–0	2–1	2–2	2–2	1–0	1–1	2–3
11 Hertford Town	2–3	3–2	3–1	0–2	0–0	1–2	1–2	1–2	4–0	4–6	*	3–1	2–2	1–0	0–2	3–3	1–0	0–1	0–3	1–1
12 Hornchurch	1–3	2–0	0–1	1–1	1–2	0–0	1–0	0–1	3–0	5–2	0–0	*	2–1	3–1	0–0	1–1	0–0	1–2	0–1	2–0
13 Horsham	0–1	2–2	2–3	3–0	0–2	1–0	1–0	2–1	6–0	2–1	0–2	3–1	*	5–3	1–1	2–3	0–1	1–1	1–2	2–4
14 Kingsbury Town	0–1	4–0	0–0	3–1	0–0	1–3	0–4	0–3	3–2	2–1	4–1	2–1	3–0	*	1–0	1–1	3–1	1–0	1–1	1–3
15 Leighton Town	1–0	6–0	4–2	2–0	1–3	4–2	3–2	3–3	4–1	3–1	1–2	1–1	2–3	0–0	*	4–1	4–1	2–0	1–1	2–2
16 Northwood	1–1	4–3	3–1	2–0	1–2	0–1	2–3	1–0	2–2	5–4	2–1	4–3	5–1	3–2	1–1	*	5–0	1–1	2–1	3–2
17 Petersfield United	0–3	0–0	1–0	1–1	0–2	0–0	0–4	1–1	3–0	0–6	2–5	3–3	2–3	2–5	1–2	1–3	*	0–4	0–5	1–1
18 Royston Town	0–1	9–0	1–0	2–1	0–3	1–0	0–0	2–1	2–0	6–0	1–2	3–0	1–1	1–0	2–2	3–2	1–2	*	2–3	1–0
19 Thame United	2–2	9–0	1–1	1–1	2–0	3–0	2–0	2–0	3–3	1–0	1–1	1–0	4–1	1–1	3–2	0–2	8–0	0–0	*	0–1
20 Tring Town	0–2	4–1	0–1	1–1	2–3	1–6	2–2	1–2	3–1	2–0	0–0	1–1	4–1	2–3	1–1	3–3	0–2	3–1	3–1	*

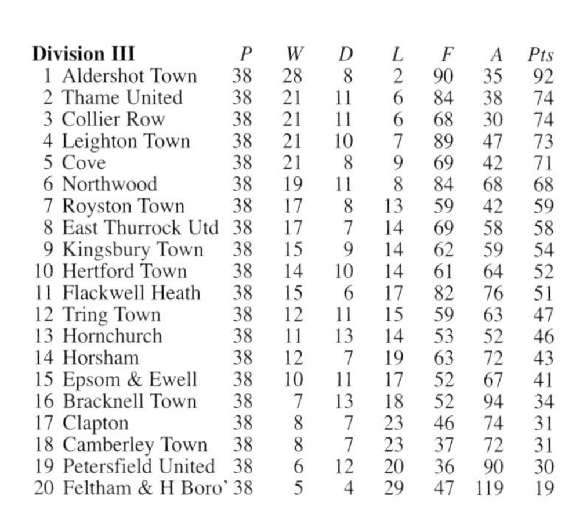

Division III	*P*	*W*	*D*	*L*	*F*	*A*	*Pts*
1 Aldershot Town	38	28	8	2	90	35	92
2 Thame United	38	21	11	6	84	38	74
3 Collier Row	38	21	11	6	68	30	74
4 Leighton Town	38	21	10	7	89	47	73
5 Cove	38	21	8	9	69	42	71
6 Northwood	38	19	11	8	84	68	68
7 Royston Town	38	17	8	13	59	42	59
8 East Thurrock Utd	38	17	7	14	69	58	58
9 Kingsbury Town	38	15	9	14	62	59	54
10 Hertford Town	38	14	10	14	61	64	52
11 Flackwell Heath	38	15	6	17	82	76	51
12 Tring Town	38	12	11	15	59	63	47
13 Hornchurch	38	11	13	14	53	52	46
14 Horsham	38	12	7	19	63	72	43
15 Epsom & Ewell	38	10	11	17	52	67	41
16 Bracknell Town	38	7	13	18	52	94	34
17 Clapton	38	8	7	23	46	74	31
18 Camberley Town	38	8	7	23	37	72	31
19 Petersfield United	38	6	12	20	36	90	30
20 Feltham & H Boro'	38	5	4	29	47	119	19

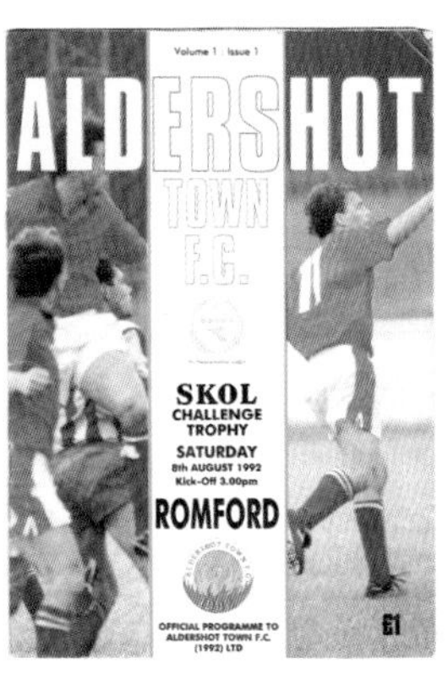

Two of the season's new clubs

Left: the programme for Aldershot Town's first ever match, at home to Romford, before starting life as Isthmians.

Right: the programme for Leighton Town against Horsham.

1993–94 - It was a season of fixture congestion due to the bad weather which caused most clubs to lose several matches to waterlogged pitches. Stevenage Borough were worthy champions, claiming the Premier Division title and promotion to the GM Vauxhall Conference in their second season in the top division, five points clear of runners-up Enfield who improved by one place from the previous year. Marlow enjoyed their highest League position since gaining promotion in 1987 and previous champions Chesham United finished fourth. At the other end Dorking, after just one season in the Premier Division, Basingstoke Town and Wivenhoe Town were relegated to Division One. Returning to the Premier Division after two seasons' absence were champions of Division One Bishop's Stortford together with Purfleet and Walton & Hersham who just pipped Tooting & Mitcham United for third place. Relegated to Division Two were Chalfont St. Peter, Windsor & Eton and Croydon, who had a disastrous season conceding a record 198 goals. Division Two was effectively a three-horse race with the championship not decided until the last week of the season when Newbury Town bettered Chertsey Town by one point with both clubs scoring well over one hundred goals. Aldershot Town were third, achieving back-to-back promotions. At the foot of the table Lewes, Collier Row, after just one season, and Rainham Town were relegated to Division Three although the latter had resigned from the League. In a close championship Bracknell Town won the Division Three championship by two points from Cheshunt with Oxford City third, just beating Harlow Town for the final promotion place.

At the Annual General Meeting Slough Town, relegated from the GM Vauxhall Conference, were elected to replace champions Stevenage Borough. Canvey Island (Essex Senior League) and Bedford Town (South Midlands League) were elected to Division Three replacing Rainham Town and Royston Town who had resigned from the League.

Premier Division	1	2	3	4	5	6	7	8	9	10	11	12	13	14	15	16	17	18	19	20	21	22
1 Aylesbury United	*	4–4	2–1	3–0	0–2	2–0	1–3	1–0	0–1	0–1	1–0	2–3	1–1	3–6	1–5	2–1	1–2	0–1	1–2	3–0	3–0	1–1
2 Basingstoke Town	2–3	*	1–3	0–2	3–3	0–0	0–1	1–2	0–0	1–1	4–1	0–1	1–3	1–1	1–3	1–2	0–1	1–2	0–0	6–2	1–2	1–1
3 Bromley	0–0	3–0	*	0–2	1–2	2–1	3–2	1–2	0–2	0–3	0–0	3–3	0–0	2–2	2–3	0–1	2–0	1–2	1–4	6–0	1–0	2–1
4 Carshalton Athletic	1–3	2–0	2–1	*	1–1	1–2	0–1	0–3	3–0	2–1	2–0	3–0	1–4	1–4	2–1	0–1	3–3	2–0	1–0	4–3	1–0	2–0
5 Chesham United	1–4	2–1	5–0	2–1	*	3–0	2–1	2–3	2–1	3–0	0–1	2–1	0–3	1–0	1–3	0–1	0–0	1–2	1–0	5–1	3–0	3–2
6 Dorking	1–4	1–2	0–3	1–4	3–4	*	0–1	1–3	3–3	4–3	0–1	1–2	3–1	2–0	2–3	3–1	1–2	1–5	1–3	4–1	1–3	4–3
7 Dulwich Hamlet	2–0	1–1	1–2	2–1	0–2	1–1	*	2–2	2–3	1–2	3–2	0–1	0–0	1–7	2–3	1–0	1–2	0–2	0–3	0–1	2–2	1–1
8 Enfield	4–0	0–1	2–0	1–1	0–1	6–0	3–0	*	1–0	2–0	2–0	1–0	0–3	3–0	0–0	3–0	1–1	3–0	1–0	8–0	1–0	0–0
9 Grays Athletic	2–0	2–0	3–2	1–1	0–2	4–0	4–0	1–4	*	0–1	0–1	0–3	0–2	0–3	4–7	1–2	0–1	1–2	1–0	1–0	0–3	2–1
10 Harrow Borough	0–1	4–0	0–0	3–0	0–4	3–2	2–1	1–1	1–1	*	3–3	2–1	1–1	2–4	2–0	1–1	0–0	1–0	0–1	3–0	1–1	1–0
11 Hayes	0–0	4–0	3–1	3–3	1–1	3–2	1–2	0–1	1–3	1–1	*	1–1	2–2	2–1	2–0	3–0	2–1	1–3	1–8	0–2	1–2	0–1
12 Hendon	2–2	6–0	2–1	1–1	0–1	3–1	2–1	0–2	2–1	0–2	0–2	*	2–4	0–0	0–1	2–0	1–0	1–2	0–1	0–2	1–1	5–2
13 Hitchin Town	5–1	1–0	1–0	1–0	2–1	2–3	2–3	2–3	2–3	0–1	3–2	0–0	*	1–3	2–1	2–0	1–3	1–3	0–0	6–2	1–0	4–2
14 Kingstonian	2–1	5–0	3–0	0–2	1–2	2–2	3–0	1–2	3–0	7–0	4–1	1–3	3–5	*	1–1	0–0	0–1	3–5	0–2	8–1	5–0	1–2
15 Marlow	1–0	2–0	3–4	0–6	0–2	2–1	4–2	2–1	3–1	0–1	4–3	2–1	1–0	3–3	*	2–1	4–2	0–0	3–2	3–1	3–1	1–1
16 Molesey	1–2	0–0	2–3	0–1	1–1	3–0	0–0	0–1	0–2	0–0	3–2	2–3	1–2	1–1	1–1	*	2–1	1–2	0–0	4–0	2–0	0–0
17 St. Albans City	1–1	6–1	2–0	1–3	1–1	3–0	4–3	2–1	5–3	3–1	4–0	0–0	2–1	1–4	1–2	4–1	*	1–2	0–0	9–1	2–0	1–1
18 Stevenage Borough	4–0	0–0	0–1	2–4	0–0	4–3	2–0	0–1	1–0	3–0	2–1	3–0	1–2	4–1	4–2	4–2	3–0	*	3–2	6–0	1–0	4–1
19 Sutton United	3–1	5–0	3–0	2–2	3–1	3–0	0–3	1–1	1–0	3–1	0–1	0–1	2–0	2–1	2–2	4–1	4–1	0–0	*	5–0	1–0	1–1
20 Wivenhoe Town	0–4	1–2	0–0	0–8	1–1	1–0	3–4	1–2	0–4	2–3	0–6	0–4	0–7	1–1	2–3	3–4	0–3	0–1	0–3	*	3–2	2–4
21 Wokingham Town	0–3	0–0	2–1	0–4	2–0	3–1	0–1	1–1	3–0	0–1	0–1	0–2	2–0	1–3	0–6	1–1	1–3	0–1	0–1	1–0	*	1–2
22 Yeading	1–2	3–1	2–3	2–1	0–2	1–2	0–0	1–2	1–1	2–0	2–3	1–1	2–1	2–3	2–0	3–0	1–1	0–2	0–0	4–1	1–3	*

Premier Division	*P*	*W*	*D*	*L*	*F*	*A*	*Pts*
1 Stevenage Borough	42	31	4	7	88	39	97
2 Enfield	42	28	8	6	80	28	92
3 Marlow	42	25	7	10	90	67	82
4 Chesham United	42	24	8	10	73	45	80
5 Sutton United	42	23	10	9	77	31	79
6 Carshalton Athletic	42	22	7	13	81	53	73
7 St. Albans City	42	21	10	11	81	54	73
8 Hitchin Town	42	21	7	14	81	56	70
9 Harrow Borough	42	18	11	13	54	56	65
10 Kingstonian	42	18	9	15	101	64	63
11 Hendon	42	18	9	15	61	51	63
12 Aylesbury United	42	17	7	18	64	67	58
13 Hayes	42	15	8	19	63	72	53
14 Grays Athletic	42	15	5	22	56	69	50
15 Bromley	42	14	7	21	56	69	49
16 Dulwich Hamlet	42	13	8	21	52	74	47
17 Yeading	42	11	13	18	58	66	46
18 Molesey	42	11	11	20	44	62	44
19 Wokingham Town	42	11	6	25	38	67	39
20 Dorking	42	9	4	29	58	104	31
21 Basingstoke Town	42	5	12	25	38	86	27
22 Wivenhoe Town	42	5	3	34	38	152	18

Left: the programme for Billericay Town's match at home to Leyton which they lost by the odd goal in seven!

Right: the programme for Champions Stevenage Borough's match at home to Harrow Borough which they won 3-0.

Division I	1	2	3	4	5	6	7	8	9	10	11	12	13	14	15	16	17	18	19	20	21	22
1 Abingdon Town	*	0–1	1–0	0–3	1–0	1–1	3–1	1–1	2–1	0–0	2–1	3–1	1–1	2–0	2–1	0–1	1–0	0–3	3–3	1–2	1–0	3–3
2 Barking	1–1	*	0–0	2–2	3–2	0–0	0–2	1–0	0–2	3–2	1–2	1–1	0–3	1–1	3–2	1–2	0–3	4–2	0–1	5–0	3–0	0–1
3 Berkhamsted Town	3–2	0–0	*	0–2	0–1	1–1	3–2	2–1	14–1	3–3	1–1	0–2	1–5	0–1	4–1	0–4	3–4	2–3	1–3	2–2	2–1	2–0
4 Billericay Town	2–0	1–0	1–1	*	0–0	1–0	0–1	3–4	3–0	0–4	3–4	3–2	2–2	6–1	0–5	0–1	2–0	3–1	0–1	3–4	1–1	0–0
5 Bishop's Stortford	2–0	4–0	3–0	1–2	*	1–0	5–2	4–0	9–1	0–0	2–2	1–1	2–3	3–0	3–1	2–2	1–2	1–0	3–1	5–1	5–0	2–0
6 Bognor Regis Tn	1–0	1–2	4–2	0–1	0–0	*	2–2	4–1	8–0	1–2	3–2	2–1	2–2	1–0	3–1	1–1	1–0	0–1	0–4	4–1	0–1	0–0
7 Boreham Wood	1–1	2–3	0–0	1–1	0–0	0–0	*	0–1	10–0	2–1	1–2	2–0	0–2	3–1	1–1	2–1	1–0	0–0	0–0	1–0	2–2	3–1
8 Chalfont St. Peter	0–1	1–1	0–2	1–3	1–1	0–0	1–1	*	4–0	1–1	0–6	0–2	1–2	0–2	0–5	2–1	1–2	1–1	2–1	0–1	3–0	0–3
9 Croydon	0–9	4–1	0–4	0–1	1–4	1–2	1–5	2–2	*	0–0	1–3	0–3	1–4	2–7	0–14	0–7	1–4	1–4	1–2	3–7	1–2	0–7
10 Heybridge Swifts	0–0	2–3	4–1	3–1	2–3	2–0	1–2	4–1	6–0	*	3–2	2–1	0–0	0–0	0–0	0–1	4–2	1–2	2–2	3–0	1–0	2–1
11 Leyton	2–3	0–2	1–3	0–2	0–1	2–1	1–1	3–2	3–1	1–2	*	1–1	2–1	2–0	5–3	0–1	4–0	5–1	4–1	6–1	3–3	1–1
12 Maidenhead Utd	0–1	3–2	1–0	0–2	1–1	1–1	0–2	3–1	4–0	1–0	0–1	*	1–1	1–2	0–1	1–1	0–0	0–1	0–0	4–0	4–1	1–2
13 Purfleet	4–0	2–1	1–1	3–2	0–2	2–0	0–2	1–0	2–4	0–0	1–0	1–0	*	2–1	4–0	1–0	0–3	0–0	0–0	0–1	3–1	1–1
14 Ruislip Manor	0–2	2–2	1–2	1–1	1–1	2–0	1–2	1–2	0–0	1–2	1–0	3–1	2–3	*	0–6	3–0	0–0	0–1	2–0	0–2	1–2	2–1
15 Staines Town	0–0	1–3	2–0	1–1	0–0	0–2	1–1	2–0	3–0	0–1	2–3	3–1	0–1	4–0	*	3–0	4–1	0–0	3–2	1–0	2–0	2–1
16 Tooting & M Utd	3–0	3–1	3–0	1–1	0–1	0–1	3–3	0–0	6–0	2–0	2–2	0–0	3–1	1–0	4–2	*	1–0	1–0	1–4	1–0	2–0	1–1
17 Uxbridge	1–0	2–2	6–0	0–1	0–1	2–2	4–2	2–1	3–1	0–1	1–2	0–0	1–2	0–0	2–0	0–2	*	2–3	0–3	0–0	2–1	1–1
18 Walton & Hersham	1–3	3–3	2–1	1–2	2–2	3–0	3–1	1–0	6–2	2–1	5–2	2–2	2–2	5–0	1–1	1–1	1–0	*	2–1	2–1	3–1	1–2
19 Wembley	4–5	3–0	3–0	3–2	0–1	0–1	1–2	1–0	7–0	0–1	1–1	0–2	1–1	2–0	2–0	0–1	2–0	1–1	*	1–4	0–1	2–4
20 Whyteleafe	0–1	1–4	2–1	0–0	1–1	2–4	1–2	3–2	6–1	3–2	1–2	1–3	0–1	6–2	3–3	2–0	0–2	1–4	1–1	*	3–1	3–2
21 Windsor & Eton	1–2	2–3	1–3	0–4	0–1	2–2	0–0	1–1	5–3	1–4	2–3	1–0	1–4	1–0	2–3	1–1	1–4	1–4	0–2	4–3	*	2–3
22 Worthing	0–1	3–0	1–0	1–2	0–1	1–1	2–1	4–1	5–0	2–3	2–1	2–2	2–1	6–0	0–1	0–0	5–1	1–0	0–0	5–1	2–0	*

1993-94 Division I	P	W	D	L	F	A	Pts
1 Bishop's Stortford	42	24	13	5	83	31	85
2 Purfleet	42	22	12	8	70	44	78
3 Walton & Hersham	42	22	11	9	81	53	77
4 Tooting & M Utd	42	21	12	9	66	37	75
5 Heybridge Swifts	42	20	11	11	72	45	71
6 Billericay Town	42	20	11	11	70	51	71
7 Abingdon Town	42	20	10	12	61	50	70
8 Worthing	42	19	11	12	79	46	68
9 Leyton	42	20	8	14	88	66	68
10 Boreham Wood	42	17	15	10	69	50	66
11 Staines Town	42	18	9	15	85	56	63
12 Bognor Regis Tn	42	15	14	13	57	48	59
13 Wembley	42	16	10	16	66	52	58
14 Barking	42	15	11	16	63	69	56
15 Uxbridge	42	15	8	19	57	58	53
16 Whyteleafe	42	15	6	21	71	90	51
17 Maidenhead Utd	42	12	13	17	52	48	49
18 Berkhamsted Town	42	12	9	21	65	77	45
19 Ruislip Manor	42	10	8	24	42	79	38
20 Chalfont St. Peter	42	7	10	25	40	79	31
21 Windsor & Eton	42	8	7	27	47	94	31
22 Croydon	42	3	3	36	37	198	12

Left: the programme for Bromley's 1993-94 campaign.

Right: the Worthing programme for the same season.

Division II	1	2	3	4	5	6	7	8	9	10	11	12	13	14	15	16	17	18	19	20	21	22
1 Aldershot Town	*	2–1	1–2	1–0	1–1	1–0	3–0	3–2	3–0	2–0	3–1	1–0	4–0	1–2	3–1	1–0	2–0	1–0	0–0	2–0	4–0	1–0
2 Aveley	1–0	*	1–0	2–2	2–3	2–1	1–2	4–0	1–0	0–3	3–2	0–2	2–1	1–0	0–1	1–2	6–2	0–0	1–5	2–1	4–1	0–1
3 Banstead Athletic	0–0	2–2	*	0–3	4–3	2–0	1–3	1–0	2–0	0–0	3–2	3–0	1–0	1–1	0–1	0–1	4–1	0–2	3–1	3–1	1–0	1–1
4 Barton Rovers	0–1	2–0	1–0	*	1–0	3–0	5–4	4–1	1–1	0–0	2–0	1–0	4–0	0–2	1–0	0–0	3–0	0–1	2–2	2–0	3–2	0–3
5 Chertsey Town	3–2	3–2	4–0	3–2	*	10–2	1–1	0–0	2–0	5–1	4–2	6–2	5–0	3–0	5–1	3–2	4–0	5–2	5–0	1–0	3–0	5–1
6 Collier Row	1–3	1–2	2–3	1–0	2–3	*	2–2	3–1	0–1	0–1	1–1	2–1	0–0	0–3	2–2	0–3	0–2	3–2	3–2	0–3	1–3	0–2
7 Edgware Town	0–2	2–2	1–1	0–1	2–3	5–1	*	3–4	1–1	3–1	2–2	1–1	2–3	1–2	1–3	1–3	4–1	4–1	2–2	3–1	3–0	3–4
8 Egham Town	0–0	1–0	0–1	1–1	1–2	0–0	2–7	*	0–2	1–0	0–5	1–1	4–0	0–1	2–1	0–0	3–0	0–3	0–2	3–0	1–1	3–1
9 Hampton	0–3	4–0	2–1	0–1	0–2	2–1	1–2	0–1	*	1–1	1–0	2–3	1–1	1–4	0–1	1–1	2–0	0–3	0–3	1–2	3–1	0–5
10 Hemel Hempstead	0–1	0–1	2–3	0–3	2–0	2–1	1–1	0–2	0–1	*	5–0	1–1	2–1	1–1	1–3	0–3	2–0	3–1	0–1	2–0	3–0	1–1
11 Hungerford Town	0–0	3–1	1–0	2–3	2–1	3–1	2–1	0–1	2–0	0–3	*	4–0	3–1	1–2	1–4	0–1	1–0	0–2	1–1	4–0	0–0	0–1
12 Leatherhead	0–5	2–3	1–2	0–2	1–5	0–1	0–2	2–0	1–0	0–1	2–0	*	1–0	1–0	2–1	3–6	6–0	0–1	0–8	0–0	0–2	1–2
13 Lewes	1–3	1–2	0–0	0–1	1–3	1–0	1–1	2–1	0–4	0–0	1–0	1–1	*	1–1	1–3	1–4	2–0	2–0	0–2	3–2	1–2	2–3
14 Malden Vale	1–2	1–1	1–1	0–1	2–0	0–2	0–2	1–0	2–0	0–0	2–0	2–1	6–1	*	2–2	1–2	5–1	3–2	2–1	3–4	3–1	1–1
15 Metropolitan Police	1–3	5–1	1–3	1–1	0–1	2–0	0–2	0–3	2–1	0–0	5–1	5–0	4–2	1–1	*	1–1	0–1	2–1	0–0	4–1	0–0	1–1
16 Newbury Town	0–3	4–1	2–0	3–0	5–2	6–0	3–1	4–1	4–2	1–0	2–1	6–0	2–1	2–0	2–0	*	7–0	6–1	3–3	4–2	4–0	5–1
17 Rainham Town	1–2	0–1	1–4	0–4	0–3	1–1	1–2	0–3	0–3	1–0	0–3	0–4	0–0	1–7	1–2	1–2	*	3–0	1–6	2–3	0–5	0–1
18 Saffron Walden Tn	2–2	0–1	3–0	0–1	0–1	1–1	0–4	5–1	2–0	1–0	2–2	3–2	7–1	0–0	1–5	0–0	1–0	*	2–2	3–1	3–0	2–1
19 Thame United	3–0	0–1	0–1	3–2	1–3	3–0	7–0	0–0	5–0	2–2	2–1	3–0	1–0	1–2	1–3	1–2	2–1	2–0	*	0–1	2–2	1–1
20 Tilbury	1–2	2–1	3–0	3–4	1–2	2–0	1–5	1–2	0–2	1–0	1–2	5–2	1–2	1–2	2–3	1–1	2–1	0–1	2–2	*	5–1	1–0
21 Ware	0–2	1–0	3–1	0–1	0–2	0–0	2–1	3–2	2–1	0–3	1–1	4–2	1–1	2–1	0–3	0–1	2–0	1–0	1–2	2–1	*	0–2
22 Witham Town	2–2	1–3	1–1	0–0	0–1	2–1	3–1	1–0	4–1	0–3	1–0	0–0	1–1	4–0	2–0	1–5	2–0	2–0	1–2	2–0	5–2	*

Division II	P	W	D	L	F	A	Pts
1 Newbury Town	42	32	7	3	115	36	103
2 Chertsey Town	42	33	3	6	121	48	102
3 Aldershot Town	42	30	7	5	78	27	97
4 Barton Rovers	42	25	8	9	68	37	83
5 Witham Town	42	21	10	11	68	51	73
6 Malden Vale	42	20	10	12	70	49	70
7 Thame United	42	19	12	11	87	51	69
8 Metropolitan Police	42	20	9	13	75	54	69
9 Banstead Athletic	42	19	9	14	56	53	66
10 Aveley	42	19	5	18	60	66	62
11 Edgware Town	42	16	10	16	88	76	58
12 Saffron Walden Tn	42	17	7	18	61	62	58
13 Hemel Hempstead	42	14	11	17	47	43	53
14 Egham Town	42	14	8	20	48	65	50
15 Ware	42	14	7	21	48	76	49
16 Hungerford Town	42	13	7	22	56	66	46
17 Tilbury	42	13	3	26	59	81	42
18 Hampton	42	12	5	25	42	70	41
19 Leatherhead	42	10	6	26	46	92	36
20 Lewes	42	8	10	24	38	85	34
21 Collier Row	42	7	8	27	37	88	29
22 Rainham Town	42	4	2	36	24	116	14

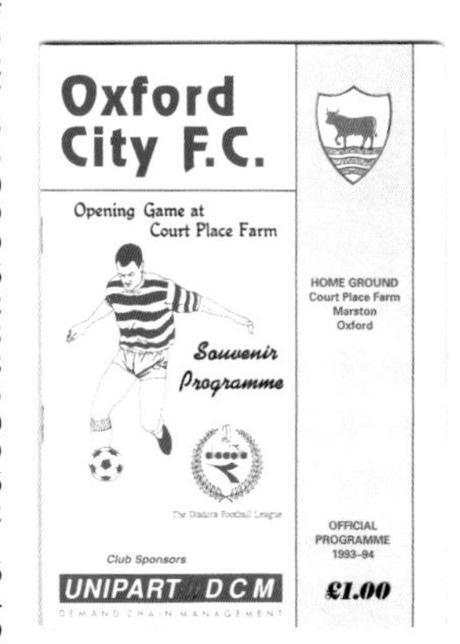

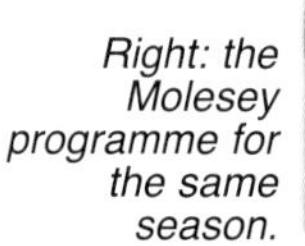

Left: the programme for Oxford City's first game at their new Court Place Farm ground against Oxford United.

Right: the Molesey programme for the same season.

Division III	1	2	3	4	5	6	7	8	9	10	11	12	13	14	15	16	17	18	19	20	21
1 Bracknell Town	*	1–1	2–0	1–0	3–1	4–2	3–2	0–1	2–2	3–2	2–3	6–0	3–0	3–0	2–2	2–0	1–1	4–0	2–0	2–1	2–0
2 Camberley Town	0–1	*	1–1	2–0	5–1	4–0	0–0	2–0	2–0	1–1	0–1	3–1	3–0	3–1	1–1	0–0	1–0	2–1	1–0	3–1	3–1
3 Cheshunt	0–0	1–0	*	0–0	0–1	1–3	1–0	2–0	1–1	0–1	0–0	2–2	2–1	4–3	1–1	2–0	4–1	2–0	1–0	2–1	2–1
4 Clapton	1–0	2–0	1–3	*	1–1	3–2	2–0	4–2	1–1	1–1	2–3	3–1	0–2	2–1	1–1	3–0	0–1	1–3	3–0	0–1	4–0
5 Cove	0–3	1–0	0–2	4–3	*	2–1	2–5	2–2	5–1	0–0	2–0	1–2	4–1	2–1	1–4	5–2	3–3	1–2	2–0	5–2	1–0
6 East Thurrock Utd	1–1	1–2	1–1	1–1	5–0	*	2–4	2–3	1–3	1–2	0–0	1–1	2–0	3–0	2–2	5–0	4–4	1–1	1–1	2–2	2–0
7 Epsom & Ewell	0–1	3–1	0–1	1–0	3–1	2–2	*	0–2	4–0	3–2	1–1	3–1	2–1	1–0	1–1	1–2	2–5	2–3	2–0	0–3	1–1
8 Feltham & H Boro'	1–2	3–0	1–3	3–0	1–1	5–1	2–1	*	0–1	0–1	0–0	3–2	1–2	5–0	1–2	0–3	5–2	3–1	0–0	1–2	2–1
9 Flackwell Heath	1–0	1–0	0–0	1–1	0–0	1–5	2–2	2–1	*	1–4	1–2	1–2	0–1	1–1	1–4	1–1	1–5	1–4	1–2	0–2	1–4
10 Harefield United	0–1	1–0	1–3	1–1	1–0	0–0	0–1	2–2	1–1	*	2–3	0–0	2–0	1–0	1–0	0–1	2–2	1–5	1–1	1–1	1–3
11 Harlow Town	3–0	2–0	0–1	2–1	1–0	1–0	2–0	3–0	3–0	1–1	*	1–0	0–1	1–1	2–3	4–2	1–1	1–2	1–0	2–2	1–1
12 Hertford Town	1–0	2–1	0–2	5–1	1–2	3–2	4–2	3–0	3–1	1–2	2–3	*	0–2	4–2	2–3	1–1	1–0	2–1	0–2	1–1	1–0
13 Hornchurch	0–0	0–0	0–2	0–1	2–1	0–1	2–0	3–1	1–2	1–1	0–3	1–2	*	3–2	3–1	1–1	2–1	2–1	1–2	0–1	3–4
14 Horsham	0–6	0–5	1–1	3–0	3–1	3–1	2–5	1–3	1–3	0–1	0–2	0–1	1–1	*	0–0	3–2	3–1	1–2	0–0	1–3	1–2
15 Kingsbury Town	0–0	1–4	1–3	2–3	1–2	1–0	2–3	1–0	4–1	3–0	0–0	0–1	1–0	1–1	*	0–0	2–0	1–1	1–2	1–2	1–1
16 Leighton Town	1–2	4–0	1–4	2–1	4–0	2–3	2–1	2–1	1–3	5–0	1–3	2–0	0–0	2–0	1–0	*	2–2	1–3	0–0	1–1	1–1
17 Northwood	0–5	5–1	2–2	4–0	2–1	1–1	2–4	1–1	0–1	3–3	2–1	0–6	2–1	3–1	2–3	2–0	*	3–2	1–2	2–1	1–0
18 Oxford City	1–0	4–1	1–2	5–0	2–3	2–0	3–0	1–1	4–0	0–0	3–0	6–4	3–1	3–1	2–1	2–0	4–4	*	3–2	3–0	5–0
19 Royston Town	0–1	0–1	3–0	1–0	1–0	0–2	0–0	3–1	2–0	4–1	0–1	1–1	1–1	2–1	2–2	1–1	2–0	3–1	*	1–0	1–2
20 Southall	1–6	6–0	0–1	3–3	2–0	0–0	1–1	3–0	4–3	2–1	1–1	2–1	1–1	0–0	2–1	3–0	1–2	1–2	4–2	*	0–0
21 Tring Town	0–1	1–2	2–3	1–0	2–0	1–1	0–0	1–2	2–2	0–2	1–2	1–2	5–1	2–3	2–1	3–0	0–5	2–2	0–0	0–2	*

1993-94 Division III	P	W	D	L	F	A	Pts
1 Bracknell Town	40	25	8	7	78	29	83
2 Cheshunt	40	23	12	5	62	34	81
3 Oxford City	40	24	6	10	94	55	78
4 Harlow Town	40	22	11	7	61	36	77
5 Southall	40	17	12	11	66	53	63
6 Camberley Town	40	18	7	15	56	50	61
7 Hertford Town	40	18	6	16	67	65	60
8 Royston Town	40	15	11	14	44	41	56
9 Northwood	40	15	11	14	78	77	56
10 Epsom & Ewell	40	15	9	16	63	62	54
11 Harefield United	40	12	15	13	45	55	51
12 Cove	40	15	6	19	59	74	51
13 Kingsbury Town	40	12	14	14	57	54	50
14 Feltham & H Boro'	40	14	7	19	60	63	49
15 Leighton Town	40	12	11	17	51	64	47
16 East Thurrock Utd	40	10	15	15	65	64	45
17 Clapton	40	12	9	19	51	65	45
18 Hornchurch	40	12	8	20	42	60	44
19 Tring Town	40	10	11	19	48	64	41
20 Flackwell Heath	40	9	11	20	44	83	38
21 Horsham	40	6	8	26	43	86	26

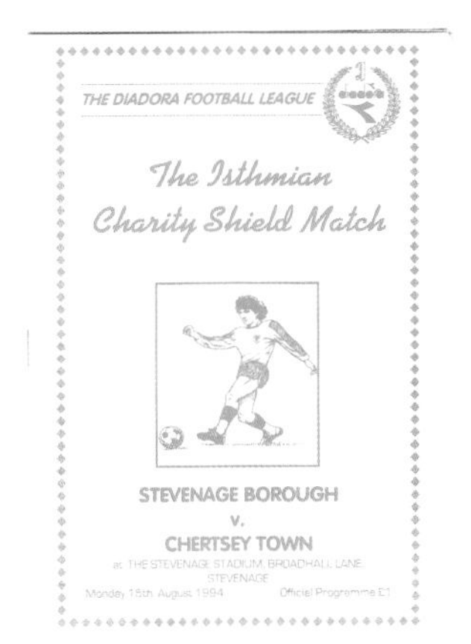

Above left: the programme for Charity Shield match between Champions Stevenage Borough and League Cup winners Chertsey Town.
Above right: Bedford Town's programme for the 1994-95 season.

1994–95 - After being runners-up three times in the last four seasons Enfield finally secured the Premier Division title beating Slough Town, their nearest challengers, by fourteen points. However, they were unable to meet the financial part of the Conference criteria and their place went to runners-up Slough Town. The three clubs relegated to Division One were all Berks & Bucks affiliated clubs, namely Chesham United, Marlow and Wokingham Town. Boreham Wood romped home with the Division One championship twenty-two points clear of second placed Worthing with the third promotion place going to Chertsey Town, their second successive promotion and only achieved by a superior goal-difference to fourth placed Aldershot Town. The three clubs relegated to Division Two were Newbury Town who made an immediate return to the Division Two following the previous year's promotion, Wivenhoe Town and Dorking who were both relegated in successive years following demotion the previous season from the Premier Division. In Division Two Thame United were crowned champions finishing eleven points ahead of runners-up Barton Rovers with Oxford City in third just beating Bracknell Town by two points thus gaining successive promotions. Relegated to Division Three were Windsor & Eton, Aveley and Malden Vale with the latter resigning from the League while in Division Three Collier Row gained an immediate return to Division Two with the championship and also promoted were Canvey Island and Bedford Town who both were playing in their first season.

Below: the programme for The FA Trophy Semi Final Second Leg between Enfield and Woking which finished all square, as did the aggregate scores, therefore requiring a decider at Wycombe, which Enfield lost 3-0.

During this season a kick-in experiment was conducted throughout the season on behalf of FIFA. When the ball went out of play over the touch line a player could either throw or kick the ball into the field of play. A questionnaire was sent out to club officials, players, managers and supporters but the 'kick-in' proved hugely unpopular although the League received much publicity during the experiment.

At the end of the season Diadora UK decided not to take up a further contract to sponsor the League after four years as the League's main sponsor which achieved substantial success.

At the Annual General Meeting Yeovil Town, relegated from the GM Vauxhall Conference, replaced Slough Town while Wingate & Finchley, from the South Midlands League, and Wealdstone, transferring from the Southern League, were elected to Division Three replacing Malden Vale and Feltham & Hounslow Borough who resigned at the end of the season.

Above: the Heybridge Swifts programme for their FA Cup tie with Gillingham.

Premier Division	1	2	3	4	5	6	7	8	9	10	11
1 Aylesbury United	*	3–0	3–2	5–0	5–1	5–3	3–3	2–0	3–0	2–0	1–0
2 Bishop's Stortford	2–1	*	2–1	3–4	0–3	3–3	1–1	0–1	0–2	2–2	1–2
3 Bromley	3–2	0–1	*	0–1	1–3	0–2	2–0	2–1	1–0	2–0	1–1
4 Carshalton Athletic	1–3	1–2	0–3	*	1–1	2–1	1–3	0–1	3–4	0–0	3–0
5 Chesham United	0–2	1–1	0–3	6–2	*	2–1	0–3	1–1	2–0	2–3	3–1
6 Dulwich Hamlet	4–3	0–2	2–2	1–2	1–0	*	1–2	1–1	2–3	4–2	1–0
7 Enfield	2–2	1–0	3–1	2–1	1–1	8–1	*	2–1	3–0	0–1	5–1
8 Grays Athletic	0–2	2–3	0–3	3–4	5–0	0–0	2–3	*	1–1	0–3	2–1
9 Harrow Borough	3–0	2–0	2–0	2–1	1–0	1–2	0–1	1–2	*	0–1	2–4
10 Hayes	2–0	1–0	2–2	5–0	2–0	1–1	1–4	1–2	1–1	*	1–1
11 Hendon	2–1	1–1	1–1	0–1	2–1	4–0	1–3	3–3	1–2	0–0	*
12 Hitchin Town	3–1	1–1	3–3	0–1	4–3	0–1	0–3	0–0	0–0	0–0	2–0
13 Kingstonian	2–0	1–0	1–0	0–1	5–1	0–1	3–2	1–0	3–1	1–1	1–2
14 Marlow	3–2	3–1	1–2	1–1	1–4	0–4	2–2	1–4	2–0	1–3	0–0
15 Molesey	1–3	4–0	1–1	4–1	1–2	1–0	0–2	1–1	2–0	0–2	1–1
16 Purfleet	0–3	3–3	2–1	4–4	3–1	1–2	2–2	0–3	4–2	1–2	3–3
17 St. Albans City	2–1	5–0	1–2	3–1	4–2	3–2	1–2	1–1	1–0	1–1	3–2
18 Slough Town	1–0	1–0	4–1	3–3	5–2	1–1	1–4	2–0	1–1	3–1	2–2
19 Sutton United	1–3	5–0	1–2	3–2	1–2	4–2	0–2	2–2	2–1	3–3	3–1
20 Walton & Hersham	2–0	5–2	2–3	2–4	1–1	4–1	1–3	2–1	1–2	3–1	2–0
21 Wokingham Town	0–1	0–0	1–1	2–3	2–1	0–1	0–3	0–1	0–2	1–2	1–1
22 Yeading	4–2	1–1	1–3	3–2	1–1	1–1	4–2	1–1	0–3	1–1	0–1

Premier Division	12	13	14	15	16	17	18	19	20	21	22
1 Aylesbury United	2–1	2–0	0–0	2–4	1–1	0–0	3–3	3–0	4–0	4–1	1–2
2 Bishop's Stortford	1–0	2–1	2–0	3–1	2–5	1–2	2–2	1–1	0–2	5–1	2–0
3 Bromley	0–2	3–1	0–6	4–3	2–2	2–2	1–1	4–4	5–0	3–1	3–1
4 Carshalton Athletic	2–4	0–0	3–1	2–0	2–2	2–0	1–3	2–1	1–0	2–2	1–1
5 Chesham United	2–2	0–5	1–0	0–3	1–1	1–6	0–1	1–3	1–0	5–1	1–1
6 Dulwich Hamlet	0–1	1–5	3–2	3–2	2–2	4–1	0–2	4–2	4–3	1–1	1–3
7 Enfield	4–1	1–1	5–0	1–1	3–1	3–1	0–1	2–1	1–1	6–0	3–0
8 Grays Athletic	1–3	0–0	2–1	0–0	1–2	2–2	3–3	2–2	1–1	2–0	1–3
9 Harrow Borough	2–4	1–1	3–1	5–2	3–5	2–1	0–3	1–3	4–2	3–0	1–1
10 Hayes	0–0	1–0	2–0	3–2	4–1	1–1	3–1	2–1	2–0	1–0	1–3
11 Hendon	4–1	0–0	3–0	3–1	1–0	1–1	1–2	0–1	1–6	2–0	2–2
12 Hitchin Town	*	1–1	4–2	1–3	3–2	2–0	1–0	1–1	3–1	1–0	1–3
13 Kingstonian	3–1	*	2–1	0–1	0–1	3–5	0–3	1–1	2–5	5–0	0–1
14 Marlow	0–4	1–0	*	3–0	1–0	4–4	0–2	1–3	2–2	1–1	1–0
15 Molesey	0–0	1–2	2–1	*	1–2	3–2	0–2	1–1	2–1	1–0	1–0
16 Purfleet	1–3	0–3	3–1	0–1	*	0–4	3–0	2–2	2–5	4–3	2–2
17 St. Albans City	3–3	8–3	3–2	0–2	2–0	*	3–1	3–2	2–2	6–2	1–1
18 Slough Town	3–2	2–1	4–0	3–1	2–4	1–1	*	3–2	0–0	1–0	5–3
19 Sutton United	0–0	4–1	1–2	2–3	1–2	5–1	1–1	*	0–0	0–2	2–0
20 Walton & Hersham	4–1	0–2	1–1	1–2	2–2	3–2	3–3	1–0	*	0–1	1–1
21 Wokingham Town	1–3	0–1	1–2	1–1	5–1	2–2	2–0	0–1	3–2	*	0–3
22 Yeading	0–1	1–0	0–0	0–4	1–0	7–2	0–0	2–1	0–1	1–1	*

1994-95

Premier Division	P	W	D	L	F	A	Pts
1 Enfield	42	28	9	5	106	43	93
2 Slough Town	42	22	13	7	82	56	79
3 Hayes	42	20	14	8	66	47	74
4 Aylesbury United	42	21	6	15	86	59	69
5 Hitchin Town	42	18	12	12	68	59	66
6 Bromley	42	18	11	13	76	67	65
7 St. Albans City	42	17	13	12	96	81	64
8 Molesey	42	18	8	16	65	61	62
9 Yeading	42	14	15	13	60	59	57
10 Harrow Bough	42	17	6	19	64	67	57
11 Dulwich Hamlet	42	16	9	17	70	82	57
12 Carshalton Athletic	42	16	9	17	69	84	57
13 Kingstonian	42	16	8	18	62	57	56
14 Walton & Hersham	42	14	11	17	75	73	53
15 Sutton United	42	13	12	17	74	69	51
16 Purfleet	42	13	12	17	76	90	51
17 Hendon	42	12	14	16	57	65	50
18 Grays Athletic	42	11	16	15	57	61	49
19 Bishop's Stortford	42	12	11	19	53	76	47
20 Chesham United	42	12	9	21	60	87	45
21 Marlow	42	10	9	23	52	84	39
22 Wokingham Town	42	6	9	27	39	86	27

Left: the programme for Aylesbury United's home match with Hayes, which The Ducks won 2-0.

Right: the programme for Feltham & Hounslow Borough.

Division I	1	2	3	4	5	6	7	8	9	10	11	12	13	14	15	16	17	18	19	20	21	22
1 Abingdon Town	*	0–2	2–1	1–3	2–2	2–2	1–1	2–3	3–1	3–1	2–0	2–2	2–1	3–0	2–2	2–3	2–1	2–2	0–3	4–2	5–1	1–0
2 Aldershot Town	3–0	*	1–3	1–0	2–0	1–0	3–0	3–1	3–2	7–0	0–1	2–0	1–3	3–0	3–2	2–2	3–4	3–0	2–1	1–1	2–0	1–4
3 Barking	3–1	2–1	*	2–0	0–1	4–0	1–2	0–1	1–6	0–2	0–2	2–2	2–0	2–2	3–2	2–2	0–3	1–1	1–4	4–2	4–0	0–2
4 Basingstoke Town	2–4	1–1	1–0	*	2–0	1–2	0–1	0–1	2–2	6–1	3–2	4–2	2–2	3–1	2–2	2–3	1–1	1–1	0–0	3–2	2–2	1–2
5 Berkhamsted Town	1–1	0–3	2–2	2–3	*	3–1	0–0	1–3	1–4	2–3	2–1	1–3	1–1	0–3	3–2	0–0	2–1	1–0	0–3	1–0	2–1	5–4
6 Billericay Town	3–0	0–1	0–3	1–0	1–0	*	0–0	1–1	0–2	4–1	4–2	1–0	3–5	1–1	2–0	2–5	1–2	0–0	1–1	2–0	1–2	1–0
7 Bognor Regis Tn	0–1	1–4	0–4	5–2	1–1	4–1	*	3–2	1–1	1–1	0–1	1–0	1–1	5–3	1–1	3–4	2–1	2–3	0–1	2–1	1–0	1–1
8 Boreham Wood	4–0	2–0	3–2	4–0	1–1	0–0	2–0	*	0–0	4–0	3–1	4–1	4–2	1–0	3–0	2–0	1–0	3–0	1–0	4–0	5–1	0–4
9 Chertsey Town	3–1	4–1	3–1	2–1	1–1	1–2	2–0	1–2	*	8–0	1–3	4–1	3–0	3–0	4–1	1–1	1–3	5–1	3–3	5–1	1–1	1–3
10 Dorking	0–4	1–6	2–3	0–3	2–3	0–3	1–2	2–1	0–6	*	0–3	3–4	0–1	0–2	1–1	1–5	0–1	2–6	1–8	3–4	2–2	2–5
11 Heybridge Swifts	5–0	2–1	4–3	0–1	3–5	1–5	3–3	2–3	3–2	5–0	*	0–1	3–2	1–1	2–1	1–1	1–2	1–1	1–0	2–3	2–0	0–1
12 Leyton	0–2	1–1	2–0	2–3	3–0	1–2	2–3	0–1	2–2	2–1	0–1	*	0–0	1–1	4–0	3–1	0–1	3–2	1–1	4–0	3–1	2–2
13 Maidenhead Utd	0–2	2–2	5–2	1–3	0–1	1–1	2–1	0–1	2–8	6–1	2–2	3–2	*	1–1	4–3	4–2	2–0	3–0	0–5	1–2	3–2	1–0
14 Newbury Town	1–1	1–0	0–2	0–2	1–4	0–5	1–1	0–3	1–0	4–1	2–1	0–2	2–2	*	2–2	4–4	2–0	0–5	0–0	1–2	3–2	2–0
15 Ruislip Manor	2–1	2–0	4–1	2–2	1–0	0–2	1–0	2–5	1–1	9–2	3–0	5–2	1–0	1–1	*	0–4	1–3	0–0	2–6	0–1	3–0	1–1
16 Staines Town	1–1	1–0	1–2	2–1	3–1	1–2	2–1	0–0	1–2	5–2	3–0	1–2	2–2	1–3	1–2	*	0–0	1–2	1–1	3–0	3–0	1–1
17 Tooting & M Utd	1–2	0–1	1–1	0–2	2–1	0–0	0–0	3–2	3–3	4–0	1–1	1–2	1–1	2–2	3–0	0–1	*	2–1	1–1	0–0	1–0	2–2
18 Uxbridge	1–0	2–3	1–4	3–2	1–1	1–3	1–0	0–1	0–2	2–0	1–4	0–2	1–1	1–1	0–2	2–1	2–0	*	2–1	1–1	1–0	2–1
19 Wembley	1–1	2–1	2–0	3–6	0–1	0–4	1–1	0–2	3–0	2–0	4–2	2–2	0–5	3–1	0–3	1–4	0–4	1–0	*	2–0	1–2	1–1
20 Whyteleafe	2–0	1–2	1–2	4–2	2–1	3–2	2–3	1–2	0–3	4–0	5–3	2–0	3–0	0–3	1–1	3–2	1–1	1–1	2–0	*	3–2	1–1
21 Wivenhoe Town	1–1	0–2	2–1	2–4	1–0	0–2	1–1	1–4	2–4	5–1	2–2	2–0	1–1	0–5	0–2	0–4	1–0	0–1	1–2	4–1	*	1–4
22 Worthing	3–1	4–1	4–4	2–2	2–0	2–0	3–2	4–0	1–1	7–0	4–0	1–1	3–0	0–0	2–0	5–0	2–2	0–2	1–0	0–5	4–1	*

Division I	P	W	D	L	F	A	Pts
1 Boreham Wood	42	31	5	6	90	38	98
2 Worthing	42	21	13	8	93	49	76
3 Chertsey Town	42	21	11	10	109	57	74
4 Aldershot Town	42	23	5	14	80	53	74
5 Billericay Town	42	20	9	13	68	52	69
6 Staines Town	42	17	12	13	83	65	63
7 Basingstoke Town	42	17	10	15	81	71	61
8 Tooting & M Utd	42	15	14	13	58	48	59
9 Wembley	42	16	11	15	70	61	59
10 Abingdon Town	42	16	11	15	67	69	59
11 Whyteleafe	42	17	7	18	70	78	58
12 Maidenhead Utd	42	15	12	15	73	76	57
13 Uxbridge	42	15	11	16	54	62	56
14 Leyton	42	15	10	17	67	66	55
15 Barking	42	16	7	19	74	77	55
16 Heybridge Swifts	42	16	6	20	73	78	54
17 Ruislip Manor	42	14	11	17	70	75	53
18 Bognor Regis Tn	42	13	14	15	57	63	53
19 Berkhamsted Town	42	14	10	18	54	70	52
20 Newbury Town	42	12	15	15	58	71	51
21 Wivenhoe Town	42	8	7	27	47	94	31
22 Dorking	42	3	3	36	40	163	12

Left: the programme for Boreham Wood's 1994-95 campaign.

Right: the programme for Staines Town's 3-2 victory at Abingdon Town.

Division II	1	2	3	4	5	6	7	8	9	10	11	12	13	14	15	16	17	18	19	20	21	22
1 Aveley	*	0–4	1–3	0–1	2–1	0–3	3–1	1–5	1–1	0–0	0–0	1–3	4–2	2–2	3–4	0–2	0–1	0–1	2–3	1–2	2–1	1–1
2 Banstead Athletic	2–1	*	3–1	1–3	1–1	4–0	2–1	2–1	2–3	2–2	1–0	1–0	1–1	0–0	5–0	1–2	2–3	1–2	2–0	3–2	0–3	0–7
3 Barton Rovers	3–0	4–0	*	0–2	4–1	6–0	1–2	0–2	2–1	2–3	2–0	1–0	3–0	3–1	1–1	0–0	1–1	1–0	4–1	2–1	1–1	3–2
4 Bracknell Town	9–0	2–1	0–4	*	0–2	4–1	3–1	3–1	1–1	1–2	5–1	3–0	3–2	0–0	1–2	1–2	1–1	1–2	4–1	3–1	0–0	2–3
5 Chalfont St. Peter	4–1	0–0	2–1	1–1	*	2–3	1–3	0–1	2–0	1–1	2–0	1–1	2–3	2–2	3–4	3–1	3–0	2–4	2–0	1–1	3–0	0–1
6 Cheshunt	5–1	1–1	2–2	0–2	1–1	*	1–1	2–2	3–1	0–2	1–1	2–3	0–3	2–0	3–4	0–2	2–0	2–1	2–2	5–0	1–1	1–0
7 Croydon	4–1	2–1	1–2	0–2	1–1	2–1	*	4–2	4–2	3–0	2–0	4–0	1–1	4–0	2–3	0–4	3–0	3–1	2–0	1–2	1–0	3–3
8 Edgware Town	3–2	1–4	1–4	0–3	1–1	5–2	4–2	*	0–2	0–3	3–1	2–0	1–1	2–1	3–3	1–2	1–1	0–1	1–2	5–0	5–1	1–1
9 Egham Town	3–0	1–2	1–2	2–2	1–1	2–2	3–1	3–0	*	0–0	0–1	2–1	0–2	0–2	4–2	1–3	1–1	0–2	3–2	1–1	4–2	0–2
10 Hampton	2–1	3–4	2–1	3–1	1–3	1–1	2–7	0–2	3–2	*	1–0	2–1	7–1	8–1	1–1	2–3	0–2	1–3	2–1	1–0	1–0	2–2
11 Hemel Hempstead	3–0	0–5	1–1	0–2	1–2	1–1	1–0	2–2	1–1	3–5	*	3–2	1–1	0–2	0–0	3–2	1–1	1–3	2–1	2–1	2–3	1–3
12 Hungerford Town	0–1	1–1	2–5	2–3	2–0	0–3	2–1	0–2	2–1	2–3	0–3	*	3–3	3–0	0–1	2–3	3–1	0–1	3–1	1-4	2–1	1–0
13 Leatherhead	1–0	1–1	1–3	1–3	2–1	0–2	1–1	0–2	3–2	3–2	2–0	4–3	*	3–1	0–0	3–1	4–1	1–4	4–0	2–2	3–2	2–0
14 Malden Vale	0–2	0–5	2–2	1–5	0–3	1–1	0–2	4–3	1–1	2–3	4–1	0–1	2–2	*	2–2	1–3	1–2	2–4	0–3	1–2	0–2	4–1
15 Metropolitan Police	1–0	1–0	1–3	0–0	1–2	4–1	0–3	0–1	0–1	1–1	3–0	2–0	1–1	6–1	*	3–1	3–2	4–3	10–1	3–1	3–2	1–2
16 Oxford City	3–1	0–2	3–1	1–1	2–2	3–2	2–3	1–1	1–1	5–0	3–0	0–0	2–1	3–0	1–1	*	0–1	0–2	4–1	5–1	4–1	0–2
17 Saffron Walden Tn	3–1	1–0	2–4	0–0	3–1	2–0	2–1	3–0	2–1	1–1	2–2	2–0	2–2	3–2	0–2	1–1	*	1–1	5–1	2–0	1–2	0–0
18 Thame United	4–1	3–1	0–3	2–1	0–2	5–0	2–1	1–0	2-1	3–1	1–2	2–2	2–0	4–0	3–1	1–0	3–2	*	6–1	4–1	4–1	5–2
19 Tilbury	0–3	0–0	3–1	2–0	1–2	6–0	1–0	2–1	0–0	2–3	1–1	2–2	1–0	1–0	2–2	1–1	1–1	1–1	*	3–1	2–0	3–2
20 Ware	3–2	1–1	0–1	0–3	1–0	1–3	3–2	0–1	2–4	2–0	1–0	5–2	2–0	5–0	1–1	0–2	3–1	1–2	0–3	*	3–1	0–2
21 Windsor & Eton	1–3	1–2	3–2	1–2	1–2	0–2	3–5	0–0	1–1	3–0	1–2	2–2	5–1	3–1	0–1	0–6	2–2	2–1	1–2	1–1	*	3–2
22 Witham Town	1–3	3–2	1–3	2–3	0–1	2–2	2–0	1–1	1–1	1–2	3–1	2–1	1–3	4–2	1–0	0–1	3–0	2–1	2–1	3–3	2–0	*

1994-95 Division II	P	W	D	L	F	A	Pts
1 Thame United	42	30	3	9	97	49	93
2 Barton Rovers	42	25	7	10	93	51	82
3 Oxford City	42	24	8	10	86	47	80
4 Bracknell Town	42	23	9	10	86	47	78
5 Metropolitan Police	42	19	12	11	81	65	69
6 Hampton	42	20	9	13	79	74	69
7 Croydon	42	20	5	17	85	65	65
8 Banstead Athletic	42	18	10	14	73	59	64
9 Saffron Walden Tn	42	17	13	12	64	59	64
10 Chalfont St. Peter	42	17	12	13	67	54	63
11 Witham Town	42	18	9	15	75	64	63
12 Leatherhead	42	16	12	14	71	75	60
13 Edgware Town	42	16	10	16	70	66	58
14 Tilbury	42	15	9	18	62	82	54
15 Cheshunt	42	13	13	16	66	81	52
16 Ware	42	14	7	21	61	81	49
17 Egham Town	42	11	14	17	60	65	47
18 Hemel Hempstead	42	10	11	21	45	76	41
19 Hungerford Town	42	11	7	24	55	81	40
20 Windsor & Eton	42	10	8	24	58	84	38
21 Aveley	42	9	5	28	48	95	32
22 Malden Vale	42	5	9	28	46	108	24

Left: the programme for Leighton Town's 1994-95 campaign.

Right: the programme for Saffron Walden Town.

Division III	1	2	3	4	5	6	7	8	9	10	11	12	13	14	15	16	17	18	19	20	21
1 Bedford Town	*	1–0	2–4	2–2	1–2	4–0	1–1	2–1	1–2	5–0	2–2	5–0	3–0	4–2	2–3	1–1	2–2	3–1	3–2	0–0	1–1
2 Camberley Town	0–1	*	0–1	0–0	0–1	2–1	5–0	2–2	5–0	1–0	1–2	0–2	0–0	3–2	1–0	3–1	0–1	3–2	0–0	5–1	2–2
3 Canvey Island	2–1	1–0	*	2–1	1–0	4–0	2–1	2–1	0–2	4–1	2–1	4–0	5–0	3–1	3–3	1–1	2–0	2–0	1–1	1–1	0–1
4 Clapton	3–3	2–1	2–1	*	0–1	3–1	2–0	2–2	6–0	2–1	1–2	1–1	1–1	1–2	1–1	3–3	0–1	4–0	2–1	1–2	1–2
5 Collier Row	1–1	3–0	2–0	3–0	*	3–0	1–1	5–1	2–0	4–1	4–0	1–1	2–0	0–0	4–1	2–1	0–1	5–1	4–1	3–0	1–0
6 Cove	1–2	0–2	0–2	6–0	0–2	*	0–1	1–0	1–4	1–1	1–3	0–1	1–1	1–2	2–4	2–5	0–3	3–1	1–2	0–2	0–0
7 East Thurrock Utd	2–3	1–0	1–2	3–1	0–1	5–2	*	1–4	5–3	1–3	0–3	0–1	4–0	2–1	1–3	1–1	2–1	3–2	0–1	2–5	1–1
8 Epsom & Ewell	0–2	1–3	1–3	0–3	1–0	5–1	1–1	*	1–1	3–1	6–1	2–2	0–1	0–1	1–2	3–3	1–1	0–1	2–0	1–5	1–1
9 Feltham & H Boro'	2–4	2–2	2–3	2–1	0–2	3–1	1–3	1–2	*	2–2	2–1	0–0	3–1	1–2	2–3	0–2	1–2	1–0	1–3	3–4	4–3
10 Flackwell Heath	1–3	2–1	1–4	0–4	1–0	3–3	4–0	0–2	2–4	*	1–2	3–1	1–2	1–3	1–4	0–2	0–1	3–0	2–1	1–5	1–1
11 Harefield United	1–2	0–2	0–1	3–0	0–5	0–0	1–1	1–1	3–1	1–3	*	0–3	2–1	1–2	0–4	1–2	5–1	1–1	3–1	1–0	0–3
12 Harlow Town	3–2	1–1	2–1	4–3	0–3	1–0	0–3	0–1	1–4	4–2	3–0	*	2–2	5–1	0–4	1–2	1–4	0–1	1–5	0–4	1–2
13 Hertford Town	0–2	0–2	1–3	3–1	0–3	3–1	4–0	1–2	3–1	3–1	2–3	4–2	*	1–1	1–0	1–1	1–2	2–2	1–2	0–3	4–2
14 Hornchurch	1–3	0–2	1–3	1–1	0–1	2–0	1–2	0–1	4–1	4–2	4–0	2–3	1–1	*	2–0	0–2	0–0	4–0	1–5	2–1	3–0
15 Horsham	1–1	4–0	0–2	2–6	2–1	3–1	5–3	5–0	0–2	2–1	2–1	4–3	3–1	4–0	*	2–3	1–3	3–2	0–2	1–1	1–1
16 Kingsbury Town	1–2	0–0	2–1	0–1	1–2	3–2	1–1	1–0	2–0	6–0	4–1	1–1	3–2	2–2	0–1	*	4–3	2–0	0–1	1–3	1–0
17 Leighton Town	1–2	0–2	3–1	0–1	2–3	1–0	0–0	0–1	1–0	4–0	0–0	4–0	0–0	2–3	3–0	1–1	*	4–0	2–4	2–1	6–1
18 Lewes	0–5	1–3	0–2	1–4	1–3	2–1	2–3	0–4	2–1	1–0	1–1	0–0	2–5	1–1	0–3	0–3	0–1	*	0–2	0–4	4–2
19 Northwood	1–0	0–1	3–2	0–0	1–2	3–2	4–0	0–0	2–0	3–2	3–0	0–1	4–2	1–2	1–1	3–2	1–1	6–0	*	3–2	4–0
20 Southall	1–4	1–2	1–6	1–1	1–1	2–0	5–1	2–1	3–2	3–0	4–2	2–1	1–1	1–2	0–2	4–0	2–1	4–1	1–1	*	2–2
21 Tring Town	2–2	0–2	2–4	2–1	1–3	4–0	1–3	3–2	2–3	2–1	2–2	5–0	6–0	1–1	2–0	2–1	0–1	3–1	2–2	1–2	*

Division III	P	W	D	L	F	A	Pts
1 Collier Row	40	30	5	5	86	23	95
2 Canvey Island	40	28	4	8	88	42	88
3 Bedford Town	40	22	11	7	90	50	77
4 Northwood	40	22	8	10	80	47	74
5 Horsham	40	22	6	12	84	61	72
6 Southall	40	21	8	11	87	59	71
7 Leighton Town	40	20	8	12	66	43	68
8 Camberley Town	40	19	8	13	59	39	65
9 Kingsbury Town	40	18	11	11	72	54	65
10 Hornchurch	40	17	8	15	64	63	59
11 Clapton	40	14	11	15	69	61	53
12 Tring Town	40	13	12	15	68	69	51
13 East Thurrock Utd	40	14	8	18	60	79	50
14 Epsom & Ewell	40	13	10	17	58	62	49
15 Harlow Town	40	13	8	19	53	83	47
16 Harefield United	40	12	8	20	51	79	44
17 Hertford Town	40	11	10	19	56	78	43
18 Feltham & H Boro'	40	13	4	23	64	87	43
19 Flackwell Heath	40	8	4	28	50	99	28
20 Lewes	40	6	5	29	34	104	23
21 Cove	40	3	5	32	37	94	14

Left: the programme for Kingsbury Town's 1-0 victory over visitors Tring Town.

Right: the programme for Chalfont St. Peter's 3-1 FA Cup victory over Lowestoft Town.

1995–96 - The Isthmian League had a new sponsor for this season as sports manufacturer ICIS signed an agreement to take over as title sponsors. Prior to the start of the season, Newbury Town, League members since 1983, folded because of severe financial difficulties and therefore Division Two comprised 21 clubs. In one of the closest Premier Division championships for years, the title was decided on the last day of the season with Hayes, by virtual of a better goal difference, clinching the championship from second placed Enfield with subsequent promotion to the GM Vauxhall Conference. Boreham Wood, Yeovil Town and Dulwich Hamlet were all in contention up to the final couple of weeks of the season. At the foot of the table Surrey Clubs Molesey and Walton & Hersham were relegated to Division One along with Worthing who returned after just one season. In Division One Oxford City clinched the championship by three points from runners-up Heybridge Swifts, who would be competing in the Premier Division for the first time, with Staines Town gaining the final promotion place. Relegated to Division Two were Ruislip Manor, Wembley and Barking with the former resigning from the League due to financial difficulties. In Division Two Canvey Island won the championship and back-to-back promotions and were joined by runners-up Croydon and Hampton who finished in third place. No clubs were relegated to Division Three as Dorking, who would have become the first club relegated from the Premier Division to Division Three in successive seasons, were reprieved along with Hungerford Town due to League resignations. In Division Three Horsham beat Leighton Town to the championship by three points with Windsor & Eton gaining the third promotion place ten points ahead of fourth placed Wealdstone. At the Annual General Meeting Dagenham & Redbridge, relegated from the GM Vauxhall Conference, replaced champions Hayes. However, Ruislip Manor, Saffron Walden Town, Harefield United and Cove all resigned from the League, while Braintree Town, transferring from the Southern League, were elected to Division Three, which would contain just 17 clubs. In addition, Division One club Collier Row FC merged with Romford FC of the Essex Senior League to become Collier Row & Romford FC.

1995-96

Premier Division	1	2	3	4	5	6	7	8	9	10	11	12	13	14	15	16	17	18	19	20	21	22
1 Aylesbury United	*	0–0	1–3	3–0	0–1	2–0	0–3	2–3	2–2	2–0	1–3	1–0	2–1	0–2	1–1	1–0	1–1	4–1	0–0	1–1	1–1	3–1
2 Bishop's Stortford	3–6	*	0–2	1–1	0–2	3–1	1–2	0–1	2–0	2–3	1–2	3–1	2–2	2–3	4–0	1–1	3–2	1–3	2–0	0–0	3–1	2–2
3 Boreham Wood	2–2	0–1	*	3–1	2–3	2–0	2–2	4–1	2–0	3–2	0–0	4–0	1–0	0–0	0–1	2–1	2–0	0–1	1–1	3–1	1–1	0–2
4 Bromley	0–3	0–2	0–1	*	1–2	3–3	0–2	0–1	2–2	5–1	0–1	2–5	0–2	1–1	1–3	0–2	1–0	2–3	3–2	3–2	1–0	1–5
5 Carshalton Athletic	3–1	2–0	0–0	0–0	*	3–1	2–2	1–1	3–1	0–1	0–3	1–1	1–1	0–3	4–0	3–1	1–1	1–2	5–2	4–0	2–0	2–1
6 Chertsey Town	0–3	3–0	0–3	0–2	0–1	*	0–1	0–3	2–0	1–6	1–3	3–1	2–1	2–1	3–0	2–1	1–2	1–1	1–3	2–1	1–1	1–3
7 Dulwich Hamlet	1–0	4–1	0–2	4–1	2–1	0–0	*	1–1	3–5	3–2	1–1	1–0	3–3	1–3	2–0	1–1	3–1	2–2	1–1	4–1	3–0	2–1
8 Enfield	3–3	0–1	0–2	5–0	4–0	0–0	1–0	*	3–0	3–0	1–1	2–0	3–0	2–1	2–0	3–0	2–2	0–2	4–0	5–1	2–0	2–1
9 Grays Athletic	2–0	0–2	1–2	0–3	1–0	2–1	1–4	0–3	*	0–2	3–3	0–0	1–0	1–1	1–0	2–0	0–3	1–2	3–1	6–0	0–0	0–2
10 Harrow Borough	3–3	0–0	1–1	1–3	0–1	3–1	1–2	3–1	3–0	*	1–1	2–2	1–2	2–1	3–1	2–2	0–0	0–0	2–3	3–1	4–1	0–1
11 Hayes	0–1	3–1	1–1	5–1	1–2	4–0	2–2	3–1	5–1	2–1	*	3–1	1–1	2–1	2–0	2–1	0–0	0–0	2–0	2–0	0–0	1–1
12 Hendon	4–2	1–1	1–1	2–0	0–0	0–0	1–2	0–1	0–0	0–2	0–2	*	1–2	0–3	2–0	2–4	1–2	0–4	4–0	3–0	1–1	1–3
13 Hitchin Town	0–3	1–1	1–2	2–1	2–5	2–0	1–3	1–0	1–0	1–5	1–3	0–1	*	1–1	0–1	2–0	0–0	1–0	0–2	2–2	0–3	1–2
14 Kingstonian	1–1	2–1	1–0	0–1	2–1	0–2	0–2	0–1	1–0	0–1	1–0	0–1	0–1	*	1–1	1–1	4–1	2–2	1–0	1–1	3–1	2–2
15 Molesey	1–4	2–1	1–2	3–2	0–1	2–0	1–2	1–4	0–0	0–0	0–2	1–2	2–1	0–2	*	2–3	1–1	0–5	2–2	3–1	1–2	2–3
16 Purfleet	1–2	1–2	1–0	1–1	2–1	1–3	3–1	1–1	1–0	0–1	0–0	2–3	1–1	1–3	0–2	*	0–1	2–1	2–1	3–1	1–2	0–3
17 St. Albans City	2–0	3–0	0–0	5–0	3–0	2–0	4–1	1–0	1–1	0–2	0–3	3–1	5–1	1–2	1–0	3–0	*	2–2	3–0	2–0	0–1	2–2
18 Sutton United	2–3	2–1	0–3	1–3	2–1	2–1	1–1	2–4	0–0	4–0	2–2	2–3	4–0	0–1	2–0	1–0	0–1	*	2–1	3–1	2–2	1–1
19 Walton & Hersham	2–1	0–2	0–4	3–1	0–1	0–1	0–2	0–1	1–4	1–2	0–1	1–0	4–1	0–2	3–3	1–2	1–2	1–1	*	1–0	0–0	1–3
20 Worthing	1–3	0–1	0–2	2–2	2–3	1–2	1–3	0–1	1–1	1–2	0–3	0–5	2–0	0–5	4–4	1–2	1–5	5–2	0–2	*	2–1	3–2
21 Yeading	0–0	2–4	0–3	3–0	1–3	1–3	5–3	1–1	0–1	1–2	0–1	0–0	2–0	0–2	2–2	3–1	2–1	2–2	3–0	1–0	*	1–1
22 Yeovil Town	3–2	1–3	0–1	4–3	2–1	1–0	5–3	0–1	1–0	0–0	3–0	4–1	1–1	1–1	3–2	2–1	1–1	0–0	4–1	3–1	2–0	*

Premier Division	*P*	*W*	*D*	*L*	*F*	*A*	*Pts*
1 Hayes	42	24	14	4	76	32	86
2 Enfield	42	26	8	8	78	35	86
3 Boreham Wood	42	24	11	7	69	29	83
4 Yeovil Town	42	23	11	8	83	51	80
5 Dulwich Hamlet	42	23	11	8	85	59	80
6 Carshalton Athletic	42	22	8	12	68	49	74
7 St. Albans City	42	20	12	10	70	41	72
8 Kingstonian	42	20	11	11	62	38	71
9 Harrow Borough	42	19	10	13	70	56	67
10 Sutton United	42	17	14	11	71	56	65
11 Aylesbury United	42	17	12	13	71	58	63
12 Bishop's Stortford	42	16	9	17	61	62	57
13 Yeading	42	11	14	17	48	60	47
14 Hendon	42	12	10	20	52	65	46
15 Chertsey Town	42	13	6	23	45	71	45
16 Purfleet	42	12	8	22	48	67	44
17 Grays Athletic	42	11	11	20	43	63	44
18 Hitchin Town	42	10	10	22	41	74	40
19 Bromley	42	10	7	25	52	91	37
20 Molesey	42	9	9	24	46	81	36
21 Walton & Hersham	42	9	7	26	42	79	34
22 Worthing	42	4	7	31	42	106	19

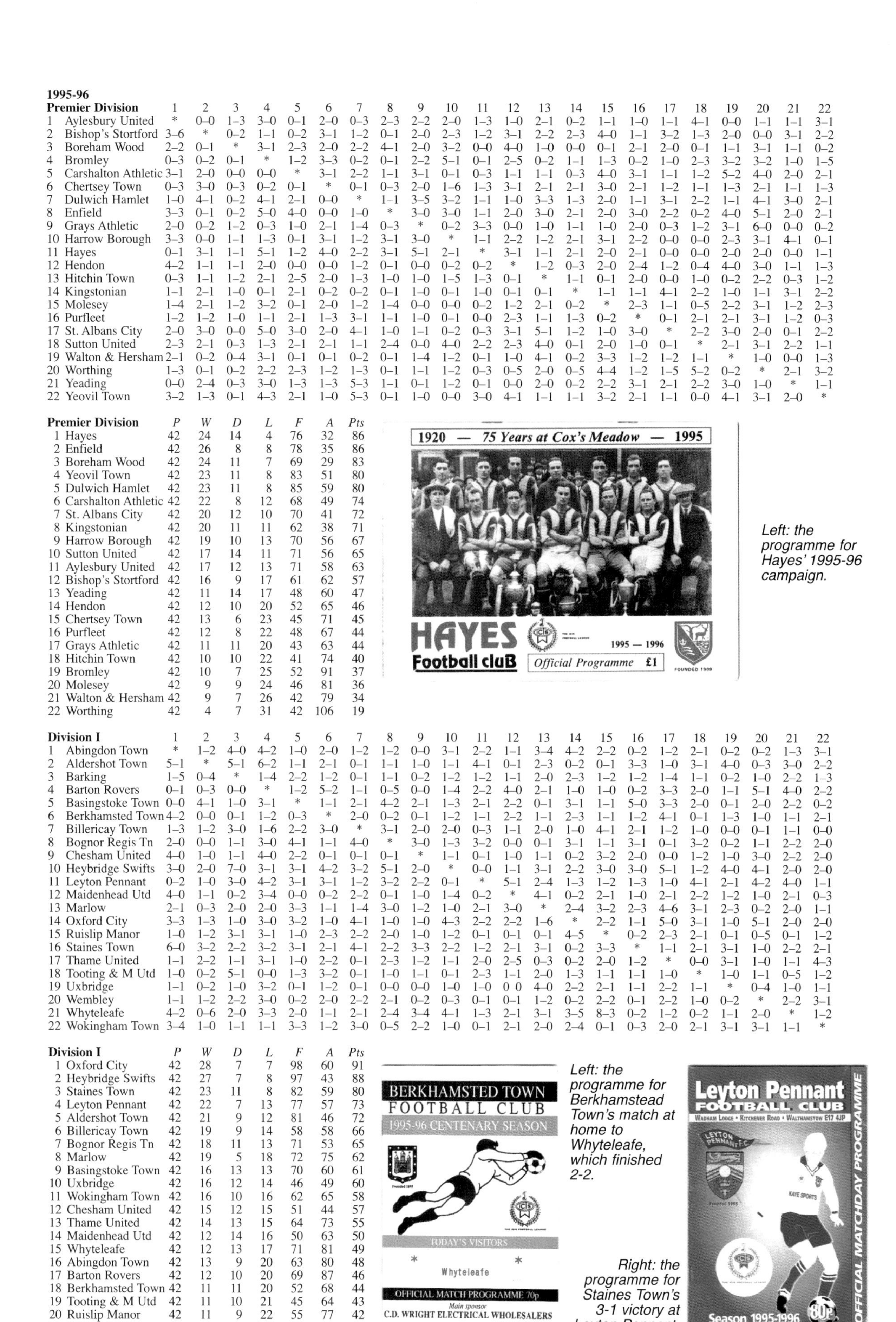

Left: the programme for Hayes' 1995-96 campaign.

Division I	1	2	3	4	5	6	7	8	9	10	11	12	13	14	15	16	17	18	19	20	21	22
1 Abingdon Town	*	1–2	4–0	4–2	1–0	2–0	1–2	1–2	0–0	3–1	2–2	1–1	3–4	4–2	2–2	0–2	1–2	2–1	0–2	0–2	1–3	3–1
2 Aldershot Town	5–1	*	5–1	6–2	1–1	2–1	0–1	1–1	1–0	1–1	4–1	0–1	2–3	0–2	0–1	3–3	1–0	3–1	4–0	0–3	3–0	2–2
3 Barking	1–5	0–4	*	1–4	2–2	1–2	0–1	1–1	0–2	1–2	1–2	1–1	2–0	2–3	1–2	1–2	1–4	1–1	0–2	1–0	2–2	1–3
4 Barton Rovers	0–1	0–3	0–0	*	1–2	5–2	1–1	0–5	0–0	1–4	2–2	4–0	2–1	1–0	1–0	0–2	3–3	2–0	1–1	5–1	4–0	2–2
5 Basingstoke Town	0–0	4–1	1–0	3–1	*	1–1	2–1	4–2	2–1	1–3	2–1	2–2	0–1	3–1	1–1	5–0	3–3	2–0	0–1	2–0	2–2	0–2
6 Berkhamsted Town	4–2	0–0	0–1	1–2	0–3	*	2–0	0–2	0–1	1–2	1–1	2–2	1–1	2–3	1–1	1–2	4–1	0–1	1–3	1–0	1–1	2–1
7 Billericay Town	1–3	1–2	3–0	1–6	2–2	3–0	*	3–1	2–0	2–0	0–3	1–1	2–0	1–0	4–1	2–1	1–2	1–0	0–0	0–1	1–1	0–0
8 Bognor Regis Tn	2–0	0–0	1–1	3–0	4–1	1–1	4–0	*	3–0	1–3	3–2	0–0	0–1	3–1	1–1	3–1	0–1	3–2	0–2	1–1	2–2	2–0
9 Chesham United	4–0	1–0	1–1	4–0	2–2	0–1	0–1	0–1	*	1–1	0–1	1–0	1–1	0–2	3–2	2–0	0–0	1–2	1–0	3–0	2–2	2–0
10 Heybridge Swifts	3–0	2–0	7–0	3–1	3–1	4–2	3–2	5–1	2–0	*	0–0	1–1	3–1	2–2	3–0	3–0	5–1	1–2	4–0	4–1	2–0	2–0
11 Leyton Pennant	0–2	1–0	3–0	4–2	3–1	3–1	1–2	3–2	2–2	0–1	*	5–1	2–4	1–3	1–2	1–3	1–0	4–1	2–1	4–2	4–0	1–1
12 Maidenhead Utd	4–0	1–1	0–2	3–4	0–0	0–2	2–2	0–1	1–0	1–4	0–2	*	4–1	0–2	2–1	1–0	2–1	2–2	1–2	1–0	2–1	0–3
13 Marlow	2–1	0–3	2–0	2–0	3–3	1–1	1–4	3–0	1–2	1–0	2–1	3–0	*	2–4	3–2	2–3	4–6	3–1	2–3	0–2	2–0	1–1
14 Oxford City	3–3	1–3	1–0	3–0	3–2	1–0	4–1	1–0	1–0	4–3	2–2	2–2	1–6	*	2–2	1–1	5–0	3–1	1–0	5–1	2–0	2–0
15 Ruislip Manor	1–0	1–2	3–1	3–1	1–0	2–3	2–2	2–0	1–0	1–2	0–1	0–1	0–1	4–5	*	0–2	2–3	2–1	0–1	0–5	0–1	1–2
16 Staines Town	6–0	3–2	2–2	3–2	3–1	2–1	4–1	2–2	3–3	2–2	1–2	2–1	3–1	0–2	3–3	*	1–1	2–1	3–1	1–0	2–2	2–1
17 Thame United	1–1	2–2	1–1	3–1	1–0	2–2	0–1	2–3	1–2	1–1	2–0	2–5	0–3	0–2	2–0	1–2	*	0–0	3–1	1–0	1–1	4–3
18 Tooting & M Utd	1–0	0–2	5–1	0–0	1–3	3–2	0–1	1–0	1–1	0–1	2–3	1–1	2–0	1–3	1–1	1–1	1–0	*	1–0	1–1	0–5	1–2
19 Uxbridge	1–1	0–2	1–0	3–2	0–1	1–2	0–1	0–0	0–0	1–0	1–0	0 0	4–0	2–2	2–1	1–1	2–2	1–1	*	0–4	1–0	1–1
20 Wembley	1–1	1–2	2–2	3–0	0–2	2–0	2–2	2–1	0–2	0–3	0–1	0–1	1–2	0–2	2–2	0–1	2–2	1–0	0–2	*	2–2	3–1
21 Whyteleafe	4–2	0–6	2–0	3–3	2–0	1–1	2–1	2–4	3–4	4–1	1–3	2–1	3–1	3–5	8–3	0–2	1–2	0–2	1–1	2–0	*	1–2
22 Wokingham Town	3–4	1–0	1–1	1–1	3–3	1–2	3–0	0–5	2–2	1–0	0–1	2–1	2–0	2–4	0–1	0–3	2–0	2–1	3–1	3–1	1–1	*

Division I	*P*	*W*	*D*	*L*	*F*	*A*	*Pts*
1 Oxford City	42	28	7	7	98	60	91
2 Heybridge Swifts	42	27	7	8	97	43	88
3 Staines Town	42	23	11	8	82	59	80
4 Leyton Pennant	42	22	7	13	77	57	73
5 Aldershot Town	42	21	9	12	81	46	72
6 Billericay Town	42	19	9	14	58	58	66
7 Bognor Regis Tn	42	18	11	13	71	53	65
8 Marlow	42	19	5	18	72	75	62
9 Basingstoke Town	42	16	13	13	70	60	61
10 Uxbridge	42	16	12	14	46	49	60
11 Wokingham Town	42	16	10	16	62	65	58
12 Chesham United	42	15	12	15	51	44	57
13 Thame United	42	14	13	15	64	73	55
14 Maidenhead Utd	42	12	14	16	50	63	50
15 Whyteleafe	42	12	13	17	71	81	49
16 Abingdon Town	42	13	9	20	63	80	48
17 Barton Rovers	42	12	10	20	69	87	46
18 Berkhamsted Town	42	11	11	20	52	68	44
19 Tooting & M Utd	42	11	10	21	45	64	43
20 Ruislip Manor	42	11	9	22	55	77	42
21 Wembley	42	11	8	23	49	66	41
22 Barking	42	4	12	36	35	90	24

Left: the programme for Berkhamstead Town's match at home to Whyteleafe, which finished 2-2.

Right: the programme for Staines Town's 3-1 victory at Leyton Pennant.

Leyton Pennant FC took the place of Leyton FC.

1995-96 Division II	1	2	3	4	5	6	7	8	9	10	11	12	13	14	15	16	17	18	19	20	21
1 Banstead Athletic	*	2–0	1–1	0–3	6–1	0–0	2–4	1–0	2–2	2–2	3–1	1–1	2–1	6–0	2–1	0–0	2–0	1–1	3–0	3–0	2–0
2 Bedford Town	0–6	*	1–1	1–7	3–0	4–2	0–3	2–0	3–1	4–1	3–0	1–1	1–0	1–0	6–1	0–0	0–0	5–0	2–2	0–1	3–2
3 Bracknell Town	0–1	3–1	*	2–1	1–0	4–0	0–3	0–2	1–0	2–3	1–1	3–5	4–2	4–1	1–3	1–0	2–1	1–1	5–0	1–0	6–0
4 Canvey Island	1–0	2–2	0–0	*	2–0	1–1	2–1	0–0	4–0	2–0	5–1	3–3	1–0	3–0	1–1	2–0	1–0	3–2	4–1	2–0	3–3
5 Chalfont St. Peter	1–1	1–0	0–0	1–2	*	4–1	1–1	0–1	2–2	2–0	1–1	2–0	0–1	3–0	2–2	1–2	1–3	1–0	0–0	0–0	0–3
6 Cheshunt	1–2	3–0	2–1	0–0	1–1	*	0–2	0–5	2–0	1–6	1–0	0–3	0–0	3–2	2–3	2–4	0–4	1–1	0–2	1–1	1–4
7 Collier Row	0–3	1–1	0–2	1–3	5–2	2–2	*	1–2	3–1	1–0	4–0	0–1	1–1	2–1	4–2	1–1	2–0	2–0	0–6	9–0	1–1
8 Croydon	0–0	4–1	2–1	0–2	4–0	3–2	1–3	*	2–1	0–1	1–0	1–0	2–0	3–0	2–1	4–1	2–0	2–1	5–2	2–0	1–2
9 Dorking	0–2	1–3	2–3	2–3	0–6	3–3	1–3	0–3	*	0–1	2–1	3–1	1–4	1–6	2–0	2–0	0–3	1–3	0–1	0–2	3–0
10 Edgware Town	1–2	3–1	3–1	1–1	2–1	0–3	1–1	1–4	7–0	*	0–2	4–0	0–0	2–2	2–3	2–0	1–1	0–0	5–0	1–0	3–1
11 Egham Town	1–0	0–2	0–4	0–4	3–1	2–4	0–1	2–3	1–0	3–2	*	0–2	2–2	0–1	1–4	0–2	1–0	2–1	0–2	2–1	0–1
12 Hampton	5–4	3–0	1–0	0–0	1–0	2–2	0–0	5–3	2–1	1–0	1–0	*	2–3	1–0	3–3	2–0	1–1	4–0	3–1	2–1	2–0
13 Hemel Hempstead	0–0	0–3	3–1	0–2	1–4	1–2	0–1	0–0	1–1	1–2	1–0	3–3	*	3–0	2–2	1–3	0–2	2–1	4–0	2–3	0–3
14 Hungerford Town	0–2	0–0	1–2	2–5	3–2	0–3	0–2	0–3	5–0	2–2	0–4	1–1	1–0	*	2–3	1–3	0–1	2–0	0–1	0–0	2–2
15 Leatherhead	0–2	1–1	1–3	2–4	2–2	2–2	0–1	2–2	2–3	2–3	2–0	1–2	4–0	3–0	*	0–2	0–1	4–2	3–0	1–0	0–1
16 Metropolitan Police	2–1	3–1	0–3	1–1	1–1	3–0	0–0	1–0	3–1	7–1	1–2	0–2	2–0	2–1	2–5	*	1–1	2–0	3–1	2–0	0–0
17 Saffron Walden Tn	0–0	1–2	1–1	1–4	2–2	7–1	1–3	2–3	1–1	3–0	0–2	1–0	1–2	2–3	2–2	2–1	*	1–1	2–1	2–4	1–2
18 Tilbury	2–0	0–2	2–1	0–5	1–1	3–1	1–0	2–0	5–0	1–3	2–1	0–3	1–1	1–1	2–0	0–0	3–1	*	4–0	1–1	2–2
19 Ware	0–1	2–5	1–1	1–0	2–4	2–2	0–2	2–2	3–4	3–2	0–1	1–0	2–1	0–1	3–3	2–0	2–2	3–2	*	2–0	2–1
20 Witham Town	0–1	0–1	2–1	0–0	3–5	2–4	0–0	0–0	0–2	2–2	4–3	0–1	0–2	0–2	2–0	1–1	3–1	0–2	2–2	*	0–1
21 Wivenhoe Town	4–3	1–1	2–0	6–2	0–2	4–0	2–2	3–4	7–0	3–2	5–2	0–2	2–1	3–1	3–0	0–1	1–1	2–1	1–0	4–0	*

Division II	*P*	*W*	*D*	*L*	*F*	*A*	*Pts*
1 Canvey Island	40	25	12	3	91	36	87
2 Croydon	40	25	6	9	78	42	81
3 Hampton	40	23	10	7	74	44	79
4 Banstead Athletic	40	21	11	8	72	36	74
5 Collier Row	40	21	11	8	73	41	74
6 Wivenhoe Town	40	21	8	11	82	57	71
7 Metropolitan Police	40	18	10	12	57	45	64
8 Bedford Town	40	18	10	12	67	59	64
9 Bracknell Town	40	18	8	14	69	50	62
10 Edgware Town	40	16	9	15	72	67	57
11 Tilbury	40	12	11	17	52	62	47
12 Ware	40	13	8	19	55	80	47
13 Chalfont St. Peter	40	11	13	16	58	63	46
14 Leatherhead	40	12	10	18	71	77	46
15 Saffron Walden Tn	40	11	12	17	56	58	45
16 Cheshunt	40	10	12	18	56	90	42
17 Hemel Hempstead	40	10	10	20	46	62	40
18 Egham Town	40	12	3	25	42	74	39
19 Witham Town	40	8	10	22	35	68	34
20 Hungerford Town	40	9	7	24	44	79	34
21 Dorking	40	8	5	27	44	104	29

Left: the programme for Collier Row's FA Vase victory at Burgess Hill Town, who were to become members of the League on 2004.

Right: the programme for Witham Town's match with Hemel Hempstead.

Division III	1	2	3	4	5	6	7	8	9	10	11	12	13	14	15	16	17	18	19	20	21
1 Aveley	*	3–2	3–0	0–0	2–1	0–2	1–1	3–2	0–1	0–0	1–1	0–2	1–1	0–1	2–1	4–0	0–1	1–0	1–1	0–0	4–3
2 Camberley Town	1–2	*	1–0	0–1	0–4	0–2	2–0	1–2	1–3	4–3	0–1	0–2	1–1	1–5	2–1	0–1	0–0	0–3	1–2	1–1	0–2
3 Clapton	0–3	1–3	*	0–1	3–2	2–4	0–2	2–1	0–0	3–0	1–2	1–3	2–2	1–2	2–0	0–2	4–2	5–0	1–10	0–5	3–0
4 Cove	0–2	0–0	1–0	*	0–2	2–2	1–2	1–1	1–1	2–0	2–0	0–5	0–0	0–3	1–0	0–2	3–0	1–1	1–9	0–4	3–1
5 East Thurrock Utd	0–1	4–1	5–1	3–0	*	1–1	2–1	4–1	2–2	0–2	3–0	3–0	2–2	1–1	2–0	1–0	2–0	0–1	0–3	1–4	1–2
6 Epsom & Ewell	2–2	4–0	2–1	6–0	1–1	*	4–3	2–0	2–2	1–1	1–4	1–2	2–2	1–2	0–0	3–0	5–0	11–1	0–2	4–1	7–1
7 Flackwell Heath	1–0	1–4	1–1	3–2	1–1	1–2	*	3–0	0–1	2–3	1–3	2–1	1–2	1–0	2–4	1–2	4–2	1–0	0–0	0–3	1–2
8 Harefield United	1–3	2–1	1–0	2–1	2–0	0–0	2–4	*	1–3	1–3	1–0	0–6	0–1	1–4	0–1	2–2	0–0	0–2	1–2	1–3	4–3
9 Harlow Town	4–3	2–2	2–1	3–1	1–0	1–1	2–3	1–1	*	8–4	2–1	2–3	3–2	3–0	4–3	1–1	0–2	3–0	3–0	3–3	2–0
10 Hertford Town	0–2	1–3	5–2	3–1	2–3	1–4	3–4	0–2	1–3	*	2–4	1–3	0–4	0–3	1–2	2–3	5–0	5–0	1–2	1–4	1–7
11 Hornchurch	2–2	1–3	0–0	1–1	0–0	0–1	2–2	1–2	3–5	2–1	*	1–4	0–2	1–2	2–1	2–2	1–2	6–1	1–1	1–4	0–2
12 Horsham	3–1	6–0	2–1	5–1	1–1	3–1	1–3	5–2	3–0	1–0	2–1	*	0–1	1–3	2–0	1–0	3–1	2–0	2–1	1–1	1–0
13 Kingsbury Town	3–2	2–2	2–2	1–0	1–3	1–1	5–0	0–0	2–1	0–2	0–1	3–3	*	1–0	1–1	3–1	2–0	1–0	0–0	1–1	4–0
14 Leighton Town	2–1	6–0	1–0	3–0	2–3	3–1	3–1	5–1	2–1	4–1	5–0	3–3	2–0	*	3–0	5–0	5–0	2–0	0–2	4–3	0–1
15 Lewes	3–2	2–3	4–2	1–1	1–0	2–3	3–0	3–3	1–2	4–2	1–0	2–1	1–1	0–3	*	0–2	1–0	2–1	0–4	2–0	2–2
16 Northwood	3–1	2–2	6–1	3–2	3–0	4–2	2–1	3–1	4–0	1–1	7–1	1–1	4–1	0–0	1–2	*	2–1	0–2	0–5	1–1	2–2
17 Southall	2–1	2–1	0–3	2–1	0–1	1–1	1–3	3–2	0–2	2–6	1–2	2–6	3–1	0–3	1–1	0–3	*	0–0	0–7	0–3	1–2
18 Tring Town	0–0	2–2	0–0	1–1	2–0	1–1	3–1	1–2	1–2	1–1	2–6	0–1	1–3	0–1	5–1	0–2	0–1	*	1–0	0–3	3–1
19 Wealdstone	3–4	0–0	2–1	4–0	3–0	1–1	4–0	3–1	0–2	7–0	4–0	0–1	2–0	1–1	3–2	0–4	9–0	3–1	*	1–5	1–1
20 Windsor & Eton	2–1	3–0	0–1	5–3	2–0	7–2	7–0	7–0	5–2	2–5	2–1	0–2	2–1	2–0	5–1	2–0	6–1	4–0	0–2	*	3–1
21 Wingate & Finch	1–3	1–0	7–0	8–1	0–2	1–4	3–2	2–3	2–2	2–2	1–0	0–1	1–1	1–1	1–0	2–0	3–0	2–3	2–0	1–2	*

Division III	*P*	*W*	*D*	*L*	*F*	*A*	*Pts*
1 Horsham	40	29	5	6	95	40	92
2 Leighton Town	40	28	5	7	95	34	89
3 Windsor & Eton	40	27	6	7	117	46	87
4 Wealdstone	40	23	8	9	104	39	77
5 Harlow Town	40	22	10	8	85	62	76
6 Northwood	40	20	9	11	76	56	69
7 Epsom & Ewell	40	18	14	8	95	57	68
8 Kingsbury Town	40	15	16	9	61	48	61
9 East Thurrock Utd	40	17	8	15	61	50	59
10 Aveley	40	16	10	14	62	53	58
11 Wingate & Finch	40	16	7	17	74	70	55
12 Lewes	40	14	7	19	56	72	49
13 Flackwell Heath	40	14	5	21	60	84	47
14 Hornchurch	40	11	8	21	55	77	41
15 Harefield United	40	11	7	22	49	89	40
16 Tring Town	40	10	8	22	40	78	38
17 Camberley Town	40	9	9	22	45	81	36
18 Hertford Town	40	10	5	25	72	103	35
19 Cove	40	8	10	22	37	89	34
20 Clapton	40	9	6	25	48	89	33
21 Southall	40	9	5	26	34	104	32

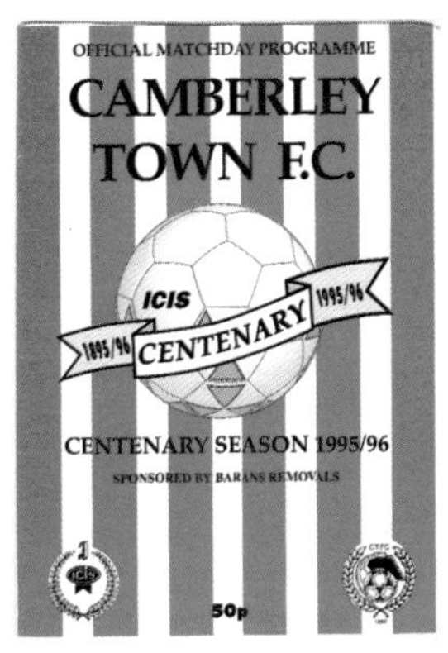

Left: the programme for Camberley Town's centenary season.

Right: the programme for Wealdstone's FA Vase match at home to Hampton.

1996–97 - At the start of the season it was speculated that the Premier Division would be one of the closest championships in recent times but in the end it turned out to be a two-horse race. Yeovil Town, after a two-year absence, won promotion to the GM Vauxhall Conference by gaining the championship six points clear of nearest challengers Enfield. When the clubs met at Yeovil in February an attendance of 8,007, the largest League crowd for many years, witnessed a 2–2 draw. Sutton United, who finished third, were a massive twenty-eight points behind runners-up Enfield with Dagenham & Redbridge, Yeading, St. Albans City and Aylesbury United closely following. At the foot of the table Staines Town, after one season, Grays Athletic and Chertsey Town made the drop to Division One. A superb season by Chesham United saw them secure the Division One championship. Runners-up were Basingstoke Town with Walton & Hersham, returning after one season, just eclipsing Hampton and Billericay Town for the final promotion place. Moving in the opposite division were Canvey Island, Marlow and Tooting & Mitcham United, all relegated to Division Two.

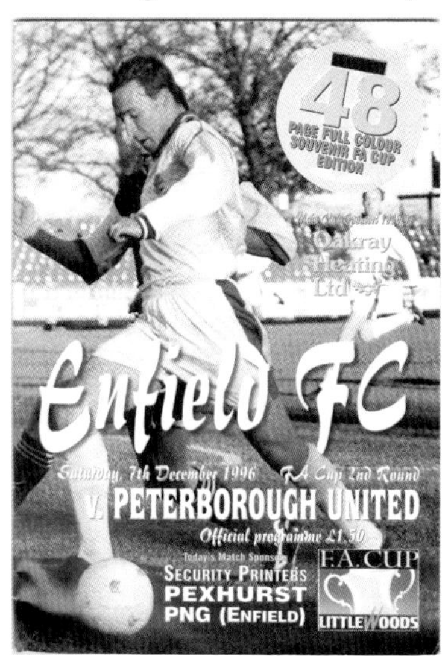

Two clubs dominated Division Two with the newly merged club Collier Row & Romford gaining the championship by one point from runners-up Leatherhead while the third promotion place went to the wire with Wembley securing promotion just ahead of nearest challengers Barking and Horsham. At the foot of the table Hertfordshire clubs Ware and Hemel Hempstead, joined by Dorking who were reprieved from relegation the previous season, were relegated to Division Three.

The Division Three championship race was between former Southern League clubs Wealdstone and Braintree Town with the former securing the title by one point while Northwood gained the third promotion place, pipping Harlow Town.

At the Annual General Meeting Gravesend & Northfleet switched from the Southern League replacing League champions Yeovil Town while Corinthian–Casuals (Combined Counties), Croydon Athletic (London-Spartan) and Ford United (Essex Senior) were elected to fill vacancies, increasing Division Three from seventeen to twenty clubs. Division Two champions Collier Row & Romford reverted back to Romford for the start of the season.

Premier Division	1	2	3	4	5	6	7	8	9	10	11	12	13	14	15	16	17	18	19	20	21	22
1 Aylesbury United	*	2–2	2–0	1–1	3–1	2–1	0–1	2–0	1–3	3–0	2–0	1–2	1–0	2–1	2–5	6–1	0–2	2–1	2–1	3–3	2–2	0–0
2 Bishop's Stortford	2–0	*	0–0	4–3	2–1	3–1	2–0	0–1	1–3	0–0	0–1	2–1	0–0	1–2	2–2	2–2	2–3	1–1	1–0	2–5	1–1	0–1
3 Boreham Wood	1–1	4–1	*	2–2	3–0	1–2	3–1	2–2	1–1	2–1	2–0	1–2	0–0	4–0	0–0	3–2	0–1	0–2	3–0	1–0	1–1	0–3
4 Bromley	0–2	2–1	2–0	*	2–0	5–1	1–0	0–0	0–2	1–2	1–2	2–2	1–1	3–2	2–2	3–0	2–1	1–1	1–2	2–1	5–1	1–2
5 Carshalton Athletic	3–1	1–0	1–2	3–2	*	2–0	0–0	0–0	0–1	6–0	2–1	0–2	4–1	1–2	1–3	1–1	2–1	2–0	2–0	3–3	0–0	0–1
6 Chertsey Town	0–0	0–3	1–1	3–1	2–3	*	0–3	0–2	1–1	0–6	2–2	1–0	3–5	0–5	0–3	2–4	0–1	0–5	3–2	1–1	2–1	0–2
7 Dagenham & R	0–2	3–0	2–1	0–2	0–1	2–1	*	1–1	0–2	2–1	3–1	1–1	3–0	1–1	2–0	4–2	2–0	0–1	3–0	2–1	1–2	0–1
8 Dulwich Hamlet	1–1	2–0	2–1	2–1	4–1	3–0	0–2	*	0–1	3–0	0–0	2–1	1–3	2–2	1–2	0–1	2–1	1–2	0–2	0–1	0–1	4–1
9 Enfield	3–0	1–1	3–0	4–3	2–0	5–0	0–1	2–3	*	4–0	1–0	2–2	1–2	1–0	3–0	3–3	3–0	1–0	4–0	3–1	1–1	3–0
10 Grays Athletic	2–0	0–1	2–4	1–0	0–1	0–2	0–3	1–1	0–2	*	3–2	0–0	0–1	2–2	1–1	1–1	0–1	1–2	1–2	1–1	1–2	2–3
11 Harrow Borough	0–0	1–1	2–0	2–0	1–1	1–0	1–1	2–1	1–1	1–0	*	2–2	3–3	3–1	1–2	2–3	3–1	0–1	0–2	2–1	0–1	2–3
12 Hendon	0–3	3–1	1–2	4–1	2–2	1–0	2–1	2–2	0–3	0–1	2–1	*	1–1	1–0	2–1	2–0	2–3	0–2	1–1	1–2	1–1	1–3
13 Heybridge Swifts	1–3	0–0	0–2	4–3	0–2	4–1	4–1	1–1	0–0	3–0	0–0	1–1	*	2–1	2–1	2–1	1–3	2–1	2–1	3–3	0–5	0–0
14 Hitchin Town	2–1	3–0	1–2	5–2	3–2	2–1	0–0	0–0	0–3	0–2	2–4	1–2	1–2	*	4–1	4–2	2–0	1–1	2–1	2–5	3–1	0–1
15 Kingstonian	0–1	0–1	5–1	1–1	1–1	2–0	2–3	4–2	0–1	5–2	4–4	2–1	1–0	3–1	*	4–1	3–2	0–1	3–3	2–3	4–2	0–3
16 Oxford City	3–2	4–1	0–0	2–3	1–1	0–2	2–2	1–1	1–4	1–1	2–1	2–0	1–2	5–1	3–1	*	1–2	3–2	1–0	1–3	0–1	0–2
17 Purfleet	0–1	3–0	1–1	2–0	2–0	2–0	2–2	1–4	1–3	2–4	2–0	0–0	3–3	1–1	3–2	2–2	*	2–2	2–0	3–2	2–2	1–1
18 St. Albans City	0–0	1–1	0–2	0–3	0–0	4–5	0–2	2–2	1–4	4–2	2–2	1–0	4–2	2–1	2–0	0–1	2–1	*	3–0	1–1	0–0	2–3
19 Staines Town	3–1	0–0	2–1	3–0	2–0	0–0	0–0	1–3	0–2	3–1	1–1	0–3	2–2	1–2	2–1	1–2	1–3	1–2	*	2–3	2–3	1–1
20 Sutton United	3–3	2–1	1–1	2–2	2–0	4–2	2–1	2–0	1–1	1–1	3–3	3–1	0–2	4–3	5–2	1–2	0–0	2–3	2–0	*	3–0	0–3
21 Yeading	0–1	3–0	2–1	1–0	0–0	0–0	1–1	3–0	1–1	3–0	1–2	2–1	1–0	0–1	5–1	4–1	1–1	0–3	1–0	1–2	*	0–0
22 Yeovil Town	3–2	1–0	0–0	1–0	3–0	4–0	0–0	6–1	2–2	2–0	2–1	2–0	1–0	1–0	2–3	4–1	4–3	3–1	3–1	3–2	2–0	*

Premier Division	*P*	*W*	*D*	*L*	*F*	*A*	*Pts*
1 Yeovil Town	42	31	8	3	83	34	101
2 Enfield	42	28	11	3	91	29	95
3 Sutton United	42	18	13	11	87	70	67
4 Dagenham & Red	42	18	11	13	57	43	65
5 Yeading	42	17	14	11	58	47	65
6 St. Albans City	42	18	11	13	65	55	65
7 Aylesbury United	42	18	11	13	64	54	65
8 Purfleet	42	17	11	14	67	63	62
9 Heybridge Swifts	42	16	14	12	62	62	62
10 Boreham Wood	42	15	13	14	56	52	58
11 Kingstonian	42	16	8	18	79	79	56
12 Dulwich Hamlet	42	14	13	15	57	57	55
13 Carshalton Athletic	42	14	11	17	51	56	53
14 Hitchin Town	42	15	7	20	67	73	52
15 Oxford City	42	14	10	18	67	83	52
16 Hendon	42	13	12	17	53	59	51
17 Harrow Borough	42	12	14	16	58	62	50
18 Bromley	42	13	9	20	67	72	48
19 Bishop's Stortford	42	10	13	19	43	64	43
20 Staines Town	42	10	8	24	46	71	38
21 Grays Athletic	42	8	9	25	43	78	33
22 Chertsey Town	42	8	7	27	40	98	31

Left: the programme for the Associate Members Trophy Final at Hitchin, which Leighton Town won 1-0.

Right: the programme for Dagenham & Redbridge's 3-1 victory over visitors Harrow Borough.

1996-97 Division I	1	2	3	4	5	6	7	8	9	10	11	12	13	14	15	16	17	18	19	20	21	22
1 Abingdon Town	*	0–0	2–0	1–1	3–1	2–1	0–3	2–2	0–1	1–0	0–1	2–1	0–0	2–1	0–1	0–0	1–0	6–0	0–0	0–1	2–1	4–1
2 Aldershot Town	3–1	*	3–1	1–0	0–0	1–1	1–0	1–2	2–2	1–0	1–1	2–2	3–0	0–1	1–3	1–0	2–2	2–0	1–1	5–2	1–0	0–2
3 Barton Rovers	0–0	0–0	*	1–4	1–0	0–0	0–3	2–0	0–1	0–1	3–1	2–1	2–1	0–1	1–1	0–0	3–1	2–1	0–1	0–1	0–0	1–1
4 Basingstoke Town	3–0	2–0	3–0	*	2–0	2–2	2–2	2–1	4–0	2–1	0–2	2–1	2–0	6–1	2–2	3–0	1–0	0–2	0–0	4–1	0–2	1–1
5 Berkhamsted Town	1–1	0–3	1–0	1–3	*	2–0	2–0	1–4	2–2	0–2	0–4	2–3	0–3	1–0	2–1	3–0	0–1	4–1	1–1	1–1	1–0	0–2
6 Billericay Town	2–1	2–2	1–1	1–1	3–0	*	0–0	2–0	1–2	2–0	0–0	4–3	2–2	0–2	0–1	2–0	4–1	2–1	2–1	2–1	3–1	4–0
7 Bognor Regis Tn	2–2	0–5	0–1	0–2	1–0	4–1	*	1–0	4–1	1–0	1–1	2–0	1–0	3–0	0–1	2–2	3–0	2–1	0–0	2–2	3–0	2–1
8 Canvey Island	1–0	0–1	1–2	1–1	2–2	1–3	1–1	*	0–3	3–0	1–0	1–2	4–2	2–2	0–1	3–3	2–1	0–0	0–0	1–4	0–1	2–2
9 Chesham United	2–1	1–3	4–0	2–1	5–2	1–2	1–0	4–0	*	2–2	1–0	2–1	2–1	3–0	4–0	3–2	4–0	1–0	1–1	0–1	2–0	2–1
10 Croydon	2–0	1–1	1–0	0–2	1–0	2–0	0–5	2–2	0–1	*	0–2	2–2	0–2	2–1	0–1	3–0	3–1	0–3	3–3	1–2	1–2	0–1
11 Hampton	2–1	1–1	3–2	1–0	1–1	3–1	3–0	3–1	1–1	2–1	*	4–3	3–4	1–0	1–2	2–1	0–2	2–2	0–0	1–0	2–0	2–0
12 Leyton Pennant	1–0	4–2	4–0	1–6	0–5	2–2	3–0	1–1	1–2	0–0	0–0	*	1–1	5–0	2–3	2–4	4–1	1–1	2–2	2–1	1–1	2–0
13 Maidenhead Utd	0–1	1–1	1–0	1–1	2–0	0–1	3–0	1–1	2–1	1–2	1–2	2–0	*	2–3	0–2	1–0	1–1	1–0	1–1	4–3	4–0	1–3
14 Marlow	0–1	3–1	1–1	1–0	0–2	1–3	0–2	2–1	2–0	1–1	2–1	0–1	2–0	*	0–2	2–2	1–1	1–7	0–2	1–2	0–2	3–1
15 Molesey	0–1	0–2	1–3	1–2	2–1	1–2	0–1	1–2	0–1	2–1	1–1	1–1	1–2	4–2	*	3–2	0–2	1–1	1–4	1–1	0–0	1–1
16 Thame United	0–3	0–2	2–0	1–2	3–2	2–2	1–1	1–0	3–2	3–1	1–2	2–1	1–0	6–1	0–2	*	1–0	0–3	1–1	0–3	1–1	1–1
17 Tooting & M Utd	1–1	0–1	4–0	0–4	1–0	1–3	0–3	3–1	0–4	1–1	0–1	1–2	1–5	0–0	0–1	1–3	*	0–2	2–3	0–5	1–1	2–1
18 Uxbridge	0–0	3–3	1–1	2–2	1–0	1–1	1–0	1–1	0–0	0–0	1–1	2–2	2–0	4–0	2–2	4–2	5–0	*	2–1	1–3	0–2	1–1
19 Walton & Hersham	2–0	3–1	5–0	0–2	2–1	2–1	3–0	2–0	1–2	2–1	1–0	1–2	2–2	2–1	1–0	0–2	4–0	0–3	*	2–1	0–3	4–0
20 Whyteleafe	0–2	1–0	0–0	1–1	3–3	0–1	0–3	4–2	1–3	1–0	1–0	2–1	1–2	3–1	2–0	2–0	2–5	1–3	1–2	*	1–2	3–4
21 Wokingham Town	3–0	0–1	0–1	2–2	0–1	0–1	1–2	1–2	2–1	0–0	1–1	2–3	0–0	2–0	1–2	1–0	1–0	0–1	0–2	1–1	*	2–0
22 Worthing	1–0	2–5	1–0	1–1	1–1	1–2	2–3	3–3	2–3	1–2	0–3	2–0	4–0	3–1	1–0	1–4	2–2	0–0	1–2	4–5	1–2	*

Division I	*P*	*W*	*D*	*L*	*F*	*A*	*Pts*
1 Chesham United	42	27	6	9	80	46	87
2 Basingstoke Town	42	22	13	7	81	38	79
3 Walton & Hersham	42	21	13	8	67	41	76
4 Hampton	42	21	12	9	62	39	75
5 Billericay Tow	42	21	12	9	69	49	75
6 Bognor Regis Tn	42	21	9	12	63	44	72
7 Aldershot Town	42	19	14	9	67	45	71
8 Uxbridge	42	15	17	10	65	48	62
9 Whyteleafe	42	18	7	17	71	68	61
10 Molesey	42	17	9	16	50	53	60
11 Abingdon Town	42	15	11	16	44	42	56
12 Leyton Pennant	42	14	12	16	71	72	54
13 Maidenhead Utd*	42	15	10	17	57	57	52
14 Wokingham Town	42	14	10	18	41	45	52
15 Thame United	42	13	10	19	57	69	49
16 Worthing	42	11	11	20	58	77	44
17 Barton Rovers	42	11	11	20	31	58	44
18 Croydon	42	11	10	21	40	57	43
19 Berkhamsted Town	42	11	9	22	47	66	42
20 Canvey Island	42	9	14	19	52	71	41
21 Marlow	42	11	6	25	41	84	39
22 Tooting & M Utd	42	8	8	26	40	85	32

** Maidenhead U had three points deducted.*

Left: the League handbook for 1996-97.

Right: the programme for Canvey Island's 2-1 home defeat by visitors Barton Rovers.

Division II	1	2	3	4	5	6	7	8	9	10	11	12	13	14	15	16	17	18	19	20	21	22
1 Banstead Athletic	*	0–1	1–2	0–3	3–1	4–2	2–2	3–0	1–2	2–0	3–0	1–1	5–2	1–2	0–0	1–2	2–3	2–0	1–0	3–0	1–2	1–2
2 Barking	1–1	*	0–0	2–1	1–2	4–0	0–1	4–2	1–1	2–0	2–1	1–0	4–0	2–1	3–1	1–0	2–2	1–0	2–2	1–3	1–0	3–0
3 Bedford Town	2–3	0–0	*	5–4	1–3	6–0	0–1	1–1	0–3	1–0	1–0	0–1	2–0	3–0	2–1	0–0	1–0	4–1	1–3	1–2	3–0	1–3
4 Bracknell Town	1–0	2–2	2–1	*	1–1	0–0	0–0	3–2	1–2	6–1	7–1	0–0	3–3	2–4	0–0	4–4	5–1	4–3	1–2	2–0	5–1	0–3
5 Chalfont St. Peter	0–2	0–1	2–1	1–1	*	4–0	2–2	1–1	0–1	2–0	0–0	1–1	1–3	0–3	2–1	3–0	2–1	3–2	0–0	1–1	2–0	2–1
6 Cheshunt	0–2	1–1	0–4	0–3	1–0	*	0–1	4–2	1–3	0–1	0–1	0–2	3–5	2–5	0–1	1–0	2–5	2–2	1–4	1–2	1–0	1–2
7 Collier Row & Rm	2–0	2–4	1–1	1–0	3–0	1–0	*	3–1	2–3	3–0	9–2	1–1	3–0	2–1	4–1	2–1	4–2	1–0	1–0	2–0	0–0	4–0
8 Dorking	0–3	0–4	0–3	2–1	0–3	3–1	0–2	*	1–6	0–2	2–3	3–3	0–3	0–3	1–0	2–0	0–2	0–2	1–2	0–2	0–3	2–1
9 Edgware Town	4–1	0–0	3–0	0–1	1–0	3–1	1–1	2–0	*	1–1	4–0	1–1	1–1	2–3	1–1	1–2	1–0	3–6	1–1	1–1	1–0	2–0
10 Egham Town	0–4	4–1	0–3	3–2	4–2	0–2	0–3	2–1	1–1	*	0–0	2–1	3–0	1–4	1–2	1–3	1–4	1–0	0–6	0–1	2–2	1–3
11 Hemel Hempstead	0–2	0–2	0–6	0–4	0–1	2–3	0–4	1–5	0–1	1–1	*	2–1	0–1	0–3	0–1	1–4	2–4	0–0	1–4	1–4	0–1	1–4
12 Horsham	3–2	0–0	0–2	4–1	4–0	1–0	1–2	5–0	1–0	1–0	5–1	*	3–1	1–2	3–1	1–1	0–1	3–2	4–2	3–1	6–3	0–2
13 Hungerford Town	1–3	3–1	2–3	1–0	1–1	2–1	1–1	1–0	2–2	6–4	3–0	0–3	*	0–4	0–0	3–0	4–2	2–2	1–1	0–0	1–1	1–1
14 Leatherhead	3–1	0–1	0–2	4–1	7–0	3–1	2–2	3–0	5–1	4–0	9–0	1–1	2–0	*	2–0	3–0	5–2	2–1	1–1	4–2	0–3	1–0
15 Leighton Town	2–1	0–3	1–1	2–0	1–0	4–1	2–2	4–0	5–2	2–1	5–0	1–1	2–2	2–2	*	2–0	2–3	3–1	1–2	1–1	2–0	2–1
16 Metropolitan Police	0–1	4–0	1–1	4–0	2–0	3–0	0–4	5–1	2–4	2–1	10–4	1–2	2–3	2–4	0–1	*	1–4	0–0	3–2	3–1	2–3	0–2
17 Tilbury	0–0	1–1	2–1	0–1	2–2	1–2	0–4	3–0	0–2	1–1	1–1	2–3	1–1	0–1	1–3	2–1	*	3–1	0–1	1–2	1–2	2–4
18 Ware	0–1	0–0	0–0	0–2	0–4	0–1	0–2	1–0	2–1	1–2	1–1	0–1	2–4	3–2	2–1	4–1	1–3	*	0–4	0–1	0–2	0–3
19 Wembley	4–3	1–2	3–1	4–0	2–0	7–0	2–2	1–1	1–1	1–0	4–2	1–2	3–1	0–2	2–2	1–3	3–1	3–1	*	3–0	0–0	3–0
20 Windsor & Eton	0–2	2–0	0–4	1–2	2–2	6–0	2–2	1–1	2–2	1–1	2–0	1–1	2–1	1–4	2–0	2–2	4–3	3–1	1–1	*	2–1	1–1
21 Witham Town	0–1	0–5	0–4	0–1	2–2	1–0	0–1	1–3	0–0	2–2	1–3	0–1	2–0	1–4	0–0	1–0	1–0	1–1	0–3	2–3	*	0–0
22 Wivenhoe Town	2–5	2–2	0–2	6–1	1–1	0–1	1–3	2–2	1–2	2–2	0–2	5–2	3–2	1–1	2–1	1–1	0–1	3–1	0–2	1–0	3–0	*

Division II	*P*	*W*	*D*	*L*	*F*	*A*	*Pts*
1 Collier Row & Rm	42	28	12	2	93	33	96
2 Leatherhead	42	30	5	7	116	45	95
3 Wembley	42	23	11	8	92	45	80
4 Barking	42	22	13	7	69	40	79
5 Horsham	42	22	11	9	78	48	77
6 Edgware Town	42	20	14	8	74	50	74
7 Bedford Town	42	21	8	13	77	43	71
8 Banstead Athletic	42	21	5	16	75	52	68
9 Windsor & Eton	42	17	13	12	65	62	64
10 Leighton Town	42	17	12	13	64	52	63
11 Bracknell Town	42	17	9	16	78	71	60
12 Wivenhoe Town	42	17	9	16	69	62	60
13 Chalfont St. Peter	42	14	13	15	53	61	55
14 Hungerford Town	42	14	13	15	68	77	55
15 Metropolitan Police	42	14	7	21	72	75	49
16 Tilbury	42	14	7	21	68	77	49
17 Witham Town	42	11	10	21	39	67	43
18 Egham Town	42	10	9	23	47	86	39
19 Cheshunt	42	9	3	30	37	101	30
20 Ware	42	7	8	27	44	80	29
21 Dorking	42	7	6	29	40	100	27
22 Hemel Hempstead	42	5	6	31	34	125	21

Collier Row FC and Romford FC (Essex Senior League) amalgamated to form Collier Row & Romford FC.

Left: the programme for Banstead Athletic's 1996-97 season.

Right: the programme for Boreham Wood's FA Cup tie at Luton Town.

1996-97 Division III	1	2	3	4	5	6	7	8	9	10	11	12	13	14	15	16	17
1 Aveley	*	1–2	1–2	1–2	0–4	4–1	1–1	3–1	3–1	5–0	2–0	1–0	2–2	4–1	2–0	1–1	1–1
2 Braintree Town	3–2	*	0–0	6–0	7–1	4–1	6–0	0–0	6–1	4–0	5–3	6–1	1–0	3–0	0–1	2–0	6–0
3 Camberley Town	0–2	0–1	*	1–0	8–3	2–2	3–1	0–1	3–0	2–1	2–0	0–1	3–1	1–1	0–2	0–3	4–2
4 Clapton	0–2	1–11	0–1	*	0–1	0–1	3–1	0–2	0–2	0–0	0–0	2–0	1–1	1–2	5–1	0–1	0–0
5 East Thurrock Utd	0–0	3–2	2–0	3–0	*	3–2	4–0	1–3	4–2	0–1	4–2	3–0	0–0	3–0	2–2	0–1	2–0
6 Epsom & Ewell	3–5	2–5	2–3	1–2	1–3	*	5–0	1–3	3–1	0–3	1–1	1–1	2–3	2–0	4–3	2–3	4–7
7 Flackwell Heath	0–7	0–3	2–5	0–2	0–0	2–1	*	3–1	1–1	0–3	0–1	2–0	1–1	0–1	5–0	4–0	1–0
8 Harlow Town	3–0	1–1	3–1	1–3	3–2	3–1	3–0	*	2–3	2–1	2–1	0–2	1–3	2–0	1–2	2–1	5–3
9 Hertford Town	0–1	0–1	3–0	1–2	5–1	2–1	2–2	0–2	*	3–1	0–1	4–0	0–1	1–1	4–2	0–2	3–3
10 Hornchurch	0–1	1–5	2–2	0–1	1–1	2–2	2–1	0–2	3–1	*	1–0	2–2	1–0	0–1	2–0	0–3	0–1
11 Kingsbury Town	1–3	1–0	1–2	0–1	3–0	1–3	0–2	3–0	2–3	1–1	*	2–1	0–1	3–1	1–4	0–0	3–0
12 Lewes	6–2	1–1	1–1	3–1	2–3	2–5	0–1	2–2	0–0	1–0	4–1	*	1–1	4–0	1–1	0–1	2–0
13 Northwood	2–0	2–2	1–1	0–0	0–0	2–1	4–1	1–0	7–3	4–0	4–1	4–1	*	3–2	4–1	1–3	1–0
14 Southall	0–4	0–3	2–1	2–2	0–2	2–3	3–1	0–3	1–5	2–3	0–2	0–1	0–1	*	4–0	1–1	0–2
15 Tring Town	0–2	0–2	0–1	0–2	0–2	2–1	2–1	2–3	2–2	0–1	1–2	1–3	1–2	2–0	*	0–3	0–3
16 Wealdstone	1–0	6–0	3–1	2–0	4–1	2–1	3–0	0–2	5–1	2–0	5–0	2–1	0–2	1–0	7–0	*	3–2
17 Wingate & Finch	1–1	0–1	0–5	2–0	2–0	2–2	4–3	1–1	2–1	2–3	1–4	3–1	1–1	5–1	2–1	0–3	*

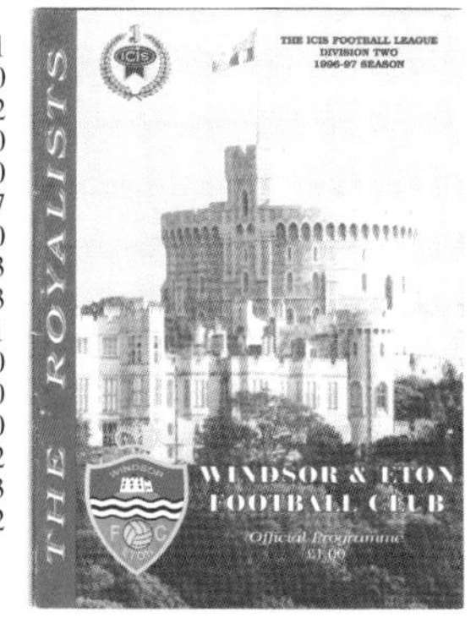

Division III	*P*	*W*	*D*	*L*	*F*	*A*	*Pts*
1 Wealdstone	32	24	3	5	72	24	75
2 Braintree Town	32	23	5	4	99	29	74
3 Northwood	32	18	10	4	60	31	64
4 Harlow Town	32	19	4	9	60	41	61
5 Aveley	32	17	6	9	64	39	57
6 East Thurrock Utd	32	16	6	10	58	51	54
7 Camberley Town	32	15	6	11	55	44	51
8 Wingate & Finch	32	11	7	14	52	63	40
9 Hornchurch	32	11	6	15	35	51	39
10 Clapton	32	11	6	15	31	49	39
11 Lewes	32	10	8	14	45	53	38
12 Kingsbury Town	32	11	4	17	41	54	37
13 Hertford Town	32	10	6	16	55	65	36
14 Epsom & Ewell	32	8	5	19	62	78	29
15 Flackwell Heath	32	8	5	19	36	71	29
16 Tring Town	32	7	3	22	33	74	24
17 Southall	32	6	4	22	28	69	22

Above: the Windsor & Eton edition for the 1996-97 campaign.

Left: the programme for Braintree Town's three goal victory over visitors Southall at Cressing Road in September 1996.

Below right: the Puma Cup Final programme between Basingstoke Town and Hendon.

Below left: Ford United's programme for their first season.

1997–98 - Kingstonian, who recruited Geoff Chapple as manager prior to the start of the season, won their first League championship since 1937 and with it promotion to the GM Vauxhall Conference. Boreham Wood were runners-up, eight points behind, with Sutton United in third.

At the foot of the table Hitchin Town and Oxford City were relegated to Division One, along with Yeading, whose goal difference was worse than both Aylesbury United and Bishop's Stortford, who thus escaped the drop. In Division One, at the fourth time of asking, Aldershot Town clinched the championship and promotion to the Premier Division. The runners-up were Billericay Town, with Hampton just pipping Maidenhead United for the final promotion place.

At the other end of the table Wokingham Town, Abingdon Town and Thame United were relegated to Division Two. In Division Two the championship was not decided until the final day of the season and was won by Canvey Island on goal difference, after Braintree Town lost 0–1 at home to basement club Cheshunt.

The third promotion place went to Wealdstone who, like Braintree Town, gained successive promotions. Relegated to Division Three were Tilbury, Egham Town and Cheshunt. A closely fought title race in Division Three ended with Hemel Hempstead securing the title by four points from Hertford Town, with Harlow Town in third.

At the Annual General Meeting, Hastings Town were going to switch from the Southern League to fill the vacancy left by Kingstonian, but Slough Town were expelled from the Football Conference (previously GM Vauxhall Conference) and were elected in Hastings' place. With no other clubs seeking election the constitution remained at 86 clubs for season 1998–99.

Premier Division	1	2	3	4	5	6	7	8	9	10	11	12	13	14	15	16	17	18	19	20	21	22
1 Aylesbury United	*	1–2	2–0	2–2	1–2	4–1	0–0	1–2	0–0	1–1	0–2	1–0	3–0	1–3	1–0	2–0	4–1	0–2	1–2	1–1	4–0	1–1
2 Basingstoke Town	1–0	*	3–1	2–2	0–3	1–2	2–0	1–2	4–3	0–0	2–1	2–2	1–1	2–0	3–0	0–0	2–1	0–2	3–1	1–1	1–2	1–2
3 Bishop's Stortford	1–0	1–1	*	3–1	2–0	4–3	4–2	1–1	1–1	0–2	1–2	1–2	1–2	2–2	0–2	0–1	0–1	2–0	1–0	0–1	3–1	2–1
4 Boreham Wood	2–1	5–0	1–0	*	0–0	2–2	3–1	0–0	4–0	2–1	4–1	2–2	1–2	2–3	0–0	0–1	3–1	3–1	2–3	2–2	3–0	3–1
5 Bromley	3–0	0–2	3–2	1–2	*	3–0	1–2	2–0	1–1	3–1	2–0	2–1	0–0	2–2	0–0	0–2	1–2	2–3	1–1	1–1	0–1	0–2
6 Carshalton Athletic	2–3	1–2	1–2	0–2	1–0	*	0–1	0–2	2–3	2–0	1–1	3–0	3–1	1–1	1–2	1–1	2–0	1–0	0–2	1–5	1–2	1–0
7 Chesham United	4–2	0–1	1–1	1–1	2–3	3–0	*	0–0	5–1	1–2	4–2	1–5	4–1	0–3	3–3	1–1	6–0	1–1	1–2	3–3	2–0	3–1
8 Dagenham & Red	2–3	2–1	2–1	1–1	2–1	2–0	2–0	*	2–1	0–2	2–0	1–2	1–1	6–2	1–0	2–2	7–0	2–2	1–1	0–2	4–2	1–1
9 Dulwich Hamlet	2–1	0–1	5–0	0–1	3–3	0–3	3–1	0–2	*	2–0	1–1	1–0	1–2	1–2	2–2	2–1	3–2	2–1	1–2	1–0	1–3	2–1
10 Enfield	2–1	2–1	4–1	0–3	1–1	3–0	0–1	1–2	0–0	*	1–2	3–5	3–3	4–2	2–1	0–1	2–0	0–0	0–2	0–2	3–0	2–0
11 Gravesend & Nth	6–0	3–0	1–2	1–1	1–0	3–3	3–2	2–2	0–1	1–3	*	3–0	4–0	1–0	2–0	1–2	3–2	0–0	2–1	2–2	1–2	1–2
12 Harrow Borough	1–1	2–0	2–1	1–0	2–3	1–3	1–0	0–5	1–2	5–2	2–1	*	0–0	0–2	1–1	0–2	0–3	3–0	1–0	0–2	2–0	2–1
13 Hendon	3–0	2–1	3–0	2–1	1–0	4–0	3–0	3–0	2–1	0–3	1–2	2–1	*	0–2	0–2	1–1	1–0	1–1	2–1	4–2	4–0	5–0
14 Heybridge Swifts	5–1	5–1	1–0	2–1	2–2	0–0	0–3	2–5	3–1	4–1	2–2	1–0	1–1	*	1–2	1–3	3–0	0–1	3–2	1–1	0–1	2–2
15 Hitchin Town	2–3	1–2	2–4	0–2	1–1	1–2	1–2	0–1	2–0	1–1	4–0	2–2	1–1	1–1	*	0–0	0–0	3–3	1–1	0–3	1–0	0–2
16 Kingstonian	3–0	2–0	1–0	2–5	4–1	5–1	3–1	0–2	2–1	0–0	3–1	5–2	2–1	3–0	2–0	*	0–0	2–2	5–0	0–0	7–0	0–1
17 Oxford City	2–2	0–1	1–0	0–1	1–1	1–1	2–1	2–0	1–2	1–2	2–1	2–4	0–2	0–2	2–2	0–1	*	0–0	0–0	1–2	0–1	0–3
18 Purfleet	0–2	1–2	3–1	0–2	2–0	1–2	3–2	4–0	2–2	4–0	2–0	2–2	1–0	1–1	1–0	1–1	2–1	*	0–1	0–6	1–0	1–3
19 St. Albans City	1–3	2–2	2–1	0–2	0–1	3–0	1–1	2–0	1–0	0–4	1–0	0–0	1–2	0–3	4–1	0–3	4–1	3–2	*	4–2	0–1	0–1
20 Sutton United	2–1	1–1	2–4	1–2	1–0	3–1	2–4	2–1	1–1	0–5	3–1	2–1	2–1	4–1	2–0	3–3	2–1	3–0	3–1	*	2–0	2–1
21 Walton & Hersham	3–0	1–1	3–0	1–4	0–2	3–4	1–1	2–1	1–0	3–1	0–1	0–0	2–2	1–0	2–1	1–4	1–0	2–4	1–0	1–1	*	1–1
22 Yeading	1–0	2–2	0–2	0–1	1–1	0–0	2–0	0–2	2–2	0–2	4–3	2–2	0–2	0–3	1–2	1–3	1–1	0–0	0–2	3–1	2–4	*

1997-98

Premier Division	P	W	D	L	F	A	Pts
1 Kingstonian	42	25	12	5	84	35	87
2 Boreham Wood	42	23	11	8	81	42	80
3 Sutton United	42	22	12	8	83	56	78
4 Dagenham & Red	42	21	10	11	73	50	73
5 Hendon	42	21	10	11	69	50	73
6 Heybridge Swifts	42	18	11	13	74	62	65
7 Enfield	42	18	8	16	66	58	62
8 Basingstoke Town	42	17	11	14	56	60	62
9 Walton & Hersham	42	18	6	18	50	70	60
10 Purfleet	42	15	13	14	57	58	58
11 St. Albans City	42	17	7	18	54	59	58
12 Harrow Borough	42	15	10	17	60	67	55
13 Gravesend & Nth	42	15	8	19	65	67	53
14 Chesham United	42	14	10	18	71	70	52
15 Bromley	42	13	13	16	53	53	52
16 Dulwich Hamlet	42	13	11	18	56	67	50
17 Carshalton Athletic	42	13	9	20	54	77	48
18 Aylesbury United	42	13	8	21	55	70	47
19 Bishop's Stortford	42	14	5	23	53	69	47
20 Yeading	42	12	11	19	49	65	47
21 Hitchin Town	42	8	15	19	45	62	39
22 Oxford City	42	7	9	26	35	76	30

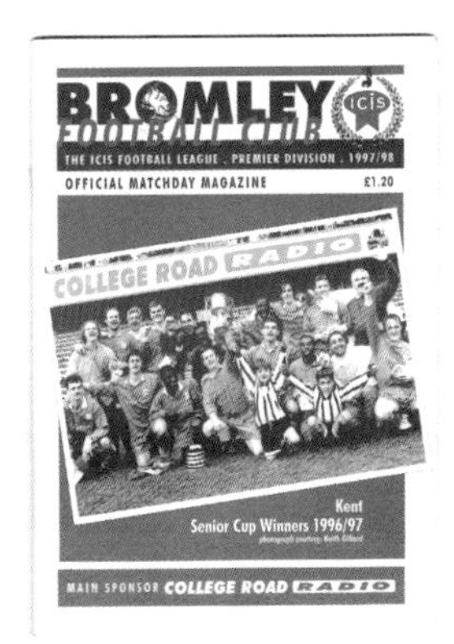

Left: the programme for Bromley's 1997-98 season.

Right: the programme for Gravesend & Northfleet's game with Braintree Town.

Division I	1	2	3	4	5	6	7	8	9	10	11	12	13	14	15	16	17	18	19	20	21	22
1 Abingdon Town	*	0–2	3–3	0–2	0–1	1–3	0–2	1–2	0–2	0–2	1–2	0–4	1–4	0–3	1–6	2–0	1–0	1–2	2–0	1–0	2–2	3–0
2 Aldershot Town	3–1	*	1–0	3–0	1–0	1–1	0–1	1–1	2–1	2–0	1–0	8–1	0–2	3–1	2–0	2–0	1–1	4–0	3–1	3–0	4–0	3–1
3 Barton Rovers	1–2	1–1	*	2–2	2–0	1–1	0–0	1–0	1–2	1–1	4–4	0–0	1–0	3–0	2–4	0–0	3–0	0–1	0–0	3–0	0–3	1–4
4 Berkhamsted Town	0–1	4–2	1–0	*	1–5	3–2	3–1	1–0	1–0	1–2	2–1	3–3	5–0	2–2	2–4	4–2	3–3	0–2	1–2	1–3	1–1	0–0
5 Billericay Town	3–1	1–2	4–0	1–1	*	0–2	1–5	2–1	2–1	1–1	1–0	1–2	0–2	2–1	2–1	2–0	4–0	1–1	4–0	4–1	3–0	4–0
6 Bognor Regis Tn	7–0	1–2	4–0	0–0	4–2	*	2–3	0–1	2–0	1–2	2–0	0–2	2–1	4–1	3–0	1–1	4–0	2–1	1–2	2–0	3–0	1–2
7 Chertsey Town	1–1	2–0	3–2	4–2	1–3	1–1	*	5–1	3–3	1–1	3–4	1–1	0–2	1–1	2–4	4–0	3–0	1–3	4–1	1–3	4–1	1–4
8 Croydon	3–1	2–1	3–5	1–0	1–3	0–0	0–0	*	1–2	2–1	3–2	2–1	2–1	0–0	1–2	1–2	1–1	0–1	0–1	1–0	2–0	1–0
9 Grays Athletic	7–1	2–1	2–2	2–0	2–1	2–2	3–0	1–1	*	1–2	3–1	1–2	1–0	2–0	2–2	0–1	2–0	2–3	2–0	1–1	1–1	1–0
10 Hampton	4–2	1–1	1–2	3–2	0–2	2–1	2–2	2–2	2–2	*	2–0	3–1	1–0	1–0	1–0	3–1	4–1	1–0	1–1	2–1	3–3	2–0
11 Leatherhead	3–4	0–0	2–1	3–0	1–1	0–1	2–1	1–1	1–1	0–0	*	1–2	2–1	1–0	3–1	1–0	1–2	5–2	0–0	2–0	2–1	5–1
12 Leyton Pennant	2–1	3–3	2–0	0–1	2–3	0–0	1–1	2–0	1–2	1–0	1–3	*	1–2	3–1	3–1	1–2	4–1	4–0	2–1	1–1	2–2	1–3
13 Maidenhead Utd	2–1	0–2	3–0	2–1	1–0	1–0	4–1	6–1	0–1	1–1	2–1	0–0	*	1–1	1–3	3–0	5–0	2–1	4–0	5–0	2–1	1–2
14 Molesey	1–0	0–1	2–1	0–1	2–3	5–0	2–4	3–2	1–0	1–1	0–2	0–1	0–3	*	1–1	3–2	2–3	2–3	0–0	0–0	1–0	1–0
15 Romford	3–2	1–2	6–1	2–1	1–2	1–2	2–2	3–1	3–3	0–1	1–0	0–0	0–1	0–0	*	2–1	3–1	3–1	1–2	1–0	3–0	4–0
16 Staines Town	2–1	2–5	2–3	3–2	0–2	3–0	0–1	3–1	1–4	2–2	1–1	1–0	0–4	2–3	1–4	*	4–1	0–1	1–1	3–1	3–0	1–1
17 Thame United	3–0	1–4	1–1	0–1	0–2	0–3	1–6	1–2	2–0	0–5	0–3	0–0	0–0	2–1	0–1	1–1	*	0–1	1–1	0–2	0–0	3–2
18 Uxbridge	5–2	1–2	2–1	3–1	0–0	2–1	1–1	2–1	3–2	1–2	1–1	1–0	1–1	1–0	3–2	0–0	3–1	*	3–0	1–3	1–0	2–1
19 Wembley	1–0	0–1	0–1	1–0	1–0	0–5	2–2	0–0	0–1	1–3	1–1	2–3	0–2	1–1	3–3	0–0	5–0	1–3	*	0–0	2–1	1–3
20 Whyteleafe	0–3	0–4	1–1	0–1	1–3	2–2	4–1	2–1	0–3	1–1	0–3	3–5	1–2	2–2	2–8	2–2	4–0	3–2	0–0	*	2–1	0–1
21 Wokingham Town	1–1	0–3	4–0	0–1	0–1	0–2	0–2	1–1	1–2	3–4	2–2	2–1	0–1	2–1	1–1	1–3	0–1	2–1	0–2	1–2	*	2–1
22 Worthing	7–2	3–2	0–2	3–1	1–1	0–2	2–1	2–0	1–7	2–2	0–3	1–0	2–1	4–1	0–4	0–1	3–1	3–0	1–1	4–0	0–1	*

Division I	P	W	D	L	F	A	Pts
1Aldershot Town	42	28	8	6	89	36	92
2Billericay Town	42	25	6	11	78	44	81
3Hampton	42	22	15	5	75	47	81
4Maidenhead Utd	42	25	5	12	76	37	80
5Uxbridge	42	23	6	13	66	59	75
6Grays Athletic	42	21	10	11	79	49	73
7Romford	42	21	8	13	92	59	71
8Bognor Regis Tn	42	20	9	13	77	45	69
9Leatherhead	42	18	11	13	70	51	65
10Leyton Pennant	42	17	11	14	66	58	62
11Chertsey Town	42	16	13	13	83	70	61
12Worthing	42	17	6	19	64	71	57
13Berkhamsted Town	42	15	8	19	59	69	53
14Staines Town	42	13	10	19	54	71	49
15Croydon	42	13	10	19	47	64	49
16Barton Rovers	42	12	11	13	53	72	46
17Wembley	42	10	15	17	38	61	45
18Molesey	42	10	11	21	47	65	41
19Whyteleafe	42	10	10	22	48	83	40
20Wokingham Town	42	7	10	25	41	74	31
21Abingdon Town	42	9	4	29	47	101	31
22Thame United	42	7	9	26	33	96	30

Romford previously Collier Row & Romford.

Left: the programme for Romford's 2-2 draw with visitors Chertsey Town in April 1998.

Right: the Walton & Hersham programme showing Ryman sponsorship of the club.

Division II	1	2	3	4	5	6	7	8	9	10	11	12	13	14	15	16	17	18	19	20	21	22
1 Banstead Athletic	*	1–2	0–2	3–1	0–0	2–2	1–2	3–2	2–2	1–0	1–2	0–4	1–3	1–2	3–1	1–1	5–2	1–1	4–1	2–1	0–0	1–3
2 Barking	3–1	*	1–2	3–3	1–3	0–4	1–1	0–0	0–0	2–1	0–1	4–2	0–1	1–0	0–2	1–1	0–3	1–2	2–1	3–0	2–2	4–3
3 Bedford Town	2–0	2–0	*	1–1	0–1	2–3	0–0	3–1	3–2	2–0	0–0	2–0	1–0	0–1	1–0	4–0	3–0	2–0	0–0	3–0	1–0	1–1
4 Bracknell Town	1–0	1–2	2–0	*	1–4	1–1	1–2	1–1	0–0	3–1	3–2	4–1	1–2	3–2	2–0	2–4	1–2	1–2	3–4	5–3	1–1	1–8
5 Braintree Town	4–0	1–1	3–0	4–2	*	2–1	4–1	0–1	1–1	4–1	5–1	3–1	4–0	5–3	7–0	4–0	4–1	3–0	0–1	3–0	1–0	4–4
6 Canvey Island	1–2	6–0	1–0	5–1	1–1	*	4–0	3–0	3–2	6–1	2–0	7–2	2–0	3–1	1–1	4–0	5–1	3–0	2–0	5–1	3–0	3–3
7 Chalfont St. Peter	2–1	2–2	0–0	5–5	1–4	0–5	*	0–0	0–3	4–2	1–0	1–2	2–0	2–0	1–1	3–1	1–1	2–0	1–1	4–0	0–1	2–0
8 Cheshunt	0–1	1–2	0–1	1–0	1–2	1–2	0–2	*	2–2	0–3	0–0	2–3	1–1	3–5	0–3	0–0	0–2	0–3	0–2	0–3	0–0	0–2
9 Edgware Town	2–0	2–2	0–0	0–1	2–2	3–0	2–1	8–0	*	3–1	5–2	2–1	1–2	3–2	3–4	3–1	2–1	2–2	0–2	0–4	0–2	2–1
10 Egham Town	0–4	1–0	1–2	2–0	0–2	4–3	0–2	2–2	1–0	*	3–2	2–0	0–0	2–0	0–3	2–0	2–2	1–4	3–5	0–1	1–2	2–2
11 Horsham	0–4	1–2	1–0	0–1	1–1	0–3	2–2	2–3	1–3	2–0	*	1–1	4–0	3–0	0–2	0–1	5–2	2–1	0–2	3–0	3–1	0–1
12 Hungerford Town	4–1	0–2	1–1	1–2	2–3	1–1	1–1	1–0	1–0	7–1	2–4	*	4–0	1–2	1–3	1–3	2–0	1–3	1–1	1–2	3–1	2–2
13 Leighton Town	0–2	2–2	0–0	1–0	0–4	2–4	2–0	3–2	0–3	2–0	2–1	2–1	*	2–1	1–3	1–3	2–3	1–3	0–1	1–1	2–0	1–3
14 Marlow	0–3	5–2	2–0	2–1	1–3	1–3	1–3	3–1	1–3	2–1	2–2	1–1	2–0	*	2–1	1–2	1–0	4–3	0–2	4–1	4–2	0–1
15 Metropolitan Police	3–1	5–1	0–1	5–0	4–4	1–2	1–4	3–1	2–2	1–0	1–7	4–2	3–0	3–2	*	2–1	2–0	0–1	1–0	0–2	2–1	1–2
16 Northwood	3–1	1–1	0–3	2–1	1–2	1–2	3–1	6–0	1–0	2–1	2–2	1–1	2–1	1–1	3–3	*	4–2	1–1	0–0	1–4	1–2	0–3
17 Tilbury	0–0	2–1	1–1	3–4	1–4	1–2	1–2	2–1	3–4	1–1	1–1	1–0	3–2	1–1	2–2	1–2	*	1–1	1–2	0–0	2–2	1–3
18 Tooting & M Utd	2–0	1–1	0–0	2–3	1–1	0–1	0–3	1–2	3–0	4–0	1–2	1–1	3–0	2–0	1–0	0–1	1–2	*	2–2	2–1	1–0	1–0
19 Wealdstone	1–1	4–2	0–1	2–0	1–1	1–1	2–0	5–1	3–1	4–2	4–2	3–1	2–1	5–0	0–2	1–1	3–1	2–0	*	2–0	1–1	1–1
20 Windsor & Eton	0–2	2–3	0–4	4–2	3–3	0–3	3–0	3–0	2–3	7–1	1–0	0–0	2–2	2–1	1–1	2–4	5–0	1–0	1–2	*	3–1	5–1
21 Witham Town	1–1	1–2	1–1	3–0	2–3	1–2	1–1	1–1	2–4	3–1	3–3	1–2	0–2	0–1	2–2	1–2	2–1	5–1	3–4	0–0	*	2–1
22 Wivenhoe Town	0–2	1–3	1–3	2–2	2–3	1–1	1–1	1–0	3-1	5–0	6–2	2–2	3–1	0–0	0–2	3–1	2–2	2–1	2–1	0–3	2–1	*

1997-98 Division II	P	W	D	L	F	A	Pts
1 Canvey Island	42	30	8	4	116	41	98
2 Braintree Town	42	29	11	2	117	45	98
3 Wealdstone	42	24	11	7	81	46	83
4 Bedford Town	42	22	12	8	55	25	78
5 Metropolitan Police	42	21	8	13	80	65	71
6 Wivenhoe Town	42	18	12	12	84	66	66
7 Edgware Town	42	18	10	14	81	65	64
8 Chalfont St. Peter	42	17	13	12	63	60	64
9 Northwood	42	17	11	14	65	69	62
10 Windsor & Eton	42	17	7	18	74	72	58
11 Tooting & M Utd	42	16	9	17	58	56	57
12 Barking	42	15	12	15	62	75	57
13 Banstead Athletic	42	15	9	18	60	63	54
14 Marlow	42	16	5	21	64	78	53
15 Horsham	42	13	9	20	67	75	48
16 Bracknell Town	42	13	8	21	68	93	47
17 Leighton Town	42	13	6	23	45	78	45
18 Hungerford Town	42	11	11	20	66	77	44
19 Witham Town	42	9	13	20	55	68	40
20 Tilbury	42	9	12	21	57	88	39
21 Egham Town	42	9	5	28	47	101	32
22 Cheshunt	42	4	10	28	31	90	22

Left: Horsham's programme for their 3-0 victory over visitors Windsor & Eton.

Right: the programme for Bracknell Town's 4-0 victory over visitors Barking.

Division III	1	2	3	4	5	6	7	8	9	10	11	12	13	14	15	16	17	18	19	20
1 Aveley	*	1–3	2–1	3–0	2–1	2–0	0–1	1–2	1–3	2–2	3–4	2–0	3–0	2–0	2–1	1–1	1–0	1–1	0–1	2–0
2 Camberley Town	1–3	*	3–0	1–0	0–1	7–2	0–2	1–1	4–0	1–2	2–3	2–1	1–0	4–0	2–1	5–0	2–1	6–0	1–0	2–0
3 Clapton	0–3	0–3	*	3–3	1–1	1–0	0–1	4–2	2–2	1–3	4–5	0–3	1–0	1–0	2–1	3–0	1–0	2–2	0–2	3–0
4 Corinthian-Casuals	3–1	4–2	1–3	*	3–2	3–0	0–0	0–1	1–1	0–2	1–3	0–1	2–4	0–2	3–0	1–1	1–2	2–4	3–2	2–0
5 Croydon Athletic	3–2	1–4	0–1	1–3	*	7–1	1–2	5–2	2–1	0–1	1–1	1–1	0–3	2–1	2–1	3–1	1–2	1–4	2–2	5–1
6 Dorking	3–2	1–4	2–0	3–2	1–0	*	1–4	4–3	0–3	3–3	0–2	0–0	0–3	0–5	2–2	3–1	2–1	2–3	2–2	1–2
7 East Thurrock Utd	1–1	0–1	1–0	3–0	3–0	3–0	*	3–1	3–1	1–0	1–2	0–2	0–0	2–1	1–2	3–0	1–1	3–0	3–1	0–2
8 Epsom & Ewell	4–2	1–1	0–1	0–1	3–1	2–1	7–2	*	1–0	0–1	2–3	2–1	1–2	2–2	2–0	4–0	6–0	1–2	1–2	2–0
9 Flackwell Heath	1–1	1–3	1–1	3–1	0–0	4–1	0–3	0–3	*	2–3	1–3	1–3	3–2	2–3	3–0	2–1	2–1	2–1	0–2	1–1
10 Ford United	1–1	0–1	6–0	1–1	1–0	3–1	1–1	6–1	8–0	*	1–1	0–6	0–1	3–1	8–0	5–0	1–1	3–2	3–0	6–0
11 Harlow Town	1–1	2–2	2–0	2–0	1–1	3–0	2–0	1–1	0–0	1–3	*	0–1	2–4	1–0	2–0	2–1	4–1	1–0	2–0	2–2
12 Hemel Hempstead	1–0	1–1	2–1	3–0	3–0	2–1	6–0	1–0	7–0	3–1	2–2	*	1–2	2–1	3–0	2–0	2–1	1–0	1–1	3–0
13 Hertford Town	3–1	0–1	1–0	0–1	2–1	2–0	2–2	2–1	2–0	0–0	1–1	1–1	*	6–1	4–2	3–0	2–0	5–0	4–2	1–0
14 Hornchurch	4–2	3–3	1–1	0–3	3–1	0–0	1–2	1–1	0–0	1–0	0–3	2–4	0–4	*	0–2	2–0	2–1	4–2	1–1	4–4
15 Kingsbury Town	1–2	2–3	2–1	0–2	1–2	4–4	0–3	0–1	0–1	0–2	1–5	3–2	0–1	0–2	*	1–1	2–0	0–3	0–4	0–2
16 Lewes	0–3	1–4	2–0	1–3	2–1	3–1	0–5	1–2	1–4	0–3	0–1	0–1	3–0	1–2	4–1	*	2–2	2–1	1–6	1–0
17 Southall	3–2	1–7	2–1	1–1	1–4	2–0	1–2	1–0	2–2	1–3	0–1	0–7	0–1	1–0	1–0	2–0	*	2–3	1–7	2–2
18 Tring Town	0–2	1–1	0–1	0–4	1–1	2–0	0–2	1–1	3–1	0–2	2–2	0–1	0–3	2–1	4–1	3–1	1–2	*	1–3	1–1
19 Ware	2–0	4–2	2–1	0–1	1–0	0–4	3–3	2–3	5–0	0–2	1–2	0–2	0–5	1–2	3–1	1–1	4–1	1–0	*	1–0
20 Wingate & Finch	4–5	2–2	0–4	1–3	0–3	2–3	0–3	1–2	1–2	0–0	3–6	1–3	0–1	2–2	4–1	2–0	5–0	0–1	1–0	*

Division III	P	W	D	L	F	A	Pts
1 Hemel Hempstead	38	27	6	5	86	28	87
2 Hertford Town	38	26	5	7	77	31	83
3 Harlow Town	38	24	11	3	81	43	83
4 Camberley Town	38	24	7	7	93	43	79
5 Ford United	38	23	9	6	90	34	78
6 East Thurrock Utd	38	23	7	8	70	40	76
7 Epsom & Ewell	38	17	6	15	69	57	57
8 Ware	38	17	6	15	69	57	57
9 Aveley	38	16	7	15	65	57	55
10 Corinthian-Casuals	38	16	6	16	59	57	54
11 Hornchurch	38	12	9	17	55	68	45
12 Clapton	38	13	6	19	46	61	45
13 Flackwell Heath	38	12	9	17	50	76	45
14 Croydon Athletic	38	12	7	19	58	63	43
15 Tring Town	38	12	7	19	51	69	43
16 Southall	38	10	6	22	41	85	36
17 Dorking	38	9	6	23	49	94	33
18 Wingate & Finch	38	7	8	23	46	80	29
19 Lewes	38	7	5	26	34	88	26
20 Kingsbury Town	38	5	3	30	35	93	18

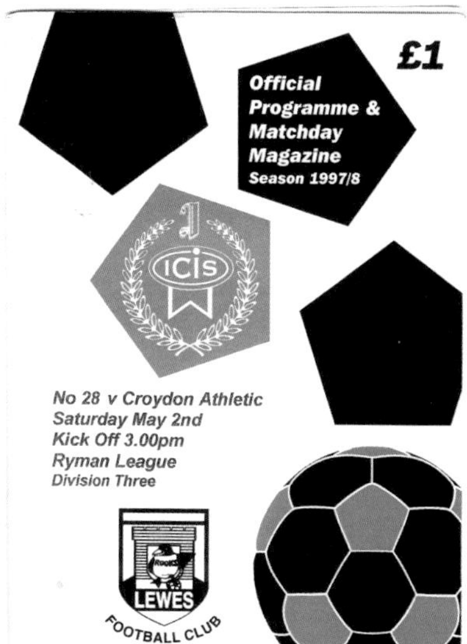

Right: The Lewes programme for their 2-1 victory over visitors Croydon Athletic.

1998–99 - In the early part of the season the top spot was shared by Aylesbury United and Aldershot Town but as the season progressed Sutton United got a grip and ended the season as worthy champions, gaining promotion to the Football Conference. Aylesbury United had to settle for runners-up four points clear of Dagenham & Redbridge and Purfleet with Enfield finishing in fifth while early pacesetters Aldershot Town were seventh. Relegation saw only two clubs, namely Bishop's Stortford and Bromley, relegated to Division One as Carshalton Athletic were reprieved due to Wealdstone's ineligibility to be promoted. Canvey Island achieved successive League titles, having secured the Division One championship by five points from nearest challengers Hitchin Town. Wealdstone, who finished third, were not promoted to the Premier Division as work on their ground was not completed by the 1st April deadline.

At the foot of the table Molesey, Wembley and Berkhamsted Town suffered relegation to Division Two. Bedford Town, who narrowly missed promotion the previous year, secured the Division Two championship with Harlow Town runners-up and Thame United, relegated the previous season, securing an immediate return to Division One. At the other end of the table Hertford Town, Bracknell Town and Abingdon Town, with the latter conceding 124 goals and suffering successive demotions, were relegated to Division Three. The Division Three championship was won by Ford United who were promoted, with runners-up Wingate & Finchley and third placed Cheshunt, to Division Two.

Farnborough Town, relegated from the Football Conference, were elected at the Annual General Meeting to replace champions Sutton United while Division Three was increased to twenty-one clubs by the election of Essex club Great Wakering Rovers.

Hampton changed their name to Hampton & Richmond Borough for the 1999–2000 season.

1998-99

Premier Division	1	2	3	4	5	6	7	8	9	10	11	12	13	14	15	16	17	18	19	20	21	22
1 Aldershot Town	*	0–1	0–1	0–1	5–0	6–0	3–0	4–0	0–0	4–3	3–1	3–1	3–0	5–0	5–2	0–2	1–1	1–1	1–2	1–1	1–2	7–2
2 Aylesbury United	0–1	*	3–2	3–0	4–2	0–0	2–1	2–0	0–3	0–1	3–0	1–2	2–0	3–0	2–0	1–0	0–1	2–1	0–0	0–0	1–4	1–0
3 Basingstoke Town	2–1	2–1	*	0–1	3–1	1–1	1–1	2–1	4–0	1–1	2–1	1–0	2–2	1–0	2–1	1–1	2–2	3–2	1–2	0–2	1–2	0–0
4 Billericay Town	1–1	0–3	0–0	*	3–2	1–0	2–2	2–0	3–0	1–2	1–0	0–1	0–2	2–0	2–2	2–1	2–1	0–1	3–3	1–2	1–2	1–0
5 Bishop's Stortford	0–8	0–3	0–0	1–1	*	2–0	1–3	1–2	5–2	0–3	2–1	1–2	3–1	0–2	0–3	0–3	1–3	0–0	1–1	0–1	1–2	1–0
6 Boreham Wood	1–1	1–6	1–1	0–0	1–2	*	0–3	4–4	0–0	0–2	4–0	3–2	3–1	4–2	1–0	2–0	1–1	2–1	1–1	1–0	2–0	0–0
7 Bromley	1–1	0–1	1–3	2–2	2–4	2–2	*	2–3	0–1	0–0	0–3	2–1	0–1	0–0	3–0	1–4	6–1	2–1	0–1	2–1	1–1	1–1
8 Carshalton Athletic	0–2	3–3	1–0	3–1	1–0	1–1	1–1	*	0–1	0–0	2–0	2–1	1–2	2–4	1–2	1–3	1–2	2–1	1–1	0–3	1–0	1–3
9 Chesham United	0–0	1–0	0–2	3–3	0–1	2–5	3–1	3–0	*	2–5	0–0	2–0	3–2	2–2	1–4	0–2	1–0	3–3	2–1	1–0	0–3	1–2
10 Dagenham & Red	0–1	1–0	2–0	1–2	1–1	1–1	3–3	5–0	0–0	*	1–0	3–3	0–0	4–0	1–0	6–0	3–0	0–1	2–2	3–0	0–0	3–1
11 Dulwich Hamlet	4–3	0–1	2–0	2–4	1–1	2–0	2–0	0–0	3–2	1–2	*	0–1	1–0	2–1	0–2	3–1	4–3	1–2	2–2	2–2	2–1	3–2
12 Enfield	4–0	2–3	3–2	1–0	2–1	1–3	3–0	1–0	2–2	4–0	2–1	*	0–2	0–0	5–0	2–1	4–1	1–2	0–0	2–1	1–1	3–2
13 Gravesend & Nth	2–1	1–2	1–0	0–0	4–1	3–2	1–2	3–1	0–2	2–0	0–1	0–3	*	3–0	2–0	0–1	3–2	1–1	0–1	1–2	2–1	2–0
14 Hampton	0–0	0–0	2–1	0–0	0–0	3–3	2–1	1–1	0–1	1–2	0–0	0–2	1–0	*	0–0	3–1	4–0	2–3	1–2	2–2	0–3	2–0
15 Harrow Borough	1–0	1–4	0–2	3–3	2–2	3–0	2–0	8–2	5–4	2–1	3–2	0–0	0–1	4–0	*	2–2	2–0	5–0	0–0	0–2	0–3	0–1
16 Hendon	1–1	3–3	2–1	2–0	5–3	0–1	2–1	1–1	2–1	2–2	1–1	2–0	0–0	1–2	1–2	*	6–1	1–2	4–3	5–2	0–3	0–3
17 Heybridge Swifts	1–1	1–1	3–9	1–0	1–2	2–0	2–1	0–2	0–4	1–2	0–2	2–2	3–0	3–0	2–4	1–0	*	0–0	0–3	2–1	2–4	1–0
18 Purfleet	1–1	0–0	2–1	0–2	3–1	2–1	1–0	4–2	3–0	3–0	2–1	0–1	2–1	4–0	4–0	4–0	2–0	*	1–0	0–4	1–3	6–1
19 St. Albans City	1–1	2–1	4–2	1–0	5–1	1–2	4–1	1–0	2–3	2–2	1–1	2–1	0–2	3–1	1–1	4–2	1–1	2–0	*	3–3	2–2	1–1
20 Slough Town	2–2	1–0	0–1	1–1	2–2	0–3	2–1	1–1	3–1	0–1	1–0	2–2	4–0	3–0	0–3	1–1	0–1	2–3	1–0	*	1–2	3–0
21 Sutton United	5–0	1–2	1–2	4–1	2–0	2–1	2–0	3–0	2–0	3–1	2–0	1–1	1–1	3–2	2–1	4–1	1–1	2–1	2–3	0–1	*	5–0
22 Walton & Hersham	0–4	0–2	2–1	3–4	2–2	1–1	1–0	3–2	9–1	0–1	3–1	0–4	1–3	0–1	2–2	0–3	0–1	1–0	1–0	2–0	0–2	*

Premier Division	*P*	*W*	*D*	*L*	*F*	*A*	*Pts*
1 Sutton United	42	27	7	8	89	39	88
2 Aylesbury United	42	23	8	11	67	38	77
3 Dagenham & Red	42	20	13	9	71	44	73
4 Purfleet	42	22	7	13	71	52	73
5 Enfield	42	21	9	12	73	49	72
6 St. Albans City	42	17	17	8	71	52	68
7 Aldershot Town	42	16	14	12	83	48	62
8 Basingstoke Town	42	17	10	15	63	53	61
9 Harrow Borough	42	17	9	16	72	66	60
10 Gravesend & Nth	42	18	6	18	54	53	60
11 Slough Town	42	16	11	15	60	53	59
12 Billericay Town	42	15	13	14	54	56	58
13 Hendon	42	16	9	17	70	71	57
14 Boreham Wood	42	14	15	13	59	63	57
15 Chesham United	42	15	9	18	58	79	54
16 Dulwich Hamlet	42	14	8	20	53	63	50
17 Heybridge Swifts	42	13	9	20	51	85	48
18 Walton & Hersham	42	12	7	23	50	77	43
19 Hampton	42	10	12	20	41	71	42
20 Carshalton Athletic	42	10	10	22	47	82	40
21 Bishop's Stortford	42	9	10	23	49	90	37
22 Bromley	42	8	11	23	50	72	35

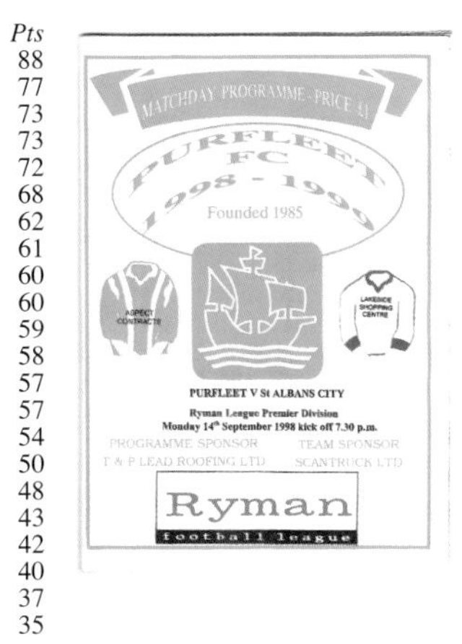

Left: Purfleet programme for their game with St. Albans City which The Fleet won 1-0.

Right: Aylesbury United's programme for their game with Aldershot Town, which the visitors won 1-0.

Division I	1	2	3	4	5	6	7	8	9	10	11	12	13	14	15	16	17	18	19	20	21	22
1 Barton Rovers	*	2–0	0–2	1–3	0–1	1–1	2–0	0–1	0–0	0–0	0–2	1–1	2–1	0–0	1–1	0–0	1–0	0–3	0–1	2–0	0–0	2–1
2 Berkhamsted Town	2–1	*	1–2	0–2	1–3	3–3	2–2	1–4	1–2	3–2	2–0	0–3	0–1	0–2	3–3	5–0	0–0	4–1	1–1	2–1	0–1	0–3
3 Bognor Regis Tn	1–0	1–3	*	4–0	0–0	3–1	1–2	0–1	6–1	3–0	0–1	3–1	0–0	0–1	1–1	1–0	2–0	2–0	4–1	3–1	1–2	1–3
4 Braintree Town	1–1	6–0	2–3	*	0–2	1–2	3–2	1–1	2–0	0–0	8–2	2–2	0–0	1–2	1–3	4–0	2–4	1–0	0–1	2–0	4–0	1–0
5 Canvey Island	0–2	3–0	2–0	2–1	*	2–0	2–1	2–1	3–0	3–0	6–1	0–4	2–1	2–0	0–2	2–0	1–0	4–2	3–0	1–1	2–0	3–1
6 Chertsey Town	2–1	0–4	3–1	0–3	1–1	*	2–0	2–2	1–3	1–0	1–1	2–2	0–2	0–1	2–2	1–1	2–1	0–1	1–1	2–0	2–2	2–0
7 Croydon	1–0	2–0	2–1	0–0	3–0	1–4	*	2–0	1–4	2–0	2–1	0–0	2–4	2–0	1–1	2–0	2–2	2–3	0–0	0–2	1–2	2–1
8 Grays Athletic	2–2	1–0	1–3	1–1	0–1	1–0	4–0	*	1–0	4–0	2–3	0–2	1–0	1–0	0–1	1–2	1–0	1–1	4–1	2–0	1–0	3–0
9 Hitchin Town	1–1	1–0	4–0	1–0	3–0	3–1	0–1	4–0	*	2–1	1–0	2–2	1–0	3–3	0–0	1–0	2–1	3–1	3–0	3–2	5–0	2–1
10 Leatherhead	4–2	2–0	1–0	0–1	1–2	1–2	7–3	1–1	1–1	*	1–0	0–1	0–3	2–2	4–1	0–1	2–0	0–1	1–1	4–1	1–0	2–0
11 Leyton Pennant	3–0	1–2	1–2	0–3	1–1	1–1	1–1	1–1	0–4	2–1	*	3–1	2–2	2–1	2–2	4–1	2–3	1–2	0–0	0–1	1–2	2–1
12 Maidenhead Utd	0–2	2–1	0–0	0–2	0–2	0–0	0–0	2–3	1–0	1–3	1–2	*	1–1	2–2	0–2	2–1	0–2	0–2	0–1	1–1	0–0	0–1
13 Molesey	0–6	0–3	0–0	2–1	0–0	0–0	0–0	1–1	0–0	1–0	1–4	0–4	*	0–0	0–1	1–1	0–4	2–0	0–0	0–0	3–4	1–1
14 Oxford City	2–0	2–1	2–2	3–0	2–1	0–0	0–2	0–0	1–2	3–2	3–2	0–1	2–1	*	2–2	2–2	1–3	3–1	3–0	0–1	2–2	2–2
15 Romford	2–2	2–2	0–1	0–1	1–0	0–1	1–1	2–2	0–3	4–1	3–2	0–3	0–0	1–0	*	1–0	0–0	0–4	3–4	3–1	2–1	3–4
16 Staines Town	0–0	2–0	1–1	1–1	0–3	1–3	2–1	1–0	1–1	0–0	1–1	1–1	1–0	0–0	1–2	*	0–1	2–2	2–1	1–0	0–1	0–0
17 Uxbridge	1–0	1–1	1–3	1–2	1–2	4–2	0–0	0–1	1–2	0–0	2–2	1–1	0–0	0–3	2–3	2–2	*	0–1	4–0	5–0	1–2	2–0
18 Wealdstone	5–2	5–2	2–0	2–2	3–0	2–2	0–1	1–2	2–1	1–1	1–0	0–3	2–2	2–0	1–0	3–1	2–1	*	1–0	2–1	4–1	2–0
19 Wembley	1–1	1–0	0–2	0–3	1–2	0–3	1–5	0–1	0–1	1–0	1–4	0–0	1–1	4–1	2–0	2–0	1–2	0–2	*	2–1	1–2	1–1
20 Whyteleafe	3–4	4–1	1–1	2–3	5–5	2–1	0–1	1–0	0–3	1–0	0–2	3–2	1–3	0–1	2–1	3–0	3–0	0–2	1–0	*	1–1	1–3
21 Worthing	0–0	3–2	1–0	2–2	0–2	1–1	0–0	2–1	1–1	0–1	1–1	0–1	1–1	2–4	3–0	0–1	0–0	1–2	5–3	1–2	*	0–1
22 Yeading	0–1	3–0	0–2	1–2	1–3	1–2	0–0	1–1	1–1	4–1	1–1	0–2	3–0	0–0	2–2	1–2	0–1	0–1	3–0	2–1	3–0	*

Division I	*P*	*W*	*D*	*L*	*F*	*A*	*Pts*
1 Canvey Island	42	28	6	8	76	41	90
2 Hitchin Town	42	25	10	7	75	38	85
3 Wealdstone	42	26	6	10	75	48	84
4 Braintree Town	42	20	10	12	75	48	70
5 Bognor Regis Tn	42	20	8	14	63	44	68
6 Grays Athletic	42	19	11	12	56	42	68
7 Oxford City	42	16	14	12	58	51	62
8 Croydon	42	16	13	13	53	53	61
9 Chertsey Town	42	14	16	12	57	57	58
10 Romford	42	14	15	13	58	63	57
11 Maidenhead Utd	42	13	15	14	50	46	54
12 Worthing	42	13	13	16	47	61	52
13 Leyton Pennant	42	13	12	17	62	70	51
14 Uxbridge	42	13	11	18	54	51	50
15 Barton Rovers	42	11	15	16	43	49	48
16 Yeading	42	12	10	20	51	55	46
17 Leatherhead	42	12	9	21	48	59	45
18 Whyteleafe	42	13	6	23	51	72	45
19 Staines Town	42	10	15	17	33	57	45
20 Molesey	42	8	20	14	35	52	44
21 Wembley	42	10	10	22	36	71	40
22 Berkhamsted Town	42	10	7	25	53	81	37

Left: Maidenhead United's programme for their game with Wealdstone which finished 1-1.

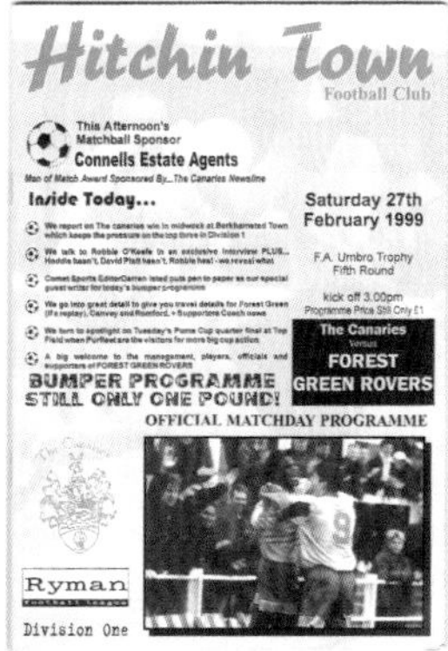

Right: the programme for Hitchin Town's FA Trophy Fifth Round tie with Forest Green Rovers.

1998-99 Division II	1	2	3	4	5	6	7	8	9	10	11	12	13	14	15	16	17	18	19	20	21	22
1 Abingdon Town	*	1–2	0–0	0–3	0–1	2–2	0–2	3–2	2–5	4–1	3–2	0–4	2–2	0–4	2–4	1–4	2–6	0–2	1–6	2–3	2–4	1–1
2 Banstead Athletic	4–1	*	1–0	3–1	3–1	5–1	1–1	2–2	0–4	5–1	4–4	1–1	0–1	4–1	2–0	2–0	1–3	1–1	1–0	0–1	4–1	1–3
3 Barking	4–2	2–2	*	1–1	0–2	2–0	1–0	0–0	0–3	4–0	3–2	1–0	2–3	0–3	0–1	0–1	1–1	4–3	1–0	2–2	1–2	1–2
4 Bedford Town	1–0	1–1	1–1	*	2–1	3–0	2–1	5–0	2–2	5–0	2–0	2–0	0–1	2–1	1–0	6–0	4–0	2–0	3–0	1–0	0–0	4–1
5 Bracknell Town	0–5	3–0	4–0	1–2	*	4–4	0–4	1–4	1–1	3–1	0–1	3–2	2–3	0–1	1–1	0–2	1–2	0–0	0–1	1–5	1–4	1–2
6 Chalfont St Peter	6–2	0–2	3–1	1–2	3–2	*	2–4	1–4	0–0	4–1	1–1	0–0	3–1	0–0	2–0	2–3	0–2	0–0	3–2	1–0	5–2	1–2
7 Edgware Town	2–1	2–5	4–1	0–1	4–0	1–1	*	0–3	1–1	4–0	0–2	2–2	1–1	0–2	1–1	0–4	0–1	1–2	2–2	2–2	1–2	3–0
8 Harlow Town	3–1	2–1	1–0	3–0	7–1	2–0	6–0	*	1–3	2–1	3–1	0–0	1–4	6–1	3–0	3–0	5–1	7–0	1–1	4–0	3–0	1–1
9 Hemel Hempstead	3–0	0–1	3–0	2–1	2–2	4–1	2–1	6–0	*	3–1	3–0	2–1	2–1	3–1	4–1	1–1	0–0	4–5	1–3	2–2	1–2	1–2
10 Hertford Town	3–2	6–2	3–2	0–2	1–0	0–2	0–1	0–2	1–4	*	0–1	0–3	2–1	1–0	0–1	1–3	0–0	0–1	2–1	0–3	3–1	0–1
11 Horsham	3–1	2–3	2–0	0–2	1–0	0–1	0–1	2–1	1–5	1–2	*	2–3	2–0	6–2	3–0	1–3	4–2	3–0	3–0	3–1	1–3	7–0
12 Hungerford Town	2–0	3–2	1–1	1–4	0–0	1–2	4–1	0–4	4–2	7–2	3–1	*	1–1	0–0	0–2	1–1	1–0	2–1	0–1	0–1	1–2	1–0
13 Leighton Town	3–0	2–0	5–3	1–4	2–0	2–2	1–2	1–1	2–0	0–0	2–2	1–0	*	4–2	0–2	0–1	0–5	1–2	1–1	3–2	1–4	2–1
14 Marlow	9–1	1–0	2–2	0–2	2–2	0–2	4–2	1–1	2–3	2–1	0–0	3–1	0–0	*	4–3	2–0	4–2	1–2	2–2	1–3	1–2	2–1
15 Metropolitan Police	0–1	0–5	4–0	2–4	7–1	1–1	1–2	1–1	1–1	2–0	2–0	1–0	1–0	1–0	*	2–1	0–2	0–2	0–1	3–3	5–2	3–0
16 Northwood	5–0	0–2	2–1	1–1	2–1	2–2	2–1	1–2	1–1	2–3	0–3	3–1	1–1	3–1	0–3	*	0–2	4–2	0–7	2–0	4–1	4–1
17 Thame United	4–0	3–3	1–0	1–2	3–0	4–0	2–2	3–0	1–0	2–0	2–2	3–3	2–1	0–2	2–1	2–0	*	0–2	4–1	5–3	4–1	2–1
18 Tooting & M Utd	4–0	0–1	3–1	1–5	1–1	1–1	2–1	0–2	2–2	3–1	1–1	4–0	1–0	0–2	1–0	0–1	1–2	*	1–6	1–1	2–1	4–0
19 Windsor & Eton	6–0	4–0	1–2	2–1	5–2	1–2	3–0	0–1	1–0	4–1	0–2	1–0	2–1	2–1	2–0	4–1	1–1	2–1	*	2–1	1–4	1–4
20 Witham Town	2–2	1–0	1–1	0–0	0–2	4–0	1–4	1–2	0–2	1–3	2–0	1–1	4–1	1–1	2–2	0–0	0–1	1–1	1–1	*	3–1	4–2
21 Wivenhoe Town	0–0	1–3	1–1	0–2	2–2	1–5	0–3	1–2	0–0	3–1	4–1	2–2	1–2	3–1	1–1	1–2	1–3	0–1	2–3	1–1	*	7–1
22 Wokingham Town	0–1	0–3	2–3	2–0	0–0	0–3	0–0	1–2	1–2	2–1	2–1	1–2	0–1	0–3	0–1	3–0	0–3	0–2	1–0	1–0	2–0	*

Division II	*P*	*W*	*D*	*L*	*F*	*A*	*Pts*
1 Bedford Town	42	29	7	6	89	31	94
2 Harlow Town	42	27	8	7	100	47	89
3 Thame United	42	26	8	8	89	50	86
4 Hemel Hempstead	42	21	12	9	90	50	75
5 Windsor & Eton	42	22	6	14	84	55	72
6 Banstead Athletic	42	21	8	13	83	62	71
7 Northwood	42	20	7	15	67	68	67
8 Tooting & M Utd	42	19	9	14	63	62	66
9 Chalfont St. Peter	42	16	12	14	70	71	60
10 Metropolitan Police	42	17	8	17	61	58	59
11 Leighton Town	42	16	10	16	60	64	58
12 Horsham	42	17	6	19	74	67	57
13 Marlow	42	16	9	17	72	68	57
14 Edgware Town	42	14	10	18	65	68	52
15 Witham Town	42	12	15	15	64	64	51
16 Hungerford Town	42	13	12	17	59	61	51
17 Wivenhoe Town	42	14	8	20	71	83	50
18 Wokingham Town	42	14	4	24	44	79	46
19 Barking	42	10	11	21	50	75	41
20 Hertford Town	42	11	2	29	44	96	35
21 Bracknell Town	42	7	10	25	48	92	31
22 Abingdon Town	42	6	6	30	48	124	24

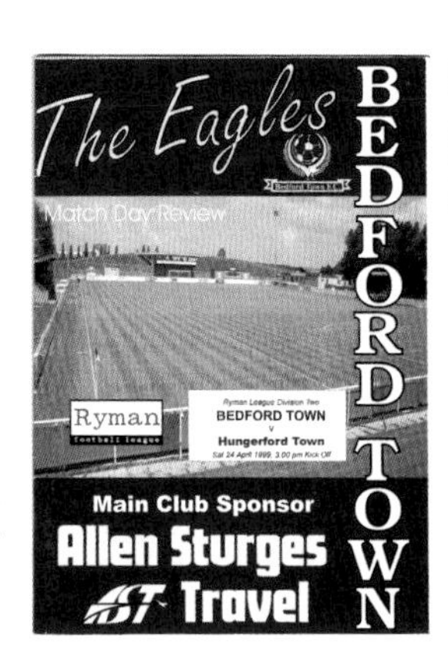

Left: Bedford Town's programme for the 1998/99 season.

Right: Thame United's edition for the same season.

Hemel Hempstead changed their name to Hemel Hempstead Town.

Division III	1	2	3	4	5	6	7	8	9	10	11	12	13	14	15	16	17	18	19	20
1 Aveley	*	0–1	2–1	2–4	2–3	0–1	2–1	2–0	1–0	1–1	0–0	1–1	2–0	1–0	0–2	1–2	0–1	3–3	1–3	2–3
2 Camberley Town	4–2	*	1–3	2–2	2–3	3–0	4–0	2–3	9–0	2–1	2–1	1–0	1–0	1–1	1–2	3–3	1–6	3–0	2–1	1–2
3 Cheshunt	3–1	6–2	*	2–0	2–2	4–2	3–0	3–3	2–1	1–1	2–0	0–0	1–0	2–1	2–0	2–0	3–1	3–0	2–1	2–2
4 Clapton	2–0	0–1	0–0	*	0–1	2–1	1–2	1–0	0–3	0–4	2–1	1–9	2–3	4–1	0–2	0–4	3–1	5–2	0–4	0–4
5 Corinthian-Casuals	5–1	1–4	3–0	4–2	*	4–4	0–1	1–1	1–4	3–0	2–1	2–3	5–1	2–1	3–3	2–3	3–4	2–0	0–5	0–1
6 Croydon Athletic	0–0	2–1	2–2	4–2	3–1	*	2–3	0–2	0–1	2–3	2–2	6–2	2–1	5–1	1–0	5–1	1–3	9–1	2–2	0–1
7 Dorking	1–1	3–0	0–1	0–3	0–2	1–5	*	1–1	0–4	2–2	2–4	2–7	1–3	0–1	1–5	0–5	1–1	3–0	2–5	2–1
8 East Thurrock Utd	3–0	1–1	0–1	1–1	1–0	0–0	2–2	*	2–2	2–4	4–1	1–1	2–3	4–0	0–1	2–2	3–2	6–0	4–1	2–0
9 Egham Town	0–1	2–0	1–2	2–2	1–0	1–1	1–1	1–1	*	0–2	3–0	2–3	2–2	2–0	1–2	1–1	0–4	7–2	3–1	1–2
10 Epsom & Ewell	1–0	1–1	0–0	3–0	1–2	2–0	2–1	1–2	1–0	*	4–2	0–5	2–0	4–0	1–0	1–2	0–5	3–0	1–2	0–2
11 Flackwell Heath	3–4	6–0	2–0	1–1	0–1	1–1	4–2	3–2	0–1	1–6	*	1–2	0–0	4–2	2–0	1–1	0–3	4–0	2–1	0–4
12 Ford United	4–2	5–0	7–0	1–0	4–1	4–1	2–1	4–2	3–0	1–2	2–0	*	1–1	3–0	2–0	5–1	1–1	5–1	2–0	2–3
13 Hornchurch	1–4	1–0	1–4	1–3	1–1	1–4	3–0	0–2	1–5	3–0	1–1	1–4	*	2–1	1–3	3–1	2–2	3–2	1–1	0–2
14 Kingsbury Town	5–2	2–2	1–2	1–2	1–2	1–0	4–2	0–4	1–4	2–3	1–1	1–4	2–0	*	1–2	1–4	1–3	1–2	0–3	1–6
15 Lewes	4–1	6–2	3–2	9–0	2–0	1–1	6–1	3–3	4–1	0–1	1–0	3–0	2–1	2–0	*	2–1	3–0	3–1	1–0	1–2
16 Southall	0–1	2–0	0–2	1–1	6–2	2–3	4–4	1–2	1–2	0–1	1–4	0–3	0–0	2–1	5–0	*	3–1	3–1	2–1	1–1
17 Tilbury	0–1	1–1	0–1	3–1	2–0	2–2	0–1	1–2	1–1	2–1	1–1	0–1	4–3	2–0	0–1	4–1	*	2–1	3–1	0–1
18 Tring Town	0–3	1–1	1–1	1–0	3–3	1–5	1–3	4–0	2–1	2–1	1–3	1–3	0–0	1–2	2–4	0–2	0–4	*	0–0	0–4
19 Ware	4–3	2–4	0–3	3–1	0–2	0–2	4–2	4–2	2–3	2–0	2–0	0–2	4–1	5–1	2–1	3–0	3–3	1–0	*	3–2
20 Wingate & Finch	0–0	3–0	0–0	5–0	2–1	0–1	2–1	2–2	0–1	1–0	6–2	3–2	0–2	4–0	3–2	0–1	3–1	2–1	0–3	*

Division III	*P*	*W*	*D*	*L*	*F*	*A*	*Pts*
1 Ford United	38	27	5	6	110	42	86
2 Wingate & Finch	38	25	5	8	79	38	80
3 Cheshunt	38	23	10	5	70	41	79
4 Lewes	38	25	3	10	86	45	78
5 Epsom & Ewell	38	19	5	14	61	51	62
6 Ware	38	19	4	15	79	60	61
7 Tilbury	38	17	8	13	74	52	59
8 Croydon Athletic	38	16	10	12	82	59	58
9 East Thurrock Utd	38	15	13	10	74	56	58
10 Egham Town	38	16	8	14	65	58	56
11 Corinthian-Casuals	38	16	7	15	70	71	55
12 Southall	38	14	9	15	68	66	51
13 Camberley Town	38	14	8	16	66	77	50
14 Aveley	38	12	7	19	50	67	43
15 Flackwell Heath	38	11	9	18	59	70	42
16 Hornchurch	38	10	9	19	48	73	39
17 Clapton	38	11	6	21	48	89	39
18 Dorking	38	8	7	23	52	98	31
19 Kingsbury Town	38	6	3	29	40	98	21
20 Tring Town	38	5	6	27	38	108	21

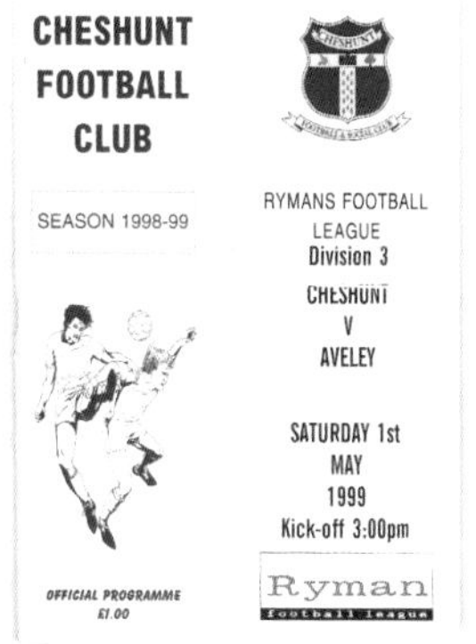

Left: the Cheshunt programme for the 1998/99 season.

Right: East Thurrock United's edition for the same season.

1999–2000 - This season started with at least eight clubs who looked strong enough to win the Premier Division championship but in the end Dagenham & Redbridge won the title by 24 points from nearest challengers Aldershot Town. Chesham United had an enjoyable season finishing in third while Purfleet again finished in fourth with Canvey Island in their first Premier Division campaign securing fifth place. At the bottom Boreham Wood and Walton & Hersham were relegated to Division One along with Aylesbury United who finished on level points with Carshalton Athletic, Basingstoke Town and Harrow Borough but had an inferior goal-difference. After several mediocre seasons Croydon were champions of Division One, returning to the Premier Division for the first time since 1989. Joining Croydon in the top flight were runners-up Grays Athletic and Maidenhead United, finishing on level points, while Thame United just missed out in fourth place by two points. Only two clubs were relegated to Division Two, namely Chertsey Town and Leyton Pennant, with Leatherhead earning a reprieve as Division Two champions Hemel Hempstead Town's excellent season was spoilt by not having the correct ground grading criteria by the deadline. However runners-up Northwood and third placed Ford United were both promoted. Division Three was dominated by Essex based clubs with East Thurrock United securing the championship from runners-up Great Wakering Rovers, who gained promotion in their first season as members of the League, with Tilbury gaining the final promotion place six points ahead of Hornchurch. At the foot of the table basement club Southall became the first club relegated from the League since Letchworth Garden City in 1989.

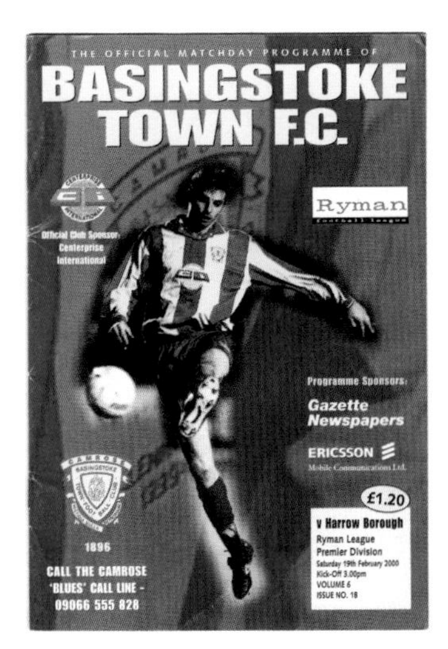

At the Annual General Meeting Sutton United, after only one season, were relegated from the Football Conference and would replace League champions Dagenham & Redbridge while Arlesey Town were elected from the South Midlands League with Ashford Town (Middlesex), who gained promotion from the Combined Counties League to replace relegated Southall, increasing the constitution to the full complement of eighty-eight clubs for the first time since 1990.

Premier Division	1	2	3	4	5	6	7	8	9	10	11	12	13	14	15	16	17	18	19	20	21	22
1 Aldershot Town	*	1–1	5–2	0–1	1–0	3–1	4–0	4–1	1–0	3–2	0–4	1–0	2–1	1–1	1–2	2–1	0–1	5–1	0–2	0–2	2–0	3–0
2 Aylesbury United	3–0	*	3–0	0–1	0–1	3–3	3–2	3–2	0–2	2–3	1–0	1–2	4–1	2–2	3–1	2–3	2–2	3–1	0–3	0–2	2–2	1–0
3 Basingstoke Town	2–1	4–2	*	2–0	1–1	0–1	2–0	0–1	0–4	2–0	2–1	2–2	2–0	2–0	2–0	1–1	2–2	1–1	2–2	0–2	1–0	1–3
4 Billericay Town	3–2	5–0	1–0	*	1–0	0–0	2–0	2–1	0–4	3–5	0–0	0–3	3–3	1–0	5–0	1–1	1–2	1–1	1–1	3–1	3–1	0–3
5 Boreham Wood	2–5	2–2	3–4	0–2	*	3–2	0–2	1–3	0–1	0–0	1–0	1–1	3–4	0–4	0–1	0–2	0–0	0–0	1–1	2–3	1–3	1–0
6 Canvey Island	2–1	2–3	3–1	3–0	0–1	*	1–0	2–1	3–1	0–1	1–0	2–0	4–1	1–2	2–0	0–0	6–1	0–3	2–0	0–1	2–0	1–1
7 Carshalton Athletic	3–0	2–1	3–3	3–3	3–0	3–1	*	0–3	1–1	0–5	2–2	1–1	1–2	1–1	3–1	0–1	1–1	2–0	0–0	0–1	1–1	0–2
8 Chesham United	2–0	1–1	1–1	1–1	5–0	2–1	0–0	*	0–3	1–2	1–0	2–1	1–1	1–0	1–2	2–1	1–1	2–1	1–0	3–4	3–0	2–1
9 Dagenham & Red	3–1	4–1	1–0	2–1	2–0	2–0	3–1	1–1	*	3–0	4–0	3–2	2–1	5–0	4–1	4–0	2–0	4–1	3–1	2–1	2–1	2–0
10 Dulwich Hamlet	1–2	3–0	3–2	1–2	1–2	2–0	1–3	1–2	0–0	*	0–0	1–3	1–5	2–0	2–0	1–0	2–1	1–2	3–2	3–2	2–3	1–0
11 Enfield	1–4	3–1	2–0	1–1	1–1	1–1	3–2	2–2	1–1	3–2	*	3–0	0–1	2–3	0–3	5–3	3–2	1–1	1–2	4–0	1–3	4–1
12 Farnborough Town	0–0	3–1	3–0	2–0	0–2	1–2	4–1	0–1	2–1	2–0	1–1	*	3–2	0–1	0–0	0–1	0–1	1–1	1–1	1–0	0–1	1–2
13 Gravesend & Nth	1–1	5–0	1–0	2–2	3–0	0–1	0–5	3–2	1–2	3–1	1–2	5–1	*	0–0	4–1	1–0	1–1	1–1	1–2	1–2	1–0	1–1
14 Hampton & R Bor	0–1	2–1	2–1	1–2	1–1	0–2	0–1	0–1	2–3	3–0	2–1	1–0	1–0	*	3–1	1–2	1–4	2–1	1–1	2–2	1–1	0–2
15 Harrow Borough	0–1	4–1	1–1	1–1	1–3	1–3	0–0	0–2	1–1	1–0	1–2	1–3	6–0	3–0	*	2–1	2–0	4–0	2–3	0–2	0–1	0–1
16 Hendon	1–2	1–0	4–3	3–2	2–1	3–2	2–0	4–2	0–1	1–2	2–2	5–3	2–0	1–0	0–1	*	2–0	1–1	1–3	0–3	1–1	2–2
17 Heybridge Swifts	1–3	0–0	2–0	1–2	0–1	3–0	0–2	2–1	5–4	1–1	2–1	1–2	2–4	2–2	1–2	1–2	*	2–3	0–0	2–1	1–1	5–1
18 Hitchin Town	1–2	4–3	2–0	4–0	1–3	3–3	3–2	0–2	0–2	2–0	2–1	1–1	1–0	2–2	4–0	1–0	1–2	*	1–0	2–2	1–2	0–2
19 Purfleet	2–4	0–2	1–2	2–2	3–2	2–0	1–1	0–0	2–0	1–1	4–2	4–0	0–0	0–0	1–1	4–1	1–0	3–0	*	3–3	2–0	3–1
20 St. Albans City	0–1	1–1	4–1	1–2	0–0	2–5	4–0	1–1	1–3	4–1	5–0	0–0	0–1	1–1	3–2	3–0	2–0	2–1	2–4	*	0–1	1–1
21 Slough Town	0–0	1–2	1–4	4–0	2–3	1–2	2–1	2–0	2–3	2–1	2–1	1–2	2–1	1–1	2–3	1–1	2–1	3–0	3–0	0–3	*	3–1
22 Walton & Hersham	0–1	0–3	1–0	0–1	3–1	0–3	0–2	1–2	0–2	0–3	0–2	0–0	2–2	1–3	3–1	1–2	0–1	4–3	0–3	1–1	2–2	*

Premier Division	*P*	*W*	*D*	*L*	*F*	*A*	*Pts*
1 Dagenham & Red	42	32	5	5	97	35	101
2 Aldershot Town	42	24	5	13	71	51	77
3 Chesham United	42	20	10	12	64	50	70
4 Purfleet	42	18	15	9	70	48	69
5 Canvey Island	42	21	6	15	70	53	69
6 St. Albans City	42	19	10	13	75	55	67
7 Billericay Town	42	18	12	12	62	62	66
8 Hendon	42	18	8	16	61	64	62
9 Slough Town	42	17	9	16	61	59	60
10 Dulwich Hamlet	42	17	5	20	62	68	56
11 Gravesend & Nth	42	15	10	17	66	67	55
12 Farnborough Town	42	14	11	17	52	55	53
13 Hampton & R Boro	42	13	13	16	49	57	52
14 Enfield	42	13	11	18	64	68	50
15 Heybridge Swifts	42	13	11	18	57	65	50
16 Hitchin Town	42	13	11	18	59	72	50
17 Carshalton Athletic	42	12	12	18	55	65	48
18 Basingstoke Town	42	13	9	20	56	71	48
19 Harrow Borough	42	14	6	22	54	70	48
20 Aylesbury United	42	13	9	20	64	81	48
21 Boreham Wood	42	11	10	21	44	71	43
22 Walton & Hersham	42	11	8	23	44	70	41

Hampton changed their name to Hampton & Richmond Borough.

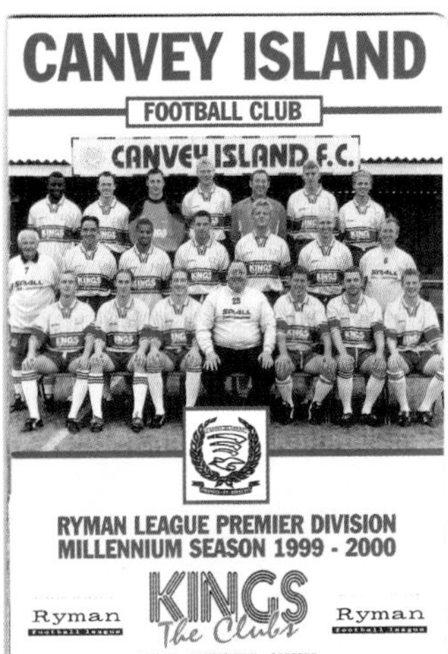

Right: matchday programmes from both Aldershot Town and Canvey Island.

1999-2000 Division I	1	2	3	4	5	6	7	8	9	10	11	12	13	14	15	16	17	18	19	20	21	22
1 Barton Rovers	*	0–1	2–3	3–1	1–1	1–2	0–3	2–1	0–2	0–3	2–1	0–2	1–1	3–1	3–2	0–1	1–0	1–1	2–1	1–0	2–2	4–1
2 Bedford Town	1–0	*	1–0	2–1	1–1	1–2	2–2	1–0	1–1	3–3	1–1	1–0	2–2	2–0	0–1	0–2	0–2	1–0	4–0	0–1	2–3	1–0
3 Bishop's Stortford	1–2	2–3	*	0–0	0–0	0–2	3–1	1–0	0–1	2–1	0–1	2–0	1–1	0–3	0–0	2–3	0–3	1–2	3–0	4–2	4–4	0–0
4 Bognor Regis Tn	2–2	1–1	0–1	*	0–1	0–0	1–0	1–2	1–3	0–1	1–3	2–2	1–2	2–1	1–2	0–1	1–2	2–1	1–1	0–0	1–3	1–1
5 Braintree Town	2–2	3–1	3–0	4–0	*	2–2	2–1	0–2	0–1	2–1	2–1	3–2	2–2	1–3	3–3	1–1	0–0	1–0	2–1	2–1	1–2	4–0
6 Bromley	4–1	0–2	0–2	3–2	1–3	*	2–0	3–2	1–2	1–1	1–1	1–0	0–0	2–1	2–1	1–2	0–1	4–1	4–1	3–2	1–4	2–2
7 Chertsey Town	2–1	2–1	3–5	1–1	4–1	0–0	*	2–4	2–1	1–3	0–1	1–2	1–2	2–0	2–5	0–4	2–2	0–1	1–3	0–3	2–3	0–1
8 Croydon	1–2	1–1	1–1	0–2	6–1	3–1	3–2	*	0–0	1–0	2–2	3–0	2–2	2–0	1–1	2–1	2–4	1–1	2–2	3–0	1–0	2–0
9 Grays Athletic	4–1	3–0	1–3	0–0	4–0	5–0	1–2	3–4	*	2–2	2–2	4–0	2–2	1–0	2–1	1–0	0–2	1–0	0–1	4–1	3–1	1–1
10 Harlow Town	2–3	0–5	2–2	0–3	1–1	2–2	5–2	1–4	4–4	*	0–1	1–0	1–1	0–1	0–1	1–1	3–2	1–3	0–0	0–1	1–1	1–1
11 Leatherhead	1–2	2–0	0–2	0–2	4–1	0–2	1–1	1–2	1–3	2–5	*	2–1	1–3	1–2	1–1	1–2	2–2	1–0	0–2	0–0	1–2	0–1
12 Leyton Pennant	0–3	1–0	2–2	0–1	1–5	2–0	1–0	1–4	0–3	2–2	1–1	*	0–3	1–5	2–1	0–0	1–2	0–1	0–2	0–4	0–2	2–2
13 Maidenhead Utd	2–2	2–1	0–1	1–1	4–3	3–2	2–0	1–0	3–1	2–0	1–1	1–3	*	0–1	4–0	3–2	0–1	2–2	2–0	0–1	1–1	2–1
14 Oxford City	2–0	1–2	5–0	0–1	2–0	3–1	1–0	0–2	2–1	0–2	5–0	1–1	1–3	*	0–3	1–0	2–4	1–1	2–1	0–1	0–1	1–0
15 Romford	1–2	2–2	0–1	1–2	2–1	2–1	3–2	0–2	0–1	0–2	2–1	2–1	1–3	1–2	*	1–1	1–1	0–2	1–3	1–2	0–3	0–1
16 Staines Town	2–2	1–1	0–0	1–4	3–2	4–1	4–0	2–6	1–1	2–1	0–2	1–0	1–0	2–2	3–1	*	3–1	0–0	2–1	1–3	1–0	2–2
17 Thame United	2–0	0–1	3–2	1–2	3–0	1–0	0–2	0–0	2–1	3–0	2–2	5–1	1–0	3–1	1–1	1–1	*	1–0	1–1	1–1	0–0	0–0
18 Uxbridge	5–1	0–1	5–1	3–2	3–1	2–0	1–0	1–2	1–1	6–0	5–0	3–0	0–4	1–0	1–3	0–1	0–0	*	1–1	2–3	0–1	1–1
19 Wealdstone	4–1	1–1	0–2	0–0	2–0	1–3	0–1	1–2	0–2	3–1	1–1	2–2	0–1	2–1	2–0	0–2	1–0	1–1	*	3–1	2–1	1–3
20 Whyteleafe	4–2	2–1	0–1	1–0	1–2	1–1	4–1	1–2	0–5	3–1	2–1	4–0	1–1	2–1	0–1	2–0	0–1	0–0	2–1	*	1–1	0–0
21 Worthing	8–2	3–4	3–2	1–2	2–0	0–2	3–1	2–3	1–1	1–5	3–1	3–0	1–1	1–1	4–0	3–1	2–0	1–1	1–1	1–1	*	1–5
22 Yeading	3–4	3–3	2–0	1–1	3–1	1–2	2–1	0–2	1–1	1–2	1–1	0–0	1–2	2–1	2–2	3–1	1–0	1–1	1–1	0–2	2–0	*

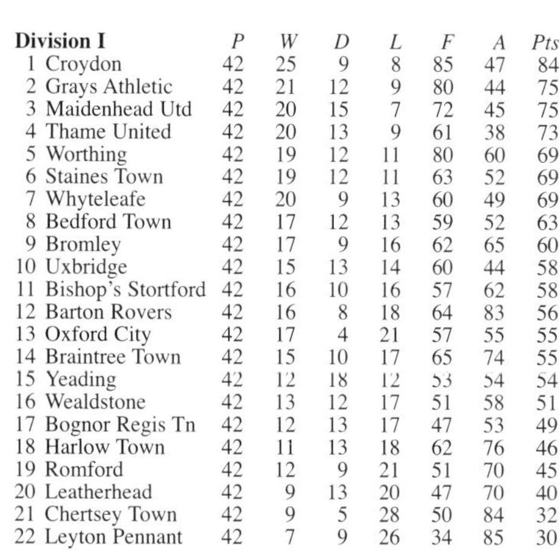

Division I	P	W	D	L	F	A	Pts
1 Croydon	42	25	9	8	85	47	84
2 Grays Athletic	42	21	12	9	80	44	75
3 Maidenhead Utd	42	20	15	7	72	45	75
4 Thame United	42	20	13	9	61	38	73
5 Worthing	42	19	12	11	80	60	69
6 Staines Town	42	19	12	11	63	52	69
7 Whyteleafe	42	20	9	13	60	49	69
8 Bedford Town	42	17	12	13	59	52	63
9 Bromley	42	17	9	16	62	65	60
10 Uxbridge	42	15	13	14	60	44	58
11 Bishop's Stortford	42	16	10	16	57	62	58
12 Barton Rovers	42	16	8	18	64	83	56
13 Oxford City	42	17	4	21	57	55	55
14 Braintree Town	42	15	10	17	65	74	55
15 Yeading	42	12	18	12	53	54	54
16 Wealdstone	42	13	12	17	51	58	51
17 Bognor Regis Tn	42	12	13	17	47	53	49
18 Harlow Town	42	11	13	18	62	76	46
19 Romford	42	12	9	21	51	70	45
20 Leatherhead	42	9	13	20	47	70	40
21 Chertsey Town	42	9	5	28	50	84	32
22 Leyton Pennant	42	7	9	26	34	85	30

Left: Yeading's programme for the 1999/2000 season.

Right: Farnborough Town's edition for the same season.

Division II	1	2	3	4	5	6	7	8	9	10	11	12	13	14	15	16	17	18	19	20	21	22
1 Banstead Athletic	*	0–1	3–1	4–1	3–0	2–0	0–0	1–2	1–0	1–1	0–0	3–2	1–0	2–1	1–3	0–0	0–2	1–0	1–0	7–1	0–1	1–1
2 Barking	1–1	*	2–2	0–0	0–0	1–1	1–3	0–1	3–1	2–0	2–4	6–0	1–0	3–0	3–1	2–2	0–1	1–2	3–1	2–0	1–1	1–3
3 Berkhamsted Town	3–1	1–3	*	0–0	2–1	3–1	2–0	0–2	4–1	3–2	4–0	3–1	1–0	1–0	1–1	4–3	4–1	4–4	2–1	1–0	3–0	1–3
4 Chalfont St. Peter	1–1	2–2	1–3	*	1–2	0–3	0–6	0–1	2–3	2–3	2–3	3–0	3–3	2–4	0–3	0–6	1–0	1–2	0–2	0–0	0–2	1–4
5 Cheshunt	1–1	1–4	0–2	2–1	*	3–1	2–2	0–0	1–2	1–1	3–2	0–1	0–2	1–4	2–3	2–0	0–0	1–1	0–1	0–0	3–3	2–1
6 Edgware Town	1–2	0–0	2–2	4–0	1–1	*	1–1	0–8	3–0	2–1	5–1	2–4	3–0	2–2	1–1	4–3	1–1	0–0	2–3	2–1	1–3	0–1
7 Ford United	2–0	1–1	3–1	8–1	2–0	2–1	*	0–0	4–0	6–0	3–1	2–0	2–0	4–2	1–1	1–0	2–1	3–1	6–1	4–0	3–1	0–1
8 Hemel Hempstead	8–0	3–0	3–1	2–1	3–0	3–0	1–0	*	3–1	1–1	4–1	1–0	7–1	3–0	2–2	5–2	2–0	0–0	2–1	4–1	4–2	5–1
9 Horsham	4–0	1–2	1–2	5–2	2–2	0–2	2–5	2–3	*	2–1	1–1	1–1	5–2	0–0	2–5	3–0	4–1	1–2	2–2	5–3	2–1	0–0
10 Hungerford Town	3–0	0–2	0–4	3–2	0–2	1–1	1–4	0–0	2–1	*	5–0	3–2	2–0	1–4	1–3	2–1	1–1	1–2	4–0	6–2	2–2	0–1
11 Leighton Town	2–2	2–0	0–1	5–0	1–1	2–3	1–3	0–1	1–2	2–1	*	2–5	1–3	3–3	0–5	0–1	1–2	0–2	4–1	4–1	0–2	2–0
12 Marlow	2–1	3–0	1–0	10–0	1–0	2–1	0–2	0–1	3–0	1–2	2–0	*	2–2	4–1	0–0	3–0	0–3	0–2	3–1	0–2	0–3	5–1
13 Metropolitan Police	1–2	2–0	2–0	2–0	2–0	3–0	3–1	1–5	1–3	4–2	3–2	3–2	*	4–2	1–2	5–2	0–0	0–0	2–2	2–0	1–0	3–2
14 Molesey	0–0	0–3	2–0	1–1	0–1	2–3	2–2	1–2	1–2	1–2	1–1	1–3	1–1	*	0–3	3–0	0–2	2–1	4–0	0–0	1–0	1–1
15 Northwood	2–0	6–2	1–0	7–2	4–0	1–0	0–3	0–0	2–0	7–1	2–3	1–0	2–0	2–0	*	4–2	2–1	3–0	7–2	5–0	2–1	4–0
16 Tooting & M Utd	1–2	1–1	0–0	2–0	3–2	2–1	2–2	0–1	3–1	1–2	2–2	3–0	6–5	3–2	0–1	*	1–2	0–2	3–1	3–0	1–0	1–1
17 Wembley	0–1	2–2	0–1	2–1	1–4	2–0	1–6	0–1	3–1	2–0	0–1	2–1	2–1	1–1	0–0	0–1	*	0–1	1–0	3–0	0–2	1–1
18 Windsor & Eton	2–1	1–1	1–1	3–3	2–1	3–2	4–0	1–1	2–1	3–1	3–5	3–4	0–0	2–0	3–2	1–4	1–1	*	2–0	4–0	1–2	1–2
19 Wingate & Finch	2–1	1–2	1–1	4–1	0–1	0–9	4–2	3–1	0–0	2–1	1–1	2–5	0–3	1–2	1–1	2–1	1–1	0–2	*	5–2	0–1	3–1
20 Witham Town	2–1	0–4	0–5	2–1	2–7	0–4	1–3	1–0	2–2	0–0	2–1	0–6	1–0	0–2	1–3	1–3	2–2	1–1	4–2	*	0–1	1–1
21 Wivenhoe Town	1–1	0–3	1–0	3–0	1–0	1–1	0–1	1–0	2–0	0–0	0–2	1–1	4–2	2–0	2–2	0–1	2–1	2–2	2–0	2–1	*	5–2
22 Wokingham Town	0–5	0–2	3–1	2–0	2–3	3–1	0–3	1–2	1–0	1–1	0–1	2–6	0–5	0–0	1–3	4–2	2–1	0–3	4–0	2–2	2–1	*

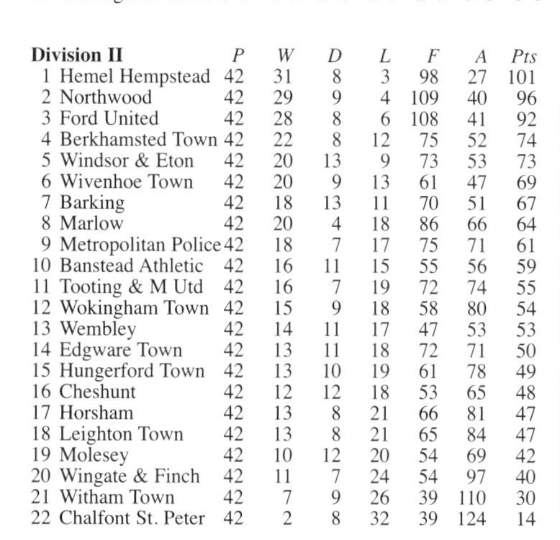

Division II	P	W	D	L	F	A	Pts
1 Hemel Hempstead	42	31	8	3	98	27	101
2 Northwood	42	29	9	4	109	40	96
3 Ford United	42	28	8	6	108	41	92
4 Berkhamsted Town	42	22	8	12	75	52	74
5 Windsor & Eton	42	20	13	9	73	53	73
6 Wivenhoe Town	42	20	9	13	61	47	69
7 Barking	42	18	13	11	70	51	67
8 Marlow	42	20	4	18	86	66	64
9 Metropolitan Police	42	18	7	17	75	71	61
10 Banstead Athletic	42	16	11	15	55	56	59
11 Tooting & M Utd	42	16	7	19	72	74	55
12 Wokingham Town	42	15	9	18	58	80	54
13 Wembley	42	14	11	17	47	53	53
14 Edgware Town	42	13	11	18	72	71	50
15 Hungerford Town	42	13	10	19	61	78	49
16 Cheshunt	42	12	12	18	53	65	48
17 Horsham	42	13	8	21	66	81	47
18 Leighton Town	42	13	8	21	65	84	47
19 Molesey	42	10	12	20	54	69	42
20 Wingate & Finch	42	11	7	24	54	97	40
21 Witham Town	42	7	9	26	39	110	30
22 Chalfont St. Peter	42	2	8	32	39	124	14

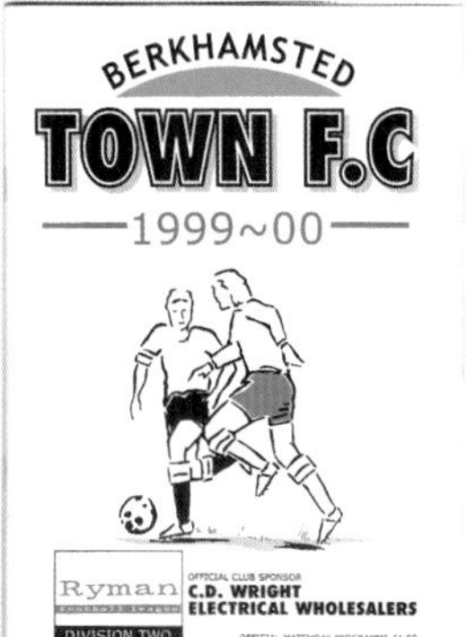

Left: Berkhamsted Town's programme for the 1999/2000 season.

Right: Barton Rovers' edition for the same season.

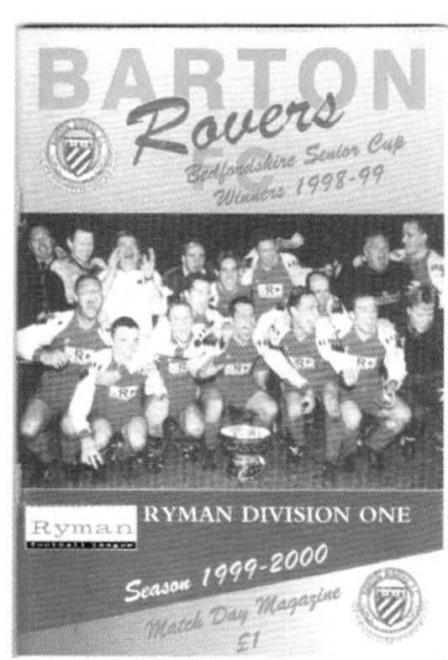

1999-2000 Division III	1	2	3	4	5	6	7	8	9	10	11	12	13	14	15	16	17	18	19	20	21
1 Abingdon Town	*	1–2	0–1	0–1	1–1	0–0	1–3	0–4	2–2	1–0	1–2	0–1	1–0	1–2	1–1	2–2	1–5	0–2	2–1	2–1	1–0
2 Aveley	1–2	*	1–1	6–1	4–0	0–3	1–1	2–0	0–1	2–2	0–1	2–1	2–1	2–2	4–1	5–1	0–1	3–0	4–3	0–0	3–3
3 Bracknell Town	1–1	3–3	*	3–1	5–1	1–1	2–0	1–1	0–2	5–2	1–3	3–1	2–3	1–2	2–1	3–3	2–1	1–1	1–0	2–2	1–0
4 Camberley Town	0–0	0–2	2–2	*	2–0	3–1	0–3	0–2	0–1	1–2	1–0	2–2	1–2	1–4	2–1	3–4	1–1	2–0	2–2	1–0	1–0
5 Clapton	1–2	1–2	0–6	3–2	*	3–1	2–4	1–0	0–1	1–1	1–2	3–3	0–4	0–1	0–0	3–1	0–2	4–0	1–2	1–0	0–3
6 Corinthian-Casuals	1–1	5–1	2–2	0–1	3–0	*	3–1	0–0	0–2	1–0	0–3	1–2	1–2	1–0	3–1	1–3	4–1	3–1	0–3	1–2	2–1
7 Croydon Athletic	1–1	5–1	5–3	3–0	6–0	0–1	*	1–1	3–4	2–1	4–1	1–2	0–0	4–2	2–2	2–1	1–1	4–0	1–2	3–0	4–3
8 Dorking	1–0	1–2	4–4	5–1	1–2	0–0	3–2	*	2–2	1–0	2–1	1–0	0–1	1–5	0–0	0–1	1–2	4–0	0–1	5–0	1–2
9 East Thurrock Utd	2–1	4–1	1–1	3–0	3–2	2–0	1–2	5–0	*	2–0	0–4	3–0	2–1	2–1	3–0	6–2	1–0	6–0	3–0	2–2	3–1
10 Egham Town	0–5	2–4	1–1	3–1	3–0	3–1	3–0	3–1	0–0	*	1–0	3–0	1–2	0–1	0–1	2–0	1–0	1–1	0–1	0–0	0–0
11 Epsom & Ewell	1–1	0–0	1–1	2–1	2–2	1–1	1–0	3–2	2–1	0–0	*	2–1	3–1	2–2	0–1	1–1	3–3	4–0	6–1	3–3	3–0
12 Flackwell Heath	3–1	6–2	4–2	3–0	3–5	1–4	0–3	2–1	1–0	1–1	2–1	*	1–0	1–1	6–2	5–0	1–6	2–1	0–1	3–0	2–4
13 Great Wakering R	3–3	2–0	2–2	1–0	5–0	2–2	1–1	3–1	0–3	0–1	3–1	2–1	*	3–1	4–1	4–0	2–1	5–0	1–1	3–1	2–1
14 Hertford Town	2–1	1–3	1–1	4–1	1–1	0–1	3–3	2–1	2–1	2–2	0–0	0–1	0–3	*	1–3	2–0	1–2	4–1	0–0	0–2	2–4
15 Hornchurch	2–1	2–0	2–3	2–2	3–3	3–1	1–1	3–2	2–1	0–1	3–0	3–2	1–0	3–1	*	4–0	3–2	3–0	0–0	4–1	3–1
16 Kingsbury Town	2–0	0–3	1–3	3–0	2–0	0–2	0–3	2–2	3–3	0–1	2–1	3–1	1–3	0–1	1–1	*	1–1	7–2	0–2	0–2	1–1
17 Lewes	4–1	1–0	4–1	1–1	2–1	1–1	0–2	1–1	5–2	1–1	0–2	2–1	1–3	3–1	1–1	4–0	*	2–0	0–0	1–0	0–1
18 Southall	2–3	2–3	1–5	1–2	4–5	0–3	1–1	3–1	0–3	1–1	0–3	1–3	1–1	1–4	1–3	0–3	1–6	*	1–4	0–1	0–3
19 Tilbury	4–2	0–0	1–0	3–0	1–0	2–1	2–1	5–0	1–1	2–0	1–1	2–1	1–2	2–2	1–1	2–0	2–0	5–0	*	2–0	2–3
20 Tring Town	1–1	2–1	1–0	1–3	2–1	0–1	0–1	2–0	0–3	0–4	0–1	2–2	0–1	1–0	0–0	0–2	2–3	2–3	1–1	*	3–1
21 Ware	1–3	1–1	1–2	3–1	3–1	2–2	1–1	3–0	1–2	1–1	2–0	5–1	1–3	0–2	3–4	5–2	3–1	3–0	1–1	2–0	*

Division III	*P*	*W*	*D*	*L*	*F*	*A*	*Pts*
1 East Thurrock Utd	40	26	7	7	89	42	85
2 Great Wakering R	40	25	7	8	81	41	82
3 Tilbury	40	21	12	7	67	39	75
4 Hornchurch	40	19	12	9	72	57	69
5 Croydon Athletic	40	19	11	10	85	52	68
6 Epsom & Ewell	40	18	12	10	67	46	66
7 Lewes	40	18	10	12	73	51	64
8 Bracknell Town	40	15	16	9	81	64	61
9 Aveley	40	17	10	13	73	64	61
10 Corinthian-Casuals	40	16	10	14	59	51	58
11 Flackwell Heath	40	17	6	17	74	76	57
12 Ware	40	16	8	16	74	62	56
13 Egham Town	40	14	13	13	48	43	55
14 Hertford Town	40	15	10	15	63	60	55
15 Abingdon Town	40	10	12	18	48	64	42
16 Kingsbury Town	40	11	8	21	55	86	41
17 Camberley Town	40	11	7	22	44	79	40
18 Tring Town	40	10	9	21	37	64	39
19 Dorking	40	9	10	21	53	69	37
20 Clapton	40	9	7	24	50	93	34
21 Southall	40	3	5	32	33	123	14

Left: the Great Wakering programme for their match against East Thurrock United, which the visitors won 3-0.

Right: the programme for Croydon Athletic's match at home to Egham Town, which they won 2-1.

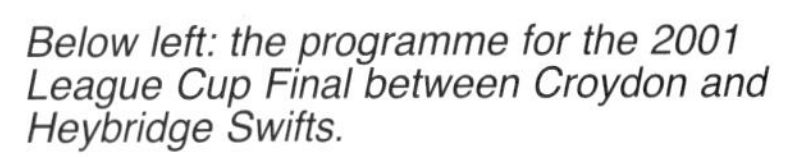

Below left: the programme for the 2001 League Cup Final between Croydon and Heybridge Swifts.

Below right: the Dulwich Hamlet programme for the season.

2000–01 - This year was by far the worst season since 1963 as far as the weather was concerned with virtually continuing rain from September to April causing many floods throughout the country and the end result was that five League fixtures (three in the Premier Division and two in Division Three) remained unplayed after an extension to the season was rejected by the majority of clubs at a special meeting. Farnborough Town won the championship by ten points from Canvey Island, although the 'Islanders' had to play fourteen games in the final three weeks of the season. Basingstoke Town finished ten points behind Canvey Island with Aldershot Town fourth. At the foot of the table Slough Town, Carshalton Athletic and Dulwich Hamlet were relegated to Division One.

The Division One championship was dominated by clubs beginning with the letter 'B' as a tight championship eventually saw Boreham Wood secure the League title just ahead of runners-up Bedford Town with Braintree Town in third place just beating Bishop's Stortford. The relegation issues saw Leatherhead, reprieved the previous year, relegated along with Romford and Barton Rovers with the latter only winning two matches all season.

In Division Two the promoted clubs were all returning to a higher division where they played in previous seasons with Tooting & Mitcham United gaining the championship six points clear of Windsor & Eton and Barking, the former securing runners-up by virtual of a better goal-difference, with Berkhamsted Town and Wivenhoe Town two points behind and just missing out. At the other end of the table Edgware Town, Leighton Town and Wokingham Town, the latter having played in the Premier Division a few seasons ago, were relegated to Division Three.

Arlesey Town, who in their first season gained 108 points and scored 138 goals, won the Division Three championship by twelve points. Runners-up Lewes, who had played a game less, and fellow new club Ashford Town (Middlesex) gained the other promotion places. At the bottom of the table Chalfont St. Peter completed a miserable season by finishing bottom, conceding 150 goals and gaining only thirteen points while founder-members Clapton finished next to bottom with twenty four points, eight points behind Camberley Town.

At the end of the season Barking merged with Essex Senior Leaguers East Ham United to become Barking & East Ham United.

At the Annual General Meeting Kingstonian were elected to replace champion club Farnborough Town who secured promotion to the Football Conference while there were no suitable clubs eligible for promotion from the feeder leagues and so no clubs were relegated.

Right: the programme for Grays Athletic's FA Cup tie at future members Chelmsford City.

2000-2001

Premier Division	1	2	3	4	5	6	7	8	9	10	11	12	13	14	15	16	17	18	19	20	21	22
1 Aldershot Town	*	1–0	NP	1–0	4–0	1–0	4–0	1–0	2–1	1–1	1–0	6–0	2–2	3–0	1–1	2–1	2–0	2–1	3–0	1–0	2–3	1–1
2 Basingstoke Town	2–1	*	1–1	0–0	1–1	2–1	1–1	2–2	4–0	0–1	4–0	1–0	1–0	2–2	5–0	3–2	2–1	2–1	1–2	3–2	2–1	1–0
3 Billericay Town	2–2	2–2	*	2–1	0–0	1–1	0–0	3–0	0–2	1–2	1–0	3–1	3–1	1–1	2–0	5–1	3–1	2–0	1–1	0–0	2–1	0–5
4 Canvey Island	1–1	0–0	2–1	*	3–2	2–1	5–0	3–2	4–1	0–1	1–1	1–0	1–0	3–0	3–2	3–0	2–2	1–0	1–0	1–0	3–1	6–2
5 Carshalton Athletic	2–1	1–0	5–0	1–4	*	0–4	4–2	3–1	2–1	0–5	1–3	1–0	0–3	1–1	1–2	1–1	0–5	1–0	1–0	0–1	1–1	0–1
6 Chesham United	0–3	1–2	2–0	1–1	3–1	*	4–1	2–0	0–0	1–4	3–0	3–1	1–0	1–1	4–1	2–3	3–0	2–1	5–0	2–0	2–0	0–3
7 Croydon	2–2	2–2	1–2	2–1	3–0	2–1	*	1–1	2–2	0–1	1–2	1–0	1–1	2–0	2–0	1–2	5–1	0–2	0–0	4–1	0–1	2–1
8 Dulwich Hamlet	2–4	0–2	0–1	2–3	1–0	0–1	1–4	*	1–1	0–2	0–2	1–2	1–1	0–1	0–3	1–0	0–2	2–3	1–1	2–2	1–0	2–1
9 Enfield	1–0	1–4	1–0	3–0	2–1	3–1	1–0	1–1	*	0–3	0–1	2–1	2–2	1–2	0–2	1–1	2–5	3–1	2–1	1–1	2–3	2–2
10 Farnborough Town	1–0	1–1	3–0	1–2	3–0	0–0	3–1	3–0	1–1	*	1–0	3–0	1–1	3–1	2–0	0–1	3–0	4–1	3–2	1–1	4–0	2–1
11 Gravesend & Nth	2–0	0–2	1–1	1–2	3–0	3–2	2–0	2–1	1–0	2–1	*	0–1	3–4	2–1	2–1	0–0	3–0	0–1	1–0	1–2	1–0	2–2
12 Grays Athletic	1–1	0–0	2–3	0–3	3–1	0–2	2–2	1–1	2–0	0–3	2–1	*	1–3	1–1	3–2	1–0	2–1	2–1	1–1	1–0	6–0	1–2
13 Hampton & R Bor	1–0	3–2	1–2	2–2	4–2	3–1	3–0	4–0	4–0	1–0	1–0	0–0	*	3–3	0–2	2–1	2–4	1–0	2–0	2–0	1–2	3–1
14 Harrow Borough	1–1	1–4	4–2	0–2	2–2	3–2	0–1	2–1	2–1	2–3	0–6	1–2	4–5	*	1–4	1–1	1–4	1–2	1–2	1–0	2–2	2–1
15 Hendon	0–5	2–3	0–2	2–1	1–0	2–2	4–0	4–0	3–0	0–2	1–2	1–1	2–0	NP	*	1–4	4–0	2–1	1–2	2–1	0–1	0–1
16 Heybridge Swifts	2–1	1–1	2–2	1–1	2–1	3–1	1–2	3–1	2–0	2–3	2–2	4–0	3–2	4–2	2–2	*	0–0	4–0	4–3	3–2	0–1	2–2
17 Hitchin Town	2–5	0–1	2–1	4–1	3–0	1–2	7–3	1–0	2–1	1–2	1–2	2–0	2–0	3–6	3–3	0–2	*	0–2	0–1	3–0	0–0	3–0
18 Maidenhead Utd	3–0	3–2	1–2	0–2	2–0	0–2	3–1	1–0	2–1	0–1	1–3	3–2	0–0	4–1	1–2	1–3	0–1	*	1–2	1–0	1–0	0–2
19 Purfleet	2–2	0–0	1–1	0–1	3–0	1–2	3–0	1–1	3–0	0–2	1–0	3–1	2–2	4–2	0–0	1–1	0–1	1–1	*	2–0	1–3	2–1
20 Slough Town	0–1	0–2	2–3	0–1	3–1	0–2	1–0	1–1	3–1	0–2	2–0	1–0	1–1	1–2	1–0	1–1	0–3	1–0	3–2	*	1–2	4–4
21 St. Albans City	0–1	0–3	0–0	1–4	0–1	1–5	2–2	2–1	0–1	2–4	0–2	1–2	5–0	1–0	1–3	3–0	2–0	3–1	0–2	1–0	*	0–1
22 Sutton United	1–1	2–0	1–4	0–1	3–1	2–3	2–1	7–1	2–3	1–0	1–4	2–3	2–2	3–3	NP	1–2	1–1	2–0	2–2	1–1	4–2	*

NP = Not Played

Premier Division	*P*	*W*	*D*	*L*	*F*	*A*	*Pts*
1 Farnborough Town	42	31	6	5	86	27	99
2 Canvey Island	42	27	8	7	79	41	89
3 Basingstoke Town	42	22	13	7	73	40	79
4 Aldershot Town	41	21	11	9	73	39	74
5 Chesham United	42	22	6	14	78	52	72
6 Gravesend & Nth	42	22	5	15	63	46	71
7 Heybridge Swifts	42	18	13	11	74	60	67
8 Billericay Town	41	18	13	10	62	54	67
9 Hampton & R Boro	42	18	12	12	73	60	66
10 Hitchin Town	42	18	5	19	72	69	59
11 Purfleet	42	14	13	15	55	55	55
12 Hendon	40	16	6	18	62	62	54
13 Sutton United	41	14	11	16	74	70	53
14 St. Albans City	42	15	5	22	50	69	50
15 Grays Athletic	42	14	8	20	49	68	50
16 Maidenhead Utd	42	15	2	25	47	63	47
17 Croydon	42	12	10	20	55	77	46
18 Enfield	42	12	9	21	48	74	45
19 Harrow Borough	41	10	11	20	62	91	41
20 Slough Town	42	10	9	23	40	62	39
21 Carshalton Athletic	42	10	6	26	40	85	36
22 Dulwich Hamlet	42	4	10	28	33	84	22

Left: Enfield's programme for the 2000-01 campaign.

Right: Chesham United's edition for the same season.

UNPLAYED MATCHES
Aldershot Town v Billericay Town, Hendon v Harrow Borough, Sutton United v Hendon.

Division I	1	2	3	4	5	6	7	8	9	10	11	12	13	14	15	16	17	18	19	20	21	22
1 Aylesbury United	*	0–0	3–0	1–2	2–0	2–2	1–2	1–4	1–1	1–3	1–0	5–1	1–0	0–1	0–4	1–2	3–0	0–1	0–2	5–1	1–2	5–1
2 Barton Rovers	0–4	*	0–1	0–1	2–2	0–2	0–3	1–2	0–1	1–3	0–1	0–1	0–0	2–1	0–1	1–2	1–3	0–0	0–1	0–2	2–4	0–3
3 Bedford Town	1–0	1–1	*	3–1	1–1	1–0	2–2	3–0	2–3	4–0	3–0	6–1	2–1	3–1	4–4	1–0	0–0	2–1	4–1	1–1	1–0	5–1
4 Bishop's Stortford	2–3	2–2	2–3	*	2–4	4–0	5–3	0–1	4–0	4–3	4–0	1–3	1–2	3–2	2–1	1–0	2–1	4–3	2–2	4–1	4–2	5–1
5 Bognor Regis Tn	2–1	2–0	0–1	2–5	*	0–2	2–0	1–2	2–3	1–1	5–0	2–2	2–0	5–0	4–5	1–1	1–0	2–3	2–3	1–1	1–0	2–1
6 Boreham Wood	3–2	2–0	3–0	0–3	3–1	*	1–4	1–0	1–1	6–3	2–1	2–0	1–1	3–0	2–0	1–0	2–3	3–0	2–1	0–3	4–2	6–2
7 Braintree Town	3–2	2–1	2–1	1–1	2–1	0–3	*	5–0	2–4	2–1	4–0	1–2	3–1	10–0	4–1	4–1	3–0	5–1	1–1	5–0	2–2	3–1
8 Bromley	3–2	0–2	1–1	3–0	0–1	2–4	0–6	*	1–3	1–1	1–0	0–4	2–3	1–0	0–1	1–1	3–2	1–3	4–0	2–3	0–3	2–0
9 Ford United	2–0	4–2	1–1	0–0	0–0	1–1	0–3	3–1	*	0–3	2–1	2–0	0–0	1–0	3–0	1–3	2–2	0–2	2–1	5–1	1–2	0–3
10 Harlow Town	0–0	3–0	0–0	2–2	0–0	1–1	0–0	3–1	3–2	*	3–0	3–2	0–2	2–2	1–3	0–0	1–1	3–2	3–1	2–1	3–2	1–0
11 Leatherhead	3–0	2–1	0–2	1–2	2–1	0–2	1–2	3–3	0–2	1–1	*	1–5	1–0	4–1	3–1	0–2	0–2	5–1	1–0	1–3	1–1	0–6
12 Northwood	1–3	1–0	2–2	7–3	2–2	1–1	3–2	3–2	2–3	4–2	4–1	*	1–1	2–0	1–0	1–5	0–1	5–3	3–1	4–1	2–4	1–2
13 Oxford City	0–2	5–1	0–0	2–2	2–1	2–2	1–0	3–2	1–1	1–1	3–0	2–5	*	0–1	5–0	0–0	0–1	2–2	3–0	1–2	4–1	0–1
14 Romford	0–1	2–2	0–6	1–2	1–4	0–4	2–4	2–3	1–3	5–2	2–0	3–1	3–2	*	1–0	2–4	2–6	2–3	0–2	0–3	3–1	1–1
15 Staines Town	0–3	3–1	1–5	2–3	3–3	1–2	2–2	1–1	0–0	0–1	3–0	3–1	0–2	3–0	*	2–1	0–2	1–1	4–1	1–0	0–1	0–0
16 Thame United	1–0	11–3	0–0	3–2	2–1	1–0	4–1	1–0	1–4	2–2	4–0	1–2	1–1	3–1	0–4	*	5–0	1–3	4–0	0–1	3–1	2–1
17 Uxbridge	2–0	8–2	2–2	1–0	3–0	1–0	3–1	3–1	0–2	2–1	3–0	3–0	4–0	2–4	0–1	4–1	*	1–2	0–2	1–2	1–1	0–2
18 Walton & Hersham	0–2	1–0	1–1	2–4	5–2	1–0	0–4	1–4	1–1	3–2	0–0	1–2	1–1	1–0	2–0	0–2	0–2	*	0–2	0–0	0–1	2–5
19 Wealdstone	1–3	2–0	1–1	1–2	2–0	2–3	2–3	4–1	3–1	2–2	0–1	2–2	0–1	3–3	1–1	0–4	1–0	2–3	*	1–2	0–1	0–0
20 Whyteleafe	1–0	4–1	1–2	5–4	2–4	0–1	2–1	3–1	1–0	0–0	0–1	1–2	0–2	2–1	2–0	1–5	2–1	2–1	2–0	*	0–3	2–2
21 Worthing	0–3	1–1	0–1	2–3	3–3	1–2	0–3	2–2	3–3	4–1	5–0	1–1	1–5	2–0	0–1	3–0	3–1	1–0	0–1	0–0	*	3–1
22 Yeading	1–0	0–0	1–1	0–3	1–0	1–2	5–2	2–4	3–2	0–3	0–1	2–2	0–2	7–2	1–2	2–2	0–1	3–2	2–2	3–1	4–0	

Division I	*P*	*W*	*D*	*L*	*F*	*A*	*Pts*
1 Boreham Wood	42	26	7	9	82	49	85
2 Bedford Town	42	22	16	4	81	40	82
3 Braintree Town	42	25	6	11	112	60	81
4 Bishop's Stortford	42	24	6	12	103	76	78
5 Thame United	42	22	8	12	86	54	74
6 Ford United	42	19	12	11	70	58	69
7 Uxbridge	42	21	5	16	73	55	68
8 Northwood	42	20	8	14	89	81	68
9 Whyteleafe	42	20	6	16	62	69	66
10 Oxford City	42	16	13	13	64	49	61
11 Harlow Town	42	15	16	11	70	66	61
12 Worthing	42	16	9	17	69	69	57
13 Staines Town	42	16	8	18	60	66	56
14 Aylesbury United	42	17	4	21	65	55	55
15 Yeading	42	15	9	18	72	74	54
16 Bognor Regis Tn	42	13	11	18	71	71	50
17 Walton & Hersham	42	14	8	20	59	80	50
18 Bromley	42	14	6	22	63	86	48
19 Wealdstone	42	12	9	21	54	73	45
20 Leatherhead	42	12	4	26	37	87	40
21 Romford	42	9	4	29	53	113	31
22 Barton Rovers	42	2	9	31	30	94	15

Left: Braintree Town's programme for the 2000-01 campaign.

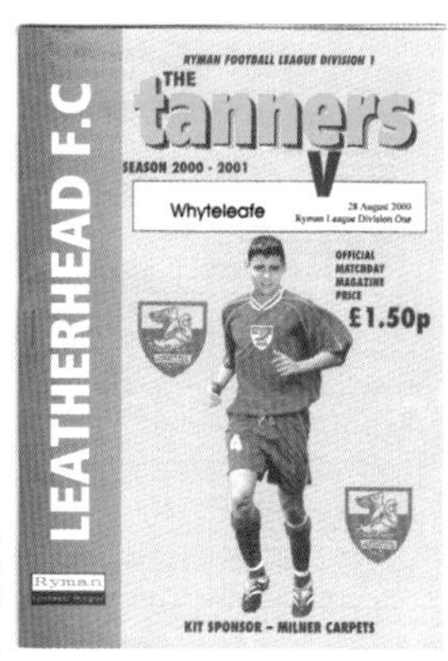

Right: the Leatherhead programme for the season.

2000-01 Division II	1	2	3	4	5	6	7	8	9	10	11	12	13	14	15	16	17	18	19	20	21	22
1 Banstead Athletic	*	1–1	0–3	4–0	1–4	0–2	1–2	1–0	0–1	2–0	2–0	2–0	0–1	2–2	6–1	0–1	3–0	0–3	3–1	0–2	1–2	2–1
2 Barking	2–0	*	1–6	2–1	2–1	2–2	4–1	2–0	1–0	2–1	2–0	1–1	3–2	2–1	2–0	0–0	3–5	3–1	2–0	2–1	2–2	3–0
3 Berkhamsted Town	1–1	0–0	*	2–0	5–0	4–0	5–0	5–2	2–2	2–1	0–1	4–2	1–1	4–1	3–0	4–1	2–0	2–0	0–1	0–3	1–2	5–2
4 Chertsey Town	3–1	2–4	2–3	*	2–2	0–0	1–0	0–1	1–1	0–0	4–2	4–1	3–0	2–1	2–1	1–0	3–0	1–1	0–2	0–1	0–0	2–0
5 Cheshunt	2–1	1–2	1–1	1–0	*	2–4	3–1	1–2	0–3	1–0	0–0	1–4	2–1	2–3	0–4	0–3	3–1	1–2	0–1	1–2	1–2	1–1
6 East Thurrock Utd	1–1	2–1	0–0	3–1	3–1	*	2–1	1–1	1–2	1–1	2–1	4–2	1–2	3–2	4–2	0–1	0–1	0–1	2–1	2–2	1–3	4–1
7 Edgware Town	2–1	0–0	1–3	1–2	1–2	3–1	*	2–1	1–2	0–1	1–2	1–1	2–1	0–2	0–1	1–1	2–4	2–2	0–2	1–2	1–5	2–1
8 Great Wakering R	1–1	1–1	1–4	2–1	2–1	4–2	1–1	*	0–0	1–1	4–0	3–0	3–1	2–1	3–3	0–0	3–0	2–2	3–1	0–1	2–1	7–0
9 Hemel Hempstead	2–1	0–1	0–2	0–2	1–3	3–3	2–0	2–0	*	1–1	1–1	3–1	3–1	1–2	2–2	3–1	1–0	0–3	2–1	2–1	2–2	4–0
10 Horsham	1–4	4–0	1–6	6–0	4–0	2–1	2–0	3–0	0–2	*	2–0	2–0	3–0	3–2	0–1	2–2	2–2	3–2	1–1	0–3	3–1	3–3
11 Hungerford Town	0–3	0–3	1–4	1–0	3–1	2–1	1–1	1–1	1–4	0–4	*	0–2	0–1	0–2	1–1	2–0	0–3	0–4	0–1	1–2	1–4	2–2
12 Leighton Town	2–0	0–3	1–3	2–2	1–1	4–3	0–1	1–5	0–0	1–5	1–0	*	1–1	0–1	0–3	1–3	1–2	0–3	0–0	0–0	4–1	1–1
13 Leyton Pennant	1–3	1–3	0–2	0–0	0–2	1–3	2–0	2–0	1–6	1–1	0–1	4–0	*	0–0	0–2	2–1	3–3	0–3	0–0	0–2	2–4	1–0
14 Marlow	3–4	2–2	2–0	1–3	1–1	3–0	2–1	1–2	0–4	4–1	1–3	1–1	1–1	*	1–0	1–0	2–1	1–2	0–0	1–3	0–0	1–1
15 Metropolitan Police	0–1	2–0	1–4	1–2	2–1	0–1	3–2	5–3	1–0	1–6	1–1	2–1	4–2	0–4	*	1–3	3–0	0–5	1–0	1–2	0–3	3–2
16 Molesey	1–1	1–2	0–0	1–0	2–0	1–5	3–0	1–2	1–3	4–2	1–3	0–1	0–0	2–2	2–1	*	1–0	0–2	1–2	3–3	4–1	2–0
17 Tilbury	3–2	2–1	1–1	1–2	1–2	1–1	2–3	3–0	2–0	2–1	0–0	3–2	2–1	0–1	4–3	2–1	*	1–1	3–2	0–1	0–1	3–2
18 Tooting & M Utd	3–0	2–2	3–0	1–1	2–0	1–1	1–1	1–1	2–0	2–3	2–1	4–0	3–3	1–0	2–0	4–0	4–0	*	2–1	1–0	5–0	2–1
19 Wembley	1–2	2–2	3–2	2–4	2–1	1–0	1–1	1–1	0–1	0–4	0–0	2–1	0–3	1–0	1–4	1–0	0–1	0–3	*	0–3	0–2	0–0
20 Windsor & Eton	0–3	2–2	1–2	5–0	2–1	1–0	0–0	1–0	1–2	2–1	2–3	3–0	2–2	2–1	1–0	4–2	1–0	1–1	2–0	*	0–2	0–0
21 Wivenhoe Town	2–2	2–2	1–0	1–3	1–0	1–5	4–0	0–0	1–1	4–0	2–0	3–0	3–0	2–2	0–1	1–0	1–0	3–1	4–2	2–2	*	1–1
22 Wokingham Town	0–0	2–7	2–1	1–2	1–0	0–0	0–1	3–2	0–5	0–3	1–4	2–3	1–2	2–3	0–2	1–2	1–2	0–2	2–2	1–1	0–1	*

Division II	P	W	D	L	F	A	Pts
1 Tooting & M Utd	42	26	11	5	92	35	89
2 Windsor & Eton	42	24	10	8	70	40	82
3 Barking	42	23	13	6	82	54	82
4 Berkhamsted Town	42	24	8	10	99	49	80
5 Wivenhoe Town	42	23	11	8	78	52	80
6 Hemel Hempstead	42	22	10	10	74	44	76
7 Horsham	42	19	9	14	84	61	66
8 Chertsey Town	42	18	9	15	59	59	63
9 Great Wakering R	42	16	13	13	69	59	61
10 Tilbury	42	18	6	18	61	67	60
11 Banstead Athletic	42	17	8	17	69	58	59
12 East Thurrock Utd	42	16	11	15	72	64	59
13 Metropolitan Police	42	18	4	20	64	77	58
14 Marlow	42	15	11	16	62	61	56
15 Molesey	42	14	9	19	53	61	51
16 Wembley	42	12	10	20	39	63	46
17 Hungerford Town	42	11	9	22	40	73	42
18 Leyton Pennant	42	10	11	21	47	74	41
19 Cheshunt	42	11	6	25	48	77	39
20 Edgware Town	42	9	9	24	41	77	36
21 Leighton Town	42	8	10	24	44	87	34
22 Wokingham Town*	42	3	12	27	39	94	20

** Wokingham Town had one point deducted*

Left: the St. Albans City programme for their match with Sutton United in September 2000.

Right: Whyteleafe's edition for their game with Worthing in the same month.

Division III	1	2	3	4	5	6	7	8	9	10	11	12	13	14	15	16	17	18	19	20	21	22
1 Abingdon Town	*	0–5	0–3	1–6	3–1	2–1	1–0	1–1	0–4	3–2	3–1	0–1	2–1	1–4	2–2	2–3	1–3	1–1	1–1	1–2	1–3	2–4
2 Arlesey Town	5–0	*	2–0	2–1	2–1	4–1	9–1	3–0	4–0	2–1	3–3	3–0	2–1	2–3	8–1	3–3	5–1	1–1	6–0	4–3	3–1	2–0
3 Ashford Town (Mx)	1–2	1–2	*	2–1	2–2	3–0	8–0	3–2	2–0	2–2	5–1	1–1	0–1	0–1	1–1	3–0	5–1	1–3	3–4	3–0	1–2	3–1
4 Aveley	4–0	1–1	0–4	*	6–1	1–0	3–1	3–1	1–3	2–0	3–1	2–0	0–1	0–3	5–2	2–1	5–2	0–1	4–2	1–0	1–1	0–1
5 Bracknell Town	4–1	0–3	2–2	2–2	*	2–1	3–0	2–1	2–2	3–3	0–3	3–3	2–3	3–2	2–0	0–1	3–1	3–1	0–2	3–2	5–1	6–3
6 Camberley Town	2–1	1–3	0–4	2–0	1–5	*	4–2	0–3	2–4	2–2	2–2	1–1	0–4	1–2	1–3	0–5	1–2	0–5	2–3	0–3	5–2	1–1
7 Chalfont St. Peter	1–2	0–5	2–3	1–5	0–6	0–2	*	3–0	0–1	1–2	2–1	1–1	1–2	0–5	1–2	0–3	1–2	0–3	0–2	1–4	2–1	1–2
8 Clapton	1–1	2–8	0–4	2–4	1–0	1–3	2–0	*	1–1	1–3	3–1	1–2	0–4	2–6	2–2	2–2	0–2	0–1	2–4	1–5	0–5	1–5
9 Corinthian-Casuals	4–0	0–6	0–1	3–0	2–2	3–2	4–0	8–1	*	3–2	0–0	1–0	0–1	2–0	3–1	1–1	3–1	0–0	2–2	1–3	2–1	1–0
10 Croydon Athletic	0–1	0–2	0–2	4–1	NP	5–1	4–0	3–1	0–0	*	4–0	2–2	0–1	2–2	1–1	2–2	4–1	3–0	4–0	5–0	0–2	2–1
11 Dorking	3–2	2–3	1–3	1–2	0–5	3–2	2–1	1–0	0–2	0–3	*	2–1	0–2	4–3	4–3	0–1	4–4	2–7	1–3	4–4	3–2	0–3
12 Egham Town	2–1	3–2	1–2	2–1	1–2	0–1	7–0	1–1	1–1	4–2	1–1	*	1–2	0–1	4–0	0–4	0–1	1–1	1–2	0–0	2–1	1–2
13 Epsom & Ewell	1–2	0–2	1–2	3–1	0–2	4–0	1–2	5–0	1–2	0–1	3–0	1–2	*	1–1	3–1	4–1	2–2	1–2	3–1	2–1	0–4	4–0
14 Flackwell Heath	2–2	1–1	2–3	1–2	4–0	2–1	4–0	2–2	2–0	2–2	2–2	2–1	3–0	*	3–1	1–0	2–1	1–0	4–0	2–0	3–0	2–0
15 Hertford Town	1–3	0–3	0–3	2–3	0–3	3–3	6–1	2–1	0–1	1–3	3–1	1–2	2–3	2–0	*	0–3	3–2	0–1	0–1	1–4	1–0	1–3
16 Hornchurch	5–1	0–3	4–0	0–2	2–0	1–2	4–1	1–3	0–3	2–2	0–0	4–0	2–2	2–2	0–1	*	3–2	0–1	0–1	1–2	3–0	1–1
17 Kingsbury Town	6–2	2–3	0–5	3–1	0–3	1–1	5–2	1–1	1–5	5–0	2–1	2–2	1–2	2–2	1–1	3–2	*	0–4	0–1	2–3	2–3	1–2
18 Lewes	3–0	1–1	4–4	0–1	3–0	6–0a	13–0	5–1	1–1	4–0	4–2	3–0	0–1	1–0	NP	3–3	4–2	*	2–2	4–0	2–0	0–0
19 Tring Town	2–3	0–3	1–2	0–2	1–2	1–1	1–0	2–1	2–4	2–0	1–1	0–1	1–1	1–2	5–1	1–1	1–1	0–1	*	2–0	2–2	0–2
20 Ware	1–0	1–5	1–3	0–3	2–2	4–0	2–1	1–1	2–3	3–3	0–1	0–2	1–2	1–1	3–1	2–0	1–0	1–3	1–2	*	3–0	3–0
21 Wingate & Finch	4–0	0–1	0–1	1–2	1–1	4–3	8–0	5–1	2–3	0–0	1–0	1–3	1–0	1–2	2–2	1–1	5–3	1–1	2–1	1–6	*	2–1
22 Witham Town	1–1	0–1	1–1	3–1	2–2	0–0	5–0	6–1	2–0	1–0	1–0	1–2	4–2	5–4	2–2	1–1	1–0	0–4	2–0	4–0	2–1	*

NP = Not Played

a = Lewes v Camberley Town was abandoned after 75 minutes - result stood.

Division III	P	W	D	L	F	A	Pts
1 Arlesey Town	42	34	6	2	138	37	108
2 Lewes	41	25	11	5	104	34	86
3 Ashford Town (Mx)	42	26	7	9	102	49	85
4 Flackwell Heath	42	24	10	8	93	51	82
5 Corinthian-Casuals	42	24	10	8	83	50	82
6 Aveley	42	24	3	15	85	61	75
7 Epsom & Ewell	42	23	4	15	76	52	73
8 Witham Town	42	21	9	12	76	57	72
9 Bracknell Town	41	19	10	12	90	70	67
10 Croydon Athletic	41	15	12	14	78	63	57
11 Ware	42	17	6	19	75	76	57
12 Tring Town	42	16	9	17	60	71	57
13 Egham Town	42	15	11	16	60	60	56
14 Hornchurch	42	14	13	15	73	60	55
15 Wingate & Finch	42	15	7	20	75	75	52
16 Kingsbury Town	42	11	8	23	74	100	41
17 Abingdon Town*	42	12	7	23	53	102	40
18 Dorking	42	10	9	23	59	99	39
19 Hertford Town	41	9	8	24	57	97	35
20 Camberley Town	42	8	8	26	53	107	32
21 Clapton	42	5	9	28	48	121	24
22 Chalfont St. Peter	42	4	1	37	30	150	13

** Abingdon Town had three points deducted.*

UNPLAYED MATCHES: Croydon Athletic v Bracknell Town, Lewes v Hertford Town.

Left: the programme from Ashford Town (Middlesex) for the 2000-01 campaign.

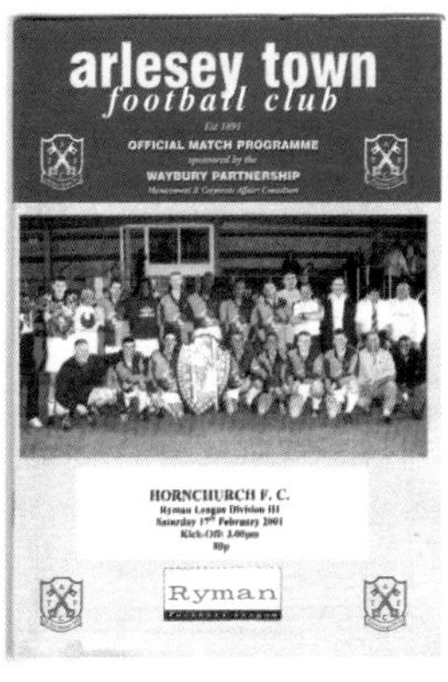

Right: the Arlesey Town edition for the same season.

2001–02 - With the championship race not being decided until the final Saturday of the season, Gravesend & Northfleet won 1–0 at Bedford Town in front of 1,700 spectators to take the title by four points from Canvey Island who had to settle for runners-up for the second successive season. Aldershot Town, who were twenty-two points behind Canvey Island, finished third on goal difference from Braintree Town with Purfleet in fifth. At the bottom only one club relegated, Croydon, whose short spell back in the Premier Division ended when they finished bottom of the table. Division One was another tight championship not decided until the final Saturday when Ford United, needing a win, duly obliged with a 2–1 victory over mid-table Uxbridge to secure the championship by just one point from Bishop's Stortford who had to settle for runners-up with Aylesbury United claiming the remaining promotion place by finishing third, six points clear of fourth placed Bognor Regis Town. Due to the League's restructuring no clubs were relegated. In Division Two, although there was no promotion and relegation, there was plenty of pride at stake with Lewes ending one of their most successful seasons with the championship six points clear of Sussex rivals Horsham who finished runners-up. At the foot of the table Romford had a disappointing season finishing in last place. In Division Three there were six promotion places up for grabs and Croydon Athletic, who gained maximum points at home, secured their first League championship from Essex clubs Hornchurch and Aveley who finished second and third respectively whilst Bracknell Town, Epsom & Ewell and Egham Town were the remaining clubs to gain promotion.

At the Annual General Meeting, Hayes were elected to replace Gravesend & Northfleet who had won promotion to the Football Conference as League champions while Romford had already given notice of their intention to resign from the League. Wingate & Finchley, the club finishing seventh in Division Three, thus gained the last promotion place. Leyton were elected to Division Two keeping the constitution of the League at 88 clubs.

Also at the Annual General Meeting, a proposal was made to change the League's constitution, the first major restructuring of divisions since 1991. The proposal was that there would be a Premier Division, two Division Ones – split geographically into North and South – all consisting of 24 clubs, with the remaining 16 placed in Division Two, which would be at the same level as the feeder leagues. After much discussion, the proposal was carried by a majority vote and would be in operation for the 2002–03 season. As a result of ground grading criteria, Cheshunt and Hungerford Town would be relegated to Division Two, while Corinthian–Casuals and Hertford Town, who finished 10th and 11th respectively, would take their places in the regionalised Division Ones.

Premier Division	1	2	3	4	5	6	7	8	9	10	11	12	13	14	15	16	17	18	19	20	21	22
1 Aldershot Town	*	2–2	4–0	1–1	0–2	4–0	1–3	1–0	2–0	3–1	1–2	0–1	4–1	2–1	2–1	3–3	1–2	3–0	4–1	4–1	1–1	1–0
2 Basingstoke Town	1–1	*	1–1	0–1	1–0	1–2	0–4	1–1	1–0	2–0	1–4	0–2	1–1	2–1	2–1	1–3	2–3	2–1	1–2	2–2	3–1	1–0
3 Bedford Town	1–2	3–0	*	3–4	2–0	2–0	1–3	2–0	3–2	2–2	0–1	4–0	4–1	3–4	0–5	5–2	0–1	2–1	1–2	1–0	0–1	0–1
4 Billericay Town	2–0	3–0	0–0	*	0–1	2–4	0–3	0–0	2–0	3–2	1–3	3–2	2–0	1–1	4–6	1–2	1–1	1–1	2–2	2–0	1–5	2–1
5 Boreham Wood	1–3	0–0	1–0	1–1	*	1–2	0–3	2–1	1–1	1–3	0–2	2–2	3–2	1–2	1–2	2–4	2–1	1–3	2–1	1–0	0–1	1–2
6 Braintree Town	2–0	3–2	2–1	1–0	2–0	*	2–1	2–0	2–1	2–3	0–2	2–3	3–2	0–0	2–0	2–0	0–1	1–0	2–1	2–2	2–1	3–0
7 Canvey Island	1–3	5–1	3–3	3–0	2–1	3–2	*	2–1	3–0	3–1	0–2	1–2	1–1	3–0	3–1	6–1	5–3	2–0	2–0	3–0	3–2	1–1
8 Chesham United	2–1	1–1	1–1	2–0	1–0	4–1	1–5	*	2–1	0–0	2–2	3–5	2–1	5–0	0–2	3–0	5–5	0–0	1–0	0–0	3–2	2–0
9 Croydon	1–2	1–3	3–3	0–0	0–5	0–4	2–1	0–1	*	0–2	3–4	1–0	0–0	2–1	1–3	2–3	1–2	4–0	0–2	0–1	2–1	1–2
10 Enfield	1–1	3–0	1–0	0–2	0–1	1–2	0–3	0–3	3–1	*	1–5	1–2	0–2	1–2	0–6	4–2	0–5	2–2	0–2	0–1	0–0	2–2
11 Gravesend & N	2–1	0–0	4–1	1–0	0–1	3–0	0–1	1–4	6–1	3–0	*	2–0	2–1	2–2	3–0	1–1	2–0	2–0	3–2	0–0	3–2	3–1
12 Grays Athletic	3–1	0–0	2–1	0–0	3–2	3–0	0–1	2–1	1–0	0–0	2–0	*	1–1	2–1	2–0	1–3	2–1	2–0	0–1	1–3	3–2	3–3
13 Hampton & R	1–1	1–1	1–1	1–2	1–2	0–2	1–5	0–2	6–0	2–1	0–2	0–0	*	0–1	0–0	1–1	6–3	0–0	2–1	1–1	0–5	2–1
14 Harrow Borough	2–3	3–3	2–4	0–2	2–3	1–2	1–1	2–1	2–0	2–4	0–3	1–1	1–1	*	0–2	1–3	1–1	1–3	0–3	1–2	2–6	1–6
15 Hendon	0–1	1–3	1–2	1–3	2–1	3–0	0–1	1–2	0–1	2–0	1–1	1–0	1–0	0–1	*	1–0	2–2	2–0	1–1	1–0	1–0	4–3
16 Heybridge Swifts	1–2	5–1	1–1	2–3	0–2	1–1	0–7	2–1	2–0	4–2	1–2	1–1	1–3	1–1	1–6	*	3–1	1–1	2–0	3–3	0–2	2–0
17 Hitchin Town	0–3	0–1	2–2	3–2	4–1	1–1	2–1	2–3	2–2	1–2	0–4	2–4	2–4	3–0	3–0	1–0	*	0–0	1–0	0–3	2–4	0–2
18 Kingstonian	2–1	1–1	3–0	4–1	1–1	0–2	2–1	1–0	3–0	0–2	0–1	2–3	3–0	1–0	1–2	1–2	2–2	*	1–0	1–5	4–2	1–1
19 Maidenhead Utd	1–2	2–2	2–1	0–2	2–0	2–0	0–1	0–4	0–1	0–1	0–3	2–1	2–1	4–2	3–1	1–0	1–1	0–1	*	1–3	2–1	2–2
20 Purfleet	2–1	0–0	1–1	1–1	0–1	3–2	0–0	2–2	5–1	1–0	2–0	2–0	3–0	0–3	2–0	3–1	3–1	1–1	5–2	*	2–2	1–1
21 St. Albans City	0–3	2–0	0–0	0–0	1–0	3–1	2–4	3–1	5–0	1–1	0–3	2–1	1–3	1–0	1–1	1–2	1–2	2–2	1–0	0–1	*	2–0
22 Sutton United	2–0	2–1	2–2	2–2	2–2	3–1	1–4	0–1	2–0	1–1	0–1	2–2	2–0	1–1	2–1	4–1	2–4	0–0	2–1	0–0	1–1	*

Premier Division	*P*	*W*	*D*	*L*	*F*	*A*	*Pts*
1 Gravesend & N	42	31	6	5	90	33	99
2 Canvey Island	42	30	5	7	108	41	95
3 Aldershot Town	42	22	7	13	76	51	73
4 Braintree Town	42	23	4	15	66	61	73
5 Purfleet	42	19	15	8	67	44	72
6 Grays Athletic	42	20	10	12	65	55	70
7 Chesham United	42	19	10	13	69	53	67
8 Hendon	42	19	5	18	66	55	62
9 Billericay Town	42	16	15	13	59	60	61
10 St. Albans City	42	16	9	17	71	60	57
11 Hitchin Town	42	15	10	17	73	81	55
12 Sutton United	42	13	15	14	62	63	54
13 Heybridge Swifts	42	15	9	18	68	85	54
14 Kingstonian	42	13	13	16	50	56	52
15 Boreham Wood	42	15	6	21	50	62	51
16 Maidenhead Utd	42	15	5	22	51	63	50
17 Bedford Town	42	12	12	18	64	69	48
18 Basingstoke Town	42	11	15	16	50	68	48
19 Enfield	42	11	9	22	48	77	42
20 Hampton & R Boro	42	9	13	20	51	71	40
21 Harrow Borough	42	8	10	24	50	89	34
22 Croydon	42	7	5	30	36	93	26

Left: Billericay Town unveil plans for a new stadium back in 2002 through their matchday programme against Basingstoke Town.

Right: Thame United's edition for the same campaign.

2001-02 Division I	1	2	3	4	5	6	7	8	9	10	11	12	13	14	15	16	17	18	19	20	21	22
1 Aylesbury United	*	3–2	3–3	2–2	3–1	2–1	3–3	3–4	1–0	3–2	1–4	4–0	2–1	2–0	3–2	0–0	4–2	2–2	0–0	3–2	1–1	4–1
2 Barking & EHU	2–1	*	0–4	1–2	2–2	1–2	1–0	1–4	0–6	0–5	1–1	0–1	2–0	2–3	2–1	2–3	3–3	2–1	3–0	2–4	1–3	3–4
3 Bishop's Stortford	2–2	3–1	*	1–3	3–0	2–1	2–2	4–1	4–1	1–2	2–0	3–2	2–0	3–0	5–0	2–4	2–0	7–1	3–0	2–0	1–1	6–4
4 Bognor Regis Tn	1–1	8–3	0–0	*	2–0	1–1	1–0	1–1	0–0	3–1	3–1	0–0	0–2	2–1	3–1	0–1	3–3	0–1	2–0	2–1	1–1	3–1
5 Bromley	0–2	3–2	1–1	1–1	*	0–1	1–0	1–2	1–3	2–0	1–0	0–3	0–1	1–1	1–3	1–0	2–1	1–2	0–0	1–0	0–2	2–2
6 Carshalton Athletic	2–1	1–1	2–0	0–2	3–0	*	0–0	2–1	1–2	1–1	3–2	2–1	1–0	2–2	2–3	4–1	3–2	3–0	2–0	2–2	0–2	2–5
7 Dulwich Hamlet	3–3	7–1	1–2	2–1	5–3	0–3	*	0–5	1–1	1–4	1–2	0–0	0–1	2–2	0–2	1–1	0–3	3–2	0–3	3–1	1–2	2–0
8 Ford United	0–3	2–1	2–1	1–3	1–1	1–1	2–2	*	0–2	2–0	5–0	0–2	2–1	4–2	1–1	2–1	6–1	2–1	2–2	4–2	2–1	3–2
9 Harlow Town	1–3	3–1	1–2	4–0	0–1	2–2	1–2	4–1	*	3–2	1–2	1–4	2–2	2–2	0–1	2–2	0–1	2–0	2–0	1–0	2–1	2–1
10 Northwood	3–2	2–2	2–2	5–1	2–2	1–1	1–3	1–2	2–1	*	4–1	1–1	4–3	3–1	3–4	2–0	3–5	3–1	5–0	0–1	2–0	4–1
11 Oxford City	0–2	0–1	1–0	2–2	2–0	1–1	0–0	0–2	1–2	2–2	*	3–0	3–1	1–1	1–0	1–1	2–3	4–2	3–2	2–0	1–0	2–1
12 Slough Town	3–4	2–1	0–1	0–1	3–0	1–1	3–2	1–2	4–0	2–1	1–2	*	2–0	1–1	3–1	3–0	0–3	6–0	0–0	3–0	0–1	3–3
13 Staines Town	2–1	2–1	0–0	1–1	0–0	0–0	0–0	2–4	1–3	1–3	0–0	0–1	*	0–0	1–3	1–2	3–1	1–1	0–0	3–0	4–3	0–2
14 Thame United	0–1	10–2	0–2	1–1	4–1	0–0	4–2	1–2	1–4	2–1	3–0	3–0	0–1	*	0–0	1–0	3–3	4–2	3–0	1–0	0–1	3–4
15 Tooting & M Utd	2–4	5–0	2–3	2–3	2–0	1–1	1–1	0–4	2–4	1–1	3–0	1–1	4–1	2–2	*	0–1	1–0	3–2	2–3	2–1	0–0	4–4
16 Uxbridge	3–1	3–1	1–3	2–0	1–0	2–0	0–3	1–2	2–3	0–2	3–1	3–1	2–3	1–3	1–1	*	3–4	1–0	2–0	5–3	2–3	6–1
17 Walton & Hersham	1–1	4–0	0–1	1–0	2–4	2–2	1–1	0–2	1–1	0–0	1–2	1–1	0–1	2–1	1–2	2–1	*	1–2	1–2	4–0	2–0	0–1
18 Wealdstone	1–0	2–2	2–2	2–3	4–1	1–2	1–3	1–1	1–1	2–2	3–0	2–1	1–0	1–3	0–1	2–1	3–3	*	1–1	1–1	1–1	0–2
19 Whyteleafe	1–2	2–4	2–4	1–5	1–1	0–0	2–1	1–0	1–1	1–3	4–2	0–2	1–1	2–2	3–0	0–1	2–5	1–2	*	1–0	2–1	2–2
20 Windsor & Eton	1–3	4–0	1–7	3–4	2–1	1–2	3–0	1–5	4–2	0–3	1–4	3–3	1–2	0–1	0–0	0–1	1–2	3–3	4–0	*	0–1	1–2
21 Worthing	2–0	2–2	2–4	0–2	2–3	2–3	6–2	1–2	6–1	0–1	2–2	0–3	4–2	0–2	1–2	3–2	1–2	0–2	0–3	2–0	*	7–1
22 Yeading	1–2	5–2	3–2	3–1	3–3	4–1	1–4	0–1	1–3	3–3	0–1	0–0	1–0	1–1	3–2	1–1	0–1	2–1	4–0	3–1	1–1	*

Division I	P	W	D	L	F	A	Pts
1 Ford United	42	27	7	8	92	56	88
2 Bishop's Stortford	42	26	9	7	104	51	87
3 Aylesbury United	42	23	10	9	96	64	79
4 Bognor Regis Tn	42	20	13	9	74	55	73
5 Northwood	42	19	11	12	92	64	68
6 Carshalton Athletic	42	17	16	9	64	53	67
7 Harlow Town	42	19	11	14	77	65	66
8 Slough Town	42	17	11	14	68	51	62
9 Uxbridge	42	18	6	18	68	65	60
10 Oxford City	42	17	9	16	59	66	60
11 Thame United	42	15	14	13	75	61	59
12 Tooting & M Utd	42	16	11	15	70	70	59
13 Walton & Hersham	42	16	10	16	75	70	58
14 Yeading	42	16	10	16	84	90	58
15 Worthing	42	15	8	19	69	65	53
16 Staines Town	42	12	11	19	45	60	47
17 Dulwich Hamlet	42	11	13	18	64	76	46
18 Wealdstone	42	11	12	19	60	82	45
19 Bromley	42	10	11	21	44	74	41
20 Whyteleafe	42	10	11	21	46	86	41
21 Barking & EHU	42	8	7	27	61	123	31
22 Windsor & Eton	42	7	5	30	53	93	26

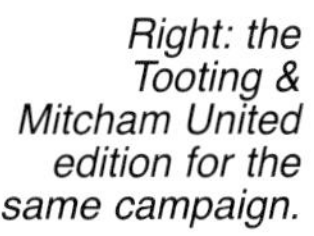

Left: the Windsor & Eton programme for 2001-02.

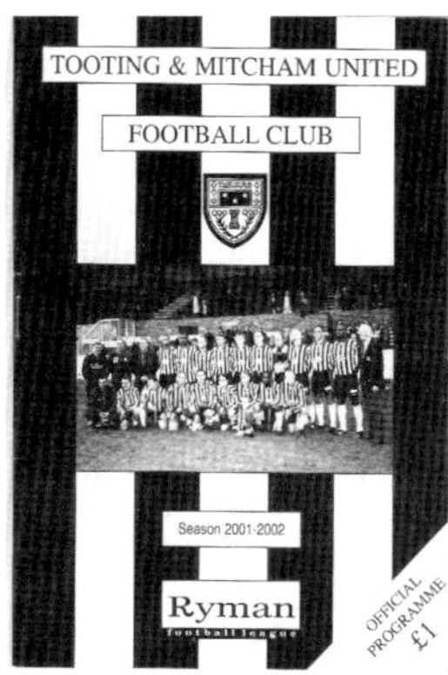

Right: the Tooting & Mitcham United edition for the same campaign.

Division II	1	2	3	4	5	6	7	8	9	10	11	12	13	14	15	16	17	18	19	20	21	22
1 Arlesey Town	*	0–2	2–2	3–3	0–2	2–1	2–3	2–0	3–2	2–0	4–5	2–1	1–0	1–0	1–1	1–1	5–2	6–0	1–1	5–1	4–1	5–0
2 Ashford Town (Mx)	2–2	*	2–2	1–2	1–0	2–2	1–1	1–0	1–3	0–1	2–1	2–0	1–3	1–0	2–2	3–3	2–1	1–2	3–1	1–2	4–1	0–0
3 Banstead Athletic	1–0	0–2	*	3–1	2–1	4–1	6–0	2–0	0–1	4–3	1–0	1–1	1–1	0–1	1–3	3–3	0–3	2–1	6–1	1–0	5–0	1–2
4 Barton Rovers	0–1	0–1	1–2	*	0–1	3–3	2–0	0–1	1–3	4–2	0–1	2–1	3–1	0–0	1–2	1–3	0–1	2–0	2–0	2–0	1–0	3–1
5 Berkhamsted Town	3–1	8–1	2–3	3–1	*	2–1	2–2	1–1	0–1	1–1	1–0	0–2	3–0	1–5	3–1	2–2	2–0	7–2	2–0	2–1	1–0	1–1
6 Chertsey Town	2–6	2–0	1–1	2–2	0–5	*	2–3	1–2	2–0	6–3	0–6	4–1	2–1	1–4	2–2	3–3	1–5	3–0	1–1	3–4	2–2	1–1
7 Cheshunt	0–3	0–0	1–2	1–2	1–2	1–2	*	1–2	0–0	2–4	3–3	1–2	3–1	1–2	3–2	2–3	2–2	0–1	3–3	2–2	0–0	1–1
8 East Thurrock Utd	0–2	2–2	0–4	1–1	1–1	5–1	3–0	*	0–0	3–0	2–1	3–0	1–2	0–3	0–0	2–1	3–0	4–1	1–0	2–1	3–2	1–5
9 Great Wakering R	1–0	3–0	3–0	3–1	3–1	0–0	3–1	1–2	*	0–1	0–0	4–1	3–0	1–3	0–1	1–2	1–1	2–0	3–0	1–1	4–0	6–2
10 Hemel Hempstead	1–2	1–2	1–0	1–1	2–2	2–2	1–2	6–0	3–2	*	3–1	2–0	0–0	2–2	1–5	4–0	4–1	3–1	1–0	0–2	5–0	3–3
11 Horsham	3–0	3–1	2–1	3–1	3–0	4–0	6–1	3–1	3–0	0–0	*	2–2	3–0	0–1	3–2	1–1	1–0	3–1	3–0	4–2	2–0	7–0
12 Hungerford Town	0–3	2–2	2–1	2–0	1–2	1–1	2–2	1–3	0–1	0–0	0–0	*	1–3	1–1	2–1	2–1	1–5	3–0	1–4	2–1	2–0	1–1
13 Leatherhead	0–3	2–0	0–1	0–1	1–3	4–0	1–0	1–3	1–0	2–2	1–4	3–0	*	0–0	4–1	1–2	0–0	2–1	3–1	3–1	1–1	4–0
14 Lewes	4–0	2–0	3–0	3–0	1–1	7–1	3–1	1–2	1–0	3–0	1–1	3–2	5–1	*	2–0	1–1	6–2	4–0	4–1	3–0	3–2	5–0
15 Leyton Pennant	2–1	2–1	1–1	1–2	4–1	6–4	3–0	3–1	2–1	0–4	1–3	2–0	2–0	1–1	*	3–2	1–0	2–0	3–0	1–3	2–1	5–1
16 Marlow	1–0	1–2	1–1	3–0	1–1	2–2	3–0	2–6	0–1	2–0	3–4	1–0	2–1	1–0	1–1	*	3–2	2–0	2–0	1–2	0–2	1–1
17 Metropolitan Police	4–1	4–4	2–3	0–1	0–1	2–2	2–3	1–1	1–0	5–1	1–2	3–0	3–2	2–2	0–4	1–4	*	5–1	3–0	4–0	2–0	4–3
18 Molesey	0–1	0–1	1–4	1–0	0–1	1–1	1–0	1–1	0–2	0–3	1–1	2–4	3–1	0–5	1–1	1–1	4–1	*	1–0	1–3	0–0	2–1
19 Romford	0–6	4–0	0–3	0–2	2–2	1–5	0–3	0–1	1–1	1–4	0–4	1–2	0–1	2–5	2–3	2–3	1–6	4–1	*	2–3	3–3	1–1
20 Tilbury	0–1	0–2	1–2	2–2	0–3	5–0	1–0	2–0	0–1	0–3	1–2	2–4	0–0	0–3	2–0	2–0	0–0	1–3	2–0	*	2–2	1–0
21 Wembley	1–3	4–1	0–4	1–1	1–2	0–2	0–0	1–2	1–1	2–1	2–2	3–4	0–3	1–2	0–4	0–1	2–0	3–1	1–0	6–1	*	2–0
22 Wivenhoe Town	2–1	2–1	3–2	2–2	1–3	6–3	1–1	3–1	0–1	1–3	3–4	0–2	1–9	0–3	2–1	1–3	2–3	2–3	0–2	0–1	1–3	*

Division II	P	W	D	L	F	A	Pts
1 Lewes	42	29	9	4	108	31	96
2 Horsham	42	27	9	6	104	44	90
3 Berkhamsted Town	42	23	10	9	82	51	79
4 Arlesey Town	42	23	6	13	89	55	75
5 Banstead Athletic	42	22	8	12	83	54	74
6 Leyton Pennant	42	22	8	12	84	60	74
7 Great Wakering R	42	21	8	13	64	37	71
8 East Thurrock Utd	42	21	8	13	67	59	71
9 Marlow	42	18	13	11	73	63	67
10 Hemel Hempstd	42	18	10	14	82	66	64
11 Leatherhead	42	17	6	19	72	62	57
12 Ashford Town (Mx)	42	15	11	16	58	71	56
13 Metropolitan Police	42	16	7	19	84	84	55
14 Barton Rovers	42	15	9	18	54	60	54
15 Hungerford Town	42	14	9	19	56	75	51
16 Tilbury	42	15	6	21	55	74	51
17 Chertsey Town	42	10	14	18	79	112	44
18 Wembley	42	9	10	23	51	82	37
19 Molesey	42	10	6	16	40	93	36
20 Cheshunt	42	7	13	22	51	84	34
21 Wivenhoe Town	42	8	9	25	55	111	33
22 Romford	42	4	7	31	42	105	19

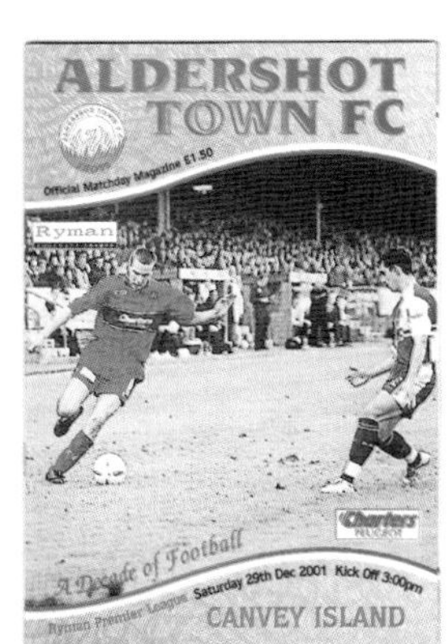

Left: the programme for Aldershot Town's 3-1 home defeat by Canvey Island.

Right: the Tring Town programme for the same season.

2001-02 Division III	1	2	3	4	5	6	7	8	9	10	11	12	13	14	15	16	17	18	19	20	21	22
1 Abingdon Town	*	1–2	3–1	2–0	1–2	4–0	1–1	1–2	2–2	0–3	0–1	0–2	1–0	0–3	0–2	3–1	0–0	1–1	1–3	1–0	1–1	4–0
2 Aveley	5–1	*	3–1	3–0	2–1	6–1	2–2	0–3	1–1	5–0	3–1	2–2	4–0	7–0	1–2	4–4	4–3	3–1	4–1	1–3	7–0	7–1
3 Bracknell Town	3–0	2–0	*	5–0	6–0	5–1	2–0	3–2	3–0	3–1	3–1	1–2	2–0	3–2	0–2	4–0	3–0	2–2	2–1	2–2	2–0	3–1
4 Camberley Town	2–0	1–3	1–1	*	2–2	0–0	1–1	1–1	1–1	3–2	1–3	1–4	1–1	3–2	0–2	3–1	1–0	1–2	0–4	0–3	2–1	1–2
5 Chalfont St. Peter	3–4	2–0	3–2	1–0	*	3–1	0–1	0–3	6–2	2–0	0–1	0–4	2–3	3–6	1–3	1–0	2–1	0–2	1–4	0–0	1–1	4–1
6 Clapton	1–0	0–2	3–4	1–0	3–1	*	0–2	0–7	1–2	4–2	0–2	0–1	0–2	1–4	0–5	1–1	2–1	1–2	1–0	1–4	1–1	2–3
7 Corinthian-Casuals	1–0	3–0	1–0	2–1	3–1	5–0	*	1–1	2–1	0–1	3–3	0–0	0–0	4–2	1–2	0–1	4–0	0–0	3–0	1–2	3–1	3–0
8 Croydon Athletic	4–0	5–2	4–1	2–0	2–0	8–1	4–2	*	4–0	3–0	3–0	4–2	6–1	6–0	3–0	5–2	2–0	8–0	2–1	2–0	1–0	5–2
9 Dorking	2–1	2–1	1–1	4–1	2–1	4–1	0–3	2–1	*	4–2	1–1	2–2	1–2	2–0	2–6	5–2	0–2	3–0	0–0	4–0	0–0	1–0
10 Edgware Town	0–5	2–2	2–0	2–2	1–3	0–1	1–1	0–3	1–4	*	1–4	1–1	1–2	1–2	3–1	1–2	7–1	6–3	2–3	3–4	2–5	1–1
11 Egham Town	0–0	1–2	0–1	3–1	2–1	1–0	1–1	1–1	2–2	3–0	*	1–1	1–0	3–2	2–1	2–1	3–0	2–1	1–1	4–2	3–1	1–4
12 Epsom & Ewell	3–1	1–2	3–3	2–1	5–1	3–0	1–0	2–2	2–2	3–1	0–0	*	1–0	1–1	2–2	2–2	1–1	1–2	2–0	0–1	1–1	1–1
13 Flackwell Heath	4–1	0–3	3–5	1–2	5–3	0–5	1–1	3–7	0–3	0–3	1–2	1–2	*	0–8	1–3	4–2	2–2	1–1	0–2	1–3	2–4	2–0
14 Hertford Town	3–1	0–2	0–2	3–0	1–2	5–1	0–0	0–0	1–1	0–2	5–2	3–2	2–1	*	2–0	2–2	3–1	3–0	2–1	1–1	6–2	3–2
15 Hornchurch	2–2	2–1	0–0	5–1	6–3	6–0	4–0	3–2	3–0	2–3	2–0	0–0	1–1	1–1	*	1–0	1–1	4–1	1–0	4–2	1–1	5–1
16 Kingsbury Town	4–2	0–3	1–2	3–1	0–3	0–2	0–0	3–2	1–2	3–2	2–2	2–3	1–3	1–2	1–1	*	1–1	0–1	1–1	1–4	2–4	1–1
17 Leighton Town	0–3	1–2	2–2	3–0	1–0	5–2	0–3	0–6	3–3	1–1	0–2	1–2	3–1	3–1	3–2	1–2	*	0–0	4–4	1–4	1–1	2–6
18 Tring Town	4–0	3–0	1–1	3–0	2–4	6–1	1–0	1–0	0–3	3–3	0–3	2–0	0–0	1–0	1–2	2–1	3–1	*	4–2	1–2	2–0	2–2
19 Ware	3–0	0–4	4–2	6–0	1–1	4–2	5–2	0–4	0–0	6–1	5–1	1–3	3–2	1–2	0–2	2–2	0–0	0–1	*	1–1	1–1	0–5
20 Wingate & Finch	1–4	0–0	0–1	2–0	2–0	5–2	2–1	3–2	1–3	2–0	2–2	0–2	0–0	2–3	1–1	3–0	4–1	0–0	2–1	*	2–3	5–0
21 Witham Town	0–3	1–2	0–1	5–0	2–3	0–0	0–2	3–1	3–1	2–0	4–2	0–3	4–1	1–0	1–1	1–0	4–3	1–2	0–2	3–2	*	3–0
22 Wokingham Town	3–6	0–2	2–6	1–1	4–2	2–1	2–6	0–5	2–2	2–0	0–2	5–2	3–1	5–2	1–2	2–4	1–2	0–0	7–0	2–1	2–0	*

Division III	P	W	D	L	F	A	Pts
1 Croydon Athletic	42	30	5	7	138	41	96
2 Hornchurch	42	25	11	6	96	46	86
3 Aveley	42	26	6	10	109	55	84
4 Bracknell Town	42	25	8	9	96	54	83
5 Epsom & Ewell	42	20	15	7	81	51	75
6 Egham Town	42	21	11	10	72	59	74
7 Wingate & Finch	42	20	9	13	80	60	69
8 Dorking	42	18	14	10	77	66	68
9 Tring Town	42	19	11	12	64	62	68
10 Corinthian-Casuals	42	18	13	11	69	44	67
11 Hertford Town	42	20	7	15	88	74	67
12 Witham Town	42	15	10	17	66	72	55
13 Ware	42	14	10	18	74	76	52
14 Chalfont St. Peter	42	15	4	23	69	92	49
15 Wokingham Town	42	14	6	22	79	107	48
16 Abingdon Town	42	13	7	22	61	75	46
17 Leighton Town	42	8	12	22	56	95	36
18 Kingsbury Town	42	8	11	23	58	91	35
19 Edgware Town	42	9	7	26	65	101	34
20 Flackwell Heath*	42	9	8	25	53	99	32
21 Clapton	42	9	4	29	45	118	31
22 Camberley Town	42	7	9	26	37	95	30

** Flackwell Heath had three points deducted.*

Left: the League's handbook for 2002-03.

Right: Billericay Town's programme for that season.

2002–03 - Aldershot Town, under the guidance of manager Terry Brown, secured the Premier Division championship and subsequent promotion to the Football Conference by thirteen points from nearest challengers Canvey Island who for the third year running finished as runners-up. Hendon, who enjoyed their best League position for several years, finished third closely followed by St. Albans City, Basingstoke Town and Sutton United. At the foot of the table four clubs were relegated, namely Chesham United, Boreham Wood, eight-times champions Enfield and Hampton & Richmond Borough. In Division One North a close championship saw Northwood, who scored over 100 goals pip Hornchurch, who were in Division Three the previous season, by one point while in the South Division Carshalton Athletic won the title by four points from Sussex clubs Bognor Regis Town and Lewes with the former having a better goal-difference to claim promotion to the Premier Division. At the bottom of the table Hertford Town were relegated to Division Two after their brief stay in Division One North while Chertsey Town were relegated from Division One South. The third relegation place saw Metropolitan Police defeat Wembley on aggregate in a play-off. In Division Two Cheshunt, who were relegated the previous season, bounced straight back after making the relevant ground improvements and were joined by Leyton, in their first season, and South Midlands League champions Dunstable Town.

At the Annual General Meeting Kettering Town were elected to replace Aldershot Town who won promotion to the Football Conference while Dunstable Town were elected to Division One North from the Spartan-South Midlands League.

Premier Division	1	2	3	4	5	6	7	8	9	10	11	12	13	14	15	16	17	18	19	20	21	22	23	24
1 Aldershot Town	*	1–0	0–3	2–1	0–0	0–0	1–0	3–0	1–0	1–2	2–0	2–1	2–1	4–0	0–1	1–0	6–2	2–0	1–0	2–1	1–1	1–0	5–1	3–2
2 Aylesbury United	3–2	*	1–1	1–1	0–1	1–2	3–3	1–1	1–6	2–1	4–1	2–0	3–2	3–0	0–0	3–0	0–1	2–1	2–2	1–0	0–0	1–1	0–3	0–4
3 Basingstoke Town	0–1	2–2	*	2–1	2–0	3–1	1–1	2–1	2–1	2–1	2–3	3–0	3–1	3–1	1–2	3–1	0–2	2–2	3–0	0–1	3–2	2–1	3–1	1–0
4 Bedford Town	1–2	4–0	0–0	*	2–0	3–1	0–4	1–0	2–1	0–4	8–2	0–2	1–0	1–0	1–1	2–1	2–3	1–2	2–1	5–2	0–0	2–0	2–0	2–1
5 Billericay Town	0–1	1–1	1–0	4–0	*	1–1	0–0	1–2	2–1	1–0	0–1	1–3	4–1	0–2	1–0	1–1	0–0	2–0	1–2	0–2	2–0	1–3	1–0	2–0
6 Bishop's Stortford	1–1	2–2	3–1	1–1	1–0	*	1–4	1–1	1–2	2–1	1–0	0–1	1–3	2–1	4–0	2–3	4–1	2–0	2–3	2–2	3–4	2–2	0–2	1–0
7 Boreham Wood	0–1	1–2	1–5	0–1	1–3	1–1	*	1–2	1–3	0–0	2–1	3–2	0–2	0–0	2–2	2–0	1–1	0–0	2–2	2–1	0–3	0–0	1–0	3–0
8 Braintree Town	2–1	2–2	0–3	2–0	1–0	1–3	0–1	*	2–4	1–2	1–3	1–0	1–1	3–1	2–4	0–1	1–2	3–0	1–3	1–2	1–2	0–0	2–2	0–1
9 Canvey Island	0–1	2–1	4–0	1–1	3–0	0–4	1–0	1–1	*	4–1	10–1	3–1	2–0	4–0	2–1	2–2	4–4	4–1	3–1	1–1	3–2	2–2	6–1	1–1
10 Chesham United	1–3	1–3	3–2	1–3	0–2	3–1	3–1	1–1	2–4	*	2–2	2–2	2–1	1–0	1–1	2–3	1–1	3–0	2–1	0–4	0–0	1–1	1–3	2–0
11 Enfield	1–2	0–0	3–1	1–2	1–1	0–2	1–0	1–1	1–2	1–0	*	1–1	1–1	2–0	0–1	0–1	0–0	2–3	0–5	2–2	1–1	1–0	0–1	1–4
12 Ford United	2–3	1–2	2–3	2–0	0–2	3–2	1–1	3–0	1–3	2–0	3–1	*	1–0	3–0	2–0	3–3	1–3	3–3	2–2	2–2	0–3	1–1	1–1	3–4
13 Grays Athletic	0–0	3–1	1–2	0–0	1–0	1–0	2–1	1–2	1–2	1–0	3–0	1–2	*	1–1	4–1	1–0	0–2	0–2	1–1	1–1	1–4	2–1	0–1	0–0
14 Hampton & Rich	1–3	2–1	0–0	0–2	1–1	1–0	0–4	0–1	0–2	1–3	0–1	2–3	1–1	*	0–2	1–1	1–1	1–1	0–2	2–2	1–1	1–1	2–3	1–3
15 Harrow Borough	0–2	2–2	1–2	0–2	1–2	2–2	2–0	2–2	1–2	3–0	2–0	4–0	0–4	1–0	*	1–3	1–3	2–1	2–0	2–1	1–1	1–2	0–4	0–1
16 Hayes	1–0	1–1	1–0	2–0	0–2	2–0	0–0	1–3	2–1	1–0	4–0	2–0	1–0	2–1	6–0	*	0–0	2–2	2–1	2–2	0–2	1–2	3–0	2–2
17 Hendon	1–3	3–1	2–1	0–2	2–1	0–3	0–2	2–0	1–0	0–1	3–0	3–1	1–0	3–3	1–1	2–0	*	0–0	2–1	1–1	1–1	1–2	0–2	0–2
18 Heybridge Swifts	0–4	1–0	2–4	1–0	1–1	3–3	1–0	2–0	0–2	0–0	2–1	4–4	1–1	1–0	0–1	1–0	0–4	*	31	2–4	0–0	0–2	3–3	1–3
19 Hitchin Town	1–3	2–3	1–0	2–1	1–0	0–1	2–1	0–0	2–3	1–1	7–1	2–2	3–3	1–1	1–0	2–3	2–2	0–1	*	0–0	2–3	1–1	1–2	2–0
20 Kingstonian	0–2	1–0	2–1	2–2	2–0	31	0–0	1–4	0–4	5–1	4–2	0–2	1–0	1–1	1–3	1–1	0–1	4–0	0–0	*	2–0	0–1	0–2	2–1
21 Maidenhead Utd	1–2	2–1	2–2	3–2	1–0	2–3	2–1	2–3	1–1	5–0	3–3	0–4	0–2	1–1	2–0	1–1	0–1	2–2	1–2	4–4	*	1–0	0–1	4–1
22 Purfleet	1–2	1–0	1–0	3–0	0–0	2–1	0–0	1–1	3–2	6–0	5–2	2–2	3–1	5–2	4–2	1–2	1–0	1–2	0–1	0–1	1–0	*	1–0	0–2
23 St. Albans City	2–0	3–1	1–2	1–2	1–1	3–2	2–0	2–4	2–1	1–0	0–0	3–2	1–2	2–0	1–0	1–1	1–4	2–0	0–1	2–2	1–3	2–2	*	2–1
24 Sutton United	1–1	3–2	1–1	0–0	1–2	2–1	3–2	3–1	0–2	3–2	2–1	4–1	2–0	1–0	3–0	2–1	2–3	2–0	3–1	1–1	2–2	1–1	2–4	*

2002-03

Premier Division		P	W	D	L	F	A	Pts
1	Aldershot Town	46	33	6	7	81	36	105
2	Canvey Island	46	28	8	10	112	56	92
3	Hendon	46	22	13	11	70	56	79
4	St. Albans City	46	23	8	15	73	65	77
5	Basingstoke Town	46	23	7	16	80	60	76
6	Sutton United	46	22	9	15	77	62	75
7	Hayes	46	20	13	13	67	54	73
8	Purfleet	46	19	15	12	68	48	72
9	Bedford Town	46	21	9	17	66	58	72
10	Maidenhead Utd	46	16	17	13	75	63	65
11	Kingstonian	46	16	17	13	71	64	65
12	Billericay Town	46	17	11	18	46	44	62
13	Bishop's Stortford	46	16	11	19	74	72	59
14	Hitchin Town	46	15	13	18	69	67	58
15	Ford United	46	15	12	19	78	84	57
16	Braintree Town	46	14	12	20	59	71	54
17	Aylesbury United	46	13	15	18	62	75	54
18	Harrow Borough	46	15	9	22	54	75	54
19	Grays Athletic	46	14	11	21	53	59	53
20	Heybridge Swifts	46	13	14	19	52	80	53
21	Chesham United	46	14	10	22	56	81	52
22	Boreham Wood	46	11	15	20	50	58	48
23	Enfield	46	9	11	26	47	101	38
24	Hampton & R Boro	46	3	14	29	35	86	23

Left: the Canvey Island programme for 2002-03.

Right: the Bishop's Stortford edition for the same campaign.

Division I North		1	2	3	4	5	6	7	8	9	10	11	12	13	14	15	16	17	18	19	20	21	22	23	24
1	Arlesey Town	*	0–0	0–0	1–0	2–2	2–0	0–4	1–2	0–0	6–0	2–2	3–1	0–0	2–3	1–0	1–0	3–3	0–2	0–1	3–3	3–2	0–0	1–1	2–1
2	Aveley	3–3	*	1–2	2–1	0–3	1–0	1–1	1–0	1–1	1–0	0–2	0–1	1–0	1–2	0–0	1–1	1–2	2–0	2–1	1–2	2–0	1–0	3–1	1–1
3	Barking & EHU	3–1	1–3	*	0–3	3–5	4–0	0–4	3–1	0–1	1–0	1–1	2–0	1–2	0–0	0–0	2–1	2–1	1–0	0–1	2–0	1–5	0–2	3–4	2–3
4	Barton Rovers	1–0	1–1	1–2	*	0–0	0–4	0–0	1–0	2–0	2–1	0–1	0–1	1–2	3–2	1–2	2–2	1–0	2–3	1–0	0–1	1–2	0–3	1–0	2–0
5	Berkhamsted Town	1–2	1–2	2–2	3–1	*	3–0	4–2	2–2	1–0	4–0	1–1	2–0	1–4	3–4	4–2	3–1	2–3	3–0	0–1	1–5	3–1	1–0	6–2	3–2
6	East Thurrock Utd	2–1	0–1	0–4	2–5	1–1	*	5–0	0–0	2–0	5–1	4–3	0–1	3–3	2–3	2–1	0–2	1–1	3–1	1–0	2–2	5–0	2–0	3–3	3–2
7	Great Wakering R	2–3	1–1	4–3	2–1	1–1	0–4	*	1–1	0–1	2–0	3–3	2–0	0–0	2–0	0–1	2–2	0–0	0–1	0–3	2–1	5–0	1–1	3–2	3–2
8	Harlow Town	3–1	2–1	3–2	0–0	1–1	1–0	2–0	*	0–2	0–2	0–0	0–0	2–1	1–3	0–0	2–2	2–0	2–0	0–1	0–1	2–1	0–2	3–1	2–0
9	Hemel Hempstead	1–1	0–1	2–1	2–1	2–3	4–1	2–3	0–2	*	3–1	1–3	2–1	1–0	3–2	1–0	2–2	3–1	3–2	1–3	2–1	2–1	1–0	1–0	2–1
10	Hertford Town	2–4	0–3	1–3	0–4	2–2	0–1	1–1	1–2	0–2	*	1–2	2–2	2–6	0–5	0–1	1–3	1–3	0–1	1–3	3–2	2–0	3–3	0–1	2–0
11	Hornchurch	4–3	0–1	5–1	1–1	5–3	1–1	2–1	1–2	2–2	2–1	*	2–1	0–3	1–0	3–1	3–2	1–1	2–0	0–0	3–0	6–0	1–0	0–0	1–1
12	Leyton Pennant	0–1	0–2	1–2	1–0	1–1	0–2	1–2	0–1	0–2	2–3	0–0	*	1–1	1–3	0–1	0–2	0–1	2–3	2–4	1–2	2–1	1–0	0–0	2–1
13	Marlow	1–0	4–3	1–2	3–1	0–0	1–4	0–0	4–1	0–2	4–1	2–3	4–0	*	1–0	1–2	2–3	2–1	2–0	0–0	2–0	0–1	2–2	2–1	1–4
14	Northwood	6–0	1–1	1–2	2–1	2–0	4–2	4–0	1–4	2–1	5–1	2–0	5–1	1–3	*	2–1	5–1	2–0	5–1	0–1	2–1	6–1	4–1	1–0	3–3
15	Oxford City	0–1	0–0	4–1	2–1	0–2	2–0	1–2	3–2	1–1	3–0	1–1	2–1	2–0	0–3	*	1–1	1–1	5–0	1–0	0–3	1–1	2–2	5–0	2–2
16	Slough Town	3–0	1–1	3–1	1–0	3–2	2–0	4–0	1–1	0–1	2–2	1–1	5–1	2–0	2–1	3–0	*	2–0	5–1	1–1	1–1	2–1	0–3	4–0	0–2
17	Thame United	2–1	1–1	2–1	1–0	1–1	1–3	2–0	0–0	8–2	0–0	0–1	3–1	4–0	0–1	1–0	1–1	*	3–0	4–0	4–2	5–0	0–1	7–0	0–1
18	Tilbury	1–4	1–1	0–1	3–1	2–1	1–1	1–1	3–2	1–0	2–1	1–2	1–1	0–2	0–3	0–0*	3–0	1–6	*	1–4	2–0	2–1	1–3	0–3	3–5
19	Uxbridge	2–0	2–0	1–1	5–0	1–2	1–1	0–0	3–1	1–0	4–1	0–1	3–2	0–0	0–0	1–0	0–1	2–1	1–4	*	1–0	2–1	1–1	1–0	3–1
20	Wealdstone	1–3	0–2	2–2	2–3	3–0	3–0	4–2	1–1	0–2	4–0	1–0	1–0	2–0	4–4	4–0	3–2	1–2	4–1	2–1	*	1–1	3–2	3–2	2–0
21	Wembley	0–3	2–6	2–2	2–3	0–2	1–1	2–3	1–5	1–1	3–1	0–4	0–1	1–1	2–2	0–2	2–2	2–4	4–2	2–1	0–0	*	4–1	2–3	0–3
22	Wingate & Finch	1–2	1–2	0–3	1–0	0–4	3–0	3–0	1–4	1–4	2–3	0–1	4–1	4–3	1–2	1–1	2–3	1–0	2–1	1–1	5–2	1–1	*	1–1	2–2
23	Wivenhoe Town	3–1	2–1	1–2	1–2	1–1	4–1	0–1	1–3	0–2	3–1	1–5	1–2	1–3	0–0	0–1	1–2	2–2	1–1	2–0	1–4	2–2	2–3	*	0–3
24	Yeading	2–1	3–5	1–1	1–1	0–1	5–1	0–1	2–1	1–2	5–1	1–2	2–1	2–1	1–0	1–0	0–2	1–1	1–1	1–0	1–1	2–1	3–2	1–1	*

** Tilbury v Oxford City was awarded 0–0 by the Board of Directors.*

Division I North		P	W	D	L	F	A	Pts
1	Northwood	46	28	7	11	109	56	91
2	Hornchurch	46	25	15	6	85	48	90
3	Hemel Hempstead	46	26	7	13	70	55	85
4	Slough Town	46	22	14	10	86	59	80
5	Uxbridge	46	23	10	13	62	41	79
6	Aveley	46	21	14	11	66	48	77
7	Berkhamsted Town	46	21	13	12	92	68	76
8	Thame United	46	20	12	14	84	51	72
9	Wealdstone	46	21	9	16	85	69	72
10	Harlow Town	46	20	12	14	66	53	72
11	Marlow	46	19	10	17	74	63	67
12	Barking & EHU	46	19	9	18	73	76	66
13	Yeading	46	18	11	17	77	69	65
14	Great Wakering R	46	17	14	15	64	70	65
15	Oxford City	46	17	13	16	55	51	64
16	Arlesey Town	46	17	12	17	69	71	63
17	East Thurrock Utd	46	17	10	19	75	79	61
18	Wingate & Finch	46	15	11	20	70	74	56
19	Barton Rovers	46	15	7	24	53	65	52
20	Tilbury	46	14	7	25	55	96	49
21	Wivenhoe Town	46	9	11	26	56	94	38
22	Leyton Pennant	46	9	7	30	38	81	34
23	Wembley	46	7	11	28	57	111	32
24	Hertford Town	46	6	6	34	46	119	24

Left: the Dulwich Hamlet programme for 2002-03.

Right: the Tilbury programme for the same campaign.

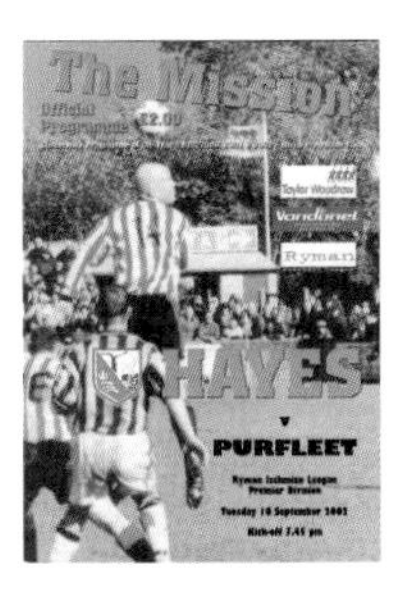

2002-03

Division I South	1	2	3	4	5	6	7	8	9	10	11	12	13	14	15	16	17	18	19	20	21	22	23	24
1 Ashford Town (Mx)	*	0–0	0–1	0–0	1–1	0–2	2–0	1–1	1–0	0–2	0–5	1–3	1–1	0–1	0–1	0–3	2–1	1–2	0–0	1–1	2–1	1–1	0–3	4–0
2 Banstead Athletic	2–3	*	0–1	0–1	3–3	0–2	3–1	4–0	2–3	0–1	4–1	3–2	4–0	1–1	1–1	1–1	1–0	2–5	0–1	2–1	0–4	1–0	1–2	0–0
3 Bognor Regis Tn	8–0	1–0	*	0–1	1–1	1–0	6–0	1–1	3–1	2–0	0–1	3–1	3–0	1–3	0–0	0–2	4–0	1–1	3–0	3–0	3–0	3–0	2–1	3–0
4 Bracknell Town	1–1	1–1	3–1	*	2–1	1–4	4–2	3–2	2–2	0–3	0–4	0–1	0–3	1–2	5–2	1–2	1–2	0–3	0–0	2–2	0–1	0–1	1–0	1–4
5 Bromley	2–1	2–2	2–1	2–0	*	0–3	4–1	2–0	3–1	0–1	1–1	1–2	1–0	1–0	1–0	3–2	2–3	0–2	2–2	2–3	3–0	1–1	0–0	1–3
6 Carshalton Athletic	1–0	1–0	1–0	2–2	1–4	*	1–0	2–2	1–0	2–1	2–0	0–1	2–0	2–1	2–0	4–1	2–0	1–1	1–1	2–3	1–2	2–1	1–0	2–1
7 Chertsey Town	0–5	1–0	0–2	1–1	1–4	0–2	*	0–1	4–1	1–2	1–2	1–2	0–3	1–1	2–8	1–5	1–2	2–2	0–1	0–7	1–6	1–4	1–2	0–1
8 Corinthian-Casuals	1–2	0–1	0–3	0–0	0–0	1–2	5–0	*	1–1	1–1	1–2	0–4	1–0	1–2	3–0	1–2	1–0	0–3	1–0	0–3	1–1	1–1	1–0	1–1
9 Croydon	2–1	0–0	0–6	1–1	1–1	1–2	3–1	0–3	*	1–1	1–0	3–1	0–0	0–2	1–2	1–3	1–0	1–0	3–1	0–1	2–2	2–0	0–2	4–1
10 Croydon Athletic	0–1	1–1	1–0	0–1	1–2	0–1	2–0	0–4	3–0	*	0–2	2–1	1–1	0–5	1–1	2–2	1–1	1–3	1–1	1–5	2–0	2–3	2–3	0–0
11 Dulwich Hamlet	2–0	0–0	0–0	2–2	0–2	1–0	3–1	4–2	0–1	2–1	*	2–0	3–1	3–1	3–2	2–2	1–1	1–0	1–0	4–0	1–1	2–3	2–0	2–2
12 Egham Town	0–3	0–0	1–6	0–3	1–0	1–1	3–3	3–1	1–0	1–1	3–0	*	0–3	1–0	1–1	1–5	0–0	2–1	2–1	2–0	3–3	0–1	1–1	3–0
13 Epsom & Ewell	3–0	1–3	1–1	3–2	1–2	1–4	3–0	0–0	4–0	1–0	3–3	1–0	*	1–1	2–1	0–7	1–0	1–0	1–0	2–2	1–0	1–3	4–0	1–5
14 Horsham	1–0	2–0	1–2	3–3	1–1	0–1	4–0	0–1	6–1	2–2	1–0	1–2	2–1	*	1–2	2–2	2–0	6–2	0–2	3–3	0–1	4–2	1–0	3–3
15 Leatherhead	2–0	2–2	0–0	1–1	1–1	0–3	3–3	2–2	5–2	4–2	3–1	0–2	1–1	0–2	*	0–1	6–2	0–1	0–1	1–1	4–0	1–0	2–0	1–0
16 Lewes	5–2	0–2	2–2	2–0	1–0	3–1	7–0	5–0	0–2	3–2	2–0	2–0	1–0	1–0	0–0	*	1–1	3–2	2–2	0–1	1–1	1–1	6–2	0–2
17 Metropolitan Police	1–1	1–3	0–2	2–2	2–2	1–2	2–1	2–1	3–2	3–0	1–1	2–3	0–1	0–1	2–1	0–3	*	0–2	2–2	0–2	0–2	0–1	0–2	2–1
18 Molesey	0–2	0–2	1–5	1–1	2–1	1–1	1–2	1–0	1–2	0–4	0–1	0–0	0–1	0–1	4–1	0–7	3–1	*	1–2	0–2	0–1	1–0	1–1	1–1
19 Staines Town	0–2	1–1	0–3	1–0	1–2	2–2	2–2	2–0	2–1	1–0	0–0	5–0	2–2	1–1	4–1	1–1	1–2	4–1	*	1–2	0–7	0–0	1–0	0–0
20 Tooting & M Utd	3–1	1–2	4–0	2–3	0–1	0–2	5–0	0–1	1–2	1–1	0–2	1–2	3–4	1–4	2–0	1–1	2–4	1–1	3–2	*	1–3	1–2	3–3	0–4
21 Walton & Hersham	0–2	1–1	0–0	3–1	2–1	3–0	5–2	1–1	2–0	3–1	1–3	4–2	0–0	2–3	1–3	2–2	2–0	3–0	1–2	2–2	*	2–2	0–2	2–4
22 Whyteleafe	0–1	1–0	3–1	0–1	1–2	3–1	3–3	5–0	4–1	0–0	0–0	2–1	2–2	4–1	1–0	2–2	1–0	1–2	3–0	1–2	2–2	*	2–0	4–1
23 Windsor & Eton	1–1	5–0	0–2	2–0	0–1	1–1	1–0	1–1	2–3	0–1	1–0	3–2	4–3	3–1	0–2	0–0	1–1	3–1	2–1	5–2	1–4	1–2	*	2–0
24 Worthing	5–0	3–2	1–1	2–2	0–1	2–0	3–1	3–1	5–2	0–1	2–3	0–0	1–3	2–1	1–3	2–1	1–3	3–1	4–3	0–2	0–3	0–0	4–3	*

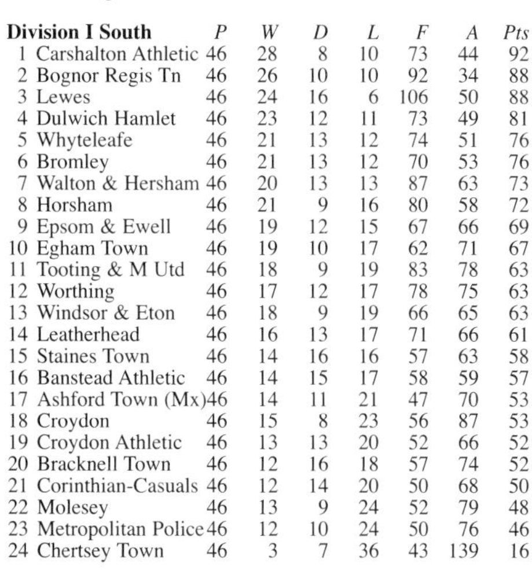

Division I South	P	W	D	L	F	A	Pts
1 Carshalton Athletic	46	28	8	10	73	44	92
2 Bognor Regis Tn	46	26	10	10	92	34	88
3 Lewes	46	24	16	6	106	50	88
4 Dulwich Hamlet	46	23	12	11	73	49	81
5 Whyteleafe	46	21	13	12	74	51	76
6 Bromley	46	21	13	12	70	53	76
7 Walton & Hersham	46	20	13	13	87	63	73
8 Horsham	46	21	9	16	80	58	72
9 Epsom & Ewell	46	19	12	15	67	66	69
10 Egham Town	46	19	10	17	62	71	67
11 Tooting & M Utd	46	18	9	19	83	78	63
12 Worthing	46	17	12	17	78	75	63
13 Windsor & Eton	46	18	9	19	66	65	63
14 Leatherhead	46	16	13	17	71	66	61
15 Staines Town	46	14	16	16	57	63	58
16 Banstead Athletic	46	14	15	17	58	59	57
17 Ashford Town (Mx)	46	14	11	21	47	70	53
18 Croydon	46	15	8	23	56	87	53
19 Croydon Athletic	46	13	13	20	52	66	52
20 Bracknell Town	46	12	16	18	57	74	52
21 Corinthian-Casuals	46	12	14	20	50	68	50
22 Molesey	46	13	9	24	52	79	48
23 Metropolitan Police	46	12	10	24	50	76	46
24 Chertsey Town	46	3	7	36	43	139	16

Left: the Croydon programme for 2002-03.

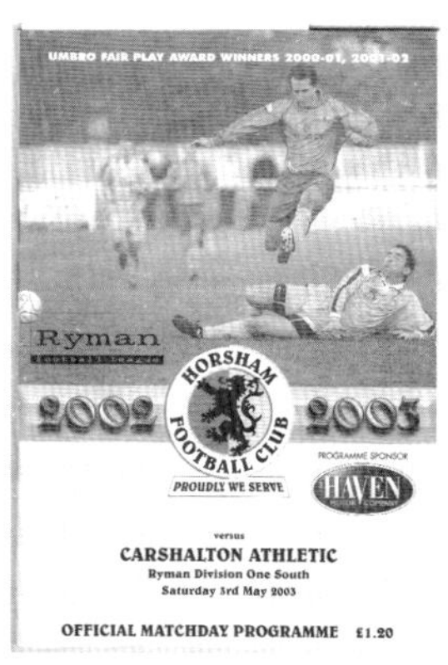

Right: the Horsham edition for the same campaign.

Below right: the Hitchin Town programme for the season.

Division II	1	2	3	4	5	6	7	8	9	10	11	12	13	14	15	16
1 Abingdon Town	*	4–0	3–1	1–2	2–2	2–1	1–1	2–3	0–0	1–1	3–1	5–1	6–1	1–0	0–0	2–0
2 Camberley Town	0–3	*	1–4	2–3	1–2	2–0	0–0	0–2	1–3	0–1	0–2	1–1	0–3	2–0	0–1	1–3
3 Chalfont St. Peter	1–2	0–1	*	0–4	0–3	1–0	1–3	1–4	1–2	3–0	5–3	1–3	2–1	0–3	0–0	2–2
4 Cheshunt	4–1	2–1	3–0	*	3–0	1–0	6–1	3–1	0–0	7–0	2–1	1–1	3–2	2–1	3–1	4–1
5 Clapton	2–2	2–1	2–0	0–5	*	3–3	0–5	2–4	2–0	0–1	0–2	1–1	3–1	3–0	1–1	2–1
6 Dorking	2–2	2–0	2–2	3–6	0–1	*	1–2	1–2	1–1	1–1	2–1	0–7	0–1	1–2	4–0	5–0
7 Edgware Town	0–3	0–1	0–4	1–3	0–1	3–6	*	3–0	0–1	1–6	1–0	3–1	2–3	2–1	3–1	9–1
8 Flackwell Heath	0–4	3–2	1–0	0–2	2–1	3–0	3–1	*	1–3	2–0	1–0	0–2	3–2	2–1	1–2	0–1
9 Hungerford Town	1–1	1–0	5–1	1–3	3–0	2–0	3–2	1–2	*	2–2	1–0	0–2	1–1	1–1	1–1	2–2
10 Kingsbury Town	1–1	1–1	2–2	2–0	2–1	0–0	1–0	2–2	0–0	*	1–1	0–2	3–1	0–1	2–0	0–1
11 Leighton Town	3–3	2–1	2–0	0–5	0–1	3–0	8–0	3–3	2–3	5–2	*	0–1	0–1	2–1	2–0	2–3
12 Leyton	8–0	3–0	4–0	5–2	1–0	4–0	3–1	3–0	3–2	0–0	1–3	*	1–0	2–0	3–0	5–0
13 Tring Town	2–0	3–0	1–1	1–6	0–2	3–1	2–1	0–2	3–1	7–1	2–7	0–2	*	2–3	2–1	1–1
14 Ware	3–5	0–0	2–1	1–4	3–2	4–2	3–1	2–1	1–1	3–2	0–3	0–0	3–1	*	1–2	3–3
15 Witham Town	0–4	7–2	2–0	0–0	1–0	3–2	1–3	0–0	1–1	2–1	0–1	2–1	2–2	4–2	*	1–0
16 Wokingham Town	1–1	3–2	2–0	1–2	2–1	1–9	0–0	0–4	2–6	1–3	0–2	0–6	0–0	1–2	1–4	*

Division II	P	W	D	L	F	A	Pts
1 Cheshunt	30	25	3	2	91	29	78
2 Leyton	30	21	5	4	77	22	68
3 Flackwell Heath	30	17	3	10	52	44	54
4 Abingdon Town	30	14	11	5	65	42	53
5 Hungerford Town	30	12	12	6	49	36	48
6 Leighton Town	30	14	3	13	61	43	45
7 Witham Town	30	12	8	10	40	43	44
8 Ware	30	12	5	13	47	53	41
9 Clapton	30	12	5	13	40	47	41
10 Tring Town	30	11	5	14	49	58	38
11 Kingsbury Town	30	9	11	10	38	48	38
12 Edgware Town	30	10	3	17	49	65	33
13 Wokingham Town	30	7	7	16	34	81	28
14 Dorking	30	6	6	18	49	63	24
15 Chalfont St. Peter	30	6	5	19	34	63	23
16 Camberley Town	30	4	4	22	23	61	16

Left: the Cheshunt programme for 2002-03.

Right: the Carshalton Athletic edition for the same campaign.

2003–04 - Following the Football Association's decision to restructure the game below the Football League, of which details can be found elsewhere in this book, season 2003-04 proved to be the last in the present format with no less than 15 clubs moving to the new Conference South at the end of the season.

Two weeks before the season opened, the League was notified of the immediate resignation of Tring Town from Division Two due to financial problems suffered during the close season. The League decided that due to the shortage of matches for clubs from the division, clubs would play each other three times giving them a total of 42 League games.

After three years of being the bridesmaid, Canvey Island finally claimed the Premier Division championship by 19 points and scoring 106 goals including 42 by prolific marksman Lee Boylan. Sutton United, who last won the championship in 1998 finished runners-up, two points ahead of Purfleet and Hendon, with Hornchurch, who had progressed through the divisions, ending their first season in the Premier Division in fifth place. In Division One North, Yeading won the title by seven points from Leyton with Cheshunt in third while in Division One South a closer finish ensued with Lewes finishing ahead of Sussex rivals Worthing by two points, closely followed by Windsor & Eton and Slough Town. In Division Two a two-horse race developed between Leighton Town and Dorking resulting in the former winning the championship by two points.

During the close season a lot of activity took place with clubs switching from leagues in the first phase of restructuring as follows: Canvey Island were promoted to the Football Conference and Kettering Town promoted to Conference North with Sutton United, Thurrock *(previously Purfleet)*, Hornchurch, Grays Athletic, Carshalton Athletic, Hayes, Bognor Regis Town, Bishop's Stortford, Maidenhead United and Ford United automatically promoted to Conference South with St. Albans City and Lewes joining them via a series of play-offs. Hendon opted not to join the new set-up and were subsequently replaced by Basingstoke Town who finished in the next available place. Leyton, Cheshunt, Chesham United, Dunstable Town, Hemel Hempstead Town moved up from Division One North and Worthing, Windsor & Eton, Slough Town, Hampton & Richmond Borough and Staines Town from Division One South. There was one remaining place still available; seventh placed Wealdstone from Division One North met seventh placed Dulwich Hamlet from Division One South in a play-off match which resulted in a win for Wealdstone on penalties after a 2–2 drawn game.

At the end of the season a further 27 clubs switched to the Southern League and the League welcomed 16 new clubs into their constitution including 13 transferred from the Southern League. Division Two would remain under the League's constitution as a Step Five League and Ilford opted to join the division switching from the Essex Senior League. However Wokingham Town had resigned from the League, opting to merge with Embrook, and would be known as Wokingham Town & Embrook competing in the Hellenic League.

Premier Division	1	2	3	4	5	6	7	8	9	10	11	12	13	14	15	16	17	18	19	20	21	22	23	24
1 Aylesbury United	*	0–3	3–3	3–2	0–1	1–0	0–0	0–2	1–1	3–2	0–3	0–1	0–1	1–1	0–0	1–4	0–2	0–2	0–0	1–3	1–2	0–2	0–6	2–4
2 Basingstoke Town	2–0	*	2–0	0–1	1–2	0–1	3–0	1–2	1–2	1–0	0–2	0–1	0–2	1–4	1–1	2–3	0–3	2–2	2–1	2–1	2–0	1–1	0–5	0–3
3 Bedford Town	4–1	5–2	*	2–1	0–3	8–0	2–0	2–4	1–0	1–1	0–4	2–0	1–2	0–2	3–1	1–2	2–1	2–3	0–0	1–2	1–4	1–0	2–1	0–0
4 Billericay Town	2–2	3–1	0–0	*	1–0	1–1	0–1	0–3	0–1	1–0	0–1	0–1	0–2	1–2	1–2	1–3	2–0	3–1	1–2	0–1	1–4	1–1	0–1	1–1
5 Bishop's Stortford	4–4	0–1	3–1	3–0	*	0–0	2–3	2–0	0–3	4–0	1–2	1–1	0–0	2–0	0–1	3–0	2–1	4–1	2–1	2–1	6–0	2–2	1–1	1–3
6 Bognor Regis Tn	4–0	1–3	0–0	2–0	0–1	*	4–1	0–0	0–1	3–2	2–1	3–1	4–0	1–2	2–0	2–0	1–3	1–0	2–0	0–3	5–2	2–2	0–2	6–1
7 Braintree Town	2–0	0–1	0–2	2–2	2–0	0–3	*	0–3	0–1	1–2	0–5	0–2	1–2	1–3	1–3	2–0	1–3	0–1	0–1	1–2	2–5	2–4	0–3	1–0
8 Canvey Island	4–0	3–1	3–1	0–2	5–1	3–1	4–1	*	3–0	3–1	1–1	1–1	2–1	1–0	2–0	4–0	3–2	1–1	6–1	3–1	1–1	4–0	1–3	4–3
9 Carshalton Athletic	3–0	0–2	2–1	2–1	1–2	1–1	2–1	0–2	*	1–1	0–2	3–2	2–0	1–3	4–1	2–1	0–0	3–2	2–1	3–2	1–0	1–1	2–2	0–3
10 Ford United	4–1	1–1	1–1	2–1	3–0	2–0	3–0	0–3	2–1	*	3–0	1–3	0–0	0–1	5–3	3–0	0–0	2–0	0–1	1–1	3–0	2–2	2–4	2–3
11 Grays Athletic	2–1	3–1	1–1	1–1	3–1	6–0	1–1	1–1	0–0	2–0	*	2–2	4–0	1–0	4–0	2–0	0–0	1–1	1–0	1–1	2–1	9–1	3–2	1–1
12 Harrow Borough	0–2	1–1	2–1	2–1	1–0	0–1	2–3	0–1	0–0	1–1	0–0	*	1–0	1–2	0–0	0–2	0–0	1–2	0–1	1–1	2–2	3–1	2–4	1–2
13 Hayes	3–0	2–1	1–0	1–1	1–0	0–1	0–0	2–1	1–0	1–1	1–1	1–1	*	3–1	2–0	5–1	1–1	0–1	1–0	0–1	1–1	1–0	0–0	1–2
14 Hendon	1–1	0–1	1–0	3–0	2–5	2–2	1–0	1–0	1–2	2–2	1–0	2–0	3–2	*	0–1	3–0	1–0	1–2	2–0	3–1	1–1	1–1	0–2	1–1
15 Heybridge Swifts	1–2	0–3	0–0	1–4	1–0	1–2	1–2	1–4	4–0	4–1	3–0	2–3	1–2	0–0	*	4–2	1–1	1–0	0–2	0–0	3–2	0–2	2–2	0–3
16 Hitchin Town	2–2	2–2	1–3	2–5	0–2	2–2	2–0	1–3	0–3	1–1	1–0	3–2	0–2	1–4	1–2	*	0–2	1–1	3–0	2–0	1–2	1–0	2–4	0–0
17 Hornchurch	1–0	2–0	1–0	1–1	2–0	3–0	2–1	0–0	2–0	1–0	2–0	2–1	0–2	0–2	0–2	4–0	*	1–1	1–0	1–0	3–1	0–1	3–0	2–0
18 Kettering Town	2–2	0–3	0–0	1–0	3–2	3–1	1–2	1–4	0–3	0–3	0–0	1–1	0–3	4–1	4–1	1–1	3–2	*	1–1	3–1	2–1	2–0	0–1	2–1
19 Kingstonian	0–0	2–0	0–0	0–0	1–1	1–1	2–2	1–2	0–1	0–2	3–1	1–1	1–0	0–1	1–1	1–1	0–1	1–0	*	3–1	0–1	1–2	1–2	1–1
20 Maidenhead Utd	4–2	0–2	2–1	1–0	0–4	0–2	4–0	0–0	0–0	1–1	1–4	1–0	1–0	0–1	2–4	2–1	1–1	1–2	0–4	*	3–1	4–2	2–0	1–4
21 Northwood	1–1	0–0	3–1	4–5	2–3	1–2	3–1	1–5	0–4	2–3	1–1	3–1	3–4	0–1	2–1	1–0	0–1	1–2	2–0	0–0	*	3–4	1–2	0–3
22 St. Albans City	3–1	0–3	1–3	0–2	3–2	2–2	0–0	4–1	0–4	2–0	0–3	0–1	1–1	0–4	0–0	1–2	1–1	0–1	0–1	1–2	3–0	*	2–0	0–2
23 Sutton United	2–2	2–2	1–1	1–1	2–2	1–0	1–2	0–1	6–0	2–3	1–0	3–0	4–1	2–0	5–1	0–3	3–1	2–1	4–1	0–3	0–0	4–2	*	0–3
24 Thurrock	5–0	0–0	1–1	1–0	1–1	4–1	0–1	1–2	2–3	0–0	2–0	3–0	2–0	2–0	1–1	2–0	1–3	0–2	4–1	3–1	6–0	2–0	0–1	*

Premier Division	*P*	*W*	*D*	*L*	*F*	*A*	*Pts*
1 Canvey Island	46	32	8	6	106	42	104
2 Sutton United	46	25	10	11	94	56	85
3 Thurrock	46	24	11	11	87	45	83
4 Hendon	46	25	8	13	68	47	83
5 Hornchurch*	46	24	11	11	63	35	82
6 Grays Athletic	46	22	15	9	82	39	81
7 Carshalton Athletic	46	24	9	13	66	55	81
8 Hayes	46	21	11	14	56	46	74
9 Kettering Town	46	20	11	15	63	63	71
10 Bognor Regis Tn	46	20	10	16	69	67	70
11 Bishop's Stortford	46	20	9	17	78	61	69
12 Maidenhead Utd	46	18	9	19	60	68	63
13 Ford United	46	16	14	16	69	63	62
14 Basingstoke Town	46	17	9	20	58	64	60
15 Bedford Town	46	14	13	19	62	63	55
16 Heybridge Swifts	46	14	11	21	57	78	53
17 Harrow Borough	46	12	14	20	47	63	50
18 Kingstonian	46	12	13	21	40	56	49
19 St. Albans City	46	12	12	22	55	83	48
20 Hitchin Town	46	13	8	25	55	89	47
21 Northwood	46	12	9	25	65	95	45
22 Billericay Town	46	11	11	24	51	66	44
23 Braintree Town	46	11	6	29	41	88	39
24 Aylesbury United	46	5	14	27	41	101	29

** Hornchurch had one point deducted for fielding an ineligible player.*

PROMOTION PLAY-OFFS

FIRST ROUND
Yeading 0–1 Lewes

SEMI-FINALS
Basingstoke Town 1–4 Lewes
Bedford Town 3–1 Hitchin Town
Harrow Borough 0–0 Kingstonian
(AET: Kingstonian won 5–3 on penalties)
Heybridge Swifts 3–4 St. Albans City

FINALS
Bedford Town 4–5 St. Albans City
Lewes 1–0 Kingstonian

Right: the Barking & East Ham United programme for 2003-04.

Right: the Wingate & Finchley edition for the same campaign.

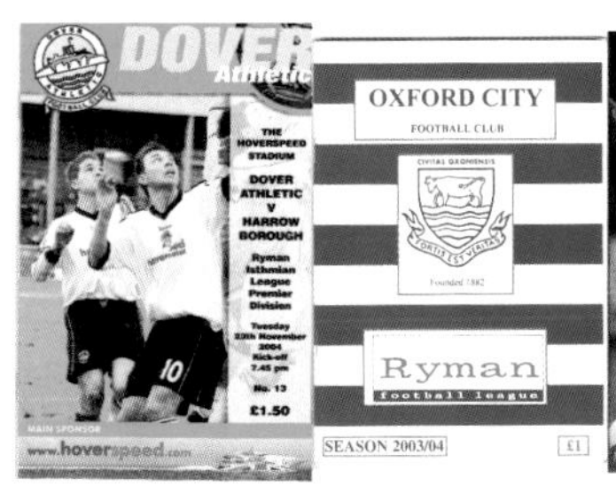

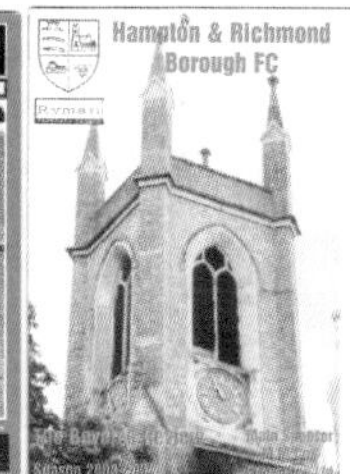

2003-04

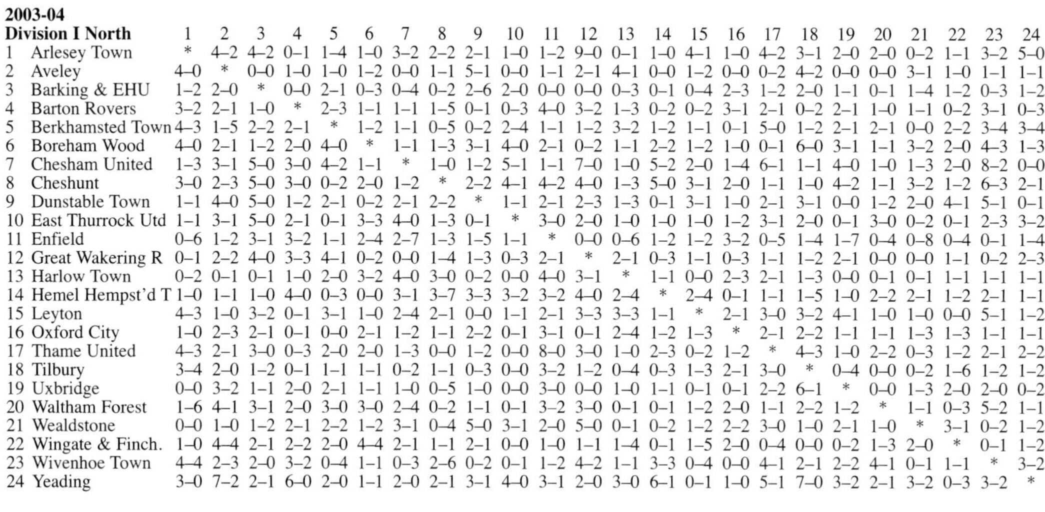

Division I North	1	2	3	4	5	6	7	8	9	10	11	12	13	14	15	16	17	18	19	20	21	22	23	24
1 Arlesey Town	*	4–2	4–2	0–1	1–4	1–0	3–2	2–2	2–1	1–0	1–2	9–0	0–1	1–0	4–1	1–0	4–2	3–1	2–0	2–0	0–2	1–1	3–2	5–0
2 Aveley	4–0	*	0–0	1–0	1–0	1–2	0–0	1–1	5–1	0–0	1–1	2–1	4–1	0–0	1–2	0–0	0–2	4–2	0–0	0–0	3–1	1–0	1–1	1–1
3 Barking & EHU	1–2	2–0	*	0–0	2–1	0–3	0–4	0–2	2–6	2–0	0–0	0–0	0–3	0–1	0–4	2–3	1–2	2–0	1–1	0–1	1–4	1–2	0–3	1–2
4 Barton Rovers	3–2	2–1	1–0	*	2–3	1–1	1–1	1–5	0–1	0–3	4–0	3–2	1–3	0–2	0–2	3–1	2–1	0–2	2–1	1–0	1–1	0–2	3–1	0–3
5 Berkhamsted Town	4–3	1–5	2–2	2–1	*	1–2	1–1	0–5	0–2	2–4	1–1	1–2	3–2	1–2	1–1	0–1	5–0	1–2	2–1	2–1	0–0	2–2	3–4	3–4
6 Boreham Wood	4–0	2–1	1–2	2–0	4–0	*	1–1	1–3	3–1	4–0	2–1	0–2	1–1	2–2	1–2	1–0	0–1	6–0	3–1	1–1	3–2	2–0	4–3	1–3
7 Chesham United	1–3	3–1	5–0	3–0	4–2	1–1	*	1–0	1–2	5–1	1–1	7–0	1–0	5–2	2–0	1–4	6–1	1–1	4–0	1–0	1–3	2–0	8–2	0–0
8 Cheshunt	3–0	2–3	5–0	3–0	0–2	2–0	1–2	*	2–2	4–1	4–2	4–0	1–3	5–0	3–1	2–0	1–1	1–0	4–2	1–1	3–2	1–2	6–3	2–1
9 Dunstable Town	1–1	4–0	5–0	1–2	2–1	0–2	2–1	2–2	*	1–1	2–1	2–3	1–3	0–1	3–1	1–0	2–1	3–1	0–0	1–2	2–0	4–1	5–1	0–1
10 East Thurrock Utd	1–1	3–1	5–0	2–1	0–1	3–3	4–0	1–3	0–1	*	3–0	2–0	1–0	1–0	1–0	1–2	3–1	2–0	0–1	3–0	0–2	0–1	2–3	3–2
11 Enfield	0–6	1–2	3–1	3–2	1–1	2–4	2–7	1–3	1–5	1–1	*	0–0	0–6	1–2	1–2	3–2	0–5	1–4	1–7	0–4	0–8	0–4	0–1	1–4
12 Great Wakering R	0–1	2–2	4–0	3–3	4–1	0–2	0–0	1–4	1–3	0–3	2–1	*	2–1	0–3	1–1	0–3	1–1	1–2	2–1	0–0	0–0	1–1	0–2	2–3
13 Harlow Town	0–2	0–1	0–1	1–0	2–0	3–2	4–0	3–0	0–2	0–0	4–0	3–1	*	1–1	0–0	2–3	2–1	1–3	0–0	0–1	0–1	1–1	1–1	1–1
14 Hemel Hempst'd T	1–0	1–1	1–0	4–0	0–3	0–0	3–1	3–7	3–3	3–2	3–2	4–0	2–4	*	2–4	0–1	1–1	1–5	1–0	2–2	2–1	1–2	2–1	1–1
15 Leyton	4–3	1–0	3–2	0–1	3–1	1–0	2–4	2–1	0–0	1–1	2–1	3–3	3–3	1–1	*	2–1	3–0	3–2	4–1	1–0	1–0	0–0	5–1	1–2
16 Oxford City	1–0	2–3	2–1	0–1	0–0	2–1	1–2	1–1	2–2	0–1	3–1	0–1	2–4	1–2	1–3	*	2–1	2–2	1–1	1–1	1–3	1–3	1–1	1–1
17 Thame United	4–3	2–1	3–0	0–3	2–0	2–0	1–3	0–0	1–2	0–0	8–0	3–0	1–0	2–3	0–2	1–2	*	4–3	1–0	2–2	0–3	1–2	2–1	2–2
18 Tilbury	3–4	2–0	1–2	0–1	1–1	1–1	0–2	1–1	0–3	0–0	3–2	1–2	0–4	0–3	1–3	2–1	3–0	*	0–4	0–0	0–2	1–6	1–2	1–2
19 Uxbridge	0–0	3–2	1–1	2–0	2–1	1–1	1–0	0–5	1–0	0–0	3–0	0–0	1–0	1–1	0–1	0–1	2–2	6–1	*	0–0	1–3	2–0	2–0	0–2
20 Waltham Forest	1–6	4–1	3–1	2–0	3–0	3–0	2–4	0–2	1–1	0–1	3–2	3–0	0–1	0–1	1–2	2–0	1–1	2–2	1–2	*	1–1	0–3	5–2	1–1
21 Wealdstone	0–0	1–0	1–2	2–1	2–2	1–2	3–1	0–4	5–0	3–1	2–0	5–0	0–1	0–2	1–2	2–2	3–0	1–0	2–1	1–0	*	3–1	0–2	1–2
22 Wingate & Finch.	1–0	4–4	2–1	2–2	2–0	4–4	2–1	1–1	2–1	0–0	1–0	1–1	1–4	0–1	1–5	2–0	0–4	0–0	0–2	1–3	2–0	*	0–1	1–2
23 Wivenhoe Town	4–4	2–3	2–0	3–2	0–4	1–1	0–3	2–6	0–2	0–1	1–2	4–2	1–1	3–3	0–4	0–0	4–1	2–1	2–2	4–1	0–1	1–1	*	3–2
24 Yeading	3–0	7–2	2–1	6–0	2–0	1–1	2–0	2–1	3–1	4–0	3–1	2–0	3–0	6–1	0–1	1–0	5–1	7–0	3–2	2–1	3–2	0–3	3–2	*

Division I North	P	W	D	L	F	A	Pts
1 Yeading	46	32	7	7	112	54	103
2 Leyton	46	29	9	8	90	53	96
3 Cheshunt	46	27	10	9	119	54	91
4 Chesham United	46	24	9	13	104	60	81
5 Dunstable Town	46	23	9	14	86	61	78
6 Hemel Hempstd	46	22	12	12	75	72	78
7 Wealdstone	46	23	7	16	81	51	76
8 Arlesey Town	46	23	7	16	95	70	76
9 Boreham Wood	46	20	13	13	82	59	73
10 Harlow Town	46	20	10	16	75	51	70
11 Wingate & Finch.	46	19	13	14	68	63	70
12 East Thurrock Utd	46	19	11	16	62	54	68
13 Uxbridge	46	15	14	17	59	57	59
14 Aveley	46	15	14	17	67	71	59
15 Thame United	46	16	9	21	72	83	57
16 Waltham Forest	46	15	13	18	62	60	55
17 Wivenhoe Town	46	15	10	21	79	104	55
18 Barton Rovers	46	16	6	24	52	80	54
19 Oxford City	46	14	11	21	55	65	53
20 Berkhamsted Town	46	12	10	24	66	88	46
21 Great Wakering R	46	10	13	23	47	97	43
22 Tilbury	46	10	9	27	56	100	39
23 Barking & EHU	46	8	7	31	37	100	31
24 Enfield	46	5	7	34	44	138	22

Left: the Dunstable Town programme for season 2003-04.

Right: the Epsom & Ewell programme for the same season.

Leyton Pennant changed their name to Waltham Forest.

Division I South	1	2	3	4	5	6	7	8	9	10	11	12	13	14	15	16	17	18	19	20	21	22	23	24
1 Ashford Town (Mx)	*	2–0	4–1	1–1	2–1	0–2	2–0	1–1	1–0	2–0	0–0	1–2	2–2	2–3	1–1	3–1	1–2	1–2	0–2	2–3	2–2	4–2	3–0	1–1
2 Banstead Athletic	0–1	*	1–0	1–2	0–1	1–4	1–1	1–1	5–1	4–1	0–1	1–2	1–3	6–1	1–0	1–1	0–2	1–2	0–1	2–1	0–1	2–0	0–3	1–1
3 Bracknell Town	0–0	3–0	*	0–1	5–0	5–4	1–0	1–2	3–2	2–0	0–4	2–1	1–3	0–3	1–1	0–3	4–0	4–2	3–4	0–6	2–1	10–1	0–0	4–2
4 Bromley	2–3	1–1	4–0	*	3–0	2–0	2–2	2–2	1–2	2–0	2–0	1–3	2–0	1–2	0–2	1–1	4–0	0–4	2–1	1–0	0–3	2–2	1–0	0–0
5 Corinthian-Casuals	0–2	1–6	0–3	0–1	*	0–4	1–3	0–3	4–2	0–1	1–1	1–1	3–2	2–4	2–4	1–1	0–1	4–1	0–0	0–3	1–2	0–5	0–3	1–3
6 Croydon	2–2	3–1	0–2	0–1	4–3	*	0–2	2–2	0–2	0–2	0–3	4–2	3–1	0–4	2–4	0–1	3–1	1–0	0–4	2–2	1–1	0–1	0–1	1–1
7 Croydon Athletic	1–0	3–0	1–2	0–2	3–2	1–0	*	2–2	2–1	3–0	2–4	1–2	3–2	1–2	2–0	4–2	4–1	1–0	0–3	0–2	2–0	5–1	0–0	0–0
8 Dulwich Hamlet	4–0	1–2	2–2	0–4	3–2	2–0	1–0	*	1–0	3–1	2–1	1–0	4–2	4–1	3–1	1–1	1–3	2–4	2–2	1–1	1–4	1–3	2–2	2–1
9 Egham Town	2–2	1–2	1–2	1–4	1–1	3–2	1–3	0–0	*	1–0	2–2	0–2	2–3	2–4	0–0	3–0	1–2	2–3	2–1	1–1	0–1	2–3	0–1	0–2
10 Epsom & Ewell	0–5	1–1	0–2	1–1	4–1	1–2	1–1	0–2	1–2	*	0–2	0–3	1–2	0–4	0–3	2–5	2–0	1–4	0–2	2–3	0–3	0–1	2–4	2–2
11 Hampton & R Boro	1–0	2–1	1–1	1–3	2–0	2–0	1–1	1–3	1–1	2–1	*	1–0	1–2	4–3	1–0	3–0	3–1	4–0	2–0	2–1	1–1	2–2	0–1	1–2
12 Horsham	1–0	3–1	4–1	1–2	1–1	2–2	1–2	0–1	1–3	5–0	3–1	*	2–3	0–2	3–0	2–2	5–0	1–4	0–3	2–3	0–0	1–0	0–1	1–2
13 Leatherhead	2–2	6–0	2–2	0–5	2–0	2–2	3–2	0–2	2–1	1–2	0–3	0–1	*	5–4	3–1	3–3	2–2	2–3	1–0	1–0	2–2	0–1	1–0	0–1
14 Lewes	2–0	2–2	4–0	3–1	3–2	2–0	1–2	4–0	4–1	2–0	2–2	6–1	2–2	*	3–0	2–1	3–0	3–2	1–1	1–2	3–0	2–1	1–2	2–2
15 Marlow	0–2	0–1	2–1	1–0	4–0	2–0	0–0	0–0	1–1	4–1	1–1	2–0	3–4	1–2	*	2–0	0–1	0–0	3–1	1–0	1–2	1–0	0–0	0–5
16 Metropolitan Police	0–1	0–2	1–2	1–3	2–0	1–1	1–1	0–0	2–0	2–2	1–3	1–1	1–2	1–4	1–1	*	1–0	1–3	1–3	2–2	1–2	6–2	2–2	0–2
17 Molesey	0–2	1–0	4–3	1–2	2–3	1–1	0–2	0–0	2–0	2–0	0–1	1–1	0–2	2–2	3–0	0–2	*	0–3	0–2	0–3	1–1	0–2	0–1	0–2
18 Slough Town	1–1	5–1	4–1	4–2	2–1	3–1	1–0	1–2	3–1	7–1	1–1	3–2	3–1	1–0	1–2	3–0	3–1	*	2–2	2–0	1–1	3–1	1–3	1–1
19 Staines Town	5–1	0–0	3–0	3–1	0–2	5–2	1–0	3–2	1–0	2–0	1–0	0–0	3–2	3–1	3–0	4–2	2–1	1–3	*	1–2	0–0	2–1	1–1	3–3
20 Tooting & M Utd	2–3	2–0	3–2	4–3	3–0	0–0	2–1	1–2	4–1	3–3	0–2	2–2	4–0	0–4	0–1	2–1	1–3	0–2	2–0	*	2–1	2–1	1–1	1–2
21 Walton & Hersham	0–0	0–1	2–0	3–3	3–2	2–1	2–1	0–1	3–1	8–0	1–3	1–1	1–1	1–0	3–0	2–0	2–1	3–1	2–4	1–1	*	3–0	0–1	0–2
22 Whyteleafe	1–2	1–3	0–2	1–1	2–1	2–1	1–4	0–3	3–2	5–2	1–4	2–3	1–2	0–0	2–0	0–1	3–2	2–0	1–2	3–2	2–0	*	1–3	1–3
23 Windsor & Eton	5–1	0–1	2–0	1–0	1–0	2–0	1–1	0–0	4–2	1–1	0–1	3–1	4–2	1–2	0–0	2–0	2–0	1–4	2–0	3–1	5–3	2–0	*	1–1
24 Worthing	2–1	4–0	2–1	2–1	2–0	4–0	1–0	1–2	2–1	1–1	1–3	1–1	2–0	0–3	4–0	4–1	2–1	2–0	2–0	3–2	2–2	0–1	2–2	*

2003-04

Division I South	P	W	D	L	F	A	Pts
1 Lewes	46	29	7	10	113	61	94
2 Worthing	46	26	14	6	87	46	92
3 Windsor & Eton	46	26	13	7	75	39	91
4 Slough Town	46	28	6	12	103	63	90
5 Hampton & R Boro	46	26	11	9	82	45	89
6 Staines Town	46	26	9	11	85	52	87
7 Dulwich Hamlet	46	23	15	8	77	57	84
8 Bromley	46	22	10	14	80	58	76
9 Walton & Hersham	46	20	14	12	76	55	74
10 Croydon Athletic	46	20	10	16	70	54	70
11 Tooting & M Utd	46	20	9	17	82	68	69
12 Ashford T (Mdx)	46	18	13	15	69	62	67
13 Leatherhead	46	19	9	18	83	88	66
14 Bracknell Town	46	19	6	21	81	87	63
15 Horsham	46	16	11	19	71	69	59
16 Marlow	46	16	11	19	50	64	59
17 Whyteleafe	46	17	4	25	66	93	55
18 Banstead Athletic	46	15	8	23	56	73	53
19 Molesey	46	12	6	28	45	84	42
20 Metropolitan Police	46	9	14	23	58	84	41
21 Croydon	46	10	10	26	57	88	40
22 Egham Town	46	8	8	30	55	92	32
23 Corinthian-Casuals	46	6	6	34	48	110	24
24 Epsom & Ewell	46	5	8	33	40	117	23

PROMOTION PLAY-OFF: Dulwich Hamlet 2–2 Wealdstone (AET: Wealdstone won 5–4 on penalties).

Division II	1	2	3	4	5	6	7	8	9	10	11	12	13	14	15
1 Abingdon Town	*	3–2, 1–2	3–0	0–1, 0–2	7–1	1–2, 2–2	2–4	1–2, 3–1	2–3	5–5, 2–0	2–7	1–2, 2–1	5–3	4–1, 1–1	0–0
2 Camberley Town	2–1	*	3–2, 2–0	0–0	2–3, 4–0	1–3	0–1, 0–1	2–1	0–2, 0–2	2–1	0–1, 1–0	1–1	0–0, 0–1	1–2	2–0, 1–3
3 Chalfont St Peter	1–1, 0–3	2–4	*	1–1, 6–1	4–3	0–4, 1–3	2–3	2–3, 0–2	0–1	0–3, 2–2	0–1	1–1, 2–1	2–2	0–3, 0–2	7–2
4 Chertsey Town	4–1	2–1, 2–0	0–1	*	0–4, 1–1	0–1	2–1, 2–2	1–0	1–1, 1–0	1–0	2–1, 2–2	1–1	3–0, 1–1	2–3	1–0, 1–2
5 Clapton	1–1, 0–5	1–2	3–0, 3–0	0–6	*	1–1, 1–7	0–2	2–4, 0–3	1–6	3–1, 0–2	0–4	2–2, 1–7	0–1	0–1, 1–3	1–2
6 Dorking	2–1	3–0, 1–0	2–1	4–1, 3–2	3–2	*	3–1, 6–1	1–0	5–3, 0–3	3–0	1–2, 0–2	1–0	3–0, 1–0	1–0	4–0, 1–0
7 Edgware Town	6–3, 3–4	0–1	1–2, 1–3	2–6	2–1, 10–0	2–2	*	0–1, 1–3	0–4	1–1, 0–2	0–3	0–0, 3–2	0–1	3–1, 1–1	1–2
8 Flackwell Heath	1–0	3–1, 0–4	1–0	1–3, 0–1	3–3	4–1, 0–1	1–0	*	1–3, 1–0	3–1	3–1, 2–2	3–2	4–0, 3–1	1–3	3–1, 1–1
9 Hertford Town	0–3, 3–0	0–1	1–2, 1–1	1–0	0–2, 2–0	1–1	3–0, 4–0	2–1	*	4–1, 1–1	0–1	1–1, 0–0	2–0	2–0, 3–1	2–1
10 Kingsbury Town	2–0	3–0, 2–2	0–1	0–3, 1–4	3–0	4–1, 2–2	0–1	0–0, 2–1	2–4	*	0–2, 3–2	2–1	0–0, 3–0	2–0	1–1, 3–1
11 Leighton Town	3–2, 1–0	8–0	3–0, 8–0	3–1	9–0, 1–2	2–1	2–0, 4–1	1–0	1–1, 1–1	1–2	*	3–2, 1–1	3–2	2–0, 2–0	9–0
12 Ware	0–1	2–4, 2–2	1–2	0–1, 3–1	1–2	1–1, 1–3	2–1	0–1, 2–1	0–1	5–1, 1–0	1–0	*	3–1, 4–2	2–3	4–1, 4–1
13 Wembley	2–0, 1–0	0–0	2–0, 3–2	1–4	4–0, 1–0	0–1	1–0, 1–1	0–2	0–1, 0–0	1–0	0–5, 1–2	0–2	*	1–1, 5–0	1–4
14 Witham Town	3–1	5–1, 2–0	4–2	1–1, 1–2	6–1	1–1, 3–1	5–0	3–3, 1–0	1–0	1–1, 1–1	1–1	3–0, 0–1	2–0	*	3–0, 1–1
15 Wokingham Town	0–2, 4–7	4–0	1–3, 0–2	2–4	4–0, 2–1	0–0	1–4, 4–1	0–3	1–3, 0–2	1–0	0–3, 1–1	2–0	2–2, 1–4	2–1	*

Clubs played each other three times.

Division II	P	W	D	L	F	A	Pts
1 Leighton Town	42	28	7	7	111	36	91
2 Dorking	42	27	8	7	87	47	89
3 Hertford Town	42	24	9	9	74	35	81
4 Chertsey Town	42	22	9	11	75	53	75
5 Flackwell Heath	42	22	5	15	71	53	71
6 Witham Town	42	20	10	12	75	54	70
7 Kingsbury Town	42	14	11	17	60	64	53
8 Ware	42	14	10	18	67	60	52
9 Abingdon Town	42	15	6	21	83	81	51
10 Camberley Town	42	15	6	21	51	71	51
11 Wembley	42	13	9	20	46	67	48
12 Wokingham Town	42	12	7	23	53	94	43
13 Edgware Town	42	12	6	24	62	88	42
14 Chalfont St. Peter	42	12	6	24	57	89	42
15 Clapton	42	8	5	29	47	129	29

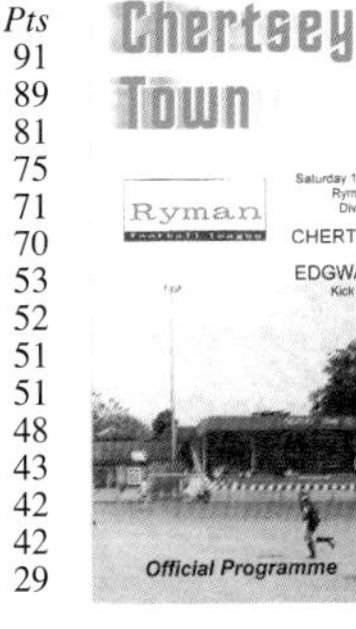

2004–05 - The first season under restructuring, which coincided with the League's Centenary, proved to be an exciting one with clubs also competing for play-off places. In the Premier Division the championship went to Yeading – who won Division One North the previous season – by six points from Billericay Town, Eastleigh, Braintree Town and Leyton, with the latter pipping Hampton & Richmond Borough on goal difference for the final place. Eastleigh defeated Leyton 2–1 in the final to join champions Yeading in Conference South. At the foot of the table Cheshunt should have been relegated to Step 4, but were reprieved because another club elected to drop down to that level. The three clubs going down were Kent's Tonbridge Angels and Dover Athletic, along with Kingstonian, who endured a difficult season both on and off the pitch. In Division One AFC Wimbledon in their first season in the League won the championship losing only three League games. Walton & Hersham secured the second automatic promotion spot by ten points from nearest challengers Horsham, who had to settle for the play-offs, along with Bromley, Metropolitan Police and Cray Wanderers. In the play-offs Bromley travelled to Horsham and defeated the home club 3–1 to gain promotion. At the other end, Dorking and Croydon were both relegated to Division Two. In Division Two, the re-formed Ilford club – in their first season back in the Isthmian League – won the title by three points from Enfield, who also gained promotion to Step 4, with Brook House in third place. At the bottom, Clapton again had a disappointing season and finished four points adrift of Kingsbury Town. Abingdon Town had indicated they would be resigning from the League at the end of the season and would be joining the Hellenic League.

At the Annual General Meeting the constitution for the 2005–06 season was confirmed as follows:

Premier Division: AFC Wimbledon, Billericay Town, Braintree Town, Bromley, Chelmsford City, East Thurrock United, Fisher Athletic, Folkestone Invicta, Hampton & Richmond Borough, Harrow Borough, Hendon, Heybridge Swifts, Leyton, Maldon Town, Margate, Redbridge *(previously Ford United)*, Slough Town, Staines Town, Walton & Hersham, Wealdstone, Windsor & Eton and Worthing.

Division One: Ashford Town, Banstead Athletic, Bashley, Burgess Hill Town, Corinthian–Casuals, Cray Wanderers, Croydon Athletic, Dover Athletic, Dulwich Hamlet, Fleet Town, Hastings United, Horsham, Kingstonian, Leatherhead, Lymington & New Milton, Metropolitan Police, Molesey, Newport IOW, Ramsgate, Tonbridge Angels, Tooting & Mitcham United, Walton Casuals, and Whyteleafe.

Division Two: Brook House, Camberley Town, Chalfont St. Peter, Chertsey Town, Clapton, Croydon, Dorking, Edgware Town, Egham Town, Epsom & Ewell, Flackwell Heath, Hertford Town, Kingsbury Town, Ware, Wembley and Witham Town.

2004-05

Premier Division	1	2	3	4	5	6	7	8	9	10	11	12	13	14	15	16	17	18	19	20	21	22
1 Billericay Town	*	1–0	1–2	4–1	2–0	2–0	0–0	2–0	1–0	1–1	4–1	6–1	0–3	2–1	0–0	2–0	2–1	1–1	1–0	2–1	0–0	1–1
2 Braintree Town	5–0	*	1–1	1–2	1–1	1–1	0–0	3–1	2–0	1–0	3–0	5–1	2–0	0–0	2–2	2–1	1–2	0–0	1–0	1–0	3–0	0–0
3 Chelmsford City	1–3	1–1	*	2–2	5–2	2–2	2–1	2–1	1–0	0–1	5–2	3–2	3–5	1–0	1–3	3–0	1–2	2–1	1–0	0–1	2–1	1–2
4 Cheshunt	3–2	0–3	0–3	*	5–2	2–4	0–0	0–0	0–0	2–1	2–1	1–5	0–0	2–2	2–2	1–0	0–3	1–1	0–1	1–1	1–0	1–2
5 Dover Athletic	1–1	1–3	1–1	2–1	*	1–2	0–1	2–0	2–2	0–1	1–2	1–2	2–2	0–1	2–1	3–1	3–1	2–1	2–4	1–0	1–2	0–3
6 Eastleigh	1–1	0–0	3–0	1–0	1–0	*	1–1	3–3	1–1	7–1	1–0	6–3	1–0	4–2	3–0	0–4	4–0	2–0	1–2	0–0	3–0	1–1
7 Folkestone Invicta	1–0	2–2	1–0	4–3	1–0	2–2	*	0–2	1–0	0–1	1–3	3–0	2–1	0–0	3–1	3–1	0–3	2–0	3–0	2–2	1–2	1–2
8 Hampton & R Boro	0–3	0–0	1–1	2–1	1–0	5–1	2–1	*	2–0	1–0	1–2	2–1	2–1	1–0	3–2	2–2	2–0	2–2	2–1	2–1	2–1	2–1
9 Harrow Borough	0–3	1–1	1–1	1–3	1–4	1–2	1–0	1–0	*	1–3	1–2	2–2	2–1	1–1	3–2	1–2	1–0	1–0	2–1	1–1	2–0	1–2
10 Hendon	1–3	1–3	0–0	2–1	1–0	2–1	2–1	2–1	1–0	*	3–0	1–0	0–0	0–1	1–2	0–0	0–2	0–0	1–4	2–1	0–1	1–2
11 Heybridge Swifts	0–1	2–1	1–2	2–2	2–1	1–2	2–0	3–1	1–3	5–2	*	3–0	1–2	6–1	1–2	5–2	0–3	0–0	1–1	3–2	0–0	4–1
12 Kingstonian	1–3	0–1	2–3	0–3	0–0	0–3	1–5	0–1	1–0	3–4	1–2	*	1–2	1–0	0–4	0–4	0–1	1–2	0–0	0–1	1–1	0–1
13 Leyton	0–6	2–2	2–0	2–1	1–1	2–2	0–4	4–2	1–2	1–0	0–2	3–1	*	3–2	3–2	0–1	1–3	1–0	4–0	4–0	1–0	1–2
14 Northwood	1–1	1–4	3–1	2–0	1–0	0–3	3–0	2–4	0–0	2–0	2–0	0–1	1–4	*	0–3	1–0	2–0	1–3	2–0	1–3	0–3	2–3
15 Salisbury City	1–0	0–0	0–2	1–0	0–0	0–0	1–0	2–1	1–2	2–1	1–1	1–0	0–2	1–4	*	0–0	1–3	1–0	3–1	5–1	1–2	1–3
16 Slough Town	0–6	3–0	0–2	2–0	3–2	1–4	1–1	0–1	2–0	1–3	1–3	2–3	1–2	1–1	1–0	*	1–0	2–0	1–0	3–1	1–1	2–2
17 Staines Town	3–1	0–0	0–0	1–3	1–3	0–1	0–0	0–0	2–0	1–1	1–1	3–2	0–2	3–1	2–2	4–0	*	1–3	3–3	1–3	2–1	0–1
18 Tonbridge Angels	0–2	2–1	2–1	1–6	3–2	0–3	3–2	3–2	0–0	4–1	0–4	1–1	3–2	2–3	2–3	2–2	0–3	*	0–1	0–1	1–0	1–2
19 Wealdstone	2–3	2–4	3–2	3–1	0–1	1–4	3–0	2–1	0–3	2–3	2–2	4–5	1–2	1–2	4–2	1–1	3–1	1–1	*	1–1	1–0	2–3
20 Windsor & Eton	1–1	1–2	0–0	1–3	1–1	1–1	2–1	1–5	2–0	0–1	3–3	1–0	0–0	1–0	2–1	0–4	2–1	4–1	0–0	*	0–2	1–1
21 Worthing	1–1	0–3	2–2	1–1	1–0	3–0	3–0	0–1	2–1	0–0	2–1	2–0	1–3	1–0	5–1	1–4	0–0	4–0	0–1	1–1	*	2–1
22 Yeading	3–1	1–1	2–0	3–0	3–2	3–2	1–0	0–0	0–1	3–2	1–1	2–0	1–1	2–0	1–2	3–3	1–2	2–1	2–1	3–2	1–1	*

PROMOTION PLAY-OFFS

SEMI-FINALS
Billericay Town 0–2 Leyton
Eastleigh 2–0 Braintree Town

FINAL
Eastleigh 2–1 Leyton

Premier Division	*P*	*W*	*D*	*L*	*F*	*A*	*Pts*
1 Yeading	42	25	11	6	74	48	86
2 Billericay Town	42	23	11	8	78	40	80
3 Eastleigh	42	22	13	7	84	49	79
4 Braintree Town	42	19	17	6	67	33	74
5 Leyton	42	21	8	13	71	57	71
6 Hampton & R Boro	42	21	8	13	64	53	71
7 Heybridge Swifts	42	18	9	15	76	65	63
8 Chelmsford City	42	17	11	14	63	58	62
9 Staines Town	42	17	9	16	59	53	60
10 Worthing	42	16	11	15	50	45	59
11 Hendon	42	17	7	18	48	60	58
12 Salisbury City	42	16	9	17	60	64	57
13 Slough Town	42	15	10	17	61	66	55
14 Folkestone Invicta	42	14	10	18	51	53	52
15 Windsor & Eton	42	12	14	16	48	62	50
16 Harrow Borough	42	13	10	19	41	54	49
17 Northwood	42	14	7	21	49	66	49
18 Wealdstone	42	13	8	21	60	73	47
19 Cheshunt	42	12	11	19	58	71	47
20 Tonbridge Angels	42	11	10	21	47	73	43
21 Dover Athletic	42	10	9	23	50	66	39
22 Kingstonian	42	7	5	30	43	93	26

Right: the Ashford Town (Kent) programme for their match against Burgess Hill Town.

Left: the Dulwich Hamlet programme for the 2004-05 season.

Right: the Braintree Town edition for the season.

Left: the Billericay Town programme for the season.

Division I	1	2	3	4	5	6	7	8	9	10	11	12	13	14	15	16	17	18	19	20	21	22
1 AFC Wimbledon	*	5–1	2–0	0–0	1–0	2–0	1–1	3–0	3–0	2–2	3–0	2–0	3–0	3–1	4–1	2–2	1–0	4–0	5–0	2–2	3–1	1–2
2 Ashford Town (Kt)	1–4	*	1–1	4–1	1–1	1–2	0–4	2–2	3–2	2–2	2–2	2–2	1–0	1–1	2–2	2–1	0–0	2–1	2–0	3-2	0–1	0–2
3 Banstead Athletic	1–3	1–0	*	0–3	0–1	0–3	2–1	1–1	6–0	1–3	3–0	1–2	1–2	0–1	2–3	2–2	1–1	0–0	2–3	1–1	2–2	1–3
4 Bashley	1–2	1–1	0–1	*	0–3	2–2	0–0	1–5	4–0	0–0	1–2	1–1	1–0	2–2	2–3	4–2	1–3	0–2	2–2	2–0	2–3	1–0
5 Bromley	1–1	3–0	0–1	3–5	*	1–0	1–1	3–2	4–3	1–1	1–0	2–0	2–0	1–2	4–1	1–1	1–1	4–0	2–2	1–2	1–0	4–0
6 Burgess Hill Town	1–3	2–1	1–1	4–5	3–2	*	5–1	1–2	0–1	1–2	4–1	1–0	2–0	1–0	1–2	0–4	0–1	3–0	5–0	2–0	1–0	4–1
7 Corinthian-Casuals	0–3	4–0	2–1	2–1	1–1	3–0	*	0–5	0–2	0–0	2–1	3–1	2–2	3–2	0–2	2–3	2–1	1–1	0–3	1–1	0–1	4–1
8 Cray Wanderers	2–0	2–2	0–1	4–4	5–2	1–1	2–0	*	0–0	1–2	3–3	1–1	3–2	2–1	1–2	2–2	4–1	2–1	5–0	1–1	1–2	1–1
9 Croydon	0–3	2–1	2–3	1–2	1–2	1–2	0–2	0–2	*	3–1	2–1	2–2	1–3	2–2	0–1	1–3	0–2	1–1	1–2	1–1	1–3	1–3
10 Croydon Athletic	1–3	2–0	1–1	3–5	1–0	5–3	0–1	2–2	1–1	*	3–1	0–1	5–0	1–1	1–2	1–2	2–1	1–1	3–1	2–4	3–2	3–3
11 Dorking	0–2	0–2	2–1	2–1	0–1	2–2	0–3	0–3	1–1	0–0	*	2–1	2–1	1–1	2–3	0–2	1–0	4–2	2–2	0–0	0–1	0–6
12 Dulwich Hamlet	0–1	2–1	2–3	1–1	0–1	1–2	4–1	1–3	2–0	2–0	1–1	*	1–1	4–0	3–2	1–2	1–3	1–1	3–3	0–1	2–0	2–3
13 Fleet Town	1–3	2–0	2–0	2–3	0–1	1–3	2–1	3–2	0–0	0–1	4–3	0–3	*	3–2	1–1	1–2	0–3	0–1	1–0	1–1	0–4	1–3
14 Hastings United	1–1	1–0	2–1	1–1	1–0	1–0	2–0	0–2	5–1	1–1	2–0	2–2	4–1	*	0–3	0–1	3–0	1–1	3–4	0–0	0–1	1–2
15 Horsham	2–3	5–0	2–1	2–0	0–4	1–2	5–0	2–2	2–1	3–0	7–0	1–1	2–1	1–2	*	4–1	1–1	2–1	1–0	2–2	1–4	5–0
16 Leatherhead	1–1	1–0	1–1	4–2	3–0	2–2	1–3	0–0	1–1	3–0	0–0	2–1	2–0	5–1	0–1	*	2–1	1–2	2–1	1–3	1–4	1–0
17 Metropolitan Police	1–1	3–2	3–1	1–1	0–2	2–1	1–0	1–2	4–0	3–3	2–1	2–1	4–1	1–0	4–3	2–2	*	3–1	1–0	2–1	1–0	2–0
18 Molesey	0–1	3–0	0–4	1–0	3–0	3–0	1–0	0–5	2–0	2–1	0–1	3–3	1–3	0–1	3–2	0–1	0–3	*	3–3	1–3	0–1	2–0
19 Newport IOW	1–2	0–0	1–0	1–1	1–1	1–4	0–2	0–6	4–0	0–2	2–2	3–2	0–2	0–1	2–3	1–1	1–4	1–0	*	1–6	0–1	2–0
20 Tooting & M Utd	1–1	8–3	2–0	2–0	0–1	2–2	3–2	2–2	4–0	3–3	4–2	2–2	6–1	3–1	1–2	1–2	3–2	4–2	1–2	*	2–1	4–1
21 Walton & Hersham	4–0	2–1	2–0	2–3	0–1	2–0	0–0	3–4	2–0	1–0	5–0	0–0	2–1	1–0	1–0	1–1	3–1	1–0	1–0	2–1	*	1–0
22 Whyteleafe	0–1	3–0	1–0	0–1	0–3	1–0	2–1	0–0	1–1	1–1	3–1	2–1	3–1	0–2	1–0	3–2	1–0	2–0	3–0	2–2	0–1	*

PROMOTION PLAY-OFFS
SEMI-FINALS
Bromley 1–1 Metropolitan Police (AET: Bromley won 4–3 on penalties)
Horsham 3–1 Cray Wanderers

FINAL
Horsham 1–3 Bromley

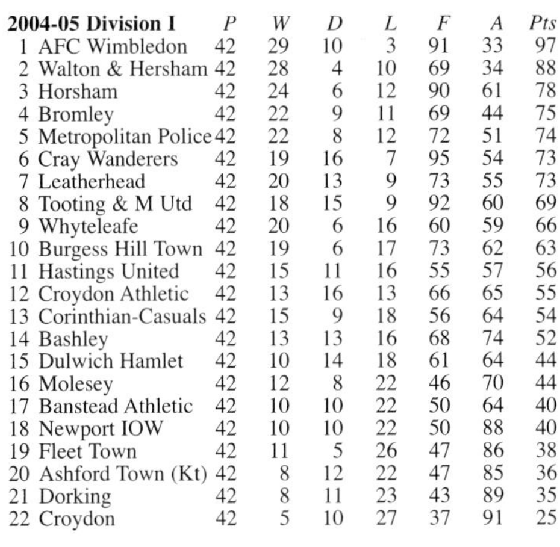

2004-05 Division I	*P*	*W*	*D*	*L*	*F*	*A*	*Pts*
1 AFC Wimbledon	42	29	10	3	91	33	97
2 Walton & Hersham	42	28	4	10	69	34	88
3 Horsham	42	24	6	12	90	61	78
4 Bromley	42	22	9	11	69	44	75
5 Metropolitan Police	42	22	8	12	72	51	74
6 Cray Wanderers	42	19	16	7	95	54	73
7 Leatherhead	42	20	13	9	73	55	73
8 Tooting & M Utd	42	18	15	9	92	60	69
9 Whyteleafe	42	20	6	16	60	59	66
10 Burgess Hill Town	42	19	6	17	73	62	63
11 Hastings United	42	15	11	16	55	57	56
12 Croydon Athletic	42	13	16	13	66	65	55
13 Corinthian-Casuals	42	15	9	18	56	64	54
14 Bashley	42	13	13	16	68	74	52
15 Dulwich Hamlet	42	10	14	18	61	64	44
16 Molesey	42	12	8	22	46	70	44
17 Banstead Athletic	42	10	10	22	50	64	40
18 Newport IOW	42	10	10	22	50	88	40
19 Fleet Town	42	11	5	26	47	86	38
20 Ashford Town (Kt)	42	8	12	22	47	85	36
21 Dorking	42	8	11	23	43	89	35
22 Croydon	42	5	10	27	37	91	25

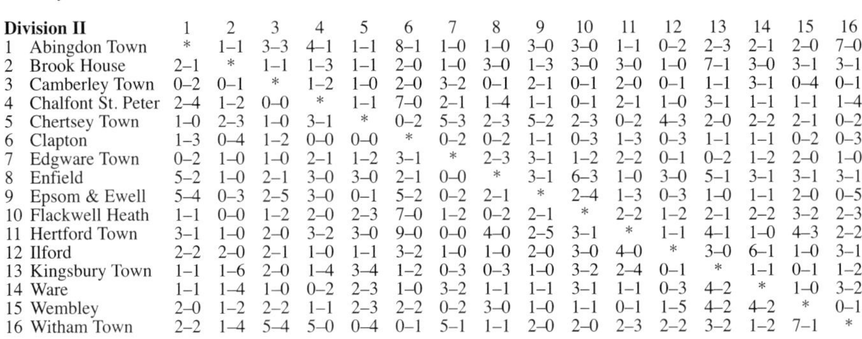

Division II	1	2	3	4	5	6	7	8	9	10	11	12	13	14	15	16
1 Abingdon Town	*	1–1	3–3	4–1	1–1	8–1	1–0	1–0	3–0	3–0	1–1	0–2	2–3	2–1	2–0	7–0
2 Brook House	2–1	*	1–1	1–3	1–1	2–0	1–0	3–0	1–3	3–0	3–0	1–0	7–1	3–0	3–1	3–1
3 Camberley Town	0–2	0–1	*	1–2	1–0	2–0	3–2	0–1	2–1	0–1	2–0	0–1	1–1	3–1	0–4	0–1
4 Chalfont St. Peter	2–4	1–2	0–0	*	1–1	7–0	2–1	1–4	1–1	0–1	2–1	1–0	3–1	1–1	1–1	1–4
5 Chertsey Town	1–0	2–3	1–0	3–1	*	0–2	5–3	2–3	5–2	2–3	0–2	4–3	2–0	2–2	2–1	0–2
6 Clapton	1–3	0–4	1–2	0–0	0–0	*	0–2	0–2	1–1	0–3	1–3	0–3	1–1	1–1	0–2	0–3
7 Edgware Town	0–2	1–0	1–0	2–1	1–2	3–1	*	2–3	3–1	1–2	2–2	0–1	0–2	1–2	2–0	1–0
8 Enfield	5–2	1–0	2–1	3–0	3–0	2–1	0–0	*	3–1	6–3	1–0	3–0	5–1	3–1	3–1	3–1
9 Epsom & Ewell	5–4	0–3	2–5	3–0	0–1	5–2	0–2	2–1	*	2–4	1–3	0–3	1–0	1–1	2–0	0–5
10 Flackwell Heath	1–1	0–0	1–2	2–0	2–3	7–0	1–2	0–2	2–1	*	2–2	1–2	2–1	2–2	3–2	2–3
11 Hertford Town	3–1	1–0	2–0	3–2	3–0	9–0	0–0	4–0	2–5	3–1	*	1–1	4–1	1–0	4–3	2–2
12 Ilford	2–2	2–0	2–1	1–0	1–1	3–2	1–0	1–0	2–0	3–0	4–0	*	3–0	6–1	1–0	3–1
13 Kingsbury Town	1–1	1–6	2–0	1–4	3–4	1–2	0–3	0–3	1–0	3–2	2–4	0–1	*	1–1	0–1	1–2
14 Ware	1–1	1–4	1–0	0–2	2–3	1–0	3–2	1–1	1–1	3–1	1–1	0–3	4–2	*	1–0	3–2
15 Wembley	2–0	1–2	2–2	1–1	2–3	2–2	0–2	3–0	1–0	1–1	0–1	1–5	4–2	4–2	*	0–1
16 Witham Town	2–2	1–4	5–4	5–0	0–4	0–1	5–1	1–1	2–0	2–0	2–3	2–2	3–2	1–2	7–1	*

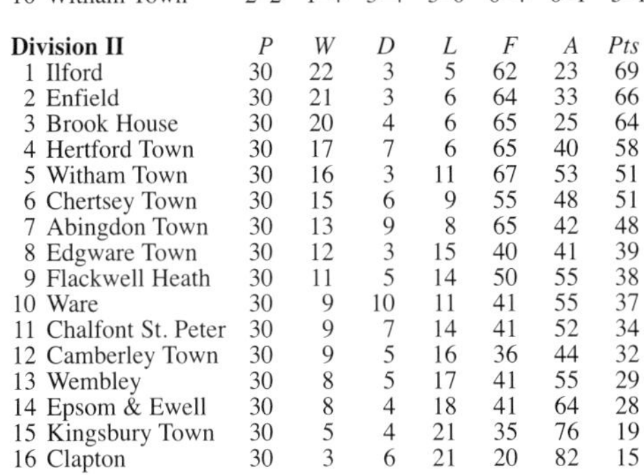

Division II	*P*	*W*	*D*	*L*	*F*	*A*	*Pts*
1 Ilford	30	22	3	5	62	23	69
2 Enfield	30	21	3	6	64	33	66
3 Brook House	30	20	4	6	65	25	64
4 Hertford Town	30	17	7	6	65	40	58
5 Witham Town	30	16	3	11	67	53	51
6 Chertsey Town	30	15	6	9	55	48	51
7 Abingdon Town	30	13	9	8	65	42	48
8 Edgware Town	30	12	3	15	40	41	39
9 Flackwell Heath	30	11	5	14	50	55	38
10 Ware	30	9	10	11	41	55	37
11 Chalfont St. Peter	30	9	7	14	41	52	34
12 Camberley Town	30	9	5	16	36	44	32
13 Wembley	30	8	5	17	41	55	29
14 Epsom & Ewell	30	8	4	18	41	64	28
15 Kingsbury Town	30	5	4	21	35	76	19
16 Clapton	30	3	6	21	20	82	15

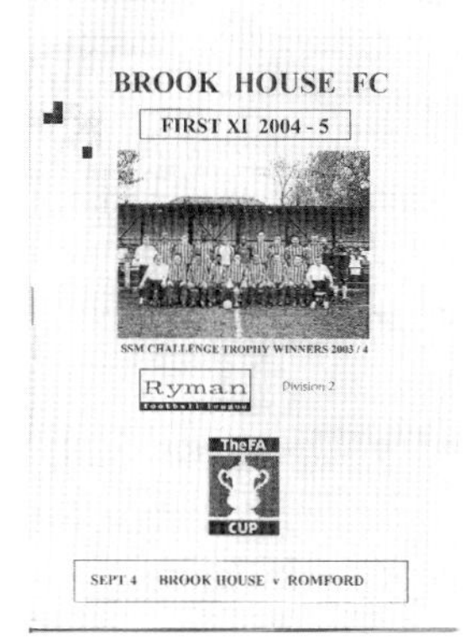

Pictured here are a number of member clubs' matchday programmes for the one hundredth anniversary season.

CHAPTER FOUR

The Elite Eleven Clubs

It is very difficult to know where to start in selecting ten Clubs to represent the first hundred years of the League. We started by ignoring the Super Six founder members and then felt that we could not ignore two of the three Clubs which joined the League just two years after the commencement of fixtures. Then there became a mixture of justification for inclusion as to length of service in the League and achievement whilst in membership.

Even in setting out fairly strict criteria which eliminated the likes of Bromley, Hendon and Sutton United it was impossible to get to ten so we went back to the "eleven a side" ethos of our sport and allowed an elite eleven!

Inevitably there will be some disappointed Clubs and supporters but to those we say that we hope that the honour of taking part in the League will be sufficient, thus emulating our founders. To those whose exploits are set out below, thank you for your contributions.

Dulwich Hamlet FC - Having joined the League in its third year of operation, the Club with the famous pink and blue shirts were once the giants of the amateur game.

The Hamlet story began in 1893, when Lorraine Wilson was handed the small sum of one shilling and eight pence by a couple of keen young footballers and asked to start a Dulwich Hamlet Football Club. "Pa", as Mr Wilson was affectionately known, tackled the task with great relish and over the next 30 years he helped to nurse, nudge and build Hamlet into a powerful force.

Life in the early days was fairly tough. The club's original ground in Woodwarde Road had no changing facilities. For matches, the players walked half a mile through the streets of Dulwich Village to get from their dressing room to the pitch, usually carrying the goalposts, crossbars and corner flags with them. One consolation was that their route took them through the gardens of the local inn where, no doubt, they paused on their return journey for a post-match drink or two!

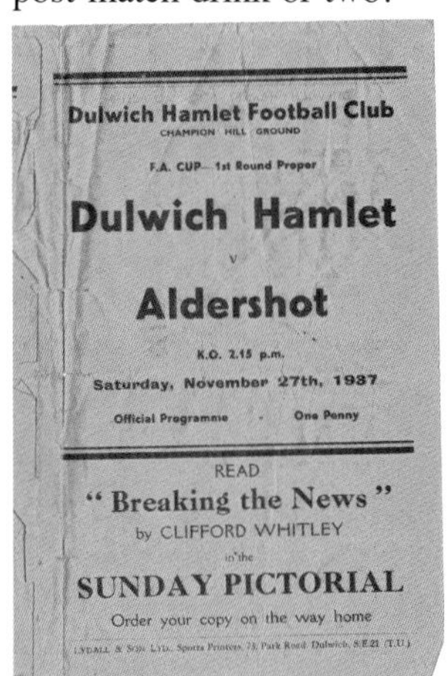

Dulwich joined the local Camberwell League in 1894 and achieved senior status in 1900. Five years later they lifted the Surrey Senior Cup for the first time. It is a competition they have now won on a record 16 occasions.

The Hamlet were founder members of the Spartan League and on 28 September 1907, Dulwich played their first ever game in the Isthmian League, at home to the London Caledonians. Some 3,000 spectators basked in the sunshine that afternoon as Dulwich beat the eventual champions 3–0, after long-serving defender Arthur Knight had ventured forward to open the scoring. Despite this encouraging start, Dulwich were only able to finish fifth out of six teams in their debut season. The club continued to progress though and in 1909 they were FA Amateur Cup semi-finalists. Two players, Charlie Tyson and George Shipway, won England Amateur International caps in the years before World War 1.

Dulwich's finest years came between the wars, when their record was second to none. Amateur Cup winners four times, they also won the London Senior Cup twice, six Surrey Senior Cups, eight London Charity Cups, as well as the Isthmian League championship on three occasions. Reg Anderson, Bill Caesar, Bill Davis, George Goodliffe, Taffy Hamer, Hyden Hill, Jack Hugo, Dick Jonas, Leslie Morrish, Cecil Murray, Sid Nicol and Horace Robbins were just a few of the Hamlet's leading players of that period.

However, the man who played the greatest part in Dulwich's triumphs was the legendary Edgar Kail, one of the finest forwards ever to grace the non-league game. During his brilliant 14-year career with the Hamlet, Kail netted 427 goals and played three times for the full England side, scoring twice on his debut against France. Another Hamlet star of that era was goalkeeper Bert Coleman who gained a full England cap in 1921, keeping a clean sheet against Wales.

The FA Amateur Cup victories were an obvious highlight. Tufnell Park were defeated 1–0 in the 1920 final at Millwall and Marine (Liverpool) were thumped 7–1 at West Ham some 12 years later. That equalled the record score for an Amateur Cup Final. Hamlet went on to beat Leyton in the 1934 and 1937 finals, 2–1 and 2–0 respectively.

That 1919–20 season saw Dulwich complete a notable "double", as they also lifted the Isthmian League championship for the first time. But it was a close run thing as they only pipped Nunhead on goal average. Dulwich's next Isthmian title success, in 1925–26, was more emphatic. A tremendous run-in produced seven straight victories and they won by a four-point margin.

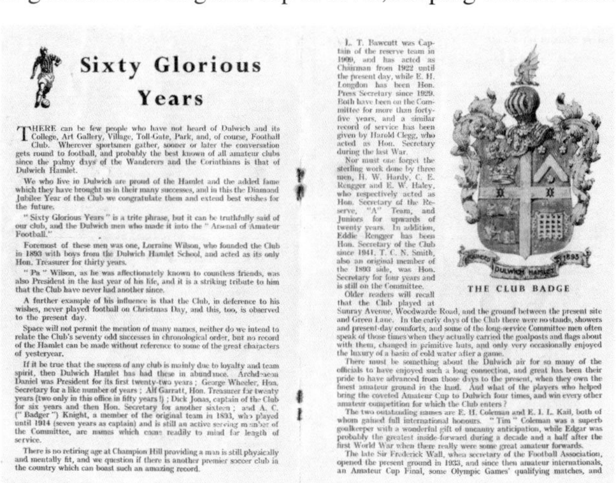
Sixty Glorious Years

THE CLUB BADGE

A third Isthmian championship followed in 1932–33 and, as with the first, it was achieved in a nail-biting finish. Faced with a backlog of fixtures, Hamlet had to take maximum points from their last five games to win the title, which they duly did, but only on goal average!

After World War 2, Dulwich finished runners-up to Leytonstone in 1946–47. Two years later, they went one better, winning the title for a fourth time. Again there was an exciting climax, as Wimbledon were defeated 4-0 before a 7,000 crowd at Champion Hill to enable Dulwich to pip Walthamstow Avenue to the title, yet again on goal average! One of the stars of that championship-winning side was flying left-winger Tommy Jover whose career goals tally for Dulwich has only been bettered by Edgar Kail. Tommy has now completed nearly seventy years magnificent service to the club, first as player, then official and, latterly, club President.

In 1949–50 Dulwich won the London Senior Cup again, and it was in the same season that full-back Reg Merritt embarked upon a long career during which he made a club record 576 appearances.

Dulwich reached The FA Amateur Cup semi-finals in 1956 and were runners-up to Wimbledon in the Isthmian League in 1958–59. But they then went through a very lean spell – apart from three good seasons in the mid-1970s – which culminated in relegation from the top division. However, they bounced straight back under manager Alan Smith (who later managed Crystal Palace), winning the Division One championship in 1977–78. Midfield dynamo Chris Lewington was ever-present that season and he repeated the feat in each of the next four seasons to complete a remarkable 290 consecutive appearances – another club record.

Since the phasing out of amateur football, Dulwich have been a semi-professional club, but further success has proved elusive. There were a couple of occasions when they challenged strongly for the Premier Division title, finishing third in 1979–80 and fifth in 1995–96, but generally League results have been disappointing and the club have spent the last few years in Division One. Recent cup honours have been limited to London Senior Cup wins in 1984 and 2004, a 14th appearance in The FA Cup first round proper in 1998 and a London Challenge Cup win in 1999.

Back in 1993 Dulwich celebrated their centenary by moving into a new stadium, built on the site of their famous old ground. When the former Champion Hill opened in 1931, Dulwich's Isthmian League match against local rivals Nunhead attracted a crowd of 17,000 – the biggest gate ever for an amateur League game.

Enfield FC - Enfield Football Club is undoubtedly one of the most famous names in non-league football. Founded in August 1893 as Enfield Spartans, by 1912 the club had established itself as a force in amateur football in the London League and was invited to become founder members of the Athenian League. The E's moved to a new ground in Southbury Road in 1936, but despite sporadic success in the Cups and the odd good League season the club led a fairly unremarkable existence until 1959, when George Ludford built a magnificent side that won almost every honour open to it. Led by the club's record goalscorer Tommy Lawrence, Enfield swept to successive Athenian League titles in 1961–62 and 62–63.

Enfield, together with Hendon, Hitchin Town and Sutton United, joined the Isthmian League in 1963–64. The E's were members for 18 seasons before joining the Alliance Premier League in 1981–82, but such was their domination in this spell that they were involved in the title race 16 times, winning seven championships – including two hat-tricks.

The E's first Isthmian League championship was won in 1967–68, despite playing for much of the season without injured ace goal scorer Ray Hill. Under manager Tommy Lawrence, the team remained unbeaten at home and suffered just two defeats all season to rack up a League record 64 points.

Enfield retained the title in 1968–69, scoring more than 100 League goals including an 8–0 win at Dulwich Hamlet, although it was the excellence of defender Phil Fry that consistently caught the eye, leading to him joining the long list of England Amateur internationals to play for the Club.

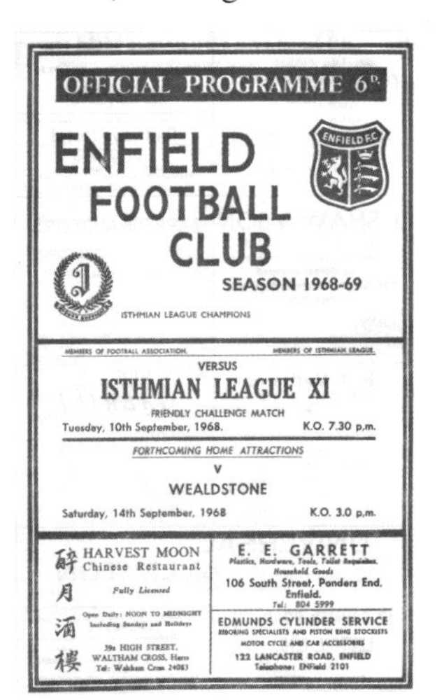

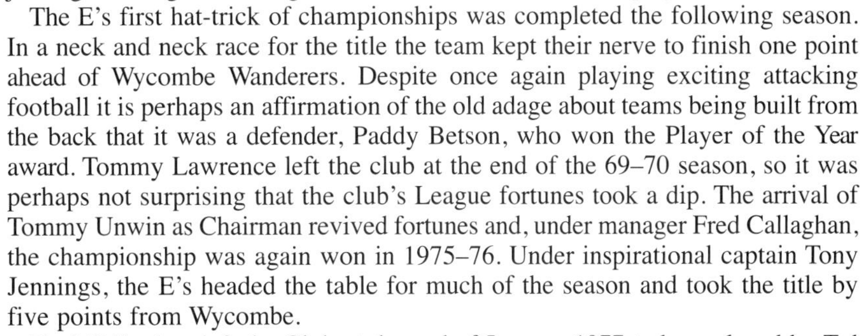

The E's first hat-trick of championships was completed the following season. In a neck and neck race for the title the team kept their nerve to finish one point ahead of Wycombe Wanderers. Despite once again playing exciting attacking football it is perhaps an affirmation of the old adage about teams being built from the back that it was a defender, Paddy Betson, who won the Player of the Year award. Tommy Lawrence left the club at the end of the 69–70 season, so it was perhaps not surprising that the club's League fortunes took a dip. The arrival of Tommy Unwin as Chairman revived fortunes and, under manager Fred Callaghan, the championship was again won in 1975–76. Under inspirational captain Tony Jennings, the E's headed the table for much of the season and took the title by five points from Wycombe.

Fred Callaghan left the Club at the end of January 1977 to be replaced by Ted Hardy in the manager's seat, but despite a number of changes on and off the field, the E's retained the title by a point from Wycombe.

Enfield's best season in the Isthmian League was undoubtedly 1977–78. A 4–1 victory at Bishop's Stortford on the final Saturday of the season saw them set a new points record. Enfield finished 31 points clear of their nearest challengers, amassing 110 points from the 42 games, having won 35, drawn five and lost only two. The 1979–80 championship could not have been won in more exciting circumstances. Enfield welcomed second-placed Walthamstow Avenue to Southbury Road on the last day of the season, enjoying a three-point lead and a superior goal difference of three. Walthamstow thus needed to win by two clear goals to take the title. In front of more than 1,500 spectators, the biggest League crowd for many seasons, few gave much for the E's chances when Walthamstow led 3–1 after 70 minutes, but Ted Hardy's side battled back for a 3–3 draw to take their seventh Isthmian League title.

This 18-year spell in the League also saw the Middlesex club enjoy plenty of cup glory. The E's claimed The FA Amateur Cup in 1966–67 and 1969–70, coupled with two further Final appearances, in 1963–64 and 1971–72. Tragedy befell the club in 1967 when a FA Amateur Cup quarter final at Highgate United *(see programme left)* was halted when a home player was struck by lightning during the game. Enfield also won the European Amateur Cup in 1970, the Isthmian League Cup twice and the Middlesex & London Senior Cups on many occasions. The E's most famous FA Cup exploits came in 1980–81. During that run to the fourth round, Enfield beat Hereford United and Port Vale before losing 3–0 to Barnsley, in front of 35,244 spectators at White Hart Lane, following a 1–1 draw at Oakwell.

An invitation to what was then the Alliance Premier League saw continued success with two titles and two victories in The FA Trophy. However a dip in fortunes saw the E's return to the Isthmian fold for the 1990–91 season and they immediately made their stamp, finishing runners up in three of the next four seasons before winning their eighth Isthmian League title in 1994–95. In winning the League by 14 points the team set a new Club record of 15 consecutive wins but promotion to the Conference was denied on financial grounds. In 1995–96, Enfield and Hayes finished level on points at the top of the table, but the E's were pipped for the championship by just one goal. The following season the E's enjoyed another remarkable run of success but finished runners-up yet again. They suffered just three defeats, scored more goals and conceded fewer than any club in the division and remained unbeaten away from home. Despite all this Yeovil Town beat them to the title.

Their Southbury Road home was sold for development in 1999. Homeless, the Club played its matches at a variety of venues for the rest of that season before ground-sharing at Boreham Wood. The acrimony caused by the sale of Southbury Road caused a split in the ranks with most of the supporters and directors leaving to form a new club, Enfield Town. This uncertainty and acrimony unsurprisingly affected the team and they were relegated from the Premier Division and – a couple of seasons later – the First, too. However, the rot stopped and in their only season in Division Two, they won promotion – albeit, courtesy of The FA realignment, into the Southern League, Division One East. One highlight that season was an FA Vase victory against Enfield Town, a tie and result which attracted national media attention. Thereafter The E's played home games at Ware – a few miles north up the A10 from their home borough. Enfield may have declined from those heady days of the sixties and seventies, but it is perhaps fitting that when they left their Southbury Road home for the last time the team once again stood proudly at the top of the Isthmian League table.

Kingstonian FC - Kingstonian Football Club became members of the Isthmian League on 14 June 1929, after a successful ten-year spell in the Athenian League, when they were unanimously elected at the League's Annual General Meeting to fill the vacancy created by the resignation of Civil Service.

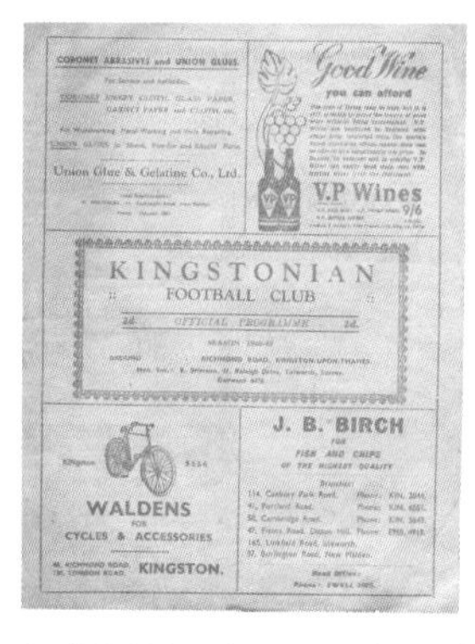

Although the Kingstonian club can trace its roots back to 1885, they first took to the field under the Kingstonian name when they joined the Athenian League in 1919, the first full season after World War One. After early years of struggle, the Ks – as they soon became known – won the League in 1924 and 1926 and quickly developed a reputation as one of England's leading Amateur sides. The Ks finished third in their first Isthmian League season. And they soon enhanced their reputation with their FA Amateur Cup performances, semi-finalists in 1932 and winners in 1933, then by their success in winning the Isthmian League in 1934 and 1937.

Kingstonian's clown supporter at Dulwich

The 1934 success, when they finished two points ahead of Dulwich Hamlet, was based on the wily skills of veteran Ks and Army striker "Gunner" Frank Macey and the prolific goalscoring of Douglas "Jock" Whitehead, who averaged more than a goal a game over the season. After something of a blip in 1936 when they finished second from bottom, Ks were champions once more in 1937, this time finishing two points ahead of Nunhead. Whitehead's goals were again a significant contribution, alongside colleague Doug Smale, who signed professional forms for Chelsea two months before the season's end.

Kingstonian could not play any competitive football during World War Two as their Richmond Road ground had been requisitioned by the Services. In the first season after hostilities ceased, Ks struggled greatly with a side of inexperienced youngsters alongside veterans of the 1930s. They were forced to seek re-election having finished last.

They were re-elected and, within two years, were back challenging for the title, coming second by the narrowest of margins to Leytonstone in 1948. A notable member of this side was Ted Croker, who later found international fame through his various leading roles with The Football Association.

Ks finished third in 1950 but spent the rest of the decade in mid-table, despite the record-breaking goalscoring exploits of Northumbrian forward Johnny Whing. Kingstonian lost a heartbreaking 1960 Amateur Cup final to Hendon, who scored twice in the final three minutes to snatch the trophy. A tight battle for the title that season saw Ks finish fourth, but just three points behind champions Tooting & Mitcham United.

Three years later, they came even closer after a battle royal with neighbours Wimbledon, falling two points short after exasperating home defeats in their last two League fixtures and finishing third.

Following a serious injury to top scorer Johnny McCormack – who replaced Whing and was to become an equally prolific forward – in 1965, Ks fell into gradual decline. And they weren't to challenge for the title again for another quarter of a century. The 1970s was an unhappy decade for the club. They finished in the lower reaches of the League table every season, bar a creditable eighth place in 1972–73. And they were spectacularly relegated to Isthmian League Division One in 1979, winning only three League games all season with none after Christmas. Not the best way for Ks to commemorate their 50th season in the League.

The highlight of their time in Division One was a memorable run to the final of the League's Hitachi Cup competition in 1982. Forward Jim Baptie scored after just over four seconds of the second leg of their semi-final against Premier Division giants Wycombe Wanderers. Although Ks were 5-3 down within 37 minutes, they drew the tie on aggregate and won the replay 2-1, with Baptie netting the winner. An all-conquering Leytonstone–Ilford side awaited them in the final and they completed a League and Cup double with a 2-0 win over Ks in the final at Boreham Wood.

Promotion back to the Premier Division was gained just in time for the Club's centenary in 1985. But it came in controversial circumstances. Having finished in third place, on goal difference behind Leatherhead, Ks were awarded the second of two promotion spots a week after the season's end when Leatherhead were deducted three points for fielding an ineligible player. Ks took advantage of their good fortune to consolidate their position back amongst the Isthmian League's elite, finishing eighth in their centenary season 1985–86. And they were back challenging for the title in 1990 and 1991, the first two seasons at their new Kingsmeadow Stadium ground.

Kingstonian had played their final Isthmian League game at Richmond Road – their fondly remembered home since 1919 – on 23 January 1988, losing by the only goal to then leaders Bromley. As Ks spent 18 months ground-sharing, fans watched an entertaining new team develop under the management of non-league legend Chris Kelly.

The 1990 and 1991 title challenges both faltered in the last month of the season. Kelly moved to a chief executive role, and a string of managerial changes during the mid-90s failed to halt the slide. In 1996 Billy Smith's Ks side memorably won the League Cup (now sponsored by Guardian Insurance) against Aldershot at the Shots' own Recreation Ground. But Smith was soon to be one of four managers sacked by Ks before the end of the year.

In 1997, Ks fortunes took an upswing with the appointment of former Woking manager Geoff Chapple. A run of 15 wins and two draws in their last 18 matches gave Ks the League title by eight points over nearest challengers Boreham Wood, and promotion to the Conference. But Ks were unable to sustain the costs associated with national football, despite consecutive FA Trophy wins. Relegation back to Isthmian ranks in 2001 was quickly followed by administration. Further practical relegation followed in 2004, as the Conference expanded to two divisions and Ks remained in the Ryman Premier Division. Actual relegation back to Division One followed in 2005.

Leytonstone FC - To younger sports fans, Leytonstone is famous for being the birthplace of two England captains, the cricketer Graham Gooch and the footballer David Beckham. Cedars FC were founded in 1886 before becoming Leytonstone FC in 1892. Founder members of the Spartan League in 1907–08, they left after just one season, accepting an invitation to become members of the Isthmian League, where they were to remain for 71 years. In their first season as Isthmian members, they reached the Amateur Cup quarter-finals, where Clapton beat them 8–1.

Although Leytonstone were twice runners-up in their first three Isthmian League campaigns, the title would prove elusive for 30 years – apart from a wartime success in 1918–19. There were, however, cup successes, notably the Essex Senior Cup in 1904–05, the London Charity Cup in 1909–10 and the London Senior Cup in 1919–20. That same season, Leytonstone also reached the quarter-final of the Amateur Cup, where Stanley United ended their interest. Twelve months later, they advanced to the semi-final, but Swindon Victoria

EUROPEAN
AMATEUR
CUP
WINNERS'
CUP
FINAL
– 1st Leg

LEYTONSTONE
(ENGLAND)
v
S.T.E.F.E.R. Rome
(ITALY)

Friday, September 27th, 1968
Leyton Stadium
Kick-off 7.30 p.m.

Official souvenir programme - One Shilling

won 3–1 at neutral Reading. Leytonstone made three European tours in this era, to the Netherlands in 1914 and 1923 and to Germany in 1926. An early star of this era was Albert Barrett, who won England Amateur International caps at Leytonstone before making one full international appearance for England, against Northern Ireland in 1930, after turning professional with Fulham. After hanging up his boots in the 1930s, Barrett returned to Granleigh Road as a coach, before emigrating.

Runners-up for a third time in 1932–33, the championship finally came to Granleigh Road in 1937–38. Leytonstone retained their title the following season, but World War II put paid to any hopes of a hat-trick. They did enjoy success in the Amateur Cup, reaching the semi-final for the second time. The most successful club in Amateur Cup history, Bishop Auckland, came out on top – 1–0 – in a replay at Darlington after the teams had drawn 1–1 at Wimbledon.

In 1946–47, not only was a third championship celebrated, but also the first of three FA Amateur Cup successes was enjoyed, together with a second consecutive Essex Thames-side Trophy. After Enfield and Barnet had been overcome in the Amateur Cup quarter-final and semi-final, respectively, fellow Isthmians Wimbledon provided the opposition in the Final at Highbury. It was the Dons who took the lead through Stannard, but Leytonstone hit back quickly, equalising through Noble before Smith scored the winner before halftime. A brilliant save by Jarvis denied Stannard a second goal as Leytonstone prevailed.

A year later, Leytonstone swept all before them, winning the Isthmian League, Amateur Cup, Essex Senior Cup and London Senior Cup. The Amateur Cup run was impressive because, after beating Hendon 4–1 away in the quarter-final, Leytonstone travelled up to Middlesbrough and trounced Bishop Auckland 5–0 in the last four. The final at Stamford Bridge, pitted the cup-holders against Athenian League champions Barnet, Amateur Cup winners in 1945–46. A crowd of almost 60,000 watched a very tight encounter settled by a solitary goal from Groves. It was enough to send the Cup back to Granleigh Road. Over the next 20 years, Leytonstone would suffer four semi-final defeats in the Amateur Cup. Leytonstone did not enjoy a huge amount of success in The FA Cup. They made only ten appearances in the competition proper and Football League clubs were beaten just twice – Watford 2–1 at home in 1948 and Shrewsbury 2–0, also at home in 1951. Of the ten FA Cup defeats in the competition proper, Walsall were responsible three times and Newport County twice. The last appearance was in 1973–74, when Hendon won an all-Isthmian encounter 3–0 at Claremont Road.

Barry East

In 1965–66, Leytonstone had another four-trophy season, claiming the Isthmian League for the eighth and final time, the Essex Senior Cup, Essex Thames-side Trophy and London Senior Cup. Leytonstone won their third, and last, Amateur Cup in 1967–68. Any hopes of winning the Isthmian Championship foundered on an exhaustive cup season because Leytonstone played six ties in The FA Cup – including a 3–0 defeat of Chesham United in the first qualifying round – and the same number from the last eight of the Amateur Cup. Two goalless quarter-final draws with Enfield were followed by a 1–0 victory, which set up a semi-final against Sutton United. After another goalless draw Leytonstone won the replay 3–1. Their final opponents were the surprising Chesham, and it proved to be a dramatic occasion. Leytonstone lost Hames to a leg injury inside ten minutes. Ten minutes later substitute Albon broke his leg, leaving the Stones to play with ten men for 70 minutes. The only goal came courtesy of two England amateur internationals, Ken Gray scoring on the rebound after Les Tilley's effort had been parried by the Chesham goalkeeper. Leytonstone still had to survive a penalty from Chesham, Hadlow saving from Kent to preserve the victory. This victory brought entry to the inaugural two-legged Barassi Cup or European Amateur Cup Winners Cup. A 1–1 draw at home to Stefer Roma was followed by a 2–2 draw in Italy, which meant the Cup came to England on the away goals rule. Granleigh Road was a unique, quirky stadium, shoe-horned into a tiny space, directly below the westbound platform of Leytonstone High Road Station on the Barking to Gospel Oak railway line. Spectators stood above the action at that end, below it at the other, while a large terrace stood in front of a small stand down the station side. The other side allowed no spectators, as gardens from the adjoining street ran almost to the touchline. Taking corners was always a precise art because players had no run-up. In 1978, Ilford became tenants at Granleigh Road, but it was also a season which saw relegation for Leytonstone. Struggling financially, Leytonstone and Ilford merged for the start of the 1979–80 season.

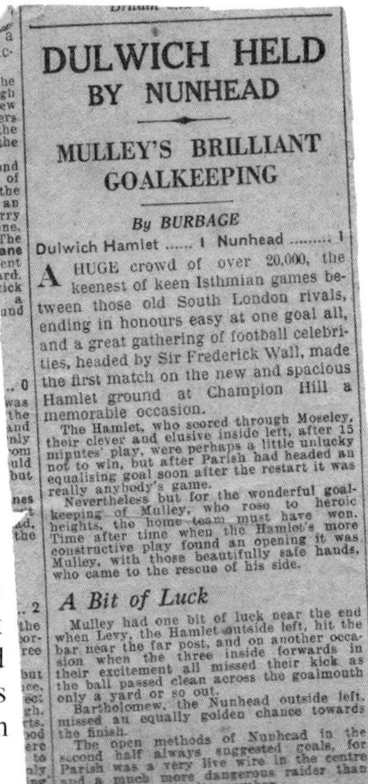

DULWICH HELD
BY NUNHEAD

MULLEY'S BRILLIANT
GOALKEEPING

By BURBAGE

Dulwich Hamlet ...... 1 Nunhead 1

A HUGE crowd of over 20,000, the keenest of keen Isthmian games between those old South London rivals,
ending in honours easy at one goal all,
and a great gathering of football celebri-
ties, headed by Sir Frederick Wall, made
the first match on the new and spacious
Hamlet ground at Champion Hill a
memorable occasion.

The Hamlet, who scored through Moseley,
their clever and elusive inside left, after 15
minutes' play, were perhaps a little unlucky
not to win, but after Parish had headed an
equalising goal soon after the restart it was
really anybody's game.

Nevertheless but for the wonderful goalkeeping of Mulley, who rose to heroic
heights, the home team must have won.
Time after time when the Hamlet's more
constructive play found an opening it was
Mulley, with those beautifully safe hands,
who came to the rescue of his side.

A Bit of Luck

Mulley had one bit of luck near the end
when Levy, the Hamlet outside left, hit the
bar near the far post, and on another occasion when the three inside forwards in
their excitement all missed their kick as
the ball passed clean across the goalmouth
only a yard or so out.

Bartholomew, the Nunhead outside left,
missed an equally golden chance towards
the finish.

The open methods of Nunhead in the
second half always suggested goals, for
Parish was a very live wire in the centre
and a much more dangerous raider than

Nunhead FC - Nunhead, originally known as Wingfield House, were founded in 1888 as a club for working boys by a number of gentlemen connected with the Stock Exchange. As time went on the club was divided into two sections, Eastern and Western, and in 1895–96 the Eastern used to meet Dulwich Hamlet, Dulwich St Peters and Clapham in the Camberwell and Brixton League, and Western played Clapham Hawthorne, Willow Dene and Wimbledon Old Centrals in the Clapham League.

In 1898 Wingfield House merged their two sections and the single club joined the Southern Suburban League, playing their home matches at Hyde Park, Balham, having previously been forced to ground-share with a number of different landlords. In 1900 they moved to Poplar Walk, Loughborough Junction but, two years later, made yet another move, this time to Wavertree Road, Streatham Hill. In 1904–05 Wingfield House amalgamated with Honor Oak FC – a club itself which had been the result of a merger between St. Aidans FC and Dulwich Village FC – and the new Club took the name of Nunhead FC. Playing at the Ivy Ground in their inaugural season, Nunhead won the Southern Suburban League shield and the Surrey Senior Cup, as well as being London Charity Cup finalists. Nunhead went on to win the Southern Suburban League in both 1905–06 and 1906–07, thus completing a hat-trick of championships.

Price ONE PENNY

Nunhead Football Club

Headquarters - NUNHEAD SPORTS GROUND

SATURDAY, DECEMBER 29th, 1934

NEWS AND NOTES.

N.F.C. SUPPORTERS' ASSOCIATION

Season 1907–08 was a ground-breaking one for Nunhead. After almost 20 nomadic seasons, the Club moved to the famous Brown's ground, Nunhead. It was to be their home until they disbanded. Brown's had been the home of Southern United of the Southern League and later Deptford Invicta FC. The ground was of unusual historic interest because King Edward VII – when he was the Prince of Wales – shot there regularly and Dr WG Grace often played cricket there. On the pitch, as founder-members of the Spartan League, they finished third of six clubs. However, it was their only season in that competition. In the first decade of the 20th century, South London was a hotbed of amateur football, but Nunhead's record made them stand out as one of the best. This, no doubt, was one of the reasons why, in 1908, Nunhead were invited to join the Isthmian League. Of the Elite Eleven in this chapter, their time in the Isthmian League is one of the shortest, but they did enjoy plenty of success, particularly in cup competitions, and they were also two-time League champions.

The best of their six pre-War seasons was 1913, when they finished runners-up in the Isthmian League, defeated Dulwich Hamlet 1–0 in the London Charity Cup Final and reached the final of the London Senior Cup, losing 2–0 to Ilford after a 1–1 draw. In The FA Cup, after beating Croydon 2–0, Redhill 7–0, Kingston 4–0 and West Norwood 3–1, they lost to professional Gillingham 2–0. After the War, Nunhead took almost a decade to return to their glory days just before commencement of hostilities. Seasons 1928–29 and 1929–30 were probably the most successful in the club's history. In both campaigns Nunhead won the Isthmian League championship, and in the latter were only just beaten by Bristol Rovers in The FA Cup.

Sadly, the Nunhead story would come to an end after less than 60 years in existence. It was not just the locals, but all of London amateur football which suffered a loss when Nunhead, owing to great ground difficulties, were unable to carry on after the end of World War II. In their first quarter-century as members of the Isthmian League, they were not only one of the strongest but one of the most popular clubs in membership. Their form did decline during the mid to late 1930s. However, Nunhead did enter war-time competition, playing in the eight-team South-Eastern Combination in 1939–40 and 1940–41, finishing fourth and seventh, respectively. Unfortunately, this latter campaign proved to be their final playing season.

However, club stalwart Eric Mulley – the former England international goalkeeper – did try to resurrect Nunhead after the end of the War, but he was unable to obtain either a suitable ground of their own or one in a ground-share arrangement. The Brown's Ground was owned by the Haberdashers' Company and Mulley tried unsuccessfully to get Nunhead's lease on the ground renewed. Ever-optimistic, Nunhead continued to be members of The Football Association until 1949. The greatest of all Nunhead players was Albert Cox, who played in the half-backs, normally in the middle. Albert began his long career with Nunhead at the age of just 14 in 1909 and continued playing until 1931–32 – a wonderful record of 23 years' continuous service.

Another Nunhead stalwart of those days was the tall, powerfully built full-back, Dan Hooton, who was frequently appointed captain of both the Surrey and Civil Service representative sides. Other famous players to wear the Nunhead colours included the Corinthian footballer and Surrey cricketer Johnnie Lockton, Billy Hill, Billy Warnes, Welsh amateur international Emrys Ellis, Norman Sidey, Irish Amateur international Dick Tarrant and speedy winger, Yuno Dimmock. Like several other Isthmian League clubs in the first quarter of the century, Nunhead did a considerable amount of missionary work abroad, many tours being undertaken in Germany and Luxembourg. Haberdasher Aske's playing field remains standing today, a crescent-shaped plot of land, shoe-horned between a railway line and Ivydale Road, Nunhead, just across the road from the famous Nunhead Cemetery.

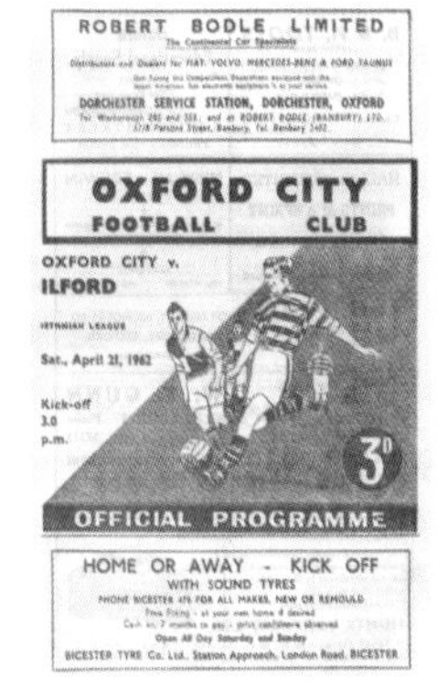

Oxford City FC - Records show that Oxford City was formed in 1882 but, unfortunately, there is no account of matches until 1893. Mr GW Gordon was instrumental in forming the Club on a firm standing on Tuesday 17 October 1893. Three of the clubs City met in those earliest days were New College, Marlow and Newbury.

Oxford first entered The FA Amateur Cup in 1894–95 season, when they beat Slough in a replay 8–0 and Newbury in the next round, before losing to near neighbours Maidenhead.

In 1901–02, City reached the first round proper of The FA Cup, but lost to Lincoln City in a replay. A season later, City reached the final of the Amateur Cup, where they met Stockton at Reading. The match ended in a draw, but Oxford lost the replay 1–0 at Darlington. Three seasons later, Oxford went one better and won the Amateur Cup for the first time, beating Bishop Auckland, 3–0 at Stockton. On the way to the final they defeated Dulwich Hamlet 4–0, Uxbridge 5–1, Cheshunt 4–1 and New Crusaders 4–2 in the semi-final. For the 1907–08 season, Oxford were invited to join the Isthmian League. Their first match was on 4 September 1907, against West Norwood, at the White House Ground. City won 5-2. City again reached the Amateur Cup Final in 1910–11, but lost to South Bank after a replay.

Amateur Cup success continued after World War One. On 3 January 1920, City visited Charlton Athletic and won 2–1. They eventually went out to Dulwich Hamlet in the fourth round, before a record crowd at the White House Ground of 5,500. Season 1922–23 was a disappointing one when Oxford had to apply for re-election to the Isthmian League for the first time. A season later, City were involved in controversy in The FA Amateur Cup. Oxford lost 6–4 at the Casuals, but lodged a protest because they believed the Casuals team contained as many as four ineligible players. The FA upheld the appeal and ordered the tie to be replayed at Oxford. However, as the White House was under water, the match was staged at the Varsity rugby ground, City won 1–0, in front of 7,000 spectators. Although they did not lose the tie, The FA nonetheless punished Oxford with a £2 2s (2 guineas) fine for failing to notify them of the change of venue. The Isthmian League resumed after World War Two and, in 1945–46, City enjoyed their highest finish as League members, ending runners-up to Walthamstow Avenue. Season 1953–54 saw City finish bottom and although they were re-elected, Oxford were warned by Isthmian League Chairman Syd Donaldson to improve their record the next season.

"Well done, lads. Bet you're thrilled and excited at your win!" "Should auld acquaintance..."

Jumping ahead to 1971–72, City entered the Guinness Book of Records when meeting Alvechurch over six matches in The FA Cup's 4th qualifying round. Matches were played at both clubs' grounds, St. Andrews (Birmingham City), twice at Oxford United's Manor Ground and finally at Villa Park, where City lost by the only goal of the game. This record is unlikely ever to be beaten as all FA Cup ties are now decided after just one replay. In December 1979 City became a limited company and, the following year, England's 1966 World Cup captain Bobby Moore was appointed manager, with Harry Redknapp as his assistant. Bobby remained manager for 18 months.

Ex-England skipper to manage ailing Oxford club

Moore signs up for City

Flashback . . . the Oxford Mail's front page December 12, 1979

Oxford were relegated twice from the top division of the Isthmian League in the first ten years of the multiple-division format, but things got much worse when City were forced to resign from the Isthmian League in 1988 Brasenose College, the landlords, terminated the lease of the ground due to a contravention of the terms of the lease. City were unable to play because they could not use a ground commensurate with their standing. However, they continued to meet as a Club. In 1989 a City youth side was formed and, for 1990–91, a senior side was elected to the South Midlands League. They gained promotion to the Premier Division at the first attempt, but had to move to better facilities at the Roman Way ground. At the end of their second season, they won the Championship and were eligible to move back into the Isthmian League. It meant another move, and a completely new ground was a necessity. With the help of the Oxford City Council, a site was found and developed in double quick time to meet the deadline and, more importantly, League requirements. The opening game at Court Farm Park was a friendly against Oxford United, won by City 3–1 in front of 1,800 spectators.

In 1995, Oxford City, multiple finalists in The FA Amateur Cup in the days before it was built, finally got to play at Wembley Stadium. It came in the final of FA Vase but, unfortunately, there was no fairy-tale finish as they lost 2–1 to Arlesey Town. The following season saw City win their first-ever Isthmian League title, the Division One championship, earning promotion back to the Premier Division. After relegation and FA re-structuring, City moved to the Southern League for season 2004–05. It was another sad season, as Oxford suffered relegation back to the Spartan South Midlands League. City have won the Oxon Senior Cup 33 times and been runners up 15 times. The Club has had ten English Amateur Internationals, one Welsh International and numerous others who wore the blue and white hoops before moving on to play in the Football League.

St. Albans City FC - Founded on 13 April 1908, St. Albans City competed in the Herts County and Spartan Leagues before winning the Athenian League twice between 1920 and 1923. The club won election into the Isthmian League on 1 June 1923, outpolling the departing West Norwood by 19 votes to four. A fine of £25 was incurred from the Athenian League, due to the Club's late withdrawal, while Club chairman Frederick Martin resigned in protest at the switch. Life in the Isthmian League kicked off with four defeats in six games and but Saints were then undefeated for the remaining 20 matches to clinch their first championship. The club also brought honour to the League by staging a North v South international trial match at Clarence Park in February 1924. A month later, Harold (Ted) Miller gained an Amateur England international cap. Leading St. Albans' attack was fellow England international Wilfred 'Billy' Minter; in November 1922 he scored seven times in a FA Cup replay at Dulwich Hamlet only for City to lose a historic match 8–7.

FOR UTMOST VALUE
IN
MEN'S & BOYS' OUTFITTING
Suits and Overcoats to measure, or ready-to-wear at keenest Prices.
SPORTS OUTFITTING A SPECIALITY.
W. S. GREEN, CHEQUER ST., ST. ALBANS.
St. Albans City Football Club.
OFFICIAL PROGRAMME
ONE PENNY.
Published by the Proprietors of The Hertfordshire News.
For Best Football Reports read the Herts News Tuesdays—One Penny.
THE "RELIANCE" CHARS-A-BANCS
AVAILABLE FOR
Football and Private Parties.
Reliability—Comfort—Moderate Charges.
Sole Proprietor: ALFRED BARNES, St. Peter's St., St. Albans.

The championship was beyond City's reach for the next two seasons but the Isthmian League was won for a second time in 1926–27 with Minter setting the club record of 36 League goals in one season. Twelve months later St. Albans retained the title for a fifth championship success in eight remarkable years. Inevitably, the team was ageing with Minter and club captain Harold Figg – 362 and 370 appearances respectively – moving into their 30s and, despite success in several cups, the Club floundered in the League, finishing bottom for the first time, in 1938. However, in Charlie Bunce, the club discovered the perfect replacement for Minter; in two seasons Bunce scored exactly 100 times in all competitions.

The post-war era began badly; in November 1946 City suffered an 11–0 rout at Clarence Park by Wimbledon. An influx of summer signings in 1954 almost secured a fourth Isthmian title *(pictured left is the team which finished runners-up)*, but Saints were pipped by Walthamstow Avenue. The following season City slumped to the foot of the table, not winning a single League match until January.

Fortunes were revived during the 1960s with the introduction of local players such as Phil Wood, Dave Lawrence and John Butterfield. That trio made 1,754 appearances for the club (1,119 in the League) with Wood and Butterfield gaining England Amateur international honours whilst Lawrence – then with Bishop's Stortford – became the last captain to lift the Amateur Cup in 1974.

The appointment of Sid Prosser as manager in 1967 preceded a five-year period of sustained success. By the time Prosser resigned in 1972 the Saints had finished third in the Isthmian League, suffered a fourth Amateur Cup semi-final defeat, taken Walsall to a FA Cup 2nd round replay, and played in a dozen cup finals, winning ten. A rapid decline followed and in 1974, City, along with Corinthian–Casuals, were the first clubs to be relegated in the now two-division Isthmian League. Twelve years later the Saints slipped down to Division Two North.

City turned to their former striker John Mitchell, who left to join Fulham in exchange for £500 in 1972. Under his leadership a side brimming with local talent won promotion to Division One at the first attempt. Two years later Mitchell orchestrated a second promotion with a 7–1 win at Lewes on the last day of the season.

ST. ALBANS CITY		BISHOP STORTFORD
R. WHITEAKER	1	D. MOLLISON
D. LAWRENCE	2	D. HAGGAR
L. BURGESS	3	T. KING
P. WOOD	4	S. HILL
D. GIBBS	5	D. GOUGH
D. NEVILLE	6	B. HEWITT
M. HARMAN	7	C. DUGGAN
R. CHILDS	8	N. HAMMOND
J. BUTTERFIELD	9	B. CHEESEWRIGHT
W. RATTY	10	B. NESBIT
W. BROOMFIELD	11	P. PHILLIPS

Mitchell stepped down in 1987, but returned, four years later, to stave off relegation from the Premier Division and with a rebuilt side City, in 1992–93, were title-contenders right up to the final day of the campaign. That disappointment was offset by a run through to the 1st round of The FA Cup and success in two other competitions. With champions Chesham United unable to accept promotion, St. Albans were put forward but were denied when it was stated that the Football Conference ruled that the 140-year old oak tree growing out of the Hatfield Road terrace was unsuitable for their League. Over the next ten years, four more title challenges were mounted, although twice during that time the club dismissed its manager when holding a top-three position. With Garry Hill as manager, St. Albans' national cup competition semi-final jinx struck again in 1998–99 when Forest Green Rovers, in The FA Trophy, overturned a 3–1 first-leg deficit to win 4–3 on aggregate. A year later saw the departure of another truly great goalscorer as Steve Clark, for nine years the Clubs' top marksman, left. In addition to coming within one goal of equalling Minter and Bunce's record of 36 League goals in one season, Clark was also the second St. Albans player to score a double hat-trick in The FA Cup.

The future of the club was in serious doubt in 1998, just 48 hours from closure. To save the club a new board were left with little alternative than to accept the terms of a particularly onerous financial arrangement.

By 2001 the club's board of directors could not maintain payment of both its ongoing and inherited debts. That failure to maintain all payments led to the Isthmian League suspending the club from its competition for five weeks in 2002. With the club's future again threatened, the then Chairman wrote off his loans and gave away his shareholding so that the club's future could be secured by new owners.

On the pitch, though, City struggled to move forward and, in 2004, avoided relegation by just three points, but fortuitously squeezed into the play-offs for a place in the newly-formed Conference South. After two wins at Heybridge Swifts and Bedford Town, St. Albans City said farewell to the Isthmian League after 81 years.

Walthamstow Avenue - The original Walthamstow Avenue Football Club was formed by former students of Pretoria Avenue School in 1900 as Pretoria Avenue Old Boys. Legend has it that a club rule decreed all members had to reside in thoroughfares with "Avenue" in the name! After one season, they changed their name to Avenue United and, two years later, became Walthamstow Avenue. After much success at local level, Avenue disbanded during World War I.

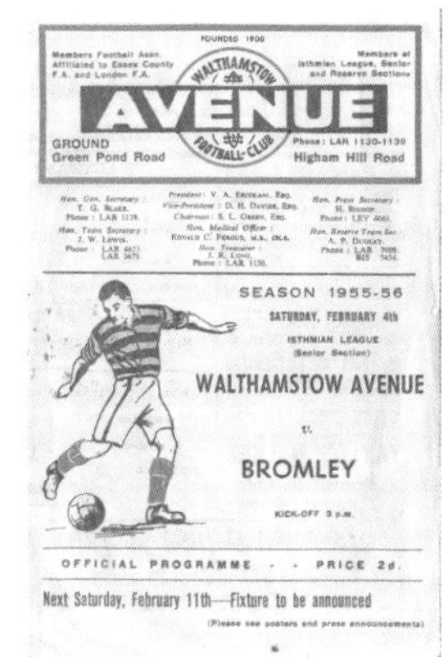

A second Walthamstow Avenue emerged after the War ended, and they enjoyed the palatial surroundings of the ground at Higham Hill, one of the finest in amateur football. Even at the end of its days in the 1980s, Green Pond Road was was an outstanding place to watch football, with plenty of covered accommodation both seated and standing and large terraces on three sides. After World War II, Walthamstow joined the Isthmian League and the Avenue celebrated their debut season with a championship. Their first decade as members of the Isthmian League was stunningly successful, with three championships and seven top-four finishes. The star of the team was Jim Lewis, who was a regular for England and Great Britain. Walthamstow were equally competitive in cup competitions. After a semi-final loss to Bishop Auckland in 1945–46, Avenue reached the Final in 1951–52, never venturing further afield than Southall or Tilbury. Their opponents at Wembley were even more local: Leyton, whose Lea Bridge Road ground was barely two miles from Green Pond Road. In a dramatic Final, watched by 100,000 spectators, Lewis opened the scoring for the Avenue after Trevor Bailey (the international cricketer) had seen his shot pushed against a post by Leyton goalkeeper Sullivan. Skipp equalised for Leyton before half-time and there was no more scoring until the dying moments of extra time, when Hall scored the winner for Walthamstow. This Amateur Cup success brought automatic entry into The FA Cup proper and, after beating Wimbledon, Watford and Stockport County, they had a fourth round tie against the reigning Football League Champions, Manchester United, at Old Trafford. The first contest ended all-square, 1–1, and the replay was staged at Highbury, where United eventually triumphed 5–2. For Lewis, a member of the 1948 Olympic Games squad, those ties gave him a chance to play against the side managed by his coach, Matt Busby.

The following season, Walthamstow Avenue knocked out Gillingham in The FA Cup and reached the Amateur Cup semi-final, where Crook Town won a replay at Sunderland after a draw at Tottenham. Twelve months later, Walthamstow enjoyed their last victory over Football League opposition, beating Queens Park Rangers.

There was a gradual decline thereafter, save for the 1960–61 season, when West Auckland Town were defeated at Wembley in the Amateur Cup Final and second place was achieved in the League. Once again, the Avenue were fortunate in not having to venture too far from home on their run to the final, Harwich being their longest trip. In the final, Avenue were effectively down to ten men because of an first-minute injury to Saggers, but Lewis, a colossus of the amateur game in the post-war era, was again to the fore, hitting the post before Groves knocked in the rebound to cancel out an early strike from West Auckland's Douglass. In a torrential second half downpour, a cross from Dave Andrews was dropped by West Auckland keeper Bowmaker and Lewis finished with aplomb.

In 1963–64 Walthamstow finished outside the top ten for the first time. Inconsistency became a byword at Green Pond Road. Twice a 13th-place finish was followed by a runners-up berth.

The arrival of semi-professionalism in 1974 – as much as the economics of the time – helped to signal the death knell for many clubs, particularly those in and around London. Players became more upwardly mobile and thus were able to travel further afield for their football; in addition, they could negotiate contracts as they wished and with clubs far beyond the local area. Furthermore, with the population growing rapidly, the demand for housing grew, especially in and around London. Not surprisingly, football grounds – often quite dilapidated and with repair bills far beyond the means of the clubs playing there – became prime targets for property developers.

Walthamstow's fortunes fluctuated wildly over the next few years. This was best illustrated by a four-year spell from 1980. In 1979–80, the Avenue finished second in the Isthmian League, just three points behind champions Enfield. Twelve months later, they were in 20th place, although Enfield and Dagenham's defection to the Alliance Premier League meant that no teams were relegated from the Premier Division that season. The roller-coaster continued over the next two seasons, too, with a fifth place being followed by 18th in 1982–83.

In 1986–87, Leytonstone-Ilford moved in as tenants at Green Pond Road after leaving Granleigh Road (and, in the case of Ilford a few years earlier, Lynn Road). That same season the unthinkable happened for the Avenue: they managed just four victories, scraped together just 18 points, and finished bottom of the table. For the first time since the 1920s, they failed to win at least ten times; the Avenue were 15 points from 21st place and 26 from safety. After one season in Division One, an anonymous 15th place finish, they dropped out of the Isthmian League, merging into Leytonstone–Ilford, who soon became Redbridge Forest. It was a sad end to a once-famous club. Three years later, even Green Pond Road was gone, sold for housing, as Redbridge Forest went to Victoria Road, Dagenham, with whom they would also eventually merge.

Wimbledon FC - Wimbledon's connection with the Isthmian League stretches back to the years just after the First World War. In 1921, the competition was expanded from 12 to 14 clubs and the Dons resigned from the Athenian League to join. At first they found it hard to get out of the bottom half of the table but led by Jack Meadows, who later became President, and assisted by Frank Headicar they gradually began to improve.

Wimbledon were champions for the first time in 1931 and repeated the feat the following season. After a gap of two years they managed to win successive titles again in 1935 and 1936. During their heyday the great Dons team of the 1930s also won the London Senior Cup twice, the London Charity Cup, the Surrey Senior Cup, the Surrey Charity Shield twice, the Surrey Combination Cup and in 1934-35 they reached the final of The FA Amateur Cup, only to be beaten by Bishop Auckland after a drawn game at Middlesbrough. The outstanding players of those days were defender Fred Gregory, Bobbie Goodchild in midfield and WW (Doc) Dowden at centre forward.

However the club were unable to reach the same heights after the Second World War despite reaching the Amateur Cup Final again in 1947. They generally finished mid-table and even had to suffer the ignominy of having to apply for re-election at the end of the 1953–54 season. They fared poorly again the following year despite winning the Surrey Senior Cup. Matters came to a head in the summer of 1955 when new chairman Sydney Black brought in Les Henley as coach. It was the start of a successful partnership that was to propel the club to undreamt of heights. At first, however, the improvement was slow as the Dons continued to languish in the wrong half of the table.

WIMBLEDON FOOTBALL CLUB

CLUB NOTES

EVERYTHING FOR MEN AT THE MAN'S SHOP
CAWDELLS of Wimbledon

Then, in 1959, the title was won, for the first time in 23 years, as the club finished five points clear of Dulwich Hamlet.

By the early 1960s Wimbledon were one of the best amateur sides in the country and proved it by winning the Isthmian League title in three successive years – 1962, 1963 and 1964 – as well as beating Sutton United at Wembley in 1963 to finally secure the Amateur Cup. The hero of the hour was Eddie Reynolds who became the only man to score four goals with his head at the famous old stadium. Other stars of that era included inside left Geoff Hamm, right back John Martin and captain and centre half Roy Law.

Sydney Black had correctly foreseen that the amateur era was coming to an end and proposed a move into the ranks of the semi-professional clubs. Thus the Dons joined the Southern League in June 1964 and the rest, as they say, is history.

The Dons claimed three successive Southern League championships in the mid 1970s which, together with some astonishing success in The FA Cup, saw the club elected into the Football League. The highlight of The FA Cup run was a pair of matches against First Division Leeds United. The first game ended goalless, while the replay was decided only by a penalty. Many of that team became household names, including the hero of the two ties, goalkeeper Dickie Guy. Wimbledon built slowly and carefully, but by the mid 1980s, incredibly, they had climbed to the very top, finishing their inaugural season in Division One in sixth position – five places ahead of Manchester United.

Wimbledon held their place among the elite for 14 seasons, capturing the 1988 FA Cup, deservedly beating Liverpool – with another Dons goalkeeper earning FA Cup fame, this time Dave Beasant becoming the first keeper to save a penalty in the Final – and becoming founder members of the Premiership. However in the process they had left behind their historic roots at Plough Lane and rumours of a move out of London were never far away. The financial demands proved too much and when the Dons were finally relegated in 2000 they succumbed to a hostile takeover bid. The FA allowed the club to relocate to Milton Keynes outraging supporters who vowed to start again.

In the summer of 2002 a new club – AFC Wimbledon – was formed by the fans and immediately applied to join the Isthmian (now Ryman) League. At the League's AGM in June they failed to secure the support required. Undaunted the club joined the Combined Counties League instead. After narrowly missing out on promotion in their inaugural season, an unbeaten 2003–04 campaign saw them clinch promotion to a Ryman League they had left 40 years before. They immediately topped Division One at their first attempt. For long term supporters like Michael Renwick the wheel has turned full circle. It was on 30th August 1958, as a 17-year-old, that he first went to Plough Lane. The Dons won a thrilling Isthmian League encounter with Woking 5–4 and he has been hooked ever since. "We've seen some wonderful times," says the now 65-year-old. "Who would have thought that my little Wimbledon would go right to the top and then start all over again?"

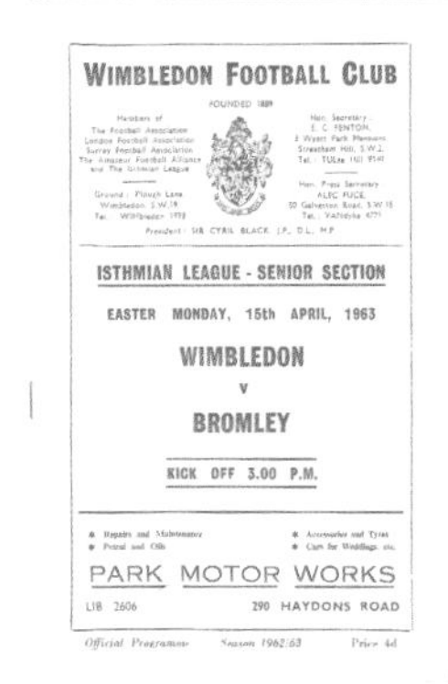

The original club, now known as MK Dons, played at the National Hockey Stadium in Milton Keynes whilst a new ground was built to enable the club to battle its way back up the Football League.

How long will it be before the MK Dons play AFC Wimbledon in a competitive match? And what a match that will be!

Woking FC - Woking Football Club, almost universally known as The Cards (from the Cardinal red of the red and white halves of their shirts), was formed in 1889. The club joined the West Surrey League in 1895–96, winning the title by one point on the final day of the season. However, within 21 years of being formed, the club was in danger of folding for financial reasons. The turning point came when, in January 1908, Woking played Bolton Wanderers in the first round of The FA Cup, having battled through five qualifying rounds. Despite losing the away game 5–0, the club made it into the national press. Bolton Wanderers, impressed by the minnows they had defeated, travelled to Woking for a friendly match the following season, which kept the club solvent.

The Cardinals made an inauspicious start to their days in the Isthmian League, finishing bottom in the 1913–14 season. Wartime saw the loss of possibly Woking's greatest-ever player, full England international Evelyn Lintott, killed in the Battle of the Somme. Post-war saw high crowds and lots of goals, including a 9–4 defeat by Wycombe Wanderers in the 1922–23 season, the club's first at their new Kingfield ground. The 1926–27 season was undoubtedly the high point of the decade, with the Club finishing fifth in the League, drawing a crowd of over 8,000 for an FA Cup tie with Charlton Athletic and winning the Surrey Senior Cup before a crowd of over 7,000. The 1930–31 season saw the club reach the semi-finals of the Amateur Cup, being beaten by the eventual winners, Wycombe. However, the immediate pre-war seasons saw the club struggling again on the field.

When football resumed there were high attendances and the club was boosted by its purchase of the freehold of the ground. Respectable mid-table positions followed before the club moved into a golden era in the mid-1950s culminating in the winning of the Amateur Cup in 1958, when the Cardinals beat Ilford 3–0 before a crowd of 71,000 at Wembley. Woking were part of a little piece of history that day, for it was the last time that the Amateur Cup Final was televised live. Great names from those days still echo round Kingfield: Charlie Mortimore, Roy Littlejohn, Geoff Hamm and Reg Stratton amongst others. Phil Ledger, who made over 100 appearances in goal in the 1953–57 seasons, is the present director of football. Preceding that Amateur Cup triumph, Woking had won the Surrey Senior Cup for the second time in 1955-56 and claimed the runners-up spot in the League in 1957, when the Cards scored a record 104 goals.

It was perhaps not surprising that the Wembley triumph could not be sustained as the team gradually disintegrated. The club, which remained true to its amateur status, increasingly found that it could not hold onto the young players who continued to come through its ranks. The mid-1960s saw falling attendances, although a highlight was the erection of floodlights in the 1964–65 season. However, at the end of that season the club had to apply for re-election to the League. The remaining seasons in that decade saw the club occupying lower mid-table positions.

Sadly, the club then went into decline, culminating in a first-ever relegation in 1982–83. By the end of the 1984–85 season the club had plunged further down the football ladder, being relegated to Division Two South of the Isthmian League. It was during that season that former player Geoff Chapple was appointed as manager. Although he was not able to save the club from relegation, the renaissance was under way. Just missing out on promotion at the first attempt, the club clinched the Division Two South title in 1986–87 and, after two third place finishes in Division One, they were promoted back to the Premier Division at the end of the 1989–90 season.

The next season saw the club become part of FA Cup folklore. Entering the competition at the fourth qualifying round, they beat Conference opposition in the shape of Bath City, Kidderminster Harriers and Merthyr Tydfil to set up a third round tie away to West Bromwich Albion. Recovering from being a goal behind, Woking triumphed 4–2, thanks to a superb team effort and a never to be forgotten hat-trick from Tim Buzaglo. To be drawn out of the hat with a home game against Everton was beyond everyone's wildest dreams. The tie was switched to Goodison Park and, against a team packed with internationals, the sides were separated only by a solitary Kevin Sheedy goal. Over 34,000 people remained in the ground to give the players a rapturous standing ovation.

Promotion to the Conference was achieved in 1991–92. Such was Woking's dominance that the Isthmian League title was clinched in early April, with seven games still to be played. Nearest rivals Enfield had been swept aside 5–0 in a scintillating display of flowing, attacking football and the season ended with the club 18 points clear of the North Londoners.

Wycombe Wanderers FC - Before the formation of Wycombe Wanderers Football Club, there had been several attempts to establish a football team in the town. Football had been flourishing in High Wycombe since 1863, while Marlow, only seven miles away, had been represented at the inaugural meeting of The FA Cup in 1871 and had reached the semi-finals in 1882. Sadly, there are no surviving documents covering the early years of the development of the club that was to become Wycombe Wanderers FC.

However, it is thought the inspiration for the name of the club came from the original Wanderers, five time winners of The FA Cup who had visited the town in December 1877 for a second round FA Cup match against the old High Wycombe club. It is believed that, in the early 1880s, a group of young men living in the Wheelers Field district of the town, got together to talk of playing football. Most of the lads worked in the chair shops of the area hence the nickname of "Chairboys".

In 1884 they decided to form a club to play against some of the villages in the area but, in 1887, they felt they might do well if they went into junior football and played against better clubs. A name had to be agreed upon. North Town Wanderers was proposed but rejected because most of the players came from other areas; eventually it was agreed to call the club Wycombe Wanderers Football Club.

At the start of the 1893–94 season the club decided to rent Spring Meadow to get away from the difficult conditions on the Rye where the club was playing. They had no control over crowds where playing space was limited. In July 1894 a decision was taken to become a senior club and to enter The FA Amateur Cup and The FA Cup.

The next substantial move was to the famous Loakes Park, which, in those days, was an open space for those who occupied the Abbey as a residence. The first match was played at Loakes Park on 7 September 1895. Receipts in that first season were nearly four times those at the previous ground and following on from this the club joined the Southern League.

The new century saw demand for a stand and this was erected in November–December 1903. Unfortunately at this time, the club recorded poor results in the Southern League and, in 1908, withdrew from the Southern League to join the Great Western Suburban League. Just before the outbreak of World War One, Wycombe's application to join the Spartan League was accepted. After the resumption of competitive football in 1919, Wanderers entered teams in both the Spartan League and the Great Western Suburban League. Success followed success, extensions were made either side of the stand in the early 1920s and, for the start of the 1923–24 season, new dressing rooms were opened. Of equal importance was the fact that Wycombe Wanderers had been elected as members of the Isthmian League.

The early years in the Isthmian League did not see any championships. However, one of the highlights of Wanderers' first 100 years came in 1931, when the Amateur Cup was won for the only time with Hayes beaten at Highbury.

Immediately after World War Two, Wanderers were presented with the deeds to Loakes Park by Frank Adams, who had been club captain when they joined the Isthmian League. In 1954–55 Wycombe claimed their first championship. Having got their taste for success, the Chairboys repeated the feat a season later. In 1956–57, Wanderers lost to Bishop Auckland in The FA Amateur Cup.

If the 1950s had been a purple patch in the Club's history, it was dwarfed by the teams of the 1970s. Brian Lee took over as manager in 1969 and under his astute guidance, Wanderers won the Isthmian League championship four times in five seasons between 1971 and 1975. Wycombe then finished runners-up to Enfield in 1976 and 1977. There was also success in The FA Cup, most notably in 1974–75, when First Division Middlesbrough escaped with a draw at Loakes Park *(pictured)* and narrowly won the replay at Ayresome Park.

With Alan Gane and Paul Bence in charge, a seventh Isthmian League Championship was finally secured in 1985, as a result of which the club took promotion to the then Gola League. Relegation followed at the end of that first season, but for Wycombe it proved to be the signal for one final Isthmian League campaign as Wanderers clinched an immediate return to the Conference on the back of their eighth League championship.

The first club from the County of Buckinghamshire to reach the Football League, Wycombe have continued to move forward, on two occasions playing at the third level of English professional football. Then in 2001, Wycombe Wanderers became the first club to appear in the semi-finals of The FA Amateur Cup, FA Trophy and FA Cup.

Some of the legendary players to appear for Wycombe in the Isthmian League days include: Frank Adams, the first Isthmian League captain; Jock McCallum, who scored 224 goals in 348 appearances either side of World War Two; forward Paul Bates and winger Len Worley, from the great sides of the 1950s; three stars from the Brian Lee era, goalkeeper John Maskell, defender John Delaney and striker Tony (Bodger) Horseman who holds the club records for appearances and goals – 749 and 416, respectively – and, finally, striker Mark West, whose career encompassed the Isthmian League, Conference and Football League.

CHAPTER FIVE

Off The Field

The Isthmian League is, of course, mainly about the players and the Clubs in membership, but no celebration of the League's centenary would be complete without a short chapter on some of the most important men who shaped and directed it over its long and glorious history. The Isthmian League has come a long way since the three founders met in Bishopsgate back in the early years of the 20th century.

FOUNDERS

Thomas H Kirkup - Thomas H Kirkup was born in Durham in 1864, but moved down to the South-East as a young man. A fine administrator, by 1895 he was Honorary Secretary of the South Essex League, and was elected a member of the Essex County Football Association Executive the following year.

At the end of 1896, Kirkup was co-opted as a member of Division 3 of the London Football Association. In 1897 he helped to co-found the Essex Branch of the Referees Association and he was elected to the Council of the London FA.

Upon being appointed as a Divisional Secretary of the London FA in 1898, Kirkup resigned from the Essex FA. He became a clerk with Charles Squire (then London FA Secretary), and succeeded him as Secretary of the London Football Association in 1903, which office he held until his retirement in 1947, by which time he was well into his 80s. In May 1904 he was appointed to the Council of The Football Association, was made a Life Member in 1941 and remained on the Council until his death in 1951.

With JR Schumacher, Kirkup was also joint-founder of the Spartan League in 1907 as well as assisting in the formation of the Football Combination in 1915, remaining as Secretary of that competition until 1947.

George J Clarke - George J Clarke was elected on to the Ilford Executive Committee in 1890, and the following year jointly – with W Johnson – took over the position of Hon Financial Secretary continuing in that office until 1915. Clarke then succeeded H Bailey as Club Treasurer, until his retirement in 1947.

He was elected a Life Member of Ilford in 1948 and he died on 28 August 1950. George Clarke was also a member of the London Football Association from 1905 until retiring in 1914. He was elected to the Essex County Football Association in 1919, receiving their long service award in 1929.

He served as an auditor for the Isthmian League and Essex County Football Association for many years.

Frank Evans - Frank Evans can certainly be described as one of Clapton FC's most celebrated servants and, with a history as illustrious as theirs, there have been many important and remarkable individuals involved at one time or another.

He was, amongst other things, a long-serving Hon Secretary at a time when this job involved virtually the everyday running of the Club, arranging its fixtures and the many cup-ties that teams played before organised leagues were formed. It should also be remembered that these were the days when communication, whether between points on a compass or between people, was not always easy.

Evans was one of the leading lights of the movement to recognise the importance of providing competitive league football and, as a result of the increasing ground-swell in this regard, the Isthmian League was finally formed in 1905.

Frank would have been immensely proud of the fact that the Club he loved so much was the only one to remain members of the Isthmian League throughout its first 100 years.

OFFICERS

William A Brown - Chairman 1907–26 - William Brown was the first Hon Treasurer of London Caledonians and continued to act in that capacity until succeeding Hugh Scott McPherson – founder of the Caleys – as Hon Secretary in 1896. He remained in the position for almost six years, resigning in 1901. In recognition of his 15 years' service he was elected the club's first life member.

In 1907, Brown, who was the London Caledonians' representative at Isthmian League Council meetings, was elected as League Chairman, succeeding Percy Timbs, who had resigned the position. Brown served the Isthmian League as Chairman until 1926 when he resigned due to ill-health, subsequently being elected as a Life Member of the League. He was also a Vice-President of the London Football Association from 1899 to 1926. He died in 1940 after a short illness.

Henry Huband, JP - Hon Secretary and Treasurer 1905–35, Chairman 1946–52 and President 1936–52 - Henry Huband was born on 6 September 1868. Educated at Eton College, he represented the school at football, cricket and tennis. He went on to play for the Old Hampden Gurney Football Club, and was Hon Secretary of the Club from 1891 to 1902.

In 1893, at the age of 24, he was elected as a member of the Council of the London Football Association. It was the start of a long involvement with the county and he did an immense amount of work for the Association, being Chairman from 1921 and President from 1923. He was also a member of the Middlesex County Football Association for a number of years, but his greatest contribution to football administration came with The Football Association. Huband was a member of The FA Council from 1907 until his death in 1952, and was Treasurer from 1934. He also served on several committees, including Finance and Amateur Cup.

In 1905, before becoming an FA Councillor, Huband was approached to act as the Hon Secretary and Treasurer of the newly-formed Isthmian League, a position he accepted and held until 1935, when he resigned, having taken over as FA Treasurer. He accepted the League's invitation to become President the following year, a position he held until his death. In 1946, Huband returned to his roots, as it were, and became Chairman of the Isthmian League. Away from football, after World War One, Huband joined the Inland Revenue and was the Assessor of Taxes for the Mayfair Districts. He was also a keen golfer and was a member of the Brent Valley Golf Club.

Sidney A Donaldson - Hon Referees and Fixture Secretary 1934–49, Hon. Secretary and Treasurer 1949–53 and Chairman 1953–64 - Sydney Donaldson's involvement with the Isthmian League is almost unique. His first career began on the pitch, as a player with both Tufnell Park and Ilford. A long and highly successful second career followed from 1921, still on the pitch, but this time as a referee. Donaldson officiated at many notable matches, including Football League, Amateur and full internationals.

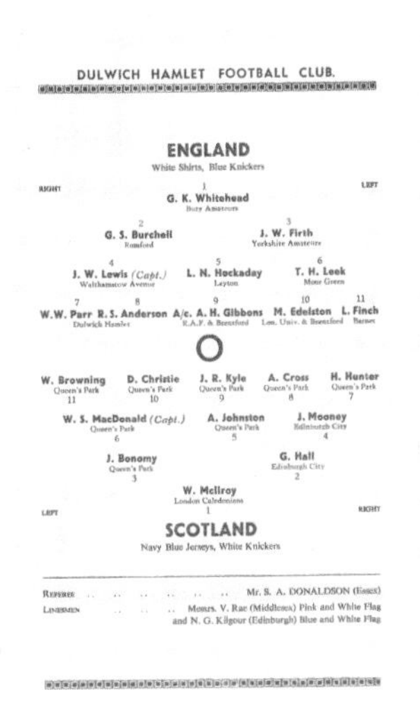
DULWICH HAMLET FOOTBALL CLUB.

ENGLAND
White Shirts, Blue Knickers

RIGHT — LEFT

1 G. K. Whitehead

2 G. S. Burchell, Romford — 3 J. W. Firth, Yorkshire Amateurs

4 J. W. Lewis *(Capt.)*, Walthamstow Avenue — 5 L. N. Hockaday, Leyton — 6 T. H. Leek

7 W.W. Parr, Dulwich Hamlet — 8 R. S. Anderson — 9 A/c. A. H. Gibbons, R.A.F. & Brentford — 10 M. Edelston, Lon. Univ. & Brentford — 11 L. Finch

W. Browning, Queen's Park, 11 — D. Christie, Queen's Park, 10 — J. R. Kyle, Queen's Park, 9 — A. Cross, Queen's Park, 8 — H. Hunter, Queen's Park, 7

W. S. MacDonald *(Capt.)*, Queen's Park, 6 — A. Johnston, Queen's Park, 5 — J. Mooney, 4

J. Bonomy, Queen's Park, 3 — G. Hall, 2

W. McIlroy, London Caledonians, 1

LEFT — RIGHT

SCOTLAND
Navy Blue Jerseys, White Knickers

REFEREE .. .. Mr. S. A. DONALDSON (Essex)
LINESMEN .. .. .. Messrs. V. Rae (Middlesex) Pink and White Flag and N. G. Kilgour (Edinburgh) Blue and White Flag

In 1934 he began his third Isthmian career, this one in administration, succeeding Stanley (later Sir Stanley) Rous in the position of Hon Referees and Fixture Secretary of the League, after Rous had been appointed Secretary of The Football Association. Donaldson took on the role of Hon Secretary and Treasurer following the sudden death of Andrew Ralston in 1949, and he remained in that position until 1953 when he succeeded Henry Huband – who had died the previous year – as Chairman. He retired after 11 years as Chairman and was President from 1965 until his death on 15 October 1968.

Sidney Donaldson was also a member of the Councils of both The FA, which included a spell as Treasurer from 1962 to 1968, and the London Football Association, which he joined in 1947 as a representative of Clapton.

Donald W McKenzie - Hon Assistant Referees and Fixture Secretary 1948–49, Hon Referees and Fixture Secretary 1949–53, Hon Secretary and Treasurer 1953–64, Chairman 1964–72, Chairman and President 1969–72, President 1969–79 - Donald McKenzie, who had served on the Referee's List of the League, was recommended to replace LWS Guy, who had resigned due to business commitments as Hon Assistant Referees and Fixture Secretary in 1948. The following year, he moved up to become Hon Referees and Fixture Secretary, a position he held for four years. When Sidney Donaldson was elected Chairman in 1953, McKenzie took over his former post as Hon Secretary and Treasurer, remaining in that position for 11 years, when he again succeeded Donaldson, this time as Chairman. Following Donaldson's death in 1968, it was proposed that the offices of President and Chairman should be combined, McKenzie was elected to serve in the dual role from 1969. In 1972 McKenzie resigned as League Chairman, but he remained President of the League until his death on 26 November 1979. McKenzie also served on the Council of The Football Association and London Football Association for a number of years.

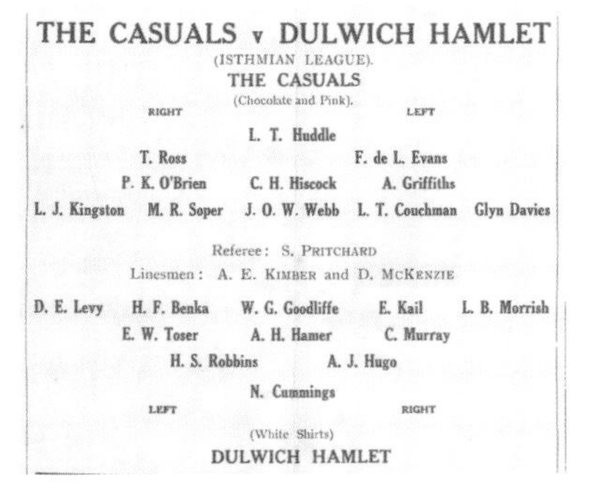
THE CASUALS v DULWICH HAMLET
(ISTHMIAN LEAGUE).

THE CASUALS
(Chocolate and Pink).

RIGHT — LEFT

L. T. Huddle

T. Ross — F. de L. Evans

P. K. O'Brien — C. H. Hiscock — A. Griffiths

L. J. Kingston — M. R. Soper — J. O. W. Webb — L. T. Couchman — Glyn Davies

Referee: S. PRITCHARD
Linesmen: A. E. KIMBER and D. MCKENZIE

D. E. Levy — H. F. Benka — W. G. Goodliffe — E. Kail — L. B. Morrish

E. W. Toser — A. H. Hamer — C. Murray

H. S. Robbins — A. J. Hugo

N. Cummings

LEFT — RIGHT

(White Shirts)
DULWICH HAMLET

Andrew T Ralston - Vice-Chairman 1926–35 and Hon Secretary and Treasurer 1935–49 - Andrew Ralston joined London Caledonians in 1899, and played regularly for 25 years, a wonderful record of service to the Club. Elected Vice-Captain in 1902–03, he was Club Captain from 1903 for six successive years. Ralston stepped up to become Vice-President in 1909, a role he fulfilled for three years, before becoming the Club's Hon Secretary, a position he held from 1912 to 1934. His representative honours as a player were many fold – for both the London and Middlesex Football Associations – and he was awarded a huge collection of medals, caps and badges. He also made occasional appearances for Watford, Tottenham Hotspur and Aston Villa.

His playing days behind him, Ralston was elected to the Isthmian League as Vice-Chairman in 1926, succeeding Sir Arthur Holmes who had resigned. He served in that position for ten years, until taking over as Hon Secretary from Henry Huband, who had been appointed Treasurer of The Football Association. Ralston remained as Hon Secretary until ill-health caused his sudden resignation in 1949. He died shortly afterwards. In addition to his work for the Isthmian League, Ralston had been elected to The FA Council during World War Two and, when Amateur international fixtures resumed, he became a member of the Amateur International Selection Committee.

Barry D East - Vice-Chairman 1971–72, Chairman 1972–82, President 1980–96 - Barry East was a great Isthmian who made a substantial contribution to the League. He was connected with Leytonstone, a Club he joined shortly after World War Two, holding a variety of offices, including Hon Secretary and Trustee, as well as President from 1960.

As with Sydney Donaldson and Andrew Ralston, East began his association with the League as a player. He gained his colours at Brighton College, for football and athletics, before assisting Corinthian–Casuals FC.

After retiring as a player, East represented Leytonstone FC at Isthmian League Council meetings and was elected League Vice-Chairman in 1971. One season later, he assumed the role of Chairman, guiding the League over ten tumultuous seasons. In this time, the Isthmian League expanded from one to three divisions as well as entering into its first sponsorship deal –with Rothman's. He played a major role in the negotiations for the sponsorship deal. In 1980 he added the role of League President, but stepped down as Chairman two years later. In recognition for his services to the League he was elected a Life Member.

East, who was a Vice-President of the Essex County Football Association, was also active in other sporting fields. He was a Vice-President of Essex County Cricket Club and was a former member of the British Olympic Committee as well as being involved in the National Playing Fields Association. He remained President of Dagenham & Redbridge FC – the successors to his beloved Leytonstone – until his death on Boxing Day 1996 when he was taken ill during a League match with Heybridge Swifts.

Stanley F Rous (Later Sir Stanley Rous CBE) - Hon Referees' and Fixture Secretary 1926–34 - Stanley Rous was born in Watford on 25 April 1895. During his early years, he played in goal for Lowestoft. After completing his studies at St. Lukes College, Exeter he became a master at Watford Grammar School – during which time, strangely, football was dropped from the curriculum and rugby was installed. Rous discovered he was a more talented referee than a player and soon became a top referee, officiating at 36 internationals and the 1934 FA Cup Final between Manchester City and Portsmouth.

In 1926 Isthmian League Hon Secretary Henry Huband offered Rous his first administrative post, that of Hon Referees and Fixture Secretary. He accepted the invitation and served in that role until he was appointed Secretary of The Football Association in 1934. Rous was subsequently made a Life Member of the Isthmian League.

His talents as an administrator included the revision of the Laws of the Game in the 1930s, making them far more accessible to the average football fan. And, in the late 1940s, Stanley Rous became Sir Stanley Rous, receiving a Knighthood from King George VI, not only for his services to football, but also for his efforts in organising the Olympic Games when they were held in London in 1948.

He was Secretary at The FA until 1962. Then, on 28 September that year, Rous was elected to succeed Arthur Drewry as President of FIFA, the highest position in world football. He served as President of FIFA for a dozen years, until 1974, when the Brazilian candidate, Dr Joao Havelange, outpolled him with a two-thirds majority vote. In recognition of his services to FIFA, he was immediately elected a lifetime Honorary President. Sir Stanley Rous died in London on 18 July 1986.

JR "Dick" Schumacher - Hon Referees & Fixtures Secretary 1909–26 - Dick Schumacher, a schoolmaster, was elected to represent St. Marks College, Chelsea, on the London Football Association Council in 1897. He was the Association's first Referee's Secretary, holding the post from 1900 to 1905, and was a Vice-President of the Association in the period 1905–14.

Along with Thomas Kirkup – a co-founder of the Isthmian League in 1905 – Schumacher was joint-founder of the Spartan League in 1907 and served as the Spartans in a variety of roles: Hon Secretary and Treasurer, 1907–22; Hon Treasurer, 1923–27; Vice-President, 1925–33; Vice-Chairman, 1927–32 and Chairman, 1932–33. He was, simultaneously, Referees & Fixture Secretary of the Isthmian League between 1909 and 1926, at which time he retired due to ill health and was honoured – along with William Brown – by being made first Life Members of the League.

Dick Schumacher had been a top-class referee and was in charge of the 1912 Cup Final at Crystal Palace between Barnsley and West Bromwich Albion and the replay at Bramall Lane. He was also President of the Walthamstow & District League and Chairman of the London Commercial League. He was also a good cricketer as well as enjoying playing bowls and chess. He died on 6 June 1933.

Alan CF Turvey - Hon Fixture Secretary 1978–1979, Hon. Secretary 1979–1982, Chairman 1982–Present, President 2000–Present - Alan Turvey was born in Essex on 12 November 1933. Following service in the Royal Air Force Police during the years 1952–56, he joined the Southend on Sea Borough Police Force and played for the Police Team until he decided to become a Referee in 1959.

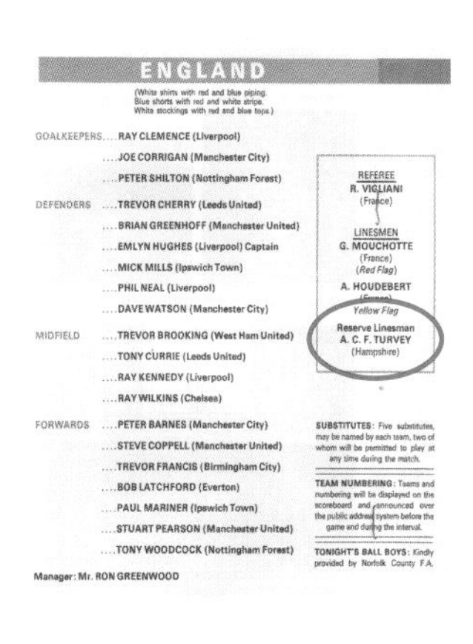

ENGLAND

(White shirts with red and blue piping. Blue shorts with red and white stripe. White stockings with red and blue tops.)

GOALKEEPERS....RAY CLEMENCE (Liverpool)
....JOE CORRIGAN (Manchester City)
....PETER SHILTON (Nottingham Forest)

DEFENDERS ....TREVOR CHERRY (Leeds United)
....BRIAN GREENHOFF (Manchester United)
....EMLYN HUGHES (Liverpool) Captain
....MICK MILLS (Ipswich Town)
....PHIL NEAL (Liverpool)
....DAVE WATSON (Manchester City)

MIDFIELD ....TREVOR BROOKING (West Ham United)
....TONY CURRIE (Leeds United)
....RAY KENNEDY (Liverpool)
....RAY WILKINS (Chelsea)

FORWARDS ....PETER BARNES (Manchester City)
....STEVE COPPELL (Manchester United)
....TREVOR FRANCIS (Birmingham City)
....BOB LATCHFORD (Everton)
....PAUL MARINER (Ipswich Town)
....STUART PEARSON (Manchester United)
....TONY WOODCOCK (Nottingham Forest)

Manager: Mr. RON GREENWOOD

REFEREE
R. VIGLIANI
(France)

LINESMEN
G. MOUCHOTTE
(France)
(Red Flag)
A. HOUDEBERT
Yellow Flag

Reserve Linesman
A. C. F. TURVEY
(Hampshire)

SUBSTITUTES: Five substitutes may be named by each team, two of whom will be permitted to play at any time during the match.

TEAM NUMBERING: Teams and numbering will be displayed on the scoreboard and announced over the public address system before the game and during the interval.

TONIGHT'S BALL BOYS: Kindly provided by Norfolk County F.A.

In 1960 Alan was appointed to the Isthmian League Reserve Section panel of linesmen and, in 1963, was appointed a Class I Referee. Two years later, Alan was appointed as a Referee on the Senior Section of the Isthmian Football League, where he continued to Referee until about 1977. In 1967 Alan was appointed to The Football League as a linesman and subsequently onto the National List of Referees officiating at all levels of the game, including Anglo Italian Competition matches and Senior Linesman on a European Champions Cup Match between the champions of Norway and the Soviet Union.

In 1978 Alan was appointed Isthmian League Hon Fixture Secretary (Division 2) and in 1979 was elected Hon Secretary of the League, a position he held until 1982, when he succeeded Barry East as League Chairman. In 1989 Alan was appointed a Life Member and, in 2000, President of the League. He remains both Chairman and President at the time of publication of this book.

During his period of administration with the League, Alan has been very innovative in terms of major sponsorship and worked closely with Nick Robinson who followed him as Secretary of the Competition in 1982.

In 1991, Alan was elected to The Football Association Council as the Representative for Full Member Clubs in Division 9, another position he still holds at this time. In 1999, following re-organisation of The Football Association, Alan was elected to the Main Board of The Association and retired on reaching the compulsory age in 2005. During his time as an FA Councillor, Alan has served on the Commercial, Discipline, Representative Matches, Leagues, Membership and FA Trophy Committees.

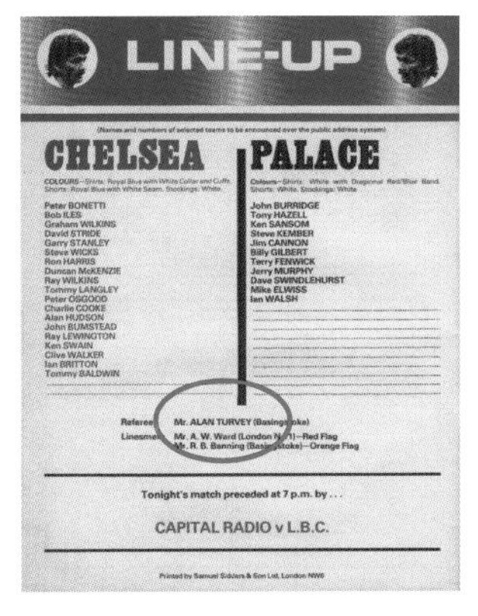

LINE-UP

(Names and numbers of selected teams to be announced over the public address system)

CHELSEA	PALACE
COLOURS—Shirts: Royal Blue with White Collar and Cuffs. Shorts: Royal Blue with White Seam. Stockings: White	Colours—Shirts: White with Diagonal Red/Blue Band. Shorts: White. Stockings: White
Peter BONETTI	John BURRIDGE
Bob ILES	Tony HAZELL
Graham WILKINS	Ken SANSOM
David STRIDE	Steve KEMBER
Garry STANLEY	Jim CANNON
Steve WICKS	Billy GILBERT
Ron HARRIS	Terry FENWICK
Duncan McKENZIE	Jerry MURPHY
Ray WILKINS	Dave SWINDLEHURST
Tommy LANGLEY	Mike ELWISS
Peter OSGOOD	Ian WALSH
Charlie COOKE	
Alan HUDSON	
John BUMSTEAD	
Ray LEWINGTON	
Ken SWAIN	
Clive WALKER	
Ian BRITTON	
Tommy BALDWIN	

Referee Mr. ALAN TURVEY (Basing[illegible]oke)
Linesmen Mr. A. W. Ward (London N[illegible]1)—Red Flag
Mr. R. B. Banning (Basin[illegible]stoke)—Orange Flag

Tonight's match preceded at 7 p.m. by...

CAPITAL RADIO v L.B.C.

Alan is currently Chairman of the Membership Committee and a Member of the Discipline and Protocol Committees. In 2003, Alan received the "50 Year Service to Football Award" from The FA Chairman in recognition of his services to Association Football. In addition to Alan's football interest, in latter years he has become actively involved in bowling and has been Secretary and President of Hampshire Indoor Bowls Association and a Member of the National Executive of the English Indoor Bowling Association.

In 2006, Alan was elected President of the English Indoor Bowling Association, a position he managed to combine with his football duties within the Isthmian Football League and The FA.

Alan would like to be remembered as a true Isthmian and is most conscious of maintaining the traditions of the Isthmian League set by his predecessors. He is proud of his record as the longest serving Chairman in the League's 100-year history.

Ingram Whittingham - Hon Assistant Secretary 1963–64, Hon Fixture Secretary 1964–71, Hon Secretary & Treasurer 1971-73, Hon Secretary 1973–77 and Vice-Chairman 1977–89 - Ingram Whittingham was born on 6 June 1917 and has been associated with the League for more than 40 years. Ingram was Hon Secretary of Dorking Football Club, a position he held until 1960, when he was asked by the Corinthian League Chairman to act as that competition's Secretary, which he duly accepted. In 1963 when the Corinthian League was taken over by the Athenian League he was offered a position as Secretary but declined and instead accepted an invitation from Isthmian League Chairman Donald McKenzie to act as Hon Assistant Secretary. The following season he took on the role of Hon. Fixture Secretary from AW Peacock, a role he fulfilled until 1971. From 1971 to 1977 Whittingham was Hon Secretary, simultaneously holding the post of Hon Treasurer as it was a dual position at that time. Ingram has since acknowledged that while the League had expanded during his term of office from one division of twenty clubs, it still only had forty-four member clubs when he retired. In 1977 he was elected Vice-Chairman, a position which he held until retiring in 1989. He was made a Life Member of the Isthmian League in 1984. Whittingham was also a Council member of the London Football Association from 1971 until 1977 and was subsequently made an Honorary Vice-President. He was elected Life President of Dorking in 1997. Away from football, Ingram worked as Personnel Officer at the Chemical Industries Association until retiring in 1982.

Nick Robinson - Hon Secretary 1982 – 2005, Company Secretary 1989 - present - Nick was born on 2 September 1952 and has been connected with the Isthmian League for nearly 50 years as his father was Treasurer of Dulwich Hamlet up to 1963 and, as Nick says, he was taken down to Champion Hill from the time that he could walk – so that his mother got a break!

In 1975, after returning from Chester where he studied for his law exams, Nick accepted an invitation to become the General Secretary of Dulwich Hamlet, a post which he held for seven years, until 1982. As Club Secretary, he was a member of the League's Council *(see below)* and in 1982 was elected Hon Secretary of the Isthmian League. Nick held the office until the end of the Centenary Season in 2005. He qualified as a Solicitor in 1977 and his legal background was advantageous and saved the League legal fees on many an occasion.

When the League became the first league outside the Football League to convert to a limited company, Nick was appointed the first Company Secretary, a position which he still holds. He was a member of the National Joint Liaison Committee and Treasurer to that organisation as well as being Treasurer to the Inter League (GMAC) Cup during its short existence.

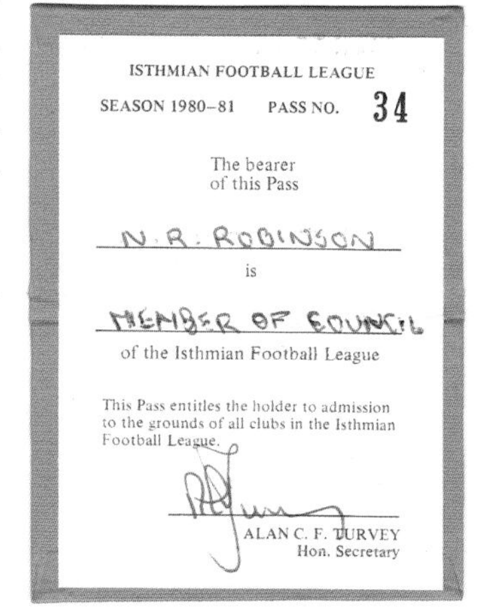

ISTHMIAN FOOTBALL LEAGUE
SEASON 1980–81 PASS NO. 34
The bearer of this Pass
N. R. ROBINSON
is
MEMBER OF COUNCIL
of the Isthmian Football League
This Pass entitles the holder to admission to the grounds of all clubs in the Isthmian Football League.
ALAN C. F. TURVEY
Hon. Secretary

When the Alliance Committee was established by the four senior leagues, Nick was, with Chairman Alan Turvey, a founding member, working with the sister leagues for Non-League football. Through his position with the League, Nick has sat on a number of working parties with The Football Association, including the group which agreed the terms of the players' contract and the sub-committees which have worked on ground requirements and the standardisation of League Rules. Nick also represented the League on The FA Leagues Committee for one season in 2003–04.

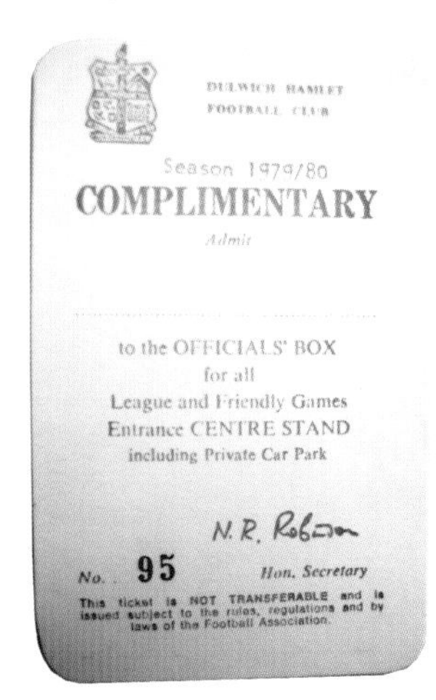

DULWICH HAMLET FOOTBALL CLUB
Season 1979/80
COMPLIMENTARY
Admit
to the OFFICIALS' BOX
for all
League and Friendly Games
Entrance CENTRE STAND
including Private Car Park
N.R. Robinson
No. 95 Hon. Secretary
This ticket is NOT TRANSFERABLE and is issued subject to the rules, regulations and by laws of the Football Association.

More recently Nick was elected as League Vice Chairman and the representative of the League on The Football Association Council, succeeding Alan Boon and joining Alan Turvey on the game's governing body.

Nick became a qualified referee with Surrey County FA in 1999 and continues to officiate on Sunday mornings. On one occasion, when there was a shortage, he found himself running the line as an assistant referee at Chertsey Town! Nick is also a qualified rugby referee and a member of the RFU panel of touch judges.

In 2000, the Isthmian League conferred a Life Membership on Nick Robinson in recognition of his 25 years of service to the League.

OFFICERS PAST AND PRESENT

President:
1905–1908 Rt Hon Alfred Lyttleton, KC
1908–1935 Rt Hon Earl of Rosebery, KG, KT, DSO, MC
1936–1952 Henry J Huband, JP
1953–1965 Max Woosnam
1965–1968 S A Donaldson
1969–1979 D W McKenzie
1980–1997 B D East
2000–present A C F Turvey

Chairman:
1905–1907 P A Timbs, MC
1907–1926 W A Brown
1926–1946 Sir A W Holmes, KBE
1946–1952 Henry J Huband, JP
1953–1964 S A Donaldson
1964–1972 D W McKenzie
1972–1982 B D East
1982–present A C F Turvey

Vice Chairman:
1919–1926 Sir A W Holmes, K B E
1926–1935 A R Ralston
1935–1949 S J Meadows
1949–1963 G W Drane
1971–1972 B D East
1972–1977 F M Wilson
1977–1989 M I Whittingham
2000–present P K Rogers

Hon Secretary & Treasurer:
1905–1935 Henry J Huband, JP
1935–1949 A T Ralston
1949–1953 S A Donaldson
1953–1964 D W McKenzie
1964–1971 F M Wilson
1971–1973 M I Whittingham

Hon Secretary:
1973–1977 M I Whittingham
1977–1979 E S G Bray
1979–1982 A C F Turvey
1982–2005 N R Robinson

Company Secretary:
1989–present N R Robinson

Competition Secretary:
2005–present B A Badcock

Hon Treasurer:
1973–1982 V T B Gurling
1982–1987 B K Robinson

Hon Referees' Secretary:
1963–1964 F M Wilson
1964–1975 J McCulloch
1975–1979 E S G Bray
1979–1986 H J Williams
1986–1988 R E Parker
1988–1999 B W Simmons

Hon Assistant Referees' Secretary:
1973–1975 E S G Bray
1976–1979 H J Williams
1979–1981 A S Barnes
1981–1986 R E Parker
1986–1987 T D Powell
1987–1988 B W Simmons

Hon Registration Secretary:
1970–1973 W Varrall
1973–1976 K Sharp
1976–1977 L C Fensom
1977–1985 J E Wallington
1985–1987 B W Hitchings

Hon Fixture Secretary:
1963–1964 A W Peacock
1964–1971 M I Whittingham
1971–1976 V T B Gurling
1976–1978 K Sharp
1980–1982 R L Reader
1982–1984 D J York
1984–1987 B W Simmons

Hon Fixture Secretary: (Prem Div)
1978–1980 L C Fensom

Hon Fixture Secretary: (Div One)
1978–1980 R L Reader

Hon Fixture Secretary: (Div Two)
1978–1979 A C F Turvey
1979–1980 D J York

Hon Asst Referees' & Fixture Sec:
1946–1948 L W S Guy
1948–1949 D W McKenzie
1951–1953 A W Peacock
1953–1955 J N Smith
1955–1960 R C Davies
1960–1963 F M Wilson

Hon Assistant Secretary:
1963–1964 M I Whittingham
1964–1970 W Varrall
1980–1984 D J York

Hon Referees' & Fixture Secretary:
1909–1926 J R Schumacher
1926–1934 S E Rous (later Sir Stanley Rous, CBE)
1934–1949 S A Donaldson
1949–1953 D W McKenzie
1953–1963 A W Peacock

Hon Assistant Fixture Secretary:
1977–1978 L C Fensom

Hon Reserve Section Secretary:
1970–1971 V J B Gosling

Administration Secretary
1987–2003 C M B Moyse
2003–2005 First Eleven Sports Agency

Referees' Administrator:
1999–2002 D W Cook

MANAGEMENT COMMITTEE/BOARD OF DIRECTORS TO 2005

MEMBER	CLUB	DATES
Alldridge, Derek, MBE	Metropolitan Police	1983–1985
Andrews, Dave	Dagenham & Redbridge	1997–1998
Barratt, Terry	Hitchin Town	1995–2004
Blackman, Rex	Bishop's Stortford	1992–1993
Boon, Alan	Staines Town	1992–2005
Buck, Cyril	Hitchin Town	1984–1989
Cooper, John	Bromley	1988–1997
Eede, Martin	Dulwich Hamlet	2004–2005
Fisher, Dean	Croydon Athletic	2004–2005
Flanders, Des	Metropolitan Police	2004–2005
Geary, Charles	Hendon	1986–1988
Gibson, Mick	Heybridge Swifts	1995–2005
Goodchild, Les	Oxford City	1981–1987
Goodwin, John	Bishop's Stortford	2003–2004
Greig, Gordon	Slough Town	1981–1983
Hermitage, Dave	Sutton United	1991–1995
Jones, Freddie	Kingstonian	1981–1990
Knight, David	Basingstoke Town	1992–2003
Ledger, Phil	Woking	1991–1992
Lee, Brian	Wycombe Wanderers	1981–1985
Molloy, Peter	Sutton United	1981–1986
Morgan, David	Hitchin Town	1981–1984
Moss, Norman	Walthamstow Avenue	1983–1991
O'Neill, Bill	Boreham Wood	1981–1991
Palmer, William	Walthamstow Avenue	1981–1983
Pearce, Jack	Bognor Regis Town	2001–2004
Pembroke, David	Chesham United	1989–1990
Philpin, Fred	Hendon	1991–1992
Reed, Roger	Enfield	1998–2001
Rogers, Peter	Harrow Borough	1985–2005
Rowlands, Stan	Bognor Regis Town	1985–1990
Sophocleous, Costas	Leyton	2003–2004
Stephenson, Wally	Carshalton Athletic	1987–1991
Stonell, Neil	Aylesbury United	1990–1992
Stott, Kevin	Windsor & Eton	2004–2005
Swindley, Nick	Chertsey Town	1993–1995
Tominey, Bernard	St. Albans City	1990–1997
Walters, David	Hastings United	2005–2005
Woodley, Mike	Oxford City	1997–2003

CHAPTER SIX

The Dream Team

The idea for this chapter was simply to find a team of eleven of the best players to play in the League. However, criteria soon had to be agreed upon to decide what qualities a player had to have, other than simply playing in the League; was it the number of games, medals won, international caps or other achievements which would entitle the individual to be selected? Originally it was decided that players could be divided into two teams, those who dignified the League and those who made it to greater things in the sport. However it soon became clear that to select just eleven players from the hundreds who "made it" was an almost impossible task. The Dream Team is therefore revealed and will be a contentious selection. Many views have been taken, dozens of players were considered but discarded. Players were selected for their contribution to the League as much as the honours they won. They are not all Internationals but they all certainly played a major part in the history of the League.

SUBSTITUTES: ERIC MULLEY (GK), LARRY PRITCHARD, TOMMY JOVER, JOHN BUTTERFIELD, PETER DEADMAN

MANAGER: TED HARDY

In alphabetical order:

PAUL GIGGLE (Hitchin Town) - Mention the name Paul Giggle at Hitchin Town and you will inevitably be bombarded with stories of the little man's near two-decade reign as the hero of the Top Field faithful.

Giggle, an ebullient character, was a fine footballer who inspired the Canaries to some of their greatest FA Cup exploits in the mid-1970s. He played 750 first team games for Hitchin, scoring over 200 goals and was widely considered to be one of the best players in the Isthmian League during his long career. Giggle was eyed by a number of Football League clubs in his early days at Hitchin and he guested for Chelsea and Luton Town's youth teams during the late 1960s. He made his debut for the Canaries in the 1968-69 season but the club's manager at the time, Vince Burgess, carefully nurtured his young starlet and refused to thrust him into action too soon. Nevertheless, in the 1969-70 season, Giggle played his part in the club's London Senior Cup triumph. Throughout the 1970s, Giggle's status of folk-hero at Hitchin was rarely threatened, although he had two short and unsuccessful spells away from the club, at Slough and Bishop's Stortford. "It never worked out at other clubs for

me - Hitchin was where I was always happiest," he recalls. "And I had a special relationship with the club's fans."

His career finally ended in the 1986-87 season in which he came back briefly to help nurture the club's youngsters. Even today, Hitchin's fans smile at the mention of his name, however, which was a headline writer's dream - "Giggle has the last laugh!"

ROD HAIDER (Hendon, Kingstonian and Corinthian–Casuals) - Rod Haider was born on 23 January 1943 and was one of the finest players ever to appear in the Isthmian League and, as captain of Hendon and England, a great ambassador for the amateur game. In his storied career at Hendon, encompassing around 600 appearances, he received precisely one caution. His record of 65 Amateur international caps is a record that is unlikely ever to be beaten in the semi-professional game. Haider started at Corinthian–Casuals but was quickly signed by Kingstonian who recognised his undoubted talent. Within a couple of seasons, he was selected for England Amateurs and he collected ten caps whilst at Richmond Road. In the summer of 1966, Haider decided to join Hendon. The Greens had taken the Isthmian League by storm, winning the title once and finishing runners-up twice, to say nothing of appearing in consecutive Amateur Cup finals. Physically, Haider was unexceptional, but he was blessed with exceptional vision, an outstanding brain and unsurpassed energy levels. He played in the centre of midfield, where he roamed effortlessly, but to great effect. As good at stopping the opposition playing as creating openings, Haider filled a role not dissimilar to Martin Peters, in that he suddenly appeared in places defenders didn't expect and his goal scoring record was exceptional. In modern football, if a striker scores 20 goals, he is a hot commodity; Haider regularly exceeded that figure coming out of midfield – and his tally was never padded out by penalty kicks. Hendon probably under-achieved a little in terms of championships and major cup triumphs in the late 1960s and early 70s, but this can be attributed to their general success and the usual fixture backlog that grew out of reaching the latter stages of various cups – if not the finals themselves. This was an era, remember, when not all clubs had floodlights and cup ties took up many Saturday afternoons. In 1972, Hendon won the Amateur Cup for the third time, beating Enfield in the Final. A year later, Haider was at the fulcrum of a Hendon team which did not lose an Isthmian League match until the title had long since been clinched.

Haider became a national celebrity in January 1974 when Hendon met Newcastle United at St James's Park in The FA Cup third round proper. Midway through the second half, with the Greens trailing 1–0, Iam McFaul failed to hold a shot and in came Haider to sweep home the equaliser, *pictured above*. Newcastle won the replay 4–0. It was the last hurrah in Hendon's great quarter-century. A chronic fixture backlog and player discontent meant the title was lost to Wycombe Wanderers (had it been two points for a win and goal average, then the Greens would have retained their crown). That great team broke up with only Haider staying loyal to the club. He was briefly player-manager, but it was not a successful appointment and he was relieved of his managerial duties. Although the club desperately wanted him to remain as a player, he decided to join Hayes, where his playing career wound down.

TONY HORSEMAN (Wycombe Wanderers) - Born at Wycombe on 12th May 1961, Tony made 749 appearances scoring 416 goals for Wycombe Wanderers during a lengthy career with the Loakes Park club. He played minor football for East End, then had two seasons with Wallaby Sports before signing for Wycombe in 1961. He made his debut at Oxford City on 23rd October 1961 and scored in the 3-2 Isthmian League defeat. He kept his place for the rest of the season, mainly on the left wing, before moving to inside-forward the following season. He finished leading scorer with 20 goals, including all five in the Isthmian League win over Clapton at Loakes Park. He kept a regular place in the team for the next fourteen seasons, finishing leading scorer in half of them, and broke the club's scoring record with 60 goals in 1966-67. Despite being on the small size for a striker at 5ft 8ins, he was good in the air and deadly in the six-yard box. At the start of the 1976-77 season, Wycombe signed Ian Pearson and Tony found his appearances limited, but, on Pearson's departure to Millwall, he once more gained a regular place the following season, which was to be his last at Loakes Park, when he scored 13 goals. During his career at Wycombe, the club won four Isthmian League championships and were runners-up twice. He made an FA Amateur Cup semi-final appearance in 1972, took part in several memorable FA Cup runs as well as winning the Berks & Bucks Senior Cup and other honours. He also retired three times in 1964, 1969 and 1972, and quickly returned to the game each time. He gained personal honours with various FA XI's, Isthmian League and the Berks & Bucks Football Association, but was never selected to play for his Country. The nearest he came to an international honour was 45 minutes for the Great Britain Olympic team against Germany in 1967. On finishing with Wycombe, he had short spells at both Tring Town and Flackwell Heath.

Tony Horseman: A career with Wycombe which spanned from 1961 to 1978. The Club's all-time record number of appearances holder and top goalscorer.

TONY JENNINGS (Hendon & Enfield) - Tony Jennings' career straddled the amateur and professional eras and although his playing days ended in what is now the Nationwide Conference, it is as an Isthmian League player that he is best known. He was the first southern-based player to win both FA Amateur Cup and FA Trophy winners medals – doing so ten years apart. He started his career as a right-back at Leytonstone and then joined Hendon in time to be an integral part of their Amateur Cup-winning team of 1972, when Enfield were beaten. A stocky full-back, he was deceptively quick and wingers rarely got the better of him. His occasional forays forward brought him a few goals, normally with powerful shots from distance. Jennings stayed at Claremont Road for three seasons, by which time he had collected his first Isthmian League champions medal, Amateur International caps and enjoyed the spotlight of The FA Cup third round. A few weeks after playing for Hendon against Newcastle United in an FA Cup third round replay, *see picture*, Jennings, along with Derek Baker and Phil Fry, left Hendon for Enfield. Their departure probably cost the Greens the chance of winning back-to-back titles. Enfield, however, were just starting another decade-long run of success.

Jennings' ability to read the game, calm, unflappable temperament, and sound tackling technique made him a natural for the middle of the back four and he soon took up that position. Runners-up to Wycombe Wanderers in 1975, the Es ran off a hat-trick of championships and four in five years, including, in 1977–78, when they set a points record of 110 and had a 31-point margin between themselves and runners-up Dagenham. This was a team without noticeable weakness; they dropped just 16 points, from five draws and two defeats, scored 18 more and conceded 14 fewer goals than any other team in the division. And Jennings was the rock at the heart of this defence. Enfield's finest FA Cup run came at this time with Barnsley being held to a draw at Oakwell before the Tykes, in front of 35,000+ at White Hart Lane, won the replay. Jennings was a regular in the England Semi-Professional team, but games were few and far between, unlike in the Amateur era. Enfield, along with Dagenham, left the Isthmian League in 1981 to join the Alliance Premier League – now the Conference. In Enfield's debut season, they finished runners-up, but had the consolation of winning The FA Trophy. Although Jennings was only a substitute, it was he who was given the honour of leading the team up the famous steps at Wembley to lift the cup. A season later the E's won the title. In 1983–84 Jennings returned to the Isthmian League and played a few games for Dulwich Hamlet, helping them to win the London Senior Cup in a replay against Kingstonian. He moved into coaching, briefly spending time at Hendon, before becoming England's Semi-Professional team coach. Jennings was then appointed manager of Dagenham and he held the dual roles for a couple of seasons in the mid to late 1980s.

BERNARD JOY (The Casuals) - Bernard Joy will, almost certainly, go down in history as the last Isthmian League player to represent England in a full international match and the last amateur to achieve that honour. He is listed below with Dulwich Hamlet's Horrie Robbins in the 1937 England side against New Zealand. Born in Fulham on 29 October 1911, Joy attended London University and played for the institution's football team. Upon leaving university, Joy joined The Casuals and, while retaining his amateur status he played in the Football League for both Southend United and Fulham.

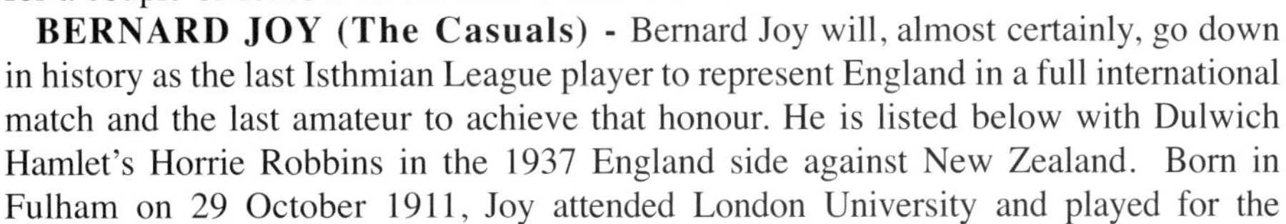

ENGLAND V NEW ZEALAND
CARLAW PARK—JUNE 19, 1937

ENGLAND (WHITE)	NEW ZEALAND (BLACK)
Goal: A. H. Woolcock (2)	Goal: F. Cameron (1)
Full Backs: G. A. Strasser (3), H. S. Robbins (5)	Full Backs: R. Haggett (2), S. Cawtheray (3)
Half Backs: J. Lewis (7), B. Joy (6), J. Sutcliffe (9)	Half Backs: F. Blackie (4), A. Sutherland (5) Capt., E. Jefferey (6)
Forwards: S. Eastham (18), L. C. Thornton (15), W. Parr (17), R. Matthews (11), L. C. Finch (14)	Forwards: A. McCallum (8), R. Scott (10), L. Woods (7), J. Leslie (9), M. Kay (11)
Referee: Mr. A. Kyle.	Linesmen: Messrs. E. Parkinson and L. T. Huddle.

Season 1935–36 was certainly memorable one for Joy. As a triallist from The Casuals, he made three appearances for Arsenal, including in The FA Charity Shield. Joy also won an FA Amateur Cup-winners' medal with the Casuals as they beat Ilford after a replay at West Ham United's

Upton Park ground in an all Isthmian League Final. A few weeks later, he earned his England full international call-up for the short tour of Austria and Belgium. Joy was not in the England team which lost 2–1 to Austria in Vienna, but on 9 May 1936, at Brussels, he played at centre-half. Sadly, England's defence was found wanting against the Belgians, who ran out 3–2 winners. It proved to be Joy's only full international appearance. However, later that summer he was invited to join the Great Britain squad for the Olympic Games in Berlin, Germany. Great Britain lost to Poland in the second round. Joy's career continued to blossom and he left the Casuals to join the Corinthians briefly before Arsenal came calling again. At the time, Arsenal had a number of nursery sides in the south of England, including Golders Green (now Hendon) and Margate and Joy is photographed as part of the Margate squad for the 1937–38 season, although he appeared in 26 of Arsenal's 42 Football League matches. The following season, he was an almost ever-present for Arsenal playing in 39 League games.

When World War Two broke out, Joy joined the Royal Air Force and he was based at RAF Henlow, in Buckinghamshire (coincidentally where Slough Town played a few Isthmian League matches in the 1970s), reaching the rank of Flight-Lieutenant. After the War, Joy continued to play for Arsenal, albeit briefly and his final competitive fixture was against Sheffield United, on 2 November 1946, like his England appearance a 3–2 defeat. He officially retired from playing at the age of 36 in 1948. He made 95 appearances for the Gunners, a number that would have been significantly higher if not for the six seasons lost to the hostilities. One of the final matches of Joy's Arsenal career was a friendly against Moscow Dynamo at Highbury, when Sir Stanley Matthews made a guest appearance for the Gunners. After retiring as a player, Joy moved to Fleet Street and became a much respected journalist writing for the Evening Standard. He also wrote three books, Play Better Football (1951), Forward Arsenal! (1952) and Soccer Tactics (1956), as well as a preview booklet for the 1966 World Cup finals. Joy died in Kenton, Middlesex, on 18 July 1984, aged 72.

EDGAR KAIL (Dulwich Hamlet) - Edgar Kail was the player who made the biggest single contribution towards the club's glory days in amateur football between the two world wars. He was the biggest attraction ever at Champion Hill, at a time when thousands used to flock to watch Dulwich play.

He was certainly one of the greatest forwards in the history of amateur football. Some idea of the greatness of the little wizard can be obtained from a glance at his wonderful record. In addition to gaining a complete set of medals for all the amateur competitions in which the club took part, he was capped 21 times for England Amateurs and, in 1929, he won three caps for the FULL England side, against France, Belgium and Spain, scoring twice on his debut. In fact, he was the last amateur player to play for England in a full international whilst exclusively with an amateur club. Kail's other honours included two appearances for The Rest v England in a full international trial; three times a reserve in full internationals, against Scotland, Ireland and Wales; he played for the Amateurs v Professionals nine times; for the Isthmian League 26 times; together with many appearances for FA Representative XIs, London and Surrey. A prolific goalscorer, he netted 53 goals for Dulwich in season 1925-26 and amassed a total of 427 goals at a rate of almost a goal a game during his Hamlet career – both still stand as first team records for the club and will take some beating! Despite the many tempting offers that were extended to him from several of the country's top Football League teams, he remained with Dulwich throughout his career. Had he turned professional he could have had the highest honours the game can bestow upon a player, but he was not out for distinction and simply played for enjoyment.

Born on 26th November 1900, he was already showing great promise as a footballer when in 1915 he played for England Schoolboys. He joined Dulwich Hamlet at the tender age of 16 during the First World War when the club's ground was in the hands of the Camberwell Gun Brigade who had appropriated it as a parade ground. When the Brigade was drafted abroad, Kail and a number of other keen young footballers who had just left school used to meet on the ground on most evenings. Encouraged by the club's officials, the lads quickly formed a team and played on the ground regularly each Saturday. Along with the other players, he helped roll and mark the pitch, thus enabling the club to keep going until the war ended. In 1920, when Dulwich won The FA Amateur Cup for the first time,

ODD NOTES ON QUEEN'S PARK *Extract from the programme Dulwich Hamlet v Queens Park*

Edgar Kail has the distinction of being the only Englishman to ever play for Queen's Park by invitation and although Edgar possesses two Amateur Cup medals, three full caps, twenty-one Amateur caps and probably more honours than any other amateur he very much values the Queen's Park jersey which was presented to him after that game.

beating Tufnell Park in the Final at Millwall, it was Kail who scored the only goal of the game in extra-time. Five years later he was at it again with both goals in the club's first-ever London Senior Cup Final triumph. He would have had a hat-trick, only the referee blew the final whistle as another shot from Kail was on its way into the net! When the club's second FA Amateur Cup success came in 1932, Kail was again in exhilarating form and scored twice in a record equalling 7-1 win over Marine (Liverpool) at West Ham.

Although only slight in build, Kail was a natural footballer with uncanny control of a ball, and able to shrug off the attentions of physically stronger opponents. He also had an excellent shot in both feet. He may not have possessed as many tricks as the great Arsenal inside-forward of that era, Alex James, but Kail had in his favour that he made direct for the opponents' goal and did not 'wander'. To see him travelling at full speed with the ball at his toe beating the oncoming defenders with apparent ease was a real treat. He was a most attractive player to watch and received more publicity than all the other Dulwich players put together. This, despite the fact that at times he used to irritate the rather critical Champion Hill crowd by his tendency to try to do too much on his own. This habit was probably due to his great confidence in his own ability and was certainly justified by results, for time and again he actually won matches off his own boots. On occasions, though, he could be the most unselfish of players. When Kail retired from playing in 1933 he gained further fame as a football writer with the *Daily Sketch* newspaper. Later he served on the Dulwich Hamlet committee for a number of years, passing on the benefits of his vast experience to future generations of Dulwich players.

Kail died in 1976, aged 75. When the club's present stadium was built in the early 1990s it was decided to name the approach road "Edgar Kail Way", thus ensuring that his memory lived on.

JIM LEWIS SENIOR (Walthamstow Avenue) - Signed from Eton Manor Old Boys during the 1929-30 season, Lewis was an all round sportsman. He had international caps for England at table tennis, won the Senior Federation of Boys' Clubs Boxing title and was a notable cricketer, with a news cutting showing that in one match he scored 102 not out. It was however, football for which he was renowned.

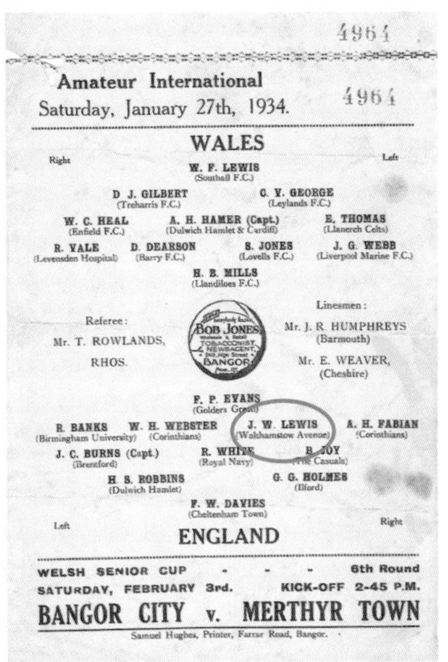

He played his first game for Walthamstow Avenue in an FA Amateur Cup tie against local opposition Walthamstow Grange, a club who had wanted to sign him. This was the beginning of eighteen years in the club colours, including 17 as captain. During this time he made 645 appearances, scoring 339 goals, and at one time was averaging 25 goals per season. Remember they were only playing 26 League fixtures in a season plus cup ties at that time. Jim was awarded 22 England Amateur International Caps and played three times for the full England team in unofficial internationals, twice with an England XI in South Africa in 1939 and then as a half time substitute in a war-time friendly against Wales at Cardiff on 11th November 1939.

He played, in total, 130 representative matches for which he received an illuminated address from The Football Association and played his last game in 1947 in a club friendly against Sing Tao Sports, a visiting top side from China.

He carried his vast experience to work for the Club as manager and secretary and served on the London Football Association until his death in 1976. Sir Stanley Rous, Football Association, stated in 1939, that Lewis was probably the finest all-round player in the game.

League Life Member Norman Moss says: *"I had the honour of being asked to take Jim's place on the London Football Association when he passed away, where I have served since and also as Chairman."*

CHARLIE MORTIMORE (Woking) - Over the years Woking and Aldershot have often swapped and traded many fine players. Kevan Brown, Dave Puckett and Grant Payne immediately spring to mind from recent seasons. But few can have made such a long lasting impact on Kingfield as Charlie Mortimore. Since the Cards had reached The FA Amateur Cup semi-final in 1931 there had been very little to get excited about at Kingfield. This was all about to change when Woking signed the 25 year-old England Amateur International, Charlie, and his 18 year-old brother, John, from Aldershot FC in August 1953.

Charlie had been a regular as an amateur for the Shots from 1949 to 1952, scoring 27 goals in 69 Football League Division 3 (South) appearances. He still jointly holds the AFC individual goal scoring record of five goals in one game – in the 7-2 defeat of Leyton Orient in February 1950. His brother, John, made five England Amateur International appearances while at Woking and was later to sign for Chelsea as a professional in 1957. Mortimore's style of play was to make an immediate impact at Woking. The unassuming schoolteacher played the game with a smile on his face and

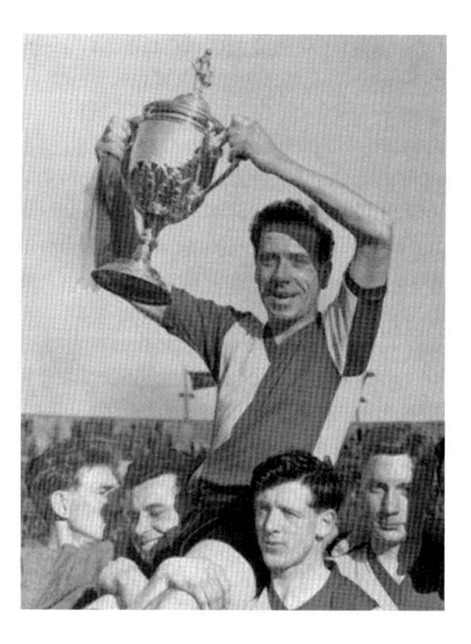

the ball on the ground. He was elected captain in his first season and kept the position until his retirement in 1968. Charlie's goalscoring record with Woking was to become legendary. He still holds three club goalscoring records. He scored 9 goals in his first 7 senior appearances and he eventually amassed a total of 250 goals in 362 games in the cardinal and white halves between 1953 and 1968. He also holds the individual goal scoring record by scoring 9 goals in a 10-3 Surrey Senior Shield victory over Dorking in 1963. Charlie also went on to make another 15 England Amateur International appearances while at Woking between 1957 and 1959, to add to the five he gained while an amateur at Aldershot.

Charlie Mortimore's greatest moment of his career at Woking *(see right)* was to come on 12 April 1958, his 30th birthday, when he captained the victorious Amateur Cup Final team, a victory which is still talked about and remembered proudly today. It was the first – and, for thirty six years, the only – time the Cardinals had played at Wembley. For many older Cards fans the image of Mortimore lifting the Amateur Cup while being hoisted around Wembley, as the Woking section of the 71,000 crowd sang "Happy Birthday To You", will remain in their memories for ever.

As captain and later as coach and manager, Charlie Mortimore represented all that was good about Woking Football Club. He remains a life member of the Club well into his seventies and still visits Kingfield a couple of times a season.

In June 2001 Charlie Mortimore was awarded the MBE in recognition of his services to young people in sport: a just reward for a man who was a real gentleman on the pitch and, to this day, remains the same off it.

WILF MINTER (St. Albans City) - Born in St. Albans on 11 February 1898, Wilfred Harry Minter signed for St. Albans City from Hatfield Road Old Boys in January 1921, and so began the career of the greatest goalscorer ever to play for the club.

Between making his debut in an Athenian League match on 5 February 1921 and his final appearance 16 years later during an Isthmian League game at Nunhead on 29 April 1937, Minter scored 356 times in 362 games. With three Amateur England appearances, Minter, pictured in his England shirt, is St. Albans City's most capped player and with 57 goals for the county he is also Hertfordshire's most prolific marksman of all time.

Throughout the 1920s, with Minter leading the attack, St. Albans City were one of the most respected, and feared, amateur clubs in the country. After two Athenian League championships in three years, the Saints were elected into the Isthmian League in 1923 and within the next five years the championship flag flew at Clarence Park on three occasions. Minter's goals also carried St. Albans through to three semi-final appearances in the Amateur Cup but the club was unable to cement its golden era with a much-coveted place in the final.

Minter, who worked with his father at their grocery store in Culver Road, St. Albans, and latterly at De Havilland in Hatfield, fell just four goals short of the 200 mark in 204 Isthmian League games; by the end of the 1928-29 season Minter had scored 233 times in just 198 Athenian and Isthmian League matches. In all competitions he scored an incredible 52 hat-tricks including 21 in the Isthmian League alone: nine times he notched four goals in a game, six times five goals and once seven.

Yet, for all his triumphs in the Isthmian League, it was an FA Cup tie that secured Wilf Minter a place in the history books. Following a 1-1 draw at Clarence Park, St. Albans City travelled to Champion Hill on 22 November 1922 for a fourth qualifying round replay against Dulwich Hamlet. Edgar Kail scored a hat-trick for Hamlet that day but was outshone by his England team-mate as Minter scored seven times. What clinched Minter a place in the record books is the fact that, remarkably, he was on the losing side as he gained the unwanted distinction of scoring the most goals by a player on the losing side of an FA Cup tie as City went down 8-7.

Such a prolific forward, who was also noted for his unselfishness close to goal and would willingly pass to a team-mate if he were better placed to score, was obviously going to be in demand and his list of representative appearances is phenomenal. In addition to his three Amateur England games he played 37 games for Hertfordshire, 15 for the Isthmian League (13 goals), eight for the Athenian League (2g), four for an FA XI (3g), and two each for The Amateurs at Highbury and Maine Road (2g), The South (3g) and The Rest of England against England (1g).

Minter passed away in St. Albans on 29 December 1984 at the age of eighty-six.

JOHN SWANNELL (Hendon) - John Swannell was England's most capped Amateur International goalkeeper with 61 caps, all won while at Hendon in the 1960s and early 70s. Like many of Swannell's contemporaries, he was certainly good enough to have made it in the professional game. He played a game each for Stockport County – when at Manchester University – and Crystal Palace, but he chose to stay in the unpaid ranks.

Not the tallest of goalkeepers, although of above average height at the time, Swannell would be considered significantly undersized in the modern game. But there was a presence about him, one that made him look taller and generally bigger than his actual measurements. Swannell was an exceptional shot-stopper and a superb organiser of his defence in front of him. Proof of this came when Hendon won the Isthmian League title in 1972–73; the rearguard was so solid that none of the 18 goals the Greens conceded came from a corner. Born in Surrey on 26 January 1939, and an England Schoolboys representative in the 1950s, Swannell went to Manchester University before signing for Corinthian–Casuals, the perennial whipping boys of the Isthmian League. There was probably no better place for a goalkeeper to learn the ropes. He joined Hendon for their Isthmian bow in 1963 and immediately became first choice at Claremont Road, making his Amateur International debut in 1964. Swannell's second season was undoubtedly the Greens' finest, winning both the Isthmian League and The FA Amateur Cup. In his first ten years at Hendon, Swannell would never finish a season outside the top six of the Isthmian League table, clinching two titles, two Amateur Cup winners medals and one Amateur Cup runners-up medal. In 1978, he also picked an FA Trophy runners-up medal with Leatherhead.

In addition to 61 England and two Semi-Professional caps, Swannell played in the Great Britain team in Olympic Games qualifying matches. He visited 39 countries with England, Great Britain and Middlesex Wanderers – for whom he was a regular. In 71 England/GB appearanes he conceded 50 goals.

In The FA Cup, Swannell twice played in the third round proper. For Hendon it was against Newcastle United in 1974, when the Magpies needed a replay to finally advance. Then, having left Hendon to join Leatherhead later that year, he was the Tanners' goalkeeper when they lost 3–2 to Leicester City at Filbert Street.

Coincidentally, one of Swannell's finest games for Hendon had come in a 1960s Amateur Cup tie at Leatherhead. The Tanners were awarded a penalty, which Swannell not only saved and held, but also he threw the ball downfield for a Hendon player to run onto and quickly score. The local newspaper's headline summed up the situation: "Leatherhead win penalty, but Hendon score." After a few seasons as Fetcham Grove, Swannell – approaching 40 – returned to Hendon, but he lost his place midway through his first season back. As further testament to his fitness level, Swannell was still playing veterans football in Surrey in the 1990s.

JOHN WOODLEY (Oxford City) - John (Jack) began his career with Oxford City at the age of 15 in 1957-58 playing in the Colts, as the youth side was then known. He began playing in the reserve team on a regular basis in the 1959-60 season, scoring 10 goals from the outside left position. His first appearance in the first team came on 16 October 1960 at the Richmond Road home of Kingstonian. His goal scoring prowess started in 1962-63 when he scored 54 goals from the same number of matches. In 1963-64 he scored another 45 goals and more were to come the following season when he broke the Club goal scoring record, achieving 64 goals in just 55 appearances. Oxford City visited Belgium club Romal FC during the 1965-66 season, winning the match 3-2 with John scoring a hat-trick. A representative of Standard Liege approached John about playing in Belgium but there were no further developments. That was good news for Oxford City and the Isthmian League. John played for the representative side of the League three times and several times for The FA Amateur XI which took the form of international trials but regrettably never won an England cap. He had trials at Aston Villa in 1959 and then at Tottenham Hotspur in 1961. One of his most memorable games was against Bristol Rovers in The FA Cup at Oxford City's White House ground on 26 November 1966 when he scored the first City goal with a 30-yarder. Oxford City subsequently pulled another goal back to level the score at 2-2 and John nearly won the game with a header which cannoned off the crossbar in the closing seconds of the match. This would have given City a famous victory over a team from the Football League but the replay at Eastville was lost.

In the next four seasons Oxford City reached the Competition Proper of The FA Challenge Cup and John scored against Luton Town, Swansea Town (as they then were), twice, and Bournemouth. John then moved from centre forward to centre half and became captain of the side. He was never sent off in his career and received just three cautions including one from a certain Mr Alan Turvey! He played 904 games in his illustrious career with Oxford City before retiring at the end of season 1979-80 having scored just over 500 goals in the process. He secured a testimonial match against Oxford United which drew a crowd of 800 plus. In the side representing Oxford City that day were both Bobby Moore and Harry Redknapp. John married Carol, the daughter of City secretary (Mac) McGowan in 1963. After finishing his football career he played in local cricket for a number of years before turning to golf which he still enjoys. Always a dedicated player who gave great service to Oxford City as a one-club man.

TED HARDY (Manager) In a long and distinguished career, Ted Hardy earned a place amongst the greatest amateur and semi professional football managers of all time. If one word was used to describe Ted's management style, it would be "passionate". There have been few people anywhere in football who have been as committed, dedicated and in love with the sport as the East Londoner, who won pretty much everything there was to win in Non-League football.

Born in the 1930s, Ted – whose job outside the game was working in a London fruit market – was not only a footballer, but also an amateur boxer. He began his football career at Arsenal before being loaned out to Blackpool, where Stan Mortensen and (later Sir) Stanley Matthews were clubmates. At Leyton in 1964, Ted's playing career ended abruptly with a knee injury. Unable to play and with no manager, the then Athenian League club asked Ted to look after the first team for a couple of weeks. He turned around the club's fortunes and Leyton invited him to take on the job permanently. He agreed and it was the start of a 36-year career with success at almost every turn.

No one would ever describe Ted's teams as the prettiest to watch, but few would argue that they played to their strengths, were uncompromising, very effective and – most importantly – extremely difficult to beat. He instilled in his players a very strong team spirit and players would run, unquestioning, through brick walls for him.

Ted left Leyton to manage Dagenham in 1966 and it was at Victoria Road where he began to make his name, taking the Athenian League side to two Amateur Cup finals. At this time, the Athenian League was clearly second-best in comparison with the Isthmian League and when Bishop's Stortford, who had joined the Isthmians in 1971, approached Ted, he accepted the challenge.

Stortford didn't manage to win the Isthmian League under Hardy – they did come third in their second season in the League – but had the honour of being the last winners of The FA Amateur Cup in 1974, defeating Ilford 4–1 in the Final. One of his on-field lieutenants that day was John Still, who has himself gone on to a long and successful career in management.

Isthmian League titles did come Ted's way in his next job, that of Enfield manager. He was at the helm as the North London club dominated the Isthmian League in the late 1970s, before enjoying big success in the Alliance Premier League (now Conference). With players such as Tony Jennings, Peter Burton, Tony Gibson, John Knapman, John Bishop and Steve King, they were far too good for the competition. Enfield's 1977–78 record of 35 wins, five draws and two defeats bettered Hendon's mark of five years earlier by two points (Hendon won 34 and drew six).

But for all of Ted's great success with already very good teams, arguably his finest achievement was not in winning a League championship or cup, but that of keeping Hendon out of the First Division of the Isthmian League in 1985–86.

Hardy took over in January 1986 with an under-performing squad, lacking talent in many areas and already bottom of the table. It took a while for his philosophies to get through to a number of players and he signed and released many who couldn't adapt. After a 5–0 shellacking at Farnborough, Hendon found themselves with 11 matches remaining and nine points adrift of 20th–placed Epsom & Ewell, who also had eight games in hand. The Greens went undefeated in that spell, recording six victories and five draws to jump out of the bottom two. He was able to attract a number of players who had been with him at Enfield, and other places, and turned around the club's fortunes. In 1986–87, Hendon reached the finals of both the Isthmian League and Premier Inter-League Cups. Another spell at Enfield followed, but this time the circumstances were different and the Es struggled in the Conference, eventually being relegated back to the Isthmian League.

Hardy returned to Victoria Road in the spring of 1996 but could not prevent Dagenham & Redbridge, as they had been known since the 1992 merger, finishing at the foot of the Conference table. A year later, however, he was leading them put at Wembley as they became the first Isthmian team for sixteen years to reach The FA Trophy final. Ted's old guard of players were now retired, but he moulded this new squad into a formidable team. A feature of this team was that every member was technically very sound: a reliable goalkeeper, solid in defence, fluid in midfield and clinical in attack. Defenders in Ted Hardy's teams knew how to tackle properly and legally and they were not afraid of doing so inside their own penalty area, when the punishment for an error in timing is so great.

Ted had already announced that the 1998–99 season would be his last at Dagenham – he had been taken ill a few years earlier and had to cut back on his time at football – but the Daggers hastened his departure by a couple of weeks. His final match in charge was a typical Dagenham performance, a 1–0 victory at Victoria Road.

After the match, he was asked about the performance and mused that he was not totally happy with the award for the man of the match going to Paul Gothard, his and England's goalkeeper. "He only did what I pay him to do," he said gruffly, before acknowledging that Gothard's performance had been exceptional.

Ted also possessed an innate instinct for the game. In his managing days, he would be out two and three nights a week watching games and players. He could be watching a match, talking to somebody as play was going on and give both his correspondent and the match in progress his full concentration. He would break off a conversation to say "goal", a couple of seconds before the ball entered the net, or berate a player he was managing and then continue his always interesting story as if nothing had happened.

Ted still gets around to football, watches the games with a passion and is never afraid to make trenchant comments about what he is watching. Nobody would get more out of this Isthmian League Dream Team than Ted Hardy.

Those who made the dream come true!

The previous section featured a team of Isthmian League legends. The original plan was to counterbalance that list with one containing those players who rose from the Isthmian League. What was clear, however, was that so many players deserved inclusion that the second list was changed to around 100 players who went from the Isthmian League to the Football League (or Premiership). You won't find Peter Crouch (four appearances for Dulwich Hamlet) here, simply because his time in the Isthmian League was only as a loan player. Similarly, a player such as Jay Demerit did not merit inclusion because his only games for Northwood were preseason friendlies. It was decided that a player had to have spent a significant time in Isthmian League first-team football to gain inclusion and then to have had a noteworthy Football League career. The statistics comprise Football League, FA Cup and League Cup starts, + substitute appearances, and then goals scored.

Zema Abbey - Hitchin Town - CAMBRIDGE UNITED (18+7, 5), NORWICH CITY (32+31, 8), BOSTON UNITED (3+2, 1), WYCOMBE WANDERERS (3+2, 0), BRADFORD CITY (6+0, 1), TORQUAY UNITED (2+4, 1) - A product of the Hitchin Town youth set-up, striker Zema Abbey was signed by Cambridge United on a free transfer in February 2000 and was immediately loaned back to the Canaries for the rest of that season. After four months of the following season, Norwich City signed him for £350,000, and put him straight in the first team. Unfortunately he managed a solitary goal for Norwich that season, albeit the only one in a game against QPR. Injuries blighted his career thereafter and he was on short term contracts at Wycombe, Bradford and Torquay after his contract at Norwich expired in 2004. He joined Forest Green Rovers in the summer of 2005.

Carl Asaba - Dulwich Hamlet - BRENTFORD (47+5, 25), COLCHESTER UNITED (9+3, 2), READING (31+1, 8), GILLINGHAM (65+12, 36), SHEFFIELD UNITED (52+15, 23), STOKE CITY (40+30, 9), MILLWALL (17+4, 3) - A total of 106 Football League goals from 261 starts is a superb return and that was Carl Asaba's record in 12 seasons. He was 20 years old when he left Dulwich Hamlet following a very successful 1993–94 season at Champion Hill. Brentford signed him for nothing and loaned him out to Colchester for a couple of months in February 1995, but the Bees were more than happy to accept £800,000 when Reading offered it in August 1997. He had scored 25 goals in 47 starts for Brentford. The move to Reading was not a complete success and he missed one-third of the Royals' campaign, scoring just eight times. Gillingham invested £590,000 in him and he repaid the Kent club with 36 goals in 77 League appearances. Still only 28, Sheffield United paid almost £100,000 just before the 2001 transfer deadline and he gave the Blades two good seasons of service, averaging a dozen goals per term in all competitions. He was released in 2003 and signed for Stoke City on a Bosman, but the goals rather dried up, with just 10 in 75 games in all competitions over two seasons – of which 31 were off the bench. Carl's final season was back in London, at Millwall, where he scored just three goals in the Lions' relegation season.

Peter Anderson - Hendon - LUTON TOWN (178+3, 34), SHEFFIELD UNITED (28+2, 12), MILLWALL (30+2, 4), Tampa Bay Rowdies (USA, 2 spells), Royal Liege (Belgium) - A goalscoring winger, Peter Anderson didn't just have brains in his boots as proved by the fact that he completed his qualification as a chartered accountant while he was a professional footballer. Anderson was not an out and out winger, in that he scored more than his fair share of goals, and it was his ability to create as well as take chances that attracted Luton to the 21-year-old. In the summer of 1975 he moved to Belgium, where he spent a couple of seasons before trying his luck in the NASL with the Tampa Bay Rowdies. At the end of the 1978 NASL season he returned to England and completed that season with Sheffield United. Now more an orthodox midfielder, he averaged a goal every two-and-a-half games for the Blades. Another spell in Tampa Bay followed at the end of that season and Peter's last club was Millwall. His nephew, Alan, briefly played for Hendon before he accepted a football scholarship at the University of South Florida in Tampa Bay.

Dean Austin - St. Albans City - SOUTHEND UNITED (102+0, 3), TOTTENHAM HOTSPUR (144+10, 0), CRYSTAL PALACE (149+18, 6) - Dean Austin left Hendon's youth set-up for St. Albans and quickly advanced into the Saints first team. After six months at Clarence Park, Southend United paid £12,000 for the full-back's transfer and it began a 12-year career that included six seasons in the Premier League. Austin was the subject of a £375,000 transfer in the summer of 1992 when he moved to Tottenham Hotspur and he stayed with Spurs for six seasons before a "Bosman" move to Crystal Palace in July 1998. The Eagles released Austin in November 2002 and he joined Woking, where he finished the season. In 2004, Austin was appointed manager of Farnborough Town, but left the job after less than a season.

Joe Bacuzzi - Tufnell Park - FULHAM (283, 2) - Giuseppe Luigi Davide (Joe) Bacuzzi was born in London during World War I. He made it into the Tufnell Park team soon after leaving school. The full-back quickly showed his class and it was not long before the 19-year-old was snapped up by Fulham. At Craven Cottage, he became a legend, completing 19 seasons with the club, interrupted, of course, by World War II. He continued to play football during the war and actually won 13 caps for England, but all were during the conflict and were thus unofficial. His only representative honour was one appearance for the Football League XI.

Paul Barrowcliff - Hendon, St. Albans City, Hayes, Wycombe Wanderers, Dagenham & Redbridge, Sutton United, Aldershot Town, Stevenage Borough - BRENTFORD (5+6, 0) - Paul Barrowcliff had played in the upper echelons of Non-League football for more than a decade before Brentford took a chance on the then 28-year-old midfielder, paying £60,000 to take him from Stevenage Borough in August 1997. Sadly Paul's League career lasted just the one season and it included a month back at Broadhall Way on loan. However, after the year at Griffin Park, he returned to Non-League football and, in his late 30s, performed consistently for the Metropolitan Police.

Warren Barton - Redbridge Forest - MAIDSTONE UNITED (41+1, 0), WIMBLEDON (178+2, 10), NEWCASTLE UNITED (142+22, 4), DERBY COUNTY (52+0, 0), QUEENS PARK RANGERS (2+1, 0), MK DONS (5+0, 0) - Warren Barton's long and storied career went full circle when he retired after two substitute appearances for Dagenham & Redbridge, the successors to the club from which he left Non-League for the professional game, Redbridge Forest. Warren signed for Maidstone United in the summer of 1989 for £10,000 and soon made an impression in the professional game when he was an ever-present for the Stones in 1989–90 season, when they just missed out on the play-offs. In the summer of 1990, Newcastle United manager Ossie Ardiles offered Maidstone £250,000 for Barton, but he joined Wimbledon instead after they had put in a higher bid of £300,000. Barton spent five seasons at the Dons, averaging 36 League games and two goals per campaign. He was also selected to play for England against the Republic of Ireland in February 1995, the match abandoned because of crowd trouble. It would be his only full international appearance. Newcastle United finally got their man in June 1995, but it cost them £4,500,000. He gave the Magpies almost seven years of service before joining Derby County for 20 months in February 2002, by which time he was almost 33 years old. Brief spells followed at Queens Park Rangers and Wimbledon, before the last hurrah at Victoria Road. Warren is now a regular radio and television football pundit.

LEYTONSTONE ILFORD
(Red & Blue Striped
(Royal Blue Shorts)
(Light Blue Socks)

1. Dave MALLETT
2. Warren BARTON
3. Paul WATTS
4. Alan CAMPBELL
5. Mark DENTON

Dave "Harry" Bassett - Hendon, Walton & Hersham, Wimbledon - WIMBLEDON (35, 0) - Dave Bassett's career turned when he broke his leg in a Sunday match just days after the man he would have replaced at Hendon, Jimmy Quail, had done the same. By the time Harry's leg had healed, he couldn't get into the Hendon team and tried his luck south of the river at Walton & Hersham. Here Bassett enjoyed much success, earning not only England amateur international caps, but also winning The FA Amateur Cup in 1973. Problems at Stompond Lane in the summer resulted in that team breaking up and Bassett turned professional at Wimbledon, where he was part of the famous Dons team that held Leeds United to a draw in The FA Cup. After retiring as a player, he moved into management and his second career has included spells at Wimbledon, Watford, Sheffield United, Crystal Palace, Nottingham Forest, Barnsley, Leicester City and Southampton.

Walter Bellamy - Barking - CHELSEA (35, 1), PLYMOUTH ARGYLE (41, 1), Chelmsford City, LEYTON ORIENT (0, 0), CHESTER (12, 1), WREXHAM (2, 0) - Full-back Wally Bellamy grew up during World War II and started his amateur career with Barking. He wasn't at Vicarage Field for long because, at the age of 20, he was signed by Chelsea. He didn't make it into the first team in his first season, but when he made his debut it was for the defending Football League champions. After more than four years at Chelsea, Wally left and joined Plymouth where, in 18 months, he made half a dozen more appearances than he had with the Pensioners. But Argyle released him in the summer of 1959 and he returned to Non-League football, with Chelmsford City. Midway through his second season there, he was signed by Leyton Orient, but didn't play for them, instead being transferred to Chester at the end of the 1960–61 campaign. Bellamy made only 12 appearances for Chester in the season and moved to Wrexham, where he wound down his professional career after just two matches.

Greg Berry - East Thurrock United - LEYTON ORIENT (68+12, 14), Grebbstaad (Sweden), WIMBLEDON (6+1, 1), MILLWALL (23+11, 1), Woking, BRIGHTON & HOVE ALBION (6+0, 2) LEYTON ORIENT (4+3, 0) - Greg Berry was just 18 when Leyton Orient signed him from East Thurrock United for the princely sum of £2,000. The left-winger made 80 appearances for the Os over the next three seasons, before joining Wimbledon, who paid £250,000 for his services. Unfortunately for Greg, he was struck by the injury bug and made just half a dozen appearances in his two years with the Dons before a £200,000 transfer took him to Millwall. Greg played in just 34 matches for the Lions in his three seasons and this included a trio of loan spells at Woking, Brighton & Hove Albion and back at Leyton Orient. Staying close to his Grays birthplace, Greg returned to Non-League football with Purfleet.

Kevin Blackwell - Bedford Town, Barton Rovers, Boston United, Barnet - SCARBOROUGH (57+0), NOTTS COUNTY, TORQUAY UNITED (18+0), HUDDERSFIELD TOWN (4+2), PLYMOUTH ARGYLE (27+0) - Goalkeeper Kevin Blackwell was almost 28 years old when he made his Football League debut for Scarborough, having played in almost every senior League in England, Bedford Town in the Southern League, Barnet in the Conference, Boston United in the Northern Premier League and Barton Rovers in the Isthmian League. His career would continue for more than a decade after his League bow, although the only team to buy him with a transfer fee, Notts County (who paid Scarborough £15,000 for his services) didn't actually play him. He left Plymouth in his 40th year and signed contracts at Bury, then Sheffield United, both as cover. A move into management at Barton Rovers didn't last long, but he did take over at Leeds United in 2005 and took them all the way to the play off final in 2006.

Jimmy Bullard - Corinthian (Kent League), Dartford, Gravesend & Northfleet - WEST HAM UNITED (0+0), NORWICH CITY (0+0), PETERBOROUGH UNITED (62+0, 11), WIGAN ATHLETIC (144+1, 10) - Midfielder Jimmy Bullard's rise up the football pecking order was not the most ordered there's ever been. After jumping from Corinthian to Dartford, then Gravesend & Northfleet, the midfielder's career stalled after West Ham spent £30,000 on him. He spent 30 months at Upton Park, apart from a brief spell at Norwich, without ever seeing Football League action. He was allowed to go to Peterborough United on a free transfer, where he played under Barry Fry and blossomed. After less than two seasons with the Posh,Wigan Athletic splashed out £200,000 to take him up north and his performances for the Latics transformed the club from a Division Two outfit into members of the Barclaycard Premiership. He made more than 150 appearances for Wigan, as the club twice won promotion and reached the 2006 League Cup Final. Sadly, in September 2006, four games into his new Fulham career – the transfer fee was £2.5 million – he damaged knee ligaments and missed the best part of a year.

Viv Busby - Wycombe Wanderers - LUTON TOWN (64+13, 16), NEWCASTLE UNITED (4+0, 2), FULHAM (114+4, 29), NORWICH CITY (22+0, 11), STOKE CITY (33+17, 10), SHEFFIELD UNITED (3+0, 1), Tulsa Roughnecks (USA, 2 spells), BLACKBURN ROVERS (8+0, 1),YORK CITY (9+10, 4) - Brian Lee knew he had unearthed a diamond when he persuaded Viv Busby, the older brother of Martyn, to sign for Wycombe Wanderers. The Chairboys were already potent up front with Tony Horseman banging in the goals, but now they were even more dangerous. Unfortunately, they couldn't keep him and he turned professional at Luton Town. He scored 74 goals in his Football League career, and it would have been many more had he been able to stay fit. Only his 114-game spell at Fulham came when he was a regular. He was at Luton for 30 months, Norwich for two seasons, Stoke for three years, Sheffield United for six months, Blackburn for four months and York for two seasons.

George Butcher - St. Albans City - WEST HAM UNITED (34+0, 8), LUTON TOWN (121+0, 24) - George Butcher came late to professional football, signing for West Ham United soon after football resumed in 1919. He was almost 30 years old and had lost the prime of his career to the War. However, he was quick to make up for lost time, scoring 8 times in 34 matches for the Irons. In 1920, he left West Ham and joined Luton, where he finished his career four years later.

Richard Cadette - Wembley - ORIENT (19+2, 4), SOUTHEND UNITED (90+0, 49), SHEFFIELD UNITED (26+2, 7), BRENTFORD (67+20, 20), BOURNEMOUTH (4+4, 1), Falkirk (Scotland), MILLWALL (19+5, 5), Shelbourne (Ireland), Clydebank (Scotland) - Richard Cadette never lacked in self-confidence. The mercurial striker banged in loads of goals for Wembley, and was spotted by Orient, who signed him. He found it hard to make his mark and Southend signed him on a free transfer. The coastal air certainly appeared to agree with him because he scored at a rate of better than a goal every other game, netting 56 in 105 matches in all competitions, Sheffield United paid the Shrimpers £130,000 for Cadette's services and Brentford followed, a year later, with £80,000 to bring him back to London. He was never quite as prolific, his 20 goals in 87 matches was not a bad return, but after a loan spell at Bournemouth didn't lead to a permanent move, Cadette decided to try his luck in Scotland, at Falkirk. It worked because he scored plenty of goals and even won the Scottish PFA Player of the Year for Division One in 1993–94. Millwall paid the Scottish club £135,000 for him, but the move was not a big success and Cadette was soon off on his travels, finishing his career at Shelbourne in Dublin and Clydebank. He was later manager of a few clubs in the Ryman League, most recently at Tooting & Mitcham United.

D J Campbell - Chesham United, Stevenage Borough, Aldershot Town, Yeading - BRENTFORD, BIRMINGHAM CITY - The phrase "falling on one's feet" might well become DJ Campbell's motto, given his meteoric rise from Ryman League Division One in January 2004 to the Barclaycard Premiership in January 2006. Campbell had always been a dangerous striker, but he wasn't consistent. That was until he came under the wing of a manager with a similar footballing ethos. Johnson Hippolyte had, to be kind to him, been around the block a bit, scoring goals with regularity but never staying at a club for long. Campbell's talents were harnessed by "Drax" and his assistant Dereck Brown and, suddenly, the livewire striker was consistently on. His time at Yeading saw almost continuous success, culminating in the Ryman Premier Division title and a narrow, but very high profile FA Cup defeat against Newcastle United. A move to Brentford followed and the shock transfer of the January 2006 window was Campbell's move to Birmingham. That's quite a rise.

Simon Clark - Boston, Holbeach United, King's Lynn, Hendon, Stevenage Borough - PETERBOROUGH UNITED (102+5, 3), LEYTON ORIENT (98+0, 10), COLCHESTER UNITED (52+3, 0), Woodlands Wellington (Singapore), King's Lynn, Chelmsford City, Leyton, Maldon Town - In January 2005, Simon Clark's career completed a full circle as he resigned for King's Lynn, 14 years after making his first appearance for the Linnets. Clark moved to London in 1991 and joined Hendon, where he stayed until January 1994. A move to Stevenage brought him not only an Isthmian League champion's medal, but also a transfer to Peterborough United, where he spent three seasons. Simon then moved to Leyton Orient, where he became a prolific goalscorer by centre-half standards, netting a goal every 10 Football League games, either with his head or a very powerful left foot. He was also in the Leyton Orient team which lost to his old club Hendon in the 1997 FA Cup. In 2000, Simon moved to Colchester United where he stayed for just over a season before trying his luck in the Far East, before returning to England. He had a brief spell as manager of Leyton FC in autumn 2005, but continued playing into his 40th year.

Leon Constantine - Edgware Town - MILLWALL (0+1, 0), LEYTON ORIENT (9+1, 3), Partick Thistle (Scotland), BRENTFORD (2+15, 0), SOUTHEND UNITED (40+3, 21), PETERBOROUGH UNITED (5+6, 1), TORQUAY UNITED (34+8, 10), PORT VALE - Leon Constantine walked out on Hendon Reserves because he thought he could play a higher standard. He joined Edgware Town, whose first team were three divisions lower down the Ryman League ladder, but he was getting his wish for first team football. His drive and passion got him his wish in 2000, with a move to Millwall. Division One was probably a bit too much for him so he went to Leyton Orient, then Partick Thistle in Scotland, both on loan. A move to Brentford didn't work for him as he spent most of his time sitting on the bench, starting just two of his 17 appearances. Southend took a gamble on him and he repaid their faith with 21 goals in 43 appearances. Barry Fry took him to Peterborough, but again he was mostly a substitute, so he jumped at the chance of going on loan at Torquay. He settled well in Devon and his goals helped to keep the club in the Football League. But for 2005–06, he was back on the move, this time going to Port Vale, where he has again been a regular scorer.

Geoff Cooper - Bognor Regis Town - BRIGHTON & HOVE ALBION (2+5, 0), BARNET (55+13, 4), Wycombe Wanderers - Midfielder turned full-back Geoff Cooper rose to play in the Football League on two occasions. First he was signed by Brighton & Hove Albion after a successful spell at Bognor Regis Town. Then, after being released by the Seagulls in 1988, he joined Barnet, where he stayed for eight seasons, apart from a week's spell at Wycombe in 1993. During that time the Bees won the Conference and joined the Football League. In the spring of 1995, aged 35, Barnet released him and he returned to Bognor.

Leon Cort - Harlow Town, Dulwich Hamlet - MILLWALL (0+0), Forest Green Rovers, Stevenage Borough, SOUTHEND UNITED (135+2, 11), HULL CITY (85+1, 10), CRYSTAL PALACE - Leon Cort, the younger brother of Carl Cort, had a much tougher football upbringing, scoring plenty of goals for Harlow Town and Dulwich Hamlet before being signed by Millwall in January 1998. Millwall converted him into a defender and he learned his new position with loan spells at both Forest Green Rovers and Stevenage Borough in the Nationwide Conference. In the summer of 2001 Southend took him and he rapidly developed into a quality defender, playing almost every game over the next three seasons. When his contract was up, Peter Taylor took him to Hull City in 2004 and he was part of their promotion squad that went into the Championship in the summer of 2005. He was a regular at the KC Stadium as the Tigers strove for promotion to the Premiership, but came up just short. When Taylor left Hull for Crystal Palace in the summer of 2006, he spent £2.5 million of the Eagles' money to continue working with Cort.

Ian Cox - Carshalton Athletic - CRYSTAL PALACE (3+15, 1), BOURNEMOUTH (197+0, 16), BURNLEY (121+9, 5), GILLINGHAM (106+3, 2) - Ian Cox spent the summer of 2006 in Germany, as a member of the Trinidad & Tobago squad in the FIFA World Cup, a far cry from his days at Carshalton, where the Croydon-born defender began his career. A £35,000 transfer to Crystal Palace in March 1994, after seven months at Colston Avenue, saw the beginning of a Football League career which has seen Cox play more than 100 competitive matches for three different clubs. Cox's time at Selhurst Park was not a huge success and, after three starts in two years, he was the subject of a free transfer – a deadline-day move to Bournemouth. In February 2000, Burnley paid the Cherries £500,000 for his services and, three years later, he made a "Bosman" move to Gillingham. In January 2000, Cox was selected to play for Trinidad & Tobago – his parents' home nation – in a match against Mexico. After a couple of years, he briefly retired from international football to concentrate on his club career, but he returned to duty in 2004 and played in six of T&T's 2006 World Cup qualifiers. Sadly, Cox didn't get to play in the World Cup finals as T&T went out at the group stage.

Ted Croker - Dartford, Carshalton Athletic, Kingstonian - CHARLTON ATHLETIC (8+0, 0) - Ted Croker's contribution to professional football came long after he had hung up his boots. Born in 1924, his football career was put on hold during World War II, but he did enough, especially at Kingstonian, to persuade Charlton Athletic to give him a chance in the professional game. He made just eight appearances for Charlton, before dropping back down to Non-League football, with Kidderminster Harriers and then Headington (now Oxford) United. In retirement, he worked hard as a football administrator, rising to be the most powerful man in English football, as the Secretary of The Football Association.

David Crown - Grays Athletic, Walthamstow Avenue - BRENTFORD (44+2, 8), PORTSMOUTH (25+3, 2), EXETER CITY (6+1, 3), READING (87+1, 14), CAMBRIDGE UNITED (106+0, 45), SOUTHEND UNITED (113+0, 61), GILLINGHAM (83+3, 38) - David Crown began his career in the Athenian League with Grays Athletic and stepped up to the Isthmian League with Walthamstow Avenue, where his pace and anticipation made him a feared goalscoring winger. At the age of 22, he joined Brentford, where he spent 15 months before joining Portsmouth. Pompey sent him out on loan to Exeter City. But it was when he moved to Reading in the summer of 1983 that his career really blossomed. He was a fan favourite at Elm Park and was practically an ever-present in his two seasons there. A move to Cambridge brought a new facet to his game. His previous goalscoring record of 27 goals in 169 games is not bad for a winger; 45 in 106 is phenomenal and that was Crown's feat. The goals came with even greater regularity at Southend where, by now an out and out striker, he found the target 61 times in 113 games. He finished his pro career at Gillingham and returned to Non-League football with Dagenham & Redbridge (who had swallowed up the Avenue during David's pro days) and then Purfleet.

John Crumplin - Bognor Regis Town - BRIGHTON & HOVE ALBION (173+34, 7) - Striker or winger John Crumplin scored lots of goals for Bognor Regis Town and was signed by Brighton for the start of the 1986 season. At Brighton, John played out wide and was very much a creator of goals rather than a taker, given his return of seven goals from more than 200 Football League appearances. Nevertheless he gave the Seagulls seven seasons of service before he was released. John returned to Non-League Football with Conference club Woking.

Jermaine Darlington - CHARLTON ATHLETIC (1+1, 0) - Hendon, Enfield, Aylesbury United - QUEENS PARK RANGERS (70+1, 2), WIMBLEDON (97+8, 3), WATFORD (25+1, 0), CARDIFF CITY (7+2) - Jermaine Darlington left Charlton Athletic, having failed to make the grade, and joined Dover Athletic, then Hendon, believing he was a winger. After a brief spell at Enfield, he joined Aylesbury United, where the present Crystal Palace Director of Football Bob Dowie was manager. He was convinced that Darlington's best position was wing-back and how right he was. After a season at Buckingham Road, QPR paid £25,000 to bring Darlington back to the full-time ranks. Given a second chance, he took it with both hands. After two seasons, Wimbledon, later MK Dons, paid QPR £250,000 for his services and he played for the club during their transitional three seasons. Given a free transfer in 2004, he joined Watford, where he played for a season, before moving on to Cardiff City.

Roy Davies - Slough Town, Hendon, Slough Town - READING (37+0, 2), TORQUAY UNITED (65+5, 6), WIMBLEDON (6+3, 0) - Roy Davies' indefatigable style made him a fan favourite wherever he went, especially with those supporters who recognised a player who never gave less than complete effort. He had been a good midfielder for a few seasons in the Isthmian League, playing for Slough Town (in two spells) and Hendon, before joining Reading where he stayed for almost all of the 1977 season. The following season saw Roy at Torquay in the old Division Four. Roy spent two seasons at Plainmoor, being a regular in the first team. A move to Wimbledon in 1980 proved to be the last of Roy's Football League career after which he joined Wealdstone in the Southern League.

John Delaney - Slough Town, Wycombe Wanderers - BOURNEMOUTH (25+0, 0) - Wycombe Wanderers, Hayes, Sutton United, Oxford City - John Delaney came very close to making the first part of this chapter as one of the Dream Team. However, he makes it into this volume on the back of Wycombe Wanderers' FA Cup run of 1972–73, when they very nearly beat Bournemouth. The Cherries were so impressed with the performance of the commanding centre-half that they offered him professional terms in the summer of 1973, despite the fact that he was already 31 years old. John played parts of two seasons for Bournemouth, before returning to the Chairboys, a move made possible by the ending of the professional/amateur designations in the summer of 1974.

Alan Devonshire - Southall & Ealing Borough - WEST HAM UNITED (345+13, 29), WATFORD (23+2, 1) - Winger or midfielder Alan Devonshire took the Isthmian League by storm at the start of the 1976–77 season and it was not long before West Ham United signed him for £5,000. Alan went on to appear in 358 League matches for West Ham in a 13-year career, which included an FA Cup winner's medal in 1980 and a Second Division champion's medal a year later. On the international stage, Alan was unlucky in that the Hammers spent a large part of his time at Upton Park languishing in the old Division Two and it was also an era where the England coach often preached perspiration ahead of inspiration. Nevertheless, Alan still won eight full England caps. After 14 years at Upton Park, Alan was transferred to Watford, where he stayed for just one season. Devonshire was appointed manager of Maidenhead United in the summer of 1996 and won the Full Members Cup in his first season. He resigned as Maidenhead boss in spring 2003 season, taking up a similar role with Hampton & Richmond Borough.

Iain Dowie - Hertford Town, St. Albans City, Hendon - LUTON TOWN (53+13, 16), FULHAM (5+0, 1), WEST HAM UNITED (12+0, 4), SOUTHAMPTON (115+7, 30), CRYSTAL PALACE (19+0, 6), WEST HAM UNITED (59+10, 9), QUEENS PARK RANGERS (16+15, 2) - Iain Dowie studied rocket engineering while employed by BAE Systems in his home town of Hatfield, and playing football for the local club before moving on to Hertford Town and St. Albans City. Dowie joined Hendon from St. Albans in autumn 1986 and played for the Greens for a little more than two years. A big, bustling, awkward striker, Dowie blossomed under the tutelage of the late Ron Duke, Hendon coach of the time. He scored almost 30 goals in all competitions in three months of the 1988–89 season, before Luton Town signed him in December in a deal worth £30,000. Iain could not continue his prolific scoring in the Football League, but remained a solid player, excellent at holding up play and setting up other players for goals. He had to have had something about him as West Ham bought him twice, for £480,000 in March 1991 and £500,000 in September 1995. Southampton also paid the Hammers £500,000 for him in September 1991 and Crystal Palace bought him for £400,000 in January 1995. Iain made his international debut for Northern Ireland in 1990 as a substitute against Norway and went on to earn 59 caps for his country. After retiring as a player at QPR, he took charge of the reserve team at Loftus Road, before being appointed as assistant coach and – shortly thereafter – manager of Oldham Athletic. Dowie employed his brother Bob as a Non-League scout and the pair unearthed a number of diamonds, such as Jermaine Darlington and Fitz Hall. He was appointed manager of Crystal Palace in December 2003 – with Bob as Director of Football – gaining promotion to the Premiership.

Stanley Earle - Clapton - ARSENAL (4+0, 3), WEST HAM UNITED (258+0, 56), CLAPTON ORIENT (15+0, 1) - Stan Earle made a late start to his football career because the Isthmian League went into wartime hibernation one day after his 18th birthday. Once peace had returned and the Isthmian League resumed operations for the 1919–20 season, Stan joined Clapton. He did not spend long at the Old Spotted Dog, because Arsenal signed him in 1921. He could not make much of an impact on the first-team squad, playing just four times in three seasons, even though he found the net three times. A move to West Ham was perfect for the inside forward and he spent seven seasons at Upton Park, playing more than 250 games. At the age of 35, Stan moved to Clapton Orient where he played for part of the season before retiring.

Freddie Eastwood - Grays Athletic - SOUTHEND UNITED (73+8, 45) - Freddie Eastwood was heartbroken when West Ham United released the 19-year-old. Five years on, it looks like the Hammers might have let a gem slip through their hands. Freddie didn't sulk in the summer of 2003, he dedicated himself to getting better and, more importantly, back to the Football League. He joined Grays Athletic, who were training on a daily basis, so technically were full-time. It suited him and he showed his gratitude by scoring goals by the bucket-load. In November 2004, with Grays on course for the Nationwide Conference, Southend gave him that second chance, taking him on loan. Four weeks, four games and four goals later, a nominal fee made the deal permanent. In the subsequent 18 months at Roots Hall, he has already clocked up more than 50 goals in all competitions, including the decisive one that saw the Shrimpers move up to the League One in the 2005 Playoff Final against Lincoln City at Cardiff, and went on to become a Welsh international after joining Wolverhampton Wanderers.

Nathan Ellington - Walton & Hersham - BRISTOL ROVERS (76+40, 35), WIGAN ATHLETIC (130+4, 59), WEST BROMWICH ALBION (21+18, 7) - Unsurprisingly nicknamed "Duke", Nathan Ellington has proved to be something of a hit wherever he has played. A callow teenager at Walton & Hersham, he was at Stompond Lane for just six months, when Bristol Rovers stumped up £150,000 for his services. Good goalscorers are hard to find and the Pirates were convinced they had a steal. With 35 goals from 76 starts (and 40 sub appearances), they weren't wrong and, when Wigan offered them £1.2 million for the 20-year-old, Rovers weren't going to say no. Ellington continued to score goals, helping

Wigan Athletic all the way to the Premiership. Nathan, however, was not able to join the Latics on their Premiership voyage of discovery. He had been signed by West Bromwich Albion just as the season started, but it took £3 million to prise him away. There are few 25-year-olds who have risen from Non-League football, been the subject of two million-pound transfers, made more than 300 League and Cup appearances and scored in excess of 120 goals.

John Faulkner - Sutton United - LEEDS UNITED (2+0, 0), LUTON TOWN (209+0, 6), Memphis Rogues (USA) - John Faulkner was one of two players Leeds United took from Sutton United following their FA Cup meeting in 1969 – Dario Gradi was the other. Groomed as the replacement for Jack Charlton, Faulkner's first-team career at Elland Road was tragically short; he scored an own goal on his debut and broke his leg in the other game. His rehabilitation took a long time and in 1972, he left Leeds to join Luton. John gave the Hatters five good seasons, making more than 200 appearances. After moving to America to play in the North American Soccer League, Faulkner returned to England and, still in the South Midlands, became manager of Barton Rovers in the 1990s.

Les Ferdinand MBE - Viking Sports, Southall, Hayes - QUEENS PARK RANGERS (152+11, 80), BRENTFORD (3+0, 0), Besiktas (Turkey), NEWCASTLE UNITED (67+1, 41), TOTTENHAM HOTSPUR (97+21, 33), WEST HAM UNITED (12+2, 2), LEICESTER CITY (20+9, 12), BOLTON WANDERERS (1+11, 1), READING (4+8, 1) - Les Ferdinand started his career with Viking Sports before moving to Southall as a teenager. He played for the club in the 1986 FA Vase Final, having a goal disallowed in the 3–0 defeat against Halesowen Town. He joined Hayes later that summer, making 39 appearances and scoring 19 goals for the Missioners, before a dream move to Queens Park Rangers for £30,000 in March 1987. He would stay with Rangers for eight years, making 163 League appearances and scoring 80 goals, as well as going to both Brentford and Turkish club Besiktas on loan. Ferdinand moved to Newcastle United for £6 million in June 1995. In two seasons on Tyneside he made 68 League appearances and scored 41 goals. He returned to London in 1997, signing for Tottenham Hotspur for another £6 million fee. He remained with Spurs six years, scoring 33 times in 118 League matches. Les also played a big role in Spurs' League Cup-winning run in 1999. Aged 36, Les became something of a hired gun, briefly appearing for four clubs: West Ham United, Leicester City, Bolton Wanderers and Reading. Les won 17 full England international caps and scored 5 goals. He was voted PFA player of the year in 1996 and awarded an MBE in the Queen's Birthday Honours list in 2005.

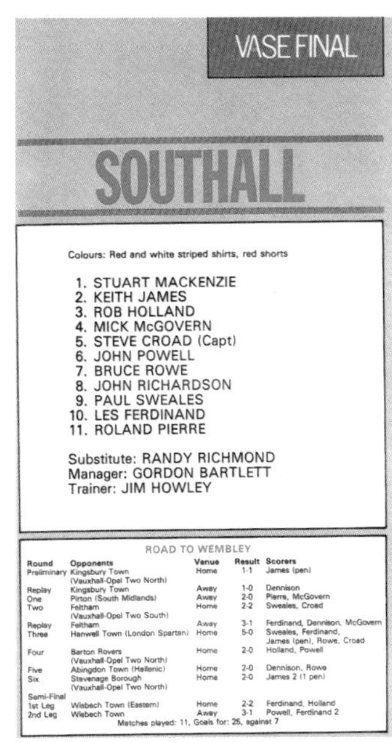
VASE FINAL

SOUTHALL

Colours: Red and white striped shirts, red shorts

1. STUART MACKENZIE
2. KEITH JAMES
3. ROB HOLLAND
4. MICK McGOVERN
5. STEVE CROAD (Capt)
6. JOHN POWELL
7. BRUCE ROWE
8. JOHN RICHARDSON
9. PAUL SWEALES
10. LES FERDINAND
11. ROLAND PIERRE

Substitute: RANDY RICHMOND
Manager: GORDON BARTLETT
Trainer: JIM HOWLEY

ROAD TO WEMBLEY

Round	Opponents	Venue	Result	Scorers
Preliminary	Kingsbury Town (Vauxhall-Opel Two North)	Home	1-1	James (pen)
Replay	Kingsbury Town	Away	1-0	Dennison
One	Pirton (South Midlands)	Away	2-0	Pierre, McGovern
Two	Feltham (Vauxhall-Opel Two South)	Home	2-2	Sweales, Croad
Replay	Feltham	Away	3-1	Ferdinand, Dennison, McGovern
Three	Hanwell Town (London Spartan)	Home	5-0	Sweales, Ferdinand, James (pen), Rowe, Croad
Four	Barton Rovers (Vauxhall-Opel Two North)	Home	2-0	Holland, Powell
Five	Abingdon Town (Hellenic)	Home	2-0	Dennison, Rowe
Six	Stevenage Borough (Vauxhall-Opel Two North)	Home	2-0	James 2 (1 pen)
Semi-Final 1st Leg	Wisbech Town (Eastern)	Home	2-2	Ferdinand, Holland
2nd Leg	Wisbech Town	Away	3-1	Powell, Ferdinand 2

Matches played: 11, Goals for: 26, against 7

Scott Fitzgerald - Northwood - WATFORD (29+26, 11), SWANSEA CITY (0+3, 0), LEYTON ORIENT (1+0, 0), BRENTFORD (7+5, 4) - Scott Fitzgerald was a prolific goalscorer for Northwood as they rose up the Ryman League in the late 1990s–early 2000s and it was no surprise that Watford, on the look-out for a Non-League bargain, gave him a chance to show what he could do. He made more than 50 appearances for the Hornets, as well as going on loan to both Swansea City and Leyton Orient for a month, but almost half of his appearances were as a substitute. Nonetheless in just over 70 total appearances, he still scored 15 times. In late 2005, he took on coaching duties too, looking after Brentford's Under-18s and masterminding a shock FA Youth Cup defeat of Arsenal.

Lee Flynn - Wingate & Finchley, Romford, Hendon, Hayes - BARNET (76+5, 3) - Left-back Lee Flynn played in the lower levels of the Isthmian League before joining Hendon in the summer of 1994. He was at Claremont Road for only four months before moving to Hayes, and helping them to win the 1996 Isthmian League Championship. A solid, dependable defender, it was nonetheless a surprise when Barnet signed him in January 2001. His Football League career didn't last long, only because Barnet were relegated from the League four months later, but he stayed loyal to the Bees, leaving in May 2003. He stayed at Conference level, having seasons at Stevenage Borough and Dagenham & Redbridge.

Howard Forinton - Oxford City, Yeovil Town - BIRMINGHAM CITY (0+5, 1), PLYMOUTH ARGYLE (8+1, 3), PETERBOROUGH UNITED (34+16, 10), TORQUAY UNITED (1+0, 0) - Howard Forinton couldn't quite make the grade at Oxford United, so he moved up the road to Oxford City, where he was a frequent goalscorer and crowd favourite. Yeovil Town, who had been Isthmian League Premier Division rivals of Oxford for a season and watched him at first hand, signed him for their push out of the Conference, but Birmingham City snatched him for £75,000. He didn't start a Football League match for the Blues, but did score for them off the bench, before going on loan to Plymouth Argyle, then being transferred to Peterborough United. In 50 matches, starting 34, he scored ten goals, but was injured for a long time. He dropped back into Non-League football, with Stevenage Borough, Farnborough Town and Banbury United, where he returned to form as a goalscorer.

Leo Fortune-West - Bishop's Stortford, Dagenham, Hendon, Bishop's Stortford, Stevenage Borough - GILLINGHAM (48+19, 18), LEYTON ORIENT (1+4, 0), LINCOLN CITY (7+2, 1), ROTHERHAM UNITED (5+0, 4), BRENTFORD (2+9, 0), ROTHERHAM UNITED (59+0, 28), CARDIFF CITY (53+39, 23), DONCASTER ROVERS (44+19, 17) - The term itinerant striker would not be insulting when used to describe Leo Fortune-West. A player who had implacable faith in his own ability to find the net, he was 24 years old when Gillingham took a chance on him in July 1995. In the decade that followed, Leo rarely spent more than a couple of seasons at any one place, but he did notch almost 100 League goals in just over 300 appearances. Exceptionally tall, he is similar to Peter Crouch in that he is deceptively clever on the ground and hard to dispossess, with heading probably one of his weaknesses. Nevertheless, strikers who score goals will always find it easy to get work, even if they have to move from time to time.

Robin Friday - Walthamstow Avenue, Hayes - READING (121+0, 46), CARDIFF CITY (20+1, 6) - Robin Friday was the subject of a biography from Reading football fan and former Oasis guitarist Paul McGuigan and Paolo Hewitt, entitled *The Greatest Footballer You Never Saw*. Those football fans lucky enough to watch the Isthmian League in the early 1970s knew all about Robin Friday, a player and a man for whom controversy was a constant companion. Whether his transfer to Reading was from either Hayes or Enfield was only resolved by The Football Association, but the Elm Park crowd didn't care a hoot where he came from. He was a genius in football boots, capable of sublime pieces of skill, with two good feet and a stunning shot. Tragically, he had an addictive personality and, after four seasons at Reading and one at Cardiff City, he abruptly retired at the age of 24. In the 1970s, counselling and rehabilitation were hard to find and addicted to drugs and alcohol, Friday was soon penniless. He died in 1991, aged 38, a life and talent so sadly wasted.

Barry Friend - Leatherhead - FULHAM (2+1, 0) - Wimbledon, Leatherhead, Slough Town, Carshalton Athletic - Barry Friend was a highly talented winger, good enough to play for England at Amateur level in the last years of the designation, but not quite able to make it as a professional. He had two bites of the cherry, both times at Fulham. The Cottagers released him as an 18-year-old, after which he joined Leatherhead as they enjoyed their seasons in the limelight with Chris Kelly and Peter McGillicuddy two other stars. Fulham resigned Friend in 1973, but he made just three appearances before being released a second time. This time he returned to Non-League Football for good, winning a Isthmian League winner's medal with Slough Town.

Paul Furlong - Enfield - COVENTRY CITY (32+11, 5), WATFORD (88+0, 41), CHELSEA (52+26, 14), BIRMINGHAM CITY (119+29, 56), QUEENS PARK RANGERS (136+19, 55), SHEFFIELD UNITED (4+0, 2) - Paul Furlong has been a defender's nightmare for around 20 seasons. A prolific goalscorer for Enfield, Coventry City spent a then incredible £130,000 to bring him into the First Division from Non-League football and whilst his return of five goals from 43 appearances for the Sky Blues was not great, Watford, Chelsea, Birmingham City and Queens Park Rangers haven't had much to complain about. After a £250,000 move to Vicarage Road in 1992, Furlong netted 41 times in 88 starts, attracting a £2.5 million bid from Chelsea in 1994. Two seasons at Stamford Bridge ended after 14 goals from 52 starts and a £1.5 million transfer to Birmingham City. The Blues kept him for six seasons, during which time he topped the 50-goal mark. After a second loan spell at QPR, Birmingham let him stay at Loftus Road permanently, where he continued to score at better than a goal every three appearances.

William "Viv" Gibbins - Clapton - WEST HAM UNITED (129+0, 58), BRENTFORD (8+0, 5), BRISTOL ROVERS (37+0, 15), SOUTHAMPTON (2+0, 0) - In modern football Viv Gibbins would be called a striker. However, when he played Gibbins was either an inside or centre-forward. Whatever the term, he liked to score goals and was very good at it too. He began his football career just after the end of World War I, playing for Clapton. After three seasons, West Ham United showed an interest and he moved from Upton Lane to Upton Park, where he spent most of the next eight seasons, earning two England international caps. A move to Brentford in 1931, when he was already 30 years old, didn't work, but he then joined Bristol Rovers, where was very productive. His professional career ended at Southampton, but he returned to the Amateur game in 1934, playing for Leyton in the Athenian League and Catford Wanderers.

Jon Goodman - Bromley - MILLWALL (97+12, 35), WIMBLEDON (28+32, 11) - When Millwall signed Jon Goodman from Bromley in August 1990, paying £30,000 – with a further £20,000 in incentives - a few eyebrows were raised. A promising young striker, many felt there were better players available in the Isthmian League at that price, but the Lions management knew what they were looking at and he made more than 100 appearances for them, averaging a goal every three games. In November 1994, Wimbledon, then in the Premiership signed him in a joint deal with Kenny Cunningham, a transfer valued at £1.3 million. Injuries blighted Jon's career with the Dons as he averaged only a dozen games a season, and then it was mainly as a substitute. He did, however, represent the Republic of Ireland four times in full internationals.

Andy Gray - Corinthian–Casuals, Dulwich Hamlet - CRYSTAL PALACE (91+7, 27), ASTON VILLA (34+3, 4), QUEEN'S PARK RANGERS (11+0, 2), CRYSTAL PALACE (87+3, 12), TOTTENHAM HOTSPUR (23+10, 3), SWINDON TOWN (3+0, 0), Athletico Marbella (Spain), Falkirk (Scotland), BURY (21+0, 1), MILLWALL (12+0, 1) - Andy Gray made the most of his career, spending 13 seasons in professional football. He earned one full England international cap, having earlier collected two at under-21s level. A season at Corinthian–Casuals led to a move to Dulwich Hamlet, where his performances soon attracted a legion of scouts.

Gray chose Crystal Palace, scoring on his debut against Grimsby. Initially a striker, Gray blossomed as a midfielder. He had two spells at the club, the second of which was highlighted by the Eagles' run to the 1991 FA Cup Final when he and Geoff Thomas bossed the midfield and Mark Bright and Ian Wright banged in the goals. In all competitions for Palace, he made 242 appearances and scored 51 goals, a more than respectable strike rate. After a less successful spell at Spurs, Gray tried his luck in both Spain and Scotland, before winding down his career at Bury and finally, near to his football roots, at Millwall.

Phil Gridelet - Hendon, Barnet - BARNSLEY (3+3, 0), ROTHERHAM UNITED (9+0, 0), SOUTHEND UNITED (151+26, 9) - Phil Gridelet was released by Watford as a teenager and joined Hendon. He made his debut in a Middlesex Charity Cup Final as a 17-year-old. The following season, playing at sweeper, he was almost an ever-present and it was clear, from this very young age, that he was an exceptional talent. In an era when almost every England Non-League international was a Conference player, Gridelet earned his first two England caps at Hendon, making his debut in Italy. A move to Barnet was followed by a change of position, to ball-winning midfielder, a role to which Phil was ideally suited and he blossomed further, earning a £175,000 transfer to Barnsley. Unfortunately a serious ankle injury derailed his career and after a spell at Rotherham, he returned to the south of England, at Southend. He spent five seasons with the Shrimpers, making almost 200 appearances. He then joined Woking, before returning to Hendon for a season, then Harrow Borough, where he became assistant manager.

Leroy Griffiths - Hampton & Richmond Borough - QUEENS PARK RANGERS (26+10, 3) - Leroy Griffiths terrified Ryman League defenders with his power and pace while at Hampton & Richmond Borough. After two seasons with the Beavers, Queens Park Rangers paid £40,000 for his services. Leroy spent two seasons at Loftus Road, with loan periods at both Margate and Farnborough Town, having never been able to cement a regular first-team place. He found it hard to score goals against better defences, managing only three in 36 appearances, before dropping back to Non-League football. After playing for several clubs he earned a brief return to the Football League with Gillingham.

Vic Groves - Leytonstone - TOTTENHAM HOTSPUR (4+0, 3), Walthamstow Avenue, LEYTON ORIENT (42+0, 24), ARSENAL (185+0, 31) - Vic Groves played for England at four different levels, Youth, Amateur, Under-23 and "B", thus coming close to appearing at every available level. A member of the all-conquering Leytonstone team of the immediate post-World War II era, Vic earned England Youth and Amateur international caps before joining Spurs as an amateur. He left White Hart Lane after scoring three times in four matches but his spell at Walthamstow Avenue was very brief as Leyton Orient came calling. Vic spent a couple of seasons at Brisbane Road, continuing his fine goalscoring record with 24 goals in 42 games. This persuaded Arsenal to bid what was, in 1955, a very high £23,000 for his services. The Os couldn't say no and Groves moved to Highbury. He couldn't repeat his scoring feat in the First Division, though injuries played a big part in this. Nevertheless, in all competitions he did find the target 37 times in 201 games for the Gunners, including a spell as club captain. Groves was also a part of the London XI which competed in the inaugural Inter-Cities Fairs Cup and appeared in the Final against Barcelona.

Fitz Hall - Aylesbury United, Chesham United - OLDHAM ATHLETIC (41+0, 4), SOUTHAMPTON (7+4, 0), CRYSTAL PALACE (75+0, 3), WIGAN ATHLETIC (5+0, 0) - This central defender, who has been blessed with one of the most imaginative nicknames in all of football, "One Size", first came to notice playing for Aylesbury United under Bob Dowie. When Dowie took over at Chesham, Hall followed him and when Bob's brother Iain was looking for talent from Non-League football as he took charge of Oldham Athletic, Fitz went off to Boundary Park for £20,000. He took to the professional game like a duck to water and, after little more than a season, Southampton signed him for £250,000. An injury-hit season at St Mary's resulted in Hall playing in only 11 matches, but his value was not diminished, judging by the £1.5 million Iain Dowie paid for his services in August 2004. After two seasons with Palace, Wigan Athletic took him back to the Premiership, paying £3million for him.

Paul Harding - Sutton United, Whyteleafe, Epsom & Ewell, Carshalton Athletic, Dulwich Hamlet, Barnet - NOTTS COUNTY (45+9, 1), SOUTHEND UNITED (2+3, 0), WATFORD (1+1, 0), BIRMINGHAM CITY (19+3, 0), CARDIFF CITY (36+0, 0) - Midfielder Paul Harding worked incredibly hard for the chance to be a professional footballer, playing at half a dozen clubs, including five in the Isthmian League, before finally getting his chance when Notts County signed him from Barnet for £60,000 at the age of 26. The Magpies sent him out on loan to both Southend United and Watford at the end of his four-season stint before Birmingham City paid £50,000 for his services just before Christmas 1993. Paul spent almost two seasons as an occasional player at St Andrews, before a two-year stay at Cardiff City – which included a loan spell at Kettering Town – completed his full-time career, by which time he was 33 years old. After playing at Worcester City and Halesowen, Harding's last club was back in the Isthmian League, with Harrow Borough, where he played for former Birmingham team-mate David Howells.

Rashid Harkouk - Feltham - CRYSTAL PALACE (51+3, 20), QUEENS PARK RANGERS (15+5, 3), NOTTS COUNTY (124+20, 39) - Crystal Palace signed the firebrand centre-forward Rashid Harkouk from Feltham unaware that he was about to serve a huge ban from the Middlesex County FA for indiscretions while playing on a Sunday for Pinner Gas. He played and scored in an FA Cup tie against rivals Brighton & Hove Albion, but the ban was cancelled on a very belated appeal and he was able to resume his professional career. Palace officials were somewhat surprised to find out that Rashid was called up for international duties, but not many Algerians were playing in the Football League in the mid-1970s. After two seasons with Palace, Harkouk moved to Queens Park Rangers, but the bulk of his career was spent at Notts County, where he played from 1980 to 1985, scoring more than 40 goals in just over 150 games.

Greg Heald - Hendon, Norwich City, Enfield - PETERBOROUGH UNITED (101+0, 6), BARNET (141+0, 13), LEYTON ORIENT (9+0, 1), ROCHDALE (39+0, 3) - One of almost two dozen players to appear for Hendon at youth or reserve level without getting into an Isthmian League game yet still going on to have a long Football League career, Greg Heald was a teenager when he played in a London Senior Cup tie. He then joined Norwich City as a YTS, but the Canaries released him before he made his League debut and Greg joined Enfield, his local club. He played for England at Non-League level before Peterborough paid The E's £35,000 to give the tall, dominant centre-half a second chance at professional level. He took it with both hands, making more than 100 appearances for the Posh, before he returned to London and Barnet. He was with the club for almost six full seasons – including a couple of seasons after the Bees were relegated – and was club captain when Leyton Orient signed him just before the 2003 transfer deadline passed. After a year with the O's, he moved to Rochdale, where he spent a full season before dropping down to play in the Nationwide Conference.

Andy Hessenthaler - Dartford, Corinthian, Redbridge Forest - WATFORD (195+0, 12), GILLINGHAM (273+30, 20), HULL CITY (6+4, 0), BARNET (23+1, 2) - Andy Hessenthaler has had an unusual career, proving again that lack of height is not a barrier to a successful football life. Charlton Athletic signed the teenager from Dartford, but he could not break into the first team and was released. Andy then joined Corinthian of the Kent League before returning to Dartford and moving on to Redbridge Forest. In 1991 Watford paid Redbridge Forest £65,000 for the diminutive Hessenthaler, generously listed at 5ft 7in tall, but he was big enough for the hustle and bustle of the Football League, making more than 200 appearances for both the Hornets and later Gillingham – who laid out £235,000 to take him to the Priestfield Stadium. When he was with the Gills, Andy was made player-manager, succeeding to Peter Taylor. After four seasons at the helm, he gave up the management side, but continued to play, and was soon loaned out to Peter Taylor-managed Hull City. He continues to play, aged 41, having made in excess of 600 first team appearances for Football League clubs.

Kevin Hitchcock - Barking - MANSFIELD TOWN (182+0, 0), CHELSEA (92+4, 0), NORTHAMPTON TOWN (17+0, 0) - Goalkeeper Kevin Hitchcock was seeing duty for Barking in three teams at once, under-18s, reserves and first team, vying with Dave Root for the No.1 shirt with the Blues. Root only saw regular action once Nottingham Forest boss Brian Clough had taken Hitchcock up to the County Ground. He never got to play in a first team game for the legendary manager, going to near neighbours Mansfield for a very successful loan spell in 1983. Kevin became a Stag on a permanent basis in 1984 and spent four seasons with the club, the highlight being a Wembley penalty shoot-out victory in the ZDS Cup against Bristol City. Chelsea brought him back to London in 1987 and Kevin spent 11 seasons with the Blues – albeit with a couple of spells out on loan – mainly as a back-up, but he did have a couple of runs as first choice and made more than a century of appearances in all competitions.

Gavin Holligan - Walton & Hersham, Kingstonian - WEST HAM (0+1, 0), LEYTON ORIENT (2+0, 0), EXETER (3+0, 0), WYCOMBE (27+23, 10) - Gavin Holligan's prolific debut season at Walton & Hersham in 1997–98 resulted in a transfer to Kingstonian, who sold him to West Ham United for £150,000 in November 1998. After one substitute appearance for the Hammers and short loan spells at Leyton Orient, Exeter City and back at Ks, Holligan joined Wycombe Wanderers where, in three seasons at Adams Park he made 50 League and cup appearances and scored ten goals. His contract was not renewed in the summer of 2004 and he returned to non-League football.

Dean Hooper - Marlow, Hayes - SWINDON TOWN (0+4, 0), PETERBOROUGH UNITED (4+0, 0), Hayes, Kingstonian, PETERBOROUGH UNITED (99+14, 2) - Dean Hooper retired from football at 18 in 1989, after captaining Hendon's youth team. He took a couple of years to realise how much he missed football and returned, playing for his home-town Marlow side. Hayes signed him and, in March 1995 Swindon paid the Missioners £15,000 for him to join the Robins. His debut could hardly have been higher profile, coming on as a substitute in a League Cup semi-final. However, he wasn't quite ready for the Football League as loans at Peterborough United and now Conference Hayes suggested. Dean then joined Kingstonian, but Barry Fry took him back to London Road, this time for good and he spent four seasons with Peterborough completing his century of Football League starts for the Posh. When Aldershot released Hooper in 2004, he was 33 and, no doubt, musing that unretiring had been a good career decision.

David Howell - Hillingdon Borough, Hounslow, Harrow Borough, Enfield - BARNET (57+0, 3), SOUTHEND UNITED (6+0, 0), BIRMINGHAM CITY (2+0, 0) - A superb central defender who earned England Non-League international recognition, David Howell waited 13 years to make his Football League debut following his release by

Fulham at the age of 20 in 1978. However, he was a part of the Barnet team which climbed out of the Conference and Dave spent two seasons with the Bees in the Football League before joining Southend United. Injuries were now beginning to take a toll on the 35-year-old, but Barry Fry, his manager at Barnet, persuaded him to join him at Birmingham City. He did make two appearances for the Blues before dropping back to Non-League football with a brief spell at Stevenage Borough. He returned to Harrow Borough in the early 2000s and became manager in 2003.

Alan Hull - Basildon United, Barking - LEYTON ORIENT (45+25, 16) - Redbridge Forest, Basildon United, Enfield, Dagenham, Heybridge Swifts, Great Wakering Rovers - Alan Hull was released by Southend United without making a first-team appearance and joined Basildon United, before moving to Barking, where his goals attracted the attention of Leyton Orient, for whom he signed in 1987. His Football League career lasted four seasons, during which time he scored 16 times in 70 appearances. After returning to the Non-League circuit, he played for a number of clubs before becoming manager of Great Wakering Rovers in 2001.

Chris Hutchings - Southall & Ealing Borough, Harrow Borough - CHELSEA (83+4, 3), BRIGHTON & HOVE ALBION (153+0, 4), HUDDERSFIELD TOWN (110+0, 10), WALSALL (40+0, 0), ROTHERHAM UNITED (76+2, 4) - Southend United released full-back Chris Hutchings when he was just 17, but he went on to prove the Shrimpers were horribly wrong in their decision. After spells at Southall & Ealing Borough and Harrow Borough, Chelsea took a chance on the 23-year-old in 1980 and it proved a wise choice. He averaged almost 30 games in each of his three seasons at Stamford Bridge before moving down to the south coast and Brighton & Hove Albion, where he played in their 1983 FA Cup Final side. Four seasons at Brighton were followed by another three at Huddersfield and one at Walsall, where the consistency of his performances remained undiminished despite the fact that he was well into his 30s. In fact, Rotherham happily signed the 34-year-old, who went on to play more than 80 games for the Millers before hanging up his boots.

Andrew Impey - Yeading - QUEENS PARK RANGERS (178+10, 13), WEST HAM UNITED (25+1,0), LEICESTER CITY (132+20, 2), NOTTINGHAM FOREST (33+3, 1), MILLWALL (0+5, 0), COVENTRY CITY (4+12, 0) - Andy Impey came through Yeading's successful youth policy and had been with the club for five seasons, scoring 5 goals in his 39 first team appearances for the club, and was also a member of the club's successful FA Vase team. Andy was still only 18 when Gordon Bartlett, the manager at Yeading, sold him to Queens Park Rangers for £35,000 in June 1990. He went on to make 188 League appearances, scoring 13 goals, before being transferred across London to West Ham United in September 1997 for £120,000. While with Rangers Impey was awarded an England Under-21s international cap. Andy made just 26 League appearances at Upton Park before a move to the East Midlands where he signed for Leicester City for £160,000 in November 1998. Impey spent six years with Leicester City before going on to Nottingham Forest in February 2004. The move to the City Ground was made permanent and he made 33 appearances there, scoring once. Impey completed the 2005 season at Millwall on loan and, after a long summer in the USA, resumed his Football League career at Coventry City.

Gordon Jago - Dulwich Hamlet - CHARLTON ATHLETIC (137+0, 1) - Gordon Jago is one of the very few Isthmian League footballers to receive an honour from Her Majesty The Queen for services to football. His playing career, as a centre-half began with Dulwich Hamlet, but he left Champion Hill for a professional contract at Charlton Athletic. He spent eight seasons at The Valley, before moving into coaching. He was manager of Millwall briefly before being wooed by the United States Soccer Federation and became national coach in 1969. He did not last long in that spell in the United States – the team lost the two matches he was in charge – returning to take charge of Queens Park Rangers from 1970 to 1975. But America called again, and this time he stayed for more than 20 years, coaching in the North American Soccer League. He was made president of the World Indoor Soccer League before it merged with the Major Indoor Soccer League and it was for his services to international youth football that he was awarded an MBE in 2006.

Steve Jones - Billericay Town - WEST HAM UNITED (8+8, 4), BOURNEMOUTH (71+23, 26), WEST HAM UNITED (5+3, 0), CHARLTON ATHLETIC (28+24, 8), BOURNEMOUTH (5+0, 4), BRISTOL CITY (29+8, 7), BRENTFORD (6+2, 0), SOUTHEND UNITED (0+0, 2), WYCOMBE WANDERERS (5+0, 0) - Steve Jones scored lots of goals for Billericay Town, earning him a transfer to West Ham United, where he knocked in four goals from 16 appearances. Dropping down a couple of divisions in 1994, Jones found his shooting boots at Bournemouth, finding the net 26 times in 71 starts. A brief return to West Ham was followed by a three-year spell at Charlton, where he made 52 appearances, but scored just eight times. A loan period on the South Coast did appeal because Jones scored four times in five outings for Bournemouth. This spurt of scoring persuaded Bristol City to take a chance on Jones, who responded with seven goals in 29 starts, interspersed with loan spells at Brentford, Southend and Wycombe. He returned to Non-League football with Hornchurch in 2000.

Chris Kelly - Leatherhead - MILLWALL (9+2, 0) - Chris Kelly's career was not one hidden away in obscurity, the self-styled "Leatherhead Lip" ensured that. Kelly was a very talented and entertaining striker in an exceptional Leatherhead team which was one of the top teams in amateur football for a brief spell in the early 1970s. They enjoyed a fantastic FA Cup run in 1974–75, culminating in a 3–2 defeat at the hands of Leicester City after First Division Burnley had been ousted in the Third Round, courtesy of a spectacular Kelly goal. Unfortunately, the professional game didn't come up to Kelly's expectations and he left Millwall after fewer than a dozen matches. After retiring from playing, Kelly became manager then chief executive of Kingstonian.

David Kemp - Slough Town - CRYSTAL PALACE (32+3, 10), PORTSMOUTH (63+1, 30), CARLISLE UNITED (60+1, 22), PLYMOUTH ARGYLE (82+2, 39), GILLINGHAM (9+0, 2), BRENTFORD (3+0, 1) - David Kemp made the most of his chance when Crystal Palace took the striker from Slough Town in 1974. He scored goals at a more than presentable rate everywhere he played, netting more than 100 in just over 250 appearances. His longest spell was at Plymouth Argyle, where he was also at his most prolific, averaging almost a goal every other game. After leaving Argyle in 1982, he moved to America before returning to join Wimbledon. However, he did not break into their League team and instead concentrated on the coaching side. He was part of the management team in 1988 when the Dons won The FA Cup, and has since returned to the US to continue coaching.

Marlon King - Dulwich Hamlet - BARNET (36+17, 14), GILLINGHAM (82+19, 40), NOTTINGHAM FOREST (40+10, 10), LEEDS UNITED (4+5, 0), WATFORD (47+1, 23) - It would be fair to say that Marlon King is not everyone's cup of tea. Rumours of dressing room unpopularity and other stories have followed King around, but as he is very good at scoring goals in the Football League, clubs desperately short in that category will swallow their pride and sign him. Barnet signed him from Dulwich Hamlet after the striker had spent one season as a 17-year-old at Champion Hill. Marlon scored 14 goals in 53 games before Gillingham signed him in the summer of 2000 and he spent three and a half years at the Priestfield Stadium, passing 100 League appearances and scoring 40 goals. It persuaded Nottingham Forest to splash out £950,000 for his services, but they got only 10 goals at a rate of one goal in five games. He went to Leeds and Watford on loan, in the latter case regaining his scoring touch to such an effect that they paid Forest half a million pounds to bring him to Vicarage Road permanently.

Dave Kitson - Arlesey Town - CAMBRIDGE UNITED (110+5, 45), READING (80+14, 46) - Dave Kitson's flaming red hair will make him one of the most recognisable players in the Premier League, although he has admitted the attention given to it disturbs him. However, his penchant for scoring goals has disturbed defenders more and taken him from Arlesey Town, via Cambridge United, to Reading, where he has been part of the Royals' surge up the football ladder. Kitson left Arlesey in March 2001 – their debut season in the Isthmian League – and spent almost three seasons at the Abbey Stadium scoring 45 times at better than a goal every three games. Reading paid £150,000 to sign him in December 2003 and he has rewarded his new club with an even better strike rate, 46 goals in 80 starts.

John Lacy - Kingstonian - FULHAM (164+4, 7), TOTTENHAM HOTSPUR (99+5, 2), CRYSTAL PALACE (24+3, 0) - A small piece of football history was created when Spurs signed John Lacy from Fulham in July 1978. It was the first time that an independent transfer tribunal was used to set the price for a player and, at £200,000, the Liverpool-born central defender made the move across London. Lacy had been a student at the London School of Economics and whilst representing London Universities had impressed their coach, ex-England and Fulham star George Cohen. He also played for Kingstonian and attracted plenty of scouts to Richmond Road. The tall defender signed for Cohen's old club Fulham in 1972 and spent five seasons with the Cottagers, before his landmark move. Lacy had four successful seasons at White Hart Lane, even though his arrival was overshadowed by Spurs's signings of Ricardo Villa and Osvaldo Ardiles immediately after their Argentina team had won the 1978 World Cup. John moved to Crystal Palace for a season before going to play in Norway for a period and returned to England, signing for Barnet, who were then in the Alliance Premier League, before dropping another level, into the Isthmian League, with St. Albans City and Wivenhoe Town.

Richard Langley - Dulwich Hamlet, Hendon, Corinthian Casuals - FULHAM (43+7, 0) - One of the more remarkable 50-game Football League careers belongs to full-back Richard Langley. Released as a junior by Charlton Athletic, Langley went to Gravesend & Northfleet, Dulwich Hamlet, Hendon, back to Dulwich and then dropped down a couple of divisions to join Corinthian–Casuals, all the moves happening in four seasons. From there, he jumped straight back to the Football League, with Fulham, where he stayed for four years. He made exactly 50 appearances, including seven as a substitute, before injuries ended his professional career at the age of 25 in 1990. He tried unsuccessfully to make a comeback with Kingstonian.

Rob Lee - Hornchurch - CHARLTON ATHLETIC (274+24, 59), NEWCASTLE UNITED (292+11, 44), DERBY COUNTY (47+1, 2), WEST HAM UNITED (12+4, 0) OLDHAM ATHLETIC, WYCOMBE WANDERERS (34+4) - Rob Lee was 17 when he broke into the Hornchurch side, but his stay with the Urchins was very brief because Charlton Athletic manager Lennie Lawrence signed him in 1983. The Addicks were still in their nomadic era, but Lee was worth travelling to watch. One of the best midfielders in the country, he was unlucky that his surrounding cast did not match his talent and he found himself back in the old Division Two. After nine years of loyal service, and to ease Charlton's debts, Lee was sold to Newcastle United in September 1992 for £700,000. Rob would give Newcastle even greater service, staying on Tyneside for a full decade, during which time he earned 21 full England caps and made one appearance in the 1998 World Cup finals in France. He got involved in a contract dispute at the end of 2001 and, in February 2002, Rob joined Derby County for

£250,000, where he stayed for 18 months before signing for the club he supported as a boy, West Ham United. Now 37, Rob could not hold down a regular place with the Hammers and spent a short time at Oldham, without making a League appearance, before going to Wycombe Wanderers in 2004. In all, Rob made 703 apperances in the Football League.

Junior Lewis - FULHAM (2+4, 0), Hayes, Hendon, GILLINGHAM (47+12, 8), LEICESTER CITY (24+6, 1), BRIGHTON & HOVE ALBION (14+1, 3), SWINDON TOWN (13+0, 0), HULL CITY (44+8, 3), BRENTFORD (11+3, 0), MK DONS. - Junior Lewis owes most of his Football League career to one man, Peter Taylor, his manager at Dover Athletic, Gillingham, Leicester City, Brighton & Hove Albion (on loan) and Hull City. He began his career at Fulham, but the Cottagers released him after he had made half a dozen League appearances and Junior dropped into Non-League football at Dover Athletic, Hayes and Hendon. He was the Greens' goalscorer when they recorded a famous FA Cup victory at Leyton Orient and, ably assisted by Paul Whitmarsh, scored more than 70 goals in just under three full seasons. A "Bosman" free agent, Junior was given a chance by Taylor, who had just taken over at Gillingham, and he repaid the Gills by putting in a number of stellar performances, helping them to the Division Two Playoff Final, where they lost to Manchester City. Taylor left for Leicester City after the following season, when Gillingham reached what is now the Championship, and Junior followed his mentor up the M1 some nine months later. His time at Leicester was less successful and he went out on loan a number of times. In 2003, Junior and Taylor were reunited at Hull City and the pair again enjoyed promotion. In 2005 Junior returned to London and was at Brentford before turning his eye to coaching in 2006 at MK Dons.

Scott McGleish - Edgware Town - CHARLTON ATHLETIC (0+6, 0), LEYTON ORIENT (4+2, 1), PETERBOROUGH UNITED (3+10, 0), COLCHESTER UNITED (10+5, 6), CAMBRIDGE UNITED (10+0, 7), LEYTON ORIENT (36+0, 7), BARNET (106+28, 36), Ancona (Italy), COLCHESTER UNITED (118+26, 38), NORTHAMPTON TOWN (89+4, 35) - Scott McGleish, whose father Jock played for Hendon in the 1970s and 1980s, left the Greens while a member of the same youth team as fellow future League players Micah Hyde, Junior Hunter and Darren Currie (only Hunter ever made it to the Hendon first team). He went to Edgware and was in their first team as a 17-year-old, playing for his father, who carefully guided his early career. Charlton came calling and Scott went off to The Valley, but made only six substitute appearances in the Football League, although he did score his first League goal on loan at Leyton Orient. A move to Peterborough United followed, but not regular first team football, because two loan spells at Colchester United and one at Cambridge United ensued – during which time he showed his goalscoring prowess, netting 13 goals in 20 loan starts. Scott scored only seven League goals in 36 when Leyton Orient signed him. When he was released in 1997, people had to realise that he was only 23. Barnet took a chance on the tall striker and he repaid their faith with 36 goals in four seasons, but Scott left the Bees when they were relegated back to the Conference. After a trial at Ancona in Italy, Scott had another spell at Colchester, much more successfully, and then went to Northampton, where his strike rate is just about a goal every two and a half starts.

Jermaine McSporran - Oxford City - ARSENAL (0+0, 0), WYCOMBE WANDERERS (117+41, 30), WALSALL (2+4, 0), DONCASTER ROVERS (17+11, 1), BOSTON UNITED (0+2, 0), CHESTER CITY (0+1, 0) - Jermaine McSporran made his name at Oxford City, briefly playing alongside Howard Forinton. Arsenal offered him a trial in 1998, but nothing came of it. However, later in the year Wycombe did likewise, but they paid Oxford City £75,000 for his services and he stayed at Adams Park for five seasons, making more than 150 League appearances for the Chairboys. A late-season move to Walsall in 2004 proved to be a short-term deal, as he played just six matches for the Saddlers before joining Doncaster Rovers, where he spent two seasons, including a spell on loan at Boston United.

Steve Milton - Epsom & Ewell, Croydon, Kingstonian, Whyteleafe - FULHAM (39+19, 9) - West Ham United released striker Steve Milton just after his 18th birthday, but he was not prepared to accept his professional career was over. He went to Redhill in the dying days of the Athenian League, before moving to the Isthmian with a succession of Surrey clubs: Epsom & Ewell, Croydon, Kingstonian and Whyteleafe. Steve never stopped scoring goals at any of his stops and in 1989, Fulham took on the 26-year-old. Milton was only with the Cottagers for three seasons, but he made 58 appearances in the Football League. After leaving Fulham, Steve returned to Non-League football, first with Woking, then back at Whyteleafe.

Charlie Ntamark - Boreham Wood - WALSALL (296+21, 13) - At the age of 25, Charlie Ntamark, Paddington-born, but of Cameroon ancestry, turned up at Hendon FC and asked for a trial, claiming to be a full international for his parents' homeland. After a couple of utterly unconvincing reserve team appearances he was shown the door. Boreham Wood were equally sceptical about his talent until he made a couple of useful first-team appearances. Ntamark joined Walsall for the 1990–91 season, where his career took off, literally. Within a few weeks he was in the Saddlers first team and back in the Indomitable Lions squad. He was no flash in the pan, because Ntamark, a member of Cameroon's 1988 African Cup of Nations' winning team, made more than 300 appearances for Walsall before being released just short of his 33rd birthday.

Emeka Nwajiobi - Dulwich Hamlet - LUTON TOWN (59+13, 17) - Emeka Nwajiobi came to England as a young boy and quickly displayed his talent on the football pitch, earning England Schoolboy international caps.

He joined Dulwich Hamlet and scored lots of goals at Champion Hill, attracting plenty of scouts to South London. Luton Town were the ones who took the gamble and signed Emeka in 1983. Although he spent four seasons at Kenilworth Road, Emeka's appearances were somewhat limited; he did make more than 70 in the Football League, scoring 17 times, but the Hatters faithful remember him more as a creator of chances for others than a finisher in his own right.

Andy Pape - Feltham - QUEENS PARK RANGERS (1+0, 0), CHARLTON ATHLETIC (0+0, 0), Ikast (Denmark), CRYSTAL PALACE (0+0, 0), Harrow Borough, Enfield, BARNET (40+0, 0) - Andy Pape's Football League career was disappointingly short, given his undoubted talent. But the pro game's loss was Non-League's gain and his record of 15 consecutive appeances for England Non-League in the mid- to late-1980s will probably never be beaten, especially considering that England rarely play as many as six matches in a season at this level. Andy played for Feltham before joining Queens Park Rangers, where he made his Football League debut in 1979, before his 18th birthday. Unsuccessful spells at Charlton Athletic and Crystal Palace bookended a spell in Denmark, before Andy joined Harrow Borough in time to win an Isthmian League winner's medal. Moves to Enfield and Barnet cemented his reputation and Andy finally became a Football League regular when the Bees won promotion. After three seasons, Andy dropped back to the Isthmian League, playing for Enfield, Sutton United and Aldershot, before retiring at the age of 42. In February 2005, he joined fellow goalkeeper Gary McCann in becoming assistant manager and manager, respectively, of Hendon.

Alan Pardew - Corinthian–Casuals, Dulwich Hamlet, Yeovil Town - CRYSTAL PALACE (111+17, 8), CHARLTON ATHLETIC (98+6, 24), TOTTENHAM HOTSPUR, BARNET (64+3, 0) - The man who managed West Ham United back to the Premier League in 2005 has his roots in Non-League football. After leaving Corinthian–Casuals for Dulwich Hamlet during the mid-1980s, the elegant, hard-working midfielder proved his class and earned a call-up for the England Non-League squad. A £5,000 move to Yeovil Town followed in February 1986 and then, 13 months later, a transfer to Crystal Palace for £7,000. At Selhurst Park, Alan went on to play for Palace in the 1990 FA Cup Final against Manchester United, having scored the semi-final winning goal against Liverpool. Charlton Athletic signed the now 30-year-old Pardew in November 1991, and he gave the Addicks four good seasons. Alan went to Spurs on loan before signing for Barnet in 1995. After two seasons at Underhill, Alan returned to Dulwich briefly in September 1999, making a further three appearances for the club. A month later he took the job as manager of Reading, where he remained for four years. In October 2003, he was appointed manager of West Ham United.

Steve Perrin - Wycombe Wanderers - CRYSTAL PALACE (45+3, 13), PLYMOUTH ARGYLE (33+1, 6), PORTSMOUTH (18+10, 3) NORTHAMPTON TOWN (22+0, 5) - Queens Park Rangers didn't think Steve Perrin was quite good enough for the Football League, so released the 18-year-old in 1970. Perrin, who went to college to become a teacher, joined Wycombe Wanderers and became a member of one of the finest teams in Isthmian League history, playing alongside legends such as John Delaney, John Maskell and Tony Horseman. Perrin certainly did not pale into insignificance in their shadows. Indeed, Crystal Palace thought enough of him to sign him and he partnered former Slough Town striker David Kemp for a couple of seasons before moving to Plymouth Argyle in 1977. Unfortunately injuries hampered Steve's career in the West Country and after just 34 matches in three seasons, he left for Portsmouth. Three goals in 28 games (10 as a substitute) was not a good return at Fratton Park and he was released in 1980. Steve joined Hillingdon Borough, but quickly returned to the Football League with Northampton Town, where he scored five times in 22 matches. At the age of 30, Steve returned to Non-League football, playing for Wycombe, Hillingdon and St. Albans City before retiring.

Cyrille Regis - Molesey, Hayes - WEST BROMWICH ALBION (233+4, 82), COVENTRY CITY (231+6, 47), ASTON VILLA (46+6, 12), WOLVERHAMPTON WANDERERS (8+11, 2), WYCOMBE WANDERERS (30+5, 9), CHESTER CITY (29+0, 7) - Cyrille Regis's goal celebration, arm raised with one finger pointing skywards, was a regular feature in the 1980s as the French Guyanan striker hit the net more than 140 times in the old First Division. His top-flight career lasted 16 seasons, but he didn't hang up his boots when Aston Villa sold him to Wolves in August 1993. Cyrille would go on to play three more seasons, with Wycombe Wanderers and Chester City, before retiring at the age of 39. Chelsea had a look at him while Cyrille was at Molesey, but after they rejected him, he went to Hayes, where he blossomed. West Bromwich Albion paid £5,000 for him and got seven excellent seasons from him, teaming up most notably with the silky-skilled Laurie Cunningham. He, Regis and full-back Brendan Batson were nicknamed the Three Degrees. Cyrille won his five England caps while a Baggie, but in November 1984 he moved across the Midlands to Coventry for £250,000. By strange coincidence, he made 237 appearances for both clubs, the big difference being the goal returns: 82 at West Brom, 47 at Coventry. A season and a bit at Aston Villa was followed by an injury-hit campaign at Wolves (the only top-flight West Midlands club Cyrille didn't play for was Birmingham City).

In 1994, the 36-year-old Regis signed for Football League newcomers Wycombe Wanderers, before rounding off his career at Chester City. In all competitions, Cyrille played in more than 750 matches and scored more than 200 goals.

Robbie Reinelt - Wivenhoe Town - GILLINGHAM (41+23, 8), COLCHESTER UNITED (29+26, 14), BRIGHTON & HOVE ALBION (37+11, 9), LEYTON ORIENT (2+9, 1) - Braintree Town, Ford United/Redbridge - Striker or midfielder Robbie Reinelt will probably never have to buy a drink or a meal in Brighton. He began his career at Wivenhoe Town and was quickly snapped up by Gillingham, where he stayed for two seasons before moving on to Colchester United. After two years at Layer Road, the struggling Seagulls bought him for £15,000, and it was his goal against Hereford United on 3 May 1997 that saved Brighton from relegation from the Football League. His last League club was Leyton Orient, but he continued to enjoy success in Non-League for another half-dozen years.

Carl Richards - Dulwich Hamlet, Enfield - AFC BOURNEMOUTH (57+14, 16), BIRMINGHAM CITY (18+1, 2), PETERBOROUGH UNITED (16+4, 5), BLACKPOOL (32+9, 8), MAIDSTONE UNITED (4+0, 2) - Jamaican-born Carl Richards was discovered by Dulwich Hamlet playing Sunday football. The Isthmian League discovered Richards the day he made his debut, coming on as a second half substitute and scoring a hat-trick. His goals fuelled an excellent season for the Hamlet, but they couldn't hold onto him when Enfield came calling. Carl banged in the goals in the Alliance Premier League too, and it was no surprise that he turned professional in 1986, signing for AFC Bournemouth. He was already 26 at this stage and much of the rawness remained, certainly the raw speed that terrified defenders. He spent a little over two seasons at Bournemouth before moving to Birmingham City, where he made almost 20 appearances, then moved to Peterborough United for another 20-game spell. Carl joined Blackpool in 1989, but injuries affected him at Bloomfield Road and although he averaged a goal every four starts, they were limited to just 32 in three seasons, during which time he also went on loan to Maidstone United. He returned to Non-League football to finish his career, seeing service at Enfield, Bromley and Tooting & Mitcham United.

Gary Roberts - Wembley - BRENTFORD (180+7, 45) - Gary Roberts moved to London as a teenager and was playing for Wembley when Brentford snapped up the striker. He stayed six seasons at Griffin Park, averaging 30 starts and more than seven goals per campaign, a pretty good return. After leaving the Brentford Bees, Roberts joined the Underhill Bees and was a member of the Barnet team that pushed for promotion to the Football League. He left them before they achieved that aim, and joined Baldock Town where he became manager. The best player he signed at Baldock was a youngster just released by Watford. He groomed Kevin Phillips into one of the best English strikers of the last decade. Since then Gary has managed St. Albans City and Cambridge City.

Jason Roberts - Dunstable Town, Hayes - WOLVERHAMPTON WANDERERS (0+0, 0), TORQUAY UNITED (13+1, 6), BRISTOL CITY (1+2, 1), BRISTOL ROVERS (73+5, 38), WEST BROMWICH ALBION (75+14, 24), PORTSMOUTH (4+6, 1), WIGAN ATHLETIC (93+0, 37), BLACKBURN ROVERS - It is a great shame that sell-on clauses on profits in transfer deals can't be carried over for the whole of a player's career, because Hayes would be pretty well off now. Unfortunately for the Missioners, Wolves' September 1997 deal for £250,000 took him to the West Midlands and his next move – after a combined 14 loan starts at Torquay and Bristol City – was to Bristol Rovers, also for £250,000. Jason's career really took off with the Pirates, scoring 48 goals in 88 appearances for them in all competitions. Two years later, in July 2000, West Bromwich Albion spent £2 million to take him to the Hawthorns, and he made 101 appearances in three and a half seasons, as well as ten more in three months on loan at Portsmouth. Wigan Athletic paid West Brom £1.4 million for Jason to spearhead their push to the Premiership and it worked perfectly. Then in summer of 2006, Blackburn paid £3 million for his services. For those Missioners fans just wondering, that's £6.4 million in transfers since his second move after leaving Hayes.

Simon Rodger - Bognor Regis Town - CRYSTAL PALACE (282+39, 12) MANCHESTER CITY (8, 1), STOKE CITY (5, 0), Woking, BRIGHTON & HOVE ALBION (34+2, 2) - Simon Rodger enjoyed a long Football League career, mainly with Crystal Palace, after leaving Bognor Regis following a single season at Nyewood Lane. The midfielder moved to Selhurst Park for a bargain £1,000 in July 1990 and, apart from three months on loan at Stoke City and Manchester City in 1996–97, spent 12 seasons at Selhurst Park. Released by Palace in 2002, Rodger spent a month at Woking before Brighton & Hove Albion signed him. Playing close to his Shoreham birthplace did wonders for Rodger, whose career was extended by another two seasons.

Paul Rogers - Sutton United - SHEFFIELD UNITED (120+5, 10), NOTTS COUNTY (21+2, 2), WIGAN ATHLETIC (92+8, 5), BRIGHTON & HOVE ALBION (105+14, 15) - It is strange how many players' careers end at one of the clubs where they started on the long road through the Football League. Paul Rogers is another of these, the midfielder leaving Sutton United soon after their glorious FA Cup victory over Coventry City, by which time he was already 26 years old. Paul's career had started at Chipstead, but he really moved forward at Sutton, helping them to win promotion to the Conference. Sheffield United paid £35,000 to take him to Bramall

Lane in January 1992, and he stayed with the Blades until Christmas 1995, when he moved to Notts County on a free transfer. Fifteen months at Meadow Lane were followed by a very successful loan spell at Wigan Athletic, where Paul scored three times in nine League appearances. Amazingly, after signing on for a £50,000 transfer fee, he notched just two goals in 91 games. Aged 34, Paul joined Brighton, and stayed for four seasons, passing the 100 League appearance mark for his third different club. He finished his career with brief spells at Worthing and finally Sutton United, where it had all begun more than a decade earlier.

Simon Royce - Heybridge Swifts - SOUTHEND UNITED (147+2, 0), CHARLTON ATHLETIC (8+0, 0), LEICESTER CITY (16+3, 0), BRIGHTON & HOVE ALBION (6+0, 0), QUEENS PARK RANGERS (16+0, 0), CHARLTON ATHLETIC (1+0, 0), LUTON TOWN (2+0, 0), QUEENS PARK RANGERS (43+0, 0) - Simon Royce could be described as one of the ultimate "hired hands", a goalkeeper who is good enough to hold onto the No. 1 jersey whereever he goes, but also someone who spends much of his time sitting on the bench. Heybridge Swifts were very happy with him and it took a £10,000 transfer fee from Southend United to prise him away from Scraley Road. In seven seasons, however, Simon made only 150 appearances, less than half of the Shrimpers' matches in that period. It was also the only transfer fee that his services have attracted. Two seasons at Charlton Athletic brought eight matches, three at Leicester 16 and, during his time with the Foxes, he had four loan spells including one at Manchester City where he didn't play at all. Two more seasons at Charlton brought him one Premiership start and his third loan spell at Queens Park Rangers and one at Luton Town. Then, in May 2005, QPR signed him on a permanent deal. Unfortunately a long-term injury kept him out of for most of the 2005–06 seasons but, in a typically nomadic goalkeeping career, Simon is on his way to completing 300 appearances in all competitions.

Ashley Sestanovich - Hampton & Richmond Borough - SHEFFIELD UNITED (0+2, 0), Scarborough (12, 3), GRIMSBY TOWN (21+5, 2) - Known as Sir Stan, Ashley Sestanovich turned up for pre-season training at Hampton & Richmond Borough in July 2002, having previously played in Ireland and on the European continent. The scouts flooded to the Beveree and Sheffield United won the bidding war, with a £10,000 offer in March 2003. The Blades rarely used him but instead sent him out on loan to Scarborough, where he starred in their 2003-04 FA Cup run. A further loan period at Grimsby Town brought him a couple of dozen more appearances, but following two months at Chester, he was released and signed for Gravesend & Northfleet.

Efetobor Sodje - Stevenage Borough - MACCLESFIELD TOWN (83+0, 6), LUTON TOWN (5+4, 0), COLCHESTER UNITED (3+0, 0), CREWE ALEXANDRA (86+12, 3), HUDDERSFIELD TOWN (61+6, 5), YEOVIL TOWN (23+2, 3), SOUTHEND UNITED (12+1, 1) - Efe Sodje was the first of a family of Sodjes to make their mark in the Football League, but he began his career in England at Stevenage Borough, as part of the side Paul Fairclough guided out of the Isthmian League and into the Conference, from where they nearly progressed to the Football League themselves. However, Sodje made the jump himself, Macclesfield Town paying £30,000 to take him up to Moss Rose. Amazingly for a player who has appeared for so many clubs, it was the only time he was ever the subject of a transfer fee, all his other moves being either as a "Bosman" free agent or on loan. It hasn't stopped him appearing in 350 first team matches with Football League clubs. Both Sam Sodje and Akpo, Efe's brothers, also played at Stevenage Borough before going into the Football League, but Borough were a Conference side at the time. Sam did play a few Isthmian games for Grays Athletic.

Alex Stepney - Tooting & Mitcham United - MILLWALL (137+0, 0), CHELSEA (1+0, 0), MANCHESTER UNITED (433+0, 2) - Alex Stepney's first brush with fame came when he was a squad member of the famous Tooting & Mitcham team of the late 1950s which had memorable FA Cup runs, including taking eventual winners Nottingham Forest to a replay. He made only 35 appearances for the Terrors before joining Millwall in May 1963. Alex was a regular at the Den before signing for Chelsea in May 1966 for £50,000. After a solitary appearance in the opening month of the 1966–67 season, Manchester United offered Chelsea £55,000 for Stepney's services. Making a £5,000 profit in four months was good business sense for Chelsea who already had England international Peter Bonetti on their books. As good as it was for Chelsea, it was even better for Alex. During his long career with the Reds, he made 433 appearances, and his honours included the League Championship in 1967, the European Cup in 1968 and The FA Cup in 1977. In 1973 he was also United's penalty taker and he converted two spot-kicks. Alex was named in 20 England international squads, but ended with only one cap, playing against Sweden on 22 May 1968, three weeks after the European Cup Final. Stepney went to America and joined Dallas Tornados in the summers of 1979 and 1980. Altrincham of the Alliance Premier League (now Football Conference) appointed him their goalkeeping coach but he actually played 17 games for the club. He currently works as a goalkeeping coach.

Kenny Swain - Wycombe Wanderers - CHELSEA (114+5, 26), ASTON VILLA (148+0, 4), NOTTINGHAM FOREST (112+0, 2), PORTSMOUTH (113+0, 0), WEST BROMWICH ALBION (7+0, 1) 1987, CREWE

ALEXANDRA (123+3, 1) - Kenny Swain is almost unique in that he made more than 100 League appearances for five different clubs. Was born on Merseyside but came to London and was studying at Shoreditch College when Wycombe Wanderers signed him. Playing alongside the likes of John Delaney and Tony Horseman, he enjoyed a lot of success with the Chairboys until Chelsea signed him in 1973. In five seasons at Stamford Bridge, he passed the 100 appearance mark and scored 26 goals. Normally a winger, Chelsea also played him as a central striker and a midfielder. When Aston Villa signed Kenny in 1978, they viewed him in a more defensive role and indeed much of the rest of his career was spent at full-back. Kenny's time at Aston Villa was his most successful and he won both a League champion's medal and a European Cup winner's medal with Villa. In October 1982, he moved across the Midlands to play for Brian Clough's Nottingham Forest, another club where he spent almost four seasons. This was followed by a move to the South Coast and Portsmouth. Here he helped Pompey to return to the old First Division after many seasons in the lower levels. In his final season, when Portsmouth went straight back down, he went out on loan to West Bromwich Albion. In 1988, he went back close to his roots, joining Crewe Alexandra, where he finished his career in 1991.

Scott Taylor - Staines Town - MILLWALL (13+15, 0), BOLTON WANDERERS (2+10, 1), ROTHERHAM UNITED (10+0, 3), BLACKPOOL (3+2, 1), TRANMERE ROVERS (78+30, 17), STOCKPORT COUNTY (19+9, 4), BLACKPOOL (97+19, 43), PLAYMOUTH ARGYLE (17+17, 4), MK DONS (11+13, 4) - It would not be unkind to call striker Scott Taylor a journeyman footballer, given that he has played for eight clubs, as far south-west as Plymouth, south-east as Millwall, north-west as Blackpool and north-east as Rotherham, all in 11 seasons. He came through the very successful Staines Town youth system and was in the Swans' first team at 17. At the age of 18, in 1995, he moved to Millwall – the only Football League club for whom he failed to score – and made 28 appearances, 15 off the subs' bench. This was followed by a move to Bolton Wanderers, but they loaned him out to Rotherham and Millwall before Tranmere Rovers signed him in 1998. After two seasons Scott joined Stockport County, but finished the campaign back at Blackpool, where he completed 100 League starts – if the earlier loan period is taken into account. Thereafter, he swapped the Lancashire coast for the Devon one at Plymouth before ending up at MK Dons, but still scoring goals.

Ashley Vickers - Heybridge Swifts - PETERBOROUGH UNITED (1+0, 0) - Centre half Ashley Vickers looked to be a fine prospect at Heybridge Swifts and, although he picked up a red card in Swifts' 1997 FA Cup tie at Bournemouth, Peterborough signed him. His Football League career was remarkably short, lasting just 84 minutes before he was red-carded. A serious injury ended his season, after which his contract was not renewed. He joined St. Albans City in 1999 and then moved to Dagenham & Redbridge.

Damien Webber - Bognor Regis Town - MILLWALL (52+13, 4) - Standing 6ft 4in tall and weighing 14st, Damien Webber was the ultimate big centre-half. He did a pretty good job at the heart of the Bognor Regis defence, so much so that Millwall came in for the then 26-year-old. Damien spent four seasons at Millwall without ever being an automatic first choice. But he was certainly reliable enough for the Lions to give him more than 50 Football League appearances. When he left Millwall, Damien went back to Sussex, this time with Worthing and he played for them in the 1998 Puma Cup Final, when the First Division team lost out to Hendon.

Tony Weston - Maidstone United, Bromley - GILLINGHAM (162+0, 3) - Tony Weston was born a month before the end of World War Two. He grew up in Kent and, amazingly, spent his whole career with Kent clubs, from Bromley in the London suburbs to Folkestone on the Channel coast. His first club was Maidstone United, but he left them to step up to the Isthmian League with Bromley before his 18th birthday. In less than a year, Gillingham had invited the full-back to join them and he turned professional in 1963. Tony spent the rest of the decade with the Gills before dropping down to play for a variety of clubs in the hop county.

Darron Wilkinson - Wokingham Town - BRIGHTON & HOVE ALBION (34+4, 3) - Darron Wilkinson was part of the very good Wokingham Town team which went very close to winning the Isthmian League championship in the early 1990s. He joined Brighton & Hove Albion in 1992 and stayed for two seasons, making more than 40 League appearances and scoring three goals. Darron then tried his luck in Hong Kong with Kuitan Sports, before returning to England, where he joined Hayes, then Woking, both in the Conference. After leaving the Cards, Darron went to Slough Town, where he continued to play in his late 30s and in October 2006 he was appointed assistant manager of the Rebels.

Tommy Williams - Walton & Hersham - WEST HAM UNITED, PETERBOROUGH UNITED (32+4, 2), BIRMINGHAM CITY (4+0, 0), QUEENS PARK RANGERS (26+5, 1), PETERBOROUGH UNITED (20+1, 1), BARNSLEY (38+1, 0) - Walton & Hersham have got a surprisingly good reputation for sending players to the Football League, the finest of recent times being Nathan Ellington. However, one who is often forgotten is full-back Tommy Williams, who went to West Ham in the spring of 2000. He had not made it into the Football League team at Upton Park before he joined Peterborough United for the first of two spells. Under Barry Fry's tutelage, Tommy progressed enough to make it into the Premiership with Birmingham City, albeit for a handful of appearances before he dropped down a division to join Queens Park Rangers, first on loan, then as a permanent signing. He left Rangers to return to Peterborough and, in 2004, moved again, this time to Barnsley.

Paul Wilson - Billericay Town, Barking - BARNET (240+23, 24) - Paul Wilson was at the West Ham academy as a youngster, but didn't quite make the grade. However, he persevered and after a spell at Billericay Town, he joined Barking, where his performances caught the attention of Barnet, who were looking to climb out of the Conference. Paul joined the Bees in 1988 and, three years later, the club achieved its ambition of Football League status. Paul was an integral part of the team and stayed loyal to the club even when it went through turmoil in 1993. He actually stayed with Barnet for more than a decade, only leaving in 1999, at the age of 35, having made more than 250 League appearances for the Bees. Paul then went to Boston United, but had left them just before they won promotion to the Football League.

Tony Witter - Grays Athletic - CRYSTAL PALACE, QUEENS PARK RANGERS (1+0, 0), PLYMOUTH ARGYLE (3+0, 1), READING (4+0, 0), MILLWALL (99+3, 2), NORTHAMPTON TOWN (1+3, 0), TORQUAY UNITED (4+0, 0), Welling United, SCUNTHORPE UNITED (14+0, 0) - Defender Tony Witter stood out like a beacon in the Grays Athletic defence in the late 1980s/1990 in that he was an accomplished, football-playing defender when the usual tactics for the Club at the time were to launch the ball as far away from danger as possible. After trying to make it at Crystal Palace, Queens Park Rangers, Plymouth Argyle and Reading, where he made a combined eight League appearances, he joined Millwall in 1994 and found a niche. Tony completed a century of appearances, but brief spells at Northampton Town and Torquay United followed his time at Millwall and he then dropped down to play for Welling United. However, he was given another chance in the Football League in February 1999 when Scunthorpe United signed him. He stayed at Glandford Park until the end of the season, but that concluded his full-time career.

Jeff Wood - Harlow Town - CHARLTON ATHLETIC (147), HJK Helsinki, Oulu Palloaseura, Happy Valley, EXETER CITY (33), Rabat Ajax - goalkeeper Jeff Wood made his name with Harlow Town before joining Charlton Athletic, where he spent half a dozen seasons. After being released in 1980, he went to Finland playing for HJK Helsinki. A brief spell at Colchester, without a League appearance, was followed by a return to Finland, this time with Oulo Palloaseura, then to Hong Kong with Happy Valley. In 1984, Wood returned to England and Exeter City, but he left at the end of the season and went to Morocco and Rabat Ajax. He became assistant manager of Brighton & Hove Albion in 1996 and stepped up to manage the club in 1999 after Brian Horton joined Port Vale, but was sacked after only thirteen games.

Eric Young - Staines Town, Slough Town - BRIGHTON & HOVE ALBION (126+0, 10), WIMBLEDON (96+3, 9), CRYSTAL PALACE (161+0, 15), WOLVERHAMPTON WANDERERS (31+0, 2) - A no-nonsense centre-half, Eric Young, who was born in Singapore – which made him eligible to play for Wales on the international stage – left Staines for Slough Town in 1981. The Rebels sold him to Brighton & Hove Albion for £10,000 in November 1982, when Eric was already 22, and he went on to enjoy five productive seasons on the south coast. A £70,000 move to Wimbledon in 1987 which saw Eric join the "Crazy Gang" was a huge bargain and he was in the Dons team which won the 1988 FA Cup Final. In August 1990, Crystal Palace paid £850,000 to bring Eric back to London and he continued to be a regular first-teamer for five seasons, before moving to Wolves as a 35-year-old. He continued to play for two seasons and hung up his boots having played in more than 500 first-team games.

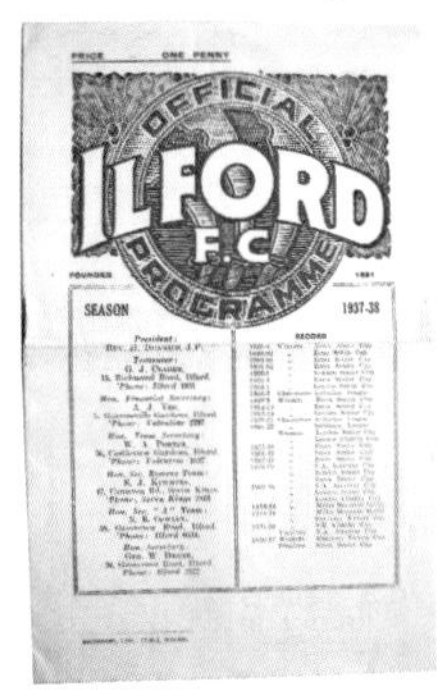

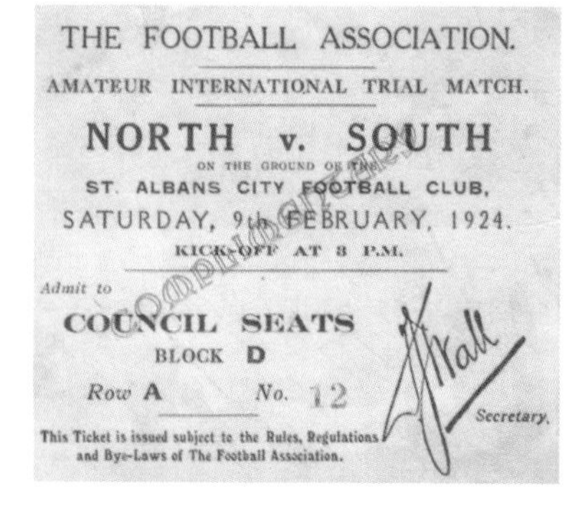
THE FOOTBALL ASSOCIATION.
AMATEUR INTERNATIONAL TRIAL MATCH.
NORTH v. SOUTH
ON THE GROUND OF THE
ST. ALBANS CITY FOOTBALL CLUB,
SATURDAY, 9th FEBRUARY, 1924.
KICK-OFF AT 3 P.M.
Admit to
COUNCIL SEATS
BLOCK D
Row A No. 12
Secretary.
This Ticket is issued subject to the Rules, Regulations and Bye-Laws of The Football Association.

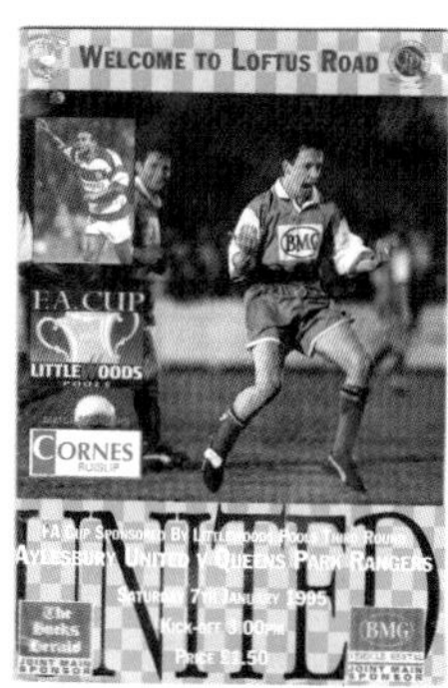

THE MANAGERS

Until the 1960's most Clubs had a selection committee and a trainer who was manager and coach but gradually the trainer became the manager and the spongeman became the trainer.

This section is to make glorious that species of man which referees hate more than all others. The men who are now penned into a technical area and for whom The Football Association have issued specific guidelines as to what being banned from the touchline actually means!

This section is limited to those who have achieved success and/or notoriety as a manager of a Club or Clubs in the Isthmian League. The feats of those whose management achievements have come exclusively with Football League clubs, such as Alan Pardew, Kevin Blackwell, Dave Bassett and Iain Dowie, have been recorded in the player's section.

Allan Batsford - Allan Batsford is a legend at two clubs, both of which he took to unthought-of heights, though maybe his finest job was in the Isthmian League before he became a national name. As manager of Southern League Wimbledon, Allan was the mastermind behind an FA Cup campaign that made a hero out of Dickie Guy, the goalkeeper who saved a Peter Lorimer penalty in a goalless draw against Leeds United at Plough Lane. He was also at the helm as Wimbledon entered the Football League, although he left soon after. A few years later, Allan was at Wealdstone, helping them to reach the Alliance Premier League and, in 1985, win the double of APL and FA Trophy. But what is less well known is that a large part of the Wimbledon team that swept all aside was similar to the one which won The FA Amateur Cup in 1973 as Batsford led Walton & Hersham to their greatest ever days, including a 4–0 rout of Brighton & Hove Albion, managed by Brian Clough no less, in The FA Cup. Players such as Dave Bassett, Roger Connell, Dave Donaldson, Billy Edwards, Keiron Somers and Richard Teale all moved from Stompond Lane to Plough Lane, although Somers didn't actually play in the Football League. Allan stayed true to his Non-League recruits with a number of other recruits to the Dons for that 1977–78 debut season in the Football League, taking players from Tooting & Mitcham United, Sutton United, Leatherhead and Dulwich Hamlet too. The Wealdstone team he built in the 1980s was very different, using uncompromising rocks Paul Bowgett and Denis Byatt in central defence and flying wide players Neil & Alan Cordice to feed the lethal George Duck.

George Borg - There are few managers who have enjoyed as long and distinguished a career in management as George Borg. He has been managing for almost twenty years, never lower than at level 3 of Non-League football. After his professional playing career ended, he was a tough, uncompromising (no surprise there) full-back, deadly from the penalty spot, with Wycombe Wanderers, then Barking, where he was player-manager. George's famous rants have got him in trouble on countless occasions and resulted in many touchline bans. While he was manager of Chesham United, the Generals came up with an imaginative way for him to view matches from almost pitchside, but without sitting in the stand. They built a box on top of the stand which George reached via a ladder and he was able to give his inimitable advice whilst enjoying an almost perfect vantage point directly over the halfway line. After a spell at Harrow Borough, a move to Enfield brought an Isthmian League championship in 1995, but that club's financial problems denied him promotion to the Conference. That championship was followed by successive second-place finishes and gave George a reputation as something of a nearly-man. When George went to Aldershot Town, he wasted little time in getting them promoted. George then spent brief spells at both Billericay and Hornchurch before moving to Braintree Town in 2004. In his first season he secured a play-off place for the Cressing Road club and secured the championship twelve months later.

Terry Brown - Terry Brown was a combative and effective centre-forward, whose career included stops at both Hayes and Slough Town, where he scored a League Cup Final goal in 1975. As manager of Hayes, he built the team slowly and carefully, finishing in a Club-best third place in the Premier Division in 1994. A season later, at the climax of one of the closest title races in Isthmian League history, Terry's Hayes team came out on top by dint of a +44 goal difference compared to Enfield's +43 after both teams garnered 86 points, with Boreham Wood in third on 83 points and Yeovil Town and Dulwich Hamlet on 80. In April 2002, Terry was appointed manager of Aldershot Town, too late for them to have an impact on that season's championship race. However, Terry used the experience he had gained at Church Road to great effect at the Rec. There was little doubt from midway through the season that Aldershot Town would be champions in 2003 and they finished 13 points clear of Canvey Island. The Shots have now given the town an emotional return to the Football League, less than 20 years after their exit.

Paul Fairclough - Paul Fairclough is very unusual in this list of managers because his reputation was built at one Club, Stevenage Borough, although he is now in a very select band of men who have won the Conference title twice. A Liverpudlian and a former schoolteacher, Paul was in charge of Stevenage Borough even before they reached the Isthmian League Premier Division. In 1991, Borough won Division Two North by 25 points; the First Division title arrived a year later with an incredible home record of 19 wins and two draws from 21 games. It took him two seasons to win the Isthmian League championship, but a long unbeaten run in the second half made the title a formality long before it was actually clinched. And the success continued in the Conference with a championship there and a famous FA Cup battle with Newcastle United into the bargain. Unfortunately for Paul, the Borough board tried to defy the Football League over ground grading regulations and lost, so his title did not mean promotion. Paul then became manager of the England Non-League team, a post he continued to hold not only after succeeding Martin Allen as Barnet manager, but also winning the Conference and this time becoming a Football League manager.

Dario Gradi - was born in Italy on 8 July 1941. He played for Sutton United, including The FA Cup tie against Leeds United in 1970, and Tooting & Mitcham United as well as gaining one England Amateur Cap. After a period of teaching, Gradi turned to football coaching, becoming assistant coach at Chelsea in 1971. This was followed by coaching and management posts at Sutton United, Derby County and Wimbledon with two years as youth coach at Leyton Orient. In January 1978 he became manager of Wimbledon, winning promotion from the then Fourth Division in 1978-79. In February 1981 Dario accepted an offer to manage Crystal Palace but his time at Selhurst Park was short lived as he failed to prevent relegation and after a poor start the following season, he resigned. In January 1983 he became manager of Crewe Alexandra and after six years guided the club to promotion in 1988-89. They suffered relegation two years later but promotions to Division Two in 1994 and Division One in 1997 were acheived. Players such as David Platt, Danny Murphy and Neil Lennon started their professional careers at Crewe during Gradi's reign.

Garry Hill - Garry Hill first came to prominence in the Isthmian League with Heybridge Swifts. He did not enjoy immediate success, but his fast, direct style combined with solid and unspectacular defenders soon made the Swifts a difficult team to beat. Garry then moved on to St. Albans City and took the Clarence Park club to within one match of Wembley in The FA Trophy, before Dagenham & Redbridge came calling. Here he enjoyed great success, taking the Daggers into the Conference and close to a Football League position via the playoffs. Staying in Essex, Garry moved to Hornchurch. The Urchins missed out on the Isthmian League title as Canvey Island ran away with it, but they were steamrollering their way to the Conference South title when the money ran out and most of the team were allowed to become free agents. Garry moved out of the area altogether, taking over at Weymouth, another club whose off-field problems had overshadowed what was happening on the pitch. This time, however, Garry didn't let it affect him and he took the Terras to the Conference South title in 2006.

Brian Lee - Wycombe Wanderers were among the two or three biggest Clubs in the Isthmian League around the time amateur status ended and much of the credit for that belongs to their manager Brian Lee. It was an era of huge success for Berks & Bucks clubs with Chesham United reaching the 1968 FA Amateur Cup Final and Slough Town doing likewise three years later. Wycombe, however, got no closer than a couple of semi-final appearances, but in the Isthmian League, the Chairboys were utterly dominant. With numerous Amateur internationals, John Maskell, Tony Brothers, Geoff Reardon, Tony Horseman, John Delaney and others, Wycombe were practically without weakness, especially at Loakes Park, where the huge slope running along the pitch and fervent local support was worth a goal's start in practically every match. There was certainly no more intimidating an atmosphere in the Isthmian League than at Loakes Park on a midweek evening and Lee's teams absolutely thrived on it.

Eddie McCluskey - When Barking won the Isthmian League championship in 1979 it broke the decade-long stronghold exerted by Enfield, Wycombe Wanderers and, to a lesser extent, Hendon. They were managed by quiet, reserved school-teacher Eddie McCluskey – well, quiet and reserved when not in the thick of a battle at Mayesbrook Park or Southbury Road when he took over as Enfield boss. Eddie's passion may not have matched a couple of other Enfield bosses mentioned elsewhere in this book, but he cared just as passionately. He brought along players such as Nicky Ironton, Peter Burton and Bryn Key, the first of whom went on to play many times for England, the second of whom scored Enfield's goal in their famous FA Cup fourth round draw with Barnsley and the latter whose career was side-tracked by work engagements which took him back to his native South Africa. After leaving Enfield, Eddie spent a few years out of football, but he returned to work at Harlow Town, who came very close to returning to the Isthmian League Premier Division in the 1990s.

Jack Pearce - Bognor Regis Town joined the Isthmian League in 1981 and spent 24 seasons as Members. During that time the Rocks had just one manager: Jack Pearce; and, on occasion, their coach driver was Jack Pearce, their chairman was Jack Pearce. In fact, pretty much everything except the tea bar and turnstiles at Nyewood Lane were in Jack's remit and they couldn't be because the team needed him more. Bognor never won the Isthmian League Premier Division title; in fact their only major success came in the GMAC (Isthmian League) Cup in 1987, which they won, 3–2 against Hendon, at Stag Meadow. The Rocks did little in The FA Trophy, but they did enjoy many FA Cup runs, taking a few Football League scalps into the bargain. It is a testament not only to Jack's loyalty but his astute football mind that Bognor have continued to play the same way throughout his tenure. With Jack loyalty is a two-way street, as a look through a Bognor Regis Town programme and the player appearances page will prove. More often than not, there will be at least three players with more than 200 appearances and some with 400 and maybe even 500. After all the Pullen brothers, Paul and Mark, mustered around 1,700 between them in all competitions.

John Rains - John Rains' loyalty to Sutton United comes close to that of Jack Pearce at Bognor Regis Town, but John was a stalwart player before he managed the Us, and he cut his teeth at Molesey before returning to Gander Green Lane. John and Tony Rains played well over 1,000 games in the amber and chocolate colours, winning pretty much everything there was to win at their level. League titles, League Cups, Full Members' Cups and FA Cup glory all came their way, while a young John played in the 1981 FA Trophy Final defeat against Bishop's Stortford. In their around 20 seasons of Isthmian Football from 1980 to 2004, Sutton were, almost invariably in the top half of the table and, rarely out of the top eight. Sutton United have always believed in doing things the right way, and this administrative punctilliousness is matched on the field too, as John learned as a player under Barrie Williams and took on when he was in the dugout. He managed Worthing, Dorking and Carshalton Athletic before, predictably, taking charge at Gander Green Lane. Strong on discipline, Sutton's players have rarely encountered trouble with referees and controversial stories, or even rumours, emanating from Gander Green Lane are practically unheard of. Being a defender himself, John built his teams from the back, but he allowed his teams to display plenty of flair and dull games were a distinct rarity.

Graham Roberts - If one word could describe Graham Roberts' career, it would probably be "colourful". Not many players get three chances to make it as a professional footballer, but Graham did. He was released by Southampton as a 16-year-old and joined Sholing Sports for a couple of seasons, before AFC Bournemouth and Portsmouth took a look at him. Graham dropped back into Non-League football with Dorchester Town and their near-neighbours Weymouth before Tottenham Hotspur signed him in 1980. At the third time of asking, his career took off. Graham played more than 200 times for Spurs, spent two seasons at Glasgow Rangers, a couple more at Chelsea, before winding down his pro career at West Bromwich Albion, by which time he was almost 32 and the possessor of six full England international caps. His first club in his third spell in Non-League was Enfield, where he was player-manager, as they finished as League runners-up in 1994. A brief move to Hertford Town was followed by the job at Yeovil Town, where he again enjoyed success – and incidentally, ended his playing career. Graham then took over at Boreham Wood and took them back to the Isthmian League Premier Division, but was controversially sacked in the off-season. Graham also enjoyed spells managing both Carshalton Athletic and Braintree Town. In January 2006, Graham masterminded Clyde FC's shock Scottish FA Cup victory over Celtic, but this job ended in August the same year.

Alan Smith - Former Crystal Palace boss Alan Smith cut his managerial teeth in the Isthmian League with a four-year spell at Dulwich Hamlet. After his playing career had been cruelly cut short by injury, Smith was appointed to the coaching staff at Wimbledon. During the summer of 1977 he became manager of Dulwich after the famous old club had been relegated from the Isthmian's top division. He set about reviving the Hamlet's fortunes and was immediately successful, the first nine games of the season all being won. By the end of that campaign Dulwich had been crowned as Division One champions and had regained their place in the Premier Division, the first club to do so at the first attempt. Under Smith's guidance, Dulwich also won the Surrey Centenary Shield that season. Smith was determined that the Hamlet would not be also-rans in the top flight and with a few additions to the squad he quickly established them as one of the leading sides in the League. 1978-79 saw Dulwich finish fourth, then twelve months later they came third when at one stage the championship itself appeared within their grasp. Smith also took the Hamlet to the League Cup semi-finals and, in 1979-80, The FA Trophy quarter-finals, the one and only time the club has reached the last eight. His boundless enthusiasm and thorough professionalism not only singled him out as arguably Dulwich's most successful ever manager, but also earned him the opportunity to manage the Isthmian League representative team. Sadly, injuries to key players during the early part of season 1980-81 saw Dulwich slip down the table and with his outside business commitments taking up an increasing amount of time, Smith stepped down at the end of that season. A few years later, he gave up his business and joined the Crystal Palace coaching staff, being appointed as assistant manager to Steve Coppell. He eventually replaced Coppell as manager and in his first season guided the Palace to the Division One championship and promotion back to the Premiership. Unfortunately, Palace failed to survive in the top flight and it cost Smith his job. He later became manager at Wycombe Wanderers, then had a second spell in the Palace hot seat in 2000-01, but both stays were short and less successful than Alan would have liked.

Billy Smith - Billy Smith was an artful midfielder in the great Leatherhead teams of Billy Miller in the early 1970s. He took that grounding to heart and became an excellent manager in his own right. He did a fantastic job at Carshalton Athletic, taking perennial strugglers and making them tough Isthmian League opposition, especially at their sloping Colston Avenue ground. Billy's job was certainly made easier by the goalscoring talent of Jimmy Bolton. He also instilled a resolution in defence that had been lacking previously and a certain steel in midfield. Kingstonian realised what a gem they had close at hand and Billy was taken by the Ks in a bid to get them promoted to the Conference. He laid the groundwork, but was no longer at the club when the Ks, under Geoff Chappell, finally took the step up.

John Still - John Still's career as a player made him a candidate for the Dream Team earlier in this section. His success in the dugout – with Leytonstone-Ilford/Redbridge Forest, Dartford, Maidstone, Barnet and Dagenham & Redbridge ensures that his career is duly noted. John was a very solid centre-half, whose career highlight came in 1974 when he played in the Bishop's Stortford team that won the last ever FA Amateur Cup. As a manager in Non-League Football, there is practically no trophy he hasn't won, including the Conference title – with Maidstone. When the Stones moved into the Football League, John stepped down because he did not wish to go full-time, but he didn't move far, taking over at Maidstone's landlords Dartford. Within four years both clubs had ceased to exist, but John's career was on an upward curve, as evidenced by his move to Peterborough United, where he spent just over a season working with Barry Fry. Eighteen months later, John returned to the Football League with Barnet, where he was in charge for three and a half years, winning as many games as he lost in the Football League. He left in November 2000 but his replacement, Tony Cottee, was unsuccessful and Barnet plummeted down the table. Still returned in March 2001, with the Bees desperately trying to avoid the drop back into the Conference. Despite his best efforts, Barnet were relegated and John tried vainly to engineer their immediate return to the Football League. In 2004, John went back to Dagenham & Redbridge and led them into the Football League.

Peter Taylor - Peter Taylor is the only Isthmian League manager to take charge of the full England side, doing so in the 2000–01 season between the departure of Kevin Keegan and the arrival of Sven Goran Eriksson. It was Taylor who made David Beckham England captain. As a player, mainly with Crystal Palace and Tottenham Hotspur, Peter was good enough to earn five full England caps. As he wound down his playing career, he became one of the select band to earn caps at full and Non-League level, playing at Maidstone. Peter was made player-manager of Enfield the season after they were relegated from the Conference and he spent one season there before accepting the job of assistant manager at Watford. When he left Watford in May 1993, he took on the job at Hendon, rejecting the chance to become Glenn Hoddle's assistant at Chelsea. His time at Claremont Road was disappointingly short, just seven months, before his home club, Southend United, approached him to be their manager. It was not a successful move and Peter was sacked after barely a year at Roots Hall. His next job was back in Non-League football, with Dover Athletic in the Conference League, but again his stay was short, this time because Glenn Hoddle as England manager wanted Peter to take over as coach of the Under-21s, a role he has made his own. Gillingham offered Taylor the chance to return as a Football League manager and this time he took the opportunity with both hands, guiding the Gills first to a heart-breaking Playoff Final loss to Manchester City at Wembley, then, 12 months on, to promotion to what is now the Championship. Leicester City, who had just lost Martin O'Neill, made Peter his successor, but his style and that of his predecessor were so completely different, he couldn't win over the dressing room. The Foxes were relegated and Taylor was out. But a short spell at Brighton & Hove Albion was more successful, as another promotion from the old Division Two was achieved. Hull City, in the bottom division offered him a brand-new stadium and boundless potential, something that the Withdean Stadium couldn't match, so Peter, never one to shirk a challenge, went to Humberside and gave the Tigers fans two seasons of promotions. While managing Hull, Peter returned to his role with The FA and the England Under-21s, once again ensuring they won their European Under-21s qualifying group. In the summer of 2006, Peter's career came full circle as he replaced another former Hendon and Crystal Palace player as Eagles boss, Iain Dowie. Even more strangely, his director of football was a man whom he had signed as a Hendon player, Bob Dowie.

George Wakeling - It seems as if George Wakeling has been in a football dugout for ever. He first came to prominence with Leyton–Wingate, taking the Hare & Hounds Club into the Isthmian League Premier Division in the mid-1980s, just a few years after they left the Athenian League. George moved across London, to Bromley, and gave the Lilywhites many seasons of good service, on a fluctuating budget – though normally on the small side – with the concomitant problems of relegation and promotion battles. A strong believer in work ethic, George's teams are always hard to beat, well organised and determined to play for the full 90 minutes. In 1999, George went further south, joining Hastings of the Southern League, where he took them to the first round of The FA Cup in 2002. Unfortunately a rash of injuries led to the club's relegation and George returned to Bromley, where he worked his magic to get the Club promoted back to the Ryman League Premier Division.

Barrie Williams - Barrie Williams' finest moment as a manager came while Sutton United were members of the Conference, but that should in no way lessen his inclusion in this chapter. Barrie spent more than a dozen seasons at Gander Green Lane, taking Sutton to two Isthmian League titles in the 1980s.

A pipe-smoking school-teacher, Barrie took an academic interest in football, his programme columns being works of literary art, if a bit impenetrable for the average football fan! He was a firm believer in good football, passing to feet, solid and uncomplicated defending, with a big striker off whom others could feed. After leaving Sutton, Barrie spent a brief spell coaching the England Ladies team and had a less successful six months at Hendon.

In other fields

CRICKET

Trevor Bailey - Pegasus, Walthamstow Avenue - Trevor Bailey's sporting career has had many facets. In his youth, he was good enough to play cricket for Cambridge University, Essex and England as a solid, middle-order batsman and swing bowler; as a footballer, he was good enough for Walthamstow Avenue to arrange for him to take three flights from the Caribbean (where he was touring with England) to appear in an FA Amateur Cup Final replay – sadly bad weather resulted in him arriving just too late to be named in the starting eleven but in enough time to watch the game from the stands. After retiring as a player, Trevor worked as a journalist for *The Financial Times*, being their football and cricket correspondent, and also for the BBC as a colour analyst on the ever-popular *Test Match Special*.

Denis Compton - his football career started at Nunhead – he also played for Golders Green, who became Hendon in 1946 – and could have made him eligible for the earlier part of this chapter, but he belongs more appropriately here. Denis was born in Hendon on 23 May 1918 – almost six years after his brother and fellow Arsenal and Middlesex dual sportsman Leslie. Denis is probably the finest sportsman ever to come out of the old London Borough of Hendon. A left winger, he was aged only 15 when he signed for Nunhead. But Denis made a big impression at Nunhead, earning Isthmian League representative honours before his 18th birthday. Arsenal were well aware of his talent with brother Leslie already on their books and it was no surprise that he joined the Gunners in 1936. A knee injury severely curtailed his football career and, without it, he would almost certainly have joined the ranks of dual internationals. As it was Denis played football for England only in unofficial wartime internationals. However, for all of his undoubted football talents, Denis is best known as a cricketer and as the face of Brylcreem hair products. Not only the finest batsman of his generation, the "Brylcreem Boy" was the first British sportsman to become a marketing front man. Denis's football career was over by 1950, but he continued to play cricket until the end of the 1950s, appearing in 78 Test matches and scoring 5,807 runs at an average of more than 50. He played for Middlesex from 1936 to 1958, missing, of course, the War years. His finest achievements for Middlesex came in 1947, when he set batting records that will never be broken, those of 18 centuries and 3,816 runs in first-class cricket. He also hit the fastest ever first-class triple-century, on England's tour to South Africa in 1948–49.

Mike Gatting - Hendon - Mike Gatting spent parts of three seasons with Hendon, all while a teenager, as a bustling centre-forward. A lack of inches, however, rather reduced his effectiveness and he was more or less a regular in the reserve team. He found playing football a very useful way of keeping fit in the offseason, in the few years he was not required for an international tour. Quite how far Mike could have gone in the football world is something that will never be known because he was a regular in the Middlesex CCC team from 17 and, within a couple of years, a tourist with England in the winter. After leaving Hendon, Mike played park football sporadically. His brother, Steve, was the opposite to Mike in that he had to end his cricket career – he was an excellent wicket-keeper/batsman who might have gone on to enjoy a long County career, had his football commitments not limited him to two months of cricket per season.

Doug Insole - Pegasus, Walthamstow Avenue - Doug was President of the MCC and is an FA Councillor. He, too, was a fine footballer and was a regular in the all-conquering Walthamstow Avenue side of the early 1950s. He played in the 1952 FA Amateur Cup Final and was also in the side that met Manchester United in the following season's FA Cup, losing only after a replay. An excellent cricketer, Doug played for Essex and England before becoming a member of the England selection committee. Doug still attends matches on the London–Essex border.

Graham Roope - Corinthian–Casuals, Woking, Kingstonian - As a cricketer, Graham Roope had few peers as a slip fielder for both Surrey CCC and England. A regular at The Oval for 15 years, Graham's international career was of the stop-start variety as he was vying with a number of other talented upper middle-order batsmen, though few could boast his versatility as a bowler and top fieldsman too. Although a little short for a goalkeeper, he was an excellent shot-stopper. However, Graham, like all cricketer-footballers, had reduced careers due to their unavailability until mid-September, frequent overseas tours with club or country and March departure for pre-season training.

Mickey Stewart OBE - Corinthian–Casuals, Hendon - Unlike his Chelsea-supporting son, Alec, Mickey Stewart was lucky enough to play his sport in an era where he was able to serve both Surrey CCC and amateur football clubs. An excellent slip fielder and top-order batsman, Mickey didn't quite have Alec's cricket ability but was certainly good enough to hold down a place in the Surrey team – and captain them – for more than a decade, during which time he won the County Championship. He gained 8 England caps and mananged the national side.

Derek Ufton - Dulwich Hamlet, CHARLTON ATHLETIC (263+0, 0) - Derek Ufton played several games for Dulwich Hamlet during the latter part of the Second World War and in the first season afterwards, 1945–46. After serving in the Forces, he had a short period with Bexleyheath & Welling before joining Charlton Athletic in 1949. He soon established himself in the first team at centre-half and went on to make 263 Football League appearances during his ten years with Charlton. Amazingly, however, even for a defender in those days, he failed to score a single goal. He did, nevertheless, earn a full international cap for England, playing in the prestigious fixture against the Rest of Europe at Wembley in 1953. Derek was also an accomplished county cricketer, playing for Kent in the 1950s as a top order batsman and occasional wicket-keeper, deputising behind the stumps for Godfrey Evans when he was away on England duty. His son Jonny was a top-class rugby player, making numerous appearances for Wasps.

WH "Tadge" Webster - Corinthian–Casuals - Tadge Webster was a high-quality player for Casuals – just before their merger with Corinthians – who earned England Amateur international caps. His first love, however, was cricket and he was a fine administrator at the Marylebone Cricket Club, in the days when the MCC basically defined how cricket would be played around the world. Such was his authority that he joined such luminaries as Sir Tim Rice, HRH the Duke of Norfolk and HRH Prince Philip in having a one-year term as President of the MCC. He died in the early 1980s.

EDUCATION

Sir Alan Davies - Wembley, Finchley - Alan Davies played football as a hobby at the end of the Amateur and start of the "players" eras. He was a solid, unspectacular full-back, one of hundreds who played football for fun in that time. He moved into coaching and was manager of Finchley briefly in the early 1980s, and a coach/scout at Hendon later in the decade. However, his work as a teacher was far more notable and his work in a number of schools with problems earned him a knighthood. He was made headmaster of the Copland Community School in Wembley in 2003.

MUSIC

MC Harvey - Lewes, Ford United, AFC Wimbledon - Rapper MC Harvey showed his football ability in Sky TV's *The Match* and was soon signed by Lewes. Playing out wide, MC is equally adept as a wing-back or orthodox winger. For all his talent, however, he has struggled to make a consistent impact, but this probably has much to do with his off-field activities making it hard for him to train with his teams.

ACTING

Ralf Little - Edgware Town, Chertsey Town, Windsor & Eton - Unlike most actors who are football "wannabes", Ralf Little is a bona fide footballer, who has played in the Isthmian League for a couple of seasons when his acting appearances permit. A left-back, Ralf made his debut for Edgware Town at Ilford in a 2004–05 Associate Members' Cup tie after starring in Sky's *The Match*. He left Edgware when offered a contract by Chertsey Town before moving on to play in the Premier Division for struggling Windsor & Eton in 2005–06. Quiet and unassuming, he has been a good club man, turning up to away matches even when not selected.

BROADCASTING

Martin Tyler - Corinthian–Casuals - Sky Television's senior commentator Martin Tyler learned about football the hard way. He was a member of the consistently unsuccessful Corinthian–Casuals teams of the early 1960s before hanging up his boots and moving into journalism, where his football experience proved invaluable. In the 1970s he was part of the ITV team and moved to Sky in the 1990s. He has been Sky Sports' No. 1 football commentator since the satellite broadcaster gained exclusive rights to show live football in the Premiership.

Maurice Edelston - FULHAM (3+0, 0) Wimbledon, BRENTFORD (21+0, 6), Corinthians, READING (202+0, 70), NORTHAMPTON TOWN (40+0, 17) - To younger football fans, the name Maurice Edelston means absolutely nothing, but for those who grew up in the 1960s and 1970s, Maurice Edelston was one of the most well-known voices in football. He was one of the main BBC radio commentators and his background was impeccable. He was an amateur at Fulham before joining Wimbledon in the Isthmian League in 1937. After a short spell at the Dons, but remaining an amateur, he moved to Brentford, earning England Amateur international caps in the process. Maurice then joined Corinthians in their final season before their merger with Casuals and, turning professional, signed for Reading a few months before the outbreak of World War II. He didn't leave Elm Park until 1951, during which time he earned further international recognition, albeit Wartime England caps. He finished his career with Northampton before moving into broadcasting. He died at the age of 58 in 1976.

CHAPTER SEVEN

Referees

The Laws of the Game specify the equipment needed for a match but the most obvious thing which is needed for a senior match is a referee with, hopefully, two assistant referees or linesmen as they were known for the vast majority of the history of the League.

It has often been said that if a spectator has not noticed the referee then he has had a good game but until probably forty years ago the referee was rarely noticed, he certainly did not occupy the spotlight which his present day counterparts enjoy.

However, in the 1920's Stanley Rous was not only an active referee on the League but was the Honorary Referees' Secretary at Surrey FA and Fixture Secretary of the League from 1926 to 1934. This was the start of a career in administration for Mr Rous who subsequently became not only Secretary of The Football Association but President of FIFA until 1974 when he was succeeded by Mr Joao Havelange. He was rewarded for his services to football with a knighthood.

Rous' successor as Referees' and Fixture Secretary on the League was referee Sid Donaldson who refereed the England v Scotland Amateur International played at Dulwich Hamlet's Dog Kennel Hill ground in 1939. It can be seen therefore that referees have played an important part in the development of the League and many of the officials over the history of the League were former referees. Indeed, it could be said that in the way that match officials went on to become League officials this reflected the way that, historically, former players became club officials in scores of amateur clubs up and down the country and the Isthmian League was no exception.

There has also been a career path for match officials and the Isthmian League has always occupied a significant position in the development of those officials.

The system today is very much as it has always been although the designation of a referee has changed somewhat in the last few years.

There is, typically, a three tier structure for those wanting to referee senior football; there are currently ten levels of referees whereas until the late 1990's there were only three Classes so that when a referee first took up his whistle and passed his exam he would be a Class 3 (now Level 7) official and he would then have to prove himself by serving on a League or Leagues and be assessed as to his competency, progressing by Class 2 (Level 6) to Class 1 (Level 5).

Once a referee had Class 1 he was able to progress in senior football whereas now he has to achieve fitness levels and be accepted into a system which sees him go up through Level 4 (Supply League) through to Level 1 (National List). From there, a select few will be appointed to the FIFA List of Referees and be able to officiate at European and International matches, culminating for a very select band in appearance at the pinnacle of football, the FIFA World Cup.

Graham Poll was England's sole referee representative in Germany in 2006, having officiated for many years in the Isthmian League.

A match official has always had a career path; he refereed at one level and 'ran the line' at the next level and so it is today. The Isthmian League's divisions are at Steps 3 and 4 in football below the Football League and are what are called Contributory Leagues as opposed to Leagues at Steps 5 & 6 which are termed Supply Leagues. The way the system operates is that the referees at Isthmian matches will also act as assistant referees at the next Step (Conference) and the assistant referees will be referees on a Step 5 League.

The performance of each referee is marked by each Club participating in the match he is appointed to and often he will be "assessed" by an independent assessor from a panel of present and past match officials who have been trained for the task. When a referee does well on Club marks and Assessor reports he will hope to be promoted at the end of one season to the next level for him which is the next Step in football. In this way referees will hope to progress to the Football League and on to the Premiership.

In the past, however, the Isthmian League, as with other leagues, maintained its own list of referees and occupied a higher place in the pecking order of referees. The League promoted direct so that referees on the Isthmian League List would act as linesmen/assistant referees on Football League matches and would be promoted direct to that League.

The League is fortunate to have had probably more than its fair share of men promoted to the League List and beyond. David Elleray, received his grounding as an Isthmian referee and the destiny of officials has been in the hands of a select few referees' secretaries who have been former referees and while understanding the pressures referees are under, have in many cases been their harshest critics. In the recent past many of today's member clubs will remember Eddy Bray, John Williams, Ray Parker and Barry Simmons but they were preceded by a distinguished band of men such as Donald Mackenzie, A W Peacock, Frank Wilson and John McCulloch.

The League produced good football and a stern test for aspiring referees and so the League was seen to have a substantial number of its members promoted to the Football League, present Chairman Alan Turvey being a great example of this. Sadly the League no longer has its own referees' list because this was taken over by The Football

Association in 2002 and has been administered by the Association centrally since then. No longer can a referee claim to have come from one league but, in future, all referees will officiate at a match at the level they have attained, irrespective of the league.

A high proportion of the most senior referees have been former Isthmians and whilst that number will now decline because of the new system, at the time of writing six of the referees on the Premier League are former Isthmians and from the FIFA List we can boast Rob Stiles, Steve Bennett and Mark Halsey alongside Graham Poll.

Current (and recent past) members of Premiership and Football League Panels who had been on the Isthmian League Panel were approached to contribute something to this chapter; some declined, some did not respond but the great majority were pleased to have an opportunity to add their piece.

We are placing the list in the time honoured tradition of alphabetical order to avoid arguments from Rob Stiles as to why he should be placed before Steve Bennett!

Paul Armstrong

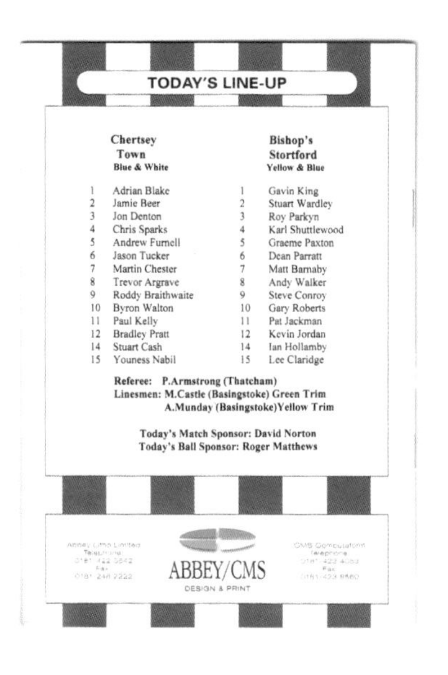

TODAY'S LINE-UP

	Chertsey Town Blue & White		Bishop's Stortford Yellow & Blue
1	Adrian Blake	1	Gavin King
2	Jamie Beer	2	Stuart Wardley
3	Jon Denton	3	Roy Parkyn
4	Chris Sparks	4	Karl Shuttlewood
5	Andrew Furnell	5	Graeme Paxton
6	Jason Tucker	6	Dean Parratt
7	Martin Chester	7	Matt Barnaby
8	Trevor Argrave	8	Andy Walker
9	Roddy Braithwaite	9	Steve Conroy
10	Byron Walton	10	Gary Roberts
11	Paul Kelly	11	Pat Jackman
12	Bradley Pratt	12	Kevin Jordan
14	Stuart Cash	14	Ian Hollamby
15	Youness Nabil	15	Lee Claridge

Referee: P.Armstrong (Thatcham)
Linesmen: M.Castle (Basingstoke) Green Trim
A.Munday (Basingstoke)Yellow Trim

Today's Match Sponsor: David Norton
Today's Ball Sponsor: Roger Matthews

ABBEY/CMS

After progressing through the North Berks and Hellenic Leagues, Paul was invited to join the Isthmian League as an Assistant Referee for the 1987-88 season. His first appointment was at Maidenhead United when the hosts beat Ruislip Manor 3-0. He remained on the Assistants list for a further four seasons, making a total of 94 appearances. A 95th appearance did follow some nine seasons later in his last season on the League, when Paul covered a line due to a shortage of officials, on the Premier Division clash between Hitchin Town and Hampton.

At the commencement of the 1992–93 season, Paul was promoted to the Referees' list. His first 'middle' was at Bracknell Town who entertained Northwood (making their first appearance in the League) in August 1992 and Paul went on to referee a total of 180 matches, with his last appointment being a League Cup semi-final between Oxford City and Purfleet in May 2001. Paul refereed the 1995–96 Carlton Trophy Final between Banstead Athletic and Canvey Island, a representative match between the Isthmian League and an FA XI in December 1999, and the 1999–2000 season Isthmian League Cup Final between Farnborough Town and Maidenhead United.

Paul's career saw him complete 149 matches as a National List Assistant, the highlight being appointment to the last Football League Cup Final staged at the 'old' Wembley Stadium between Leicester City and Tranmere Rovers in February 2000; he proceeded to the National List of Referees in August 2000, and has now spanned more than 200 'middles' with a highlight being his appointment to referee the 2006 FA Vase Final.

Steve Bennett

Steve qualified as the old Class 1 in January 1984, progressing via the Winstonlead Kent League, Isthmian League and GM Vauxhall Conference to the Football League in 1995 and then to The FA Premier League in 1999. Steve was appointed as a Football League Linesman in 1992, Premier League Linesman in 1993 and FIFA Linesman in 1995. He became a FIFA Referee in January 2001.

Steve has had so many honours it is difficult to know where to begin but he is currently a full time referee with a contract from The Football Association. He was a linesman in the 1995 FA Challenge Cup Final between Manchester United and Everton as well as officiating in the same role for the Division One Play Off Final between Reading and Bolton Wanderers; in 2000 he refereed The FA Youth Cup Final between Arsenal and Coventry City and the following year was fourth official for the Cup Final between Liverpool and Arsenal. He has refereed The FA Community Shield (2003) and the Varsity Match (2006) as well as seeing Chelsea victorious in the Carling Cup Final at Cardiff in 2005 (famously sending Jose Mourinho to the stands for his "Shhh" gesture) and in the first FA Cup Final back at the new Wembley in 2007. He continues to officiate at the highest level.

Phil Crossley

Phil didn't take up the whistle until he was 29, thereafter made rapid steps through the Suburban, Isthmian and Panel Leagues until his promotion to the National List of referees in 2002. Was 4th official for the 2005 FL Cup Final and has refereed The FA Women's Cup Final, FA Vase Final, and a FL League One Play Off Final as well as matches in the Premier League. He missed season 2007-08 due to injuries sustained in a game at Derby County.

Darren Deadman

Aged 34, Darren is a civil servant in Peterborough and is married with two children. He progressed to the National List via the Isthmian League and Panel Leagues, joining the National List of assistant referees in 2000 and the referees' list in 2005. No major appointments are listed within his profile, and his hobbies include his family and horse racing.

Andy D'Urso

Andy was appointed to the League's linesman's list for season 1985-86 and then promoted to the referees list for season 1989–90, serving on the League as a referee for 7 seasons. He was promoted to the Football League linesman's list for season 1990–91 and became a Panel League referee in season 1992-93. Andy achieved membership of the National list of referees in 1994-95 and then went onto The FA Premier League Referees' list for season 1999. In addition, Andy was a FIFA referee from January 2001 until December 2005. Over the past 7 seasons Andy officiated as Referee at the Final of the UEFA Under 16 Championships in 2001 as well as the 2001 F A Community Shield and the 2004 F A Youth Cup Final; he has refereed 3 FA Cup quarter finals and the 2002 League Cup semi final as well as officiating in a number of countries in Europe on FIFA/UEFA competitions.

When asked to comment on his time with the League, Andy said "I have many fond memories from my refereeing on the Isthmian League during which time I refereed the League Representative side versus an FA XI in season 1994-95 and at the end of that season refereed the Carlsberg Cup Final. I made many friends during my time on the League – referees, linesman and club officials. I enjoyed the banter in the boardrooms/bar with club officials, managers and players with some great characters like George Wakeling, Jack Pearce and many others."

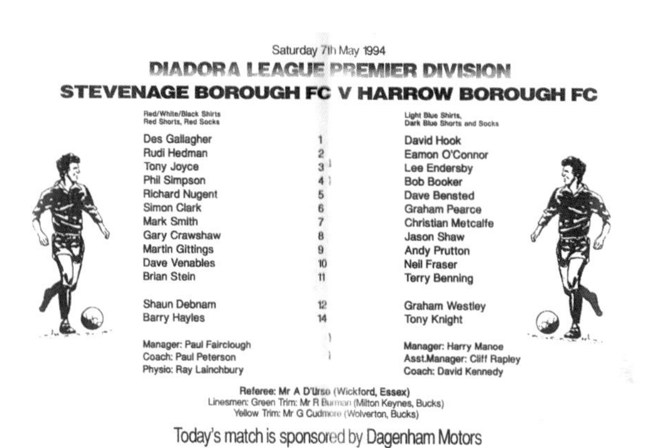

Saturday 7th May 1994

DIADORA LEAGUE PREMIER DIVISION

STEVENAGE BOROUGH FC V HARROW BOROUGH FC

Red/White/Black Shirts Red Shorts, Red Socks		Light Blue Shirts, Dark Blue Shorts and Socks
Des Gallagher	1	David Hook
Rudi Hedman	2	Eamon O'Connor
Tony Joyce	3	Lee Endersby
Phil Simpson	4	Bob Booker
Richard Nugent	5	Dave Bensted
Simon Clark	6	Graham Pearce
Mark Smith	7	Christian Metcalfe
Gary Crawshaw	8	Jason Shaw
Martin Gittings	9	Andy Prutton
Dave Venables	10	Neil Fraser
Brian Stein	11	Terry Benning
Shaun Debnam	12	Graham Westley
Barry Hayles	14	Tony Knight
Manager: Paul Fairclough		Manager: Harry Manoe
Coach: Paul Peterson		Asst.Manager: Cliff Rapley
Physio: Ray Lainchbury		Coach: David Kennedy

Referee: Mr A D'Urso (Wickford, Essex)
Linesmen: Green Trim: Mr R Burman (Milton Keynes, Bucks)
Yellow Trim: Mr G Cudmore (Wolverton, Bucks)

Today's match is sponsored by Dagenham Motors

David Elleray

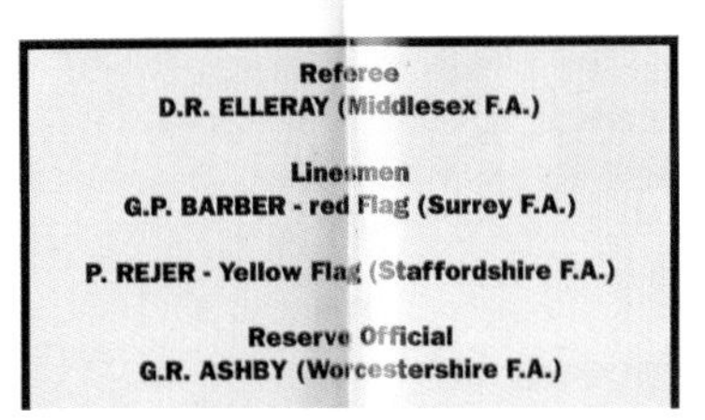

FA CUP 1994
ONE HUNDRED AND THIRTEENTH
© THE FOOTBALL ASSOCIATION

Referee
D.R. ELLERAY (Middlesex F.A.)

Linesmen
G.P. BARBER - red Flag (Surrey F.A.)

P. REJER - Yellow Flag (Staffordshire F.A.)

Reserve Official
G.R. ASHBY (Worcestershire F.A.)

As you would expect of a schoolmaster, David wrote his own article and we can do no better than to reproduce it here.

"The ten seasons I spent officiating on the Isthmian League were hugely enjoyable but also extremely instructive as I 'cut my teeth' in the world of professional football.

When I moved from Oxford University to Harrow I applied for a linesman's position to both the Isthmian and Southern Leagues. The Southern ignored my letter but the Isthmian accepted me. I later learned that this was the wrong way to have done things and recommendations were supposed to go via the County FA!

My Isthmian career began at Wembley (Vale Farm not Wembley Stadium, unfortunately!) when I ran the line for Wembley v Horsham in August 1977. I spent three seasons on the linesmen's list, officiating in 42 matches, my first experience of the Premier Division being Southall v Kingstonian in April 1978. I also refereed and lined in the Isthmian League Youth Cup (we were put in teams of three and alternated between refereeing and lining) and I was delighted to line on the Final in May 1980 when Tring beat Wokingham 2-0. I can still remember that match vividly. I was promoted to the Supplementary List of Referees for Season 1980–81. I refereed my first game at Willesden on 16 August 1980. Although only 25 years old, it was the 800th match of my career and I marked the occasion by sending off Mickey Stock of Willesden for a head butt in the 80th minute! I remember that Willesden were extremely hospitable hosts whatever the result and it was not easy driving home if you spent too long in the boardroom after a game! My 20 games must have gone well as I was promoted to the Full Referees list for season 1981–82 and on 11 November 1981 I refereed my first Premier Division match: Dulwich Hamlet v Hayes. It was an exciting afternoon for me not only because it was my first Premier Division match but because it was at Dulwich Hamlet's legendary Dog Kennel Hill ground. I refereed 22 matches that season and was 4th in the merit order and devastated when I did not get promotion to the Football League line; I did not realise that you had to do two seasons before you could move up.

Undeterred, I worked hard and the next three seasons saw successive promotions to the Football League line, Panel League middle and then, on the basis of my Isthmian League marks, I was called for interview to become a Football League referee. The interview was successful and I became a Football League referee for season 1986–87.

I was fortunate that you could stay on your Contributory League for one year after promotion so I continued officiating until the end of season 1986-7. My last middle was Kingstonian v Dulwich Hamlet but, in a nice twist, my last appearance on the League was as a linesman. I had been appointed as senior linesmen for the European Cup quarter final between Red Star Belgrade and Read Madrid. I decided that I need to brush up my lining technique so the League helped out and I ran the line on a cold evening for Staines v Stevenage in front of a few hundred people. A fortnight late I lined in sub-zero temperatures in Yugoslavia in front of 90,000!

I have many memories of my Isthmian days, not least the camaraderie at the fitness tests and the terrifying diktats from Alan Turvey at our meetings! I learned a very important lesson on the 5 January 1985 when, after 12 minutes, I abandoned the Wycombe Wanderers v Sutton United match because of frost. I had inspected the pitch at noon, 1.00 pm and 2.00 pm and it seemed playable. However, I made two miscalculations: I failed to take account of the fact that from about 2.00 pm onwards in winter the temperature drops and conditions can only get worse. I also allowed myself to be influenced by one of the teams who were desperate to play. The pitch was solid when we kicked off and the game quickly became a farce and conditions very dangerous so I abandoned the game to hoots of derision from the fans but the grateful thanks of the players. I got a terrific telling off from Alan Turvey for starting the game in the first place and for the rest of my career if ever there was a doubt about a frozen pitch I erred on the side of caution. Indeed it was the 'Wycombe experience' which helped me when I postponed a Sky live Boxing Day match between Leicester and Arsenal, even though their 'tent' seemed to have protected quite a lot of the pitch. I learned a great deal from my decade on the Isthmian League – the experiences were valuable and, I believe, contributed to the enjoyment and success I had in the years that followed."

The Teams

ENFIELD		AYLESBURY
Andy Pape	1	Gary Phillips
Gary Blackford	2	Naseem Bashir
Jimmy Carstairs	3	Mickey Danzey
Paul Turner	4	Gary Simpson
Steve Terry	5	Matt Hayward
Andy Kerr	6	Allan Pluckrose
Billy Goldstone	7	Paul Hobbs
Andy Sayer	8	Steve Heard
Gary Abbott	9	Cliff Hercules
John Richardson	10	John Caesar
Justin Gentle	11	Gary Smith
Paul Cobb	12	Steve Shea
Dave Flemming	14	Gary Cobb
Danny Adams	15	Keith Dirke

HUNTER VEHICLES LTD.

THE OFFICIALS
Referee: M. HALSEY

COMING SOON
DULWICH HAMLET

THE OTHER MATCHES

Mark Halsey

Former Non-League goalkeeper, spent twelve years playing before he commenced refereeing in 1989. In December 1984 he played for Barnet before joining St. Albans City. Progressed through the Isthmian League to the Football League. Refereed the 1999 Football League One Play-Off Final between Gillingham and Manchester City at Wembley. Then joined the Select Group Referees list on its formation in 2001. Appointed to the FIFA International Referees list in 2000 and was appointed as fourth official in the 2002 FA Cup Final. In 2004 he took control of his first major FIFA appointment between Belgium and France.

Graham Horwood

A married man with two young children, Graham started refereeing at fifteen years of age and reached the National list of assistant referees in 2001 after progressing through the South Midlands and Isthmian Leagues. He was promoted to the List of Panel referees in 2005 and the National List of referees in 2007, the year in which he refereed a Conference Play Off Semi-final.

Ray Lewis

LEATHERHEAD Colours : Green/White		DULWICH HAMLET Colours : Pink/Blue
1. John SWANNELL		1. Allan THOMAS
2. Dave SARGEANT		2. Paul WEBB
3. Barry WEBB		3. Steve ROGERS
4. John COOPER	Our Team chooses	4. Peter MILLS
5. Dave REID	CHAPMANS MENSWEAR	5. Rodney BROOKES
6. Derek WELLS	Walton and Weybridge	6. Peter SMITH
7. Colin WOFFINDEN		7. Trevor BLADON
8. Peter LAVERS		8. Ken JELLEY
9. Peter McGILLICUDDY		9. John BAKER
10. Willie SMITH		10. Dave BARKER
11. John DOYLE		11. Alex JACKSON
12. Peter PAGE		12. Chris PULLEY
Referee : M. J. Holland		Linesmen : Red R. S. Lewis, Orange T. G. Giles

Above: the appearance of Ray Lewis as senior linesman in the 1975 Surrey Senior Cup Final.

Ray, famously known as the ref from Great Bookham, is now the Chairman of The FA Referees Committee, having had the honour of refereeing an FA Cup Final and serving on the Football League. Less happily, Ray was the referee for the ill-fated FA Cup Semi-Final at Hillsborough in 1989 between Liverpool and Nottingham Forest.

Of his career, he says: I was appointed to the Isthmian League Reserve Section linesman's list in 1965. My first match was at Woking where Dougie Burns was the referee. I will always remember his instruction "The centre circle is all mine".

I enjoyed my association with the League and will always be grateful for the constructive advice from colleagues, clubs and players especially John McCulloch, the referees' secretary at the time. From this I was able to form a strong foundation, which helped me climb the refereeing tree. I have many happy memories of games in the Isthmian days. I had just become a father and visited St. Albans City where Dick East, the secretary, had got to know my good news. I left the ground that Saturday evening at 10.45pm and was taken to Watford Junction then onto Euston and Waterloo before catching the night train back to Bournemouth. Fellowship is as strong now as it was then with my peer group.

Clive Penton

Married with two children Clive is a support officer in the communications industry and started refereeing in 1986. Progressing through the Sussex County League and the Isthmian League, he reached the National List of assistant referees in 1997. After three years on the list of Panel Referees he was promoted to the National List of referees in 2001. Hobbies include walking, gardening and swimming.

Graham Poll

Graham started refereeing in August 1980 and became a National List Assistant Referee in 1986 while on the Isthmian list and then progressed to the National List of Referees in 1991, moving to the Premier League two years later. He was appointed by FIFA at the beginning of 1996 and then joined the FIFA Elite List after just two years. At the time of writing, Graham has just retired having officiated at 22 International matches, 41 Champions League Matches and 296 matches in the Premier League. In addition he has received the "plum" appointments at the Finals of the UEFA Cup, The FA Cup, the Worthington Cup, FA Vase and the 1998 Charity Shield. He was the sole representative of England in Germany in 2006 for the World Cup following on from his appointment in Japan in 2002 for Croatia v Italy.

TEAM CHECK

SATURDAY 27th JANUARY 1990

WOKINGHAM TOWN		BROMLEY
Gary WESTWOOD	1	Curtis HAYES
Chris HODGE	2	Mark DENTON
Phil ALEXANDER	3	Gary FIORE
Tony CARTER	4	Jim CANNON
Bobby PURSER	5	Paul COATES
David COX	6	Gary BOWYER
Darron WILKINSON	7	Martin MORGAN
Brian BROOME	8	Martin COATES
David PEARCE	9	Paul McMENEMY
Paul SWANNACK	10	Steve GRENFELL
Dave THOMPSON	11	Graham LANE
Darren BARNARD	12	Jerry DOLKE
Roy ATKIN	14	Paul LOUGHLIN

RESULT	HALF-TIME			FULL TIME		

OFFICIALS

REFEREE:

G. POLL (Berkhamsted)

LINESMEN:

R. GREY (Thatcham) K.R. PARSONS (Newbury)

Just prior to refereeing the 2006 FA Cup Semi Final between Chelsea and Liverpool, Graham commented "My memories of the Isthmian League are quite simply that my 10 years on the list were the happiest of my 26 years as a referee to date. The football was of a high standard and in my mind remains the highest level of football which is still played as a sport and not a business. This may of course have changed but Julia and I still talk of the frequent visits we made to Kingstonian, Carshalton, Staines, Bishop's Stortford and Windsor & Eton amongst others where Julia was made to feel particularly welcome and we always had a drink and a chat after the game whatever the result. Clubs were more like extended families, there were so many characters that saw me grow and develop as a man and a referee.

Men such as Jack Pearce, George Borg and Chris Kelly certainly tested me whilst players like Phil Gridelet, Ian Dowie and Les Ferdinand helped prepare me for the bigger stage. I started as a linesman in 1984, aged 21, and did my last game in 1993 when I had graduated to The FA Premier League – without a doubt those who remember my early days will remember a particularly brash young man who was never short on confidence. Without the grooming of John Williams, Ray Parker and Barry Simmons I would never have made it to the level I now officiate at and I will always be grateful for that."

Mick Russell

Married with three children, forty one year old Mick is a gas service engineer who started refereeing in the early 1990's, progressing through the South Midlands League to reach the National List of assistant referees in 2000 and was promoted to the referees' list in 2004. Enjoys a game of golf and spending what spare time he has with his family, and is a licensed FA Coach.

Rob Styles

Is now in his mid-forties and has 3 children – James, Aimee and Alexandra. He is a company director in a groundwork and civil engineering business as well as being a full time referee and admits to enjoying the occasional round of golf.

His career path as a referee began when he qualified to Class 3 in Portsmouth in 1987, progressing to Class 2 in 1988 and on to Class 1 in 1989. He then served on the Hampshire League as a Referee in 1990, moving to the Wessex League middle and the Isthmian League line in 1992. He was quickly promoted to the Isthmian Referees List in 1993 and made it as a National List Assistant and Panel Referee in 1994.

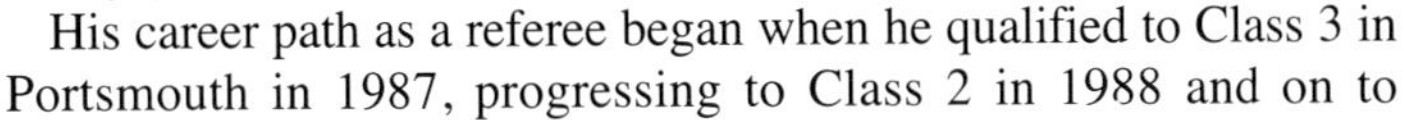

1996 saw Rob promoted as a National List Referee and The FA Premier League welcomed him as a Referee in 2000. He progressed to the International List in 2002.

His major plum appointments have been: Hampshire Senior Cup Final and Isthmian League Cup Final Referee (1995), FA Trophy Reserve Referee (2000), Football League Div II Play Off Final Referee (2000), Auto Windscreen Shield Final Reserve Referee (2000), FA Youth Cup Final Referee (2003), FA Cup Final Referee (2006).

Paul Taylor

Paul Taylor commenced refereeing in 1977 and progressed via the Herts County League; the Isthmian League and the Panel League competitions. He was appointed as a Football League Linesman in 1986 and promoted to Referee in 1989. In season 2000-01, he "made it" as an FA Premier League Referee. Paul has refereed the Hertfordshire Senior County Cup Final, various Isthmian Cup Finals and Representative matches, The FA Sunday Cup Final and several International matches at Youth and Semi-Professional level. Paul has also officiated in the Football League play-offs on five occasions including the Division One Final between Ipswich Town and Barnsley at Wembley in May 2000. Other notable appointments include refereeing Cheltenham Town's first game in the Football League and Southampton's last match at The Dell (vs Arsenal). His overseas appointments include the 2000-01 Champions League fixture between Dynamo Kiev and Red Star Belgrade. He refereed his first senior FIFA International between Nigeria and Venezuela in August 2003. In 2004 he was fourth official at The FA Trophy Final. In 2005 Paul became a County Accredited Referees Instructor and has subsequently qualified as a National Licensed Instructor. In 2006 he refereed the Channel Islands Cup Final in Guernsey.

Paul writes "I had watched my local team Cheshunt playing in the Isthmian League during my teens and was delighted when the League gave me my 'break' into officiating senior football. Whilst the football was extremely competitive and an ideal preparation for my subsequent progression to the higher echelons of the game, the post-match invitation for match officials to the boardroom exemplified the warm and friendly ethos of the League. I made and retained many friends and it was a pleasure to have served. I wish the League every success over the coming years".

Mike Tingey

Mike Tingey is a commercial director and married to Andrea with one son, Marcus. He commenced refereeing at 16 years of age on High Wycombe Leagues. Progressed via the Hellenic League to the Isthmian League Referees' List in 1991; aged 24. Appointed to Football League as a linesman in 1993 and to the Premier League in the same capacity the following Season. Selected as FIFA Assistant Referee from January 2004. Mike has officiated as an Assistant Referee for: 1999 FA Youth Cup Final, 2001 FA Cup Final, 2001 Division 3 Play-Off Final, 2002 Division One Play-Off Final, 2004 Community Shield & 2005 UEFA Cup Final in Lisbon.

Mike recalls "From when I started as a match official on the Isthmian League in 1986 as a linesman (aged 19), and then as a referee from 1991, generally I have fond memories of the games that I have been appointed to. I particularly recall competitive encounters at Aldershot Town, Enfield, St. Albans and Kingstonian, to name a few, with a number of local derbies played over the Bank Holiday periods through the years. Whilst there have been challenging matches during my 20 year association with the League, I have generally found the football to be fair and well-disciplined. I have developed mutual respect and a friendly working relationship with even some of the most notable characters within the Isthmian League, whether players, managers or club officials."

Alan Turvey

Alan began refereeing on the Isthmian League Reserve Section in 1960 and rose to become a Football League referee in 1977, when he hung up his whistle and took up his pen to become an administrator. *Right: a letter of confirmation of fixture from Bishop's Stortford during Alan's refereeing days.*

Gavin Ward

Gavin is one of the latest recruits having been born in 1979. He is a Business Relationship Manager with RBS Insurance and is currently single. He qualified in April 1992 in Kent and progressed through the Kent League in 1999-2000, the Isthmian League in 2000-01 then on to the Panel in 2004-05 as a referee. Gavin became a Football League assistant in 2002-03, and is now on the Football League Referees' List and the Premier League Assistants' List. Due to his age his major matches are hopefully in front of him but, to date, he has refereed the Kent Senior Cup Final, Bromley v Gravesend & Northfleet in April 2006, and has also acted as an Assistant in the Champions League for the match FC Haka (Finland) v Valarenga (Norway) He gives this insight into the mysteries of appointment of match officials: "I remember during my season as an assistant referee hearing stories about Barry Simmons (Referees' Secretary – responsible for the appointment of officials) regarding late 'additional' appointments and his phone calls. I thought the stories were a wind up by the guys, only to receive a call on a Sunday evening from Barry, it went something like this:

Barry: *Gavin it's Barry Simmons from the Isthmian League.*
Gavin: *Hello Barry, how are you?*
Barry: *Yeah alright, got a game for you.......*
Gavin: *Oh ok, where and when?*
Barry: *Tuesday night at Tilbury, you're not shown as closed, so I'm sure you're ok to do the game aren't you?*
Gavin: *Yeah I think I'm ok.*
Barry: *I know so.*
Gavin: *Oh right.*
Barry: *Good.*
Barry hangs up - no goodbye or thank you!

Gavin also recalls an incident from a League Cup match at Barking:

"The game was in extra time and I had quite a few cautions at this point, then an Arlesey player who was already cautioned committed a reckless foul, so I awarded a free kick, then called the player towards me, I then informed him that I was going to caution and then dismiss him, so I showed him a second yellow card followed by a red. His response was to walk closer towards raising his arms and hands, so I started to back pedal, he then started to run after me and ended up chasing me across half the pitch. The sort of thing you would see on *You've Been Framed* and laugh your head off! It was not funny at the time but I can laugh about it now!"

	Dulwich Hamlet (Yellow and Blue)		Southall (White)
1	Alan Thomas	1	Alan Jarrett
2	Chris Lewington	2	Micky Heath
3	Steve Rogers	3	Keith Baker
4	Trevor Bladon (Capt.)	4	Harry Manoe
5	Rodney Brookes	5	Duncan Clough
6	Eric Allinson	6	Chris Mullen
7	Peter Mills	7	Cliff Rapley
8	Hugh Wilson	8	Alan Devonshire
9	John Dear	9	Alan Clarke
10	Brian West	10	Ray Knowles
11	Alec Jackson	11	Derek Harris
12	Fred Pudney	12	Gordon Towers

Referee: ... ... Mr. A. W. Ward (New Southgate)
Linesmen: ... ... Messrs. N. S. Butler and B. Pleasance (Red flag) (Orange flag)

Tony Ward

Tony progressed to the Football League list in 1981 having served on the Isthmian League for many years, by which time he had officiated in both an FA Vase Final and an FA Cup semi-final.

His last Isthmian match was the 1981 Hitachi Cup Final which saw Slough Town defeat Walthamstow Avenue 4-2 at Hayes.

Iain Williamson

Head of Sales for a company within the financial sector, Iain is married with one young son and first qualified as a referee in 1991 at age fifteen. He progressed via the Isthmian League list, on which he served from 1997 to 1999, and then to the National List of Assistant Referees in 1999. He reached the Referees' List three years later. Has officiated on the Football League Play Off Semi Finals as assistant, fourth official and Referee since 2002. His hobbies include golf, horseracing and spending time with his family.

CUP & CHARITY SHIELD REFEREES

	League Cup	*Full Members Cup*	*Associate Members Trophy*	*Charity Shield*
1974-75	A.C.F. Turvey (1st leg)			
	B. Daniels (2nd leg)			
1975-76	V. McCowan			
1976-77	J. Martin			
1977-78	A. Cox			
1978-79	T. Maber			A. Ward
1979-80	B. O'Leary			A. Buksh
1980-81	A. Ward			A. Rogers
1981-82	A. Buksh			D. Keen
1982-83	R. Bigger			M. Cotton
1983-84	A. Rogers			B. O'Leary
1984-85	D. Keen			D. Keen
1985-86	R. Wiseman			K. Wenham
1986-87	A. Williams			M. Brown
1987-88	K. Wenham			P. Helsby
1988-89	P. Taylor			A. Williams
1989-90	G. Poll			D. Orr
1990-91	G. Willard	P. Taylor	E. Green	P. Vosper
1991-92	D. Orr	G. Poll	J. Smyth	J. Smyth
1992-93	C. Henderson	M. Stobbart	P. Gage	E. Green
1993-94	S. Tomlin	G. Barber	J. Pettitt	G. Poll
1994-95	M. Stobbart	A. D'Urso	J. Ross	A. Schneider
1995-96	S. Bennett	M. Halsey	P. Armstrong	M. Halsey
1996-97	J. Ross	W. Jordan	M. Ebbage	J. Pettitt
1997-98	K. Reynolds	R. Styles	C. Penton	D. Crick
1998-99	W. Jordan	J. Moore	A. Harvey	M. Dearing
1999-2000	P. Armstrong	S. Rubery	J. Pearce	C. Penton
2000-01	P. Crossley	P. Vosper	R. Evans	A. Wilkins
2001-02	J. Pearce			D. Deadman
2002-03	K. Pyke		S. Briffitt	P. Crossley
2003-04	A. E. Rayner			B. D. Baker
2004-05	M. Darlow		S.A. Child	M. Bull

CHAPTER EIGHT

Representative Matches

Over the 100 years the League has played 229 representative matches with the first being played on 4 May 1912 and the last being a celebration of 100 years on 7 March 2005. It will be seen therefore that the League has always been keen to take part in representative matches. It was a keen participant in the Inter League Cup matches of the late 70s. Initially representative matches were seen to be an honour and players would have welcomed the opportunity to play against other leagues as well as nations. However, over the history of the League the attitude of society changed and with the loss of "honor sufficit", the loss of amateur status and the greater rewards brought about from increasingly competitive football the importance of representative matches waned. Instead of many thousands turning up to see matches as was the case before the Second World War, attendances were numbered in their hundreds in the latter part of the 20th century.

The Football Association decreed in the early 21st century that they would no longer provide a team to play the annual match against the League. The League therefore felt that the cost of the representative team could not be justified simply for one match against the Combined Services and, apart from the Centenary Match in March 2005, no representative match has been played since 5 February 2003. The likelihood of future representative matches is remote – until our next milestone!

THE FIRST 100 YEARS OF ISTHMIAN REPRESENTATIVE FOOTBALL

Year	Date	Opponents	Score
1912	4 May	Spartan League	4-3
	7 September	Spartan League	6-1
1920	27 December	Corinthian F.C.	3-1
1921	14 September	Spartan League	6-2
	29 October	Athenian League	3-1
	26 December	Corinthian F.C.	8-5
1922	5 April	Southern Amateur League	2-2
	16 September	Spartan League	6-0
	30 September	Athenian League	1-3
	7 December	Oxford University	3-1
	26 December	Corinthian F.C.	2-2
1923	18 April	Southern Amateur League	6-2
	12 September	Spartan League	2-2
	27 October	Athenian League	5-1
	20 November	Oxford University	0-2
	22 December	Corinthian F.C.	4-4
1924	2 April	Southern Amateur League	7-0
	18 September	Spartan League	7-3
	18 October	Athenian League	3-2
	13 November	South Africa	2-4
	26 December	Corinthian F.C.	2-2
1925	22 January	Southern Amateur League	5-1
	19 February	London League	1-2
	5 March	Middlesex County League	1-2
	1 April	Royal Navy & R.M.	4-2
	1 October	Spartan League	7-1
	22 October	Athenian League	2-3
	26 December	Corinthian F.C.	0-3
1926	28 January	London League	2-2
	3 March	Royal Navy & R.M.	7-0
	30 September	Spartan League	6-2
	21 October	Athenian League	1-7
	27 December	Corinthian F.C.	5-6
1927	27 January	London League	3-2
	3 March	Royal Navy & R.M.	4-2
	24 March	France	4-2
	2 October	Athenian League	4-1
1928	15 February	Spartan League	6-1
	3 March	Corinthian F.C.	1-3
	14 March	Royal Navy & R.M.	0-0
	13 May	Berlin F.A.	1-2
	19 September	Spartan League	4-0
	10 October	Athenian League	3-4
	20 October	Berlin F.A.	1-4
	21 November	London League	3-1
	26 December	Corinthian F.C.	2-4
1929	20 March	Royal Navy & R.M.	1-5
	19 September	Spartan League	2-2
	16 October	Athenian League	3-7
	26 December	Corinthian F.C.	2-5
1930	6 February	Middlesex County League	2-0
	19 March	Royal Navy & R.M.	4-3
	17 September	Spartan League	3-5
	16 October	Athenian League	1-3
	27 November	London League	6-4
	26 December	Corinthian F.C.	3-9
1931	4 February	Middlesex County League	3-0
	19 March	Royal Navy & R.M.	1-3
	12 September	Spartan League	3-4
	28 November	Athenian League	7-2
	26 December	Corinthian F.C.	5-3
1932	3 February	Middlesex County League	5-0
	9 March	Royal Navy & R.M.	1-5
	15 September	Spartan League	1-2
	17 November	London League	4-2
	3 December	Athenian League	2-3
	26 December	Corinthian F.C.	3-3
1933	15 March	Royal Navy & R.M.	2-1
	2 December	Athenian League	3-5
	26 December	Corinthian F.C.	4-2
1934	3 March	Royal Navy & R.M.	4-2
	27 October	Spartan League	6-3
	26 December	Corinthian F.C.	4-0
1935	2 February	Secondary Schools' Old Boys League	2-1
	2 March	London League	0-0
	26 December	Corinthian F.C.	1-6
1936	1 February	Secondary Schools' Old Boys League	12-2
	29 February	Athenian League	2-3
	21 March	Royal Navy & R.M.	1-2
	5 December	Spartan League (H)	3-1
	26 December	Corinthian F.C. (H)	1-3
1937	20 March	London League (A)	1-2
	6 May	France (Amateurs) (A)	2-1
	4 December	Athenian League (H)	4-0
	27 December	Corinthian F.C. (A)	2-4
1938	12 March	Royal Navy & R.M. (H)	4-1
	3 April	France (Amateurs) (A)	1-2
	28 September	Spartan League (A)	1-2
	22 October	Corinthian F.C. (H)	0-1
	30 November	London League (H)	8-2
1939	28 January	Secondary Schools' Old Boys League (H)	4-3
	8 March	Royal Navy & R.M. (H)	2-1
	8 April	Athenian League (A)	1-1
1940	6 April	Athenian League (H)	1-3
1946	16 March	Spartan League (H)	6-2
	13 April	Athenian League (H)	1-2
	18 September	Spartan League (A)	4-1
	3 October	Icelandic Sports Assoc (H)	5-3
	4 December	London League (H)	5-3
	26 December	Athenian League (A)	3-1
1947	15 March	Royal Navy & R.M. (H)	3-2
	2 June	Nykjobing Boldklubben AF 1901	4-1
	5 June	Naestved Idraets Forening	1-2
	7 June	Svendborg Boldklub	0-2
	10 June	Aarbus Gymnastikfotening	2-3
	12 June	Horsens Forende Boldklubber	2-1
	4 September	Sing Tao Sports Club (Hong Kong) (H)	1-2
	18 September	Corinthian League (H)	1-2
	1 October	Athenian League (H)	3-2
	3 December	London League (A)	3-1
1948	13 March	Royal Navy & R.M. (H)	3-2
	21 August	Indian Olympic XI (H)	1-3
	1 September	Spartan League (H)	5-4
	16 September	Corinthian League (A)	5-3
	29 September	Athenian League (A)	3-5
1949	5 March	Royal Navy & R.M. (H)	3-1
	31 August	Spartan League (A)	2-4

continued overleaf ...

Year	Date	Opponent	Score
1949	10 September	Nigerian XI (H)	5-1
	15 September	London League (H)	0-2
	28 September	Athenian League (H)	3-2
1950	11 March	Royal Navy & R.M. (H)	3-0
	13 September	Athenian League (A)	1-6
1951	10 March	Royal Navy FA (H)	4-0
	18 April	Corinthian League (H)	1-1
	1 September	Gold Coast A.FA (H)	10-1
1952	1 March	Royal Navy FA (H)	2-1
	24 April	Corinthian League (H)	4-3
1953	28 February	Royal Navy FA (H)	3-2
	22 April	Athenian League (H)	3-3
	16 September	Athenian League (A)	3-0
1954	27 February	Royal Navy FA (H)	3-0
	8 September	Corinthian League (H)	1-2
	2 October	FA Amateur XI (H)	4-4
1955	5 March	Royal Navy FA (H)	5-4
	21 April	Athenian League (H)	0-1
	19 September	Athenian League (A)	1-2
1956	23 February	Royal Navy FA (H)	5-1
	11 April	Corinthian League (A)	3-2
	12 September	Athenian League (H)	2-1
	29 September	Uganda XI (H)	2-2
1957	13 March	Royal Navy FA (H)	2-0
	8 April	Millwall F.C. (A)	4-1
	1 May	Corinthian League (H)	6-2
	18 September	Athenian League (A)	3-1
	28 October	Millwall F.C. (A)	1-5
1958	13 October	Millwall F.C. (A)	1-5
	26 December	Athenian League (H)	1-3
1959	25 February	Royal Navy FA (H)	4-1
	10 September	Caribbean XI (H)	3-1
	12 October	Millwall F.C. (A)	3-1
1960	24 February	Royal Navy FA (H)	3-1
	27 September	Japan FA XI (H)	6-1
	31 October	Millwall F.C. (A)	0-4
	9 November	Athenian League (A)	5-0
1961	18 September	Iceland FA (H)	4-0
1962	10 April	Athenian League (H)	2-1
	1 October	Kenya (in Uganda)	3-3
	7 October	Ghana (in Uganda)	2-2
	8 October	Buganda (in Uganda)	1-1
1963	17 October	Civil Service (H)	3-0
1964	22 April	Athenian League (H)	6-3
	29 September	Athenian League (H)	3-2
1965	24 August	Wimbledon (A)	1-2
	28 September	Athenian League (A)	1-2
1966	7 May	Hitchin Town (A)	7-0
	1 November	Athenian League (H)	2-1
1967	9 May	Bromley	3-4
	25 September	Athenian League (A)	7-0
1969	29 April	Athenian League (H)	0-2
1970	28 April	Athenian League (A)	2-0
1971	5 May	Athenian League (H)	2-3
1972	21 May	Italian FA Amateur XI (A)	1-0
1974	22 May	Hellenic League (H)	5-0
	2 September	Oxford City (A)	2-3
1976	20 October	Rothmans Hellenic League (A)	1-1
1977	17 April	Rothmans Western League (A)	1-1
1979	29 April	Southern League (A)	0-3
	20 November	British Police (A)	1-0
	9 December	Western League (A)	1-2
1980	17 January	Southern League (H)	0-2
	31 March	FA XI (H)	3-0
1982	22 November	Oxford City (A)	3-3
1984	22 February	Hendon (A)	1-3
	24 September	Bognor Regis Town (A)	1-2
	24 October	FA XI (H)	1-2
1985	24 April	Hemel Hempstead (A)	1-0
	25 September	Horsham (A)	5-0
	20 November	FA XI (H)	4-2
1986	26 January	Multipart League (A)	1-0
	7 May	Leytonstone-Ilford (A)	1-1
	18 September	Hungerford Town (A)	3-1
	3 December	FA XI (H)	1-4
1987	15 March	Multipart League (H)	2-2
	27 October	British Police (A)	2-0
1988	13 January	FA XI (H)	1-2
	28 April	Dan Air League (H)	2-1
	7 December	FA XI (H)	3-0
1989	8 March	Dan Air League (A)	0-0
	2 April	HFS Loans League (A)	0-1
	10 April	Combined Services (H)	1-0
	19 December	FA XI (H)	1-3
1990	6 February	Combined Services (A)	4-0
	11 March	HFS Loans League (H)	0-1
	28 March	Slough Town (A)	4-1
1991	23 January	FA XI (H)	0-4
	5 February	Combined Services (A)	0-1
1992	21 January	FA XI (H)	1-7
	4 February	Combined Services (A)	1-3
	24 November	FA XI (H)	1-6
1993	9 February	Combined Services (H)	0-2
	7 December	FA XI (H)	2-1
1994	8 February	Combined Services (A)	3-1
	15 March	English Universities (H)	2-1
	7 December	FA XI (H)	0-1
1995	6 February	Combined Services (A)	5-0
	14 November	Maidenhead United (A)	0-0
1996	10 December	FA XI (H)	1-0
1997	5 February	Combined Services (H)	2-1
	10 December	FA XI (H)	0-2
1998	4 February	Combined Services (H)	3-0
	9 December	FA XI (H)	1-1
1999	3 February	Combined Services (A)	4-1
	8 December	FA XI (H)	1-3
2000	2 February	Combined Services (A)	2-2
	22 November	FA XI (H)	1-3
2001	21 November	FA XI (H)	2-0
2002	6 February	Combined Services (A)	1-0
2003	5 February	Combined Services (H)	1-0
2005	7 March	FA XI (H)	2-3

However, one can look back over more than 200 occasions and see not only many matches against other Leagues but also regular matches against clubs such as the Corinthians as well as matches against representative teams from France, Nigeria, the Gold Coast, Uganda, Japan and Italy. Latterly the League representative side played matches to mark centenaries of many clubs before celebrating its own centenary with a representative match.

Many famous Isthmian managers have taken charge of the representative side – and there have been many managers who thought that they ought to have taken charge of the side! When Jack Pearce was made a Vice President of the League in 2004 it was to recognise not only his personal contribution at his own Bognor Regis Town Football Club but also his contribution to the League as a Director and as the Representative Team Manager for three years.

It is impossible to give details of all the matches played. Therefore it was decided to list the full playing record of the League Representative team and produce the verbatim reports of just five matches.

The style of the reporting is different to that of today. These are not typographical errors which were missed on proof reading but are verbatim newspaper reports.

Reproduced below is a report from the first-ever match, which was played in aid of the fund established for the survivors of the *Titanic* disaster which occurred in April 1912.

Spartan League 3, Isthmian League 4
At Aylesbury United Football Club on 4th May 1912
Report from The Buckingham and Aylesbury News

The Football Association having granted permission to football clubs to play matches until Saturday 4th May in aid of the Titanic disaster fund that Aylesbury United Football Club arranged for a match to take place at Aylesbury on Saturday between representatives of teams of the Isthmian and Spartan Leagues. Although the Printing Works ground had been closed for the cricket season Messrs. Hazell, Walters, Viney kindly gave permission for the match to be played on the ground. As the proceeds of the match were to be donated to the Titanic fund and the players who had promised to appear included three amateur internationals and 13 county men, a large number of tickets were sold. Rain fell in the morning and early part of the afternoon and fears were held out that this would seriously affect the "gate" but Aylesbury supporters were not to be so easily denied witnessing what promised such an excellent game and by the time for the kick-off a crowd of some 700 spectators had assembled. The printing works band which very kindly turned out and under the conductorship of Mr R Payne marched down the high street playing selections and also played in the ground, their services being highly appreciated.

The teams did not turn out quite as advertised, Barrett of the 2nd Coldstream Guards could not play for the Spartans, his place being taken by his partner Leach. Nicholls of West Norwood also did not appear for the Isthmians, Stevens of the Aylesbury United Reserves having to be requisitioned at the last hour. The Isthmians were the first to take the field in their white shirts and after they had a few minutes shooting practice, the appearance of the blue and white colours of the Spartans were greeted with loud applause. The teams were captained by Louch of Shepherd's Bush for the Isthmians, and Smith of Sutton Court for the Spartans. Smith won the toss for the Spartans and chose to kick towards the band stand goal, with the drizzling rain at their backs. Hegasi kicked off for the Isthmians and from their breakaway the ball went into touch near the corner flag. From the throw-in the ball was worked near the goal, but Hearn cleared with a strong kick. Mann sent Horne away at the other end and he finished his run with a good cross. The ball again came to Mann who was following close up and taking a first time shot while running at fall speed, he banged the ball into the net scoring a lovely goal, which was loudly applauded. The Isthmians broke away but were repulsed by Hearn. Some pretty and tricky play on the part of Wingfield the Spartan centre-half resulted in Horne having a shot at goal, the ball just hitting the wrong side of the post. Smith then tested Thompson with a good shot, the latter clearing with a tremendous kick. A pretty combined run by the Isthmian forwards threatened the downfall of the Spartans goal, but Hearn stepped in, in the nick of time and averted the danger. Stevens then got away and after beating Hearn finished with a lovely centre from which Leese brought off a magnificent save close in, by which he earned considerable applause. On two occasions the Spartans broke away, the final shots just missing by inches only, Melhuish made a brilliant run finishing with a fine centre, the ball just alighting on the wrong side of the cross-bar. At this point the Spartan forwards who were playing a strong game together got away and Horne finished the run by centreing right into the goal mouth. Smith getting his head neatly to the ball and netting but the goal was ruled offside. Some clever work on the Isthmians right-wing threatened danger but the final shot just missed at the other end from one of Horne's passes Leech just put over with a lovely shot. The Isthmians outside-right then got away and after one of his clever runs sent in a ripping shot which Leece had to measure his length on the ground to save. At this point Leese was loudly applauded for three splendid saves in quick succession. Melhuish sent in a lightning shot from a distance of about three yards but Leese promptly caught the ball and kicked away amidst applause. The Spartans responded and following some nice combination on the right-wing, Leech finished the effort by sending in a splendid first time shot, which the goalie no chance to save. It was a fine goal and very similar to the first one. The next event was a penalty awarded to the Isthmians for a foul on the part of the Spartans left-back. Although Leese was noted for saving penalties, he failed to save this one, for Louch netted with a very fast shot, which evidently deceived the custodian. Shortly before half-time the Spartans were awarded a penalty. Tommy Hearn was deputed by his captain to take the kick, but he failed to get the ball anywhere between the posts. Half-time then arrived with the Spartans leading 2-1.

Upon the restart the Isthmians took up the running and Louch forced Hearn to concede a corner. Hegasi the clever Dulwich Hamlet centre-forward then put in two fine shots from some distance out, which just missed the desired Haven. The Isthmians outside-right who was hearabouts playing a great game and delighting the crowd by his runs, centred well, from which Leese was obliged to concede a corner. From the resultant kick, Leese effected a smart save and the pressure was relieved by Louch shooting wide. Horne then had a try and got in a good shot which just hit the side of the post. Later Louch got through but Hearn ran across and cleared. Hegasi received the ball and beat Leese with a ripping shot. The teams were now on level terms and a struggle ensued for the lead. A minute afterwards Horne broke away and centred from which Mann scored a good goal. A sharp run between Hegasi and Louch resulted in a fruitless corner being forced. Oscar again beat his man and got in a good centre from which some pretty work in front of goal resulted in which Horne narrowly missed scoring, but the pressure was relieved by Jones heading away. The Isthmians now began to assume superiority of the game, their finesse appearing more. Their clever combination was much admired, and in the last quarter of an hour the Spartans defence had a very busy time. After the forwards had nicely worked the ball near to the goal, Mallett sent in a fast cross shot, which although Leese got his hands to entered the corner of the net. The game was then stopped though Horne receiving a knock on the head why lying on the ground but he was soon able to resume playing. Oscar beat the opposing half and finished with a shot which just missed the post. Hegasi neatly placed the ball to Louch who got through and tested Leese with a good shot which he failed to hold. The forwards kept up the pressure and gave Leese a busy time. The Spartans tried hard towards the close of the game to draw on level terms, but after the ball had crossed and re-crossed the goalmouth several times Horne shot at goal but the custodian jumped and caught the ball and averted danger. This proved to be the extent of the scoring and the game ended with the Isthmians winners by 4 goals to 3. The game was thoroughly interesting throughout and played in good spirit, the absence of fouls being a noticeable feature. Mr JR Schumacher who refereed in this year's final of the English FA Cup gave every satisfaction in the discharge of his duties and kept the teams well together.

Isthmian League: JW Thompson (Dulwich Hamlet), TC Burn (London Caledonians), A A Farquharson (Dulwich Hamlet), D Davidson (Shepherd's Bush), JH Jones (Shepherd's Bush), J Langland (London Caledonians), HW Melhuish (London Caledonians), LA Louch (Shepherd's Bush), H Hegazi (Dulwich Hamlet), HJ Mallet (West Norwood), Stevens (Aylesbury United).

Note: *Stevens was a guest player.*

After the end of the First World War a Christmas match was established with Corinthians FC which continued until the Second World War. It is fair to say that the League lost more than they won and on Boxing Day 1924 honours were even at Clarence Park, St. Albans, when the 1920's equivalent of Walter Gammie of the Times filed this report:

Isthmian League 2, Corinthians 2
At St. Albans City Football Club on 26th December 1924
Report from The Times

The Corinthians played a drawn game with the Isthmian League at St. Albans City, with the score being two goals each. He result was the same as it had been the previous season, but the goals on that occasion were 4-4.

The Corinthians should certainly have won have the forwards taken advantage of a number of exceedingly opportunities. They had all the better of the play in the first half and Hartley, Hilleary and Doggart should have scored, but there was an apparent lack of finish. The game was an exceedingly hard one. The Isthmian League were without Edar Kail for the greater part of the first half as a result of an injury. There was a good breeze blowing down the ground when play began immediately after the kick-off the Isthmian League looked dangerous but Howard Baker cleared. The Corinthians playing with the wind played a prolonged attack and did everything but get the ball into the net. Doggart, Hartley, Ashden and Hilleary all had plenty of opportunities, but either shot over or wide of the goal. Several of these chances were to open goals.

The Isthmian League were the first to score after a very clever forward movement, which resulted in a goal scored by WH Minter. It was a good shot and gave Howard Baker no chance of saving. There was no more scoring before half-time, although the Corinthians had several chances of equalising. After the interval the Corinthians attacked strongly. CMR Cannon kept goal very well, even though he must be said to have been lucky on several occasions. It from a pass that originated from Ewer that Hilleary got away and passed across to Jenkins, who equalised. This was the first occasion on which RG Jenkins had played for the Corinthians.

After this goal the play became more vigorous. The Corinthians took the lead, Jenkins getting well away and swinging the ball across to Capel-Slaughter, who scored. The Isthmian League then made desperate efforts to equalise, and they were rewarded by a gaol, headed through by Minter, after Bellamy had made a very good run on the left wing. The Corinthians should even then had won, for Jenkins got away again with no one except the goalkeeper to beat, but he shot wide.

Isthmian League: CMR Cannon (St. Albans City), EA Penstone (Clapton), FJ Holland (St. Albans City), AL Cox (Nunhead), AF Barrett (Leytonstone), JW Booker (Nunhead), J McCree (London Caledonians), E Kail (Dulwich Hamlet), WH Minter (St. Albans City), RB Miller (St. Albans City), WR Bellamy (Tufnell Park).

At the beginning of the 50s, Dulwich Hamlet's magnificent Champion Hill Stadium hosted a match against the Gold Coast (subsequently to become Ghana after independence) AFA and it will be seen that the guests played without boots in conditions they would not have been used to.

Isthmian League 10, Gold Coast Amateur Football Association 1.
At Dulwich Hamlet Football Club on 1st December 1951
Report from The Times

DULWICH HAMLET FOOTBALL CLUB

NOTES

In placing this ground at the disposal of the Isthmian League Council this afternoon, the Dulwich Hamlet Football Club particularly extend a very hearty welcome to the officials and players of the United Gold Coast Football Association on the occasion of their visit to London and trust they will have a very happy tour. They have already played in Northern Ireland and in Eire, in Wales and last Wednesday at Romford, but this will be their first match in the Capital. In their first match at Belfast, they had the misfortune to lose their goalkeeper, who had his leg broken and will therefore take no further part in the tour—may we take this opportunity of wishing him a speedy recovery and at the same time express the hope that they will have no further serious mishaps. Had the accident been a broken toe we should not have been so surprised, for we understand that most of their team play in bare feet. We think our visitors will be interested to know that they are playing on the largest amateur ground in England, with a holding capacity of 40,000. Amongst other games played here have been Amateur Internationals, England v. Scotland, England v. Wales, the final of the Football Association Amateur Cup, finals of the London Senior Cup and Surrey Senior Cup and a host of other representative games. Two years ago we had the pleasure of entertaining the Nigerian team and previous to that the Sing Tao team from Hong Kong. The ground was used during the last Olympic games by the Korean and Mexico teams. After the match today, both teams will be entertained to dinner at the Grove Tavern.

The Isthmian League was founded in 1905. Mr. Henry J. Huband, J.P., the Hon. Treasurer of the Football Association, has held office since its inception—first as Hon. Secretary and Hon. Treasurer, he is at present President and Chairman. Incidentally Mr. Huband has not enjoyed the best of health recently, but we trust that he will be present this afternoon. The Hon. Secretary of the Isthmian League is Mr. Syd A. Donaldson, who was a well-known referee and took the England v. Scotland Amateur International on this ground in 1939.

The Isthmian League is probably unique inasmuch as there is no trophy of any kind for the winners of the Championship. Their crest bears the motto "Honor Sufficit."

Owing to the colours of both teams being similar, decision as to change of colour will be announced.

ISTHMIAN LEAGUE.

D. H. JARVIS (Leytonstone): Has many Amateur International Caps, also represented his County Essex and Isthmian League on many occasions. Has been appointed Captain today, this being his farewell representative game.

A. MAGGS (Wimbledon): First appearance in Isthmian League representative side.

H. RAWLINS (St. Albans): Represented Herts County and Isthmian League.

D. MUNDAY (Wimbledon): First appearance in Isthmian League representative side.

L. BRAHAM (Walthamstow Avenue): Played for F.A. XI's and represented his County Essex and Isthmian League.

DULWICH HAMLET FOOTBALL CLUB

ISTHMIAN LEAGUE

(Green, White and Gold)

Right — Left

1 D. H. JARVIS (Leytonstone)

2 A. MAGGS (Wimbledon) — 3 H. RAWLINGS (St. Albans City)

4 D. MUNDAY (Wimbledon) — 5 L. BRAHAM (Walthamstow Avenue) — 6 H. E. DODKINS (Ilford)

8 A. W. NOBLE (Leytonstone) — 10 A. ZIMMER (Kingstonian)

7 H. BROOKS (Romford) — 9 J. L. LEWIS (Walthamstow Avenue) — 11 T. R. JOVER (Dulwich Hamlet)

O

O. GESPAR 11 — R. AGGREY 10 — W. JOHNSON 9 — C. GYAMFI 8 — H. MACAULEY 7

J. J. NELSON 6 — G. B. WOODE 5 — V. A. ESSAKA 4

E. C. BRIANDT 3 — O. ADDY 2

V. BEESHER

Left — Right

GOLD COAST

A.F.A. XI

(Green and White)

Referee .. .. Mr. A. S. MELTON (Essex)

Linesmen .. Messrs. L. J. WARNE (Surrey), R. C. DAVIES (Essex)
(Pink Flag) (Blue Flag)

FORTCOMING FIXTURES:

Sept. 15th—DULWICH HAMLET v. WALTHAMSTOW AVENUE (A)

Sept. 15th—DULWICH HAMLET RES. v. WIMBLEDON RES. (H) K.O. 3.30 p.m.

Sept. 22nd—DULWICH HAMLET v. WOKING (H). K.O. 3.30 p.m.

NEXT SATURDAY'S GAME ON THIS GROUND

Dulwich Hamlet v Ilford

K.O. 3.30 p.m.

In unfamiliar conditions the Gold Coast A F A X1 were beaten by the Isthmian League by 10 goals to 1 at Dulwich Hamlet's ground. Playing bare footed suits their style of play on dry ground, when their manner of bringing the ball under control can be delighted to watch. But it is a tremendous handicap in the wet, and how it rained all through this miserable afternoon!

From the time Jover scored the League's first goal 10 minutes from the start it became obvious that the tourists had no chance whatever of preventing the match becoming rout. Without unduly exerting themselves the League scored four more goals before half-time, Smith getting two and Zimmer and Noble one each, and although the Gold Coast did make one excellent effort to score, when Jarvis just managed to read a curling shot from Gespar, as a rule their forwards were completely mastered by the bigger Isthmian defenders.

Like the forwards, the Gold Coast defenders never stopped trying, but they were unable to turn on the slippery ground, and Addy, their centre-half, who had kept a firm grip on England's centre-forward Lewis in the first half, tired perceptibly after the interval. After Lewis had got his side sixth goal Gyfami, after clever play by Gespar, at last managed to reduce the lead, but when Noble replied with another a minute later the Isthmians once more took control of the game and Lewis scored two more goals and Smith one before the tired Africans were at last relieved when the final whistle blew.

Isthmian League: DH Jarvis (Leytonstone), A Maggs (Wimbledon), H Rawlings (St. Albans City), D Munday (Wimbledon), L Braham (Walthamstow Avenue), HE Dodkins (Ilford), A Smith (Ilford), AW Noble (Leytonstone), JL Lewis (Walthamstow Avenue), A Zimmer (Kingstonian), TR Jover (Dulwich Hamlet).

Isthmian League 3, Civil Service 0
At Ilford Football Club on 17 October 1963
Report from The Times

To celebrate the 100th anniversary of their foundation, Civil Service FC last night played a representative match against a strong Isthmian League XI on Ilford's ground at Newbury Park. Conditions were ideal for good football, but the game was too one-sided to be real interesting.When one had had time to analysis the various changes in the published teams, it could be guessed that the match would in all probability resolve itself into a contest between the League forwards, with their three internationals, and the Civil Service defence, with Cakebread, the Brentford goalkeeper as a strong last line of resistance. So it proved, but the League made things easier for themselves by scoring the first goal within a few minutes of the start. King, the right-half, took the ball up field and as the Civil Service defence retreated to the edge of their penalty area, he made a shrewd cross pass to Harvey and, from his accurately placed centre, Browning shot firmly into the corner of the net.

Both right-half backs were prominent, and Harvey was able to test Cakebread twice from good movements which started on the right side of the field. The League continued to hold the upper hand, and after 25 minutes, Quail found himself in possession 20 yards from goal, realised that all his colleagues were well marked, quickly pivoted from one foot to the other and then shot a goal which surprised Cakebread, and everybody else, as it rocketed into the top corner of the net. Encouraged and well promptly by Robertson, the centre-half, and Turner, the right-half, Civil Service fought hard to reduce this two-goal lead before half-time, but to many final passes went astray.

In the second half, the three inside-forwards of the Civil Service faded right out and they seldom found a way past a reliable League defence. In fact, the best Service attacker was their tall blond right-half from Blackpool, NST Turner, one of the two professional players on their side. Everything he did had the stamp of class about it, whether it was tackling, heading or shooting. He was without doubt, the outstanding player of the evening. Their was one perfect half-volley of his compelled Barr to dive full length. A goal at this time might have given Civil Service the encouragement they so badly needed. The game gradually slowed down as the League began to take things easily, but suddenly Quail produced one of his devastating through passes which Browning cleverly anticipated! The Tooting centre-forward dashed though the gap to make the result certain with a well placed ground drive into the corner of the net. It was only the persistence of their half-back line which kept the Civil Service in the game during the quarter of an hour, but the comfortable win for the League was a fair result to a pleasant but not over skilful or exciting game.

Isthmian League: J Barr (Ilford), K Holden (Tooting & Mitcham United), R Wood (Leytonstone), B King (Hitchin Town), S Turner (Barking), A Knox (Hendon), D Hyde (Hendon), K Gray (Leytonstone), M Browning (Tooting & Mitcham United), J Quail (Hendon), B Harvey (Walthamstow Avenue).

Finally here is a report of the Centenary Match, at Dulwich Hamlet, this time at the new Champion Hill ground. It is a sign of the times that *The Times* did not attend and did not include a report other than the scoreline.

Isthmian League 2, Football Association XI 3
At Dulwich Hamlet Football Club on 7th March 2005
Report from the Ryman League bulletin

A late goal from Kieran Knight secured a victory for The Football Association in a thrilling match to celebrate the centenary of the Isthmian League at Dulwich Hamlet. The match was a hard fought contest played in good spirit. Lee Clark put the Football Association ahead after only eight minutes, a lead which they held until just before half-time when Billericay's Ross Wareham equalised. The second half was just as competitive as the first with both sides making substitutions it was Ross Wareham who put the Isthmians in front with his second goal (56) only for substitute Stuart Booth to equalise (74) before Knight's late winner.

Isthmian League XI: P Nicholls (Chelmsford City), L Hopkins (Chelmsford City), A Stanley (Yeading), L Hunter (Billericay Town), S Mangodza (Chelmsford City), P Sappleton (Billericay Town), L Collins (Worthing), F Manuella (Staines Town), R Wareham (Billericay Town), R Jolly (Wealdstone), R Ursell (AFC Wimbledon). ***Subs:*** *R Tolfrey (Dulwich Hamlet) for Nicholls, M Shinn (Heybridge Swifts) for Jolly, K Beaney (Dulwich Hamlet (for Hunter), P Scott (Whyteleafe) for Wareham, R Martin (Dulwich Hamlet) for Collins*

CHAPTER NINE

Sponsorship

In the 1960s and 70s, Barry East, a great supporter of Dagenham Football Club – then members of the Athenian League – was also Chairman of the Isthmian League as well being a very successful businessman. He had the idea of linking product advertising with football in the form of sponsorship of a League. He made his proposal to the Isthmian League Hon Secretary, Ingram Whittingham, who also thought this was a fine idea and he contacted a well-known sporting personality and businessman who had links with the League, former Corinthian–Casuals and Walthamstow Avenue player Doug Insole, better known as a cricketer with Essex County Cricket Club and England and latterly an international team selector.

On 2 February 1973 Ingram wrote to Doug asking if he would be interested in helping to set up a sponsorship deal for the Isthmian League, which appeared to be growing in reputation within the Non-League football world. Ingram also wondered if television analyst Jimmy Hill might be persuaded to help.

Jimmy agreed to become involved – on a professional basis – and, before the next Isthmian Council meeting, Doug sent him some guidelines regarding the proposed sponsorship from the League's viewpoint. Both men agreed that, if sponsorship could make Isthmian League football more exciting, enjoyable and sporting, then Clubs might attract more spectators, be more successful in national competitions and everyone connected with Clubs and the League itself would get more enjoyment and satisfaction from their football, to say nothing of raising the profile of the sponsor.

After a meeting with the League Council, Doug and Jimmy discussed how they would put the proposals to potential sponsors. Mr Hill drew up a list of awards that included prize money for the League champions and runners up, incentives for scoring goals, rewards for good sportsmanship, plus an administrative pool for the League which would allow the match fees of Isthmian League referees to be doubled. In addition it was proposed to change the points system, which had been in place throughout world football since the English Football League began in 1888, allocating three for a win and one to each team for a draw. A full proposal was drawn up and a meeting was arranged with the first of the potential sponors, Carreras Rothmans, who were one of the era's leading tobacco companies.

ROTHMANS ISTHMIAN LEAGUE

This is the first Representative Match played by the Rothmans Isthmian League X1; and with Hendon as reigning Champions providing the opposition what better start could there be to the season.

We at Rothmans, are extremely excited about the months ahead, and judging by the consistant demands for cleaner and more attractive football from the National Press, the League appears to be way out in front for progressive ideas backed by strong administrative support.

Sports writer of the Year, John Morgan recently wrote in the Daily Express, "What we want is less niggling, less of the negative, boring 4-4-2 formation stuff devised by frightened men whose only aim is survival, a return to the individual skills for which the British footballer was once famed, and constant obediance for the referee".

His words could well have been the brief to which the Isthmian League, Doug Insole, Jimmy Hill and Rothmans were working when this seasons sponsorship incentives were drawn up.

We are all working hard to produce a league where good competitive football can be played in the right spirit.

There can never be any sympathy for players 'cautioned' for dissent or retaliation, and if these unnecessary offences alone are completely cut out, all the league clubs will qualify for a share of the sportsmanship pool!

The Rothmans Isthmian League committee aim to stamp out the brutal players, and allow ball players to express themselves once again without fear of intimidation

Everyone will enjoy their football more if the emphasise is on open, attractive, attacking, sporting play; and the aims of the awards this season are to produce just that.

With one voice our football writers are demanding a change of attitude in the Football League, so we hope they will watch the progress of the Rothmans Isthmian League throughout the season.

Rothmans are determined to help the league committee to ensure that what they see will prove the point:-

That the Rothmans Isthmian League is without doubt the most progressive in the country, and at least it is one competition where football is enjoyed by players, officials and spectators alike!

L. E. BREFFITT
Director of Carreras Rothmans

An introduction to their sponsorship ideals from new League sponsors - Rothmans

Rothmans had already ventured into football sponsorship, backing the best-selling annual, *The Rothmans Football Yearbook*. A member of Carreras Rothmans' Public Relations Department was Tony Williams, the founder/editor of the *Yearbook*. Tony had a long history with the Isthmian League, having played for Corinthian-Casuals, Kingstonian, Dulwich Hamlet and – very briefly – Tooting & Mitcham United and Wycombe Wanderers, and with his playing career over, he had worked with Greg Tesser on his *Amateur Footballer* magazine, before being made Editor of *Jimmy Hill's Football Weekly*, a company which also published a magazine called *Non–League Football*. When the owners of the company sold up, Tony became the founder-editor of the Rothmans Football Yearbook and then joined Carreras Rothmans.

Carreras Rothmans' main cigarette brand was Rothmans Kingsize, but they also produced Piccadilly, Dunhill, Peter Stuyvesant, Guards and a wide variety of cigars, as well as regularly launching new tobacco brands. These names were well known through sponsorships in a wide variety of sports, each of which had a marketing manager in a department headed up by John King.

Tony, who then lived in Hungerford, Berkshire, had already encouraged regional company budget holders to help the Hellenic League, the parent competition of his local club Hungerford Town, but his dream was that Carreras Rothmans might sponsor the famous Isthmian League, with him having the task of administering the whole operation for the Company. They were delighted to agree to the proposal first dreamed up by Barry East and carried forward by Ingram Whittingham, Doug Insole and Jimmy Hill.

In just a few meetings everything was sorted out and this is Jimmy's record of that final meeting, when the official sponsorship of the Isthmian League was drawn up. It should be noted that the sponsorship of the League was the first of its kind in senior football; it has become the template for deals that are agreed from the Premier League down to the lowest levels of non-League football.

ISTHMIAN LEAGUE SPONSORSHIP SCHEME

Following my original proposition it was decided after discussion with Mr. Tony Williams, representing Rothmans, Mr. Doug Insole, representing the Isthmian League and myself that in the general interest the scheme should be finalised on the lines set out in this document.

A method has been found of applying the various incentives to both divisions of the Isthmian League, embracing 38 teams, 22 in the First and 16 in the Second.

1. ATTACKING FOOTBALL

The points system in both Divisions of the League to be changed so that three points are given for a win and only one for a draw.

2. GOAL INCENTIVES

Weekly Awards

If a club wins a match by three clear goals, i.e. either 4-1, 3-0 etc., it will be paid a bonus of £40 in the First Division and £25 in the Second. It is estimated that this will happen 90 times in the 1st and 60 times in the 2nd and at that rate will cost £3,600 in the 1st Division + £1,500 in the 2nd Division. It must be appreciated that this cannot be a fixed figure and if this incentive worked it would increase the number of times that a team won by three clear goals. It would prove more expensive, but it would enable the sponsor to capitalize on the immense publicity value in full measure.

Approximate total cost £5,100

Cont'd...

Cont'd.... - 2 -

2. GOAL INCENTIVES cont'd...

Seasons Awards

These awards will apply to clubs who have not received a cash prize for finishing first, second or third in their respective divisions and will be as follows:-

	Highest Scorers	2nd Highest Scorers	3rd Highest Scorers
DIVISION 1	300	200	100
DIVISION 2	150	100	50

.... £900

3. SPORTSMANSHIP POOL

This will be £2,000 in the 1st Division and £1,000 in the 2nd. Teams will lose four points if a player is sent off and one if he is cautioned. If a team loses eight points or more in the course of a season it will not qualify for a share of the Sportsmanship Pool. Teams who qualify to share the Pool, i.e. by not accumulating eight points against them, will receive a pro rata share of the Pool according to the number of points lost. This scale will be carefully devised so that it is understood by all clubs at the outset.
Total cost........... £3,000

4. REFEREES FEES

Referees fees to be increased to £8 per match in the 1st Division only. £4 of this fee will be paid by the club and £4 by the sponsor.

Total cost £2,000

Cont'd..

Cont'd..... - 3 -

5. INCENTIVES TO WIN THE LEAGUE

The incentives for 1st, 2nd and 3rd place will be as follows:-

	1st	2nd	3rd
DIVISION 1	1,000	500	300
DIVISION 2	500	250	150

.... £2,700

N.B. If a team finishing 1st, 2nd and 3rd loses eight disciplinary points on the scale set out above, i.e. four points for a sending off and one for a caution, then it will not qualify for the prize money. The money instead will go towards increasing the SPORTSMANSHIP POOL in its division.

6. REVISED BUDGET

GOALS INCENTIVES - Weekly Awards	5,100
GOALS INCENTIVES - Seasons Awards	900
SPORTSMANSHIP POOL	3,000
REFEREES FEES	2,000
INCENTIVES TO WIN THE LEAGUE	2,700
ADMINISTRATIVE COSTS	2,000
	£15,700

There was terrific media coverage of the sponsorship deal, see the details above, and most of it was very positive. However, some cynics thought the initial reaction and the ideals and rewards for good conduct would soon be forgotten and players would revert to the win-at-all-costs mentality and strong-arm tactics that had become all too prevalent within the League in previous seasons.

However, the scheme was a resounding success and before long Rothmans had decided to expand their sponsorship to other leagues, in areas where their King Size brand was being outsold by other, cheaper brands. The Northern, Western and Hellenic Leagues were invited to join the "Rothmans family" and an encouraging spirit of camaraderie developed between the competitions and their officials.

The Isthmian League's leadership was recognised by The Football Association.

Referees certainly noticed the difference, as they faced less confrontation and dissent, and were glad to see retaliation diminish significantly. As a consequence, they started to give the benefit of doubt to players. In short, everyone enjoyed their football more than before.

The performances of clubs from sponsored leagues in various cup competitions also improved, maybe the referees in these games appreciating the players' less confrontational attitude. Carrreras Rothmans, with cigarette machines in clubhouses, opened more new accounts than they had through any other sponsorship.

Quite simply, everyone involved in football at this level was happy!

Enfield v Hendon

ISTHMIAN SPORTSMANSHIP SCHEME 1973–77

Clubs started each season with eight Sportsmanship points. In League matches, every caution received by a player counted as one point against the club, each dismissal was four points. If a club reached eight points the club would forfeit any positional prize money, which was added to the Sportsmanship pool and shared amongst those clubs which had not reached eight points. The following is the overall Sportsmanship Table.

	Total disciplinary points				*Final finishing positions*			
	C	*D*	*Total*	*No. of times 8 pts lost In season*	*73–74*	*74–75*	*75–76*	*76–77*
Wycombe Wanderers	5	0	5	0	1	1	2	2
Sutton United	8	0	8	0	12	10	11	16
Hitchin Town	10	0	10	0	13	12	16	9
Dagenham	13	0	13	0	**1**	3	3	3
Bishop's Stortford	14	4	18	0	3	11	12	20
Hendon	14	4	18	0	2	13	6	4
Leatherhead	23	0	23	1	5	6	8	10
St. Albans City	20	4	24	1	21	**6**	**7**	**13**
Slough Town	20	4	24	1	**2**	9	10	8
Kingstonian	25	0	25	1	15	19	18	17
Corinthian Casuals	20	8	28	2	22	**18**	**18**	**16**
Chesham United	24	4	28	1	**4**	**5**	**5**	**12**
Wokingham Town	24	4	28	3	**16**	**14**	**13**	**10**
Horsham	18	12	30	2	**8**	**8**	**11**	**6**
Oxford City	28	4	32	1	11	8	21	**8**
Carshalton Athletic	25	8	33	2	**11**	**16**	**3**	**2**
Woking	28	8	36	2	7	15	14	19
Maidenhead United	28	8	36	2	**7**	**9**	**19**	**19**
Leytonstone	25	12	37	2	8	18	20	12
Hertford Town	34	4	38	3	**3**	**12**	**21**	**18**
Tilbury	27	12	39	2	**6**	**3**	**1**	5
Staines Town	32	8	40	2	**10**	**1**	9	11
Aveley	32	8	40	4	**5**	**17**	**17**	**15**
Southall & Ealing Borough	36	8	44	2	**15**	**2**	19	14
Dulwich Hamlet	32	12	44	3	4	5	5	21
Walton & Hersham	33	12	45	3	6	21	**14**	**14**
Ilford	38	8	46	2	9	7	4	22
Hampton	38	8	46	3	**12**	**10**	**6**	**9**
Harwich & Parkeston	31	16	47	3	**9**	**4**	**5**	**3**
Barking	31	16	47	3	14	17	15	13
Finchley	36	12	48	4	**14**	**15**	**15**	**21**
Harlow Town	43	8	51	4	**13**	**7**	**18**	**17**
Enfield	36	16	52	2	17	2	1	1
Walthamstow Avenue	49	4	53	4	18	14	13	7
Tooting & Mitcham United	42	16	58	3	16	4	7	6
Hayes	35	24	59	3	10	16	17	18
Bromley	61	12	73	4	19	22	**16**	**7**
Clapton	67	28	95	4	20	20	22	**20**
Croydon	14	0	14	1	–	**11**	**2**	15
Boreham Wood	39	12	51	2	–	**13**	**8**	**1**
Harrow Borough	18	0	18	1	–	–	**9**	**5**
Hornchurch	17	4	21	1	–	–	**10**	**11**
Ware	11	4	15	1	–	–	**20**	**22**
Wembley	13	4	17	1	–	–	**12**	**4**

Bold print denotes Division 1 clubs and statistics.

The deal with Carreras Rothmans lasted for four seasons, ending after the conclusion of the 1976–77 season. The League faced a period without financial support but, early in the 1977–78 season, Barry East secured the help of a firm of Estate Agents, Michael Lawrie & Partners, and a separate deal was struck with Radio Luxembourg which broadcast the results of the day each Saturday at 6.30pm. This was a stopgap deal before another major sponsor was found; it lasted only until the end of that season.

BERGER PAINTS

The League then negotiated an arrangement with Berger Paints Ltd for a sponsorship which spanned the next four seasons and the following is the press release which was issued to announce the arrangement.

SPONSORSHIP OF THE LEAGUE – A SCHEME FOR 1978–79 AND 1979–80

Berger Paints Ltd have agreed to sponsor the League and the League Youth Cup by the provision of £25,000 per annum for two years with an option for a third year. The option will be reviewed at the end of the 1978–79 season. The incentives and awards have been agreed with the company as follows:

1. INCENTIVES TO WIN THE LEAGUE AND DIVISIONAL CHAMPIONSHIP

	CHAMPIONS	**RUNNERS–UP**	**THIRD PLACE**
PREMIER DIVISION	£1,500	£1,000	£500
DIVISION 1	£1,000	£600	£300
DIVISION 2	£600	£400	£200

2. GOALSCORING INCENTIVES SEASONS AWARDS

There will be one award for each division and these will be available to clubs who have not qualified for an award under paragraph 1:

Highest scorers

PREMIER DIVISION	£500
DIVISION 1	£300
DIVISION 2	£200

3. GOALSCORING INCENTIVES MATCH AWARDS

If a club wins a match by 3 clear goals ie 3–0, 4–1, 5–2 etc it will be paid a bonus of:

PREMIER DIVISION	£40
DIVISION 1	£30
DIVISION 2	£20

ESTIMATED TOTAL COST £6,970

The bonuses will be paid to clubs by the League on a bi–monthly basis. If the actual cost over the season exceeds the estimate, the balance will be paid from the contribution to administration (see paragraph 5). If the actual cost falls below the estimate, the balance will be shared equally between all 62 member clubs by way of a rebate on Isthmian News payments (see paragraph 6).

4. SPONSORSHIP POOL

This will provide cash awards for the clubs with the best sportsmanship records in League matches. A points system will operate on the following scale:

Any player cautioned by the referee – one point
Any player sent–off for persisting in misconduct after being cautioned – three points
Any player sent off without having being cautioned – five points

If a team collects 12 or more points in the course of the season it will not qualify for a share of the sportsmanship pool. Qualifying clubs, i.e. those with less than 12 points at the end of the League season, will receive a pro–rata share of the pool according to the number of points collected.

The amounts to be shared in each division are:

PREMIER DIVISION	£2,500
DIVISION 1	£2,000
DIVISION 2	£1,500
TOTAL	£6,000

5. CONTRIBUTION TOWARDS LEAGUE'S ADMINISTRATION COSTS
6% of the sportsmanship money will be paid into League funds as a contribution towards the additional expenditure which will be incurred by the officers in administering the scheme.

TOTAL COST £1,500

6. ISTHMIAN NEWS
In order to ensure an immediate benefit to each and every club in the League, a payment will be made to the Isthmian News, equal to 15% of the annual charge to clubs for their 200 copies per issue.

TOTAL COST £930

7. BERGER YOUTH CUP INCENTIVES TO WIN

To each of the eight losing clubs in the first round	–	£50
To each of the four losing clubs in the second round	–	£150
To each of the two losing clubs in the semi–finals	–	£300
To the losing finalists	–	£400
To the Cup winners	–	£500
Total Cost	–	£2,500

The disciplinary point system as in paragraph 4 will apply to the Berger Youth Cup and for each point collected a club's prize money will be reduced on the scale: up to and including the first round, £5; second round, £15; semi-finals, £20; and Final, £25.

8. DISQUALIFICATION
If a club collects 12 or more disciplinary points on the scale set out in paragraph 4, it will not qualify for any of the prize money under paragraphs 1 and 2. The money will instead go, after the deduction of 10% for administrative costs, towards increasing the sportsmanship pool in its division.

9. SPONSORSHIP BUDGET

Incentives to win the League (Paragraph 1)	–	£6,100
Goalscoring Incentives – season awards (Paragraph 2)	–	£1,000
Goalscoring Incentives – match awards (Paragraph 3)	–	£6,970
Sportsmanship pool (Paragraph 4)	–	£6,000
Administrative costs (Paragraph 5)	–	£1,500
Isthmian News discount to clubs (Paragraph 6)	–	£930
Berger Youth Cup (Paragraph 7)	–	£2,500
TOTAL COST	–	£25,000

If you thought our Spot-the-Ball was difficult, try finding your team's result in most Sunday newspapers.

Every week The Mail on Sunday is the only national paper to give the Vauxhall-Opel League tables and results in full. In fact, when it comes to sports coverage in general, we like to think we're a great all-rounder.

Match reports, news and comment combine to make our sports section one of the most authoritative you're likely to come across. Read Patrick Collins' column and Joe Melling on football, Ivor Herbert on the racing scene and John Taylor's news and views.

Every Sunday our Pools Guide includes a Formcast for future matches and a coupon check for the previous day's results. We're now offering a special introductory discount for Vauxhall-Opel League supporters when they place a regular order for The Mail on Sunday each week.

Apart from increasing your chances in our Spot-the-Ball competition, you'll also soon discover why over 5 million people read The Mail on Sunday each week – and some of them don't even like sport!

You'll find a whole range of fascinating features with something for everyone. YOU Magazine is a colourful collection of articles and pictures on who's in the news, our Cartoon Section is full of favourite characters the kids will love, plus occasional partwork series for you to collect. To get your introductory discount just fill in the coupon below and hand it into your newsagent when you place your order.

80p off for Vauxhall-Opel league supporters.

Take this coupon to your newsagent and when you order The Mail on Sunday* you'll get 80p off your first 4 weeks bill. You will also be entitled to 12 extra crosses on The Mail on Sunday Spot-the-Ball Game for one week only. Just fill in your newsagent's name and address on the Spot-the-Ball coupon overleaf.

Please deliver/reserve The Mail on Sunday, with YOU Magazine and the Cartoon Section.

Name ....

Address ....

.... Postcode .... Tel No ....

Offer closes 18th May 1987. Only one coupon per household.

To the newsagent: Stamp this coupon and send it to the Newsagent Federation Services Ltd., FREEPOST, London EC4B 4LP for full refund plus 10p handling allowance.

The Mail ON SUNDAY

Over the years the League has embarked on a number of marketing initiatives. When The Mail on Sunday was first published it provided an in-depth results service and the League had an agreement with the newspaper for a spot-the-ball competition (see left and right) which also gave a money-off voucher for the newspaper.

Play The Mail on Sunday Spot-the-Ball and win a Philips Radio Cassette Recorder.

Game 3

Please fill in the details below and send your completed entry to: The Mail on Sunday Spot-the-Ball Competition, PO Box 73, Mitcham, Surrey CR4 2XU.

Closing date for entries for Game 3 is 6/3/87. All entrants must be 18 years of age or over.

Name ....

Address ....

.... Postcode .... Tel No ....

Newsagent where you placed your order (if applicable)

Name ....

Address ....

The Mail on Sunday has always taken a keen interest in non-league football, and now here's a competition specially for all you Vauxhall-Opel League supporters.

Every week this season we'll be putting your very own Spot-the-Ball contest in every match programme.

The game will change four times over the season and you can play every week. All you have to do is place three crosses on the picture where you think the ball should be.

What's more, if you place a regular order for The Mail on Sunday not only will you get a special introductory discount, but it will also entitle you to an extra 12 crosses for that week only. Just think, over the whole season you could have up to 108 chances to make X mark the spot.

Before each game commences our panel of judges will have decided where, in their opinion, the ball is most likely to be. The three winners for each game will be those whose opinion most closely coincides with that of the judges.

The first prize winner will receive a Philips Radio Cassette Recorder *plus* the chance to give his team some real support – we will donate a new match ball to the Vauxhall Opel League team of his choice.

There are also two runners-up prizes for each game of Konica Pop Cameras.

SERVOWARM

After Berger Paints had renewed their agreement once, they declined to do so again and the search was on for another sponsor. Central heating company Servowarm stepped forward and agreed to become title sponsors of the League.

The company was the country's largest installers of gas central heating systems and the announcement was made on 6 October 1982, from which date the League officially became known as the Servowarn Isthmian League.

A total package worth in excess of £32,000 was agreed for the first season (1982-83) with an option for two more seasons. The League Champions received £2,500, with a further £3,700 being divided between the next five clubs. This formula was repeated in the other divisions but with less money. A total of £14,600 was paid to the 24 clubs finishing in the first six places in the four division and a further £8,250 was allocated to a pool to be shared by all clubs winning a match by four goals or more.

NEWS RELEASE

SW/02/82

SERVOWARM ARE NEW SPONSORS OF ISTHMIAN LEAGUE

Servowarm, the country's largest installers of gas central heating systems, have become sponsors of the Isthmian Football League for the 1982-83 season, it was announced in London today (Wednesday, 6 October 1982).

The league will be known officially as the Servowarm Isthmian Football League from the day of the announcement, with full approval of the Football Association.

Although operating on a fully national basis, Servowarm has particular strength in the area around London and Greater London where the majority of member clubs of the Servowarm Isthmian Football League are located, and the company intends to work closely with clubs through its local branches and sales centres.

The Operations Director and General Manager of Servowarm, Syd Starkie explained that, despite almost daily approaches from organisations seeking sponsorship, this was the first time that the company had entered into any form of sponsorship agreement.

"There were very special reasons involved in our deciding to sponsor the League: of course we are a commercial enterprise, and it was essential that we could see there being value for money in this relationship and the location of league clubs fits our trading pattern superbly. Equally, as a responsible company, we took the view that we were entering into a two-way partnership and it was therefore essential that Servowarm should help the League, and football, in a positive way.

...../

In addition to the financial rewards, the League managed to obtain from the sponsor a payment for each club based on sales.

As part of the sponsorship agreement, each member club was encouraged to provide the League sponsor with sales leads in return for additional sponsorship payments.

A leaflet was placed within every member club's matchday programme and for every Servowarm central heating system installed as a direct result of this leaflet fifty pounds was given by Servowarm to the club involved.

The sponsorship continued the idea of rewarding substantial margins of victory in matches, but increased the threshold to four-goal victories as opposed to the previous three-goal victories.

A substantial four-figure investment was also made available for youth football and the Isthmian Youth Cup was initiated under the Servowarm banner. The League was very grateful to have the whole-hearted support of Syd Starkie and the active involvement of Jim Douglas from the company.

VAUXHALL MOTORS SPONSORSHIP

At the end of season 1984-85 car giants Vauxhall saw the opportunity to promote the Opel side of their European business and the League dropped the 'Isthmian' name for the first time. The League became known as the Vauxhall-Opel League and subsequently the Vauxhall League. Vauxhall's associated parts compant AC Delco sponsored the League Cup which had, since 1977, been sponsored by Japanese electronics company Hitachi.

The original agreement was for three seasons with an option for a further three–year period. The package, worth £250,000 over three years at the time, was one of the largest in non–league football. The following is taken from the press release issued to announce the sponsorship arrangement.

"In the first season the total cash awards will be £44,000, in the second £50,000 and in the third £56,000. The cash awards will consist of prize money for League positions from champions to sixth place in each division, League goal scoring awards (four-goal win margins and highest goal scorers in a season from each division) and awards for the most successful clubs in The FA Cup, FA Trophy and FA Vase competitions as well as cash prizes for success in the AC Delco Cup. In additions clubs will receive promotional material support from Vauxhall Motors to the value of at least £26,000 in the first year, £20,000 in the second and £14,000 in the third. A sum will also be made available for League administration."

SPONSONSHIP BREAKDOWN – 1985–86 SEASON

Division	Champions	Second	Third	Fourth	Fifth	Sixth
Premier	£3,500	£2,000	£1,250	£1,000	£750	£500
One	£2,000	£1,250	£1,000	£750	£500	£300
Two North	£1,300	£800	£600	£450	£300	£200
Two South	£1,300	£800	£600	£450	£300	£200
Total	£8,100	£4,850	£3,450	£2,650	£1,850	£1,200
Grand Total		£22,100				

LEAGUE GOAL SCORING AWARDS

(i) For each win by 4 goals or more the club has a share of its divisional pool:

Premier Division	£3,000	
Division 1	£2,250	
Division 2 North	£1,500	
Division 2 South	£1,500	
Total		£8,250

(ii) The club in each division scoring the most goals in a season receives:

Premier Division	£850	
Division 1	£550	
Division 2 North	£300	
Division 2 South	£300	
Total		£2,000

AWARDS FOR SUCCESS IN FA COMPETITIONS

FA Cup	£750
FA Trophy	£500
FA Vase	£250
Total	£1,500

AC DELCO LEAGUE CUP

Winners (one at £1,600)	£1,600
Losing finalists (one at £1,000)	£1,000
Losing semi–finalists (two at £600)	£1,200
Losing quarter finalists (four at £400)	£1,600
Clubs losing in third round (eight at £200)	£1,600
*Special Associate Member Club payment	£400
Total	£7,400

*The Associate Member Club i.e. one in either Division Two North or Division Two South going the furthest in the competition will receive £400. The award will be shared if two or more Associate Member Clubs are eligible for it.

Contribution to League administration expenses	£2,750
Grand Total	**£44,000**

DIADORA

This was the first time the famous old title "Isthmian" had been dropped from the name of the League and the headline name simply used the name of the sponsor.

As a result of European rebranding by General Motors, "Opel" was dropped and the League became the Vauxhall League in 1989. It was at this time the League incorporated as a Limited Company and the name was protected by the formation of The Isthmian Football League Limited. In future, the Company would *trade as* a league using the sponsors name. Vauxhall was that first name and remained until the end of the sponsorship in 1991 when the Italian sportswear company Diadora agreed to become the sixth sponsors of the League. This was a successful era for the League and for the Italian sportswear company Diadora who were seeking to establish themselves in the English market.

They were not the first company to realise that such an aim could be achieved through this type of sponsorship. The Chairman of Diadora was the world renowned athlete Seb (now Lord) Coe and he always found time to support the League and to attend functions. On one famous occasion he simply could not get back to England to attend the annual Banquet and Ball and sent a video to be played at the event.

After their first season, the sponsors also agreed to add their name to the League Cup, which had been without a sponsor during the inaugural Diadora season. During the sponsorship, the League agreed to introduce Diadora's own matchball in place of the Mitre Multiplex which was the ball favoured by most clubs.

Prior to this time the League had not stipulated a ball to be used in all League and League Cup matches. Although the ball was used in Serie A in Italy, it was less warmly received by Isthmians. Every match had to commence with the appropriate Diadora ball, but most teams finished with another maker's product!

The value of the sponsorship increased considerably and by the end of the agreement, the company were paying over one hundred thousand pounds each season to the League.

ICIS

Eventually Diadora were the subject of commands from Italy and in 1995 they reluctantly withdrew from active involvement in England for a short while. This meant that the League was once again seeking the support of an interested party. That support came in the shape of ICIS, another sportswear company which saw the potential which Diadora had used to its benefit. The Company was based in Aspatria, Cumbria and the Chairman Bill Wilson won the hearts of the Clubs when, at the AGM introducing the Company, he agreed to not only supply a set of home shirts free of charge, but also agreed to give every Club a set of away shirts in addition. This proved to be the downfall of the Company and cashflow was a great problem. The 1997-98 season commenced under the ICIS banner but matters were coming to a head and, with lawyers involved, the agreement was terminated by the League.

RYMAN

Once again the search was on for a backer. That search was made easy when Chairman Alan Turvey, by now the full time Managing Director of the League, received a call from Theo Paphitis offering help. Theo was a director of member Club Walton & Hersham as well as being an entrepreneur who was engaged in rescuing the famous name of Ryman the Stationer. Theo saw that one way to attain brand awareness quickly was to have the name liberally used across the sports pages of the national papers and so he agreed to enter into what has become one of the longest running sponsorships in sport. The name Ryman has become synonymous with the Isthmian League and Clubs have not only received direct support through rewards for success, each Member Club has received a discount card for the Ryman group of Companies which has pleased and benefited many of our lady supporters through the La Senza and Contessa chains!

When the League lost Guardian Insurance as the sponsor of the League Cup in 1998, it was Ryman which agreed to take over that commitment as well as the League sponsorship for three years. Theo Paphitis and Malcolm Cooke were honoured by the League in 2000 when they were both elected as Vice Presidents of the League to recognise the great contribution each had made to the continuing success of the League and its member Clubs.

Over the years the sponsorship monies have increased. The sponsor stood by the League when The FA reorganisation took effect. Although monies were initially reduced to reflect the fact that the League had effectively dropped a Step in the System, there has been a positive reaction to the efforts of Member Clubs by the sponsors who have reinstated the value of the sponsorship to what it was before the reorganisation.

Ryman
football league

The **Ryman** Football League

Ryman Sponsorship
of
The Isthmian League

Ryman Ltd, the leading high street stationery retailer, has signed a deal to sponsor the Isthmian Football League from immediate effect through until the end of season 1999-2000.

The Ryman Football League sponsorship is an ideal fit for Ryman, operating as it does within the Ryman heartland of the south east. With Ryman stores close to the majority of clubs, the local as well as national benefits for both parties are large.

Both the league and Ryman are long established institutions in the south east with almost 200 years of service between them.

The league sponsorship will give Ryman the opportunity for many new innovative promotional and marketing developments. The Isthmian League will also benefit by being able to further develop its close links with the local community through the Ryman connection.

The sponsorship package agreed today is worth over £200,000 to the league and was put together in conjunction with sponsorship and marketing agency Movie & Media Sports Ltd.

Both parties will benefit from the package with Ryman being able to take advantage of increased multi media opportunities and an audience of 14 million from over 88 clubs spread throughout southern England. The Ryman league logo will appear on all publicity material issued by the league, the weekly league information sheet and all clubs' match programmes.

For further information please contact Diana, Ailsa or Ben at
The London PR Company on 0171 580 8147.

Movie & Media Sports, 262 The Broadway,
Wimbledon, SW19 1SB. Telephone number 0181 544 9482.

Ryman
football league

SPONSORS

ISTHMIAN LEAGUE

Sponsor	Years
Rothmans of Pall Mall	1973–77
Michael Lawrie & Partners	1977–78
Berger Paints	1978–82
Servowarm	1982–85
Vauxhall Motors	1985–91
Diadora UK	1991–95
ICIS Sportswear	1995–97
Ryman the Stationer	1997–date

LEAGUE CUP

Sponsor	Years
Hitachi	1977–85
AC Delco	1985–91
Diadora UK	1992–95
Guardian Insurance	1995–98
Ryman the Stationer	1998–2001
Bryco	2002–05
Westview Rail	2005

FULL MEMBERS CUP

Sponsor	Years
Loctite	1990–92
Carlsberg	1993–95
Carlton TV	1995–96
Puma UK	1997–99

ASSOCIATE MEMBERS TROPHY

Sponsor	Years
Loctite	1990–92
Carlsberg	1993–95
Carlton TV	1995–96
Vandanel	1997–00

YOUTH CUP

Sponsors	Years
Berger Paints	1977–82
Servowarm	1982–85
Loctite	1990–92
Westview Rail	2005

CHARITY SHIELD

Sponsors	Years
Dylon International	1978–86
One 2 One (now T Mobile)	1999–03

MANAGER OF THE MONTH/SEASON

Sponsors	Years
MacKenzie Scotch Whisky	1984–85
Hunting Gate Homes	1985–91
William Hill	1991–99
in association with Sandoms Solicitors	*1993-97*
Spall Sports	1999–03
Score Team Wear	2001–05

SAFE HANDS

Sponsors	Years
Guardian Insurance	1996–98
Ryman the Stationer	1998–99
Umbro International	1999–02
Endsleigh Insurance	2002–06

GOALSCORERS

Sponsors	Years
Radio Luxembourg	1976–77
Mitre	1989–97
Puma UK	1997–98
Spall Sports	1999–06

FAIR PLAY

Sponsors	Years
Carlsberg	1995-97
Umbro International	1997-date

TEAM OF THE MONTH

Sponsors	Years
GX Soccer	2003-05

Note: In addition to the above, Chryso and ICIS Clubwear have sponsored the match football and bench kit respectively. ClubCall have provided the League telephone line for many years.

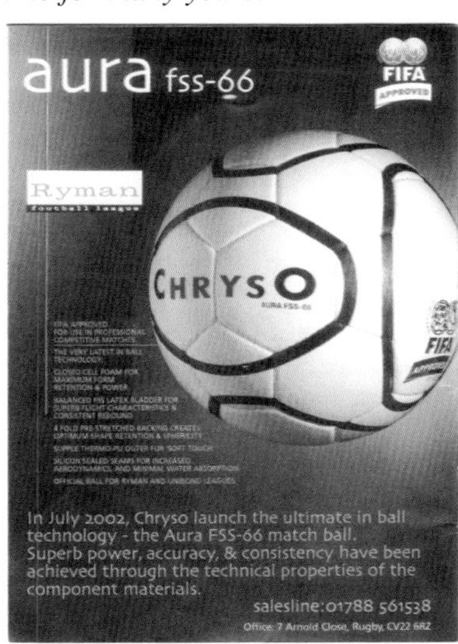

When it comes to stationery and office supplies, there's only one winner...

Official sponsors of the Ryman Football League
www.ryman.co.uk

LOCTITE®
Stick with the best

CHAPTER TEN

Success in FA Competitions

The greatest Cup competition in the world! That is how The FA Cup is described by so many people. The League has had its fair share of Cup successes and the purpose of this part of the chapter is to recognise all the matches played by Clubs whilst in membership of the League against clubs which were members of the Football League or The FA Premier League at the time of the match. Pictured below is the trophy which was used between 1911 and 1991 when it was retired to protect it and replaced with that used today.

One of the great representatives of the League who has done so much for The FA Cup is Tony Williams and he was asked to contribute an item about his recollections of the League in The FA Cup. This is what he says:

The first game of senior football remembered by young lads in the fifties, sixties and seventies was usually The FA Cup Final. Many adopted the winners as 'their club' for life and the mystique and excitement of The FA Cup Final with all its glamour and wonderful traditions became a special highlight of the sporting year which could not be missed.

So imagine the excitement when a young footballer making his way into senior amateur or semi-professional football found out that his club was actually playing in The FA Cup. Not everyone realises that the competition starts in August and five or six preliminary and qualifying rounds can be played before the first round proper welcomes the Football League clubs from the bottom two divisions.

In my early seasons in the Isthmian League with Corinthian–Casuals we missed out on the national knock-out competition. The club didn't enter until 1965, so my first FA Cup experience was with Kingstonian and the first tie at home to Walton & Hersham in the 1st qualifying round of the 1960-61 season. I was in the RAF and wasn't able to train regularly on Tuesdays and Thursdays so couldn't challenge for a regular place in the team. Peter Gleeson had built a good squad and I was thrilled to get a chance in the cup match. We won 5-0 and I scored but missed a couple of others and didn't do enough to keep my place.

I will never forget the thrill, I was playing in the famous FA Cup and that goal was special - even if I did get dropped! Having played my early football in the Isthmian League with Casuals, K's, Dulwich Hamlet and, for a very short time when stationed at RAF Halton, with Wycombe Wanderers, I obviously have great affection for the competition. I was also with Hungerford Town when they were invited into the Isthmian League and have some wonderful memories of those days.

Isthmian clubs had enjoyed some great moments in The FA Cup before I was aware of their inclusion but the first real excitement involving a team I knew well was Tooting & Mitcham United's cup run in 1958-59. They were the current Isthmian champions and had one of amateur football's best known players in Irish International Paddy Hasty.

In the first round they drew Third Division club Bournemouth and won 3-1 at Sandy Lane, then another home draw brought them a 2-1 victory over Fourth Division Northampton Town *(see programme)*. The third round draw couldn't come quickly enough.

TOOTING AND MITCHAM UNITED
FOOTBALL CLUB

Member of the Football Association. Affiliated to London F.A. and Surrey F.A.

T.&M.U.F.C.

Hon. Secretary: G. A. COVINGTON, 17 St. Georges Road, Mitcham, Surrey.

OFFICIAL PROGRAMME — No. 18 — THREEPENCE

Saturday, 6th December, 1958

F.A. CUP SECOND ROUND PROPER

TOOTING & MITCHAM UTD.
v.
NORTHAMPTON TOWN

KICK-OFF 2.15 p.m.

RANDOM NOTES

For the second time in three years we find ourselves in the second round of the F.A. Cup. On 8th December, 1956, we lost to Q.P.R. John Harlow, George Edwards, Gordon Holden, Paddy Hasty, Tony Slade, Jimmy O'Neill and Johnny Blizzard (now starting training again) were with us then as now. Lessons they learnt on that day may be useful against our redoubtable football league professional opponents this afternoon from Northampton. We extend a hearty welcome to our "Cobbler" visitors—officials, players and supporters—and hope they have pleasant memories of their visit to Mitcham. We hope to avenge our fellow Isthmian leaguers, Wycombe Wanderers, whom they defeated in the 1st round.

We have arrived at this round as follows: Bromley (H) 5-1, after a 2-2 draw away, Redhill (H) 7-1, Sutton United (A) 8-1, Horsham (H) 4-0, Bournemouth and Boscombe Athletic (H) 3-1. With a goal average of 29-6, the following have contributed: P. Hasty 7, A. Viney, A. Slade and A. Grainger 5 each, Eric Parker 3, Jimmie O'Neill 2, D. Flanagan and E. Murphy 1 each.

The team is the same as last round except that John Harlow returns to enable George Edwards to revert to left-back vice Norman Pilgrim.

Many disappointed patrons please note that they could have had their tickets sent to them by post simply by paying £2 5s. for a reserved and numbered seat. Moreover for this moderate sum they can see all league and friendly games on this

[Continued on back page

Everyone with an interest in football in those days would find a radio at mid day on the Monday. A dream came true- "Tooting & Mitcham United (at least they were drawn at home) ... will play ... Nottingham Forest!"

South London was buzzing and a 14,300 crowd squashed into Sandy Lane to watch a brilliant cup tie. There was a thin covering of snow on the pitch and both Tooting's senior goalkeepers were injured so a youngster called Ray Secker had to step in for an incredibly nerve-wracking experience.

Paddy Hasty crashed a shot against the bar before Albert Grainger gave Tooting the lead, heading home after a goalmouth mix-up. Before half-time midfield dynamo Ted Murphy had crashed in another from 35 yards and the Tooting supporters could hardly believe their luck as their heroes held on to a 2-0 lead at the interval.

Just eight minutes after the restart, hero Murphy passed back to his young keeper who fumbled and Forest were given a lifeline. Secker redeemed himself with a brilliant diving save and then got knocked out after a collision but he couldn't save the penalty given just thirteen minutes from the end after the ball had appeared to brush against Murphy's shoulder. There were questions about the refereeing even in those days!

In the replay 42,000 saw Forest in control for most of the game and, although first-choice keeper Wally Pearson returned, the Division One club won comfortably by 3-0. A wonderful cup run was over, but a very good amateur side had written a special chapter in their club's history.

Tooting & Mitcham United: *Secker; Harlow, Edwards; Holden, Bennett, Murphy; Grainger, Viney, Hasty, Slade and Flanagan. Replay: Same team with Pearson for Secker in goal.*

The Isthmian League has played a large part in my lifetime involvement with non-league football and, after playing in the competition when there was just one division of sixteen clubs, I enjoyed my time helping Hungerford Town to develop as a club and had five wonderful years running the Rothmans sponsorship of the Isthmian League, later expanded by the addition of Northern, Western and Hellenic Leagues under the Rothmans umbrella. In more recent years I enjoyed my time as a director of Yeovil Town as they passed through the Isthmian League for a short spell before returning to the Conference. In all these periods of my football experience The FA Cup kept providing special memories.

During my time as General Manager at Hungerford Town the club proudly took its place in the Isthmian League Division Two and between 1979 and 1982 finished third in three consecutive seasons. In the first of these, under the guidance of Jimmy Kelman, who went on to manage Wycombe Wanderers, we reached the fourth qualifying round of The FA Cup for the first time and drew Bridgend, a powerful Southern League club, away from home.

A 1-1 draw played on a sloping quagmire was a test of character and a late Andy Young penalty gave Hungerford a home replay that attracted a fifth of Hungerford's official 5,000 inhabitants. This time heavy rain on the grassy pitch encouraged fast exciting football and it turned out to be the Berkshire club's night. An early Keith Curtis goal was followed by a memorable hat trick from ace goalscorer Ian Farr and a late tap in from centre half Paul Duffy to make it a 5-1 scoreline and probably the club's greatest result.

Bridgend went on to win the Southern League championship that year, whilst Hungerford avoided Portsmouth, Oxford United and Plymouth Argyle in the first round draw, but had to make the short trip across the county to Slough where they lost 1-3 after an early Farr goal. A disappointing end to a great cup run.

Hungerford Town v Bridgend: *Greenwood; W.Angel, Turner, Duffy, I.Farmiloe; T.Ingram, Curtis, McMahon; Phillips, Farr, Young.*

I had the pleasure of running the first sponsorship of an English football league for Rothmans and the Isthmians under Chairman Barry East were the front runners in setting up the scheme. It was a vintage time for the clubs from the sponsored leagues as they were all aware of the sportsmanship incentives, which encouraged member clubs to cut out rough tactics, retaliation and dissent. Many critics suggested that this would give them a disadvantage in full-blooded cup battles against clubs not 'hampered' by sporting 'ethics'. But it was just the opposite, as clubs giving referees less grief and showing better discipline tended to concentrate on the game more and - dare we say it - probably got the appreciative referees' vote in doubtful situations.

One of the first Isthmian clubs to benefit from a 'disciplined' cup run was Hendon in 1973-74. With a team full of amateur internationals the thought of taking on Malcolm Macdonald's famous FA Cup fighters Newcastle United at St James' Park was an amazing challenge that needed the strongest possible show of character, especially when it was watched by a fanatical crowd of 32,000.

England's goalkeeper John Swannell and his defence weathered the initial burst from the home club but after twenty minutes McFaul saved well from Fry and the Isthmians gradually edged back into the game. Full-time professionals often show their extra fitness against part-timers just before the break and from a long throw defender Pat Howard gave the First Division club the lead on half-time.

With nothing to lose and some non-league legends such as Swannell, England's most capped amateur Rod Haider and Tony Jennings, who was to go on to become arguably the most successful non-league player of all time, it was no surprise that the Isthmians came into the game. Derek Baker brought a great save from McFaul and then after a free kick the same player nodded the cross to his skipper Haider who slammed in a wonderful equalizer.

This was a great story for the press and a wonderful boost to new sponsors Rothmans, who managed to blow up a photo of Hendon's goal and frame it for a presentation before the replay, which was held at Watford the following week. There was a limit on all power in the country at the time so the game was played in the afternoon but 15,000 still turned up at Vicarage Road although this time, despite tremendous early pressure from Hendon, the First Division club took the lead with a disputed goal after 24 minutes and then grabbed three more as the amateurs tired at the end of the game.

It was a wonderful performance over 180 minutes against one of the country's best clubs. Possibly Hendon's greatest!

Hendon: *Swannell; Jennings, Hand; Deadman, Phillips, Haider; Baker D, Childs, Baker J, Somers and Fry, with Connell sub for the replay.*

The 1974-75 season saw five non-league clubs reach the third round proper of The FA Cup. The Rothmans Isthmian League provided their champions Wycombe Wanderers, at home to Division One leaders Middlesbrough, and Leatherhead, inspired by John Swannell in goal and the charismatic Chris Kelly up front, who were away to Brighton.

The Northern Premier League had the experienced cup fighters Altrincham playing at Everton and Stafford Rangers at home to Rotherham United while the Southern League had Wimbledon travelling to take on First Division Burnley.

On probably non-league football's best ever FA Cup day not one of the five were beaten and not one conceded a goal from open play!

Everton scored a penalty in a 1-1 draw with Alty and Stafford drew 0-0. Wimbledon recorded a glorious 1-0 victory at Turf Moor and it was another spectacular Kelly goal that saw Leatherhead through in front of 20,491 at the Goldstone Ground.

In the last minute at Loakes Park, Wanderers central defender Alan Phillips just failed to win the game in which Brian Lee's amateurs had deserved to go through. I was privileged to be with the club for the replay against Jack Charlton's high flying team of stars and it was only a very late goal by Armstrong that gave Boro a 1-0 victory in front of 30,128.

Wycombe Wanderers: *Maskell; Birdseye, Hand; Mead, Phillips, Rearden; Perrin, Kennedy, Searle, Holifield and Horseman. Sub: Evans in first game, Dylan in replay.*

Altrincham lost their replay which was played at Old Trafford in front of 35,000 by a respectable 0-2 scoreline and Stafford Rangers lost by the same score at Rotherham, but Leatherhead had more glory to come.

'The Tanners' had beaten Colchester United in the Second Round with a goal from Johnny Doyle and were welcomed to Brighton by a packed stadium with a wonderful cup tie atmosphere. Chris Kelly, only recently back after injury, was inspired on the day and his individual dribble and shot provided one of television archives' best-ever recordings as the commentator became more and more excited the closer 'The Leatherhead Lip' came to the goal.

A confident finish brought him a trip to the Match of the Day studios that Saturday evening and a memorable interview conducted after his evening of celebrations!

Non-League football was full of characters at that time with the amateurs of the Isthmian giants and indeed many from the famous North Eastern clubs, such as Blyth Spartans, holding their own with the part-time professionals of clubs like Altrincham and Wimbledon.

The third round draw paired Leatherhead with First Division Leicester City and they ran out in front of a 32,000 crowd. The news went round the country that the little Surrey club were leading 2-0 at half-time with goals from McGillicuddy and Kelly - was there to be another massive giant killing?

Within minutes of the restart Kelly rounded the keeper but delayed his angled shot and the Leicester defence cleared off the line. A three-goal lead would probably have been too much for the Foxes but this escape lifted them and by the end goals from Sammels, Earle and Weller had saved the match for Leicester and the Isthmians were left with great memories of a wonderful cup run.

Leatherhead: *Swannell; Sargent, Webb; Cooper, Reid, McGillicuddy; Woffinden, Lavers, Kelly, Smith and Doyle. Sub Wells (for Brighton match).*

One of the best individual FA Cup performances by an Isthmian player was produced by Woking's Tim Buzaglo, who hit a splendid hat-trick against West Bromwich Albion at the Hawthorns in their 4-2 third round victory in the 90-91 season. Substitute Worsfold came on in the 87th minute and scored Woking's fourth.

Woking v WBA: *Read; Mitchell,Cowler; Pratt, Baron, Wye. S.; Brown, Biggins, Franks (Worsfold), Buzaglo, Wye. L., Mulvaney came on for Franks against Everton.*

I was thrilled to see that exciting display which was even more creditable as Buzaglo was marked by Graham Roberts, an ex-England international, in front of 14,516. The centre half later became a popular manager of Yeovil Town, where he had more mixed FA Cup experiences, as well as Carshalton Athletic.

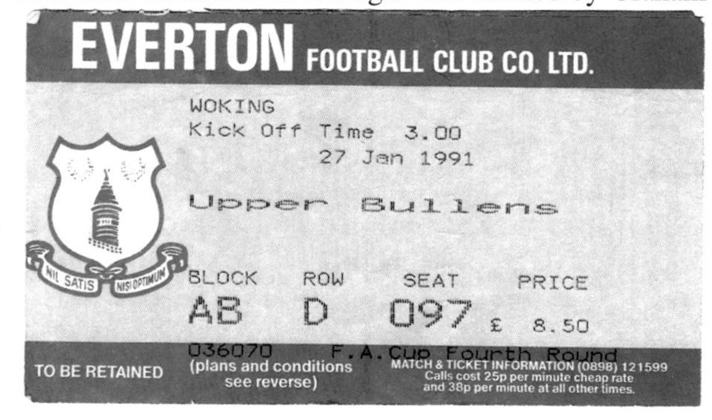

Once again this Isthmian victory was a success achieved with fast-flowing passing football and brought great credit to the management team of Geoff Chapple and Colin Lippiatt and their squad who were rewarded with a trip to Everton in the fourth round.

The atmosphere created by 34,724 at Goodison Park must have been intimidating for the Woking lads, but they were up for it and enjoyed the surrounding publicity including a story about melons and centre half Bradley Pratt! A great defensive display kept the home side at bay until the 58th minute when Sheedy scored the only goal of the game. Their manager had many more exciting days to come in The FA Trophy and Cup, but I'm sure this cup run will always be special for everyone concerned.

My final Isthmian connection with The FA Cup was as a director at Yeovil Town, when Graham Roberts had built a new squad capable of promotion back to the Conference. In the two seasons between 1995 and 1997 there was no giant killing, but probably the luck of the draw may well have indirectly laid the foundations for the club's excellent push into the Football League just six years later.

The Western League was sponsored by Screwfix, a local company owned and run by the Goddard-Watts family. Mr Goddard-Watts senior had never taken an interest in football before, but his home town of Yeovil were drawn to play two of his League's senior clubs - at home to Taunton Town (0-0) and the replay (5-3) and Tiverton Town (2-0 away). Yeovil were knocked out in the fourth qualifying round that year, but he thoroughly enjoyed the atmosphere, excitement, friendliness and hospitality, especially at Yeovil's lovely facilities, where chairman Brian Moore and his directors made him and his wife especially welcome.

The crowds were lively with the replay at Taunton being especially eventful, while lady referee Wendy Toms was tested to the full in a bloodcurdling atmosphere which lifted the supporters to hysterical levels of excitement. As a man in his seventies Mr Goddard-Watts got the football bug late in life and his investment was to prove the most important aspect of Yeovil Town pulling away into the Football League. He has recently sold his shares in the club to David Webb, so has recouped his investment and hopefully he has considered it a happy part of his very successful life. So not only has The FA Cup given many Isthmian clubs great moments to remember, but the competition may actually have helped shape their future.

Those with cup memories will enjoy them all their lives and if you look carefully, the competition can live up to its reputation and then, for the believers, there really is magic in The FA Challenge Cup!

We now present an exhaustive list of all matches played by Isthmian Clubs against opposition from the Football League or The FA Premier League:

ISTHMIANS AGAINST THE PROFESSIONALS IN THE FA CHALLENGE CUP
THE RESULTS IN FULL

Aldershot Town

20.11.99	Exeter City	A	L0-2	
18.11.00	Brighton	H	L2-6	
17.11.01	Bristol Rovers	H	D0-0	
27.11.01	Bristol Rovers	A	L0-1	

Aylesbury United

18.11.89	Southend United	H	1-0	
09.12.89	Northampton Town	A	0-0	
12.12.89	Northampton Town	H	0-1	*aet*
17.11.90	Walsall	H	0-1	
07.12.91	Hereford United	H	2-3	

Barking

16.12.78	Aldershot	H	L1-2	
24.11.79	Oxford United	H	W1-0	
15.12.79	Reading	A	L1-3	
15.12.81	Gillingham	A	D1-1	
02.01.82	Gillingham	H	L1-3	*aet*
Played at Gillingham				
10.12.83	Plymouth Argyle	A	L1-2	

Barton Rovers

22.11.80	Torquay United	A	L0-2	

Basingstoke Town

09.12.89	Torquay United	H	L2-3	
15.11.97	Wycombe Wanderers	A	D2-2	
25.11.97	Wycombe Wanderers	H	D2-2	*aet*
won 5-4 on penalties				
06.12.97	Northampton Town	A	D1-1	
16.12.97	Northampton Town	H	D0-0	*aet*
Northampton won 4-3 on penalties				
14.11.98	Bournemouth	H	L1-2	

Bedford Town

17.11.01	Peterborough United	H	D0-0	
27.11.01	Peterborough United	A	L1-2	

Bishops Stortford

09.12.72	Peterborough United	H	D2-2	
11.12.72	Peterborough United	A	L1-3	
13.12.75	Aldershot	A	L0-2	
20.11.82	Reading	A	W2-1	
08.01.83	Middlesbrough	A	D2-2	
11.01.83	Middlesbrough	H	L1-2	
17.11.84	Brentford	A	L0-4	
16.11.85	Peterborough United	H	D2-2	
20.11.85	Peterborough United	A	L1-3	
15.11.86	Colchester United	H	D1-1	
18.11.86	Colchester United	A	L0-2	
08.11.03	Mansfield Town	A	L0-6	

Bognor Regis Town

17.11.84	Swansea City	A	D1-1	
21.11.84	Swansea City	H	W3-1	
08.12.84	Reading	A	L2-6	
14.11.87	Torquay United	H	L0-3	
19.11.88	Exeter City	H	W2-1	
10.12.88	Cambridge United	H	L0-1	
02.12.95	Peterborough United	A	L0-4	

Boreham Wood

07.12.96	Luton Town	A	L1-2	
15.11.98	Luton Town	H	L2-3	
16.11.02	Torquay United	A	L0-5	
08.11.03	Blackpool	A	L0-4	

Bracknell Town

18.11.00	Lincoln City	A	L0-4	

Bromley

20.11.76	Swindon Town	A	L0-7	

Camberley Town

14.11.98	Brentford	A	L0-5	

Canvey Island

12.11.95	Brighton	H	D2-2	
21.11.95	Brighton	A	L1-4	
19.11.00	Port Vale	H	D4-4	
28.11.00	Port Vale	A	W2-1	*aet*
10.12.00	Southend United	H	L1-2	
Played at Southend				
17.11.01	Wigan Athletic	A	W1-0	
09.12.01	Northampton Town	H	W1-0	
05.01.02	Burnley	A	L1-4	
08.11.03	Southend United	A	D1-1	
19.11.03	Southend United	H	L2-3	

Carshalton Athletic

11.12.82	Torquay United	A	L1-4	
13.11.93	Barnet	A	L1-2	

Chesham United

20.11.76	Brentford	A	L0-2	
05.01.80	Cambridge United	H	L0-2	

Clapton

28.11.25	Norwich City	H	W3-1	
09.01.26	Swindon Town	H	L2-3	
Played at Upton Park				
27.11.26	Brentford	H	D1-1	
01.12.26	Brentford	A	L3-7	
30.11.27	Luton Town	A	L0-9	
16.11.57	QPR	H	D1-1	
18.11.57	QPR	A	L1-3	

Corinthian-Casuals

13.11.65	Watford	H	L1-5	
19.11.83	Bristol City	H	D0-0	
Played at Dulwich Hamlet				
23.11.83	Bristol City	A	L0-4	

Croydon

15.12.79	Millwall	H	D1-1	
Played at Selhurst Park				
18.12.79	Millwall	A	L2-3	*aet*

Dagenham

24.11.73	Aldershot	H	L0-4	
26.11.77	Walsall	A	L0-1	
25.11.78	Watford	A	L0-3	
22.11.80	Gillingham	A	L1-2	

Dagenham & Redbridge

06.12.97	Peterborough United	A	L2-3	

Dorking

14.11.92	Plymouth Argyle	H	L2-3	

Dulwich Hamlet

28.11.25	Southend United	A	L1-5	
27.11.26	Southend United	H	L1-4	
24.11.28	Merthyr Town	A	L2-4	
30.11.29	Plymouth Argyle	H	L0-3	
29.11.30	Newport County	H	D2-2	
04.12.30	Newport County	A	L1-4	
26.11.32	Swindon Town	A	L1-4	
25.11.33	Newport County	H	D2-2	
30.11.33	Newport County	A	L2-6	
24.11.34	Torquay United	H	L1-2	
30.11.35	Torquay United	A	L2-3	
28.11.36	Swindon Town	A	L0-6	
27.11.37	Aldershot	H	L1-2	
27.11.48	Northampton Town	A	L1-2	

Enfield

Date	Opponent	Venue	Result	
16.11.63	Reading	A	D2-2	
19.11.63	Reading	H	L2-4	*aet*
07.01.67	Watford	H	L2-4	
18.12.67	Swansea Town	A	L0-2	
15.11.69	Brighton	A	L1-2	
21.11.70	Cambridge United	H	L0-1	
11.12.71	Peterborough United	A	L0-4	
11.12.76	Crystal Palace	A	L0-4	
26.11.77	Wimbledon	H	W3-0	
17.12.77	Northampton Town	A	W2-0	
16.12.78	Swindon Town	A	L0-3	
13.12.80	Hereford United	H	W2-0	
03.01.81	Port Vale	A	D1-1	
06.01.81	Port Vale	H	W3-0	
24.01.81	Barnsley	A	D1-1	
28.01.81	Barnsley	H	L0-3	
Played at White Hart Lane				
16.11.91	Aldershot	A	W1-0	
07.12.91	Barnet	H	L1-4	
13.11.93	Cardiff City	H	D0-0	
30.11.93	Cardiff City	A	L0-1	
12.11.94	Cardiff City	H	W1-0	
03.12.94	Torquay United	H	D1-1	
13.12.94	Torquay United	A	W1-0	
07.01.95	Leicester City	A	L0-2	
07.12.96	Peterborough United	H	D1-1	
17.12.96	Peterborough United	A	L1-4	
14.11.98	York City	H	D2-2	
24.11.98	York City	A	L1-2	
30.10.99	Chesterfield	A	W2-1	
20.11.99	Preston North End	A	D0-0	
30.11.99	Preston North End	H	L0-3	
Played at Clarence Park, St. Albans				

Farnborough Town

Date	Opponent	Venue	Result
17.11.84	Hereford United	A	L0-3
15.11.86	Swindon Town	A	L0-4
14.11.87	Cambridge United	A	L1-2

Ford United

Date	Opponent	Venue	Result
14.11.98	Preston North End	A	L0-3
08.11.03	Port Vale	A	D2-2
19.11.03	Port Vale	H	L1-2

Gravesend & Northfleet

Date	Opponent	Venue	Result
08.12.00	Notts County	H	L1-2
17.11.01	Huddersfield Town	A	L1-2

Grays Athletic

Date	Opponent	Venue	Result
18.11.00	Reading	A	L0-4

Hampton & Richmond Borough

Date	Opponent	Venue	Result
18.11.00	Barnet	A	L1-2

Harlow Town

Date	Opponent	Venue	Result
15.12.79	Southend United	A	D1-1
18.12.79	Southend United	H	W1-0
05.01.80	Leicester City	A	D1-1
08.01.80	Leicester City	H	W1-0
26.01.80	Watford	A	L3-4
22.11.80	Charlton Athletic	H	L0-2
16.11.91	Peterborough United	A	L0-7

Harrow Borough

Date	Opponent	Venue	Result
10.12.83	Newport County	H	L1-3
18.11.00	Wycombe Wanderers	A	L0-3

Hayes

Date	Opponent	Venue	Result
18.11.72	Bristol Rovers	H	W1-0
09.12.72	Reading	A	D0-0
11.12.72	Reading	H	L0-1
14.11.87	Swansea City	H	L0-1
19.11.88	Aldershot	A	L0-1
18.11.89	Peterborough United	A	D1-1
21.11.89	Peterborough United	H	L0-1
17.11.90	Cardiff	A	D0-0
21.11.90	Cardiff	H	W1-0
08.12.90	Bournemouth	A	L0-1
15.11.91	Fulham	A	W2-0
14.11.92	Brighton	A	L0-2
11.11.95	Northampton Town	A	L0-1

Hendon

Date	Opponent	Venue	Result
14.11.64	Port Vale	A	L1-2
26.11.66	Reading	H	L1-3
21.11.70	Aldershot	H	L0-2
18.11.72	Plymouth Argyle	A	L0-1
05.01.74	Newcastle United	A	D1-1
09.01.74	Newcastle United	H	L0-4
Played at Vicarage Rd			
22.11.75	Reading	H	W1-0
13.12.75	Swindon Town	H	L0-1
26.11.77	Watford	A	L0-2
19.11.88	Reading	A	L2-4
16.11.96	Cardiff City	A	L0-2
15.11.97	Leyton Orient	H	D2-2
25.11.97	Leyton Orient	A	W1-0
06.12.97	Cardiff City	A	L1-3
15.11.98	Notts County	H	D0-0
01.12.98	Notts County	A	L0-3
20.11.99	Blackpool	A	L0-2

Heybridge Swifts

Date	Opponent	Venue	Result
11.11.94	Gillingham	H	L0-2
Played at Layer Rd Colchester			
15.11.97	Bournemouth	A	L0-3
16.11.02	Bristol City	H	L0-7

Hitchin Town

Date	Opponent	Venue	Result	
23.11.74	Cambridge United	H	D0-0	
26.11.74	Cambridge United	A	L0-3	
11.12.76	Swindon Town	H	D1-1	
21.12.76	Swindon Town	A	L1-3	*aet*
25.11.78	Bournemouth	A	L1-2	
12.11.94	Hereford United	A	D2-2	
22.11.94	Hereford United	H	W4-2	
03.12.94	Wycombe Wanderers	H	L0-5	
11.11.95	Bristol Rovers	H	W2-1	
02.12.95	Gillingham	A	L0-3	

Hornchurch

Date	Opponent	Venue	Result
09.11.03	Darlington	H	W2-0
06.12.03	Tranmere Rovers	H	L0-1

Ilford

Date	Opponent	Venue	Result
10.12.27	Exeter City	A	L3-5
30.11.29	Watford	H	L0-3
29.11.30	Brentford	H	L1-6
26.11.32	Newport County	A	L2-4
25.11.33	Swindon Town	H	L2-4
28.11.36	Reading	H	L2-4
15.11.58	Norwich City	A	L1-3
14.12.74	Southend United	H	L0-2

BARKING F.C.
F.A. CUP
2nd ROUND
Barking v Aldershot
16th DECEMBER OR WHEN PLAYED AT
MAYESBROOK PARK, LODGE AVENUE, DAGENHAM
PRICE £1·50
BLOCK 'A' ROW C SEAT 13
ENTRANCE 1

Kingstonian

26.11.32	Luton Town	A	D2-2	
30.11.32	Luton Town	H	L2-3	
25.11.33	Bristol City	H	L1-7	
14.11.92	Peterborough United	H	D1-1	
25.11.92	Peterborough United	A	L1-9	
FA ordered match to be replayed behind closed doors after Kingstonian goalkeeper was hit by coins.				
04.12.92	Peterborough United	A	L0-1	
12.11.94	Brighton	H	W2-1	
03.12.95	Plymouth Argyle	H	L1-2	

Leatherhead

14.12.74	Colchester United	H	W1-0	
04.01.75	Brighton	A	W1-0	
25.01.75	Leicester City	H	L2-3	
Played at Filbert Street				
22.11.75	Cambridge United	H	W2-0	
20.11.76	Northampton Town	H	W2-0	
26.11.77	Swansea City	H	D0-0	
29.11.77	Swansea City	A	L1-2	
16.12.78	Colchester United	H	D1-1	
18.12.78	Colchester United	A	L0-4	
22.11.80	Exeter City	A	L0-5	

Lewes

18.11.01	Stoke City	H	L0-2	
Played at Britannia Stadium Stoke				

Leyton Wingate

16.11.85	Swansea City	A	L0-2	

Leytonstone

30.11.46	Walsall	H	L1-6	
29.11.47	Bristol Rovers	A	L2-3	
27.11.48	Watford	H	D1-1	
Abandoned after 63 minutes- fog				
04.12.48	Watford	H	W2-1	
11.12.48	Newport County	H	L3-4	*aet*
24.11.51	Shrewsbury Town	H	W2-0	
15.12.51	Newport County	H	D2-2	
20.12.51	Newport County	A	L0-3	
22.11.52	Watford	H	L0-2	
09.12.67	Walsall	H	L0-1	
16.11.68	Walsall	H	L0-1	

Leytonstone Ilford

12.11.81	Aldershot	A	L0-2	

London Caledonians

18.01.13	Wolverhampton W	A	L1-3	
10.01.14	Huddersfield Town	A	L0-3	
27.11.26	Luton Town	A	L2-4	
14.01.28	Crewe Alexandra	H	L2-3	
Played at Stamford Bridge				

Marlow

16.11.91	West Bromwich Albion	A	L0-6	
02.01.93	Tottenham Hotspur	H	L1-5	
Played at White Hart Lane				
13.11.93	Plymouth Argyle	H	L0-2	
16.11.94	Oxford United	H	W2-0	
07.01.95	Swindon Town	A	L0-2	

Nunhead

30.11.29	Bristol Rovers	H	L0-2	
30.11.35	Watford	H	L2-4	

Oxford City

17.12.21	Norwich City	H	D1-1	
21.12.21	Norwich City	A	L0-3	
25.11.33	Gillingham	H	L1-5	
26.11.66	Bristol Rovers	H	D2-2	
29.11.66	Bristol Rovers	A	L0-4	
09.12.67	Luton Town	H	L1-2	
Played at Kenilworth Road				
16.11.68	Swansea Town	H	L2-3	
06.12.69	Swansea Town	H	L1-5	
21.11.70	Bournemouth	H	D1-1	
23.11.70	Bournemouth	A	L1-8	
30.10.99	Wycombe Wanderers	A	D1-1	
09.11.99	Wycombe Wanderers	H	D1-1	
Abandoned				
16.11.99	Wycombe Wanderers	H	L0-1	
Played at the Manor Ground Oxford				

Romford

17.11.45	Brighton	A	L1-3	
24.11.45	Brighton	H	D1-1	

Slough Town

24.11.73	Reading	A	L0-3	
23.11.74	Brentford	H	L1-4	
20.11.82	Millwall	H	W1-0	
07.12.85	Orient	A	D2-2	
10.12.85	Orient	H	L2-3	
06.12.86	Swansea City	A	L0-3	
12.11.94	Birmingham City	H	L0-4	
Played at St. Andrews				
14.11.98	Macclesfield Town	A	D2-2	
24.11.98	Macclesfield Town	H	D1-1	*aet*
Macclesfield won 9-8 on penalties				
13.11.04	Walsall	H	W2-1	

St. Albans City

07.12.68	Walsall	H	D1-1	
10.12.68	Walsall	A	L1-3	
13.12.80	Torquay United	H	D1-1	
17.12.80	Torquay United	A	L1-4	
07.12.96	Bristol City	A	L2-9	
16.11.02	Stockport County	A	L1-4	

Sutton United

16.11.63	Aldershot	H	L0-4	
24.01.70	Leeds United	H	L0-6	
22.11.75	Bournemouth	H	D1-1	
26.11.75	Bournemouth	A	L0-1	
15.12.81	Swindon Town	A	L1-2	
16.11.91	Maidstone United	A	L0-1	
14.11.92	Hereford United	A	L1-2	
13.11.93	Colchester United	A	W4-3	
04.12.93	Torquay United	A	W1-0	
08.01.94	Notts County	A	L2-3	
02.12.95	Hereford United	A	L0-2	

Thurrock

07.11.03	Luton Town	H	D1-1	
18.11.03	Luton Town	A	L1-3	

Tilbury

07.01.78	Stoke City	A	L0-4	

Right: the Newcastle United programme for their FA Cup tie with Hendon.

Tooting & Mitcham United

Date	Opponent	Venue	Result	
08.12.56	Queens Park Rangers	H	L0-2	
15.11.58	Bournemouth	H	W3-1	
06.12.58	Northampton Town	H	W2-1	
10.01.59	Nottingham Forest	H	D2-2	
24.01.59	Nottingham Forest	A	L0-3	
27.11.74	Crystal Palace	H	L1-2	
03.01.76	Swindon Town	A	D2-2	
06.01.76	Swindon Town	H	W2-1	
24.01.76	Bradford City	A	L1-3	
26.11.77	Northampton Town	H	L1-2	

Walthamstow Avenue

Date	Opponent	Venue	Result	
08.12.45	Brighton	H	D1-1	
15.12.45	Brighton	A	L2-4	
11.12.48	Oldham Athletic	H	D2-2	aet
18.12.48	Oldham Athletic	A	L1-3	
26.11.49	Northampton Town	A	L1-4	
25.11.50	Mansfield Town	A	L0-1	
06.12.52	Watford	H	D1-1	
10.12.52	Watford	A	W2-1	aet
10.01.53	Stockport County	H	W2-1	
31.01.53	Manchester United	A	D1-1	
05.02.53	Manchester United	H	L2-5	
Played at Highbury				
21.11.53	Gillingham	H	W1-0	
12.12.53	Ipswich Town	A	D2-2	
16.12.53	Ipswich Town	H	L0-1	
20.11.54	Queens Park Rangers	A	D2-2	
25.11.54	Queens Park Rangers	H	D2-2	aet
29.11.54	Queens Park Rangers	N	W4-0	
Played at Highbury				
11.12.54	Darlington	H	L0-3	
17.11.56	Crystal Palace	A	L0-2	
16.11.57	Coventry City	A	L0-1	
14.11.59	Bournemouth	H	L2-3	
05.11.60	Queens Park Rangers	A	L2-3	
06.01.68	Bournemouth	H	L1-3	

Walton & Hersham

Date	Opponent	Venue	Result
18.11.72	Exeter City	H	W2-1
24.11.73	Brighton	H	D0-0
28.11.73	Brighton	A	W4-0
15.12.73	Hereford United	A	L0-3
22.11.75	Crystal Palace	A	L0-1
21.11.94	Swansea City	H	L0-2

Wealdstone

Date	Opponent	Venue	Result
13.11.65	Millwall	A	L1-3

Whyteleafe

Date	Opponent	Venue	Result
30.10.99	Chester City	H	D0-0
09.11.99	Chester City	A	L1-3

Wimbledon

Date	Opponent	Venue	Result
30.11.30	Fulham	A	D1-1
03.12.30	Fulham	H	L0-6
28.11.31	Norwich City	H	L1-3
08.12.34	Southend United	H	L1-5
29.11.47	Mansfield Town	H	L0-1
03.11.62	Colchester United	H	W2-1
24.11.62	Bristol City	A	L1-2

Windsor & Eton

Date	Opponent	Venue	Result
12.11.82	Brentford	H	L0-7
Played at Griffin Park			
13.12.83	Bournemouth	H	D0-0
19.12.83	Bournemouth	A	L0-2
17.11.84	Gillingham	A	L1-2
16.11.85	Torquay United	H	D1-1
19.11.85	Torquay United	A	L0-3

Woking

Date	Opponent	Venue	Result	
27.11.26	Charlton Athletic	H	L1-3	
24.11.28	Newport County	A	L0-7	
15.11.58	Southampton	A	L1-4	
16.11.68	Brentford	A	L0-2	
16.12.78	Swansea City	A	D2-2	
19.12.78	Swansea City	H	L3-5	aet
19.11.88	Cambridge United	H	L1-4	
09.12.89	Cambridge United	A	L1-3	
05.01.91	West Bromwich Albion	A	W4-2	
27.01.91	Everton	A	L0-1	
04.01.92	Hereford United	H	D0-0	
14.01.92	Hereford United	A	L1-2	aet

Wokingham Town

Date	Opponent	Venue	Result
20.11.82	Cardiff City	H	D1-1
23.11.82	Cardiff City	A	L0-3

Worthing

Date	Opponent	Venue	Result
11.12.82	Oxford United	A	L0-4
12.11.94	Bournemouth	A	L1-3
30.10.99	Rotherham United	A	L0-3

Wycombe Wanderers

Date	Opponent	Venue	Result
26.11.32	Gillingham	A	D1-1
30.11.32	Gillingham	H	L2-4
15.11.58	Northampton Town	A	L0-2
05.12.59	Watford	A	L1-5
24.11.73	Newport County	H	W3-1
15.12.73	Peterborough United	H	L1-3
14.12.74	Bournemouth	H	D0-0
18.12.74	Bournemouth	A	W2-1
04.01.75	Middlesbrough	H	D0-0
07.01.75	Middlesbrough	A	L0-1
13.12.75	Cardiff City	A	L0-1
11.12.76	Reading	H	L1-2
22.11.80	Bournemouth	H	L0-3
20.11.82	Bristol Rovers	A	L0-1

Yeading

Date	Opponent	Venue	Result
13.11.93	Gillingham	H	D0-0
Played at Hayes FC			
30.11.93	Gillingham	A	L1-3
12.11.94	Colchester United	H	D2-2
22.11.94	Colchester United	A	L1-7
09.01.05	Newcastle United	H	L0-2
Played at QPR			

Yeovil Town

Date	Opponent	Venue	Result
16.11.85	Hereford United	H	L2-4
05.12.87	Cambridge United	A	W1-0
09.01.88	Queens Park Rangers	H	L0-3

The Longest FA Cup tie

FA CUP Fourth Qualifying Round: November 6, 1971

ALVECHURCH 2 OXFORD CITY 2

(Attendance 1,300)

ALVECHURCH looked like cruising through at the first attempt after taking an early two goal lead through Arthur Horne and Bobby Hope. But goals a minute either side of half-time from Bobby McCrae and John Woodley ensured a draw for Oxford on a heavy pitch. Oxford enjoyed the better of the second period but could not find a way through.

❑ ❑ ❑

1st Replay: November 9

OXFORD CITY 1 ALVECHURCH 1

(Attendance 1,100)

THE game was a bruising affair in which Oxford took a third minute lead through Tommy Eales but a goalkeeping error by Oxford keeper Peter Harris allowed Geoff Green to notch a 37th minute equaliser for Alvechurch. Harris made up for his error with a string of fine saves to deny Church victory in extra-time.

❑ ❑ ❑

2nd Replay: November 15

ALVECHURCH 1 OXFORD CITY 1

(Played at Birmingham City FC, Attendance 3,600)

IT WAS Alvechurch's turn to go in front when Graham Allner turned home a cross by Bobby Hope. But again Oxford equalised within a minute of the second half, this time through a Goucher header. By the end of the game the players were dropping with cramp and exhaustion.

❑ ❑ ❑

3rd Replay: November 17

ALVECHURCH 0 OXFORD CITY 0

(Played at Oxford United FC, Attendance 2,300)

THE closest thing to a winner came in the final minute of extra-time, the 449th minute of the tie. Oxford's Tommy Eales headed the ball powerfully towards goal but the ball agonisingly struck the underside of the crossbar, leaving hundreds of fans shaking their heads in disbelief. The game had started with exciting football but descended into a catalogue of mistakes.

❑ ❑ ❑

4th Replay: November 20

ALVECHURCH 0 OXFORD CITY 0

(Played at Oxford United FC, Attendance 1,900)

THE tie was played in bitterly cold weather with sleet and snow lashing the ground. Allner nearly won it for Alvechurch by striking the crossbar but the match was marred by the sad death of an Alvechurch fan who collapsed in the street moments after the end.

❑ ❑ ❑

5th Replay: November 22

ALVECHURCH 1 OXFORD CITY 0

(Played at Aston Villa FC, Attendance 1,952)

BOBBY Hope finally ended the record-breaking 11-hour stalemate with an 18th minute strike. Oxford's best chance fell to Tommy Eales who struck the bar from just three yards out.

The Longest FA Cup tie

THE FA AMATEUR CUP

The Isthmian League and The FA Amateur Cup were inextricably entwined in the 69 years the two competitions were simultaneously extant. Thirty victories for member clubs, plus more than a dozen for past or future teams, show just how much the clubs enjoyed this competition.

In the 1904–05 final, Clapton – who had already agreed to join the new League as one of the six founder members – lost 3–2 to West Hartlepool. In the first season, neither the Casuals, nor eventual champions London Caledonians made it to the first round proper. But Clapton did again and won an all-Isthmian tie 3–0 over Civil Service. Ilford fell to Cheshunt, but Ealing Association overcame Gosport United. Sadly the Isthmian interest ended in round two as Clapton lost to Cheshunt in a replay, while New Crusaders crushed Ealing 5–1. The eventual winners would join the Isthmian League just two years later – Oxford City.

F.A. AMATEUR CUP
(1893-1974)

Winners and Finalists whilst in membership of the League

Season	Club	Season	Club
1906-07	Clapton – winners	1951-52	Walthamstow Ave. – winners
1908-09	Clapton – winners	1955-56	Corinthian Cas. – runners-up
1910-11	Bromley – winners	1956-57	Wycombe Wand. – runners-up
1912-13	Oxford City – runners- up	1957-58	Woking – winners
1914-15	Clapton – winners		Ilford – runners-up
1919-20	Dulwich Hamlet – winners	1959-60	Kingstonian – runners-up
	Tufnell Park – runners-up	1960-61	Walthamstow Ave. – winners
1922-23	London Caledonians – winners	1962-63	Wimbledon – winners
1923-24	Clapton – winners	1963-64	Enfield – runners-up
1924-25	Clapton – winners	1964-65	Hendon – winners
1928-29	Ilford – winners	1965-66	Wealdstone – winners
1929-30	Ilford – winners		Hendon – runners-up
1930-31	Wycombe Wand. – winners	1966-67	Enfield – winners
1931-32	Dulwich Hamlet – winners	1967-68	Leytonstone – winners
1932-33	Kingstonian – winners	1968-69	Sutton United – runners-up
1933-34	Dulwich Hamlet – winners	1969-70	Enfield – winners
1934-35	Wimbledon – runners-up	1971-72	Hendon – winners
1935-36	The Casuals – winners		Enfield – runners-up
	Ilford – runners-up	1972-73	Walton & Hersham – winners
1936-37	Dulwich Hamlet – winners	1972-73	Slough Town – runners-up
1946-47	Leytonstone – winners	1973-74	Bishops Stortford – winners
	Wimbledon – runners-up		Ilford – runners-up
1947-48	Leytonstone – winners		
1948-49	Romford – runners-up		

In 1906–07, Clapton went all the way and goals from Russell and Rance were enough to give the Tons a 2–1 victory over Stockton – whose scorer was Chambers – at Stamford Bridge. Two years later, Clapton won the Cup again, this time crushing Eston United, a team of ironstone mineworkers, 6–0 in the final at Ilford.

Clapton reached the semi-final the following season but fell to South Bank. Future Isthmians Bromley won the Cup in 1911 while, two years later, Oxford City lost a second final, this time to South Bank of Middlesbrough after a replay.

In 1915, with many clubs already closed down for the First World War effort, Clapton, Ilford and London Caledonians reached the semi-finals. Sadly only Clapton advanced, but they did win another Cup, beating Bishop Auckland 1–0 at New Cross. Sherwood scored after 18 minutes, the Bishops having already missed a penalty and hit a post.

The first post-war Amateur Cup final pitted two Isthmian Clubs, Dulwich Hamlet and newcomers Tufnell Park, at Millwall. The game went into extra time and a goal from Edgar Kail was enough to give Hamlet the trophy.

Northern clubs dominated the next three seasons, but London Caledonians became the third Isthmian winners of the Cup in 1923, overcoming Evesham Town in another match requiring the extra 30 minutes. Sloan of Caleys and S. Jones had scored in the first half, but the winner came after 115 minutes, McGubbin finding the target for Caledonians.

Clapton recorded wins number four and five in the following two seasons, beating Erith & Belvedere 3–0 and Southall 2–1, both finals being played at Millwall. The Tons' fifth Amateur Cup in 18 years was to be their lot. After yet another future Isthmian club, Leyton, had won two in a row, in 1927 and 1928, Ilford denied them a hat-trick by winning the final in 1929. Drane, Peploe and Potter scored for Ilford, all in the first half at Highbury, where a then-record Amateur Cup final crowd of 35,000 watched with interest.

Ilford retained the trophy in 1930, beating Bournemouth Gasworks Athletic in the final at West Ham. Peploe was again on target – twice this time – and he was joined on the score sheet by team-mates Dellow, Welsh and Potter, while Pettey replied for the Hampshire club. Their hat-trick dreams were comprehensively ended in round three by Bishop Auckland, 6–2. But Wycombe Wanderers made it three in a row for the Isthmian League, overcoming Hayes courtesy of a Britnell goal in the final at Highbury.

The Chairboys saw their defence end in Yorkshire as Yorkshire Amateur crushed them 4–0 in round three. Liverpool club Marine made it to the final, but they were no match for Dulwich Hamlet, who equalled the Amateur Cup final record with a 7–1 victory at West Ham. Twelve years after the scoring the only goal in Hamlet's previous triumph Kail was on target again, twice, but he was overshadowed by Moseley, who grabbed a four-timer.

Kingstonian continued the great run for Isthmian clubs, winning the final in 1932–33, in a replay at Darlington. The Amateur Cup actually stayed at Dulwich a little longer than usual because Champion Hill was the venue for the first game. After a 1–1 draw, Ks made no mistake, winning 4–1 at Feethams. The 1934 final went to West Ham and Dulwich Hamlet collected the Amateur Cup for the third time, beating Leyton 2–1 in a dramatic contest. Hamlet finished with only seven fit players, but goals from Robbins and Court were enough for them to win the game.

Wimbledon could not make it seven straight for the Isthmians, losing to Bishop Auckland in the 1935 final. After a goalless first game at Middlesbrough, the Bishops scored twice after Dowden had given the Dons the lead. Wimbledon hit the woodwork twice in the second half, but they couldn't find an equaliser.

An all-Isthmian final in 1936 went the way of Casuals as they beat Ilford 2–0 in a replay at West Ham, after a 1–1 draw at Crystal Palace. More than 52,000 people watched the two games, the second of which was decided by goals from Shearer and Amateur International "Tadge" Webster – later President of the MCC.

Dulwich Hamlet and Leyton met for the second time in three years in 1937, also at West Ham. Amazingly, only four players, Morrish, Murray, Robbins and Toser – all of the Hamlet – were in the teams for both games, with Morrish scoring both goals as Dulwich won their fourth Amateur Cup in four finals. Another oddity in this final was that both teams missed a penalty.

That was the end of the Isthmians' great run of success. In 1938, Dulwich went out at the quarter-final stage, although Bromley did win the trophy against Erith & Belvedere. A year later, Leytonstone lost a semi-final replay against Bishop Auckland, who beat Willington at Sunderland to record their seventh win in the final. Thanks to the outbreak of the Second World War in 1939, it would be ten years between Isthmian clubs holding the Amateur Cup.

The Amateur Cup resumed in 1945 and goals flew in. Three future Isthmian Clubs, Aylesbury United, Harrow Town (later Borough) and Edgware Town all reached double figures in the first qualifying round, although none made it to the competition proper in January 1946. In the first round, at Richmond Road, Kingstonian held Wycombe Wanderers to a 1–1 draw. When the sides went to Loakes Park for the replay, it all went horribly wrong for the Ks, who shipped in 10 goals, six from Avery, while netting just one themselves. The 11-goal aggregate from that replay was surpassed in the next round when Walthamstow Avenue needed two bites of the cherry to beat Wycombe. A 1–1 draw at Loakes Park was followed by a 7–5 victory for the Avenue at Green Pond Road.

Wimbledon's Amateur Cup Finalists, 1946-47. Back row, left to right: Dowden (manager), Jones, Walker, Head, Haydock, Lober, Magill, Price (coach). Front row: Clark, Nash, Wallis, Lemmer, Cousins, Stannard, Edelston.

Walthamstow, who had already beaten Dulwich Hamlet in the first round, ended the hopes of Bromley in round three and Ilford in the quarter-final. But their run ended in the semi-final when Bishop Auckland beat them 2–1 at Darlington. The Bishops were beaten by Athenian League Barnet in a five-goal thriller of a final at Chelsea.

The Isthmian League Amateur Cup headline makers from 1945–46 exited quietly, Walthamstow losing to Leytonstone and Wycombe to Enfield, both in the first round. It was a south-east dominated season, with only Lowestoft and Bishop Auckland making the last eight from outside the region.

There were three four-goal victories at this stage, Barnet and the Bishops beating Lowestoft and Bromley 5–1, but the eyebrow-raiser was at Plough Lane, where Tilbury scored four times but still were hammered in a 12-goal spectacular. The two finalists from 1946 lost to Isthmian opposition in the semi-finals, Leytonstone topping Barnet at Brentford and Wimbledon seeing off Bishop Auckland at Dulwich.

The final was a very tight affair. Stannard gave the Dons an early lead, but the Stones hit back with goals from Noble and Smith to reach half-time with a narrow lead. Wimbledon threw everything at Leytonstone, but they came up just short, a brilliant save by Jarvis denying Stannard a second goal, their best effort.

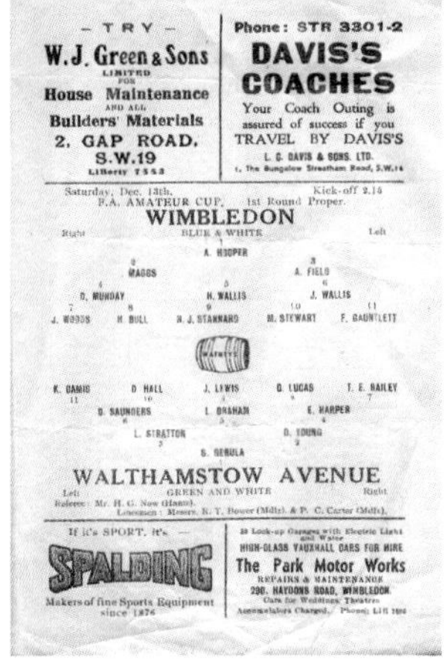

Above: the teams that lined up for Wimbledon's FA Amateur Cup match with Walthamstow Avenue during the early fifties.

Leytonstone retained their trophy in 1948, beating their predecessors Barnet in the final. Without the advantage of a home tie on their way to the final, at least Leytonstone didn't have to travel far – Wealdstone and Erith & Belvedere being their longest trips. Dulwich Hamlet and Wycombe Wanderers were the only other Isthmian League clubs to make the quarter-finals and they fell, away at Barnet and Bishop Auckland respectively.

A crowd of almost 60,000 was crammed into Stamford Bridge to witness the Stones and Bees locked in a dour defensive struggle. The breakthrough was made by Reg Groves and his solitary strike was enough to keep the Amateur Cup in east London.

The 1948–49 competition was a watershed in The FA Amateur Cup. It heralded the entry of Pegasus, a joint Oxford–Cambridge University squad, which eschewed league competition, but still won the Amateur Cup twice. In addition, the final was moved to a new, permanent home, Wembley Stadium – the largest in the land.

Pegasus reached the quarter-finals without meeting Isthmian opposition in the competition proper. When they did, Bromley – who had brushed aside Maidenhead, Wimbledon and Barking – came out victorious, 4–3 at Iffley Road. They beat Leytonstone 2–0 in the semi-finals at Stamford Bridge and faced Romford at Wembley in the final. A crowd of 93,000 turned up, attracting gate receipts of more than £20,000 – both records for amateur football in England – and they were treated to a close final, decided by Hopper's goal from Bromley midway through the opening half. Romford laid siege to the Bromley goal in the second half but could not find an equaliser. The 1950s was a rather barren decade for Isthmian clubs in the Amateur Cup. There were only two victories to celebrate in ten competitions and four other teams were runners-up. Bromley opened their defence in style, hammering Thameside Amateurs 11–2 in round one, but they were upset by Cheshunt Sports in the next round. Barking and Wycombe Wanderers reached the semi-finals in 1949–50, but both fell at that stage, to Willington at Middlesbrough and Bishop Auckland at Brentford, respectively. Willington crushed the Bishops 4–0 in the Final.

Bromley, Oxford City and Wimbledon made it to the quarter-finals in 1950–51, but only Bromley advanced, beating Barnet. Wimbledon went out after a replay against Hendon, while Pegasus saw off near neighbours Oxford City. Bishop Auckland overcame Bromley 3–2 at Leeds to reach the final, where Pegasus beat them, this after they had seen Hendon miss a penalty in the last minute of the semi-final before winning a replay.

Walthamstow Avenue finally won the Amateur Cup in 1952. But they and Wimbledon were the only two Isthmian clubs to reach the last eight. The Dons fell to the Avenue at the quarter-final stage, albeit in a second replay at Highbury after a goalless draw at Plough Lane and a 1–1 stalemate at Higham Hill. In the Final, in front of 100,000 fans, Leyton, in their 13th game of the competition excluding an abandonment in the qualifying rounds, found it a step too far. Jim Lewis and Hall scored, the latter late in extra time to give Walthamstow victory.

Pegasus regained the trophy in 1953, hammering Harwich & Parkeston 6–0 in the Final. It was the first time in half a century that none of the Northern, Athenian or Isthmian Leagues had a representative in the final, Leytonstone, Tooting & Mitcham United and Romford all falling in the quarter-final.

The 1953–54 competition took a while to be completed because there were many close ties. Leytonstone and Wycombe Wanderers needed two replays to sort out their second-round tie, the Chairboys prevailing at Dulwich. Walthamstow Avenue went out at the semi-final stage, losing to Crook Town in a replay at Sunderland, after beating Finchley at the second attempt in the previous round. Crook needed no second bidding in the last eight as they put ten past Hitchin Town. The final was a different matter and Crook finally overcame Bishop Auckland in a second replay at Middlesbrough after draws at Wembley and Newcastle. The combined attendance for the Final was more than 192,000.

Bishop Auckland made no mistake the following year, beating Hendon 2–0 in the Final, the last one to attract a 100,000 gate. Walthamstow crushed Ware 11–0 in the second round, but fell to Hendon a round later, the same stage at which Kingstonian were routed 12–3 by the eventual winners. Wycombe were the sole Isthmian representatives in the semi-final; Wimbledon had bowed out against Hendon in the last eight.

Corinthian–Casuals flew the flag proudly for the Isthmian League in 1955–56, losing a final replay against Bishop Auckland at Middlesbrough after a draw at Wembley. Three out of the four semi-finalists were from the Isthmian League, with Dulwich losing to the Casuals and Kingstonian, although improving by five goals on their 1955 performance, were still 5–1 losers to Bishop Auckland. In the final Kerruish gave Corinthian–Casuals the lead, but McKenna equalised with 12 minutes to go. Micky Stewart, on tour with the England cricket team in the West Indies, fell victim to the vagaries of 1950s air travel and failed to arrive at Ayresome Park in time. Fellow England cricketer Doug Insole – not selected for the tour –

had played in the first game, but although Citron gave the Casuals an early lead, Bishop Auckland hit back with four unanswered goals to win 4–1.

The balance of power in the Amateur Cup was definitely moving south, although Bishop Auckland completed a hat-trick – their last victory – in 1956–57. Five quarter-finalists were Isthmian clubs – and a sixth, Hayes, would join within 15 years – and two would reach the last four. Unfortunately, Corinthian–Casuals and Wycombe Wanderers met in the semi-final and the Chairboys went through 4–2 at Highbury. Hayes fell to Bishop Auckland at Newcastle. Two of the Bishops' stalwarts, Bob Hardisty and Jimmy Nimmins, were appearing in their sixth final, and fourth in a row. And this experience helped them to win 3–1 against the first-time finalists from Buckinghamshire. Smith cancelled out Russell's opener, but Lewin restored the advantage within two minutes and Bradley added a third later on.

The 1958 Final was an all-Isthmian affair, Woking beating Ilford 3–0 in a rather one-sided affair at Wembley. Corinthian–Casuals had enjoyed a 10–0 round victory over Salts, before losing at home to Crook Town in a replay. But the fairy-tale came from Wokingham Town, who lost to Crook in the quarter-final, this after finding out that one of their players in the previous round – against West Auckland Town – had been ineligible, so they had to replay the game. The Cardinals' hero was inside-right Hebdon, who scored twice. In between Ilford battled hard, but conceded a goal on the break to Stratton. It was Woking's first Amateur Cup win.

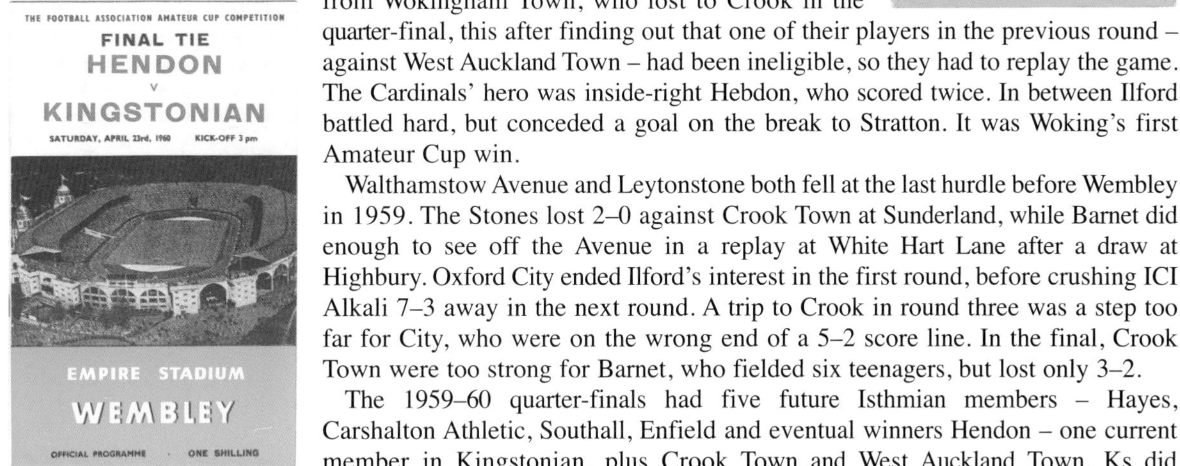

Walthamstow Avenue and Leytonstone both fell at the last hurdle before Wembley in 1959. The Stones lost 2–0 against Crook Town at Sunderland, while Barnet did enough to see off the Avenue in a replay at White Hart Lane after a draw at Highbury. Oxford City ended Ilford's interest in the first round, before crushing ICI Alkali 7–3 away in the next round. A trip to Crook in round three was a step too far for City, who were on the wrong end of a 5–2 score line. In the final, Crook Town were too strong for Barnet, who fielded six teenagers, but lost only 3–2.

The 1959–60 quarter-finals had five future Isthmian members – Hayes, Carshalton Athletic, Southall, Enfield and eventual winners Hendon – one current member in Kingstonian, plus Crook Town and West Auckland Town. Ks did magnificently to see off Carshalton 4–0 and Crook Town 2–1, at Newcastle, but were robbed at the very death in the final. Johnny Whing capitalised on an error from Charlie Murphy to give Kingstonian the lead in the final. It stayed 1–0 until the 87th minute, when Laurie Topp equalised. Within a matter of seconds, Terry Howard had given Hendon the lead, but the Dons had to survive a close shave in injury time as Oakes hit a post.

No less than nine first-round ties in 1960–61 required replays, though Leytonstone were the only Isthmians to need a second chance to advance, which they took, 5–0 against Bungay Town. Walthamstow Avenue won a replay against Hendon at the White City to end the holders' interest and they took on their mantle too. Dulwich Hamlet were embarrassed 7–1 at Harwich & Parkeston in the second round, but the Avenue gained Isthmian revenge almost as emphatically at Dovercourt, winning 7–2. Victory at Wimbledon in the quarter-final was followed by another trip to White City for the Avenue, this time in the last four. And the West London venue was to their liking again as Hitchin were sent packing 1–0. West Auckland, who had ended Leytonstone's interest in the other semi-final, were in uncompromising mood in the Final. Avenue inside left Saggers was left a passenger in the opening minute and Douglass gave Wests a lead. Reg Groves equalised, pouncing on a rebound after Jim Lewis had hit a post. Bad weather hit Wembley in the second half, but the Avenue would not be denied, Lewis scoring the winner after Dave Andrews' cross had been dropped.

No Isthmian team made it to the last four in 1962, with Bromley – after a replay – Wimbledon and Leytonstone all falling by the wayside. The biggest shock for some years had come in the first round when Aetolian League Ford United had dumped holders Walthamstow out of the competition, 2–0 at Higham Hill. At the same stage, Pegasus made their last appearance in the competition proper, losing a replay 6–1 to Hendon, whose goals came from Miles Spector and David Bell, both hat-tricks. A year later and Pegasus was no more. Hounslow, Bromley's conquerors, were the only southern team in the semi-finals, and they made it to the final too, but Crook Town – with future European Cup winner Frank Clark in their squad - took the Cup 4–0 after a replay.

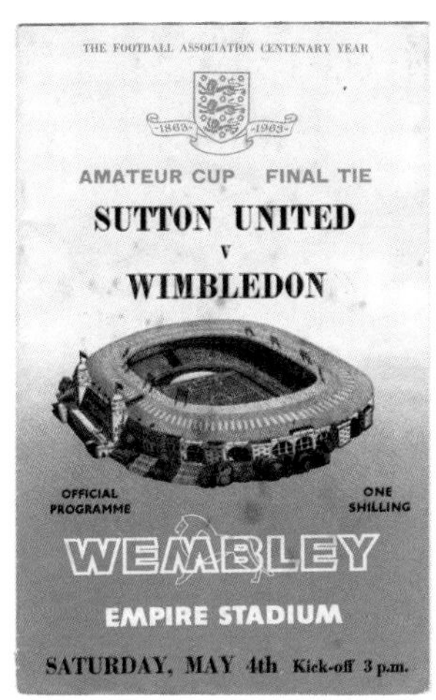

The dismal winter of 1962–63 meant a chaotic competition, which somehow was completed by 4 May, albeit a couple of weeks behind schedule. And the less bad weather in the south certainly seemed to be advantageous, with Hitchin Town and Bishops Stortford being the most northerly quarter-finalists. Two Isthmian teams reached the Final – one in membership, the other already accepted as a newcomer for 1963–64. Sutton United were in their first Final, while Wimbledon were in their third, but first for 16 years. This game will be remembered for ever more as the Eddie Reynolds Final because the Wimbledon centre-forward did something that remains probably unique in all senior football. He scored four times, all with his head, and all in the second half too, as the Dons won 4–2. Only one other player, Denis Wilshaw, had ever scored four times at Wembley before Reynolds.

Another of the Isthmian newcomers for 1963–64 were finalists that season, Enfield, who lost 2–1 to Crook Town. Holders Wimbledon, in their final season in the amateur ranks, went out to the E's at Southbury Road, 2–0 in round three. The busiest team in the competition proper was Walthamstow Avenue who, after winning 5–0 at Eastbourne, needed three replays to beat Bromley in the second round, a second go to beat Carshalton at the next stage and then had nothing left for a quarter-final replay at Crook Town. The north-easterners saw off Barnet in one semi-final at Newcastle; the other between Enfield and Kingstonian needed two goes, before Enfield advanced. In the final, Roger Day gave Enfield the lead, but they lost goalkeeper Mitchell with a broken arm before half-time, Thomas going in goal. The handicap proved too much, as Goodfellow and Brown netted for Crook.

Hendon won their first Amateur Cup as Isthmian League members in 1965, beating first-time finalists Whitby Town 3–1 in the Final. Kingstonian made the early-round headlines, beating Callenders Athletic 10–0 away in round one and Speenymoor United 11–2 at Richmond Road at the next stage. A goalless draw at Bromley was followed by a 4–2 replay victory, making it an aggregate of 25–2. Alas for them, Finchley won a quarter-final at Kingston, 2–0. Hounslow Town also scored ten in round one, beating Alton Town, but they fell at the next hurdle, 4–1 at Carshalton. After overcoming Sutton United, Leytonstone and Carshalton, Hendon then made the long trip to Whitley Bay, fostering a friendship that lasted for more than 25 years. A semi-final victory over Finchley gave the Greens a final berth against Enfield's conquerors, Whitby Town. Once again all the action came in the second half. David Hyde scored twice and Jimmy Quail – the only Dons survivor from the 1960 Final – once, while Mulvaney was on target for the north Yorkshire club. In addition Danny Lakey of Hendon and Mulvaney hit the goal frame after the interval.

Wealdstone denied Hendon the rare privilege of being successful defenders of their crown, winning the 1966 Final 3–1. Sutton United scored seven and five goals against Clapton and Dagenham, respectively, in reaching round three, where Bishop Auckland were despatched by a more mundane 2–1 at Gander Green Lane. Whitley Bay ended the Us interest at the last eight stage, only to fall again to Hendon, also in the North-East, but at Sunderland. Wealdstone had beaten Hitchin Town, Tow Law and Barking to reach the quarter-final, where they ended Leatherhead's surprising run. A semi-final victory over Alvechurch put them in their first final. Geoff Riddy gave Hendon a perfect start, scoring after four minutes, but Bobby Childs – who would win another Amateur Cup with Hendon in 1972 – equalised just before half-time. Billy Bremer gave Wealdstone the lead in the 88th minute and Childs rounded off a famous day for Wealdstone with a stoppage-time third goal.

Enfield finally got their hands on the trophy in 1966–67, but it was hard work for the north Londoners, tinged with tragedy. Their first three matches were relatively unremarkable, Sutton United, Wembley and Leytonstone – after a replay – were beaten to set up a quarter-final tie at Highgate United from the Midlands. The match will be remembered for the thunderstorm that hit the ground in the second half and the bolt of lightning that took the life of Highgate midfielder Tony Allden. The match was abandoned, with the replay at Villa Park. There, in front of more than 30,000 fans, Enfield made no mistake, winning 6–0. Wealdstone's defence ended in round three, where Skelmersdale United won at Lower Mead. Three other Isthmian clubs made the quarter-finals, Hendon, who beat Leatherhead 3–0 at Fetcham Grove and Walthamstow Avenue, who crushed Kingstonian 5–0. Enfield beat Walthamstow 1–0 in one semi-final, while Hendon lost an epic to Skelmersdale 3–1 in a second replay at West Bromwich. In the second game at Birmingham City – the first, at Derby, ended goalless – Hendon defender Mickey Cooper equalised in the dying moments of extra time with a hopeful downfield kick that eluded everyone and ended up in the net to make it 2–2. The Final at Wembley ended goalless, with Ian Wolstenholme the E's hero, saving a penalty from Alan Bermingham in the last minute of normal time. Enfield made no mistake in the replay at Maine Road, winning 3–0, with Hill scoring twice after John Connell had given them the lead.

EMPIRE STADIUM · WEMBLEY
The Football Association
AMATEUR
CHALLENGE CUP COMPETITION
FINAL TIE
Saturday, April 22, 1967
KICK-OFF 3 p.m.
SOUTH TERRACE 10/-
ENTER K TURNSTILE | ENTRANCE 40 | ROW 10 | SEAT 235

Chesham United showed what was possible in the 1967–68 competition, going all the way from the preliminary round to the final, where they fell to Leytonstone in a dramatic game. Their 17 matches included ties against Hemel Hempstead Town, Didcot Town, Hazells (Aylesbury), Marlow and Soham Town Rangers, just to reach the first round proper. Thereafter, Maidenhead United, Dulwich Hamlet, Corinthian-Casuals and Oxford City all fell after replays to the Generals. In the semi-final, at Fulham, a single goal was enough to give Chesham a place in the final. After beating Clapton and Southall, Leytonstone hammered Bishop's Stortford 7–2 at Granleigh Road to reach the quarter-finals, where they needed three games to finally end Enfield's interest. The Stones also needed a replay in the semi-final to overcome Sutton United. At Wembley, Leytonstone used their substitute Albon after just a few minutes because Hamer was injured. Sadly the substitute then broke his leg, leaving the Stones with only ten men. The only goal came after 70 minutes, Kenny Gray converting a Les Tilley cross after Chesham goalkeeper Wells had dropped the ball. In the last minute, Hadlow saved Kent's penalty to preserve Leytonstone's lead and give them the Cup.

A new name was guaranteed to go on the Amateur Cup in 1968–69 as Sutton United made their second appearance in the final playing North Shields, in their first final. Enfield's run was ended by Skelmersdale, who gained revenge for their Final defeat 22 months earlier with a quarter-final victory at Southbury Road. The E's had needed replays in each of their three earlier rounds, beating Leatherhead at the third attempt, and Cheshunt and Harwich & Parkeston, both at the second. Wealdstone made even heavier weather of their first round tie with Hertford, finally prevailing 1–0 in a fourth replay. They eventually went out in the quarter-final. Five Isthmian clubs were in the quarter-finals, but only Sutton, conquerors of Leytonstone, made it to the last four. Barking were crushed by Whitley Bay, who then lost 4–2 to Sutton at Birmingham. In the Final, Micky Mellows gave Sutton the lead after four minutes but Hall equalised for North Shields and Brian Joicey scored the winner for them.

Two Isthmian teams made it to the semi-finals in 1969–70, Enfield and St. Albans City. Saints needed two replays to beat Wembley in round one, which was where the holders fell, North Shields losing to Evenwood, also in a second replay. Replays were the order of the day, with eight first-round ties, five in the second round, three in the third and a semi-final ending in stalemate. Evenwood's run ended at Hendon, 4–2, in a round two replay – a tie which saw the Greens go to the north-east three times: first for an abandonment while leading 2–1, then for a postponement and finally for a 1–1 draw. A strange feature of this season's competition was that, in the last 19 matches, only five times did both teams score and in three of those the matches ended in draws. Enfield were the team to concede in winning games on both occasions, winning 5–2 at Alton Town, then 5–1 over Dagenham in the final at Wembley. The final was a disappointment, because Enfield were simply too canny for the Daggers. John Connell scored twice, with other goals coming from Feely, Adams and a Daniels own goal; Rod Brookes got Dagenham's consolation.

In 1970–71, Isthmian clubs spent much of the competition knocking each other out. St. Albans saw off Bromley, Wycombe ousted Wealdstone, Leytonstone did for Sutton and Walthamstow Avenue overcame Ilford, and that was just in the first round. In round two, Hendon beat Barking, Leytonstone got past Kingstonian, while Wycombe ended holders Enfield's interest. It meant that by the quarter-finals, only Wycombe remained, and they were beaten by Skelmersdale at Loakes Park. Five future members also reached the last eight, Aveley losing to Slough Town at Mill Field, Dagenham overcoming Whitley Bay and Leatherhead advancing after a replay against Hayes. Dagenham needed a replay to end Slough's interest in the last four, while Skelmersdale downed Leatherhead in the other game. The Cheshire side were too strong for the Daggers in the final, winning 4–1 with Dickin scoring a hat-trick, two in the first half. Tony Bass reduced the arrears 12 minutes into the second half, but Windsor made it 3–1 before Dickin added a fourth late on.

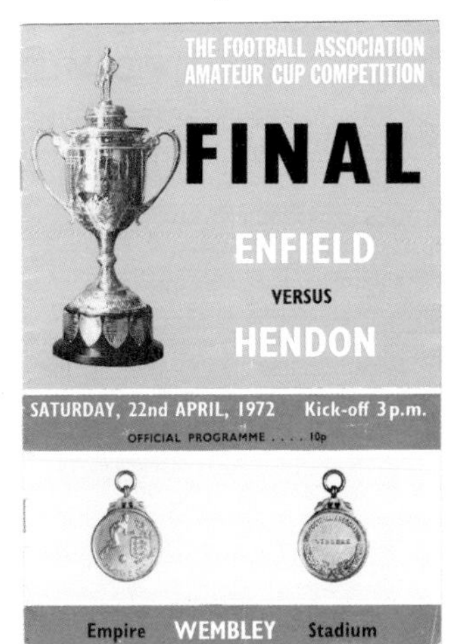

In 1971–72, Isthmian newcomers Hayes joined Enfield, Hendon, Hitchin Town and Wycombe Wanderers in the quarter-finals, along with Leatherhead and Slough Town, who would join in 1972–73 and 1973–74, respectively. The outsiders were Blyth Spartans, who would fall to Enfield in the semi-final. Hendon ended Hitchin's interest in the last eight and were somewhat surprising winners of the semi-final against Wycombe at Brentford. It set up another all-Isthmian final and, not unusually, an intra-county battle too, this time the all-Middlesex contest between Hendon and Enfield. Enfield did most of the pressing but after Mick

Smith had deflected John Baker's shot past Andy Williams after 33 minutes, it was in a losing cause. In the last couple of minutes, Hendon broke quickly, won a corner and Bobby Childs' inch-perfect delivery was headed home by Tony Bass, who thus scored in consecutive finals for different teams.

In 1972–73, Walton & Hersham set a new Amateur Cup record by winning the competition without conceding a goal. Two of the semi-finalists from 1972 met in the second round, with Blyth Spartans ending Hendon's interest in a replay at Claremont Road, after a draw at Croft Park. Bishop's Stortford and Walton & Hersham, two of the newcomers to the Isthmian League, were the only two representatives to make it to the last eight, with both advancing, albeit after replays against Dagenham and Spennymoor United, respectively. It could not be an all-Isthmian final because the two teams met in the semi-final, though there was the next best thing with Slough Town, three months from their League bow, advancing to meet Walton at Wembley. The game was a very tight affair on a foul afternoon and it looked certain to go to extra time, until Roger Connell headed home to give the Swans their first Amateur Cup.

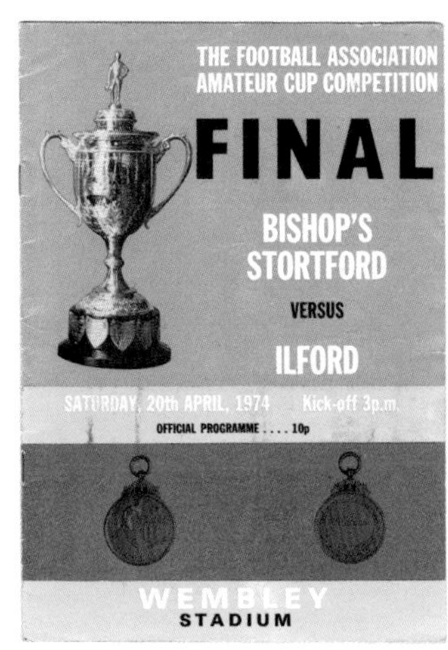

The last season of the competition produced another all-Isthmian final, with Bishop's Stortford claiming the honour of being the last winners after trouncing Ilford 4–1. Hendon played nine matches in the competition, but didn't make it past the third round, losing a second replay to Leatherhead at Wycombe after needing four games to beat Harwich & Parkeston and two more to see off Tilbury. The Tanners made it all the way to the semi-final, where Ilford ended their run. Other Isthmian quarter-finalists were Woking, Dulwich Hamlet and Sutton United. Ilford were the season's surprise packets, having struggled in the League for much of the season, but were resurgent under Hendon's 1972 Cup-winning boss John Evans. But, in the final, the canny Ted Hardy led a powerful and very experienced Bishops Stortford outfit to a comprehensive victory. Dave Lawrence opened the scoring for the Bishops and Murphy extended the lead before John Drabwell reduced the arrears for Ilford. But Leakey restored the two-goal lead and Smith converted a late penalty to make it 4–1. It was the last goal in the Amateur Cup.

THE FA TROPHY

There is a myth that Isthmian League clubs fared poorly in the first five seasons of what is now the premier knock-out competition in Non-League Football. This is untrue, because until the 1974–75 competition, no Isthmian League clubs even entered. The reason for this is quite simple: as has been seen earlier in this volume, Isthmian League clubs were amateur until the designation was removed in the summer of 1974, and all clubs played in The FA Amateur Cup until then.

It would, however, be perfectly fair to say that Isthmian League clubs have not enjoyed anything like the success they had in The FA Amateur Cup, but the quality of opposition was significantly higher in The FA Trophy, with clubs from the Southern League and Northern Premier League and, latterly the Alliance Premier League/Conference participating. Nevertheless, there have been a few memorable moments for Isthmian League clubs.

F.A. CHALLENGE TROPHY
(inaugurated 1969)

Winners and Finalists whilst in membership of the League

1976-77	Dagenham – runners-up
1977-78	Leatherhead – runners-up
1979-80	Dagenham – winners
1980-81	Bishops Stortford – winners
	Sutton United – runners-up
1996-97	Dagenham & Redbridge – runners-up
2000-01	Canvey Island - winners
2003-04	Canvey Island - runners-up

In that first season of "open" football, three Isthmian League clubs reached the last 16 of The FA Trophy, but both Enfield and Ilford bowed out at that stage, against Scarborough and Matlock Town, respectively, the latter in a replay. They turned out to be the two finalists, too, with Matlock triumphing 4–0 at Wembley. Dagenham, those sturdy cup-fighters, were the last survivors, but they fell in the quarter-finals at home to Burton Albion.

In 1975–76, the last 16 again contained three Isthmian League clubs, Harwich & Parkeston (from Division Two as it was then), Slough Town and Enfield, again. Bedford Town and Runcorn saw off Harwich and Slough, but Enfield advanced to the semi-finals, where a solitary goal from eventual winners Scarborough at Seamer Road was enough to decide the two-legged tie.

The first Isthmian League finalists appeared in 1977 and it was Dagenham who flew the flag at Wembley. Slough also reached the last 16, and indeed the last four.

However hopes of an all-Isthmian League final were dashed by the draw which pitted the Rebels and Daggers together. The other semi-final saw Scarborough and Altrincham meet four times before the Yorkshire club advanced to their third straight final. Dagenham all but booked their final berth in the first leg, winning 3–0 at Victoria Road; the second led ended 3–2 in their favour too. Sadly the final may be remembered more for two deaths than the football. Moments after Dagenham had taken a first-half lead through Terry Harris, the father-in-law of Laurie Wilkinson, the Daggers' manager, collapsed and died of a heart attack. Scarborough attacked strongly in the second half and Harry A Dunn converted a late penalty to equalise. In stoppage time Abbey grabbed a winner for the Yorkshire side. And, 48 hours later, one of the Scarborough team died of a seizure.

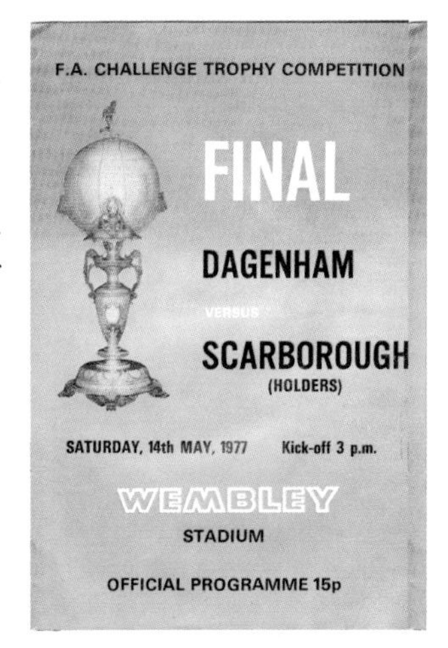

Twelve months later, Dagenham went out in the quarter-finals and the new standard bearers were Leatherhead, who went all the way to Wembley after beating Spennymoor United 3–2 on aggregate in the semi-final, winning the Fetcham Grove first leg 2–0 and hanging on up in the North East. Sadly Altrincham were too strong in the final, winning 3–1. Alty scored after two minutes through Rogers and Johnson added a second before half-time. Chris Kelly watched an effort bounce off the Altrincham woodwork before John King scored their third goal. Micky Cook got a consolation for the Tanners late on.

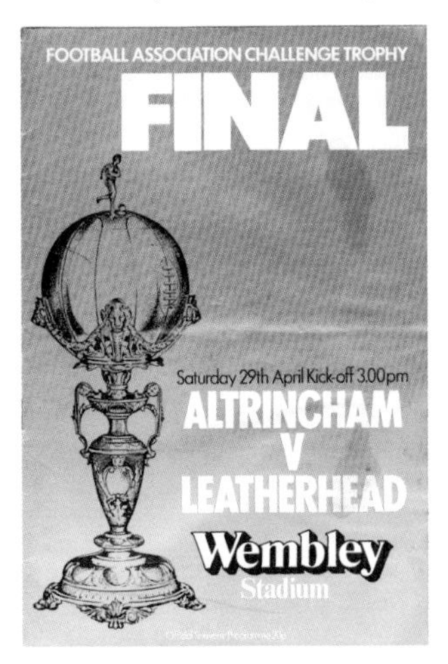

Getting four clubs into the last 16 was finally achieved in 1978–79 and the League went one better with five. Enfield crushed Cheltenham Town 4–0 at Whaddon Road, Dagenham overcame Witton Albion in a second replay, Hayes needed two games to see off Wycombe Wanderers, while Leatherhead were the other losers, in an all green-and-white match against Yeovil Town. The quarter-finals were a step too far for Enfield, who went out in a replay, and Hayes, while Dagenham lost to eventual runners-up Kettering Town in the semi-final. A solitary goal in the second leg, at Rockingham Road, was enough to settle the tie.

The first Isthmian League winners were Dagenham, who triumphed in 1980. They were one of three in the last 16, Woking and Dulwich Hamlet were the other two, and they all reached the quarter-finals. The Hamlet did the hard work against Boston United, drawing at York Street, but they lost the replay at Champion Hill. Dagenham and Woking both advanced to the last four, the Daggers 3–2 at home to Nuneaton Borough, the Cards 2–0 winners against Barrow at Kingfield. Once again, the draw pitted the two Isthmian League clubs together and the Daggers greater Trophy experience probably stood them in good stead as they won 3–1 at Kingfield and 4–1 at Victoria Road. In the Final, Mossley provided the opposition and it provided cracking entertainment. Veteran goalscorer George Duck got the Daggers' first with a header, but Mossley equalised through Smith. The winner came from 21-year-old Chris Maycock, who finished off a mazy run with a powerful shot into the roof of the Mossley net.

Any thoughts that shenanigans were being used to keep Isthmian League teams apart in the final were finally disproved in 1980–81. Hitchin Town, Bishop's Stortford, Carshalton Athletic, Sutton United and Leytonstone/Ilford all made it to the last 16 and they were all kept apart. Sutton and Stortford were the only survivors and they both won their quarter-finals too. The semi-finals pitted Sutton United with Bangor City and Dartford with Bishop's Stortford, with the Isthmian clubs travelling in the first leg, where they achieved draws. Both then won their home legs to set up the all-Isthmian League final. Sadly, familiarity rather bred contempt, because the game was nothing to write home about. Indeed, the only mercy was that Joe Sullivan's winner came in the 88th minute and not the 118th! For Bishop's Stortford it was a case of lucky 13, because the final was their 13th match in the competition that season. John Radford the Stortford striker became the first player to win an FA Trophy medal after winning both Football League Championship and FA Cup winners' medals.

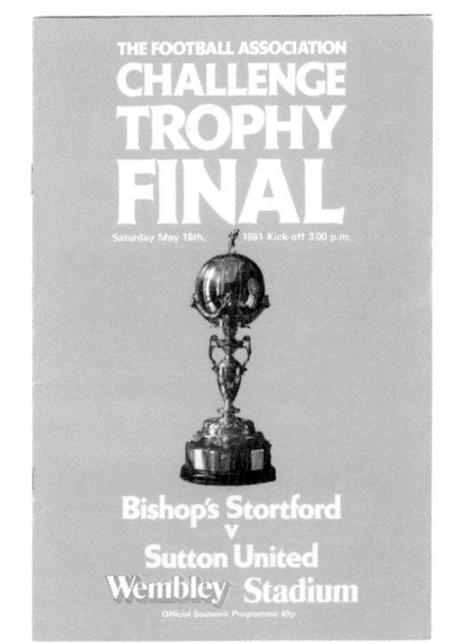

The Alliance Premier League was now clearly the strongest league in the country and for the Northern Premier League, Southern League and Isthmian League, success in The FA Trophy became a very rare treasure. With Enfield and Dagenham having defected to the Alliance, there were nonetheless four Isthmian League teams in the last 16, defending champions Bishop's Stortford, Slough Town, Sutton United and Wycombe Wanderers. Sutton and Slough perished in replays, while the other two advanced. Stortford went out in the quarter-finals, Wycombe in the semis and it was former Isthmian League powerhouse Enfield who clinched the Trophy, beating Altrincham 1–0 on Paul Taylor's goal. Tony Jennings lifted the Trophy after the game and he became only the second player to win both FA Amateur Cup and FA Trophy winners' medals, having played for Hendon – against Enfield coincidentally – in the 1972 Amateur Cup.

Harrow Borough and Tilbury were the only two Isthmian League representatives in the last 16 in 1982–83 and the Dockers went out to cross-Thames rivals Dartford at that stage. Borough, however, needed two replays to finally see off Barrow and they reached the semi-final too. The first leg, against Telford United, was at the Bucks Head and Harrow won 2–0. Two minutes into the second leg at Earlsmead they scored again, thus taking a 3–0 aggregate lead. Incredibly they continued to attack with reckless abandon and Telford gradually picked them off, scoring their third of the afternoon in the final minutes of normal time. In extra time Telford got a fourth and a fifth. Harrow exited, broken-hearted. Twelve months later, a much more negative Harrow Borough team won the Isthmian League title. There's a moral in there somewhere!

The tenth season of Isthmian League involvement in The FA Trophy saw the worst performance to date. Dulwich Hamlet were the sole representatives in the last 16 and they went out to eventual winners Northwich Victoria in a second replay at that stage.

If anything, things got even worse a year later. Harrow Borough were the only Isthmian League members to reach the last 16, although three former clubs did so, and Borough were crushed 6–1 at home by Enfield. Maidstone lost to Enfield in quarter-finals, and the E's went down to eventual Trophy winners Wealdstone in the final. Wealdstone also completed the first Conference/Trophy double – beating Boston United in the Final – but could not rise to the Football League.

In 1985–86, Worthing and Bishop's Stortford reached the last 16 but exited there after replays of 0–0 draws, to Kettering Town and Cheltenham Town, respectively. Former and future Isthmians Wycombe, who would rejoin the League in 1986–87, lost to Kettering in the quarter-finals. Enfield lost in the semis to eventual winners Altrincham.

This miserable lack of success continued in 1986–87, with only Aylesbury United making it to the last 16, where they lost in a replay to Dagenham. In fact, it was pretty bad for former clubs too, with Dagenham and Maidstone United both losing in the quarter-finals. Kidderminster Harriers won the Trophy, needing a replay to beat Burton Albion after an awful goalless draw at Wembley.

There was another dire Wembley showpiece a year later, with Enfield beating Telford United 3–2 in a replay after a goalless first game. Telford had been too strong for the last Isthmian representatives, Wokingham Town, winning the two-legged semi-final 1–0 at Finchampstead Road and 2–0 at the Bucks Head. Leyton Wingate had also made it to the last 16, but they fell to Macclesfield.

In 1988–89, Woking and Windsor & Eton both reached the last 16, but Newcastle Blue Star and Hyde United defeated them, the latter in a replay. Telford United won the Trophy again, beating Macclesfield Town with a solitary goal in the Final.

Northern domination continued the following year as Barrow – who ended Kingstonian's hopes in the quarter-finals – crushed Leek Town 3–0 in the final. Stafford Rangers – conquerors of Redbridge Forest in the last 16 – and Colne Dynamoes were the other two teams in the last four.

Redbridge Forest made it back to the last 16 in 1990–91, but Horwich RMI won 2–1 at home to end their dreams for another season. The other Isthmian League Club at this stage were Wivenhoe Town, who were drawn away to Colchester United in a local derby. The Conference club won 3–0 at Layer Road. But there was joy for a former Isthmian Club as Wycombe Wanderers overcame Kidderminster Harriers 2–1 in the final.

For a third season running, Redbridge Forest were the last Isthmian League representative standing, and in 1991–92 they made it to the quarter-finals, where a home defeat in a replay against Marine saw the end of their hopes. Colchester United completed a Conference/FA Trophy double beating Witton Albion 3–1 in the final.

Two Isthmian members reached the last 16 for the first time in 1992–93 when Chesham United and Grays Athletic got to this stage. Sutton United saw off the Generals at the Meadow, while Grays lost a replay at Gateshead after a 1–1 draw at the Recreation Ground. Wycombe Wanderers became the latest team to win both The FA Trophy – they beat Sutton in the semi-final and Runcorn 4–1 in the final – and the Conference championship.

Long-time Isthmians Woking, by now in the Conference, won The FA Trophy in 1993–94, having ended Enfield's interest in the semi-finals. The Es' performance was the best since Wokingham Town reached the last four, six years earlier. A 1–1 draw at Kingfield gave Enfield the advantage but, at Southbury Road, the Cards held out for a 0–0 draw and won a replay 3–0. Woking went on to beat Runcorn 2–1 in the final.

Enfield were, once again, the best performing Isthmian League club a season later, reaching the last eight. Unfortunately for them, they met Rushden & Diamonds and lost in a replay at Nene Park, 4–3 after extra time. The match at Southbury Road had ended in a 1–1 draw. Boreham Wood had reached the last 16, where they lost to Marine. Former Isthmian members Stevenage – in the first season in the Conference – lost to Woking at the same stage, 3–0 at Broadhall Way. And Woking went on to retain the Trophy, this time beating Kidderminster Harriers after extra time at Wembley.

The 1995–96 season was pretty dismal for southern clubs again. In fact, the last four all came from within about 30 miles of each other – winners Macclesfield Town and runners-up Northwich Victoria from Cheshire and Hyde United and Chorley from slightly further north. Stevenage Borough had been the only southern club in the last eight, while Isthmian League interest had ended in the last 16 with the exits of Boreham Wood, in a replay at Chorley, and Carshalton Athletic, at Hyde United.

The following season saw an Isthmian League Trophy finalist for the first time since the early 1980s, with the Ted Hardy-managed Dagenham & Redbridge facing former Isthmians Woking. The Daggers had been the lone standard-bearers since the quarter-finals, which was where Heybridge Swifts exited, 1–0 at home to Woking. The Cards reached Wembley by beating Stevenage Borough in a replayed semi-final, 2–1 in the decider, while Dagenham & Redbridge also needed three games to beat Gloucester, also 2–1. In the final, Dagenham had Tony Rogers sent off in normal time, but the game was goalless for the full 90 minutes. In extra-time, however, a goal from Darran Hay was enough to give Woking their third Trophy success in four seasons.

Boreham Wood were the only current Isthmians in the last 16 of the 1997–98 edition, but they lost to one of three former Isthmian members also at this stage, Slough Town, who were shortly to return to the fold. Hayes lost to eventual winners Cheltenham Town in the quarter-finals, while Slough, who saw off Stevenage Borough in the last eight, succumbed to Southport, crucially losing the home leg of the semi-final before drawing at Haig Avenue.

Former Isthmians Kingstonian, managed by Geoff Chapple, the master of FA Trophy successes, beat Forest Green Rovers 1–0 in the final. The Gloucestershire club had ended Isthmian interest at the semi-final stage by beating St. Albans City 4–3 on aggregate. The teams had shared two goals at Clarence Park but at The Lawn the Conference side came back from 2-0 down to just shade a five-goal thriller. Hendon made it to the last 16 for the first time in 25 attempts, but Conference champions-in-waiting Cheltenham Town saw them off 3–0 at Whaddon Road. Hitchin Town were the other team to reach this stage, but they fell to Forest Green.

Kingstonian retained the Trophy in the first final of the 21st century, beating Kettering Town 3–2 in an exciting game at Wembley, the last final at the famous old venue. Sutton United had carried the Isthmian League hopes into the semi-final, but a Surrey derby was unceremoniously decided in the second leg at Kingsmeadow, Ks running out 6–0 winners, 7–1 on aggregate. Sutton had ploughed a lonely furrow after Heybridge Swifts had exited at the hands of Runcorn in the last 16.

After a gap of 20 years, an Isthmian Club won the 2000–01 FA Trophy. In fact, in a testament to the domination of the Conference, it would have been equally accurate to say after a gap of 20 years, a non-Conference Club won The FA Trophy. Canvey Island took this competition, but paid the price in a manic end-of-season fixture pile-up which cost them a most-deserved League title. Forest Green Rovers lost their second final in three years, again to a solitary goal, this time coming from the Gulls central defender Ben Chenery, who headed home a Mark Stimson corner after 16 minutes. Former England international Tony Daley was Forest Green's most dangerous player, but Canvey deservedly held on for what was inaccurately considered a big upset. The only other Isthmian League club to make it as far as the last 16 was Billericay Town, but they went out at that stage, 3–2 at home to Telford United.

Canvey Island's defence of the Trophy lasted to round five, the last 16. They lost 3–2 at Huish Park to eventual Trophy winners, Yeovil Town. Braintree Town's 2–1 home replay defeat at the hands of Margate ensured there would be no Isthmian League interest in the quarter-finals, although two former members Yeovil and Stevenage Borough met in the final, Yeovil winning 2–0.

Canvey Island's success in 2001 was actually a shifting in the sands. Two years later, unheralded Burscough won The FA Trophy, beating Tamworth 2–1 in the final. The last 16 contained a large number of non-Conference sides: Aylesbury United, who beat Windsor & Eton on penalties after a replay, and went on to reach the semi-finals; Wakefield & Emley, who were crushed 5–0 at Burscough; Gloucester City, conquerors of Southport, who fell to Aylesbury in the last eight; and Havant & Waterlooville, who trounced Hayes 3–0 at West Leigh Park and then beat Forest Green Rovers in the quarter-finals. Aylesbury had home advantage in the first leg of the semi-final against Burscough, but could only draw 1–1 at Buckingham Road. The second leg ended 1–0 to Burscough.

Canvey Island and Aldershot Town, fierce Isthmian League rivals a couple of seasons earlier, both made it to the 2003–04 semi-finals. The Shots went down to Hednesford Town, after losing 2–0 at the Rec in the first leg, but the Gulls advanced after a penalty shoot-out against Telford United after a pair of draws. Arlesey Town, FA Vase winners in 1995, had dreams of an amazing double as they reached the last 16, but Exeter City pricked that bubble 3–0 at St James' Park. Hornchurch took on and knocked out Burton Albion at Bridge Avenue, but they succumbed to Hednesford in the quarter-finals 3–1. Maidenhead United went up to Yorkshire and beat Halifax Town 2–0 at The Shay, before Canvey Island sent them packing, 4–0 at Park Lane, in the last eight.

The FA Trophy
in partnership with Carlsberg
Canvey Island v Hednesford Town

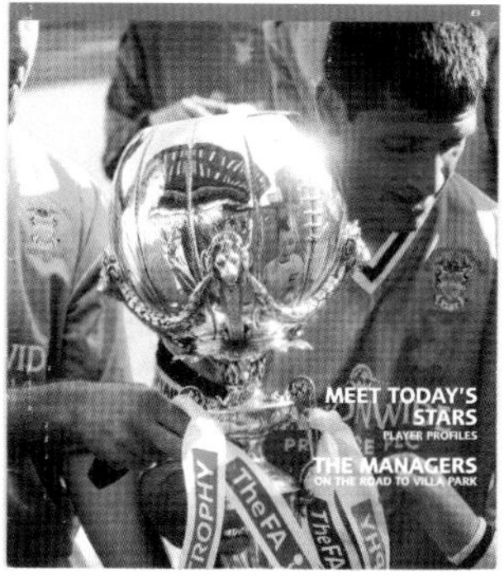

The new-look Isthmian League had two former members in the semi-finals. Grays Athletic and Bishop's Stortford, who had been promoted to the new Conference South division for 2004–05, avoided each other in the last four, but Stortford couldn't avoid defeat at the hands of Hucknall Town, losing both legs. But Grays made no mistake against Burton Albion, winning the first leg 5–0 at the Recreation Ground. They won 2–0 at Eton Park for good measure to reach the final. The final will be most remembered for the grisly broken leg suffered by Hucknall player-manager Dean Barrick. John Martin scored for Grays early in the second half, Bacon equalised ten minutes later, and that was the end of the scoring. The Grays hero in the penalty shoot-out was goalkeeper Ashley Bayes, who made the crucial sudden-death save as it ended 6–5 in the shoot-out. The only current members of the Isthmian League to reach the last 16 were Slough Town, who lost 3–2 away to Gravesend & Northfleet.

While few Isthmian Clubs won The FA Trophy while members, the roll of honour contains 10 who at one time graced the League. Congratulations, therefore, to Dagenham, Bishop's Stortford and Canvey Island who won as members, and to those who triumphed as formers members: Enfield, Wealdstone, Wycombe Wanderers, Woking, Kingstonian, Yeovil Town and Grays Athletic.

THE FA VASE

The Football Association instituted The FA Vase in 1974 as the successor to the highly-prized FA Amateur Cup, which had become effectively redundant, at least nominally, once the amateur/professional designations were removed. The Vase has always been the third-ranked of The FA's competitions, behind The FA Cup and FA Trophy. Only clubs at a certain level are eligible to enter, and it took a quarter of a century for it to be sorted out once and for all. It has been a fair rule of thumb that clubs in the two top divisions of the Isthmian League, Southern League and Northern Premier League will have entered The FA Trophy and those clubs below that level and in almost all other feeder leagues will play in The FA Vase (there were exceptions with some clubs in the Northern League playing The FA Trophy and some in Division One of the Southern League and Isthmian playing in The FA Vase).

Sad to say that while the Isthmian League was undoubtedly the pre-eminent competition in The FA Amateur Cup's final 15 years, it has never been the case with The FA Vase. Indeed few clubs enjoyed much success in the competition's first 30 seasons.

F. A. CHALLENGE VASE
(inaugurated 1974)

Winners and Finalists whilst in membership of the League

1985-86	Southall – runners-up
1989-90	Yeading – winners
1994-95	Oxford City – runners-up
2000-01	Berkhamsted Town - runners-up

Isthmian League clubs did not enter the competition until the 1977–78 season, the first one with three divisions of members. Future Isthmian League members did rather well in these early years with Epsom & Ewell losing to Hoddesdon Town in the inaugural season's final and Billericay winning it in 1975–76, 1976–77 and 1978–79. In 1977–78 Barton Rovers lost to Newcastle Blue Star in the final, while the last Isthmian member Club in the competition was Eastbourne United, who went out to Burnham in the last 16. Hungerford Town, who lost to Barton in the semi-final, joined the Isthmian League for the following season but they failed to make it past round two. Cheshunt, Eastbourne United and Worthing all made it to the last 16, but only Eastbourne advanced and they were eliminated by the eventual winners.

In 1979–80, Barton Rovers, Billericay Town and Epsom & Ewell were all Isthmian League members, but the most successful FA Vase club this season was Hungerford Town – quarter-final conquerors of Billericay – who suffered a second semi-final exit, going out 5–3 on aggregate against eventual runners-up Guisborough Town. Billericay had seen off Molesey in the last 16 as three Isthmian League clubs again reached that stage.

The following season was pretty disastrous for Isthmian League Clubs with only Hungerford reaching the last 16, where they fell to future Isthmians Windsor & Eton, themselves semi-final losers to eventual cup-winners Whickham. Cheshunt were the only other club to get as far as the last 32, and lost at home to Alma Swanley at that stage.

No less than four clubs reached the last 16 in 1981–82, Barton Rovers, semi-final losers to Rainworth Miners Welfare – the runners-up to Forest Green Rovers in the Final – Cheshunt, who fell to Newcastle Blue Star in the quarter-finals after an all-Isthmian League round five tie against Hemel Hempstead, and Molesey who, like Barton, went out to the Nottinghamshire miners' club.

It was back to famine in 1982–83, with only Windsor & Eton making it to the last 16, where they fell to eventual runners-up Halesowen Town – 1–0 losers to VS Rugby in the Final. Two future Isthmian League members, Wivenhoe Town and Bracknell Town, also failed to advance to the last eight from this stage.

Corinthian–Casuals and Isthmian League newcomers Leyton Wingate flew the flag in 1983–84, the former falling to eventual runners-up Stamford in the last 16, the latter going a round further, but Whickham ended their interest. Stansted won an exciting final, 3–2.

The chances for Isthmian League success should have grown in 1984–85 as the League expanded to include a second Division Two. However, not a single one of the 39 eligible teams reached the last 16, Harefield United, Cheshunt, Egham Town, Berkhamsted Town and Finchley all going out in round four. Halesowen Town beat Fleetwood Town in the final.

The first Isthmian League club to reach the final was Southall, who lost 3–0 to Vase-holders Halesowen Town, 3–0, at Wembley in April 1986. Four teams had made it to the last 16, including Whyteleafe and Stevenage Borough who met to guarantee at least one Isthmian representative in the quarter-finals. It turned out to be Stevenage who won 4–1. Despite having almost double the support of the home team, Borough fell in the 2–0 quarter-finals to Southall at Western Road. Camberley Town were less fortunate, going down 5–1 at Halesowen. The goals of Les Ferdinand had played a big part in the Fowlers' run to the Final, but he had a goal disallowed for offside when Halesowen, against the run of play, led 1–0. Then two goals in the final 18 minutes sealed Southall's fate.

Collier Row and Heybridge Swifts were the only Isthmian Clubs to reach the last 16 in 1986–87 and the Romford club made it all the way to the semi-finals. Heybridge, however, lost an East Anglian derby to Haverhill Rovers in round five, going

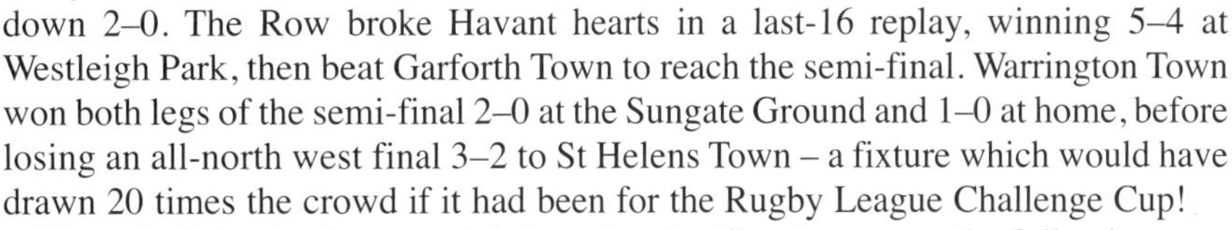

down 2–0. The Row broke Havant hearts in a last-16 replay, winning 5–4 at Westleigh Park, then beat Garforth Town to reach the semi-final. Warrington Town won both legs of the semi-final 2–0 at the Sungate Ground and 1–0 at home, before losing an all-north west final 3–2 to St Helens Town – a fixture which would have drawn 20 times the crowd if it had been for the Rugby League Challenge Cup!

The only Isthmian League club to make significant progress the following year was Chertsey Town, and they lost 3–1 at home to Bashley in the quarter-finals. There was another all-northern final, this time Colne Dynamoes seeing off Emley with a solitary extra-time goal.

Those old Vase warhorses Hungerford Town were at it again in 1988–89, reaching the semi-final. They had been the lone representatives in the last 16, overcoming Hailsham Town and Thatcham Town to get to the last four. However, after being held to a goalless draw at home in the first leg, Hungerford were blown away by Sudbury Town in the return, going down 6–0. Sudbury lost in the final, albeit after a replay, to Tamworth.

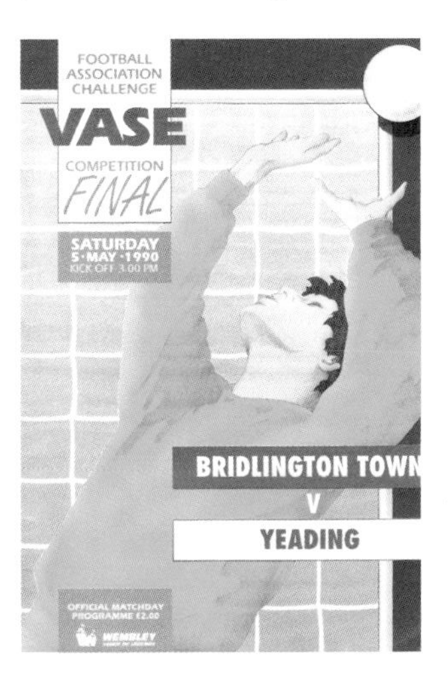

The only Isthmian League winners of The FA Vase were Yeading, who completed an FA Vase/Isthmian League Division Two South championship double in 1989–90. Abingdon Town, Billericay Town and Harefield United had joined the Ding in the last 16, but Abingdon fell to Hythe after a replay. Yeading, after seeing off Paulton Rovers, beat Harefield 3–0 in the quarter-finals at the Warren. Billericay, however, could not repeat their success of the late 1970s and, just four seasons after losing their Isthmian Premier place, went out 1–0 to Bridlington Town at New Lodge. In the semi-final, Yeading overcame a 3–2 first leg deficit to beat Hythe Town 4–3 on aggregate to set up a final against Bridlington. Three members of the Southall team which had lost the 1986 final were in Yeading's team for Wembley: goalkeeper Stuart MacKenzie, centre-back Steve Croad and striker Paul Sweales. Out wide was a youngster who, like Les Ferdinand at Southall, would go on to play for both QPR and England – albeit only at Under-21 level – Andrew Impey. The game at Wembley was playing in stiflingly hot conditions and very tight, ending goalless after 120 minutes. The replay at Elland Road, Leeds, was decided by a single, spectacular strike from the late Paul Sweales and his 25-yarder dipping drive brought The FA Vase to an Isthmian League member.

Yeading could not defend their trophy in 1990–91, having been promoted, and Isthmian League clubs went out with barely a whimper, only Saffron Walden reaching the last 16, where they exited to Buckingham Town, 2–1 at Catons Lane. Guiseley and Gresley Rovers put on a spectacle in the Wembley final, sharing eight goals. The replay brought half that return, but Guiseley got three of them to take home the Vase.

Four teams made it to the last 16 the following season, Metropolitan Police and Hungerford from the new Division Two and Edgware Town and Chertsey Town from Division Three. And it was the Curfews who were the last ones standing, going out in the quarter-finals to Bamber Bridge, after West Midlands Police had overcome Hungerford, Diss Town saw off Metropolitan Police and Guiseley outplayed Edgware. Wimborne Town were too good for Guiseley in the Final, winning 5–3 in another Wembley goalfest.

The only Isthmian League Club to reach the quarter-finals in 1992–93 were Banstead Athletic, who went down 1–0 to eventual winners Bridlington Town. Future Isthmian League members Canvey Island reached the semi-final, but Tiverton Town won 2–1 on aggregate.

A very strong Isthmian League Division Two sent two representatives to the quarter-finals, Aldershot Town and Newbury Town. No other clubs had reached the last 16. The Shots – conquerors of Wimborne Town – lost a second replay to Atherton Laburnum Rovers, while Newbury – who had won at Hinckley Athletic – went down 2–0 at Taunton Town. The Somerset club advanced to the Final, where Diss Town beat them 2–1.

Oxford City, who had not won The FA Amateur Cup as members of the Isthmian League, despite making almost 60 attempts, almost won The FA Vase in 1995. They lost 2–1 in the Final to Arlesey Town, who would become fellow members a few years later. This season's competition saw a large number of past, present or future Isthmian Clubs in the last eight. Former members Basildon United lost to Raunds Town, present members Metropolitan Police fell to Belper Town at Imber Court, while Canvey Island went out to Oxford City. Oxford came from a goal down after the first leg to see off Belper Town, 3–2 on aggregate, while Arlesey emulated Telford's performance in The FA Trophy against Harrow Borough, despite being three goals behind. They, however, lost the first leg 3–0 and won the second leg 5–0, but also needed extra time for the decisive goals. Arlesey took the lead after 26 minutes of the final but Chris Fontaine set up brother Steve for Oxford's equaliser just four minutes later. An 18-yard strike from Sandor Gyalog was enough to send the Vase to Bedfordshire.

The 1995–96 season was another one where success was rather limited. Collier Row and Canvey Island were the last Isthmian League clubs standing, going out to eventual winners Brigg Town 2–0 away and Flixton, 3–0 also away, respectively, in the quarter-final. Banstead Athletic and Wivenhoe Town had both also reached the last 16 but Peacehaven & Telscombe won at Merland Rise, while the Dragons fell in a replay at Mangotsfield United.

A season later, Banstead went a stage further, reaching the semi-final, after ending Herne Bay and Northwood's interest in the two previous rounds. Whitby Town, who lost to Hendon in the 1964 FA Amateur Cup Final, went one better in The FA Vase 33 years later. They got to Wembley courtesy of a priceless victory at Merland Rise, drew the second, home, leg 1–1, progressing 2–1 on aggregate, and brushed aside North Ferriby United 3–0 in a one-sided final. The merged Collier Row & Romford and Barking both went out at the last 16 stage, Bedlington Terriers needing a replay to beat the former, while one-time FA Trophy winners Mossley defeated Barking.

It was a tale of woe for Isthmian League clubs in 1997–98, with only Great Wakering Rovers making it as far as the last 16. They lost to future Isthmian members Potters Bar Town, who lost to Kidsgrove in the quarter-finals, who in turn fell to eventual winners Tiverton Town – conquerors of Tow Law Town 1–0 in the final.

In 1998–99, things looked very promising with five of the last 16 coming from the Isthmian League. Unfortunately, Bedford Town lost 2–1 at home to Tiverton Town, Northwood were beaten 5–2 at Taunton Town, Ford United were upset 2–1 at home to Bedlington Terriers and Camberley Town fell 2–1 at Woodbridge Town. The only survivors were Thame United, who made it all the way to the semi-finals, but they were thumped 5–0 at Bedlington in the first leg and there was no way back at the Windmill Ground in the second leg, the game ending goalless. Bedlington then lost 1–0 to Tiverton in the final.

Success was non-existent in the following season as only the Metropolitan Police made it to the last 16, and they were beaten 5–2 by Deal Town – the eventual winners – at Imber Court. Future Isthmian members Ramsgate did get to the quarter-finals but their interest ended there at the hands of Newcastle Town.

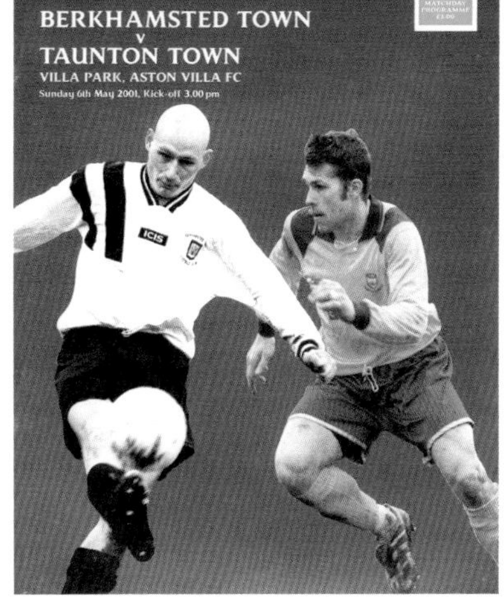

One-quarter of the last 16 in the 2000–01 FA Vase competition were members of the Isthmian League and one of them, Berkhamsted Town, made it all the way to the Final. Berko knocked out 1987 winners St Helens Town in the last 16, but that's where the ride ended for Marlow – 1–0 at home to Marske United – and former winners Arlesey Town – 2–1 at eventual winners Taunton Town. Tooting & Mitcham United fell to the Somerset powerhouses in the quarter-finals, after they had seen off Stourport Swifts in round five.

Berkhamsted were too strong for Brigg Town in the quarter-finals and beat 1999 finalists Bedlington Terriers 5–1 on aggregate in the semi-final. Steve Bateman's team made things easy for the home second leg by going up to the north-east and returning with a 3–0 victory under their belts. A 2–1 victory in the second leg set up a final against Taunton Town at Villa Park, Birmingham. Berko started brightly but conceded two goals before half-time. They fought back well and scored a penalty to set up a grandstand finish, but they couldn't find a second goal and had to settle for runners-up medals.

Three Isthmian League teams made it to the last 16 in 2002, Arlesey Town, Great Wakering Rovers and Lewes, but only the last-named progressed, Clitheroe winning 3–0 at Arlesey and Great Wakering falling 2–1 at the newly merged AFC Sudbury. It was the Suffolk club, who would join the expanded Isthmian League in 2006, who ended Lewes's interest in the quarter-finals, winning 2–1 at the Dripping Pan. The final pitted Whitley Bay and Tiptree United, with the Tyne & Wear club triumphing 1–0.

The realignment of the Isthmian League for the 2002–03 season meant that only 16 member Clubs entered The FA Vase. Unfortunately, only one club made it as far as the last 32, and Ware fell to a solitary Clitheroe goal at Wodson Park to exit. Brigg Town went on to win the Vase, beating AFC Sudbury 2–1 in the Final.

One season later, things improved slightly, with two teams in the last 16. However, Chertsey could not make home advantage count against Bideford and the Devon club returned from Alwyns Lane celebrating a 1–0 victory. Leighton Town, on their way to promotion from Division Two, went to Andover, but they were on the wrong end of a 3–1 scoreline. AFC Sudbury again made the final, but they again found one too good for them, this time Winchester City and the prolific Andy Forbes, as the Hampshire side prevailed 2–0.

The Isthmian League centenary season didn't bring much in the way of joy. Enfield, bidding to become the first Club to win The FA Amateur Cup, FA Trophy and FA Vase, reached the last 16 – having seen off their breakaway neighbours Enfield Town in a high-profile third round tie and Brislington at the next stage – but Bedlington Terriers won 3–0 at Wodson Park. Brook House also made it to the last 16 in their debut season as Isthmian League members, but they were also beaten, 3–0 at Frome Town. The last eight contained two future Isthmian League members, Bury Town and AFC Sudbury. Bury lost 2–1 at Didcot Town, who eventually saw off AFC Sudbury, too, but it was the Suffolk club's third consecutive defeat in the Final, this time 3–2 at White Hart Lane, Tottenham.

Under any other circumstances, the history of Isthmian Clubs in The FA Vase would end with the centenary season. However, as the 2005–06 competition was the last with Isthmian Clubs entering – Division Two ceased to exist after the season's end and the clubs joined other Level Five Leagues – it is worth completing the history.

Sadly, it was an almost unrelenting tale of woe. In the first qualifying round, Camberley Town, Flackwell Heath, Chertsey Town, Hertford Town and eventual champions Ware all went out. The second qualifying round was the end of the road for Clapton and Wembley. Croydon and Epsom & Ewell fell in round one and Egham Town and Witham Town did likewise at the next stage. This left just Brook House, Chalfont St Peter, Dorking and Kingsbury Town still in the competition and neither Chalfont nor Kingsbury could get past round three. And round four was the end of the Isthmian League involvement in The FA Vase as Mildenhall Town won 3–1 at the Meadowbank Ground to end Dorking's hopes, while eventual runners-up Hillingdon Borough won a Middlesex derby against Brook House, 2–0 at Breakspear Road North. Hillingdon would lose 3–1 to Nantwich Town in the Final at St Andrews, Birmingham.

Heartiest congratulations must go to the sole Isthmian League members to win The FA Vase –Yeading – and to the three finalists – Southall, Oxford City and Berkhamsted Town. It must be remembered that the level of clubs entering The FA Vase was never as high as The FA Amateur Cup and other past, future or present Isthmian League members enjoyed success, winning the Vase or at least reaching the Final. So, congratulations, too, to: AFC Sudbury, Arlesey Town, Barton Rovers, Billericay Town and Epsom & Ewell.

CHAPTER ELEVEN

League Cup Competitions

ISTHMIAN LEAGUE CUP

The Isthmian League Cup competition was introduced for the 1974–75 season as the Subsidiary Cup. Only the 18 clubs in Division 2 were eligible to enter and it was to compensate them for their lack of League fixtures – they had only 34. Much as the Associate Members' Cup for the 16-club Division Two in more recent seasons, the inaugural competition comprised regionalised pools in round one, but only the winners of each pool progressed to the semi–finals.

Here Tilbury beat Southall 4–2 at home whilst Croydon travelled to Finchley and needed an extra time goal to secure their place in the Final. The Final was played over two legs, both of which Tilbury won, 2–1 at Croydon – thanks to goals from Worrall and Walder, with Woozley replying for the home side – and 1–0 in the second leg with a goal from Heale.

A year later the competition was re–named the Isthmian League Cup and opened to Division 1 Clubs, although entry was not compulsory and several opted not to enter. Holders Tilbury, who had secured the Division 2 championship, again reached the Final, this time – and for the next few years – a one-off game at a neutral venue. The Dockers failed to complete a double as Slough Town won 4–0 at Church Road, Hayes FC, with goals from Gordon Bartlett (2), Terry Brown and an own goal.

Entry was compulsory in 1976–77 season and Hendon became the first winners on this basis, defeating Barking 1–0 with a goal scored by Rod Haider in the Final at Earlsmead. Laurie Abrahams, in his last match for the Blues before turning professional, smashed a second-half penalty against the bar and knocked in the rebound without another player touching the ball, so the goal was disallowed. It was the worst of a host of misses by Barking who totally dominated the game.

Japanese electrical giants Hitachi agreed to sponsor the competition in 1977–78 and it became known as The Hitachi Cup *(as detailed below)*. Dagenham beat Leatherhead 1–0 in the Final at Champion Hill, Dulwich Hamlet FC, with Mal Harkins scoring the Daggers' winning goal.

Enfield won the Hitachi Cup in consecutive seasons, 1979–80. Goals from Nicky Glover and Ward were enough for a 2–1 success against Hayes, for whom Bobby Wiles replied, at Slough Town FC in the first of those finals. A year later, the Es completed an Isthmian League and Cup double, beating Sutton United 3–2 in the Final at Harrow Borough FC. Steve King and John McCombe (2) scored for the Es, John Rains and Paul McKinnon for the Us.

The Value of Hitachi

While the F.A. Trophy and the F.A. Cup will always be the prestigious competitions for non-league clubs, Isthmian League clubs must now see the Hitachi Cup as the most important cup competition in the calendar.

The F.A. Trophy is the competition every Isthmian League club should aim to win and the F.A. Cup is the 'glamour', the means of gaining some much sought after publicity; but when it comes to hard financial reality today's competition is at the top of the tree.

The League campaign must always remain the 'bread and butter' for any Isthmian League side, but the introduction of the Hitachi Cup has given every club a chance of taking a share in rewards albeit large or small.

With Premier Division sides excluded until the First Round proper, the First and Second Division sides are the first ones to have the opportunity of collecting Hitachi awards. And Hertford Town and Worthing have shown just how it can be done.

First and Second Division sides winning through to the First Round proper earn themselves a Hitachi portable television and from then on the road to the Final is paved with cash and electrical goods as reward for their efforts.

Dependent upon the disciplinary points position, today's winners will have earned themselves £1,160 with a number of valuable Hitachi products to boost the overall prize.

This has been the first year of the competition but the Japanese Electrical giants have already agreed to continue next season and have been so pleased with this season's effort they have increased the value of their sponsorship.

The Hitachi Cup awards are as follows: –

To the 16 winning Clubs in the 1st Round Proper ...	£40 each
To the 8 winning Clubs in the 2nd Round Proper ...	£70 each
To the 4 winning Clubs in the 3rd Round Proper ...	£150 each
To the 2 winning Clubs in the Semi-Finals	£300 each
To the winning Club in the Final tie	£600

A disciplinary points scheme will apply and for each point awarded a Club's prize money will be reduced on the scale:–

1st and 2nd Rounds–	£10
3rd Round–	£20
Semi-Finals–	£30
Final tie–	£40

Equipment Awards

To the Division 2 Club going furthest in the Competition – a Hitachi Colour Television or Music Centre to the value of £340.

To the Division 1 Club going furthest in the Competition – a Hitachi Colour Television or Music Centre to the value of £340.

To the Club with the best aggregate score from any four Isthmian League and Hitachi Cup matches (at least one of which must be a Hitachi Cup match) in the period from the date of the first Hitachi Cup match to the completion of the 3rd Round Proper – a Hitachi Colour Television or Music Centre to the value of £340.

To each of the 10 winning Clubs from the Qualifying Competition – a Hitachi product to the value of £70.

Hitachi radio sets will be presented to the players in the Semi-Finals and Finals.

There was a slight change to the Hitachi Cup format from the 1980–81 competition in that the semi–finals would be decided over two legs. Slough Town emulated Enfield by winning the competition for the second time in 1981, beating Walthamstow Avenue 4–2 in the Final at Hayes FC.

The following year Leytonstone–Ilford became the second team to do the Isthmian League and Cup double when they defeated Kingstonian 2–0 in the Final at Boreham Wood FC. In 1982–83, the competition reverted to a single-game semi–final, but with the Final being played on a home and away basis. Sutton United and Wycombe Wanderers reached the Final in successive seasons, with the Surrey club holding sway both times.

The Us won the first leg of the 1983 Final, at Loakes Park, 1–0 with John Rains scoring the only goal. The return at Gander Green Lane ended in a 1–1 draw, so Sutton prevailed 2–1 on aggregate. In the 1984 Final, the first leg was again at Loakes Park and it ended in a 1–1 draw. Back at Gander Green Lane, Sutton made no mistake winning 2–0 on the night and 3–1 on aggregate.

Sutton's hopes of completing a hat-trick were dashed by Division One champions-elect Farnborough Town at the semi-final stage, but Wycombe did make it three Finals in a row. This time they made no mistake, returning from the first leg at Cherrywood Road with a commanding 3–0 lead. The last match of the Hitachi Cup competition was the second leg, and Wycombe won it 2–1 to take the Final 5–1 on aggregate.

Carparts manufacturer AC Delco – part of the Vauxhall Motors group now sponsoring the League competition – became the title sponsors from 1985–86 and the Isthmian League's knock-out competition returned to the previous format of a two-legged semi–final and a one-off Final played at a neutral venue. The first AC Delco Cup winners – with great political incorrectness it was known as the ACDC Cup – Sutton United completed the Isthmian League and Cup double by beating Division 1 Club Uxbridge 3–1 in the Final at Imber Court, Metropolitan Police FC.

There was an all-Premier Division Final in 1987, played at Windsor & Eton FC, with Bognor Regis Town beating Hendon 3–2 with goals from Pat Clements, Paul Marriner and Russell Burtenshaw. Hendon replied with two Dermot Drummy goals including a penalty.

The 1988 Final was won by Yeovil Town, who joined the list of those Clubs completing an Isthmian League and Cup double by beating Hayes 3 –1 in the Final at Basingstoke Town FC. A year later, Bishop's Stortford inflicted a second Cup Final defeat on Farnborough Town, this time it was 1–0, with the only goal of the game – at Hayes FC – being scored by Andy Weddell.

Aveley's AC Delco Cup success in 1990 must be considered the biggest Final upset in the League Cup's history. Members of Division 2 North, they reached the Final at Victoria Road, Dagenham FC, where Premier Division St. Albans City provided the opposition. The Essex club triumphed in one of the more comprehensive and one-sided Finals, winning 3–0. Graham Daly and Bobby Moyce added to an opening own goal.

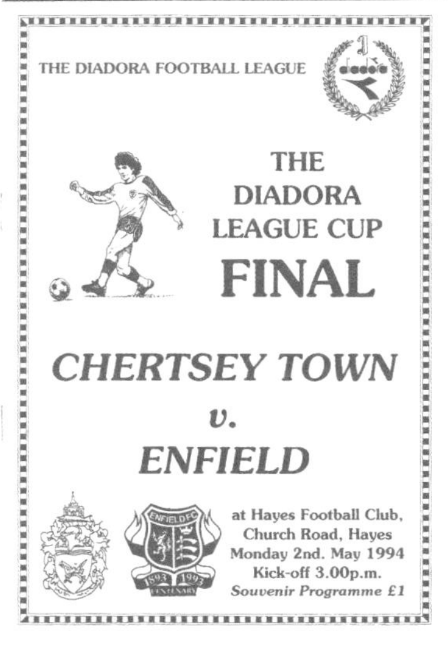

In the last year as the AC Delco Cup, the 1991 Final was an all Surrey affair, with Woking defeating Carshalton Athletic 2–1 at Kingstonian FC. Paul Mulvaney and Trevor Baron scored the Cards' goals; Gary Bowyer netted for the Robins.

Vauxhall Motors' sponsorship of the Isthmian League ended in 1991, so the 1991–92 League Cup reverted to the name of the Isthmian League Cup. The Final, at Dagenham FC, saw Grays Athletic – in their first final – against two-time winners Enfield, and it was the Essex club who were victorious, with goals from Winston Whittingham, John Campbell and an own goal to set up a 3–1 win. Enfield's solitary goal came from Mark Kane.

In 1992–93, the Isthmian League's headline sponsors, Diadora, agreed also to sponsor the League Cup competition, which would be known as the Diadora League Cup. The first Diadora League Cup Final was played at the Recreation Ground, Aldershot Town FC, and featured two first-time finalists in Premier Division Marlow and Division 1 Molesey. It ended 2–1 to the Buckinghamshire club, with Garfield Blackman and Mark Watkins scoring for them, while Micky Rose converted a penalty for the Moles.

It was decided that from the 1993–94 Diadora League Cup Final, instead of a second game, Final ties level after 120 minutes would be decided by means of a penalty shoot-out. Ten years later, all replays were done away with, a decision every Club Secretary celebrated. There was something of an upset in that season's Final when Chertsey Town, the Division 2 champions, defeated Premier Division runners–up Enfield 3–0 at Hayes FC. But the Curfews were no ordinary Division Two team as is evidenced by their goalscorers: former FA Youth-cup winner Josh Price, future Football League player Lee Charles and a penalty from the man who ended 2006 as England's most capped full-back, with 86 full international appearances, Kenny Sansom.

The 1994–95 Diadora League Cup Final was decided on penalties for the first time when Aylesbury United defeated Slough Town 7–6. The all Berks & Bucks FA match was played at the Alfred Davis Memorial Ground, Marlow FC, and Slough players scored both goals in the regulation 120 minutes, Trevor Baron putting the ball into his own net and Andy Clements at the right end.

Guardian Insurance became League Cup sponsors in 1995, the competition being known as the Guardian Insurance Cup. The first Final of this competition pitted Division One Aldershot Town against Premier Division Kingstonian. The Ks were happy to travel to the Recreation Ground for the Final and comfortably overcame the Shots' home advantage with a 4–1 victory. Kingstonian's goals came from Jimmy Bolton (2), Eddie Akuamoah and Dale Jasper, while Danny Holmes scored for Aldershot.

There was nearly a shock in the 1996–97 Guardian Insurance Cup competition. Braintree Town, who were members of Division Three, reached the Final after knocking out Premier Division Sutton United in the last four. Premier Division Boreham Wood made sure there would be no shock in the Final, winning 1–0, albeit after extra time, courtesy of Tony Samuels.

The final year of the Guardian Insurance Cup provided the highest score in a League Cup Final when Sutton United trounced Oxford City in the Final 6–1. It was a special night for Us striker Joff Vansittart, who scored five times at Earlsmead, Harrow Borough FC. Nassim Akrour scored Sutton's other goal while Ian Concannon scored Oxford City's consolation.

The League Cup had a new sponsor for 1998–99 when Isthmian League headline sponsors Ryman the Stationer agreed also to sponsor the League Cup and the competition would be known as the Ryman League Cup. The first Ryman League Cup Final, at Wexham Park, Slough Town FC, went the way of Aldershot Town who defeated Boreham Wood 2–1, with Gary Abbott scoring a brace for the Shots and Tony Samuels – his second League Cup Final goal in three seasons – netting for the Wood.

The following year's Final also went to extra time and it was Farnborough Town's Keith Dublin who scored the only goal of the game against Maidenhead United at Basingstoke Town FC.

Heybridge Swifts were first-time finalists in 2001, while their opponents at the Thurrock Hotel, Purfleet FC, were Croydon, who were in their first League Cup Final for 26 years. Goals from Simon Parker, Kris Lee and Colin Wall gave the Essex Club a comfortable 3–0 victory.

Although Ryman the Stationer remained the Isthmian League's headline sponsor, they opted not to continue to sponsor the League Cup and the 2001–02 competition reverted to the Isthmian League Cup. The Final, hosted by St. Albans City FC, was a close affair between two Middlesex clubs, Premier Division Hampton & Richmond Borough, and First Division Northwood. It was the latter who triumphed, winning 3–2 after extra time with Andy Cook scoring twice and Lawrence Yaku getting the other. Neil Gough and Richard O'Connor got on the score sheet for Hampton & Richmond Borough.

The Isthmian League Cup became known as the Bryco Cup from 2002–03 after a new sponsorship agreement was secured. The first winners under the new name were Yeading who defeated Premier Division runners–up Canvey Island at Hornchurch FC with Errol Telemaque and Danny Jordan goals in a 2–0 win.

Replayed League Cup-ties became a thing of the past from the 2003–04 competition – except for matches abandoned after 90 minutes or during extra-time – with penalty shoot-outs deciding matches level after 120 minutes. The competition had another first – a more unwanted one – when the 2003–04 Final had to be held over until the start of the 2004–05 season because the original match – scheduled for Bridge Avenue, Hornchurch FC – was postponed due to a waterlogged pitch. The re–arranged match was played at Bishop's Stortford FC, with Thurrock enjoying a comfortable 5–1 victory over Division 1 North opponents Dunstable Town, in their first appearance in the competition.

Adding to the confusion, The FA's realignment of Non-League Football for the 2004–05 season and the birth of the Conference South, meant that neither Dunstable (Southern League Premier Division) nor Thurrock (Conference South) were actually members of the Isthmian League when the match was played. Nevertheless Lee Hodges, Cliff Akurang (2), Tresor Kandol and Jimmy McFarlane scored for Thurrock while Grant Carney replied for Dunstable Town.

The 2004–05 Final saw Slough Town, whose last appearance in the Final had been ten seasons earlier, meet 2001–02 finalists Hampton & Richmond Borough at Staines Town FC. The Rebels won the Final 3–1 thanks to a brace of goals from Ian Hodges and one from Josias Carbon. Dudley Gardner was on target for the Beavers.

THE ISTHMIAN LEAGUE CUP - RESULTS IN FULL

1974–75

NORTHERN POOL

		1	2	3	4
1	Boreham Wood	*	1–5	0–1	1–0
2	Corinthian–Casuals	1–0	*	2–3	3–1
3	Finchley	2–1	3–3	*	3–1
4	St. Albans City	0–0	1–2	0–1	*

		P	*W*	*D*	*L*	*F*	*A*	*Pts*
1	Finchley	6	5	1	0	13	7	16
2	Corinthian–Casuals	6	4	1	1	16	9	13
3	Boreham Wood	6	1	1	4	3	9	4
4	St. Albans City	6	0	1	5	3	10	1

EASTERN POOL

		1	2	3	4	5
1	Aveley	*	1–4	0–1	3–3	1–4
2	Harlow Town	0–2	*	2–2	0–1	2–2
3	Harwich & Parkeston	1–3	1–3	*	2–1	2–1
4	Hertford Town	0–1	1–4	2–0	*	0–0
5	Tilbury	2–1	2–1	4–1	2–1	*

		P	*W*	*D*	*L*	*F*	*A*	*Pts*
1	Tilbury	8	5	2	1	17	9	17
2	Harlow Town	8	3	2	3	16	12	11
3	Aveley	8	3	1	4	12	15	10
4	Harwich & Parkeston	8	3	1	4	10	16	10
5	Hertford Town	8	2	2	4	9	12	8

SOUTHERN POOL

		1	2	3	4
1	Carshalton Athletic	*	0–1	2–2	2–1
2	Croydon	1–1	*	2–0	1–1
3	Horsham	1–3	1–2	*	0–1
4	Staines Town	0–1	2–1	0–0	*

		P	*W*	*D*	*L*	*F*	*A*	*Pts*
1	Croydon	6	3	2	1	8	5	11
2	Carshalton Athletic	6	3	2	1	9	6	11
3	Staines Town	6	2	2	2	4	4	8
4	Horsham	6	0	2	4	4	10	2

WESTERN POOL

		1	2	3	4	5
1	Chesham United	*	0–0	1–1	1–3	2–2
2	Hampton	5–1	*	2–1	0–2	0–2
3	Maidenhead United	2–2	2–2	*	0–1	1–1
4	Southall	4–2	2–0	3–1	*	0–1
5	Wokingham Town	1–2	1–0	0–2	1–0	*

		P	*W*	*D*	*L*	*F*	*A*	*Pts*
1	Southall	8	6	0	2	15	6	18
2	Wokingham Town	8	4	2	2	9	7	14
3	Hampton	8	2	2	4	9	11	8
4	Maidenhead United	8	1	4	2	10	12	7
5	Chesham United	8	1	4	2	11	18	7

SEMI–FINALS
Finchley 0, Croydon 1 aet
Tilbury 4, Southall 2

FINAL
Croydon 1, Tilbury 2
Tilbury 1, Croydon 0 (3–1 agg)

1975–76

***NB** Bishop's Stortford, Corinthian–Casuals, Dagenham, Dulwich Hamlet, Enfield, Harwich & Parkeston, Hendon, Leatherhead, St. Albans City, Sutton United, Tooting & Mitcham United and Wokingham Town did not enter.*

FIRST ROUND
Barking 2, Leytonstone 0
Boreham Wood 2, Horsham 1
Carshalton Athletic 2, Hitchin Town 1
Croydon 1, Aveley 0
Hampton 1, Slough Town 3
Harrow Borough 2, Kingstonian 1
Hertford Town 3, Finchley 2
Hornchurch 0, Ilford 1
Maidenhead United 3, Staines Town 1 aet
Oxford City 0, Wycombe Wanderers 1
Tilbury 3, Bromley 0
Walthamstow Avenue 2, Clapton 0
Walton & Hersham 3, Chesham United 4
Ware 4, Harlow Town 4 aet
Wembley 1, Southall & Ealing Borough 0
Woking 3, Hayes 0
FIRST ROUND REPLAY
Harlow Town 2, Ware 0

SECOND ROUND
Barking 0, Carshalton Athletic 2
Harlow Town 2, Walthamstow Avenue 1
Ilford 2, Croydon 0
Slough Town 2, Maidenhead United 0
Tilbury 3, Hertford Town 2
Walton & Hersham 3, Chesham United 0
Wembley 0, Harrow Borough 3
Wycombe Wanderers 3, Boreham Wood 2

THIRD ROUND
Harlow Town 2, Carshalton Athletic 1
Harrow Borough 2, Slough Town 3
Tilbury 3, Ilford 2
Walton & Hersham 1, Wycombe Wanderers 2

SEMI–FINAL
Tilbury 3, Harlow Town 1
Wycombe Wanderers 1, Slough Town 0 aet

FINAL
Slough Town 4, Tilbury 0
At Hayes FC

1976–77

FIRST ROUND
Bishop's Stortford 1, Barking 3
Chesham United 0, Boreham Wood 1
Corinthian–Casuals 0, Carshalton Athletic 1
Harrow Borough 0, Hampton 1
Hendon 5, Wokingham Town 1
Hertford Town 0, Dulwich Hamlet 2
Hornchurch 1, Croydon 4
Ilford 8, Clapton 1
Maidenhead United 0, Woking 6
Oxford City 0, Slough Town 5
Tilbury 1, Dagenham 2
Walton & Hersham 1, Horsham 2

SECOND ROUND
Barking 6, Harwich & Parkeston 0
Bromley 0, Dagenham 5
Dulwich Hamlet 6, Ware 0
Enfield 2, Aveley 0
Finchley 3, Carshalton Athletic 2
Hampton 0, Staines Town 3
Harlow Town 1, Ilford 0
Hendon 2, Slough Town 1
Hitchin Town 2, Boreham Wood 3
Horsham 0, St. Albans City 1
Kingstonian 2, Hayes 0
Leytonstone 2, Croydon 5
Southall 1, Sutton United 1 aet
Walthamstow Avenue 2, Tooting & Mitcham United 1
Woking 4, Wembley 0
Wycombe Wanderers 1, Leatherhead 0
SECOND ROUND REPLAY
Sutton United 5, Southall 0

THIRD ROUND
Barking 3, Finchley 1
Croydon 1, Walthamstow Avenue 0
Dulwich Hamlet 3, Harlow Town 2
Enfield 0, Dagenham 2
St. Albans City 0, Woking 1 aet
Staines Town 2, Boreham Wood 1
Sutton United 2, Hendon 3
Wycombe Wanderers 3, Kingstonian 0

FOURTH ROUND
Croydon 0, Barking 1
Dagenham 3, Dulwich Hamlet 1
Staines Town 3, Wycombe Wanderers 1 aet
Woking 0, Hendon 2

SEMI–FINAL
Barking 2, Dagenham 0
Hendon 5, Staines Town 0

FINAL
Hendon 1, Barking 0
At Harrow Borough FC

1977–78

FIRST QUALIFYING ROUND
Camberley Town 1, Farnborough Town 3
Chesham United 3, Egham Town 1
Clapton 1, Aveley 0
Corinthian–Casuals 1, Bromley 3
Dulwich Hamlet 3, Metropolitan Police 0
Eastbourne United 1, Horsham 3
Epping Town 2, Ware 2 aet
Epsom & Ewell 1, Hampton 2
Feltham 0, Molesey 1
Hertford Town 1, Finchley 0
Hornchurch 3, Rainham Town 3 aet
Ilford 0, Cheshunt 1
Letchworth Garden City 0, Tring Town 2 aet
St. Albans City 0, Harrow Borough 1
Walton & Hersham 1, Maidenhead United 2
Wembley 2, Willesden 0
Wokingham Town 3, Oxford City 2
Worthing 3, Lewes 1
FIRST QUALIFYING ROUND REPLAYS
Rainham Town 4, Hornchurch 2
Ware 2, Epping Town 4

SECOND QUALIFYING ROUND
Chesham United 2, Maidenhead United 4
Cheshunt 3, Clapton 2
Dulwich Hamlet 2, Bromley 1
Farnborough Town 3, Wokingham Town 0
Hemel Hempstead 1, Epping Town 0
Molesey 4, Hampton 3
Rainham Town 2, Harwich & Parkeston 3
Tring Town 1, Hertford Town 3
Wembley 0, Harrow Borough 1
Worthing 2, Horsham 0

FIRST ROUND
Barking 2, Croydon 0
Boreham Wood 2, Hitchin Town 1
Carshalton Athletic 2, Cheshunt 1
Dagenham 4, Harwich & Parkeston 0
Dulwich Hamlet 2, Sutton United 2 aet
Enfield 1, Hertford Town 3
Farnborough Town 2, Hayes 1
Hemel Hempstead 3, Bishop's Stortford 2
Hendon 1, Harrow Borough 0
Kingstonian 4, Worthing 5
Leatherhead 2, Molesey 0
Leytonstone 3, Tooting & Mitcham United 2
Maidenhead United 1, Southall & Ealing Borough 0
Slough Town 0, Woking 1
Walthamstow Avenue 1, Tilbury 0
Wycombe Wanderers 3, Staines Town 1
FIRST ROUND REPLAY
Sutton United 0, Dulwich Hamlet 3

SECOND ROUND
Barking 2, Leytonstone 0
Boreham Wood 2, Woking 1
Farnborough Town 0, Worthing 1
Hemel Hempstead 1, Dagenham 4
Hertford Town 2, Carshalton Athletic 0
Leatherhead 1, Hendon 0
Walthamstow Avenue 2, Dulwich Hamlet 1
Wycombe Wanderers 1, Maidenhead United 0

THIRD ROUND
Dagenham 4, Barking 1
Hertford Town 3, Walthamstow Avenue 0
Leatherhead 1, Wycombe Wanderers 0
Worthing 0, Boreham Wood 0 aet
THIRD ROUND REPLAY
Boreham Wood 2, Worthing 0

SEMI–FINAL
Boreham Wood 0, Leatherhead 1
Dagenham 1, Hertford Town 1 aet
SEMI–FINAL REPLAY
Hertford Town 0, Dagenham 0 aet
SEMI–FINAL SECOND REPLAY
Dagenham 4, Hertford Town 1

FINAL
Dagenham 1, Leatherhead 0
At Dulwich Hamlet FC

1978–79

FIRST ROUND
Aveley 0, Finchley 3
Camberley Town 1, Farnborough Town 4
Epping Town 0, Harlow Town 0 aet
Epsom & Ewell 6, Lewes 1
Hampton 1, Chesham United 3
Harrow Borough 2, Hungerford Town 1
Harwich & Parkeston 2, Cheshunt 1
Hertford Town 4, Letchworth Garden City 1
Hornchurch 1, Feltham 1 aet
Horsham 1, Walton & Hersham 0
Ilford 3, Willesden 0
Metropolitan Police 4, Corinthian–Casuals 0
Molesey 2, Eastbourne United 0
Rainham Town 0, Wembley 1
St. Albans City 0, Hemel Hempstead 1
Southall & Ealing Borough 2, Clapton 1
Tring Town 4, Egham Town 5
Ware 1, Bishop's Stortford 4
Wokingham Town 2, Maidenhead United 1
Worthing 1, Bromley 3
FIRST ROUND REPLAYS
Feltham 3, Hornchurch 1
Harlow Town 2, Epping Town 1

SECOND ROUND
Bishop's Stortford 3, Harwich & Parkeston 0
Bromley 2, Horsham 0
Egham Town 2, Chesham United 1
Feltham 0, Hertford Town 3
Harrow Borough 3, Farnborough Town 0
Hemel Hempstead 2, Finchley 1
Metropolitan Police 3, Epsom & Ewell 0
Molesey 0, Wokingham Town 1
Southall & Ealing Borough 2, Ilford 2 aet
Wembley 1, Harlow Town 2
SECOND ROUND REPLAY
Ilford 2, Southall & Ealing Borough 1

THIRD ROUND
Barking 3, Leytonstone 1
Bishop's Stortford 0, Harrow Borough 2
Boreham Wood 2, Hitchin Town 0
Croydon 4, Hemel Hempstead 0
Dagenham 6, Oxford City 2
Dulwich Hamlet 3, Woking 1
Egham Town 0, Enfield 4
Harlow Town 1, Wokingham Town 2
Hayes 4, Hertford Town 1
Ilford 2, Hendon 1
Kingstonian 0, Tooting & Mitcham United 4
Metropolitan Police 1, Bromley 2
Slough Town 3, Staines Town 0
Sutton United 2, Walthamstow Avenue 0
Tilbury 3, Carshalton Athletic 1
Wycombe Wanderers 1, Leatherhead 2

FOURTH ROUND
Bromley 5, Barking 4 aet
Dagenham 1, Croydon 5
Dulwich Hamlet 3, Leatherhead 0
Harrow Borough 2, Slough Town 0
Sutton United 1, Ilford 0
Tilbury 2, Boreham Wood 1
Tooting & Mitcham United 1, Enfield 3
Wokingham Town 1, Hayes 2
FOURTH ROUND REPLAY
Barking 1, Bromley 1 aet
FOURTH ROUND SECOND REPLAY
Bromley 4, Barking 3

FIFTH ROUND
Bromley 0, Enfield 4
Croydon 0, Harrow Borough 3
Dulwich Hamlet 4, Sutton United 3
Tilbury 1, Hayes 3

SEMI–FINAL
Enfield 0, Dulwich Hamlet 0 aet
Harrow Borough 1, Hayes 2
SEMI–FINAL REPLAY
Dulwich Hamlet 0, Enfield 0 aet
SEMI–FINAL SECOND REPLAY
Enfield 3, Dulwich Hamlet 2

FINAL
Enfield 2, Hayes 1
At Slough Town FC

1979–80

PRELIMINARY ROUND
Billericay Town 2, Barton Rovers 1

FIRST ROUND
Billericay Town 1, St. Albans City 1 aet
Bromley 2, Molesey 3
Camberley Town 1, Maidenhead United 0
Corinthian–Casuals 0, Epsom & Ewell 7
Cheshunt 0, Bishop's Stortford 3
Egham Town 0, Hampton 1
Farnborough Town 4, Tring Town 3
Harwich & Parkeston 2, Hemel Hempstead 1 aet
Hertford Town 5, Epping Town 1
Hornchurch 0, Clapton 2
Horsham 1, Lewes 2
Kingstonian 2, Hungerford Town 1
Letchworth Garden City 4, Ware 1
Leytonstone 2, Feltham 0
Rainham Town 0, Finchley 6
Walton & Hersham 2, Eastbourne United 3
Wembley 0, Southall & Ealing Borough 1
Willesden 2, Aveley 3
Wokingham Town 0, Chesham United 4
Worthing 0, Metropolitan Police 0 aet
FIRST ROUND REPLAYS
Metropolitan Police 1, Worthing 2
St. Albans City 1, Billericay Town 0

SECOND ROUND
Aveley 0, Bishop's Stortford 3
Camberley Town 1, Chesham United 2
Clapton 1, Finchley 2
Farnborough Town 1, Epsom & Ewell 2
Hampton 2, Kingstonian 3
Harwich & Parkeston 1, St. Albans City 0
Hertford Town 3, Leytonstone 2
Letchworth Garden City 1, Wembley 2
Molesey 1, Eastbourne United 1 aet
Worthing 1, Lewes 1 aet
SECOND ROUND REPLAYS
Eastbourne United 2, Molesey 3 aet
Lewes 1, Worthing 2

THIRD ROUND
Bishop's Stortford 1, Epsom & Ewell 3
Boreham Wood 2, Hitchin Town 0
Croydon 1, Walthamstow Avenue 2
Dagenham 3, Harrow Borough 2
Harlow Town 4, Wycombe Wanderers 3
Harwich & Parkeston 5, Worthing 1
Hayes 1, Leatherhead 2
Hertford Town 2, Hendon 2 aet
Molesey 3, Dulwich Hamlet 4
Oxford City 0, Sutton United 3
Slough Town 4, Chesham United 0
Staines Town 2, Finchley 2 aet
Tilbury 0, Barking 1
Tooting & Mitcham United 2, Carshalton Athletic 2 aet
Wembley 0, Enfield 2
Woking 2, Kingstonian 1
THIRD ROUND REPLAYS
Carshalton Athletic 2, Tooting & Mitcham United 2 aet
Hendon 1, Hertford Town 0
Finchley 2, Staines Town 2 aet
THIRD ROUND SECOND REPLAYS
Staines Town 0, Finchley 2
Tooting & Mitcham United 2, Carshalton Athletic 0

FOURTH ROUND
Barking 2, Hendon 0
Boreham Wood 1, Leatherhead 0
Dagenham 6, Harlow Town 1
Dulwich Hamlet 5, Slough Town 2
Enfield 2, Walthamstow Avenue 0
Epsom & Ewell 1, Harwich & Parkeston 2
Sutton United 3, Finchley 3 aet
Tooting & Mitcham United 1, Woking 1 aet
FOURTH ROUND REPLAYS
Finchley 0, Sutton United 2
Woking 2, Tooting & Mitcham United 1

FIFTH ROUND
Barking 1, Sutton United 4
Boreham Wood 1, Woking 6
Dulwich Hamlet 1, Harwich & Parkeston 0
Enfield 2, Dagenham 1 aet

SEMI-FINAL
Enfield 2, Dulwich Hamlet 1
Sutton United 1, Woking 1 aet
SEMI-FINAL REPLAY
Woking 1, Sutton United 3

FINAL
Enfield 3, Sutton United 2
At Harrow Borough FC

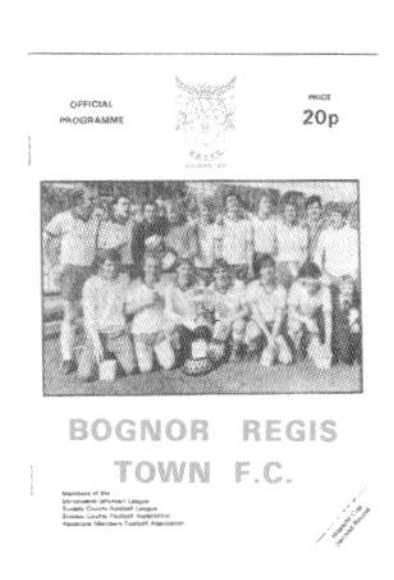

1980–81

FIRST ROUND
Aveley 1, Harwich & Parkeston 0
Billericay Town 2, Metropolitan Police 2 aet
Bishop's Stortford 3, Bromley 2
Boreham Wood 3, Barking 1
Camberley Town 1, Maidenhead United 2
Cheshunt 5, Leatherhead 0
Croydon 1, Farnborough Town 0
Dulwich Hamlet 3, Epping Town 0
Enfield 4, Clapton 0
Hampton 2, Finchley 1
Harrow Borough 1, Sutton United 2
Hayes 2, Wycombe Wanderers 1
Hemel Hempstead 3, Dagenham 7
Hertford Town 1, Carshalton Athletic 0
Hitchin Town 1, Southall 0
Hornchurch 0, Hendon 5
Hungerford Town 2, Chesham United 1
Kingstonian 1, Barton Rovers 1
Letchworth Garden City 0, Harlow Town 4
Lewes 3, Walthamstow Avenue 4
Leytonstone–Ilford 4, Dorking 0
Molesey 0, Ware 5
Oxford City 1, Eastbourne United 2
Rainham Town 1, Epsom & Ewell 4
Slough Town 2, Horsham 1
Staines Town 1, Feltham 0
Tooting & Mitcham United 2, Walton & Hersham 0
Tring Town 1, Tilbury 1 aet
Wembley 3, Egham Town 1
Willesden 0, Worthing 0 aet
Woking 9, Corinthian–Casuals 0
Wokingham Town 0, St. Albans City 1
FIRST ROUND REPLAYS
Barton Rovers 2, Kingstonian 2 aet
Metropolitan Police 1, Billericay Town 2
Tilbury 1, Tring Town 3
Worthing 6, Willesden 1
FIRST ROUND SECOND REPLAY
Barton Rovers 2, Kingstonian 1

SECOND ROUND
Aveley 1, Hungerford Town 2
Barton Rovers 3, Staines Town 2
Billericay Town 3, Boreham Wood 3 aet
Croydon 3, Ware 0
Dulwich Hamlet 1, Sutton United 3
Eastbourne United 0, Bishop's Stortford 1
Hampton 1, Hendon 2
Hayes 3, Harlow Town 1
Hitchin Town 0, Enfield 1
Maidenhead United 0, Leytonstone–Ilford 3
St. Albans City 3, Woking 4
Slough Town 3, Dagenham 1
Tooting & Mitcham United 2, Cheshunt 0
Walthamstow Avenue 2, Tring Town 1
Wembley 2, Hertford Town 1
Worthing 2, Epsom & Ewell 2 aet
SECOND ROUND REPLAYS
Boreham Wood 3, Billericay Town 1
Epsom & Ewell 1, Worthing 0

THIRD ROUND
Bishop's Stortford 2, Leytonstone–Ilford 1 aet
Croydon 2, Hendon 0
Enfield 3, Sutton United 0
Hayes 1, Epsom & Ewell 0
Hungerford Town 4, Wembley 4 aet
Slough Town 3, Barton Rovers 1
Tooting & Mitcham United 1, Boreham Wood 0
Woking 2, Walthamstow Avenue 4

THIRD ROUND REPLAY
Wembley 1, Hungerford 2

FOURTH ROUND
Bishop's Stortford 1, Tooting & Mitcham United 1 aet
Hayes 1, Hungerford Town 0
Slough Town 1, Enfield 0
Walthamstow Avenue 6, Croydon 3
FOURTH ROUND REPLAY
Tooting & Mitcham United 4, Bishop's Stortford 5 aet

SEMI–FINAL - FIRST LEG
Bishop's Stortford 1, Slough Town 1
Hayes 1, Walthamstow Avenue 3
SEMI–FINAL - SECOND LEG
Slough Town 2, Bishop's Stortford 1 (3–2 agg)
Walthamstow Avenue 1, Hayes 1 (4–2 agg)

FINAL
Slough Town 4, Walthamstow Avenue 2
At Hayes FC

1981–82

FIRST ROUND
Barking 1, Kingstonian 1 aet
Barton Rovers 1, Dorking 0 aet
Bishop's Stortford 1, Billericay Town 0
Bognor Regis Town 0, Metropolitan Police 2
Boreham Wood 0, Tooting & Mitcham United 1
Camberley Town 1, Hampton 4 aet
Cheshunt 2, Wokingham Town 1 aet
Croydon 2, Harlow Town 1 aet
Egham Town 1, Eastbourne United 3
Epsom & Ewell 2, Aveley 1 aet
Farnborough Town 1, Tring Town 0
Feltham 3, Bromley 0 (at Bromley FC)
Finchley 0, Hornchurch 1
Harrow Borough 2, Dulwich Hamlet 1
Harwich & Parkeston 0, Slough Town 1
Hayes 1, Leytonstone–Ilford 3
Hemel Hempstead 2, Southall 2 aet
Hendon 2, Staines Town 0
Hertford Town 1, Chesham United 0 aet
Hungerford Town 4, Horsham 1
Letchworth Garden City 0, Leatherhead 3
Maidenhead United 0, Carshalton Athletic 0 aet
Molesey 2, Corinthian Casuals 0
Rainham Town 0, Wycombe Wanderers 1
Oxford City 2, Walthamstow Avenue 1
St. Albans City 1, Hitchin Town 3 aet
Sutton United 6, Clapton 1
Tilbury 5, Lewes 3
Walton & Hersham 1, Ware 2
Wembley 2, Woking 1
Windsor & Eton 4, Basildon United 1
Worthing 3, Epping Town 3 aet
FIRST ROUND REPLAYS
Carshalton Athletic 2, Maidenhead United 2 aet
Epping Town 1, Worthing 1 aet
Kingstonian 2, Barking 0
Southall 1, Hemel Hempstead 0
FIRST ROUND SECOND REPLAYS
Maidenhead United 0, Carshalton Athletic 2
Worthing 1, Epping Town 0

SECOND ROUND
Barton Rovers 2, Leytonstone–Ilford 3
Croydon 1, Hampton 0
Eastbourne United 0, Worthing 3
Epsom & Ewell 1, Tooting & Mitcham United 0
Farnborough Town 4, Ware 0
Harrow Borough 0, Bishop's Stortford 1
Hendon 1, Wembley 2
Hitchin Town 4, Molesey 1
Hornchurch 0, Kingstonian 2
Hiungerford Town 2, Feltham 1
Latherhead 0, Sutton United 0 aet
Metropolitan Police 1, Oxford City 0
Slough Town 3, Windsor & Eton 0
Southall 2, Hertford Town 0
Tilbury 0, Carshalton 1
Cheshunt 1, Wycombe Wanderers 4
SECOND ROUND REPLAY
Sutton United 2, Leatherhead 1

THIRD ROUND
Bishop's Stortford 0, Carshalton Athletic 2
Croydon 1, Kingstonian 2
Farnborough Town 1, Epsom & Ewell 0
Hungerford Town 0, Hitchin Town 2
Slough Town 2, Wycombe Wanderers 3
Sutton United 1, Leytonstone–Ilford 3
Wembley 3, Southall 0
Worthing 5, Metropolitan Police 1

FOURTH ROUND
Carshalton Athletic 0, Wycombe Wanderers 3
Kingstonian 1, Worthing 0
Leytonstone–Ilford 5, Hitchin Town 0
Wembley 1, Farnborough Town 2

SEMI–FINAL - FIRST LEGS
Farnborough Town 0, Leytonstone–Ilford 1
Kingstonian 2, Wycombe Wanderers 0
SEMI–FINAL - SECOND LEGS
Wycombe Wanderers 5, Kingstonian 3 aet (5–5 agg)
Leytonstone–Ilford 1, Farnborough Town 2 aet (2–2 agg)
SEMI–FINAL - REPLAYS
Kingstonian 2, Wycombe Wanderers 1
Farnborough Town 0, Leytonstone–Ilford 1

FINAL
Leytonstone–Ilford 2, Kingstonian 0
At Boreham Wood FC

1982–83

PRELIMINARY ROUND
Uxbridge 2, Leyton–Wingate 2 aet
PRELIMINARY ROUND REPLAY
Leyton–Wingate 0, Uxbridge 1

FIRST ROUND
Aveley 0, Barking 3
Barton Rovers 1, Wokingham Town 0
Bognor Regis Town 2, Wembley 1
Boreham Wood 0, Basildon United 1
Bromley 2, Dorking 1
Cheshunt 2, Eastbourne United 1 aet
Clapton 2, Kingstonian 2 aet
Corinthian–Casuals 0, Hertford Town 1
Dulwich Hamlet 3, Epsom & Ewell 0
Epping Town 0, Woking 1
Farnborough Town 3, Uxbridge 1
Finchley 1, Walthamstow Avenue 2
Hampton 3, Southall 0
Hendon 3, Hemel Hempstead 1
Hitchin Town 5, Tring Town 1
Horsham 0, Chesham United 1
Hungerford Town 0, Hayes 3
Leatherhead 0, Molesey 2
Letchworth Garden City 1, Hornchurch 3
Leytonstone–Ilford 0, Walton & Hersham 1
Lewes 1, Harlow Town 4
Maidenhead United 3, Windsor & Eton 4
Metropolitan Police 4, Bishop's Stortford 1
Oxford City 1, Feltham 0
Rainham Town 2, Carshalton Athletic 3
St. Albans City 4, Croydon 2
Staines Town 2, Egham Town 2 aet
Sutton United 6, Ware 1
Tilbury 1, Billericay Town 2
Tooting & Mitcham United 1, Slough Town 0
Worthing 8, Harwich & Parkeston 0
Wycombe Wanderers 2, Harrow Borough 1
FIRST ROUND REPLAYS
Egham Town 0, Staines Town 3
Kingstonian 4, Clapton 1

SECOND ROUND
Barking 2, Bromley 2 aet
Billericay Town 3, Basildon United 2
Carshalton Athletic 3, Wycombe Wanderers 4
Chesham United 1, Barton Rovers 0
Dulwich Hamlet 2, Tooting & Mitcham United 0 aet
Harlow Town 0, Farnborough Town 2
Hayes 3, St. Albans City 0
Hendon 2, Walthamstow Avenue 0
Hertford Town 1, Hitchin Town 0
Hornchurch 2, Woking 1
Kingstonian 1, Cheshunt 0
Molesey 1, Hampton 2
Staines Town 0, Metropolitan Police 4
Walton & Hersham 2, Bognor Regis Town 4
Windsor & Eton 3, Oxford City 1
Worthing 1, Sutton United 2
SECOND ROUND REPLAY
Bromley 1, Barking 0

THIRD ROUND
Billericay Town 1, Farnborough Town 2 aet
Bromley 4, Dulwich Hamlet 2
Chesham United 0, Kingstonian 1
Hendon 4, Bognor Regis Town 4 aet
Hornchurch 3, Hayes 0
Sutton United 3, Hertford Town 0
Windsor & Eton 4, Hampton 1
Wycombe Wanderers 3, Metropolitan Police 2
THIRD ROUND REPLAY
Bognor Regis Town 3, Hendon 1

FOURTH ROUND
Bognor Regis Town 2, Hornchurch 1aet
Farnborough Town 1, Bromley 1
Kingstonian 0, Wycombe Wanderers 1
Windsor & Eton 3, Sutton United 4
FOURTH ROUND REPLAY
Bromley 1, Farnborough Town 0

SEMI–FINAL
Bromley 0, Wycombe Wanderers 2
Sutton United 2, Bognor Regis Town 0

FINAL - FIRST LEG
Wycombe Wanderers 0, Sutton United 1
FINAL - SECOND LEG
Sutton United 1, Wycombe Wanderers 1 (2–1 agg)

1983–84

PRELIMINARY ROUND
Grays Athletic 2, Newbury Town 0
Horsham 1, Finchley 2

FIRST ROUND
Barking 2, Tring Town 1
Barton Rovers 1, Bromley 2
Basildon United 6, Ware 0
Bognor Regis Town 2, Walthamstow Avenue 0
Boreham Wood 2, Chesham United 0
Clapton 4, Uxbridge 3
Croydon 2, Cheshunt 3
Dulwich Hamlet 0, Egham Town 0 aet
Eastbourne United 3, Hemel Hempstead 1
Farnborough Town 2, Corinthian–Casuals 3
Feltham 1, Hayes 2
Finchley 1, Aveley 2
Hampton 2, Epping Town 1
Harlow Town 3, Billericay Town 2
Harrow Borough 3, St. Albans City 1
Hendon 4, Dorking 3
Hitchin Town 1, Bishop's Stortford 2
Leatherhead 6, Hungerford Town 1
Leyton–Wingate 2, Hertford Town 0
Lewes 2, Kingstonian 3
Molesey 0, Staines Town 1
Oxford City 2, Carshalton Athletic 1
Tilbury 0, Slough Town 4
Tooting & Mitcham United 3, Epsom & Ewell 1
Sutton United 3, Southall 1
Walton & Hersham 0, Grays Athletic 1
Wembley 3, Hornchurch 2
Windsor & Eton 2, Maidenhead United 1
Wokingham Town 6, Rainham Town 1
Woking 0, Metropolitan Police 0 aet
Worthing 3, Leytonstone–Ilford 1
Wycombe Wanderers 6, Letchworth Garden City 0
FIRST ROUND REPLAYS
Egham Town 2, Dulwich Hamlet 5
Metropolitan Police 2, Woking 0

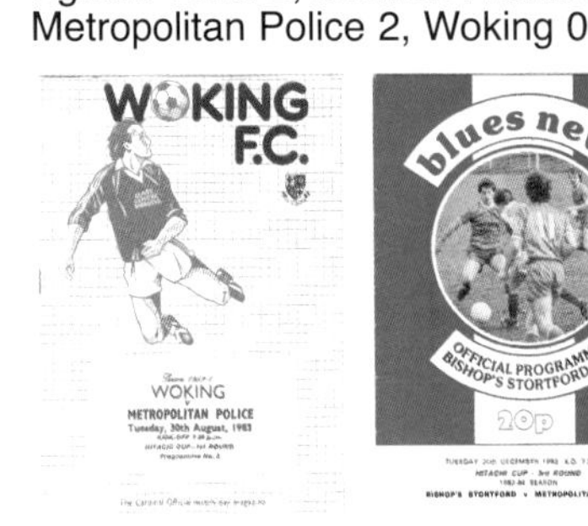

SECOND ROUND
Aveley 1, Leatherhead 0
Basildon United 1, Boreham Wood 0
Bishop's Stortford 0, Cheshunt 0 aet
Bognor Regis Town 7, Kingstonian 0
Clapton 1, Slough Town 0
Grays Athletic 2, Leyton–Wingate 0
Hampton 0, Staines Town 2
Harrow Borough 1, Bromley 2
Hayes 0, Wycombe Wanderers 1
Hendon 2, Dulwich Hamlet 2 aet
Metropolitan Police 4, Eastbourne United 0
Oxford City 5, Barking 1
Sutton United 4, Worthing 0
Tooting & Mitcham United 4, Harlow Town 3
Wembley 1, Corinthian–Casuals 0
Wokingham Town 2, Windsor & Eton 1
SECOND ROUND REPLAYS
Cheshunt 0, Bishop's Stortford 5
Dulwich Hamlet 1, Hendon 0

THIRD ROUND
Aveley 0, Wembley 2
Bishop's Stortford 3, Metropolitan Police 1
Bromley 1, Sutton United 2
Clapton 2, Basildon United 3
Dulwich Hamlet 2, Oxford City 4
Grays Athletic 0, Wycombe Wanderers 1
Staines Town 1, Wokingham Town 2
Tooting & Mitcham United 2, Bognor Regis Town 1

FOURTH ROUND
Basildon United 1, Sutton United 2
Oxford City 2, Tooting & Mitcham United 1
Wembley 1, Bishop's Stortford 0
Wycombe Wanderers 1, Wokingham Town 0

SEMI–FINAL
Sutton United 4, Wembley 1
Wycombe Wanderers 1, Oxford City 0

FINAL - FIRST LEG
Wycombe Wanderers 1, Sutton United 1
FINAL - FIRST LEG
Sutton United 2, Wycombe Wanderers 0 (3–1 agg)

1984–85

PRELIMINARY ROUND
Bracknell Town 2, Saffron Walden Town 0
Chertsey Town 2, Marlow 0
Cheshunt 3, Petersfield United 0
Dorking 1, Wolverton Town 0
Eastbourne United 1, Heybridge Swifts 2
Epping Town 4, Banstead Athletic 2
Feltham 0, Finchley 1
Flackwell Heath 1, Chalfont St Peter 2
Harefield United 1, Camberley Town 1 aet
Haringey Borough 3, Ruislip Manor 1
Hemel Hempstead 3, Egham Town 4
Horsham 2, Kingsbury Town 1
Hungerford Town 2, Tring Town 2 aet
Letchworth Garden City 1, Rainham Town 0
Leyton–Wingate 3, Newbury Town 0
Royston Town 1, Grays Athletic 0
Southall 2, St. Albans City 3
Stevenage Borough 6, Molesey 1
Uxbridge 2, Barton Rovers 3 aet
Ware 1, Berkhamsted Town 2 aet
Whyteleafe w/o Corinthian-Casuals scr
PRELIMINARY ROUND REPLAYS
Camberley Town 0, Harefield United 0 aet
Tring Town 0, Hungerford Town 3

PRELIMINARY ROUND SECOND REPLAY
Camberley Town 2, Harefield United 1

FIRST ROUND
Barton Rovers 2, Oxford City 1 aet
Berkhamsted Town 2, Stevenage Borough 3
Bishop's Stortford 1, Barking 0
Bognor Regis Town 1, Hayes 2
Chalfont St Peter 0, Aveley 1
Cheshunt 1, Wokingham Town 3
Clapton 2, Farnborough Town 3
Croydon 4, Bromley 3
Dorking 0, Epsom & Ewell 4
Egham Town 1, Leyton–Wingate 4
Epping Town 4, Royston Town 0
Hampton 1, Kingstonian 2
Haringey Borough 0, Finchley 2
Harrow Borough 1, Basildon United 0
Hendon 0, Hornchurch 0 aet
Hertford Town 2, Lewes 3
Heybridge Swifts 1, Hitchin Town 1 aet
Leatherhead 4, Harlow Town 1
Letchworth Garden City 4, Horsham 1
Maidenhead United 4, Leytonstone–Ilford 0
Metropolitan Police 3, Chesham United 1
St. Albans City 2, Billericay Town 4
Slough Town 0, Staines Town 1
Sutton United 2, Worthing 2 aet
Tilbury 1, Carshalton Athletic 0
Tooting & Mitcham United 0, Boreham Wood 1
Walthamstow Avenue 3, Dulwich Hamlet 1
Walton & Hersham 4, Chertsey Town 1
Wembley 1, Camberley Town 0
Whyteleafe 5, Woking 1
Windsor & Eton 5, Hungerford Town 0
Wycombe Wanderers 3, Bracknell Town 3 aet
FIRST ROUND REPLAYS
Bracknell Town 0, Wycombe Wanderers 4
Hitchin Town 1, Heybridge Swifts 2
Hornchurch 1, Hendon 2
Worthing 1, Sutton United 2

SECOND ROUND
Aveley 2, Metropolitan Police 1
Barton Rovers 2, Epping Town 0
Billericay Town 2, Wycombe Wanderers 3
Epsom & Ewell 2, Windsor & Eton 1
Farnborough Town 5, Hayes 0
Harrow Borough 2, Finchley 1 aet
Hendon 3, Walton & Hersham 0
Lethworth Garden City 3, Leatherhead 1
Lewes 4, Whyteleafe 1
Leyton–Wingate 4, Walthamstow Avenue 1
Maidenhead United 0, Bishop's Stortford 1
Staines Town 2, Croydon 0
Stevenage Borough 4, Boreham Wood 2 aet
Sutton United 5, Tilbury 0
Wembley 0, Heybridge Swifts 1
Wokingham Town 1, Kingstonian 1 aet
SECOND ROUND REPLAY
Kingstonian 0, Wokingham Town 1

THIRD ROUND
Aveley 0, Lewes 1
Barton Rovers 1, Hendon 2
Epsom & Ewell 3, Heybridge Swifts 2
Farnborough Town 2, Wokingham Town 0
Leyton–Wingate 1, Harrow Borough 1 aet
Staines Town 2, Letchworth Garden City 0
Sutton United 4, Stevenage Borough 1
Wycombe Wanderers 4, Bishop's Stortford 0
THIRD ROUND REPLAY
Harrow Borough 2, Leyton–Wingate 0

FOURTH ROUND
Epsom & Ewell 0, Staines Town 1 aet
Hendon 0, Farnborough Town 1
Lewes 0, Sutton United 1 aet
Wycombe Wanderers 2, Harrow Borough 0

SEMI–FINAL
Staines Town 0, Wycombe Wanderers 2
Sutton United 0, Farnborough Town 3

FINAL - FIRST LEG
Farnborough Town 0, Wycombe Wanderers 3
FINAL - SECOND LEG
Wycombe Wanderers 2, Farnborough Town 1 (5–1 agg)

1985–86
PRELIMINARY ROUND
Banstead Athletic 2, Hemel Hempstead 0
Barton Rovers 0, Wolverton Town 1
Camberley Town 1, Heybridge Swifts 1 aet
Cheshunt 0, Stevenage Borough 1
Clapton 0, Flackwell Heath 6
Dorking 4, Berkhamsted Town 3
Egham Town 1, Bracknell Town 3
Feltham 4, Rainham Town 3 aet
Harefield United 3, Letchworth Garden City 1
Hertford Town 3, Ruislip Manor 3 aet
Hungerford Town 3, Haringey Borough 2
Metropolitan Police 4, Horsham 0
Newbury Town 4, Marlow 1
Petersfield United 3, Eastbourne United 1
Royston Town 1, Saffron Walden Town 2
Southwick 2, Kingsbury Town 1
Tring Town 3, Molesey 0
Ware 0, Southall 2
Whyteleafe 2, Chalfont St Peter 4
Woking 5, Vauxhall Motors 3 aet
PRELIMINARY ROUND REPLAYS
Heybridge Swifts 3, Camberley Town 1
Ruislip Manor 2, Hertford Town 1

FIRST ROUND
Billericay Town 3, Leytonstone–Ilford 2
Bishop's Stortford 2, Basildon United 0
Carshalton Athletic 3, Bracknell Town 0
Croydon 1, Hungerford Town 0
Dorking 3, Banstead Athletic 1
Dulwich Hamlet 2, Saffron Walden Town 1
Farnborough Town 9, Harlow Town 3
Feltham 1, Hendon 3
Grays Athletic 2, Worthing 1
Hampton 3, Tooting & Mitcham United 0
Harefield United 0, Whyteleafe 1
Hayes 5, Aveley 0
Heybridge Swifts 2, Chalfont St Peter 3
Hornchurch 0, Flackwell Heath 1
Leatherhead 4, Boreham Wood 3
Lewes 2, Windsor & Eton 1
Leyton–Wingate 1, Chesham United 0
Metropolitan Police 1, Hitchin Town 0
Newbury Town 0, Finchley 0 aet
Oxford City 3, Wokingham Town 2
Petersfield United 4, Tring Town 3 aet
Ruislip Manor 1, Epsom & Ewell 2 aet
Slough Town 3, Bromley 1 aet
Southall 0, Harrow Borough 3
Staines Town 3, Wolverton Town 1
Stevenage Borough 1, Barking 4
Sutton United 3, Bognor Regis Town 3 aet
Tilbury 3, Walthamstow Avenue 3 aet
Uxbridge 2, Woking 1
Walton & Hersham 2, Southwick 1
Wembley 2, Kingstonian 4
Yeovil Town 2, Maidenhead United 2 aet
FIRST ROUND REPLAYS
Bognor Regis Town 1, Sutton United 3
Finchley 3, Newbury Town 2
Maidenhead United 3, Yeovil Town 1 aet
Walthamstow Avenue 3, Tilbury 1

SECOND ROUND
Barking 0, Hampton 1
Carshalton Athletic 2, Slough Town 2 aet
Croydon 2, Leyton–Wingate 1
Dorking 1, Billericay Town 0
Epsom & Ewell 3, Bishop's Stortford 1
Farnborough Town 3, Grays Athletic 2
Flackwell Heath 1, Dulwich Hamlet 3
Hayes 1, Finchley 0 aet
Leatherhead 2, Kingstonian 1
Lewes 2, St. Albans City 1
Maidenhead United 3, Sutton United 5
Oxford City 4, Walthamstow Avenue 1
Petersfield United 0, Harrow Borough 1
Uxbridge 1, Hendon 0
Staines Town 3, Walton & Hersham 2
Whyteleafe 1, Metropolitan Police 2 aet
SECOND ROUND REPLAY
Slough Town 0, Carshalton Athletic 2

THIRD ROUND
Carshalton Athletic 0, Sutton United 2
Croydon 1, Hayes 3
Epsom & Ewell 3, Dulwich Hamlet 2 aet
Farnborough Town 7, Staines Town 1
Hampton 3, Lewes 2
Harrow Borough 5, Dorking 1
Leatherhead 5, Metropolitan Police 3
Oxford City 1, Uxbridge 3

FOURTH ROUND
Epsom & Ewell 1, Uxbridge 1 aet
Harrow Borough 3, Sutton United 5
Hayes 1, Farnborough Town 2
Leatherhead 0, Hampton 0 aet
FOURTH ROUND REPLAYS
Hampton 2, Leatherhead 0 aet
Uxbridge 4, Epsom & Ewell 2

SEMI–FINAL - FIRST LEGS
Uxbridge 4, Farnborough Town 2
Hampton 1, Sutton United 0
SEMI–FINAL - SECOND LEGS
Farnborough Town 1, Uxbridge 2 (3–6 agg)
Sutton United 2, Hampton 1 aet (2–2 agg)
SEMI–FINAL - REPLAY
Sutton United 3, Hampton 1

FINAL
Sutton United 3, Uxbridge 1
at Metropolitan Police FC

1986–87

PRELIMINARY ROUND
Aveley 2, Barton Rovers 2 aet
Banstead Athletic 3, Royston Town 1
Chesham United 3, Egham Town 2
Collier Row 1, Newbury Town 3
Dorking 4, Wolverton Town 3 aet
Eastbourne United 2, Hornchurch 6
Flackwell Heath 0, Chalfont St Peter 3
Haringey Borough 0, Kingsbury Town 2
Hemel Hempstead 2, Harlow Town 1
Hertford Town 7, Cheshunt 1
Heybridge Swifts 2, Camberley Town 0
Hungerford Town 4, Berkhamsted Town 2
Letchworth Garden City 7, Molesey 1
Metropolitan Police 0, Chertsey Town 2
Petersfield United 0, Tring Town 4
Rainham Town 1, Stevenage Borough 1 aet
Ruislip Manor 0, Feltham 3 aet
Saffron Walden Town 1, Horsham 0
Vauxhall Motors 1, Harefield United 2
Ware 0, Southall 0 aet
Whyteleafe 2, Marlow 1
Wivenhoe Town 2, Clapton 1
Woking 2, Bracknell Town 0
PRELIMINARY ROUND REPLAYS
Barton Rovers 0, Aveley 2
Southall 1, Ware 2
Stevenage Borough 2, Rainham Town 2 aet
PRELIMINARY ROUND SECOND REPLAY
Rainham Town 2, Stevenage Borough 1

FIRST ROUND
Basildon United 1, Banstead Athletic 0
Bishop's Stortford 1, Croydon 2 aet
Bromley 1, Dorking 1 aet
Chalfont St Peter 0, Bognor Regis Town 2
Chertsey Town 5, Letchworth Garden City 4 aet
Dulwich Hamlet 5, Lewes 1
Epsom & Ewell 0, Southwick 2
Farnborough Town 6, Aveley 2
Hampton 2, Boreham Wood 0
Harefield United 1, Grays Athletic 2
Harrow Borough 6, Finchley 2
Hemel Hempstead 3, Wivenhoe Town 2
Hendon 2, Whyteleafe 1
Hertford Town 2, Uxbridge 0
Heybridge Swifts 1, Kingstonian 0
Hitchin Town 1, Billericay Town 0
Hungerford Town 3, Chesham United 4 aet
Leytonstone–Ilford 4, Walthamstow Avenue 0
Leyton–Wingate 2, Wembley 1
Maidenhead United 4, Tooting & Mitcham United 0
Oxford City 1, Tilbury 4
Newbury Town 0, Windsor & Eton 2
Rainham Town 0, Hayes 3
St. Albans City 4, Wokingham Town 4 aet
Slough Town 2, Ware 1
Staines Town 2, Barking 4
Walton & Hersham 1, Feltham 0
Tring Town 0, Carshalton Athletic 3
Woking 2, Leatherhead 2 aet
Worthing 2, Saffron Walden Town 2 aet
Wycombe Wanderers 3, Hornchurch 2 aet
Yeovil Town 3, Kingsbury Town 3 aet
FIRST ROUND REPLAYS
Dorking 0, Bromley 0 aet
Kingsbury Town 1, Yeovil Town 2 aet
Leatherhead 2, Woking 1
Saffron Walden Town 0, Worthing 3
Wokingham Town 0, St. Albans City 1
FIRST ROUND SECOND REPLAY
Dorking 6, Bromley 1

SECOND ROUND
Barking 2, Hemel Hempstead 0
Basildon United 1, Leatherhead 1 aet
Bognor Regis Town 4, Harrow Borough 2
Carshalton Athletic 4, Farnborough Town 5
Chertsey Town 2, Grays Athletic 0
Croydon 2, Hendon 4
Hertford Town 0, Dulwich Hamlet 2
Hitchin Town 3, Heybridge Swifts 1
Leytonstone–Ilford 1, Tilbury 0
Leyton–Wingate 0, Hampton 1
St. Albans City 1, Windsor & Eton 2
Slough Town 2, Dorking 0
Southwick 0, Maidenhead United 0 aet
Walton & Hersham 2, Hayes 0
Wycombe Wanderers 2, Worthing 1
Yeovil Town 7, Chesham United 1
SECOND ROUND REPLAYS
Leatherhead 1, Basildon United 3
Maidenhead United 5, Southwick 0

THIRD ROUND
Bognor Regis Town 3, Dulwich Hamlet 0
Farnborough Town 3, Walton & Hersham 1
Hampton 0, Chertsey Town 1
Hitchin Town 4, Barking 3
Leytonstone–Ilford 3, Hendon 5
Slough Town 0, Basildon United 2
Windsor & Eton 0, Maidenhead United 1
Wycombe Wanderers 1, Yeovil Town 2

FOURTH ROUND
Basildon United 2, Maidenhead United 0
Hendon 1, Chertsey Town 0 aet
Hitchin Town 0, Bognor Regis Town 2
Yeovil Town 6, Farnborough Town 3 aet

SEMI–FINAL - FIRST LEGS
Bognor Regis Town 1, Basildon United 2
Yeovil Town 0, Hendon 2
SEMI–FINAL - FIRST LEGS
Basildon United 2, Bognor Regis Town 5 aet (4–6 agg)
Hendon 2, Yeovil Town 0 (4–0 agg)

FINAL
Bognor Regis Town 3, Hendon 2
At Windsor & Eton FC

1987–88

PRELIMINARY ROUND
Banstead Athletic 3, Yeading 4 aet
Berkhamsted Town 2, Flackwell Heath 0
Chertsey Town 1, Eastbourne United 0
Chesham United 4, Tilbury 3
Clapton 2, Tring Town 0
Finchley 1, Witham Town 2
Hemel Hempstead 2, Epsom & Ewell 0
Hertford Town 2, Harefield United 2 aet
Hornchurch 4, Hungerford Town 2
Maidenhead United 2, Feltham 1
Metropolitan Police 2, Collier Row 1
Molesey 0, Dorking 1,
Newbury Town 1, Horsham 1 aet
Petersfield United 1, Heybridge Swifts 0
Rainham Town 1, Egham Town 2
Royston Town 3, Camberley Town 3 aet
Ruislip Manor 3, Aveley 0
Southall 2, Saffron Walden Town 2 aet
Vauxhall Motors 0, Haringey Borough 1
Ware 0, Chalfont St Peter 1
Whyteleafe 0, Woking 3
Wivenhoe Town 1, Harlow Town 2
Wolverton Town (MK) 1, Barton Rovers 0

PRELIMINARY ROUND REPLAYS
Camberley Town 2, Royston Town 1
Harefield United 2, Hertford Town 0
Horsham 0, Newbury Town 2
Saffron Walden Town 3, Southall 0

FIRST ROUND
Barking 2, Woking 0
Basildon United 1, Maidenhead United 2
Basingstoke Town 0, Kingstonian 2
Berkhamsted Town 2, Chertsey Town 0
Billericay Town 2, Metropolitan Police 1
Bracknell Town 0, Ruislip Manor 3
Bromley 3, Egham Town 1
Carshalton Athletic 2, Leatherhead 1
Chesham United 5, Worthing 1
Croydon 0, Bishop's Stortford 1
Dulwich Hamlet 0, Wokingham Town 1
Harefield United 0, Hampton 2
Haringey Borough 3, Hitchin Town 2
Harlow Town 0, Bognor Regis Town 0 aet
Harrow Borough 1, Grays Athletic 2
Hayes 6, Newbury Town 0
Hemel Hempstead 0, Wembley 2
Hornchurch 0, Kingsbury Town 1 aet
Lewes 0, Hendon 3
Leytonstone–Ilford 3, Witham Town 0
Leyton–Wingate 6, Petersfield United 1
Oxford City 0, Marlow 1
Royston Town 2, Clapton 1
Saffron Walden Town 0, Farnborough Town 3
St. Albans City 7, Dorking 0
Southwick 3, Slough Town 1
Stevenage Borough 1, Chalfont St Peter 2
Tooting & Mitcham United 3, Yeading 2
Walthamstow Avenue 0, Yeovil Town 5
Walton & Hersham 1, Boreham Wood 0
Windsor & Eton 2, Uxbridge 1
Wolverton Town (MK) 0, Staines Town 2
FIRST ROUND REPLAY
Bognor Regis Town 3, Harlow Town 0

SECOND ROUND
Barking 3, Farnborough Town 0
Berkhamsted Town 1, Maidenhead United 0
Billericay Town 5, Windsor & Eton 2 aet
Bognor Regis Town 2, Chalfont St Peter 1
Chesham United 0, Yeovil Town 3
Grays Athletic 0, Bishop's Stortford 0 aet
Hampton 4, Walton & Hersham 3
Hayes 7, Haringey Borough 0
Kingsbury Town 2, Hendon 1 aet
Kingstonian 3, Leyton–Wingate 1
Leytonstone–Ilford 1, St. Albans City 0
Marlow 1, Wembley 2
Royston Town 1, Carshalton Athletic 5
Ruislip Manor 2, Wokingham Town 3
Staines Town 2, Southwick 1 aet
Tooting & Mitcham United 0, Bromley 4
SECOND ROUND REPLAY
Bishop's Stortford 3, Grays Athletic 1

THIRD ROUND
Barking 5, Wembley 2
Berkhamsted Town 0, Wokingham Town 0 aet
Billericay Town 2, Bognor Regis Town 4
Hampton 3, Carshalton Athletic 2
Hayes 5, Bromley 4
Kingsbury Town 1, Staines Town 1 aet
Kingstonian 1, Bishop's Stortford 0
Yeovil Town 2, Leytonstone–Ilford 0
THIRD ROUND REPLAYS
Staines Town 3, Kingsbury Town 4 aet
Wokingham Town 3, Berkhamsted Town 1

FOURTH ROUND
Barking 0, Hayes 3
Bognor Regis Town 1, Kingstonian 2
Hampton 0, Yeovil Town 2
Kingsbury Town 0, Wokingham Town 3

SEMI–FINAL - FIRST LEGS
Wokingham Town 1, Hayes 1
Yeovil Town 2, Kingstonian 0
SEMI–FINAL - SECOND LEGS
Hayes 3, Wokingham Town 0 (4–1 agg)
Kingstonian 0 Yeovil Town 1 (0–3 agg)

FINAL
Yeovil Town 3, Hayes 1
At Basingstoke Town FC

1988–89

PRELIMINARY ROUND
Banstead Athletic 4, Hertford Town 1 aet
Barton Rovers 1, Purfleet 0
Berkhamsted Town 1, Epsom & Ewell 2
Billericay Town 0, Aveley 0
Camberley Town w/o Haringey Borough scr
Chertsey Town 0, Dorking 2
Collier Row 3, Eastbourne United 0
Egham Town 1, Harlow Town 1 aet
Feltham 2, Maidenhead United 2 aet
Flackwell Heath 1, Wolverton Town (MK) 0
Harefield United 2, Molesey 3
Heybridge Swifts 1, Hemel Hempstead 0
Hornchurch 2, Vauxhall Motors 3 aet
Horsham 4, Finchley 0
Hungerford Town 2, Letchworth Garden City 1
Petersfield United 2, Clapton 1 aet
Royston Town 0, Witham Town 2
Ruislip Manor 0, Chalfont St Peter 2
Southall 1, Newbury Town 2
Stevenage Borough 0, Metropolitan Police 1
Tring Town 0, Whyteleafe 2
Ware 6, Saffron Walden Town 1
Wivenhoe Town 3, Rainham Town 0
Yeading 0, Tilbury 0 aet
PRELIMINARY ROUND REPLAYS
Aveley 0, Billericay Town 2
Harlow Town 2, Egham Town 2 aet
Maidenhead United 1, Feltham 4
Tilbury 1, Yeading 0
PRELIMINARY ROUND SECOND REPLAY
Egham Town 1, Harlow Town 2

FIRST ROUND
Barking 3, Slough Town 0
Barton Rovers 0, Hitchin Town 2
Basildon United 0, Lewes 2
Basingstoke Town 2, Feltham 2 aet
Bishop's Stortford 4, Windsor & Eton 2 aet
Bracknell Town 0, Worthing 1
Camberley Town 1, Farnborough Town 6
Chesham United 4, Bognor Regis Town 1
Dulwich Hamlet w/o Oxford City scr
Harlow Town 1, Boreham Wood 0
Harrow Borough 2, Hayes 0
Hendon 2, Wembley 0 aet
Heybridge Swifts 1, Croydon 2
Hungerford Town 4, Flackwell Heath 0
Kingsbury Town 1, Newbury Town 0
Kingstonian 3, Grays Athletic 1
Leytonstone–Ilford 3, Collier Row 1
Molesey 1, Banstead Athletic 0
Petersfield United 2, Horsham 1
St. Albans City 5, Epsom & Ewell 0
Southwick 1, Marlow 0
Staines Town 5, Dagenham 0
Tilbury 4, Chalfont St Peter 1
Tooting & Mitcham United 1, Leyton–Wingate 2
Uxbridge 3, Bromley 2 aet
Vauxhall Motors 0, Dorking 2 aet
Walton & Hersham 2, Billericay Town 1
Ware 0, Hampton 1
Whyteleafe 0, Woking 3
Witham Town 0, Carshalton Athletic 2
Wivenhoe Town 0, Leatherhead 1
Wokingham Town 3, Metropolitan Police 1
FIRST ROUND REPLAY
Feltham 1, Basingstoke Town 3

SECOND ROUND
Bishop's Stortford 3, Molesey 1
Carshalton Athletic 2, Tilbury 1
Croydon 1, Chesham United 1 aet
Dorking 2, Walton & Hersham 1
Dulwich Hamlet 1, Wokingham Town 1 aet
Farnborough Town 2, Basingstoke Town 1
Hampton 2, Hendon 1 aet
Harlow Town 2, Leyton–Wingate 4 aet
Harrow Borough 1, Leatherhead 0
Hitchin Town 1, Barking 3
Hungerford Town 1, St. Albans City 2
Kingstonian 4, Lewes 1
Petersfield United 0, Woking 2
Staines Town 1, Southwick 0
Uxbridge 0, Kingsbury Town 2 aet
Worthing 3, Leytonstone–Ilford 2 aet
SECOND ROUND REPLAYS
Chesham United 0, Croydon 0 aet
Wokingham Town 4, Dulwich Hamlet 2 aet
SECOND ROUND SECOND REPLAY
Croydon 1, Chesham United 0 aet

THIRD ROUND
Bishop's Stortford 1, Hampton 0
Carshalton Athletic 2, Woking 0
Croydon 2, Leyton–Wingate 1
Dorking 2, Kingstonian 1 aet
Farnborough Town 3, Wokingham Town 0
Kingsbury Town 1, Harrow Borough 1 aet
Staines Town 1, St. Albans City 0
Worthing 0, Barking 2
THIRD ROUND REPLAY
Harrow Borough 2, Kingsbury Town 3

FOURTH ROUND
Barking 1, Farnborough Town 2 aet
Bishop's Stortford 4, Croydon 1
Dorking 1, Carshalton Athletic 2 aet
Kingsbury Town 0, Staines Town 2 aet

SEMI–FINAL - FIRST LEGS
Bishop's Stortford 1, Staines Town 0
Farnborough Town 1, Carshalton Athletic 1
SEMI–FINAL - SECOND LEGS
Carshalton Athletic 1, Farnborough Town 2 (2–3 agg)
Staines Town 0, Bishop's Stortford 0 (0–1 agg)

FINAL
Bishop's Stortford 1, Farnborough Town 0
At Hayes FC

BISHOP'S STORTFORD
v
FARNBOROUGH TOWN

AC DELCO CUP FINAL – 1989

Church Road, Hayes
Monday, 1st May, 1989 – 3.00 p.m.

AC Delco 50p CUP FINAL

1989–90

PRELIMINARY ROUND
Abingdon Town 0, Purfleet 1
Basildon United 2, Hemel Hempstead 3
Billericay Town 1, Saffron Walden Town 0
Camberley Town 1, Ware 2
Dorking w/o Newport County scr
Egham Town 3, Ruislip Manor 1
Epsom & Ewell 1, Collier Row 1 aet
Feltham 1, Bracknell Town 2 aet
Finchley 1, Banstead Athletic 0
Flackwell Heath 1, Barton Rovers 2
Harlow Town 2, Hertford Town 1
Hornchurch 1, Clapton 1 aet
Letchworth Garden City 1, Witham Town 2
Maidenhead United 1, Whyteleafe 2
Malden Vale 1, Aveley 2
Molesey 3, Tilbury 2
Newbury Town 1, Berkhamsted Town 0
Petersfield United 3, Eastbourne United 1
Rainham Town 2, Harefield United 1
Royston Town 0, Stevenage Borough 1
Southall 0, Hungerford Town 1
Tring Town 2, Chertsey Town 4 aet
Vauxhall Motors 3, Horsham 0
Yeading 2, Heybridge Swifts 3
PRELIMINARY ROUND REPLAYS
Clapton 1, Hornchurch 0
Collier Row 4, Epsom & Ewell 3

FIRST ROUND
Aveley 1, Chertsey Town 0
Aylesbury United 3, Croydon 0
Basingstoke Town 2, Rainham Town 0
Boreham Wood 1, Barton Rovers 0
Bracknell Town 1, Dorking 2
Chalfont St Peter 3, Harrow Borough 2
Chesham United 4, Egham Town 1
Clapton 2, Heybridge Swifts 0
Collier Row 1, Bishop's Stortford 2
Dulwich Hamlet 0, Molesey 1
Finchley 1, Grays Athletic 0
Hampton 1, Barking 2
Harlow Town 1, Ware 2
Hayes 0, Wokingham Town 0 aet
Hendon 3, Metropolitan Police 2
Hungerford Town 1, Vauxhall Motors 2
Kingsbury Town 3, Hemel Hempstead 0
Leyton–Wingate 3, Hitchin Town 2
Newbury Town 0, Uxbridge 1
Petersfield United 3, Leatherhead 5 aet
Purfleet 2, Billericay Town 0
Redbridge Forest 2, Dagenham 3
St. Albans City 2, Witham Town 0
Slough Town 2, Lewes 1
Staines Town 2, Kingstonian 3
Stevenage Borough 0, Carshalton Athletic 1
Tooting & Mitcham United 1, Woking 5
Walton & Hersham 0, Windsor & Eton 0 aet
Whyteleafe 2, Marlow 1
Wivenhoe Town 2, Southwick 1
Worthing 2, Wembley 3 aet
FIRST ROUND REPLAYS
Windsor & Eton 2, Walton & Hersham 1
Wokingham Town 2, Hayes 0

SECOND ROUND
Aveley 1, Windsor & Eton 0
Aylesbury United 6, Leyton–Wingate 2
Barking 2, Boreham Wood 1
Bishop's Stortford 2, Slough Town 0
Bromley 0, St. Albans City 3
Chesham United 2, Basingstoke Town 1
Dagenham 0, Uxbridge 1
Dorking 0, Carshalton Athletic 1
Finchley 2, Leatherhead 1
Kingsbury Town 2, Chalfont St Peter 1
Purfleet 0, Molesey 0 aet
Wembley 4, Ware 1
Whyteleafe 0, Vauxhall Motors 1
Wivenhoe Town 0, Hendon 2
Woking 8, Clapton 1
Wokingham Town 2, Kingstonian 1
SECOND ROUND REPLAY
Molesey 2, Purfleet 0

THIRD ROUND
Aveley 1, Hendon 1 aet
Barking 1, Woking 1 aet
Bishop's Stortford 0, Wokingham Town 1
Carshalton Athletic 3, Wembley 0
Chesham United 3, Vauxhall Motors 0
Molesey 0, Kingsbury Town 2
St. Albans City 2, Aylesbury United 0
Uxbridge 3, Finchley 2
THIRD ROUND REPLAYS
Hendon 1, Aveley 2
Woking 3, Barking 0

FOURTH ROUND
Chesham United 1, St. Albans City 2
Kingsbury 0, Woking 0 aet
Uxbridge 0, Aveley 3
Wokingham Town 0, Carshalton Athletic 0 aet

FOURTH ROUND REPLAYS
Carshalton Athletic 0, Wokingham Town 3
Woking 2, Kingsbury Town 1

SEMI–FINAL - FIRST LEGS
Aveley 2, Wokingham Town 1
St. Albans City 1, Woking 1
SEMI–FINAL - SECOND LEGS
Woking 1, St. Albans City 2 (2–3 agg)
Wokingham Town 0, Aveley 0 (1–2 agg)

FINAL
Aveley 3, St. Albans City 0
At Dagenham FC

1990–91

PRELIMINARY ROUND
Abingdon Town 0, Flackwell Heath 0 aet
Banstead Athletic 1, Billericay Town 0
Barton Rovers 0, Ware 2
Berkhamsted Town 2, Cove 0
Bracknell Town 2, Horsham 3 aet
Camberley Town 0, Petersfield United 1
Chertsey Town 0, Hemel Hempstead 3
Edgware Town 5, Maidenhead United 2
Feltham 1, Molesey 2
Finchley 0, Egham Town 2
Hampton 3, Rainham Town 1 aet
Harefield United 2, Hungerford Town 1
Hertford Town 0, Witham Town 3
Heybridge Swifts 3, Vauxhall Motors 1
Kingsbury Town 0, Yeading 4
Malden Vale 4, Eastbourne United 1
Newbury Town 4, Clapton 1
Purfleet 3, Epsom & Ewell 2
Royston Town 0, Southall 1
Ruislip Manor 1, Aveley 2
Saffron Walden Town 3, Collier Row 4
Stevenage Borough 2, Hornchurch 1
Tilbury 2, Basildon United 3 aet
Tring Town 2, Leatherhead 0
PRELIMINARY ROUND REPLAY
Flackwell Heath 0, Abingdon Town 1

FIRST ROUND
Basildon United 2, Newbury Town 1
Basingstoke Town 0, Aveley 2
Bishop's Stortford 3, Dorking 0
Boreham Wood 2, Hampton 2 aet
Bromley 2, Leyton–Wingate 0
Chalfont St Peter 1, Lewes 2
Collier Row 2, Banstead Athletic 1
Croydon 2, Berkhamsted Town 2 aet
Dagenham 4, Hemel Hempstead 1
Dulwich Hamlet 1, Horsham 0
Edgware Town 0, Marlow 3
Egham Town 0, Woking 2
Harefield United 1, Abingdon Town 2
Harlow Town 2, Aylesbury United 2 aet
Harrow Borough 3, Metropolitan Police 4 aet
Hayes 3, Heybridge Swifts 4
Hendon 1, Chesham United 1 aet
Kingstonian 3, Whyteleafe 1
Malden Vale 1, Southwick 0
Purfleet 2, Walton & Hersham 1
Southall 1, Carshalton Athletic 2
Staines Town 0, Redbridge Forest 2
Stevenage Borough 1, Grays Athletic 2
Uxbridge 3, Hitchin Town 2
Ware 1, Molesey 3
Wembley 5, Tring Town 0
Windsor & Eton 5, Bognor Regis Town 1
Witham Town 1, Barking 3 aet
Wivenhoe Town 2, Tooting & Mitcham United 1 aet
Wokingham Town 1, Enfield 3
Worthing 3, Petersfield United 4 aet
Yeading 3, St. Albans City 2 aet
FIRST ROUND REPLAYS
Aylesbury United 1, Harlow Town 2
Berkhamsted Town 0, Croydon 2
Chesham United 1, Hendon 3
Hampton 1, Boreham Wood 0

SECOND ROUND
Barking 0, Redbridge Forest 2
Bishop's Stortford 3, Woking 3 aet
Dagenham 1, Collier Row 0
Enfield 0, Bromley 1
Grays Athletic 3, Aveley 2
Harlow Town 3, Abingdon Town 0
Heybridge Swifts 3, Basildon United 1
Kingstonian 3, Malden Vale 1
Marlow 5, Petersfield United 2
Metropolitan Police 0, Dulwich Hamlet 2
Molesey 2, Hendon 0
Purfleet 0, Hampton 1
Uxbridge 4, Croydon 1 aet
Wembley 0, Windsor & Eton 0 aet
Wivenhoe Town 3, Lewes 2
Yeading 0, Carshalton Athletic 1
SECOND ROUND REPLAYS
Windsor & Eton 2, Wembley 3
Woking 2, Bishop's Stortford 1

THIRD ROUND
Bromley 0, Carshalton Athletic 3
Dulwich Hamlet 0, Wivenhoe Town 1
Harlow Town 1, Kingstonian 0
Heybridge Swifts 0, Dagenham 2
Marlow 1, Woking 3
Molesey 1, Grays Athletic 0
Redbridge Forest 4, Wembley 1 aet
Uxbridge 2, Hampton 1

FOURTH ROUND
Carshalton Athletic 3, Harlow Town 0
Molesey 1, Woking 2 aet
Redbridge Forest 3, Uxbridge 0
Wivenhoe Town 1, Dagenham 2

SEMI–FINAL - FIRST LEGS
Redbridge Forest 1, Carshalton Athletic 4
Woking 2, Dagenham 1
SEMI–FINAL - SECOND LEGS
Carshalton Athletic 0, Redbridge Forest 2 (4–3 agg)
Dagenham 1, Woking 1 (2–3 agg)

FINAL
Woking 2, Carshalton Athletic 1
At Kingstonian FC

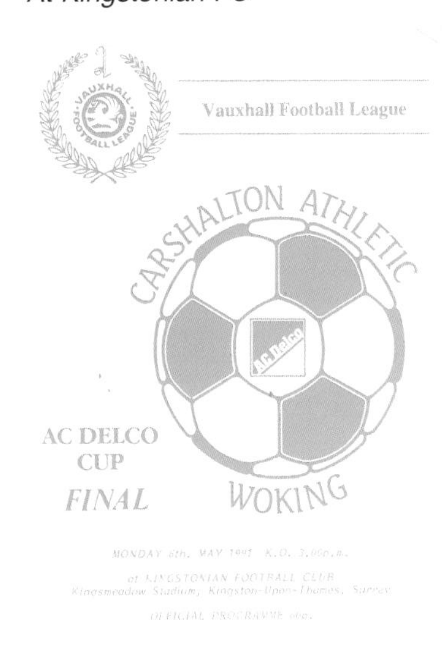

1991–92

PRELIMINARY ROUND
Abingdon Town 2, Hemel Hempstead 0
Barton Rovers 3, Clapton 2
Billericay Town 4, Petersfield United 1
Bracknell Town 0, Harefield United 1
Chertsey Town 1, Tring Town 0
Collier Row 1, Ruislip Manor 4
Eastbourne United 2, Southwick 2 aet
Edgware Town 0, Ware 1 aet
Hertford Town 2, Purfleet 1
Horsham 4, Feltham & Hounslow Borough 1
Hungerford Town 2, Berkhamsted Town 4
Leatherhead 1, Banstead Athletic 2
Lewes 0, Hornchurch 0 aet
Maidenhead United 2, Kingsbury Town 3 aet
Malden Vale w/o Vauxhall Motors scr
Rainham Town 4, Epsom & Ewell 2
Saffron Walden Town 2, Newbury Town 2 aet
Southall 3, Metropolitan Police 1
Stevenage Borough 3, Cove 0
Thame United 1, Camberley Town 2
Tilbury 1, Hampton 0
Witham Town 1, Flackwell Heath 2 aet
Worthing 1, Egham Town 1 aet
PRELIMINARY ROUND REPLAYS
Egham Town 4, Worthing 2
Hornchurch 2, Lewes 3
Newbury Town 0, Saffron Walden Town 2
Southwick 6, Eastbourne United 0

FIRST ROUND
Abingdon Town 2, Harefield United 0
Aveley 1, Hayes 3
Barking 4, Southwick 3
Banstead Athletic 1, Grays Athletic 2
Barton Rovers 1, Woking 3
Basingstoke Town 1, Dagenham 0
Bishop's Stortford 1, Hertford Town 2 aet
Carshalton Athletic 3, Croydon 2
Chalfont St Peter 4, Hendon 6 aet
Chertsey Town 2, Aylesbury United 0
Chesham United 2, Tooting & Mitcham United 2 aet
Dorking 2, Malden Vale 1
Egham 2, Boreham Wood 0
Harrow Borough 2, Walton & Hersham 1
Heybridge Swifts 1, Kingstonian 0
Hitchin Town 1, Billericay Town 2 aet
Lewes 3, Camberley Town 0
Leyton–Wingate 1, Bromley 2
Marlow 2, Wokingham Town 1
Molesey 1, Kingsbury Town 0
Rainham Town 1, Bognor Regis Town 0
Royston Town 0, Berkhamsted Town 2
Saffron Walden Town 0, Enfield 2
Southall 1, Tilbury 3
Staines Town 2, Flackwell Heath 0
Sutton United 2, Stevenage Borough 1
Uxbridge 0, Harlow Town 3
Ware 2, Horsham 2 aet
Whyteleafe 2, Wivenhoe Town 1
Windsor & Eton 4, Wembley 1
Yeading 2, Dulwich Hamlet 1 aet
FIRST ROUND REPLAYS
Horsham 1, Ware 2
Tooting & Mitcham United 2, Chesham United 3

SECOND ROUND
Abingdon Town 2, Lewes 0
Barking 2, Heybridge Swifts 1
Berkhamsted Town 1, Carshalton Athletic 6
Chertsey Town 1, Enfield 4
Dorking 3, Molesey 3 aet
Egham Town 0, Billericay Town 1
(Billericay Town removed from competition)
Harlow Town 0, Grays Athletic 4
Harrow Borough 1, Basingstoke Town 0
Hayes 1, Yeading 0
Hertford Town 0, Sutton United 5
Marlow 3, Windsor & Eton 4 aet
St. Albans City 4, Bromley 1
Staines Town 0, Chesham United 1
Tilbury 3, Hendon 0
Ware 2, Whyteleafe 1
Woking 4, Rainham Town 1
SECOND ROUND REPLAY
Molesey 0, Dorking 2

THIRD ROUND
Abingdon Town 1, Sutton United 2
Chesham United 1, Woking 2
Dorking 3, Grays Athletic 4
Enfield 3, Hayes 0
Harrow Borough 0, Carshalton Athletic 1
St. Albans City 5, Tilbury 0
Ware 2, Barking 0
Windsor & Eton 0, Egham Town 0 aet
THIRD ROUND REPLAY
Egham Town 0, Windsor & Eton 0 *(Abandoned at 90 mins)*
THIRD ROUND SECOND REPLAY
Egham Town 3, Windsor & Eton 1

FOURTH ROUND
Carshalton Athletic 2, Ware 2 aet
Egham Town 1, Grays Athletic 4
Sutton United 2, St. Albans City 3 aet
Woking 0, Enfield 2

FOURTH ROUND REPLAY
Ware 1, Carshalton Athletic 0

SEMI–FINAL - FIRST LEGS
St. Albans City 2, Grays Athletic 2
Ware 1, Enfield 2
SEMI–FINAL - SECOND LEGS
Enfield 0, Ware 0 (2–1 agg)
Grays Athletic 1, St. Albans City 0 (3–2 on agg)

FINAL
Grays Athletic 3, Enfield 1
At Dagenham FC

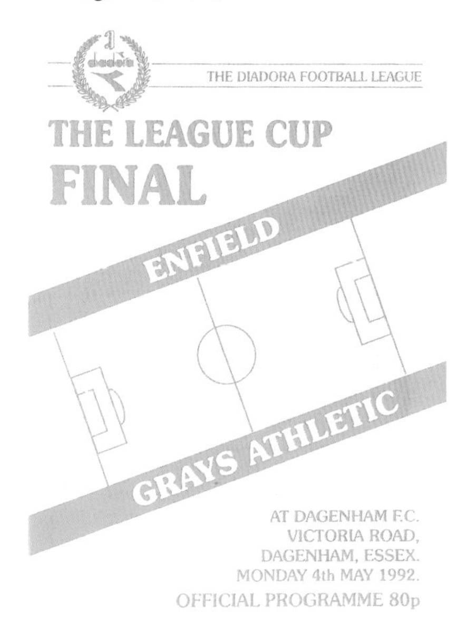

1992–93

PRELIMINARY ROUND
Billericay Town 2, East Thurrock United 0
Bracknell Town 0, Banstead Athletic 3
Camberley Town 1, Edgware Town 0
Cove 3, Berkhamsted Town 2
Feltham & Hounslow Borough 2, Barton Rovers 1
Flackwell Heath 1, Chertsey Town 3
Hemel Hempstead 3, Lewes 1
Hertford Town 3, Southall 1,
Hungerford Town 1, Metropolitan Police 5
Kingsbury Town 2, Harefield United 0
Leatherhead 1, Aldershot Town 1 aet
Leighton Town w/o Farnham Town scr
Northwood 4, Collier Row 1
Petersfield United 2, Horsham 3
Purfleet 3, Royston Town 1
Rainham Town 1, Hampton 5
Saffron Walden Town 2, Newbury Town 0
Thame United 3, Epsom & Ewell 0
Tilbury 2, Ruislip Manor 4 aet
Tring Town 1, Egham Town 2
Ware 1, Malden Vale 2
Witham Town 1, Clapton 0
Worthing 2, Hornchurch 0
PRELIMINARY ROUND REPLAY
Aldershot Town 3, Leatherhead 2

FIRST ROUND
Abingdon Town 3, Camberley Town 1
Aylesbury United 4, Aveley 2
Barking 1, Wivenhoe Town 6
Basingstoke Town 3, Walton & Hersham 0
Bognor Regis Town 1, Metropolitan Police 3
Boreham Wood 4, Feltham & Hounslow Borough 1 aet
Chalfont St Peter 2, Saffron Waldem Town 1
Chertsey Town 2, Egham Town 3 aet
Cove 0, Hayes 5
Croydon 3, Carshalton Athletic 3 aet
Dulwich Hamlet 1, St. Albans City 0 aet
Enfield 7, Whyteleafe 0
Grays Athletic 2, Windsor & Eton 3
Hampton 1, Dorking 0 aet
Harrow Borough 3, Bromley 0
Hemel Hempstead 1, Marlow 4
Hendon 7, Hertford Town 0
Horsham 2, Staines Town 4
Kingstonian 3, Malden Vale 2
Kingsbury Town 0, Aldershot Town 1
Leighton Town 2, Tooting & Mitcham United 3
Leyton 2, Chesham United 1
Maidenhead United 1, Yeading 1 aet
Molesey 2, Bishop's Stortford 1
Purfleet w/o Harlow Town scr
Ruislip Manor 3, Heybridge Swifts 0
Stevenage Borough 1, Billericay Town 2
Sutton United 2, Hitchin Town 0
Thame United 3, Wembley 1
Uxbridge 0, Northwood 1
Wokingham Town 2, Witham Town 0
Worthing 3, Banstead Athletic 1 aet
FIRST ROUND REPLAYS
Carshalton Athletic 0, Croydon 1
Yeading 4, Maidenhead United 1

SECOND ROUND
Abingdon Town 3, Molesey 3 aet
Aldershot Town 5, Hampton 2 aet
Aylesbury United 3, Thame United 3 aet
Basingstoke Town 0, Metropolitan Police 1
Boreham Wood 2, Purfleet 0
Dulwich Hamlet 1, Worthing 3
Hayes 2, Croydon 1
Hendon 2, Ruislip Manor 1
Kingstonian 1, Billericay Town 0 aet
Leyton 2, Tooting & Mitcham United 3
Marlow 5, Egham Town 1
Northwood 2, Windsor & Eton 3
Staines Town 0, Yeading 1
Sutton United 4, Chalfont St Peter 1
Wivenhoe Town 2, Harrow Borough 1
Wokingham Town 0, Enfield 1
SECOND ROUND REPLAYS
Molesey 1, Abingdon Town 0 aet
Thame United 2, Aylesbury United 3 aet

THIRD ROUND
Aylesbury United 1, Enfield 2
Hendon 2, Aldershot Town 1
Marlow 3, Yeading 1
Metropolitan Police 1, Wivenhoe Town 2
Molesey 3, Tooting & Mitcham United 0
Sutton United 3, Boreham Wood 0
Windsor & Eton 0, Hayes 1
Worthing 1, Kingstonian 2

FOURTH ROUND
Hendon 1, Enfield 1 aet
Kingstonian 0, Marlow 4
Molesey 2, Hayes 0
Wivenhoe Town 1, Sutton United 2

FOURTH ROUND REPLAY
Enfield 2, Hendon 0

SEMI–FINAL - FIRST LEGS
Enfield 1, Molesey 0
Sutton United 0, Marlow 2

SEMI–FINAL - SECOND LEGS
Marlow 2, Sutton United 1 (4–1 agg)
Molesey 5, Enfield 0 (5–1 agg)

FINAL
Marlow 2, Molesey 1
At Aldershot Town FC

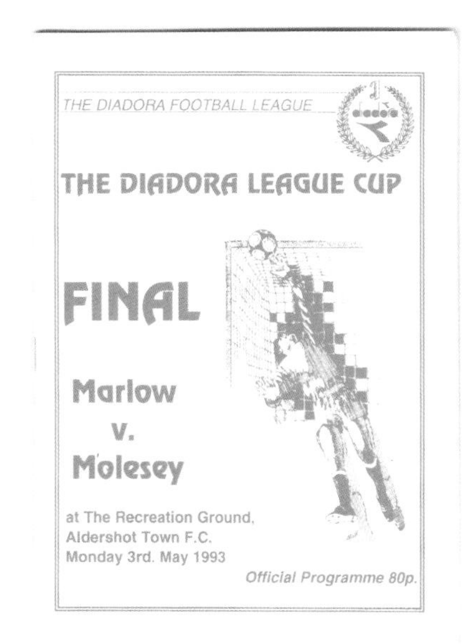

1993–94

PRELIMINARY ROUND
Aldershot Town 5, Clapton 1
Aveley 0, Ruislip Manor 0 aet
Banstead Athletic 1, Edgware Town 0
Barton Rovers 1, Harlow Town 2
Bracknell Town 1, Cheshunt 2
Chertsey Town 1, Royston Town 0
Cove 5, Flackwell Heath 3 aet
Epsom & Ewell 1, Hungerford Town 0
Feltham & Hounslow Borough 2, Thame United 3
Hampton 0, Berkhamsted Town 1
Harefield United 0, Collier Row 1
Hertford Town 1, Lewes 3
Horsham 2, East Thurrock United 1
Leatherhead 1, Hornchurch 0
Leighton Town 0, Tring Town 1
Malden Vale 2, Tilbury 1
Metropolitan Police 3, Rainham Town 0
Newbury Town 2, Kingsbury Town 0
Northwood 1, Witham Town 1 aet
Oxford City 3, Egham Town 0
Saffron Walden Town 4, Southall 2
Ware 0, Camberley Town 2
Worthing 3, Hemel Hempstead 2 aet
PRELIMINARY ROUND REPLAYS
Ruislip Manor 3, Aveley 1
Witham Town 1, Northwood 2

FIRST ROUND
Aldershot Town 0, Kingstonian 4
Aylesbury United 2, Cheshunt 1 aet
Barking 1, Wembley 3
Banstead Athletic 0, Bishop's Stortford 6
Berkhamsted Town 1, Chesham United 4
Billericay Town 3, Tring Town 0
Bognor Regis Town 2, Hayes 0
Camberley Town 1, Maidenhead United 3
Carshalton Athletic 5, Wivenhoe Town 1
Chalfont St Peter 1, Leyton 5
Collier Row 1, Whyteleafe 2
Cove 1, Enfield 5
Croydon 1, Thame United 2
Epsom & Ewell 1, Chertsey Town 2 aet
Grays Athletic 4, Dulwich Hamlet 2
Harlow Town 1, Dorking 2 aet
Hendon 2, Boreham Wood 3 aet
Heybridge Swifts 1, Basingstoke Town 2
Horsham 2, Worthing 3
Hitchin Town 4, Uxbridge 3
Leatherhead 1, Staines Town 3
Malden Vale 2, Oxford City 3
Marlow 2, Yeading 0
Metropolitan Police 3, Wokingham Town 4
Molesey 1, Newbury Town 1 aet
Northwood 1, Windsor & Eton 3
Ruislip Manor 1, Harrow Borough 3
Saffron Walden Town 2, Stevenage Borough 0
St. Albans City 2, Bromley 1 aet
Sutton United 2, Purfleet 0
Tooting & Mitcham United 2, Lewes 1
Walton & Hersham 2, Abingdon Town 1
FIRST ROUND REPLAY
Newbury 2, Molesey 3

SECOND ROUND
Aylesbury United 1, Grays Athletic 4
Billericay Town 1, Maidenhead United 1 aet
Boreham Wood 2, Chertsey Town 3
Dorking 1, Enfield 4
Kingstonian 4, Hitchin Town 3 aet
Leyton 3, St. Albans City 4
Molesey 0, Staines Town 1
Oxford City 1, Basingstoke Town 3
Saffron Walden Town 2, Windsor & Eton 1
Sutton United 1, Bognor Regis Town 3
Thame United 4, Harrow Borough 4 aet
Tooting & Mitcham United 0, Carshalton Athletic 3
Walton & Hersham 0, Worthing 1
Wembley 2, Marlow 2 aet
Whyteleafe 2, Bishop's Stortford 7
Wokingham Town 2, Chesham United 1
(Wokingham Town removed from competition)
SECOND ROUND REPLAYS
Harrow Borough 3, Thame United 3 aet
(Harrow Borough won 5–4 on penalties)
Maidenhead United 1, Billericay Town 0
Marlow 2, Wembley 1

THIRD ROUND
Basingstoke Town 1, Marlow 1 aet
Bognor Regis Town 2, Enfield 3
Carshalton Athletic 1, Bishop's Stortford 0
Chertsey Town 3, Worthing 0
Chesham United 3, Grays Athletic 2
Kingstonian 6, Harrow Borough 1
Saffron Walden Town 3, Maidenhead United 1
Staines Town 0, St. Albans City 1
THIRD ROUND REPLAY
Marlow 3, Basingstoke Town 2 aet

FOURTH ROUND
Chertsey Town 5, St. Albans City 0
Chesham United 0, Marlow 3
Enfield 3, Saffron Walden Town 1 aet
Kingstonian 0, Carshalton Athletic 1

SEMI–FINAL - FIRST LEGS
Carshalton Athletic 0, Chertsey Town 3
Marlow 1, Enfield 1
SEMI–FINAL - SECOND LEGS
Chertsey Town 2, Carshalton Athletic 1 (5–1 agg)
Enfield 2, Marlow 1 aet (3–2 agg)

FINAL
Chertsey Town 3, Enfield 0
At Hayes FC

1994–95

PRELIMINARY ROUND
Aldershot Town 3, Bracknell Town 1
Barton Rovers 2, Egham Town 4
Chalfont St Peter 4, Kingsbury Town 1
Chertsey Town 2, Oxford City 3
Cheshunt 0, Ware 1
Clapton 2, Hemel Hempstead 3 aet
East Thurrock United 2, Banstead Athletic 0 aet
Epsom & Ewell 0, Hornchurch 0 aet
Feltham & Hounslow Borough 0 Leighton Town 0 aet
Hampton 1, Edgware Town 3
Harefield United 1, Hungerford Town 2
Hertford Town 1, Camberley Town 3
Horsham 2, Cove 0
Leatherhead 1, Canvey Island 2 aet
Lewes 1, Aveley 1 aet
Malden Vale 2, Harlow Town 4
Newbury Town 3, Metropolitan Police 0
Northwood 0, Bedford Town 1
Southall 2, Saffron Walden Town 6
Tilbury 1, Flackwell Heath 1 aet
Tring Town 1, Collier Row 3 aet
Windsor & Eton 3, Croydon 1
Witham Town 5, Thame United 4 aet
PRELIMINARY ROUND REPLAYS
Aveley 1, Lewes 1 aet *(Lewes won 5–4 on penalties)*
(Lewes were removed from competition)
Flackwell Heath 3, Tilbury 0
Hornchurch 3, Epsom & Ewell 0
Leighton Town 1, Feltham & Hounslow Borough 1 aet
(Leighton Town won 3–2 on penalties)

FIRST ROUND
Aldershot Town 4, Basingstoke Town 2
Aylesbury United 4, Whyteleafe 2
Barking 2, Wokingham Town 0
Bedford Town 2, Dulwich Hamlet 3 aet
Billericay Town 1, Purfleet 2
Bishop's Stortford 2, Marlow 6
Bognor Regis Town 4, Hemel Hempstead 1
Bromley 0, Oxford City 1
Carshalton Athletic 6, Flackwell Heath 0
Chalfont St Peter 2, Saffron Walden Town 3
Chesham United 2, Aveley 1 aet
Collier Row 2, Yeading 0
Dorking 1, Ware 0
East Thurrock United 2, Uxbridge 0
Edgware Town 3, Enfield 4
Egham Town 1, Wembley 2
Grays Athletic 2, Harlow Town 1
Hayes 0, Slough Town 1
Heybridge Swifts 2, Boreham Wood 0
Hitchin Town 3, Berkhamsted Town 1
Kingstonian 1, Abingdon Town 2
Leighton Town 0, Staines Town 2
Leyton 4, Camberley Town 0
Maidenhead United 0, Walton & Hersham 2
Molesey 1, Newbury Town 2
Ruislip Manor 2, Horsham 1 aet
St. Albans City 2, Harrow Borough 1
Sutton United 1, Canvey Island 1 aet
Tooting & Mitcham United 2 Hornchurch 0
Witham Town 3, Windsor & Eton 1
Wivenhoe Town 0, Hungerford Town 2
Worthing 3, Hendon 3 aet
FIRST ROUND REPLAYS
Canvey Island 2, Sutton United 4 aet
Hendon 2, Worthing 2 aet *(Hendon won 3–1 on pens)*

SECOND ROUND
Abingdon Town 2, St. Albans City 3
Aldershot Town 2, Walton & Hersham 1 aet
Carshalton Athletic 7, Dorking 0
Grays Athletic 5, Saffron Walden Town 1
Heybridge Swifts 1, Aylesbury United 2
Hungerford Town 0, Dulwich Hamlet 6
Leyton 2, Hendon 1 aet
Marlow 2, Newbury Town 1 aet
Oxford City 2, Chesham United 1
Purfleet 2, East Thurrock United 0
Ruislip Manor 1, Sutton United 3
Slough Town 4, Collier Row 0
Staines Town 4, Barking 1
Tooting & Mitcham United 1, Hitchin Town 2
Wembley 2, Bognor Regis Town 1
Witham Town 0, Enfield 5

THIRD ROUND
Aldershot Town 3, Staines Town 2
Aylesbury United 2, Grays Athletic 0
Carshalton Athletic 3, Enfield 1
Dulwich Hamlet 3, Wembley 2
Leyton 1, Marlow 2
Oxford City 1, St. Albans City 2
Purfleet 1, Hitchin Town 2 aet
Slough Town 5, Sutton United 1

FOURTH ROUND
Aldershot Town 1, Aylesbury United 2
Carshalton Athletic 1, Dulwich Hamlet 1 aet
Marlow 2, Hitchin Town 0
St. Albans City 3, Slough Town 4
FOURTH ROUND REPLAY
Dulwich Hamlet 5, Carshalton Athletic 1

SEMI–FINAL - FIRST LEGS
Aylesbury United 4, Marlow 0
Slough Town 3, Dulwich Hamlet 1
SEMI–FINAL - SECOND LEGS
Dulwich Hamlet 1, Slough Town 2 (5–2 agg)
Marlow 2, Aylesbury United 2 (2–6 agg)

FINAL
Aylesbury United 1, Slough Town 1 aet
(Aylesbury United won 7–6 on penalties)
At Marlow FC

1995–96

PRELIMINARY ROUND
Banstead Athletic 2, East Thurrock United 0
Bedford Town 2, Metropolitan Police 1
Bracknell Town 3, Cheshunt 1
Collier Row 0, Canvey Island 0 aet
Croydon 4, Camberley Town 0
Dorking 3, Aveley 2
Edgware Town 2, Harlow Town 1
Egham Town 2, Hertford Town 0
Epsom & Ewell 2, Barton Rovers 3
Flackwell Heath 2, Wingate & Finchley 1
Hemel Hempstead 3, Tilbury 1 aet
Horsham 3, Oxford City 6
Hungerford Town w/o Newbury Town scr
(Newbury Town suspended by Football Association)
Kingsbury Town 2, Cove 0
Leatherhead 3, Clapton 2 aet
Leighton Town 1, Hampton 2 aet
Lewes 1, Witham Town 2
Northwood 0, Harefield United 1
Saffron Walden Town 1, Hornchurch 2
Thame United 0, Chalfont St Peter 1
Ware 3, Tring Town 5
Windsor & Eton 2, Southall 1 aet
Wivenhoe Town 2, Wealdstone 5
PRELIMINARY ROUND REPLAY
Canvey Island 0, Collier Row 2
(Collier Row were removed from competition)

FIRST ROUND
Aldershot Town 3, Chertsey Town 2
Aylesbury United 3, Maidenhead United 0
Banstead Athletic 6, Windsor & Eton 1
Berkhamsted Town 1, Kingsbury Town 2
Billericay Town 3, Hampton 1
Bracknell Town 3, Wokingham Town 5
Chesham United 4, Harrow Borough 1
Croydon 3, Witham Town 0
Dorking 1, Barton Rovers 5
Edgware Town 0, Bishop's Stortford 2
Egham Town 1, Ruislip Manor 1 aet
Enfield 4, Leyton Pennant 2
Flackwell Heath 1, Dulwich Hamlet 3 aet
Harefield United 0, Bromley 3
Hayes 0, Grays Athletic 1
Hitchin Town 4, Canvey Island 1
Hornchurch 1, Bedford Town 4
Kingstonian 2, Abingdon Town 1
Leatherhead 2, Hungerford Town 1
Marlow 2, Hemel Hempstead 1
Molesey 0, Basingstoke Town 1
Purfleet 0, Boreham Wood 1
St. Albans City 2, Worthing 3
Staines Town 3, Oxford City 1 aet
Sutton United 2, Tring Town 0
Tooting & Mitcham United 4, Wealdstone 3
Uxbridge 0, Barking 1
Walton & Hersham 2, Chalfont St Peter 2 aet
Wembley 1, Carshalton Athletic 3
Whyteleafe 1, Heybridge Swifts 2
Yeading 0, Bognor Regis Town 3
Yeovil Town 1, Hendon 3
FIRST ROUND REPLAYS
Chalfont St Peter 3, Walton & Hersham 5 aet
Ruislip Manor 2, Egham Town 0

SECOND ROUND
Aldershot Town 2, Grays Athletic 1
Barking 0, Kingstonian 6
Barton Rovers 0, Dulwich Hamlet 1
Basingstoke Town 2, Ruislip Manor 2 aet
Bedford Town 3, Tooting & Mitcham United 2
Bishop's Stortford 3, Staines Town 1
Bromley 3, Boreham Wood 3 aet
Carshalton Athletic 2, Bognor Regis Town 0
Chesham United 2, Aylesbury United 3 aet
Hendon 0, Croydon 1 aet
Heybridge Swifts 4, Billericay Town 3
Kingsbury Town 1, Walton & Hersham 1
(Abandoned in extra time)
Leatherhead 0, Marlow 2
Sutton United 0, Hitchin Town 1
Wokingham Town 0, Banstead Athletic 3
(Banstead Athletic removed from the competition)
Worthing 1, Enfield 4
SECOND ROUND REPLAYS
Boreham Wood 1, Bromley 0
Ruislip Manor 2, Basingstoke Town 3
Walton & Hersham 3, Kingsbury Town 1

THIRD ROUND
Aldershot Town 1, Boreham Wood 0
Aylesbury United 3, Carshalton Athletic 1
Basingstoke Town 6, Marlow 0
Bedford Town 1, Wokingham Town 2
Croydon 2, Walton & Hersham 1
Enfield 2, Kingstonian 2 aet
Heybridge Swifts 3, Dulwich Hamlet 2 aet
Hitchin Town 4, Bishop's Stortford 1 aet
THIRD ROUND REPLAY
Kingstonian 3, Enfield 0

FOURTH ROUND
Aldershot Town 1, Basingstoke Town 0
Aylesbury United 2, Croydon 1 aet
Heybridge Swifts 2, Kingstonian 2 aet
Wokingham Town 2, Hitchin Town 3
FOURTH ROUND REPLAY
Kingstonian 2, Heybridge Swifts 0

SEMI–FINAL - FIRST LEGS
Aylesbury United 1, Kingstonian 3
Hitchin Town 0, Aldershot Town 1
SEMI–FINAL - FIRST LEGS
Aldershot Town 2, Hitchin Town 0 (3–0 agg)
Kingstonian 2, Aylesbury United 1 (5–2 agg)

FINAL
Aldershot Town 1, Kingstonian 4
At Aldershot Town FC

1996–97

PRELIMINARY ROUND
Banstead Athletic 1, Camberley Town 0
Chalfont St Peter 0, Leighton Town 1
Cheshunt 1, Horsham 3
East Thurrock United 1, Clapton 0 aet
Egham Town 0, Collier Row & Romford 2
Epsom & Ewell 3, Wivenhoe Town 2
Flackwell Heath 1, Bedford Town 4
Hemel Hempstead 5, Barking 2
Hertford Town 1, Edgware Town 2
Hungerford Town 2, Metropolitan Police 1
Leatherhead 2, Harlow Town 2 aet
Lewes 0, Dorking 2
Northwood 2, Windsor & Eton 1
Southall 0, Tilbury 1
Tring Town 1, Braintree Town 6
Ware 0, Aveley 2
Wealdstone 1, Kingsbury Town 0
Wembley 1, Bracknell Town 0
Witham Town 0, Wingate & Finchley 1
PRELIMINARY ROUND REPLAY
Harlow Town 2, Leatherhead 3 aet

FIRST ROUND
Aldershot Town 0, Enfield 3
Aveley 5, Leatherhead 1
Aylesbury United 1, Braintree Town 4
Banstead Athletic 3, Northwood 1
Barton Rovers 0, Bedford Town 1
Berkhamsted Town 5, Harrow Borough 6
Billericay Town 2, Basingstoke Town 1
Bognor Regis Town 6, East Thurrock United 2 aet
Boreham Wood 3, Edgware Town 2 aet
Canvey Island 1, Sutton United 2
Carshalton Athletic 6, Whyteleafe 0
Chesham United 3, Epsom & Ewell 3 aet
Collier Row & Romford 4, Bromley 3 aet
Croydon 0, Leighton Town 1
Dagenham & Redbridge 3, Marlow 0
Dorking 1, Hitchin Town 0
Dulwich Hamlet 0, Yeading 1
Grays Athletic 1, Hornchurch 0
Hemel Hempstead 1, Abingdon Town 0
Hendon 1, Wembley 0 aet
Hungerford Town 0, Walton & Hersham 1
Kingstonian 2, Tilbury 1
Leyton Pennant 1, Purfleet 4
Maidenhead United 1, Heybridge Swifts 2
Oxford City 2, Chertsey Town 3 aet
Staines Town 1, Uxbridge 0
Thame United 4, Hampton 1
Wealdstone 4, Horsham 2 aet
Wingate & Finchley 1, St. Albans City 6
Wokingham Town 2, Bishop's Stortford 1
Worthing 0, Tooting & Mitcham United 3
Yeovil Town 6, Molesey 1
FIRST ROUND REPLAY
Epsom & Ewell 1, Chesham United 2

SECOND ROUND
Banstead Athletic 6, Wealdstone 0
Bedford Town 1, Chertsey Town 0
Billericay Town 1, Collier Row & Romford 1 aet
Bognor Regis Town 2, Staines Town 1
Boreham Wood 1, Dagenham & Redbridge 0
Carshalton Athletic 1, Braintree Town 2
Chesham United 3, Thame United 2 aet
Dorking 0, Heybridge Swifts 4
(Match ordered to be replayed)
Harrow Borough 3, Enfield 2
Kingstonian 3, Hemel Hempstead 2 aet
Leighton Town 1, Hendon 0
Purfleet 3, Sutton United 6
St. Albans City 3, Aveley 1
Walton & Hersham 0, Grays Athletic 3
Wokingham Town 3, Tooting & Mitcham United 0
Yeading 1, Yeovil Town 1 aet
SECOND ROUND REPLAYS
Collier Row & Romford 4, Billericay Town 3 aet
(Collier Row & Romford removed from the competition)
Heybridge Swifts 8, Dorking 0
Yeovil Town 0, Yeading 1

THIRD ROUND
Bedford Town 2, Heybridge Swifts 1 aet
Braintree Town 3, Billericay Town 1
Grays Athletic 1, Chesham United 2
Kingstonian 2, Banstead Athletic 1 aet
Leighton Town 0, Boreham Wood 2
St. Albans City 2, Harrow Borough 4
Sutton United 3, Yeading 2
Wokingham Town 1, Bognor Regis Town 2
(Bognor Regis Town removed from the competition)

FOURTH ROUND
Braintree Town 2, Bedford Town 1 aet
Chesham United 2, Sutton United 1
(Chesham United removed from the competition)
Harrow Borough 1, Boreham Wood 3
Kingstonian 2, Wokingham Town 0

SEMI–FINAL - FIRST LEGS
Braintree Town 1, Sutton United 0
Kingstonian 1, Boreham Wood 1
SEMI–FINAL - SECOND LEGS
Boreham Wood 3, Kingstonian 2 aet (4–3 agg)
Sutton United 1, Braintree Town 2 (1–3 agg)

FINAL
Boreham Wood 2, Braintree Town 0 aet
At Dagenham & Redbridge FC

1997–98

PRELIMINARY ROUND
Aveley 3, Epsom & Ewell 0
Bedford Town 1, Windsor & Eton 0
Camberley Town 1, Witham Town 0
Cheshunt 0, Marlow 5
Corinthian–Casuals 2, Wingate & Finchley 2 aet
Croydon Athletic 3, Ware 3 aet
East Thurrock United 2, Ford United 4 aet
Egham Town 2, Braintree Town 4
Flackwell Heath 1, Lewes 2 aet
Hemel Hempstead 4, Kingsbury Town 2 aet
Hertford Town 1, Clapton 1 aet
Horsham 2, Harlow Town 4
Hungerford Town 2, Northwood 1 aet
Leatherhead 0, Canvey Island 1
Metropolitan Police 2, Barking 1
Southall 1, Hornchurch 2 aet
Tilbury 2, Chalfont St Peter 1
Tooting & Mitcham United 5, Dorking 2
Tring Town 0, Bracknell Town 2 aet
Wealdstone 2, Edgware Town 1
Wembley 2, Leighton Town 1
Wivenhoe Town 3, Banstead Athletic 0
PRELIMINARY ROUND REPLAYS
Clapton 2, Hertford Town 0
Ware 0, Croydon Athletic 1
Wingate & Finchley 2, Corinthian–Casuals 0

FIRST ROUND
Aldershot Town 4, Croydon Athletic 0
Aveley 4, Abingdon Town 2
Basingstoke Town 3, Dulwich Hamlet 1
Bedford Town 1, Whyteleafe 0
Berkhamsted Town 1, Walton & Hersham 2
Billericay Town 5, Hornchurch 2 aet
Bracknell Town 0, Sutton United 2
Bromley 3, Bishop's Stortford 1
Camberley Town 2, Kingstonian 1
Carshalton Athletic 3, Hungerford Town 2
Chesham United 1, Boreham Wood 4
Croydon 4, Metropolitan Police 0
Enfield 1, St. Albans City 2 aet
Ford United 1, Dagenham & Redbridge 3
Gravesend & Northfleet 1, Aylesbury United 0
Harrow Borough 0 Canvey Island 3
Hitchin Town 2, Wembley 0
Lewes 0, Clapton 4
Leyton Pennant 2, Uxbridge 2 aet
Maidenhead United 1, Romford 2
Marlow 1, Harlow Town 4
Molesey 0, Hampton 4
Oxford City 4, Braintree Town 1
Staines Town 1, Hendon 8
Thame United 1, Heybridge Swifts 2
Tilbury 0, Bognor Regis Town 2 aet
Wealdstone 4, Barton Rovers 1
Wingate & Finchley 1, Chertsey Town 2 aet
Wivenhoe Town 0, Purfleet 2
Wokingham Town 1, Grays Athletic 0
Worthing 0, Tooting & Mitcham United 1
Yeading 3, Hemel Hempstead 2
FIRST ROUND REPLAY
Uxbridge 3, Leyton Pennant 0

SECOND ROUND
Aldershot Town 0, Dagenham & Redbridge 1
Basingstoke Town 1, Aveley 1 aet
Billericay Town 0, Purfleet 0 aet
Boreham Wood 4, Bognor Regis Town 3 aet
Carshalton Athletic 1, Yeading 0
Clapton 1, St. Albans City 2
Croydon 1, Bedford Town 2
Gravesend & Northfleet 3, Wokingham Town 2 aet
(Gravesend & Northfleet removed from the competition)
Hampton 2, Walton & Hersham 3
Harlow Town 2, Bromley 3
Hendon 2, Canvey Island 4
Heybridge Swifts 0, Oxford City 1
Hitchin Town 4, Wealdstone 4 aet
Romford 4, Chertsey Town 1
Sutton United 3, Uxbridge 0
Tooting & Mitcham United 0, Camberley Town 2
SECOND ROUND REPLAYS
Aveley 1, Basingstoke Town 3
Purfleet 1, Billericay Town 2 aet
Wealdstone 2, Hitchin Town 6

THIRD ROUND
Boreham Wood 1, Dagenham & Redbridge 0
Camberley Town 0, Oxford City 3
Canvey Island 2, Hitchin Town 0
Carshalton Athletic 1, Billericay Town 0
Romford 3, Bromley 1
St. Albans City 1, Bedford Town 1 aet
Sutton United 2, Basingstoke Town 2 aet
Wokingham Town 1, Walton & Hersham 0
THIRD ROUND REPLAYS
Basingstoke Town 1, Sutton United 3
Bedford Town 3, St. Albans City 3 aet
(St. Albans City won 4–2 on penalties)

FOURTH ROUND
Boreham Wood 2, Canvey Island 0
Carshalton Athletic 0, Oxford City 1
Romford 2, Sutton United 2 aet
Wokingham Town 0, St. Albans City 3
FOURTH ROUND REPLAY
Sutton United 5, Romford 3 aet

SEMI–FINAL - FIRST LEGS
Oxford City 2, Boreham Wood 1
Sutton United 0, St. Albans City 0
SEMI–FINAL - SECOND LEGS
Boreham Wood 0, Oxford City 3 (1–5 agg)
St. Albans City 0, Sutton United 3 (0–3 agg)

FINAL
Oxford City 1, Sutton United 6
At Harrow Borough FC

1998–99

PRELIMINARY ROUND
Abingdon Town 2, Epsom & Ewell 1
Aveley 2, Ford United 2 aet
Banstead Athletic 1, Witham Town 0
Barking 0, Harlow Town 4
Bedford Town 2, Braintree Town 1
Bracknell Town 0, Tooting & Mitcham United 4
Camberley Town 2, Tring Town 0
Corinthian–Casuals 4, Horsham 0 aet
Dorking 2, Croydon Athletic 3 aet
East Thurrock United 2, Wokingham Town 0
Egham Town 1, Clapton 1 aet
(Egham Town withdrew from the competition)
Hemel Hempstead Town 1, Edgware Town 0
Hertford Town 1, Lewes 2
Hornchurch 1, Cheshunt 1 aet
Kingsbury Town 0, Leighton Town 3
Marlow 5, Flackwell Heath 2 aet
Metropolitan Police 3, Tilbury 3 aet
Southall 0, Hungerford Town 1
Ware 0, Thame United 0 aet
Wealdstone 4, Northwood 1 aet
Wingate & Finchley 1, Chalfont St Peter 2
Wivenhoe Town 1, Windsor & Eton 2
PRELIMINARY ROUND REPLAYS
Cheshunt 3, Hornchurch 1
(Cheshunt removed from competition)
Ford United 2, Aveley 0
Thame United 0, Ware 2
Tilbury 0, Metropolitan Police 2 aet

FIRST ROUND
Abingdon Town 0, Slough Town 1
Aylesbury United 1, Leyton Pennant 4 aet
Barton Rovers 2, Camberley Town 1
Bedford Town 6, Ford United 2
Bognor Regis Town 2, Chesham United 2 aet
Boreham Wood 2, Enfield 0
Bromley 3, Tooting & Mitcham United 0
Carshalton Athletic 4, Banstead Athletic 3
Chertsey Town 3, Chalfont St Peter 2
Clapton 1, Marlow 5
Croydon 2, Basingstoke Town 4 aet
Croydon Athletic 2, Harlow Town 2 aet
Dulwich Hamlet 2, Sutton United 3
Grays Athletic 1, Metropolitan Police 2
Harrow Borough 3, East Thurrock United 2 aet
Hemel Hempstead Town 0, Romford 1
Heybridge Swifts 3, Walton & Hersham 2
Hitchin Town 0, Aldershot Town 1
Hornchurch 0, Canvey Island 3
Leatherhead 2, Corinthian–Casuals 1
Leighton Town 0, Uxbridge 2
Maidenhead United 3, Lewes 1 aet
Molesey 1, Bishop's Stortford 2
Purfleet 4, Oxford City 2 aet
St. Albans City 1, Hendon 4
Staines Town 1, Yeading 0
Ware 1, Dagenham & Redbridge 2
Wealdstone 4, Berkhamsted Town 1 aet
(Wealdstone removed from the competition)
Wembley 1, Hampton 1 aet
Whyteleafe 0, Gravesend & Northfleet 5
Windsor & Eton 0, Hungerford Town 1
Worthing 0, Billericay Town 1
FIRST ROUND REPLAYS
Chesham United 2, Bognor Regis Town 1
Hampton 5, Wembley 0
Harlow Town 1, Croydon Athletic 1 aet
(Croydon Athletic won 5–4 on penalties)

SECOND ROUND
Berkhamsted Town 3, Canvey Island 1
Bishop's Stortford 5, Basingstoke Town 4 aet
(Bishop's Stortford removed from the competition)
Boreham Wood 3, Hungerford Town 1
Carshalton Athletic 1, Uxbridge 2
Chertsey Town 4, Aldershot Town 4 aet
Chesham United 3, Dagenham & Redbridge 1 aet
Croydon Athletic 0, Maidenhead United 2
Harrow Borough 1, Bedford Town 0
Hendon 2, Gravesend & Northfleet 1
Heybridge Swifts 1, Bromley 2 aet
Leatherhead 6, Leyton Pennant 4
Metropolitan Police 3, Marlow 4
Purfleet 5, Hampton 0
(Purfleet removed from the competition)
Romford 1, Barton Rovers 2
Staines Town 1, Slough Town 3
Sutton United 4, Billericay Town 0
SECOND ROUND REPLAY
Aldershot Town 5, Chertsey Town 0

THIRD ROUND
Barton Rovers 0, Boreham Wood 3
Berkhamsted Town 3, Aldershot Town 3 aet
Chesham United 0, Bromley 3
Hampton 2, Leatherhead 5
Maidenhead United 4, Slough Town 2
Marlow 2, Hendon 1
Sutton United 2, Basingstoke Town 0
Uxbridge 1, Harrow Borough 0
THIRD ROUND REPLAY
Aldershot Town 1, Berkhamsted Town 0

FOURTH ROUND
Boreham Wood 5, Marlow 1
Leatherhead 0, Aldershot Town 1
Maidenhead United 5, Sutton United 4 aet
Uxbridge 2, Bromley 0

SEMI–FINAL - FIRST LEGS
Bromley 1, Aldershot Town 3
Maidenhead United 2, Boreham Wood 3
SEMI–FINAL - SECOND LEGS
Aldershot Town 1, Bromley 2 aet (4–3 agg)
Boreham Wood 1, Maidenhead United 0 (4–2 agg)

FINAL
Aldershot Town 2, Boreham Wood 1
At Slough Town FC

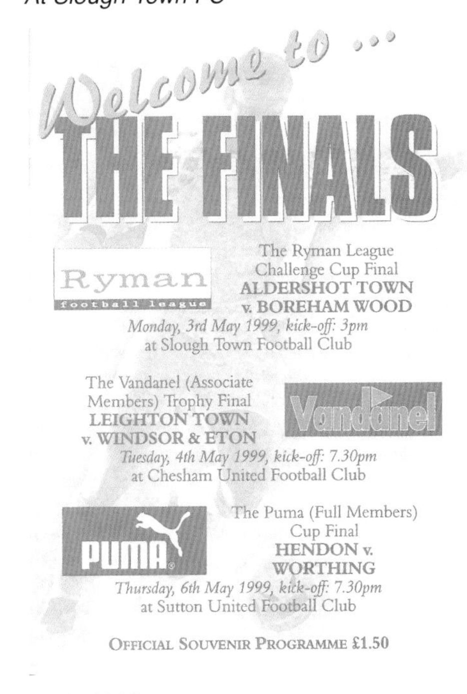

1999–2000

PRELIMINARY ROUND
Aveley 0, Wingate & Finchley 1
Banstead Athletic 3, Ford United 4
Bracknell Town 2, Berkhamsted Town 1
Camberley Town 1, East Thurrock United 0
Cheshunt 3, Harlow Town 2
Clapton 0, Epsom & Ewell 4
Dorking 4, Windsor & Eton 7 aet
Edgware Town 0, Tring Town 2
Flackwell Heath 1, Egham Town 0
Hemel Hempstead Town 3, Barking 0
Hertford Town 1, Corinthian–Casuals 0
Hungerford Town 5, Ware 3
Kingsbury Town 1, Leighton Town 3
Marlow 5, Hornchurch 4 aet
Metropolitan Police 1, Abingdon Town 2 aet
Molesey 1, Bedford Town 2
Northwood 0, Tilbury 0 aet
Southall 1, Chalfont St Peter 1 aet
Thame United 3, Croydon Athletic 1 aet
Tooting & Mitcham United 1, Wembley 3
Witham Town 2, Lewes 4 aet
Wivenhoe Town 5, Horsham 2
Wokingham Town 2, Great Wakering Rovers 4 aet
PRELIMINARY ROUND REPLAYS
Chalfont St Peter 3, Southall 3 aet
(Southall won 4–2 on penalties)
Tilbury 0, Northwood 5

FIRST ROUND
Abingdon Town 2, Cheshunt 1
Basingstoke Town 3, Walton & Hersham 1
Bedford Town 0, Oxford City 2
Billericay Town 3, Wembley 2
Boreham Wood 0, Bishop's Stortford 2
Bracknell Town 0, Great Wakering Rovers 1
Braintree Town 3, Aylesbury United 1
Bromley 1, Maidenhead United 2
Camberley Town 0, Lewes 1
Canvey Island 1, Romford 3
Carshalton Athletic 0, Bognor Regis Town 0 aet
Chertsey Town 5, Southall 3 aet
Croydon 5, Dagenham & Redbridge 0
Dulwich Hamlet 6, Wivenhoe Town 2
Enfield 1, Barton Rovers 2 aet
Epsom & Ewell 1, Staines Town 1 aet
Farnborough Town 2, Yeading 0
Ford United 2, Flackwell Heath 1
Gravesend & Northfleet 1, Hendon 2 aet
Hampton & Richmond Borough 0, St. Albans City 2
Hemel Hempstead Town 1, Aldershot Town 3 aet
Hertford Town 3, Wealdstone 4
Heybridge Swifts 5, Harrow Borough 1
Hungerford Town 1, Tring Town 2
Leyton Pennant 2, Thame United 0
Marlow 1, Leatherhead 0
Northwood 3, Chesham United 3 aet
Purfleet 2, Leighton Town 0
Slough Town 1, Grays Athletic 0
Uxbridge 1, Hitchin Town 2
Windsor & Eton 2, Worthing 1
Wingate & Finchley 0, Whyteleafe 5
FIRST ROUND REPLAYS
Bognor Regis Town 0, Carshalton Athletic 2
Chesham United 2, Northwood 1 aet
Staines Town 3, Epsom & Ewell 0

SECOND ROUND
Abingdon Town 0, Aldershot Town 3
Barton Rovers 3, Hendon 1
Bishop's Stortford 2, Tring Town 2 aet
Dulwich Hamlet 1, Croydon 2
Ford United 0, Chesham United 5
Heybridge Swifts 2, Windsor & Eton 1
Hitchin Town 3, Farnborough Town 3 aet
(Hitchin Town removed from the competition)
Lewes 1, Billericay Town 3
Maidenhead United 2, Basingstoke Town 1
Oxford City 5, Marlow 1
Purfleet 2, Chertsey Town 1
Romford 0, Braintree Town 0 aet
St. Albans City 4, Great Wakering Rovers 2
Slough Town 0, Carshalton Athletic 1
Wealdstone 1, Leyton Pennant 0
Whyteleafe 3, Staines Town 2 aet
SECOND ROUND REPLAYS
Braintree Town 1, Romford 1 aet
(Braintree Town won 5–4 on penalties)
Tring Town 1, Bishop's Stortford 2

THIRD ROUND
Aldershot Town 1, Farnborough Town 2
Barton Rovers 5, Carshalton Athletic 0
Billericay Town 1, St. Albans City 2 aet
(St. Albans City removed from the competition)
Chesham United 1, Purfleet 0
Croydon 0, Bishop's Stortford 2
Heybridge Swifts 3, Braintree Town 1
Wealdstone 0, Oxford City 1
Whyteleafe 1, Maidenhead United 2

FOURTH ROUND
Chesham United 0, Billericay Town 2
Farnborough Town 2, Heybridge Swifts 7
(Heybridge Swifts removed from the competition)
Maidenhead United 2, Bishop's Stortford 1
Oxford City 0, Barton Rovers 0 aet
FOURTH ROUND REPLAY
Barton Rovers 1, Oxford City 1 aet
(Barton Rovers won 2–1 on penalties)

SEMI–FINAL - FIRST LEGS
Barton Rovers 1, Farnborough Town 1
Billericay Town 1, Maidenhead United 1
SEMI–FINAL - SECOND LEGS
Farnborough Town 2, Barton Rovers 0 (3–1 agg)
Maidenhead United 0, Billericay Town 0 aet (1–1 agg)
(Maidenhead United won 4–3 on penalties)

FINAL
Farnborough Town 1, Maidenhead United 0 aet
At Basingstoke Town FC

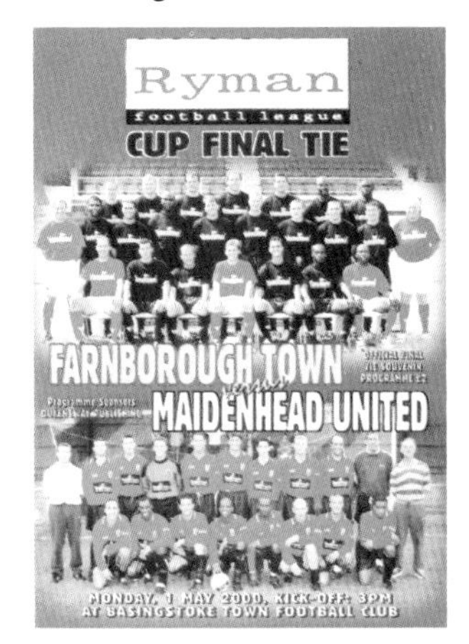

2000–01

PRELIMINARY ROUND
Ashford Town (Middlesex) 5, Croydon Athletic 3
Aveley 4, Tooting & Mitcham United 2 aet
Banstead Athletic 4, Bracknell Town 2 aet
Barking 0, Arlesey Town 0 aet
Berkhamsted Town 2, Flackwell Heath 3
Chalfont St Peter 2, Northwood 4
Chertsey Town 0, East Thurrock United 3
Clapton 0, Corinthian–Casuals 1
Dorking 1, Hungerford Town 2
Edgware Town 0, Metropolitan Police 0 aet
Egham Town 2, Hemel Hempstead Town 2 aet
Ford United 1, Hornchurch 0
Great Wakering Rovers 2, Tilbury 0
Hertford Town 4, Witham Town 0
Leatherhead 1, Romford 0
Leighton Town 1, Epsom & Ewell 2
Lewes 5, Kingsbury Town 0
Leyton Pennant 2, Abingdon Town 1
Marlow 1, Wivenhoe Town 0
Molesey 0, Cheshunt 0 aet
Tring Town 0, Wingate & Finchley 2
Ware 2, Windsor & Eton 1
Wembley 4, Camberley Town 0
Wokingham Town 1, Horsham 3
PRELIMINARY ROUND REPLAYS
Arlesey Town 3, Barking 1
Cheshunt 1, Molesey 2
Hemel Hempstead Town 3, Egham Town 1 aet
Metropolitan Police 0, Edgware Town 1

FIRST ROUND
Arlesey Town 3, Hendon 4
Ashford Town (Middlesex) 1, Bromley 3
Banstead Athletic 0, Horsham 2
Bedford Town 1, Epsom & Ewell 0
Billericay Town 3, Barton Rovers 1
Bishop's Stortford 3, Canvey Island 5 aet
Bognor Regis Town 5, Harlow Town 3
Carshalton Athletic 1, Hitchin Town 0 aet
Corinthian–Casuals 1, Sutton United 0
Dulwich Hamlet 5, Aveley 2 aet
East Thurrock United 1, Braintree Town 2 aet
Edgware Town 0, Basingstoke Town 1
Farnborough Town 2, Enfield 1 aet
Flackwell Heath 1, Slough Town 3
Ford United 0, Heybridge Swifts 2
Gravesend & Northfleet 6, Hungerford Town 1
Grays Athletic 0, Northwood 4
Harrow Borough 2, Croydon 3
Hemel Hempstead Town 2, Great Wakering Rovers 0 aet
Hertford Town 2, Oxford City 3
Lewes 0, Aylesbury United 0 aet
Leyton Pennant 0, Hampton & Richmond Borough 4
Maidenhead United 1, Leatherhead 3
Molesey 2, Ware 4
St. Albans City 1, Boreham Wood 1
Thame United 4, Wealdstone 3
Uxbridge 2, Purfleet 3
Walton & Hersham 2, Aldershot Town 1 aet
Wembley 2, Staines Town 1
Whyteleafe 2, Worthing 3 aet
Wingate & Finchley 1, Chesham United 3
Yeading 0, Marlow 1 aet
FIRST ROUND REPLAYS
Aylesbury United 2, Lewes 1
Boreham Wood 2, St. Albans City 3

SECOND ROUND
Aylesbury United 4, Ware 0
Billericay Town 4, Corinthian–Casuals 0
Bromley 1, Chesham United 3
Canvey Island 2, Gravesend & Northfleet 0
Croydon 3, Wembley 0
Dulwich Hamlet 1, Carshalton Athletic 2 aet
Farnborough Town 5, Hemel Hempstead Town 1 aet
Hampton & Richmond Borough 3, Bognor Regis Town 2
Hendon 3, Braintree Town 2 aet
Heybridge Swifts 3, Oxford City 0
Marlow 0, Slough Town 2
(Slough Town removed from the competition)
Purfleet 4, Horsham 0
St. Albans City 3, Leatherhead 1
Thame United 0, Basingstoke Town 4
Walton & Hersham 0, Bedford Town 5
Worthing 0, Northwood 2

THIRD ROUND
Aylesbury United 0, Purfleet 1
Carshalton Athletic 0, Hampton & Richmond Borough 3
Croydon 5, Canvey Island 0
Farnborough Town 1, Basingstoke Town 3
Hendon 2, Chesham United 3
Heybridge Swifts 3, Bedford Town 0
Northwood 4, Billericay Town 3
St. Albans City 3, Marlow 1

FOURTH ROUND
Basingstoke Town 0, Croydon 2
Heybridge Swifts 3, Chesham United 1
Northwood 4, Purfleet 1
St. Albans City 3, Hampton & Richmond Borough 3 aet
FOURTH ROUND REPLAY
Hampton & Richmond Borough 3, St. Albans City 0

SEMI–FINAL - FIRST LEGS
Hampton & Richmond Borough 2, Croydon 3
Heybridge Swifts 4, Northwood 1
SEMI–FINAL - SECOND LEGS
Croydon 3, Hampton & Richmond Borough 2 (6–4 agg)
Northwood 1, Heybridge Swifts 2 (2–6 agg)

FINAL
Heybridge Swifts 3, Croydon 0 *At Purfleet FC*

2001–02

PRELIMINARY ROUND
Abingdon Town 3, Ashford Town (Middx) 1
Arlesey Town 4, Wingate & Finchley 0
Aveley 2, Corinthian–Casuals 3
Banstead Athletic 3, Barton Rovers 3 aet
Berkhamsted Town 2, Leighton Town 3 aet
Camberley Town 1, Chertsey Town 0
Clapton 0, Epsom & Ewell 2
Croydon Athletic 4, Ware 3
Dorking 2, Hertford Town 4
Egham Town 2, Wivenhoe Town 0
Flackwell Heath 2, Marlow 5 aet
Hemel Hempstead Town 5, East Thurrock United 1
Hornchurch 0, Wokingham Town 0 aet
Hungerford Town 2, Cheshunt 1
Kingsbury Town 1, Barking & East Ham United 2
Leatherhead 2, Leyton Pennant 3
Lewes 4, Witham Town 0
Metropolitan Police 2, Great Wakering Rovers 1
Romford 1, Molesey 3
Tilbury 3, Tring Town 2 aet
Tooting & Mitcham United 3, Bracknell Town 2
Wealdstone 5, Edgware Town 2
Wembley 2, Horsham 0
Windsor & Eton 1, Chalfont St Peter 0
PRELIMINARY ROUND REPLAYS
Barton Rovers 1, Banstead Athletic 0
Wokingham Town 0, Hornchurch 4

FIRST ROUND
Aldershot Town 5, Croydon 1
Aylesbury United 1, Metropolitan Police 3
Barking & East Ham Utd 3, Hampton & Richmond B 8
Basingstoke Town 2, Kingstonian 0
Boreham Wood 1, Leyton Pennant 2
Braintree Town 2, Abingdon Town 2 aet
Bromley 2, Billericay Town 0
Canvey Island 3, Lewes 2
Carshalton Athletic 0, Worthing 2
Chesham United 2, St. Albans City 0
Corinthian–Casuals 2, Whyteleafe 1
Enfield 4, Egham Town 1
Ford United 1, Epsom & Ewell 0
Gravesend & Northfleet 2, Arlesey Town 1
Grays Athletic 5, Bedford Town 1
Harlow Town 1, Northwood 2 aet
Harrow Borough 3, Camberley Town 0
Hemel Hempstead Town 1, Croydon Athletic 3 aet
Hertford Town 0, Hendon 3
Hitchin Town 8, Walton & Hersham 2
Hornchurch 5, Bognor Regis Town 2
Hungerford Town 0, Maidenhead United 3
Marlow 1, Barton Rovers 2
Molesey 4, Leighton Town 1
Oxford City 0, Bishop's Stortford 4
Purfleet 0, Yeading 1
Staines Town 2, Heybridge Swifts 0
Sutton United 5, Dulwich Hamlet 3 aet
Thame United 1, Windsor & Eton 0 aet
Uxbridge 1, Tooting & Mitcham United 1 aet
Wealdstone 6, Tilbury 1 aet
Wembley 4, Slough Town 6

FIRST ROUND REPLAY
Abingdon Town 0, Braintree Town 4
Tooting & Mitcham United 3, Uxbridge 1

SECOND ROUND
Bishop's Stortford 2, Canvey Island 4
Braintree Town 4, Molesey 1
Bromley 0, Corinthian–Casuals 1
Chesham United 0, Enfield 2
Ford United 4, Barton Rovers 1
Gravesend & Northfleet 4, Basingstoke Town 1 aet
Hampton & Richmond Borough 5, Maidenhead United 3
Harrow Borough 1, Northwood 4
Hendon 0, Aldershot Town 2
Hornchurch 0, Leyton Pennant 2 aet
Metropolitan Police 1, Wealdstone 2 aet
Slough Town 0, Hitchin Town 1
Staines Town 0, Grays Athletic 2
Thame United 1, Sutton United 3
Tooting & Mitcham United 2, Croydon Athletic 0
Yeading 3, Worthing 2 aet

THIRD ROUND
Aldershot Town 3, Corinthian–Casuals 0
Braintree Town 3, Canvey Island 5
Enfield 4, Hitchin Town 0
Gravesend & Northfleet 1, Tooting & Mitcham United 2
Leyton Pennant 0, Northwood 1
Sutton United 1, Grays Athletic 7
Wealdstone 3, Ford United 2
Yeading 1, Hampton & Richmond Borough 3

FOURTH ROUND
Grays Athletic 2, Aldershot Town 3 aet
Hampton & Richmond Borough 1, Enfield 0
Northwood 3, Canvey Island 1
Wealdstone 0, Tooting & Mitcham United 1

SEMI–FINAL - FIRST LEGS
Aldershot Town 2, Hampton & Richmond Borough 2
Northwood 4, Tooting & Mitcham United 2
SEMI–FINAL - SECOND LEGS
Hampton & Richmond B 1, Aldershot Town 0 aet (3–2 agg)
Tooting & Mitcham United 1, Northwood 1 (3–5 agg)

FINAL
Northwood 3, Hampton & Richmond Borough 2 aet
At St. Albans City FC

2002–03

FIRST ROUND
Aveley 4, Bracknell Town 0
Banstead Athletic 2, Tring Town 0
Barton Rovers 4, Croydon Athletic 1
Berkhamsted Town 4, Arlesey Town 4 aet
Chertsey Town 3, Camberley Town 2
Cheshunt 6, Hertford Town 0
Clapton 2, Whyteleafe 2 aet
Corinthian–Casuals 3, Edgware Town 1
East Thurrock United 3, Wokingham Town 1
Epsom & Ewell 1, Ashford Town (Middx) 4
Great Wakering Rovers 0, Bromley 1
Hemel Hempstead Town 1, Leyton 3 aet
Horsham 1, Abingdon Town 1 aet
Kingsbury Town 0, Wembley 6
Leighton Town 0, Chalfont St Peter 2
Lewes 3, Wivenhoe Town 0
Leyton Pennant 0, Flackwell Heath 1
Metropolitan Police 2, Hornchurch 6
Molesey 4, Barking & East Ham United 3
Tilbury 2, Hungerford Town 3
Ware 0, Marlow 1
Windsor & Eton 5, Egham Town 2
Wingate & Finchley 6, Dorking 5 aet
Witham Town 3, Leatherhead 0
FIRST ROUND REPLAYS
Abingdon Town 0, Horsham 3
Arlesey Town 3, Berkhamsted Town 2
Whyteleafe 1, Clapton 0

SECOND ROUND
Ashford Town (Middx) 3, Heybridge Swifts 1
Aveley 2, Marlow 0
Barton Rovers 1, Braintree Town 3
Billericay Town 5, Enfield 0
Bromley 0, Bedford Town 1
Chalfont St Peter 1, Arlesey Town 2
Chesham United 2, Sutton United 3 aet
Cheshunt 1, Aldershot Town 0
Corinthian–Casuals 2, Carshalton Athletic 1
Croydon 2, Banstead Athletic 0
Dulwich Hamlet 2, Chertsey Town 0
Flackwell Heath 0, Aylesbury United 3
Ford United 3, Purfleet 0
Harlow Town 1, Grays Athletic 2
Hayes 0, Canvey Island 1
Hendon 4, Staines Town 2
Horsham 1, Boreham Wood 3
Hungerford Town 0, Bishop's Stortford 0 aet
Lewes 3, Maidenhead United 3 aet
Leyton 3, Wealdstone 0
Molesey 0, Hampton & Richmond Borough 1
Northwood 4, Hornchurch 2
Slough Town 1, Kingstonian 3 aet
St. Albans City 3, Bognor Regis Town 2 aet
Thame United 2, East Thurrock United 3 aet
Tooting & Mitcham United 1, Worthing 4
Uxbridge 1, Basingstoke Town 2
Walton & Hersham 0, Hitchin Town 1
Wembley 5, Oxford City 3
Whyteleafe 0, Yeading 3
Windsor & Eton 0, Harrow Borough 4
Witham Town 1, Wingate & Finchley 2 aet

SECOND ROUND REPLAYS
Bishop's Stortford 7, Hungerford Town 1
Maidenhead United 0, Lewes 1

THIRD ROUND
Ashford Town (Middx) 1, St. Albans City 2
Aveley 2, Northwood 1
Aylesbury United 3, Sutton United 2
Bishop's Stortford 3, Basingstoke Town 1
Braintree Town 1, Harrow Borough 3
Cheshunt 1, Canvey Island 5
Croydon 1, Wingate & Finchley 3
East Thurrock United 0, Grays Athletic 1
Ford United 1, Billericay Town 3
Hendon 2, Arlesey Town 1
Hitchin Town 4, Boreham Wood 0
Kingstonian 3, Worthing 0
Lewes 6, Hampton & Richmond Borough 0
Leyton 3, Bedford Town 4 aet
Wembley 0, Dulwich Hamlet 2
Yeading 4, Corinthian–Casuals 0

FOURTH ROUND
Bedford Town 1, Yeading 2
Billericay Town 1, Bishop's Stortford 1 aet
Grays Athletic 1, Aylesbury United 0
Harrow Borough 2, Lewes 3
Hendon 5, Wingate & Finchley 2 aet
Hitchin Town 1, Canvey Island 3
Kingstonian 3, Aveley 1
St. Albans City 1, Dulwich Hamlet 2
FOURTH ROUND REPLAY
Bishop's Stortford 3, Billericay Town 0

FIFTH ROUND
Bishop's Stortford 1, Yeading 4
Canvey Island 6, Grays Athletic 0
Dulwich Hamlet 4, Lewes 1
Hendon 1, Kingstonian 0 aet

SEMI–FINAL - FIRST LEGS
Canvey Island 4, Hendon 2
Dulwich Hamlet 1, Yeading 3
SEMI–FINAL - SECOND LEGS
Hendon 2, Canvey Island 2 (4–6 agg)
Yeading 3, Dulwich Hamlet 3 (6–4 agg)

FINAL
Yeading 2, Canvey Island 0
At Hornchurch FC

2003–04

FIRST ROUND
Arlesey Town 3, Abingdon Town 0
Banstead Athletic w/o Tring Town scr
Chalfont St Peter 5, Ware 1
Clapton scr Bracknell Town w/o
Dorking 0, Worthing 1
Dunstable Town 7, Wivenhoe Town 1
East Thurrock United 2, Croydon 1
Epsom & Ewell 0, Waltham Forest 1
Flackwell Heath 1, Egham Town 5
Great Wakering Rovers 2, Barton Rovers 1
Harlow Town 2, Hertford Town 0
Kingsbury Town 0, Wealdstone 8
Leatherhead 1, Croydon Athletic 4
Leighton Town 0, Ashford Town (Middx) 2
Marlow 2, Barking & East Ham United 2 aet
(Marlow won 5–4 on penalties)
Metropolitan Police 2, Corinthian–Casuals 1 aet
Molesey 3, Windsor & Eton 1
Oxford City 1, Cheshunt 3
Staines Town 4, Witham Town 4 aet
(Witham Town won 5–4 on penalties)
Tooting & Mitcham United 1, Lewes 2 aet
Wembley 0, Camberley Town 1
Wingate & Finchley 2, Chertsey Town 0
Wokingham Town 2, Tilbury 4
Yeading 5, Edgware Town 1

SECOND ROUND
Arlesey Town 0, Hornchurch 2
Basingstoke Town 2, Aylesbury United 0
Bedford Town 1, Bognor Regis Town 0
Berkhamsted Town 0, Ashford Town (Middx) 2
Billericay Town 1, East Thurrock United 2
Bracknell Town 5, Chalfont St Peter 0
Braintree Town 1, Thurrock 2
Camberley Town 0, Northwood 1
Canvey Island 0, Hendon 3
Carshalton Athletic 0, Harlow Town 1
Chesham United 1, Lewes 0
Dulwich Hamlet 3, Hampton & Richmond Borough 3 aet
(Hampton & Richmond Borough won 4–3 on pens)
Egham Town 4, Tilbury 2
Ford United 2, Bishop's Stortford 1
Great Wakering Rovers 2, Banstead Athletic 1
Harrow Borough 2, Bromley 0
Heybridge Swifts 2, St. Albans City 1
Horsham 2, Witham Town 1
Kingstonian 2, Croydon Athletic 0
Leyton 4, Enfield 1
Maidenhead United 3, Hayes 2
Marlow 3, Boreham Wood 2
Molesey 0, Walton & Hersham 0 aet
(Molesey won 4–2 on penalties)
Slough Town 1, Cheshunt 4
Sutton United 2, Metropolitan Police 0
Thame United 1, Hitchin Town 2
Uxbridge 1, Dunstable Town 2
Waltham Forest 0, Aveley 2
Whyteleafe 0, Grays Athletic 2
Wingate & Finchley 2, Wealdstone 0
Worthing 2, Kettering Town 0
Yeading 2, Hemel Hempstead Town 1

THIRD ROUND
Aveley 0, Hornchurch 5
Basingstoke Town 0, Ashford Town (Middx) 0 aet
(Ashford Town (Middx) won 3–2 on penalties)
Bracknell Town 4, Hendon 3 aet
Chesham United 6, Molesey 1
East Thurrock United 1, Wingate & Finchley 2
Egham Town 0, Grays Athletic 1
Ford United 0, Northwood 1
Harlow Town 3, Great Wakering Rovers 1
Heybridge Swifts 3, Harrow Borough 2 aet
Hitchin Town 1, Marlow 3
Horsham 0, Bedford Town 3
Leyton 1, Hampton & Richmond Borough 2
Sutton United 2, Dunstable Town 3
Thurrock 1, Kingstonian 0
Worthing 2, Maidenhead United 0
Yeading 4, Cheshunt 4 aet *(Cheshunt won 9–8 on pens)*

FOURTH ROUND
Bracknell Town 2, Worthing 1 aet
Chesham United 2, Ashford Town (Middx) 0
Dunstable Town 1, Grays Athletic 0
Hampton & Richmond Boro 4, Wingate & Finchley 2
Heybridge Swifts 3, Cheshunt 4
Hornchurch 0, Harlow Town 0 aet
(Harlow Town won 4–2 on penalties)
Marlow 2, Northwood 0
Thurrock 4, Bedford Town 1

FIFTH ROUND
Bracknell Town 1, Hampton & Richmond Borough 2
Dunstable Town 4, Harlow Town 1
Marlow 1, Cheshunt 2
Thurrock 2, Chesham United 1

SEMI–FINAL - FIRST LEGS
Cheshunt 0, Thurrock 2
Dunstable Town 2, Hampton & Richmond Borough 1
SEMI–FINAL - SECOND LEGS
Hampton & Richmond B 1, Dunstable Town 3 (2–5 agg)
Thurrock 1, Cheshunt 2 (3–2 agg)

FINAL
Thurrock 5, Dunstable Town 1
At Bishop's Stortford FC

2004–05

FIRST ROUND
AFC Wimbledon 2, Flackwell Heath 0
Bashley 4, Abingdon Town 0
Brook House 3, Molesey 2 aet
Chalfont St Peter 3, Clapton 4
Chertsey Town 1, Burgess Hill Town 3
Cray Wanderers 5, Camberley Town 1
Croydon Athletic 4, Dorking 1
Dulwich Hamlet 6, Corinthian–Casuals 0
Edgware Town 3, Horsham 4
Epsom & Ewell 1, Witham Town 2
Hertford Town 1, Bromley 0
Ilford 1, Kingsbury Town 2
Leatherhead 1, Newport (IOW) 0
Metropolitan Police 5, Hastings United 1
Tooting & Mitcham United 2, Ashford Town 1
Walton & Hersham 7, Banstead Athletic 1
Ware 2, Enfield 3 aet
Wembley 0, Croydon 2

SECOND ROUND
Burgess Hill Town 3, Whyteleafe 0
Clapton 0, Walton & Hersham 1
Cray Wanderers 2, Croydon 1
Dulwich Hamlet 4, Croydon Athletic 1
Fleet Town 3, Brook House 0
Horsham 1, AFC Wimbledon 2
Kingsbury Town 3, Enfield 4 aet
Leatherhead 2, Tooting & Mitcham United 0 aet
Metropolitan Police 2, Hertford Town 3
Witham Town 2, Bashley 3

THIRD ROUND
Billericay Town 0, Heybridge Swifts 2
Cray Wanderers 1, Burgess Hill Town 0
Dover Athletic 1, AFC Wimbledon 2
Enfield 1, Bashley 4 aet
Fleet Town 0, Yeading 2
Folkestone Invicta 6, Kingstonian 1
Hampton & Richmond Boro 2, Dulwich Hamlet 1 aet
Harrow Borough 0, Braintree Town 1
Hendon 3, Leatherhead 6 aet
Hertford Town 0, Chelmsford City 1
Salisbury City 2, Leyton 0
Slough Town 1, Cheshunt 0
Walton & Hersham 2, Northwood 1
Wealdstone 3, Tonbridge Angels 0
Windsor & Eton 0, Staines Town 1
Worthing 0, Eastleigh 2

FOURTH ROUND
AFC Wimbledon 3, Cray Wanderers 2
Chelmsford City 2, Wealdstone 1
Eastleigh 1, Hampton & Richmond Borough 2
Folkestone Invicta 2, Bashley 1
Leatherhead 3, Yeading 3 aet
(Leatherhead won 4–2 on penalties)
Slough Town 3, Salisbury City 0
Staines Town 0, Heybridge Swifts 1
Walton & Hersham 0, Braintree Town 2

FIFTH ROUND
Chelmsford City 3, Leatherhead 0
Hampton & Richmond Borough 1, Braintree Town 0
Heybridge Swifts 1, Folkestone Invicta 1 aet
(Heybridge Swifts won 3–2 on penalties)
Slough Town 4, AFC Wimbledon 2

SEMI–FINAL - FIRST LEGS
Hampton & Richmond Borough 0, Chelmsford City 0
Heybridge Swifts 1, Slough Town 2
SEMI–FINAL - SECOND LEGS
Chelmsford City 0, Hampton & Richmond B 1 (0–1 agg)
Slough Town 2, Heybridge Swifts 1 (4–2 agg)

FINAL
Slough Town 3, Hampton & Richmond Borough 1
At Staines Town FC

FULL MEMBERS CUP

The Full Members Cup was a relatively short-lived competition, lasting just 11 seasons. It was contested by the Isthmian League's Full Members, i.e. those in the Premier and First Divisions, and entry was compulsory. Hendon were the most successful Club, with three victories in the Final, while Sutton won it twice.

The Full Members Cup was introduced for the 1990–91 under a two-season sponsorship deal with Loctite, who gave their name to the Cup. Bishop's Stortford were the inaugural Loctite Cup-winners, beating Chesham United on penalties at Hendon FC in the Final after a 2-2 draw in which Pat Ryan and Peter Risley scored for Bishop's Stortford and Gary Attrell and Michael Banton were on the mark for Chesham United. Bishop's Stortford won the cup 7–6 on penalties.

There were a couple of small changes to the regulations for the 1991–92 competition. Replays were replaced by a penalty shoot-out if ties were level after 120 minutes, except for the now single-game semi-final, which would go to a replay if it had not been decided in 120 minutes. In the Final, at Hayes FC, an all-Surrey affair went the way of Sutton United, 2–0 over Woking, courtesy of goals from Andy Scott and Dereck Browne.

Loctite opted not to renew their sponsorship, so the 1992–93 competition was not sponsored and it was simply called the Full Members Cup. Once again the Final was an all-Surrey affair – and all First Division too – played at Kingstonian FC. Tooting & Mitcham United beat Dorking 1–0, with the winning goal being scored by Micky Stephens.

In 1993, Carlsberg agreed to sponsor the Full Members Cup for two seasons and the competition became known as the Carlsberg Cup. The first Final was played at Marlow FC, where Hendon scored a goal late in each half to defeat Wokingham Town 2–1. Tommy Mason converted a penalty before half-time and Mark Hill scored his only goal for the Greens in the last ten minutes. Elliott Pearce – who tragically died in a car crash a few months later – netted Wokingham's equaliser.

The following year, the Final, between Staines Town and Boreham Wood, was played at Harrow Borough FC and the two teams produced a thrilling contest, with six goals shared in the 120 pulsating minutes. Craig Reilly (2) and Jim Williams were on target for the Swans, whilst Dave Hatchett, Garry Nisbet and Tony Samuels netted for the Wood. In the penalty shoot-out, it was Staines Town who triumphed, 4–2 to lift the Cup.

Carlton TV – part of Carlton Communications – sponsored the Full Members Cup in 1995–96 and it was renamed the Carlton Cup. Boreham Wood reached the Final for the second consecutive year, and were defeated on penalties again, this time 4–3, by Sutton United after a 2–2 draw at Purfleet FC. Sutton led 2–0, with goals from Jimmy Dack, a penalty, and Chris Green, before Boreham Wood hit back with late goals from Marc Liburd and Brian Stein.

In 1996–97, the Full Members Cup was not sponsored so the competition reverted to that name. Marlow FC once again hosted the Final, appropriately an all Berks & Bucks affair, between Maidenhead United from Division 1 and fellow Premier Division Aylesbury United. It ended 3–0 to the lower level Magpies, with the goals coming from Michael Creighton, Gary Attrell – who had scored for Chesham in the inaugural Final – and Francis Duku.

Puma UK agreed to sponsor the competition for two seasons from 1997–98 under the name of the Puma Cup. One Club, Hendon, claimed the Cup in both seasons. In 1997–98 they came from 1–0 down at half-time to defeat Basingstoke Town 4–1 at Chesham United FC. Ian Mancey scored for Basingstoke Town, but Hendon stormed home with goals from Tony Kelly, Junior Lewis, Curtis Warmington and Michael Banton.

The following year the Final was held at Gander Green Lane, Sutton United FC, where Division One Worthing provided the opposition. Matthew Maran's early goal was enough for Hendon to retain the Cup in a match that lacked the sparkle and atmosphere of the previous year's match.

In the final two years of the competition, there was no sponsor so it reverted to being known as the Full Members Cup. It was decided that the two finalists would toss a coin to decide home advantage and, in 2000 Purfleet guessed correctly, so entertained Croydon, from Division 1. And it was the visiting Trams who returned to Surrey with the Cup, courtesy of a 2–0 victory, the goals coming from the ever-prolific Nic McDonnell and Eben Allen, a penalty. The result meant Croydon completed a Division 1 and Full Members Cup double.

Purfleet were finalists again in 2001, but this time they had to travel, to Stonebridge Road, the home of Premier Division champions Gravesend & Northfleet. Purfleet took an early lead through Colin Simpson, but a brace from Jimmy Jackson, including a penalty, and a goal from Robert Owen resulted in a 3–1 victory for Gravesend & Northfleet.

THE FULL MEMBERS CUP - RESULTS IN FULL

1990–91

FIRST ROUND
Aveley 1, Wokingham Town 2
Barking 0, Leyton–Wingate 1
Basingstoke Town 1, Molesey 2
Chesham United 2, Enfield 1 aet
Dorking 1, Harrow Borough 4
Hayes 2, Wembley 1
Lewes 2, Whyteleafe 1
St. Albans City 0, Dagenham 1
Staines Town 1, Walton & Hersham 5
Tooting & Mitcham United 4, Bromley 3 aet
Uxbridge 2, Aylesbury United 3
Woking 4, Bognor Regis Town 1

SECOND ROUND
Chesham United 1, Walton & Hersham 0
Croydon 0, Dulwich Hamlet 3
Grays Athletic 0, Wokingham Town 0
Harrow Borough 0, Bishop's Stortford 2
Hayes 2, Aylesbury United 3
Heybridge Swifts 0, Wivenhoe Town 1 aet
Hitchin Town 2, Marlow 2 aet
Kingstonian 0, Dagenham 1 aet
Lewes 1, Boreham Wood 1 aet
Leyton–Wingate 1, Woking 0
Metropolitan Police 0, Hendon 1
Molesey 0, Carshalton Athletic 2
Redbridge Forest 1, Chalfont St Peter 0
Tooting & Mitcham United 3, Harlow Town 2
Worthing 2, Southwick 0
Yeading 0, Windsor & Eton 2

SECOND ROUND REPLAYS
Boreham Wood 1, Lewes 2
Marlow 2, Hitchin Town 4
Wokingham Town 0, Grays Athletic 1

THIRD ROUND
Aylesbury United 1, Dulwich Hamlet 0 aet
Bishop's Stortford 1, Windsor & Eton 0
Carshalton Athletic 13, Worthing 0
Dagenham 3, Grays Athletic 2
Hitchin Town 1, Wivenhoe Town 3
Lewes 0, Chesham United 1
Leyton–Wingate 1, Hendon 2
Tooting & Mitcham United 1, Redbridge Forest 8

FOURTH ROUND
Aylesbury United 4, Hendon 1
Bishop's Stortford 2, Wivenhoe Town 1
Carshalton Athletic 0, Redbridge Forest 1
Chesham United 5, Dagenham 1

SEMI–FINAL - FIRST LEGS
Aylesbury United 1, Chesham United 2
Redbridge Forest 2, Bishop's Stortford 0

SEMI–FINAL - SECOND LEGS
Bishop's Stortford 3, Redbridge Forest 0 (3–2 agg)
Chesham United 1, Aylesbury United 1 (3–2 agg)

FINAL *(at Hendon FC)*
Bishop's Stortford 2, Chesham United 2 aet *(5–4 pens)*

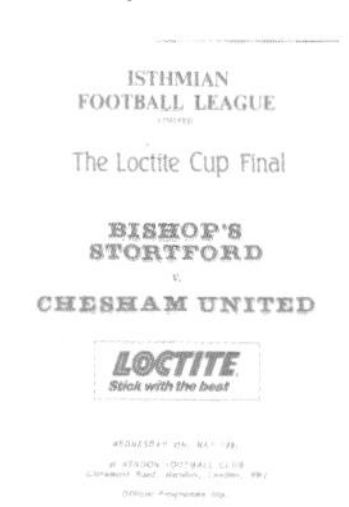

1991–92

FIRST ROUND
Aveley 1, St. Albans City 6
Aylesbury United 1, Barking 3
Basingstoke Town 1, Croydon 0
Harrow Borough 2, Heybridge Swifts 2 aet *(5–4 pens)*
Hendon 3, Chalfont St Peter 1
Hitchin Town 0, Abingdon Town 3
Tooting & Mitcham Utd 1, Stevenage Borough 2 aet
Wembley 0, Uxbridge 1
Windsor & Eton 2, Harlow Town 3
Wokingham Town 2, Bishop's Stortford 0
Yeading 3, Kingstonian 2 aet

SECOND ROUND
Barking 1, Dagenham 5
Boreham Wood 1, Yeading 2 aet
Bromley 0, Bognor Regis Town 1
Dorking 3, Harrow Borough 4
Enfield 2, Molesey 2 aet *(2–4 pens)*
Harlow Town 2, Hayes 4
Hendon 1, Abingdon Town 2
Leyton–Wingate 0, Chesham United 4
Maidenhead Utd 2, Basingstoke Town 2 aet *(2–3 pens)*
Marlow 1, Carshalton Athletic 2
St. Albans City 1, Wokingham Town 3
Staines Town 0, Dulwich Hamlet 3
Sutton United 4, Whyteleafe 0
Uxbridge 4, Grays Athletic 2 aet
Wivenhoe Town 0, Stevenage Borough 4
Woking 2, Walton & Hersham 1

THIRD ROUND
Carshalton Athletic 2, Abingdon Town 1
Chesham United 2, Woking 5
Dagenham 0, Yeading 2
Dulwich Hamlet 0, Bognor Regis Town 0 aet *(5–4 pens)*
Harrow Borough 2, Wokingham Town 0
Hayes 1, Uxbridge 3
Molesey 4, Stevenage Borough 4 aet *(3–0 pens)*
Sutton United 3, Basingstoke Town 2

FOURTH ROUND
Dulwich Hamlet 0, Sutton United 0 aet *(4–5 pens)*
Harrow Borough 2, Carshalton Athletic 2 aet *(3–1 pens)*
Molesey 1, Uxbridge 0 aet
Woking 1, Yeading 0

SEMI–FINALS
Harrow Borough 0, Woking 2
Sutton United 4, Molesey 1

FINAL *(at Hayes FC)*
Sutton United 2, Woking 0

1992–93

PRELIMINARY ROUND
Abingdon Town 1, Basingstoke Town 2
Aveley 2, Bromley 5
Aylesbury United 2, Marlow 5
Bishop's Stortford 5, Billericay Town 0
Chesham United 1, Stevenage Borough 3
Hayes 1, Wembley 0
Heybridge Swifts 0, Wivenhoe Town 1
Molesey 2, Dulwich Hamlet 0
Sutton United 3, Lewes 1
Uxbridge 0, Harrow Borough 1
Wokingham Town 2, Chalfont St Peter 0

FIRST ROUND
Barking 0, Leyton 2
Bishop's Stortford 1, Hayes 2
Bromley 3, Maidenhead United 0
Carshalton Athletic 1, Bognor Regis Town 0
Croydon 1, Wokingham Town 2
Dorking 1, Walton & Hersham 0
Grays Athletic 2, Wivenhoe Town 0
Hendon 0, Boreham Wood 0 aet *(2–4 pens)*
Marlow 3, St. Albans City 2
Molesey 2, Staines Town 0
Purfleet 2, Harrow Borough 1
Stevenage Borough 0, Enfield 2
Sutton United 2, Kingstonian 1
Tooting & Mitcham United 3, Basingstoke Town 1
Windsor & Eton 3, Whyteleafe 0
Yeading 1, Hitchin Town 2

SECOND ROUND
Boreham Wood 2, Hayes 4
Bromley 2, Dorking 4
Enfield 1, Grays Athletic 2
Hitchin Town 1, Leyton 1 aet *(4–1 pens)*
Marlow 2, Purfleet 3
Sutton United 2, Tooting & Mitcham United 3
Windsor & Eton 2, Molesey 1
Wokingham Town 2, Carshalton Athletic 2 aet *(3–4 pens)*

THIRD ROUND
Carshalton Athletic 6, Windsor & Eton 1
Dorking 2, Hitchin Town 1 aet
Hayes 2, Grays Athletic 1
Tooting & Mitcham United 1, Purfleet 1 aet *(4–2 pens)*

SEMI–FINALS
Carshalton Athletic 1, Dorking 2
Hayes 0, Tooting & Mitcham United 2

FINAL *(at Kingstonian FC)*
Tooting & Mitcham United 1, Dorking 0

1993–94

FIRST ROUND
Barking 0, Leyton 2
Berkhamsted Town 1, Yeading 2
Bishop's Stortford 3, Hayes 0
Bognor Regis Town 2, Carshalton Ath 2 aet *(1–4 pens)*
Boreham Wood 1, Hitchin Town 3
Chalfont St Peter 1, Maidenhead United 2
Chesham United 0, St. Albans City 2
Dulwich Hamlet 2, Tooting & Mitcham United 1
Marlow 2, Ruislip Manor 1
Staines Town 1, Basingstoke Town 3
Sutton United 5, Worthing 1
Whyteleafe 3, Croydon 4 aet

SECOND ROUND
Basingstoke Town 1, Wokingham Town 1 aet *(3–4 pens)*
Billericay Town 1, Bishop's Stortford 2
Bromley 3, Croydon 1
Carshalton Athletic 3, Sutton United 1
Dulwich Hamlet 2, Walton & Hersham 0
Enfield 0, Hendon 1
Grays Athletic 2, Hitchin Town 1
Harrow Borough 2, Aylesbury United 1 aet
Kingstonian 4, Abingdon Town 0
Marlow 0, Purfleet 1
Molesey 3, Maidenhead United 2 aet
St. Albans City 5, Leyton 3
Stevenage Borough 1, Heybridge Swifts 2
Wembley 1, Uxbridge 2 aet
Windsor & Eton 0, Dorking 2
Wivenhoe Town 1, Yeading 3

THIRD ROUND
Dulwich Hamlet 1, Kingstonian 0
Harrow Borough 1, Grays Athletic 4
Hendon 1, Uxbridge 0
Molesey 2, Bromley 1
Purfleet 2, Carshalton Athetic 2 aet *(8–7 pens)*
St. Albans City 3, Heybridge Swifts 3 aet *(4–3 pens)*
Wokingham Town 2, Dorking 1
Yeading 0, Bishop's Stortford 1

FOURTH ROUND
Bishop's Stortford 1, Hendon 1 aet *(1–3 pens)*
Grays Athletic 1, Dulwich Hamlet 2
Purfleet 1, Wokingham Town 1 aet *(4–5 pens)*
St. Albans City 2, Molesey 1

SEMI–FINALS
Hendon 2, Dulwich Hamlet 1 aet
St. Albans City 0, Wokingham Town 2

FINAL *(at Marlow FC)*
Hendon 2, Wokingham Town 1

1994–95

FIRST ROUND
Billericay Town 2, Barking 0
Bognor Regis Town 1, Aldershot Town 2
Boreham Wood 2, Wivenhoe Town 1
Chertsey Town 1, Newbury Town 0
Chesham United 3, Grays Athletic 1
Dorking 3, Dulwich Hamlet 1
Hitchin Town 2, Enfield 1
Maidenhead United 1, Tooting & Mitcham United 3
Uxbridge 1, St. Albans City 5
Walton & Hersham 5, Marlow 1
Whyteleafe 0, Basingstoke Town 3
Yeading 2, Wembley 1

SECOND ROUND
Berkhamsted Town 1, Bishop's Stortford 1 aet *(6–5 pens)*
Billericay Town 2, Heybridge Swifts 1 aet
Boreham Wood 3, Purfleet 1
Carshalton Athletic 2, Tooting & Mitcham United 0
Chertsey Town 2, Aldershot Town 0
Chesham United 1, Harrow Borough 5
Hendon 5, Aylesbury United 1
Hitchin Town 3, Leyton 1
Kingstonian 1, Sutton United 3
Molesey 3, Bromley 3 aet *(4–3 pens)*
St. Albans City 1, Ruislip Manor 1 aet *(2–4 pens)*
Staines Town 6, Dorking 0
Walton & Hersham 5, Abingdon Town 4 aet
Wokingham Town 1, Basingstoke Town 4
Worthing 3, Slough Town 6
Yeading 2, Hayes 3

THIRD ROUND
Basingstoke Town 3, Sutton United 5 aet
Berkhamsted Town 1, Billericay Town 1 aet *(5–4 pens)*
Chertsey Town 3, Slough Town 2 aet
Hendon 0, Boreham Wood 2
Hitchin Town 3, Harrow Borough 1
Molesey 1, Walton & Hersham 0
Ruislip Manor 1, Hayes 4
Staines Town 5, Carshalton Athletic 1

FOURTH ROUND
Berkhamsted Town 0, Boreham Wood 1
Hitchin Town 2, Hayes 2 aet *(3–4 pens)*
Staines Town 3, Molesey 0
Sutton United 2, Chertsey Town 1

SEMI–FINALS
Hayes 1, Boreham Wood 2
Sutton United 2, Staines Town 3 aet

FINAL *(at Harrow Borough FC)*
Staines Town 3, Boreham Wood 3 aet *(4–2 pens)*

1995–96

FIRST ROUND
Aldershot Town 3, Bromley 0
Aylesbury United 3, Chesham United 1 aet
Barton Rovers 3, Heybridge Swifts 2
(Match ordered to be replayed)
Barton Rovers 0, Heybridge Swifts 1
Basingstoke Town 4, Whyteleafe 1
Berkhamsted Town 0, Yeading 3
Chertsey Town 0, Yeovil Town 2
Hendon 3, St. Albans City 4
Molesey 0, Kingstonian 3
Purfleet 2, Hayes 0
Staines Town 0, Walton & Hersham 1
Thame United 4, Marlow 1
Uxbridge 1, Harrow Borough 0

SECOND ROUND
Aldershot Town 3, Maidenhead United 1
Aylesbury United 0, Purfleet 1
Bishop's Stortford 3, Hitchin Town 0
Bognor Regis Town 6, Worthing 0
Boreham Wood 3, Barking 1
Carshalton Athletic 2, Yeovil Town 1
Enfield 1, Yeading 2 aet
Grays Athletic 1, Billericay Town 2 aet
Heybridge Swifts 3, Uxbridge 1
Oxford City 1, Basingstoke Town 0
St. Albans City 1, Ruislip Manor 2
Sutton United 3, Abingdon Town 0
Thame United 3, Dulwich Hamlet 0
Tooting & Mitcham United 4, Wokingham Town 3
Walton & Hersham 1, Kingstonian 3
Wembley 2, Leyton Pennant 3

THIRD ROUND
Aldershot Town 2, Bognor Regis Town 2 aet *(3–5 pens)*
Carshalton Athletic 4, Thame United 0
Heybridge Swifts 0, Boreham Wood 2
Kingstonian 5, Oxford City 3
Leyton Pennant 5, Purfleet 1
Ruislip Manor 1, Billericay Town 4
Tooting & Mitcham United 1, Sutton United 3
Yeading 0, Bishop's Stortford 1

FOURTH ROUND
Billericay Town 0, Bishop's Stortford 2
Bognor Regis Town 1, Sutton United 2 aet
Boreham Wood 5, Leyton Pennant 1
Kingstonian 2, Carshalton Athletic 3

SEMI–FINALS
Boreham Wood 4, Bishop's Stortford 1
Sutton United 1, Carshalton Athletic 1 aet

REPLAY
Carshalton Athletic 1, Sutton United 4 aet

FINAL *(at Purfleet FC)*
Sutton United 2, Boreham Wood 2 aet *(4–3 pens)*

1996–97

FIRST ROUND
Aylesbury United 1, Boreham Wood 0
Barton Rovers 0, Canvey Island 3
Chertsey Town 3, Wokingham Town 1
Croydon 1, Carshalton Athletic 4 aet
Grays Athletic 1, Leyton Pennant 0
Hampton 2, Bromley 1
Hendon 3, Berkhamsted Town 1
Marlow 2, Staines Town 1
Molesey 3, Worthing 1
Oxford City 2, Aldershot Town 1 aet
St. Albans City 0, Hitchin Town 4
Thame United 0, Yeading 1

SECOND ROUND
Aylesbury United 2, Canvey Island 1
Basingstoke Town 2, Tooting & Mitcham United 1
Billericay Town 2, Harrow Borough 1
Bognor Regis Town 1, Dulwich Hamlet 0 aet
Chertsey Town 0, Abingdon Town 3
Dagenham & Redbridge 2, Hendon 2 aet *(5–4 pens)*
Grays Athletic 0, Chesham United 0 aet *(6–7 pens)*
Heybridge Swifts 0, Enfield 1
Kingstonian 4, Walton & Hersham 4 aet *(3–5 pens)*
Molesey 0, Maidenhead United 2
Oxford City 2, Whyteleafe 3
Purfleet 3, Hitchin Town 2
Sutton United 2, Hampton 2 aet *(5–3 pens)*
Uxbridge 0, Bishop's Stortford 3
Yeading 4, Marlow 0
Yeovil Town 2, Carshalton Athletic 0

THIRD ROUND
Aylesbury United 3, Billericay Town 0
Basingstoke Town 1, Abingdon Town 0
Bishop's Stortford 1, Yeading 2
Chesham United 3, Enfield 3 aet *(3–1 pens)*
Dagenham & Redbridge 0, Purfleet 1
Sutton United 4, Whyteleafe 0
Walton & Hersham 0, Maidenhead United 1
Yeovil Town 3, Bognor Regis Town 2

FOURTH ROUND
Aylesbury United 2, Chesham United 0
Purfleet 0, Yeading 2
Sutton United 5, Basingstoke Town 3
Yeovil Town 0, Maidenhead United 1

SEMI–FINALS
Maidenhead United 3, Sutton United 1
Yeading 2, Aylesbury United 2 aet

REPLAY
Aylesbury United 1, Yeading 0

FINAL *(at Marlow FC)*
Maidenhead United 3, Aylesbury United 0

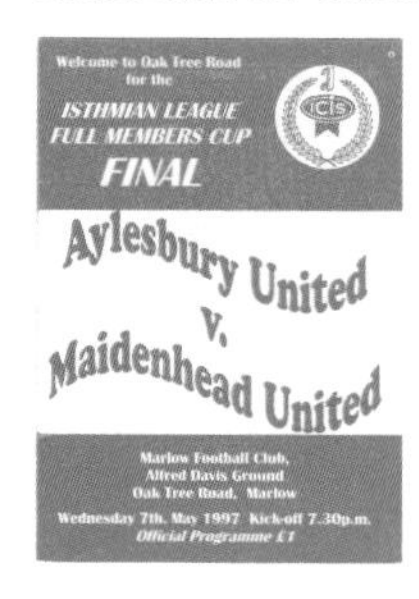

1997–98

FIRST ROUND
Abingdon Town 0, Basingstoke Town 1
Bishop's Stortford 0, Leyton Pennant 2
Bromley 2, Maidenhead United 3 aet
Chertsey Town 3, Wokingham Town 3 aet *(5–4 pens)*
Dulwich Hamlet 0, Kingstonian 3
Gravesend & Northfleet 4, Berkhamsted Town 3 aet
Hendon 3, Purfleet 0
Hitchin Town 1, Boreham Wood 2
Molesey 0, Worthing 1
St. Albans City 5, Enfield 1
Walton & Hersham 3, Staines Town 4
Wembley 2, Billericay Town 0

SECOND ROUND
Barton Rovers 0, Harrow Borough 2
Basingstoke Town 3, Kingstonian 2
Bognor Regis Town 3, Worthing 1
Boreham Wood 6, Aylesbury United 1
Carshalton Athletic 1, Aldershot Town 0
Chesham United 0, Gravesend & Northfleet 3
Croydon 0, Whyteleafe 2
Dagenham & Redbridge 3, Romford 0
Hampton 0, Maidenhead United 4
Hendon 6, St. Albans City 1
Leatherhead 2, Chertsey Town 1
Leyton Pennant 3, Grays Athletic 0
Oxford City 3, Thame United 1
Staines Town 3, Sutton United 0
Uxbridge 1, Heybridge Swifts 1 aet *(5–4 pens)*
Yeading 3, Wembley 2 aet

THIRD ROUND
Boreham Wood 2, Uxbridge 1
Carshalton Athletic 3, Bognor Regis Town 2
Dagenham & Redbridge 3, Harrow Borough 1
Hendon 1, Gravesend & Northfleet 0
Leatherhead 1, Maidenhead United 0
(Leatherhead removed from competition)
Leyton Pennant 1, Yeading 2
Oxford City 1, Basingstoke Town 2
Whyteleafe 1, Staines Town 3

FOURTH ROUND
Boreham Wood 2, Yeading 2 aet *(0–3 pens)*
Carshalton Athletic 1, Maidenhead United 2
Hendon 3, Dagenham & Redbridge 1
Staines Town 1, Basingstoke Town 4

SEMI–FINALS
Hendon 2, Maidenhead United 1
Yeading 2, Basingstoke Town 4

FINAL *(at Chesham United FC)*
Hendon 4, Basingstoke Town 1

1998–99

FIRST ROUND
Basingstoke Town 4, Croydon 1
Boreham Wood 2, Braintree Town 0
Chesham United 4, Barton Rovers 1
Enfield 2, St. Albans City 0
Grays Athletic 0, Wealdstone 1
Harrow Borough 1, Leyton Pennant 0 aet
Leatherhead 0, Whyteleafe 1
Romford 1, Staines Town 0
Slough Town 1, Bromley 0
Sutton United 1, Walton & Hersham 3
Wembley 0, Bishop's Stortford 2
Worthing 3, Maidenhead United 1

SECOND ROUND
Basingstoke Town 3, Bognor Regis Town 0
Berkhamsted Town 1, Aylesbury United 1 aet *(4–2 pens)*
Boreham Wood 1, Canvey Island 1 aet *(0–3 pens)*
Carshalton Athletic 2, Chertsey Town 0
Chesham United 2, Dagenham & Redbridge 1
Dulwich Hamlet 1, Hampton 0
Enfield 1, Bishop's Stortford 0
Harrow Borough 1, Romford 3
Hendon 2, Heybridge Swifts 1
Oxford City 2, Molesey 0
Purfleet 2, Billericay Town 1
Uxbridge 0, Hitchin Town 2
Walton & Hersham 2, Slough Town 0
Whyteleafe 2, Gravesend & Northfleet 1
Worthing 6, Aldershot Town 0
Yeading 2, Wealdstone 5

THIRD ROUND
Berkhamsted Town 0, Chesham United 5
Carshalton Athletic 2, Walton & Hersham 0
Canvey Island 0, Hendon 2
Dulwich Hamlet 3, Basingstoke Town 1
Enfield 0, Purfleet 2
Hitchin Town 3, Romford 1
Oxford City 2, Wealdstone 4
Whyteleafe 0, Worthing 2

FOURTH ROUND
Chesham United 0, Hendon 1
Dulwich Hamlet 1, Wealdstone 0
Hitchin Town 0, Purfleet 2
Worthing 3, Carshalton Athletic 0

SEMI–FINALS
Dulwich Hamlet 0, Hendon 2 aet
Purfleet 0, Worthing 1

FINAL *(at Sutton United FC)*
Hendon 1, Worthing 0

1999–2000

FIRST ROUND
Barton Rovers 0, Grays Athletic 3
Billericay Town 0, Bedford Town 2
Bromley 3, Aldershot Town 1
Croydon 0, Bognor Regis Town 0 aet *(3-2 pens)*
Dulwich Hamlet 0, Farnborough Town 3
Hampton & Richmond Borough 2, Worthing 4
Harrow Borough 3, Chertsey Town 3 aet *(2-3 pens)*
Hendon 2, Wealdstone 2 aet *(6-7 pens)*
Maidenhead United 2, Walton & Hersham 0
Purfleet 5, Bishop's Stortford 0
St. Albans City 2, Chesham United 1
Slough Town 4, Staines Town 1

SECOND ROUND
Aylesbury United 1, Oxford City 2 aet
Basingstoke Town 2, Maidenhead United 0
Braintree Town 2, Gravesend & Northfleet 5
Bromley 1, Worthing 0
Croydon 3, Farnborough Town 0
Dagenham & Redbridge 2, Romford 0
Harlow Town 1, Grays Athletic 5
Heybridge Swifts 2, Purfleet 4 aet
Hitchin Town 2, Enfield 1
Leatherhead 4, Whyteleafe 1 aet
Leyton Pennant 2, Canvey Island 1
St. Albans City 2, Bedford Town 2 aet *(3-4 pens)*
Slough Town 2, Carshalton Athletic 1
Thame United 1, Uxbridge 0
Wealdstone 3, Boreham Wood 0
Yeading 3, Chertsey Town 2 aet

THIRD ROUND
Bromley 1, Basingstoke Town 0
Croydon 1, Oxford City 0
Gravesend & Northfleet 3, Wealdstone 1
Grays Athletic 3, Purfleet 4 aet
Hitchin Town 3, Bedford Town 2
Leatherhead 0, Slough Town 3
Leyton Pennant 1, Dagenham & Redbridge 5
Yeading 2, Thame United 1

FOURTH ROUND
Croydon 2, Bromley 1
Gravesend & Northfleet 3, Slough Town 2
Hitchin Town 1, Yeading 3
Purfleet 5, Dagenham & Redbridge 2

SEMI–FINALS
Gravesend & Northfleet 1, Croydon 2
Yeading 2, Purfleet 3

FINAL *(at Purfleet FC)*
Purfleet 0, Croydon 2

2000–01

FIRST ROUND
Aylesbury United 1, Thame United 2
Braintree Town 5, Enfield 0
Carshalton Athletic 3, Basingstoke Town 3 aet *(2–3 pens)*
Harlow Town 0, Hendon 2
Harrow Borough 1, Romford 2
Heybridge Swifts 2, Billericay Town 0
Hitchin Town 2, Bedford Town 1
Purfleet 3, Boreham Wood 1
Slough Town 4, Aldershot Town 3 aet
Staines Town 4, Sutton United 4 aet *(5–6 pens)*
Walton & Hersham 1, Farnborough Town 0
Worthing 2, Hampton & Richmond Borough 0

SECOND ROUND
Basingstoke Town 2, Whyteleafe 1
Bromley 1, Slough Town 0
Chesham United 4, Braintree Town 2
Dulwich Hamlet 2, Walton & Hersham 1
Gravesend & Northfleet 4, Ford United 0
Grays Athletic 4, Bishop's Stortford 2
Heybridge Swifts 6, Hendon 5 aet
Maidenhead United 2, Leatherhead 1 aet
Northwood 3, St. Albans City 4
Purfleet 1, Canvey Island 0
Romford 0, Barton Rovers 2
Sutton United 2, Croydon 2 aet *(4–3 pens)*
Thame United 2, Oxford City 3
Wealdstone 0, Hitchin Town 3
Worthing 2, Bognor Regis Town 4
Yeading 1, Uxbridge 4

THIRD ROUND
Barton Rovers 2, Grays Athletic 0
Bognor Regis Town 2, Maidenhead United 1
Chesham United 0, St. Albans City 2
Dulwich Hamlet 0, Basingstoke Town 2
Gravesend & Northfleet 7, Hitchin Town 1
Heybridge Swifts 1, Purfleet 3
Oxford City 2, Bromley 0
Uxbridge 2, Sutton United 0

FOURTH ROUND
Barton Rovers 0, Purfleet 1
Basingstoke Town 1, Bognor Regis Town 3
Gravesend & Northfleet 1, St. Albans C 1 aet *(4–3 pens)*
Oxford City 4, Uxbridge 1

SEMI–FINALS
Bognor Regis Town 0, Gravesend & Northfleet 2
Oxford City 1, Purfleet 3

FINAL *(at Gravesend & Northfleet FC)*
Gravesend & Northfleet 3, Purfleet 1

ISTHMIAN CHARITY SHIELD (League Champions v League Cup Winners)
(1978-86 called Dylon Isthmian Charity Shield)

Season	*Winners*	*Runners-up*	*Venue*	*Score*
1978-79	Enfield	Dagenham	Enfield	2-1
1979-80	Barking	Enfield	Enfield	1-0
1980-81	Enfield	Sutton United	Enfield	2-1
1981-82	Wycombe Wanderers	Slough Town	Slough	4-1
1982-83	Leytonstone-Ilford	Sutton United	Leytonstone	3-2
1983-84	Wycombe Wanderers	Sutton United	Wycombe	1-0
1984-85	Sutton United	Harrow Borough	Harrow	3-1
1985-86	Wycombe Wanderers	Sutton United	Sutton	3-1
1986-87	Yeovil Town	Sutton United	Sutton	5-1
1987-88	Wycombe Wanderers	Bognor Regis Town	Wycombe	1-0
1988-89	Yeovil Town	Bromley	Yeovil	4-0
1989-90	Redbridge Forest	Bishop's Stortford	Bishop's Stortford	2-1
1990-91	Slough Town	Aveley	Kingstonian	2-0
1991-92	Woking	Redbridge Forest	Woking	3-1
1992-93	Woking	Grays Athletic	Sutton	5-1
1993-94	Chesham United	Marlow	Chesham	4-1
1994-95	Chertsey Town	Stevenage Borough	Stevenage	5-0
1995-96	Aylesbury United	Enfield	Enfield	2-1
1996-97	Hayes	Kingstonian	Hayes	4-2
1997-98	Yeovil Town	Boreham Wood	Yeovil	1-0
1998-99	Kingstonian	Sutton United	Sutton	6-1
1999-2000	Aldershot Town	Sutton United	Aldershot Town	2-1
2000-01	Dagenham & Redbridge	Farnborough Town	Farnborough	2-0
2001-02	Farnborough Town	Heybridge Swifts	Heybridge	4-0
2002-03	Northwood	Gravesend & Northfleet	Northwood	4-2
2003-04	Aldershot Town	Yeading	Aldershot	4-2
2004-05	Thurrock	Canvey Island	Canvey Island	3-2

ASSOCIATE MEMBERS TROPHY

The Associate Members Trophy was introduced for the 1990–91 season, with entry compulsory for the Isthmian League's Associate Members, being those clubs in Divisions Two and Three or, as in the inaugural season, i.e. the two regionalised Second Divisions. Until 1997, the sponsors of the Full Members Cup also sponsored the Associate Members Trophy.

Thus in the first two seasons, the competition was known as the Loctite Trophy. The highest aggregate score in the competition came in the opening round when Ware and Tilbury shared 12 goals. The replay, at St. Chad's Road, ended all-square, but only at 1–1, then the Hertfordshire Club just about held their nerve, winning the penalty shoot-out 6–5. Abingdon Town, who had secured the Division Two South title, reached the first Final of the competition but were denied a League and Cup double by Ruislip Manor, who won 2–1, with goals from Charlie Turlunch and Kevin Quinn. John Harvey-Lynch scored Abingdon's reply in the match, played at Chesham United FC.

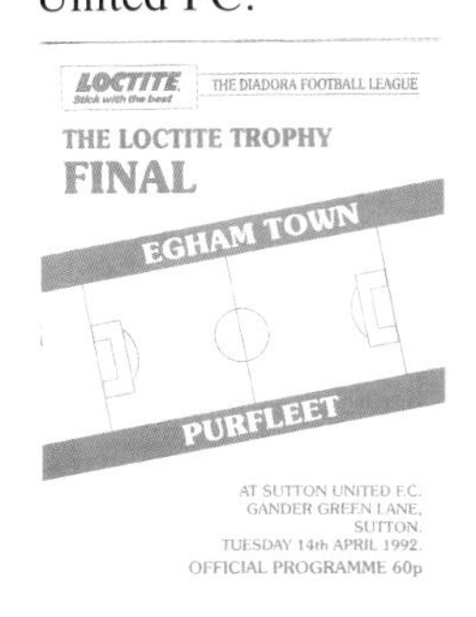

As with the Full Members Cup, the regulations for the second season varied slightly in that there would be no replays, matches level after 120 minutes going to a penalty shoot-out, and the semi-final would be a single game. There was another 12-goal spectacular in this season's competition, but little of the drama as Barton Rovers crushed Southwick 10–2. Sutton United hosted the Final in 1992 and the Loctite Trophy was won by Division Two champions Purfleet, who defeated Egham Town 3–2. Alan Brett, Nigel Jeyes and Jeff Wood scored for Fleet after the Sarnies had taken a 2-0 lead through Mark Butler and Brett Smith.

Northwood from Division Three won the Associate Members Trophy in 1992–93 in the first Final to go to extra time, overcoming Division Two Barton Rovers 3–1 at Chesham United FC. Vic Schwartz gave Northwood the lead before a last-minute goal by Graham Golds forced extra time. However, in the additional 30 minutes, goals from Rob Holland and Frank Omere sealed the win for Northwood.

In 1993–94, the first season of sponsorship by Carlsberg, the re-named Carlsberg Trophy went to Surrey as Chertsey Town – who had already secured promotion to Division One – beat Division Three strugglers Hornchurch. Lee Charles, who had also been on target in the Curfews' League Cup Final victory, scored the only goal of the game and ensured that Chertsey Town became the only Isthmian League Club to win their divisional title, the League Cup and Associate or Full Members competition in the same season.

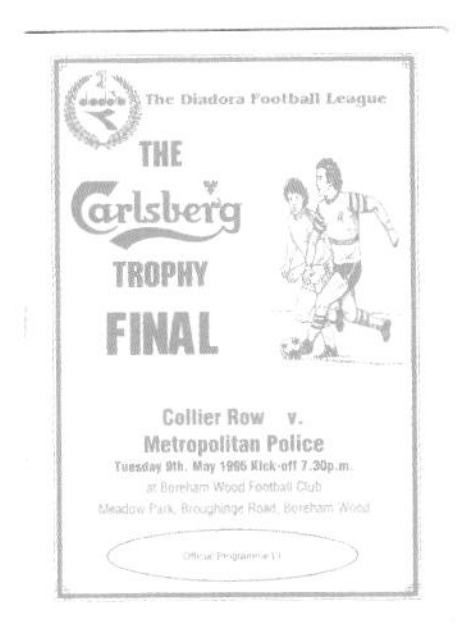

The 1994–95 Carlsberg Trophy Final was hosted by Boreham Wood FC and Metropolitan Police – from Division Two – overcame Division Three champions Collier Row, 4–3 on penalties, after the match had ended 1–1 after 120 minutes. Paul Carruth scored for the Police, while Kevin Rendell was on target for Collier Row.

The 1995–96 competition was called the Carlton Trophy, following a change in sponsorship. The final was held at Aveley FC and won by Division Two champions-elect Canvey Island, who defeated divisional rivals Banstead Athletic 2–1. Glen Pennyfather and Alan Brett – a scorer for Purfleet in the 1992 Final – put the Gulls 2–0 up, before Simon Liddle reduced the arrears for Banstead.

In 1996–97 the competition was not sponsored and it reverted back to the Associate Members Trophy. The Final was held at Hitchin Town FC and was decided by a last minute goal, which denied Wealdstone a Division Three championship and Cup double. Leighton Town were the winners, 1–0, with Paul Firth scoring the decisive goal.

Vandanel Sportwear agreed to sponsor the competition for three seasons from 1997–98, and it would be known as the Vandanel Trophy. The first Vandanel Trophy Final, in 1998, pitted Bedford Town, who had just missed out on promotion to Division One, against Division Three Epsom & Ewell. The Eagles won 2–0, with a Paul Sherlock strike and an own goal settling the match played at Hendon FC.

The following season, Leighton Town became the first club to win the competition twice when they defeated Windsor & Eton 1–0 at Chesham United FC thanks to a first-half goal from Scott Walters.

And in 1999–2000, the final year of Vandanel's sponsorship, Northwood emulated Leighton by winning their second Final, this time overcoming Barking 2–1, courtesy of two goals from Lawrence Yaku. Lee Parish netted Barking's reply at Harrow Borough FC.

The Associate Members Trophy would not be sponsored in 2000–01 and, in a rain-affected tournament, the Final had to be held over and played before the start of the following season. Marlow hosted the Final and defeated Hemel Hempstead Town, 4–0 thanks to a hat-trick from John Travis and another goal from Nicky Ryder.

There was no Associate Members Trophy in season 2001–02, but the competition was resurrected for 2002–03, though with entry limited to the 16 Division Two members to compensate them for the smaller, 30-match, League programme. To ensure all clubs played at least half a dozen extra matches, the opening round of the competition was played on a round-robin basis, with the top two clubs from each of four groups advancing to the quarter-finals.

Champions Cheshunt had to travel to the Division's runners-up, Leyton, in the Final and home advantage proved decisive, a goal in each half - from Scott Curley and Manny Williams – giving Leyton the Trophy, 2–0. Tring Town's resignation from the Isthmian League just before the start of the 2003--04 season meant that Division Two was reduced to 15 Clubs and the League Board decided that each team would play their 14 rivals three times. This rendered the Associate Members Trophy somewhat redundant, so it was decided not to run the competition in this season.

It was, however, revived in the previous form in 2004–05, and the Final was between Ilford, who had already won the Division title, and Flackwell Heath. Ilford had home advantage, but had to come from behind to defeat the Heathens 2–1 after extra time. Ryan Newman gave Flackwell Heath an early lead, but substitute Chris Stevens equalised in second-half stoppage time. Stevens also got the winner in the extra 30 minutes.

Division Two clubs left the Isthmian League after the 2005–06 season so, as with The FA Vase, for the sake of neatness the final season of this competition is recorded here, even though it was played after the completion of the League's centenary season. The Associate Members Trophy was again played on a round robin basis to give eight quarter-finalists. Brook House won their way through to the Final, where they entertained Hertford Town. The Middlesex Club were far too strong for the Blues and won 3–1, the goals coming from Papali, Booth and Jones. Phil Goss converted a late penalty for Hertford.

FULL MEMBERS CUP

Season	*Winners*	*Runners-up*	*Venue*	*Score*
1990-91	Bishop's Stortford	Chesham United	Hendon	2-2*
1991-92	Sutton United	Woking	Hayes	2-0
1992-93	Tooting & Mitcham United	Dorking	Kingstonian	1-0
1993-94	Hendon	Wokingham Town	Marlow	2-1
1994-95	Staines Town	Boreham Wood	Harrow Borough	3-3**
1995-96	Sutton United	Boreham Wood	Purfleet	2-2***
1996-97	Maidenhead United	Aylesbury United	Marlow	3-0
1997-98	Hendon	Basingstoke Town	Chesham	4-1
1998-99	Hendon	Worthing	Sutton	1-0
1999-2000	Croydon	Purfleet	Purfleet	2-0
2000-01	Gravesend & Northfleet	Purfleet	Gravesend	3-1

** (5-4 on penalties) ** (4-2 on penalties) *** (4-3 on penalties)*

ASSOCIATE MEMBERS TROPHY

Season	*Winners*	*Runners-up*	*Venue*	*Score*
1990-91	Ruislip Manor	Abingdon Town	Chesham	2-1
1991-92	Purfleet	Egham Town	Sutton	3-2
1992-93	Northwood	Barton Rovers	Chesham	3-1 (AET)
1993-94	Chertsey Town	Hornchurch	Hendon	1-0
1994-95	Metropolitan Police	Collier Row	Boreham Wood	1-1*
1995-96	Canvey Island	Banstead Athletic	Aveley	2-1
1996-97	Leighton Town	Wealdstone	Hitchin	1-0
1997-98	Bedford Town	Epsom & Ewell	Hendon	2-0
1998-99	Leighton Town	Windsor & Eton	Chesham	1-0
1999-2000	Northwood	Barking	Harrow Borough	3-0
2001-02	Marlow	Hemel Hempstead Town	Marlow	4-0
2002-03	Leyton	Cheshunt	Leyton	2-0
2004-05	Ilford	Flackwell Heath	Ilford	2-1 (AET)
2005-06	Brook House	Hertford Town	Brook House	3-1

** (4-3 on penalties)*

YOUTH CUP

(1977-82 called Berger Isthmian Youth Cup; 1982-85 called Servowarm Isthmian Youth Cup)

Season	*Winners*	*Runners-up*	*Venue*	*Score*
1977-78	Harlow Town	Maidenhead United	Walthamstow	2-1
1978-79	Croydon	Slough Town	Maidenhead	3-1 *(replay)*
1979-80	Tring Town	Wokingham Town	Tring	2-0
1980-81	Barking	Boreham Wood	Walthamstow	5-3
1981-82	Worthing	Barking	Epsom	3-2
1982-83	Woking	Hemel Hempstead	Uxbridge	3-1
1983-84	Chesham United	Farnborough Town	Hampton	1-0
1984-85	Hornchurch	Aveley	Billericay	1-0
1990-91	Epsom & Ewell	Bromley	Carshalton	4-1
1991-92	Lewes	Clapton	Bromley	3-1

THE ASSOCIATE MEMBERS TROPHY - RESULTS IN FULL

1990–91

FIRST ROUND
Barton Rovers 3, Feltham 1
Berkhamsted Town 2, Chertsey Town 1
Billericay Town 0, Abingdon Town 1
Bracknell Town 4, Malden Vale 4 aet
Edgware Town 2, Maidenhead United 4
Hampton 2, Epsom & Ewell 0
Hornchurch 3, Kingsbury Town 3 aet
Newbury Town 3, Hemel Hempstead 1
Ruislip Manor 2, Rainham Town 0
Saffron Walden Town 3, Royston Town 4 aet
Tring Town 0, Witham Town 3
Ware 6, Tilbury 6 aet
FIRST ROUND REPLAYS
Kingsbury Town 1, Hornchurch 2
Malden Vale 2, Bracknell Town 0 aet
Tilbury 1, Ware 1 aet *(5–6 pens)*

SECOND ROUND
Barton Rovers 0, Malden Vale 5
Berkhamsted Town 1, Hampton 2 aet
Collier Row 1, Vauxhall Motors 2
Eastbourne United 3, Cove 5
Flackwell Heath 7, Hertford Town 1
Hornchurch 0, Finchley 1
Horsham 2, Clapton 0
Hungerford Town 1, Maidenhead United 0
Leatherhead 3, Royston Town 0
Newbury Town 1, Banstead Athletic 0
Petersfield United 2, Harefield United 5
Purfleet 3, Camberley Town 1 aet
Ruislip Manor 2, Basildon United 1 aet
Stevenage Borough 4, Southall 2
Ware 1, Abingdon Town 2

THIRD ROUND
Abingdon Town 1, Stevenage Borough 0
Cove 2, Purfleet 1 aet
Finchley 0, Horsham 2
Flackwell Heath 0, Newbury Town 0 aet
Harefield United 0, Hampton 1
Hungerford Town 0, Malden Vale 0
Ruislip Manor 5, Leatherhead 1
Witham Town 1, Vauxhall Motors 0
THIRD ROUND REPLAYS
Malden Vale 0, Hungerford Town 3
Newbury Town 3, Flackwell Heath 0

FOURTH ROUND
Cove 0, Ruislip Manor 2
Hampton 0, Witham Town 1
Horsham 3, Newbury Town 0
Hungerford Town 0, Abingdon Town 2

SEMI–FINAL - FIRST LEGS
Ruislip Manor 3, Horsham 1
Witham Town 0, Abingdon Town 1
SEMI–FINAL - SECOND LEGS
Abingdon Town 1,Witham Town 1 (2–1 agg)
Horsham 1, Ruislip Manor 1 (2–4 agg)

FINAL *(at Chesham United FC)*
Ruislip Manor 2, Abingdon Town 1

1991–92

FIRST ROUND
Banstead Athletic 7, Eastbourne United 1
Barton Rovers 3, Horsham 2 aet
Collier Row 4, Lewes 3
Cove 4, Berkhamsted Town 0
Epsom & Ewell 3, Hertford Town 1
Hampton 2, Hornchurch 1
Hemel Hempstead 0, Harefield United 2
Leatherhead 1, Ware 3
Ruislip Manor 1, Witham Town 0
Tilbury 0, Purfleet 2
Tring Town 1, Camberley Town 2

SECOND ROUND
Banstead Athletic 0, Southall 1
Barton Rovers 10, Southwick 2
Bracknell Town 1, Newbury Town 1 aet *(2–4 pens)*
Chertsey Town 1, Kingsbury Town 3
Clapton 1, Ruislip Manor 3
Collier Row 2, Saffron Walden Town 4
Cove 2, Hampton 1
Epsom & Ewell 4, Royston Town 1
Flackwell Heath 0, Egham Town 1
Harefield United 2, Camberley Town 1
Hungerford Town 0, Malden Vale 1
Metropolitan Police 1, Feltham & Hounslow Borough 2
Petersfield United 2, Rainham Town 1
Purfleet 2, Edgware Town 0
Thame United 1, Billericay Town 0
Ware 2, Worthing 3

THIRD ROUND
Egham Town 3, Harefield United 0
Epsom & Ewell 0, Cove 1
Feltham & Hounslow Borough 1, Ruislip Manor 3
Kingsbury Town 0, Barton Rovers 2
Newbury Town 0, Purfleet 5
Petersfield United 1, Thame United 2
Saffron Walden Town 4, Southall 1
Worthing 0, Malden Vale 3

FOURTH ROUND
Cove 0, Saffron Walden Town 2
Egham Town 2, Thame United 0
Malden Vale 6, Barton Rovers 0
Purfleet 3, Ruislip Manor 0

SEMI–FINALS
Malden Vale 2, Egham Town 2 aet
Saffron Walden Town 0, Purfleet 2
SEMI–FINAL REPLAY
Egham Town 4, Malden Vale 3

FINAL *(at Sutton United FC)*
Purfleet 3, Egham Town 2

1992–93

PRELIMINARY ROUND
Aldershot Town 4, Chertsey Town 1
Banstead Athletic 1, Egham Town 1 aet *(5–4 pens)*
Barton Rovers 3, Clapton 0
Bracknell Town 0, Newbury Town 2
East Thurrock United 1, Collier Row 0
Hemel Hempstead 2, Tring Town 4 aet
Hungerford Town 0, Hampton 1
Leighton Town 2, Flackwell Heath 1
Royston Town 3, Hornchurch 0
Saffron Walden Town 1, Ware 0

FIRST ROUND
Berkhamsted Town 2, Tring Town 1
Cove 2, Banstead Athletic 3 *(Aban. in extra time - fog)*
Edgware Town 4, Hertford Town 1
Horsham 0, Aldershot Town 1
Leatherhead 1, Camberley Town 1 aet *(4–1 pens)*
Leighton Town 1, Barton Rovers 2
Metropolitan Police 4, Feltham & Hounslow Boro 0
Newbury Town 1, Hampton 1 aet *(6–5 pens)*
Northwood 3, East Thurrock United 1
Petersfield United 1 Malden Vale 3
Royston Town 1, Saffron Walden Town 2
Ruislip Manor 3, Rainham Town 1
Southall 3, Epsom & Ewell 2
Tilbury 1, Kingsbury Town 4
Thame United 2, Witham Town 1
Worthing 4, Harefield United 0
FIRST ROUND REPLAY
Banstead Athletic 0, Cove 2

SECOND ROUND
Barton Rovers 3, Ruislip Manor 0
Berkhamsted Town 0, Edgware Town 2 aet
Cove 0, Thame United 2
Kingsbury Town 4, Saffron Walden Town 3
Metropolitan Police 3, Leatherhead 2 aet
Newbury Town 3, Malden Vale 1
Southall 1, Northwood 2
Worthing 4, Aldershot Town 4 aet *(5–3 pens)*

THIRD ROUND
Kingsbury Town 0, Barton Rovers 1 aet
Newbury Town 3, Metropolitan Police 7
Northwood 3, Edgware Town 2
Thame United 0, Worthing 1

SEMI–FINAL
Barton Rovers 2, Metropolitan Police 2 aet
Northwood 3, Worthing 1 aet
REPLAY
Metropolitan Police 1, Barton Rovers 2

FINAL *(at Chesham United FC)*
Barton Rovers 1, Northwood 3 aet

1993–94

FIRST ROUND
Barton Rovers 0, Leighton Town 1
Bracknell Town 1, Leatherhead 1 aet *(4–5 pens)*
Cheshunt 2, East Thurrock United 1
Collier Row 1, Rainham Town 1 aet *(2–4 pens)*
Flackwell Heath 3, Southall 2
Harefield United 1, Camberley Town 0
Horsham 1, Feltham & Hounslow Borough 3
Hungerford Town 0, Newbury Town 1
Kingsbury Town 1, Hornchurch 2 aet
Saffron Walden Town 2, Northwood 1
Tring Town 1, Hemel Hempstead 4

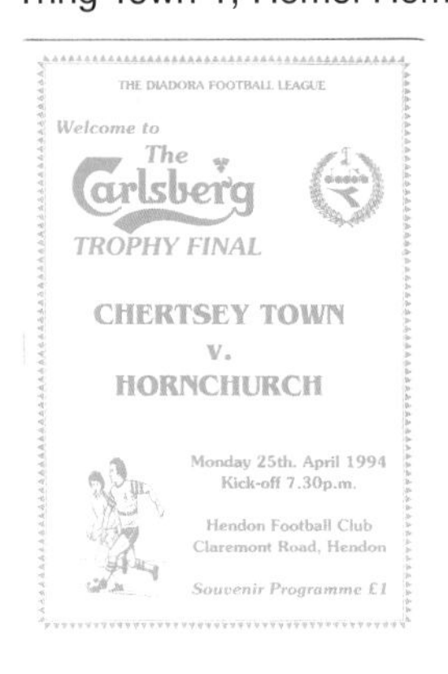

SECOND ROUND
Aldershot Town 2, Malden Vale 0
Aveley 3, Clapton 2
Banstead Athletic 2, Lewes 0
Chertsey Town 4, Metropolitan Police 0
Cheshunt 3, Ware 2
Edgware Town 2, Rainham Town 1
Egham Town 0, Newbury Town 1
Feltham & Hounslow Borough 1, Epsom & Ewell 3
Hampton 1, Leatherhead 0
Harefield United 0, Cove 2 aet
Hemel Hempstead 2, Royston Town 0 aet
Hertford Town 0, Harlow Town 2
Leighton Town 1, Hornchurch 3
Saffron Walden Town 2, Tilbury 1
Thame United 2, Oxford City 0
Witham Town 5, Flackwell Heath 1

THIRD ROUND
Aldershot Town 0, Epsom & Ewell 2
Aveley 0, Hornchurch 2 aet
Chertsey Town 7, Thame United 3
Cove 1, Banstead Athletic 3
Edgware Town 3, Harlow Town 0
Hemel Hempstead 2, Cheshunt 1
Newbury Town 3, Hampton 1
Saffron Walden Town 1, Witham Town 2

FOURTH ROUND
Epsom & Ewell 0, Chertsey Town 7
Hornchurch 5, Edgware Town 0
Newbury Town 2, Hemel Hempstead 1
Witham Town 0, Banstead Athletic 1

SEMI–FINALS
Chertsey Town 1, Banstead Athletic 0
Newbury Town 0, Hornchurch 2 aet

FINAL *(at Hendon FC)*
Chertsey Town 1, Hornchurch 0

1994–95

FIRST ROUND
Cheshunt 1, East Thurrock United 1 aet *(2–3 pens)*
Croydon 3, Leatherhead 1
Hampton 2, Metropolitan Police 3
Hertford Town 2, Barton Rovers 1
Horsham 1, Bracknell Town 2
Leighton Town 2, Tring Town 1
Lewes 5, Banstead Athletic 2 aet
Oxford City 4, Epsom & Ewell 1
Saffron Walden Town 1, Collier Row 3
Southall 4, Clapton 2
Windsor & Eton 0, Camberley Town 2

SECOND ROUND
Canvey Island 2, Witham Town 2 aet
Chalfont St Peter 1, Hungerford Town 1 aet *(1–3 pens)*
Croydon 3, Oxford City 1
(Croydon removed from competition)
Edgware Town 3, Collier Row 5 aet
Feltham & Hounslow Borough 1, Bracknell Town 3
Flackwell Heath 6, Cove 1
Harefield United 1, Egham Town 3
Harlow Town 3, Hertford Town 1
Hemel Hempstead 1, Kingsbury Town 1 aet *(5–4 pens)*
Leighton Town 1, Bedford Town 1 aet *(4–1 pens)*
Lewes 3, Malden Vale 1
Northwood 0, Metropolitan Police 1
Southall 3, East Thurrock United 0
Thame United 4, Camberley Town 1
Tilbury 3, Aveley 0
Ware 2, Hornchurch 5 aet

SECOND ROUND REPLAY
Witham Town 4, Canvey Island 2 aet

THIRD ROUND
Flackwell Heath 1, Egham Town 0
Harlow Town 1, Leighton Town 3
Hornchurch 0, Collier Row 2
Hungerford Town 1, Bracknell Town 0
Metropolitan Police 5, Lewes 3
Southall 0, Witham Town 0 aet *(6–5 pens)*
Thame United 2, Oxford City 1
Tilbury 1, Hemel Hempstead 4

FOURTH ROUND
Flackwell Heath 2, Hungerford Town 2 aet *(2–3 pens)*
Hemel Hempstead 1, Collier Row 2
Leighton Town 1, Southall 3
Thame United 1, Metropolitan Police 2 aet

SEMI–FINALS
Hungerford Town 0, Collier Row 3
Metropolitan Police 2, Southall 2 aet
SEMI-FINAL REPLAY
Southall 1, Metropolitan Police 2

FINAL *(at Boreham Wood FC)*
Metropolitan Police 1, Collier Row 1 aet *(4–3 pens)*

1995–96

FIRST ROUND
Aveley 6, Harlow Town 2
Banstead Athletic 2, Windsor & Eton 0
Bracknell Town 1, Horsham 0
Chalfont St Peter 1, Croydon 0
Cove 2, Flackwell Heath 0
Hertford Town 0, East Thurrock United 2
Newbury Town scr Metropolitan Police w/o
Southall 3, Saffron Walden Town 1
Wingate & Finchley 0, Harefield United 1
Witham Town 1, Clapton 4
Wivenhoe Town 5, Hornchurch 2

SECOND ROUND
Aveley 0, Ware 1
Banstead Athletic 6, Camberley Town 1
Bracknell Town 2, Harefield United 1 aet
Canvey Island 3, Collier Row 2
Cove 0, Hampton 4
Dorking 1, Hungerford Town 6
East Thurrock United 3, Cheshunt 2
Egham Town 1, Leatherhead 2
Epsom & Ewell 0, Lewes 1
Hemel Hempstead 3, Edgware Town 0
Kingsbury Town 2, Clapton 5
Metropolitan Police 2, Chalfont St Peter 6
Northwood 6, Southall 1
Tring Town 1, Tilbury 5
Wealdstone 1, Bedford Town 0
Wivenhoe Town 5, Leighton Town 3

THIRD ROUND
Banstead Athletic 2, Leatherhead 0
Bracknell Town 2, Lewes 0
Canvey Island 1, Clapton 0
East Thurrock United 2, Tilbury 2 *(abandoned 90 mins)*
Hungerford Town 1, Hampton 0
Northwood 0, Wealdstone 2
Ware 3, Hemel Hempstead 1 aet
Wivenhoe Town 5, Chalfont St Peter 1
THIRD ROUND REPLAY
Tilbury 2, East Thurrock United 0

FOURTH ROUND
Banstead Athletic 1, Bracknell Town 0
Tilbury 2, Ware 1
Wealdstone 1, Hungerford Town 2
Wivenhoe Town 1, Canvey Island 3

SEMI–FINALS
Banstead Athletic 2, Tilbury 1 aet
Canvey Island 1, Hungerford Town 1 aet
SEMI-FINAL REPLAY
Hungerford Town 1, Canvey Island 2

FINAL *(at Aveley FC)*
Canvey Island 2, Banstead Athletic 1

1996–97

FIRST ROUND
Aveley 2, Barking 2 aet *(2–4 pens)*
Chalfont St Peter 0, Banstead Athletic 2
Cheshunt 0, Ware 3
Dorking 0, Wealdstone 7
Epsom & Ewell 2, Lewes 0
Leatherhead 5, Northwood 3
Wembley 4, Hertford Town 1

SECOND ROUND
Barking 2, Harlow Town 0
Camberley Town 0, Horsham 3
Clapton 1, Braintree Town 6 aet
Collier Row & Romford 3, Ware 1
East Thurrock United 2, Witham Town 3
Flackwell Heath 0, Egham Town 1
Hemel Hempstead 0, Leighton Town 1
Hornchurch 1, Bedford Town 2 aet
Kingsbury Town 1, Wingate & Finchley 1
Leatherhead 3, Banstead Athletic 1 aet
Metropolitan Police 1, Epsom & Ewell 0
Tring Town 4, Southall 4 aet *(2–4 pens)*
Wealdstone 3, Bracknell Town 1
Wembley 4, Tilbury 1
Windsor & Eton 1, Hungerford Town 2
Wivenhoe Town 2, Edgware Town 0
SECOND ROUND REPLAY
Wingate & Finchley 3, Kingsbury Town 0

THIRD ROUND
Barking 2, Bedford Town 2 aet *(4–5 pens)*
Collier Row & Romford 3, Wivenhoe Town 4
Horsham 2, Egham Town 3
Hungerford Town 4, Southall 2 aet
Leatherhead 1, Wembley 0
Leighton Town 2, Braintree Town 1 aet
Wealdstone 4, Metropolitan Police 2
Witham Town 1, Wingate & Finchley 2

FOURTH ROUND
Egham Town 1, Wealdstone 2
Leatherhead 6, Hungerford Town 2
Leighton Town 1, Bedford Town 1 aet *(4–3 pens)*
Wivenhoe Town 2, Wingate & Finchley 1

SEMI–FINALS
Leatherhead 0, Wealdstone 0 aet
Wivenhoe Town 0, Leighton Town 2
SEMI–FINALS REPLAY
Wealdstone 3, Leatherhead 0

FINAL *(at Hitchin Town FC)*
Leighton Town 1, Wealdstone 0

1997–98

FIRST ROUND
Banstead Athletic 2, Camberley Town 1
Clapton 1, Ford United 4
Croydon Athletic 0, Corinthian–Casuals 2
East Thurrock United 4, Witham Town 3
Egham Town 1, Chalfont St Peter 0 aet
Flackwell Heath 3, Tring Town 1
Hertford Town 0, Canvey Island 3
Kingsbury Town 0, Braintree Town 4
Ware 2, Aveley 2 aet *(9–10 pens)*
Wingate & Finchley 1, Marlow 8

SECOND ROUND
Aveley 1, Cheshunt 0
Banstead Athletic 2, Marlow 4 aet
Barking 5, Braintree Town 4
Bracknell Town 1, Epsom & Ewell 2 aet
Canvey Island 4, Harlow Town 1
Egham Town 4, Hungerford Town 0
Flackwell Heath 2, Dorking 0
Ford United 1, Edgware Town 4
Hemel Hempstead 0, East Thurrock United 2
Leighton Town 1, Bedford Town 2 aet
Lewes 0, Horsham 2
Metropolitan Police 1, Windsor & Eton 4
Northwood 4, Wivenhoe Town 0
Southall 1, Hornchurch 1 aet *(5–4 pens)*
Tilbury 1, Wealdstone 2
Tooting & Mitcham United 0, Corinthian–Casuals 1

THIRD ROUND
Aveley 2, East Thurrock United 3
Barking 0, Bedford Town 3 aet
Corinthian–Casuals 4, Southall 1
Edgware Town 1, Wealdstone 2
Egham Town 6, Flackwell Heath 1
Epsom & Ewell 4, Windsor & Eton 1
Marlow 3, Horsham 2
Northwood 3, Canvey Island 1

FOURTH ROUND
Bedford Town 2, Northwood 1
East Thurrock United 1, Weadstone 2
Egham Town 3, Corinthian–Casuals 0
Epsom & Ewell 2, Marlow 1

SEMI–FINALS
Egham Town 0, Bedford Town 1
Wealdstone 0, Epsom & Ewell 1

FINAL *(at Hendon FC)*
Bedford Town 2, Epsom & Ewell 0

1998–99

FIRST ROUND
Barking 3, Ware 1
Bracknell Town 1, Thame United 3
Chalfont St Peter 4, Kingsbury Town 0
Dorking 1, Lewes 2
Egham Town 1, Hungerford Town 0
Harlow Town 1, Ford United 0
Tilbury 1, Northwood 2 aet
Windsor & Eton 1, Flackwell Heath 0
Wingate & Finchley 0, Leighton Town 4
Wokingham Town 0, Marlow 5

SECOND ROUND
Abingdon Town 2, Egham Town 3
Banstead Athletic 4, Camberley Town 2
Bedford Town 1, Cheshunt 0
Clapton 0, Edgware Town 2
Corinthian–Casuals 0, Metropolitan Police 1
East Thurrock United 2, Hertford Town 3 aet
Harlow Town 6, Aveley 0
Hemel Hempstead 0, Windsor & Eton 2
Hornchurch 1, Barking 3
Leighton Town 2, Northwood 1
Marlow 3, Lewes 2
Southall 2, Croydon Athletic 0
Thame United 3, Chalfont St Peter 2
Tooting & Mitcham United 4, Horsham 1
Tring Town 0, Epsom & Ewell 2
Wivenhoe Town 3, Witham Town 1

THIRD ROUND
Banstead Athletic 1, Epsom & Ewell 4 aet
Bedford Town 1, Leighton Town 3
Harlow Town 0, Edgware 1
Hertford Town 0, Windsor & Eton 2
Marlow 4, Egham Town 0
Thame United 1, Southall 3
Tooting & Mitcham United 3, Windsor & Eton 1
Wivenhoe Town 4, Barking 1

FOURTH ROUND
Leighton Town 2, Wivenhoe Town 1
Southall 0, Marlow 1
Tooting & Mitcham United 3, Epsom & Ewell 2
Windsor & Eton 4, Edgware Town 1

SEMI–FINALS
Leighton Town 3, Tooting & Mitcham United 2 aet
Windsor & Eton 3, Marlow 0

FINAL *(at Chesham United FC)*
Leighton Town 1, Windsor & Eton 0

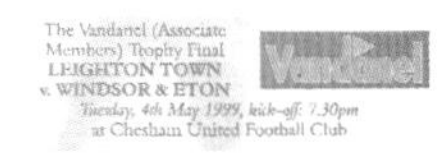

1999–2000

FIRST ROUND
Cheshunt 1, Ware 2
Clapton 0, Hertford Town 1 aet
Flackwell Heath 1, Chalfont St Peter 1 aet *(3–4 pens)*
Great Wakering Rovers 1, Aveley 1 aet *(1–3 pens)*
Horsham 2, Epsom & Ewell 6
Hungerford Town 2, Abingdon Town 2 aet *(4–2 pens)*
Leighton Town 0, Northwood 1
Marlow 2, Metropolitan Police 0
Molesey 1, Camberley Town 2
Wembley 1, Wivenhoe Town 2 aet
Windsor & Eton 3, Dorking 1

SECOND ROUND
Aveley 1, Wivenhoe Town 2
Banstead Athletic 4, Wokingham Town 0
Berkhamsted Town 2, Witham Town 0
Bracknell Town 5, Egham Town 1
Chalfont St Peter 2, Hungerford Town 1
Corinthian–Casuals 1, Windsor & Eton 2
Croydon Athletic 0 Marlow 2
East Thurrock United 1, Hornchurch 1 aet *(4–3 pens)*
Hertford Town 2, Edgware Town1
Lewes 2, Camberley Town 4
Northwood 4, Hemel Hempstead Town 1
Tilbury 0, Barking 2
Tooting & Mitcham United 4, Epsom & Ewell 1
Tring Town 0, Southall 1
Ware 5, Kingsbury Town 1
Wingate & Finchley 4, Ford United 2

THIRD ROUND
Berkhamsted Town 3, Wingate & Finchley 0
Camberley Town 1, Windsor & Eton 3 aet
Chalfont St Peter 1, Banstead Athletic 2
East Thurrock United 1, Barking 5
Marlow 1, Bracknell Town 0
Tooting & Mitcham United 4, Southall 1
Ware 2, Northwood 3
Wivenhoe Town 3, Hertford Town 0

FOURTH ROUND
Banstead Athletic 1, Marlow 1 aet *(4–5 pens)*
Berkhamsted Town 1, Barking 1 aet *(1–3 pens)*
Northwood 2, Wivenhoe Town 1 aet
Tooting & Mitcham United 3, Windsor & Eton 4 aet

SEMI–FINALS
Barking 3, Windsor & Eton 1
Northwood 3, Marlow 0

FINAL *(at Harrow Borough FC)*
Northwood 2, Barking 1

2000–01

FIRST ROUND
Abingdon Town 2, Hungerford Town 2 aet *(4–5 pens)*
Arlesey Town 4, Tring Town 0
Berkhamsted Town 1, Edgware Town 3
Bracknell Town 1, Wokingham Town 1 aet *(6–5 pens)*
Dorking 2, Croydon Athletic 1
East Thurrock United 3, Clapton 1
Flackwell Heath 3, Chalfont St Peter 0
Hertford Town 2, Cheshunt 3
Leyton Pennant 2, Wembley 1
Molesey 1, Tooting & Mitcham United 1 aet *(3–0 pens)*
Windsor & Eton 4, Ashford Town (Middx) 1
Witham Town 0, Tilbury 2

SECOND ROUND
Chertsey Town 1, Bracknell Town 2
Dorking 3, Corinthian–Casuals 2
East Thurrock United 4, Aveley 0
Edgware Town 2, Cheshunt 1
Great Wakering Rovers 1, Barking 2 aet
Hemel Hempstead Town 4, Wingate & Finchley 0
Horsham 5, Flackwell Heath 2
Hungerford Town 0, Banstead Athletic 5
Kingsbury Town 2, Leighton Town 0
Lewes 2, Epsom & Ewell 1
Leyton Pennant 2, Hornchurch 3
Marlow 4, Camberley Town 2 aet
Metropolitan Police 1, Egham Town 1 aet *(2–3 pens)*
Molesey 0, Windsor & Eton 1
Tilbury 1, Wivenhoe Town 4
Ware 2, Arlesey Town 1

THIRD ROUND
Barking 4, Kingsbury Town 0
Dorking 1, Bracknell Town 0
Edgware Town 1, Hornchurch 0
Egham Town 0, Horsham 1
Marlow 2, Banstead Athletic 1
Ware 0, East Thurrock United 4
Windsor & Eton 0, Lewes 5
Wivenhoe Town 2, Hemel Hempstead Town 4

FOURTH ROUND
Barking 0, Hemel Hempstead Town 1
Edgware Town 1, East Thurrock United 2
Horsham 3, Lewes 1
Marlow 3, Dorking 3 aet *(3–1 pens)*

SEMI–FINALS
East Thurrock United 1, Marlow 4
Hemel Hempstead Town 5, Horsham 2 aet

FINAL *(at Marlow FC)*
Marlow 4, Hemel Hempstead Town 0

2001–02 – NO COMPETITION

2002–03

	GROUP A	**1**	**2**	**3**	**4**
1	Chalfont St Peter	*	0–2	2–1	3–3
2	Flackwell Heath	2–2	*	1–1	2–0
3	Leighton Town	0–2	0–2	*	6–0
4	Wokingham Town	1–8	1–2	3–2	*

		P	*W*	*D*	*L*	*F*	*A*	*Pts*
1	Flackwell Heath	6	4	2	0	11	4	14
2	Chalfont St Peter	6	3	2	1	17	9	11
3	Leighton Town	6	1	1	4	10	10	4
4	Wokingham Town	6	1	1	4	8	23	4

	GROUP B	**1**	**2**	**3**	**4**
1	Abingdon Town	*	2–2	2–3	3–0
2	Camberley Town	1–2	*	3–1	2–2
3	Dorking	2–0	2–2	*	1–4
4	Hungerford Town	4–0	1–1	5–2	*

		P	*W*	*D*	*L*	*F*	*A*	*Pts*
1	Hungerford Town	6	3	2	1	16	9	11
2	Camberley Town	6	1	4	1	11	10	7
3	Abingdon Town	6	2	1	3	9	12	7
4	Dorking	6	2	1	3	11	16	7

	GROUP C	**1**	**2**	**3**	**4**
1	Cheshunt	*	3–0	4–0	3–0
2	Edgware Town	0–1	*	0–1	1–3
3	Kingsbury Town	0–2	4–1	*	3–2
4	Tring Town	1–3	1–2	0–2	*

		P	*W*	*D*	*L*	*F*	*A*	*Pts*
1	Cheshunt	6	6	0	0	16	1	18
2	Kingsbury Town	6	4	0	2	10	9	12
3	Tring Town	6	1	0	4	7	14	3
4	Edgware Town	6	1	0	5	4	13	3

	GROUP D	**1**	**2**	**3**	**4**
1	Clapton	*	0–2	0–2	3–0
2	Leyton	4–0	*	4–0	2–1
3	Ware	4–1	2–8	*	1–0
4	Witham Town	0–3	1–1	1–2	*

		P	*W*	*D*	*L*	*F*	*A*	*Pts*
1	Leyton	6	5	1	0	21	4	16
2	Ware	6	4	0	2	11	14	12
3	Clapton	6	2	0	4	7	12	6
4	Witham Town	6	0	1	5	3	12	1

QUARTER FINALS
Cheshunt 1, Chalfont St Peter 0
Flackwell Heath 2, Ware 1
Hungerford Town 3, Kingsbury Town 3 aet *(5-6 pens)*
Leyton 4, Camberley Town 0

SEMI–FINALS
Cheshunt 5, Kingsbury Town 0
Flackwell Heath 2, Leyton 2 aet

REPLAY
Leyton 2, Flackwell Heath 0

FINAL *(at Leyton FC)*
Leyton 2, Cheshunt 0

2003–04 – NO COMPETITION

2004–05

GROUP A	**1**	**2**	**3**	**4**
1 Enfield	*	3–2	2–1	5–1
2 Hertford Town	1–1	*	2–0	1–4
3 Ware	1–4	2–1	*	1–1
4 Witham Town	4–4	0–5	4–1	*

	P	*W*	*D*	*L*	*F*	*A*	*Pts*
1 Enfield	6	4	2	0	19	10	14
2 Witham Town	6	2	2	2	14	17	8
3 Hertford Town	6	2	1	3	12	10	7
4 Ware	6	1	1	4	6	14	4

GROUP B	**1**	**2**	**3**	**4**
1 Abingdon Town	*	4–1	2–2	1–0
2 Chalfont St Peter	1–0	*	1–2	3–1
3 Flackwell Heath	2–1	2–1	*	2–0
4 Wembley	0–0	1–3	0–2	*

	P	*W*	*D*	*L*	*F*	*A*	*Pts*
1 Flackwell Heath	6	5	1	0	12	5	16
2 Chalfont St Peter	6	3	0	3	10	10	9
3 Abingdon Town	6	2	2	2	8	6	8
4 Wembley	6	0	1	5	2	11	1

GROUP C	**1**	**2**	**3**	**4**
1 Brook House	*	2–1	3–0	3–1
2 Camberley Town	0–2	*	0–2	1–1
3 Chertsey Town	0–2	5–1	*	2–0
4 Epsom & Ewell	NP	5–2	1–1	*

	P	*W*	*D*	*L*	*F*	*A*	*Pts*
1 Brook House	5	5	0	0	12	2	15
2 Chertsey Town	6	3	1	2	10	7	10
3 Epsom & Ewell	5	1	2	2	8	9	5
4 Camberley Town	6	0	1	5	5	17	1

Epsom & Ewell v Brook House not played

GROUP D	**1**	**2**	**3**	**4**
1 Clapton	*	0–2	1–2	NP
2 Edgware Town	2–0	*	0–3	6–1
3 Ilford	3–2	1–2	*	3–1
4 Kingsbury Town	4–1	1–0	2–2	*

	P	*W*	*D*	*L*	*F*	*A*	*Pts*
1 Ilford	6	4	1	1	14	8	13
2 Edgware Town	6	4	0	2	12	6	12
3 Kingsbury Town	5	2	1	2	9	12	7
4 Clapton	5	0	0	5	4	13	0

Clapton v Kingsbury Town not played

QUARTER FINAL
Brook House 2, Witham Town 1
Enfield 5, Edgware Town 2 aet
Flackwell Heath 2, Chertsey Town 0
Ilford 2, Chalfont St Peter 1

SEMI–FINAL
Brook House 1, Flackwell Heath 2
Enfield 2, Ilford 5

FINAL *(at Ilford FC)*
Ilford 2, Flackwell Heath 1 aet

2005–06

GROUP A	**1**	**2**	**3**	**4**
1 Clapton	*	0–1	1–0	2–0
2 Hertford Town	1–2	*	4–1	3–1
3 Ware	0–1	2–3	*	6–3
4 Witham Town	5–3	2–0	5–2	*

	P	*W*	*D*	*L*	*F*	*A*	*Pts*
Hertford Town	6	4	0	2	12	8	12
Clapton	6	4	0	2	9	7	12
Witham Town	6	3	0	3	16	16	9
Ware	6	1	0	5	11	17	3

GROUP B	**1**	**2**	**3**	**4**
1 Camberley Town	*	0–1	0–3	0–3
2 Croydon	3–0	*	3–0	1–1
3 Dorking	4–0	1–3	*	2–3
4 Epsom & Ewell	2–1	1–0	0–1	*

	P	*W*	*D*	*L*	*F*	*A*	*Pts*
Croydon	6	4	1	1	11	3	13
Epsom & Ewell	6	4	1	1	10	5	13
Dorking	6	3	0	3	11	9	9
Camberley Town	6	0	0	6	1	16	0

GROUP C	**1**	**2**	**3**	**4**
1 Brook House	*	3–3	5–1	4–1
2 Chalfont St Peter	3–2	*	2–1	2–1
3 Chertsey Town	2–5	1–3	*	2–2
4 Flackwell Heath	1–2	3–1	0–0	*

	P	*W*	*D*	*L*	*F*	*A*	*Pts*
Brook House	6	4	1	1	21	11	13
Chalfont St Peter	6	4	1	1	14	11	13
Flackwell Heath	6	1	2	3	8	11	5
Chertsey Town	6	0	2	4	7	17	2

GROUP D	**1**	**2**	**3**	**4**
1 Edgware Town	*	2–2	4–1	5–0
2 Egham Town	2–1	*	0–3	2–1
3 Kingsbury Town	1–0	1–2	*	1–0
4 Wembley	1–1	0–2	2–0	*

	P	*W*	*D*	*L*	*F*	*A*	*Pts*
Egham Town	6	4	1	1	10	8	12
Edgware Town	6	2	2	2	13	7	8
Kingsbury Town*	6	3	0	3	7	8	6
Wembley	6	1	1	4	4	11	4

**Kingsbury Town 3 pts deducted for fielding an ineligible player.*

QUARTER FINAL
Brook House 3, Epsom & Ewell 2
Croydon 2, Clapton 1
Egham Town 1, Chalfont St Peter 2
Hertford Town 3, Edgware Town 0

SEMI FINAL
Chalfont St Peter 1, Brook House 2
Croydon 0, Hertford Town 1

FINAL *(at Brook House FC)*
Brook House 3, Hertford Town 1

CHAPTER TWELVE

The Complete Record Member Clubs 1905-2005 Brief Histories

Isthmian Football League

1905 - 2005

Member Clubs in the first one hundred years

Abingdon Town
AFC Wimbledon
Aldershot Town
Arlesey Town
Ashford Town (Kent)
Ashford Town (Middlesex)
Aveley
Aylesbury United
Banstead Athletic
Barking & East Ham United
Barton Rovers
Bashley
Basildon United
Basingstoke Town
Bedford Town
Berkhampstead Town
Billericay Town
Bishops Stortford
Bognor Regis Town
Boreham Wood
Bracknell Town
Braintree Town
Bromley
Brook House
Burgess Hill Town
Camberley Town
Canvey Island
Carshalton Athletic
Chalfont St Peter
Chelmsford City
Chertsey Town
Chesham United
Cheshunt
Civil Service
Clapton
Corinthian Casuals
Cove
Cray Wanderers
Croydon
Croydon Athletic
Dagenham
Dagenham & Redbridge
Dorking
Dover Athletic
Dulwich Hamlet
Dunstable Town
Ealing Association
East Thurrock United
Eastbourne United
Eastleigh
Edgware Town
Egham Town
Enfield
Epping Town
Epsom & Ewell
Farnborough Town
Farnham Town
Feltham & Hounslow Borough
Finchley
Flackwell Heath
Fleet Town
Folkestone Invicta
Gravesend & Northfleet
Grays Athletic
Great Wakering Rovers
Hampton & Richmond Borough
Harefield United
Haringey Borough
Harlow Town
Harrow Borough
Harwich & Parkeston
Hastings United
Hayes
Hemel Hempstead Town
Hendon
Hertford Town
Heybridge Swifts
Hitchin Town
Hornchurch
Horsham
Hungerford Town
Ilford
Kettering Town
Kingsbury Town
Kingstonian
Leatherhead
Leighton Town
Letchworth Garden City
Lewes
Leyton
Leytonstone
London Caledonians
Maidenhead United
Maidstone United
Malden Vale
Marlow
Metropolitan Police
Molesey
New Crusaders
Newbury Town
Newport IoW
Northwood
Nunhead
Oxford City
Petersfield United
Rainham Town
Redbridge
Redbridge Forest
Romford
Royston Town
Ruislip Manor
Saffron Walden Town
Salisbury City
Shepherds Bush
Slough Town
Southall
Southwick
St Albans City
Staines Town
Stevenage Borough
Sutton United
Thame United
Thurrock
Tilbury
Tonbridge Angels
Tooting & Mitcham United
Tring Town
Tufnell Park
Tunbridge Wells
Uxbridge
Vauxhall Motors
Waltham Forest
Walthamstow Avenue
Walton & Hersham
Ware
Wealdstone
Wembley
West Norwood
Whyteleafe
Willesden
Wimbledon
Windsor & Eton
Wingate & Finchley
Witham Town
Wivenhoe Town
Woking
Wokingham Town
Wolverton Town
Worthing
Wycombe Wanderers
Yeading
Yeovil Town

The Isthmian League has had more than 150 Clubs in membership in its first 100 years. Each Club's achievements are listed below following the same formula: Club name (years in membership); ground(s); colours; nickname(s) – if any; formation; formative years; senior leagues; Isthmian era; FA Competitions. The formation section covers the year the Club was founded or records are first known and any subsequent mergers. The Senior Leagues part describes those leagues with Senior status of which the Club was a member, highlighting if it was a founding member with the symbol *(f)* and listing any Championships won. The Isthmian era is exactly what it says but expanded to include the Divisions in which the Club competed in each season of membership, together with any championships or League competition victories. FA Competitions lists the best performance of the Club in each of The FA competitions, together with the year achieved. In the case of The FA Amateur Cup, Trophy and Vase all appearances in the last four or better are recorded.

Abingdon Town (1989–2005)
Ground: Culham Road, Abingdon, Oxfordshire
Colours: Yellow & Green shirts and Green shorts.
Nickname: The Abbots or Town.
Formation: The club was originally formed in 1870 and merged in 1898 with St. Michael's and dropped suffix Town until 1920. **Formative years:** Oxford & District 1898–1901 (champions 1899, 1900 and 1901), West Berks 1901–04, Reading Temperance 1904–09, North Berks 1909–27 and Reading & District 1927–50 (champions 1948). **Senior Leagues:** Spartan 1950–53, Hellenic *(f)* 1953–88 (champions 1957, 1959, 1960, 1987) and Spartan 1988–89 (champions 1989). **Isthmian era:** Elected to Division 2 South in 1989 winning promotion as champions in 1990–91; relegated to Division 2 in 1997–98 and Division 3 in 1998–99. Back in Division 2 following re-organisation in 2002; spent two seasons before resigning from the League at the end of 2004–05. The club were Associate Members Trophy finalists in 1990–91.

AFC Wimbledon (2004–2008)

Ground: Kingsmeadow Stadium, Jack Goodchild Way, 422a, Kingston Road, Kingston–Upon–Thames, Surrey.
Colours: Blue shirts and shorts with Yellow trim. **Nickname:** The Dons.
Formation: 2002. **Senior Leagues:** Combined Counties 2002–04 (champions 2004). **Isthmian era:** Promotion to the Isthmian League as champions of the Combined Counties League, winning the Division 1 championship the following year and promotion to the Premier Division.

Aldershot Town (1992–2003)

Ground: Recreation Ground, High Street, Aldershot.
Colours: Red shirts and shorts with Blue trim.
Nickname: The Shots.
Formation: Formed in 1992 by supporters of former Football League club Aldershot FC who folded in March 1992 due to financial problems. **Isthmian era:** The newly–formed club were immediately accepted into Division 3 in 1992, winning the championship at the first attempt, and then gained a second promotion the following season. The club spent four seasons in Division 1 before promotion as Champions in 1997–98. The club finished seventh in 1998–99, runners-up in 1999–2000, fourth in 2000–01 and third in 2001–02 before securing the championship in 2002–03 and promotion to the Football Conference, where they finished in the playoffs – fifth and fourth, respectively, in their first two seasons. The club were League Cup winners in 1998–99 and finalists in 1995–96. **FA competitions:** FA Cup second round 1999–2000, 2003–04 and 2004–05. FA Trophy semi–finalists 2003–04.

Arlesey Town (2000–2004)

Ground: Hitchin Road, Arlesey, Bedfordshire. **Colours:** Light & Dark Blue shirts and Dark Blue shorts. **Nickname:** The Blues. **Formation:** 1891. **Formative years:** Biggleswade & District 1897–1922 and 1928–29, Bedford 1926–27 and Luton & District 1932–33. **Senior leagues:** Bedfordshire County–South Midlands *(f)* 1922–26, 1927–28, 1929–32, 1936–54, 1961–82 and 1992–97 (champions Division 2 1930 & 1937 and Premier Division 1952, 1953, 1995 & 1996), United Counties 1933–36 & 1982–92 (champions 1985), Parthenon 1954–58, London 1958–60, 1960–61 not active and Spartan–South Midlands 1997–2000 (champions 1995, 1999 & 2000). **Isthmian era:** Gained promotion to Division 3 as champions of Spartan– South Midlands League in 2000, winning promotion to Division 2 as champions in 2000–01. The club were placed in Division 1 North following League re-organisation in 2002. Restructuring for 2004–05 allocated the club to the Southern League Division 1 East where they finished 13th. **FA competitions:** FA Vase winners 1994–95.

Ashford Town (2004–to date)

Ground: The Homelands, Ashford Road, Kingsnorth, Ashford, Kent. **Colours:** Light Green shirts, Navy Blue shorts. **Nickname:** Nuts & Bolts. **Formation:** 1930, out of the ashes of the former Ashford Railway Works Club. **Senior leagues:** Kent 1930–59 (champions 1949) and Southern 1959–2004. **Isthmian era:** League restructuring for 2004–05 placed the club in the Isthmian League where they finished 20th in Division 1. **FA competitions:** FA Cup 2nd round 1961-62, 1966-67 and 1996-97.

Ashford Town (Middlesex) (2000–2004)

Ground: Short Lane, Stanwell, Staines, Middlesex. **Colours:** Tangerine & White striped shirts and Black shorts. **Nickname:** Tangerines. **Formation:** 1964. **Formative years:** Hounslow & District 1964–68 absorbing Staines Youth Club FC on the way, Surrey Intermediate 1967–82, Surrey County Premier 1982–90. **Senior leagues:** Combined Counties 1990–2000 (champions 1995, 1996, 1997, 1998 & 2000). **Isthmian era:** Promoted to Division 3 as Combined Counties League champions in 2000 won promotion to Division 2 as third placed club in 2000–01 and the club were placed in Division 1 South following re-organisation in 2002. Restructuring for 2004–05 allocated the club to the Southern League Division 1 West where they reached the play–offs by finishing sixth.

Aveley (1973–2004)

Ground: Mill Field, Mill Road, Aveley, Essex. **Colours:** Royal Blue shirts and shorts. **Nickname:** The Millers. **Formation:** 1927 re–formed 1946. **Formative years:** Local Junior leagues 1927–39 and Thurrock Combination 1946–49. **Senior leagues:** London 1949–57 (Division 1 champions 1951, Premier Division 1955), Delphian 1957–1963 and Athenian 1963–73 (champions Division 1 1971) **Isthmian era:** Elected as founder-members when the Isthmian League formed Division 2 in 1973, they remained in that Division until relegation to Division 2 North in 1986. In 1989–90 the club won promotion back to Division 1 as runners-up, only to be relegated to Division 2 again in 1992–93 and to Division 3 in 1994–95. The club won promotion back to Division 2 in 2001–02 as third-placed club and played in Division 1 North following re-organisation in 2002. The club were League Cup winners in 1989–90. Restructuring for 2004–05 allocated the club to the Southern League Division 1 East where they finished 17th. **FA competitions:** FA Cup first round 1970–71.

Aylesbury United (1989–2004)

Ground: The Stadium, Buckingham Road, Aylesbury, Buckinghamshire.
Colours: Green & White shirts and White shorts.
Nickname: The Ducks.
Formation: 1897 following a merger between the Printing Works and St. Mary's Night School clubs. The club also merged with Aylesbury Rovers when Rovers lost their ground in 1899. **Formative years:** Bucks Contiguous Counties 1898–1900, Ascot 1900–03 (champions 1902 & 1903), South Eastern 1903–05 and Berks & Bucks 1903–06, Friendlies 1906–08. **Senior leagues:** Spartan 1908–51 (champions West Division in 1909, Division 1 West 1929 and Division 1 1939), Delphian League *(f)* 1951–63 (champions 1954) and Athenian 1963–76. The club turned semi-professional in 1976 and joined the Southern League replacing Bexley United. They won promotion in 1984–85 and were champions in 1987–88 winning promotion to the GM Vauxhall Conference, the same year they played the Full England XI in a pre Euro 1988 friendly. **Isthmian era:** Relegated from the Conference after only one season and allocated a place in the Isthmian League with their best position coming in 1998–99 when they were runners-up behind Sutton United. The club were relegated to Division 1 in 1999–2000, but gained promotion back to the Premier Division as the third-placed club two years later. The club were League Cup winners in 1994–95 and Full Members Cup finalists in 1996–97. Restructuring for 2004–05 allocated the club to the Southern League Premier Division where they finished tenth.
FA competitions: FA Cup third round 1994–95. FA Trophy semi–finalists 2002–03.

Banstead Athletic (1984–2006)

Ground: Merland Rise, Tadworth, Surrey.
Colours: Amber & Black shirts Amber shorts.
Nickname: The A's.
Formation: 1944; Previously Banstead Juniors 1944–46. **Formative years:** Epsom & Ewell Youth 1944–45 (champions 1945), Sutton & District 1945–46, Surrey Intermediate 1946–49 (Champions 1948 & 1949). **Senior leagues:** Surrey Senior 1949–1965 (champions 1951, 1952, 1953, 1954, 1957, and 1965), Spartan 1965–75, London–Spartan *(f)* 1975–79 and Athenian 1979–84. **Isthmian era:** The club were elected to Division 2 South in 1984 where they remained never finishing above mid-table. In 1991, Division 2 was re-organised into Divisions Two and Three based on league positions the previous season. The club were placed in Division 2 finishing fourth in 1995–96. The club were in Division 1 South following League re-organisation in 2002. The club remained in the Isthmian League following restructuring in 2004–05 finishing 17th in Division 1. The club were Associate Members Trophy finalists in 1995–96.
FA competitions: FA Vase semi–finalists 1996–97.

Barking & East Ham United (1952–2004)

Ground: Mayesbrook Park, Lodge Avenue, Dagenham, Essex.
Previous Ground: Vicarage Field *(pictured left)*, Ripple Road, Barking until 1973.
Colours: Royal Blue shirts and shorts. **Nickname:** the Blues.
Formation: c1880 under various guises including Barking Rovers (1880–c1890) and Barking Woodville (1893–c1900). The present club was formed in 1899 and previously known as Barking Institute (1899–1902), Barking (1902–1919 and again 1932–2000) and Barking Town (1919–32). The club took over and merged with East Ham United in the summer of 2001. **Formative years:** Leyton & District 1899–1900. **Senior leagues:** South Essex 1900–10, 1911–14 & 1919–21 (champions Division 2 joint 1901 and Division 2 A 1902), London *(f)* 1896–98 & 1909–26 (champions Division 1 A 1910, Premier Division 1921), Athenian *(f)* 1912, resigning after 2 matches, & 1923–52 (champions 1935). **Isthmian era:** The club accepted an invitation to join the Isthmian League in 1952, winning the championship in 1978–79. In 1990–91, they were relegated to Division 1 and again in 1995–96 to Division 2 before winning promotion back to Division 1 in 2000–01. The club competed in Division 1 North following League re-organisation in 2002. The club were League Cup finalists in 1976–77 and Associate Members Trophy finalists in 1999–2000. Restructuring for 2004–05 allocated the club to the Southern League Division 1 East where they reached the play–offs after finishing sixth.
FA competitions: FA Cup second round 1978–79, 1979–80, 1981–82 and 1983–84. FA Amateur Cup finalists 1926–27.

Barton Rovers (1979–2004)

Ground: Sharpenhoe Road, Barton–le–Clay, Nr Luton, Bedfordshire.
Colours: Royal Blue shirts and shorts with White trim.
Nickname: Rovers.
Formation: 1898 re–formed 1946.
Formative years: Local leagues and friendlies 1898–1946, Luton & District 1946–54 (champions Division 3 1948).
Senior leagues: South Midlands League 1954–79 (champions Division 2 1955, Division 1 1965 and Premier Division 1971, 1972, 1973, 1975, 1976, 1977, 1978 and 1979).
Isthmian era: Elected to Division 2 in 1979, switching to Division 2 North when regionalisation was introduced in 1984 and, with further league re-organisation in 1991 back to Division 2. In 1994–95 the club were promoted to Division 1 as runners-up where they remained until relegated back to Division 2 in 2000–01. The club played in Division 1 North following another League re-organisation in 2002 until The FA restructuring for 2004–05 saw the club allocated to the Southern League Division 1 East, where they finished eighth. The club were Associate Members Trophy finalists in 1992–93.
FA competitions: FA Cup first round 1980–81. FA Vase finalists 1977–78.

Bashley (2004–2006)

Ground: Recreation Ground, Bashley Road, New Milton, Hampshire.
Colours: Gold shirts Black shorts.
Nickname: The Bash.
Formation: 1947.
Formative years: Friendlies 1947–50 and Bournemouth 1950–83.
Senior leagues: Hampshire 1983–86 (champions Division 3 1985), Wessex *(f)* 1986–90 (champions 1987, 1988 and 1989) and Southern 1990–2004 (champions Southern Division 1990).
Isthmian era: National League restructuring for 2004–05 placed the club in Isthmian League Division 1, where they finished 14th.
FA competitions: FA Vase semi–finalists 1987–88.

Basildon United (1981–1991)

Ground: Gardiners Close, Basildon, Essex
Colours: Red shirts and White shorts.
Nickname: The Bees.
Formation: 1963 Previously Armada Sports 1963–67.
Formative years: Grays & Thurrock 1967–68, Greater London League 1968–71.
Senior leagues: Essex Senior *(f)* 1971–80 (champions 1977, 1978, 1979, 1980), Athenian 1980–81 (champions 1981).
Isthmian era: Promoted to Division 2 from the Athenian League in 1981, they were Division 2 champions in 1983–84, but relegated to Division 2 North in 1988–89. They resigned in 1991 and subsequently returned to the Essex Senior League winning the championship in 1994. The Club remain members of that competition.

Basingstoke Town (1987–2004)

Ground: Camrose Ground, Western Way, Basingstoke, Hampshire.
Colours: Yellow & Blue shirts Blue shorts.
Nickname: Stoke.
Formation: 1896 following a merger between Aldworth United and Basingstoke Albion. The local Hampshire Ironworks team merged with the club in 1909.
Senior leagues: Hampshire 1900–71 (champions North Division 1912 & 1920, Division 1 1968, 1970 & 1971), Southern (1971–87) (champions Division 1 South 1986).
Isthmian era: Switched from the Southern League to the Isthmian League in 1987 being relegated to Division 1 in their first season. The following year they won promotion back to the Premier Division only to suffer relegation again in 1993–94. The club were runners-up in 1996–97 to regain Premier Division status. The club finished third in 2000–01 and after finishing 14th in 2003–04 qualified as a founder-member of Nationwide South, where they finished sixth in 2004–05. The club were Full Members Cup finalists in 1997–98.
FA competitions: FA Cup second round 1989–90.

Bedford Town (1994–2004)

Ground: The New Eyrie, Meadow Lane, Cardington Road, Bedford, Bedfordshire.
Colours: Blue & White shirts and shorts.
Nickname: The Eagles.
Formation: A group of supporters formed the present club in May 1989 after the original club (formed 1908) was wound up in 1982 with their ground reclaimed by the Charles Wells Brewery.
Senior leagues: South Midlands 1991–94 (champions Division 1 1993 and Premier Division 1994).
Isthmian era: Elected to the Isthmian League in 1994, winning promotion at the first attempt as the third-placed club. The club were Division 2 champions in 1998–99 and gained promotion to the Premier Division in 2000–01 after finishing runners-up. Here they finished 17th and ninth in 2001–02 and 2002–03, respectively. Restructuring for 2004–05 allocated the club to the Southern League Premier Division where they reached the play–offs after finishing fifth. The club were Associate Members Trophy winners in 1997–98.
FA competitions: FA Cup first round 2001–02.

Berkhamsted Town (1984–2004)

Ground: Broadwater, Lower Kings Road, Berkhamsted, Hertfordshire.
Colours: White shirts Black shorts.
Nickname: Lilywhites.
Formation: The original Berkhamsted club was formed in 1895 but folded in 1906. The present club was formed in 1919 and were previously Berkhamsted Comrades 1919–22.
Senior leagues: Herts County 1919–22, Spartan 1922–51 (champions Division 2 A 1927), Delphian *(f)* 1951–63, Athenian 1963–66, Spartan 1966–75, London–Spartan *(f)* 1975–83 (champions 1980), returned to Athenian 1983–84.
Isthmian era: Elected to Division 2 North in 1984. League re-organisation in 1991 resulted in the club playing in Division 2. Promotion was achieved to Division 1 in 1992–93, but they were relegated back to Division 2 in 1998–99. Further League re-organisation in 2002 placed the club in Division 1 where they finished seventh in 2001–02. Restructuring for 2004–05 allocated the club to the Southern League Division 1 East where they finished 18th.
FA competitions: FA Vase finalists 2000–01.

Billericay Town (1979–to date)

Ground: New Lodge, Blunts Wall Road, Billericay, Essex.
Colours: Royal Blue shirts White shorts.
Nickname: Town or The Blues.

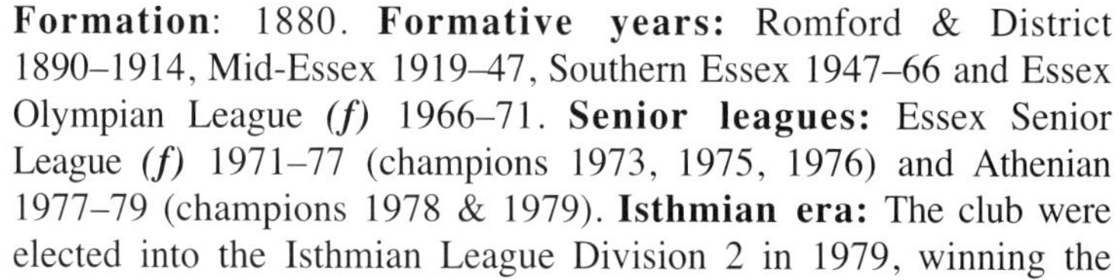

Formation: 1880. **Formative years:** Romford & District 1890–1914, Mid-Essex 1919–47, Southern Essex 1947–66 and Essex Olympian League *(f)* 1966–71. **Senior leagues:** Essex Senior League *(f)* 1971–77 (champions 1973, 1975, 1976) and Athenian 1977–79 (champions 1978 & 1979). **Isthmian era:** The club were elected into the Isthmian League Division 2 in 1979, winning the Division 1 championship at the first attempt and and gaining promotion, as runners-up, to the Premier Division the following season. The club suffered relegations to Division 1 and Division 2 North in 1985–86 and 1987–88, respectively. Following League re-organisation in 1991 they gained promotion, finishing third in 1991–92, and were Division 1 runners-up in 1997–98, thus gaining promotion to the Premier Division, where they have remained. The Club finished runners-up in 2004–05, but lost in the playoffs for promotion to the Conference South.
FA competitions: FA Cup first round 1997–98 and 2004–05. FA Vase winners 1975–76, 1976–77 and 1978–79.

Bishop's Stortford (1971–2004)

Ground: Woodside Park, Dunmow Road, Bishop's Stortford, Hertfordshire.
Previous Ground: George Wilson Stadium, Rhodes Avenue, Bishop's Stortford, until 1997.
Colours: Blue & White shirts Blue shorts.
Nickname: Blues or Bishops.
Formation: 1874, although Bishop's Stortford Wanderers (1895–97) and Bishop's Stortford Casuals (1897–1903) are included in the club's early history.
Formative years: East Herts 1896–97, 1902–06, 1913–14 & 1919–21 (champions 1920), Stansted & District 1907–19, 1925–27 & 1928–29, Herts & Essex Border 1927–28, Saffron Walden & District 1911–14 & 1927–28 (champions 1912, 1913 and 1914 joint winners).
Senior leagues: Herts County 1921–25 & 1927–28, Spartan 1929–51 (champions Division 2 East 1932), Delphian *(f)* 1951–93 (champions 1955), Athenian 1963–71 (champions Premier Division 1970).
Isthmian era: An invitation to join the Isthmian League was accepted in 1971. Relegation to Division 1 in 1977–78 was followed by promotion as champions of that division in 1980–81. In 1991–92 the club were again relegated to Division 1, returning as champions two years later. A third relegation to Division 1 occurred in 1998–99 before winning promotion as the third place club in 2001–02. The club finished 11th in 2003–04 and qualified as founder-members of Nationwide South following restructuring in 2004. The club were League Cup winners in 1989–90 and inaugural Full Members Cup winners in 1990–91. In addition they were the only Club from the League to win the Premier Inter League Cup, beating Hyde United in 1990.
FA competitions: FA Cup third round 1982–83. FA Amateur Cup winners 1973–74. FA Trophy Winners 1980–81.

Bognor Regis Town (1981–2004)

Ground: Nyewood Lane, Bognor Regis, West Sussex
Colours: White shirts with Green trim Green shorts.
Nickname: The Rocks.
Formation: 1883.
Formative years: West Sussex *(f)* 1896–1926, Brighton & Hove District 1926–27.
Senior leagues: Sussex County 1927–72 (champions Division 2 1971 & Division 1 1949, 1972), Southern 1972–81.
Isthmian era: Switched to the Isthmian League in 1981 and placed in Division 1, winning promotion as runners-up. Relegated back to Division 1 in 1991–92, where they remained until winning promotion, again as runners-up, in 2002–03. The club finished tenth in the Premier Division in 2003–04 and qualified as founder-members of Nationwide South following restructuring in 2004 where they finished ninth. The club won the League Cup in 1986–87.
FA competitions: FA Cup second round 1984–85, 1985–86, 1988–89 and 1995–96.

Boreham Wood (1974–2004)

Ground: Meadow Park, Broughinge Road, Boreham Wood, Hertfordshire.
Colours: White shirts Black shorts.
Nickname: The Wood.
Formation: 1948 following a merger between Boreham Wood Rovers and Royal Retournez.
Formative years: Mid-Herts 1948–52.
Senior leagues: Parthenon 1952–57 (champions 1957), Spartan 1957–66 (champions 1966) and Athenian 1966–74 (champions 1974).
Isthmian era: Accepted an invitation to join Division 2 in 1974, promoted as champions in 1976–77, relegated to Division 1 1981–82. Were Division 1 champions in 1994–95, relegated back to Division 1 in 1999–2000 but won promotion the following season as champions. The club was relegated again in 2002–03 to Division 1 North. Restructuring for 2004–05 allocated the club to the Southern League Division 1 East where they finished seventh. The club were League Cup winners in 1996–97 and Full Members Cup finalists in 1994–95 & 1995–96.
FA competitions: FA Cup second round 1996–97 and 1997–98.

Bracknell Town (1984–2004)

Ground: Larges Lane, Bracknell, Berkshire.
Colours: Red & White quarters shirts Red shorts.
Nickname: Robins.
Formation: 1896; Previously Old Bracknell Wanderers 1896–1949 and Bracknell 1949–62.
Formative years: Ascot 1904–49, Reading & District 1949–58.
Senior leagues: Great Western Combination 1958–63, Surrey Senior 1963–70 (champions 1970), Spartan 1970–75, London–Spartan *(f)* 1975–84 (champions Senior Division 1981 & Premier Division 1983). **Isthmian era:** Elected to Division 2 South in 1984, won promotion to Division 1 as runners-up in 1985–86, relegated back to Division 2 South in 1988–89. In 1991 following League re-organisation the club were placed in Division 3 becoming champions in 1993–94. The club were relegated back to Division 3 in 1998–99. Following League re-organisation they finished fourth in 2001–02 to secure a place in Division 1 South. Restructuring for 2004–05 allocated the club to the Southern League Division 1 West where they finished 20th.
FA competitions: FA Cup first round 2000–01.

Braintree Town (1996–2006)

Ground: Cressing Road Stadium, Braintree, Essex.
Colours: Yellow shirts Yellow shorts.
Nickname: The Iron.
Formation: 1898; Previously Manor Works 1898–1921, Crittall Athletic 1921–68 and Braintree & Crittall Athletic 1968–81.
Formative years: North Essex 1898–1925 and Essex & Suffolk Border 1925–28.
Senior leagues: Spartan 1928–35, Eastern Counties *(f)* 1935–37 (champions 1937), Essex County *(f)* 1937–38, Eastern Counties 1938–39, London 1945–52, Eastern Counties 1952–55, Essex & Suffolk 1955–64, Greater London *(f)* 1964–66, Metropolitan 1966–70, Eastern Counties 1970–91 (champions 1984 & 1985) and Southern 1991–96.
Isthmian era: Switched from the Southern League in 1996 to Division 3 winning promotion as runners-up followed by promotion to Division 1 the following year as third placed club. Promoted to the Premier Division in 2000–01 as third placed club. They reached the play–offs in 2004–05 after finishing fourth and won the championship and with it promotion to the Conference in 2005-06. The club were League Cup finalists in 1996–97.
FA competitions: FA Cup first round 2005–06.

Bromley (1908–1911 & 1952–to date)

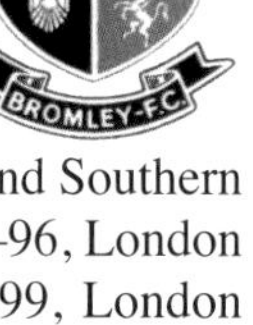

Ground: Hayes Lane, Bromley, Kent.
Colours: White with Blacks striped shirts Black shorts.
Nickname: The Lilywhites.
Formation: 1892. **Formative years:** South London 1893–96 (champions 1894), West Kent 1901–04 and Southern Suburban 1907–08. **Senior leagues:** Southern *(f)* 1894–96, London *(f)* 1896–98 (Champions Division 2 1897), Kent 1898–99, London 1899–1901, Spartan *(f)* 1907–08 (champions 1908), Kent 1911–14 and Athenian 1919–52 (champions 1923, 1949 & 1951). **Isthmian era:** First invited to join in 1908 and were champions in both 1908–09 and 1909–10. The following season, the Club had four points deducted and the Club's membership was not accepted for the following season. The club was invited to rejoin the Isthmian League in 1952. They were champions in 1953–54 and 1960–61, and runners-up in 1952–53 and 1955–56, but relegated in 1974–75. The club returned to the Premier Division in 1979–80 only to be relegated back to Division 1 in 1983–84, before winning promotion as runners-up two years later. The club were Premier Division runners-up in 1987–88, but again relegated to Division 1 in 1989–90, winning promotion back the following year as runners-up. Relegation to Division 1 occurred in 1998–99 but promotion back to the Premier Division was secured via the play–offs in 2004–05.
FA competitions: FA Cup second round 1937–38, 1938–39 and 1945–46. FA Amateur Cup winners 1910–11, 1937–38 and 1948–49.

Brook House (2004–2006)

Ground: Farm Park, Kingshill Avenue, Hayes.
Colours: Blue & White shirts Blue shorts.
Nickname: The House.
Formation: 1974 **Formative years:** Sunday Football 1974–82, South West Middlesex 1982–84, Middlesex County 1984–88. **Senior leagues:** Spartan 1988–97, Spartan–South Midlands *(f)* 1997–2004 (champions Premier South Division 1998). **Isthmian era:** After finishing Spartan–South Midlands League runners-up in 2003–04, the club decided to switch to the Isthmian League where they were third in Division 2 in their first season.

Burgess Hill Town (2004–to date)

Ground: Leylands Park, Maple Drive, Burgess Hill, West Sussex.
Colours: Yellow & Black quartered shirts Black shorts. **Nickname:** Hillians.
Formation: 1882 **Formative years:** Mid–Sussex *(f)* 1900–58 (champions 1901, 1904, 1940, 1947 & 1957). **Senior leagues:** Sussex County 1958–2003 (champions Division 1 1976, 1997, 1998, 1999, 2002, 2003 Division 2 1975), Southern 2003–04. **Isthmian era:** National League restructuring for 2004–05 placed the club in the Isthmian League where they finished tenth in Division 1.

Camberley Town (1977–1982 & 1984–2006)

Ground: Krooner Park, Krooner Road, Camberley.
Colours: Red & White striped shirts Red shorts.
Nickname: Krooners, Reds or Town.
Formation: 1896; Previously Camberley & Yorktown 1896–1946 and Camberley 1946–67 – Merged with Camberley Wanderers in 1967 to form present club. **Formative years:** East & West Surrey 1899–1902, Ascot & District 1903–09 (champions 1904), West Surrey 1910–14 (champions 1914) and Aldershot Senior 1919–22. **Senior leagues:** Surrey Senior *(f)* 1922–73 (champions 1931, 1932 & 1933), Spartan 1973–75, Athenian 1975–77 & 1982–84. **Isthmian era:** Elected as founder-members of Division 2 in 1977. Promoted in 1978–79 and relegated back in 1980–81. The club finished bottom of Division 2 in 1981–82 and were relegated to the Athenian League. Re-elected to Division 2 South in 1984 following League re-organisation where they remained until 1991. Following further re-organisation, the club were placed in Division 3.
FA competitions: FA Cup first round 1998–99.

Canvey Island (1994–2004)

Ground: Park Lane, Canvey Island, Essex.
Colours: Yellow & Blue shirts White shorts.
Nickname: The Gulls.
Formation: 1926.
Formative years: Southend & District and Thurrock & Thameside Combination 1953–57 (champion 1956).
Senior leagues: Parthenon 1957–63, London 1963–64, Greater London *(f)* 1964–71 (champions 1968 & 1969), Metropolitan–London *(f)* 1971–75 and Essex Senior 1975–94 (champions 1987 & 1993).
Isthmian era: Promoted from the Essex Senior League as third-placed club to Division 3 in 1994, the club won promotion as runners-up in their first season. Division 2 champions in 1996, but relegated the following season, the club returned to Division 1 as champions of Division 2 in 1997–98. They were promoted to the Premier Division as Division 1 champions in 1998–99. The club was Premier Division runners-up in three successive seasons 2001–03, before securing the championship in 2004 and subsequent promotion to the Football Conference where they finished 18th in their first season. The club were League Cup finalists in 2002–03 and Associate Members Trophy winners in 1995–96.
FA competitions: FA Cup third round 2001–02. FA Trophy winners 2000–01. FA Vase semi–finalists 1992–93.

Carshalton Athletic (1973–2004)

Ground: War Memorial Sports Ground, Colston Avenue, Carshalton, Surrey.
Colours: White shirts Maroon shorts.
Nickname: Robins.
Formation: 1903; Previously Mill Lane Mission 1903–07 – Merged with Carshalton St. Andrews (Formed 1897) in 1908.
Formative years: Croydon & District and Southern Suburban 1903–22.
Senior leagues: Surrey Senior *(f)* 1922–23, London 1923–46, Corinthian 1946–56 (champions 1953 and 1954) and Athenian 1956–73.
Isthmian era: Invited to join Division 2 as founder-members in 1973, the club was promoted to the Premier Division as runners-up in 1976–77. They were relegated to Division 1 in 2000–01, but after League re-organisation in 2002 they were Division 1 South champions in 2002–03 returning to the Premier Division. In 2003–04 they finished seventh and qualified as Nationwide South founder-members, but just avoided relegation in their first season. The club were League Cup finalists in 1990–91.
FA competitions: FA Cup second round 1992–83.

Casuals (1905–1907 & 1919–1939)

Grounds: Tufnell Park Road (1905–07), Essex County Ground, Leyton (1919–20), East Molesey Cricket Club (1920–21) and Crystal Palace Sports Centre (1921–25) and Kingstonian FC (1925–39).
Colours: Chocolate & Pink halves shirts Chocolate shorts.
Nickname: Casuals.
Formation: 1883.
Formative years: Friendlies 1883–1905.
Isthmian era: Founder-members in 1905, the Casuals finished third and sixth (of six clubs), respectively, in their first two seasons. However, the Club resigned in 1907 and spent seven seasons in newly-formed Southern Amateur League, where they remained until 1914. In 1919 the club was accepted back into the Isthmian League, where they remained until 1939, with a best position of runners-up, in 1935–36. Casuals FC merged with Corinthians FC in 1939 to form Corinthian–Casuals FC.
FA competitions: FA Cup first round 1884–85, 1885–86, 1886–87, 1887–88, 1890–91 and 1892–93. FA Amateur Cup winners 1935–36.

Chalfont St. Peter (1984–2006)

Ground: Mill Meadow, Gravel Hill, Amersham Road, Chalfont St. Peter, Buckinghamshire.
Colours: Red shirts Green shorts.
Nickname: The Saints.
Formation: 1926. **Formative years:** Wycombe Combination. **Senior leagues:** Great Western Combination 1948–58, Parthenon 1958–60, London 1960–62, Spartan 1962–75 (champions Senior Division 1976), London–Spartan *(f)* 1975–76 and Athenian 1976–84. **Isthmian era:** Elected to Division 2 North in 1984, the club were transferred to Division 2 South in 1986, winning the Division 2 South championship in 1987–88. They were relegated to the now single Division 2 in 1993–94 and to Division 3 in 1999–2000. The club were placed in Division 2 following League re-organisation in 2002.

Chelmsford City (2004–2008)

Ground: Chelmsford Sport & Athletic Centre, Salerno Way. (Groundshared at Billericay Town FC 2004-05).
Colours: Claret shirts and shorts.
Nickname: City or Clarets.

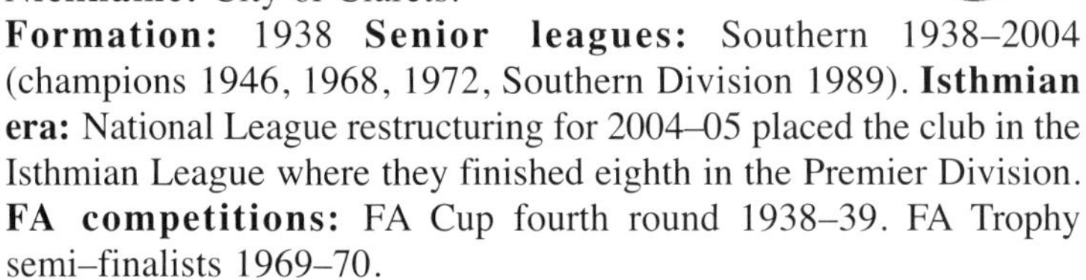

Formation: 1938 **Senior leagues:** Southern 1938–2004 (champions 1946, 1968, 1972, Southern Division 1989). **Isthmian era:** National League restructuring for 2004–05 placed the club in the Isthmian League where they finished eighth in the Premier Division. **FA competitions:** FA Cup fourth round 1938–39. FA Trophy semi–finalists 1969–70.

Chertsey Town (1984–1985 & 1986–2006)

Ground: Alwyns Lane, Chertsey, Surrey.
Colours: Blue & White striped shirts Blue shorts.
Nickname: Curfews.
Formation: 1890; Previously Chertsey 1890–1950.
Formative years: West Surrey, Surrey Junior 1899–1936, Surrey Intermediate 1936–46 (champions Division 1 West 1937). **Senior leagues:** Surrey Senior 1946–63 (champions 1960, 1962 & 1963), Metropolitan 1963–66, Greater London 1966–67, Spartan 1967–75, London–Spartan *(f)* 1975–76 and Athenian 1976–84. **Isthmian era:** Elected to Division 2 South in 1984, but relegated to the Combined Counties League in 1984–85, they returned to the Isthmian League after winning promotion the following season. The club were promoted to Division 2 as runners-up in 1991–92, then enjoyed successive promotions in 1993–94 and 1994–95. The club were relegated back to Division 1 in 1996–97 and Division 2 in 1999–2000. The club were placed in Division 1 South following re-organisation in 2002 and suffered relegation to Division 2 at the end of the 2002–03 season. The club won the double of League Cup and Associate Members Trophy in 1993–94.

Chesham United (1973–2004)

Ground: The Meadow, Amy Lane, Chesham, Buckinghamshire.
Colours: Claret & Sky Blue shirts and shorts.
Nickname: The Generals.
Formation: 1917 Merger of Chesham (Formed 1879 adding the suffix Town in 1899) and Chesham Generals (Formed 1887).
Senior leagues: Great Western Suburban 1919–20, Spartan 1919–47 (champions Division 1 1922, 1923 & 1925 Premier Division 1933), Great Western Combination *(f)* 1939–42, Corinthian 1947–63 and Athenian 1963–73.
Isthmian era: Invited as founder-members of Division 2 in 1973, they stayed in the same division until relegation in 1985–86. They were promoted back the following season as Champions. The club were Division 1 Champions in 1990–91 and secured the Premier Division title in 1992–93 but declined promotion. They were relegated in 1994–95, but in 1996–97 were Division 1 champions. The club were relegated to Division 1 North in 2002–03. Restructuring for 2004–05 allocated the club to the Southern League Premier Division where they finished twelfth. The club were inaugural Full Members Cup finalists in 1990–91.
FA competitions: FA Cup third round 1979–80. FA Amateur Cup finalists 1967–68.

Cheshunt (1977–1987 & 1993–2005)

Ground: The Stadium, Theobalds Lane, Cheshunt, Hertfordshire.
Colours: Amber & Black shirts and shorts.
Nickname: Ambers.
Formation: 1938; Previously Crossbrook Sports 1938–46 and Cheshunt Sports 1946–48. **Formative years:** North London Alliance 1941–46. **Senior leagues:** London 1946–51 (champions Division 1 1948, 1949 & 1950), Delphian *(f)* 1951–55, London 1955–59, Aetolian *(f)* 1959–62, Spartan 1962–64 (champions 1963) and Athenian 1964–77 (champions Division 1 1968 & 1976). **Isthmian era:** Elected as founder-members of Division 2 in 1977, winning promotion to Division 1 as runners-up in 1981–82. The club was relegated to Division Two North in 1983–84, then to the London–Spartan League after finishing bottom of that division in 1986–87. The club was promoted back to the Isthmian League, in Division 3, in 1993 as the third placed club in the Spartan League, and won promotion to Division 2 as runners-up after their first season back in the League. The club were again relegated to Division 3 in 1997–98, but finished third the following season to regain Division Two status. In 2002 the club were relegated to Division 2 due to ground grading, but the club won successive promotions in 2002–03 – as Division 3 champions – and 2003–04. The club narrowly escaped relegation in 2004–05, but were switched by The Football Association to the Southern League for 2005–06. The club were Associate Members Trophy finalists in 2002–03.

Civil Service (1905–1907 & 1919–1929)

Grounds: During League membership the club used several grounds including the Athletic Ground, Kensal Rise (1905–06), Coach & Horses, NW10 (1906–07), Hurlingham Polo Ground, Peterborough Road (1920–22), Hampstead Town FC, Cricklewood Lane (1922–25) and Dukes Meadow, Chiswick (1925–29).
Colours: White shirts Black shorts.
Nickname: None.
Formation: 1863 re–organised in 1892. **Formative years:** Middlesex 1899–1900. **Senior leagues:** Southern Amateur *(f)* 1907–14 (champions 1912 & 1914). **Isthmian era:** Founder-members in 1905, they finished fourth of six clubs in their first two seasons. The club resigned in 1907 to join the Amateur Football Association for seven years. In 1919 the club were accepted back into the Isthmian League, where they remained until 1929 with their best finishing position being sixth of 14 clubs in 1922–23 & 1923–24. After finishing bottom in 1928–29 the club were not re–elected and were replaced by Kingstonian. The club returned to the Southern Amateur League, becoming Division 3 champions in 1929–30, Division 2 champions the following season and Premier Division champions in 1937–38.
FA competitions: FA Cup second round 1874–75. FA Amateur Cup semi–finalists 1906–07.

Clapton (1905–2006)

Grounds: Old Spotted Dog, Upton Lane, Forest Gate, London E7. The club ground–shared with Leytonstone FC for part of 1919 as their Spotted Dog home was not available.
Colours: Red & White striped shirts Black shorts.
Nickname: Tons.
Formation: 1878; Previously Downs FC 1877–78.
Formative years: Friendlies.
Senior leagues: Southern *(f)* 1894–96, London 1896–97 (withdrew before season started).
Isthmian era: The club are the only founder-members in continuous membership since 1905. They were League champions in 1910–11 and 1922–23 as well as runners-up in 1905–06, 1907–08, 1909–10 and 1924–25. They were relegated in 1975–76 and again suffered relegation to Division 2 in 1981–82, however the following season they were promoted back as champions. Relegation to Division 2 North followed in 1984–85 where they remained until 1991 when due to League re-organisation they were placed in Division 3. The club were moved to Division 2 following further re-organisation in 2002.
FA competitions: FA Cup third round 1925–26. FA Amateur Cup winners 1905–06, 1923–24 and 1924–25.

Collier Row (1986–1996) and Collier Row & Romford (1996–1997)

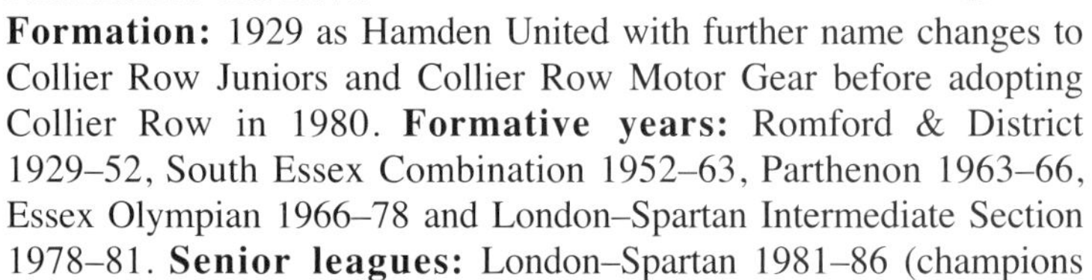

Grounds: Sungate, Collier Row Road, Collier Row, Romford, Essex.
Colours: Red & Black shirts and shorts.
Nickname: The Row.
Formation: 1929 as Hamden United with further name changes to Collier Row Juniors and Collier Row Motor Gear before adopting Collier Row in 1980. **Formative years:** Romford & District 1929–52, South Essex Combination 1952–63, Parthenon 1963–66, Essex Olympian 1966–78 and London–Spartan Intermediate Section 1978–81. **Senior leagues:** London–Spartan 1981–86 (champions Joint Senior Division 1983 and Premier Division 1984 & 1986). **Isthmian era:** Elected to Division 2 North in 1986 winning promotion to Division 1 in 1987–88 as runners-up, only to be relegated back the following season. The club were allocated in Division 3 in 1991 following League re-organisation winning promotion to Division 2 as third placed club the following season, only to be relegated in 1993–94. The club were Division 3 champions in 1994–95 and finished fifth in their final season – 1995–96. The club merged with Romford (Essex Senior League) for season 1996–97 as Collier Row & Romford, playing in Division 2, before reverting to Romford for 1997–98. Romford continued in the league until 2002. The club were Associate Members Trophy finalists in 1994–95.
FA competitions: FA Vase semi–finalists 1986–87.

Corinthian–Casuals (1939–84 & 1997–to date)

Grounds: King Georges Field, Queen Mary Close, Tolworth, Surrey. Prior to 1989 when the King Georges Field ground was secured, the club had a nomadic existence. Up until 1984 when the club failed to get re–elected the following grounds were used: Kingstonian FC (1945–46), Polytechnic Stadium, W4 (1946–47), Blackheath Rugby Club (1947–48), Motspur Park (1949–50), the Oval Cricket Ground, Kennington (1950–63), Dulwich Hamlet FC (1963–68), Tooting & Mitcham United FC (1968–83) and Molesey FC (1983–84).
Colours: Chocolate & Pink shirts Sky Blue shorts.
Nickname: Casuals.
Formation: 1939 Merger of Casuals (Formed 1883) and Corinthians (Formed 1882). **Isthmian era:** The merged club had little success in the Senior Division finishing in the lower reaches of the table most seasons. When the Isthmian League added a second Division in 1973 and introduced promotion and relegation, the club were one of the first two to be relegated in 1973–74. When a third level was added in 1977, the club again suffered relegation in that first season. They remained in Division 2 until resigning in 1984, ironically after they had finished in their highest league position, fifth. The club joined the London–Spartan League in 1984 winning the Senior Division in 1986. They remained in the London–Spartan/Spartan League until 1996, when they switched to the Combined Counties League, achieving promotion back to the Isthmian League as runners-up in their only season as members. Promotion in 2001–02 from Division 3 to Division 1 South – despite a tenth-place finish – was due to other clubs not having the correct ground grading. The club are currently members of Division 1.
FA competitions: FA Cup first round 1965–66 and 1983–84. FA Amateur Cup winners 1955–56.

Cove (1990–1996)

Ground: Oak Farm Fields, off Romayne Road, Cove, Farnborough, Hampshire.
Colours: Amber & Black shirts Black shorts.
Nickname: None.
Formation: 1897. **Formative years:** Aldershot Junior, Aldershot Intermediate 1945–48, Surrey Intermediate 1948–70. **Senior leagues:** Surrey Senior 1970–71, Aldershot Senior 1971–72, Hampshire 1972–81 (champions Division 4 1973 and Division 3 1977) and Combined Counties 1981–90. **Isthmian era:** Promoted to Division 2 South in 1990, reverting to Division 3 in 1991 due to League re-organisation. After several lowly positions (fifth in 1992–93 being their best league position) the club resigned from the league at the end of 1995–96 returning to the Combined Counties League where they remain.

Cray Wanderers (2004–to date)

Ground: Bromley FC, Hayes Lane, Bromley, Kent.
Colours: Amber shirts Black shorts.
Nickname: Wands.
Formation: 1860 **Formative years:** Friendlies 1860–94. **Senior leagues:** Kent 1894–1903, 1906–07, 1909–14, 1935–38 & 1978–2004 (champions Division 1 1902 & 1981), London *(f)* 1896–97, 1920–34 & 1951–59 (champions 1957 & 1958), Southern Suburban 1897–99, 1908–09, 1913–14 & 1919–20 (champions 1899), West Kent 1901–02 & 1903–09 (champions 1904), Kent Amateur 1938–39 & 1946–51, South London Alliance 1945–46, Aetolian *(f)* 1959–64 (champions 1963), Greater London *(f)* 1964–66 (champions 1966), Metropolitan *(f)* 1966–71, Metropolitan–London *(f)* 1971–75 (champions 1975) and London–Spartan *(f)* 1975–78 (champions 1977 & 1978). **Isthmian era:** National League restructuring in 2004–05 placed the club in the Isthmian League where they reached the play–offs as sixth placed club.
FA competitions: FA Vase semi–finalists 2003–04.

Croydon (1974–2006)

Ground: Croydon Sports Arena, Albert Road SE25.
Colours: Light & Dark Blue shirts Dark Blue shorts.
Nickname: The Trams.
Formation: 1953; Previously Croydon Amateurs 1953–73. **Senior leagues:** Surrey Senior 1953–63, Spartan 1963–64 (champions 1964) and Athenian 1964–74 (champions Division 2 1966). **Isthmian era:** Elected to Division 2 in 1974, winning promotion as runners-up without losing a match in 1975–76. They remained in the Premier Division until 1988–89 when they were relegated to Division 1, and further relegation to Division 2 in 1993–94. They won promotion to Division 1 in 1995–96 as runners-up, and were Division 1 champions in 1999–2000 securing promotion to the Premier Division. The club were relegated from the Premier Division in 2001–02 and further relegation followed at the end of 2004–05. The club were League Cup finalists in 1974–75 & 2000–01 and Full Members Cup winners in 1999–2000.
FA competitions: FA Cup second round 1979–80.

Croydon Athletic (1997–to date)

Ground: Mayfields, off Mayfield Road, Thornton Heath, Surrey.
Colours: Maroon shirts and shorts.
Nickname: The Rams.
Formation: 1986; Previously Wandsworth & Norwood 1986–90 Merger of Wandsworth (Formed 1948) and Norwood (Formed 1947). **Senior leagues:** London–Spartan/Spartan 1986–97 (champions 1995). **Isthmian era:** Promoted to Division 3 from Spartan League in 1997, they were Division 3 champions in 2001–02, winning promotion to Division 1 South following League re-organisation in 2002. The club are currently in Division 1 South.

Dagenham (1973–1981 & 1988–1992)

Ground: Victoria Road, Dagenham, Essex.
Colours: Red shirts and shorts.
Nickname: The Daggers.
Formation: 1949. **Senior leagues:** Metropolitan *(f)* 1949–51 (champions 1951), Delphian *(f)* 1951–57 (champions 1953 & 1956, 1957), Corinthian 1957–63 (champions 1959) and Athenian 1963–73 (champions Premier Division 1971), Alliance Premier/Football Conference 1981–88. **Isthmian era:** Elected as founder-members of Division 2 in 1973, they won the inaugural championship. The club were Premier Division runners-up in 1977–78 and 1978–79 before joining the Alliance Premier League in 1981. The club spent seven seasons there until relegation in 1987–88 returned them to the Isthmian League where they remained until 1992. In 1992 the club merged with Redbridge Forest to become Dagenham & Redbridge. They were League Cup winners in 1977–78.
FA competitions: FA Cup third round 1984–85. FA Amateur Cup finalists 1970 and 1971. FA Trophy winners 1980.

Dagenham & Redbridge (1996–2000)

Ground: Victoria Road, Dagenham, Essex.
Colours: Red shirts White shorts.
Nickname: Daggers.
Formation: 1992 Merger of Dagenham (Formed 1949) and Redbridge Forest (Formed 1989).
Senior leagues: Football Conference 1992–96.
Isthmian era: Relegated from the Football Conference to the Premier Division in 1995–96 finishing fourth in 1996–97 and 1997–98, third in 1998–99, before securing the Premier Division title in 1999–2000 and promotion back to the Football Conference. Since winning promotion to the Football Conference in 2000, the club finished third in 2000–01, runners-up in 2001–02 and fifth in 2002–03, which qualified the club for the play–offs, however they lost to Doncaster Rovers in the final.
FA competitions: FA Cup third round 2000–01. FA Trophy finalists 1996–97.

Dorking (1980–2006)

Ground: Meadowbank, Mill Lane, Dorking, Surrey.
Colours: Green & White hooped shirts Green shorts.
Nickname: The Chicks.
Formation: Originally formed in 1880 re–forming in 1946. The club merged with Southern Leaguers, Guildford City in 1974 following the sale of Guildford's St. Joseph's Road ground to form Guildford & Dorking United. The club went into liquidation in December 1976. The club reformed in 1977 as Dorking Town dropping the suffix Town in 1983.
Formative years: Southern Suburban 1910–22.
Senior leagues: Surrey Senior *(f)* 1922–56 (champions 1929, 1930, 1955 & 1956), Corinthian 1956–63, Athenian 1964–74, Southern 1974–77, Surrey Senior 1977–78 and Athenian 1978–81.
Isthmian era: Elected to Division 2 in 1979, switching to Division 2 South in 1984 following League re-organisation. The club were Division 2 South champions in 1988–89, and promoted to the Premier Division as third place club in 1992–93. Relegations in 1993–94, 1994–95 and 1996–97 resulted in the club playing in Division 3. The club were placed in Division 2 following League re-organisation in 2002 and immediate promotion as runners-up to Division 1 in 2002–03 before relegation again in 2004–05. The club were Full Members Cup finalists in 1992–93.
FA competitions: FA Cup first round 1992–93.

Dover Athletic (2004–to date)

Ground: Crabble Athletic Ground, Lewisham Road, Dover, Kent.
Colours: White shirts Blacks shorts.
Nickname: The Whites.
Formation: The club were formed in the summer of 1983 following the demise of Dover FC (Founded 1891) when that company was wound up. The new club took the former club's place in the Southern League.
Senior leagues: Southern 1983–1993 (champions Southern Division 1988, Premier Division 1990 & 1993), and Football Conference 1993–2004.
Isthmian era: National League restructuring for 2004–05 placed the club in the Isthmian League Premier Division following relegation from the Football Conference where they again suffered relegation.
FA competitions: FA Cup first round 2002–03. FA Trophy semi–finalists 1997–98.

Dulwich Hamlet (1907–to date)

Grounds: Champion Hill Stadium, Edgar Kail Way, Dog Kennel Hill, London, SE22.
Previous Grounds: Freemans Ground (1907–12), Champion Hill – 1 – (1912–31), Champion Hill – 2 – (1931–91) and Tooting & Mitcham United FC (1991–92).
Colours: Navy & Pink shirts and shorts.
Nickname: The Hamlet
Formation: 1893.
Formative years: Camberwell 1894–97 and Dulwich 1900–01.
Senior leagues: Southern Suburban 1897–1900 & 1901–07 (champions 1902 & 1904) and Spartan *(f)* 1907–08.
Isthmian era: The club were invited to join the Isthmian League in 1907, winning the championship in 1919–20, 1925–26, 1932–33 and 1948–49 as well as being runners-up on seven occasions, in 1921–22, 1923–24, 1929–30, 1930–31, 1933–34, 1946–47 and 1958–59. They suffered relegation to Division 1 in 1976–77 but returned as champions to the Premier Division the following year. The club were relegated to Division 1 in 1989–90, but were promoted back to the Premier Division as third place club two seasons later. They were again relegated in 2000–01 to Division 1 South following re-organisation in 2002 and are currently in Division 1 South.
FA competitions: FA Cup first round 1925–26, 1926–27, 1927–28, 1928–29, 1929–30, 1930–31, 1932–33, 1933–34, 1934–35, 1935–36, 1936–37, 1937–38, 1948–49 and 1998–99. FA Amateur Cup winners 1919–20, 1931–32, 1933–34 and 1936–37. FA Trophy semi-finalists 1997–98.

Dunstable Town (2003–2004)

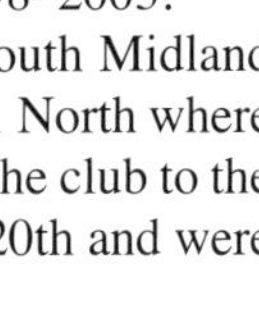

Ground: The Stadium, Creasey Park Drive, off Brewers Hill Road, Dunstable, Bedfordshire.
Colours: Blue & White striped shirts Blue shorts.
Nickname: The Blues.
Formation: 1998.
Senior leagues: Spartan–South Midlands League 1998–2003.
Isthmian era: The club won promotion as Spartan–South Midland League champions in 2003 and were placed in Division 1 North where they finished fifth. Restructuring for 2004–05 allocated the club to the Southern League Premier Division where they finished 20th and were subsequently relegated.

Ealing Association (1905–1907 and 1914–1919)

Ground: Gunnersbury Avenue, Ealing, London.
Colours: Red and Green shirts and shorts.
Nickname: None.
Formation: 1891.
Formative years: Southern Amateur *(f)* 1907–14.
Isthmian era: Founder-members in 1905 they finished fifth of six clubs in each of their first two seasons. The club resigned to join the Amateur Football Association in 1907 and although the club was invited to rejoin the Isthmian League for the 1914–15, they did not play because of the outbreak of the First World War. Following the Great War, it was thought that the club had folded. In fact they had not done so, but instead of returning to the Isthmian League rejoined the Southern Amateur League, where they were Division 1 champions in 1927 and 1947 and Division 2 champions in 1937. The club remained in the Southern Amateur League until 1970–71, when they were expelled. The club became members of the Nemean Amateur League in 1971–72, winning the Division 2 championship in 1974, then joined the Southern Olympian League in 1985.
FA competitions: FA Amateur Cup winners 1903–04.

Eastbourne United (1977–1992)

Ground: The Oval, Channel View Road, Eastbourne, East Sussex.
Colours: White shirts Black shorts.
Nickname: The U's.
Formation: 1914; Previously 1st Sussex Royal Engineers Eastbourne 1914–20, Eastbourne Royal Engineers Old Comrades 1920–21 and Eastbourne Old Comrades 1921–52. **Formative years:** East Sussex 1919–20, Eastbourne & District 1920–21. **Senior leagues:** Sussex County 1921–28, Spartan 1928–32, Brighton, Hove & District 1932–35, Sussex County 1935–56 (champions Division 1 1955 & 1956), Metropolitan 1956–64 and Athenian 1964–77 (champions Division 2 1967). **Isthmian era:** The club were elected as founder-members of Division 2 in 1977 and remained there until League re-organisation in 1984 placed the club in Division 2 South. The club finished in the lower reaches of that Division for most seasons until re-organisation in 1991, when they were placed in Division 3. The club finished bottom of Division 3 in 1991–92 and resigned from the League. The club returned to the Sussex County League where they remain. The club merged with Shinewater Association (formed 1990) in 2003 to form Eastbourne United Association.

Eastleigh (2004–2005)

Ground: Sparshotts Stadium, Ten Acres, Stoneham Lane, North Stoneham, Eastleigh, Hampshire.
Colours: White shirts & shorts with Blue trim.
Nickname: The Spitfires.
Formation: 1946; Previously Swaythling Athletic 1946–73 and Swaythling 1973–80. **Formative years:** Southampton Junior 1946–48, Southampton Senior 1948–50. **Senior leagues:** Hampshire 1950–86 (champions Division 3 West 1951 & 1954, Division 2 1970), Wessex *(f)* 1986–2003 and Southern 2003–04. **Isthmian era:** National League restructuring for 2004–05 placed the club in the Isthmian League Premier Division. They finished fourth in their first season and subsequently gained promotion to Nationwide Conference South via the play–offs.

East Thurrock United (1992–2004)

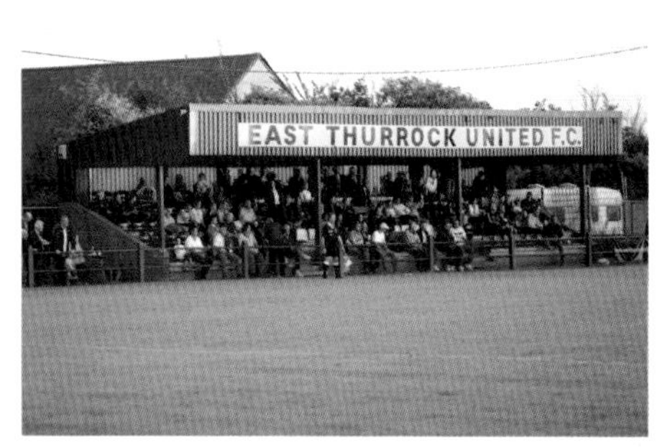

Ground: Rookery Hill, Corringham, Essex.
Colours: Amber & Black striped shirts Black shorts.
Nickname: The Rocks.
Formation: 1969. **Formative years:** Southern Essex Combination 1969–70, Greater London Intermediate Section 1970–72. **Senior leagues:** Metropolitan–London 1972–75 (champions Division 2 1973), London–Spartan *(f)* 1975–79 and Essex Senior 1979–92. **Isthmian era:** In 1992 the club were promoted to Division 3 as third placed club in the Essex Senior League. The club won promotion to Division 2 as Division 3 champions in 1999–2000 and following re-organisation in 2002 were placed in Division 1 North. Restructuring for 2004–05 allocated the club to the Southern League Division 1 East where they gained promotion as runners-up.

Edgware Town (1990–2006)

Ground: White Lion Ground, High Street, Edgware, Middlesex.
Colours: Green & White shirts Green shorts.
Nickname: The Wares.
Formation: 1939; Previously Edgware 1970–88. **Senior leagues:** West Middlesex Combination–Middlesex Senior *(f)* 1939–45 (champions 1940 & 1946 and North Division 1944 & 1945), London 1945–46 (champions Western Division 1946), Corinthian 1946–63, Athenian 1963–84 and London–Spartan/Spartan 1984–90 (champions 1988 & 1990). **Isthmian era:** The club were elected into Division 2 North in 1990 and due to League re-organisation the following season were placed in Division 3. They won promotion back to Division 2 as Division 3 Champions in 1991–92 where they stayed until 2000–01. The club again suffered relegation to Division 3 in 2000–01.

Egham Town (1977–2004)

Ground: Runnymede Stadium, Tempest Road, Egham.
Colours: Yellow shirts Green shorts.
Nickname: Sarnies.
Formation: 1877; Previously Runnymede Rovers 1877–1905 and Egham 1905–39. The present club were formed as Egham Town in 1963. **Formative years:** Hounslow & District 1896–1919, Surrey Intermediate 1919–22 (champions 1921), Surrey Senior *(f)* 1922–28 (champions 1923), Spartan 1928–33, Surrey Senior 1933–39, **Senior leagues:** Parthenon 1964–65, Surrey Senior 1965–67, Spartan 1967–74 (champions 1972) and Athenian 1974–77 (champions Division 2 1975). **Isthmian era:** The club were elected as founder-members of Division 2 in 1977 and remained there until League re-organisation in 1984 placed the club in Division 2 South. The club's best position was third in 1990–91. However, following more League re-organisation the following year, they were back in Division 2, where they remained until suffering relegation to Division 3 in 1997–98. Following further re-organisation in 2002 the club were promoted to Division 1 South in 2001–02 despite finishing sixth in Division 3. Restructuring for 2004–05 allocated the club to the Southern League Division 1 West and they were relegated at the end of 2004–05. The club were Associate Members Trophy finalists in 1991–92.

Enfield (1963–1981 and 1990–2005)

Grounds: Ware FC, Wodson Park, Wadesmill Road, Ware, Hertfordshire.
Previous Grounds: The Stadium, Southbury Road, Enfield, Middlesex until 1999, various grounds 1999–2000 and Boreham Wood FC 2001–04.
Colours: White shirts with Blue trim Blue shorts.
Nickname: The E's.
Formation: 1893; Previously Enfield Spartans 1893–1900. **Formative years:** Tottenham & District Junior Alliance, North Middlesex. **Senior leagues:** London 1903–12 (champions Division 1 1912), Middlesex 1908–12 (champions West Division 1909–10), Athenian *(f)* 1912–14, Middlesex 1919–20, London 1920–21 and Athenian 1921–63 (champions 1962 & 1963). **Isthmian era:** Accepted an invitation to join the Isthmian League in 1963 and were successful in winning the championship on seven occasions in 1967–68, 1968–69, 1969–70, 1975–76, 1976–77, 1977–78 and 1979-80, and finishing as runners-up four times, in 1964–65, 1971–72, 1974–75 and 1980–81. They were invited to join the Alliance Premier League in 1981, winning the championship twice in 1983 and 1986. They were relegated back to the Isthmian League in 1989–90 and were Premier Division runners-up in 1990–91, 1991–92 and 1993–94 before clinching their eighth championship in 1994–95. Promotion back to the Football Conference was denied and in both 1995–96 and 1996–97 they were Premier Division runners-up. In 2002 the club were relegated to Division 1 North and further relegation, to Division 2, followed a season later. In 2004–05 the club gained promotion as runners-up in Division 2 and were assigned to the Southern League Division 1 East. The club were League Cup winners in 1978–79 and 1979–80 and finalists in 1991–92 and 1993–94.
FA competitions: FA Cup fourth round 1980–81, third round 1977-78, 1981-82 and 1994-95. FA Amateur Cup winners 1966–67 and 1969–70, finalists 1963-64 and 1971–72. FA Trophy winners 1981–82 and 1987–88. European Amateur Cup Winners Cup winners 1970.

Epping Town (1977–1985)

Ground: Stonards Hill Ground, Fairfield Road, Epping, Essex.
Colours: White shirts Black shorts.
Nickname: The Town.
Formation: 1888. **Formative years:** Woodford (champions 1913, 1920), Walthamstow & District 1926–33 (champions 1928, 1930) and South Essex 1933–36. **Senior leagues:** Spartan 1936–39 & 1946–54, Parthenon 1954–55, London 1955–64 (champions 1964), Greater London *(f)* 1964–69 (champions Premier Division 1967), Metropolitan 1969–71 (champions 1971), Metropolitan–London *(f)* 1971–74 (champions Division 1 1972, 1974) and Athenian 1974–77 (champions Division 2 1976). **Isthmian era:** The club were elected as founder-members of Division 2 in 1977 and remained at that level, rarely finishing above mid-table, until League re-organisation in 1984 placed the club in Division 2 North. The club failed to fulfil all of their fixtures during 1984–85 and their record was expunged from the table, which also resulted in the club not being elected the following season it disbanded. An Epping club is now playing in the Essex Olympian League.

Epsom & Ewell (1977–2006)

Ground: Banstead Athletic FC, Merland Rise, Tadworth, Surrey.

Previous Ground: West Street, Ewell, Surrey until 1993.
Colours: Royal Blue & White hooped shirts Royal Blue shorts.
Nickname: E's.
Formation: 1918; Previously Epsom Juniors 1918–22, Epsom Town 1922-34 and Epsom FC 1934–60. **Senior leagues:** Southern Suburban 1923-24 (champions 1924), Surrey Senior 1924–27 (champions 1926 & 1927), London 1927–49 (champions 1928), Corinthian 1949–63, Athenian 1963–73, Surrey Senior 1973–75 (champions 1975) and Athenian 1975–77. **Isthmian era:** In 1977 the club were elected as founder-members of Division 2, winning the championship at the first attempt. The club gained promotion to the Premier Division as runners-up in 1983–84, only to suffer successive relegations to Division 1 in 1985–86 and Division 2 South in 1986–87. The club remained in that Division until League re-organisation in 1991 resulted in the club playing in Division 3. The club were promoted to Division 1 South in 2001–02 – despite finishing fifth – due to further League re-organisation. Relegation in 2002–03 saw the club back in Division 2. The club were Associate Members Trophy finalists in 1997–98.
FA competitions: FA Cup first round 1933–34. FA Vase finalists 1974–75.

Farnborough Town (1977–1989 & 1999–2001)

Ground: John Roberts Ground, Cherrywood Road, Farnborough, Hampshire.
Colours: Yellow and Blue or Red & White shirts and shorts.
Nickname: The Boro or Town.
Formation: 1967. **Senior leagues:** Surrey Senior 1968–72, Spartan 1972–75 (champions 1973, 1974), London–Spartan *(f)* 1975–76 (champions 1976) and Athenian 1976–77 (Division 2 champions 1977). **Isthmian era:** The club were elected as founder-members of Division 2 (Third Division) in 1977, winning the championship in 1979. Secured promotion to the Premier Division as Division 1 champions and League Cup finalists in 1984–85 and finally gained promotion to the Football Conference in 1988–89 as runners-up – the club were also League Cup finalists. Relegated from the Football Conference after just one season, they switched to the Southern League in 1990–91 and won the championship at the first attempt to make an immediate return to the Conference. After finishing fifth on their return to the Conference, they were relegated back to the Southern League in 1992–93, but bounced straight back the following year as champions. They remained in the Football Conference - seventh place was their best position in 1996–97 - until suffering a third relegation in 1998–99, this time being placed in the Isthmian League. After finishing 12th in 1999–2000 (but winning the League Cup), the club achieved promotion to the Football Conference as champions in 2000–01. They were again relegated at the end of 2004–05.
FA competitions: FA Cup fourth round 2002–03. FA Vase semi–finalists 1975–76 and 1976–77.

Farnham Town (1992)

Ground: Memorial Ground, Babbs Mead, West Street, Farnham, Surrey.
Colours: Claret & Blue striped shirts Blue shorts.
Nickname: The Town.
Formation: 1921; Previously Farnham Star 1921–29. **Formative years:** Surrey Intermediate (champions 1930 & 1931). **Senior leagues:** Surrey Senior 1947–62 & 1963–71 – due to problems with their ground they did not play during 1962–63 season (champions 1966, 1967 & 1968), Spartan 1971–75, London–Spartan 1975–80 and Combined Counties 1980–92 (champions 1991 & 1992).
Isthmian era: Although the club was elected to the Isthmian League in 1992, they did not take their place.

Feltham (1977–1991); Feltham & Hounslow Borough (1991–1995)

Ground: The Arena, Shakespeare Avenue, Feltham, Middlesex.
Colours: As Feltham, Blue & White hooped shirts Blue shorts; as Feltham & Hounslow Borough, Royal Blue & Red striped shirts Red shorts.
Nickname: The Blues or Borough.
Formations: Feltham 1946; Previously Tudor Sports 1946–63. Feltham & Hounslow Borough 1991, as merged with Hounslow Town (formed 1884). **Formative years:** West Middlesex Sunday 1946–49, Staines & District 1949–55 (champions 1951 & 1955) and Hounslow & District 1955–59. **Senior leagues:** Parthenon 1959–63, Surrey Senior 1963–68, Spartan 1968–73 and Athenian 1973–77. **Isthmian era:** The club were elected as founder-members of Division 2 in 1977, winning the championship in 1980–81. Relegated to Division 2 South in 1983–84, where they remained until 1991, with fourth place being their best position in 1986–87 and 1987–88. Following the merger with Hounslow Town, who had sold their Denbigh Road ground for development to clear debts, the new club continued in Division 3 never finishing above mid-table. The club were forced to resign in 1995 as the league had forbidden the use of artificial pitch surfaces. The club subsequently reverted to the name Feltham and were accepted into the Combined Counties League where they continue to play.

Finchley (1973–1991)

Ground: Summers Lane, Finchley, London, N12.
Colours: White shirts Blue shorts.
Nickname: The Finches.
Formation: 1874. **Formative years:** North London 1892–94, Finchley & District 1898–99 resigned, North Middlesex 1899–1902 (champions 1900 & 1901). **Senior leagues:** London 1902–12, Athenian *(f)* 1912–14, London 1914–15, 1919–21 in abeyance due to no suitable home ground, Spartan 1921–23, London 1923–29, Athenian 1929–30, London 1930–39 (champions 1937), Herts & Middlesex 1939–45 – War time competition and Athenian 1939–73 (champions 1954). **Isthmian era:** The club were elected as founder-members of Division 2 in 1973 and remained in that Division until relegation in 1981. Following League re-organisation in 1984 the club were placed in Division 2 North and immediately won promotion as runners-up to Division 1. The club suffered relegation to Division 2 North in 1986–87, switching to Division 2 South the following season and back to the North section in 1989. During 1990–91 the club was taken over by Wingate FC (founded 1946), becoming Wingate & Finchley *(see separate entry)* and they resigned from the League, having finished the season above only Tring Town. The new club was accepted into the Herts County League for 1991–92.
FA competitions: FA Cup third round 1922–23. FA Amateur Cup semi-finalists 1964–65.

Flackwell Heath (1984–2007)

Ground: Wilks Park, Magpie Lane, Flackwell Heath, Buckinghamshire.
Colours: Red shirts and shorts.
Nickname: The Heathens.
Formation: 1907. **Formative years:** Wycombe & District. **Senior leagues:** Great Western Combination 1950–64 (champions Division 2 1951, Premier Division 1958, 1963), Wycombe 1964–76, Hellenic 1976–82, Athenian 1982–84. **Isthmian era:** The club were elected to Division 2 North in 1984, switching to Division 2 South the following season, where they remained until 1991 when due to League re-organisation they were placed in Division 3. Their best position in this Division was fourth, in 2000–01. Following the 2002 re-organisation the club were placed in Division 2. They were Associate Members Trophy Finalists in 2004–05.

Fleet Town (2004–2007)

Ground: Calthorpe Park, Crookham Road, Fleet, Hampshire.
Colours: Light & Dark Blue shirts Dark Blue shorts.
Nickname: The Blues
Formation: 1890 **Formative years:** Aldershot Senior 1923–53, Basingstoke & District 1953–61. **Senior leagues:** Hampshire 1961–78 (champions Division 2 1966, Division 3 1962), Athenian 1978–84, Combined Counties 1984–86, Surrey County Premier 1986–87, Chiltonian 1987–89, Wessex 1989–95 & 2000–02 (champions 1995), Southern 1995–2000 & 2002–04. **Isthmian era:** National league restructuring in 2004–05 placed the club in the Isthmian League where they finished 19th in Division 1.

Folkestone Invicta (2004–to date)

Ground: Westbourne Stadium, Cheriton Road, Folkestone, Kent.
Colours: Black & Amber striped shirts and shorts.
Nickname: The Seasiders.
Formation: 1936 **Formative years:** Kent Amateur. **Senior leagues:** Kent Senior 1991–98 (champions Division 2 1992), Southern 1998–2004.
Isthmian era: National League restructuring in 2004–05 placed the club in the Isthmian League Premier Division where they finished 14th.

Ford United (1997–2004)

Grounds: Oakside Stadium, Station Road, Barkingside, Ilford, Essex.
Previous Ground: Ford Sports & Social Club, Rush Green Road, Rush Green, Romford, Essex until 2002.
Colours: Royal Blue shirts and shorts.
Nickname: Motormen.
Formation: 1959, after merger of Briggs Sports (previously Briggs Motor Bodies – formed 1934) and Ford Sports (formed 1932). **Senior leagues:** Aetolian *(f)* 1959–64 (champions 1960 & 1962), Greater London *(f)* 1964–71 (champions Section A 1971), Metropolitan–London *(f)* 1971–74 and Essex Senior 1974–97 (champions 1992, 1997).
Isthmian era: Elected to Division 3 in 1997 as Essex Senior League champions, the club enjoyed successive promotions, as Division 3 champions, and third in Division 2, in 1998–99 and 1999–2000, respectively. The club secured the Division 1 championship and promotion to the Premier Division 2001–02. The club announced a change of name, to Redbridge FC, during 2003–04, and qualified to be founder-members of Nationwide South in 2004–05. However, they were relegated at the end of that season.
FA competitions: FA Cup first round 1998–99 and 2003–04.

Gravesend & Northfleet (1997–2002)

Ground: Stonebridge Road, Northfleet, Kent.
Colours: Red shirts White shorts.
Nickname: The Fleet.
Formation: 1946 as merger of Gravesend United (formed 1893) and Northfleet United (formed 1890). **Senior leagues:** Southern 1946–79, Alliance Premier 1979–82 and Southern 1982–97.
Isthmian era: Switched from the Southern League in 1997, finishing in mid-table in their first three seasons, then sixth in 2000–01, before securing the Premier Division championship in 2001–02 and promotion to the Football Conference where the club now remain. The club were Full Members Cup winners in 2000–01.
FA competitions: FA Cup fourth round 1962–63.

Grays Athletic (1983–2004).

Ground: Recreation Ground, Bridge Road, Grays, Essex.
Colours: Blue shirts and shorts.
Nickname: The Blues.
Formation: The original club was formed in 1890 but merged with Grays Swifts in 1892. The present club was formed in 1903 as Grays Juniors before changing their name to Grays Athletic in 1907.
Formative years: Grays & District 1903–07. **Senior leagues:** South Essex 1907–21 (champions Division 2 B 1909), Athenian *(f)* 1912–14, London 1914–24 (champions Amateur Section 1915, 1922, 1927, 1930), Kent 1924–26, London 1926–39, Corinthian *(f)* 1945–58 (champions 1946) and Athenian 1958–83.
Isthmian era: Promoted to Division 2 as Athenian League champions in 1982–83. The club were placed in Division 2 South the following year, due to League re-organisation, and won this championship at the first attempt, gaining promotion to Division 1. The club won promotion to the Premier Division in 1987–88 as runners-up, and remained there until relegated back to Division 1 in 1996–97. Promotion, as runners-up, back to the Premier Division came in 1999–2000, and they stayed in this Division until 2004, when the club became founder-members of Nationwide South following The FA restructuring. The club secured the Nationwide South championship and promotion to the Football Conference at the first attempt. The club were League Cup winners in 1991–92.
FA competitions: FA Cup first round 1952–53, 1988–89, 2000–01 and 2003–04. FA Trophy winners 2004–05.

Great Wakering Rovers (1999–2004).

Ground: Burroughs Park, Little Wakering Hall Lane, Great Wakering, Essex.
Colours: Green & White shirts White shorts.
Nickname: The Rovers.
Formation: 1919.
Formative years: Southend & District 1919–1982, Southend Alliance 1982–89 and Essex Intermediate 1989–92.
Senior leagues: Essex Senior 1992–97 (champions 1995).
Isthmian era: Promoted to Division 3 as Essex Senior League runners-up in 1999, winning promotion to Division 2 as runners-up the following season. The club finished in ninth and seventh respectively in 2000–01 and 2001–02 before re-organisation placed the club in Division 1 North. Restructuring for 2004–05 allocated the club to the Southern League Division 1 East, where they just avoided relegation.

Hampton & Richmond Borough (1973–2007).

Ground: Beveree Stadium, Beaver Close, Hampton, Middlesex.
Colours: Red shirts with Blue trim White shorts.
Nickname: The Beavers.
Formation: 1920; Previously Hampton 1920–99.
Formative years: South West Middlesex 1921–22, Kingston & District 1922–24, South West Middlesex 1924–25, Kingston & District 1925–33 (champions 1930, 1931, 1932, 1933) and South West Middlesex 1933–59.
Senior leagues: Surrey Senior 1959–64 (champions 1964), Spartan 1964–71 (champions 1965, 1966, 1967, 1970) and Athenian 1971–73.
Isthmian era: Elected as founder-members of Division 2 in 1973 and remained in that Division (renamed Division 1) until relegation to Division 2 South in 1989–90. The club were placed in Division 3 in the 1991 League re–organisation, and won promotion as the fourth-placed club at the first attempt. Promotion to Division 1 followed in 1995–96 as the third-placed club. Two years later, Premier Division status was secured, again as the third placed club. In 2001–02 the club suffered relegation to Division 1 South and, after The FA's restructuring in 2004, won promotion back to the Premier Division. Hampton & Richmond Borough were League Cup finalists in 2001–02.
FA competitions: FA Cup first round 2000–01.

Harefield United (1984–1996).

Ground: Preston Park, Breakspear Road North, Harefield, Middlesex.
Colours: Red & White striped shirts Black shorts.
Nickname: Hares.
Formation: 1937, from merger of Harefield Old Boys and Harefield Brigade Old Boys.
Formative years: Uxbridge & District, West Herts 1938–39 and Great Western Combination 1947–64 (champions Division 2 1948, Division 1 1951).
Senior leagues: Parthenon/Middlesex Senior 1964–71 (champions 1965), Spartan 1971–75 and Athenian 1975–84.
Isthmian era: The Club were elected into Division 2 North in 1984, switched to Division 2 South in 1986, with fifth place as their best finish in 1988–89. In the 1991 League re-organisation the club were placed in Division 2, but were relegated to Division 3 in 1992–93, where they remained until 1996. The club resigned from the league and joined the Spartan League, but they finished bottom of 16 clubs in their first season. However, the Spartan and South Midlands leagues amalgamated for the 1997–98 season and Harefield were placed in the Spartan South Midlands League Premier Division South; they are currently members of the Premier Division.

Haringey Borough (1984–1988).

Ground: Coles Playing Fields, White Hart Lane, Tottenham, London, N17.
Colours: Yellow shirts Blue shorts.
Nickname: Boro.

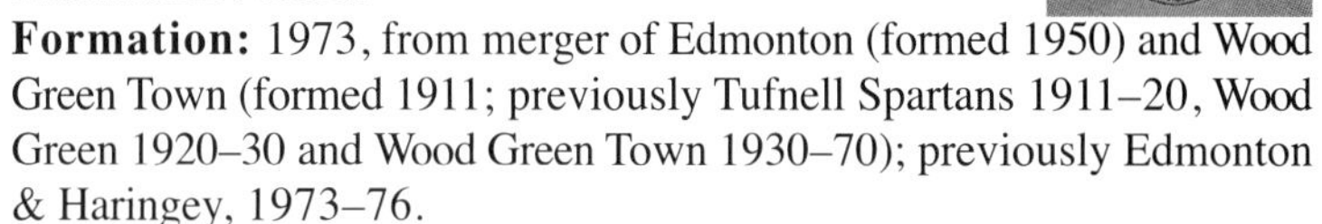

Formation: 1973, from merger of Edmonton (formed 1950) and Wood Green Town (formed 1911; previously Tufnell Spartans 1911–20, Wood Green 1920–30 and Wood Green Town 1930–70); previously Edmonton & Haringey, 1973–76.
Senior leagues: Athenian 1973–84.
Isthmian era: The club were elected into Division 2 North in 1984, finishing third in 1986–87. At the end of 1987–88, due to poor administration and ground grading, the club were not re–elected at the AGM and joined the Spartan League, where they stayed until the Spartan and South Midlands leagues amalgamated in 1997. The club were placed in the Spartan South Midlands League Premier Division South and are currently members of the Premier Division. In 1995, the club changed their name to Tufnell Park but reverted to Haringey Borough the following season.

Harlow Town (1973–2004).

Ground: Harlow Sportscentre, Hammarskjold Road, Harlow, Essex.
Colours: Red shirts with White trim White shorts.
Nickname: The Hawks.
Formation: 1879.
Formative years: East Herts *(f)* 1896–97, 1898–1900, 1903–04, 1909–25 (champions Division 1 1912, 1923) and 1927–32 (champions 1929, 1930), Stansted & District 1907–13 & 1919–29 (champions 1924, 1928), Herts & Essex Border *(f)* 1925–27.
Senior leagues: Spartan 1932–39 & 1946–54, London 1954–61, Delphian 1961–63 and Athenian 1963–73 (champions Division 1 1972).
Isthmian era: The club gained election as founder-members of Division 2 in 1973 and won promotion to the Premier from the renamed Division 1 as champions in 1978–79. They were relegated to Division 1 in 1981–82, but promoted, as runners-up, a season later. In 1984–85 and 1985–86 they suffered successive relegations to Division 1 and Division 2 North. Division 2 North champions in 1988–89, the club remained in Division 1 until 1992, when the League suspended the club's membership for the 1992–93 season because of off–field issues. The club returned to the League in 1993–94, but were placed in Division 3. They gained successive promotions, in 1997–98 as the third placed club and then as runners-up in 1998–99. Following the League's re-organisation in 2002, the club was placed in Division 1 North. The FA restructuring for 2004–05 saw the club placed in the Southern League Division 1 East, where they finished 15th.
FA competitions: FA Cup fourth round 1979–80.

Harrow Borough (1975–to date).

Ground: Earlsmead Stadium, Carlyon Avenue, Harrow, Middlesex.
Colours: Red shirts and shorts.
Nickname: The Boro.
Formation: 1933; Previously Roxonian 1933–38 and Harrow Town 1938–66. **Formative years:** Harrow & District 1933–34. **Senior leagues:** Spartan 1934–58 (champion Division 2 West 1939), West Middlesex Combination–Middlesex *(f)* 1939–45, Delphian 1958–63 and Athenian 1963–75. **Isthmian era:** The club gained election to Division 2 in 1975, winning promotion to the Premier Division as runners-up from the renamed Division 1 in 1978–79. They secured the League championship in 1983–84 and have remained members of the Premier Division ever since. **FA competitions**: FA Cup second round 1983–84. FA Trophy semi-finalists 1982–83.

Harwich & Parkeston (1973–1983).

Ground: Royal Oak Ground, Main Road, Dovercourt, Harwich, Essex.
Colours: Black & White striped shirts Black shorts.
Nickname: Shrimpers.
Formation: 1875; re–formed in 1884 as Harwich & Dovercourt and merged with Parkeston in 1889 to form Harwich & Parkeston. **Formative years:** North Essex (champions 1896, 1897, 1899), Essex & Suffolk Border 1919–34 and Southern Amateur 1934–35. **Senior leagues:** Eastern Counties *(f)* 1935–37 (joint champions 1936), Essex County *(f)* 1937–38 (champions 1938), Eastern Counties 1938–64 and Athenian 1964–73 (champions Division 2 1965). **Isthmian era:** The club gained election as founder-members of Division 2 in 1973. They remained in that Division until relegated in 1979–80. In 1983 the club finished bottom of Division 2 and were relegated to the Athenian League.

Hastings United (2004–to date).

Ground: The Pilot Field, Elphinstone Road, Hastings, East Sussex.
Colours: Claret and Blue shirts Blue shorts.
Nickname: The U's.
Formation: 1894; Previously St. Leonard's United 1894–1906, Hastings & St. Leonard's 1906–80 and Hastings Town 1980–2002. **Formative years:** East Sussex 1896–1904. **Senior leagues:** South Eastern 1904–10 (champions Division 2 1906), Southern 1905–10 & 1985–2004 (champions Southern Division 1992), Athenian 1913–14, Sussex County *(f)* 1921–27 & 1952–85 (champions Division 2 1980), Hastings 1927–52, Southern Amateur 1927–46 (champions Division 1 1935, 1936, 1937, 1939; Division 2 1928), Corinthian 1946–48. **Isthmian era:** As part of The FA's National League restructuring in 2004–05 the club was placed in Isthmian League Division 1, finishing 11th.

Hayes (1971–1996 & 2002–2004).

Ground: Townfield House, Church Road, Hayes, Middlesex.
Colours: Red & White striped shirts Black shorts.
Nickname: The Missioners.
Formation: 1909; Previously Botwell Mission 1909–29. **Formative years:** Hanwell & District 1911–14. **Senior leagues:** Great Western Suburban 1919–24 (champions 1921, 1922, 1923, 1924), Spartan 1924–30 (champions Division 1 1928), Great Western Combination *(f)* 1939–40 (champions 1940), and Athenian 1930–71 (champions 1957). **Isthmian era:** The club were invited to join the League in 1971 and remained in the top division until 1995–96, when they won the championship and gained promotion to the Football Conference. The club's best finish in the Football Conference was third, in 1998–99, but they were relegated back to the Isthmian League in 2001–02. They remained in the Premier Division until The FA restructuring in 2004, when they became founder-members of Nationwide South. The club finished 12th in their first season in this league. The club were League Cup finalists in 1978–79 and 1987–88. **FA competitions**: FA Cup second round 1972–73, 1990–91, 1991–92 and 1999–2000. FA Amateur Cup finalists 1930–31.

Hemel Hempstead Town (1977–2004).

Ground: Vauxhall Road, Adeyfield, Hemel Hempstead, Hertfordshire.
Colours: Red shirts & shorts.
Nickname: Tudors.
Formation: 1885 Apsley (1885–1947); Hemel Hempstead Town merged with Hemel Hempstead United in 1972 to form Hemel Hempstead FC, adding the suffix "Town" in 1998. **Formative years:** Wolverton 1897–98, West Herts 1898–1922 most seasons. **Senior leagues:** Herts County *(f)* 1898–1922 (champions 1900, West Division 1903, 1907), Spartan 1922–52 (champions Division 1 1934), Delphian 1952–63 and Athenian 1963–77. **Isthmian era:** The club were elected as founder members of Division 2 in 1977, and following League re-organisation were placed in Division 2 North in 1984. Following further League re-organisation the club reverted back to Division 2 in 1991, but were relegated to Division 3 in 1996–97, although they bounced back as Division 3 champions the following year. Division 2 champions in 1999–2000, the club failed to gain promotion because of ground grading issues. The club was placed in Division 1 North following further re-organisation in 2002, gaining promotion in 2003–04 as the sixth-placed club. The FA's restructuring for 2004–05 saw the club allocated to the Southern League Premier Division, but they suffered relegation at the end of that season. The club were Associate Members Trophy finalists in 2000–01.

Hendon (1963–to date).

Ground: Claremont Road, Brent Cross, London, NW2.
Colours: Green & White shirts Green shorts.
Nickname: Greens or Dons.
Formation: 1908; Previously Christchurch Hampstead 1908–09, Hampstead Town 1909–26, Hampstead 1926–33 and Golders Green 1933–46. **Formative years:** Finchley & District (champions Division 3 1909, Division 2 1910, Division 1 1911). **Senior leagues:** London 1911–14 (champions Amateur Section 1914) and Athenian 1919–63 (champions 1953, 1956, 1961). **Isthmian era:** The club were invited to join the league in 1963 and are one of the few clubs not to suffer relegation whilst members. The club were League champions in 1964–65 – beating Enfield 4–1 in a play–off after the clubs finished level on points – and 1972–73. The club were runners-up in 1963–64, 1965–66 and 1973–74. In 2003–04 the club qualified for promotion to the newly-formed Nationwide South as the fourth-placed club but subsequently declined promotion, opting to remain in the Isthmian League where they finished 11th in 2004–05. The club were League Cup winners in 1976–77, finalists in 1986–87 and Full Members Cup winners in 1993–94, 1997–98 and 1998–99. In 1987 the Club reached the inaugural final of the Premier Inter League Cup but lost to Kettering Town.
FA competitions: FA Cup third round 1973–74. FA Amateur Cup winners 1959–60, 1964–65 and 1971–72.

Hertford Town (1973–2006).

Ground: Hertingfordbury Park, West Street, Hertford, Hertfordshire.
Colours: Blue shirts and shorts.
Nickname: The Blues.

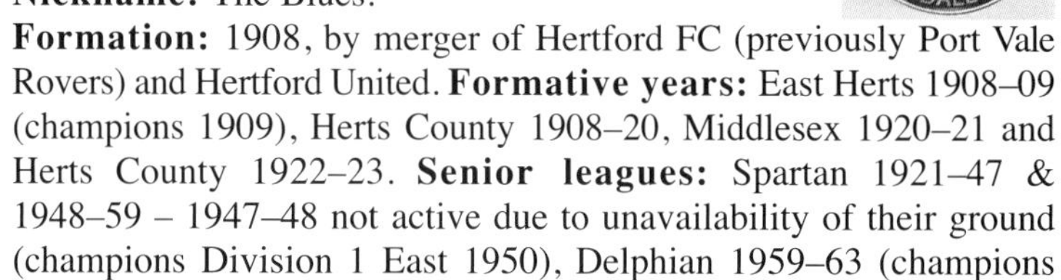

Formation: 1908, by merger of Hertford FC (previously Port Vale Rovers) and Hertford United. **Formative years:** East Herts 1908–09 (champions 1909), Herts County 1908–20, Middlesex 1920–21 and Herts County 1922–23. **Senior leagues:** Spartan 1921–47 & 1948–59 – 1947–48 not active due to unavailability of their ground (champions Division 1 East 1950), Delphian 1959–63 (champions 1961, 1962), Athenian 1963–72 and Eastern Counties 1972–73. **Isthmian era:** In 1973, the club were elected as founder-members of Division 2 and remained in the renamed Division 1, with fourth place being their best position, in 1982–83, until 1984–85, when they suffered relegation to Division 2 North. Following League re-organisation in 1991 the club were placed in Division 3. They won promotion back to Division 2 in 1997–98 as runners-up only to be relegated back to Division 3 the following season. Following League re-organisation in 2002, they were promoted to Division 1 North despite finishing only 11th. Relegation back to Division 2 occurred the following season.

Heybridge Swifts (1984–to date).

Ground: Scraley Road, Heybridge, Maldon, Essex.
Colours: Black & White striped shirts Black shorts.
Nickname: The Swifts.
Formation: 1880.
Formative years: North Essex (champions 1947), Chelmsford & District and Essex & Suffolk Border (champions 1932), South Essex.
Senior leagues: Essex Senior *(f)* 1971–84 (champions 1982, 1983, 1984).
Isthmian era: The club gained election to Division 2 North in 1984, winning promotion to Division 1 as champions in 1989–90, with further promotion to the Premier Division as runners-up in 1995–96. The club are still currently members of the Premier Division with their best league position being sixth in 1997–98. The club were League Cup winners in 2000–01.
FA competitions: FA Cup first round 1994–95, 1997–98 and 2002–03.

Hitchin Town (1963–2004).

Ground: Top Field, Fishponds Road, Hitchin, Hertfordshire.
Colours: Yellow shirts Green shorts.
Nickname: The Canaries.
Formation: 1865 Reconstituted 1928.
Senior leagues: Spartan 1928–39 (champions 1935) and Athenian 1939–63.
Isthmian era: In 1963, the club were invited to join the Isthmian League, and they remained in the top division until 1987–88, when they were relegated to Division 1. Promoted back to the Premier Division as Division 1 champions in 1992–93, they suffered a second relegation to Division 1 in 1997–98, only to bounce straight back up as runners-up the following season. The FA's restructuring for 2004–05 saw the club allocated to the Southern League Division Premier Division, where they finished 18th.
FA competitions: FA Cup second round 1981–82, 1973–74, 1976–77 and 1994–95. FA Amateur Cup semi–finalists 1960–61 and 1962–63.

Hornchurch (1975–2004).

Ground: The Stadium, Bridge Avenue, Upminster, Essex.
Colours: Red & White striped shirts Black shorts.
Nickname: The Urchins.
Formation: 1923; Previously Upminster Wanderers 1923–38, Upminster 1938–52 and Hornchurch & Upminster 1952–61.
Formative years: Romford & District 1925–27, 1928–38, 1945–46 (champions Division 2 1926, Division 1 1930, Premier Division 1931, 1946).
Senior leagues: Spartan 1938–39 & 1946–52, Delphian 1952–59 and Athenian 1959–75 (champions Division 1 1967).
Isthmian era: In 1975, the club was invited to join the Isthmian League Division 2, which was soon renamed Division 1. They were relegated to Division 2 in 1977–78, but were gained promotion back to Division 1 in 1980–81. Relegated again to Division 2 North in 1985–86, following a League re-organisation in 1991 they were placed in Division 3. In 2001–02, following another League re-organisation, they were promoted to Division 1 North as runners-up. The following season they won promotion to the Premier Division, again as runners-up. They finished in fifth place in 2003–04, qualifying as founder-members of Nationwide South. However, following financial problems and going into liquidation, the club was voted out of Conference South at the end of 2004–05. The club reformed for 2005–06 as AFC Hornchurch, competing in the Essex Senior League.
FA competitions: FA Cup second round 2003–04.

Horsham (1973–to date).

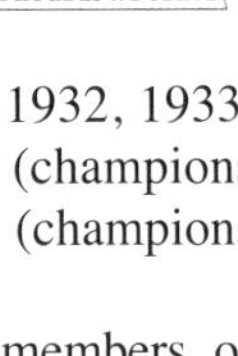

Ground: Queen Street, Horsham, West Sussex.
Colours: Amber & Green shirts Green shorts.
Nickname: Hornets.
Formation: 1885.
Formative years: West Sussex *(f)* 1896–1926.

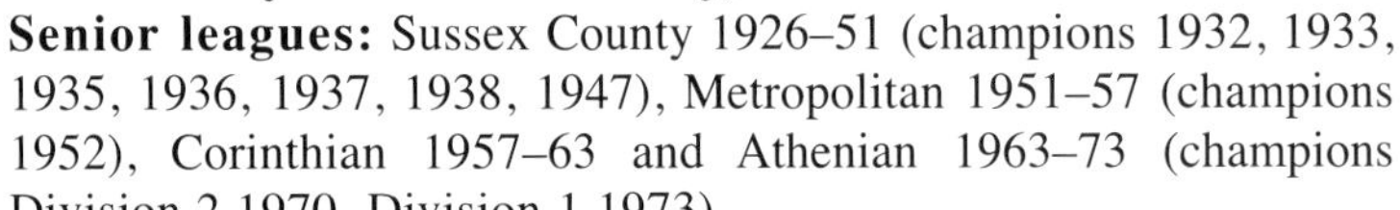

Senior leagues: Sussex County 1926–51 (champions 1932, 1933, 1935, 1936, 1937, 1938, 1947), Metropolitan 1951–57 (champions 1952), Corinthian 1957–63 and Athenian 1963–73 (champions Division 2 1970, Division 1 1973).
Isthmian era: The club gained election as founder-members of Division 2 in 1973, and remained in that Division (renamed Division 1 in 1977) until suffering relegation to Division 2 in 1979–80. They were placed in Division 2 South in 1984 following League re-organisation and were then placed in Division 3 following further League re-organisation in 1991. They secured the Division 3 championship in 1995–96 and were Division 2 runners-up in 2001–02 to climb back to Division 1. The club remain in Division 1 and in 2004–05 lost a promotion play–off final 3–1 to Bromley.
FA competitions: FA Cup first round 1947–48 and 1966–67.

Hungerford Town (1978–2003).

Ground: Town Ground, Bulpit Lane, Hungerford, Berkshire.
Colours: White shirts Navy shorts.
Nickname: Crusaders.
Formation: 1886.

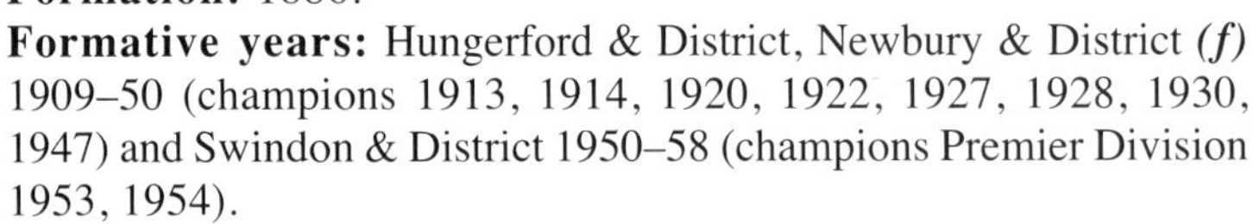

Formative years: Hungerford & District, Newbury & District *(f)* 1909–50 (champions 1913, 1914, 1920, 1922, 1927, 1928, 1930, 1947) and Swindon & District 1950–58 (champions Premier Division 1953, 1954).
Senior leagues: Hellenic 1958–78 (champions Division 1 1971).
Isthmian era: The club gained election to Division 2 in 1978, finishing third in 1979–80, 1980–81 and 1981–82. The club were placed in Division 2 South following League re-organisation in 1984 and remained there until a further League re-organisation in 1991 saw them allocated a place in Division 2. They were relegated to Division 3 in 2001–02 due to ground grading and resigned at the end of the 2002–03 season, having finished fifth in their final season. The club returned to the Hellenic League for 2003–04.
FA competitions: FA Cup first round 1979–80. FA Vase semi–finalists 1977–78, 1979–80 and 1988–89.

Ilford (1905–1979 & 2004–2005).

Ground: Cricklefield Stadium, High Road, Ilford, Essex.
Previous grounds: Lynn Road, Newbury Park, Ilford, Essex until 1977 and Leytonstone FC, Granleigh Road, Leytonstone, London, E11 1977–79.
Colours: Blue & White hooped shirts Blue shorts.
Nickname: The Foxes.
Formation: 1881; Previously Ilford Alliance 1881–83. In 1987 the club re–formed.
Senior leagues: Southern *(f)* 1894–96, London *(f)* 1896–98, South Essex 1898–1902, Metropolitan Amateur 1902–03 and Friendlies 1903–05. **Isthmian era:** Invited as founder-members in 1905, the club were League champions in 1906–07, 1920–21 and 1921–22 and runners-up in 1911–12, 1926–27, 1931–32, 1937–38 and 1938–39. The club were relegated to Division 2 in 1976–77. The club ground-shared with Leytonstone FC for two seasons from 1977, before deciding to merge with their landlords, forming Leytonstone & Ilford FC. The club finished 17th in Division 1 in 1978–79. **Re–formed Club**: In 1987 Ilford re–formed as a junior club via the Spartan League before election to the Essex Senior League in 1995. The club won promotion to the Isthmian League as champions in 2004. In their first season they were Division 2 champions, gaining promotion, and were allocated a place in the Southern League in The FA restructuring. The club also won the Associate Members Trophy in 2005.
FA competitions: FA Cup second round 1925–26, 1927–28, 1974–75. FA Amateur Cup winners 1928–29, 1929–30.

Kettering Town (2003–2004).

Ground: Rockingham Road, Kettering, Northamptonshire.
Colours: Red shirts Black shorts.
Nickname: Poppies.
Formation: 1872; Previously Kettering 1872–1925. **Senior leagues:** Midland 1892–1900 (champions 1896, 1900), United 1896–1902, Southern 1900–04, Northants 1904–10 (champions 1905), Southern 1909–12, Central Alliance 1912–23, Southern 1923–30 (champions 1928), Birmingham & District 1930–31, Northants 1931–33, East Midlands 1933–34 (champions 1934), Central Combination 1934–35, United Counties 1935–46 (champions 1939), Birmingham & District 1946–50 (champions 1948), Southern 1950–79 (champions 1957, 1973), Alliance Premier League/ Football Conference 1979–2001, Southern 2001–02 (champions 2002) and Football Conference 2002–03.
Isthmian era: Relegated from the Football Conference at the end of the 2002–03 and placed in the Isthmian League for 2003–04, they finished ninth in the Premier Division, earning promotion as founder-members of Nationwide North, from which they qualified for the play–offs in their first season.
FA competitions: FA Cup fourth round 1988–89. FA Trophy finalists 1978–79, 1999–2000.

Kingsbury Town (1984–2006).

Ground: Silver Jubilee Park, Townsend Lane, Kingsbury, London, NW9.
Colours: Yellow shirts Black shorts.
Nickname: Kings.
Formation: 1927; Previously Davis Estate Sports 1927–45. They were taken over by Sunday club 584 FC in 1967 and were briefly known as Kingsbury Town 584 but reverted back to Kingsbury Town before the season. **Formative years:** Willesden & District 1930–39 (champions Division 2 1935). **Senior leagues:** Middlesex Senior/Parthenon 1943–60 (champions 1953), Spartan 1960–75, London–Spartan *(f)* 1975–76, Athenian 1976–78, London–Spartan 1978–81 and Athenian 1981–84. **Isthmian era:** Elected to Division 2 North in 1984, and promoted as runners-up to Division 1 in 1985–86, they were relegated back to Division 2 North in 1989–90. Following League re-organisation in 1991 the club were placed in Division 3, where they rarely finished above mid-table. Following further League re-organisation in 2002, the club was placed in Division 2.

Kingstonian (1929–1998 & 2001–to date).

Ground: Kingsmeadow Stadium, Jack Goodchild Way, 422a Kingston Road, Kingston–Upon–Thames, Surrey.
Previous grounds: Richmond Road, Kingston–Upon–Thames, Surrey (until 1988) and Hampton FC, Beveree Stadium, Beaver Close, Hampton, Middlesex (1988–89).
Colours: Red & White hooped shirts Black shorts.
Nickname: The K's.
Formation: 1919, from merger of Kingston–on–Thames (formed 1885) and Old Kingstonians (formed 1908). **Senior leagues:** Athenian 1919–29 (champions 1924, 1926). **Isthmian era:** Invited to join the Isthmian League in 1929, the club were champions in 1933–34 and 1936–37 and runners-up in 1947–48 and 1962–63. They were relegated to Division 1 in 1978–79, where they stayed until gaining promotion back to the Premier Division as runners-up in 1984–85. They were Premier Division champions in 1997–98, gaining promotion to the Football Conference. In the club's three years in the Football Conference they finished eighth and fifth before suffering relegation back to the Isthmian League in 2000–01, finishing 21st. Further relegation followed in 2004–05 to Division 1. The club were League Cup winners in 1995–96 and finalists in 1981–82.
FA competitions: FA Cup second round 1994–95, 1995–96, 1998–99. FA Amateur Cup winners 1932–33. FA Trophy winners 1998–99, 1999–2000.

Leatherhead (1972–to date).

Ground: Fetcham Grove, Guildford Road, Leatherhead, Surrey.
Colours: Green shirts White shorts.
Nickname: The Tanners.
Formation: 1946 from merger of Leatherhead Rose and Leatherhead United. **Senior leagues:** Surrey Senior 1946–50 (champions 1947, 1948, 1949, 1950), Metropolitan 1950–51, Delphian *(f)* 1951–58, Corinthian 1958–63 (champions 1949, 1950, 1963) and Athenian 1963–72 (champions Division 1 1964).

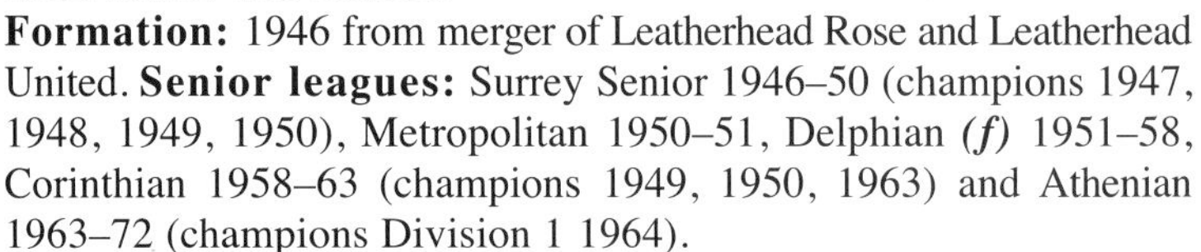

Isthmian era: Invited to join the Isthmian League in 1972, finishing third in their first season, the club remained in the top Division until being relegated to Division 1 in 1982–83. Further relegation followed to Division 2 South in 1989–90, which became Division 2 in 1991 following League re-organisation. They were promoted to Division 1 as Division 2 runners-up in 1996–97, but were relegated back in 2000–01. Following another League re-organisation in 2002, the club was placed in Division 1 South and in Division 1 in 2003–04 following The FA's restructuring, where they remain. The club were League Cup finalists in 1977–78.
FA competitions: FA Cup fourth round 1974–75. FA Amateur Cup semi–finalists 1970–71. FA Trophy finalists 1977–78.

Leighton Town (1992–2004).

Ground: Bell Close, Lake Street, Leighton Buzzard, Bedfordshire.
Colours: Red & White striped shirts Red shorts.
Nickname: Reds.
Formation: 1922, from merger of Leighton Comrades and Morgan's Ivy Leaf; Previously Leighton United 1922–63.
Senior leagues: Spartan 1922–53 (champions Division 2 1924, Division 2 A 1928), Hellenic *(f)* 1953–55, South Midlands 1955–67 (Champions Premier Division 1967, 1992), Spartan 1957–74, United Counties 1974–76 and South Midlands 1976–92.
Isthmian era: Promoted as South Midlands League champions to Division 3 in 1992, they went up to Division 2 as runners-up in 1995–96. The club failed to finish above mid-table and suffered relegation in 2000–01. Following League re-organisation in 2002, they were placed in Division 2 and won the championship in 2002–03. Restructuring by The FA for 2004–05 saw the club allocated to the Southern League Division 1 East, where they finished tenth. The club were Associate Members Trophy winners in 1996–97 and 1998–99.

Letchworth Garden City (1977–1990).

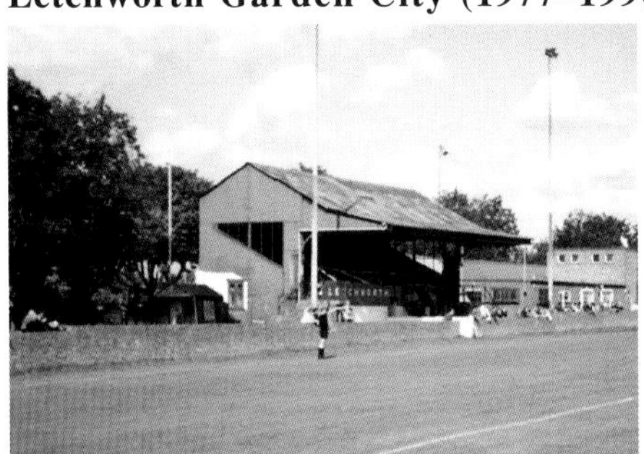

Ground: Baldock Road, Letchworth, Hertfordshire.
Colours: Blue & White shirts White shorts.
Nickname: Bluebirds.
Formation: 1906; Previously Garden City 1906–07, Letchworth Athletic 1907–14, Letchworth Town 1974–76.
Formative years: North Herts 1909–22 (champions Premier Division 1920).
Senior leagues: Herts County 1906–24 (champions North Division 1912, 1913, 1914, 1920; North & East Division 1923), Beds County *(f)* 1922–29, Spartan 1929–56 (champions Division 2 East 1930; Division 1 1954), Delphian 1956–59 (champions 1958), Corinthian 1959–63 and Athenian 1963–77 (champions Division 1 1975).
Isthmian era: Elected as founder-members of Division 2 in 1977, the club remained at that level before being placed in Division 2 North in 1984 following League re-organisation. They remained in that Division until 1989–90, when they finished bottom, lost to Horsham in a play–off, and were relegated to the South Midlands League. Renamed Letchworth FC in 1995, they stayed in that League until folding midway through the 2002–03 season.

Lewes (1977–2004).

Ground: The Dripping Pan, Mountfield Road, Lewes, East Sussex. **Colours:** Red & Black shirts Black shorts. **Nickname:** Rooks. **Formation:** 1885. **Formative years:** Mid–Sussex (champions 1911, 1914). **Senior leagues:** Sussex County *(f)* 1920–65 (champions Division 1 1965) and Athenian 1965–77 (champions Division 2 1968, Division 1 1970). **Isthmian era:** Elected founder-members of Division 2 in 1977, they won promotion to Division 1 as runners-up in 1979–80. Sixth place was their best finish – in both 1981–82 and 1988–89 – but in 1991 they were relegated to Division 2. Although promotion back to Division 1 as runners-up was achieved the following year, successive relegations followed in 1992–93 and 1993–94. The club gained promotion from Division 3 as runners-up in 2000–01 and they were back in Division 1 as Division 2 champions in 2001–02. The club was placed in Division 1 South following the League's re-organisation in 2002. After winning the Division 1 South championship in 2003–04, they qualified as founder-members of Nationwide South by winning three rounds of playoffs. The club finished fourth in Conference South 2004–05, but were denied a play–off place because of unsatisfactory ground grading. **FA competitions:** FA Cup first round 2001–02.

Leyton (1982–1995 and 2002–to date).

Ground: Hare & Hounds Ground, 282 Lea Bridge Road, Leyton, London E10. **Colours:** White shirts Navy shorts. **Nickname:** Lilywhites. **Formation:** Originally formed in 1868 as Matlock Swifts changing their name to Leyton FC in 1895. The club re–formed in 1913 and again in 1919 following professional periods. The club merged with Wingate FC (Formed in 1943) to form Leyton–Wingate in 1975. In 1992 the Wingate section split and the club reverting to Leyton. **Formative years:** Leyton & District Alliance *(f)* 1892–95 (champions 1893) **Senior leagues:** South Essex *(f)* 1895–97 (champions 1896 & 1897), London 1897–98, South Essex 1898–1903 (champions 1900), London 1902–06, Southern 1905–12, South Essex 1913–14 & 1920–21, London 1921–27 (champions Premier Division 1924, 1925 & 1926) and Athenian 1927–82 (champions 1929 & 1982 Premier Division 1966, 1967 and Division 1 1971). **Isthmian era:** Promoted to Division 2 as Athenian League champions in 1982, allocated to Division 2 North following League re-organisation in 1984 and winning the championship in that season. They won promotion to the Premier Division as runners-up in 1986–87 where they spent four seasons with seventh place being their best position in 1989–90. The club were relegated to Division 1 in 1990–91 where they remained rarely finishing above mid-table. A section of the club opted to merge with Walthamstow Pennant to form Leyton–Pennant in 1995, with the original Leyton remaining at the Hare & Hounds ground. Via the Spartan League 1997–98 and Essex Intermediate 1998–99, they joined the Essex Senior League, spending three seasons before promotion as Essex Senior League champions in 2002. In their first season back to the Isthmian League they won promotion to Division One North as runners-up. The club were Associate Members Trophy winners in 2002. **FA competitions:** FA Cup third round 1909–10. FA Amateur Cup winners 1926–27, 1927–28.

Leyton-Pennant (1995-2003) see Waltham Forest.

Leytonstone (1908–1979).

Ground: Granleigh Road, Leytonstone, London, E11. **Colours:** Red and White stripes or hooped shirts Red shorts. **Nickname:** The Stones. **Formation:** 1886; Previously Cedars 1886–92. **Formative years:** Metropolitan Amateur 1902–03. **Senior leagues:** South Essex *(f)* 1895–1900 & 1901–05 (champions 1898, 1902; Section A 1903) and Spartan *(f)* 1907–08. **Isthmian era:** Invited to join the Isthmian League in 1908, the club won the League championship on eight occasions, in 1937–38, 1938–39, 1946–47 1947–48, 1949–50, 1950–51, 1951–52 and 1965–66; they were runners-up in 1908–09, 1910–11, 1912–13, 1932–33 and 1961–62. The club were relegated to Division 1 in 1978–79 and amalgamated with Ilford to form Ilford–Leytonstone. However, shortly before the start of the 1979–80 season, the name was reversed to Leytonstone–Ilford so the club could maintain full membership of the Football Association. **FA competitions:** FA Cup 2nd round 1947–48; 1961–62. FA Amateur Cup winners 1946–47, 1947–48, 1967–68.

Leytonstone–Ilford (1979–1989).

Ground: Walthamstow Avenue FC, Green Pond Road, Higham Hill Road, Walthamstow, London, E17.
Previous ground: Granleigh Road, Leytonstone, London, E11, 1979–86.
Colours: Red shirts with Blue stripes Blue shorts.
Nickname: The Stones or The Fords.
Formation: 1979 from merger of Leytonstone (formed 1886) and Ilford (formed 1881).
Isthmian era: In their first season the amalgamated club won the Division 1 championship and, two years later, claimed the Premier Division championship. They were runners-up in 1982–83, but suffered relegation back to Division 1 in 1984–85. In 1986–87 and 1987–88, the club won back-to-back championships, of Division 1 and the Premier Division respectively. However, because of various problems regarding the ground the club was denied promotion to the Football Conference. The club won the League Cup in 1981–82. In 1988, they incorporated Walthamstow Avenue FC, changing their name to Redbridge Forest in 1989.

Leyton–Wingate (1982-1992) see Leyton.

London Caledonians (1905–1939).

Grounds: Tufnell Park Road until 1938. Park Royal Stadium 1938–1939.
Colours: Black & White hooped shirts Black shorts.
Nickname: Caleys.
Formation: 1886. **Formative years:** Cup competitions only
Isthmian era: Invited to join the Isthmian League as founder-members in 1905, they were the inaugural champions and repeated as champions in 1907–08, 1911–12, 1912–13, 1913–14 and 1924–25, while finishing as runners-up in 1906–07, 1920–21, 1925–26, 1927–28 and 1928–29. They remained members of the League until 1939. As a result of losing their ground during World War II, and being unable to find alternative facilities, the club did not resume playing after the War.
FA competitions: FA Cup third round 1886–87 and 1927–28. FA Amateur Cup winners 1922–23.

Maidenhead United (1973–2004).

Ground: York Road, Maidenhead, Berkshire.
Colours: Black & White striped shirts Black shorts.
Nickname: Magpies.
Formation: 1919, from merger of Maidenhead (formed 1870) and Maidenhead Norfolkians (formed 1884).
Senior leagues: Great Western Suburban 1919–22 (champions 1920), Spartan 1922–45 (champions Division 1 1927; Premier Division 1932, 1934), Great Western Combination *(f)* 1939–45, Corinthian *(f)* 1945–63 (champions 1958, 1961, 1962) and Athenian 1963–73. **Isthmian era:** Elected as founder members of Division 1 in 1973, finishing third in 1979–80. They were relegated to Division 2 South in 1987–88, winning promotion as runners-up in 1990–91 before securing Premier Division status as the third-placed club in 1999–2000. The club remained in the Premier Division, rarely finishing above mid-table, until restructuring in 2004. The club were founder-members of Nationwide South and finished 20th in their first season. The club were League Cup finalists in 1999–2000 and Full Members Cup winners in 1996–97.
FA competitions: FA Cup first round 1960–61, 1962–63, 1963–64 and 1971–72. FA Amateur Cup semi–finalists 1935–36.

Maidstone United (1959–1971).

Ground: Bourne Park, Central Park Complex, Eurolink Industrial Estate, Sittingbourne, Kent (Groundshare with Sittingbourne FC).
Former ground: London Road, Maidstone, Kent *(pictured left)*, until 1988.
Colours: Amber shirts Black shorts. **Nickname:** The Stones.
Formation: 1897; reformed 1992. **Senior leagues:** Kent 1897–1939, 1946–50 (champions 1899, 1900, 1901, 1922, 1923), Corinthian 1950–57 (champions 1956) and Athenian 1957–59. **Isthmian era:** Invited to join the Isthmian League in 1959, fifth place was the club's best position – in 1960–61. In 1971, they adopted professionalism, resigned from the League and were immediately elected to the Southern League, playing in Division One South. Promotion to the Premier Division was achieved in 1972–73 as Division 1 South champions. The club left the Southern League in 1979 to become founder-members of the Alliance Premier League (now Football Conference). They won the title in 1983–84 and again in 1988–89 after which they gained Football League status. They ground shared with Dartford FC, following the sale of their London Road ground but the club folded on the eve of the 1992–93 season with debts of £650,000. The club reformed in 1992 and have rejoined the League.
FA competitions: FA Cup third round 1978–79, 1980–81, 1983–84, 1986–87 and 1987–88.

Malden Vale (1989–1995).

Ground: Grand Drive, Raynes Park, London, SW20.
Colours: Royal Blue shirts and shorts.
Nickname: Vale.
Formation: 1967. **Formative years:** North Surrey Youth, Sportsman Sunday, Thameside and Surrey Combination. **Senior leagues:** Surrey Senior 1977–78 (champions 1978), London–Spartan 1978–84 and Combined Counties 1984–89 (champions 1985). **Isthmian era:** Elected to Division 2 South in 1989, the club's best finish was fourth, in 1990–91. Following League re-organisation in 1991, they were placed in Division 2. In 1994–95, they finished bottom, conceding more than 100 goals, and resigned from the League because of increased travelling costs and financial difficulties. The club returned to the Combined Counties League in 1995, at which time they merged with a local intermediate-level club, Raynes Park, and changed their name to Raynes Park Vale. They have remained members of the Combined Counties League ever since.

Marlow (1984–2004).

Ground: Alfred Davis Memorial Ground, Oak Tree Road, Marlow, Buckinghamshire.
Colours: Royal Blue shirts with White trim Royal Blue shorts.
Nickname: The Blues.
Formation: 1870; previously Great Marlow (1870–80). **Formative years:** Reading & District. **Senior leagues:** Berks & Bucks Senior 1901–02, Spartan 1908–10 – (resigned mid-way through 1910–11), – Great Western Suburban 1911–24, Reading & District 1924–28, Spartan 1928–65 (champions Division 2 West 1930; Division 1 1938), Great Western Combination *(f)* 1939–45 and Athenian 1965–84. **Isthmian era:** Elected to Division 2 South in 1984, switching to the North section the following year. They won promotion to Division 1 as runners-up in 1986–87 and secured the Division 1 championship in 1987–88. They finished third in 1993–94 but were relegated to Division 1 in 1994–95. Two seasons later, they were relegated to Division 2. Following League re-organisation in 2002–03, the club was placed in Division 1 North, switching to Division 1 South the following season. The FA restructuring in 2004 saw the club placed in Southern League Division 1 East, where they finished 13th. The club were League Cup winners in 1992–93 and Associate Members Trophy winners in 2000–01.
FA competitions: FA Cup semi-finalists 1880–81. FA Amateur Cup semi-finalists 1896–97, 1899–1900.

Metropolitan Police (1977–to date).

Ground: Imber Court Sports Club, Ember Lane. East Molesey, Surrey.
Colours: Blue shirts and shorts. **Nickname:** The Blues.
Formation: 1919. **Senior leagues:** Friendlies 1919–28, Spartan 1928–60 (champions Division 1 East 1929; Central Division 1946; Premier Division 1930, 1937, 1939, 1947, 1954, 1955), Metropolitan 1960–71 and Southern 1971–77. **Isthmian era:** Elected to Division 2 as founder-members in 1977, the club won promotion as runners-up in their first season. They finished third in 1981–82 before being relegated to Division 2 South in 1984–85. They won promotion back to Division 1, as runners-up, in 1987–88 but were again relegated to Division 2 in 1990–91. The club remained in Division 2 until 2002, when League re-organisation resulted in the club being placed in Division 1 South. The FA restructuring in 2004 saw them allocated to Division 1, where they finished in fourth place to qualify for the play-offs, but they lost in the semi-finals. The club were League Cup finalists in 1977–78 and Associate Members Trophy winners in 1994–95.
FA competitions: FA Cup first round 1931–32, 1984–85, 1993–94. FA Amateur Cup semi–finalists 1933–34.

Molesey (1977–2008).

Ground: Walton Road, West Molesey, Surrey.
Colours: White shirts Black shorts.
Nickname: The Moles.
Formation: 1953, from merger of Molesey United and West Molesey Old Boys. **Senior leagues:** Surrey Senior 1953–59 (champions 1958), Spartan 1959–73 and Athenian 1973–77. **Isthmian era:** They were elected as founder-members of Division 2 in 1977 and won promotion to Division 1 as runners-up in 1989–90. They gained promotion to the Premier Division in 1992–93, again as runners-up, and finished eighth in 1994–95, their best. Relegations, back to Division 1, in 1995–96, and to Division 2, in 1998–99, followed. The club were placed in Division 1 South following League re-organisation in 2002 and in Division One following The FA's restructuring in 2004, where they finished 16th. The club were League Cup finalists in 1992–93.
FA competitions: FA Cup first round 1993–94.

Newbury Town (1983–1995).

Ground: Town Ground, Faraday Road, Newbury, Berkshire.
Colours: Orange shirts White shorts.
Nickname: The Town.
Formation: 1887.
Formative years: Reading & District (champions 1912).
Senior leagues: Great Western Suburban 1919–27 (champions 1926), Hampshire 1927–28, Reading & District 1928–52 (champions 1929, 1930, 1932, 1938, 1950), Metropolitan & District 1952–62, Hellenic *(f)* 1953–82 (champions 1979, 1981) and Athenian 1982–83 (champions 1983).
Isthmian era: Promoted to Division 2 as Athenian League champions in 1983, they switched to Division 2 South a year later, following re-organisation. The club was placed in Division 2, following further re-organisation in 1991, bottom in the first season but were reprieved from relegation. Division 2 champions in 1993–94 and promoted to Division 1, they finished 20th out of 22 clubs, but had also declared bankruptcy and were wound up at the end of the 1994–95 season.

New Crusaders (1913–1919).

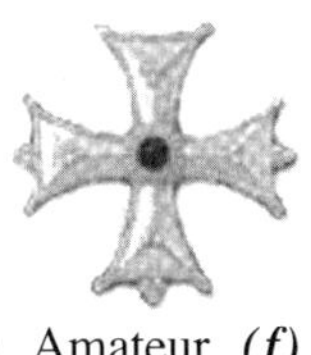

Ground: College Ground, Chislehurst Road, Sidcup, Kent.
Colours: White shirts Blue shorts.
Nickname: Crusaders.
Formation: 1905. **Formative years:** Southern Amateur *(f)* 1907–13 (champions 1908, 1909, 1910, 1911, 1912). **Isthmian era:** Invited to join the Isthmian League in 1913, they finished fifth in what proved to be their only season in the League. The club did not return to competitive action after the Great War, but they did play one final game, in 1922 at Bickley Park School, against the Kent Amateur Football Association. The club's inaugural President was Mr Samuel Farnfield, whose seven sons were all football "Blues" and played for the club at some time.
FA competitions: FA Cup first round 1905–06. FA Amateur Cup semi-finalists 1905–06.

Newport County (1989).

Ground: Somerton Park, Newport, Gwent.
Colours: Amber shirts Black shorts.
Nickname: The Ironsides.
Formation: 1912. **Senior leagues:** Southern 1912–20, Football League 1920–31, Southern 1931–32, Football League 1932–88 (champions Division 3 South 1939) and Football Conference 1988–89 – folded mid-season. **Isthmian era:** The club was expelled from the Football Conference for failing to honour fixtures and were later wound up with debts in excess of £126,000 in February 1989. They were elected to Division 2 South in 1989 but, because of various election criteria not being met, the club did not take their place.
FA competitions: FA Cup fifth round 1948–49.

Newport IoW (2004–2006).

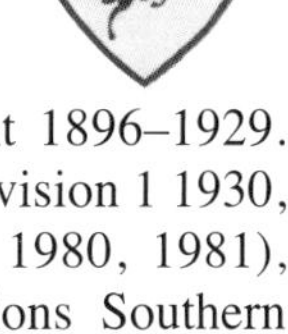

Ground: St. George's Park, St. George's Way, Newport, Isle of Wight.
Colours: Yellow shirts Blue shorts.
Nickname: The Port.
Formation: 1888 **Formative years:** Isle of Wight 1896–1929. **Senior leagues:** Hampshire 1929–86 (champions Division 1 1930, 1933, 1939, 1948, 1950, 1953, 1954, 1957, 1979, 1980, 1981), Wessex *(f)* 1986–90, Southern 1990–2004 (champions Southern Division 2001). **Isthmian era:** The Football Association's national League restructuring in 2004–05 placed the club in the Isthmian League Division 1, where they finished 18th.
FA competitions: FA Cup second round 1935–36, 1945–46.

Northwood (1992–2005).

Ground: Northwood Park, Chestnut Avenue, Northwood, Middlesex.
Colours: Red shirts and shorts.
Nickname: Woods.
Formation: 1899. **Formative years:** Harrow & Wembley 1931–69 (champions 1932, 1933, 1934, 1935, 1936, 1937, 1947, 1948, 1949). **Senior leagues:** Middlesex Senior 1969–78 (champions 1978), Hellenic 1978–84 (champions Division 1 1979) and London–Spartan/Spartan 1984–92 (champions 1992). **Isthmian era:** Promoted to Division 3 as Spartan League champions in 1992, the club won promotion to Division 2 as the third-placed finisher in 1996–97. In 1999–2000 they were promoted to Division 1 as runners-up and secured the Division 1 North title in 2002–03, winning promotion to the Premier Division. The FA restructuring in 2004 meant that, despite finishing 21st, they were not relegated at the end of the season. In 2004–05 the club finished 17th, after which FA realignment meant they were placed in the Southern League Premier Division. They won the League Cup in 2001–02 and the Associate Members Trophy in 1999–2000.

Nunhead (1908–1939).

Ground: Brown's Ground, St. Asaphs Road, Nunhead, London, SE4.
Colours: White shirts Blue shorts.
Nickname: Nuns.

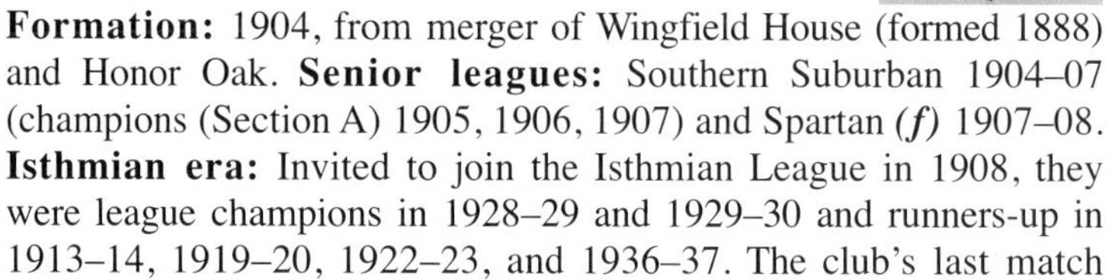

Formation: 1904, from merger of Wingfield House (formed 1888) and Honor Oak. **Senior leagues:** Southern Suburban 1904–07 (champions (Section A) 1905, 1906, 1907) and Spartan *(f)* 1907–08. **Isthmian era:** Invited to join the Isthmian League in 1908, they were league champions in 1928–29 and 1929–30 and runners-up in 1913–14, 1919–20, 1922–23, and 1936–37. The club's last match resulted in a 1–0 defeat against Tufnell Park on 26th August 1939. The club played in the South Eastern Combination – a wartime competition – between 1939 and 1941. However, as they were unable to renew the lease on their Brown's ground – and had no alternative venue available – they suspended football activities in 1941. The club remained affiliated to The Football Association until May 1949.
FA competitions: FA Cup second round 1926–27.

Oxford City (1907–1988 & 1993–2004).

Ground: Court Place Farm, Marsh Lane, Marston, Oxford, Oxfordshire.
Previous ground: White House Ground, Abingdon Road, Oxford, Oxfordshire until 1988.
Colours: Blue & White hooped shirts Blue shorts.
Nickname: City.

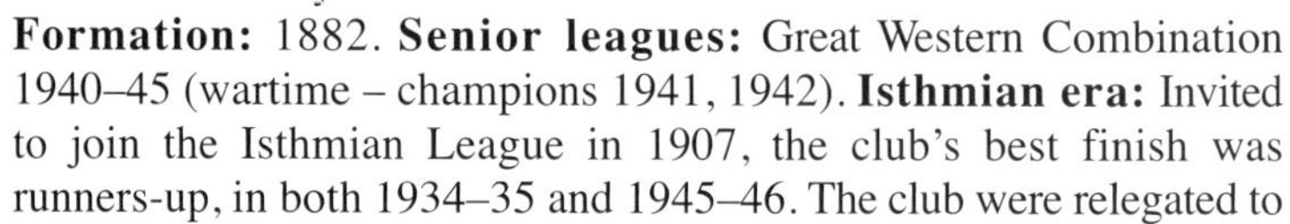

Formation: 1882. **Senior leagues:** Great Western Combination 1940–45 (wartime – champions 1941, 1942). **Isthmian era:** Invited to join the Isthmian League in 1907, the club's best finish was runners-up, in both 1934–35 and 1945–46. The club were relegated to what was then Division 2 (now Division 1) in 1975–76, but they returned to the Premier Division as runners-up after two seasons at that level. The club suffered another relegation to Division 1 in 1979–80 and remained in that Division until they were forced to resign from the league at the end of 1987–88, after the owners of their White Lion Ground terminated the lease. Their best position in that time was fourth, in 1981–82 and 1985–86. The club stayed alive, although it was not active during the 1988–89 season, and entered a side in the Oxfordshire Youth League for 1989–90. In 1990 they were elected to the South Midlands League and won the Premier Division in 1992–93, resulting in their return to the Isthmian League, albeit in Division 3. The club finished runners-up in the first season back in the League, gaining the first of three successive promotions. Runners-up in Division 2, the club won the Division 1 championship in 1995–96 – their first Isthmian League title. After two seasons, the club was relegated back to Division 1, where they remained until the League re-organisation of 2002 placed them in Division 1 North. The FA restructuring in 2004 saw the club placed in Southern League Division 1 West, but they suffered relegation in their first season and returned to the Spartan South Midlands League. The club were League Cup finalists in 1998.
FA competitions: FA Cup second round 1969–70. FA Amateur Cup winners 1905–06. FA Vase finalists 1994–95.

Petersfield United (1984–1993).

Ground: Love Lane, Petersfield, Hampshire.
Colours: Red & Black shirts White shorts.
Nickname: United or Reds.
Formation: 1889. **Formative years:** Portsmouth.
Senior leagues: Hampshire 1968–84. **Isthmian era:** Elected to Division 2 South in 1984, they remained in that division until League re-organisation in 1991 placed the club in Division 3. The club rarely finished outside the lower reaches of their division whilst in membership of the League and resigned at the end of the 1992–93 season, citing increased travelling costs. The club re–formed in 1993 as Petersfield Town, gaining election to the Wessex League. They switched to the Hampshire League in 1997, where they now remain.

Purfleet (see Thurrock).

Rainham Town (1977–1994).

Ground: Purfleet FC, Thurrock Hotel, Ship Lane, Aveley, Essex.
Previous ground: Deri Park, Wennington Road, Rainham, Essex until 1991.
Colours: Red & White striped shirts Red shorts.
Nickname: The Reds.
Formation: 1945. **Formative years:** South Essex 1945–47. **Senior leagues:** London 1947–51, Delphian *(f)* 1951–61, Metropolitan 1961–64 and Athenian 1964–77. **Isthmian era:** Elected as founder members of Division 2 (effectively the third division) in 1977, the club was placed in Division 2 South following League re-organisation in 1984. The League transferred them to the North Division the following year. Eighth place, in 1990–91, was the club's best finishing position. In 1991, the same year the club vacated their Deri Park ground, following another League re-organisation, the club was placed in Division 2, For the last three years of their League membership they were in a ground-sharing arrangement with Purfleet FC. The club finished bottom of Division 2 in 1993–94 and resigned from the league. The club folded during the summer of 1994.

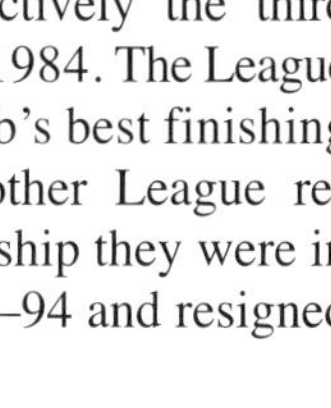

Redbridge Forest (1989–1991).

Ground: Dagenham FC, Victoria Road, Dagenham, Essex.
Colours: Red & Blue striped shirts Blue shorts.
Nickname: Reds.
Formation: 1989, from merger of Leytonstone–Ilford (formed 1979) and Walthamstow Avenue (formed 1900). **Isthmian era:** In their first season, the newly–formed club, having taken over the League Premier Division place of defending champions Leytonstone–Ilford, finished in 11th place. The following season they won the Premier Division championship, gaining promotion to the Football Conference. In 1991–92 the club finished seventh in the Football Conference, after which they merged with Dagenham FC to form Dagenham & Redbridge, who have played in the Football Conference from 1992–93 apart from four seasons back in the Isthmian League. *(see also Dagenham & Redbridge).*

Romford (1939–1959 & 1996–2002).

Ground: Brooklands Sports Ground, Romford, Essex.
Ground (reformed club): Sungate, Collier Row Road, Collier Row, Romford, Essex.
Colours: Blue & Gold shirts and shorts. **Nickname:** Boro.
Formation: 1929; reformation 1992. **Senior leagues:** London 1929–31 and Athenian 1931–39 (champions 1936, 1937). **Isthmian era:** The club were invited to join the Isthmian League in 1939, but played only one match – a 2–0 win over local rivals Ilford – before the outbreak of World War II and the cessation of League activities. However the club played in the South Essex Wartime competition of 1939–40. Following the War, the club returned to the Isthmian League and remained as members until 1959 when they elected to turn professional and joined the Southern League, gaining promotion to the Premier Division in their first season. The club won the Southern League championship in 1966–67, but were relegated to Division 1 South in 1974–75 and, in 1978, were forced to resign from the Southern League after selling their Brooklands Sports ground for redevelopment. The club reformed in 1992 and entered the Essex Senior League, winning the championship in 1996. A merger with Collier Row – who were then members of the Isthmian League – led to a renamed club and as Collier Row & Romford they won the Division 2 championship in their first season. The club reverted to the name Romford the following season, effectively completing a takeover of the old Collier Row club, which disappeared. The club were relegated back to Division 2 in 2000–01 and finished bottom of Division 2 the following year. Ongoing problems with their Sungate ground caused the club to resign from the Isthmian League and to return to the Essex Senior League, where they remain. In 2002–03, the club moved into the former Ford Sports Ground, Rush Green Road, Romford.
FA competitions: FA Cup second round 1960–61, 1961–62, 1971–72. FA Amateur Cup finalists 1948–49.

Royston Town (1984–1994).

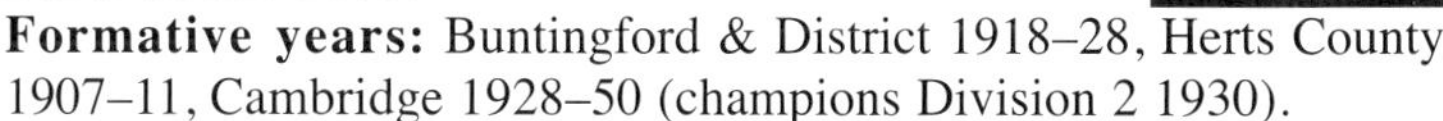

Ground: Garden Walk, Royston, Hertfordshire.
Colours: White shirts Black shorts.
Nickname: The Crows.
Formation: 1875.
Formative years: Buntingford & District 1918–28, Herts County 1907–11, Cambridge 1928–50 (champions Division 2 1930).
Senior leagues: Herts County 1950–59, South Midlands 1959–65, Herts County 1965–77 (champions 1970, 1977) and South Midlands 1977–84 (champions Division 1 1978).
Isthmian era: Elected to Division 2 North in 1984, they remained in that Division until 1991 when, following League re-organisation, they were placed in Division 3. Their best finishing position was seventh, in 1992–93. The club resigned at the end of the 1993–94 season and they returned to the South Midlands League – now Spartan–South Midlands – where they remain.

Ruislip Manor (1984–1996).

Ground: Grosvenor Vale, Off West End Road, Ruislip, Middlesex.
Colours: White shirts Black shorts.
Nickname: The Manor.
Formation: 1938.
Formative years: Uxbridge & District 1938–39, Middlesex County Amateur 1939–40.
Senior leagues: Middlesex Senior 1945–46, London 1946–58, Spartan 1958–65 and Athenian 1965–84 (champions Division 2 1973).
Isthmian era: Elected to Division 2 North in 1984, they remained in that Division until 1991 when, following League re-organisation, they were placed in Division 2. Promotion, as runners-up, to Division 1 followed in 1992–93. Unsatisfactory ground grading marks at their Grosvenor Vale ground in 1996 resulted in the club not being re–elected at that year's AGM – they would, in any case, have been relegated back to Division 2. The club was accepted into the Spartan League for 1996–97 and became members of the Spartan–South Midlands League in 1997 when the two Leagues merged. The club were the inaugural winners of the Associate Members Trophy in 1990–91.

Saffron Walden Town (1984–1996).

Ground: Catons Lane, Saffron Walden, Essex.
Colours: Red & Black striped shirts Black shorts.
Nickname: The Bloods.
Formation: 1872.
Formative years: Haverhill & District 1899–1909 & 1913–14, Stansted & District 1908–14 & 1919–24 (champions 1908, 1909, 1910, 1912, 1921, 1923, 1924), Saffron Walden & District 1911–14, Cambridgeshire 1912–13 & 1920–21, Herts & Essex Border 1925–27 (joint champions 1927), North Essex 1927–28 & 1931–33 and Essex & Suffolk Border 1928–31.
Senior leagues: Spartan 1933–54 (champions Division 2 East 1937), Parthenon 1954–55, Herts County 1955–71, Essex Senior *(f)* 1971–74 (champions 1974) and Eastern Counties 1974–84 (champions 1983).
Isthmian era: Elected to Division 2 North in 1984, they remained in that Division until 1991 when, following League re-organisation, they were placed in Division 2. The club resigned from the League after the 1995–96 season, when they finished 15th, citing increased travelling costs. They were elected the Essex Senior League in 1996, winning the championship in 1999–2000. The club attempted to switch to the Eastern Counties League in 2003 but could not cross the Pyramid, so they opted to be inactive in 2003–04. They were elected to the Eastern Counties League for the 2004–05 season.
FA competitions: FA Cup first round 1876–77.

St. Albans City (1923–2004).

Ground: Clarence Park, York Road, St. Albans, Hertfordshire.
Colours: Yellow & Blue shirts Yellow shorts.
Nickname: The Saints.
Formation: 1908.
Senior leagues: Herts County 1908–11 (champions West Division 1909, 1910), Spartan 1908–20 (champions 1912) and Athenian 1920–23 (champions 1920, 1921).
Isthmian era: The club accepted an invitation to join the Isthmian League in 1923, and won the League championship in their first season, 1923–24. Two further titles followed, in 1926–27 and 1927–28 and they were also runners-up in 1954–55. The club were relegated to what was then Division 2 – now Division 1 – in 1973–74, where they remained until 1982–83, when they suffered a second relegation, although they were promoted back to Division 1 as runners-up the following season. In 1985–86 the club were promoted back to the Premier Division as champions. The club finished as runners-up in 1992–93, but were denied promotion to the Football Conference because of a tree growing out of the terraces at one end of the ground. They remained in the Premier Division until The FA restructuring in 2004, when the club became founder-members of Nationwide South, albeit via the League play–offs, They finished 14th in their first season in Nationwide South. The club were League Cup finalists in 1989–90.
FA competitions: FA Cup second round 1968–69, 1980–81, 1996–97. FA Amateur Cup semi–finalists 1924–25, 1925–26, 1969–70. FA Trophy semi–finalists 1998–99.

Salisbury City (2004–2005).

Ground: The Raymond McEnhill Stadium, Partridge Way, Old Sarum, Salisbury, Wiltshire.
Colours: White shirts Black shorts.
Nickname: The Whites.
Formation: 1947, as Salisbury FC. "City" was added in 1992.
Senior leagues: Western 1947–68 (champions Division 1 1958, 1961; Division 2 1948), Southern 1968–2004 (champions Southern Division 1995).
Isthmian era: The FA's national league restructuring in 2004–05 placed the club in the Isthmian League Premier Division where they finished 14th. Further FA re-organisation saw the club placed back in the Southern League in 2005.
FA competitions: FA Cup second round 1959–60.

Shepherd's Bush (1908–1919).

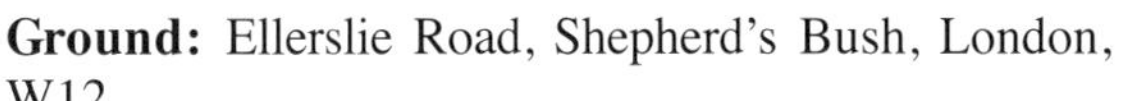

Ground: Ellerslie Road, Shepherd's Bush, London, W12.

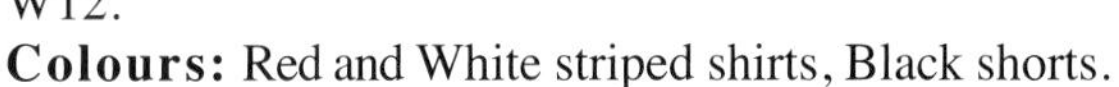

Colours: Red and White striped shirts, Black shorts.
Nickname: The Bushmen.
Formation: 1880; merged with Westminster Criterion in 1892, merged with Darfield in 1895; previously Old St. Stephen's until 1898.
Senior leagues: Southern Alliance 1892–93 (champions 1893), Southern *(f)* 1894–1902, Metropolitan Amateur 1902–06, Great Western Suburban 1906–07 (champions) and Spartan 1907–08 *(f)*.
Isthmian era: Invited to join the Isthmian League in 1908, the club remained members until 1914, when football activities ceased following the outbreak of World War 1. The club usually finished near the bottom of the table and sixth place in 1910–11 was their best position. The club did not return to the League after the Great War. Their stadium is now more commonly known as Loftus Road, the home of Queens Park Rangers FC, who took over tenancy in 1917, initially on a 21–year lease.

Slough Town (1973–1990, 1994–1995 & 1998–2007).

Ground: Windsor & Eton FC, Stag Meadow, St. Leonards Road, Windsor, Berkshire.
Previous grounds: Slough Greyhound Stadium (The Dolphin), Uxbridge Road, Slough, until 1974; Wexham Park Stadium, Wexham Park, Slough, Berkshire, until 2003.
Colours: Amber shirts Navy shorts.
Nickname: The Rebels.
Formation: 1890; previously Slough 1890–1943; a 1943 merger with Slough Centre (formed 1937) resulted in the formation of Slough United, but the clubs separated in June 1947 and the senior club resumed with "Town" added. **Formative years:** Southern Alliance 1892–93 and Berks & Bucks 1902–05. **Senior leagues:** Great Western Suburban 1905–20, Spartan 1920–39, Great Western Combination *(f)* 1939–40 & 1943–45, Corinthian *(f)* 1945–63 (champions 1951) and Athenian 1963–73 (champions Division 1 1965; Premier Division 1968, 1972, 1973). **Isthmian era:** Elected as founder-members of Division 2 (now Division 1) in 1973, they gained promotion as runners-up at the first attempt. They won the Premier Division in 1980–81 and again in 1989–90, the latter time securing promotion to the Football Conference. The club spent four seasons in the Football Conference finishing fifth in 1992–93 but 21st a season later, which resulted in relegation back to the Isthmian League. After one season, the club returned to the Football Conference, finishing as runners-up to champions Enfield – who were denied promotion because they did not meet the financial criteria for admission. Their third season back in the Conference was their most successful of the trio, finishing eighth, but it was their final one too, because the club was voted out of the League due to various financial problems. The club returned to the Isthmian League for a third spell in 1998. They were relegated to Division 1 in 2000–01 and League re-organisation in 2002 saw them placed in Division 1 North. A switch to Division 1 South followed after one season and the club gained promotion back to the Premier Division as the fourth-placed club in 2004. They won the League Cup in 1975–76 and 1980–81 and were runners-up in 1994–95. In 1980–81, they completed a League and League Cup double; in 1994–95, they were runners-up in both competitions.
FA competitions: FA Cup second round 1970–71, 1979–80, 1982–83, 1985–86, 1986–87 and 2004–05. FA Amateur Cup winners 1972–73. FA Trophy semi-finalists 1976–77 and 1997–98.

Southall (1973–2000).

Ground: Yeading FC, The Warren, Beaconsfield Road, Hayes, Middlesex.
Previous grounds: Western Road, Southall, Middlesex until 1992, Harefield United FC, Preston Park, Breakspeare Road North, Harefield, Middlesex 1992–94, Tring Town FC, Pendley Sports Centre, Cow Lane, Tring, Hertfordshire 1994–98.
Colours: Red & Black striped shirts White shorts.
Nickname: The Hall or Fowlers.
Formation: 1871; previously Southall Park 1871–c1880, known as Southall & Ealing Borough 1975–80. **Formative years:** West London 1892–93 and Middlesex 1900–01. **Senior leagues:** Southern 1896–1905, London 1904–05 (champions Division 1 1905), West Middlesex 1906–07 (champions 1907), Great Western Suburban 1907–14 (champions 1913), Metropolitan 1914–15, United Senior 1918–19; Herts & Middlesex 1939–45, and Athenian 1919–73 (champions 1927). **Isthmian era:** Elected to the old Division 2 (now Division 1) as founder-members in 1973, they won promotion to the top flight as runners-up in their second season. The club played in the Premier Division for three seasons, before suffering successive relegations, to Division 1 in 1977–78, and Division 2 a year later. In 1984, following League re-organisation, they were placed in Division 2 South, where they remained until further League re-organisation in 1991 saw the club placed in Division 2. The club was relegated to Division 3 in 1992–93, where they competed until 1999–2000. After finishing bottom of Division 3 in 2000, they were relegated to the Combined Counties League.
FA competitions: FA Cup third round 1935–36. FA Amateur Cup finalists 1924–25. FA Vase finalists 1985–86.

Southwick (1985–1992).

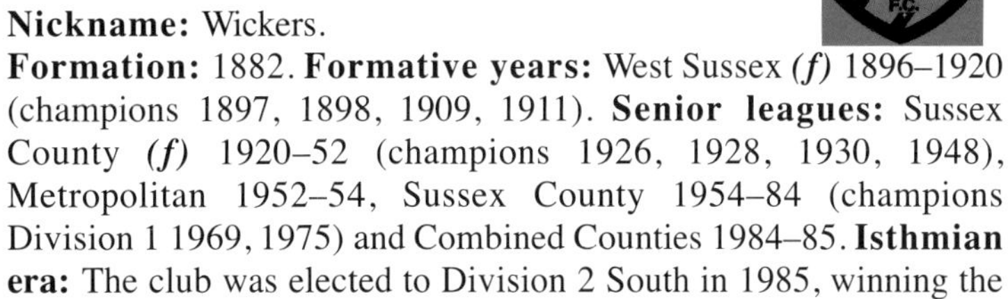

Ground: Old Barn Way, Off Manor Hall Road, Southwick, East Sussex.
Colours: Black & Red shirts Black shorts.
Nickname: Wickers.
Formation: 1882. **Formative years:** West Sussex *(f)* 1896–1920 (champions 1897, 1898, 1909, 1911). **Senior leagues:** Sussex County *(f)* 1920–52 (champions 1926, 1928, 1930, 1948), Metropolitan 1952–54, Sussex County 1954–84 (champions Division 1 1969, 1975) and Combined Counties 1984–85. **Isthmian era:** The club was elected to Division 2 South in 1985, winning the championship at the first attempt. They finished third in Division 1 in 1989–90, but were relegated back to Division 2 South the following year. In their final season the club finished 21st in Division 2 South, but a series of financial problems forced the club to resign from the league. The club was elected back into the Sussex County League.
FA competitions: FA Cup first round 1974–75.

Staines Town (1973–to date).

Grounds: Wheatsheaf Park, Wheatsheaf Lane, Staines, Middlesex. Due to various developments of their stadium, the club have entered into temporary ground-share arrangements with Chertsey Town FC, 1996–98, Walton & Hersham FC, 2001–02, and Egham Town FC, 2002–03.
Colours: Old Gold shirts with Blue trim Blue shorts.
Nickname: The Swans.
Formation: Formed 1892 (merged with St. Peters Institute in 1895); previously Staines FC 1898–1918, Staines Lagonda 1918–25 and Staines Vale 1943–46. **Formative years:** West London (champions 1900, 1901), West Middlesex (1901-1904). **Senior leagues:** Great Western Suburban *(f)* 1904–13, Hounslow & District 1913–20, Great Western Suburban 1920–24, Spartan 1924–35, *inactive 1935–43*, Middlesex Senior/Parthenon 1943–53, Hellenic *(f)* 1953–58, Spartan 1958–71 (champions 1960) and Athenian 1971–73 (champions Division 2 1972). **Isthmian era:** Elected to Division 2 as founder-members in 1973, they won promotion to the Premier Division as champions in their second season. The club had a best finish of fourth in 1981–82 but, in 1983–84, they were relegated to Division 1 because of unsatisfactory ground grading. They won promotion back to the Premier Division as Division 1 champions in 1988–89, but suffered another relegation in 1992–93, this time on League position. A third promotion to the Premier Division followed – as the third-placed club – in 1995–96 but another relegation was just a year away. Following the League's reorganisation in 2002, the club was placed in Division 1 South and they gained promotion to the Premier Division in 2003–04 as sixth-placed club as part of The Football Association restructuring of non-league football. The club were Full Members Cup winners in 1994–95.
FA competitions: FA Cup first round 1984–85.

Stevenage Borough (1984–1994).

Ground: Broadhall Way, Stevenage, Hertfordshire.
Colours: Red & White shirts Red shorts.
Nickname: Boro.
Formation: 1976. **Formative years:** Chiltern Youth 1976–79 and Wallspan Southern Combination 1979–80. **Senior leagues:** United Counties 1980–84 (champions Division 1 1981). **Isthmian era:** Elected to Division 2 North in 1984, the club won promotion to Division 1 as champions in 1985–86. After relegation back to Division 2 North in 1987–88, they won successive promotions, both times as champions, to Division 1 in 1990–91 and the Premier Division a season later. After finishing in seventh position in 1992–93, the club secured the Premier Division championship in 1993–94 and, with it, promotion to the Football Conference. In only their second season in the Football Conference they were crowned champions but the club was not allowed to progress to the Football League because ground improvement work was not completed in time. The club finished third in the Conference in 1998, and in 2004–05 lost to Carlisle United in the Conference Play-off Final.
FA competitions: FA Cup fourth round 1997–98. FA Trophy finalists 2001–02.

Sutton United (1963–1986, 1991–1999 & 2000–2004).

Ground: Borough Sports Ground, Gander Green Lane, Sutton, Surrey.
Colours: Amber & Chocolate shirts Chocolate shorts.
Nickname: The U's.
Formation: 1898, from merger of Sutton Association and Sutton Guild Rovers. **Formative years:** Surrey Junior 1898–1910. **Senior leagues:** Southern Suburban 1910–21 (champions 1910) and Athenian 1921–63 (champions 1928, 1946, 1958). **Isthmian era:** Invited to join the League in 1963, they were runners-up in 1967–68, 1970–71 and 1981–82 and were Champions in 1966–67, 1984–85 and 1985–86, when they won promotion to the Gola League (now Football Conference). In their first season in the Gola League, the club finished in seventh position, their best result. Relegation back to the Isthmian League came in 1990–91. They finished third in 1991–92, 1996–97 and 1997–98, before gaining promotion again to the Football Conference as Premier Division champions in 1998–99. The club finished bottom of the Football Conference in their first season back and returned to the Isthmian League. Three seasons of below mid-table finishes for the club was followed by a runners-up berth in 2004–05. The Football's Association's restructuring of the National Game in 2004 saw them become founder-members of Nationwide South, where they finished 15th in their first season. The club won the League Cup in 1982–83, 1983–84, 1985–86 and 1997–98, lost in the Final in 1979–80 and won the Full Members Cup in 1991–92 and 1995–96.
FA competitions: FA Cup fourth round 1969–70 and 1988–89. FA Amateur Cup finalists 1962–63 and 1968–69. FA Trophy finalists 1980–81.

Thame United (1991–2004).

Ground: Windmill Road, Thame, Oxfordshire.
Colours: Red, Black & White shirts Black shorts.
Nickname: United.
Formation: 1883; previously Thame FC. **Formative years:** Oxfordshire & District (champions 1907, 1908, 1909, 1911). **Senior leagues:** Oxfordshire Senior (champions 1930, 1931, 1955, 1956, 1957), Hellenic 1959–88 (champions Premier Division 1962, 1970) and South Midlands 1988–91 (champions 1991). **Isthmian era:** Elected to Isthmian League Division 3 in 1991 as South Midlands League champions, they gained promotion to Division 2 as runners-up in 1992–93, and to Division 1 as champions in 1994–95. They were relegated back to Division 2 in 1997–98, but won promotion back to Division 1 as the third-placed club the following season. The club just failed to win promotion to the Premier Division in 1999–2000 and, following League re-organisation in 2002, they were placed in Division 1 North. The Football Association's national restructuring in 2004 saw the club placed in Southern League Division 1 West where they finished 11th.

Thurrock (1988–2004).

Ground: Thurrock Hotel, Ship Lane, Aveley, Essex.
Colours: Yellow & Green shirts Green shorts.
Nickname: Fleet.
Formation: 1985; previously Purfleet 1985–2003.
Senior leagues: Essex Senior 1985–88 (champions 1988). **Isthmian era:** Elected to Division 2 North as Essex Senior League champions in 1988, the club won promotion to Division 1 as runners-up in their first season, only to be relegated back to Division 2 North a season later. They were promoted back to Division 1 as champions in 1991–92 and rose to the Premier Division as runners-up in 1993–94. In the Premier Division as Purfleet, the club had a best finishing position of fourth, in both 1998–99 and 1999–2000. The name change to Thurrock in 2003 preceded a best-ever finish of third place. The Football Association's restructuring of the National Game in 2004 saw the club become founder-members of Nationwide South, where they reached the inaugural season play–offs as the third placed club. The club were Full Members Cup finalists in 1999–2000 and 2000–01 and Associate Members Trophy winners in 1991–92.
FA competitions: FA Cup first round 2003–04 and 2004–05.

Tilbury (1973–2004).

Ground: Chadfields, St. Chads Road, Tilbury, Essex.
Colours: Black & White striped shirts Black shorts.
Nickname: The Dockers.
Formation: 1900.
Formative years: Grays & District 1901–12 (champions 1902, 1903, 1904, 1905, 1906).
Senior leagues: South Essex 1902–12 & 1919–27, *suspended operating 1912–19*, Kent 1927–31, London 1931–39 & 1946–50, Corinthian 1950–57, London 1957–62 (champions 1959, 1960, 1961, 1962), Delphian 1962–63 and Athenian 1963–73 (champions Division 2 1964; Division 1 1969).
Isthmian era: Elected to what was Division 2 (now Division 1) as founder-members in 1973, they won promotion as champions in 1975–76 and achieved a best ever finish of fifth place in 1976–77. The club were relegated to Division 1 in 1979–80 to Division 2 North in 1986–87, where they remained until League re-organisation in 1991. Placed in Division 3, the club won promotion to Division 2 as the third-placed club in their first season, but were relegated back to Division 3 in 1997–98. Promotion back to Division 2 was achieved in 1999–2000, again as the third-placed club. Following further League re-organisation in 2002, the club was placed in Division 1 North. The Football Association's restructuring of non-league football in 2004 saw the club placed in Southern League Division 1 East, but they finished bottom of the table and were relegated to the Essex Senior League for 2005–06. The club won the inaugural League Cup competition in 1974–75.
FA competitions: FA Cup third round 1977–78.

Tonbridge Angels (2004–to date).

Ground: Longmead Stadium, Darenth Avenue, Tonbridge, Kent.
Colours: Blue & White shirts Blue shorts.
Nickname: Angels.
Formation: 1948, as Tonbridge, adding suffix "Angels" in 1994.
Senior leagues: Southern 1948–89 & 1993–2004, Kent 1989–93 (champions 1993).
Isthmian era: National League restructuring by The Football Association in 2004–05 saw the club placed in the Isthmian League Premier Division, but they finished bottom of the table and were relegated to Division 1.
FA competitions: FA Cup first round 1950–51, 1951–52, 1952–53, 1967–68 and 1972–73.

Tooting & Mitcham United (1956–to date).

Ground: Imperial Fields, Bishopsford Road, Morden, Surrey.
Previous ground: Sandy Lane, Mitcham, Surrey, until 2002 *(pictured left)*.
Colours: Black & White striped shirts Black shorts.
Nickname: Terrors.
Formation: 1932, from merger of Tooting Town (formed 1919) and Mitcham Wanderers (formed 1912).
Senior leagues: London 1932–37 and Athenian 1937–56 (champions 1950, 1955).
Isthmian era: Invited to join the Isthmian League in 1956, they won the championship in both 1957–58 and 1959–60. The club suffered relegation to Division 1 in 1988–89 and further relegation to Division 2 in 1996–97, but won promotion back to Division 1, as champions, in 1999–2000. Following League reorganisation in 2002, the club was placed in Division 1 South and, after The Football Association's restructuring of 2004, they became members of the then Division 1. The club won the Full Members Cup in 1992–93.
FA competitions: FA Cup fourth round 1975–76.

Tring Town (1977–2003).

Ground: Pendley Sports Centre, Cow Lane, Tring, Hertfordshire.
Colours: Red shirts with White trim Red shorts.
Nickname: T's.
Formation: 1904; re–constituted 1996.
Senior leagues: Herts County 1904–07, West Herts, Great Western Combination 1948–53 (champions 1951, 1952), Spartan 1953–75 (champions 1968) and Athenian 1975–77.
Isthmian era: Elected as founder-members of then Division 2 (the League's third Division) in 1977, they had a best finishing position of fourth, in 1983–84. Following League re-organisation in 1984 the club was placed in Division 2 North, where they finished third in 1988–89. Further League re-organisation in 1991 saw the club placed in Division 3, where they rarely finished in the top half of the table. Further League re-organisation followed in 2002 saw the club placed in Division 2. Sadly, following a fire at their ground in March 2003 and mounting debts, the club resigned from the Isthmian League two weeks before the start of 2003–04 campaign. Local rivals Tring Athletic from the Spartan–South Midlands League took over the Pendley Sports Centre ground.

Tufnell Park (1919–1950) and Tufnell Park Edmonton (1950–1952).

Ground: Barrass Stadium, Edmonton, London, N18.
Previous Grounds: Tufnell Park Recreation Ground, Tufnell Park, London, N7 until 1945, Hendon FC, Claremont Road, London, NW2, 1945–1947 and Albury Ride, Cheshunt, Hertfordshire 1947–1950.
Colours: Green and White hooped shirts White shorts.
Nickname: Tuffs.
Formation: 1907.
Formative years: North Middlesex 1910–11.
Senior leagues: London 1907–14, Spartan 1910–12 and Athenian *(f)* 1912–14.
Isthmian era: Invited to join the Isthmian League after the Great War, they finished third in 1919–20, 1920–21 and 1937–38. After World War II, the club struggled and finished bottom in 1948–49 and 1949–50. The club lost their Albury Ride ground in 1950 and subsequently merged with Edmonton Borough (formed 1947) who had been members of the London League. The merged club – *Tufnell Park Edmonton* – remained in the league for only two seasons, finishing bottom on both occasions. The club failed in its bid for re-election in 1952 and became members of the Spartan League 1952–54, Delphian League 1954–63 (champions 1963, having dropped Tufnell Park from the club name in 1960) and Athenian League 1963–84. In 1973, when the club lost the use of their home ground, they merged with Haringey Borough (previously Wood Green Town) to form Edmonton & Haringey playing their home matches at Coles Park, White Hart Lane.
FA competitions: FA Amateur Cup finalists 1919–20.

Tunbridge Wells (1911–1913).

Ground: Charity Farm, Ferndale, Tunbridge Wells, Kent.
Colours: Light and Dark Blue halves shirts.
Nickname: Two Blues or Wells.
Formation: 1886.
Senior leagues: South Eastern 1905–07 and Southern Amateur 1908–11 (Champions Section 'B' 1910).
Isthmian era: Invited to join the Isthmian League in 1911, the club finished bottom in its first season and one off the bottom a season later. They failed to get re-elected to the Isthmian League, mainly due to the poor state of their ground. The club were elected to the Spartan League for 1913–14, where they finished 11th of 12 clubs in their only season. The club were to have played in the Southern Suburban League in 1914-1915 season but activity ceased during the Great War and the club subsequently disbanded.

Uxbridge (1982–2004).

Ground: Honeycroft, Horton Road, West Drayton, Middlesex.
Previous ground: Honeycroft, Cleveland Road, Uxbridge, Middlesex, 1948–78.
Colours: Red shirts White shorts.
Nickname: The Reds.
Formation: 1871; merged in 1886 with Uxbridge Crescents (formed 1880); previously Uxbridge Town 1919–46.
Senior leagues: Southern *(f)* 1894–99, Great Western Suburban *(f)* 1904–24, Athenian 1919–20, Athenian 1924–37, Spartan 1937–38, London 1938–46, Great Western Combination *(f)* 1939–45, Corinthian 1946–63 (champions 1960) and Athenian 1963–82.
Isthmian era: Elected to Division 2 after finishing third in the Athenian League in 1982, they were placed in Division 2 South as a result of League re-organisation in 1984. The club won promotion to Division 1 as runners-up in 1984–85 and remained at the second level of the Isthmian League thereafter, with a fifth-place finish in 1997–98 being their best position. In 2002, further League re-organisation placed the club in Division 1 North. The Football Association's national restructuring in 2004 saw the club placed in Southern League Division 1 East, where they reached the play–offs in their first season. The club were League Cup finalists in 1985–86.
FA competitions: FA Cup second round 1873–74. FA Amateur Cup finalists 1897–98.

Vauxhall Motors (1985–1991).

Ground: Brache Estate, Park Street, Luton, Bedfordshire.
Colours: Yellow shirts Blue shorts.
Nickname: Motors.
Formation: 1907; Previously Luton Vauxhall 1907–31.
Formative years: Beds & District 1923–28.
Senior leagues: South Midlands 1931–38 (champions Division 1 1932, 1934, 1937, 1938), Spartan 1938–74 (champions 1961, 1969), United Counties 1974–79 and South Midlands 1979–84.
Isthmian era: Elected to Division 2 North in 1985, they remained in that Division until their last season, 1990–91, when they finished runners-up to Stevenage Borough. The club – a works team playing on the company's site – was forced to resign from the Isthmian League as a result of the company's decision to lay a plastic pitch at their ground. At that time few leagues sanctioned matches on synthetic surfaces and the club did not play in 1991–92.
FA competitions: FA Cup first round 1947–48.

Waltham Forest (1995–2004).

Ground: Wadham Lodge Sports Ground, Kitchener Road, Walthamstow, London, E17.
Colours: White shirts Black shorts.
Nickname: The Stags.
Formation: 1995; Previously Leyton Pennant 1995–2003 (Leyton Pennant was itself the result of a number of mergers of clubs dating back to the 1960s).
Isthmian era: The club was elected to the League as members of Division 1 in 1995, where they stayed until relegated to Division 2 in 1999–2000. Following League re-organisation in 2002 they were placed in Division 1 North. The FA restructuring of Non-League football in 2004 saw the club placed in Southern League Division 1 East, where they finished ninth.

Walthamstow Avenue (1939–1988).

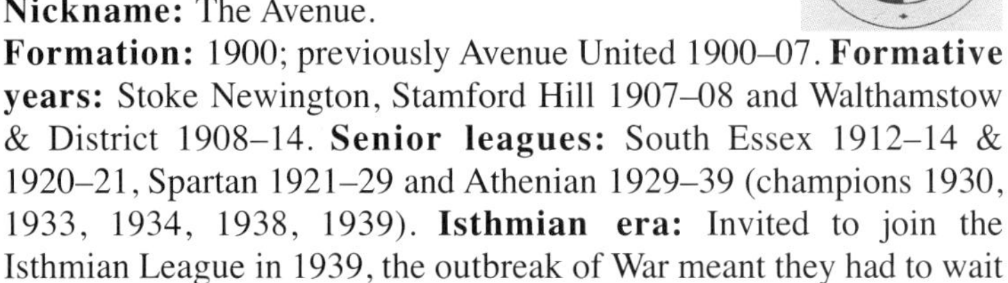

Ground: Green Pond Road, Higham Hill Road, Walthamstow, London, E17.
Colours: Light & Dark Blue shirts Blue shorts.
Nickname: The Avenue.
Formation: 1900; previously Avenue United 1900–07. **Formative years:** Stoke Newington, Stamford Hill 1907–08 and Walthamstow & District 1908–14. **Senior leagues:** South Essex 1912–14 & 1920–21, Spartan 1921–29 and Athenian 1929–39 (champions 1930, 1933, 1934, 1938, 1939). **Isthmian era:** Invited to join the Isthmian League in 1939, the outbreak of War meant they had to wait until 1945 before playing their first competitive match, but they went on to be crowned champions in their first season, 1945–46. More championships came in 1952–53 and 1954–55, while runners-up berths were achieved in 1948–49, 1950–51, 1953–54, 1960–61, 1966–67 and 1979–80. The club were relegated to Division 1 in 1986–87 and, in their final playing season, they finished 15th. In 1988 the club was incorporated into Leytonstone–Ilford FC, *see above,* and became Redbridge Forest FC a season later. Their Green Pond Road ground was sold for housing development and the merged club moved to groundshare, and later merge, with Dagenham FC. They were League Cup finalists in 1980–81.
FA competitions: FA Cup fourth round 1952–53. FA Amateur Cup winners 1951–52 and 1960–61.

Walton & Hersham (1971–to date).

Ground: Sports Ground, Stompond Lane, Walton–on–Thames, Surrey.
Colours: Red & White shirts Red shorts.
Nickname: Swans.
Formation: 1945 from merger of Walton–on–Thames (formed 1896) and Hersham (reformed 1926). **Senior leagues:** Corinthian *(f)* 1945–50 (champions 1947, 1948, 1949) and Athenian 1950–71 (champions Premier Division 1969). **Isthmian era:** Invited to join the Isthmian League in 1971, the club finished third in their first season and runners-up in 1973–74. The club were relegated to Division 1 in 1974–75 and remained in that Division until 1993–94, when they were promoted back to the Premier Division as the third-placed club. In 1995–96 they again suffered relegation to Division 1, but promotion was achieved the following season with another third place finish. The yo-yoing continued with a third relegation to Division 1 coming in 1999–2000. The League re-organisation in 2002 saw the club were placed in Division 1 South and in 2004, following The FA restructuring of the National Game, they were put back in Isthmian League Division 1, where they were runners-up in their first season and gained promotion to the Premier Division.
FA competitions: FA Cup second round 1972–73 and 1973–74. FA Amateur Cup winners 1972–73.

Ware (1975–to date).

Ground: Wodson Park, Wadesmill Road, Ware, Hertfordshire.
Previous ground: Buryfield, Park Road, Ware, Hertfordshire until 1995.
Colours: Blue & White striped shirts Blue shorts.
Nickname: The Blues.
Formation: 1892; previously Ware Town 1892–93. **Formative years:** East Herts 1896–1900 & 1902–07 (champions 1898, 1899, 1900, 1903, 1904, 1906, 1907), Middlesex & District 1907–11 (champions 1908) and East Herts 1911–12. **Senior leagues:** Herts County 1908–25 (champions East Division 1909, 1913; Central Division 1910; North & East Division 1922), Spartan 1925–55 (champions Division 2 B 1927; Division 1 1952; Premier Division 1953), Delphian 1955–63 and Athenian 1963–75. **Isthmian era:** Elected to the old Division 2 (now Division 1) in 1975, they remained at that level until 1981–82, when they were relegated to Division 2. Following League re-organisation in 1984, the club was switched to Division 2 North, with a best finish of fourth place in 1990–91. Further League re-organisation in 1991 saw the club placed in Division 2, but relegation to Division 3 in 1996–97 followed. This level was re-titled Division 2 in 2002 following more League re-organisation.

Wealdstone (1964–1971 & 1995–to date).

Ground: Edgware Town FC, White Lion Ground, High Street, Edgware, Middlesex (moving to Northwood FC, Chestnut Avenue, Northwood, Middlesex, for 2005–06 season).
Previous grounds: Lower Mead Stadium, Station Road, Harrow, until 1991 (groundshared with Watford 1991–93, Yeading 1993–95).
Colours: Blue & White shirts Blue or White shorts.
Nickname: Stones.
Formation: 1908. **Formative years:** Wealdstone & District 1908–13 (champions 1913). **Senior leagues:** London 1911–22 (champions Division 2 1913), Middlesex & District (champions 1921, 1922) 1913–22, Spartan 1922–28 and Athenian 1928–64 (champions 1952). **Isthmian era:** Invited to join the Isthmian League in 1964, they spent seven seasons as members, with a best position of fifth, in 1968–69. The club opted to turn professional in 1971 and election to the Southern League followed. The club won the First Division South title in 1973–74 and became founder-members of the Alliance Premier League (now Football Conference) in 1979, although they were relegated back to the Southern League in 1980–81. One season later, the club completed the Southern League and Cup double in 1981–82, to return to the Alliance Premier League (now Football Conference). The club won this title in 1984–85, but suffered relegation back to the Southern League in 1987–88. After selling their Lower Mead stadium for redevelopment in 1991, the club suffered financial hardships and applied to return to the Isthmian League in 1995. The club were accepted into the League, but placed in Division 3. This championship was claimed in their second season back in the Isthmian fold and promotion to Division 1 followed a season later, as the third-placed club. What would have been a third consecutive promotion, to the Premier Division (again, after finishing third), was denied because work on the ground had not been completed in time. Following League re-organisation in 2002, the club was placed in Division 1 North and The FA's restructuring in 2004 saw the club promoted to the Premier Division, albeit by winning a play-off after finishing seventh. They were Associate Members Trophy finalists in 1996–97.
FA competitions: FA Cup third round 1977–78. FA Amateur Cup winners 1965–66. FA Trophy winners 1984–85.

Wembley (1975–2006).

Ground: Vale Farm, Watford Road, Sudbury, Wembley.
Colours: Red & White shirts Red shorts.
Nickname: Lions.
Formation: 1946 Merger of Sudbury Ratepayers Association and Sudbury Rangers. **Senior leagues:** Middlesex 1946–49 (champions 1948), Spartan 1949–51 (champions Division 1 West 1951), Delphian *(f)* 1951–56, Corinthian 1956–63 and Athenian 1963–75. **Isthmian era:** Elected to the old Division 2 (now Division 1) in 1975, they remained at that level until 1995–96 – with third place in 1985–86 being their best finish – when they were relegated to Division 2. They won promotion back to Division 1 as the third-placed club the following season, but were again relegated to Division 2 in 1998–99. Following League re–organisation in 2002, the club were placed in Division 1 North, but they were relegated to Division 2 in 2002–03 following a play–off defeat against Metropolitan Police.
FA competitions: FA Cup first round 1980–81.

West Norwood (1907–1923).

Grounds: Gorringe Park, Streatham Road, off Mitcham Lane.
Previous Grounds: London County Athletic Ground, Herne Hill until 1914 *(pictured left)*.
Colours: Dark Blue and White hooped shirts.
Nickname: The Bantams.
Formation: 1887; previously Stanley FC 1887–88 and Novices 1888–89 amalgamating with Herne Hill in 1893. **Formative years:** Clapham, South London (champions Division 2 1894). **Senior leagues:** South Suburban 1897–98, London 1900–01, Southern Suburban 1902–07 and Spartan *(f)* 1907–08. **Isthmian era:** Invited to join the Isthmian League in 1907, the club very rarely finished above the bottom three. The club failed to get re-elected at the AGM in 1923, so the club rejoined the London League for 1923–24, but switched to the Athenian League, where they remained until 1927. Once more, the club failed to be re-elected and was replaced by Leyton FC. They joined the Surrey Senior League and were members of that competition from 1927 to 1939 except for the 1936–37 season, when they returned to the London League while sharing Streatham Town's ground. The club did not re–appear after World War 2.

The Bantams

Whyteleafe (1984–to date).

Ground: Church Road, Whyteleafe, Surrey.
Colours: Green & White shirts White shorts.
Nickname: The Leafe.
Formation: 1946.
Formative years: Caterham & Edenbridge, Croydon, Thornton Heath & District (champions 1952) and Surrey Intermediate 1954–58 (champions Division 1 1956).
Senior leagues: Surrey Senior 1958–75 (champions 1969), London–Spartan *(f)* 1975–81 and Athenian 1981–84.
Isthmian era: Elected to Division 2 South in 1984, they won promotion to Division 1 as runners-up in 1988–89, but rarely finished above mid-table, seventh being their best position in 1999–2000. Following League re-organisation in 2002, the club were placed in Division 1 South, but returned to Division 1 for 2004–05 as a result of The FA restructuring of Non-League football, finishing ninth.
FA competitions: FA Cup first round 1999–2000.

Willesden (1977–1981).

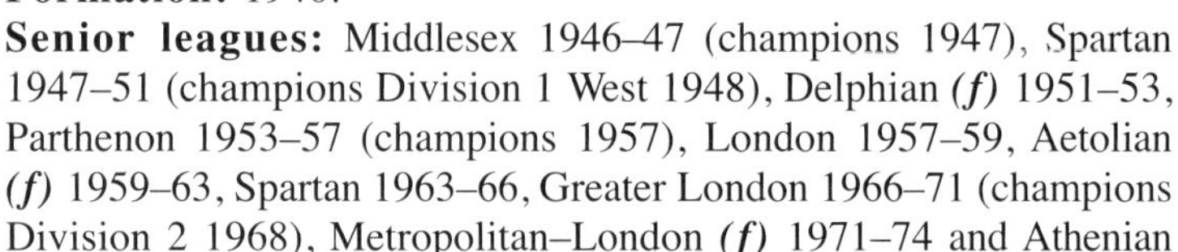

Ground: Willesden Stadium, Donnington Road, London NW10.
Colours: Red shirts and shorts. .
Nickname: None.
Formation: 1946.
Senior leagues: Middlesex 1946–47 (champions 1947), Spartan 1947–51 (champions Division 1 West 1948), Delphian *(f)* 1951–53, Parthenon 1953–57 (champions 1957), London 1957–59, Aetolian *(f)* 1959–63, Spartan 1963–66, Greater London 1966–71 (champions Division 2 1968), Metropolitan–London *(f)* 1971–74 and Athenian 1974–77. **Isthmian era:** Elected as founder-members of Division 2 (the third division) in 1977, they remained there for four years finishing in the lower half of the table on each occasion. The club resigned in 1981 when they lost the use of their ground and subsequently folded.

Wimbledon (1921–1964).

Ground: Plough Lane, Durnsford Road, Wimbledon, London, SW19, 1899–1991.
Colours: Royal Blue shirts and shorts. .
Nickname: The Dons.
Formation: 1889; Previously Wimbledon Old Centrals 1889–1905.
Formative years: South London 1894–95 (champions 1895), Clapham 1895–1904 (champions 1896, 1900), Southern Suburban 1902–08 and West Surrey 1908–09.
Senior leagues: Spartan 1909–10, *Inactive 1910–12*, Southern Suburban 1912–14, Mid–Surrey 1914–15 and Athenian 1919–21.
Isthmian era: Invited to join the Isthmian league in 1921, they were League champions on eight occasions, 1930–31, 1931–32, 1934–35, 1935–36, 1958–59, 1961–62, 1962–63 and 1963–64, finishing as runners-up in 1949–50 and 1951–52. The club opted to turn professional in 1964, resigned from the Isthmian League and were elected to the Southern League, being placed in Division One. They clinched promotion at the first attempt and won three successive Southern League championships between 1975 and 1977. This success earned them election to the Football League in 1977, replacing Workington. The club bounced between Divisions 4 and 3 for half a dozen years before starting a dramatic rise up football's hierarchy, including promotions in three seasons out of four, which saw them in Division 1 in 1986. The club won The FA Cup in 1988, and became founder members of The FA Premier League in 1992. The club left their Plough Lane home in 1991 and shared with Crystal Palace FC until 2004. In 2000 they were relegated to Football League Division 1 and, in 2004, the season they were relegated to the new League 1 (third tier of England football), the club moved to Milton Keynes and now play under the name of MK Dons.
FA competitions: FA Cup winners 1987–88. FA Amateur Cup winners 1962–63.

Windsor & Eton (1981–2004).

Ground: Stag Meadow, St. Leonards Road, Windsor, Berkshire.
Colours: Red shirts and shorts with Green trim.
Nickname: The Royalists.
Formation: 1892 from merger of Windsor Phoenix and Windsor St. Albans. The club later merged with Windsor Victoria in 1893.
Formative years: Southern Alliance 1892–93.
Senior leagues: Southern 1895–96 withdrew after one match, West Berkshire 1903–04, Great Western Suburban *(f)* 1904–22, Athenian 1922–29, Spartan 1929–39 (champions Division 1 1931), Great Western Suburban *(f)* 1939–45, Corinthian *(f)* 1945–50, Metropolitan 1950–60, Delphian 1960–63 and Athenian 1963–81 (champions 1980, 1981).
Isthmian era: Promoted to Isthmian League Division 2 as Athenian League champions in 1981, they gained successive promotions to Division 1 as runners-up in 1982–83 and the Premier Division as champions in 1983–84. After a best finishing position of fifth, in 1984–85, their fall was as steep as their rise, suffering three successive relegations – from the Premier Division to Division 3 – between 1992–93 and 1994–95. They won promotion back to Division 2 as the third-placed club in 1995–96 and, in 2000–01, were promoted to Division 1 as runners-up. Following League re-organisation in 2002, the club was placed in Division 1 South and promotion to the Premier Division was achieved in 2003–04 as the third-placed club. The club were Associate Members Trophy finalists in 1998–99.
FA competitions: FA Cup second round 1983–84. FA Vase semi-finalists 1980–81.

Wingate & Finchley (1995–2004).

Ground: The Abrahams Stadium, Summers Lane, Finchley, London, N12.
Colours: Royal Blue & White striped shirts White shorts.
Nickname: The Blues.
Formation: 1991, from merger of Wingate FC (formed 1946) and Finchley FC (formed 1874).
Senior leagues: South Midlands 1991–95.
Isthmian era: Promoted to Isthmian League Division 3 as runners-up of the South Midlands League in 1995, they won promotion to Division 2 as runners-up in 1998–99, only to drop back into Division 3 the following year. League re-organisation in 2002 saw the club promoted as the seventh-placed club to Division 1 North. Following The FA's restructuring of non-league football in 2004, the club was placed in Southern League Division 1 East, where they finished 12th in their first season.

Witham Town (1987–to date).

Ground: Spa Road, Witham, Essex.
Colours: White shirts and shorts.
Nickname: The Town.
Formation: 1947.
Formative years: Chelmsford & Mid–Essex 1947–58 (champions Division 2 1949) and Essex & Suffolk Border 1958–71.
Senior leagues: Essex Senior *(f)* 1971–87 (champions 1972, 1986).
Isthmian era: The club was elected into Division 2 North in 1987 and they achieved their best finish to date – sixth place in 1990–91 which guaranteed the club a place in Division 2 following League re-organisation that year. The club was relegated to Division 3 in 1999–2000 and following further League re-organisation in 2002 competed in Division 2.

Wivenhoe Town (1986–2004).

Ground: Broad Lane, Elmstead Road, Wivenhoe, Colchester, Essex.
Colours: Blue shirts White shorts.
Nickname: The Dragons.
Formation: 1925; previously Wivenhoe Rangers 1925–75. **Formative years:** Brightlingsea & District 1927–50 (champions 1936, 1937, 1948), Colchester & East Essex 1950–71 (champions Premier Division 1953, 1956; Division 1 1960, 1970), Essex & Suffolk Border 1971–79 (champions Division 2 1972; Division 1 1973; Premier Division 1979). **Senior leagues:** Essex Senior 1979–86. **Isthmian era:** The club were elected into Division 2 North in 1986, promoted as champions to Division 1 in 1987–88 and the Premier Division in 1989–90, again as champions. In 1993–94 and 1994–95, the club suffered successive relegations to Divisions 1 and Division 2. Following League re-organisation in 2002, the club was placed in Division 1 North. The FA's restructuring in 2004 saw them put in Southern League Division 1 East, where they reached the play–offs finishing fifth.

Woking (1911–1992).

Grounds: Kingfield Stadium, Woking, Surrey.
Previous grounds: Pembroke Road, Woking, Surrey 1911–14, Hobbs Field, Kingfield, Woking, Surrey 1919–23.
Colours: Red shirts with White trim White shorts.
Nickname: The Cardinals.

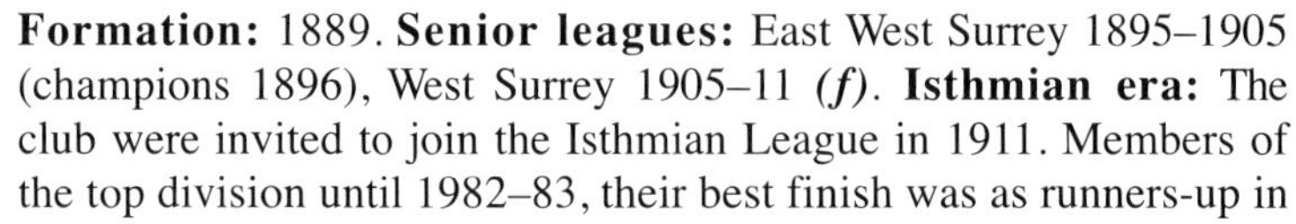

Formation: 1889. **Senior leagues:** East West Surrey 1895–1905 (champions 1896), West Surrey 1905–11 *(f)*. **Isthmian era:** The club were invited to join the Isthmian League in 1911. Members of the top division until 1982–83, their best finish was as runners-up in 1956–57. Following the 1983 relegation to Division 1, they went down again in 1985–86, dropping into Division 2 South. After finishing third in 1985–86, they were Division 2 South champions the following season, and were promoted back to the Premier Division in 1989–90 as runners-up. The club finished fourth in 1990–91 and secured the Premier Division championship in 1991–92, as well as promotion to the Football Conference. The club finished runners-up in the Football Conference in 1994–95 and 1995–96 and remain members of that competition. They were League Cup winners in 1990–91 and Full Members Cup finalists in 1991–92.
FA competitions: FA Cup fourth round 1990–91. FA Amateur Cup winners 1957–58. FA Trophy winners 1993–94, 1994–95 and 1996–97.

Wokingham Town (1973–2004).

Grounds: Egham Town FC, Runnymede Stadium, Tempest Road, Egham, Surrey.
Previous grounds: Finchampstead Road, Wokingham, Berkshire until 1999, Windsor & Eton FC, Stag Meadow, St. Leonards Road, Windsor, Berkshire 1999–2002, and Flackwell Heath FC, Wilks Park, Magpie Lane, Flackwell Heath, Buckinghamshire 2002–03.
Colours: Amber & Black shirts Black shorts.
Nickname: The Town or Satsumas.
Formation: 1875. **Formative years:** Ascot & District (champions 1911), Reading Temperance 1919–51 and Great Western Combination 1951–54 (champions 1954). **Senior leagues:** Metropolitan 1954–57, Delphian 1957–59, Corinthian 1959–63 and Athenian 1963–73. **Isthmian era:** Elected to Division 2 as founder-members in 1973, the club finished bottom in their first season. They were Division 1 champions in 1981–82, gaining promotion to the Premier Division, and finished as runners-up in 1989–90. The club then suffered three relegations to Division 1 in 1994–95, Division 2 in 1997–98 and Division 3 in 2000–01. During this spell, in 1999, the club sold its Finchampstead Road ground for redevelopment to ease crippling debts. Following League re-organisation in 2002, the club were placed in Division 2. They resigned from the League at the end of the 2003–04 season, opting to merge with Embrook FC and play in the Hellenic League for 2004–05. The club were Full Members Cup finalists in 1993–94.
FA competitions: FA Cup first round 1976–77 and 1982–83. FA Trophy semi-finalists 1987–88.

Wolverton Town (1984–1989).

Ground: The Park, Old Wolverton Road, Wolverton, Milton Keynes, Buckinghamshire. **Colours:** Green & White shirts, White shorts. **Nickname:** Wolves. **Formation:** 1890; reconstituted 1902; previously Wolverton L & NW Railway 1891–1900 and Wolverton Town & BR 1949–81. **Senior leagues:** Acott 1904–07 (champions 1905, 1907), Southern 1895–1900 (champions Division 2 1896), Northants 1902–04, 1907–14 & 1921–33 (champions 1914), North Bucks 1919–21 & 1945–46, South Midlands 1933–39 (champions Division 1 1939), Spartan 1946–61, United Counties 1961–82, London–Spartan 1982–83 and Athenian 1983–84. **Isthmian era:** Elected to Division 2 North in 1984, they gained promotion to Division 1 as runners-up in 1986–87, only to suffer relegation back to Division 2 North the following year. In their final season the club name was slightly changed – to Wolverton Town (Milton Keynes) – but they finished bottom of Division 2 North, were deducted nine points due to player irregularities and subsequently were not re–elected at the AGM. The club returned to compete in the South Midlands League for the 1989–90 season, under the title of Milton Keynes Wolverton Town. As Wolverton AFC, the following season, they were Premier Division runners-up, but the club folded midway through the 1991–92 campaign.

Worthing (1977–to date).

Ground: Woodside Road, Worthing, West Sussex. **Colours:** Red shirts and shorts with White trim. **Nickname:** The Rebels. **Formation:** 1886. **Formative years:** West Sussex *(f)* 1896–1904 (champions 1899, 1904, 1907, 1908, 1910, 1913, 1914), *Friendlies 1904–05*, West Sussex 1905–1920 and Brighton, Hove & District 1919–20. **Senior leagues:** Sussex County *(f)* 1920–48 (champions 1921, 1922, 1927, 1929, 1931, 1934, 1939, 1940), Corinthian 1948–63 and Athenian 1963–77. **Isthmian era:** Elected as founder members of Division 2 (the third level) in 1977, the club gained successive promotions as champions, to Division 1 in 1981–82, and the Premier Division in 1982–83. They were Premier Division runners-up in 1983–84 and 1984–85, but were relegated back to Division 1 in 1986–87 and down to Division 2 in 1990–91. The club bounced back to the Premier Division quickly, as Division 2 champions in 1992–93 and Division 1 runners-up in 1994–95. After one season, the club was relegated back to Division 1 and, following League re-organisation in 2002, was placed in Division 1 South, from where they won promotion to the Premier Division as runners-up in 2003–04. They were Full Members Cup finalists in 1998–99.
FA competitions: FA Cup second round 1982–83.

Wycombe Wanderers (1921–1985 & 1986–1987).

Ground: Adams Park, Hillbottom Road, Sands, High Wycombe, Buckinghamshire. **Former Ground:** Loakes Park, Queen Alexandra Road, High Wycombe, Buckinghamshire. **Colours:** Dark Blue & Sky Blue shirts Dark Blue shorts. **Nickname:** The Chairboys. **Formation:** 1887. **Senior leagues:** Southern 1896–1908, Berks & Bucks Senior 1901–03, Great Western Suburban 1908–20 and Spartan 1914–21 (champions 1920, 1921), Great Western Combination *(f)* 1939–45 (champions 1945). **Isthmian era:** Invited to join the Isthmian League in 1921, the club won back–to–back championships on three occasions in 1955–56 and 1956–57, 1970–71 and 1971–72, and 1973–74 and 1974–75, as well as finishing as runners-up in 1957–58, 1959–60, 1969–70, 1975–76 and 1976–77. After finishing third in the Premier Division in 1984–85, they were promoted to the Gola League (now Football Conference), but finished 20th and were relegated back to the Isthmian League after just one season. The following season, the club won the Premier Division title and earned an immediate return to the Football Conference. The club won the Football Conference championship in 1992–93, gaining with it promotion to the Football League. Promotion to Football League Division 2 followed in 1993–94, via play–offs. The club won the Isthmian League Cup in 1984–85, having been finalists in both 1982–83 and 1983–84.
FA competitions: FA Cup semi–finalists 2000–01. FA Amateur Cup winners 1930–31. FA Trophy winners 1990–91 and 1992–93.

Yeading (1987–2005).

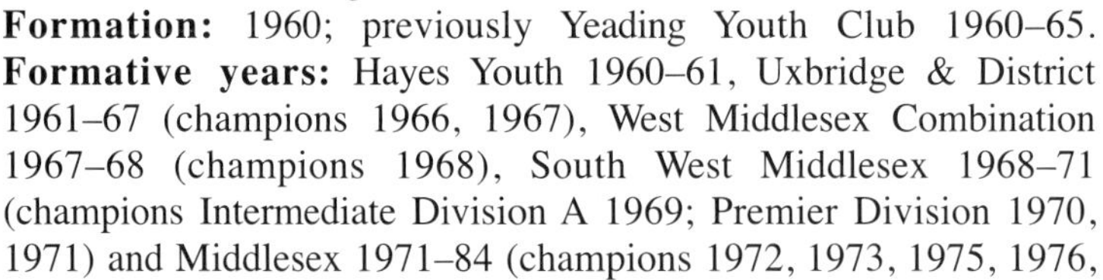

Ground: The Warren, Beaconsfield Road, Hayes, Middlesex.
Colours: Red & Black striped shirts Black shorts.
Nickname: The Ding.
Formation: 1960; previously Yeading Youth Club 1960–65. **Formative years:** Hayes Youth 1960–61, Uxbridge & District 1961–67 (champions 1966, 1967), West Middlesex Combination 1967–68 (champions 1968), South West Middlesex 1968–71 (champions Intermediate Division A 1969; Premier Division 1970, 1971) and Middlesex 1971–84 (champions 1972, 1973, 1975, 1976, 1982, 1984). **Senior leagues:** London–Spartan 1984–87 (champions 1987). **Isthmian era:** The club won promotion to Isthmian League Division 2 South as London–Spartan League champions in 1987, and won their Division championship in 1989–90. A season after finishing third in Division 1 they were promoted as runners-up to the Premier Division in 1991–92. They spent six years in the Premier Division with sixth place in 1996–97 being their highest. The club suffered relegation to Division 1 in 1997–98 and, following League re-organisation in 2002, were placed in Division 1 North where they were champions in 2003–04. The club's most successful year was in 2004–05, when they became league champions and earned promotion to the Football Conference South. The club were League Cup winners in 2002–03.
FA competitions: FA Cup third round 2004–05. FA Vase winners 1989–90.

Yeovil Town (1985–1988 & 1995–1997).

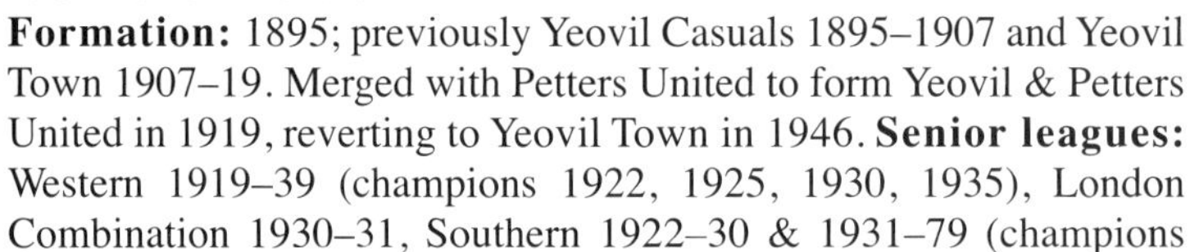

Ground: Huish Park, Lufton Way, Yeovil, Somerset.
Previous ground: Huish Sports Ground, Yeovil, Somerset until 1990.
Colours: Green & White shirts White shorts.
Nickname: Glovers.
Formation: 1895; previously Yeovil Casuals 1895–1907 and Yeovil Town 1907–19. Merged with Petters United to form Yeovil & Petters United in 1919, reverting to Yeovil Town in 1946. **Senior leagues:** Western 1919–39 (champions 1922, 1925, 1930, 1935), London Combination 1930–31, Southern 1922–30 & 1931–79 (champions 1955, 1964, 1971) and Alliance Premier League/Football Conference 1979–85. **Isthmian era:** Relegated from the Gola League to the Isthmian League in 1984–85, the club finished runners-up in both 1985–86 and 1986–87 before securing the championship in 1987–88, gaining automatic promotion to the Football Conference. They spent seven seasons in the Football Conference, with fourth being their best position in 1992–93, before suffering another relegation – as the bottom club – back to the Isthmian League in 1994–95. The championship was clinched at the second time of asking, in 1996–97, and promotion to the Football Conference. The club gained promotion to the Football League in 2002–03 after winning the Football Conference championship. In their second season in the Football League, the club gained promotion to League 1 as League 2 champions. They won the Isthmian League Cup in 1987–88.
FA competitions: FA Cup fifth round 1948–49. FA Trophy winners 2001–02.

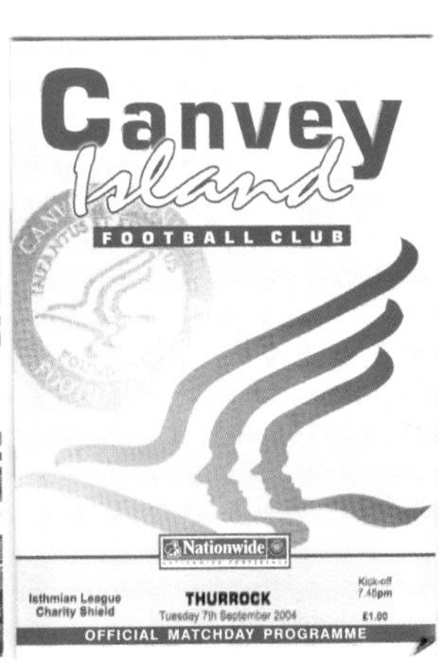

STATISTICS

WINNERS OF CHAMPIONSHIP

SENIOR SECTION

Season	*Champions*	*Runners-up*	*Season*	*Champions*	*Runners-up*
1905-06	London Caledonians	Clapton	1945-46	Walthamstow Avenue	Oxford City
1906-07	Ilford	London Caledonians	1946-47	Leytonstone	Dulwich Hamlet
1907-08	London Caledonians	Clapton	1947-48	Leytonstone	Kingstonian
1908-09	Bromley	Leytonstone	1948-49	Dulwich Hamlet	Walthamstow Avenue
1909-10	Bromley	Clapton	1949-50	Leytonstone	Wimbledon
1910-11	Clapton	Leytonstone	1950-51	Leytonstone	Walthamstow Avenue
1911-12	London Caledonians	Ilford	1951-52	Leytonstone	Wimbledon
1912-13	London Caledonians	Leytonstone	1952-53	Walthamstow Avenue	Bromley
1913-14	London Caledonians	Nunhead	1953-54	Bromley	Walthamstow Avenue
1919-20	Dulwich Hamlet	Nunhead	1954-55	Walthamstow Avenue	St. Albans City
1920-21	Ilford	London Caledonians	1955-56	Wycombe Wanderers	Bromley
1921-22	Ilford	Dulwich Hamlet	1956-57	Wycombe Wanderers	Woking
1922-23	Clapton	Nunhead	1957-58	Tooting & Mitcham United	Wycombe Wanderers
1923-24	St. Albans City	Dulwich Hamlet	1958-59	Wimbledon	Dulwich Hamlet
1924-25	London Caledonians	Clapton	1959-60	Tooting & Mitcham United	Wycombe Wanderers
1925-26	Dulwich Hamlet	London Caledonians	1960-61	Bromley	Walthamstow Avenue
1926-27	St. Albans City	Ilford	1961-62	Wimbledon	Leytonstone
1927-28	St. Albans City	London Caledonians	1962-63	Wimbledon	Kingstonian
1928-29	Nunhead	London Caledonians	1963-64	Wimbledon	Hendon
1929-30	Nunhead	Dulwich Hamlet	1964-65	Hendon	Enfield
1930-31	Wimbledon	Dulwich Hamlet	1965-66	Leytonstone	Hendon
1931-32	Wimbledon	Ilford	1966-67	Sutton United	Walthamstow Avenue
1932-33	Dulwich Hamlet	Leytonstone	1967-68	Enfield	Sutton United
1933-34	Kingstonian	Dulwich Hamlet	1968-69	Enfield	Hitchin Town
1934-35	Wimbledon	Oxford City	1969-70	Enfield	Wycombe Wanderers
1935-36	Wimbledon	The Casuals	1970-71	Wycombe Wanderers	Sutton United
1936-37	Kingstonian	Nunhead	1971-72	Wycombe Wanderers	Enfield
1937-38	Leytonstone	Ilford	1972-73	Hendon	Walton & Hersham
1938-39	Leytonstone	Ilford			

RE-TITLED: DIVISION ONE

1973-74	Wycombe Wanderers	Hendon	1975-76	Enfield	Wycombe Wanderers
1974-75	Wycombe Wanderers	Enfield	1976-77	Enfield	Wycombe Wanderers

RE-TITLED: PREMIER DIVISION

1977-78	Enfield	Dagenham	1993-94	Stevenage Borough	Enfield
1978-79	Barking	Dagenham	1994-95	Enfield	Slough Town
1979-80	Enfield	Walthamstow Avenue	1995-96	Hayes	Enfield
1980-81	Slough Town	Enfield	1996-97	Yeovil Town	Enfield
1981-82	Leytonstone & Ilford	Sutton United	1997-98	Kingstonian	Boreham Wood
1982-83	Wycombe Wanderers	Leytonstone-Ilford	1998-99	Sutton United	Aylesbury United
1983-84	Harrow Borough	Worthing	1999-2000	Dagenham & Redbridge	Aldershot Town
1984-85	Sutton United	Worthing	2000-01	Farnborough Town	Canvey Island
1985-86	Sutton United	Yeovil Town	2001-02	Gravesend & Northfleet	Canvey Island
1986-87	Wycombe Wanderers	Yeovil Town	2002-03	Aldershot Town	Canvey Island
1987-88	Yeovil Town	Bromley	2003-04	Canvey Island	Sutton United
1988-89	Leytonstone-Ilford	Farnborough Town	2004-05	Yeading	Billericay Town
1989-90	Slough Town	Wokingham Town	2005-06	Braintree Town	Heybridge Swifts
1990-91	Redbridge Forest	Enfield			
1991-92	Woking	Enfield			
1992-93	Chesham United	St. Albans City			

RESERVE SECTION

Season	*Champions*	*Runners-up*
1919-20	Leytonstone	Ilford
1920-21	Dulwich Hamlet	Leytonstone
1921-22	Wimbledon	Clapton
1922-23	Wimbledon	Dulwich Hamlet
1923-24	Wimbledon	Tufnell Park
1924-25	Wimbledon	Tufnell Park
1925-26	Wimbledon	Dulwich Hamlet
1926-27	Dulwich Hamlet	London Caledonians
1927-28	London Caledonians	Dulwich Hamlet
1928-29	Dulwich Hamlet	Oxford City
1929-30	Dulwich Hamlet	The Casuals
1930-31	Dulwich Hamlet	The Casuals
1931-32	Dulwich Hamlet	The Casuals
1932-33	Dulwich Hamlet	Clapton
1933-34	Kingstonian	Wimbledon
1934-35	Dulwich Hamlet	Woking
1935-36	Leytonstone	Dulwich Hamlet
1936-37	Woking	Dulwich Hamlet
1937-38	Ilford	Wimbledon
1938-39	Ilford	Dulwich Hamlet
1946-47	Wycombe Wanderers	Dulwich Hamlet
1947-48	Wimbledon	Dulwich Hamlet
1948-49	Dulwich Hamlet	St. Albans City
1949-50	Leytonstone	Kingstonian
1950-51	Leytonstone	Wimbledon
1951-52	Leytonstone	Romford
1952-53	Leytonstone	Bromley
1953-54	Walthamstow Ave	Dulwich Hamlet
1954-55	Dulwich Hamlet	Wycombe Wanderers
1955-56	Wycombe Wanderers	Bromley
1956-57	Wycombe Wanderers	Walthamstow Ave
1957-58	Wycombe Wanderers	Tooting & Mitcham U.
1958-59	Walthamstow Ave	Wimbledon
1959-60	Wycombe Wanderers	Corinthian Casuals
1960-61	Wimbledon	St. Albans City
1961-62	Wimbledon	St. Albans City
1962-63	Wimbledon	Walthamstow Ave
1963-64	Ilford	Hendon
1964-65	Hendon	Wealdstone
1965-66	Kingstonian	Sutton United
1966-67	Kingstonian	Sutton United
1967-68	Hendon	Hitchin Town
1968-69	Hendon	Wealdstone
1969-70	Woking	Leytonstone
1970-71	Ilford	Enfield

'A' SECTION

Season	*Champions*	*Runners-up*
1950-51	Walthamstow Avenue	Wycombe Wanderers
1951-52	Romford	Kingstonian
1952-53	Kingstonian	Barking

ISTHMIAN LEAGUE CUP

(1977-85 called Hitachi Cup; 1974-77 called Subsidiary Cup; 1985-91 called AC Delco Cup; 1974-75 open to Division 2 Clubs only)

Season	*Winners*	*Runners-up*	*Venue*	*Score*
1974-75	Tilbury	Croydon	(Two-legs)	3-1
1975-76	Slough Town	Tilbury	Hayes	4-0
1976-77	Hendon	Barking	Harrow	1-0
1977-78	Dagenham	Leatherhead	Dulwich	1-0
1978-79	Enfield	Hayes	Slough	2-1
1979-80	Enfield	Sutton United	Harrow	2-1
1980-81	Slough Town	Walthamstow Avenue	Hayes	4-2
1981-82	Leytonstone-Ilford	Kingstonian	Boreham Wood	2-0
1982-83	Sutton United	Wycombe Wanderers	(Two-legs)	2-1
1983-84	Sutton United	Wycombe Wanderers	(Two-legs)	3-1
1984-85	Wycombe Wanderers	Farnborough Town	(Two-legs)	5-1
1985-86	Sutton United	Uxbridge	Metropolitan Police	3-1
1986-87	Bognor Regis Town	Hendon	Windsor	3-2
1987-88	Yeovil Town	Hayes	Basingstoke	3-1
1988-89	Bishop's Stortford	Farnborough Town	Hayes	1-0
1989-90	Aveley	St. Albans City	Dagenham	3-0
1990-91	Woking	Carshalton Athletic	Kingstonian	2-1
1991-92	Grays Athletic	Enfield	Dagenham	3-1
1992-93	Marlow	Molesey	Aldershot	2-1
1993-94	Chertsey Town	Enfield	Hayes	3-0
1994-95	Aylesbury United	Slough Town	Marlow	1-1 *(7-6 on penalties)*
1995-96	Kingstonian	Aldershot Town	Aldershot	4-1
1996-97	Boreham Wood	Braintree Town	Dagenham	1-0
1997-98	Sutton United	Oxford City	Harrow	6-1
1998-99	Aldershot Town	Boreham Wood	Slough	2-1
1999-2000	Farnborough Town	Maidenhead United	Basingstoke Town	1-0
2000-01	Heybridge Swifts	Croydon	Purfleet	3-0
2001-02	Northwood	Hampton & Richmond Boro'	St. Albans City	3-2
2002-03	Yeading	Canvey Island	Hornchurch	2-0
2003-04	Thurrock	Dunstable Town	Bishop's Stortford	5-1
2004-05	Slough Town	Hampton & Richmond Boro'	Staines Town	3-1
2005-06	Fisher Athletic	Billericay Town	Grays Athletic	4-0

CHAMPIONS v THE REST OF THE LEAGUE

May	1912	London Caledonians	3	The Rest	2
Aug.	1960	Tooting & Mitcham United	2	The Rest	2
Oct.	1961	Bromley	2	The Rest	1
Aug.	1962	Wimbledon	1	The Rest	3
Aug.	1963	Wimbledon	3	The Rest	3
Nov.	1964	Wimbledon	3	The Rest	1
Sept.	1965	Hendon	3	The Rest	2
Aug.	1966	Leytonstone	5	The Rest	1
Oct.	1967	Sutton United	1	The Rest	1
Sept.	1968	Enfield	4	The Rest	1
Apr.	1970	Enfield	1	The Rest	2
Sept.	1970	Enfield	2	The Rest	0
Oct.	1971	Wycombe Wanderers	1	The Rest	3
Oct.	1972	Wycombe Wanderers	2	The Rest	1
Aug.	1973	Hendon	1	The Rest	2
May	1975	Wycombe Wanderers (1973-74 Champions)	4	The Rest	3
Oct.	1975	Wycombe Wanderers	0	The Rest	3
Oct.	1976	Enfield	1	The Rest	1
Oct.	1977	Enfield	1	The Rest	2

RESERVE SECTION TABLES

1919–20 Season

	P	W	D	L	F	A	Pts
1 Dulwich Hamlet	20	18	0	2	71	15	36
2 Oxford City	20	10	5	5	40	41	25
3 Civil Service	20	10	4	6	46	34	24
4 Ilford	20	8	7	5	43	26	23
5 Clapton	20	9	4	7	40	37	22
6 Leytonstone	20	8	5	7	43	47	21
7 London Caledonians	20	7	5	8	28	36	19
8 Tufnell Park	20	5	6	9	45	42	16
9 Nunhead	20	5	3	12	33	50	13
10 West Norwood	20	3	5	12	21	57	11
11 Woking	20	4	2	14	29	63	10

1920–21 Season

	P	W	D	L	F	A	Pts
1 Dulwich Hamlet	20	14	5	1	50	15	33
2 Leytonstone	20	10	4	6	69	52	24
3 Clapton	20	9	4	7	45	44	22
4 Tufnell Park	20	7	7	6	52	36	21
5 London Caledonians	20	8	3	9	35	45	19
6 Woking	20	8	3	9	35	46	19
7 Oxford City	20	7	4	9	45	47	18
8 West Norwood	20	8	2	10	44	51	18
9 Ilford	20	6	4	10	56	57	16
10 Civil Service	20	6	4	10	36	47	16
11 Nunhead	20	6	2	12	36	61	14

1921–22 Season

	P	W	D	L	F	A	Pts
1 Wimbledon	24	14	5	5	62	29	33
2 Clapton	24	14	5	5	55	51	33
3 Leytonstone	24	13	6	5	70	39	32
4 Dulwich Hamlet	24	11	9	4	58	33	31
5 Ilford	24	12	4	8	57	38	31
6 Wycombe Wanderers	24	11	5	8	76	56	27
7 Oxford City	24	11	4	9	44	36	26
8 Civil Service	24	8	7	9	29	33	23
9 Tufnell Park	24	8	4	12	35	56	20
10 Nunhead	24	6	4	14	30	61	16
11 West Norwood	24	5	5	14	30	61	15
12 London Caledonians	24	4	6	14	24	50	14
13 Woking	24	4	6	14	24	61	14

1922–23 Season

	P	W	D	L	F	A	Pts
1 Wimbledon	26	20	4	2	77	27	44
2 Dulwich Hamlet	26	15	5	6	86	32	35
3 Wycombe Wanderers	26	16	1	9	71	47	33
4 Leytonstone	26	14	5	7	57	41	33
5 Ilford	26	11	6	9	56	46	28
6 Woking	26	12	2	12	52	46	26
7 Tufnell Park	26	10	6	10	46	55	26
8 Casuals	26	10	4	12	42	52	24
9 Nunhead	26	9	4	13	50	47	22
10 London Caledonians	26	8	5	13	37	43	21
11 Oxford City	26	7	7	12	44	65	21
12 West Norwood	26	8	3	15	22	52	19
13 Clapton	26	6	5	15	36	68	17
14 Civil Service	26	6	3	17	41	76	15

1923–24 Season

	P	W	D	L	F	A	Pts
1 Wimbledon	26	18	7	1	72	25	43
2 Tufnell Park	26	17	5	4	66	33	39
3 St. Albans City	26	16	5	5	91	40	37
4 Dulwich Hamlet	26	16	5	5	83	37	37
5 Clapton	26	11	6	9	50	48	28
6 Casuals	26	10	6	10	44	38	26
7 Wycombe Wanderers	26	11	4	11	59	67	26
8 Woking	26	10	5	11	48	57	25
9 Ilford	26	10	3	13	48	58	23
10 London Caledonians	26	8	4	14	51	60	20
11 Civil Service	26	9	2	15	45	69	20
12 Nunhead	26	9	1	16	45	69	19
13 Leytonstone	26	5	4	17	42	71	14
14 Oxford City	26	2	3	21	32	104	7

1924–25 Season

	P	W	D	L	F	A	Pts
1 Wimbledon	26	19	4	3	75	23	42
2 Tufnell Park	26	15	5	6	91	45	35
3 St. Albans City	26	16	3	7	73	50	35
4 Ilford	26	14	4	8	84	59	32
5 Dulwich Hamlet	26	15	1	10	60	42	31
6 Wycombe Wanderers	26	12	5	9	82	55	29
7 Leytonstone	26	11	4	11	49	51	26
8 Woking	26	11	3	12	41	43	25
9 Oxford City	26	12	1	13	44	79	25
10 Casuals	26	10	2	14	55	60	22
11 Clapton	26	8	3	15	53	74	19
12 London Caledonians	26	8	2	16	47	71	18
13 Nunhead	26	6	1	19	30	93	13
14 Civil Service	26	4	4	18	32	71	12

1925–26 Season

	P	W	D	L	F	A	Pts
1 Wimbledon	26	19	2	5	103	52	40
2 Dulwich Hamlet	26	19	1	6	110	53	39
3 Ilford	26	15	5	6	90	59	35
4 Casuals	26	14	6	6	58	46	34
5 Wycombe Wanderers	26	14	2	10	90	77	30
6 London Caledonians	26	12	3	11	73	69	27
7 Tufnell Park	26	12	2	12	77	55	26
8 St. Albans City	26	11	4	11	66	58	26
9 Clapton	26	11	4	11	68	77	26
10 Nunhead	26	9	3	14	54	53	21
11 Leytonstone	26	9	2	15	44	91	20
12 Woking	26	7	4	15	55	81	18
13 Oxford City	26	5	3	18	56	84	13
14 Civil Service	26	4	1	21	29	118	9

1926–27 Season

	P	W	D	L	F	A	Pts
1 Dulwich Hamlet	26	19	5	2	107	38	43
2 London Caledonians	26	18	5	3	95	34	41
3 Tufnell Park	26	15	3	8	81	64	33
4 St. Albans City	26	15	2	9	88	72	32
5 Oxford City	26	14	3	9	76	53	31
6 Wimbledon	26	14	3	9	87	69	31
7 Wycombe Wanderers	26	10	4	12	92	89	24
8 Casuals	26	9	5	12	67	76	23
9 Civil Service	26	10	3	13	70	83	23
10 Ilford	26	9	3	14	52	78	21
11 Nunhead	26	9	2	15	58	73	20
12 Leytonstone	26	8	2	16	59	87	18
13 Clapton	26	6	4	16	56	98	16
14 Woking	26	2	4	20	27	101	8

1927–28 Season

	P	W	D	L	F	A	Pts
1 London Caledonians	26	21	4	1	105	39	46
2 Dulwich Hamlet	26	19	1	6	106	42	39
3 Wimbledon	26	16	3	7	72	48	35
4 Wycombe Wanderers	26	13	4	9	84	78	30
5 Tufnell Park	26	12	4	10	74	66	28
6 Ilford	26	13	2	11	62	61	25
7 St. Albans City	26	11	3	12	62	64	25
8 Leytonstone	26	10	3	13	66	71	23
9 Oxford City	26	9	3	14	51	60	21
10 Casuals	26	10	1	15	50	77	21
11 Nunhead	26	7	5	14	60	77	19
12 Clapton	26	7	5	14	53	79	19
13 Civil Service	26	4	7	15	51	90	15
14 Woking	26	7	1	18	43	87	15

1928–29 Season

	P	W	D	L	F	A	Pts
1 Dulwich Hamlet	26	18	4	4	101	37	40
2 Oxford City	26	16	5	5	73	50	37
3 Clapton	26	14	4	8	67	46	32
4 Nunhead	26	13	4	9	63	63	30
5 London Caledonians	26	13	3	10	73	54	29
6 St. Albans City	26	11	5	10	60	61	27
7 Wycombe Wanderers	26	11	5	10	75	77	27
8 Tufnell Park	26	7	9	10	49	57	23
9 Woking	26	10	2	14	68	74	22
10 Wimbledon	26	8	6	12	47	56	22
11 Civil Service	26	9	4	13	52	79	22
12 Leytonstone	26	8	3	15	52	64	19
13 Ilford	26	7	4	15	64	83	18
14 Casuals	26	7	2	17	45	88	16

1929–30 Season

	P	W	D	L	F	A	Pts
1 Dulwich Hamlet	26	17	3	6	86	48	37
2 Casuals	26	17	2	7	75	48	36
3 London Caledonians	26	13	6	7	73	51	32
4 Clapton	26	13	5	8	72	50	31
5 Oxford City	26	15	1	10	68	52	31
6 Kingstonian	26	12	5	9	67	64	29
7 Wimbledon	26	12	3	11	69	63	27
8 St. Albans City	26	11	4	11	67	66	26
9 Tufnell Park	26	12	1	13	58	56	25
10 Woking	26	8	6	12	57	76	22
11 Wycombe Wanderers	26	8	3	15	49	85	19
12 Nunhead	26	7	5	14	36	73	19
13 Leytonstone	26	4	8	14	55	78	16
14 Ilford	26	4	6	16	48	70	14

1930–31 Season

	P	W	D	L	F	A	Pts
1 Dulwich Hamlet	26	20	4	2	107	39	44
2 Casuals	26	16	3	7	74	46	35
3 Wimbledon	26	14	4	8	83	63	32
4 Nunhead	26	14	3	9	78	63	31
5 Oxford City	26	14	1	11	85	63	29
6 St. Albans City	26	10	8	8	63	57	28
7 London Caledonians	26	9	7	10	69	58	25
8 Tufnell Park	26	9	4	13	61	67	22
9 Clapton	26	10	2	14	59	79	22
10 Woking	26	9	4	13	61	87	22
11 Leytonstone	26	10	2	14	47	78	22
12 Ilford	26	8	3	15	69	73	19
13 Kingstonian	26	9	1	16	63	81	19
14 Wycombe Wanderers	26	6	2	18	49	114	14

1931–32 Season

		P	*W*	*D*	*L*	*F*	*A*	*Pts*
1	Dulwich Hamlet	26	17	2	7	124	48	36
2	Casuals	26	16	2	8	84	67	34
3	Wimbledon	26	16	0	10	96	62	32
4	Leytonstone	26	14	3	9	70	50	31
5	Kingstonian	26	13	4	9	66	63	30
6	Tufnell Park	26	12	1	13	60	65	25
7	London Caledonians	26	10	4	12	67	74	24
8	Oxford City	26	10	4	12	73	90	24
9	St. Albans City	26	11	1	14	71	75	23
10	Wycombe Wanderers	26	8	6	12	71	77	22
11	Ilford	26	10	2	14	65	78	22
12	Woking	26	10	2	14	51	85	22
13	Clapton	26	8	4	14	48	77	20
14	Nunhead	26	7	5	14	47	82	19

1932–33 Season

		P	*W*	*D*	*L*	*F*	*A*	*Pts*
1	Dulwich Hamlet	26	16	6	4	92	37	38
2	Clapton	26	14	8	4	57	36	36
3	Wycombe Wanderers	26	13	10	3	66	42	36
4	Kingstonian	26	11	4	11	63	51	26
5	St. Albans City	26	11	4	11	54	49	26
6	Leytonstone	26	11	4	11	57	54	26
7	London Caledonians	26	9	8	9	57	57	26
8	Wimbledon	26	10	6	10	50	52	26
9	Woking	26	10	6	10	48	54	26
10	Oxford City	26	12	2	12	64	78	26
11	Tufnell Park	26	10	5	11	59	61	25
12	Casuals	26	7	5	14	44	83	19
13	Ilford	26	7	4	15	56	70	18
14	Nunhead	26	5	0	21	38	81	10

1933–34 Season

		P	*W*	*D*	*L*	*F*	*A*	*Pts*
1	Kingstonian	26	15	8	3	64	44	38
2	Wimbledon	26	16	2	8	83	61	34
3	London Caledonians	26	11	9	6	56	41	31
4	Dulwich Hamlet	26	13	4	9	78	53	30
5	Ilford	26	11	7	8	77	58	29
6	Nunhead	26	13	2	11	59	50	28
7	Woking	26	11	6	9	59	57	28
8	Oxford City	26	12	4	10	59	61	28
9	Leytonstone	26	11	6	9	56	61	28
10	Wycombe Wanderers	26	10	4	12	57	70	24
11	Casuals	26	9	4	13	63	77	22
12	St. Albans City	26	6	5	15	50	63	17
13	Tufnell Park	26	7	1	18	43	69	15
14	Clapton	26	5	2	19	35	74	12

1934–35 Season

		P	*W*	*D*	*L*	*F*	*A*	*Pts*
1	Dulwich Hamlet	26	20	3	3	90	22	43
2	Woking	26	18	4	4	90	40	40
3	Wimbledon	26	16	5	5	78	43	37
4	Nunhead	26	14	5	7	49	40	33
5	St. Albans City	26	12	4	10	57	57	28
6	Oxford City	26	12	3	11	57	67	27
7	Wycombe Wanderers	26	9	7	10	63	56	25
8	Leytonstone	26	10	4	12	53	60	24
9	Casuals	26	10	4	12	51	60	24
10	Kingstonian	26	8	6	12	51	64	22
11	London Caledonians	26	5	7	14	35	58	17
12	Ilford	26	5	5	16	33	73	15
13	Clapton	26	7	1	18	34	78	15
14	Tufnell Park	26	6	2	18	55	78	14

1935–36 Season

		P	*W*	*D*	*L*	*F*	*A*	*Pts*
1	Leytonstone	26	18	1	7	58	34	37
2	Dulwich Hamlet	26	15	4	7	75	35	34
3	Nunhead	26	15	4	7	59	33	34
4	Wimbledon	26	12	5	9	74	50	29
5	Casuals	26	13	3	10	57	55	29
6	Woking	26	11	7	8	62	61	29
7	Oxford City	26	10	4	12	57	53	24
8	Wycombe Wanderers	26	10	4	12	69	70	24
9	London Caledonians	26	10	4	12	39	55	24
10	St. Albans City	26	9	5	12	34	49	23
11	Ilford	26	9	4	13	60	69	22
12	Clapton	26	8	6	12	45	65	22
13	Kingstonian	26	8	2	16	49	70	18
14	Tufnell Park	26	5	5	16	51	81	15

1936–37 Season

		P	*W*	*D*	*L*	*F*	*A*	*Pts*
1	Woking	26	17	4	5	73	40	38
2	Dulwich Hamlet	26	16	4	6	75	50	36
3	Ilford	26	14	6	6	72	50	34
4	Wimbledon	26	12	7	7	74	58	31
5	Nunhead	26	12	6	8	61	51	30
6	Clapton	26	9	8	9	60	50	26
7	St. Albans City	26	12	2	12	52	65	26
8	Wycombe Wanderers	26	9	7	10	51	61	25
9	Tufnell Park	26	10	4	12	64	70	24
10	Casuals	26	8	5	13	53	65	21
11	Leytonstone	26	7	6	13	47	53	20
12	Kingstonian	26	7	6	13	62	72	20
13	London Caledonians	26	7	6	13	31	49	20
14	Oxford City	26	6	1	19	47	79	13

1937–38 Season

		P	*W*	*D*	*L*	*F*	*A*	*Pts*
1	Ilford	26	17	4	5	72	32	38
2	Wimbledon	26	18	2	6	80	37	38
3	Leytonstone	26	15	4	7	68	49	34
4	Dulwich Hamlet	26	15	2	9	51	36	32
5	Tufnell Park	26	13	4	9	58	53	30
6	St. Albans City	26	12	6	8	47	47	30
7	Kingstonian	26	11	6	9	44	36	28
8	Nunhead	26	11	6	9	44	36	28
9	Woking	26	11	4	11	62	56	26
10	London Caledonians	26	9	3	14	45	60	21
11	Clapton	26	7	6	13	42	54	20
12	Casuals	26	6	6	14	37	60	18
13	Oxford City	26	4	3	19	35	91	11
14	Wycombe Wanderers	26	4	2	20	41	87	10

1938–39 Season

		P	*W*	*D*	*L*	*F*	*A*	*Pts*
1	Ilford	26	22	1	3	89	25	45
2	Dulwich Hamlet	26	19	3	4	74	35	41
3	Woking	26	15	2	9	75	47	32
4	Wimbledon	26	13	5	8	80	44	31
5	Wycombe Wanderers	26	13	4	9	82	78	30
6	Oxford City	26	11	5	10	54	61	27
7	Tufnell Park	26	11	4	11	52	57	26
8	Clapton	26	12	2	12	47	69	26
9	St. Albans City	26	11	3	12	66	56	25
10	Nunhead	26	8	6	12	48	57	22
11	Casuals	26	7	6	13	46	64	20
12	Leytonstone	26	8	3	15	46	68	19
13	Kingstonian	26	7	2	17	66	84	16
14	London Caledonians	26	1	2	23	22	102	4

1946–47 Season

		P	*W*	*D*	*L*	*F*	*A*	*Pts*
1	Leytonstone	26	19	2	5	92	36	40
2	Dulwich Hamlet	26	17	3	6	78	46	37
3	Romford	26	13	8	5	76	52	34
4	Walthamstow Avenue	26	13	4	9	64	37	30
5	Oxford City	26	12	6	8	70	51	30
6	Kingstonian	26	12	4	10	52	57	28
7	Wycombe Wanderers	26	9	8	9	63	62	26
8	Wimbledon	26	10	5	11	68	64	25
9	Ilford	26	7	7	12	66	78	21
10	Tufnell Park	26	8	5	13	45	69	21
11	Woking	26	7	7	12	34	62	21
12	Clapton	26	6	8	12	41	59	20
13	St. Albans City	26	7	5	14	47	79	19
14	Corinthian-Casuals	26	4	4	18	36	80	12

1947–48 Season

		P	*W*	*D*	*L*	*F*	*A*	*Pts*
1	Wimbledon	26	20	2	4	96	44	42
2	Dulwich Hamlet	26	16	4	6	88	49	36
3	Ilford	26	15	6	5	69	55	36
4	Leytonstone	26	15	2	9	74	41	32
5	Wycombe Wanderers	26	13	4	9	81	63	30
6	Walthamstow Avenue	26	12	5	9	78	50	29
7	St. Albans City	26	11	7	8	58	42	29
8	Romford	26	12	4	10	71	50	28
9	Woking	26	11	3	12	58	63	25
10	Kingstonian	26	9	4	13	48	73	22
11	Clapton	26	8	2	16	56	72	18
12	Oxford City	26	8	2	16	46	88	18
13	Corinthian-Casuals	26	7	2	17	46	96	16
14	Tufnell Park	26	1	1	24	31	114	3

1948–49 Season

		P	*W*	*D*	*L*	*F*	*A*	*Pts*
1	Dulwich Hamlet	26	16	4	4	77	39	38
2	St. Albans City	26	16	4	6	61	33	36
3	Leytonstone	26	15	5	6	58	31	35
4	Wimbledon	26	14	6	6	74	45	34
5	Walthamstow Avenue	26	14	3	9	79	44	31
6	Romford	26	12	6	8	53	46	30
7	Woking	26	12	5	9	68	49	25
8	Kingstonian	26	10	1	15	51	74	21
9	Corinthian-Casuals	26	9	3	14	43	82	21
10	Ilford	26	6	7	13	53	65	19
11	Oxford City	26	8	3	15	52	65	19
12	Wycombe Wanderers	26	9	1	16	63	90	19
13	Clapton	26	6	5	15	28	54	17
14	Tufnell Park	26	5	5	16	29	72	15

1949–50 Season

		P	W	D	L	F	A	Pts
1	Leytonstone	26	19	2	5	89	45	40
2	Kingstonian	26	17	3	6	81	47	37
3	Wimbledon	26	16	3	7	71	43	35
4	Walthamstow Avenue	26	15	3	8	73	45	33
5	Dulwich Hamlet	26	14	3	9	76	47	31
6	Romford	26	10	7	9	53	60	27
7	Wycombe Wanderers	26	11	3	12	58	57	25
8	Clapton	26	10	3	13	62	70	23
9	Ilford	26	9	4	13	52	54	22
10	Corinthian-Casuals	26	10	2	14	50	61	22
11	Woking	26	8	5	13	41	63	21
12	Oxford City	26	6	7	13	47	73	19
13	St. Albans City	26	7	2	17	43	79	16
14	Tufnell Park	26	6	1	19	34	86	13

1950–51 Season

		P	W	D	L	F	A	Pts
1	Leytonstone	26	19	5	2	70	33	43
2	Wimbledon	26	18	2	6	69	33	38
3	St. Albans City	26	14	6	6	61	48	34
4	Romford	26	14	5	7	59	48	33
5	Corinthian-Casuals	26	14	4	8	61	43	32
6	Kingstonian	26	12	5	9	55	52	29
7	Walthamstow Avenue	26	10	7	9	57	36	27
8	Wycombe Wanderers	26	12	2	12	64	57	26
9	Woking	26	9	6	11	52	57	24
10	Oxford City	26	7	6	13	45	68	20
11	Dulwich Hamlet	26	8	2	16	48	64	18
12	Clapton	26	6	3	17	37	73	15
13	Ilford	26	6	1	19	39	62	13
14	Tufnell Park Edmonton	26	5	2	19	29	72	12

Tufnell Park amalgamated with Edmonton Borough to form Tufnell Park Edmonton.

1951–52 Season

		P	W	D	L	F	A	Pts
1	Leytonstone	26	18	3	5	73	34	39
2	Romford	26	17	4	5	64	38	38
3	Oxford City	26	17	4	5	79	48	38
4	Wimbledon	26	16	3	7	79	42	35
5	Walthamstow Avenue	26	12	4	10	58	46	28
6	Dulwich Hamlet	26	11	4	11	65	55	26
7	Corinthian-Casuals	26	11	4	11	50	53	26
8	Clapton	26	9	7	10	42	54	25
9	Ilford	26	8	5	13	44	61	21
10	Woking	26	8	5	13	45	70	21
11	Wycombe Wanderers	26	8	4	14	63	78	20
12	St. Albans City	26	8	3	15	42	73	19
13	Kingstonian	26	6	3	17	56	72	15
14	Tufnell Park Edmonton	26	5	3	18	36	72	13

1952–53 Season

		P	W	D	L	F	A	Pts
1	Leytonstone	28	20	2	6	65	27	42
2	Bromley	28	16	6	6	57	35	38
3	Ilford	28	17	1	10	67	44	35
4	Wimbledon	28	15	5	8	68	45	35
5	Corinthian-Casuals	28	14	6	8	68	55	34
6	Kingstonian	28	13	6	9	76	61	32
7	Romford	28	12	5	11	53	50	29
8	Walthamstow Avenue	28	10	9	9	53	50	29
9	Barking	28	11	6	11	52	52	28
10	Dulwich Hamlet	28	11	5	12	45	59	27
11	Woking	28	10	5	13	45	63	25
12	Oxford City	28	10	2	16	50	53	22
13	Wycombe Wanderers	28	8	5	15	50	66	21
14	St. Albans City	28	8	3	17	51	72	19
15	Clapton	28	1	2	25	25	93	4

1953–54 Season

		P	W	D	L	F	A	Pts
1	Walthamstow Avenue	28	20	4	4	67	34	44
2	Dulwich Hamlet	28	18	5	5	81	46	41
3	Leytonstone	28	18	5	5	65	43	41
4	Wimbledon	28	17	3	8	72	49	37
5	Barking	28	17	2	9	65	53	36
6	Wycombe Wanderers	28	14	4	10	78	55	32
7	Oxford City	28	12	5	11	57	49	29
8	Bromley	28	11	6	11	50	50	28
9	Corinthian-Casuals	28	10	7	11	62	68	27
10	Ilford	28	8	5	15	56	66	21
11	Woking	28	8	5	15	51	69	21
12	Kingstonian	28	7	6	15	42	56	20
13	St. Albans City	28	6	4	18	45	72	16
14	Romford	28	5	4	19	51	100	14
15	Clapton	28	5	3	20	31	63	13

1954–55 Season

		P	W	D	L	F	A	Pts
1	Dulwich Hamlet	28	22	4	2	107	40	48
2	Wycombe Wanderers	28	19	4	5	76	31	42
3	Clapton	28	17	2	9	60	41	36
4	Walthamstow Avenue	28	14	5	9	59	45	33
5	Bromley	28	14	4	10	68	54	32
6	Woking	28	12	4	12	52	61	28
7	Corinthian-Casuals	28	12	2	14	49	70	26
8	Wimbledon	28	10	5	13	51	52	25
9	Leytonstone	28	10	5	13	54	58	25
10	Barking	28	9	6	13	43	55	24
11	Oxford City	28	10	4	14	48	66	24
12	St. Albans City	28	8	6	14	35	51	22
13	Kingstonian	28	9	3	16	55	69	21
14	Romford	28	6	6	16	43	79	18
15	Ilford	28	7	2	19	43	71	16

1955–56 Season

		P	W	D	L	F	A	Pts
1	Wycombe Wanderers	28	17	7	4	86	44	41
2	Bromley	28	16	7	5	80	47	39
3	Leytonstone	28	15	7	6	56	33	37
4	Walthamstow Avenue	28	15	7	6	56	33	37
5	Oxford City	28	14	7	7	83	64	35
6	Woking	28	12	7	9	57	54	31
7	Dulwich Hamlet	28	11	7	10	78	68	29
8	Barking	28	11	5	12	48	56	27
9	Ilford	28	11	2	15	53	60	24
10	Clapton	28	9	5	14	50	56	23
11	Wimbledon	28	8	7	13	60	69	23
12	Romford	28	8	6	14	39	61	22
13	Kingstonian	28	8	5	15	49	73	21
14	Corinthian-Casuals	28	7	4	17	41	83	18
15	St. Albans City	28	4	5	19	49	90	13

1956–57 Season

		P	W	D	L	F	A	Pts
1	Wycombe Wanderers	30	21	7	2	84	33	49
2	Walthamstow Avenue	30	15	9	6	71	45	39
3	Leytonstone	30	15	8	7	61	45	38
4	Dulwich Hamlet	30	15	6	9	66	54	36
5	Oxford City	30	14	7	9	77	56	35
6	Tooting & M Utd	30	14	4	12	82	65	32
7	Woking	30	14	4	12	68	57	32
8	Bromley	30	10	11	9	68	49	31
9	Barking	30	12	4	14	51	64	28
10	Romford	30	10	6	14	55	64	26
11	Wimbledon	30	12	2	16	56	72	26
12	Kingstonian	30	8	10	12	60	79	26
13	Corinthian-Casuals	30	8	8	14	59	73	24
14	Clapton	30	6	9	15	50	62	21
15	Ilford	30	7	5	18	50	91	19
16	St. Albans City	30	7	4	19	40	89	18

1957–58 Season

		P	W	D	L	F	A	Pts
1	Wycombe Wanderers	30	19	8	3	113	48	46
2	Tooting & M Utd	30	17	7	6	95	52	41
3	Dulwich Hamlet	30	16	8	6	69	58	40
4	Oxford City	30	14	8	8	78	52	36
5	Woking	30	16	3	11	63	57	35
6	Romford	30	14	6	10	62	57	34
7	Wimbledon	30	15	3	12	54	62	33
8	Clapton	30	13	5	12	54	62	31
9	Bromley	30	13	3	14	75	70	29
10	Leytonstone	30	10	9	11	46	73	29
11	Walthamstow Avenue	30	9	8	13	48	45	26
12	Barking	30	9	7	14	33	52	25
13	St. Albans City	30	6	12	12	57	66	24
14	Corinthian-Casuals	30	9	5	16	63	83	23
15	Kingstonian	30	8	4	18	61	89	20
16	Ilford	30	3	2	25	36	99	8

1958–59 Season

		P	W	D	L	F	A	Pts
1	Walthamstow Avenue	30	19	7	4	68	39	45
2	Wimbledon	30	19	4	7	91	50	42
3	Tooting & M Utd	30	17	4	9	81	62	38
4	Wycombe Wanderers	30	15	7	8	58	41	37
5	Romford	30	15	7	8	63	52	37
6	Dulwich Hamlet	30	13	7	10	80	57	33
7	Corinthian-Casuals	30	15	3	12	74	64	33
8	Woking	30	13	7	10	54	48	33
9	Clapton	30	13	5	12	66	63	31
10	Oxford City	30	13	4	13	75	65	30
11	Bromley	30	13	3	14	68	85	29
12	St. Albans City	30	11	4	15	50	64	26
13	Leytonstone	30	8	5	17	44	73	21
14	Kingstonian	30	8	5	17	43	80	21
15	Barking	30	5	4	21	42	68	14
16	Ilford	30	5	0	25	39	85	10

1959–60 Season

	P	W	D	L	F	A	Pts
1 Wycombe Wanderers	30	19	6	5	92	41	44
2 Corinthian-Casuals	30	18	6	6	79	54	42
3 Wimbledon	30	19	3	8	97	47	41
4 Walthamstow Avenue	30	15	6	9	70	47	36
5 Maidstone United	30	15	4	11	83	70	34
6 Kingstonian	30	12	9	9	75	53	33
7 Oxford City	30	13	6	11	89	73	32
8 Bromley	30	13	6	11	86	83	32
9 St. Albans City	30	14	4	12	67	67	32
10 Tooting & M Utd	30	10	11	9	81	81	31
11 Woking	30	13	4	13	58	55	30
12 Dulwich Hamlet	30	9	6	15	50	81	24
13 Ilford	30	6	12	12	44	79	24
14 Barking	30	5	7	18	37	79	17
15 Leytonstone	30	4	7	19	41	84	15
16 Clapton	30	3	7	20	36	91	13

1960–61 Season

	P	W	D	L	F	A	Pts
1 Wimbledon	30	22	4	4	93	28	48
2 St. Albans City	30	17	7	6	83	50	41
3 Wycombe Wanderers	30	18	4	8	84	63	40
4 Kingstonian	30	16	5	9	67	53	37
5 Walthamstow Avenue	30	15	6	9	69	41	36
6 Corinthian-Casuals	30	15	6	9	61	53	36
7 Ilford	30	15	5	10	59	52	35
8 Bromley	30	14	5	11	63	57	33
9 Leytonstone	30	10	5	15	49	53	25
10 Woking	30	10	5	15	49	60	25
11 Tooting & M Utd	30	9	6	15	42	55	24
12 Maidstone United	30	10	3	17	40	58	23
13 Dulwich Hamlet	30	9	5	16	50	86	23
14 Oxford City	30	7	7	16	56	71	21
15 Barking	30	6	7	17	32	75	19
16 Clapton	30	5	4	21	39	81	14

1961–62 Season

	P	W	D	L	F	A	Pts
1 Wimbledon	30	23	3	4	92	26	49
2 St. Albans City	30	18	6	6	79	46	42
3 Maidstone United	30	15	7	8	67	45	37
4 Tooting & M Utd	30	15	6	9	84	71	36
5 Leytonstone	30	14	6	10	71	53	34
6 Bromley	30	15	4	11	65	55	34
7 Kingstonian	30	15	3	12	65	64	33
8 Walthamstow Avenue	30	13	5	12	58	54	31
9 Wycombe Wanderers	30	11	5	14	74	89	27
10 Barking	30	11	4	15	51	62	26
11 Ilford	30	9	6	15	61	67	24
12 Oxford City	30	9	6	15	51	72	24
13 Dulwich Hamlet	30	9	5	16	68	83	23
14 Corinthian-Casuals	30	8	5	17	58	86	21
15 Woking	30	6	8	16	46	74	20
16 Clapton	30	8	3	19	40	83	19

1962–63 Season

	P	W	D	L	F	A	Pts
1 Wimbledon	30	23	4	3	105	31	50
2 Walthamstow Avenue	30	19	4	7	70	40	42
3 Ilford	30	14	7	9	65	45	35
4 Kingstonian	30	15	5	10	66	51	35
5 Maidstone United	30	15	3	12	73	46	33
6 St. Albans City	30	15	3	12	65	57	33
7 Oxford City	30	15	3	12	50	50	33
8 Tooting & M Utd	30	13	5	12	47	44	31
9 Barking	30	12	6	12	50	53	30
10 Bromley	30	15	0	15	62	68	30
11 Leytonstone	30	12	5	13	42	51	29
12 Wycombe Wanderers	30	10	5	15	59	66	25
13 Corinthian-Casuals	30	11	3	16	58	77	25
14 Dulwich Hamlet	30	9	5	16	38	64	23
15 Clapton	30	4	5	21	30	79	13
16 Woking	30	4	5	21	33	91	13

1963–64 Season

	P	W	D	L	F	A	Pts
1 Ilford	38	25	5	8	90	65	55
2 Hendon	38	24	6	8	101	38	54
3 Wimbledon	38	26	2	10	113	59	54
4 Wycombe Wanderers	38	21	7	10	103	72	49
5 Sutton United	38	20	6	12	87	57	46
6 Enfield	38	22	2	14	90	67	46
7 St. Albans City	38	17	8	13	77	61	42
8 Hitchin Town	38	18	6	14	77	68	42
9 Leytonstone	38	17	7	14	57	68	41
10 Walthamstow Avenue	38	17	6	15	75	69	40
11 Kingstonian	38	16	7	15	82	64	39
12 Barking	38	12	15	11	83	80	39
13 Tooting & M Utd	38	14	9	15	97	84	37
14 Maidstone United	38	11	7	20	57	85	29
15 Dulwich Hamlet	38	10	9	19	49	76	29
16 Bromley	38	10	7	21	71	89	27
17 Corinthian-Casuals	38	11	5	22	59	90	27
18 Oxford City	38	9	8	21	62	94	26
19 Woking	38	9	6	23	51	112	24
20 Clapton	38	5	4	29	38	121	14

1964–65 Season

	P	W	D	L	F	A	Pts
1 Hendon	30	25	4	1	105	31	54
2 Wealdstone	30	22	3	5	97	42	47
3 Sutton United	30	21	2	7	81	39	44
4 Leytonstone	30	19	5	6	58	37	43
5 Bromley	30	18	6	6	78	47	42
6 Enfield	30	17	2	11	69	36	36
7 Walthamstow Avenue	30	11	9	10	72	55	31
8 Woking	30	14	3	13	74	71	31
9 Kingstonian	30	14	1	15	65	56	29
10 Ilford	30	12	5	13	58	66	29
11 Hitchin Town	30	11	7	12	53	70	29
12 Tooting & M Utd	30	11	4	15	63	88	26
13 Dulwich Hamlet	30	9	7	14	47	58	25
14 Oxford City	30	10	4	16	44	61	24
15 Clapton	30	8	7	15	48	63	23
16 St. Albans City	30	8	5	17	48	75	21
17 Wycombe Wanderers	30	8	5	17	48	75	21
18 Corinthian-Casuals	30	5	10	15	45	68	20
19 Barking	30	6	8	16	38	70	20
20 Maidstone United	30	1	3	26	27	117	5

NB: Due to ground availability problems each club only played 30 games.

1965–66 Season

	P	W	D	L	F	A	Pts
1 Kingstonian	30	23	6	1	88	17	52
2 Sutton United	30	18	5	7	87	55	41
3 Bromley	30	19	3	8	89	61	41
4 Leytonstone	30	15	10	5	53	26	40
5 Walthamstow Avenue	30	17	4	9	58	44	38
6 Wealdstone	30	16	5	9	67	52	37
7 Corinthian-Casuals	30	14	6	10	59	59	34
8 St. Albans City	30	13	7	10	53	55	33
9 Oxford City	30	14	3	13	56	61	31
10 Wycombe Wanderers	30	12	6	12	54	46	30
11 Enfield	30	12	4	14	57	51	28
12 Hendon	30	10	7	13	50	54	27
13 Woking	30	10	6	14	54	66	26
14 Barking	30	9	7	14	50	58	25
15 Dulwich Hamlet	30	8	9	13	50	62	25
16 Tooting & M Utd	30	9	5	16	50	71	23
17 Clapton	30	7	5	18	37	62	19
18 Ilford	30	6	5	19	40	65	17
19 Hitchin Town	30	5	7	18	42	74	17
20 Maidstone United	30	6	4	20	41	96	16

NB: Due to ground availability problems each club only played 30 games.

1966–67 Season

	P	W	D	L	F	A	Pts
1 Kingstonian	30	18	7	5	72	39	43
2 Sutton United	30	19	5	6	67	42	43
3 Hendon	30	15	10	5	59	34	40
4 St. Albans City	30	17	5	8	81	48	39
5 Tooting & M Utd	30	17	4	9	73	41	38
6 Ilford	30	16	4	10	55	48	36
7 Walthamstow Avenue	30	15	4	11	75	50	34
8 Wealdstone	30	14	6	10	64	52	34
9 Bromley	30	15	3	12	54	58	33
10 Barking	30	14	4	12	57	59	32
11 Enfield	30	12	7	11	65	48	30
12 Leytonstone	30	12	6	12	45	48	30
13 Corinthian-Casuals	30	9	10	11	53	59	28
14 Clapton	30	9	6	15	52	67	24
15 Woking	30	9	6	15	41	64	24
16 Wycombe Wanderers	30	6	11	13	40	54	23
17 Oxford City	30	8	5	17	48	67	21
18 Dulwich Hamlet	30	7	5	18	39	69	19
19 Hitchin Town	30	5	9	16	34	74	19
20 Maidstone United	30	2	5	23	29	82	9

NB: Due to ground availability problems each club only played 30 games.

CHAMPIONSHIP PLAY–OFF (Rule 8 applied)

Kingstonian 2, Sutton United 1 (at Sutton United FC).

1967–68 Season

	P	W	D	L	F	A	Pts
1 Hendon	30	18	7	5	77	38	43
2 Hitchin Town	30	18	6	6	64	43	42
3 Sutton United	30	17	7	6	52	37	41
4 Leytonstone	30	14	11	5	50	29	39
5 Wealdstone	30	14	8	8	70	41	36
6 Wycombe Wanderers	30	12	11	7	61	53	35
7 Kingstonian	30	13	8	9	50	31	34
8 Enfield	30	12	7	11	51	50	31
9 Walthamstow Avenue	30	9	9	12	48	54	27
10 Clapton	30	7	11	12	44	56	25
11 Woking	30	9	6	15	48	70	24
12 Oxford City	30	7	10	13	41	64	24
13 Ilford	30	7	7	16	35	51	21
14 Corinthian-Casuals	30	7	7	16	41	69	21
15 Dulwich Hamlet	30	5	9	16	30	43	19
16 Bromley	30	7	4	19	43	76	18

1968–69 Season

		P	W	D	L	F	A	Pts
1	Hendon	28	18	6	4	59	24	42
2	Wealdstone	28	16	5	7	69	32	37
3	Hitchin Town	28	14	8	6	59	34	36
4	Leytonstone	28	14	7	7	52	34	35
5	Wycombe Wanderers	28	13	8	7	62	38	34
6	Clapton	28	14	6	8	50	48	34
7	Kingstonian	28	14	5	9	49	38	33
8	Walthamstow Avenue	28	14	4	10	50	31	32
9	Sutton United	28	11	6	11	39	38	28
10	Enfield	28	10	5	13	42	51	25
11	Barking	28	10	4	14	44	62	24
12	Woking	28	7	4	17	39	56	18
13	Corinthian-Casuals	28	3	9	16	29	67	15
14	Ilford	28	6	2	20	26	65	14
15	Dulwich Hamlet	28	3	7	18	29	80	13

1969–70 Season

		P	W	D	L	F	A	Pts
1	Woking	26	18	3	5	53	30	39
2	Leytonstone	26	14	7	5	54	22	35
3	Kingstonian	26	15	5	6	68	41	35
4	Sutton United	26	13	6	7	51	34	32
5	Barking	26	13	5	8	38	26	31
6	Dulwich Hamlet	26	11	8	7	38	32	30
7	Ilford	26	11	8	7	38	33	30
8	Clapton	26	10	6	10	45	41	26
9	Hitchin Town	26	8	10	8	29	29	26
10	Wealdstone	26	7	8	11	32	40	22
11	Walthamstow Avenue	26	5	5	16	36	57	15
12	Corinthian-Casuals	26	5	5	16	24	58	15
13	Enfield	26	4	6	16	26	51	14
14	Hendon	26	4	6	16	19	57	14

1970–71 Season

		P	W	D	L	F	A	Pts
1	Ilford	27	18	3	6	54	30	39
2	Enfield	27	14	7	6	49	31	35
3	Sutton United	27	11	10	6	37	34	32
4	Dulwich Hamlet	27	13	2	12	50	49	28
5	Kingstonian	27	11	4	12	42	46	26
6	Barking	27	11	4	12	44	51	26
7	Clapton	27	8	8	11	40	46	24
8	Corinthian-Casuals	27	10	4	13	28	33	24
9	Wealdstone	27	7	6	14	40	46	20
10	Bromley	27	6	4	17	34	52	16

Each Club played each other 3 times.

'A' SECTION TABLES

1950–51 Season

		P	W	D	L	F	A	Pts
1	Walthamstow Avenue	16	10	4	2	40	25	24
2	Wycombe Wanderers	16	10	3	3	50	33	23
3	Wimbledon	16	9	1	6	52	31	19
4	Leytonstone	16	5	6	5	39	33	16
5	Clapton	16	5	4	7	30	40	14
6	Tufnell Park Edmonton	16	7	0	9	29	42	14
7	Corinthian-Casuals	16	5	2	9	35	39	12
8	Woking	16	3	6	7	38	51	12
9	Ilford	16	3	4	9	17	36	10

1951–52 Season

		P	W	D	L	F	A	Pts
1	Romford	22	13	6	3	52	30	32
2	Kingstonian	22	13	5	4	86	53	31
3	Ilford	22	13	3	6	65	50	29
4	Wimbledon	22	11	5	6	79	59	27
5	Dulwich Hamlet	22	11	3	8	71	55	25
6	Walthamstow Avenue	22	9	6	7	56	42	24
7	Wycombe Wanderers	22	10	4	8	66	58	24
8	Tufnell Park Edmonton	22	7	5	10	47	54	19
9	Woking	22	6	6	10	52	77	18
10	Clapton	22	6	3	13	48	74	15
11	Leytonstone	22	5	2	15	32	65	12
12	St. Albans City	22	2	4	16	43	80	8

1952–53 Season

		P	W	D	L	F	A	Pts
1	Kingstonian	22	16	3	3	77	38	35
2	Barking	22	13	6	3	55	31	32
3	Ilford	22	12	3	7	52	32	27
4	Wimbledon	22	9	9	4	48	35	27
5	Dulwich Hamlet	22	9	4	9	64	46	22
6	Woking	22	9	4	9	57	54	22
7	Wycombe Wanderers	22	8	4	10	46	49	20
8	Walthamstow Avenue	22	6	8	8	46	54	20
9	Clapton	22	7	4	11	43	61	18
10	Romford	22	7	2	13	48	60	16
11	St. Albans City	22	5	3	14	36	82	13
12	Leytonstone	22	3	6	13	35	65	12

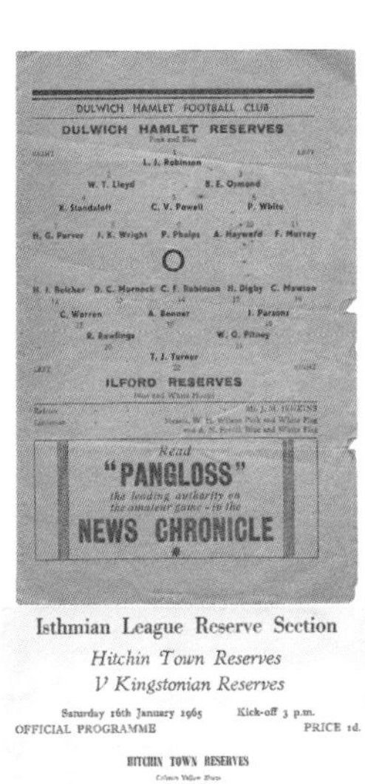

Isthmian League Reserve Section

Hitchin Town Reserves

V Kingstonian Reserves

OFFICIAL PROGRAMME

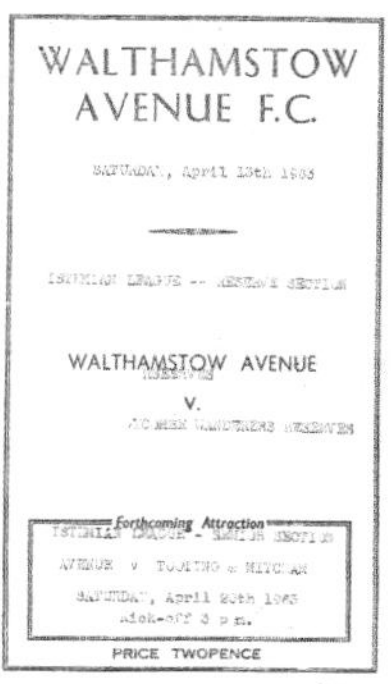

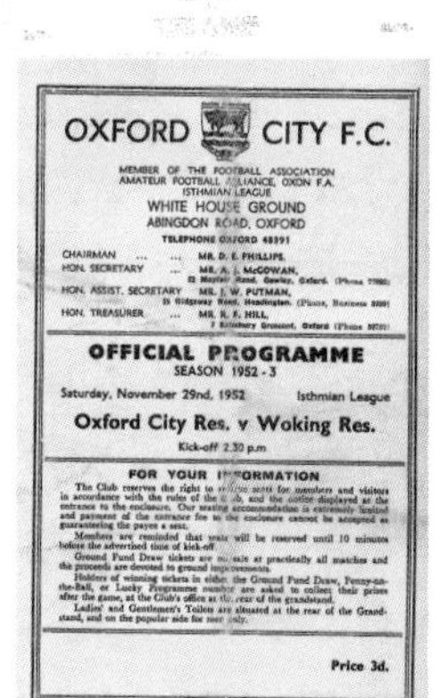

Enfield Football Club

Official Programme Price 2d

ISTHMIAN LEAGUE Res. v. SPARTAN LEAGUE Res.

OTHER CUP SUCCESSES BY MEMBER CLUBS

During the first 100 years Isthmian League clubs have been successful in many cup competitions, particularly County Senior cups, and listed below are the winners whilst in membership of the League.

AFA Senior Cup
1911–12 Oxford City
1919–20 Civil Service
1933–34 St. Albans City

AFA Invitation Cup
1955–56 Oxford City
1959–60 Wycombe Wanderers
1960–61 Wycombe Wanderers
1961–62 Oxford City
1964–65 Wycombe Wanderers
1965–66 Clapton
1966–67 Wycombe Wanderers
1967–68 Wycombe Wanderers
1970–71 Clapton*

Bedfordshire Senior Cup
1980–81 Barton Rovers
1981–82 Barton Rovers
1989–90 Barton Rovers
1992–93 Leighton Town
1994–95 Bedford Town
1995–96 Bedford Town
1997–98 Barton Rovers
1998–99 Barton Rovers
2003–04 Arlesey Town

Berks & Bucks Senior Cup
1922–23 Wycombe Wanderers
1924–25 Wycombe Wanderers
1932–33 Wycombe Wanderers
1934–35 Wycombe Wanderers
1939–40 Wycombe Wanderers
1946–47 Wycombe Wanderers
1948–49 Wycombe Wanderers
1949–50 Wycombe Wanderers
1953–54 Wycombe Wanderers
1957–58 Wycombe Wanderers
1959–60 Wycombe Wanderers
1963–64 Wycombe Wanderers
1967–68 Wycombe Wanderers
1972–73 Wycombe Wanderers
1973–74 Wycombe Wanderers
1975–76 Chesham United
1976–77 Slough Town
1977–78 Wycombe Wanderers
1978–79 Wycombe Wanderers
1980–81 Slough Town
1981–82 Hungerford Town
1982–83 Wokingham Town
1984–85 Wokingham Town
1986–87 Wycombe Wanderers
1987–88 Windsor & Eton
1988–89 Windsor & Eton
1990–91 Marlow
1991–92 Chesham United
1992–93 Chesham United
1993–94 Marlow
1995–96 Wokingham Town
1996–97 Aylesbury United
1997–98 Maidenhead United
1998–99 Maidenhead United
2000–01 Chesham United
2001–02 Maidenhead United
2002–03 Maidenhead United
2003–04 Chesham United

Berks & Bucks Benevolent Cup
1931–32 Wycombe Wanderers
1942–43 Wycombe Wanderers
1945–46 Wycombe Wanderers*

East Anglian Cup
1939–40 Walthamstow Avenue
1941–42 Walthamstow Avenue
1953–54 Barking*
1954–55 Romford
1955–56 Romford
1972–73 Hitchin Town
1981–82 Bishop's Stortford
1988–89 Aveley
1989–90 Harlow Town
1992–93 St. Albans City
1993–94 Heybridge Swifts
1994–95 Heybridge Swifts
1997–98 Romford
2001–02 Harlow Town
2002–03 East Thurrock United

Essex Senior Cup
1907–08 Ilford
1912–13 Ilford
1913–14 Leytonstone
1923–24 Ilford
1924–25 Clapton
1925–26 Clapton
1926–27 Ilford
1927–28 Ilford
1928–29 Ilford
1946–47 Romford
1947–48 Leytonstone
1948–49 Leytonstone
1952–53 Ilford
1953–54 Ilford
1954–55 Clapton
1955–56 Walthamstow Avenue
1957–58 Walthamstow Avenue
1958–59 Walthamstow Avenue
1959–60 Walthamstow Avenue
1962–63 Barking
1964–65 Leytonstone
1965–66 Leytonstone
1966–67 Leytonstone
1968–69 Walthamstow Avenue
1969–70 Barking
1971–72 Walthamstow Avenue
1973–74 Walthamstow Avenue
1974–75 Tilbury
1976–77 Walthamstow Avenue
1977–78 Dagenham
1978–79 Harlow Town
1979–80 Dagenham
1980–81 Dagenham
1981–82 Leytonstone–Ilford
1983–84 Clapton
1984–85 Walthamstow Avenue
1987–88 Grays Athletic
1989–90 Barking
1993–94 Billericay Town
1994–95 Grays Athletic
1995–96 Braintree Town
1997–98 Dagenham & Redbridge
1998–99 Canvey Island
1999–00 Canvey Island
2001–02 Canvey Island
2003–04 Thurrock

Essex Senior Trophy
1984–85 Saffron Walden Town
1987–88 Wivenhoe Town
1988–89 Clapton

Essex Thames-side Trophy
1945–46 Leytonstone
1946–47 Leytonstone
1948–49 Leytonstone
1949–50 Ilford
1950–51 Leytonstone
1951–52 Romford
1952–53 Leytonstone
1953–54 Walthamstow Avenue
1954–55 Ilford
1955–56 Romford
1956–57 Barking
1957–58 Romford
1958–59 Barking
1959–60 Ilford
1961–62 Walthamstow Avenue
1965–66 Leytonstone
1967–68 Leytonstone
1970–71 Ilford
1971–72 Walthamstow Avenue
1972–73 Leytonstone
1974–75 Dagenham
1976–77 Walthamstow Avenue
1977–78 Walthamstow Avenue
1979–80 Aveley
1982–83 Clapton
1983–84 Clapton
1984–85 Hornchurch
1985–86 Walthamstow Avenue
1986–87 Billericay Town
1987–88 Grays Athletic
1988–89 Grays Athletic
1994–95 Purfleet
1995–96 Canvey Island
1996–97 Barking
1997–98 Canvey Island
1998–99 Ford United
2000–01 Grays Athletic
2001–02 Grays Athletic
2003–04 Ford United

Hampshire Senior Cup
1981–82 Farnborough Town
1983–84 Farnborough Town
1985–86 Farnborough Town
1989–90 Basingstoke Town
1995–96 Basingstoke Town
1996–97 Basingstoke Town
1998–99 Aldershot Town
1999–00 Aldershot Town
2001–02 Aldershot Town
2002–03 Aldershot Town

Hertfordshire Senior Cup
1924–25 St. Albans City
1928–29 St. Albans City
1934–35 St. Albans City
1943–44 St. Albans City
1946–47 St. Albans City
1950–51 St. Albans City
1954–55 St. Albans City
1955–56 St. Albans City
1956–57 St. Albans City
1965–66 St. Albans City
1967–68 St. Albans City
1968–69 St. Albans City
1969–70 Hitchin Town
1972–73 Bishop's Stortford
1973–74 Bishop's Stortford
1974–75 Hitchin Town
1975–76 Bishop's Stortford
1976–77 Hitchin Town
1986–87 Bishop's Stortford
1989–90 Hertford Town
1996–97 Hitchin Town
1998–99 Boreham Wood
1999–00 St. Albans City
2001–02 Boreham Wood
2002–03 Berkhamsted Town

Hertfordshire Charity Cup
1923–24 St. Albans City
1924–25 St. Albans City
1925–26 St. Albans City
1928–29 St. Albans City
1938–39 St. Albans City
1940–41 St. Albans City*
1941–42 St. Albans City
1950–51 St. Albans City
1952–53 St. Albans City
1953–54 St. Albans City
1955–56 St. Albans City
1956–57 St. Albans City
1957–58 St. Albans City
1966–67 St. Albans City
1967–68 Hitchin Town
1968–69 St. Albans City
1969–70 St. Albans City
1970–71 St. Albans City
1971–72 St. Albans City
1973–74 Bishop's Stortford
1975–76 Hitchin Town
1976–77 Hitchin Town
1977–78 Hitchin Town
1978–79 Hitchin Town
1979–80 Hitchin Town
1980–81 Boreham Wood
1981–82 Bishop's Stortford
1982–83 Bishop's Stortford
1983–84 Boreham Wood
1984–85 Bishop's Stortford
1985–86 Boreham Wood
1986–87 St. Albans City
1987–88 Bishop's Stortford
1988–89 Boreham Wood
1989–90 Boreham Wood
1990–91 Hitchin Town
1992–93 St. Albans City
1994–95 St. Albans City
1996–97 Bishop's Stortford
1997–98 St. Albans City
1999–00 Hitchin Town
2000–01 Hitchin Town
2001–02 Berkhamsted Town
2002–03 Bishop's Stortford
2003–04 Bishop's Stortford

Hertfordshire Charity Shield
1977–78 Tring Town
1980–81 Tring Town
1982–83 Tring Town
1983–84 Hemel Hempstead
1984–85 Berkhamsted Town
1985–86 Ware
1988–89 Letchworth Garden City
1989–90 Royston Town
1990–91 Berkhamsted Town

Kent Senior Cup
1965–66 Maidstone United
1976–77 Bromley
1991–92 Bromley
1996–97 Bromley
1999–00 Gravesend & Northfleet
2000–01 Gravesend & Northfleet
2001–02 Gravesend & Northfleet

Kent Amateur Cup
1913–14 New Crusaders
1952–53 Bromley
1953–54 Bromley
1954–55 Bromley
1959–60 Bromley
1960–61 Maidstone United
1961–62 Maidstone United

London Challenge Cup
1990–91 Carshalton Athletic
1993–94 Uxbridge
1994–95 St. Albans City
1995–96 Bromley
1996–97 Uxbridge
1997–98 Boreham Wood
1998–99 Dulwich Hamlet
1999–00 Uxbridge

London Senior Cup
1907–08 London Caledonians
1908–09 Clapton
1909–10 Bromley
1910–11 Clapton
1913–14 Ilford
1914–15 London Caledonians
1919–20 Leytonstone
1921–22 Ilford
1922–23 Nunhead
1923–24 Tufnell Park
1924–25 Dulwich Hamlet
1925–26 London Caledonians
1927–28 London Caledonians
1928–29 Ilford
1929–30 Ilford
1930–31 Wimbledon
1933–34 Wimbledon
1938–39 Dulwich Hamlet
1939–40 Walthamstow Avenue
1941–42 Walthamstow Avenue
1943–44 Walthamstow Avenue
1947–48 Leytonstone
1949–50 Dulwich Hamlet
1952–53 Walthamstow Avenue*
1953–54 Ilford
1954–55 Walthamstow Avenue
1958–59 Tooting & Mitcham United
1959–60 Tooting & Mitcham United
1961–62 Wimbledon*
1962–63 Kingstonian
1963–64 Hendon
1964–65 Kingstonian
1865–66 Leytonstone
1966–67 Enfield
1968–69 Hendon
1969–70 Hitchin Town
1970–71 St. Albans City
1971–72 Enfield
1972–73 Enfield
1973–74 Bishop's Stortford
1975–76 Enfield
1977–78 Walthamstow Avenue
1978–79 Barking
1979–80 Leytonstone–Ilford
1980–81 Hayes
1981–82 Leytonstone–Ilford
1982–83 Sutton United
1983–84 Dulwich Hamlet
1985–86 Walthamstow Avenue
1986–87 Kingstonian
1997–98 Ford United
2000–01 Ford United
2001–02 Croydon
2002–03 Bromley
2003–04 Dulwich Hamlet

London Charity Cup
1905–06 London Caledonians
1906–07 London Caledonians & Casuals*
1908–09 London Caledonian
1909–10 Leytonstone
1910–11 Dulwich Hamlet & Nunhead*
1911–12 Nunhead
1912–13 London Caledonians
1913–14 Nunhead
1914–15 Nunhead
1919–20 Dulwich Hamlet
1920–21 Dulwich Hamlet
1921–22 Ilford
1922–23 Dulwich Hamlet
1923–24 Dulwich Hamlet & Clapton*
1924–25 London Caledonians
1925–26 Dulwich Hamlet
1926–27 Kingstonian
1927–28 Dulwich Hamlet
1928–29 Dulwich Hamlet
1929–30 Ilford
1930–31 Dulwich Hamlet & Kingstonian*
1931–32 Kingstonian
1932–33 Kingstonian
1935–36 Wimbledon
1937–38 Ilford
1947–48 Dulwich Hamlet
1948–49 Walthamstow Avenue
1949–50 Wimbledon
1950–51 Walthamstow Avenue
1951–52 Wimbledon
1952–53 Leytonstone
1954–55 Ilford
1955–56 Walthamstow Avenue
1956–57 Dulwich Hamlet
1957–58 Dulwich Hamlet
1961–62 Barking
1962–63 Ilford*
1965–66 Ilford
1969–70 Sutton United
1974–75 Dagenham

Middlesex Senior Cup
1909–10 Shepherd's Bush
1934–35 London Caledonians
1964–65 Hendon
1965–66 Enfield
1966–67 Hendon
1967–68 Wealdstone
1968–69 Enfield
1969–70 Enfield
1970–71 Enfield
1971–72 Hendon
1972–73 Hendon
1973–74 Hendon
1974–75 Staines Town
1975–76 Staines Town
1976–77 Staines Town
1977–78 Enfield
1978–79 Enfield
1979–80 Enfield
1980–81 Enfield
1981–82 Hayes
1982–83 Harrow Borough
1983–84 Wembley
1985–86 Hendon
1986–87 Wembley
1987–88 Staines Town
1989–90 Staines Town
1990–91 Enfield
1991–92 Yeading
1992–93 Harrow Borough
1993–94 Staines Town
1994–95 Yeading
1995–96 Hayes
1996–97 Staines Town
1997–98 Enfield
1998–99 Hendon
2000–01 Uxbridge
2001–02 Hendon
2002–03 Hendon
2003–04 Hendon
2004–05 Yeading

Middlesex Charity Cup
1943–44 Tufnell Park
1967–68 Wealdstone*
1971–72 Hayes
1972–73 Hayes
1973–74 Finchley
1974–75 Hayes
1975–76 Hendon
1976–77 Hendon
1978–79 Hendon
1979–80 Harrow Borough
1980–81 Wembley*
1982–83 Wembley
1983–84 Southall
1984–85 Hendon
1985–86 Kingsbury Town
1986–87 Wembley
1987–88 Hendon
1990–91 Hayes
1992–93 Harrow Borough
1993–94 Staines Town
1994–95 Wembley
1995–96 Hampton
1996–97 Edgware Town
1997–98 Hampton
1998–99 Hampton
2003–04 Wealdstone
2004–05 Yeading

Oxfordshire Senior Cup
1911–12 Oxford City
1928–29 Oxford City
1930–31 Oxford City
1941–42 Oxford City
1943–44 Oxford City
1944–45 Oxford City
1945–46 Oxford City
1948–49 Oxford City
1950–51 Oxford City
1953–54 Oxford City
1956–57 Oxford City
1959–60 Oxford City
1960–61 Oxford City
1961–62 Oxford City
1962–63 Oxford City
1964–65 Oxford City
1966–67 Oxford City
1967–68 Oxford City
1968–69 Oxford City
1969–70 Oxford City
1970–71 Oxford City
1971–72 Oxford City
1973–74 Oxford City
1982–83 Oxford City
1983–84 Oxford City
1985–86 Oxford City
1992–93 Thame United
1995–96 Oxford City
1996–97 Oxford City
1997–98 Oxford City
1998–99 Oxford City
1999–00 Oxford City
2000–01 Thame United
2001–02 Thame United
2002–03 Oxford City

Somerset Premier Cup
1996–97 Yeovil Town

Surrey Senior Cup
1908–09 Dulwich Hamlet
1909–10 Dulwich Hamlet
1912–13 Woking
1919–20 Dulwich Hamlet
1922–23 Dulwich Hamlet
1924–25 Dulwich Hamlet
1926–27 Woking
1927–28 Dulwich Hamlet
1929–30 Casuals
1930–31 Kingstonian
1931–32 Kingstonian
1933–34 Dulwich Hamlet
1934–35 Kingstonian
1935–36 Wimbledon
1936–37 Dulwich Hamlet
1938–39 Kingstonian
1939–40 Wimbledon
1946–47 Dulwich Hamlet
1948–49 Wimbledon
1949–50 Dulwich Hamlet
1951–52 Kingstonian
1953–54 Corinthian–Casuals
1954–55 Wimbledon
1955–56 Woking
1956–57 Woking
1957–58 Dulwich Hamlet
1958–59 Dulwich Hamlet
1959–60 Tooting & Mitcham United
1962–63 Kingstonian
1963–64 Kingstonian
1964–65 Sutton United
1966–67 Kingstonian
1967–68 Sutton United
1969–70 Sutton United
1971–72 Woking
1972–73 Walton & Hersham
1973–74 Dulwich Hamlet
1974–75 Dulwich Hamlet
1975–76 Tooting & Mitcham United
1976–77 Tooting & Mitcham United
1977–78 Tooting & Mitcham United
1978–79 Camberley Town
1979–80 Sutton United
1980–81 Epsom & Ewell
1981–82 Croydon
1982–83 Sutton United
1983–84 Sutton United
1984–85 Sutton United
1985–86 Sutton United
1988–89 Carshalton Athletic
1989–90 Carshalton Athletic
1990–91 Woking
1991–92 Carshalton Athletic
1997–98 Kingstonian
2002–03 Sutton United
2004–05 AFC Wimbledon

Surrey Charity Shield
1912–13 Woking
1924–25 Wimbledon
1925–26 Wimbledon
1926–27 Wimbledon
1929–30 Kingstonian
1930–31 Wimbledon
1931–32 Nunhead
1934–35 Wimbledon
1952–53 Woking
1953–54 Kingstonian
1956–57 Woking
1957–58 Kingstonian
1960–61 Tooting & Mitcham United
1961–62 Tooting & Mitcham United
1962–63 Woking
1965–66 Tooting & Mitcham United
1967–68 Woking
1972–73 Dulwich Hamlet
1974–75 Woking
1976–77 Carshalton Athletic

Surrey Invitation Cup
1960–61 Kingstonian
1961–62 Tooting & Mitcham United
1965–66 Kingstonian
1966–67 Woking

Sussex Senior Cup
1973–74 Horsham
1975–76 Horsham
1977–78 Worthing
1981–82 Bognor Regis Town
1982–83 Bognor Regis Town
1983–84 Bognor Regis Town
1984–85 Lewes
1986–87 Bognor Regis Town
1998–99 Worthing
2000–01 Lewes

* signifies joint winner

Nick Robinson Esq.,
The Ryman Football League,
Triumph House,
Station Approach,
Sanderstead Road,
South Croydon,
CR2 OPL

4th December, 2006.

Dear Nick,

Thank you for your letter of 30th November, 2006 telling me of your forthcoming book celebrating the Isthmian League.

I am delighted to be asked to contribute and hope that the following will be suitable:

I cannot imagine anyone who would have had the wisdom and foresight to envisage the pleasure that so many of us have enjoyed from our involvement (of one kind or another) with the Isthmian League. Thank goodness the founders' inspiration existed as they not only initiated, but powerfully nurtured a substantial growth of satisfaction over the years for so many football lovers, both on and off the field.

Those of us who have been fortunate enough to share their joy would like to register our deep-seated gratitude for it. Relishing the fun and games it has provided, together with a deposit on fitness and health for the remainder of so many lives, we sincerely re-emphasized our heartfelt thanks.

Congratulations to those whose clairvoyance and inspiration gave birth to the nature and programme of this very special league. May its future be blessed with continued joyful playing fulfillment alongside contagious sportsmanship.

Good luck and all best wishes,

Yours sincerely,

Jimmy Hill